PETER DE CUPERE

Published by stockmans.be

PETER DE CUPERE

SCENT IN CONTEXT
Olfactory Art

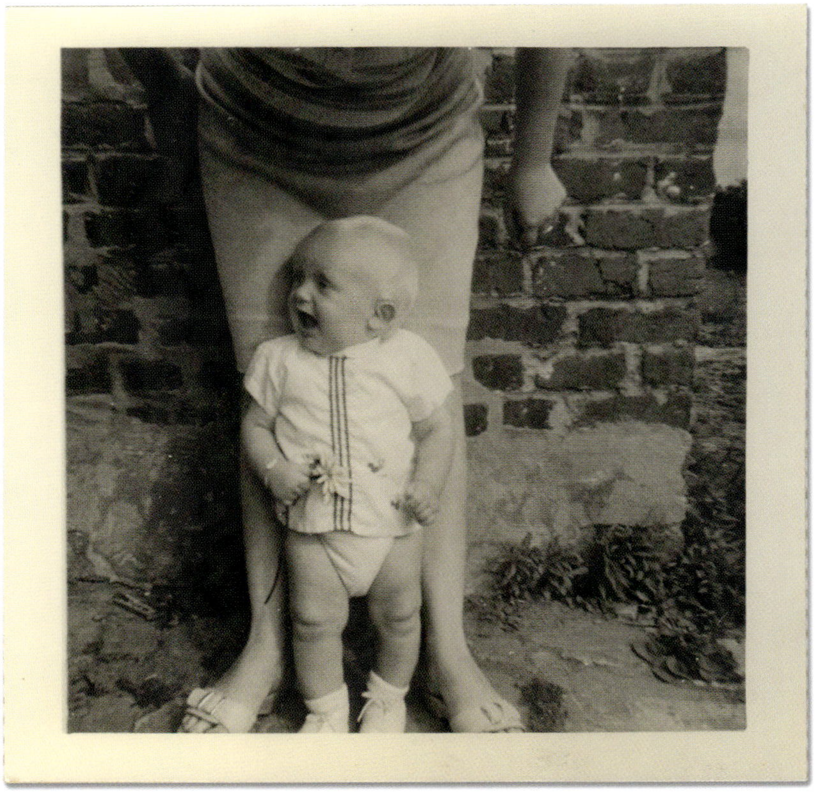

For my mother & father
with love, Peter

Peter de Cupere with his mother and a flower, 1971

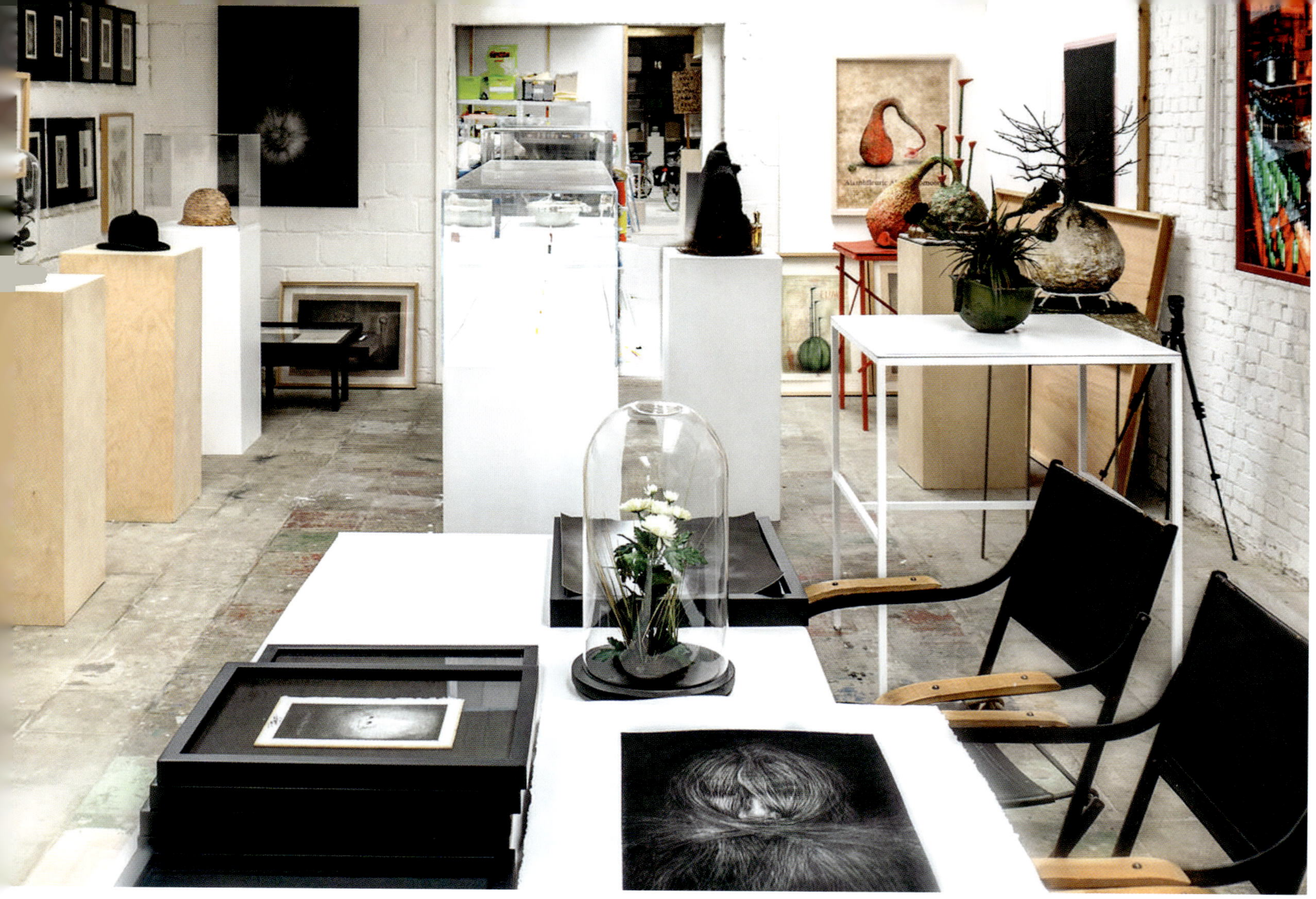

CONTENT

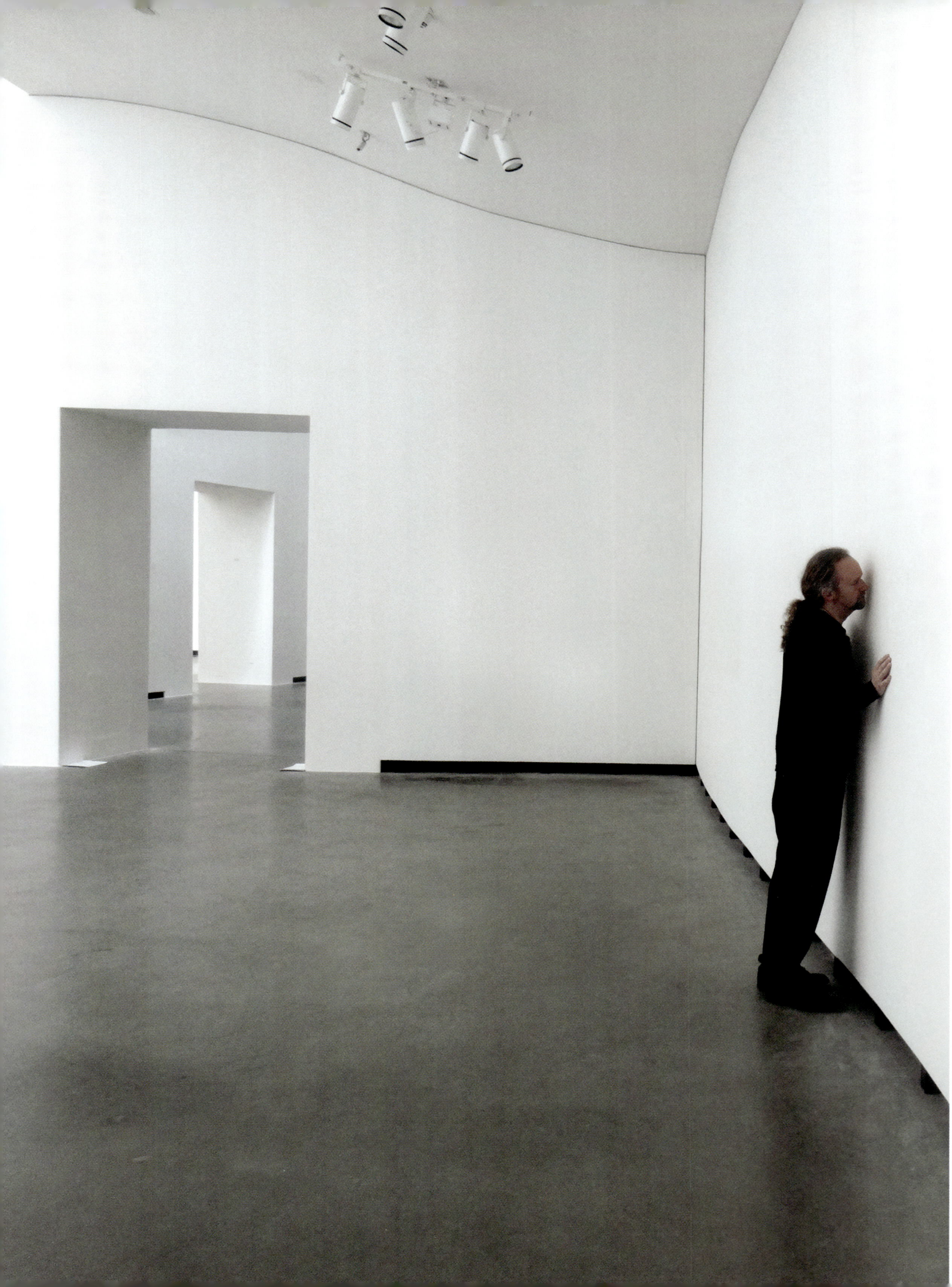

PETER DE CUPERE

THEY CALL ME A SCENT ARTIST

They call me a scent artist.

I have tried to accept this over time, yet I feel I am more of a visual artist, who uses smell/scent as the main sense/medium to give meaning to the image, so that this image does not necessarily need to be visible.
The image may also be evoked simply by the use of smell in combination with a feeling triggered, as in the piece *Scented Tears*, where the observer is moved to tears by the effect of smell in an empty room, confronted with the sorrow of others and himself. Smell may also give a cognitive meaning to, for example, a title as in the piece *Invisible (Scent) Paintings*, where titles that mean nothing are suddenly given a context by smelling scents applied to the walls of the museum using scratch & sniff technology.

In English, they use the term *Olfactory*. An *Olfactory Artist* is an artist who works with smell and scent. The term is very broad. It is used for both perfumers who regard their creations as works of art, and for artists who use smell/scent as a medium in their work and/or in combination with other mediums. You must see *Olfactory Art* in the visual arts in the meaning of *Sense of Smell*. The word 'sense' just gives an additional dimension to smell. It is not merely about the smell, but what the smell evokes. This may be a feeling, a meaning, a purpose, and/or the sensory experience in itself.

Through the translation and use of sensory perception(s) combined with a cognitive attitude, I want to say something with my work, give meaning and convey a message. So several works are a purely sensory search or a combination of factors and thoughts in which the interactions arise from my searching attitude in order to express something. I also prefer to use the word 'beelden' (to conceptualise an image) in Dutch rather than visualise, and rarely the word 'verbeelden' (to represent). To represent is usually to visualise; to conceptualise an image for me is more about suggesting, showing what I want to say in/with the image. To represent is usually more about the literal translation, while to conceptualise an image is more about providing the context. In short, that is very much what my work is about.

Smell may be an illustration, have a supporting attitude and, in addition, smell may also express and give context to an image. Smell also gives more meaning to the image than the image evokes in only a visual way. In order to achieve this and to discover the possibilities of this, I needed to research the possibilities of smell as a medium and smelling as a sensory experience of the work of art from the outset.

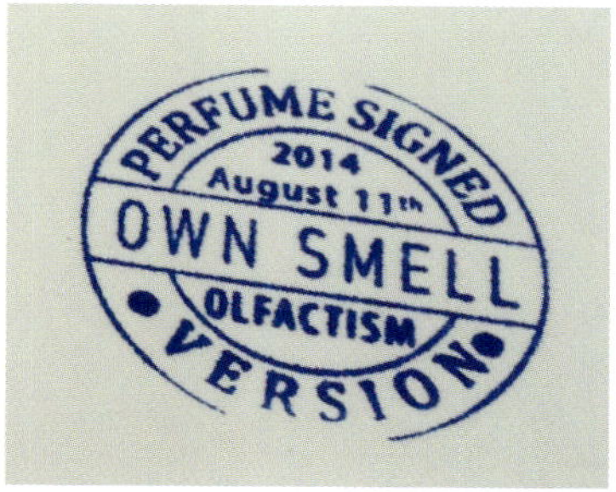

Because smell has been used so little in the art world, I had enormous freedom to test out smell as a medium. I also had to appropriate this freedom for myself as there were not many examples of artists. It was a challenging situation, as well as a difficult decision. People had difficulty in accepting my work in the beginning. They could not read it. They saw the smell as something added that for most observers was a nice additional feature, but they did not know how to look further. My first works were also very diverse and mainly researching into the possibilities of the medium. Questions, like how do you maintain a smell as long as possible, continued to pursue me. The durability of a smell is unfortunately very fleeting, but this limitation also appeared to have advantages.

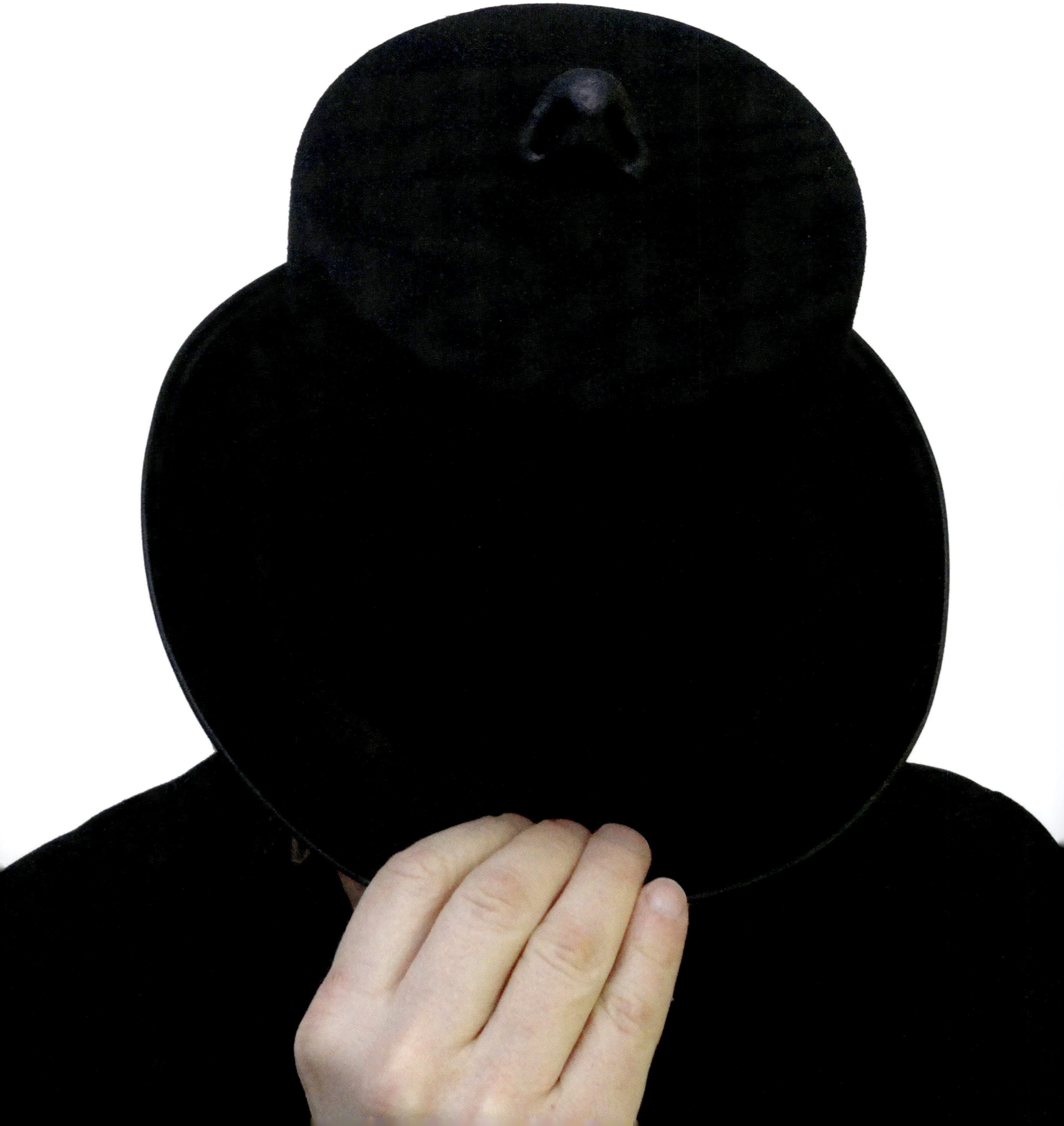

PETER DE CUPERE

A LIFE OF SMELL

Smell is the start of more than we think or more than we suspect, more than we are aware of, more than we know, more than we still have to discover, and more than we will ever discover. Smell has so many meanings, so many values, so many memories, so many languages, so many possibilities, so many 'so manies'. While the other senses are much simpler in their complexity, smell is not. Smell is not so much a medium of my work; smell is and gives the context in my work. My work is a statement made from a love of smell.

Of all the senses, smell has always been considered to be the least important sense. In recent decades, the sciences have looked more at its usefulness and particularly the importance of smell. Smell has a warning function, a memory function, a pleasure function, and above all, an awareness-raising function. This is why I use smell and ... because you can be seduced and misled by it.

Many of my works have a link with life and death. A piece like *Beauty of Birth* refers to the weight of life that you have to carry for the rest of your life.

We breathe to live. With each breath we—unconsciously—perceive the smell of the air we have breathed in. Upon your first breath at your birth, you perceive all the molecules of smell. Although it has been proven that senses already start to develop in the foetal state, you can say that from the moment when the new-born baby breathes independently, his/her first breath is an olfactory testing out of the whole world. Even before being able to see, even before opening its eyes, the sense of smell consciously starts to perceive the world.

Breathing is the start of life.

With every breath, we inhale a smell that consciously or unconsciously tells us something about our immediate environment. Every day, every minute, every second, smell gives us information to discover, experience, remember, understand, and act.

Smell may well be fleeting, but its effect on people is not so fleeting.
It is a permanent and future memory to carry with us for the rest of our life.

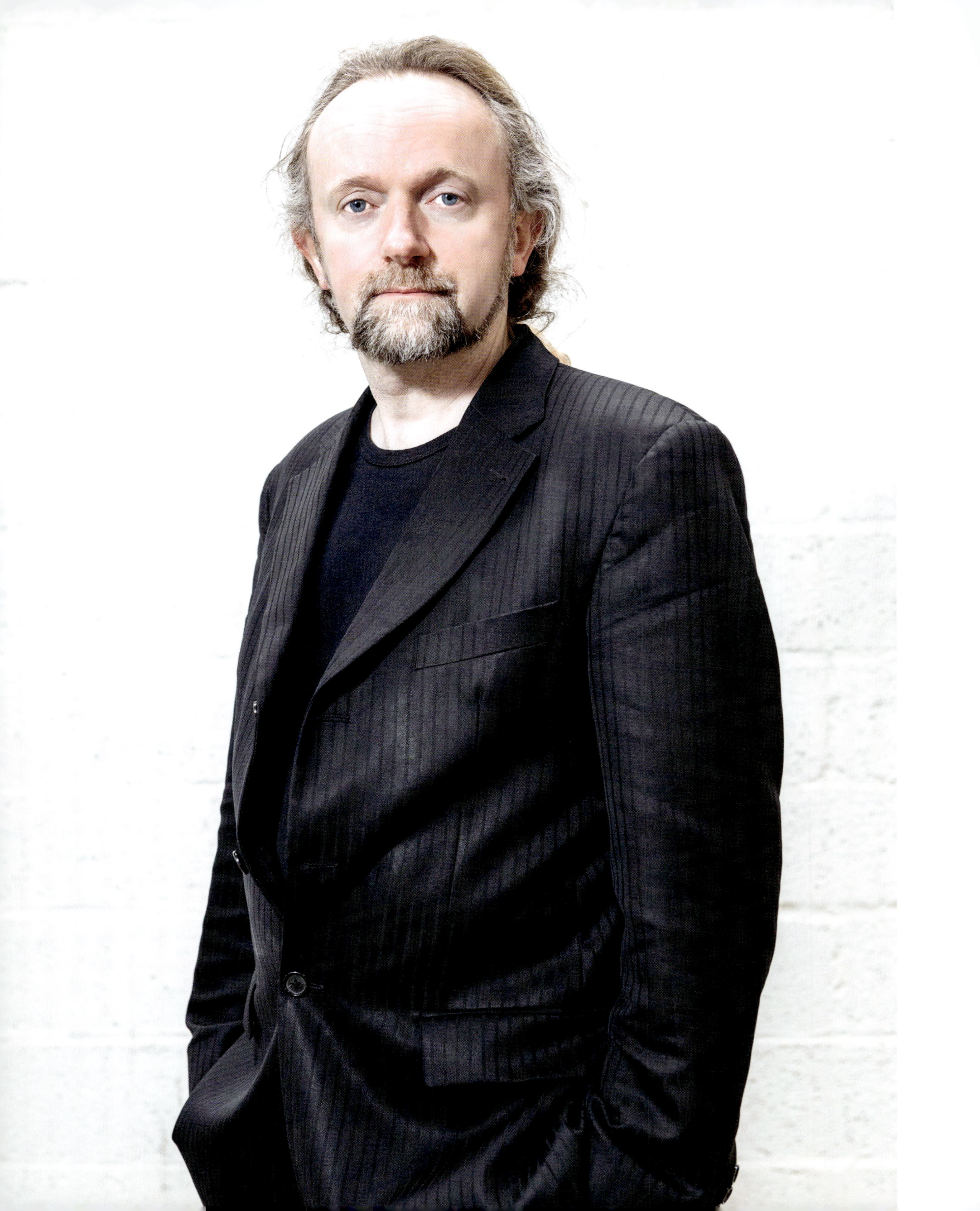

I (RE)SEARCH(ED)

For over 20 years, I have been researching the possibilities of smell as a medium for the work of art. To do this, you have to experiment a lot. The experiment was always an important part of my work.

I researched how we smell, how a smell is made up, how perfumes work, how a product retained a smell, how smells can change as the temperature fluctuates and the humidity varies. I researched how smell evokes a perception, how smell makes people happy, discredits them, how smell incites love and hate. I researched how smell determines your lifestyle, how smells differ from one culture to another, how people with a sensory impairment give smell more meaning as part of their life.

I researched how a waft of air can have an impact on a feeling, how smell made me learn and think better, but also how smell helped me sleep better, made me more alert, and could evoke a certain aggressiveness. I researched how smell can make people cry and laugh, how animals react to certain smells. I researched how I could seduce with smells. I researched how I could encourage possible buyers of my work to like a particular work unconsciously, as well as to buy it, all using pheromones.

I researched all the bodily smells of woman and men, as well as their interaction. I researched my own smell and was surprised how wonderful my smell is in my own perception and experience. I researched how you can evoke a whole world with a simple sense in combination with a smell. I researched how bad smells can become something beautiful and wonderful smells something unpleasant. I researched the molecular possibilities of smells, not that I am a chemist, but purely out of interest when it came to me. I researched the psychological effects of smell. I researched what many have already researched to find out what I did not need to research, but did want to know just for the sake of knowing it.

I researched the power of a droplet of scent compared with litres of fragrance. I researched many smells as well as the act of smelling. I researched smells of people, smelt them surreptitiously with every hello kiss. I smelt my hands after shaking hands with beautiful people. I researched how the smell of faeces, urine, sperm, vaginal secretions, and sweat could contribute to a work of art. I researched how a smell could smell different by diluting it or combining it with an object that was not obvious. I researched how observers interpret smells personally, how smell taps into memory.

I researched the strengths and weaknesses of smell and found their opposites in their counterparts. I researched the sorrow of smell and the smell of sorrow, which I still continue to search for, just as I also go on researching all these other smells.

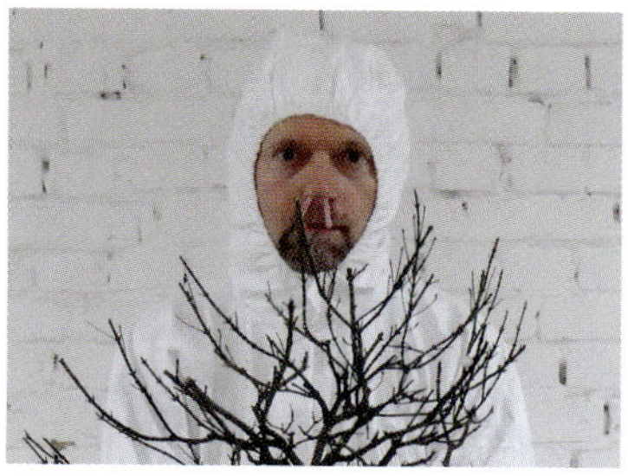

I researched the poetry of smell, but also the hard reality. I researched the illustrative nature of smell and the fanciful thoughts that accompany smells.
I researched smell; but above all, I continued to search for the context that smell can give a piece and how smell can cause this context to change.
I researched the veracity of smells and the unconscious meaning given to a smell by memories, cultural and religious backgrounds, and rituals.

I researched so much; but above all, in my artistic research, I always established that smell has so many more possibilities than can be researched. This is my longing as an artist to hold onto this searching attitude eternally. And this starts with every breath. Every molecule that I breathe is a story in itself, a meaning in itself. Every breath is meaning, is the start of the work of art as a statement, even more than seeing.

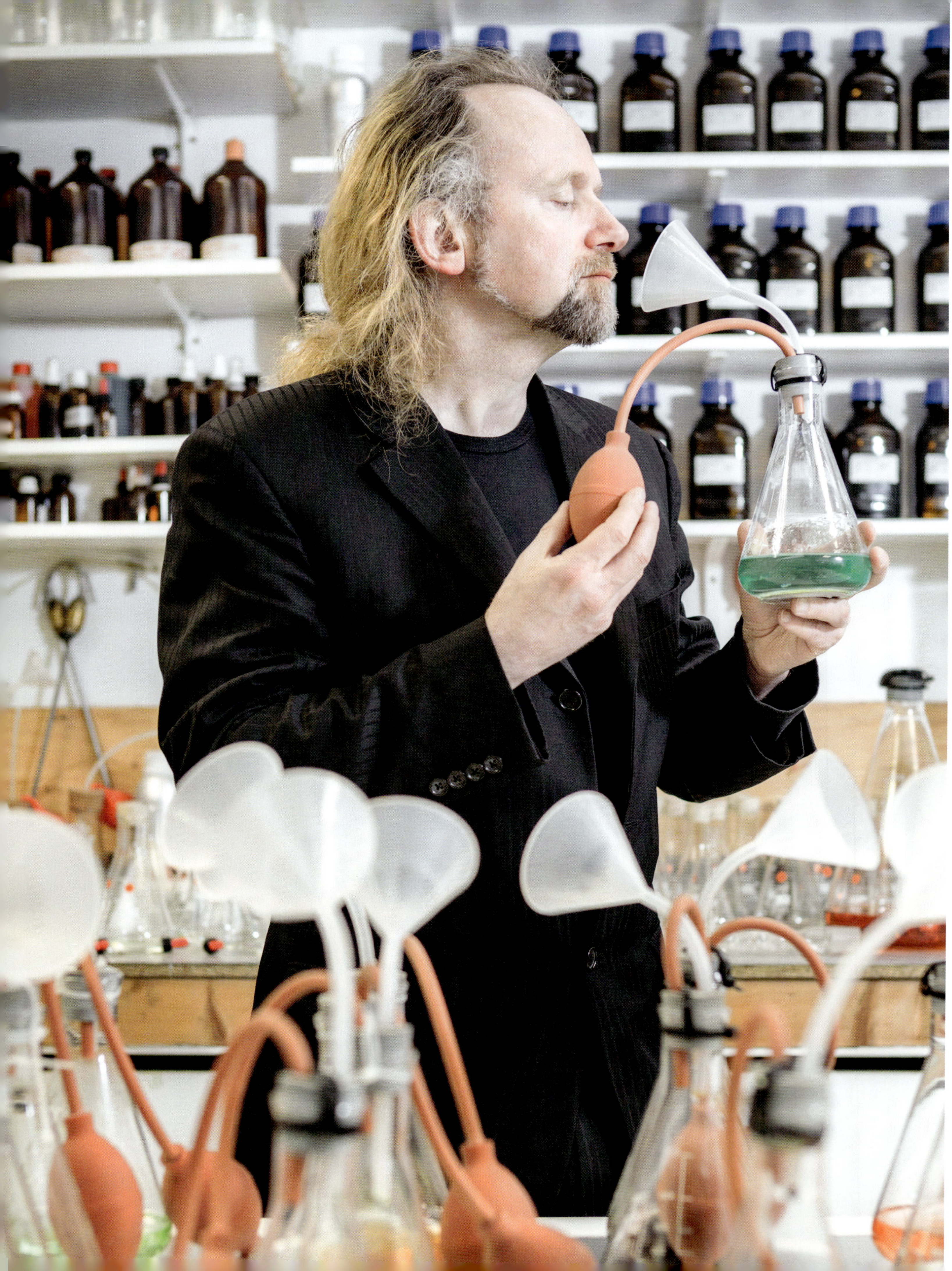

PETER DE CUPERE INTERVIEWED BY ASHRAF OSMAN

A CONVERSATION WITH PETER

Although olfactory art is beginning to attain recognition at a wider level, discussions often still emerge from a common defensive position: the historical (Western) devaluation of smell and its consequent untapped value. This value is often expressed as a reversal of smell's *primitive* status, vaunting instead its unparalleled access to memory, emotion, and other less cerebral parts of our psyche. I will not argue for this; I will assume that's already clear to you, or else you wouldn't be reading this.

I would like to present you instead with a conversation with the most prolific and proactive proponent of olfactory art, artist and curator Peter de Cupere. Even though olfactory art's origins go back nearly a century, it's still not something that most people are aware of or think of as an occupation. So I started by asking Peter how he arrived at his current vanguard position.

A O *Have you always been interested in scent? Were you particularly interested in it as a child? Do you recall any moments growing up where scent played a significant role?*

P D C I started being interested in scent when I was very little, actually, even before I was aware of it. My mother tells me the story that, when I was four years old, she gave me a little drum. At the time, I didn't love strawberries—unlike now—but I always loved the scent of them. I'm not sure if it were the scent or the excitement, but I was cutting the strawberries and putting them on the drum, making sounds with it, but also the smell was coming along. For me that's a kind of artwork, in a way, or maybe a life-statement for myself.

Another thing I liked to smell were earthworms. I would hold them and smell them from one side to the other. I remember thinking that it smelled different on one end from the other. My mother told me that I did it when I was four or five years, but I cannot remember that. I do remember that when I was eight to ten, I was still doing these experiments with them. Also, ladybugs. When a ladybug lands on your skin, it leaves a little scent. It is actually not so nice, but it was very interesting. We had a lot of ladybugs in the garden. I was curious: when you put them on your skin and you push them on their back, they leave a scent. I found it funny and wanted to show it to people, but no one dared to smell it. They said, "No, don't do that!". It was a little odd.

I also remember clearly when I was seven or eight, I hated taking the bus or train because of this mixture of scents and sweat; not everybody takes a shower in the morning. It was the smell of people who were unhappy. Back then I thought the dewdrops on the grass were its fragrance. So I would collect them when they were still dewy: I thought it was easier to get the scent out of them, because I didn't know how to distill in this period. So I would cut some grass and grind it in a vessel from the kitchen. My mother hated it because I didn't wash this tool and grass stained the vessel green. And then I would put the grass smell on me, so my skin always turned a little bit green. I hated that and tried to hide it under a scarf or something. But in the summer it was not possible; and in the summer it was the most successful because it was warmer and the smell was more intense. I liked the reaction of the people on the bus or train. I noticed people would get happy about this fragrance in the morning. This grass fragrance would make people smile in a natural way. I was looking forward to the next day to make the next production. I don't know how long I did it, but I did it quite often.

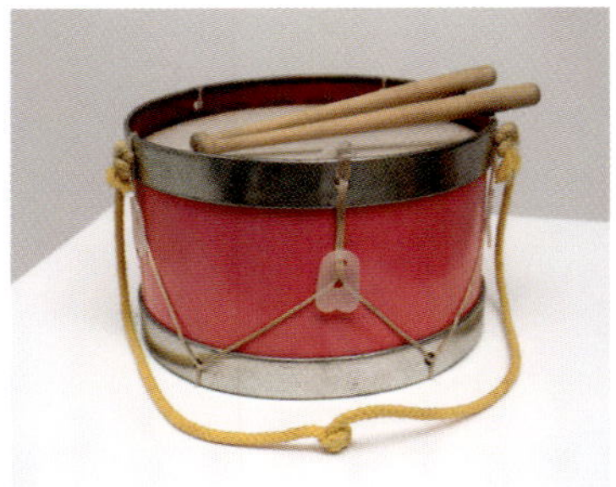

In parallel, I wanted to make perfume, but didn't know how to make it. The easiest thing to do as a child is to take perfumes from your parents or people you know, and start to mix them. It's very childish. And I always put on a lot of fragrance; my friends hated me for it. At one moment I thought I wouldn't do it anymore because everyone found it very girly. When I was a teenager, I tried to hide my love for fragrances from my friends because the reactions were not so nice. I loved to talk to girls about perfume, and they loved the way a man could appreciate that. I was afraid they would find me too girly, so I would talk more about cosmetic products: face masks against acne, to heal it in a very natural way. I was doing quite a lot of experiments with material or substances, trying different mixes. Flower honey didn't work well; it was very sticky. But cornstarch, when you put it on your face and let it dry, your skin gets very soft. These kind of things I loved to do back then.

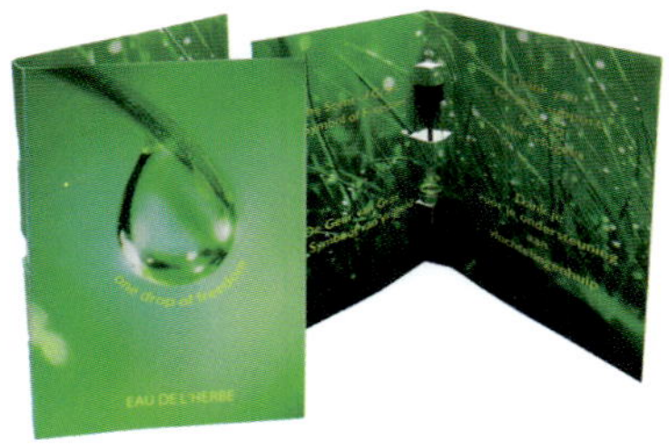

A O *How about your art education: were there any memorable moments where you were first aware of the artistic potential of scent?*

P D C I never thought it was possible to make art with scent. I think the reason why I love to work with fragrance is because I love to see. When I was eighteen, I loved to make drawings; I thought I would become an architect. Not an artist, because an artist could not make money, and I should be realistic. With architecture, it might be possible. But I never became an architect. I studied publicity, marketing, and graphic design. I had a very classical education. I have two brothers and two sisters. My oldest sister and brother were dancing ballet, and my younger sister was playing classical piano. Everyday classical music: terrible, I hated it at that time; it was a kind of reaction. But this classical idea stuck with me: I heard the story about Beethoven, that he got deaf but could still make compositions by just putting his ear on the piano and listening to the vibrations. If I became blind, I would hate it. My eyes are still very well, but as a child I was scared I would become blind.

I was looking for something totally different, and so I came up with scents: how to translate my drawings into fragrances. When I was making drawings of a tree, I would collect leaves from the tree and store them with these little drawings, for

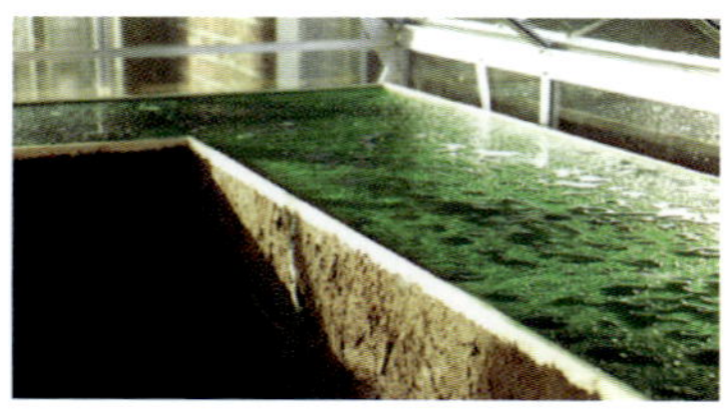

the scent. The leaves dried, but it was the idea how to capture this scent and how to include it in the drawing? But it was not for creating an artwork; it was for making a solution in case I ever became blind: how would I still enjoy my drawings?

A O *How about your practice: When did you go into art more professionally? What was the first work where you included scent?*

P D C I made the decision to become an artist when I was 26. Before this decision I made artworks using pseudonyms; I never want someone to find these out. Terrible work and I didn't qualify these as artworks. I still didn't believe in being an artist, that I could get famous via art. There were several times that I created drawings with scents, by chance. In my early twenties, a perfume bottle fell on the floor of my bedroom, covered with paper drawings. Consequently I got the idea to make drawings with perfumes. But I didn't consider this an artwork. I repeated this action when I was 26, creating drawings with different kinds of perfumes.

You almost don't capture these drawings; you have to hold them into the light to see them. I never exhibited these first artworks because at the time I didn't qualify them as a real artwork.

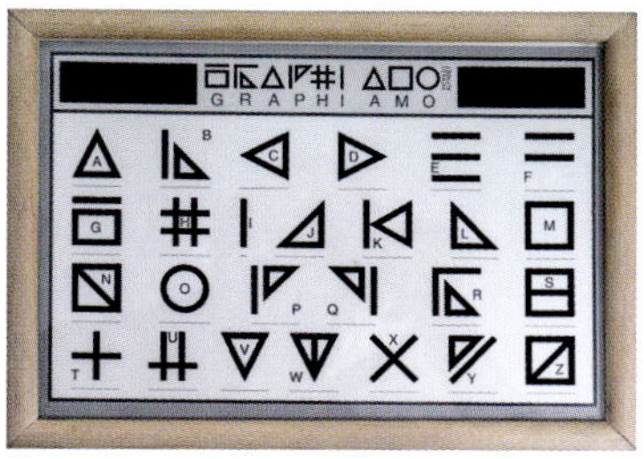

As I said, I first studied publicity and graphic design, and worked as a marketing manager for a toy company. I quickly attained a high position in the company, but I only stayed 10 months. I decided that it was not what I wanted to do and live for; it was too stressful. Everyone around me was saying, "You've changed and are not so creative anymore." It was difficult to quit because the pay wasn't bad. When I quit and decided to study fine arts, everyone said, "You're crazy to do this. There's no future in art; you cannot make money with it. And you have a good job; you should keep it." I could still work as a freelancer for that company because they couldn't find someone else with the same qualifications, and I knew a lot already. During my first year of studying fine arts, I worked in parallel for the company as a freelancer and later finished my masters in fine arts in Brussels.

A O *Was scent a prominent theme in your work during your fine arts education?*

P D C I actually did my thesis at the time on the use of computers and scent interaction. I started with printmaking, etching, and things like that. But I did it for just one semester, because I thought it's too technical, not so exciting. I wanted to do something with computers, but it wasn't possible to learn it in school at that time. There was only one teacher who was a programmer. I was talking with him and he said, "Ok, the second semester, you can come and learn with me." But I had to learn a lot by myself. It's not always apparent in my work, but a lot of my design and thinking is done by computer. For example, in printmaking, I was designing a smell-carpet totally out of herbs. I designed a print for a Persian carpet. using a letter type based on squares, triangles, and circles, and made patterns with it. I designed on the computer and realized the carpet by hand. I printed it out on a large scale on paper, and put different herbs on it. The white was composed of dried coco shavings. The result looks like a very soft carpet, very realistic.

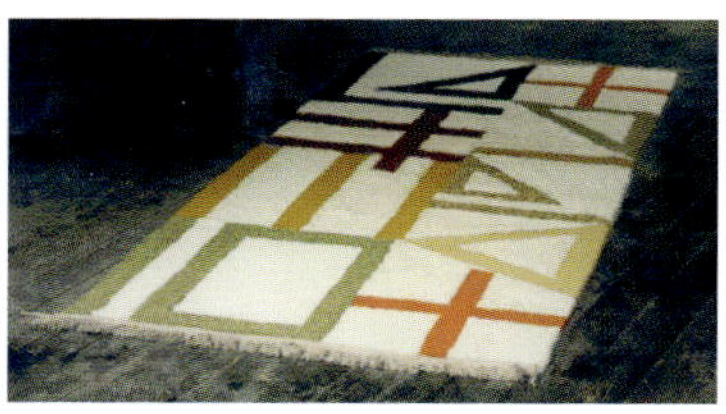

I produced another work called *Your Last Smell*. When we die, we breathe our last smell out. But in this moment you will breathe in your last scent. The artwork is a soap in a fox trap and the face fits inside of it. When you direct yourself to smell the soap, the fox trap snaps on your face. Very morbid!

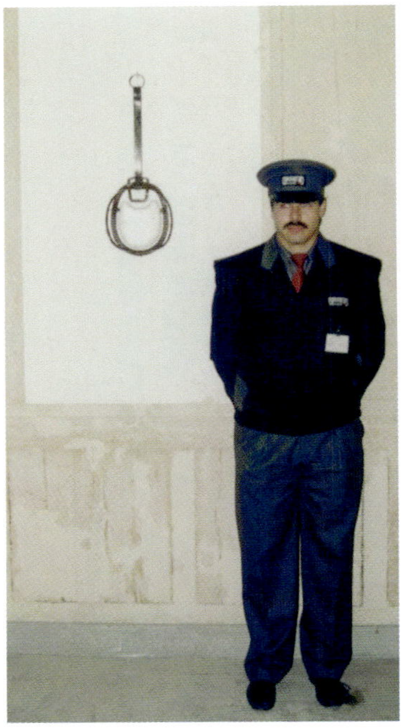

A O *So you were already experimenting with smells while studying, doing your masters. How were the reactions from your teachers at the time?*

P D C Negative. I was studying this aspect in my printmaking classes; at the jury presentation, they just let me pass: I just got enough points. Because they were reasoning computers don't produce art, and smells definitely don't belong in art.

A O *It sounds like it must have been challenging technically, and also theoretically, that they had problems with it, with your seriousness: How worthy is it? Is it really art? Did you have doubts because of these criticisms, that if you continued to work with scents you may not make it? Or did that make you want to work even more with smell?*

P D C Yes and no. I felt lucky. When I got my points at the end of this master, I was dissatisfied because I merely passed. I was so disappointed because, while studying publicity, I was one of the better students. I believe(d) very much in my artwork, so I was angry with my teachers because they were so small-minded, thinking that something done with a computer cannot be an artwork, and smell definitely was excluded from being part of an artwork.

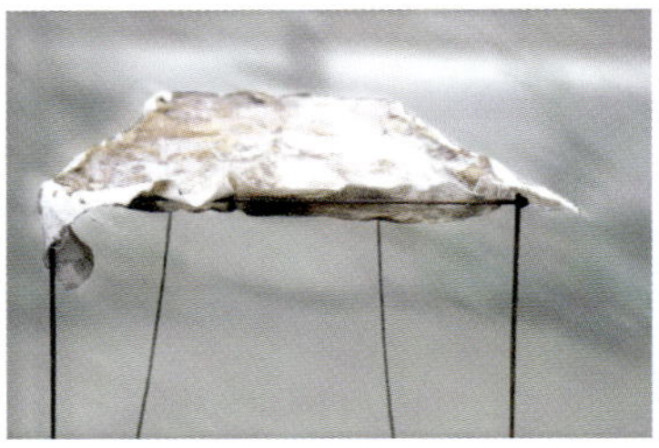

Miraculously I bought a ticket from a lottery game called *Subito*, where you can win 50.000 Belgian francs, around 1.250 euros. I was lucky: I won 50.000 Belgian francs on this same day when I got my degree! It was a paradox: being unhappy with my grade, never buying lottery tickets, winning immediately 50.000 Belgian francs. Quite a lot, especially for a student. I was so excited and phoned home, "It's a beautiful day: I got my master and I won 50.000 Belgian francs." I always think things happen, or we meet people, for a reason. I thought this event was a sign, that I should keep going on with my mission in the art world.

In this period I paid my fees by making portraits at the seaside. They were kitschy portraits, but they sold well; it was just to make money. I excused myself that I was doing this to make money, in order to make my real art. Every summer, I did it for two and a half months and gained enough to live for some months from this money. But I never saw it as an artwork. In fact, I signed the works as Piotr Noart *(No art)*. It's very funny when you receive letters at home addressed to "Cher Monsieur Noart ...". People don't see it, the play with words. In this summer I met a beautiful girl called *Fleur* (flower). She was living in Antwerp, and at the time I was living with my parents in Vertrijk, a village in the middle of Belgium. We were a couple for just one month and ten days, but it was enough to make me realize I must direct myself to Antwerp to be with her. I had to find a reason to do that.

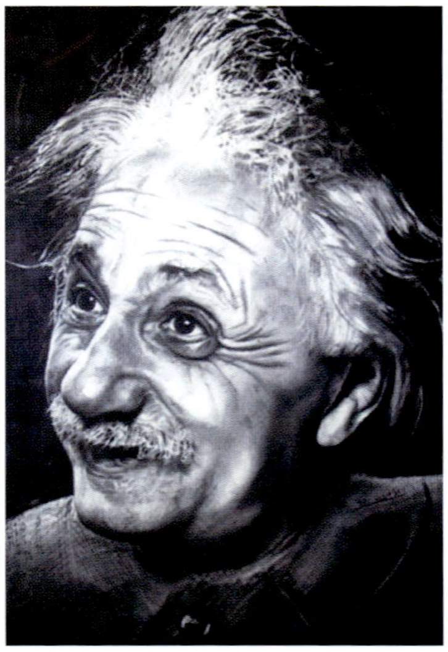

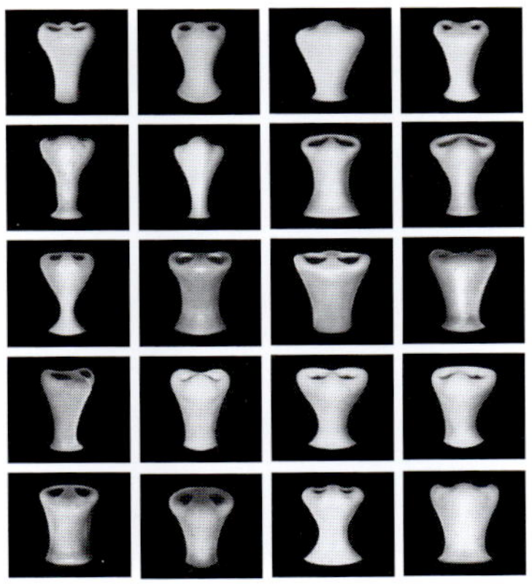

I met a Chinese artist called Lee who was also making kitschy portraits. I showed him my work with scent and computers, and he advised me to apply and get into the Higher Institute of Fine Arts (HISK) in Antwerp. At first, I was not interested but because of my encounter with this girlfriend, I contacted HISK, and they were investing in a new lab with computers for the next period. The selection would be more favorable to artists that work with computers. I made a lively dossier to get into the Institute. I included some of my artworks with scent, but the focus I put on the computer aspects of my art. I got selected!

The day I had to visit HISK to present and discuss my work, I was having dinner with my girlfriend and her parents in the evening. She played classical violin, and was playing for me in her bedroom, with her parents in the next room. She played a piece for me, *Adagio by Albinoni*—so beautiful! Then she said, "Peter, I will take the dog for a walk and won't come home before 10 pm. I hope you'll be gone by then because I want to end our relationship today. I don't know anything about art, but you aspire for it. And you say you have come to Antwerp for me, but that's not true, it's to go to this Institute." And she was actually right. She went out, and I was with her two parents crying all evening; they liked me a lot. But I stayed in Antwerp and went to the HISK and from that moment everything changed for me as an artist.

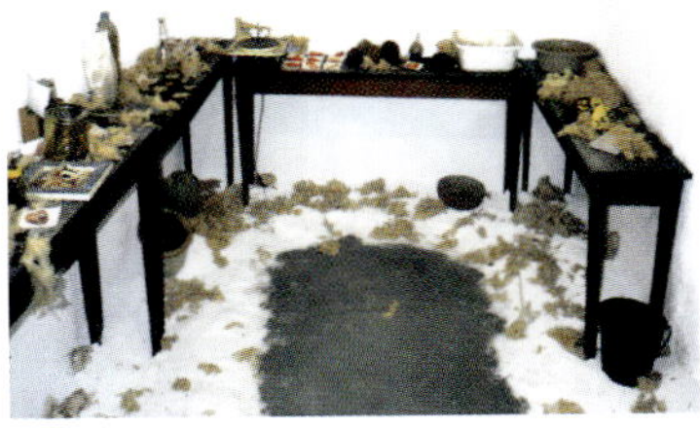

Soon I was lucky to meet Jan Hoet; he showed my work for the first time. He was the first visiting curator at the Higher Institute that believed in the possibilities of scent. He told me, "Peter, the first ten years, maybe fifteen, will be very hard for you. But if you keep going on, you'll find success and it will grow; you'll see. The art world is not ready for it, but I support you, and will buy some works that you cannot sell." These works were even difficult and hard to show at the museum: an installation totally covered with soap (it was just shown once at the opening of the new S.M.A.K. museum where he did a solo exhibition and never shown again) and installations with moldy stuff that didn't smell nice (I don't know even if they exist anymore). They also bought a smoke painting for the collection, *Please Smoke* (2mx2m), 60.000 cigarette butts. People react, "Wow! So many cigarettes; he must be a heavy smoker!". But actually I never smoked.

A O *So, you encountered some positive reactions at the Higher Institute that were more enlightened, especially from Jan Hoet. And in large part, people are more aware of olfactory art thanks to you and other artists like you. Do you feel that the art world has changed since then? Is it more ready now? Both the art world and its audience.*

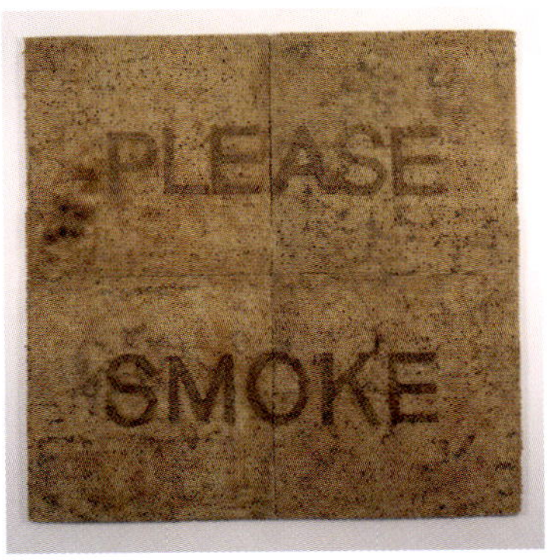

P D C The last couple of years, it is changing a lot, because there's more attention to it, thanks to organizations like yours *[Scent Culture Institute]* putting focus on scents, or *the Institute of Art and Olfaction*, or Caro Verbeek—curators that are focused on it, also writing and publishing about it. I think it is important to write and talk about it, so people can read, learn, reflect and discuss these aspects of art. I think there are still a lot of possibilities and opportunities to create platforms.

A lot of artists are starting to create work in relation to fragrances, experimenting with it. Every week I receive a question for collaboration with artists, but I cannot do that from agenda point of view. It's a pity because I can hardly finish my own works. Sometimes there are beautiful or strong proposals. The attention for olfactory art is living and growing and that is good news. But it's still hard. My advantage is that I've been working during such a long period with all aspects of olfactory art. The short term disadvantage is that I have covered and investigated a broad range and spectre. Because in producing artworks, it works better when you focus on just one part. You could compare it to a painter who has one style, and makes a series of works. I had to find my way: what is technically possible, what material can I use, how long does a material stay scented in an exhibition, how to activate it, what is the scent continuity from it, how the condition of the artwork changes with humidity, with temperature, and all these aspects you have to keep in mind when creating and presenting. And you have to find a way to deal with other artists in the exhibition next to you who are upset because your work gets more attention, just because of the scent. When scent is there, when it is intense, you get more attention; that is the power and impact of scent.

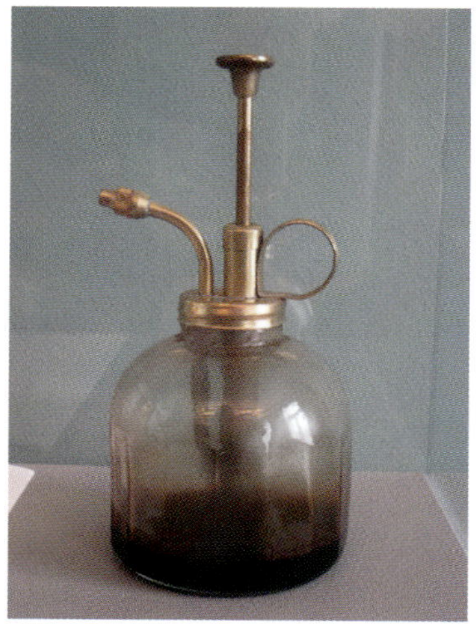

AO *That's assuming the other artworks are not scented artworks, of course; because in more recent exhibitions that have focused on olfactory art, that factor becomes a challenge also in terms of curation: how to present all these artworks together when you have competing smells. So I think this is a new challenge and, in a way, it's a good problem to have. You mentioned a few things I'd like to follow up on, such as the analogy to painting. This is a question I often ask the people in olfactory art I've interviewed: Do you see olfactory art, like painting, as a medium or a technique? Or is it a wider: a genre or a field? Or perhaps we should see it more as a movement?*

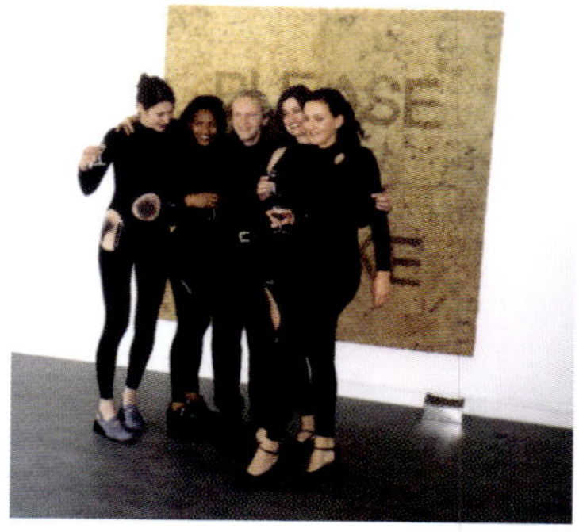

PDC I hope it's not a movement; it's more than that. Of course, it's a medium, but I think it's more than that, too. Paint can also be more than a medium. But that's the advantage of scent: scent can give context by itself. Scent is also like sound: when you hear someone who's scared, you can hear it from the sound of their voice. But when you take the tones separately, you will not hear this. With scent, if you take the molecules apart, you will also not smell it. So it's always the combination: when you smell grass, you know it's grass. But when you show an apple and there's the scent of grass, you believe that it's the scent of apple. The same with kiwi or cucumber or even banana. It's very strange how the perception of scent can be.

It also depends on the visibility. I believe it's more powerful when you combine the senses, in general. When you combine the visual and olfactory, or the knowledge (the title) with the scent, it gives meaning in both directions. It is more powerful than paint by itself. It's not exciting to just watch paintings that only illustrate something; it's more exciting to look at paintings that tell something. I think it's the same with fragrance. It's actually difficult to answer your question, in a way, and it's easy to answer. It's both: it's not that; it's this or/and that.

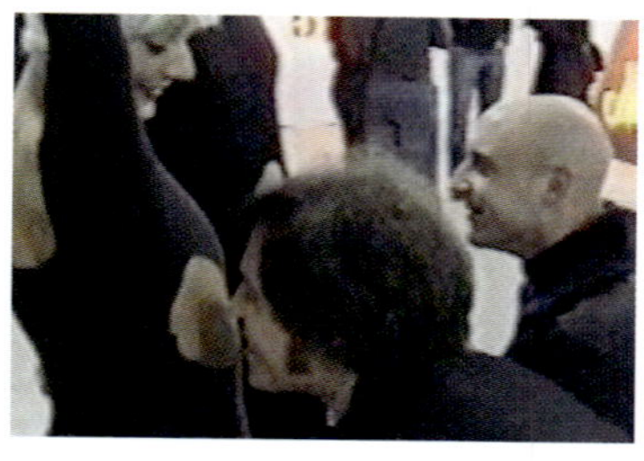

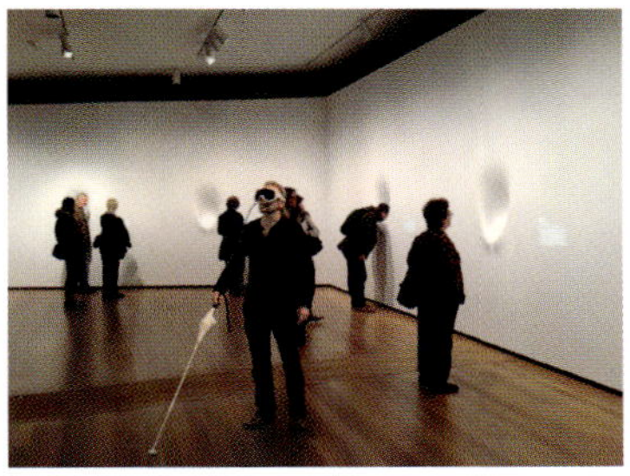

A O As part of the expansion and overlap between the fashion and art worlds in recent years, some in the perfume industry—perhaps seeking cultural legitimization—have used the term "olfactory art" for commercially available fragrances (as in The Art of Scent: 1889-2012 exhibition at the Museum of Arts and Design in New York). Do you find this usage problematic?

P D C I have mixed feelings about that. It can be: what Chandler Burr did is a nice idea, comparing perfume to other art historical *isms*. But I'm not sure you can always do that because, in a way, then you could compare everything to art. What's interesting is that it directed more attention to the use of scent in art. The perfume industry is a big industry, and we need to have scents created. We can do it by ourselves but there are a lot of scents we cannot create as artists. It's getting attention, that fragrance can be more than just perfume. It can be art when it's not something designed or functional anymore, with the purpose to make somebody feel good. It is not aromatherapy, or a scent to make someone beautiful, or give someone a certain attitude; it is more. So I have mixed feelings about it.

I don't like the word *scent artist*; because it's like a magician: an artist with scent that can only work with scent. No, I am definitely a contemporary artist and scent is a medium for me to give context. I prefer the term olfactory art because it is more than just scent. Olfactory means sense of smell, and the word sense has more meaning than just referring to a feeling. It is also about knowledge: it is content; it has a wider attitude. I think people always want to place things in narrow boxes: you're a sound artist, or video artist, etc. I'm also a video artist, I'm also a performance artist, and I'm also sometimes a painter. I'm not painting with oil paint, but with fragrances or cigarettes or soap or even my own sweat.

A O Do you still feel there are parts of this olfactory art genre that you haven't explored, that you can still create new things in it? Or do you think you've exhausted it somehow?

P D C No, I think there are still a lot of possibilities: crazy and unlimited possibilities, also crossing with the senses of touch and taste. I am now working on a tactile work, not really related to scent, but something I want to do for myself. And with scent there are a lot more possibilities; it's amazing what we can do with it. There's so much power, especially with the technology getting better and better, the possibilities for investigation and creation get easier. I am still surprised when you meet scent companies, the technology they use to put scent in buildings is mostly the same, but getting better: it's very easy, very controlled, but they're not exactly aware of the potential and total impact. It's still something of a mystery.

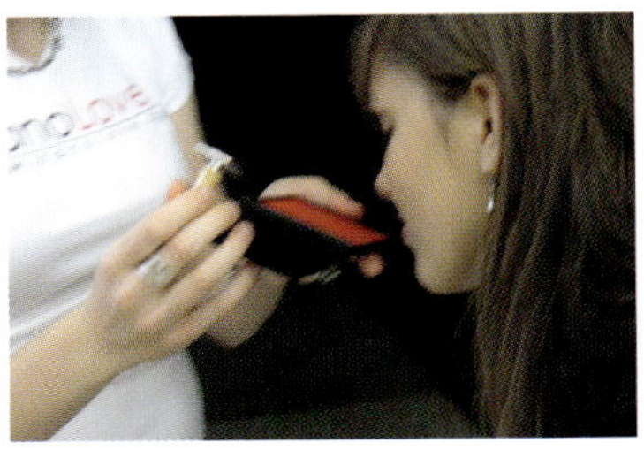

There are still a lot of opportunities to work with the body: a lot of artists do that, work around the body generally, but also the scent of the body. For example, for my *Olfactory Art Manifest* I distilled my own scent. I calculated to extract it in one year, but I didn't manage. My idea was to present my *Olfactory Art Manifest* a hundred years after the manifest of Carlo Carrà, on the 13th of August 2013. But I did it a year later, just because I was working on the scent of my own smell. I wanted to sign the manifest with my smell, to give it context: it disappears and it's there. People will understand it: in the beginning, they smell it; then the scent will disappear after a time, but it's signed with it. It was not a bad scent, but I had just a small quantity. You could save the scent, let it remain, but then you think of conservation: that's also a very interesting question. In the beginning, every year, two or three thesis students sent me questions about how to conserve applied smell. I don't care. You can totally overdo it, but it doesn't have to be. No one will ask Manzoni to open his can of shit; you know what is inside, whether it's there or not; it's the idea, the context of it is more important than the medium.

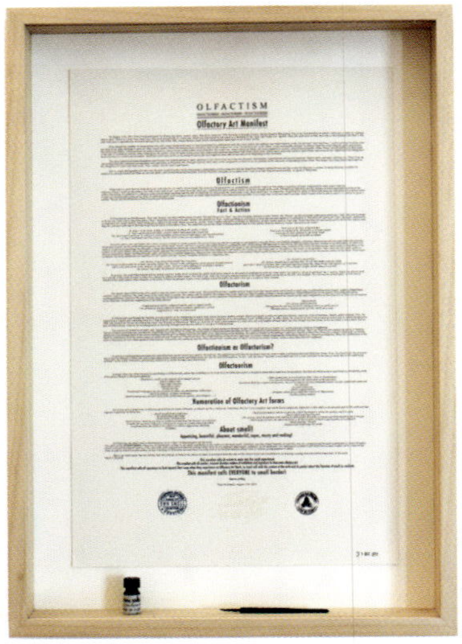

AO *I'm also contacted increasingly by artists with questions, and one thing that I noticed is that a lot of them are not very familiar with the history of olfactory art. Maybe because it's still not taught as part of most art programs around the world, there isn't even a textbook for it. But you have recently established a master's program at PXL-MAD School of Arts called Art Sense(s) Lab, which is the first of its kind to focus on the "lower" senses in art. Can you tell me a bit more about this program and how you see it in the context of your practice?*

PDC The English Master Fine Arts Programme Art Sense(s) Lab actually aims to persuade artists to start working with fragrances. It's my intention that in this master they will learn not how to distill, but how to give context, how to work with scent and the lower senses in general. The year is too short to focus on all the technical stuff; that we do in the bachelor *Open Lab*. They will learn from the beginning how to distill, how to use scents, but also touch and taste, in combination with video, performances, and other media. It is important that there are schools where people can learn it. And I hope it could be a start for other schools in the future, that they will also integrate it in their education. You can translate everything to a scent: you can translate sound, you can translate images, you can do it experimentally, or you can do it with context. You practice it on different levels. I prefer the context level but it doesn't mean that it cannot be just like a feeling, a scent-space where you enter. A kind of mood can also be an artwork when it's done the right way, when it doesn't become aromatic. For example, there are students that apply, for example, from dancing, from performance, photography. Someone that loves fragrances and hasn't worked with it before, but wants to try to combine it with photography. I find it very interesting that there are young artists or students that want to do a master to focus on scent and combine it with their practice.

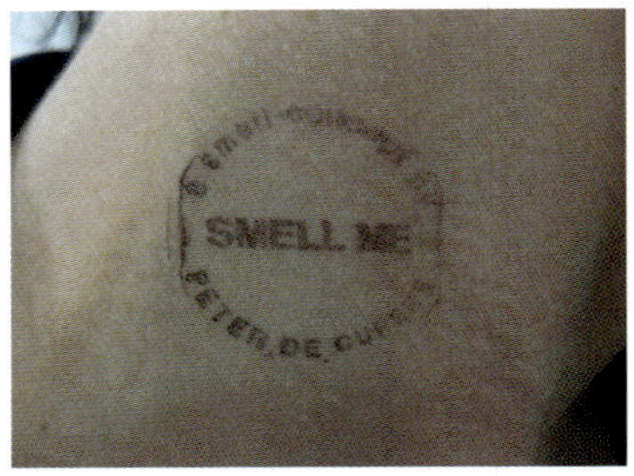

AO *That brings me back to a question about smell's resistance to digitization. Right now, with the rise of the Internet and computers, big data and the internet of things, most sight and sound aspects can be digitized. A lot of museums are going to experiential works as a way to bring in audiences: something that you have to be there in order to experience. Do you think that, in a way, the limitations of smell can actually be a positive for it in the art world, the cultural sphere, or at least the entertainment world?*

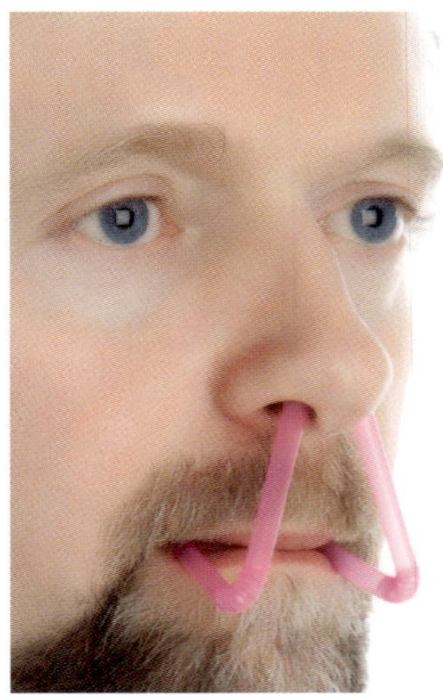

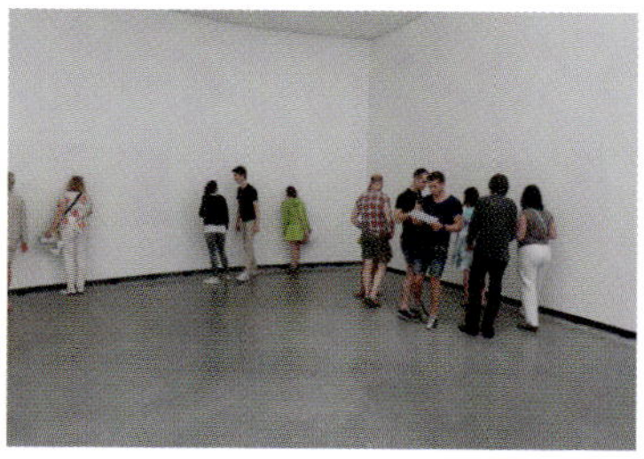

P D C Yes. I hope they don't do it only for that, that they don't show it in a museum because it's, like you said, entertainment. Art is not entertainment, it's thinking and questioning. And you see a lot of museums going into the direction of entertainment because they need a certain quantity of visitors. That's a pity in one way, but I know we cannot stop it.

Every time I present a solo exhibition I get so many visitors. There is so much attention. I think it's the power of scent, because people like to be confronted, want to experience, learn and think. Also children: a lot of families want to go; they find that it's something new. It's still new for a lot of people. And for schools it's very interesting because then they have all the senses that they can work around. In one way, it's very attractive to work with scents, and to show the result in museums. But on the other hand, I actually don't think that you go less to museums because of the Internet. The Internet is very informative, but when you see a big painting or sculpture, it's totally different when you stand in front of it than when you see it on a monitor. The Internet is a channel when you are not able to visit in person; but I try whenever I have time to visit exhibitions. It's getting less and less possible, it's a pity; the disadvantage of being busy. I did 27 projects last year. And still there are a lot of things to research and experiment, a lot of things to arrange, and of course a lot of scents to discover and to smell.

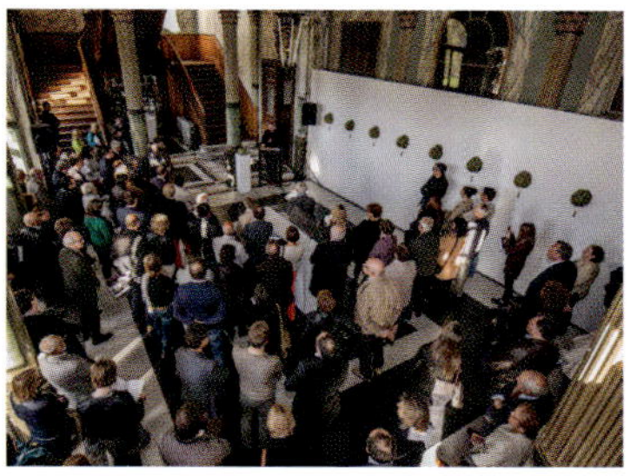

A O This conversation could have gone on a lot longer, and in fact, it did. But there's a limit to what we can include here. And as a wise person once said, "Always leave them wanting more." And conversations with Peter, like experiencing his work, does leaves one ingeniously both sated and hoping that there's still plenty more to come.

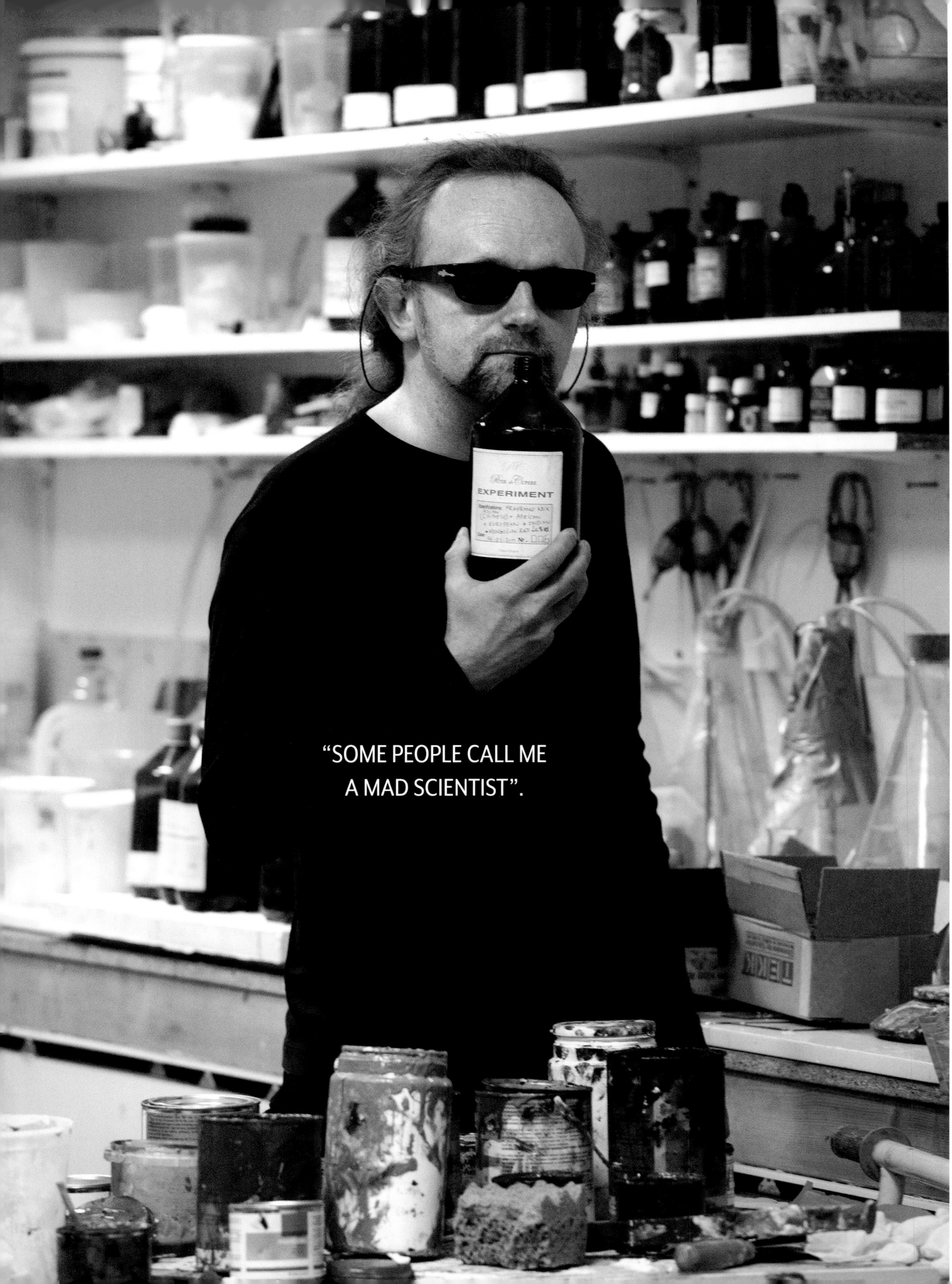

“SOME PEOPLE CALL ME
A MAD SCIENTIST”.

PETER DE CUPERE

OLFACTOLOGY LAB

ABOUT A PIPETTE, A FUNNEL AND A GLOVE

The concept 'laboratory' is an important element in my work, in which I see the world as one great laboratory with different locations that need to be analyzed olfactorily and can be translated visually into art experiments and installations.

A pipette, a funnel and a glove are for me references, symbols to our society. I use often funnels in my works where the shape is referring to the concept of a 'Flower'. The 'Flower' as both smell-producer and ideal of beauty, is for me not only important for the olfactory approach to the understanding of the flower, but also as a horn shouting towards society, a translation of my olfactory impression in a more visually aesthetical manner. For me, this flower can also be an opening in the ground or wall which emits a smell; think for example of a sewer or an air pipe in the wall; but I also see a kitchen exhaust system as the idea of a 'Flower' which spreads to the external world the smell of cooking and the bodily smells of different cultures. Other examples could be a car exhaust pipe or a factory chimney. The glands in the skin of a body, the hairs of the armpit, even genitals could also be seen as flowers in the meaning of a metamorphosis. If one can experience the notion of 'Flower' in this way, then one will understand that this idea is closely related to the relation between society and culture. The flower is seen here more as translation and distribution mechanism than as a real flower. So is a funnel also a distribution mechanism and can it stand for the 'concept' of a flower. It is the point where all smell comes together or is distributed to the world.

The pipette measures and is an important instrument in my laboratory to mix fragrances. I see the pipette as a reference to my concept of a 'laboratory' which is also an important element in my work, in which I see the world as one great laboratory with different locations that need to be analyzed olfactorily and can be translated visually into art, experiments and installations. This analysis can go from the determination of certain olfactory aspects of a city to even the registration of the olfactory differences between various cultures, and from there, eventually making a mixture which can be translated once again into a visual work. The relationship, society/culture versus nature/environment is an important area of research in my work. In addition, there are the—at first glance—more obvious investigations into smell and plants, for which mentioned is the concept 'Flower' an important starting point. The glove refers to the cleanliness and research and experimental aspects in my work. I experiment with every possible use of smells like a contemporary

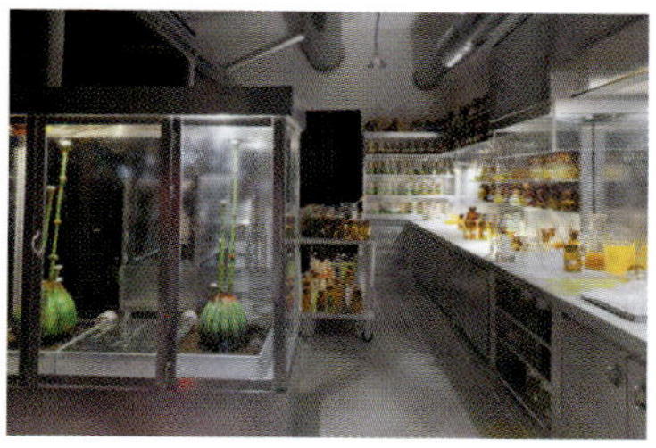

alchemist. Odorous material can vary from essences used in the composition of perfumes to aromas used in food, to odors that arise from diverse materials through experimentation. The moment I put surgical gloves on is the moment I feel one with the work I'm doing. But it's also a way to create distance between me and the object. It is a protection for my skin but also not to make the work to subjective. For this reason I find my drawings more subjective because I always use my fingertops to feel the graphite on the paper.

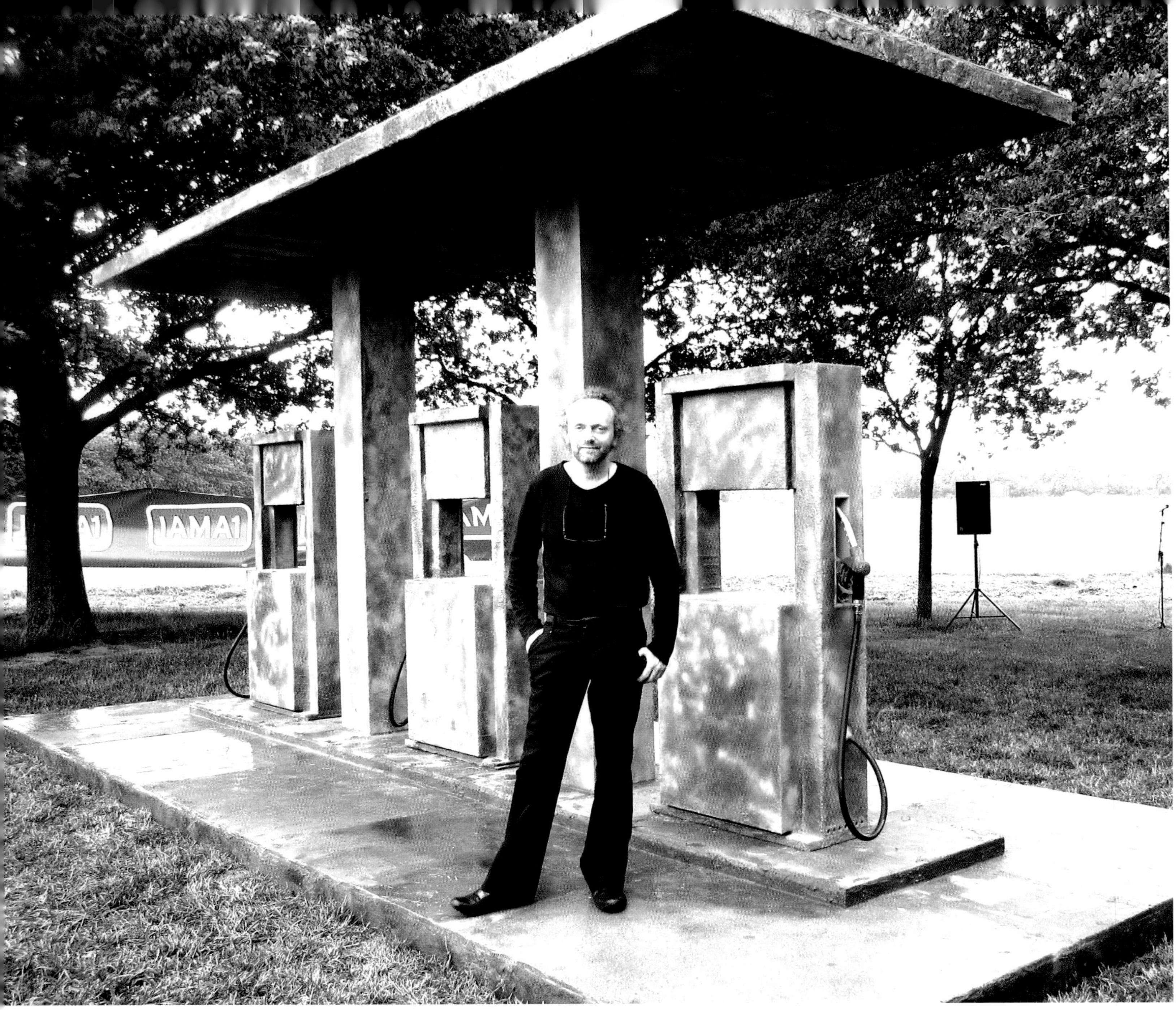

KÓAN JEFF BAYSA

A QUOTE

If there's any artist who has pushed the primacy of the olfactory sense out of the horse latitudes and into the limelight in the present, it is Peter de Cupere of Belgium, whose extraordinary scent formulations in installations and performances in museums, galleries, and innovative spaces from Belgium to Havana have made us finally come to our senses!

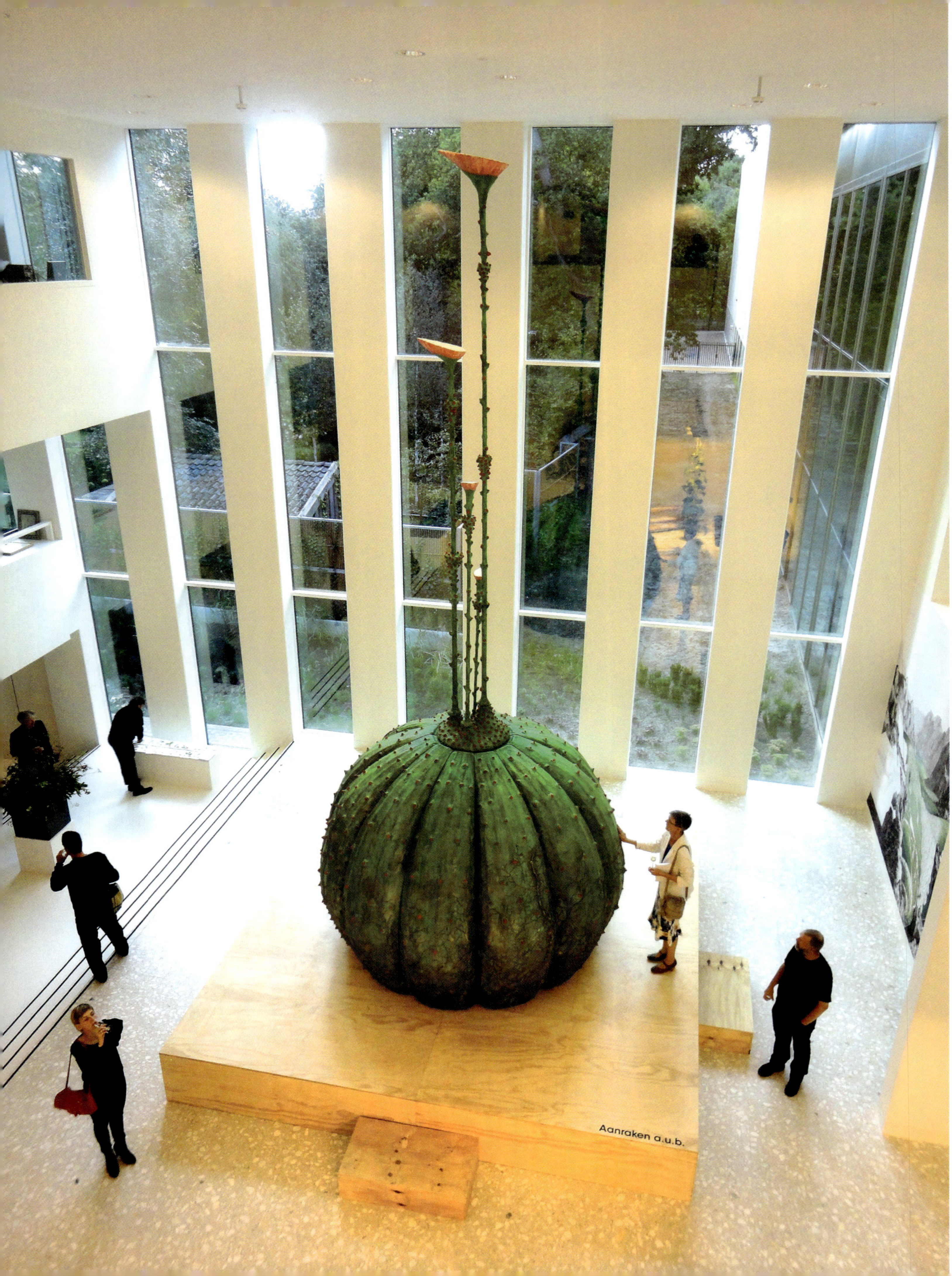
Aanraken a.u.b.

PETER DE CUPERE

THE USE OF SMELL IN ART, AN 'OLFACTOLOGY' ART RESEARCH

My passion for smell goes back to my youth and this passion has eventually expressed itself in my professionalism as a visual artist. I have been using smell as a medium in my works for several years now, and I would love to share my vision and attitude towards the use of smell in visual arts. I like to do this by means of my visual art. The use of smell in exhibitions is not always evident, since you are dependent on the conditions of the location of the exhibition.

As a visual artist working with smells for over 20 years, I have encountered several technical problems in relation to smell activation and smell continuity of a work in an exhibition.

The technical aspects are subsidiary to the context and concept of the work, but they form an important part in the success of the work since the message of the produced work stands or falls with the execution of the work.

Activation of smell at the exact moment and guaranteeing the continuity of the smell during the course of the exhibition depend on multiple factors. For instance, the choice of the (chemical) composition of the smell, i.e. is it based on oil or water, or is it in the form of powder, or is it scratch & sniff, etc. depends amongst others on the humidity, temperature, wind displacement, size and shape of the location and the material used and the interaction with other smells. Besides these technical aspects, one also has to take into account the perception of the looker or sniffer. Smell primarily works on the recollection and prior conditioning, and the social and cultural context can also determine the choice.

To promote the use of smells in visual arts, it is important that one knows how to use these technical limitations, in order not to longer see them as an obstruction, but to take this into account during the development process.

My research starts completely from my own practice. I have created over 200 works in the past 20 years and these have been exhibited with the use of active smells. I would like to show, through reference to my works, that the use of smells opens up perspectives to a broader look at art, but also to shine the light on the status of smell as art medium. It is my opinion that smell *in se* can already work visually without showing a visual piece of art. Synesthesia is not far away. By showing the different applications of smell through reference to my visual art, I hope to contribute to a broader look at the use of smells in visual arts. Smell has too long been seen as only a lower sense. I would prefer to say that 'it is a higher sense'. But how can smell be applied in visual arts? Which are the possible problems in the use of smell in exhibition models?

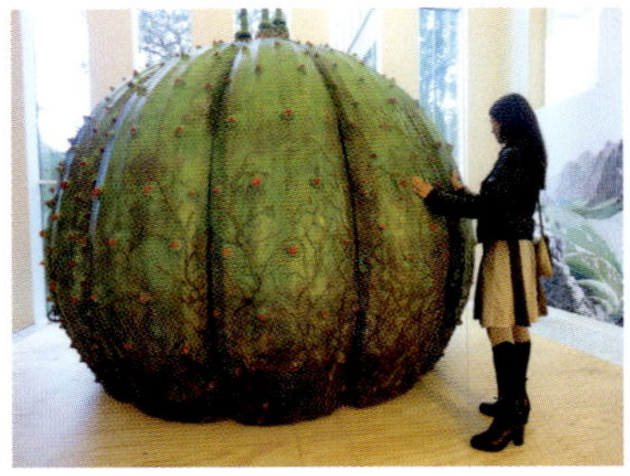

How to create a context around art through a smell? Since 1995 I have been experimenting with smells in multiple manners. I cannot imagine a work without smell and have therefore found a way to apply scents to all sorts of media such as sculptures, installations, paintings, drawings, prints, videos, happenings and performances.

A sculpture like *Flower Fragum Cardamomi* measures 9 meters high and is the first scratch & sniff sculpture in the world. The problem with scratch & sniff when it is used on a hard smooth underground like the epoxy material used to realise this flower, is that it vanishes fast. So we had to find a way to make it more resistant, so the scratch & sniff would last for years. We also managed to realize this.

The idea that scratch & sniff disappears on hard smooth surfaces when scratched a lot gave me the idea to make this work I did for an exhibition called *Ephemere*. In front of a famous painting *The Beet Harvest (De Bietenoogst, 1890)* by the Belgian artist Emile Claus, who died in 1924, I placed a safety glass with normal scratch & sniff paint on it; the paint smells like the earth on the painting. The smell is of earth from that time, not the smell of earth from our time, so without influence of pollution. Therefore when people scratch the surface to smell, the smell is taken away and they can see the painting through the glass a little bit more. It is a kind of reflection on the society, in that by hurting the surface of our mother earth, we even change the original smell such that it might eventually disappear. Outside was the same work in front of a grass field. The scratch and sniff smelled here of real unpolluted grass.

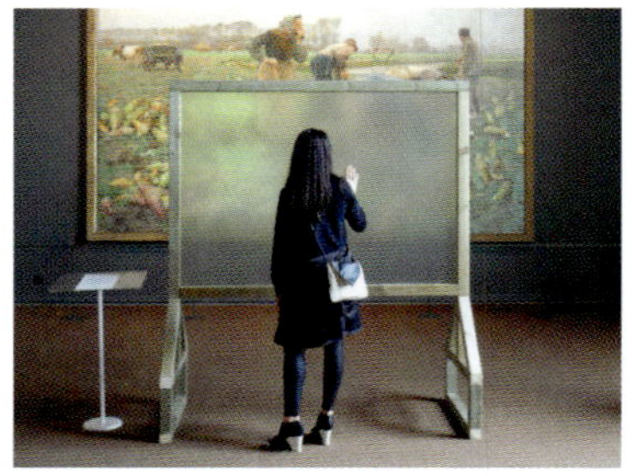

Sometimes is a work not what it seems to be.

A smell-installation like *Smoke Room*, comprising 750,000 used cigarette butts has an amazing terrible smell that only hard smokers can maybe love. But in order not to have a problem with the Belgian public health authorities we first had to take this terrible cigarette smell away and replace it with fake cigarette smoke that was more based on a mix of exhaust smoke in combination with asphalt smell and smoked bacon fragrance. The visitors, however, really believe that the smell is coming from the original cigarette butts. We did the same with the work *Smile Room*, which was a room covered with toothpaste. The problem here was to find the right toothpaste to use. We did tests with 122 different toothpastes; only one brand was usable and did not crack after some days drying in different temperature and humidity conditions. We would have needed 3,400 tubes of toothpaste to make this piece of work. Buying the toothpaste would have been possible but there was no guarantee that it would

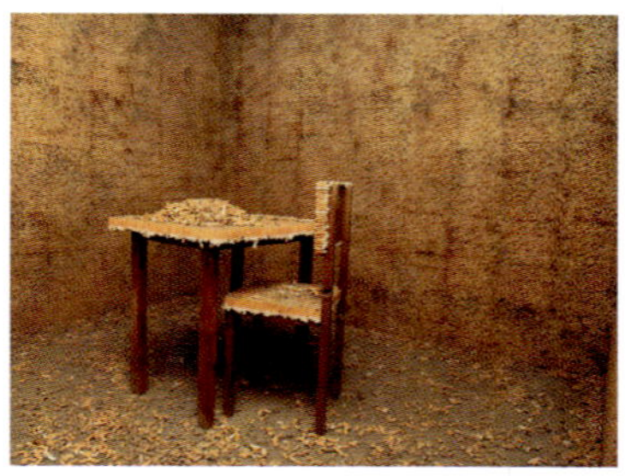

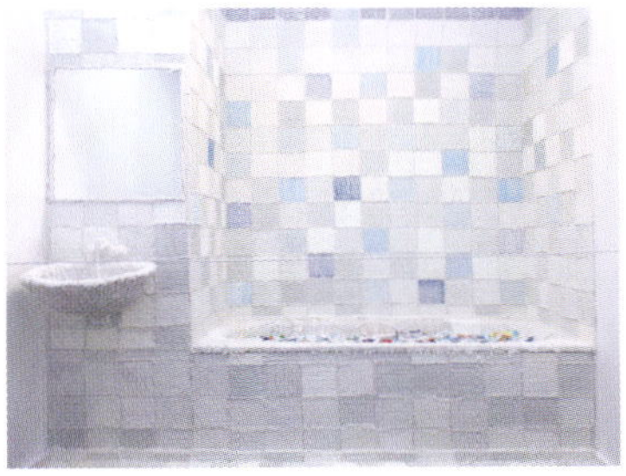

retain its dried shape and that the smell would retain its intensity after days of exhibiting. Sponsorship might have been a temporary solution. However, we decided to fake the whole installation. We made moulds of toothpaste tiles and poured our own fake toothpaste made out of PU-components to cover the room. It was much cheaper than buying the suitable brand of toothpaste. I can now show it many times without the worry that the smell will go away. The intense added peppermint fragrance makes the visitors believe that they are watching real toothpaste and they are amazed by it.

It's like a movie: if you want to enjoy it, you must believe it.

I'm extremely fascinated by the possibilities and the future of the use of smell. In 1997 I invented the *Olfactiano*, the first smell piano; there is no sound, only scents. In 2004, I presented the *Olfactiano VII*, which could play for a larger audience. IFF was the sponsor for the smells of this first smell concert I did in Brussels.

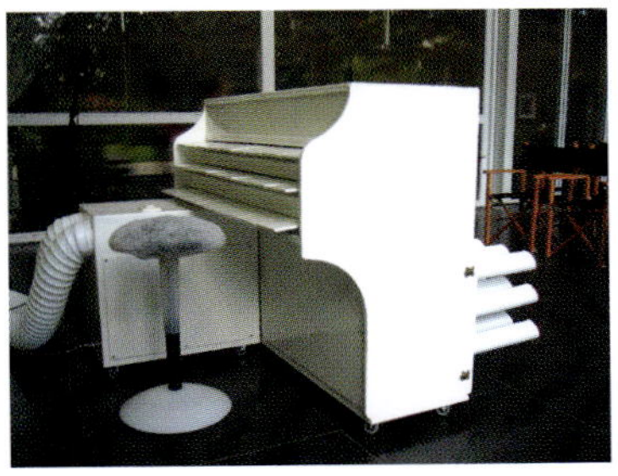

One concert might take 7 to 15 minutes, depending on the space dimensions, but also the temperature and humidity in the room. The first idea was to compose sentences with smells based on a research I have done on creating a smell alphabet. So this *Olfactiano* had 26 smell distributors and one for fresh air. 8 base notes, 9 middle notes and 9 top notes. The only problem are the people, as they are not used to just sniffing around. Most of them were more concerned about working out, 'What is this smell?' than standing open to enjoy the composition through time, because that's what it actually creates: a perfume created through the fragrances that are mixed in the room.

I find that a perfume *in se* can be a piece of art when it serves the correct context. This context can either be an aesthetic experience, linked to a social setting or anything else.

My work is mainly about environmental problems such as air pollution, like the work *Air Polluter* where visitors can decide how intensely they can pollute the air with bad and/or good smells. Or in *Garbage City Holiday Park*, where they can stay in a well/pleasantly perfumed house made of garbage that normally would smell intensively bad, but instead with a nice smell of nature. The next day they can make their own pleasant smelling garbage house in a workshop, so other people can come and stay in their creation for a night.

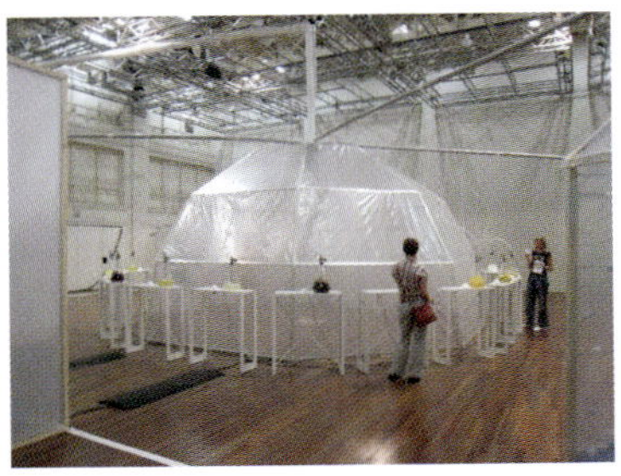

Another work that lets people reflect on pollution is *Scentedo* [2], a fake fuel station exhibited next to a highway, where visitors can smell grass, lavender, bubblegum or the nasty smell of the exhaust gasses of cars.

Other contexts of my work relate to social and cultural aspects such as respecting different races, nationalities, identities and preferences. I don't call myself a 'nose' but I am strongly interested in the study of smell and the use of it in combination with situations, materials and creations.

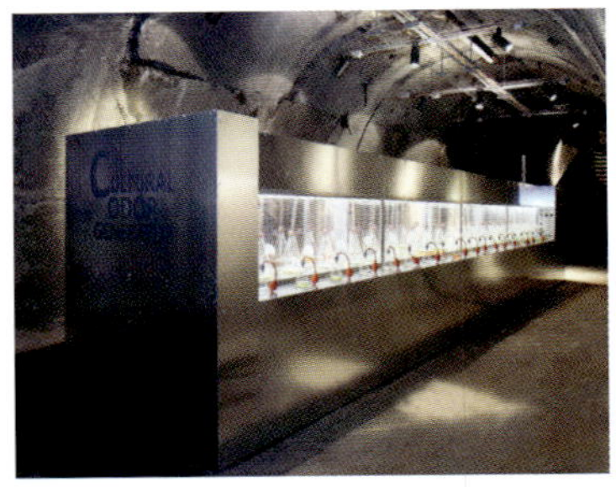

Cultural Odor Generator deals with smell integration in society and uses a collection of smells based on over 100 nationalities who inhabit Genk, a city in Belgium. Based on these nationalities, 40 smells were selected. This work remained open to visitors for 2 years in the former coal mine site, C-Mine, under the ground. Visitors could select smells based on their preferences, which mixes the previously selected smells of previous visitors, through the use of computer software. Afterwards you can fill an air balloon with this mix of smells and take it home. *Cultural Odor Generator* leaves the visitor to reflect positively about the mix of smells which was created by the different cultures which the nationalities brought with them. The main problem with this installation is the temperature and humidity in the space. Smells react differently depending on temperature and humidity, so to guarantee the intensity and quality of the fragrances, the fragrances must be checked often and the temperature must remain at the same level.

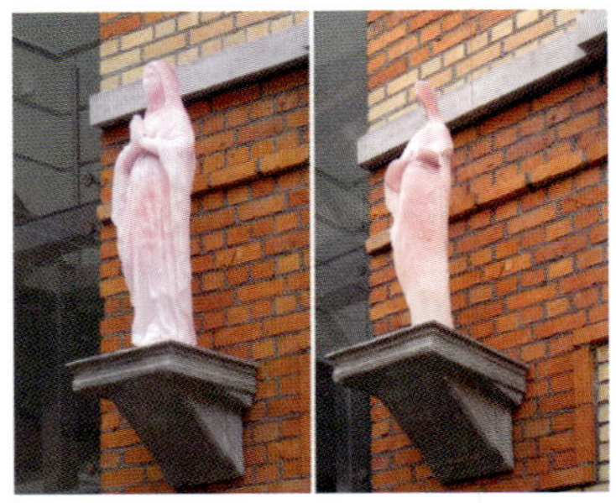

Let us therefore now have a look at a specific work where the smell of the product was used to create work with a scent.

Model for disappearing art is a Madonna that disappears in one to one and a half months when in contact with air and the warmth of the sun. So the sculpture sublimates, changes from a fixed material into a gas. During the sublimation process it almost starts to look like a work of Alberto Giacometti.

The used material is para-dichlorobenzene, better known as disinfectant urinal blocks. Para-dichlorobenzene is not easy to form into shape. This material melts at 56 °C and burns at 63 °C; 20 % evaporates. The team that realized the sculpture wore special masks and safety clothes. So don't try to make this at home!
In 2000 I made a tree of this material, called *The Right Tree*. Visitors were allowed to urinate on the tree. To exhibit such a work of 1,000 kg made out of this material requires an environmental permit. In fact we did not need a permit to show the work in the natural park in Sonsbeek in the Netherlands, but did need permission to allow people to urinate on the tree. Because too much urine at one place can be harmful to nature, we had to add an underground collection system for the urine. Some days there were more than 200 people urinating on the same tree, so you can imagine the smell. The underground collection system had to be emptied at regular intervals.
Smell has unbelievable possibilities that still need to be explored in the art world.
I love flowers and trees; they are a kind of visual reference for me. I love that people show respect for nature. What shows more respect than to start crying at seeing nature?

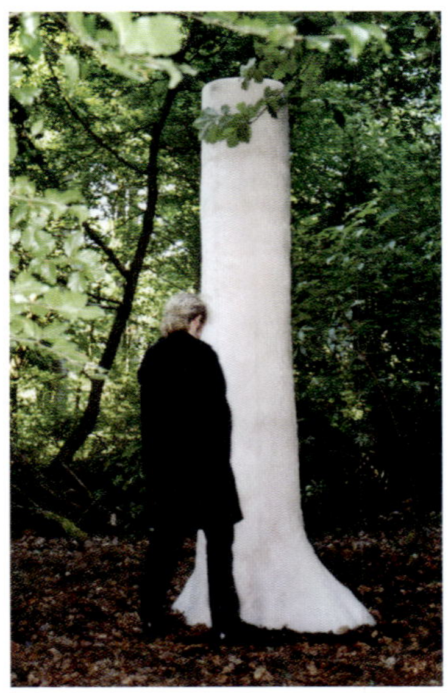

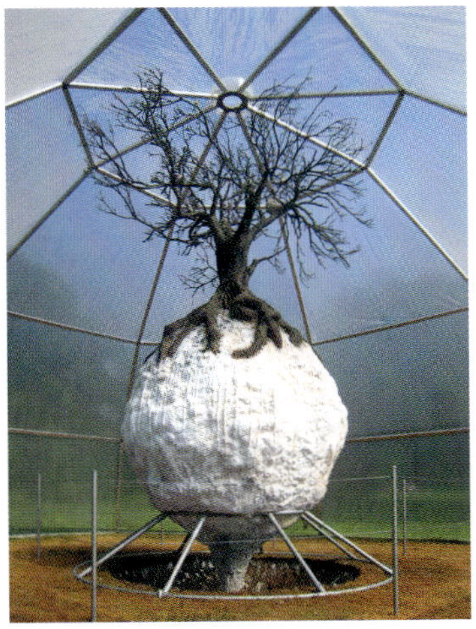

In the installation *Peppertreeduplicateballs PTDB-tree virus* people start to cry just by smelling the strong scent of peppermint. The scent is actually a combination of peppermint and black pepper together with a secret product that doesn't harm at all. The temperature inside this hemisphere must be around 39 °C to make the reaction between the fragrances and this secret product work. They are amazed that the tears are coming out of their own eyes just at seeing this work. They feel the reaction of the smell in their eyes, but can also smell that it is a fresh smell and not dangerous, so they let their tears flow. The same scent was used in the installation *Scented Tears* in *The Olfactory* in 2014 where visitors enter an empty space to see each other starting to cry. They became the artwork for each other.

Other works with trees include *The Olfactory Tree*, a tree made of epoxy and 9 metres long. This tree looks so real, not only through the visual, but more through the structure that makes people believe that this is a real tree. You can look inside the tree to see a little version of the same tree but this mini tree smells like being burnt. With the smell installation *Sick Trees* you have the opposite. This installation smells like a hospital. The smell of a disinfectant, such as a product used to clean hospitals, lets people reflect on the miss shaped forms of the trees, referring to human figures.

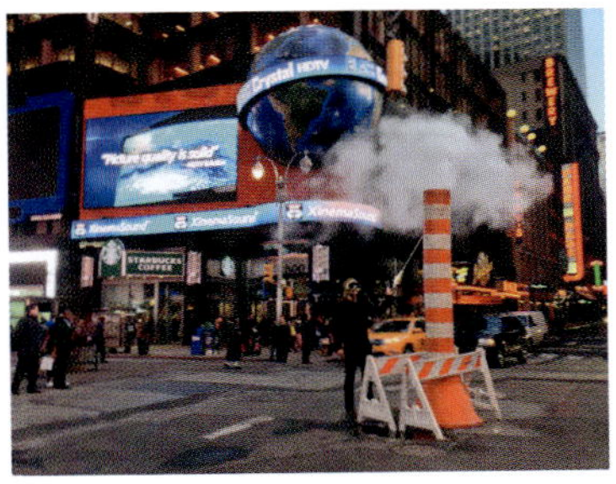

In conclusion I also want to show you the advantages that the use of smell can give to society. With the *Blind Smell Stick* and *Blind Smell Touch* people can experience a place just by navigating through smell. It offers the possibility to help blind people to find their way in the city, or to just give them a smell sign that there is something nasty like a dog faeces lying on the ground, so they won't step on it! But also imagining that every street has a specific smell. It would be great to walk on Fifth Avenue and smell not the car exhausts but the smell of grass or even the smell of a mighty flower like an orchid. And when there is a crossing you might smell some burned meat just to warn you that you have to watch out. Life would be more beautiful if smell was more educated and commonly used in society. And art can give a meaning to it. So start using smells in art and keep on smelling.

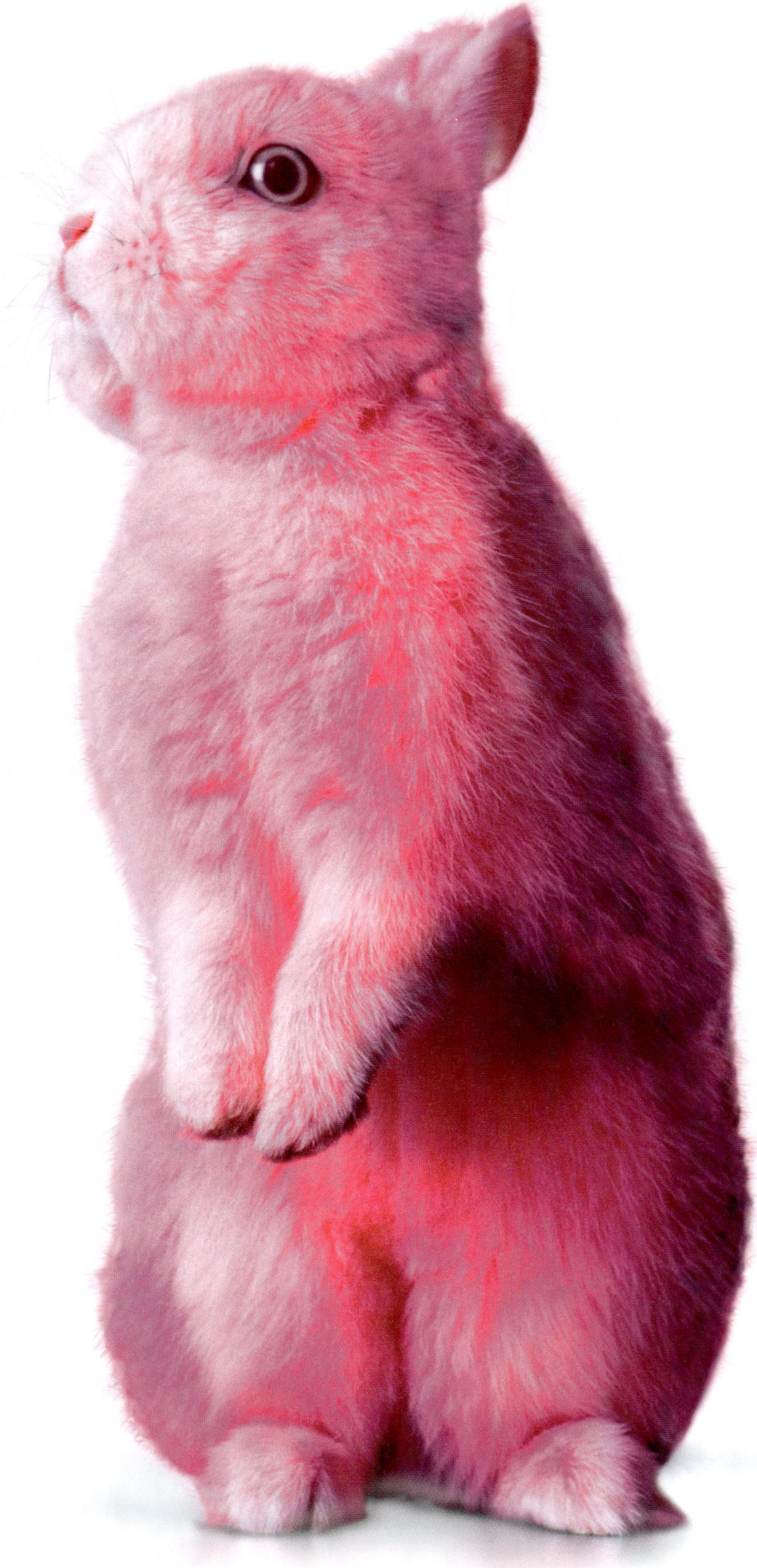

WILLEM ELIAS

PETER DE CUPERE IN EVERY COLOUR AND SCENT

INTRODUCTION

Peter de Cupere noses around the world.

Peter de Cupere is fond of the horn of plenty, though he also understands artistic austerity. This versatility in the application of earlier achievements is after all a characteristic of the generation of artists that first made their mark in the 1990s. But his work is also an exuberance, without ever going overboard. No staleness, but measured free rein.

An artist like Peter de Cupere is impossible to pigeon-hole. The 'multi' of his medium use is important. Nothing is foreign to him, it may even rot, go mouldy, evaporate, stink, have sat in ashtrays, a messy pup indeed. Among the artists who want to transform everything into art, there are many who lament being pigeon-holed, tied to their own discipline: painting, sculpture, music, theatre, dance, etc. Of course, many attempts have been made to break down these barriers. It is even an important feature of modern art and even more so of postmodern art. Nevertheless, the attempt to arrive at an all-round spectacle is invariably linked with Wagner, who gave this phenomenon the name *Gesamtkunstwerk* (synthesis of the arts), which is still in use today. The work of art that has rediscovered that its origins lie in celebration. But Wagner forgot the nose, unless the perfumed opera audience provided sufficient smells.

One all-round spectacle that did not forget the sense of smell, and which as far as I know is the oldest example of a work of art that uses the nose to see better, was performed only once on 15 October 1581 in Paris. On that day, the director Balthasar de Beaujoyeulx—a man who, it's true, had not stolen his name from Italian but had Frenchified it—put on a show for a thousand guests at a wedding party. The genre was later labelled *Ballet Comique*, not because it was full of jokes, but because it summoned one to take a joyful attitude to life. Nowadays, we would say 'You only live once'. The novelty was that he brought together all the art forms known at that time and wove them into an artistically worthwhile and attractive whole: music, song, dance, splendid set and costumes, and speeches. But the highlight was carrying onto the stage a three-part fountain from which scented water flowed. The patron, Queen Catherine de' Medici, was also seated on the same wagon.

Perhaps this historical example of using smell in art has little to do with Peter de Cupere's body of work. It does however show the rarity of the attention being paid to the sense of smell in artistic matters. His work is also not an ode to the joyful life. It is concern about the question of whether life can still be joyful? Have we not already consumed too much? We therefore have to place it in its actuality, in the very social-critical reflection of many artists, who were developing in the 1990s and who show us what we are doing to nature, or, more catastrophically, have already irrevocably done. If I look around internationally for kindred spirits, I think of the British *Saatchi artists*, including Damien Hirst, the man who exhibited parts of dead animals. His issues are indeed life and death. Or the Chapman brothers, who show all that can go wrong with genetic manipulation, so that noses become penises. Or Sarah Lucas, who became famous for her *Au Naturel*, an old mattress with an empty bucket and two melons next to a cucumber and two oranges that refer to the faded joy of the love relationship. The American artist Matthew Barney should also be mentioned. He starts from the body to build a new mythology around it through a wordless film full of music that specifically questions the boundaries of this body.

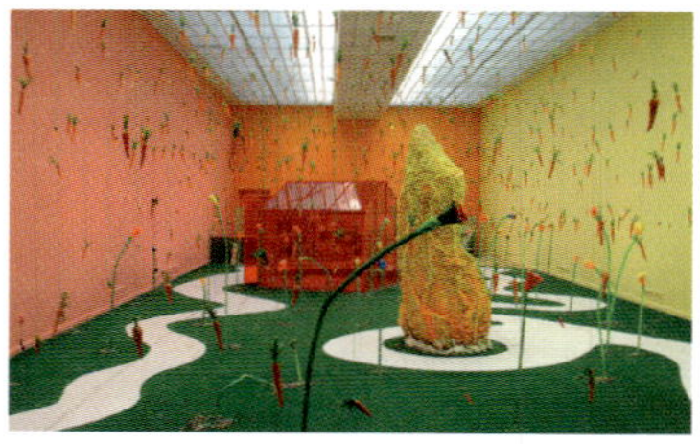

Peter de Cupere does indeed fit in with this generation of postmodern artists who do not focus on their own work on the wall that is there to look at whether or not it is valued. They tap into the whole environment that the observer, who at that time is really no more than a 'spectator', because that is a purely visually charged word, but is a 'perceiver' in an artistically activated room. The art literally surrounds the public that has become a participant. The 'installation' is within this 'environment' art and is therefore the art form of choice to generate this all-round experience. Art is no longer an initially strange thing that can be viewed from a distance. It is a foreign environment, like that of the dream that is experienced as more fictitious, or like that of the memory that is relived. The 'postmodern' in all this is indeed the frequent perspective.

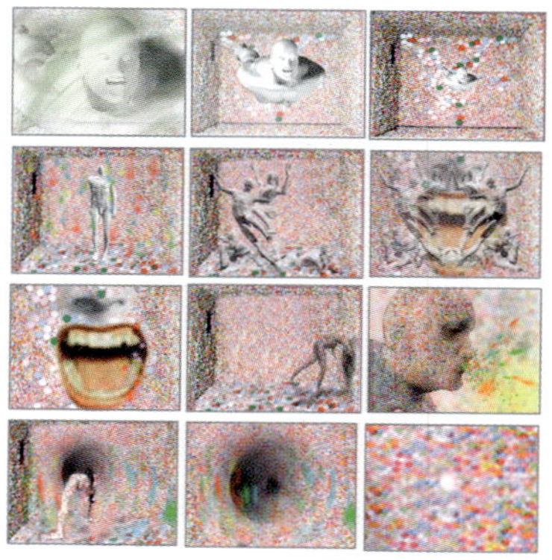

Art as a pluralism, as a refuge with its own rules is therefore closer to the celebration, to the circus even, the fancy-fair and the hall of mirrors. All places where can one can pick up trivial experiences outside, the world of the other.

Peter de Cupere prefers to situate his work in the sphere of what is called 'multimedia'. The current definition is: "multimedia is the key word, and refers to the integration of various media or telecommunications services within the limits of a single interface user." And examples of an interface are the keyboard or the mouse. De Cupere starts out on the computer, his core medium for each creation. It is here that he refines and develops his designs. These may then be implemented in installations, actions, happenings, or performances, depending on the resources available. The parts or props for these projects can also be seen as separate objects, like the *Soap paintings* for example, which are his form of painting, or the *Pipifleur*, his way of making sculpture.

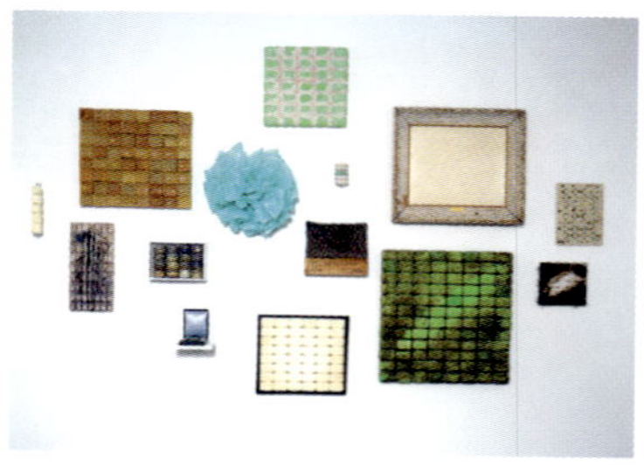

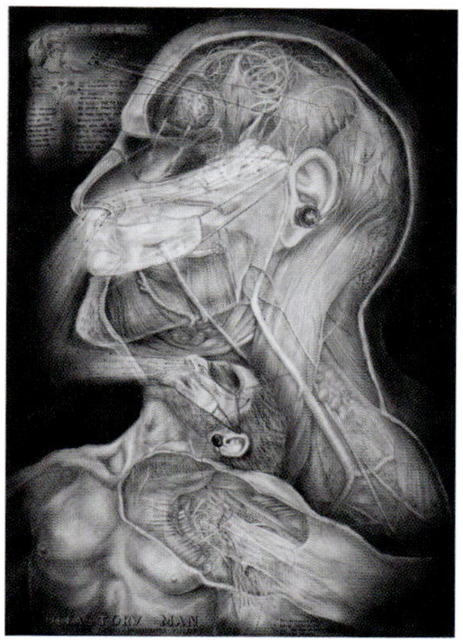

With regard to the 'multi' of the media used, it is also characteristic of de Cupere's work that he considers smell to be an exceedingly important means of artistic experience. He is not so keen on the name 'smell artist' because his assumption is that smell also opens the eyes too and after that the mind. 'Anyone with a nose can smell' seems to me to be the most suitable saying to rouse the observer's involvement. Popular wisdom itself is already a sign of the misjudgement of the sense of smell. Among the six sayings that the Dutch language can boast in which the nose makes an appearance, only the one I have quoted is about smell. The others use the nose as something that one can do harm to and on which one should not put too much faith.

SMELL

Plato did not like art. He saw real things as a reflection of perfect ideas. So art that imitates reality is therefore a reflection of a reflection and that does not take us any closer to getting to know ideas. Plato distrusted the senses as a way of learning about the world around us. It was not until the 17th century that the 'empirical' philosophers linked the acquisition of knowledge with observation.

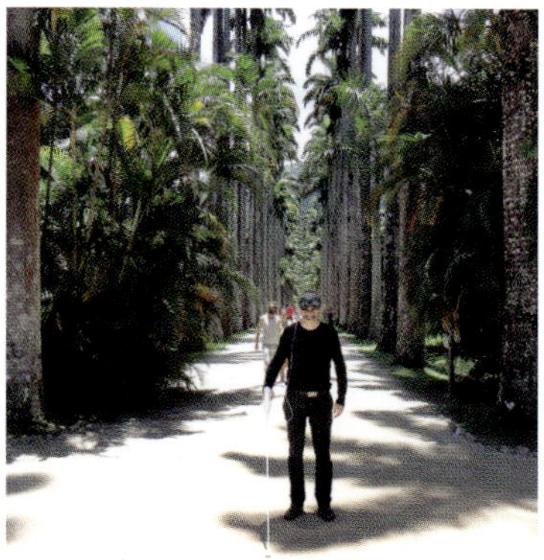

Art has always been an affair of the senses. This has sometimes made people suspicious of it. After all, the senses also lead to sensual pleasure. Yet art also has its portion of rationality. It does after all appeal primarily to the two most intellectual senses, the eye and the ear, the ones in which science also puts the most trust. Art neglects the other three means of perception. Only the blind are allowed to touch certain works of art. Although gastronomy is the art of the senses of taste and smell, it is rarely placed in the same rank as the Fine Arts. The visual and auditory arts and their combinations of them fill a space and time that is screened off by the order not to touch, and is smell- and taste-free. The latter must of course be seen literally. Three senses are excluded from the Fine Arts, and at the very most are only hinted at. The celebrated Sorbonne Professor, Etienne Souriau (1892-1979), does not include the art of taste and smell in his book dealing with the similarities between the arts.

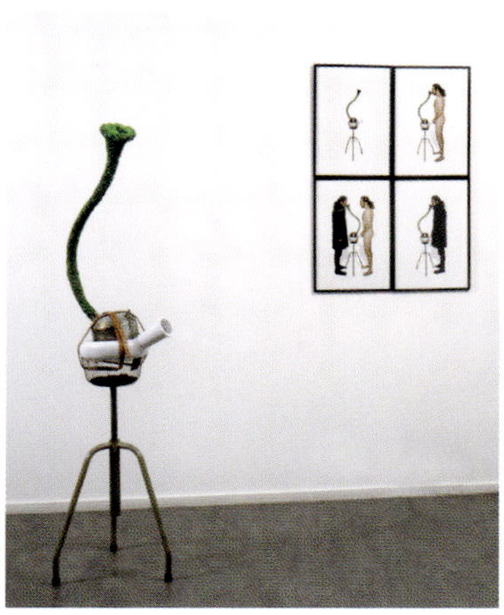

His system is limited to seven primal forms of artistic creation: lines, volumes, colours, light, movement, spoken sound, and musical sound. His definition of art is clear: "art is that which is common to a symphony or a cathedral, a sculpture and an amphora; that which makes a painting and a poem, a building or dance mutually comparable". In this example, the 'amphora' stands out: a container of tastes and smells is mentioned, but its contents count for nothing. The nose and mouth can whistle for their dinner.

As far as the appreciation of smell is concerned, religion does better than science and art. For a very long time, it has stimulated the experience of the holy by way of incense. This is how perfume came into being in Mesopotamia. After all, incense was used to make more pleasant the air of burnt animal meat, which was sacrificed to the gods. The word 'perfume' actually comes from 'per: through' and 'fumare: smoke'. In fact, magic embraces everything man believes himself to be capable of with regard to setting something in motion remotely without the aid of technology. Perfume naturally lends itself very well to this. In this matter, contact with the gods was a small matter, especially if done from the top of the Tower of Babel.

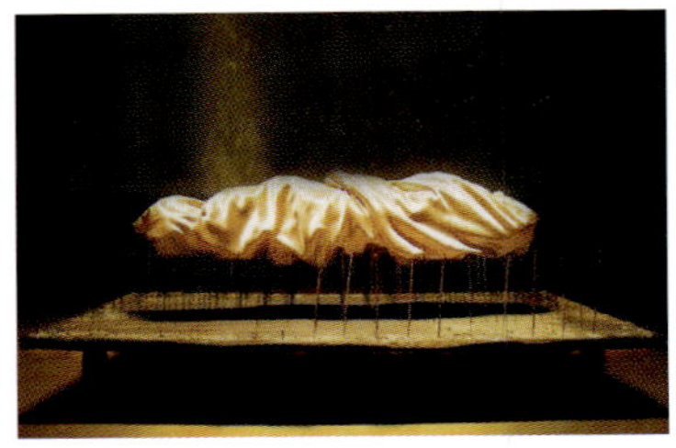

It is easier to verify the attraction perfumes bring about between people. The Egyptians were the first people we know to have cultivated the refining effects of perfumes. One could worship gods with incense, but they believed that certain scents were able to protect them from supernatural disaster, or heal them of illness, and certainly that aromatic unguents applied as make-up made them more beautiful. In addition, the Egyptians discovered what we call *enfleurage*, the extraction of essential oils from flowers using cold fat.

We also know from biology and psychology that smells are an important aspect of life itself and of the way we perceive each another. The Dutch expression 'iemand niet kunnen rieken of luchten' (I can't bear to see or smell him) is quite clear in this respect. Smells to attract or to repel, as an aphrodisiac or to mark off territory. Both functions arise from the excretion of scents called pheromones, or attractants. The finest dishes no longer have any taste when one loses one's sense of smell or suffers from what is called *anosmia*. The way a person smells is just as unique as their fingerprint. But the most important thing is the human experience of smell in relation to the memory. Smells are a distinct experience that perfume one's memories and are also able to stimulate them.

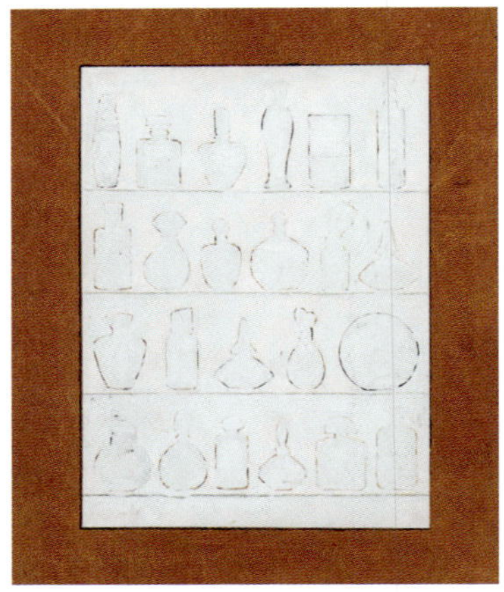

The fact that science neglects such an important area of experience is understandable because it is hard to convert it into language. There are too few descriptive words for smell to be able to create classifications. One has to refer to the thing itself (it smells like garlic, lemon, violets, roses, etc.). The only example of a word specifically for a smell that occurs to me right now is 'musty'.

Patrick Süskind would, I am sure, agree with me when I lament that, when it comes to academic dissertations, it is not customary to sniff a hundred test subjects rather than interview them. Dogs understand this better. Of course, this applies even more for art, that great challenger of sensuality.

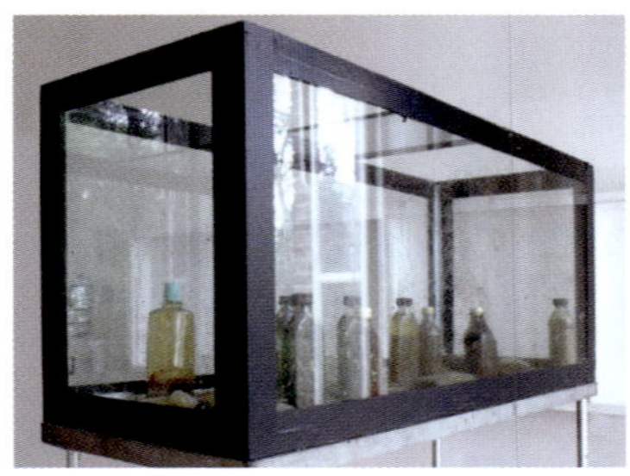

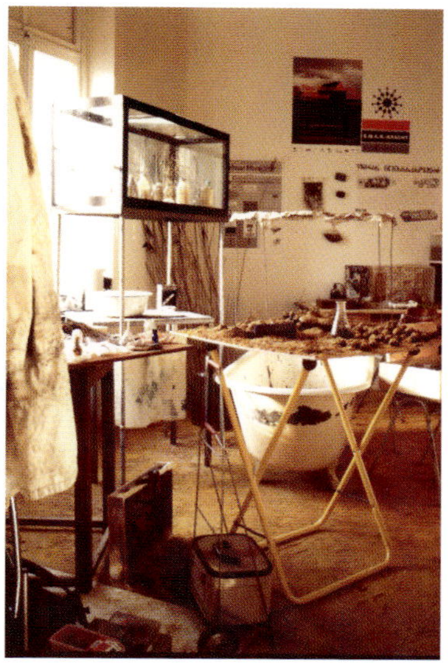

OUTLINE OF PETER DE CUPERE'S OEUVRE

Even after what the psychologists call the 'crisis in aesthetic commitment', i.e. when most children stop drawing, as a youngster Peter de Cupere continued to draw. With the skill he had acquired, he was able to earn some quick pocket money by drawing fish on a sign for a restaurateur. The fact that they also appeared in a newspaper was to boost his self-esteem. He liked to experiment, and one of his subjects was smells, lots mixed up together or a homemade aroma of grass. On the basis of this last talent, he might just as easily have become a chemist. But his virtuosity in drawing took him into art education. First to the advertising department at the College of Art (Phiko, today this is the PXL-MAD School of Arts) in Limburg, because he had a nose not only for smells but also for what appealed to the public. However, the world of advertising itself did not sufficiently enthral him, so he moved to 'Free Graphics' at St. Lucas in Brussels. There he specialised mainly, and very much as an autodidact, in creating by computer. But from an early age he had wanted to become an artist and so he had himself selected for a post-graduate course that offered the best opportunity to achieve this: the Higher Institute of Fine Arts (HISK), at the time still in an Antwerp barracks. On this course he was totally free to experiment. For example, by letting mould turn into a work of art, e.g. *Mouldy Installation* (1997-99), a thousand pots that each changed in its own way or *Mouldy Mattresses* (1998), which needs no additional description. Indeed, on the basis of a dynamic view of art (it must not solidify into a form, it must always keep moving), it is fascinating to paint a bright landscape with mouldy paint that later degenerates into an industrial landscape.

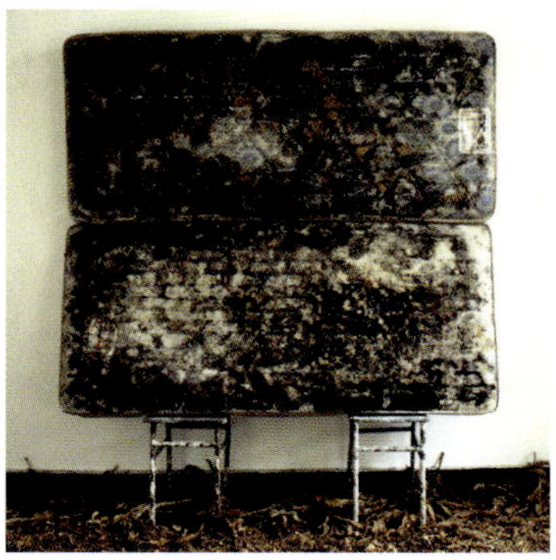

Chance also played a part in his quest for a personal contribution to the art world. Having decided to stop using smell in his expressive work for a while, he stored his preparations in pots and bottles. Some of the contents fermented and burst. He put them in an old dry aquarium so these explosions could lead a life of their own, and this is still a museum piece at the Municipal Museum of Contemporary Art (S.M.A.K.).

The *Rainworm* (1998) installation set up at HISK also refers to his curiosity in his youth. As a child, the fact that when one cuts a rain worm in half one ended up with two worms seemed almost a miracle. His *Rainworm* is made of blue checked or flowery umbrellas lying on the floor in a snaking zigzag. One can here also see the line that connects his work to surrealism: the play of images between rain worm and umbrella. Another nice bit of surrealism is his toilet bowl, made from the product of his own feces. No easy task in terms of workmanship, when one considers how unpredictably a turd can shrink when it dries, but it is certainly a life's work.

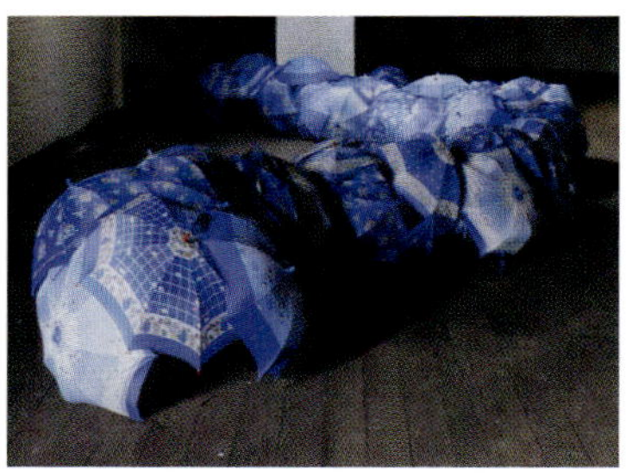

In the same spirit there is his love of fish, which he sometimes prefers when rotting. For his graduation project at HISK, called *Blue Skies* (1999,) he made an installation with an idyllic little island, sea blue painted floor with suspended above it fishing nets in which real dried fish were allowed to emit their finest smells for a certain time. Prior to that, he planted reed stems in a dilapidated Watou barn—always a good setting for installations—and added smells to it. Anyone who had the courage to walk through the smell of rotting fish was rewarded with the smell of fresh lemons, but one also had to go back the same way. This was called *Reedland* (1998). The 'fish' plays quite an extraordinary role in the formation of olfactory theory. A fish smell is without the slightest hesitation ascribed to *L'origine du monde* (The origin of the world). Experts, probably in mythology rather than biology, see the cause of the similarity between the scent of a woman's intimate parts and that of (fresh) fish in the supposed fact that all living creatures originated from the sea.

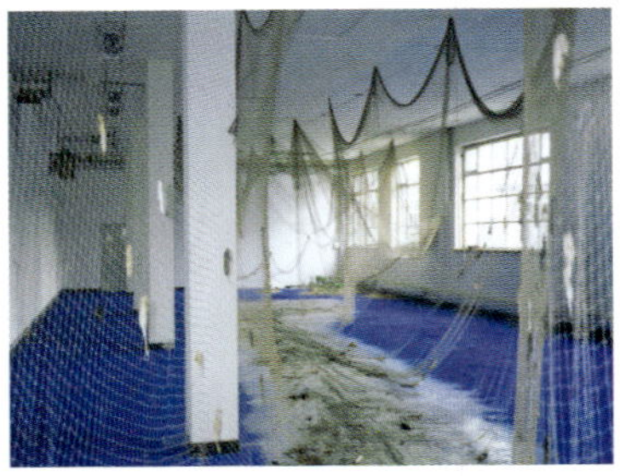

After his time at HISK Peter de Cupere led a busy artistic life. Multimedia projects followed one another in quick succession. The exciting thing about this work is also that he was part of a trend among young artists who adopted a new attitude towards the relationship between art and science. Whereas the previous generation, people like Panamarenko, played with a sort of pseudo-science as a form of poetry, science was now being taken seriously. De Cupere knows scientifically what smells are. He is a genuine computer expert. Each project is thoroughly studied. For example, the casting of sculptures in melted air fresheners (para-dichlorobenzene) was no easy matter. For *The Right Tree* (2002) he had a tree trunk cast using a thousand kilos of that substance, 320 cm high and 60 cm diameter, a favourite to pee against in the wood at Sonsbeek. There is a clear nod in the direction of the 'Fountain'/urinal of Marcel Duchamp. He had previously, on the verge of blasphemy, cast a White Madonna, which duly stood on the corner of a house, during the *Over The Edges* exhibition curated by Jan Hoet in Ghent. It is captivating to see how a perfectly cast statue gradually disappears and assumes forms that one finds in very old sculpture, eroded and worn by long term use in rituals. The title of the piece was *Model for Disappearing Art* (2000). It is also a characteristic of the social critique of the 1990s that the interpretation is left to the observer. It may be established that religion is nowadays losing importance, but it is not up to the artist to applaud or lament it. One might also point to the ongoing disappearance of distinctions. Art and life are increasingly merging into one another. But one thing is certain: that when the Madonna has vanished, because the air freshener has evaporated—peeing against it would be inappropriate and over the edge of blasphemy—she has vanished, which cannot always be said of her presence.

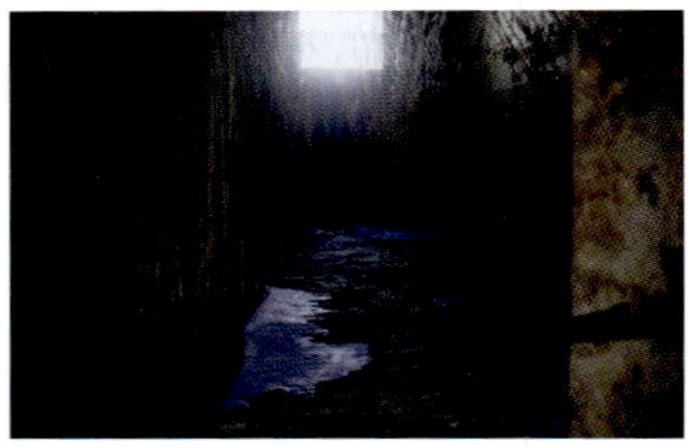

I could carry on describing the other multimedia experiments. His *Cigarette Bacon Smoke Painting* (1999) refers to the smoking and burning of meat. The work makes play of the fact that smoking can damage your health, and at the same time the hypocritical attitude of the government which allows rather unpleasant messages, like death announcements, which it prints on stimulants. De Cupere turns the message around: *Please Smoke*. A real denunciation of war crimes could be seen smelling in his exhibition *The Smell of War* (Poperinge, 2015), where the first gas attacks of WWI are commemorated.

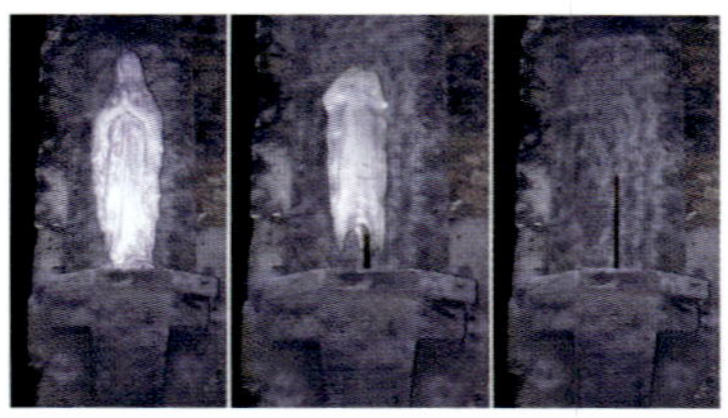

Sometimes as a criticism, sometimes as utopia, Peter de Cupere guides us sniffing through the world, the eyes open, with the request not to hold our mouth. Anyone who works with smells obviously finds soap an extremely good medium and de Cupere has indeed done soap paintings which are each about soap in their own way: the fate of everything and everyone.

Willem Elias

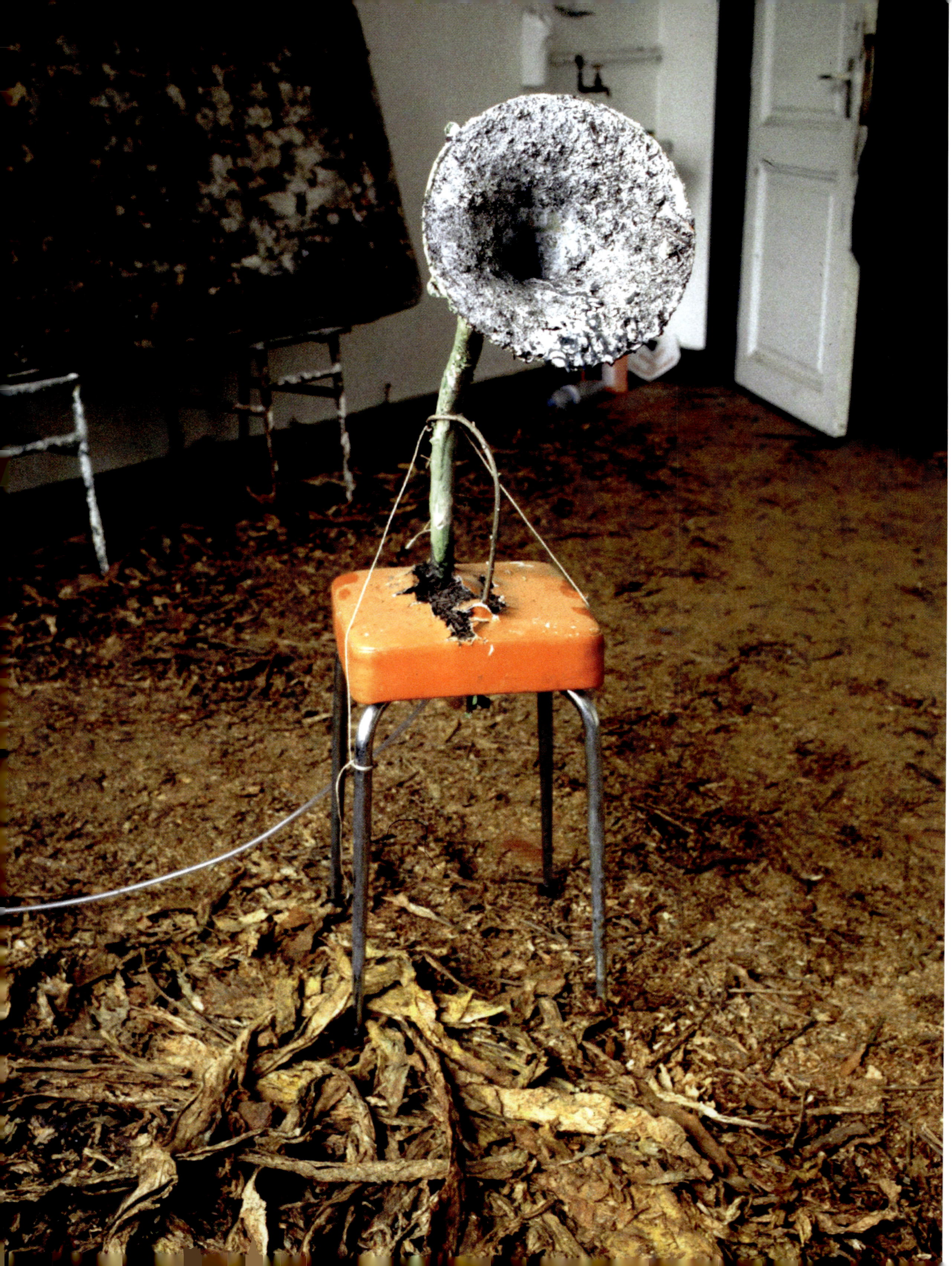

RUTH RENDERS

FASTEN YOUR NOSTRILS

An exploration of the aesthetic potential of smell in the work of Peter de Cupere

Emotion. I cannot find a better word to accurately describe my first encounter with the work of Peter de Cupere. It must have been somewhere in 1997 when, on entering his art studio in the Higher Institute of Fine Arts (HISK) in the former military hospital in Antwerp, I was overcome by a sickly, attractive sweaty smell that I could only associate with decay and fermentation processes. As far as my field of vision extended there were remains of food, mould formations, dried tobacco leaves and herbs. My cautious walk through the room felt as if it were a real quest: the floor thickly strewn with an enormous amount of dried tobacco leaves, two used and mouldy mattresses hung on a wall as if they were paintings of exceptional pictorial quality, and here and there pots and dishes of left over meals. In the middle of the room stood a work with the title *Fleur d'Anus* (Anus Blossom). A fanciful grey structure with the lines of an archetypal flower form 'growing' through the seat of an orange stool, feeding upon the faeces of the artist in a pot under the stool. The atmosphere in the room was quickly determined by a mixture of childlike attraction, fascination and aversion which we all like to share to some extent, even Jan Hoet, who enthusiastically made a way through the dried tobacco leaves alongside aluminium trays of rotten fish and other food scraps. Beauty and rancidity go hand in hand in this wonderful installation. The tone was set.

Although the use of organic materials and transient food products was not a completely new phenomenon within art history—artists like Joseph Beuys and Jan Fabre already worked with fat, butter and other organic materials such as blood in a number of their works—the aesthetic and olfactory properties of smells and scented materials, their emotional impact on people and the implicit artistic possibilities associated with them had never before been investigated as thoroughly as they were by this young artist.

A few months later Peter de Cupere took part in a group exhibition in the poetry village of Watou near Poperinge, in West Flanders. The exhibition was curated by Jan Hoet, director of the then recently opened Municipal Museum of Contemporary Art (S.M.A.K.) in Ghent. On entering the courtyard of a picturesque farm that served as one of the sites for the presentation of works of art, visitors were irresistibly attracted by an idyllic looking reed landscape in a charming open cowshed. As they unsuspectingly entered this space, they were immediately assailed by an unexpected olfactory uppercut: an overwhelming stench of rotten fish washed over this peaceful, idyllic landscape and tested the visitor to the extreme. Afterwards Peter told me about an important detail in the work that I had missed, as I raced outside again almost retching: the brave who dared keep their nostrils open until the end of the reed bed were rewarded with the fresh smell of lemon, a purification for the most resilient noses.

Like a painter putting together his colour pallet, during the early years of his artistic activity Peter de Cupere collected a pallet of various organic and inorganic materials and the corresponding processes of decay, as well as the various smells that arose during these processes. In parallel to his experiments with smells inherently present in materials, he also investigated the possibilities and availability of synthetic smells and aromas, for which he began cooperating with a few firms who develop aromas on an industrial scale. In his first own art studio, an old school building in the commercial heart of Antwerp, Peter transformed one of the rooms into a dreamlike, surreal world. The room was completely covered with cotton wool, which also completely covered the furniture and floor, and a soothing smell of baby powder caressed the epithelium of your nose as you entered it. This room in his workshop was given the title *Soft world, in honour of my mother*.

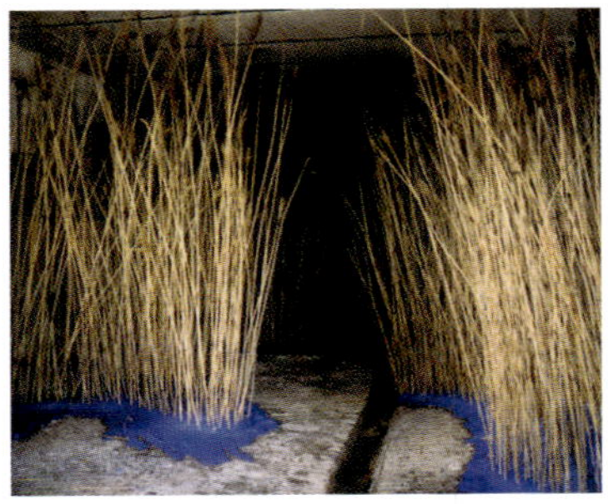

Adaptations of this installation were shown in among other places Louvain-La-Neuve and in an exhibition in Le Lieu Unique in Nantes, France. The installation there was given the title *Soft World, tv-room, relax-room* (2000) and was a square box completely covered in cotton wool, inside and out. There was only a narrow, vertical cotton wool opening which the visitor could squeeze through with some difficulty to get inside the space. The association with the womb-like experience or the 'back to the womb' feeling that was made by very many of the visitors were not of course plucked out of thin air. While the visitors made their way with great difficulty through the two vertical cotton wool wings that formed the opening, the hint of baby powder scent immediately evoked memories of their early childhood. Once inside, where a cotton wool table and a television showing pictures of a man happily frolicking around in a cotton wool costume could be seen, the visitor could lay down in an enormous cotton wool mass more than a metre high, and surrender himself to a soothing feeling of safety and uncomplicated joy.

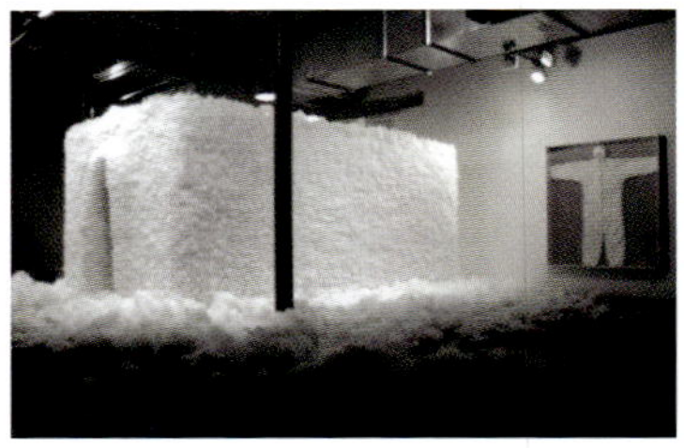

The work illustrates Peter de Cupere's masterly talent for recovering suppressed or forgotten experiences by means of works of art that some visitors experience as reminiscence sessions, elements aimed at evoking recollections that have been 'lost' in our memories like those that are often organised within the cultural heritage sector. A specific smell or a combination of smells may—whether or not in combination with other sensory elements—resurrect specific memories, whose existence we had completely forgotten up until the moment we noticed the smell.

Peter de Cupere shows us with his work the still little known possibilities of smell as an artistic medium and smelling as an aesthetic perception, equivalent to seeing and hearing. Just like early experimental photographers and filmmakers, he stresses the artistic possibilities of his medium by stressing its specific properties. The artist also uses all the other possible media and technologies that he has at his disposal. Over the past twenty years he has developed such an impressive body of work with sculptures, installations, performances, films, interactive virtual presentations, websites and even games *(Olfacio)*, in which smell always play the main role.

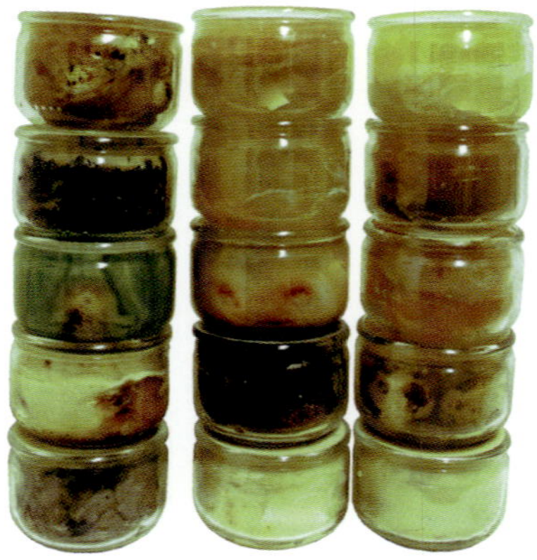

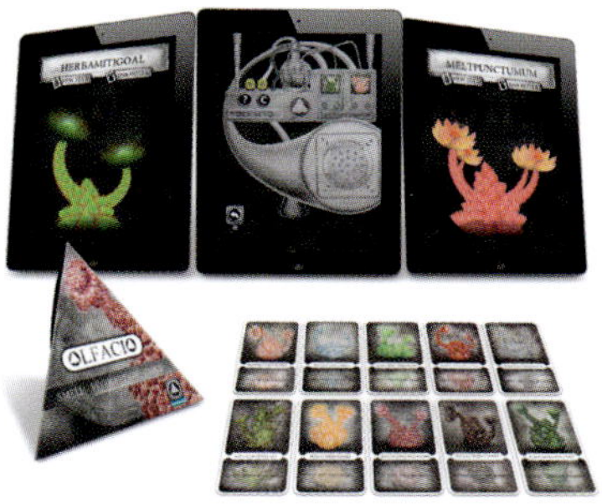

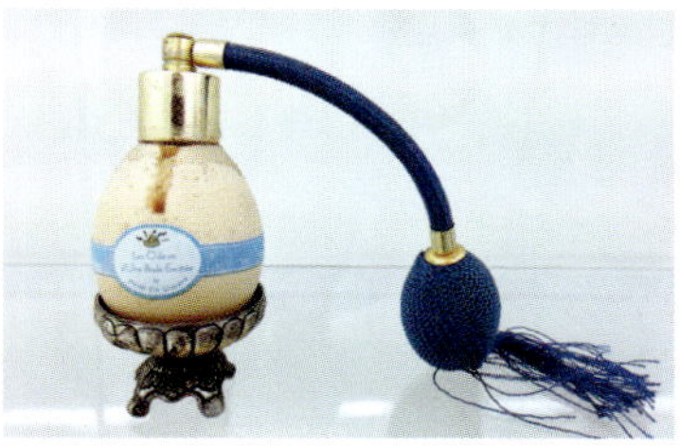

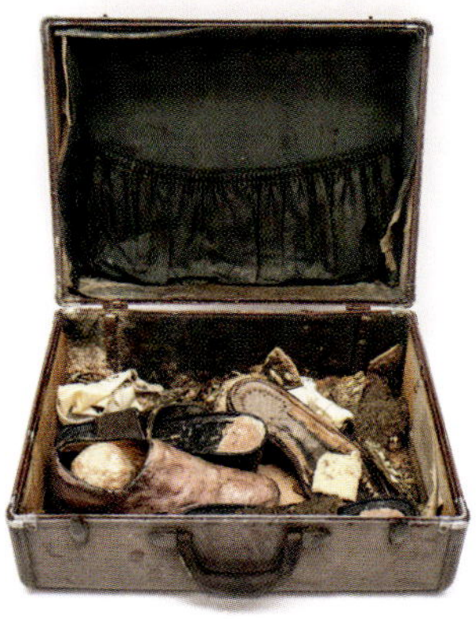

He does this with a lightness that does not refer by chance to absurdism and the institutional criticism of the Dadaists, and the often erotic humour of the surrealists is also never far away. The relationship between smells and eroticism has however also always been strong in the world of perfumes.

Odeur d'une poule excitée (Smell of an excited chicken), a perfume bottle with the body of a blown eggshell, is such a work, small in size, but rich in conceptual content and art history references. The perfume bottle contains a perfume made from the faeces of the chicken who laid the egg. In 1921, Marcel Duchamp made the work *Belle Haleine, Eau de Voilette* (Beautiful Breath, Veil Water), a perfume bottle bearing a portrait of a lady called *Rrose Sélavy*. Duchamp did in actual fact himself pose as a model for the portrait, photographed by Man Ray, and the name *Rrose Sélavy* stands for 'Eros, c'est la vie' (Eros, that's life). *Odeur d'une poule excitée*—one of de Cupere's first works with eggs and eggshells, a nod to Marcel Broodthaers—is an example of the humour and art history awareness that runs like a central thread through his further work.

Peter de Cupere continued his artistic experiments with eggs. His *Egg Paintings* (several works from 1998 to 2000) are three-dimensional 'paintings' made of dried raw eggs removed from their shells. Over the same period, he produced the work *Eggs* (1998-1999), an egg basket filled with eggs encased in pieces of chicken skin sewn together. *Untitled* (1998-99) consists of a series of stacked glass jars that each contain a raw egg from a different type of bird, over which soaps are poured with attractive fruit fragrances such as peach and strawberry. Just as in *Egg Paintings* and *Eggs* the work is the result of experiments with the transformation processes that take place in eggs. The work *Untitled* (1998-99) was based on the question of to what extent deliciously fragrant soaps and the penetrating stench of rotting eggs are assimilated in one direction or the other. Other works with soap including *Soap Bullets* (1996), *Clean Soap Flowerpot* (1997) and *Soap Cities* (2001-2004) expose the discrepancy between our associations of soap with cleanliness and attractiveness and its unhealthy, polluting aspects. Under the layer of humoristic glaze on de Cupere's work there are often subtle social and art critical notes.

With the work *My fresh feet* (1998-2003) de Cupere organised a battle between his own bodily smells and pieces of soap. The young artist regularly took with him a leather case containing a pair of shoes with pieces of soap in them, then changed his shoes for the pair with the pieces of soap in them and so activated a battle between the soap smell and the sweaty smell of his feet. The reference to the appreciation of bodily smells also occurs in *Pipifleur* (Pee Flower) (2001-2002), a bedpan from which a flower reaches like a megaphone with attached fragrance enhancer as far as the nose, so one can experience the olfactory delights of one's own pee. The flower motive also recurs in other examples, such as the poetic *Medical Flower*: a long-stemmed flower wrapped in a medical dressing that grows out of a pile of medical encyclopaedias, the head hanging from a thread to support it. Or the beautiful black flowers whose heads were hanging over the edge of a bridge in the park of Poeke castle, while from their calyx they dispersed the smell of the fish in the pond from which they grew.

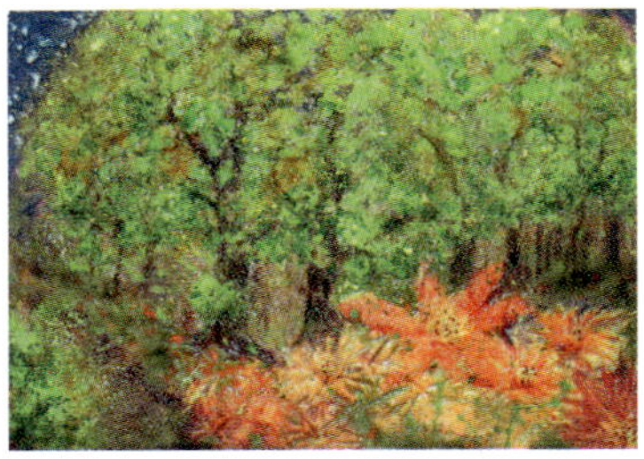

Many of the works already discussed illustrate the importance of experiment for Peter de Cupere, who regards decay as inherent in the work. It is a process that should neither be prevented nor encouraged. In this respect, Peter de Cupere is careful in his choice of words: rarely will he describe processes of change in his work as decay, but rather as transformation. After all, neither the materials nor the smells disappear. Rather they are transformed into another state. This transformation in itself forms a source of aesthetic perception.
The smell and look of the organic material changes considerably in some of his works, a phenomenon whose possibilities the artist also explores. De Cupere's experiments with moulds are examples of this process. Ten tables with 1,000 carefully arranged Petri dishes containing different culture media laid out on them together form the work *Mouldy Installation* (1997-99). Together the different types of moulds growing on the culture media form a varied colour pallet with a musty, but also familiar and even attractive smell. In the work *Evolution Painting*, a painting that was painted with blends of mixed food products, he works further on the visual possibilities of mould processes. A time-lapse video shows how the original painting of a natural landscape slowly evolves over time—as organic transformations take place—into a grey industrial-looking landscape.

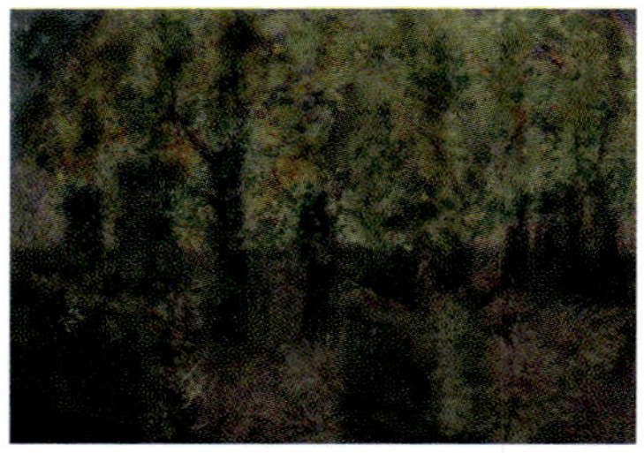

The Right Tree (2002) is a poetic and joyful work, in which de Cupere uses the qualities of a material with a specific and recognisable smell. The work leads you like a wolf in sheep's clothing, to a synthetic product in a natural environment—a beautiful park in Arnhem, where it forms part of the Sonsbeek IX exhibition. Visitors to the exhibition are invited to urinate against the work, a sparklingly white tree trunk in the park—if required using a female urination device for women. The trunk smelled like a clean urinal, and looked as if it was made of sparklingly white marble or alabaster. The trunk appeared to be cast completely from para-dichlorobenzene a substance from which disinfectant blocks in urinals are made, which is extremely toxic when heated. For this daring work de Cupere had to protect himself for several days with a gasmask and a bodysuit to protect his skin as he melted urinal air freshener blocks and cast them in the mould. Under the trunk a concealed reservoir was installed to collect the liquid waste. The interplay between nature and culture by moving smells into a different context, is one way in which Peter de Cupere draws our attention to the deeply-rooted and often unconscious associations that we make with smells, and our intuitive and/or learned reactions to them.

Through his work, Peter de Cupere clearly explores every conceivable aspect of smells. Some of his works refer to smell as a concept, in other works smell form an inherent part of the material that is used. Another way in which he brings smell into his work is by using added smells (essences, homemade smells, aromas from the food

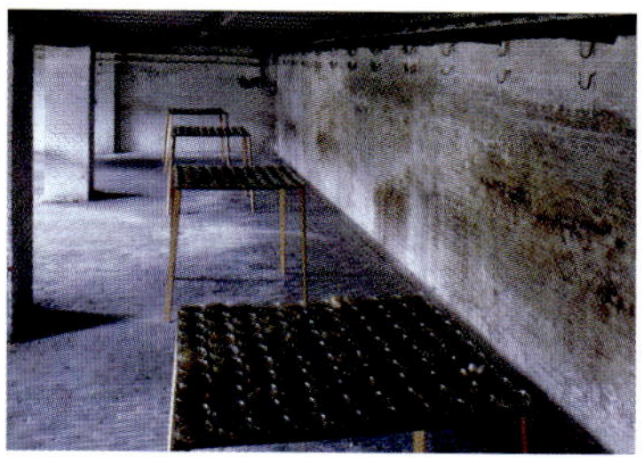

industry) where he likes to challenge our conventions relating to smells, or creates interplays between visual and olfactory elements in a work. An example of this artistic strategy that is shocking for some people is *Cigarette Bacon Smoke Painting* (1999), a 'painting' that upon closer inspection appears to be a composition of thousands of spent cigarette butts. As you the observer, fascinated by the material, take a step closer to the work, you are treated to an overpoweringly intense smell of smoked meat, a combination of a material and a smell that triggers associations between smoking cigarettes and the resultant burnt lungs.

Due to the direct impact of smells on our emotional balance, they may trigger unexpectedly violent and unpredictable reactions. Furthermore, smell is often a warning system that sets off a fight or flight reflex when we find ourselves in dangerous situations. An exhibition in the St. Lukas Stichting in Brussels in 2003 entitled *The Collector's House* generated an unexpectedly fierce reaction. The exhibition was a playfully interpreted all-round installation that presented an imaginary house of a passionate art collector in which every element was art. In the dining room stood a table on which 130 blocks of strongly smelling Hervé cheese were displayed; in the bathroom stood a bathtub filled with red wine that every 30 seconds was sucked up and sprayed downwards by the showerhead; in the 'bedroom' stood a metal bed in which an old used mattress was being cooked to make soup (*Hot Mattress*, 2003), seasoned with oregano and basil, and the toilet could be folded up and transported in a suitcase; even down to the garage everything consisted of art: there stood the work *Earth Car* (2002), a car completely covered with earth and with grass growing on the roof in which budgerigars had made their nest. Right through the exhibition, short humorous films were shown in which an actor illustrated how the imaginary art collector 'survived' among his overpowering art collection. After the health inspectorate had received a complaint from staff who worked in the building because of the presence of 'hazardous' smells, orders were given to remove the cheese table and the mattress. De Cupere commented that strangely enough the wine bath—that involved the greatest risk of unhealthy substances developing—was allowed to remain. In the end, it was decided that one block of cheese could remain, and as a compromise for the innocuous mattress that had to be removed, the artist cut the mattress into pieces and drew the 'soup' on tin cans that were offered for sale by a humorous advertising film as an art edition.

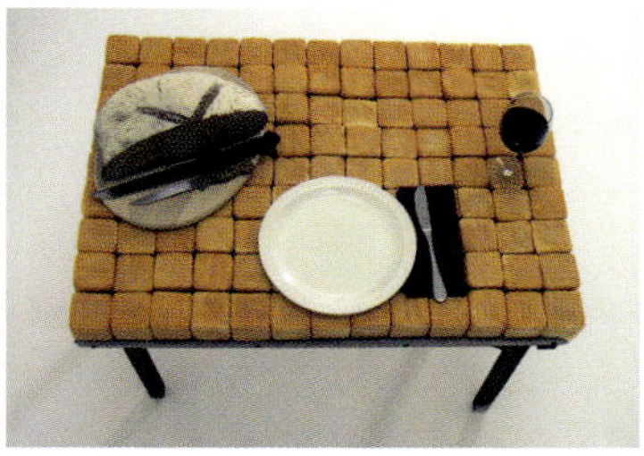

In a playful manner and through often surprising contradictions, the observer is challenged to let go of his socially and intuitively determined prejudice against smells. De Cupere's flower sculptures refer to the simple and universally known sensation of sniffing the scent of a flower, but the archetypal flower forms and various smells are shaken up together and rearranged into new, often perplexing entities. The *Flowers*—whose forms often prompt a suspicion of organic mutilations—give off smells that you would not immediately expect from the calyx of a flower. Since 2002 a series of flowers have been created based on so-called alembics. An alembic is a copper still that was used up until the beginning of the 20th century

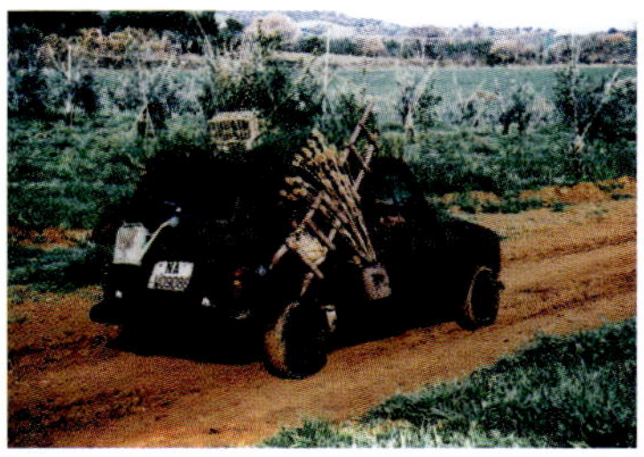

in the production of perfumes. In terms of form, you would describe *Alambfleurics*, as the name already indicates, as a cross between a flower and a still, such as for example the work *Alambfleuric Pois Feromoon 1* (2002). Alambfleurics suggest a process of scent production within their bulbous stem cavity that is released into the air via their calyx. These alambfleurics do not however give off ordinary smells but odourless pheromones. By using pheromones in this and in a few other works, the artist draws our attention to the importance of the attractants considered to be odourless that are partly responsible for the physical attraction between people. The suggestion of possible manipulation of the attraction between people can be read as a loss of our relationship with natural processes and the growing influence of scientific and technological developments on human existence, of which we are often not aware.

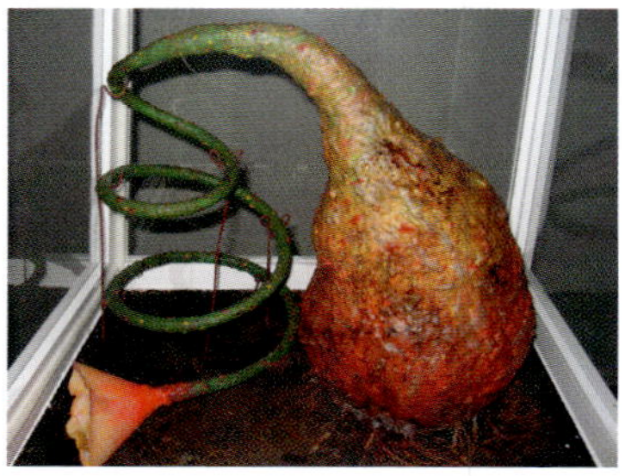

Although smell as a non-traditional art material from time to times comes up against resistance and criticism, it has meanwhile been accepted as an artistic medium in most museums and galleries. This does not however take away the fact that smells as an aesthetic perception, even among *believers* in smell as an artistic medium, raises questions about its possibilities and limitations. In their essay *The Aesthetics of Smelly Art*, art critics Larry Shiner and Yulia Kriskovets combine the theoretical aspects of olfactory art to defend it against the traditional scepticism regarding smell, where they are primarily interested in understanding the nature and limitations of smell as art: "Our concern (...) is less with whether one can classify olfactory works as 'art' (...) than with understanding their nature and limitations as artworks" (Shiner, L. & Kriskovets, Y. 2007: 277). They discuss a number of possible challenges for artists who want to use the medium of smell as an artistic medium.

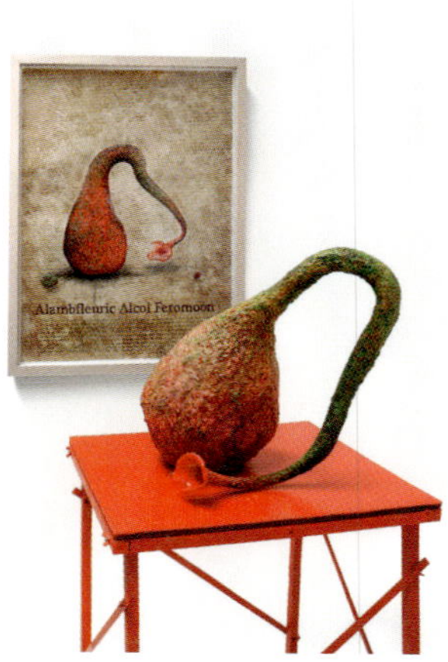

They think one of the challenges of smell as a source of aesthetic experiences lies in the fact that smells are fleeting and temporary, and that works of art based on smells are therefore less suitable than visual or auditory works for generating concentrated and repeatable attention. But, they continue, just like music, smell has a certain duration and in principle can therefore be relived in the same way. This is however only partly true. In the world of perfumes, smells are in fact also subdivided into notes—base notes, middle notes and top notes—but their properties are different in time and space, which has far-reaching consequences for the creation of aesthetic experiences with smells. A sound moves more quickly through the room and as a result is easier to delimit in time. The creation of a succession of different scent notes within a short time frame by analogy with a piece of music would create an olfactory cacophony. This is the very type of question about the medium-specific properties of smell that is the driving force for Peter de Cupere in his search for the possible aesthetic applications of the medium.

In a number of works, he researches the artistic possibilities of smell in itself. One example of this is *Smell Labyrinth* (2002) that he made in the park of Poeke castle: an enormous labyrinth whose walls consisted of neutral white sheets. To find their way through the labyrinth visitors could only rely on olfactory information.

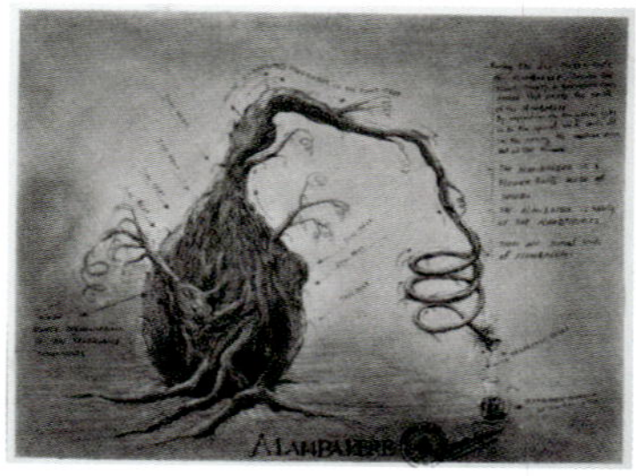

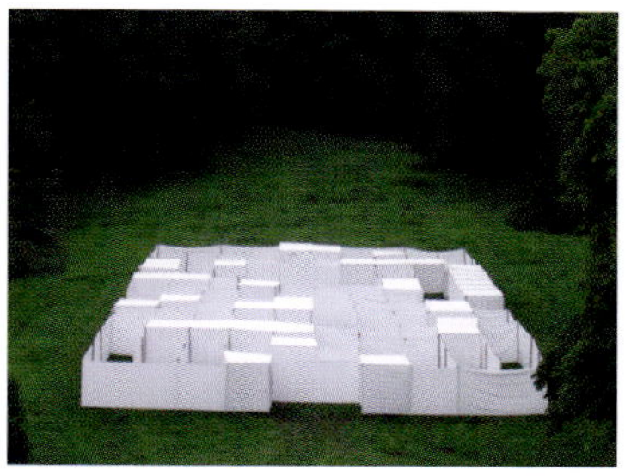

This appeared to be a particularly difficult task for many people. Five years later, in 2007 the giant installation *Air Polluter* filled the great hall in Brakke Grond, the Flemish Cultural Centre in Amsterdam. The work consisted of a large number of glass measuring cups of liquid fragrances set up in a circle and connected by means of tubes through which the fragrant vapour could be aspirated to a central dome to be drained there into a balloon. You, the visitor, could tie up the balloon filled with fragrant vapours and take it with you. Each measuring cup was filled with a 'pleasant' or 'unpleasant' smell that could be activated or deactivated by the visitor by pressing a button in a control room. Meanwhile however other visitors could press buttons next to the measuring cups themselves to change the selection again according to their own preferences and vice versa. As a result, none of the visitors had full control over the composition of the mix of smells in his or her balloon. The work is a metaphor for the subjectivity of 'pleasant' and 'unpleasant' smells, and the arbitrariness with which in daily life various smells reach our smell epithelium unasked and uncontrolled.

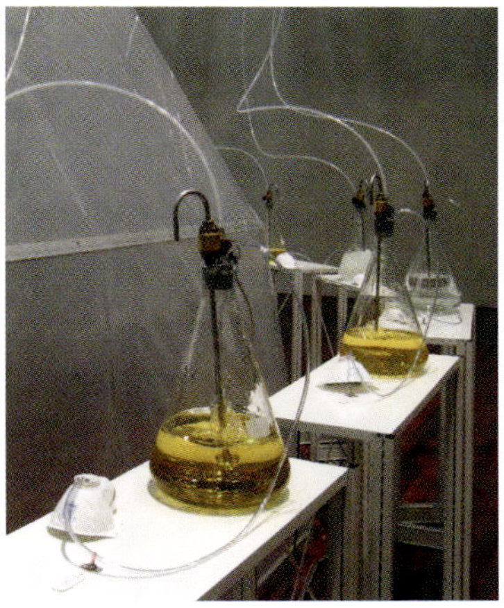

The main difficulty in the creation of art in which smells play an important part, according to Shiner and Kriskovets, remains the fact that smells are difficult to classify systematically to make complex works with them like different colours of paint or music tones and sounds. They remark that the problem is caused by a sensory limitation, namely: "the relatively low fatigue level for smelling compared with that of seeing and hearing so that the stimulus must be repeated or intensified or the nose given a rest" (Shiner, L. & Kriskovets, Y. 2007: 275). As an example of a work that has succeeded in approaching the refined aesthetic nuance of a piece of music, the authors refer to the work *Olfactiano* by Peter de Cupere. This 'smell piano' consists of 26 keys that each activate a different smell that is blown in the direction of the observers. An extra key provides the inflow of fresh air into the room, which resolves the problem of duration and mixing or accumulation of different smells.

The smells are subdivided according to base notes, middle notes and top notes, a subdivision that plays a part in the composition of smell sonatas, or as de Cupere also calls them: "time perfumes, perfumes created over time". In 2004, the artist gave his first (silent) smell concert in the Beursschouwburg in Brussels, entitled *Smell sonata for Brussels*. With his olfactianos, a collection of smell instruments that he has developed over the years, Peter de Cupere uses smells to directly evoke the associative reactions of the audience. These smell salvos evoke visual associations or mental images in the observer. Peter de Cupere also gave smell concerts for blind observers who as expected were much better able to distinguish and identify the various successive and combined smells, which shows that smelling is a skill that can be refined and developed with practice.

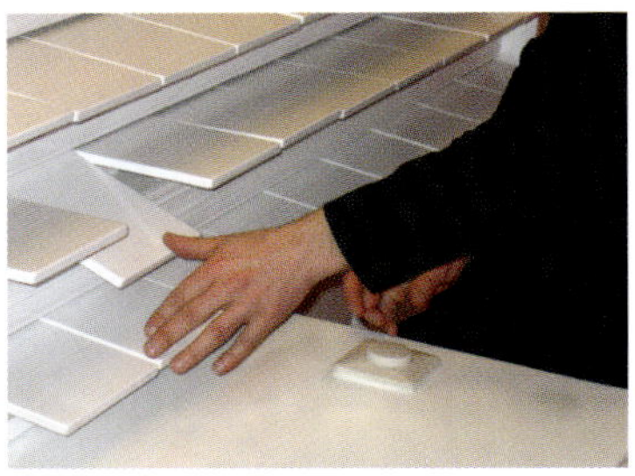

According to de Cupere, the limited development of our sense of smell has to do with the fact that in young children when they are developing their senses we first stimulate sight and hearing, and to a lesser degree also touch and taste. Less

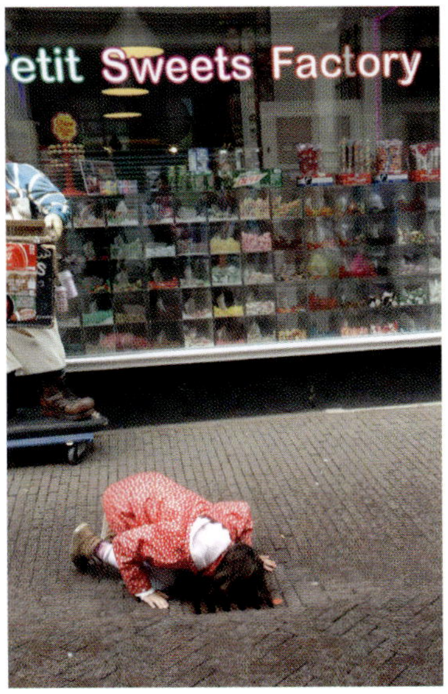

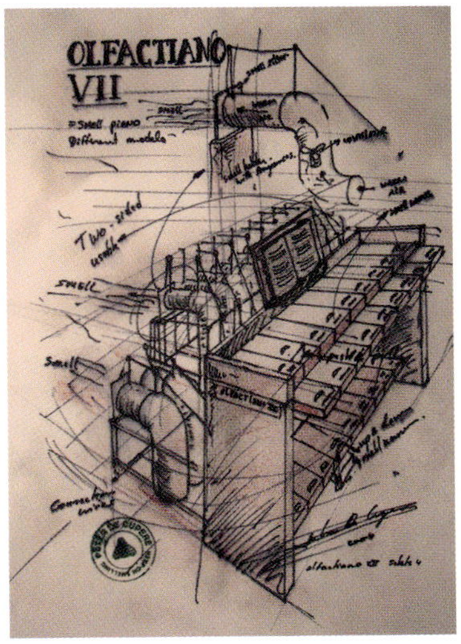

attention is paid to smell in this process, only at a later stage and mainly from a negative approach. We do after all learn to exclude intense smells. According to the artist, the result of this limited attention to the development of our olfactory skills has the result that we can only tolerate a limited number of smells within a short time span. This is where the motivation comes from for what Peter de Cupere tries to achieve via his work: the possibilities of demonstrating smells by raising our olfactory skills to a higher level and increasing our capacity to distinguish different smells. An important motivation here is to share the sensory enjoyment that he himself perceives—in particular the enjoyment that he perceives through his nose—with others.

While olfactory art is still in its infancy, and most artists only use smells sporadically in their work, Peter de Cupere has developed an impressive body of work based on smells. His work encourages us to re-educate our perception of smell and the socially and culturally determined conventions relating to sensory perception. A number of other contemporary artists were also already creating works with smells, such as for example Angela Elsworth (*Actual Odor*, 1998) or Ernesto Neto (*Wonderland*, 2010), although working with smell is a rare thing in the works of most artists. More and more artists do however seem to be finding their way to smell as an artistic medium, and there is no doubt that, with his extensive artistic applications of smells, Peter de Cupere has made a great contribution to this evolution. Or, as Shiner and Kriskovets put it so beautifully in their essay: "Peter de Cupere has created an artistic identity that is a cross between an artist and an olfactory chemist which could well become a model for olfactory artists in the future" (Shiner, L. & Kriskovets, Y. 2007: 274).

Ruth Renders, Antwerp (2008-2016)

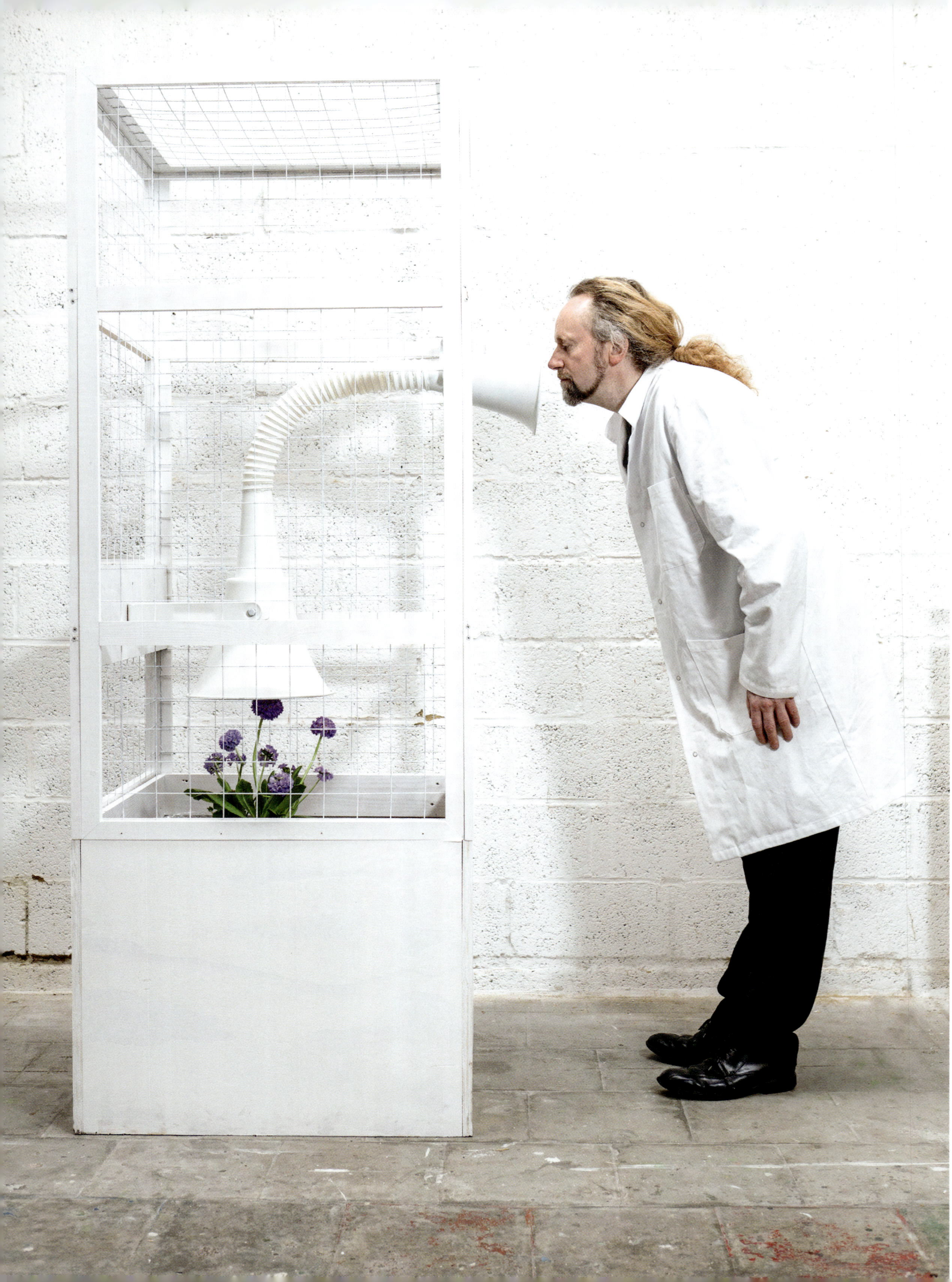

PETER DE CUPERE

WHEN SCENT MAKES SEEING, WHEN SEEING MAKES SCENTS

Olfactory Memory
"A woman can be ugly at day time and wonderful at night time." (Guerlain)

SENSE AS A MEDIUM OF CONTEXT

One could say about smell itself that it also always gives context to its own smell profile because it is always associated with the origin of the smell itself. By smell profile we mean the composition of the smell and what it refers to. So the smell of sweat will make you think of an intensive effort or a physical reaction to something. This may in itself already be an olfactory work of art when it is associated with a certain situation, fact and/or subject and in addition is more than merely an illustration. It must as a minimum aim to reinforce the message or transmit the message even better.

This could be termed a literal and/or perceptual translation of the smell of a particular fact. The meaning that this translation of smell brings to the situation/ subject of the exhibition may then be the context of the work. For example, putting the same sweaty smell into a photo exhibition on youth football clubs is experienced differently from the addition of a sweaty smell to a photo exhibition in which child labour is questioned. Ditto with an exhibition about passion compared with an exhibition about wrestling. Sweat linked to passion carries something erotic while sweat linked to wrestlers evokes a sticky less pleasant sweaty smell and this is therefore also an olfactory perception.

An extreme example with a sweaty smell would e.g. be in relation to photos of sick people with extreme injuries. Here the sweaty smell will tend to be perceived as something sickly and even more unpleasant. So the same imitated sweaty smell is experienced differently with respect to different images. It is important here that the works are not experienced together with the sweaty smell, but each separately and best, as mentioned, in a different exhibition. Obviously not every sweaty smell is the same, but since smell is translated subjectively and the smell is linked to an object to which it has a link, the observer will assume that the added smell belongs to the object exhibited.

This applies even more for unpleasant smells than for pleasant smells. In the case of unpleasant smells, one more quickly tends to want to close the nostrils and experience the smell with less olfactory analysis. The context of the images shown therefore gives quite a different perception, experience of the linked smell, but the reverse may also be true. This can therefore be termed synaesthesia, the effects of the senses on one another. And it is this very interaction between the senses that means that there are many ways of creating context. In the examples with sweat, the image gives context to the smell and the image reinforces the smell in its context.

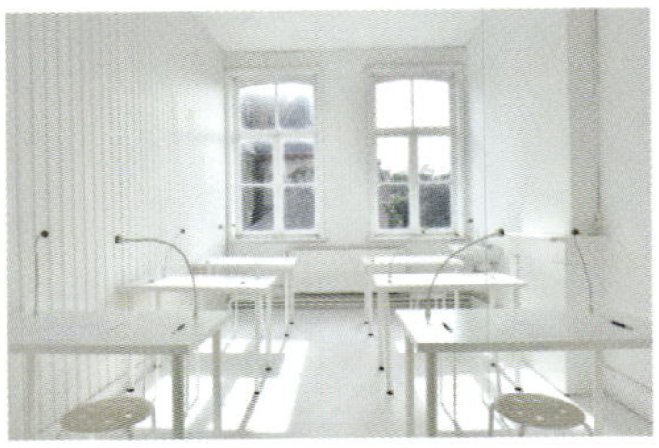

SYNAESTHESIA

The interaction between the senses to create context gives more possibilities than just focussing on one sense such as seeing. Looking at an image is always translated in our brains while smells affect the memory, emotions and physical reactions. Smells have a strong effect on our memory and are therefore also mainly subjective. Smell memories indirectly help to determine the experience and where possible are also part of the context of a work. The relation between seeing and smelling becomes an interaction whereby the experience of the work actually becomes personal thanks to one's own smell memory. In other words, the work of art will not only give a visual cognitive meaning, but also have an emotional olfactory impact. Of course, an image may also evoke an emotional reaction, but by adding a smell this will either be reinforced or actually be experienced differently. The latter may be in both a positive and a negative sense and hence cause the observer to think.
In addition, smell does of course have warning functions to protect us from danger among other things when smelling smoke, rotting processes and bad food. Even our libido and feelings of attraction to someone are largely determined by smell.

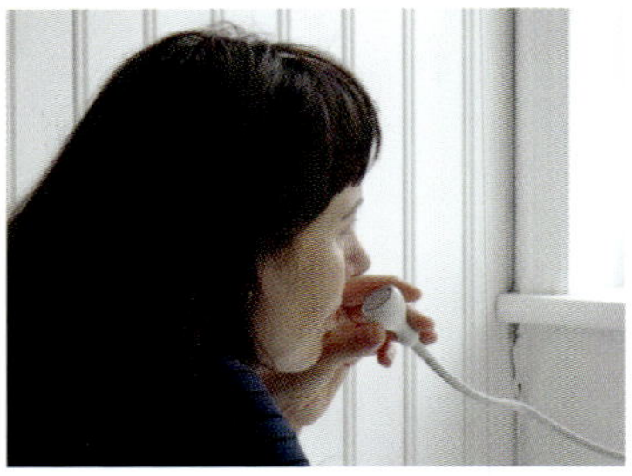

The context that smell gives or which is reinforced by the smell is in many cases determined by our own experiences of this smell. Not all smells are experienced in the same way by an observer. His own smell memory helps to determine how the observer experiences a smell. By smell memory we mean the memory, placing a smell in an earlier experience of this smell in a certain situation or context. We are not then talking here about the cultural and social identity of a smell, because every culture and even every nationality has a different meaning for some smells. We focus here on the experience of the observer himself.

THE SCENT READER, EXPERIENCING SMELLS DIFFERENTLY

In the work *The Scent Reader,* it is clear that a smell may evoke several contexts as we perceive the smell. *The Scent Reader* consists of six white tables each with two smell modules. These are set up in a white room. Visitors can smell the smells via the smell modules. On each table lies a book in which you can write down what memory the smell in question evokes or what it makes you think of. You may not state what the smell itself is. You can read the memory of previous visitors in relation to the smell that belongs to it.

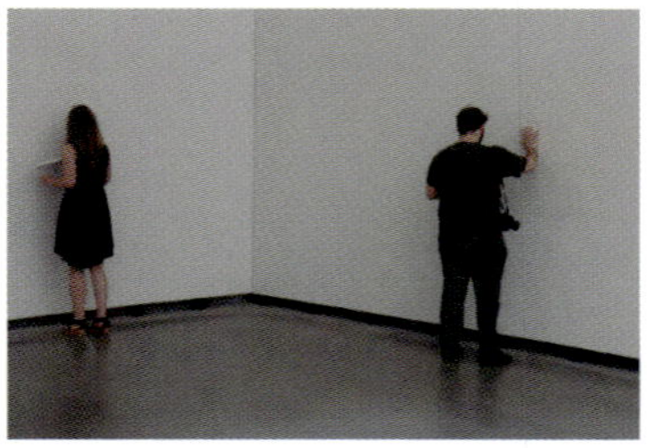

With the scent of Coca Cola candies, the following descriptions were noted amongst others:
- visit to the doctor (was mentioned multiple times)
- old attic space
- old-fashioned women
- the most delicious wild dishes of mother
- opening a bag of fruit tea with loads of sugar
- proper church scent
- incorrigible candy scent
- ...

With the scent of grass visitors mention:
- my first kiss
- chemical apple scent
- playing in the meadow behind the parental house
- in the tent during the summer holidays
- fresh sheets 40 years ago
- looking for figurines in the clouds
- the inside of the peel of an apple
- drinking a banana milkshake while studying (the description of banana scent occurred multiple times)
- bicycle ride just after rain
- spinach smoothie
- hot summer day in the park as a child
- too much love to carry
- cemetery
- party
- rose garden after the rain
- fresh cut lettuce
- ...

With the scent of mushrooms:
- the kitchen stove of my mother who is drying celery leaves and parsley
- 10 years old, playing with friends
- old little shop
- mouldy trousers
- walking in the forest
- oncoming sneeze
- sourly feeling of a sweaty summer's day
- hay stack
- memory at the point of fading
- the pantry in our previous house
- chicken dice
- sultry summer evenings at the wrong place
- nasty air, reminds me of the spot where a crime was committed
- wet tent canvas
- wet sport clothes forgotten to take them out of the bag
- mould
- laboratory of botany
- stench
- our pantry
- ...

The result is a mix of different experiences, memories, references to one and the same smell. Every smell is therefore assigned several contexts. The work encourages us to think about our awareness of smell, but also about our own life experiences and memories. In spite of the fact that most visitors do want to guess the smell themselves, many write down their emotions and memories of the smells. It is not obvious how to describe a smell without stating what the smell itself is. This is not scientific research but artistic research to see how smells are experienced and given context by an art-loving public. In addition, the intention was to create a number of new titles from these smell descriptions for a new series of invisible scent paintings where smell again gives context to a title that at first sight does not say anything. In total, more than 9,000 descriptions are given.
Clearly different contexts are given to every separate smell. The testimonials on the left clearly show that there is a big difference in the context given.

The following smells were also described: cola sweets, mushroom, lavender, cedar wood, star anise, peppermint, curry, smoked salmon, thyme, roses and strawberry.

An extra dimension for the visitors was the interaction with what other visitors had written down. As an artist this database of smell description is not only a way of experiencing how smell gives different contexts and plays them back in the memory, it is also a means of coming up with new titles for the work *Invisible Scent Paintings*.

INVISIBLE (SCENT) PAINTINGS, GIVING MEANING TO TITLES

The *Invisible (Scent) Paintings,* as the title says, are scent paintings that one cannot see. The work was exhibited in the Marta Museum in Herford (DE). The exhibition rooms of the museum, designed by Frank Gehry, appear to be completely empty.
In the empty room, you are given a plan which only lists for each of the titles, the dimensions of the work and the location where the relevant *Invisible Scent Paintings* are hung. Smells are hung on the walls like painting using scratch & sniff. The visitor first had to read the title, then scratch the wall and smell their fingers or the wall. The smell gave meaning to the title of the work. For example, you read the title *Stop being annoying*, a title that does not say much in itself unless you were to think of a particular person. By scratching the wall, you smell the scent of citronella. Citronella, a scent used to repel mosquitoes, is a well-known smell. Because of the intended use of the scent it is also easily linked with the international fight against mosquitoes. By using the scent with the title *Stop being annoying*, the title then refers indirectly to the annoying buzz and bite of mosquitoes. Another title was *Her Smile is a hidden perfume bottle* where you could perceive the smell of peppermint. In themselves, these combinations between senses and smells are not greatly appealing works of art but the perception and definition in itself gives this

sense another meaning by adding an extra dimension to the smell which makes the observer think more about the function and possibilities of smell.

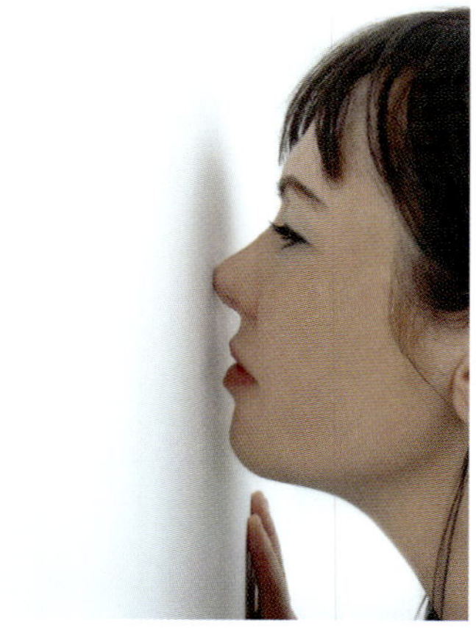

In the exhibition, there were seven *Invisible Scent Paintings*. One of these was an homage to the painting *Who's Afraid of Red, Yellow and Blue I* by Barnett Newman from 1966 and bore the same title. Three scratch & sniff smells were put up following the colour classification of this painting. The dimensions of 122 cm x 190 cm were retained, but the work was turned on its side, in other words the smell was translated horizontally instead of vertically.
The choice of the smells is as mysterious as the colour composition of the original work. The smells were baby powder, orange blossom and peppermint. In themselves, these smells are not a translation according to the colours of the painting. It would have been more logical for example to take strawberry as the smell for the red box, but actually to choose a synthetic scent of baby powder made you think more about the purpose of the work. The reason for this was to draw the observer into the incomprehension of the work of art at the time.

As an example of how a scent description from the work *The Scent Reader* evolves into a title in the work *Invisible Scent Paintings,* for the description of an observer for the smell of grass you can use the phrase 'Figuren in de wolken zoeken' (Looking for figures in the clouds) as a title for a work. The observer will not think of the idea of lying in the grass when he first reads this title, but once he has smelled the grass scent that is applied to the wall by scratch & sniff, he will think of lying peacefully in the grass and only then look for figures in the clouds. As a result, the earlier cognitive work changes into a poetic response. Another example which was not in previous smell descriptions is the smell of strawberries combined with the phrase 'My first kiss'. This may refer to a delicious kiss on lips with strawberry-flavoured lipstick, but should the scent have been garlic, the olfactory memory is not so nice, let alone if this had smelled of blood!

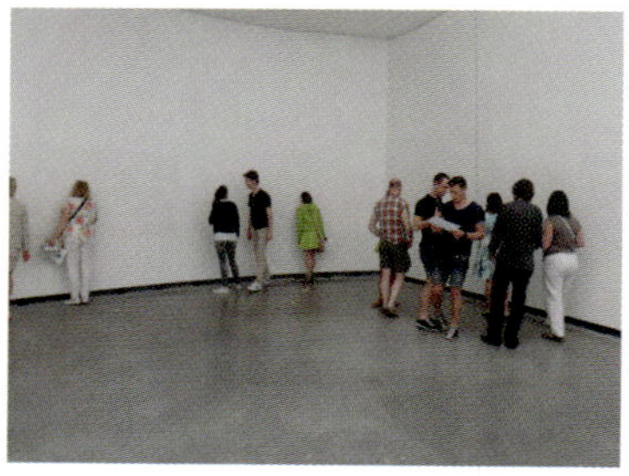

We have discussed the subjectivity of the smell. What about cultural practices of smell? If you use smell as a medium the smell profile of a particular smell may be different according to the location where the smell is used. For example, the smell of baby powder in Switzerland is different to the smell known in Belgium. As an artist it is important to know this. Composite smells like baby powder smell are not always the same. This is because it has existed for decades and in every culture has changed over the years or simply taken on a different life through attempts to imitate it.
This may therefore come over differently to the visitor when showing a work.
The choice of the right scent composition is therefore important to appeal to the visitor's credibility. But it is not only culturally determined composite smells that may differ, a smell may also differ according to the situation, location in which it is found. For example, air pollution does not smell the same everywhere. Depending on the city there may be big differences between what pollutes the air and how much the air is polluted.

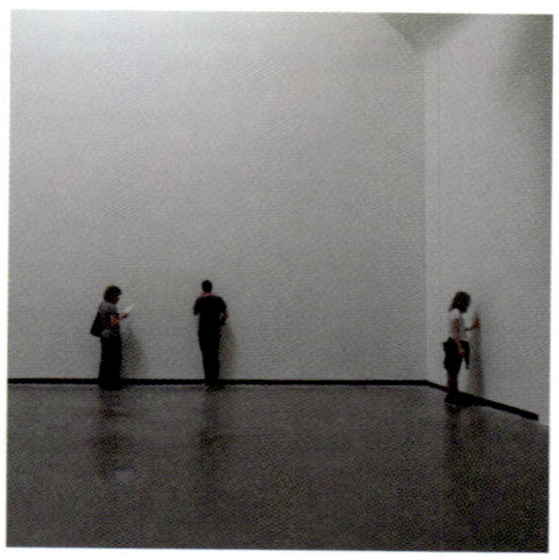

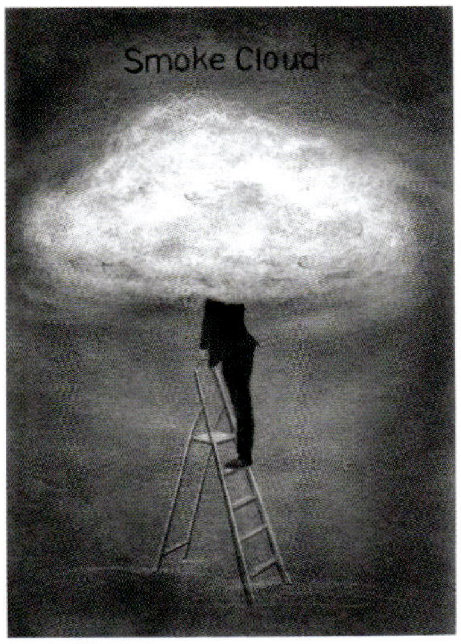

SMOKE CLOUD, SMELL AS A CONTEXT

Smoke Cloud is a big cloud made of intensely white synthetic cotton. It is suspended high in the exhibition room. Visitors can reach into the cloud via a stepladder and put their head into the opening in the cloud. The work is very appealing and most visitors also want a photo with it. Who does not like to have his/her head in the clouds! But once you have your head in *Smoke Cloud,* you will not want to stay there long. The cloud smells of air pollution. The scent differs for every exhibition where the cloud is exhibited. For example, in an exhibition in Havana the cloud smelled much more intensely than the cloud in an exhibition in the Netherlands. The smell intensity of the air pollution smell is adjusted according to the location.
The composition also differs. So the exhaust gases of cars in the Netherlands are filtered more, and the same applies for factories. In Havana, the lovely old American old-timers cause a horrible intense smell of air pollution.

People acclimatise to a smell. We are not usually aware of the smell of an environmental smell because we live in it. Only when we have been away from our environment, do we experience how it really smells. It is exactly like a perfume that you have just applied to your skin. To begin with you can smell it, after a time your nose acclimatises to the smell and you have to concentrate on smelling your skin to notice it again. But it will still not seem to smell intensely and there is a great temptation to quickly spray on some more scent. Exactly the same applies for air pollution. We know that it is there, we can smell it, but do not think it smells intensely, so it will not be so bad. When you are confronted with the smell of the city in a different setting where you do not expect it, you sometimes become aware that the situation regarding pollution is worse than expected. *Smoke Cloud* is this sort of different setting. By putting the smell of air pollution in the city in a museum context and then in a clear magical white soft innocent cloud, the contrast is even greater. But unfortunately not every resident goes to look at art. The smell here gives context to the work. Without the smell the cloud would be a beautiful virgin cloud. The aesthetic experience of the beautiful visual picture disappears into the background.

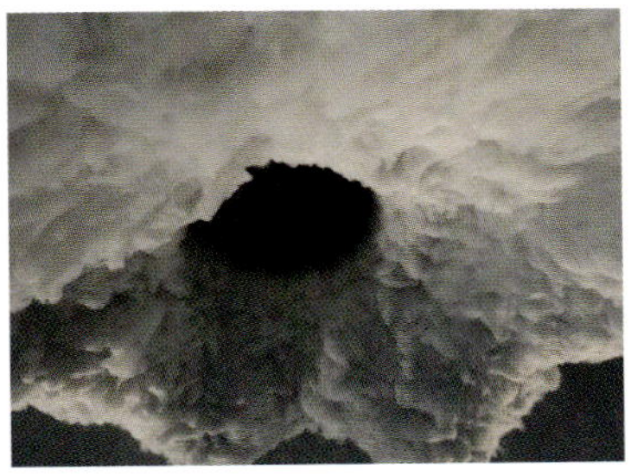

THE SMELL OF A STRANGER, SMELL AS A STATEMENT

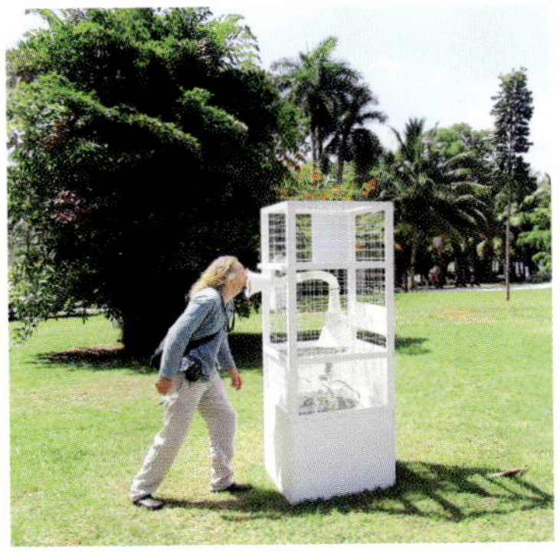

The title brings to mind the smell of a stranger, someone whom you do not know, but the work is about gene technology, nature, physicality, politics, invasion, pollution, violence, life and death and a lot more besides. The title was chosen intentionally as we do know things about these items, but not to the extent that we really know them. They attract, but they also repel. *The Smell of a Stranger* is composed of 9 modules. Each module is 90 cm x 90 cm x 200 cm h and contains a native plant. The work was shown for the first time at the Biennial in Havana (CU) in 2015.

Each plant was *scent engineered* with a different smell, smells that refer to the items referred to above. So there was the smell of blood as a reference to life, the smell of death, the smell of gunpowder as a reference to violence, the smell of cold sweat, the smell of vagina and the smell of sperm as references to physicality, sexuality and reproduction, the smell of American new dollars as a reference to the negotiations between Cuba and America and the synthetic smell of geraniums.

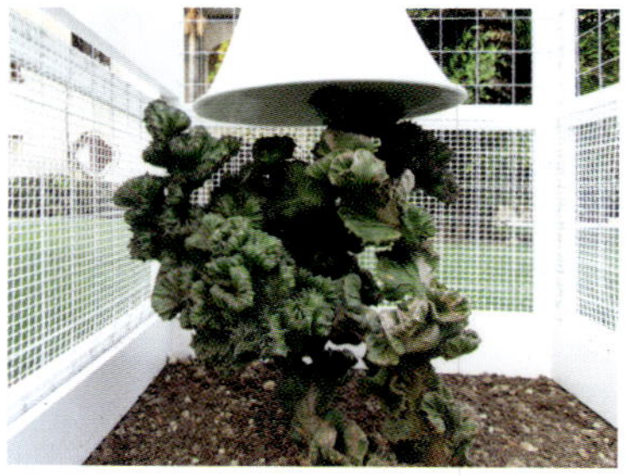

The smells were adapted to the type of plant that was chosen. So the plant *epiphytic bromeliad* smelt of American new dollars. Knowing that this plant is an epiphyte one can quickly make the link between the contribution of America in Cuba. An epiphyte is an organism that grows on a living plant without extracting food from it. You do not have to search far for a political statement here, but the way in which it is interpreted leaves sufficient freedom to begin a discourse and what better choice could be made than a parasitic plant! So this can be done for each of these *scent engineered* plants. The important thing here is that the scents are also realistic and identically imitated. I often collaborate with professional partners in the fragrance industry. The scents for *The Smell of a Stranger* were developed in partnership with IFF International.

Take away the change in smell from this work and the context is lost. The created context here is even a statement to think about. Smell therefore gives meaning to the work. In addition, scent engineering is also questioned. A still very unknown technology that is in its infancy but where *The Smell of a Stranger* gets the observer to think about the possibilities and its dangers.

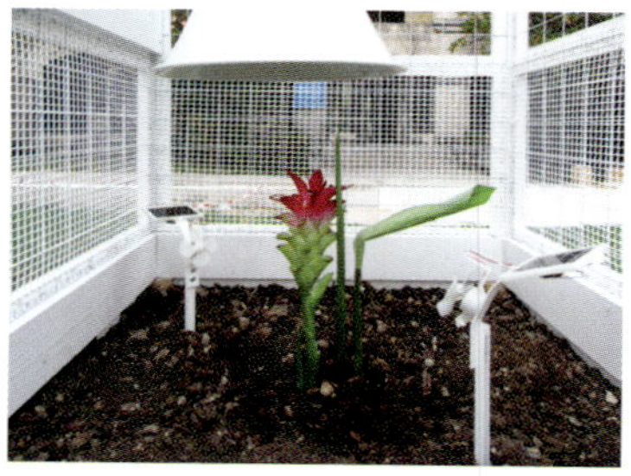

SMELL IN DISCOURSE

In the *Scent City Walk* in Palermo (IT), different scents were placed in 30 locations in relation to the place to make visitors to think about that location or about the context that the work brings with it. In a street where there was a concentration of jewellery shops, on a wall where bill posting was prohibited something was posted up, a 5 euro note and an old 5,000 lire note were stuck up. The old lire note was given the scent of new money and the 5 euro note the scent of old money. By exchanging the smell of two objects one can make a statement and tap into contemporary social sensibilities. With the arrival of the euro everything has become more expensive, many people want to go back to a national unit of currency. As an artist you simply want to start a discourse by subtly making a statement.

So replacing holy water by the smell of blood, synthetically imitated and just as transparent as water, will unexpectedly give the churchgoer another input when he enters and makes the sign of the cross with the replaced holy water and perhaps cause him to think about all the bloodshed that religions have brought with them over the course of history. But for example a holy water stoup made of vitamin C will evoke exactly the opposite thought, as if religion can actually bring healing here.

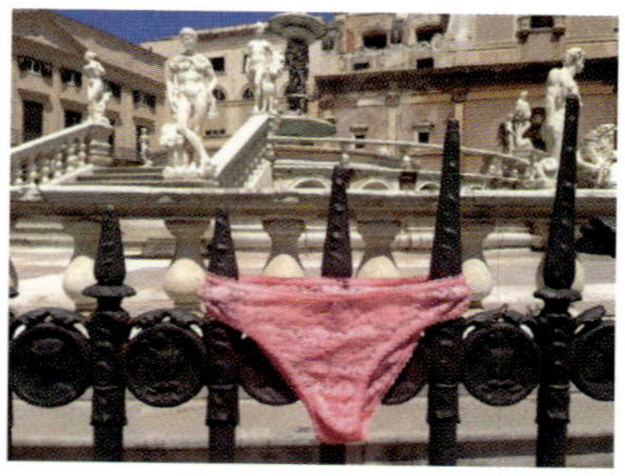

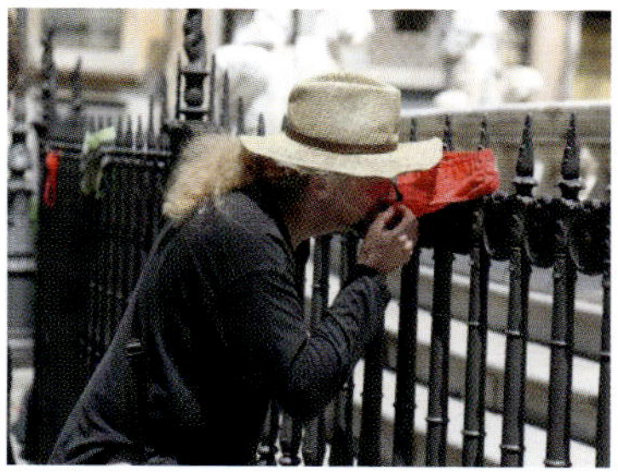

The location may therefore also be decisive for the choice of smells. In the *Scent City Trail* of Palermo, cheap colourful men's and women's briefs were hung up on the fence of the well-known *Fontana Pretoria*, known by the Sicilians as the *Fountain of Shame*. On the front or the back of the briefs, the smell of sperm or vagina was applied. This work led to many hilarious reactions among the visitors who dared to stick their noses in the underwear.

DEFLOWERING

The work *Deflowering* subtly expresses a complaint as regards the sought after and historical (and for some religions still existing today) equality of women about not being able to have their (own) sexual desires as a woman.
Deflowering consists of a small Madonna sculpture made of ice that slowly melts. The visitor has to wait for around an hour to an hour and a half before the magic begins. After this time the smell of vaginal fluid is released. The work caused a lot of commotion and had a huge number of likes and shares worldwide on social media, it was written about extensively but sometimes also experienced as insulting. How a small picture of 23 cm high was able to cause such commotion lay entirely in the smell. The smell was not just the smell of vaginal fluid, but the mix of the vaginal smell of 49 women of different nationalities and races. By cooperating in a research project and signing a confidentiality agreement, 1.7 ml of the female fluid concentrate was obtained to create this work. Knowing that such a 'scent concentrate' is not straightforward to obtain, as we are not talking about a recreated scent here, but the real essence. 1.7 ml may not seem like much, but the scent was even more heavenly. For one version a maximum of only 0.5 ml was needed to get a result.

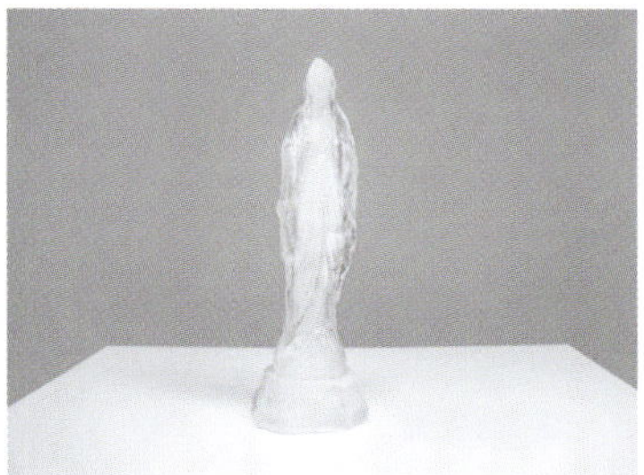

As a reaction to his own work and thanks to over a thousand emails from enthusiastic women the work *The Paintbrush of Gustave Courbet* was produced.
A paintbrush made of pubic hair with which, with the smell of vagina, a vagina was painted on a blank canvas in a stylised 'V' shape. V can also be seen here as showing the freedom symbol that one can make with the middle finger and index finger.
The freedom of being a woman.

DEAD BODY BULLETS

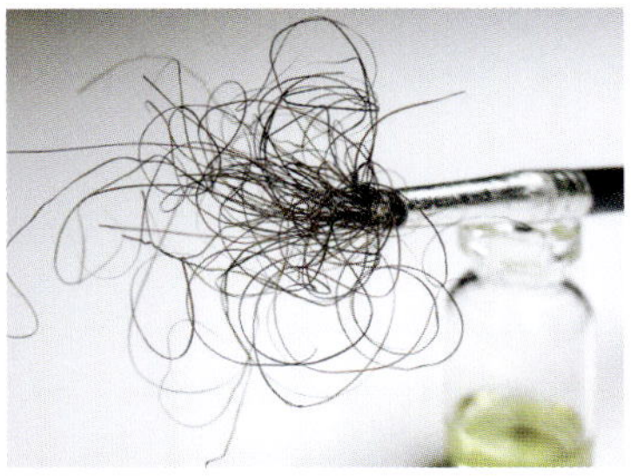

Nine glass bullets each contain a quantity of scent concentrate of the universal smell of dead bodies. The quantity of scent extract is determined according to age, sex, height and weight. So after distillation of his or her body, an adult will provide more scent concentrate than the distillate of a child or new-born baby. If one were to distil a human body after death, then the quantity of scent extract in itself would not be much. The bigger and fatter the body, the more scent extract.

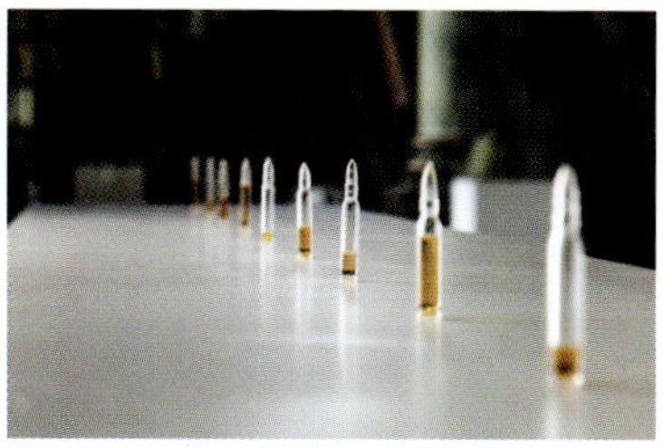

The smell is that of a person who has just died and not a person in an advanced state of decomposition. Here it was not only the smell that gave the context, but also how much smell is present in the glass bullets. The work encourages the observer to think about the futility of death.

DECISION

Smell as a statement, smell as a reaction to a social situation can sometimes encourage people to think and reflect more, but also to get the observer into discussion. An olfactory work of art must therefore be more than merely adding a smell. There must be meaning in it. This meaning may be in the smell itself, but also in relation to a given something. It is usually the interaction that actually takes it into a deeper context. Images in relation to smells and vice versa encourage people to reflect in a different way to merely one sense. The strength of smell compared with the other senses is that it may affect the memory, emotions and physical reactions due to acquired experience and so involve the observer even more and cognitively encourage them to think about the context of the work.

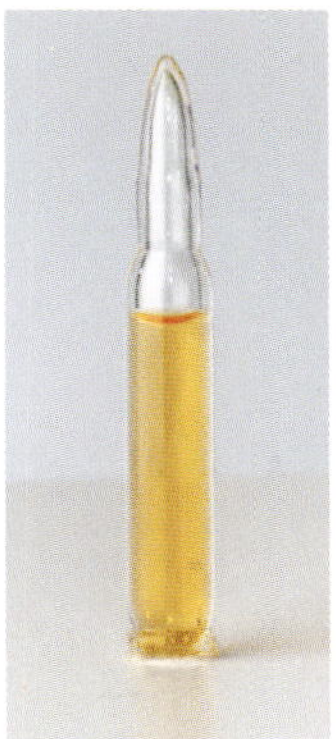

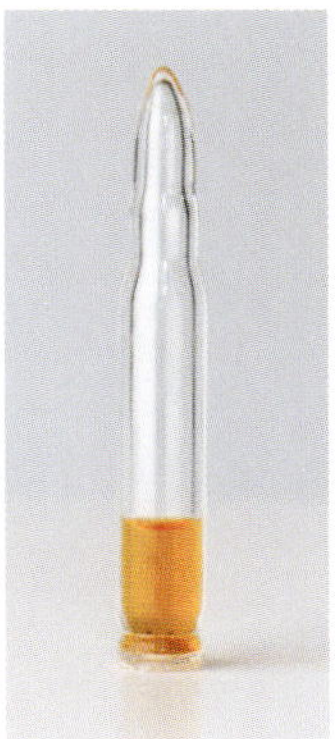

In the *Olfactory Art Manifest,* a subdivision is made according to *isms*. The works discussed here fall mainly under *Olfactionism* as there is always 'fact' in them and the observer is encouraged to 'action', to do something. This action is reflection, thinking, starting a discourse. Smell is meaning, smell is context when it has the right link with the subject and/or the title. Smell can then contribute to giving meaning to the work or is itself the carrier of meaning. Using smell as a concept of the work of art offers many future possibilities. It is up to the artist and curator to tap into this and to the observer to open their nose.

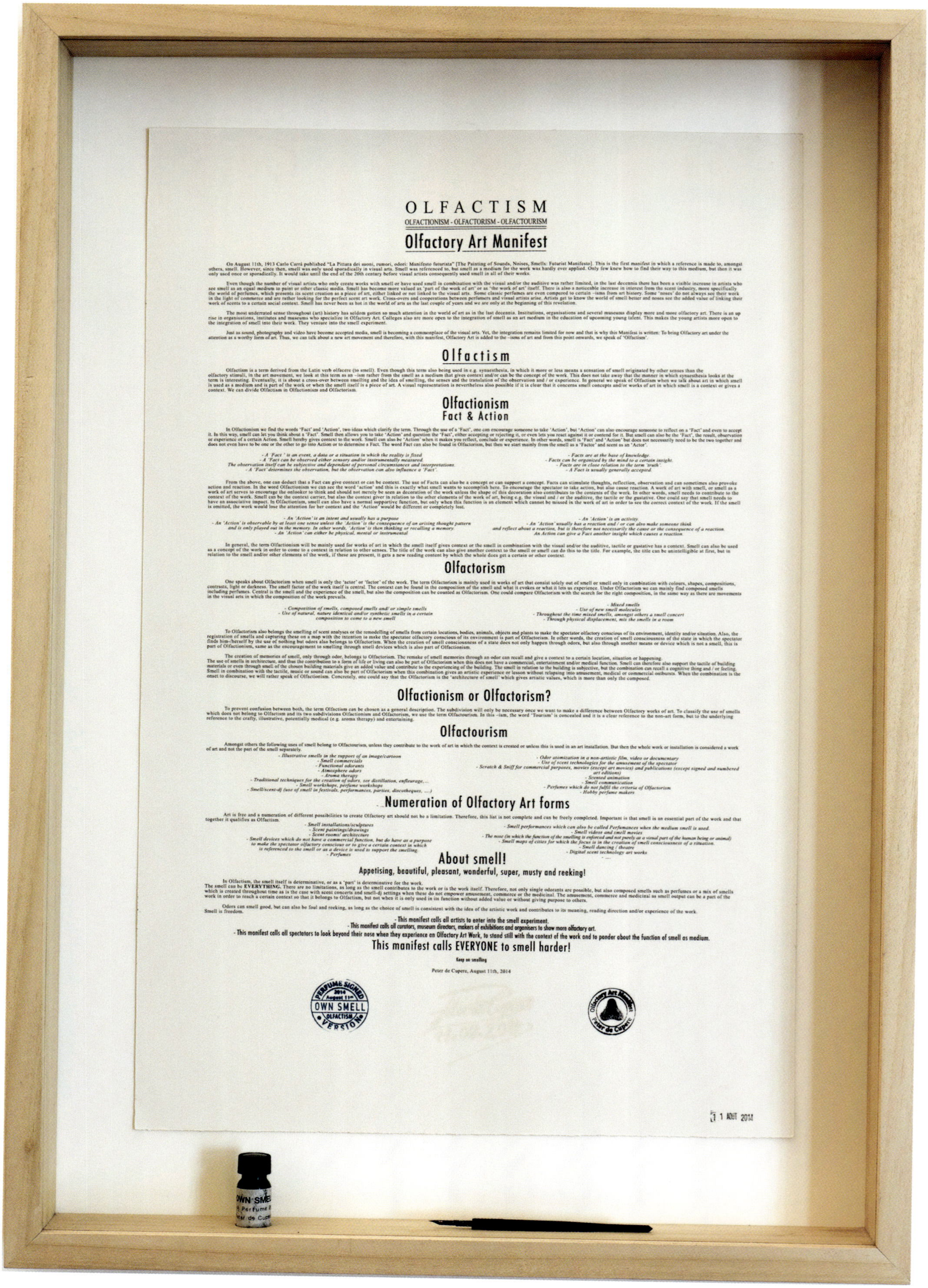
OLFACTISM
OLFACTIONISM - OLFACTORISM - OLFACTOURISM
Olfactory Art Manifest
Olfactism
Olfactionism
Fact & Action
Olfactorism
Olfactionism or Olfactorism?
Olfactourism
Numeration of Olfactory Art forms
About smell!
Appetising, beautiful, pleasant, wonderful, super, musty and reeking!
- This manifest calls all artists to enter into the smell experiment.
This manifest calls EVERYONE to smell harder!
Peter de Cupere, August 11th, 2014
OWN SMELL
1 AOUT 2014

CARO VERBEEK

“REFINE YOUR NOSTRILS!” A MANIFESTATION OF A NEW AWARENESS OF SMELL

“We have forgotten how to smell. We must refine our nostrils”.

These words were penned in around 1916—exactly a century ago—by the relatively unknown Italian artist Ennio Valentinelli in his posthumously published manifest *Arte degli Odori* (Art of Smells). The Futurist probably had not suspected that his idea of blasting smell into an art medium would have a predictive capacity. Although it would not surprise a real Futurist.

In 2014, Peter de Cupere added a new dimension to his scent performances, scent concerts, smell sculptures, scent paintings, and smell installations: the smell manifest. From the early 20th century, the manifest was the medium of choice for artists to make a statement about the unique, revolutionary qualities of their movement. Artists informed a public far outside their own national boundaries of their world-improving artistic practices using the printed pamphlet. The Futurists in particular were known for the expression of their shared ideas using the paper mass medium. So in 1909, with their *Manifesto del Futurismo (Futurist Manifesto)*, they reinforced their existence as a group. The senses were a great source of inspiration for them to establish innovative art, especially after the First World War. Only after expressing their greatest words, did they (partly) redeem their promises in practice.

De Cupere, who often deviates from the standard, does this precisely in reverse. After at least 20 years of scent practice, he puts his theories down on paper in his *Olfactory Art Manifest*. He does this with an art history awareness and indebtedness to Futurism; his argument is published a century (plus a year) after *La Pittura dei Suoni, Rumori, Odori (The Painting of Sounds, Noises, Smells)*, the very first manifest about smell and art, written by Carlo Carrà in 1913. In de Cupere’s text, we therefore find explicit and implicit references to his predecessor. The Belgian also demonstrates the embodiment of his own theory. This jack-of-all trades does not mention anything in this work that he has not already executed himself.

Olfactism, as de Cupere has named the new movement, concerns “smell as a medium that gives context and/or can be the concept of the work”. In this statement, he immediately demonstrates his first distinction from Carrà. For the Italian artist, smell (just like sound) was only a source of inspiration for ultimately arriving at a visual object.

'Olfactism' can roughly be split into *Olfactionism* and *Olfactorism*. The first category includes both 'action' and 'fact'. Smell as a fact must create a context for moving the observer (that is actually the 'smeller') to action and reaction. A good olfactory work of art loses meaning without its aromatic addition. If that were not the case, the smell would only be the garnish. A good example of this is his work *Smoke Cloud* (2014). The 'smeller' climbs a stepladder with his or her head literally reaching into the clouds. Having arrived there, the observer however does not perceive a proverbial smell of roses, but the choking smell of exhaust gases and pollution. The intellectual and detached reading of newspaper reports from our comfortable armchair has a very different impact to a physical experience. De Cupere literally forces our nose up against the facts, so that no-one can avoid it: this is what we cause with our lifestyle. And it will ultimately prevent us from breathing if we do not change it.

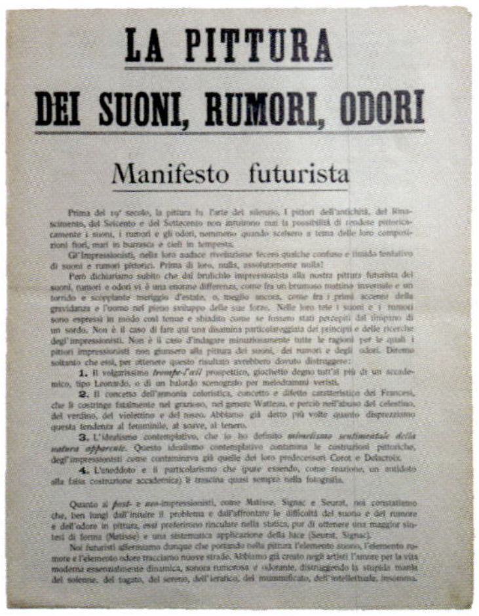
LA PITTURA
DEI SUONI, RUMORI, ODORI
Manifesto futurista

Where smell is above all an essential element in *Olfactionism,* smell occupies a central place in *Olfactorism*. In his own words, this is a concept in which the word 'factor' and 'actor' occur, "... the creation of smell consciousness of the state in which the spectator finds him/herself by the use of nothing but odours ...". So an apparently empty room can accommodate an olfactory work of art that does its work completely invisibly. The connection between scent and memory, and hence the associations and emotions that a smell can evoke, play an important part in this, according to de Cupere. Who does not know that feeling of being overwhelmed by a vivid childhood memory after inhaling a well-known smell as soon as you enter a place? The smell memory (also called the Proustian memory) is incredibly powerful. The effect does not even disappear in people with dementia. It is impossible here not to think of de Cupere's *Smelloflowers* (2007). He placed coloured, flower-shaped fragrance diffusers in the Den Ooiman nursing home in Doetinchem. Not only did the specific smells enable the elderly people to find their own room in a complex where all the corridors and doors looked the same, the scents also evoked early and vivid childhood memories. This can be very reassuring for people who are often no longer even aware of their identity.

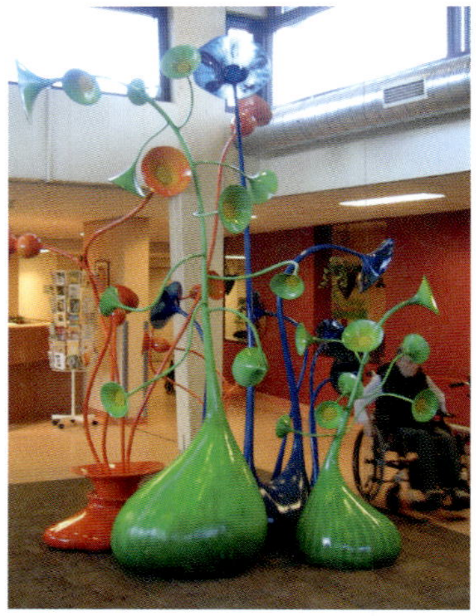

The artist also summarises what *Olfactism* is not under the term *Olfactourism*. Unless there is an artistic context or concept at the base, this does not include aromatherapy, scent and perfume workshops, aroma jockey performances, technological gadgets, advertising, perfumes that do not comply with *Olfactorism*, and smell illustrations. The fact that de Cupere creates these frameworks has to do with the confusing appropriation of the label *Olfactory Art* by various disciplines, such as perfumery and aromatherapy. The lack of clarity has less to do with the quality or otherwise of the end product than with the lack of a clear definition. The status-raising effect of the stamp also plays a part in this. Art with a capital 'A' is often equated with skill, ingenuity, quality, originality, authorship, and the exclusion of any commercial interest. Many perfumers recognise themselves in these traditional attitudes and, in this way, try to convince the public of the systematic underestimation of their profession. And this is understandable. How often are

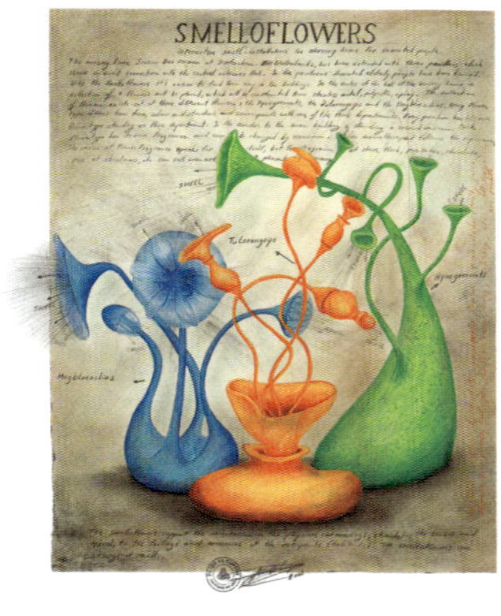

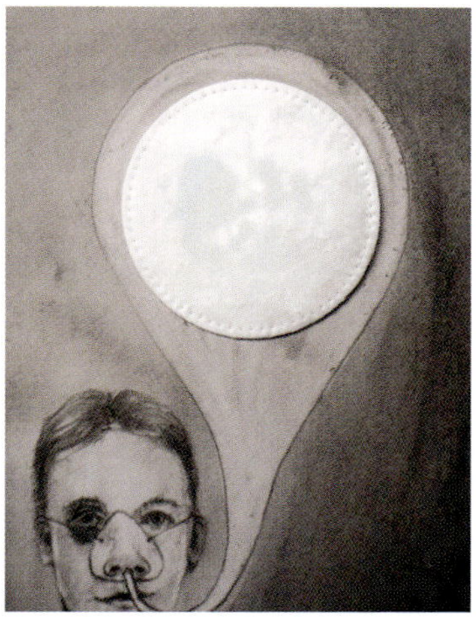

classic perfume compositions such as Coty's *Chypre* (1917), or *Chanel N°5* (1921) not treated as a 'scent'? Would one ever call a painting by Picasso a 'picture'? But although there is no conclusive definition of art, other principles will also apply within art discourse in the 20th and 21st centuries, such as asking critical questions, commitment, and a conceptual impact. These values within art are just as important as, if not even more important than, craftsmanship and pleasing the eye, or the tongue or nose. Perhaps this is why Valentinelli attaches such importance to distinguishing himself clearly from perfumers in his *Arte degli Odori* (Art of Smells). He also did that by referring to the other side of the dichotomy of smells, namely by including stench. "The complete olfactory lyricism of nature not only lies in the fragrant, it also resides in stench, in the malodorous," he said. Even de Cupere and other olfactory artists can regularly be 'caught' diffusing taboo smells. Sperm, sweat (see *Sweat*, 2010, *Life is one sweat study case*, 2015), urine, and faecal matter are not foreign to him. Yet substances identical to those of the body are also found in the undertones, or base notes of perfumes. Olfactory art distinguishes itself from perfume by the specific context in which it operates and the social questions that are asked. A cosmetic perfume could at the most be classed as applied art.

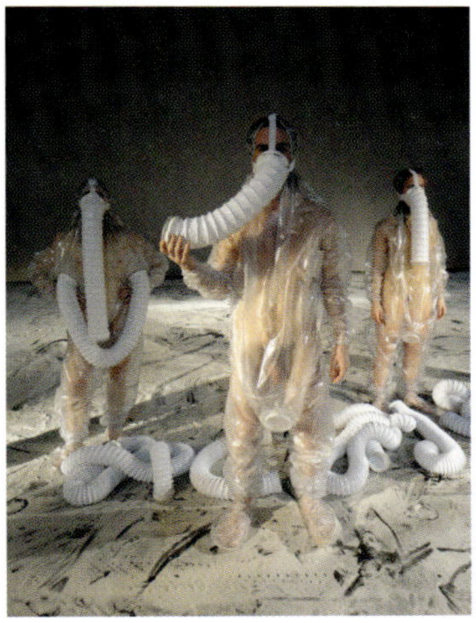

From an historical point of view, it is also interesting to note that the term *Olfactory Art* was first coined in the 19th century by the perfumer and chemist Septimus Piesse. In his treatise *De kunst van Parfumerie* (The art of Perfumery) from 1855, he describes how perfume could play an aesthetic role in smell concerts. He also comes up with explanations for synesthetic experiences for the colour and tone associations that fragrances can evoke. Piesse even mentions the possibility of an *odophone*. Finally, he mentions the lyrical sphere and universal values of which perfume can be an expression. We also need to realise that the term 'aesthetics' in the Kantian meaning still prevailing at the time did not pertain to the individual judgment of taste, but to generally applicable values that could manifest themselves in a work of art (and which would therefore have to have the same effect on everyone). Because smell evokes different associations in everyone, he argued that for this reason alone, it cannot be part of aesthetics. Added to this is the fact that smell would not be able to provide any knowledge of external objects. These ideas of course no longer apply in the present art discourse, and with his manifest de Cupere astutely wants to point us to the range and potential of smell as a medium in the hands of the artist. The Futurists were also clear about their boundaries, although their aggressive pose could be likened to that of the territorial behaviour of male gorillas. The French in particular were targeted. The Impressionists had perhaps feebly 'tried' to depict smells and sounds, but failed in this like a musician who makes sounds that are only "perceived by deaf ear drums". On the other hand, according to Carrà, they only "had to be shut up in a room with characteristic smells, such as flowers and petroleum, in order—by an obscure process—for the most expressive images to sprout from their mind". *Synaesthesia* or the translation of one sense to another, formed the basis of numerous other Futurist manifestos. In relation to smell, it only occurs on one other occasion.

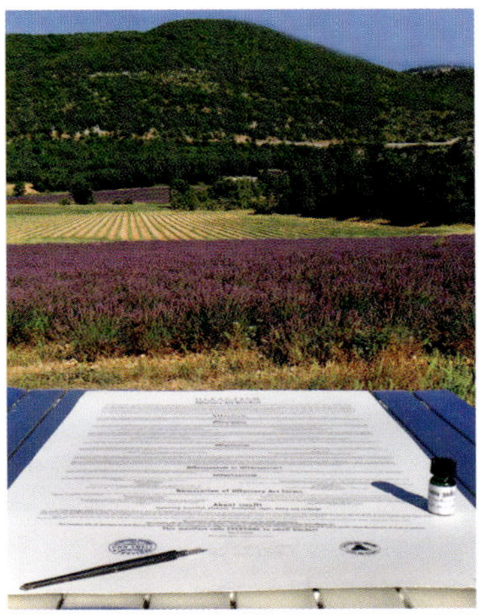

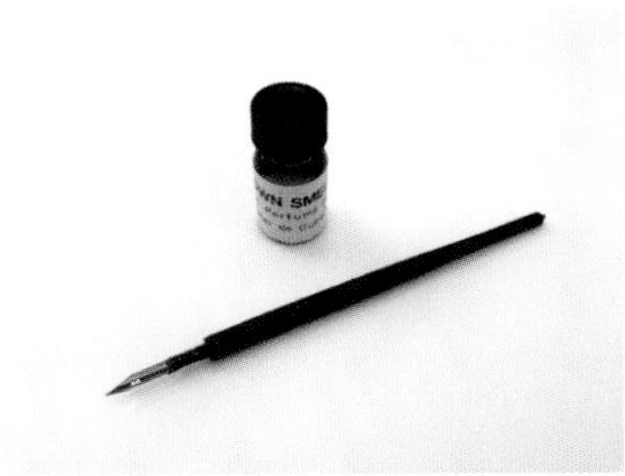

Ten years after Carrà, his Futurist colleague Fedele Azari wrote in 1924 *La Flora Futurista ed Equivalenti Plastici di Odori Artificiali* ('The Futurist Flora and Plastic Equivalents of Artificial Smells'), which perhaps still speaks to the imagination. In this, Azari writes that a stop should be put on poor innocent flower fragrances and nauseating pastel colours. It was time for acute, all-penetrating smells and bright vivid colours. Only artificial smells could sublimate imperfect nature and meet their new hunger for pronounced forms and images. The artist saw in particular the perfumes of François Coty as very suitable equivalents of the Futurist stylistic form. Heavy, powdery fragrances, not smelling of flowers, gave expression to modernity and their rejection of bourgeoisie.

For de Cupere, who from time to time called upon the striking phenomenon, synaesthesia is attractive, but did not fall so very much under Olfactism.
The direct appeal to the nose is essential for him. Although there are many common features with his historic examples, he differs on a fundamental point from the Futurists. The Belgian artist would not honour his name if he had not added an aromatic dimension to his writing. He signed the manifest with ink made from a distillate of his own body smells that he had collected over a period of two years. This biographical perfume is like the black square with which Malevich at a given moment started to sign his paintings, to identify with his work. De Cupere adds the deed to the word and gives context and meaning by using smell as a medium. His manifest not only speaks of olfactory art, but also is it. In the end, it is up to the public with their newly acquired awareness of smell, not only to refine their knowledge, but also their nostrils.

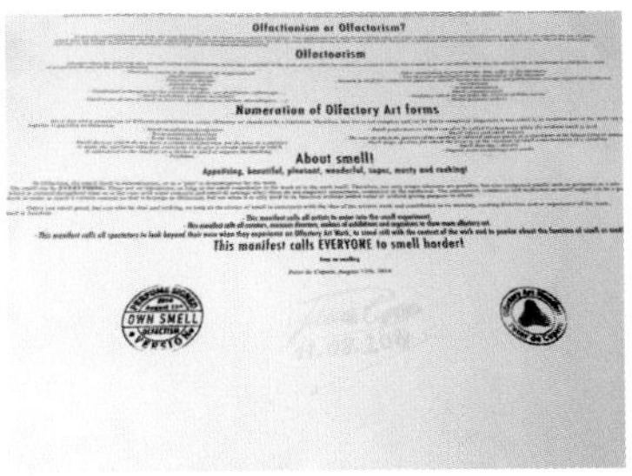
Olfactionism or Olfactorism?
Olfactoorism
Numeration of Olfactory Art forms
About smell!
Appetising, beautiful, pleasant, wonderful, super, musty and reeking!
This manifest calls EVERYONE to smell harder!

Caro Verbeek
Scent historian, Vrije Universiteit Amsterdam

Scratch & Smell the colours of this world

PETER DE CUPERE

THE ART OF SMELLING

The Art Of Smelling, Olfactory Art Research was the title of the solo exhibition in Enschede. In the light of works from the exhibition, an explanation is given of where Peter de Cupere's works originate from. As in many of Peter de Cupere's works, the visitor must actively participate in this exhibition. They themselves search for how smell may differ and provide an added value in relation to seeing.

If we generally take 'seeing' as a starting point, we discover that smells can give more of a message than merely 'sight' alone. For seeing we only use four different receptors, red, green and blue cones plus rods (for the light). Each colour can therefore be mapped in three dimensions with a different value for transparency. The assignment of a smell to a dimensional map would in a manner of speaking require an extremely large dimensional space. This is a fundamental problem of smell identification, and is thus also to speak of a pre-determined smell identification. To show this better, in the exhibition a work from 2001, *Touch & Smell the Colours of this World* [1], is processed differently in the new work *Scratch, Sniff and Imagine the Colours of this World*.
The question: 'Can the observer give his own context to a certain combination of a smell with colour?' is for this work of more paramount importance for the artist than the question: "What context does a smell give in combination with a colour?"

Why does smell have a subjective effect and is it difficult to know whether a certain context for a work is also experienced as this intended context? Can an observer identify a smell as a guide so as to identify the message of the work?

The link between smell and memory is stored in the orbitofrontal cortex. Smell is almost always stored in the long term memory. This is why we can feel certain emotions if we just smell a scent. Smell is, in addition to its primary functions, hence an element which evokes memory. It may be an event, but also a mood, a feeling from your youth.

THE 'PROUST EFFECT'

The smell memory is also called the Proust effect [2], derived from the name of the French writer Marcel Proust.
The given 'memory' plays an important part. Since a personal memory is subjective, it is also difficult to say specifically that a certain smell would give a certain context with the exception of a certain 'memory as context' in itself.

The work *Sniff and Imagine the Colours of this World* is a good example of this. The smell-colour combinations give different 'contexts' for different observers. The discourse that arises between one visitor and another about how a smell is experienced also forms a substantive part of the work.
Most contexts referred to their own memory that prompted by the combination of the smell with the particular colour. If one did not immediately identify the smell, the colour was taken first as a starting point to consider which smell would fit with this colour. The smells were chosen such that they could either go further in the memory or be based on primary functions.

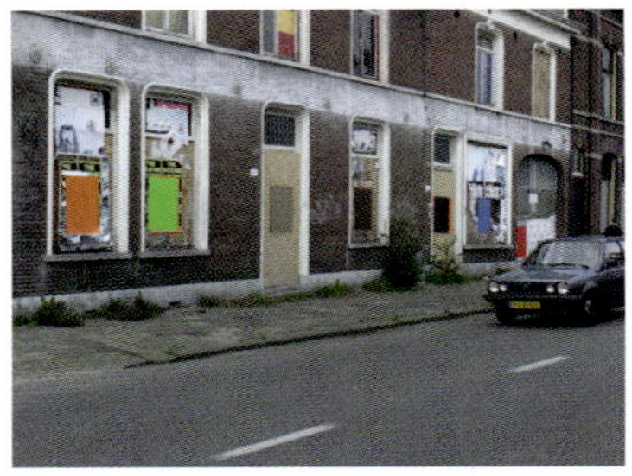

Of course, these primary functions must not be underestimated, and even form the basis of the development of smell. Smell also has a warning level.

Concretely, the function of smelling may be divided into the following, respectively:

- Primary smell as warning: the recognition of the smells of fire, smoke, poisonous and rotten food. In some animals, this function is even more extreme. They smell their enemies even before they see them.
- Smell as pleasure: the observation of scent is directly tied to the emotional brain centres (limbic system). This makes the smell sensations we can experience as pleasant very direct. Accordingly, this function is also stimulated intuitively. Scent is important for the libido. In order to enjoy sex optimally, we subconsciously perceive pheromones; hormonal substances that awaken our sex drive.
- Smell and taste: being able to recognise and enjoy food. We only have four taste buds (five including umami, cf. savoury flavour), which means that smell is important in order to properly enjoy food and drink, but also, as mentioned earlier, to recognise and avoid spoiled or bad food.
- Smell as trail: a function that we lost, but which is still widely present in animals. Following a trail or finding one's way (back) via smell.

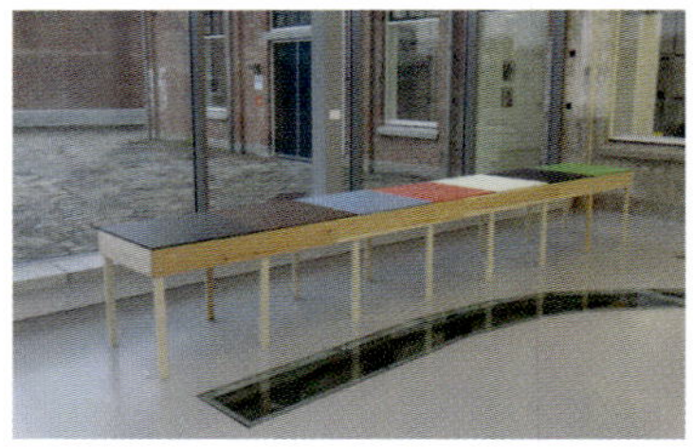

SMELL AS MEMORY

How we experience a certain smell as pleasure or warning will determine our way of remembering, and it will therefore also let us experience how we will react to a remembered scent in the future.
Nevertheless, 'scent as warning' prevails over other smell perceptions, and it may be assumed that we will also recognise this sooner as something negative (not always, the smoky smell of a barbecue is rather experienced as something positive based on the scent memory of an earlier barbecue and/or the accompanying fun).

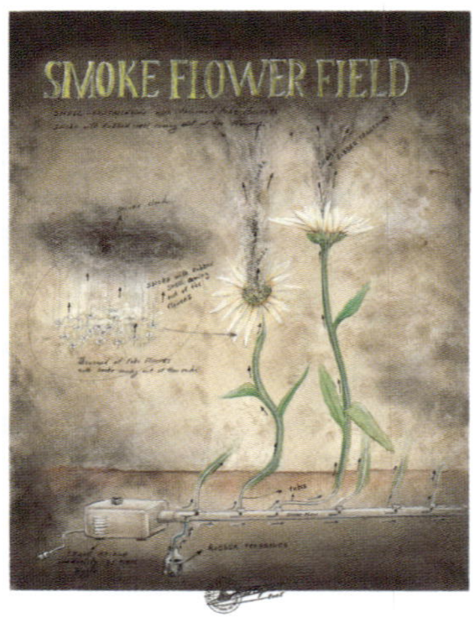

The smell of smoke and fire has such a recognisable, warning scent. These smells are used a great deal in installations where they raise questions about issues such as air pollution in combination with the visual image. For instance, in the exhibition

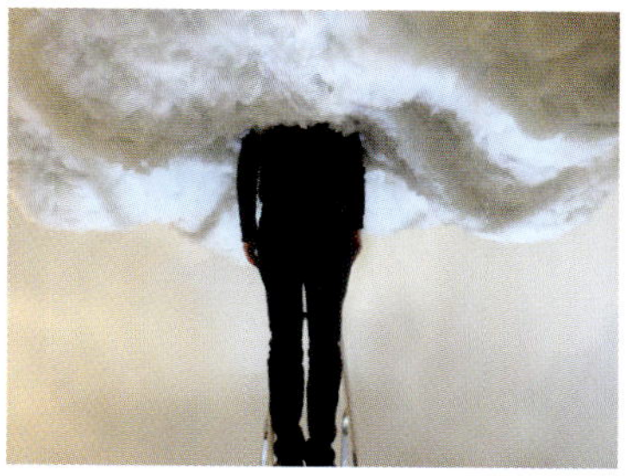

The Art of Smelling, people could see and olfactorily experience the work *Smoke Cloud* for the first time. The work later travelled across Latin-America (Havana, Buenos Aires & Rio de Janeiro) in the exhibition *The Importance of Being...*, a traveling exhibition with 40 Belgian artists, organised by Bruno Devos and curator Sara Alonso Gómez.

In Enschede, however, the smell of air pollution in the *Smoke Cloud* was combined with the smell of gunpowder, because Enschede has a strong collective memory of the explosion of a fireworks factory [3].

The environment, society and certain other issues caused by humanity are an important context of Peter de Cupere's work. The perception of how people deal with the sense of smell is important in this. Memory is a key notion, but also the way in which the smell is perceived and the perception itself. The olfactory experience of environmental problems is strongly dependent on how one perceives a scent, and how well one is aware of one's own scent recognition. The spectator must therefore be aware of his own possibilities and experiences with regard to smelling. The global spectator has too little knowledge of his own smelling capacity. He also becomes accustomed to a smell too easily [4]. In other words, he quickly gets used to the smell of air pollution, and therefore his olfactory experience of environmental problems, among other things, is too limited. As long as these smells do not disturb the domestic environment, he also doesn't look further into the future, and is, strictly speaking, only focused on his direct surroundings. He thus participates consciously in the pollution of society by not adjusting his own luxury to more environmentally friendly options.

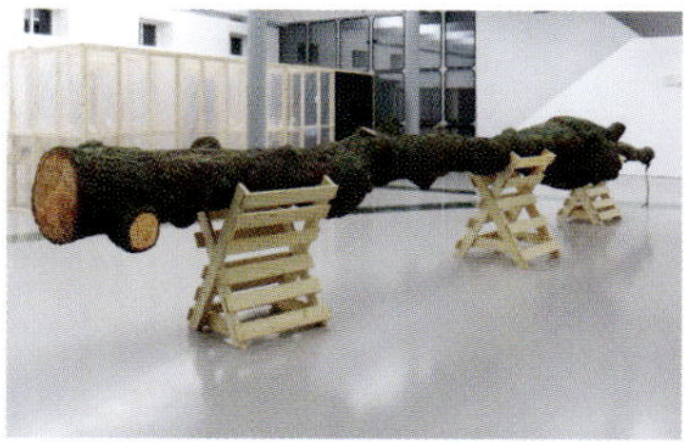

Through his scent installations, Peter de Cupere wants to inspire the spectator to think about environmental awareness by showing possible end results. These end results can be installations such as *Smoke Cloud* or *Olfactory Tree*.
The *Olfactory Tree* shows an identical tree on a scale of 1/10 in the belly (bulb) of the tree. This small tree, however, does not have the natural colours of brown and green, but is completely black and dark grey, and smells burnt. The inside forms a stark contrast with the outside. Just like in society, people only start to think when they identify the damage, and not before.

The *Olfactory Tree* is a Droste effect, because the small tree is repeated in the large tree, and therefore the small tree will also contain another small tree which has probably completely burned down and decayed. It is not pleasant to experience the burnt air, but since we love voyeurism, we will still take a look into the tree and sniffle.

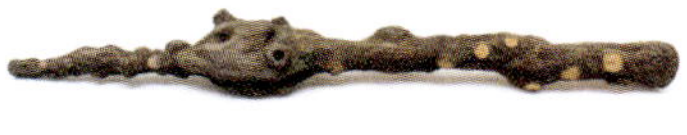

Both *Smoke Cloud* and *Olfactory Tree* refer to CO_2 emissions. Climate change is a problem that should not be underestimated, and it has been gaining attention in recent years. But as more CO_2 is emitted and the world is getting warmer, the amount of water also increases. In response to all these changes, plants emit more fragrant chemicals, called 'biogenic volatile organic compounds' (BVOC). BVOC protect the plant from plagues and make the world smell more intensely. Research has shown that plants have already started their increased emissions of BVOC, and that the world is therefore already becoming more fragrant! "The increase is exponential. It may have already increased about ten percent in the past years, and in case of a warming of two or three degrees Celsius in the next decades, it will increase about thirty or forty percent[5]."

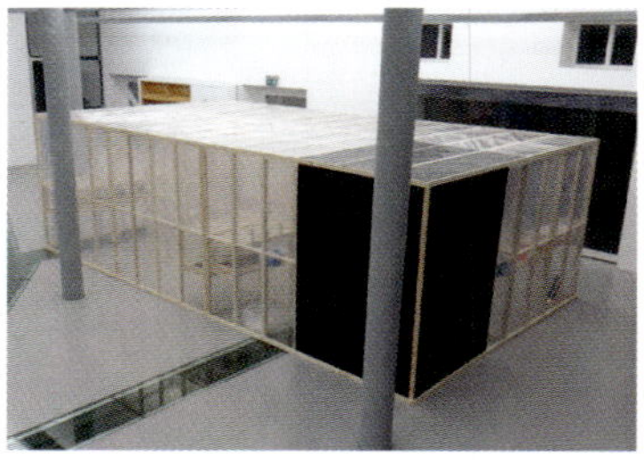

In the exhibition *The Art Of Smelling, Olfactory Art Research*, in addition to the context of environmental pollution (cf. *Smoke Cloud, Olfactory Tree*) and how the spectator depends on his own scent memory, the aspect of scent recognition and scent veracity is also dealt with.

In order to make the spectator aware of these aspects, there is the *Smell Lab*. This research lab may not look scientific, but the visitor still feels like a kind of researcher, or rather an artistic researcher. The spectator is pampered here in the role of researching artist. Visitors are also thrown back in time in a playful way. Like a curious child, they go and explore. When entering the lab, visitors must first dress in the necessary 'hygienic' lab clothing. After that, they can test their own scent awareness using two small 'smell devices'.

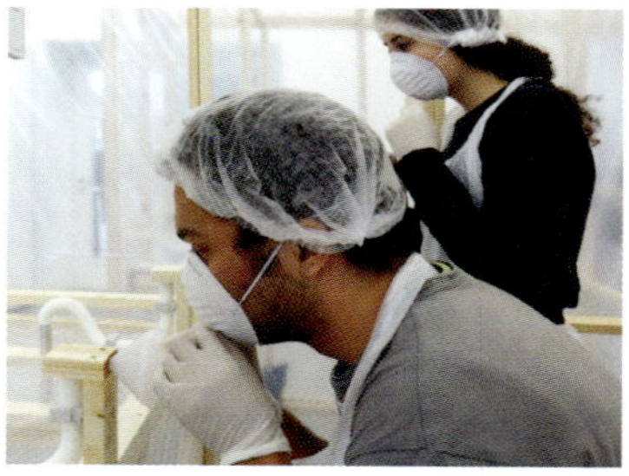

Furthermore, they can discover four different plants modified (GOM)[6] via Genetic Olfactorisation (GO). Via genetic olfactorisation, the plants have been given a smell different from their original smell. GOM offers many applications: for example, one could change the smell of sweat into the scent of roses, or make a rose smell like chocolate or strawberries. The experience is currently limited to the imaginative ability the artist provides us with here. The idea of manipulating plants is something he already started working on at the beginning of his oeuvre. The question whether possible new plant types can help the world is, therefore, always reciprocal. This question also ties into the context of offering possible solutions for environmental problems via nature itself.

As a human being, the artist does not approve of the genetic engineering of plants, and certainly not of crops we eat ourselves, but in the end, we cannot stop it. The world is evolving quickly. The global population is increasing exponentially[7], and this also has an effect on energy consumption[8]. There is no certainty that mankind will be able to decrease CO2 emissions sufficiently in order to stop climate change in the near future. The search for energy and food will only lead to more freedom for genetic engineering. Whenever the global economy gains importance, compromises keep being made. We can be scared of this, but we can also emphasise the positive side and identify any negative consequences. In this context, Peter de Cupere wants to show possible positive developments with his work as well. Concepts that are based on the possible consequences of climate change, and that will make spectators

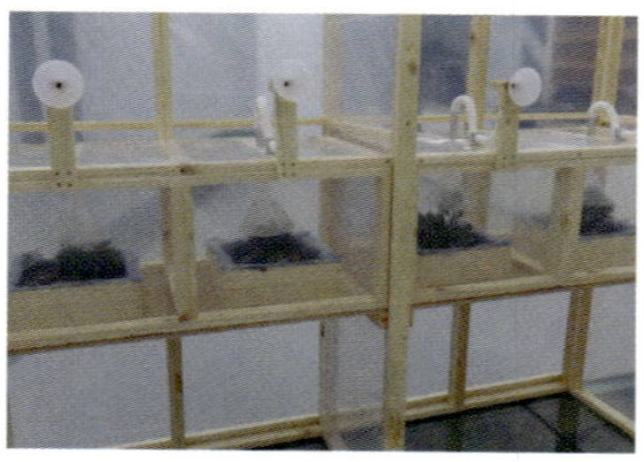

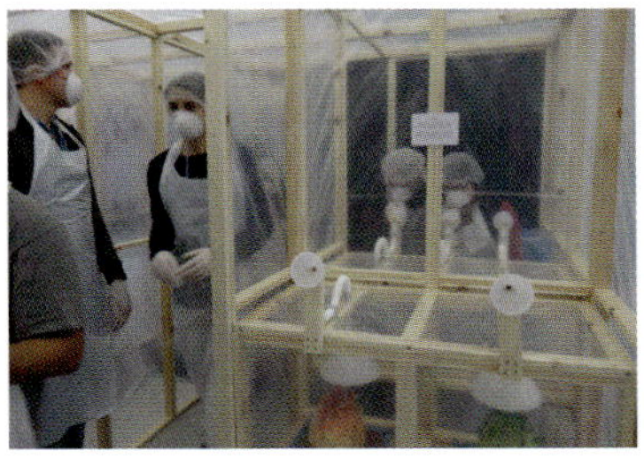

think about their future. Since smell triggers memories, people may subconsciously remember his work in the future, and may subconsciously only choose the positive output of new technologies. His work should not exclusively be seen in the context of this time, but thanks to the power of the olfactory memory, it can remind us of future-oriented solutions. Through the years, different works were created around genetic engineering. Examples are the *Alambfleurics* and the *Brewery Flowers*.

Alambfleurics are genetically modified flowers. They are shaped like an alembic[9]. During the day, the bulb of the flower is heated by the sun. In the bulb, the essence of the flower evaporates, and at night it cools down in the spiral stem of the flower in order to secrete its scent extract in the flower head. The advantage is that one no longer has to pick the flower and no longer has to get up early. It is now possible to tap the fragrance compounds at night, and at possible plantations this can be done via automatic receptacles. As the flower grows and becomes larger, the fragrance production increases in quality and quantity over the years.

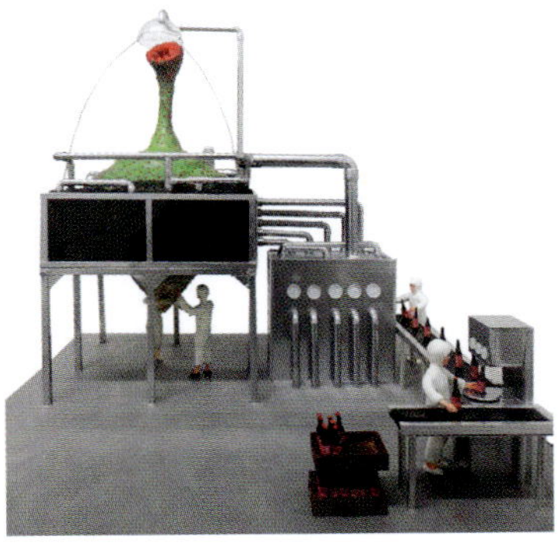

Brewery Flowers are flowers converted into a veritable factory in and of themselves via genetic modification. The plants become very large and produce enormous amounts every day. The need for polluting factories no longer exists, since these *Brewery Flowers* themselves are the factory, and work in a completely environmentally friendly way. With *Brewery Flowers*, one can create products such as beer or other beverages. The only extra addition would be water and possibly carbon dioxide gas, which can be extracted in a natural way.

Alambfleurics and *Brewery Flowers* seem like imaginative flowers, but with the fast evolution of technology, they offer possible future perspectives. For example, the artist has already approximated the form of the alambfleuric using grafting (not genetic engineering), but these tests did not last long and quickly became mouldy.

In the *Smell Lab* in the exhibition *The Art of Smelling, Olfactory Art Research*, four uncommon live plants are shown, of which the scent was modified. At least, it seems that way to the spectator. The four plants are shielded with plastic foil. Visitors can smell the plants via a tube system connected with funnels. These plants therefore smell differently than how they look or would smell from a visual perspective. The spectator also believes, or wants to believe, which of these plants really do smell differently than they would originally. Veracity is of the utmost importance in this. The fact that the visitors themselves are 'decorated' as researchers increase this veracity. The visitors also feel like researchers because they are wearing lab clothing. In order to emphasise the investigative character, they must also smell via a straw that they themselves have attached to a paper mouth mask. They have to stick the straw into the funnel for each plant, and sniff to observe the scent. The spectator standing outside the lab can follow everything through the transparent plastic. The entire setting creates a sense of scientific research, while, rather, it is an investigation into learning how to smell better and becoming aware of one's own scent perception.

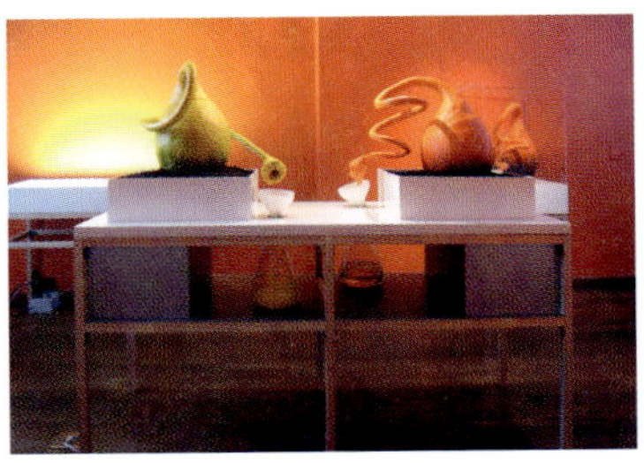

That the plants' scents have been changed using GOM (Genetic Olfactory Manipulation) may sound implausible to some, but by experiencing it themselves, they do think about whether this is or could actually be possible. Doubt is the winner here. In many of his works, the creation of veracity plays an important part in increasing awareness in the spectator and/or making him think about society, the environment and his own (scent) boundaries.

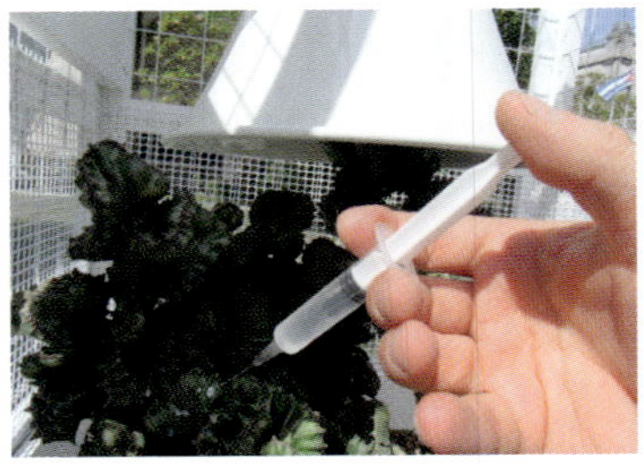

Even though the artist has been weighing the flower in relation to new genetic engineering technologies he himself invented for the benefit of a more beautiful society, scientific research in recent years has shown that this is not so far-fetched. Via 'scent engineering' [10] it is possible to give certain types of flowers a different scent, just like it is possible to give them another colour [11]. Scent engineering of plants and flowers is not yet completely developed, but we can assume that various plants will smell and even taste differently in the future. In 2015, the artist realised the work *The Smell Of A Stranger* in the XII Biennial of Havana. Here, scent engineering was pushed to extremes.

Scent adjustment of flowers can also have possible advantages for the survival of bees. For example, the scent of flowers can be made stronger, so that bees are better able to find the plants in the air-polluted world. A beautiful reference to this are the works around *Pollinators*. *Pollinators* are bees wearing a scent mask. This scent mask can be interpreted in different ways. For example, the mask can be a mini gas mask in order to purify the unhealthy air so bees can live longer. Alternatively, the mask can be a way to smell better, like a kind of actively smelling and filtering mask that leads bees to the right plants and flowers. The pollinators could also be mini drones, whose purpose is to be the 'fertilisers' of flowers and plants via scent detection. Knowing that the word 'drone' is derived from the English term for a male bee, this is not such a far-fetched thought.

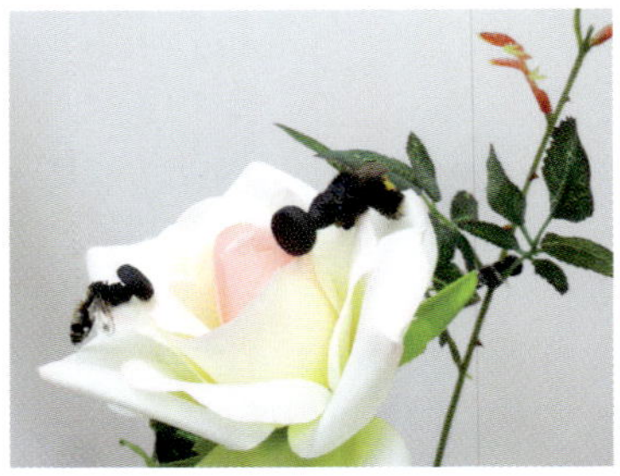

In addition to the four 'GOM Plants', there are five other non-existent plants. Two of them, *Pep & Straw*, are located in a separate plastic cell. *Pep & Straw* belong to the same plant species. They have been obtained by Creative Visualisation Genetic Olfactorisation (CVGO). In case of contact with skin, a toxic reaction may occur, but their scents are clearly recognisable as peppermint and strawberry. The two plants were developed accidentally, through the use of an incorrect Visual Genetic Modification (VGM) String.
The artist was not impressed with the plants he created, but due to the use of GOM, he felt that they gained added value. Because of their shape and scent, he named them *Pep & Straw*, referring to the scents of Peppermint and Strawberry. Again, the scents can be observed by placing the straw into the funnel. These are self-created plants that play with the story behind genetic modification. Whether the plants really exist remains a mystery. Thanks to his creative freedom as an artist, he can afford to leave it at that. In these plants, the idea of Genetic Olfactory Modification or Manipulation has been driven further. By creating two non-existent plants and

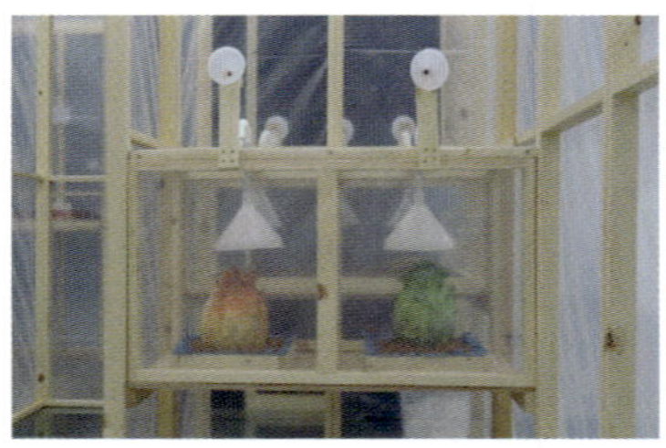

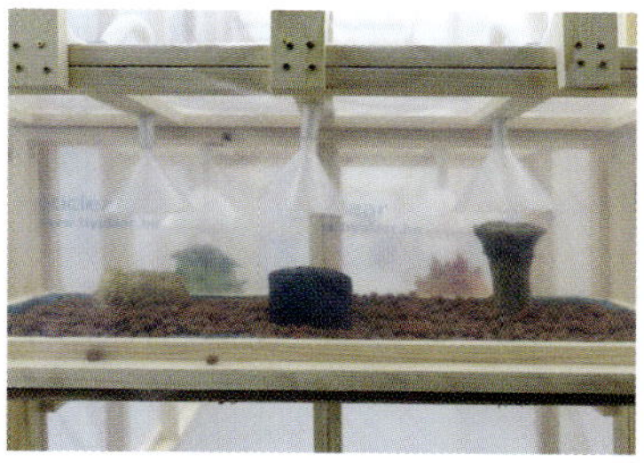

treating them with GOM, they obtain a right to exist. Here, too, veracity plays an important part. The veracity was pushed further with the three other plants, which the spectator must first smell through the straw on their mouth mask to get an idea of what kind of plants they are. The artist calls these VBS Plants, short for Visualisation by Smell.

VBS goes another step further than GOM. With VBS, spectators must create their own image of what kind of plant or flower they are smelling. Without the added scent, VBS Plants do not resemble plants at all. However, because of the addition of smell and the context in which they are shown, people do experience them as plants. Originally, VBS Plants are collected objects, shapes or waste material with an intriguing shape.

This means that the objects appealed to the artist with the idea to present them as plants, giving each of them a specific scent. In terms of veracity, the spectator is tricked entirely, but the idea stands thanks to the context. This might involve future situations in which possible doom scenarios arise, because of technological advancements and deformation of natural elements caused by pollution. Nevertheless, this is not the primary reason for creating this work. The name VBS, Visualisation by Smell, already indicates what it is about: creating an image through smell. The sense of smell is challenged here. Just as with the work *Scratch, Sniff and Imagine the Colours of this World*, the spectator must first be a 'smeller', and create his own image through the combination of the smell with the object, form and colour.

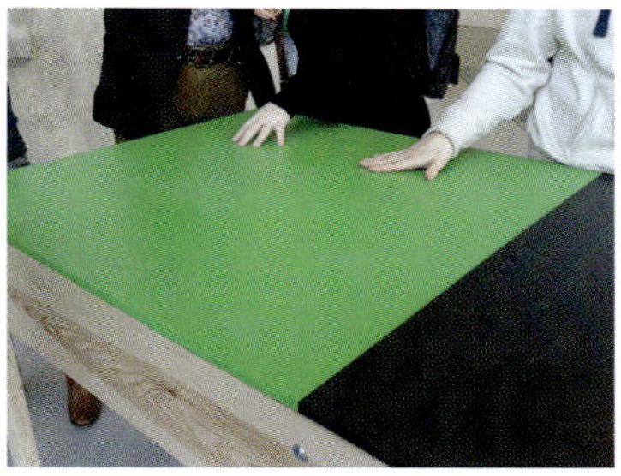

Visualisation by Smell is a challenge for the spectator to push his own smell boundaries. Not just taking the time to guess which smell it is, but to build on the instinctive reaction formed by memories and the identification of the experience elicited by the smell in combination with sight. The context of VBS lies precisely in one's own perception, ability and translation, and is partly determined by one's accumulated knowledge. The cognitive enters into a dialogue with the subjective. In order to understand the work, one must reason. Some people will not even notice that the VBS Plants that are shown, are only found objects that were given meaning by way of scent. And those who do realise this, will hopefully have enough knowledge to see more than solely the object or the scent, but will make a synthesis of both. In addition, the work emphasises the context of my art, which can be a possible outcome of environmental problems caused by pollution.

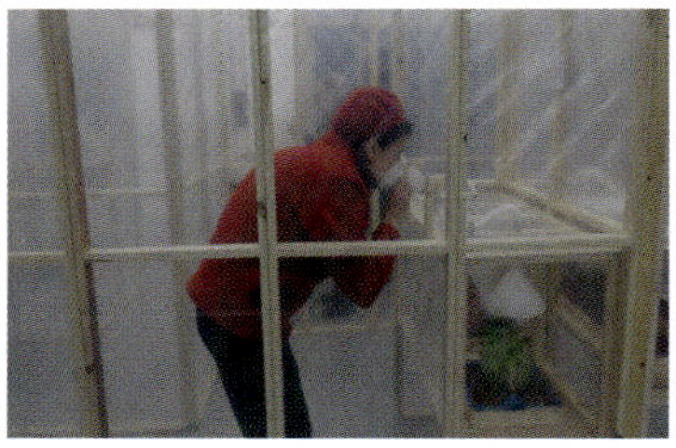

The exhibited GOM and VBS plants and flowers fit perfectly into the meaning that the concept *Flower* has to the artist. A *Flower* is more than just a flower. It is a receiver into society, an exhaust, a scream ... *Flowers* as a metaphor gives so much more meaning to the concept of a flower. Not an ideal of beauty, but a bearer of meaning. A *Flower* sends a message. It makes the spectator think and question the 'beauty' of society. The concept of *Flower* must not be seen as a purely aesthetic notion, but as a bearer of meaning.

At the end of the *Smell Lab*, the spectator will make his own concoction by selecting herbs and fluids, and filling a red test tube with them. He will then hang it in the last hallway, between the test tubes of previous visitors. The scent in the hallway is interactive, because it will always be a mix of the different scent combinations. This means that the visitor participates in the evolution of the smell in the hallway with the test tubes.

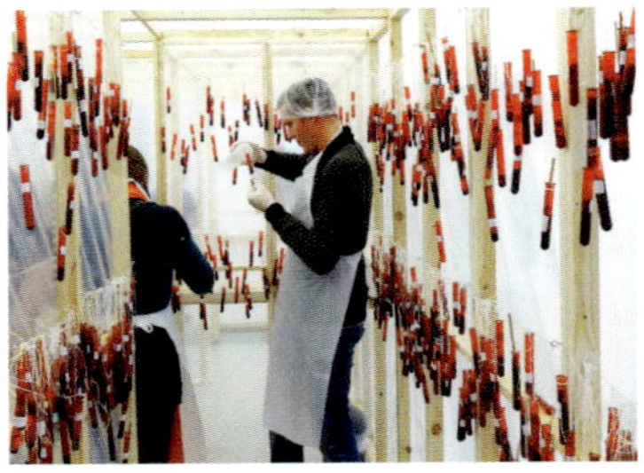

On the ground floor of the exhibition, one can also find a photo series of the 'smell devices' *Breath Odour* and *Stereo Sound Odour*, as well as *Mono Sound Odour*, which refer to the first tests one has to perform in the smell lab. Next to that is the work *Heaven*.

Heaven looks like a coffin covered by a grass mat. In the grass mat, there is a hole. When a person lies on their stomach on top of the grass mat and smells with their nose in the hole, they will smell the scent of *Heaven*. When we think of the word heaven, many people think of the metaphor of 'going to heaven when we die'. *Heaven* is a subtle parody of this, a concrete observation with a logical view. After all, people are buried or scattered after they die, and therefore go to the earth. The smell of the earth is not heavenly, but, depending on where you are buried, it smells of warm, fungus-rich soil. In the installation, the smell of mushrooms is dominant. The spectator also isn't looking up at heaven when he lies down on the grass to stick his nose into the ground.

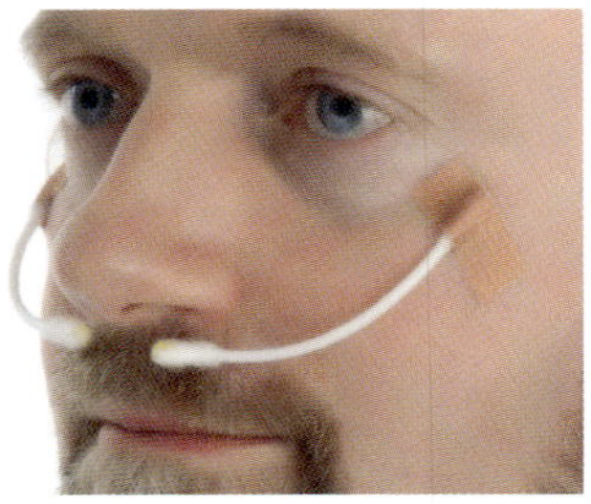

The work *Heaven* is the start or the end of the exhibition. It is the opposite of the *Smoke Cloud*, and yet they are similar in the sense that they criticise human actions. *Heaven* can also be seen as the result of the *Smoke Cloud*, which is death. This way, the work also puts human existence into perspective. Therefore, the exhibition *The Art of Smelling* is actually a kind of lifecycle, in which the spectator goes through different stages. With *Cocoon*, we are thrown back in time with the smell of baby powder, and start our own life anew. Via the *Smell Lab*, we discover ourselves and are made to reflect on truth and veracity. The *Smell Lab* actually determines how open we are to discovering the other, and to questioning ourselves. The *Olfactory Tree* is a reference to how we are ruining the world by disrespecting nature, and the *Smoke Cloud* is the *Heaven* some of us imagine, but we are then confronted with the smell of air pollution and gunpowder. Or how close heaven and hell are together, without referring to that explicitly. To an experienced spectator or reader, it will be clear that this exhibition can be about more than just the context of climate change, environmental issues and society; that it is also an underlying rebuke of religion, readable between the lines.
In addition, the exhibition included a small *Scent Space*, where one had to walk across turmeric in a small, darkened room. Turmeric is an Indian yellow root and gives curry powders its typical scent, but is also used as a colourant and as medicine [12] [13]. As a spice, turmeric has healing properties [14], but especially its scent lingers in your nasal epithelium for a long time.

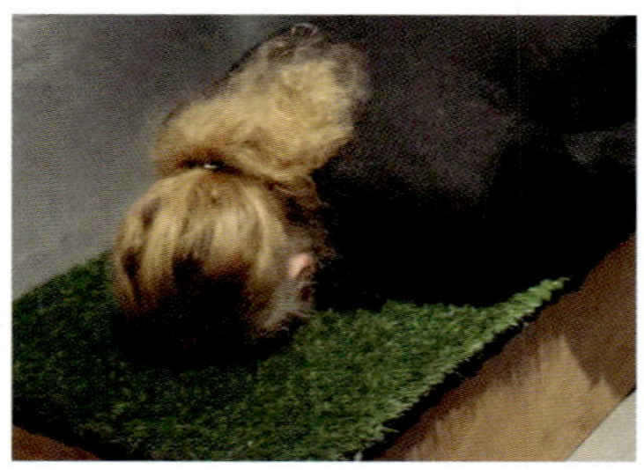

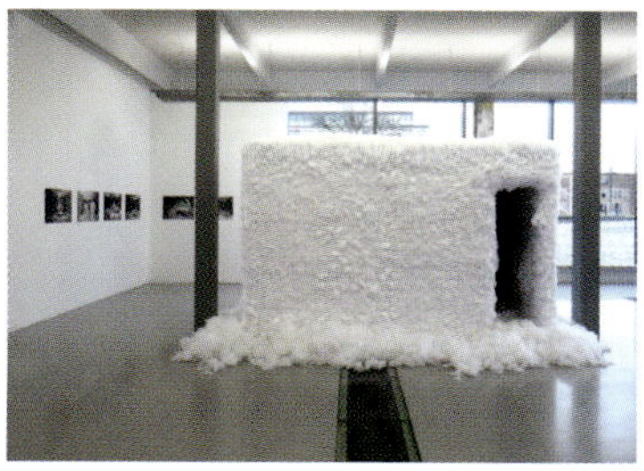

Scent Spaces appear in his work in different versions. There is the *Smoke Room*, for example, with over 750,000 used cigarette stubs, and the *Smile Room*, in which a bathroom is completely covered in toothpaste, is also a covert form of *Scent Spaces*. In *Scent Spaces*, the spectator experiences the effect of scent with his whole body. In the exhibition, you will find *Cocoon*: a space completely covered in cotton wool. Both inside and outside, synthetic white cotton wool insulates the space. *Cocoon* affects memory. The baby powder scent in the room throws you back to the time when you came into the world [15]. The installation is a reinvention of various earlier cotton wool spaces, which at the time was named *My Soft World, In Honour Of My Mother* [16]. This way, the exhibition has also become a memory of earlier scent installations.

We take too few moments for ourselves in the rushed world of technology in which we live. *Cocoon* is a flight, a mental flight at that. The softness of the cotton wool and the isolation of the space throw you back to yourself.

In addition to *Cocoon*, 7 photographs from an earlier performance [17] are shown, together with the cotton wool suit [18] in which the performance was executed. The photos show the loneliness the artist has to deal with. No matter how chaste the cotton wool space may seem, trying to live inside it is not as pleasant as being there temporarily, as the visitor pleases.

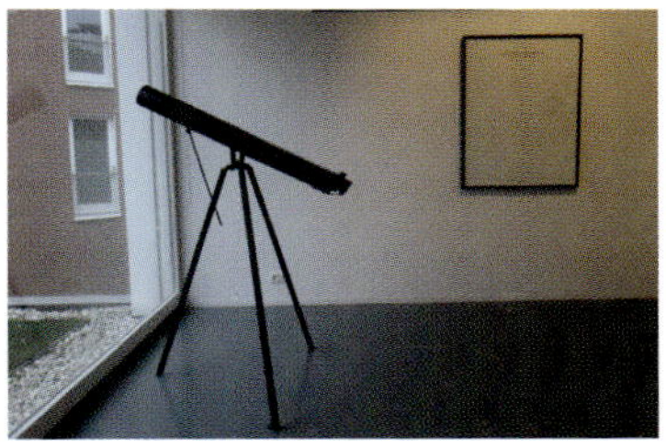

This could have been the end of the exhibition, except for the fact that another part took place on the first floor. The works on the first floor also tie into the storyline of the exhibition. Via the *Odour Telescope*, one can smell a rose from a distance. The rose is exhibited on the terrace of the top floor in the Twente Museum across the street. When one looks through the telescope, one sees and smells the rose from a distance.

In the video *Paris, Mon Amour* [19], a pink cloud is freed from an old suitcase after a walk through Paris. The cloud turned out to be created by inflating the suitcase containing a blend mix of rose petals.

It is clear that the *Odour Telescope* and the video *Paris, Mon Amour* have the rose as a common subject. There is also a link to the *Smoke Cloud*, only the cloud in the video *Paris, Mon Amour* would have a much more pleasant and poetic smell. The *Odour Telescope*, which secretly keeps an eye on a rose, is just as poetic, while giving a sense of voyeurism at the same time. In addition to the *Odour Telescope*, we also find a number of drawings illustrating the idea behind this work. The *Odour Telescope* was shown earlier in the exhibition *Kortrijk Vlaandert* [20].

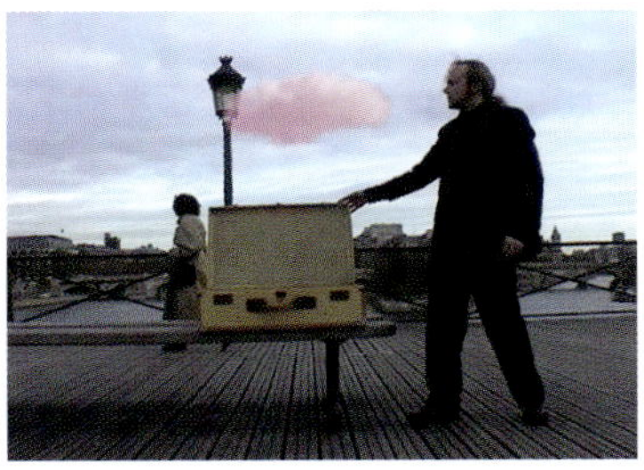

Three *Cigarettes Paintings* and a small table with a chair covered in used cigarettes are found in an adjacent room. The smell is a mix of asphalt, smoked meat aroma and the smell of exhaust gasses. Together, they give the visitor the idea that they are smelling the used cigarettes themselves. The smell of the cigarettes used originally was, therefore, removed, and replaced with the added smoke smells. The total is actually a separate smell installation in addition to the exhibition, but it is also linked to the other works. There is the reference to smoke, and the smell of smoked meat is also a hint to the burning of your own lungs. In addition, the small table and chair covered in cigarette stubs and standing in a mass of stubs on the ground are a symbolic jeer at 'innocent' youth. A youth in which many a child was confronted with the choice of whether to be cool and smoke a cigarette or not. And this is what we still have to do today: make a choice. And we must choose the preservation of our nature. Or, rather, the improvement of our nature.

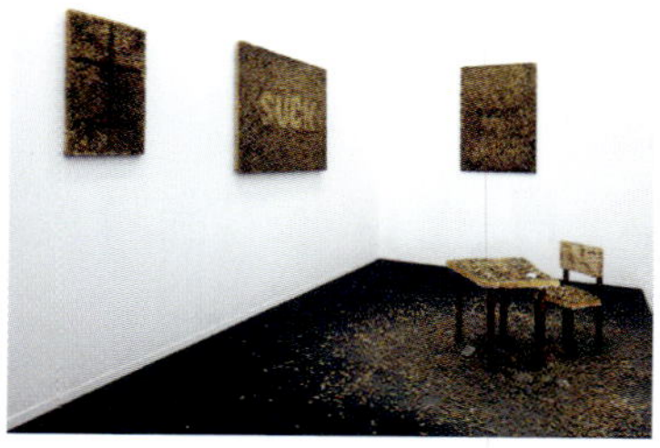

Experience from and reactions to earlier exhibitions have shown that most people sooner appreciate the work because they see so many cigarette stubs combined into one piece. Usually, people are more surprised by the number of cigarette stubs involved than that they think more deeply about the work. This happens a great deal in art, and is also found in other art forms. People often marvel about the technical abilities an artist uses in a painting, but think too little about why the artist painted this work. However, there is still the aesthetic appreciation of a work. This is, of course, not wrong; for by using the right aesthetics, you can also send a clearer message.

In the works involving thousands of cigarette butts, you also have the smell that directly attacks the spectator. Even before he can make a concrete assessment of the work, he will already have created a subconscious prejudice because of the scent [21]. This prejudice is subsequently questioned, because one thinks about it further. Because the smell is not 100 % cigarettes, but a mix of different other smoke-related smells, the prejudice about smoking is double-sided and gives the spectator more possibilities to re-evaluate the work, without even noticing.

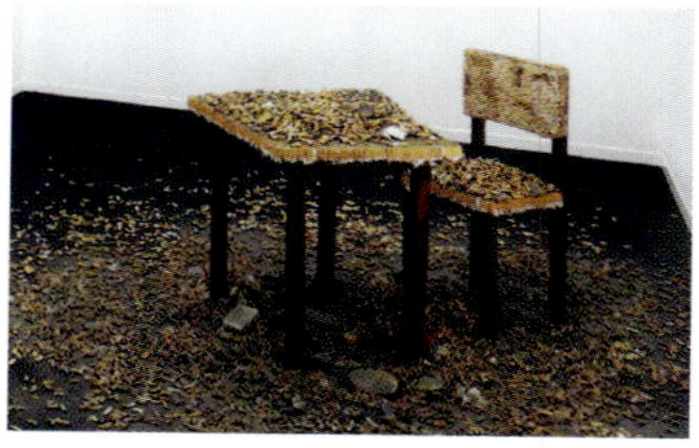

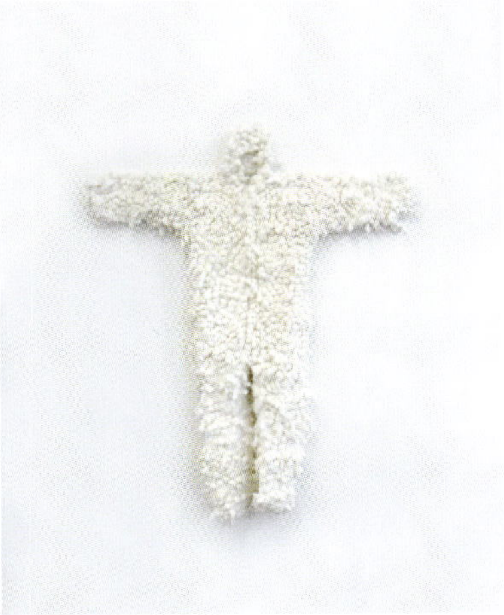

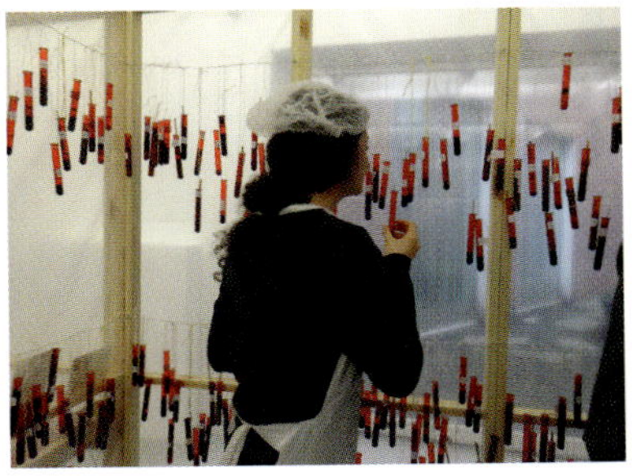

Footnotes

1 Exhibition: Silhouettes 'n' Shadows, Fundament Foundation, Tilburg, Netherlands, 01.09.2001 - 28.10.2001

2 In his book 'A la recherche du temps perdu', the main character experiences an intense sense of joy that he cannot place, after soaking a madeleine cake in lime blossom tea and eating it. This cake soaked in lime blossom tea reminds him of his happy youth.

3 On 13 May 2000, the Netherlands was startled by the explosion of the fireworks factory S.E. Fireworks in Enschede. In addition to the horrible fact that the exploding factory (located in the middle of the residential area of Roombeek) killed 23 people, the entire neighbourhood (of about 40 hectares) was blown away. http://mens-en-samenleving.infonu.nl/diversen/17939-enschede-roombeek-na-de-vuurwerkramp.html

4 Pamela Dalton, Psychophysical and Behavioral Characteristics of Olfactory Adaptation Chem. Senses (2000) 25 (4): 487-492 doi:10.1093/chemse/25.4.487 http://chemse.oxfordjournals.org/content/25/4/487.abstract

5 BVOCs and global change, BVOC emissions in a changing world: an increasingly fragrant world? Josep Peñuelas, Michael Staudt, Trends in plant science doi:10.1016/j.tplants.2009.12.005 (volume 15 issue 3 pp. 133-144)

6 GOM Genetic Olfactory Modification, term which appears frequently in Peter de Cupere's works

7 Jason Bremner, Ashley Frost, Carl Haub, Mark Mather, Karin Ringheim, And Eric Zuehlke, Population Reference Bureau, www.prb.org, Vol. 65, No. 2, July 2010, World Population Highlights: key findings from prb's 2010 world population data sheet http://www.prb.org/pdf10/65.2highlights.pdf

8 International Energy Agency, World Energy Outlook 2013, How will global energy markets evolve to 2035? http://www.worldenergyoutlook.org/media/weowebsite/factsheets/weo2013_factsheets.pdf

9 De alembic is one of the oldest chemical devices, and was already used for distillation during the time of Alexander the Great (400 B.C.). These days, the alembic is still used by old liquor distilleries or traditional perfume manufacturers (cf. Grasse). The origins of the name are not entirely clear, but are possibly derived from 'al inbiq', which means 'in the barrel' in Arabic. Over the centuries, the name was corrupted from the Latin 'alembicus', the French 'alembic' and the Old-Dutch 'alembijk' into the current 'alembic'.

10 Eran Pichersky and Natalia Dudareva, Scent engineering: toward the goal of controlling how flowers smell, http://labs.mcdb.lsa.umich.edu/labs/pichersky/references/Scentengineering.pdf

11 Tanaka, Y.; Brugliera, F.; Chandler, S. Recent Progress of Flower Colour Modification by Biotechnology. Int. J. Mol. Sci. 2009, 10, 5350-5369, http://www.mdpi.com/1422-0067/10/12/5350

12 Bharat B. Aggarwal, Anushree Kumar, Manoj S. Aggarwal, and Shishir Shishodia, Curcumin Derived from Turmeric (Curcuma longa): A Spice for All Seasons, © 2005 by CRC Press LLC, http://diyhpl.us/~bryan/papers2/longevity/Curcumin_A_Spice_For_All_Seasons.pdf

13 Mishra S, Palanivelu K. The effect of curcumin (turmeric) on Alzheimer's disease: An overview. Ann Indian Acad Neurol [serial online] 2008 [cited 2014 Jan 4]; 11:13-9. Available from: http://www.annalsofian.org/text.asp?2008/11/1/13/40220

14 B. Sasikumar, Genetic resources of Curcuma: diversity, characterization and utilization, Plant Genetic Resources: Characterization and Utilization, Volume 3, Issue 02, August 2005, pp 230-251 http://journals.cambridge.org/action/displayAbstract?fromPage=online&aid=685284
Published online: 12 February 2007

15 Meanings of certain scents can differ between cultures. When I talk about scents belonging to a certain culture, I am referring to the Western world, unless stated otherwise.

16 My Soft World in Honour of My Mother was shown for the first time during the 3° Biennale d'Art Contemporain de Louvain-La-Neuve, 13 May to 12 June, 2000 in Louvain-La Neuve.

17 Olfactory Performance: 'The Soft Man, His Table And His Chair', 2000, 7 b/w photographs, 50 cm h x 70 cm w, Ed. of 3, 2 A.P., shown for the first time in the solo exhibition at the Tim Van Laere Gallery, Antwerp, 14 September to 21 October, 2000.

18 Cotton Suit, made of 4000 natural cotton balls, shown for the first time during the 3° Biennale d'Art Contemporain de Louvain-La-Neuve, 13 May to 12 June, 2000 in Louvain-La Neuve.

19 'Paris, Mon Amour', video, colour, 7 min., http://vimeo.com/3137978

Shown for the first time in the group exhibition: Hit you with a flower, Tim Van Laere Gallery, Antwerp, Belgium, July-August, 2005, Atelier Van Lieshout, Jim Butler, Victoria Civera, Sergio De Beukelaer, Peter de Cupere, Bojan Fajfric, Nicolas Provost, Edward Lipski, Maryam Najd, Peter Rogiers, Thomas Schütte, Serse, Su-mei Tse, Juan Uslé, Franz West

20 Kortrijk Vlaandert, curator Hilde Van Canneyt, Kortrijk, BE, 04.07.2013-18.08.2013

21 Scent plays into memories (unless one has never smelled the scent before), Harth R.: Brein en Geest, Hoe het brein de geest creëert (Brain and Mind, How the brain creates the mind), Bodoni, Baarn, 1995

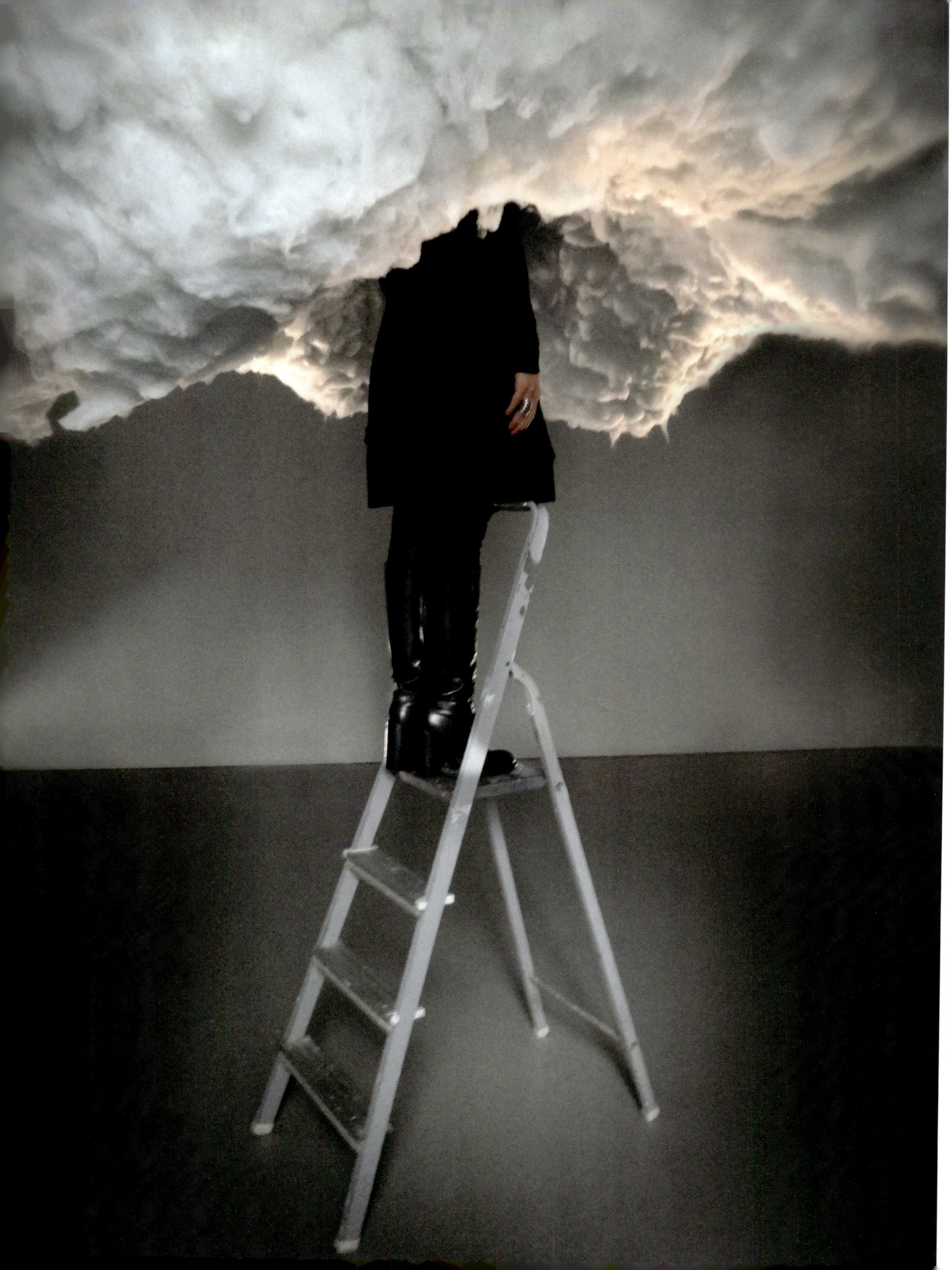

HSUAN HSU

THE SMELL OF RISK

Since the 1990s, Peter de Cupere has produced a remarkable range of olfactory artworks that experiment with the scents of sweat, genitals, candy, toothpaste, urine, garbage, pollution, grass, cardamom, peppermint, and other substances. According to the critics Larry Shiner and Yulia Kriskovets, de Cupere "has created an artistic identity that is a cross between artist and olfactory chemist that may become a model for other olfactory artists in the future." [1] While his works have addressed a wide range of smell-related themes, two works that de Cupere recently exhibited in Havana exemplify olfactory art's capacity to engage with environmental toxicity.

Unlike visual representations of pollution and toxicity, olfactory art engages with environmental risk in material as well as representational terms. Smell has long been marginalized from both aesthetic theory (because it threatens Kantian values such as autonomy and disinterestedness) and museum exhibitions (because it is volatile, and difficult to contain, and a threat to both visitors and nearby artworks). Olfactory perception has been marginalized because it manifests the potentially unruly, trans-corporeal nature of all matter: what Stacy Alaimo describes as "the material interconnections of human corporeality with the more-than-human world." [2] Yet the very qualities that once marginalized smell have made smell an intriguing medium for experimental artists since the 1960s. Artists and critics are drawn to smell not only for its immersive qualities, but also for its capacity to evoke memories and affects by acting upon the brain's limbic system. [2] As the anthropologist Mark Graham explains, smell has striking affinities with postmodern aesthetic values: "Sight has been described as the modernist sense par excellence (Levin 1993). It is the sense that discriminates, divides and orders the world into mutually exclusive categories. Smell, by contrast, has been dubbed the sense of the postmodern (Classen, Howes and Synnott 1994: 203-5), the sense that confuses categories and challenges boundaries. It is difficult to localize, hard to contain and has the character of flux and transitoriness." [3]

Transitory, mobile, and trans-corporeal in nature, air cannot function as a 'pure' aesthetic medium: to be perceived, smells must enter and interact with our bodies and surroundings in ways we cannot fully control. Air can be a medium of toxicity as well as a medium of sensation. Moreover, airborne particles with the capacity to interact with our bodies and minds may be imperceptible, and their intoxicating capacities may not be fully understood. Insofar as its transmission involves such uncertain trans-corporeal exchanges, smell transgresses the ideal of purity that governs both visual perception and conventional environmental values.

Olfactory art offers a powerful medium for aesthetic engagements with airborne toxins. As the anthropologist Timothy Choy puts it in his groundbreaking discussion of air pollution in Hong Kong, "air functions ... as a heuristic with which to encompass many atmospheric experiences. The abstraction of air does not derive from asserting a unit for comparison or a common field within which to arrange specificities, but through an aggregation of materialities irreducible to one another (including breath, humidity, SARS, particulate, and so on). Thinking about the materiality of air and the densities of our many human entanglements in airy matters also means attending to the solidifying and melting edges between people, regions, and events." [4]

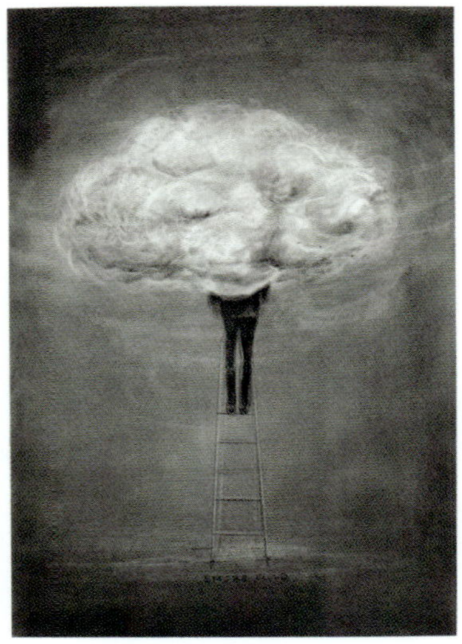

In addition to calling attention to our material interactions with multiple atmospheric substances, air embodies the frequently overlooked flow of lively materials between differentiated spaces and across geographic scales. For Choy, air is thus an important element for theorizing social relations and affect in material terms: "thinking more about air, that is, not taking it simply as solidity's opposite, might offer some means of thinking about relations and movements—between places, people, things, scales—means that obviate the usual traps of particularity and universality."

Highlighting Cuba's volatile position within the global geopolitical system, de Cupere's recent works exemplify how olfactory art can viscerally convey the environmental distinctions propagated by geographically uneven development. *Smoke Cloud* (2014), which appeared in the 2015 exhibition *The Importance of Being...* in Havana [5], consists of a ladder placed beneath a white cloud suspended from the gallery ceiling. Visitors ascend the ladder one at a time, placing their heads in the cloud and smelling the scent of air pollution. This installation interacts with visitors both visually (by presenting to others the incongruous spectacle of a body with its head in a cloud) and trans-corporeally (by introducing the scent of air pollution into the olfactor's lungs).

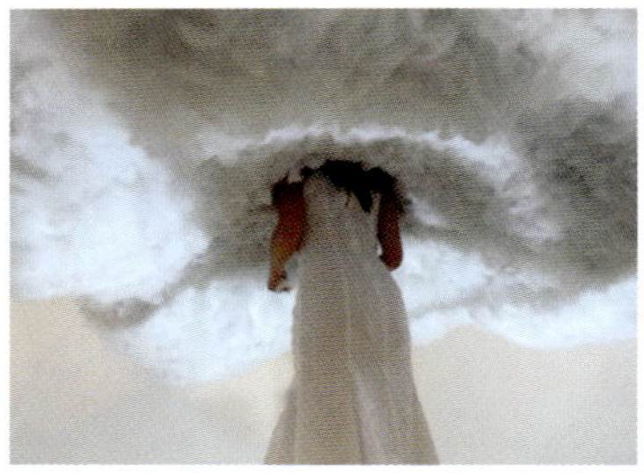

While the idiom having one's head in the clouds generally refers to a tendency towards fantasy or idealism, de Cupere's cloud of smog immerses visitors in the materiality of air: through either chemical or psychosomatic channels, the scent of smog could physically affect a visitor's mood or health. The resulting frictions between the visual and olfactory dimensions of *Smoke Cloud*—contemplation vs. smog inhalation, ascent vs. intoxication, visible beauty vs. invisible harm—interrupt the visual order of the art gallery: one at a time, visitors' heads disappear into the sculpture; for those who ascend, the gallery space itself disappears as the smell of smog sets in. According to de Cupere, the decision to fill the cloud with the scent of air pollution was inspired in part by his encounter with Havana's poor air quality, and specifically "the powerful scent of gasoline that the old Chevys and Buicks spit out." [6] The polluted air presented by *Smoke Cloud* thus references not only Cuba's urban air pollution, but also its origins in Cold War trade embargoes.

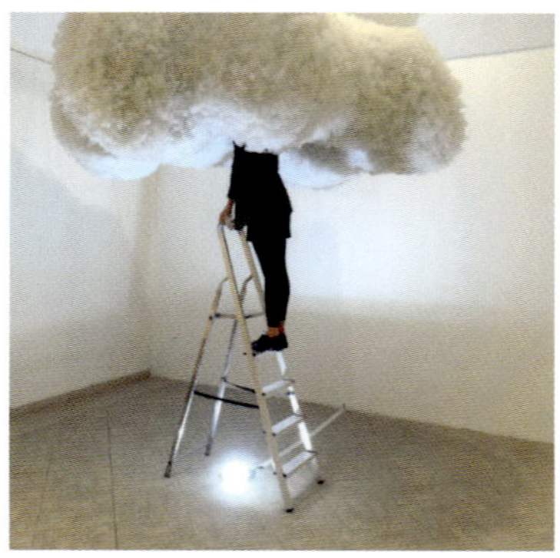

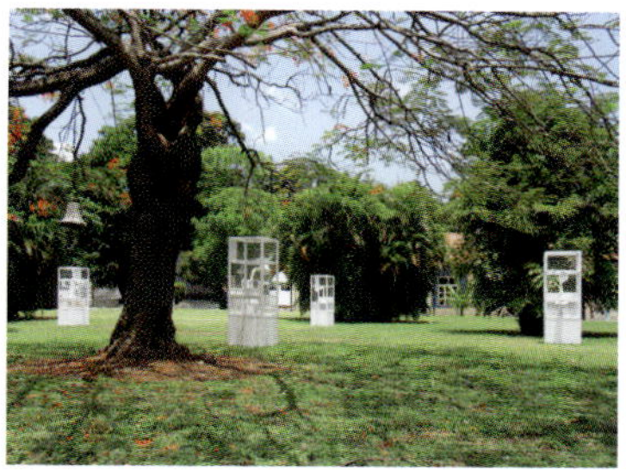

De Cupere's contribution to the XII Havana Biennial, *The Smell of a Stranger* (2015), was exhibited outdoors at the High Institute of Technology and Applied Sciences at the University of Havana. Blending scent engineering, bioengineering, and the ethos of speculative fiction, *The Smell of a Stranger* offers a cautionary allegory about both bioengineering and the 'opening' of Cuba to US commerce and diplomacy. Drawing on scents provided by International Flavors and Fragrances, de Cupere genetically modified nine local Cuban flowers and plants. While the results appear identical to natural specimens, de Cupere's flora emit a range of incongruous odors including the scents of "American New Dollars, Blood, Sperm, Vagina, Dead Body, Gun Powder, Sweat (smell of fear), Air Pollution, and Geraniums". [7] By contrasting the beauty of local plants with smells associated with sex tourism, labor exploitation, military violence, pollution, industrial food production (the artist intended to include the smells of hamburgers and Belgian fries, but these were omitted for technical reasons [8]), and death, de Cupere suggests that the opening of US-Cuba trade and diplomacy under the Obama administration may have devastating effects upon Cuba's population and environment. As the artist explains, "Western culture is slowly creeping [into Cuba] and the capital automatically follows ... Cuba has a lot of nature and a lot of cultural aspects which can be exploited with bad intentions." [9]

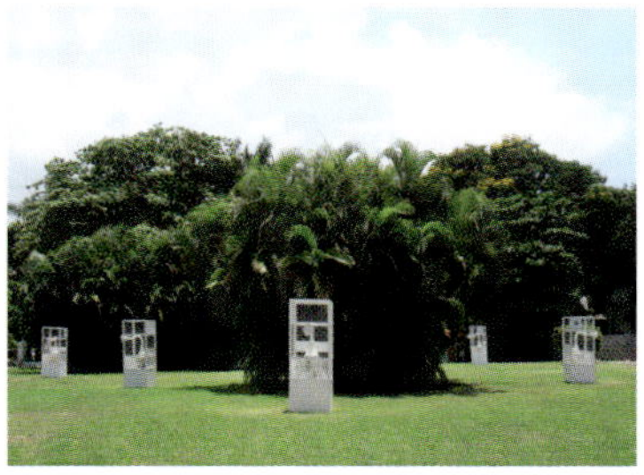

The post-natural status of bioengineered flowers indexes the broader vulnerability of Cuba's environment to capitalist incursions. *The Smell of a Stranger* violates the expectation that flowers and plants will offer up refreshing, "natural" scents, leaving olfactors disturbed—if not disgusted—by a range of visceral or unnatural scents. Different olfactors could find the scent of sperm, sweat, money, and food physically arousing or repulsive; as with *Smoke Cloud*, the scent of air pollution may be literally toxic for environmentally sensitive visitors. Such physical responses viscerally convey how the environments we produce affect our bodies, minds, and feelings through trans-corporeal exchanges. Siting this work outdoors at once underscores the plants' visual continuities with Cuba's "natural" environment and sidesteps the curatorial problems—such as unwanted exposures and scent-mixing—that would be more likely to occur in an indoor gallery.

The title of de Cupere's installation alludes to the cultural specificity of scent, or the way in which our perceptions of attractive and repulsive scents vary across cultural boundaries. [10] If smell demarcates cultural and social boundaries, 'the smell of a stranger' invokes the idea of an ethical encounter with the Other—a cross-cultural scenario in which Cubans and foreigners could become more comfortable with each other. But rather than delivering on this promise of cross-cultural olfaction, de Cupere presents visitors with another sort of 'stranger' altogether: post-natural plants that exude anthropogenic odors. Many of these scents—sperm, money, dead bodies, gunpowder, and air pollution—would not be 'strange' to either Cubans or Americans; instead, their strangeness lies in their juxtaposition with each other and with the installation's apparently 'natural' plants. Although the scents of American and Belgian food may be interpreted as a "funny reference to our Western culture

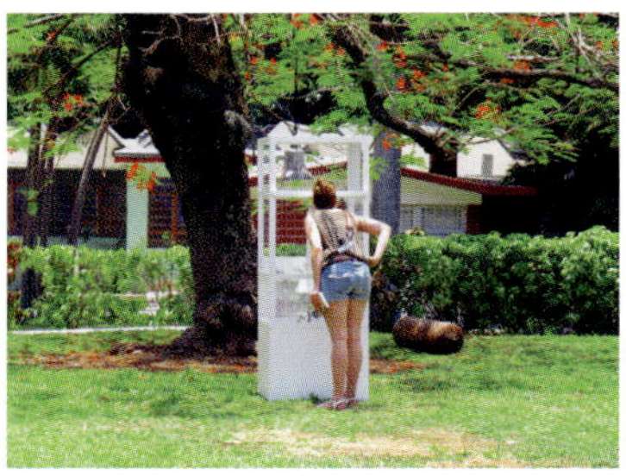

with the scent of hamburgers," [11] the references to hamburgers and fries take on darker connotations when juxtaposed with the scents of money and dead bodies. If hamburgers and Belgian fries symbolize US and Belgian culture, [12] they are also foods that, when eaten or smelled, have trans-corporeal effects upon people's bodies. Industrially produced fast food is a vehicle of malnutrition, obesity, and what Lauren Berlant calls 'slow death' [13] on a global scale; the circulation of hamburgers can be mapped as an exchange of money for premature death across unevenly developed terrains. Whether conveyed through fast food, sex tourism, capitalist exploitation, or militarization, [14] uneven development and economic imperialism threaten to bring new health risks to Cuba's citizens and more-than-human life forms. The 'stranger' here is not American culture, but the kind of place that Cuba is in danger of becoming.

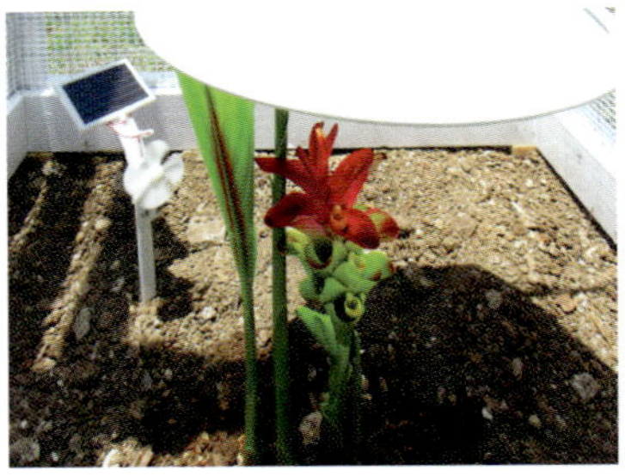

Rob Nixon's concept of 'slow violence'—a widespread form of environmental violence whose 'temporal dispersion' presents challenges to representation and political engagement—clarifies the stakes of de Cupere's dystopian scents: because the health effects of fast food, militarization, and rampant capitalism could take decades to emerge, de Cupere turns to a speculative—yet still material and viscerally trans-corporeal—form of temporal condensation as a means of manifesting future threats. [15] *The Smell of a Stranger* thus offers a powerful cautionary allegory of the stark possibilities opened up by the intensified neoliberalization of Cuba's economy, proleptically dramatizing Cuba's vulnerability to uneven transnational flows of desire, risk, and exploitation. Like the literary genre of magical realism, de Cupere's bioengineered Cuban plants register the dislocating effects of transnational contacts and capital circulation upon local reality; yet the more-than-real aspects of *The Smell of a Stranger* actually exist as material products of genetics, biotechnology, and the science of scent. Challenging the rarefied air typical of Western museums oriented by the notion of visually discrete art objects, de Cupere's olfactory artworks materially intoxicate the bodies of observers/olfactors, viscerally posing problems of environmental risk at geographic scales far beyond the 'white cube' spaces of climate-controlled galleries. They thus illustrate the distinctive capacity of olfactory aesthetics to engage with contemporary intersections between environmental risk, uneven geographies, and air's transformative mental, affective, and physical effects upon differentiated bodies and populations.

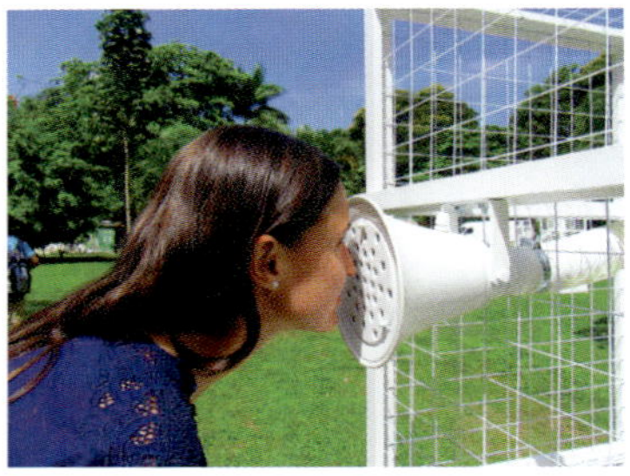

Hsuan Hsu

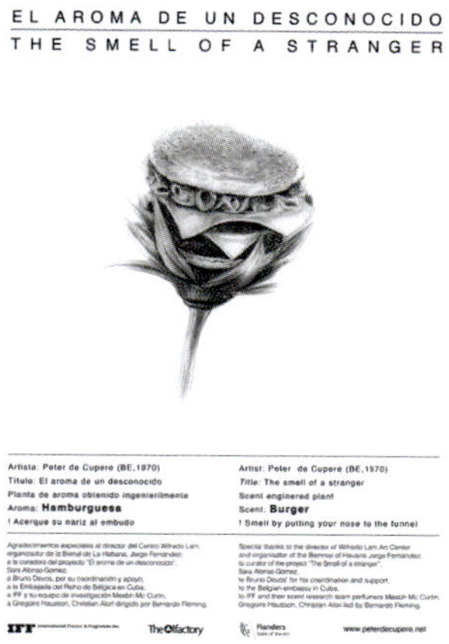

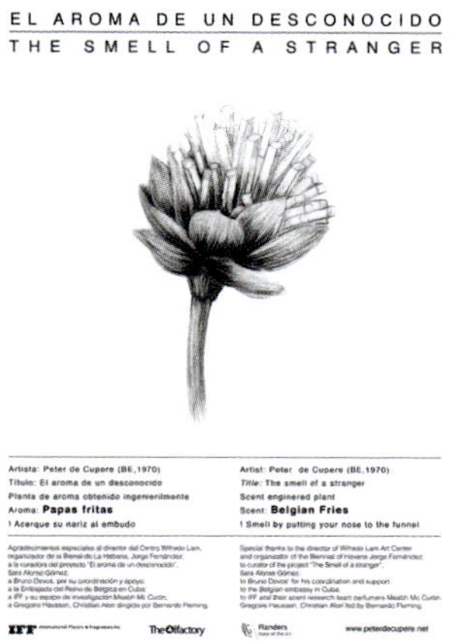

Footnotes

This essay is adapted from an article originally published in Resilience: A Journal of the Environmental Humanities. We are grateful for the permission of the University of Nebraska Press to reprint the excerpted passages.

1 Larry Shiner and Yulia Kriskovets, "The Aesthetics of Smelly Art," Journal of Aesthetics and Art Criticism 65:3 (Summer 2007), 274.

2 Stacy Alaimo, Bodily Natures: Science, Environment, and the Material Self (Bloomington, Indiana, 2010), 2.

3 Mark Graham, "Queer Smells: Fragrances of Late Capitalism or Scents of Subversion?" in The Smell Culture Reader, ed. Jim Drobnick (Oxford: Berg, 2006), 305.

4 Timothy Choy, "Air's Substantiations," in ed. Kaushik Sunder Rajan, Lively Capital: Biotechnologies, Ethics, and Governance in Global Markets (Durham: Duke University Press, 2012), 128.

5 Prior to being exhibited in Havana, Smoke Cloud was first shown in de Cupere's solo exhibition, The Art of Smelling, an Olfactory Art Research (2014), in the Netherlands. The artist has noted, however, that the smell of air pollution in Havana inspired this piece (see n° 6 below).

6 Sam Steverlynck, "A Major Exhibition of Belgian Art Opens in Havana," http://www.havana-live.com/news/2015/02/23/a-major-exhibition-of-belgian-art-opens-in-havana.html (accessed Sept 1, 2015).

7 Peter de Cupere, personal communication with author, March 20, 2016.

8 Although published accounts of the exhibit based on early interviews report that de Cupere would use "the scents of sperm, sweat, dead bodies, money, gun powder, air pollution, a hamburger, and Belgian fries," the smells of hamburger and Belgian fries (the latter intended to implicate the artist's own nation of origin) were ultimately omitted for technical reasons.
(Katherine Brooks, "Artist 'Scent Engineers' Plants to Smell Like Dead Bodies, Sperm, and Air Pollution," Huffington Post [May 13, 2015], http://www.huffingtonpost.com/2015/05/13/peter-de-cupere-scent_n_7274034.html [Accessed Sept 1, 2015]; Peter de Cupere, personal communication with author, March 20, 2016).

9 Qtd. in Brooks, "Artist 'Scent Engineers' Plants."

10 See, e.g., Gale Largey and Rod Watson, "The Sociology of Odors," in The Smell Culture Reader, ed. Drobnick, 29-40; Martin F. Manalansan IV, "Immigrant Lives and the Politics of Olfaction in the Global City," in The Smell Culture Reader 41-52; and Alan Hyde, "Offensive Bodies," in The Smell Culture Reader, 53-58.

11 Sara Alonso Gómez, "Exhibition 'The Smell of a Stranger' by Peter de Cupere" (May 23, 2015), https://www.facebook.com/events/1595498134023675 (Accessed Sept 1, 2015).

12 De Cupere explains that Belgian fries refer to his own complicity as a Belgian and European, so as "not to blame or focus only on the American eating culture. It's in a way questioning the fact that people should first see what they do wrong before blaming others. The world is not my place, it's ours. It's a pity I couldn't use these two fragrances" (Peter de Cupere, personal communication with author, March 20, 2016).

13 Lauren Berlant, "Slow Death (Sovereignty, Obesity, Lateral Agency)," Critical Inquiry 33 (Summer 2007), 754-80.

14 The smell of gunpowder here echoes several pieces that juxtaposed bullets and army helmets with the scents of dead bodies and blood that De Cupere included in his curated exhibition, The Smell of War earlier in 2015.

15 Rob Nixon, Slow Violence and the Environmentalism of the Poor (Cambridge: Harvard University Press, 2011), 3.

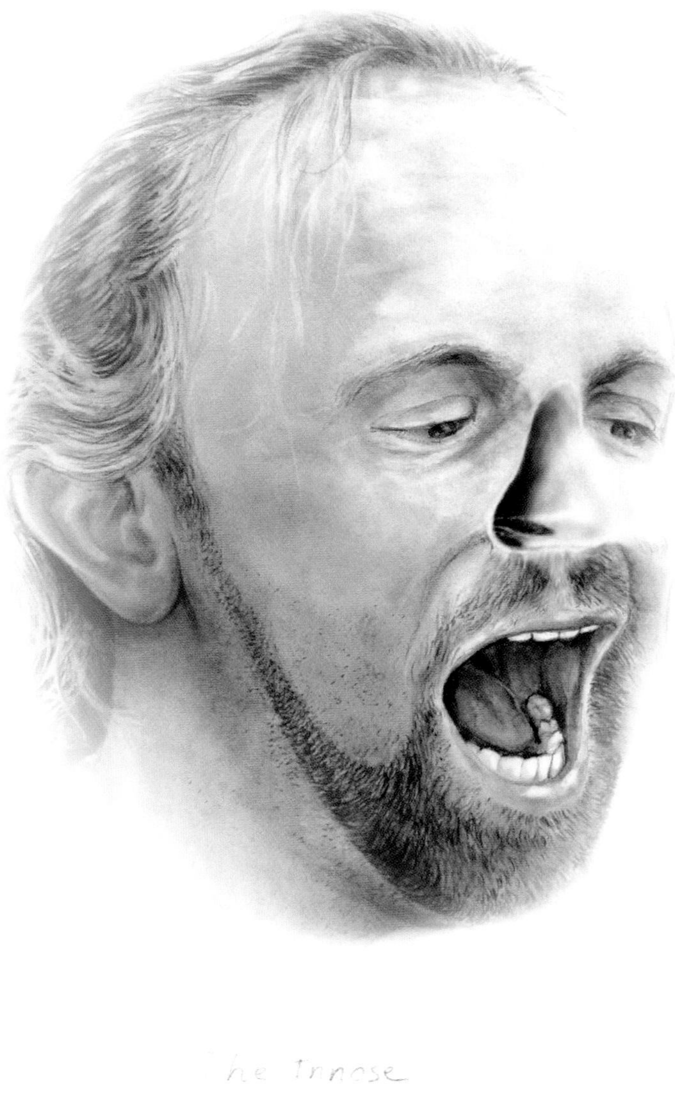
he Innose

PETER DE CUPERE

NOSES AND IN-NOSES

Imagine that people had a nose that faced into their face. A nose that is therefore not external, and which is not on the face but is in fact in the face, in other words inward facing. An exact copy of an actual nose but which is simply facing inwards. A nose that could, as it were, act as a mould for another nose. How would you breathe and smell then? Where would the olfactory nerves be? How would a connection with the limbic system be made?

How would we have sex therefore? You could have much closer contact with your partner if one of you had a an inward facing nose and the other an outward facing one. And how great would it be if one nose fitted into the other; *nosing* one another with your noses would be a wonderful part of the intimate act. Who would have an outward facing nose and who would have an inward facing nose however? Would we call them in-noses and out-noses or internal noses and external noses? Would an in-nose be able to smell as well as an out-nose or the opposite? Would the nostrils therefore smell each other and smell the inside of the nose as well as breathing on each other? What category of human would these be put in? Could we compare these noses to the penis and the vagina? Would a woman have an in-nose and a man an out-nose or would men or women have either? Would an in-nose be soft and flexible like a vagina and could an out-nose become hard like a penis? Very nice if one fitted into the other. Would nose hairs get waxed? Would there be upturned noses, hook noses, snub noses, big and small noses? What about nosebleed, blocked noses and runny noses? Would face fucking be a reality?

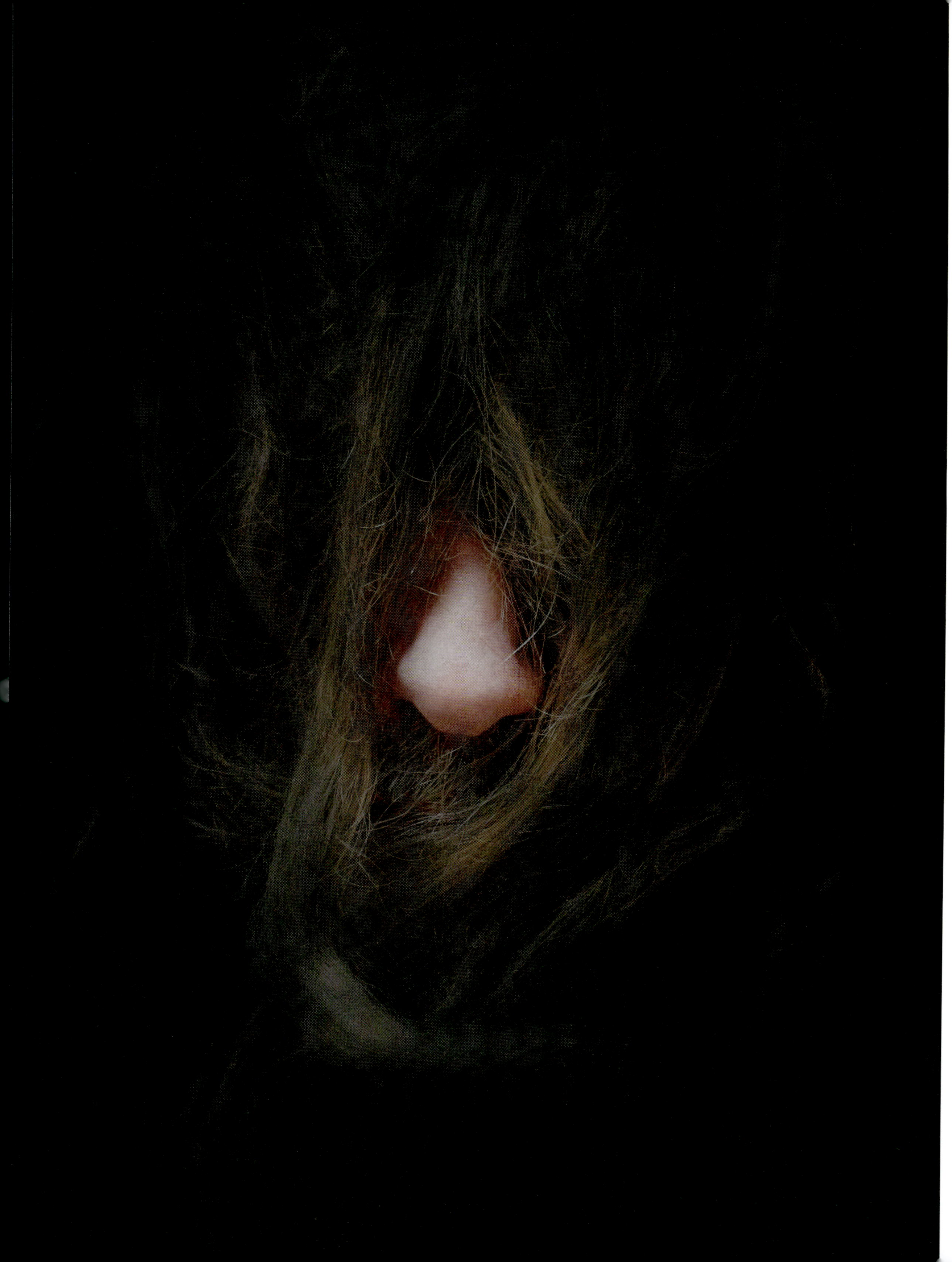

ANNELIES NAGELS

IS THIS MANKIND (2016)

In *La passion de Jeanne d'Arc*—a French silent film from 1928—we see how actress Maria Falconetti has her head shaved in the scene in which, as Joan of Arc, she is prepared for her execution. The story went around at the time that the whole film crew watched Falconetti having her head shaved and burst into tears. It is not surprising that cutting off the hair can release great emotions.

Laurent Philippon in his book about her devotes a whole chapter to 'loose hair'. Hair has a relationship with our animal past. When we tame it with brushes, combs, pins, powders and oils, we are emphasising our evolution away from the primitive and towards civilisation. But when we let it hang loose, we are freeing ourselves and returning to our natural state. As a result, our inhibitions also fall away. For many centuries and in different societies, wearing the hair loose was reserved for intimate moments. In some cultures, it is absolutely only permitted to show the hair in intimate circles. Also for a man long hair may symbolise power and manliness. Just think of the figure of Samson in the Old Testament.

When your hair is shaved off that may be forced or voluntary. In the case of voluntary shaving, this is often the start of a new life phase. It is highly charged with symbolism. Monks who enter the monastery, pilgrims on a pilgrimage, but also the shaving the head as a sign that you as a young person want to belong to a subculture. In his work *Eens was ik een mens (Is This Mankind)*, Peter de Cupere focuses attention on involuntary shaving or cutting. He links two very different situations with one another. On the one hand, he shows testimonies of cancer patients. Hair loss is a well-known side effect of chemotherapy. On the other hand, he shows testimonies of survivors of the Auschwitz extermination camp. There people had their heads shaved on arrival on the pretext of hygiene, but it was clearly a form of humiliation.

In his interviews with cancer patients and Auschwitz survivors, Peter de Cupere discusses their experiences of smell. In the cancer patients, this is about the loss of the sense of smell, or the changes in it. Some smells are perceived as stronger. Others no more. In the case of the Auschwitz survivors, the artist focuses on how smell can evoke a memory. The connection between hair and smell after all lies in the traumatic experience that is related to the loss of hair. As is apparent from research at the University of Utrecht, smell sometimes causes the return of learned fear associations.

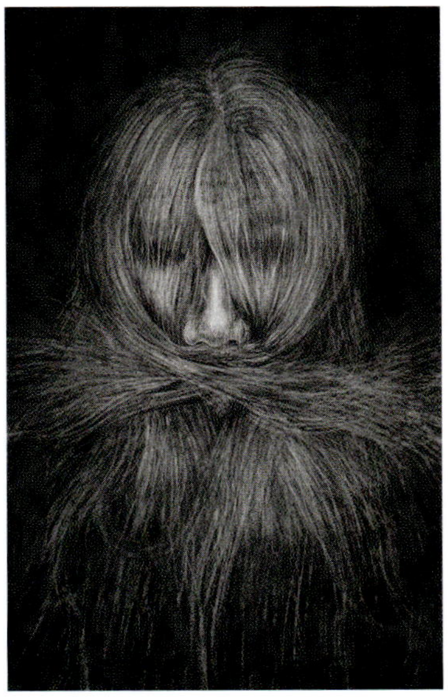

The human olfactory organ—from an anatomical point of view—is part of the hypothalamus. This is the place in the brain where smell is processed. The hypothalamus plays a crucial role in unconscious and instinctive behaviour, think for example of the regulation of emotions such as fear and the physical reaction to this. At the same time this area of the brain is involved in processing memory. There are therefore important links between the way in which fear is learned and the way in which smell information is processed. There may therefore be a strong relationship between the memory and smell, which is resistant to being wiped out. This is even more true when a smell is present at intense emotional events. Smell may serve as a key for a recollection which accompanies an emotion. This does not have to be a smell that is consciously perceived. It may also be an unknown or neutral smell. The American army has so-called 'training villages' to train their soldiers in a realistic situation. During a preparatory visit to these villages war veterans stated that without the typical penetrating smell that emanated from a combination of corpses, weaponry and open sewers there was no way what they had experienced in Iraq could be correctly reflected. Smell was experienced by them as an essential factor.

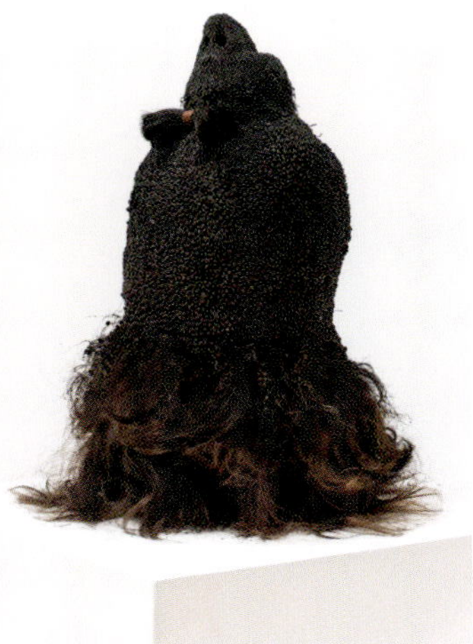

The smell of the concentration camps is of course long gone. But in addition to piles of suitcases, clothes, shoes and glasses, you can today still see mountains of hair in Auschwitz. Cut off plaits, pony tails, loose hair. A very specific smell pervades the rooms where these 'collections' can still be viewed. And after a visit to Auschwitz, this smell doubtless remains strong to the visitor.

With the title of the work—*Eens was ik een mens*—Peter de Cupere refers to the book that Primo Levi wrote in 1947 about his time in the Auschwitz concentration camp. The involuntary loss of hair is accompanied by a feeling of loss of identity. The main character in this book tells about camp life and about how the dehumanisation only continued. In a seemingly objective way, Levi reports on all the small everyday events. But between the lines there hangs a constant tension.

In this piece, the artist shows a small selection of the approx. 21,000 human ponytails in his collection. The ponytails take on their own smell, a human smell that is associated with a specific human identity. By this means Peter de Cupere wants to restore those lost identities. To bring their humanity back to the fore and allow it to prevail.

Annelies Nagels

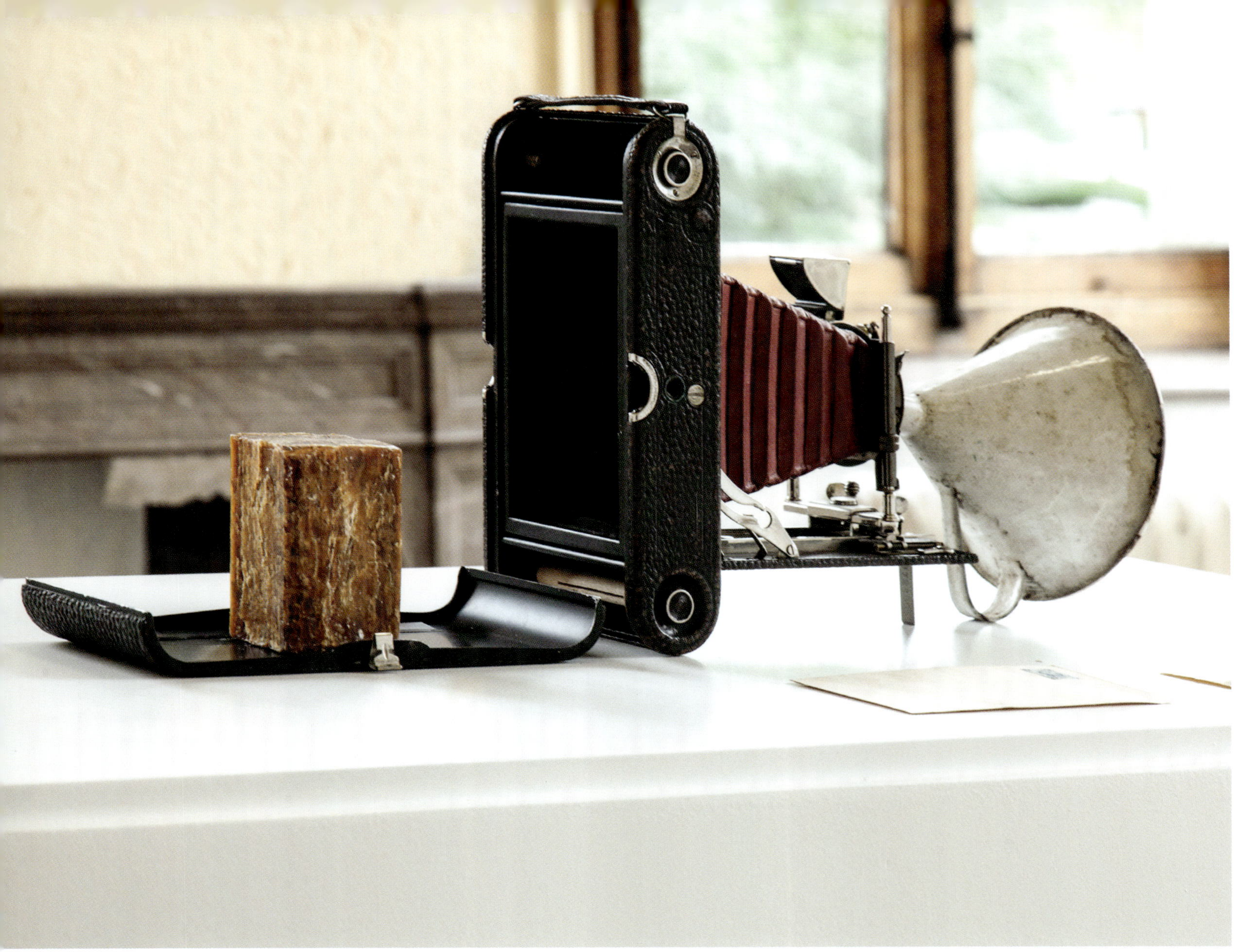

PETER DE CUPERE

IN HONOUR OF CAFLO YROT (1874-1970, UA)

The Ukrainian artist Caflo Yrot was a doctor, interpreter and teacher. He made art in his free time and in his art he mainly used scent as a medium and the idea that scent was centrally. Nevertheless, he never exposed his works. Early April 2014 Caflo's son contacted Peter de Cupere to introduce his father's works to him.

One should always place the work of Caflo Yrot in the spirit of the age. Art was end of 1800, beginning of 1900 not so extreme progressive in Ukraine. Caflo Yrot formed an exception to this.

Le Parfum de Sang (The Perfume of Blood) – As a medicine man, Caflo Yrot was strongly interested in the body and the scents of the human body. He found the most personal perfume to be the proper blood. Nevertheless blood has a rather metallic smell. Blood was life's perfume for Caflo. Without blood one cannot live, but one cannot smell their life's perfume because it is inside our body. To be able to perceive it, he came up with the idea of a perfume pump connected with a needle. By pricking in your body and dispersing the blood on your own skin, one could smell your own life's perfume. An absurd idea, but very daring for his time. And as a doctor, he probably knew what he was doing.

Tabac à Priser Rouge – His *Tabac à Priser Rouge* consisted out of different themes. He made a series of postal cards of pharmacies in which he applied the red ball in a flask. This red ball one can see as a clown's nose as is the case in other works. Another series existed out of applying a red ball to images of public buildings. He always hung these works upside down. This hanging upside down was not a pure aesthetical decision. For Caflo Yrot it meant that one should read this work differently, in other words in the opposite direction. Thus the clown's nose should be read here and something not cheerfully fun, but rather as a painful meaning. It was his way to react to certain situations. A wonderful example of this is his series with Hitler's stamps. As an extreme anti-Hitler person, he wanted to mock him by sticking a red nose on him and hanging it upside down.

Caflo Yrot liked to apply small remarks to the objects but also in magazines or books. Thus he wrote names of flowers and plants on the images of technical drawings from bullets.

More information about Caflo Yrot's work can be found on the website www.theolfactory.org, to the publication of *The Smell of War* (www.thesmellofwar.be) and in the future to the website www.cafloyrot.com.

OLFACTISM

OLFACTIONISM - OLFACTORISM - OLFACTOURISM

Olfactory Art Manifest

On August 11th, 1913 Carlo Carrá published "La Pittura dei suoni, rumori, odori: Manifesto futurista" [The Painting of Sounds, Noises, Smells: Futurist Manifesto]. This is the first manifest in which a reference is made to, amongst others, smell.

However, since then, smell was only used sporadically in visual arts. Smell was referenced to, but smell as a medium for the work was hardly ever applied. Only few knew how to find their way to this medium, but then it was only used once or sporadically. It would take until the end of the 20th century before visual artists consequently used smell in all of their works.

Even though the number of visual artists who only create works with smell or have used smell in combination with the visual and/or the auditive was rather limited, in the last decennia there has been a visible increase in artists who see smell as an equal medium to paint or other classic media. Smell has become more valued as 'part of the work of art' or as 'the work of art' itself.

There is also a noticeable increase in interest from the scent industry, more specifically the world of perfumes, which presents its scent creation as a piece of art, either linked or not linked to the visual arts. Some classic perfumes are even compared to certain –isms from art history. Some 'noses' do not always see their work in the light of commerce and are rather looking for the perfect scent art work.

Cross-overs and cooperations between perfumers and visual artists arise. Artists get to know the world of smell better and noses see the added value of linking their work of scents to a certain social context. Smell has never been as hot in the world of arts as the last couple of years and we are only at the beginning of this revelation.

The most underrated sense throughout (art) history has seldom gotten so much attention in the world of art as in the last decennia. Institutions, organisations and several museums display more and more olfactory art. There is an up rise in organisations, institutes and museums who specialize in Olfactory Art. Colleges also are more open to the integration of smell as an art medium in the education of upcoming young talent. This makes the young artists more open to the integration of smell into their work. They venture into the smell experiment.

Just as sound, photography and video have become accepted media, smell is becoming a commonplace of the visual arts. Yet, the integration remains limited for now and that is why this Manifest is written: To bring Olfactory art under the attention as a worthy form of art. Thus, we can talk about a new art movement and therefore, with this manifest, Olfactory Art is added to the –isms of art and from this point onwards, we speak of 'Olfactism'.

Olfactism

Olfactism is a term derived from the Latin verb olfacere (to smell). Even though this term also being used in e.g. synaesthesia, in which it more or less means a sensation of smell originated by other senses than the olfactory stimuli, in the art movement, we look at this term as an –ism rather from the smell as a medium that gives context and/or can be the concept of the work. This does not take away that the manner in which synaesthesia looks at the term is interesting. Eventually, it is about a cross-over between smelling and the idea of smelling, the senses and the translation of the observation and / or experience.

In general we speak of Olfactism when we talk about art in which smell is used as a medium and is part of the work or when the smell itself is a piece of art. A visual representation is nevertheless also possible if it is clear that it concerns smell concepts and/or works of art in which smell is a context or gives a context.

We can divide Olfactism in Olfactionism and Olfactorism.

Olfactionism

Fact & Action

In Olfactionism we find the words 'Fact' and 'Action', two ideas which clarify the term. Through the use of a 'Fact', one can encourage someone to take 'Action', but 'Action' can also encourage someone to reflect on a 'Fact' and even to accept it. In this way, smell can let you think about a 'Fact'. Smell then allows you to take 'Action' and question the 'Fact', either accepting or rejecting it, or even lets you react against it or contend for it. But smell can also be the 'Fact', the result, observation or experience of a certain Action. Smell hereby gives context to the work.

Smell can also be 'Action' when it makes you reflect, conclude or experience. In other words, smell is 'Fact' and 'Action' but does not necessarily need to be the two together and does not even have to be one or the other to go into Action or to determine a Fact.

The word Fact can also be found in Olfactorism, but then we start mainly from the smell as a 'Factor' and scent as an 'Actor'.

- A 'Fact ' is an event, a data or a situation in which the reality is fixed
- A 'Fact can be observed either sensory and/or instrumentally measured. The observation itself can be subjective and dependant of personal circumstances and interpretations.
- A 'Fact' determines the observation, but the observation can also influence a 'Fact'.
- Facts are at the base of knowledge.
- Facts can be organized by the mind to a certain insight.
- Facts are in close relation to the term 'truth'.
- A Fact is usually generally accepted.

From the above, one can deduct that a Fact can give context or can be context. The use of Facts can also be a concept or can support a concept.

Facts can stimulate thoughts, reflection, observation and can sometimes also provoke action and reaction.

In the word Olfactionism we can see the word 'action' and this is exactly what smell wants to accomplish here. To encourage the spectator to take action, but also cause reaction. A work of art with smell, or smell as a work of art serves to encourage the onlooker to think and should not merely be seen as decoration of the work unless the shape of this decoration also contributes to the contents of the work. In other words, smell needs to contribute to the context of the work. Smell can be the context carrier, but also the context giver in relation to the other elements of the work of art, being e.g. the visual and / or the auditive, the tactile or the gustative. One could say that smell needs to have an associative impact.

In Olfactionism, smell can also have a normal supportive function, but only when this function is an element which cannot be missed in the work of art in order to see the correct context of the work. If the smell is omitted, the work would lose the attention for her context and the 'Action' would be different or completely lost.

- An 'Action' is an intent and usually has a purpose
- An 'Action' can either be physical, mental or instrumental
- An 'Action' is an activity.
- An 'Action' is observable by at least one sense unless the 'Action' is the consequence of an arising thought pattern and is only played out in the memory. In other words, 'Action' is then thinking or recalling a memory.
- An 'Action' usually has a reaction and / or can also make someone think and reflect about a reaction, but is therefore not necessarily the cause or the consequence of a reaction. An Action can give a Fact another insight which causes a reaction.

In general, the term Olfactionism will be mainly used for works of art in which the smell itself gives context or the smell in combination with the visual and/or the auditive, tactile or gustative has a context. Smell can also be used as a concept of the work in order to come to a context in relation to other senses.

The title of the work can also give another context to the smell or smell can do this to the title. For example, the title can be unintelligible at first, but in relation to the smell and/or other elements of the work, if these are present, it gets a new reading content by which the whole does get a certain or other context.

Olfactorism

One speaks about Olfactorism when smell is only the 'actor' or 'factor' of the work. The term Olfactorism is mainly used in works of art that consist solely out of smell or smell only in combination with colours, shapes, compositions, contrasts, light or darkness. The smell factor of the work itself is central. The context can be found in the composition of the smell and what it evokes or what it lets us experience. Under Olfactorism we can mainly find composed smells including perfumes. Central is the smell and the experience of the smell, but also the composition can be counted as Olfactorism. One could compare Olfactorism with the search for the right composition, in the same way as there are movements in the visual arts in which the composition of the work prevails.

- Composition of smells, composed smells and/ or simple smells
- Use of natural, nature identical and/or synthetic smells in a certain composition to come to a new smell
- Mixed smells
- Use of new smell molecules
- Throughout the time mixed smells, amongst others a smell concert
- Through physical displacement, mix the smells in a room

To Olfactorism also belongs the smelling of scent analyses or the remodelling of smells from certain locations, bodies, animals, objects and plants to make the spectator olfactory conscious of its environment, identity and/ or situation. Also, the registration of smells and capturing these on a map with the intention to make the spectator olfactory conscious of its environment is part of Olfactorism. In other words, the creation of smell consciousness of the state in which the spectator finds him-/herself by the use of nothing but odors also belongs to Olfactorism. When the creation of smell consciousness of a state does not only happen through odors, but also through another means or device which is not a smell, this is part of Olfactionism, same as the encouragement to smelling through smell devices which is also part of Olfactionism.

The creation of memories of smell, only through odor, belongs to Olfactorism. The remake of smell memories through an odor can recall and give a context to a certain location, situation or happening.
The use of smells in architecture, and thus the contribution to a form of life or living can also be part of Olfactorism when this does not have a commercial, entertainment and/or medical function. Smell can therefore also support the tactile of building materials or even through smell of the chosen building materials give an added value and contribute to the experiencing of the building. The smell in relation to the building is subjective, but the combination can recall a cognitive thing and / or feeling.

Smell in combination with the tactile, music or sound can also be part of Olfactorism when this combination gives an artistic experience or lesson without relapsing into amusement, medical or commercial outbursts. When the combination is the onset to discourse, we will rather speak of Olfactionism.

Concretely, one could say that the Olfactorism is the 'architecture of smell' which gives artistic values, which is more than only the composed.

Olfactionism or Olfactorism?

To prevent confusion between both, the term Olfactism can be chosen as a general description. The subdivision will only be necessary once we want to make a difference between Olfactory works of art.

To classify the use of smells which does not belong to Olfactism and its two subdivisions Olfactionism and Olfactorism, we use the term Olfactourism. In this –ism, the word 'Tourism' is concealed and it is a clear reference to the non-art form, but to the underlying reference to the crafty, illustrative, potentially medical (e.g. aroma therapy) and entertaining.

Olfactourism

Amongst others the following uses of smell belong to Olfactourism, unless they contribute to the work of art in which the context is created or unless this is used in an art installation. But then the whole work or installation is considered a work of art and not the part of the smell separately.

- Illustrative smells in the support of an image/cartoon
- Smell commercials
- Functional odorants
- Atmosphere odors

- Aroma therapy
- Traditional techniques for the creation of odors, see distillation, enfleurage,...
- Smell workshops, perfume workshops
- Smell/scent-dj (use of smell in festivals, performances, parties, discotheques, ...)
- Odor atomization in a non-artistic film, video or documentary
- Use of scent technologies for the amusement of the spectator
- Scratch & Sniff for commercial purposes, movies (except art movies) and publications (except signed and numbered art editions)
- Scented animation
- Smell communication
- Perfumes which do not fulfil the criteria of Olfactorism
- Hobby perfume makers
- ...

Numeration of Olfactory Art forms

Art is free and a numeration of different possibilities to create Olfactory art should not be a limitation. Therefore, this list is not complete and can be freely completed. Important is that smell is an essential part of the work and that together it qualifies as Olfactism.

- Smell installations/sculptures
- Scent paintings/drawings
- Scent rooms/ architecture
- Smell devices which do not have a commercial function, but do have as a purpose to make the spectator olfactory conscious or to give a certain context in which is referenced to the smell or as a device is used to support the smelling.
- Perfumes
- Smell performances which can also be called Perfumances when the medium smell is used.
- Smell videos and smell movies
- The nose (in which the function of the smelling is enforced and not purely as a visual part of the human being or animal)
- Smell maps of cities for which the focus is in the creation of smell consciousness of a situation.
- Smell dancing / theatre
- Digital scent technology art works
- ....

About smell!

Appetising, beautiful, pleasant, wonderful, super, musty and reeking!

In Olfactism, the smell itself is determinative, or as a 'part' is determinative for the work.
The smell can be **EVERYTHING.** There are no limitations, as long as the smell contributes to the work or is the work itself. Therefore, not only single odorants are possible, but also composed smells such as perfumes or a mix of smells which is created throughout time as is the case with scent concerts and smell-dj settings when these do not empower amusement, commerce or the medicinal. The amusement, commerce and medicinal as smell output can be a part of the work in order to reach a certain context so that it belongs to Olfactism, but not when it is only used in its function without added value or without giving purpose to others.

Odors can smell good, but can also be foul and reeking, as long as the choice of smell is consistent with the idea of the artistic work and contributes to its meaning, reading direction and/or experience of the work. Smell is freedom.

- This manifest calls all artists to enter into the smell experiment.
- This manifest calls all curators, museum directors, makers of exhibitions and organisers to show more olfactory art.
- This manifest calls all spectators to look beyond their nose when they experience an Olfactory Art Work, to stand still with the context of the work and to ponder about the function of smell as medium.

This manifest calls EVERYONE to smell harder!

Keep on smelling
Peter de Cupere, 2014

OLFACTISME

OLFACTIONISME - OLFACTORISME - OLFACTOURISME

Olfactory Art Manifest

Op 11 augustus 1913 publiceerde Carlo Carrá "La Pittura dei suoni, rumori, odori: Manifesto futurista" [The Painting of Sounds, Noises, Smells: Futurist Manifesto]. Dit is het eerste manifest waarin o.a. verwezen wordt naar geur.

Maar sindsdien werd geur in de beeldende kunsten toch nog maar sporadisch gebruikt. Er werd wel naar geur verwezen, maar geur als medium van het werk werd heel zelden toegepast. Enkelingen wisten hun weg te vinden naar dit medium, maar het bleef bij een éénmalig of sporadisch gebruik. Het zou nog tot de laatste decennia van de 20ste eeuw duren eer beeldende kunstenaars geur als medium consequent in al hun werken hanteerden.

Al bleef het aantal beeldende kunstenaars dat alleen werken creëerde met geur of geur gebruikte in combinatie met het visuele en/of auditieve eerst beperkt. De laatste decennia is er duidelijk een toename van kunstenaars die geur als een evenwaardig medium zien zoals verf en andere klassieke media. Geur wordt als 'onderdeel van het kunstwerk' of 'geur als het kunstwerk' an sich meer ter waarde geschat.

Er is ook een duidelijke toename van interesse uit de geurindustrie, meer bepaald de parfumwereld, die hun geurcreatie naar voor brengen als een kunstwerk, gelinkt of niet gelinkt aan de beeldende kunsten. Sommige klassieke parfums worden zelfs vergeleken met bepaalde ismen uit de kunstgeschiedenis. Sommige 'neuzen' zien hun werk niet in het teken van de commercie en zoeken eerder meer naar het perfecte geurkunstwerk.

Er ontstaan cross-overs en samenwerkingen tussen parfumeurs en beeldende kunstenaars. Kunstenaars leren de wereld van de geur meer kennen en neuzen zien de meerwaarde in om hun geurwerk te linken aan een bepaalde maatschappelijke context. Geur is nog nooit zo hot geweest in de kunstwereld als de laatste jaren en we staan nog maar aan het begin van deze revelatie.

Het meest misprezen zintuig doorheen de (kunst)geschiedenis kreeg zelden zoveel aandacht in de kunstwereld als de laatste decennia. Instituten, organisaties en diverse musea tonen meer en meer olfactory art. Er ontstaan zelf organisaties, instituten en musea die zich specialiseren in Olfactory Art. Ook kunsthogescholen staan meer open voor het integreren van geur als medium van het kunstwerk in de educatie van jong aankomend geweld. Jonge kunstenaars staan hierdoor juist meer open voor het integreren van geur in hun werk. Ze durven het geurexperiment aan.

Net zoals geluid, fotografie en video aanvaarde media zijn geworden, wordt geur stilaan gemeengoed van de beeldende kunsten. Doch blijft de integratie voorlopig beperkt en daarom dit schrijven van een Manifest om Olfactory Art extra onder de aandacht te brengen als waardige kunstvorm. We kunnen zo van een nieuwe kunststroming spreken. Zo wordt met dit manifest Olfactory Art toegevoegd aan de ismen van de kunst en spreekt men over 'Olfactisme'.

Olfactisme

Olfactisme is een term afgeleid van het Latijnse werkwoord olfacere (ruiken). Ondanks dat deze term ook gebruikt wordt in bv. de synesthesie waar hij eerder de betekenis heeft van een sensatie van geur ontstaan door andere zintuigen dan de olfactory stimuli, bekijken we deze term als isme in de kunststromingen eerder vanuit hoe geur als medium context geeft en/of concept kan zijn van het werk. Maar dit neemt niet weg dat de manier hoe synesthesie naar de term kijkt ook een boeiend gegeven is. Uiteindelijk gaat het over een cross-over werking tussen ruiken of het idee van ruiken, de zintuigen en het vertalen van de waarneming en/of ervaring.

Algemeen spreken we dus van Olfactisme wanneer we het over kunst hebben waarbij geur als medium deel uitmaakt van het werk of geur an sich het kunstwerk is. Een visuele weergave is echter ook mogelijk indien het duidelijk is dat het gaat over geurconcepten en/of kunstwerken waarbij geur context is of geeft.

Men kan Olfactisme opdelen in Olfactionisme en Olfactorisme.

Olfactionisme

Fact & Action

In het woord Olfactionisme vinden we de woorden 'Fact' en 'Action' terug. Twee begrippen die de term verduidelijken. Via het gebruiken van een 'Fact' kan men iemand aanzetten tot 'Action', maar 'Action kan ook iemand aanzetten tot nadenken over een 'Fact' en zelfs tot het aanvaarden van een Fact. Zo kan geur je aldus ook laten nadenken over een 'Fact'. Geur doet je dan overgaan tot 'Action' om het 'Fact' in vraag te stellen, te aanvaarden of niet te aanvaarden of je er zelfs tegen te verzetten of ervoor te strijden. Maar geur kan ook het 'Fact' zijn, het resultaat, waarneming of ondervinding van een bepaalde Action. Geur geeft hierbij context aan het werk.

Geur kan zo ook 'Action' zijn wanneer deze je laat nadenken, vaststellen of ondervinden. Maw geur is 'Fact' en 'Action' maar hoeft niet de twee samen te zijn en hoeft zelfs niet één van de twee te zijn om over te gaan tot Action of vaststellen van een Fact.

Het woord Fact vind je ook terug in het Olfactorisme, maar daar vertrekken we voornamelijk vanuit geur als 'factor' en geur als 'actor'.

- Een 'Fact' is een gebeurtenis, gegeven of situatie waarvan de werkelijkheid vaststaat

- Een 'Fact' kan ofwel zintuiglijk worden waargenomen en/of instrumenteel gemeten worden.

De waarneming op zich kan echter subjectief zijn en afhankelijk zijn van persoonsgebonden omstandigheden en interpretaties.

- Een 'Fact' bepaalt de waarneming, maar de waarneming kan ook een 'Fact' beïnvloeden.

- Facts staan aan de basis van kennis.

- Facts kunnen door het verstand geordend worden tot een inzicht.

- Facts staan in nauw verband met het begrip waarheid.

- Een Fact wordt meestal algemeen aanvaard.

Uit bovenstaande kan men afleiden dat een Fact context kan geven of context kan zijn. Tevens kan het gebruiken van een Fact(s) concept zijn of een concept ondersteunen.

Facts zetten aan tot nadenken, reflecteren, vaststellen en soms ook tot actie en reactie.

In het woord Olfactionisme zit het woord 'action' en dit is juist wat geur hier wil bewerkstellen. De toeschouwer aanzetten tot actie, maar ook reactie. Een kunstwerk met geur of geur als kunstwerk dient de toeschouwer aan te zetten tot nadenken en mag niet louter als decoratie van het werk gebruikt worden tenzij deze vorm van decoratie ook bijdraagt aan de inhoud van het werk. Maw geur moet bijdragen aan de context van het werk. Geur kan hier de contextdrager zijn, maar kan ook de contextgever zijn in relatie met de andere elementen van het kunstwerk zijnde bv. het visuele en/of het auditieve, het tactiele of het gustatieve. Men zou hier kunnen zeggen dat geur een associatieve werking dient te hebben.

Geur kan hier echter ook gewoon een ondersteunende functie hebben, maar alleen wanneer deze functie een niet te missen element van het kunstwerk is om tot de juiste context van het werk te komen. Bij het weglaten van de geur zou het werk juist de aandacht voor haar context verliezen en ook de 'Action' zou anders zijn of zelfs volledig wegvallen.

- Een 'Action' is een intentie en heeft meestal een doel voor ogen

- Een 'Action' kan zowel lichamelijk, mentaal of instrumenteel zijn

- Een 'Action' is een handeling

- Een 'Action' is waarneembaar door minstens 1 zintuig tenzij de 'Action' het gevolg is van een ontstaan denkpatroon en deze 'Action' zich alleen afspeelt in het geheugen, maw het nadenken of het oproepen van een herinnering.

- Een 'Action' heeft meestal een reactie en/of kan ook doen nadenken, reflecteren over een reactie, maar is daarom niet noodzakelijk de oorzaak of gevolg van een reactie.

Een Action kan nl. een Fact een ander inzicht geven waardoor deze een reactie opwekt.

In het algemeen zal de term Olfactionisme vooral gebruikt worden bij kunstwerken waarbij de geur an sich context geeft of de geur in combinatie met het visuele en/of het auditieve, tactiele of gustatieve een context heeft. Geur kan ook als concept van het werk gebruikt worden om zo tot een context te komen in relatie met andere zintuigen.

De titel van het werk kan ook de geur een andere context geven of geur kan dit voor de titel doen. Zo kan bv. de titel eerst niet te begrijpen zijn, maar in relatie tot de geur en/ of de andere elementen van het werk, indien deze aanwezig zijn, een nieuwe leesinhoud krijgen waardoor het geheel wel een bepaalde of een andere context krijgt.

Olfactorisme

Men spreekt van het Olfactorisme wanneer geur alleen de 'Actor' is of 'Factor' van het werk. De term Olfactorisme wordt vooral gebruikt bij kunstwerken die alleen uit geur bestaan of geur alleen in combinatie met kleuren, vormen, composities, contrasten, licht of donkerte. De geurfactor van het werk an sich staat centraal. De context ligt hier bij hoe de geur an sich is samengesteld en wat deze oproept of doet ervaren. Onder het Olfactorisme vinden we vooral veel samengestelde geuren terug waaronder parfums. Centraal staat de geur en de ervaring van de geur, maar ook de samenstelling kan bepalend zijn om tot het Olfactorisme worden gerekend. Men zou het Olfactorisme kunnen vergelijken met het zoeken naar de juiste compositie, net zoals men bij de schilderkunst stromingen terugvindt waarbij de compositie van het werk primeert.

- Compositie van geuren, samengestelde geuren en/of enkelvoudige geuren
- Gebruikmaken van natuurlijke, natuur identieke en/of synthetische geuren in een bepaalde compositie om zo tot een nieuwe geur te komen
- Gemengde geuren
- Gebruikmaken van nieuwe geurmoleculen
- Doorheen de tijd gemengde geuren, o.a. een geurconcert
- Door lichamelijke verplaatsing in een ruimte geuren mengen
- ...

Bij het Olfactorisme hoort ook het laten ruiken van geuranalyses, of namaken van geuren van bepaalde locaties, lichamen, dieren, objecten en planten om de toeschouwer puur olfactief bewust te maken van zijn leefomgeving, identiteit en/of situatie. Tevens is ook het registreren van geuren en deze vastleggen op een kaart met bedoeling de toeschouwer olfactief bewust te maken van zijn omgeving onderdeel van het Olfactorisme. Maw het creëren van geurbewustzijn van de toestand waarin de toeschouwer zich bevindt door het gebruik van alleen geurstoffen hoort thuis bij het Olfactorisme. Wanneer het creëren van geurbewustzijn van een toestand niet alleen door geurstoffen gebeurt, maar ook door een ander gegeven of een hulpmiddel dat geen geurstof is, hoort dit thuis bij het Olfactionisme, net zoals het aanzetten tot ruiken via smell devices thuishoort bij het Olfactionisme.

Het creëren van geurherinneringen louter via een geurstof hoort thuis bij het Olfactorisme. Het namaken van geurherinneringen via een geurstof kan nl. context oproepen of geven aan een bepaalde locatie, situatie of gebeurtenis. Geurgebruik in architectuur om zo bij te dragen aan een vorm van leven of te beleven kan ook thuis horen in het olfactorisme wanneer deze geen commerciële, amusement en/ of medische functie heeft. Geur kan zo ook het tactiele van bouwmaterialen ondersteunen of zelfs via de geur van de gekozen bouwmaterialen een meerwaarde geven en bijdragen aan de ervaring van het gebouw. De geur in relatie tot het gebouw is subjectief, maar de combinatie kan een cognitief gegeven en/of gevoel oproepen.

Geur in combinatie met het tactiele, muziek of geluid kan ook deel uitmaken van het olfactorisme wanneer deze combinatie een artistieke ervaring of beleving heeft zonder te vervallen in amusement, medische of commerciële uitingen. Wanneer de combinatie aanzet tot discours zullen we echter eerder spreken van het olfactionisme.

Concreet zou je kunnen zeggen dat het Olfactorisme de 'architectuur van de geur' is dat artistieke waarden geeft, welke meer is dan alleen het samengestelde.

Olfactionisme of Olfactorisme?

Om verwarring tussen beiden te voorkomen kan de term Olfactisme als algemene omschrijving gekozen worden. De opdeling zal pas noodzakelijk zijn wanneer men een opdeling wil maken tussen olfactorische kunstwerken.

Om het gebruik van geuren die niet thuis horen bij het Olfactisme en de twee onderverdelingen, Olfactionisme en Olfactorisme, te klasseren gebruiken we de term 'Olfactourisme'. In dit isme zit het woord 'Tourism' en is een duidelijke verwijzing naar de niet kunstvorm, maar wel een onderliggende verwijzing naar het ambachtelijke, illustratieve, eventueel medische en amusement gegeven.

Olfactourisme

Bij het Olfactourisme horen o.a. volgenden thuis, tenzij ze bijdragen aan een kunstwerk waarbij er context gecreëerd wordt of tenzij deze in een kunstinstallatie gebruikt worden. Maar dan is het geheel van het werk of de installatie dat als kunstwerk wordt beschouwd en niet het geuronderdeel apart

- Illustratieve geuren voor ondersteuning van een beeldverhaal
- Geurcommercials
- Functionele geurstoffen
- Sfeergeuren

- Aromatherapie
- Traditionele technieken voor de creatie van geurstoffen, cfr. distillatie, enfleurage,...
- Geurworkshops, parfum workshops
- Geur-dj, (gebruiken van geur op festivals, optredens, fuiven, discotheken, feestjes, ...)
- Geurverstuiving bij een niet kunstfilm, video of documentaire
- Gebruikmaken van geurtechnologieën ter amusement van de toeschouwer
- Scratch & sniff voor commerciële doelen, films en publicaties
- Geuranimatie
- Geurcommunicatie
- Parfums die niet voldoen aan het Olfactorisme
- Hobby parfummakers
- ...

Opsomming van Olfactory Art soorten

Kunst is vrij en een opsomming van verschillende mogelijkheden om Olfactory Art te creëren mag geen beperking zijn, vandaar dat deze lijst niet volledig is en vrij aangevuld kan worden. Belangrijk is dat geur een noodzakelijk onderdeel van het werk moet zijn en samen voldoet aan het Olfactisme.

- Geurinstallaties
- Geurschilderijen
- Geursculpturen
- Geurtekeningen
- Geurruimtes
- Geurarchitectuur
- Smell devices welke geen commerciële functie hebben, maar wel tot doel de toeschouwer geurbewust te maken of een bepaalde context te geven waar naar geur wordt verwezen of als hulpstuk wordt gebruikt om het ruiken te ondersteunen
- Parfums
- Geurperformances welke ook Perfumances genoemd kunnen worden wanneer het medium geur gebruikt wordt.
- Geurvideos en geurfilms
- De neus (waarbij de functie van het ruiken benadrukt wordt en niet puur als visueel onderdeel van mens of dier)
- Geurkaarten van steden waarbij de focus ligt op het creëren van geurbewustheid van een situatie.
- Geurdansen
- Gedigitaliseerde geurtechnologie kunst
- ...

Over de geur!

Lekker, mooi, aangenaam, heerlijk, super, wee en stinken!

In het olfactisme is de geur 'an sich' bepalend of als 'onderdeel' bepalend voor het werk. De geur kan **ALLES** zijn. Er zijn geen beperkingen, zolang de geur bijdraagt aan het werk of zelf het werk is. Zo zijn niet alleen enkelvoudige geurstoffen mogelijk, maar ook samengestelde geuren zoals parfums of een geurmix dat gecreëerd werd doorheen de tijd zoals bij geurconcerten en geur-dj settings wanneer deze niet het amusement, de commercie of het medische bewerkstelligen. Het amusement, de commercie en het medische als geuroutput kan wel onderdeel zijn van een werk om tot een bepaalde context te komen om tot het olfactisme te horen, maar niet wanneer deze louter in hun functie gebruikt worden zonder een extra meerwaarde of doel aan derden te geven.

Geuren mogen goed ruiken, maar mogen ook wee zijn en stinken! Zolang de geurkeuze aansluit bij het idee van een artistiek werk en bijdraagt tot de betekenis, leesrichting en/of ervaring van het werk. Geur is vrij(heid).

- Dit manifest roept alle kunstenaars op om het geurexperiment aan te gaan.
- Dit manifest roept alle curatoren, museumdirecteurs, tentoonstellingsmakers en organisatoren op om meer olfactory art tonen.
- Dit manifest roept alle toeschouwers op om verder te kijken dan hun neus lang is wanneer ze een olfactory Art werk ervaren om stil te staan bij de context van het werk en welke functie geur als medium hierin heeft.

Dit manifest roept ALLEN op om harder te ruiken!

Keep on smelling

Peter de Cupere, 2014

PETER DE CUPERE

GEUR IN CONTEXT
Olfactory Art

Nederlandse tekstversie

PETER DE CUPERE

ZE NOEMEN MIJ EEN GEURKUNSTENAAR

Ze noemen mij een geurkunstenaar.

Ik heb dit doorheen de tijd proberen te aanvaarden, toch voel ik mij eerder een beeldend kunstenaar, maar gebruik geur als belangrijkste zintuig/medium om betekenis te geven aan het beeld en dit beeld hoeft daarom niet zichtbaar te zijn. Het beeld kan ook opgeroepen worden door louter het gebruik van geur in combinatie met een teweeggebracht gevoel zoals bij het werk *Scented Tears* waar de toeschouwer door toedoen van de geur in een lege ruimte begint te huilen en geconfronteerd wordt met het verdriet van anderen en zichzelf. Geur kan ook cognitief betekenis geven aan bijvoorbeeld een titel zoals bij het werk *Invisible (Scent) Paintings* waar niets beduidende titels opeens context krijgen door het ruiken van geuren die op de muren van het museum worden aangebracht via scratch & sniff technologie.

In het Engels hebben ze de term *Olfactory*. Een *Olfactory Artist* is een kunstenaar die werk maakt met geur. De term is heel breed. Men gebruikt het voor zowel parfumeurs die hun creatie als kunstwerk beschouwen, als voor kunstenaars die geur gebruiken als medium in hun werk en/of in combinatie met andere media. Je moet *Olfactory Art* in de beeldende kunsten zien in de betekenis van *Sense of Smell*. Het woord *sense* geeft juist een extra dimensie aan geur. Het gaat niet louter alleen om de geur, maar om wat de geur oproept. Dit kan een gevoel zijn, een betekenis, een doel en/of de zintuigelijke ervaring *an sich* zijn.

Via het vertalen en gebruiken van zintuigelijke waarneming(en) gecombineerd met een cognitieve attitude, wil ik met mijn werk iets zeggen, betekenis geven en een boodschap overbrengen. Zo zijn meerdere werken een puur zintuigelijk onderzoek of een combinatie van factoren en gedachten waarbij de interacties ontstaan vanuit mijn onderzoekende houding om iets te beelden. Ik gebruik ook liever het woord 'beelden' dan visualiseren, en zelden het woord verbeelden. Verbeelden is meestal visualiseren, beelden is voor mij meer het duiden, tonen wat ik wil zeggen in/met het beeld. Verbeelden is meestal eerder het letterlijk vertalen, terwijl beelden eerder context geven is. Daar gaat kort gesproken heel mijn werk over.

Geur kan een illustratie zijn, een ondersteunende houding hebben en daarnaast kan geur ook beelden, context geven aan een beeld. Geur geeft zo meer betekenis aan het beeld dan het beeld alleen visueel oproept. Om dit te bewerkstelligen en de mogelijkheden hiervan te ontdekken was ik van in het begin genoodzaakt onderzoek te doen naar de mogelijkheden van geur als medium en het ruiken als zintuigelijke ervaring van het kunstwerk. Doordat geur in de kunstwereld zo weinig gebruikt is geweest, had ik een immense vrijheid om geur als medium uit te testen. Ik moest mij ook deze vrijheid toe-eigenen daar er niet veel voorbeelden van kunstenaars waren. Het was deels een uitdagende situatie, maar ook een moeilijke beslissing. Mijn werk werd in het begin moeilijk aanvaard. Men kon het niet lezen. Men zag de geur als iets toegevoegd dat voor de meeste toeschouwers een leuke bijkomstigheid was, maar men wist niet verder te kijken. Mijn eerste werken waren ook heel divers en vooral onderzoekend naar de mogelijkheden van het medium. Vragen als "Hoe hou je een geur zo lang mogelijk vast?", bleven mij achtervolgen. De houdbaarheid van een geur is spijtig genoeg heel vluchtig, maar deze beperking bleek ook voordelen te hebben.

PETER DE CUPERE

EEN GEURLEVEN

Met geur start meer dan we denken of meer dan we vermoeden, meer dan we bewust zijn, meer dan we weten, meer dan we nog moeten ontdekken en meer dan we ooit zullen ontdekken. Geur heeft zoveel betekenissen, zoveel waarden, zoveel herinneringen, zoveel talen, zoveel mogelijkheden, zoveel zoveelheden. Terwijl de andere zintuigen veel éénvoudiger zijn in hun complexiteit, is geur dit niet. Geur is niet zomaar een medium van mijn werken, geur is en geeft de context in mijn werken. Mijn kunstwerken zijn een statement uit liefde voor de geur.

Geur is van al onze zintuigen altijd al gezien geweest als het minst belangrijkste zintuig. De laatste decennia zien de wetenschappen er wel meer het nut van in en vooral het belang van geur. Geur heeft een waarschuwingsfunctie, een herinneringsfunctie, een genotsfunctie en vooral een bewustmakingsfunctie.

Daarom gebruik ik geur en ... omdat je ermee kan verleiden en misleiden.

Veel van mijn werken hebben een link met leven en dood. Een werk zoals *Beauty of Birth* verwijst naar de zwaarte van het leven die je de rest van je leven moet meedragen.

We ademen om te leven. Bij iedere ademhaling nemen we – onbewust – de geur van de ingeademde lucht waar. Bij de eerste ademhaling bij je geboorte neem je al moleculen geur waar. Alhoewel het bewezen is dat zintuigen zich al in foetusstatus ontwikkelen, kan men zeggen dat vanaf het moment dat de geboren baby zelfstandig ademt zijn/haar eerste ademhaling de wereld al olfactief proeft. Nog voor het zien, nog voor het openen van de ogen, zet de reukzin bewust aan om de wereld waar te nemen.

Om te kunnen leven is ademen de start.

Met iedere ademhaling inhaleren we een geur die bewust of onbewust iets vertelt over onze naaste omgeving. Iedere dag, iedere minuut, iedere seconde geeft geur ons info om te ontdekken, te ervaren, te herinneren, te begrijpen en om te handelen.

Geur mag dan vluchtig zijn, maar is niet zo vluchtig in haar uitwerking op de mens. Ze is een blijvende en toekomstige herinnering om mee te dragen voor de rest van ons leven.

I (RE)SEARCH(ED)

Meer dan 20 jaar onderzoek ik de mogelijkheden van geur als medium van het kunstwerk. Om dit te doen moet je veel experimenteren. Het experiment was steeds een belangrijk onderdeel van mijn werk.

Ik onderzocht hoe we ruiken, hoe een geur in elkaar zit, hoe parfums werken, hoe een product een geur vasthoudt, hoe geuren kunnen veranderen bij temperatuurschommelingen en meer of minder luchtvochtigheid. Ik onderzocht hoe geur een beleving oproept, hoe geur mensen blij maakt, in diskrediet brengt, hoe geur aanzet tot liefde en haat. Ik onderzocht hoe geur je levensstijl bepaalt, hoe geuren verschillen van cultuur tot cultuur, hoe mensen met een zintuigbeperking geuren als onderdeel van hun leven meer zin gaven.

Ik onderzocht hoe een vleugje lucht impact kan hebben op een gevoel, hoe geur mij beter deed leren en nadenken, maar ook hoe geur mij beter deed slapen, wakkerder maken en een bepaalde agressiviteit kon oproepen. Ik onderzocht hoe geur mensen kan doen huilen en lachen, hoe dieren op bepaalde geuren kunnen reageren. Ik onderzocht hoe ik met geuren kon verleiden. Ik onderzocht hoe ik via feromonen mogelijke kopers van mijn werk onbewust kon aanzetten om van een bepaald werk te houden en dit ook te kopen.

Ik onderzocht al de geuren van een lichaam, van vrouw en man en ook hun interactie. Ik onderzocht mijn eigen geur en was verrast hoe heerlijk mijn geur is in mijn eigen perceptiebeleving. Ik onderzocht hoe je met een éénvoudige zin in combinatie met een geur een hele wereld kon oproepen. Ik onderzocht hoe slechte geuren iets moois kunnen worden en heerlijke geuren iets lelijks. Ik onderzocht de moleculaire mogelijkheden van geuren, niet dat ik een scheikundige ben, maar puur uit interesse wanneer het mij uitkwam. Ik onderzocht de psychologische effecten van geur. Ik onderzocht wat velen al hebben onderzocht om te weten wat ik niet moet onderzoeken, maar wel wilde weten gewoon om het te weten.

Ik onderzocht de kracht van een druppeltje geur t.o.v. liters geurstof. Ik onderzocht veel geuren en ook de actie van het ruiken. Ik onderzocht geuren van mensen, rook hen stiekem bij iedere hallo kus. Ik rook aan mijn handen na een handdruk met bevallige personen. Ik onderzocht hoe de geur van uitwerpselen, urine, sperma, vagina en zweet konden bijdragen aan een kunstwerk. Ik onderzocht hoe een geur anders kon ruiken door deze te verdunnen of in combinatie te brengen met een niet voor de hand liggend object. Ik onderzocht hoe toeschouwers geuren persoonlijk interpreteren, hoe geur inspeelt op de herinnering.

Ik onderzocht de zwakheden en sterktes van geur en vond in hun tegenpolen juist hun omgekeerden terug. Ik onderzocht het verdriet van geur en de geur van verdriet waar ik nog steeds blijf achter zoeken net zoals ik ook naar al die andere geuren blijf zoeken, onderzoeken. Ik onderzocht de poëzie van geur, maar ook de harde realiteit. ik onderzocht het illustratieve karakter van geur en de fantasievolle gedachten bij geuren. Ik onderzocht geur, maar bovenal zocht ik steeds naar de context die geur aan een werk kon geven en hoe geur deze context kon doen veranderen. Ik onderzocht de waarachtigheid van geuren en het onbewust betekenis geven van een geur via herinneringen, culturele en godsdienstige achtergronden en rituelen.

Ik onderzocht zoveel, maar bovenal heb ik steeds in mijn artistieke onderzoeken vastgesteld dat geur zoveel meer mogelijkheden heeft dan er te onderzoeken valt. Daar ligt mijn verlangen om als kunstenaar deze eeuwig onderzoekende houding vast te houden. En dit begint bij iedere ademhaling. Iedere molecule die ik inadem is een verhaal op zich, een betekenis op zich. Iedere adem is betekenis, is als statement de start van het kunstwerk, nog meer dan het zien.

PETER DE CUPERE GEÏNTERVIEWD DOOR ASHRAF OSMAN

EEN GESPREK MET PETER DE CUPERE

Hoewel er stilaan meer erkenning komt voor olfactorische kunst, getuigen gesprekken erover vaak nog van een vrij defensieve houding: de historische (westerse) onderwaardering van geur en de daaruit voortvloeiende onontgonnen waarde. Deze waarde wordt vaak uitgedrukt als het omgekeerde van de primitieve status van geur. Men bewierookt de ongeëvenaarde toegang die geur verleent tot het geheugen, emoties en andere minder cerebrale delen van onze psyche. Daar wil ik het echter niet over hebben. Ik veronderstel dat dit allemaal al duidelijk is voor u, anders zou u dit niet lezen.

In plaats daarvan wil ik u een gesprek laten lezen met de meest productieve en proactieve voorstander van olfactorische kunst: kunstenaar en curator Peter de Cupere. Hoewel de oorsprong van de olfactorische kunst bijna een eeuw teruggaat, beschouwen de meeste mensen deze kunstvorm nog steeds niet als een beroep. Dus begon ik met de vraag hoe Peter voortrekker werd.

A O *Heb je altijd al interesse gehad in geur? Was je er als kind reeds door geboeid? Herinner je je momenten waarop geur een belangrijke rol speelde?*

P D C Ik begon interesse te vertonen in geur toen ik nog heel klein was, zelfs voordat ik het zelf besefte. Mijn moeder vertelde me dat ze me ooit een trommeltje gaf toen ik vier jaar oud was. In die tijd vond ik aardbeien niet zo lekker – in tegenstelling tot nu – maar ik hield wel van de geur ervan. Ik weet niet zeker of het voor de geur of de opwinding was, maar ik sneed de aardbeien in stukjes en plofte ze op de trommel. Dat maakte geluid, maar er kwam ook geur vrij. Voor mij is dat een soort kunstwerk, misschien wel mijn persoonlijk *life statement*.

Iets anders dat ik graag rook, waren regenwormen. Ik hield ze vast en rook eraan, van de ene kant naar de andere. Ik weet nog dat ik vond dat het ene uiteinde anders rook dan het andere. Mijn moeder vertelde me dat ik toen vier of vijf jaar was, maar dat weet ik niet meer. Ik herinner me wel dat ik die experimenten nog steeds deed toen ik acht of tien was. Nog iets: lieveheersbeestjes. Wanneer een lieveheersbeestje landt op je huid, laat het een geur achter. Het ruikt eigenlijk niet zo lekker, maar ik vond dat heel interessant. Er waren veel lieveheersbeestjes in onze tuin. Ik was nieuwsgierig: als je ze op je huid zet en op hun rug duwt, laten ze een geur achter. Ik vond dat grappig en wilde het laten zien aan andere mensen, maar niemand durfde te ruiken. Ze zeiden: "Nee, niet doen!". Het was een beetje gek.

Ik weet ook nog heel goed dat ik het helemaal niet leuk vond om de bus of de trein te nemen, toen ik zeven of acht was. Die vreselijke mix van geuren en zweet. Niet iedereen neemt 's morgens een douche. Het was de geur van ongelukkige mensen. In die tijd dacht ik ook dat dauwdruppels op het gras de geur ervan bevatten. Ik verzamelde dus grassprieten wanneer ze nog bedauwd waren. Ik dacht dat dit een makkelijke manier was om de geur eruit te krijgen. Ik wist immers nog niet hoe ik moest distilleren. Ik sneed het gras af en vermaalde het in een pot uit de keuken. Mijn moeder haatte het omdat ik de pot niet afwaste en hij dus vol groene vlekken zat. Daarna smeerde ik de grasgeur op mij, zodat mijn huid een beetje groen werd. Ik haatte dat en probeerde het te verbergen onder een sjaal of zo. Maar in de zomer kon dat niet en dat was nu net de beste periode omdat het warmer was en de geur intenser. Ik vond de reactie van de mensen op de bus of trein leuk. Ik merkte dat de mensen 's ochtends blij werden van mijn grasgeur. Ze lachten heel spontaan. Ik keek ernaar uit om de volgende dag een nieuwe portie te maken. Ik weet niet hoe lang ik dit deed, maar in elk geval heel vaak.

Daarnaast wilde ik ook parfum maken, maar ik wist niet hoe. Als kind neem je dan gewoon de parfums van je ouders of van mensen die je kent en mengt ze. Kinderlijk eenvoudig. Ik deed ook altijd een heleboel parfum op. Mijn vrienden vonden het vreselijk. Op een gegeven moment besloot ik om dat niet meer te doen omdat iedereen het erg meisjesachtig vond. Als tiener probeerde ik mijn liefde voor geuren te verbergen voor mijn vrienden, want de reacties waren niet zo leuk. Ik praatte graag met meisjes over parfum en zij vonden het geweldig dat een man dat deed. Ik was bang dat ze mij ook meisjesachtig zouden vinden, dus schakelde ik over naar cosmetica: gezichtsmaskers tegen acne, die de huid op een natuurlijke manier hielpen te genezen. Ik deed heel wat experimenten met materialen en stoffen, probeerde verschillende mengsels uit. Bloemenhoning werkte niet goed; te plakkerig. Maar wanneer je maïzena op je gezicht aanbrengt en laat drogen, wordt je huid erg zacht. Dat waren dingen die ik toen heel leuk vond.

A O Je kunstopleiding dan. Was er een moment waarop je voor het eerst besefte dat geur artistieke mogelijkheden had?

P D C Ik had nooit gedacht dat het mogelijk was om kunst te maken met geur. Ik denk dat ik zo graag met geur werk omdat ik graag kijk. Toen ik achttien was, hield ik van tekenen. Ik wou architect worden. Geen kunstenaar, want kunstenaars verdienen geen geld en ik moest realistisch zijn. Met architectuur kon dat wel. Maar ik werd nooit architect. Ik studeerde reclame, marketing en grafisch ontwerp. Ik kreeg een zeer klassieke opleiding. Ik heb twee broers en twee zussen. Mijn oudste zus en broer deden ballet en mijn jongere zus speelde piano. Elke dag klassieke muziek: verschrikkelijk. Ik haatte het toen echt; het was een soort reactie. Maar één klassiek idee bleef me bij: het verhaal van Beethoven. Dat hij doof werd, maar nog steeds composities kon maken door zijn oor tegen de piano te leggen en te luisteren naar de trillingen. Ik zou het vreselijk vinden mocht ik blind worden. Mijn ogen zijn nog heel goed, maar als kind was ik bang dat ik blind zou worden.

Ik was op zoek naar iets totaal anders en dus dacht ik aan geuren. Ik wilde een manier vinden om mijn tekeningen te vertalen naar geuren. Wanneer ik een boom tekende, verzamelde ik bladeren van die boom en bewaarde ze bij de tekening, voor de geur. De bladeren verdroogden. Hoe kon ik de geur opvangen en integreren in mijn tekening? Het was echter niet mijn bedoeling om een kunstwerk te maken. Ik zocht een oplossing voor het geval ik ooit blind zou worden. Hoe zou ik dan nog kunnen genieten van mijn tekeningen?

A O En in de praktijk? Wanneer begon je op een professionele manier aan kunst? Wat was je eerste geurwerk?

P D C Ik besloot om kunstenaar te worden toen ik 27 was. Daarvoor maakte ik kunstwerken onder een schuilnaam. Ik hoop dat niemand die ooit terugvindt. Afschuwelijke werken. Ik beschouwde ze trouwens niet als kunst. Ik geloofde nog steeds niet in een bestaan als kunstenaar of dat ik beroemd kon worden met kunst. Het gebeurde wel eens dat ik per toeval een geurtekening maakte. Toen ik vooraan in de twintig was, viel er in mijn slaapkamer een parfumfles op de vloer, die bedekt was met papieren tekeningen. Zo kwam ik op het idee om tekeningen te maken met parfums. Maar ik zag dit niet als kunst. Toen ik 26 was, maakte ik nog eens tekeningen met verschillende soorten parfums.

Ze zijn bijna onzichtbaar; je moet ze in het licht houden om ze te zien. Ik stelde die eerste kunstwerken nooit tentoon, omdat ik ze toen niet als een echt kunstwerk beschouwde. Zoals ik al zei, studeerde ik eerst reclame en grafische vormgeving. Ik ging aan de slag als marketingmanager bij een speelgoedbedrijf. Ik bereikte snel een hoge positie in het bedrijf, maar ik bleef slechts een jaar. Ik kwam tot de vaststelling dat het niet was wat ik wilde doen en waarvoor ik wilde leven. Ik kreeg te veel stress. Iedereen om me heen zei: "Je bent veranderd, je bent niet meer zo creatief." Het was moeilijk om weg te gaan, want het loon was niet slecht. Toen ik wegging en besloot om beeldende kunsten te gaan studeren, zei iedereen: "Je bent gek. Er zit geen toekomst in kunst, je kunt er geen geld mee verdienen. Je hebt een leuke job, je blijft beter waar je bent." Ik kon nog steeds voor het bedrijf werken als freelancer, omdat ze niemand anders met dezelfde kwalificaties konden vinden en ik al veel dingen wist. Tijdens mijn eerste jaar beeldende kunsten werkte ik dus ook voor het bedrijf als freelancer en voltooide mijn master in de beeldende kunsten in Brussel.

A O Was geur een prominent thema in je werk tijdens je opleiding?

P D C Mijn thesis ging eigenlijk over het gebruik van computers en de interactie met geur. Ik ben begonnen met gravures, etsen en dat soort dingen. Maar ik deed het slechts een semester. Ik vond het te technisch, een beetje saai. Ik wilde iets met computers doen, maar dat kon toen nog niet op school. Er was slechts één leraar die programmeur was. Ik sprak met hem en hij zei: "Oké, in het tweede semester kun je bij mij komen studeren." Maar ik moest veel zelf leren. Het is niet altijd duidelijk in mijn werk, maar heel wat ontwerpen en ideeën werk ik uit met de computer. Ik maakte bijvoorbeeld een ontwerp voor een geurtapijt van kruiden. Ik ontwierp een afdruk van een Perzisch tapijt. Voor de patronen gebruikte ik een lettertype op basis van vierkanten, driehoeken en cirkels. Het ontwerp maakte ik op de computer en het tapijt vervaardigde ik met de hand. Ik drukte het af op papier, op grote schaal en legde er verschillende kruiden op. Wit maakte ik bijvoorbeeld met gedroogde kokosschilfers. Het resultaat lijkt op een heel zacht tapijt, heel realistisch.

Ik maakte nog een ander werk, getiteld *Your Last Smell*. Wanneer we sterven, ademen we onze laatste geur uit. Maar op hetzelfde moment adem je ook je laatste geur in. Het kunstwerk bestaat uit een stuk zeep in een vossenval waarin je gezicht past. Wanneer je aan de zeep wil ruiken, klapt de val dicht op je gezicht. Heel morbide!

A O Je experimenteerde dus al tijdens je masteropleiding. Hoe reageerden je leraars?

P D C Negatief. Ik bestudeerde dit aspect in mijn gravurelessen. Bij de verdediging van mijn werk liet de jury me gewoon door. Ik kreeg net een voldoende. Ze waren van oordeel dat computers geen kunst produceren en geur zeker niet thuishoort in de kunstwereld.

A O *Het klinkt alsof het technisch en theoretisch nogal een uitdaging moet zijn geweest. Ze hadden blijkbaar problemen met je ernst. Is het de moeite waard? Is het echt kunst? Twijfelde je door deze kritiek? Dacht je dat je het niet zou halen als je met geur bleef werken? Of maakte het je nog vastberadener?*

P D C Ja en neen. Ik had gewoon geluk. Toen ik mijn punten kreeg aan het einde van mijn master, was ik ontevreden omdat ik gewoon geslaagd was. Ik was teleurgesteld omdat ik tijdens mijn reclameopleiding één van de betere studenten was. Ik geloofde in mijn werk, dus ik was boos op de leraars. Ik vond ze kleingeestig, omdat ze computercreaties niet als kunst beschouwden en geurwerken nog veel minder. Wonder boven wonder kocht ik die dag een *Subito*, zo'n lotje waarmee je toen 50.000 Belgische frank, ongeveer 1.250 euro, kon winnen. Ik had geluk: ik won 50.000 Belgische frank op de dag dat ik mijn diploma kreeg! Het was compleet paradoxaal: ik was ongelukkig met mijn punten, kocht nog nooit een lotje en won dan maar meteen 50.000 Belgische frank. Dat was een hele som, zeker voor een student. Ik was enorm opgewonden en belde meteen naar huis: "Vandaag is een mooie dag: ik behaalde mijn masterdiploma en ik won 50.000 Belgische frank." Ik denk altijd dat er een reden is waarom dingen gebeuren of we bepaalde mensen ontmoeten. Ik zag dit als een teken dat ik mijn missie in de kunstwereld moest voortzetten.

In deze periode betaalde ik mijn kosten door portretten te maken aan de kust. Het waren kitscherige portretten, maar ze verkochten goed. Ik deed het gewoon om geld te verdienen. Ik vergoelijkte mezelf door te zeggen dat ik het voor het geld deed, om mijn echte kunst te kunnen maken. Ik deed het elke zomer, twee en een halve maand en verdiende tussen de 6.000 en 8.000 euro. Maar ik beschouwde het nooit als kunst. Ik signeerde de werken zelfs als Piotr Noart *(No art)*. Het is best grappig als je thuis brieven krijgt gericht aan "Cher Monsieur Noart ...". Mensen zien het woordspelletje niet. Die zomer ontmoette ik een mooi meisje dat *Fleur* ('bloem') heette. Ze woonde in Antwerpen. Ik woonde toen bij mijn ouders, in een dorp in het midden van België. We waren maar een maand en tien dagen bij elkaar, maar deze periode was genoeg om te beseffen dat ik naar Antwerpen moest gaan om bij haar te zijn. Ik moest een reden vinden om dat te doen. Ik ontmoette een Chinese kunstenaar, Lee, die ook kitscherige portretten maakte. Ik liet hem mijn werk met geur en computers zien en hij raadde me aan om me in te schrijven aan het Hoger Instituut voor Schone Kunsten (HISK) in Antwerpen. In eerste instantie was ik niet geïnteresseerd, maar toen dacht ik aan mijn vriendin en nam ik toch contact op met het HISK. Ze investeerden op dat moment in een nieuw computerlab. Ze wilden vooral kunstenaars selecteren die werkten met computers. Ik maakte een stevig dossier om te worden toegelaten aan het instituut. Ik voegde een paar van mijn geurwerken toe, maar legde de nadruk op de computeraspecten van mijn kunst. Ik werd geselecteerd!

Op de dag dat ik naar het HISK moest om mijn werk voor te stellen en te bespreken, dineerde ik 's avonds met mijn vriendin en haar ouders. Ze speelde klassieke viool en speelde voor mij in onze slaapkamer, met haar ouders in de kamer ernaast. Ze speelde het *Adagio van Albinoni* ... zo mooi! Toen zei ze: "Peter, ik maak een wandeling met de hond en kom pas om 22 uur terug. Ik hoop dat je tegen dan weg bent, want ik wil vandaag een eind maken aan onze relatie. Ik weet niets over kunst, maar jij leeft ervoor. Je zegt dat je naar Antwerpen bent gekomen voor mij, maar dat is niet waar. Het is om naar het instituut te kunnen gaan." En eigenlijk had ze gelijk. Ze ging weg en ik bleef achter met haar ouders. We huilden de hele avond; ze hadden me graag. Maar ik bleef in Antwerpen, ging naar het HISK en vanaf dat moment veranderde alles voor mij als kunstenaar.

Kort nadien had ik het geluk om Jan Hoet te ontmoeten. Hij was de eerste die mijn werk tentoonstelde. Hij was de eerste curator die een bezoek bracht aan het Hoger Instituut en geloofde in de mogelijkheden van geur. Hij zei: "Peter, de eerste tien, vijftien jaar zul je het moeilijk hebben. Maar als je blijft volhouden, zal het lukken en zul je succes hebben. Je zult het zien. De kunstwereld is er nog niet klaar voor, maar ik steun je en zal een aantal werken kopen die je niet verkocht krijgt." Het waren werken die zelfs voor het museum moeilijk waren om tentoon te stellen: een installatie volledig bedekt met zeep (ze werd slechts één keer getoond, bij de opening van het nieuwe S.M.A.K., waar ik een solotentoonstelling deed) en installaties met beschimmelde spullen die niet lekker roken. Ik weet niet eens of ze nog bestaan. Het museum kocht ook een rookschilderij voor haar collectie, *Please Smoke* (2 m x 2 m), bestaande uit 60.000 sigarettenpeuken. Mensen reageren: "Wauw! Zoveel sigaretten, dat moet een zware roker zijn!" Maar eigenlijk heb ik nooit gerookt.

A O *Je kreeg dus een aantal positieve reacties in het HISK van mensen met meer inzicht, vooral van Jan Hoet. En het is grotendeels dankzij jou en andere kunstenaars zoals jij dat mensen de olfactorische kunst beter kennen. Heb je het gevoel dat de kunstwereld sindsdien veranderd is? Zijn ze er klaar voor, de kunstwereld en zijn publiek?*

P D C De laatste jaren is er veel veranderd. Er wordt meer aandacht aan besteed, dankzij organisaties als de jouwe *[Scent Culture Institute]*, die gericht zijn op geur of het *Institute of Art and Olfaction* of Caro Verbeek, curatoren die bezig zijn met geur en er ook over schrijven. Ik denk dat het belangrijk is om erover te schrijven en te praten, zodat mensen over dit onderdeel van de kunst kunnen lezen, leren, nadenken en discussiëren. Volgens mij zijn er nog heel wat mogelijkheden en kansen om platformen te creëren.

Er zijn heel wat kunstenaars die beginnen te werken en experimenteren rond geuren. Elke week vragen kunstenaars me om samen te werken, maar mijn agenda laat dat niet toe. Jammer, maar ik kan nauwelijks mijn eigen werk afmaken. Er zijn soms mooie en interessante voorstellen bij. De aandacht voor de olfactorische kunst leeft en groeit en dat is goed nieuws. Maar het is nog steeds moeilijk. Mijn voordeel is dat ik al zo lang werk met alle aspecten van de olfactorische kunst. Een nadeel op korte termijn is dat ik binnen een heel breed bereik en spectrum heb gezocht en gewerkt. En als je met kunst werkt, is het eigenlijk beter dat je je op één onderdeel richt. Je kunt het vergelijken met een schilder die een bepaalde stijl heeft en een reeks werken maakt in die stijl. Ik moest mijn weg nog vinden: wat is technisch mogelijk, welk materiaal kan ik gebruiken, hoe lang blijft een geur behouden tijdens een tentoonstelling, hoe activeer je de geur, wat is de continuïteit ervan, welke invloed hebben vocht en temperatuur op het kunstwerk. Allemaal zaken waarmee je rekening moet houden wanneer je een werk maakt en tentoonstelt. Daarnaast moet je kunnen omgaan met andere kunstenaars op de tentoonstelling die boos zijn omdat jouw werk meer aandacht krijgt, alleen maar door de geur. Een intense geur trekt de aandacht; dat is ook de kracht en de impact van geur.

A O *Als er geen andere geurwerken zijn, uiteraard. Op recente tentoonstellingen rond olfactorische kunst bleek dit immers een uitdaging te zijn, ook voor de curatoren: hoe stellen we al deze werken met hun specifieke geuren samen tentoon? Dat lijkt me inderdaad een probleem, maar wel een leuk probleem. Je noemde een paar dingen waarover ik het nog even wil hebben, bijvoorbeeld de analogie met de schilderkunst. Het is iets wat ik vaak vraag in gesprekken over olfactorische kunst. Zie je olfactorische kunst, naar analogie met schilderen, als een medium of een techniek? Of is het breder: een genre of een domein? Of misschien moeten we het eerder zien als een beweging?*

P D C Ik hoop dat het geen beweging is. Het is meer dan dat. Natuurlijk is het een medium, maar ik denk dat het ook meer is dan dat. Verf kan ook meer zijn dan een medium. Maar het voordeel van geur is dat geur zelf een context kan creëren. Geur is zoals geluid: als iemand bang is, hoor je het aan het geluid van zijn stem. Als je echter naar elke toon afzonderlijk luistert, hoor je dat niet. Als je bij geur elke molecule apart neemt, ruik je ook niets. Het is dus altijd de combinatie: als je gras ruikt, weet je dat het gras is. Maar als je een appel ziet en de geur van gras ruikt, denk je dat het de geur van appel is. Hetzelfde geldt voor kiwi, komkommer of zelfs banaan. De perceptie van geur is iets heel vreemds.

Het hangt ook af van wat je ziet. Ik vind sowieso dat je een krachtiger effect creëert als je zintuigen met elkaar combineert. Wanneer je het visuele combineert met het olfactorische, met andere woorden kennis (de naam) met geur, krijg je betekenis in beide richtingen. Het effect is krachtiger dan bijvoorbeeld bij verf alleen. Het is saai om naar een schilderij te kijken dat gewoon iets toont. Het is boeiender wanneer dat schilderij ook iets vertelt. Zo is het ook met geur. Het is eigenlijk moeilijk om je vraag te beantwoorden, maar tegelijk ook makkelijk. Het is niet 'dit'; het is 'dit en/of dat'.

A O *De voorbije jaren zagen we een uitbreiding en overlapping van de mode- en de kunstwereld. In de parfumindustrie gebruiken sommigen – misschien zoeken ze culturele legitimatie – de term 'olfactorische kunst' voor in de handel verkrijgbare geuren (zoals bij The Art of Scent: 1889-2012 tentoonstelling in het Museum of Arts and Design in New York). Heb je daar een probleem mee?*

P D C Ik heb er gemengde gevoelens over. Wat Chandler Burr deed is een leuk idee, parfum vergelijken met andere kunsthistorische *ismen*. Maar ik weet niet of je dat altijd kunt doen, want dan zou je alles kunnen vergelijken met kunst. Het is wel interessant dat het gebruik van geur in de kunst hierdoor meer aandacht kreeg. De parfumindustrie is enorm en wij hebben geuren nodig. Een kunstenaar kan zelf een geur creëren, maar niet elke geur. Het begint door te dringen dat geur meer kan zijn dan parfum alleen. Het kan kunst zijn als het niet meer functioneel is of ontworpen om iemand een goed gevoel te geven. Het is geen aromatherapie of bedoeld om iemand mooier te maken of een bepaalde houding te geven. Het is meer. Zoals gezegd, ik heb er gemengde gevoelens over.

Ik ben geen fan van het woord geurkunstenaar, zoals ze het in België noemen. Het lijkt alsof ik een goochelaar ben, een kunstenaar die alleen met geur kan werken. Neen dus. Ik ben een hedendaagse kunstenaar en geur is een medium waarmee ik context kan creëren. Ik gebruik liever de term olfactorische kunst omdat het meer is dan alleen maar geur. Olfactorisch betekent 'met betrekking tot de reukzin'. Het woord 'zin' is meer dan alleen maar een verwijzing naar een gevoel. Het gaat ook om kennis: het is inhoud, het heeft een breder profiel. Mensen willen de dingen altijd in een hokje plaatsen. Je bent een geluidskunstenaar of een videokunstenaar enzovoort. Ik ben een videokunstenaar én een performance artist én soms ook wel eens een schilder. Ik schilder niet met olieverf, maar met geurstoffen of sigaretten of zeep.

A O *Zijn er binnen de olfactorische kunst nog aspecten die je niet hebt verkend? Kun je nog altijd nieuwe dingen creëren? Of denk je dat je het hele spectrum hebt afgewerkt?*

P D C Ik denk dat er nog heel wat mogelijkheden zijn: gekke en onbegrensde mogelijkheden, ook combinaties met de tast- en smaakzin, bijvoorbeeld. Ik ben nu bezig met een tactiel kunstwerk. Het heeft niet direct iets te maken met geur, maar het is iets wat ik wil doen voor mezelf. Met geur heb je tal van mogelijkheden. Het is verbazingwekkend wat je er allemaal mee kunt doen. Het potentieel is enorm, zeker met de technologische vooruitgang. Onderzoek en creatie worden steeds makkelijker. Ik ben altijd verbaasd wanneer ik een geurbedrijf ontmoet. De technologie die ze gebruiken om geuren te verspreiden in gebouwen is meestal dezelfde, maar wordt steeds beter.

Alles gebeurt heel vlot en gecontroleerd, maar ze zijn zich niet echt bewust van het potentieel en de impact ervan. Het heeft nog altijd iets mysterieus. Het lichaam biedt ook nog heel wat mogelijkheden. Veel kunstenaars werken rond het lichaam in het algemeen, maar ook de lichaamsgeur is interessant. Voor mijn *Olfactory Art Manifest* distilleerde ik bijvoorbeeld mijn eigen geur. Ik schatte dat ik die op een jaar zou kunnen extraheren, maar dat lukte niet. De bedoeling was om mijn *Olfactory Art Manifest* honderd jaar na het manifest van Carlo Carrà voor te stellen, op 13 augustus 2013. Maar ik deed het een jaar later, omdat ik nog bezig was met mijn eigen lichaamsgeur. Ik wilde het manifest ondertekenen met mijn geur, om het een context te geven: hij verdwijnt en toch is hij er. Mensen begrijpen het. In het begin ruiken ze de geur, na verloop van tijd verdwijnt hij, maar het manifest draagt nog steeds de handtekening ervan. Het was geen slechte geur, alleen was het niet veel. Je zou de geur kunnen opslaan zodat hij blijft, maar dan moet je nadenken over hoe je hem gaat bewaren. Dat is ook een interessante vraag. In het begin kreeg ik elk jaar de vraag van twee of drie thesisstudenten hoe ze een aangebrachte geur konden behouden. Ik lig daar niet wakker van. Je kunt daarin heel ver gaan, maar dat hoeft niet. Niemand zal Manzoni vragen om zijn blikje stront te openen. Je weet wat er in zit. Of het er nu is of niet, het is het idee dat telt. De context is belangrijker dan het medium.

A O *Ik krijg ook steeds meer vragen van kunstenaars en het valt me op dat weinigen de geschiedenis van de olfactorische kunst kennen. Misschien is de reden dat deze discipline nog niet vaak wordt onderwezen in het internationale kunstonderwijs. Er bestaat zelfs geen leerboek van. Onlangs richtte je echter een masteropleiding in aan de Hogeschool PXL-MAD: Art Sense(s) Lab. Het is de eerste in haar soort en is gericht op de 'lagere' zintuigen in de kunst. Kun je wat meer over dit programma vertellen en hoe je het ziet in de context van je praktijk?*

P D C *Het Art Sense(s) Lab* wil kunstenaars ervan overtuigen om te gaan werken met geuren. In deze master leren ze niet hoe ze moeten distilleren, maar hoe ze een context kunnen creëren, hoe ze met geur en de lagere zintuigen in het algemeen kunnen werken. Het jaar is te kort om het over alle technische aspecten te hebben. Dat gebeurt in de bachelor *Open Lab*. Daar leren ze vanaf het begin hoe je moet distilleren en geuren gebruiken. Ook de tast- en smaakzin komen aan bod, in combinatie met video, performance en andere media.

Het is belangrijk dat er scholen zijn waar je dit allemaal kunt leren. Ik hoop dat het een stimulans is voor andere scholen om de discipline ook op te nemen in hun opleidingenpakket. Je kunt alles vertalen naar een geur: geluid, beelden etc. Je kunt dat op een experimentele manier doen of binnen een context. Je kunt er op verschillende niveaus mee aan de slag. Ik werk graag met een context, maar dat kan gewoon een gevoel zijn of een geurruimte waar je binnenkomt. Een stemming kan ook een kunstwerk zijn als het goed wordt aangepakt. Het mag bijvoorbeeld niet aromatisch worden. Er zijn bijvoorbeeld studenten dans, performance, fotografie. Iemand die van geuren houdt en er nog niet mee werkte, maar het wil combineren met fotografie. Ik vind het heel interessant dat er jonge kunstenaars of studenten zijn die een master over geur willen doen om die dan te combineren met hun praktijk.

A O *Dat brengt me op het feit dat geur moeilijk kan worden gedigitaliseerd. Dankzij de opkomst van het internet, computers en opslagcapaciteit kunnen de meeste beeld- en geluidsfragmenten worden gedigitaliseerd. Veel musea gooien het over een interactieve boeg om publiek te trekken. Je moet er bij zijn om het mee te maken. Denk je dat de beperkingen van geur een positief effect kunnen hebben voor de kunstwereld, de cultuur of op zijn minst de entertainmentsector?*

P D C Ja. Ik hoop dat ze het niet alleen daarvoor doen, dat ze het niet in een museum tonen omdat het, zoals je zegt, entertainment is. Kunst is geen entertainment. Het is nadenken en vragen stellen. Je ziet veel musea inderdaad in de richting van entertainment gaan, omdat ze een bepaald aantal bezoekers moeten hebben. Dat is jammer, maar ik weet dat we die trend niet kunnen stoppen.

Mijn solotentoonstellingen krijgen enorm veel bezoekers. Er is zo veel aandacht. Ik denk dat het de kracht van de geur is. Mensen worden graag geconfronteerd met iets, ze willen ervaren, leren en denken. Er komen ook heel wat gezinnen met kinderen: het is iets nieuws voor hen. Voor veel mensen trouwens. Voor scholen is mijn werk ook heel interessant, omdat ze rond alle zintuigen kunnen werken. Enerzijds is het enorm aantrekkelijk om met geuren te werken en het resultaat te kunnen tonen in musea. Anderzijds denk ik eigenlijk niet dat mensen minder snel naar een museum gaan door het internet. Het internet is heel informatief, maar wanneer je een groot schilderij of beeldhouwwerk in het echt ziet, is dat toch iets totaal anders dan op een computerscherm. Het internet is een mogelijkheid wanneer je niet zelf kunt gaan kijken. Ik probeer toch om zelf naar een tentoonstelling te gaan als ik de tijd heb. Dat gebeurt steeds minder, helaas. Het nadeel van een drukke agenda. In 2015 deed ik 27 projecten. En er zijn nog zo veel dingen die ik wil onderzoeken en proberen, die ik moet regelen. Uiteraard zijn er ook nog heel veel geuren die ik moet ontdekken en ruiken.

A O *Dit gesprek kon nog veel langer duren. Dat was ook zo. Onze schrijfruimte is echter beperkt. En zoals een wijs persoon ooit zei: "Always leave them wanting more." [Behoud het verlangen]. Wanneer je een gesprek hebt met Peter de Cupere of kennismaakt met zijn werk, blijf je inderdaad met een wonderlijk gevoel achter, tegelijk verzadigd en uitkijkend naar meer.*

PETER DE CUPERE

OLFACTOLOGY LAB

OVER EEN PIPET, EEN TRECHTER EN EEN HANDSCHOEN

Het begrip 'laboratorium' is een belangrijk element in mijn werk. Ik zie de wereld immers als één groot laboratorium met verschillende locaties die olfactorisch moeten worden geanalyseerd en visueel kunnen worden vertaald in kunstexperimenten en installaties.

Een pipet, een trechter en een handschoen zijn voor mij referenties, symbolen voor onze samenleving. Ik gebruik vaak trechters in mijn werk. De vorm verwijst naar het concept 'bloem/*Flower*'. Als geurproducent en schoonheidsideaal is de bloem voor mij niet alleen belangrijk in de olfactorische zin van het woord, maar fungeert ze ook als een hoorn waarmee je kunt roepen naar de samenleving. Het is een vertaling van mijn olfactorische indrukken naar een eerder visueel esthetisch gegeven. Die bloem kan ook een opening in een vloer of muur zijn die een geur afgeeft. Denk bijvoorbeeld aan een rioolbuis of een luchtleiding in de muur. Ook de luchtafvoer van een keuken is voor mij een 'bloem'. Ze verspreidt dan de geur van koken en verschillende culturen naar de buitenwereld. Andere voorbeelden zijn een uitlaat van een auto of een fabrieksschoorsteen. Huidklieren, okselhaar, zelfs genitaliën kunnen worden beschouwd als bloemen in de figuurlijke zin van het woord. Als je het begrip 'bloem' op deze manier interpreteert, begrijp je dat het nauw verbonden is met de relatie tussen samenleving en cultuur. De bloem wordt hier eerder beschouwd als een vertaal- en verspreidingsmiddel dan als een echte bloem. Een trechter is ook een verspreidingsmiddel en kan staan voor het 'concept' van een bloem. Het is het punt waar alle geuren samenkomen of worden verspreid in de wereld.

De pipet is een meetinstrument en belangrijk in mijn laboratorium om geuren te mengen. Ik zie de pipet als een verwijzing naar mijn idee van een 'laboratorium', dat ook een belangrijk element is in mijn werk. Ik zie de wereld immers als één groot laboratorium met verschillende locaties die olfactorisch moeten worden geanalyseerd en visueel kunnen worden vertaald in kunst, experimenten en installaties. Deze analyse kan het determineren zijn van bepaalde olfactorische aspecten van een stad, maar ook het registreren van de olfactorische verschillen tussen verschillende culturen. Uiteindelijk dient ze als basis voor een mengsel dat opnieuw kan worden vertaald in een visueel werk. De relatie samenleving/cultuur versus natuur/milieu is een belangrijk onderzoeksgebied in mijn werk. Daarnaast zijn er de op het eerste gezicht meer logische onderzoeken naar geur en planten, waarbij het concept 'bloem' een belangrijk uitgangspunt is.

De handschoen verwijst naar de netheid, het onderzoek en de experimentele aspecten van mijn werk. Ik experimenteer op elke mogelijke manier met geuren, zoals een moderne alchemist. Geurig materiaal kan variëren van essences voor parfums tot aroma's voor voedingsmiddelen of geuren die tijdens experimenten ontstaan uit verschillende materialen. Op het moment dat ik chirurgische handschoenen aantrek, voel ik me één met het werk dat ik doe. Het is echter ook een manier om afstand te creëren tussen mezelf en het object. Het is een bescherming voor mijn huid, maar ook een middel om het werk objectief te maken. In die zin zijn mijn tekeningen subjectiever, want ik gebruik altijd mijn vingertoppen om het grafiet op het papier te voelen.

KÓAN JEFF BAYSA

CITAAT

Als er één kunstenaar is die de reukzin voor de schijnwerpers heeft gebracht, dan is het de Belgische kunstenaar Peter de Cupere. Dankzij zijn buitengewone geurformules in installaties en performances in musea, galerijen en innovatieve ruimten van België tot Havana, zijn we eindelijk tot onze zinnen gekomen!

PETER DE CUPERE

THE USE OF SMELL IN ART, AN 'OLFACTOLOGY' ART RESEARCH

Mijn passie voor geur gaat terug tot in mijn jeugd en kwam uiteindelijk tot uitdrukking in mijn beroep als beeldend kunstenaar. Ik maak intussen al jaren gebruik van geur in mijn werken en deel graag mijn visie en houding ten opzichte van het gebruik van geur in de beeldende kunsten. Ik wil dit doen door middel van mijn visuele kunst. Op een tentoonstelling is het gebruik van geur niet altijd evident, omdat je afhankelijk bent van de locatie en de omstandigheden.

Als beeldend kunstenaar die al meer dan 20 jaar werkt met geuren, kreeg ik te maken met een aantal technische problemen in verband met activering en continuïteit van de geur in een werk op een tentoonstelling.

De technische aspecten zijn ondergeschikt aan de context en het concept van het werk, maar ze vormen een belangrijk onderdeel van het succes. De boodschap van het geproduceerde werk staat of valt immers met de uitvoering ervan.

Activering van de geur op het juiste moment en gegarandeerde continuïteit tijdens de tentoonstelling zijn afhankelijk van verschillende factoren. Zo is de keuze van de (chemische) samenstelling van de geur – olie- of waterbasis, poeder, kras & ruik – onder meer afhankelijk van de vochtigheid, temperatuur, ventilatie, grootte en vorm van de locatie en het gebruikte materiaal en van de interactie met andere geuren. Naast deze technische aspecten moet men ook rekening houden met de perceptie van de toeschouwer/ruiker. Geur werkt voornamelijk op de herinnering en voorafgaande conditionering. De sociale en culturele context kunnen ook bepalend zijn voor de keuze.

Om het gebruik van geuren in de beeldende kunst te bevorderen, is het belangrijk dat je deze technische beperkingen kunt gebruiken. Je mag ze niet zien als een obstakel, maar als iets om rekening mee te houden tijdens het ontwikkelproces.

Mijn onderzoek is volledig gebaseerd op mijn eigen praktijk. Ik creëerde de voorbije 20 jaar meer dan 200 werken die werden tentoongesteld met het gebruik van actieve geuren. Via mijn werk wil ik laten zien dat het gebruik van geuren de kunst in een breder perspectief plaatst. Daarnaast wil ik de status van geur als kunstmedium in de kijker zetten. Ik ben van mening dat geur *in se* al visueel kan werken zonder een visueel kunstwerk te laten zien. Synesthesie is niet ver weg. Door de verschillende toepassingen van geur te tonen via mijn visuele kunst, hoop ik bij te dragen aan een bredere kijk op het gebruik van geuren in de beeldende kunsten. Geur werd te lang beschouwd als een lager zintuig. Ik zou eerder zeggen dat het een hoger zintuig is. Maar hoe kan geur worden toegepast in de beeldende kunsten? Wat zijn de mogelijke problemen bij het gebruik van geur op tentoonstellingen?

Hoe creëer je een context rond kunst door middel van geur? Sinds 1995 experimenteer ik op allerlei manieren met geur. Ik kan me geen werk zonder geur voorstellen. Daarom zocht ik een manier om geuren te gebruiken bij alle soorten media: sculpturen, installaties, schilderijen, tekeningen, afdrukken, video's, evenementen en performances.

Een sculptuur zoals *Flower Fragum Cardamomi* heeft een hoogte van 9 meter en is de eerste kras- & ruiksculptuur ter wereld. Het probleem met kras & ruik is dat de geur snel verdwijnt wanneer hij wordt aangebracht op een harde gladde ondergrond, zoals het epoxy dat voor deze bloem werd gebruikt. We moesten dus een manier vinden om het materiaal sterker te maken, zodat de geur jaren zou kunnen meegaan. We slaagden in ons opzet. Het feit dat de geur op een hard glad oppervlak verdwijnt wanneer er veel wordt op gekrast, gaf me inspiratie voor een werk dat ik maakte voor de tentoonstelling *Ephemere*. Voor *De Bietenoogst*, een bekend schilderij uit 1890 van de Belgische kunstenaar Emile Claus, die in 1924 overleed, plaatste ik veiligheidsglas met gewone kras- & ruikverf erop. De verf ruikt naar de aarde op het schilderij. De geur is die van aarde uit die tijd, niet die van nu. Er is dus geen sprake van vervuiling. Wanneer de mensen op het oppervlak krassen om te ruiken, verdwijnt de geur en kunnen ze het schilderij beter zien door het glas. Het is een soort van reflectie op de samenleving. Door de oppervlakte van onze moeder aarde te kwetsen, veranderen we zelfs de oorspronkelijke geur. Uiteindelijk kan hij zelfs verdwijnen. Buiten stond hetzelfde werk, maar dan tegenover een grasveld. De verf hier rook echt naar onvervuild gras.
Soms is een werk niet wat het lijkt.

Een geurinstallatie zoals *Smoke Room*, die bestaat uit 750.000 gebruikte sigarettenpeuken, heeft een afschuwelijke geur die misschien enkel nog wordt gewaardeerd door kettingrokers. Om problemen met de Belgische overheidsdienst voor volksgezondheid te vermijden, moesten we eerst de verschrikkelijke sigarettengeur verwijderen en vervangen door neprook. Deze geur bestond uit een mix van uitlaatrook, asfaltgeur en de geur van gerookt spek. De bezoekers zijn er echter van overtuigd dat de geur afkomstig is van de oorspronkelijke sigarettenpeuken. We deden hetzelfde met het werk *Smile Room*, een kamer bedekt met tandpasta. Het probleem hier was om de juiste tandpasta te vinden. We testten 122 verschillende tandpasta's. Slechts één ervan was bruikbaar en vertoonde geen barsten nadat hij was opgedroogd in verschillende temperatuurs- en vochtigheidsomstandigheden. We zouden 3.400 tubes tandpasta nodig hebben gehad voor dit stuk. We konden de tandpasta kopen, maar er was geen enkele garantie dat de vorm behouden zou blijven na uitdrogen of dat de geur zijn intensiteit zou bewaren na dagen tentoonstellen. Sponsoring kon een tijdelijke oplossing zijn geweest. We besloten echter om een nepinstallatie te maken. We maakten mallen voor tandpastategels en goten onze eigen neptandpasta uit polyurethaan erin. Daarmee bedekten we de zaal. Het was veel goedkoper dan het juiste merk tandpasta te moeten kopen. Ik kan het nu herhaaldelijk tentoonstellen zonder de zorg dat de geur verdwijnt. De intense toegevoegde pepermuntgeur laat de bezoekers geloven dat ze echte tandpasta zien en dat verbaast hen.

Het is zoals bij een film: als je wilt genieten, moet je het geloven.

Ik ben enorm gefascineerd door de mogelijkheden en de toekomst van geur. In 1997 vond ik de *Olfactiano* uit, de eerste geurpiano. Er is geen geluid, alleen geuren. In 2004 stelde ik de *Olfactiano VII* voor, die voor een groter publiek kon spelen. IFF sponsorde de geuren van het eerste geurconcert dat ik gaf in Brussel. Een concert kon 7 tot 15 minuten duren, afhankelijk van de grootte, temperatuur en vochtigheid in de ruimte. Mijn eerste idee was om zinnen te maken met geuren, op basis van een onderzoek dat ik deed voor het samenstellen van een geuralfabet. De *Olfactiano* kreeg dus 26 geurverdelers en 1 voor frisse lucht. 8 basisnoten, 9 hartnoten en 9 topnoten. Het enige probleem zijn de mensen, omdat ze niet gewend zijn om te lopen rondsnuffelen. De meesten waren meer bezig met de vraag: "Wat ruik ik?" dan open te staan voor de compositie en ervan te genieten. Want dat is wat er eigenlijk gebeurt: er wordt een parfum gecreëerd door de geuren die zich in de zaal vermengen.

Ik vind dat een parfum *in se* een kunstwerk kan zijn wanneer het in de juiste context wordt geplaatst. Dat kan een esthetische ervaring zijn, verbonden aan een sociale situatie of iets anders.

Mijn werk gaat vooral over milieuproblemen zoals luchtvervuiling. Bij het werk *Air Polluter* kunnen de bezoekers bijvoorbeeld beslissen hoe intens ze de lucht vervuilen met slechte en/of goede geuren. In *Garbage City Holiday Park* kunnen ze verblijven in een goed en aangenaam geparfumeerd huis gemaakt van afval. Normaal zou dit intens slecht moeten ruiken, maar in plaats daarvan ruiken ze een aangename geur uit de natuur. De volgende dag kunnen ze hun eigen aangenaam ruikende afvalhuis maken in een workshop, zodat andere mensen een nachtje in hun creatie kunnen doorbrengen.

Een ander werk dat mensen doet nadenken over vervuiling is *Scentedo* [2], een neptankstation naast een snelweg. Bezoekers kunnen er gras, lavendel, kauwgom of de nare geur van uitlaatgassen ruiken.

Andere contexten die ik in mijn werk gebruik, hebben betrekking op sociale en culturele aspecten zoals respect voor verschillende rassen, nationaliteiten, identiteiten en voorkeuren. Ik zie mezelf niet als een 'neus' maar ben enorm geïnteresseerd in de studie van de geur en het gebruik ervan in combinatie met situaties, materialen en creaties.

Cultural Odor Generator gaat over de integratie van geur in de samenleving. Er worden geuren gebruikt die verwijzen naar de meer dan 100 nationaliteiten die voorkomen in de Belgische stad Genk. Op basis van deze nationaliteiten werden 40 geuren geselecteerd. Het werk kan 2 jaar lang worden bezocht in C-Mine, op de site van de vroegere steenkoolmijn. De bezoekers kunnen geuren selecteren op basis van hun voorkeuren. Die worden met behulp van computersoftware vermengd met de geuren van vorige bezoekers. Achteraf kun je een ballon vullen met de geurmix en meenemen naar huis. *Cultural Odor Generator* laat de bezoeker op een positieve manier nadenken over de mix van geuren die door de verschillende culturen en nationaliteiten werd gecreëerd. Het grootste probleem met deze installatie is de temperatuur en vochtigheid in de ruimte. Geuren reageren verschillend afhankelijk van de temperatuur en vochtigheid. Om de intensiteit en kwaliteit van de geurstoffen te garanderen, moet je ze vaak controleren en moet de temperatuur constant blijven.

Laten we het daarom even hebben over een werk waar de geur van het product werd gebruikt om een geurwerk te creëren.
Model for Disappearing Art is een madonna die op één tot anderhalve maand verdwijnt wanneer ze in contact komt met lucht en zonnewarmte. De sculptuur sublimeert en verandert van een vaste stof in gas. Tijdens de sublimatie lijkt het bijna op een werk van Alberto Giacometti.

De gebruikte stof is paradichlorobenzeen, beter bekend als het ontsmettingsmiddel in urinoirblokjes. Het is niet gemakkelijk om paradichlorobenzeen vorm te geven. De stof smelt bij 56°C en vat vuur bij 63°C; 20% verdampt. Het team dat de sculptuur maakte, droeg speciale maskers en beschermende kleding. Probeer dit niet thuis!

In 2000 maakte ik een boom uit dit materiaal, *The Right Tree*. De bezoekers mochten plassen tegen de boom. Om een werk van 1.000 kg paradichlorobenzeen tentoon te stellen heb je een milieuvergunning nodig. Eigenlijk hadden we die vergunning niet nodig om het werk op te stellen in het natuurpark van Sonsbeek in Nederland, maar om de mensen te laten plassen tegen de boom. Aangezien te veel urine op een plaats schadelijk kan zijn voor de natuur, moesten we een ondergronds opvangsysteem voor de urine installeren. Soms plasten meer dan 200 mensen per dag tegen de boom. Je kunt je de geur dus wel voorstellen. De opvangbak moest regelmatig worden leeggemaakt.

Geur bezit ongelooflijke mogelijkheden die binnen de kunstwereld nog steeds moeten worden verkend. Ik hou van bloemen en bomen. Ze zijn een soort visuele referentie voor mij. Ik heb graag dat mensen respect tonen voor de natuur. Is er iets respectvoller dan beginnen huilen wanneer je de natuur ziet?

Bij de installatie *Peppertreeduplicateballs PTDB-tree virus* beginnen mensen spontaan te huilen wanneer ze de sterke pepermuntgeur ruiken. De geur is eigenlijk een combinatie van pepermunt, zwarte peper en een geheim, een volledig onschadelijk product. De temperatuur in de koepel moet ongeveer 39°C bedragen om een reactie te veroorzaken tussen de geuren en het geheim product. De bezoekers zijn verbaasd dat de tranen uit hun ogen stromen bij het zien van dit werk. Ze voelen de reactie van de geur in hun ogen, maar ruiken ook dat het een frisse, ongevaarlijke geur is, dus laten ze hun tranen vloeien. In 2014 gebruikte ik dezelfde geur in de installatie *Scented Tears* in *The Olfactory*. Hier gingen de bezoekers een lege ruimte binnen en zagen elkaar huilen. Ze werden een kunstwerk voor elkaar.

Een ander werk met een boom is *The Olfactory Tree*, een boom uit epoxy van 9 meter lang. Hij ziet er zo echt uit, niet alleen visueel maar ook door de structuur, dat mensen geloven dat het een echte boom is. In de boom zie je een miniversie van dezelfde boom die verbrand ruikt.

Bij de geurinstallatie *Sick Trees* heb je het tegenovergestelde. Deze installatie ruikt naar een ziekenhuis. De geur is die van een ontsmettingsmiddel dat wordt gebruikt om ziekenhuizen schoon te maken. Hij doet mensen nadenken over de misvormde bomen die ze zien en die verwijzen naar menselijke gedaanten.

Tot slot wil ik ook de voordelen laten zien die geur kan hebben voor de maatschappij. Met de *Blind Smell Stick* en *Blind Smell Touch* laten mensen zich enkel leiden door geur om zich een bepaalde plek te kunnen voorstellen. De werken kunnen blinde mensen helpen hun weg te vinden in de stad. Ze kunnen ook een geursignaal geven wanneer er iets vies op de grond ligt, bijvoorbeeld hondenpoep, zodat ze er niet instappen! Stel je ook eens voor dat elke straat een bepaalde geur heeft. Het zou geweldig zijn om op Fifth Avenue te lopen en geen uitlaatgassen te ruiken maar de geur van gras of een intens geurende bloem zoals een orchidee. Bij een kruispunt zou je verbrand vlees ruiken, als waarschuwing dat je moet oppassen. Het leven zou mooier zijn als geur algemeen werd gebruikt en onderwezen in de maatschappij. En kunst kan er een betekenis aan geven. Begin dus maar geuren te gebruiken in de kunst en blijf ruiken.

WILLEM ELIAS

PETER DE CUPERE IN ALLE KLEUREN EN GEUREN

INLEIDING

Peter de Cupere neuze-neust de wereld rond.

Peter de Cupere houdt van de hoorn des overvloeds, al weet hij ook wat soberheid is in de kunst. Deze veelzijdigheid van aanwenden van de verworvenheden van voordien is nu eenmaal een kenmerk van de generatie kunstenaars die in de jaren negentig opgang gemaakt hebben. Maar zijn werk is een en al exuberantie, zonder dat het ooit de spuigaten uitloopt. Geen smoezeligheden, wel afgemeten vrije loop.

Een kunstenaar als Peter de Cupere valt niet voor één gat te vangen. Het 'multi' van zijn mediumgebruik is belangrijk. Niets is hem vreemd, het mag zelfs rotten, beschimmelen, vervliegen, stinken, in asbakken vertoefd hebben, inderdaad een viespeuk. Bij de kunstenaars die alles in kunst willen herschapen zijn er velen die betreuren in een hokje te zitten, gebonden aan hun eigen discipline: schilderen, beeldhouwen, muziek, theater, dans, enz. Vele pogingen zijn dan ook ondernomen om die barrières te verwijderen. Het is zelfs een belangrijk kenmerk van de moderne kunst en nog meer van de postmoderne. Toch wordt de poging om tot een totaalspektakel te komen steevast in verband gebracht met Wagner die aan dit verschijnsel de nog gebruikelijke naam *Gesamtkunstwerk* meegegeven heeft. Het kunstwerk dat zijn oorsprong teruggevonden heeft, namelijk een feest te zijn. Maar Wagner was de neus vergeten, tenzij het geparfumeerde publiek van de opera voor voldoende odeurs zorgde.

Een totaalspektakel dat de reukzin niet vergeten was, en tevens het oudste mij bekende voorbeeld van een kunstwerk dat ook beroep doet op de neus om beter te zien, werd eenmalig opgevoerd op 15 oktober 1581 in Parijs. Op die dag bracht de regisseur Balthasar de Beaujoyeulx – een man die zijn naam weliswaar uit het Italiaans verfranst maar toch niet gestolen heeft – een vertoning voor een huwelijksfeestje met duizend aanwezigen. Het genre droeg later de naam *Ballet Comique*, niet omdat er veel gegrapt werd, maar omdat het opriep tot een levensblije levenshouding. "We leven maar één keer" zou men vandaag zeggen. Het nieuwe was dat hij de toen bekende kunstvormen samenbracht en verweefde tot een artistiek waardevol én aantrekkelijk geheel: muziek, zang, dans, prachtig decor en kostumering, toespraken. Maar het hoogtepunt was het op de scène voeren van een drieledige fontein waaruit reukwater stroomde. Op de wagen was ook de opdrachtgeefster, koningin Catharina de' Medici, gezeten.

Misschien heeft dit historisch voorbeeld van geurgebruik in de kunst weinig te maken met het oeuvre van Peter de Cupere. Het wijst wel op de zeldzaamheid van de aandacht voor de reukzin in artistieke aangelegenheden. Zijn werk is ook geen ode aan het vrolijke leven. Het is een zorg over de vraag of het leven nog wel vrolijk kan zijn? Is er al niet teveel geconsumeerd? We moeten het dan ook plaatsen in zijn actualiteit, in de zeer maatschappijkritische reflectie van vele kunstenaars, die in de jaren negentig tot ontplooiing kwamen en die ons wijzen op wat we met de natuur aan het doen zijn, of, catastrofaler, al onherroepelijk gedaan hebben. Als ik internationaal even rondkijk op zoek naar geestesverwanten dan denk ik aan de Britse *Saatchi artists*, waaronder Damien Hirst, de man die stukken dode dieren tentoonstelt. Zijn problematiek is inderdaad leven en dood. Of aan de gebroeders Chapman, die tonen wat er zo al kan misgaan bij genetische manipulatie, zodat neuzen piemels worden. Ook aan Sarah Lucas, die bekend werd met haar *Au Naturel*, een oude matras met lege emmer en twee meloenen naast een komkommer en twee sinaasappelen die verwijzen naar de uitgebluste vreugde van de liefdesrelatie. De Amerikaanse kunstenaar Matthew Barney mag er ook aan te pas komen. Hij vertrekt van het lichaam om er via een woordeloze muziekrijke film een nieuwe mythologie rond te bouwen die precies de grenzen van dit lichaam in vraag stelt.

Peter de Cupere sluit inderdaad aan bij die generatie postmoderne kunstenaars die zich niet toespitsen op een eigen werkje aan de muur dat dient om naar te kijken en al dan niet te waarderen. Zij spelen in op de ganse omgeving die de toeschouwer, die op dat ogenblik niet echt meer een 'schouwer' is want dat is een te louter visueel geladen woord, maar een 'belever' is in een artistiek geactiveerde ruimte. De kunst omgeeft letterlijk het publiek dat participant is geworden. De 'installatie' is binnen deze 'environment' kunst dan ook de kunstvorm bij uitstek om die totaalervaring op te wekken. Kunst is geen aanvankelijk vreemd ding meer dat men van op afstand bekijkt. Het is een vreemde omgeving, zoals deze van de droom die meer fictief beleeft, of zoals deze van de herinnering die men herbeleeft. Het 'postmoderne' in dit alles is inderdaad de veelvoudige invalshoek. Kunst als een pluralisme, als een vrijplaats met eigen regels staat dan ook dichter bij het feest, bij het circus zelfs, de fancy-fair en het spiegelpaleis. Allemaal plaatsen waar men buiten banale ervaringen kan opdoen, de wereld van het andere.

Peter de Cupere situeert zijn werk zelf liefst binnen wat men 'multimedia' noemt. "Multimedia is het sleutelwoord om de integratie aan te duiden van diverse media of telecommunicatiediensten binnen de grenzen van een enkele interface gebruiker", is de gangbare definitie. En zoals bekend zijn voorbeelden van *interface* het *keyboard* of 'de muis'. De Cupere vertrekt inderdaad bij elke creatie van de computer als centraal medium. Daarin concentreert en ontwikkelt hij zijn ontwerpen. Deze worden dan al dan niet gerealiseerd in installaties, acties, happenings of performances, naarmate de middelen beschikbaar zijn. De onderdelen of attributen van deze projecten kunnen ook als afzonderlijke objecten beschouwd worden, zo bijvoorbeeld de *Soap Paintings* als zijn vorm van schilderkunst, of de *Pipifleur*, zijn manier om sculpturen te maken.

Tot het 'multi' van de gebruikte media, is het ook kenmerkend voor het werk van de Cupere dat hij de geur als een bijzonder belangrijk middel van de artistieke beleving beschouwt. De naam 'geurkunstenaar' hoort hij niet zo graag, omdat hij ervan uitgaat dat de geur ook de ogen opent en nadien de geest. "Wie een neus heeft, kan rieken" lijkt me hier het gepaste gezegde om het engagement van de toeschouwer aan te wakkeren. De volkswijsheden zelf zijn reeds een teken van miskenning van de reukzin. Bij de zes spreuken, die onze taal arm is, waarin de neus voorkomt gaat enkel de geciteerde over ruiken. De andere gebruiken de neus als iets dat men kan schenden en waaraan men best niet te veel hangt.

DE GEUR

Plato hield niet van kunst. Hij zag de werkelijke dingen als een afspiegeling van volmaakte ideeën. Kunst die de werkelijkheid nabootst is dus een afspiegeling van een afspiegeling en dat brengt geen aarde aan de dijk om de ideeën te leren kennen. Plato wantrouwde de zintuigen als weg om iets te weten te komen over de wereld rondom ons. Het heeft tot in de zeventiende eeuw geduurd vooraleer de zogenaamde 'empirische' filosofen de kennisverwerving verbinden met waarnemingen.

De kunst is altijd een aangelegenheid van de zintuigen geweest. Dat heeft haar ook soms verdacht gemaakt. De zintuigen leiden immers ook naar zingenot. Toch heeft ook de kunst haar portie redelijkheid. Ze doet immers vooral beroep op de twee meest verstandelijke zintuigen, namelijk het oog en het oor, dezelfde waarop ook de wetenschap het meest vertrouwd. De kunst verwaarloost de drie andere gewaarwordingmogelijkheden. Enkel de blinden mogen sommige kunstwerken betasten. Hoewel de gastronomie de kunst is van smaak- en reukzin, wordt ze zelden op hetzelfde schap gezet van de Schone Kunsten. De visuele en auditieve kunsten en hun combinaties vullen ruimte en tijd afgeschermd door een aanrakingsverbod, geurloos en smaakloos. Dit laatste moet uiteraard letterlijk opgevat worden. Drie zintuigen worden in de Schone Kunsten uitgesloten, hoogstens gesuggereerd. De vermaarde Sorbonne professor, Etienne Souriau (1892-1979), neemt in zijn boek, dat de overeenkomsten tussen de kunsten behandelt, de kunst van het smaken en het ruiken niet op.

Zijn systeem beperkt zich tot zeven oervormen van de artistieke creatie: lijnen, volumes, kleuren, lichtgeving, beweging, gesproken klank en muzikale klank. Zijn definitie van kunst is duidelijk: "de kunst is dat wat gemeenschappelijk is aan een symphonie of aan een kathedraal, aan een beeldhouwwerk en aan een amfoor; dat wat een schilderij of een gedicht, een gebouw of de dans onderling vergelijkbaar maakt". De 'amfoor' springt in dit voorbeeld in het oog: de drager van geuren en smaken wordt vermeld, de inhoud wordt echter niet meegeteld. Neus en mond kunnen fluiten.

Wat het waarderen van de geur betreft doet de religie het beter dan de wetenschap en de kunst. Zeer lang stimuleerde de godsdienst de beleving van het sacrale via wierook. Zo ontstond in Mesopotamië het parfum. Wierook werd immers gebruikt om de lucht van verbrand dierenvlees dat aan de goden geofferd werd aangenamer te maken. Het woord 'parfum' komt dan ook van 'per: door ... heen' en 'fumare: roken'. Magie behelst eigenlijk alles waartoe de mens, zonder inbreng van technologie, in staat gelooft te zijn om vanop afstand in beweging te kunnen brengen. Parfum leent zich daar uiteraard goed toe. Contact met de goden is in deze aangelegenheid klein bier, zeker als het vanop de Toren van Babel gebeurde.

Duidelijker natrekbaar zijn de effecten die parfums op de aantrekkingskracht tussen mensen hebben. De Egyptenaren waren de eerste mensen waarvan bekend is dat ze parfums verfijnend cultiveerden. Met wierook kon men de goden vereren, maar bepaalde geuren, geloofden ze, kon hen beschermen tegen magisch onheil, of genezen bij ziekte en alleszins maakten geurhoudende zalven aangebracht als make-up hen mooier. De Egyptenaren zijn overigens de ontdekkers van de zogenaamde *enfleurage*, het winnen van etherische oliën uit bloemen met behulp van koud vet.

Uit de biologie en de psychologie weten we ook dat geuren een belangrijk aspect zijn van het leven zelf en van de wijze waarop we elkaar waarnemen. De uitdrukking 'iemand niet kunnen rieken of luchten' is daarin vrij duidelijk. Geuren dienen om aan te trekken of af te stoten, als afrodisiacum of om een territorium af te bakenen, in de volksmond 'afpissen' genaamd. Beide functies worden veroorzaakt door de geurafscheiding die men feromonen noemt, of lokstof. Het beste gerecht smaakt niet meer wanneer men de geur verliest en aan wat men 'anosmie' noemt, lijdt. De geur zou even eigen zijn aan een bepaalde mens als zijn vingerafdruk. Maar vooral belangrijk is de menselijke ervaring in de relatie met het geheugen. De geuren vormen een aparte beleving die de herinneringen als het ware parfumeren en ze ook kunnen opwekken.

Dat de wetenschap een dergelijk belangrijk ervaringsdomein verwaarloost, valt te begrijpen wegens de moeilijke omzetbaarheid in taal. Voor geur zijn te weinig beschrijvende woorden om indelingen te maken. Men moet verwijzen naar het ding zelf ("het ruikt naar look, citroen, viooltjes, rozen, enz."). 'Muf' als specifiek geurwoord is zowat het enige voorbeeld dat me te binnen schiet.

Patrick Süskind zou me allicht bijtreden wanneer ik stel het te betreuren dat het bij academische verhandelingen niet gebruikelijk is bijvoorbeeld honderd proefpersonen geregeld te besnuffelen i.p.v. hen te interviewen. De honden weten beter. Dit geldt uiteraard nog meer voor de kunst, de grote uitdager van de zintuiglijkheid.

SCHETS VAN HET OEUVRE VAN PETER DE CUPERE

Peter de Cupere tekende van jongsbeen af ook na wat de psychologen de 'crisis in de esthetische betrokkenheid' noemen, d.w.z. wanneer de meeste kinderen ophouden met tekenen. Via de aldus verworven vaardigheid kon hij vlug wat drinkgeld verdienen door voor een restauranthouder vissen te tekenen als uithangbord. Het streelde ook zijn ijdelheid dat hij met die dingen in de krant kwam. Hij experimenteerde ook graag, o.a. met geuren, vele soorten door elkaar of een zelfgemaakt grasaroma. Op basis van dit laatste talent had hij evengoed chemicus kunnen worden. Maar door zijn tekenvirtuositeit ging hij naar het kunstonderwijs. Eerst naar de publiciteitsafdeling aan de kunsthogeschool in Limburg, want behalve voor geur had hij ook een neus voor wat aanslaat bij het publiek. De publiciteitswereld op zich kon hem echter niet voldoende boeien, zodat hij 'Vrije Grafiek' ging volgen aan St. Lucas Brussel. Hier specialiseerde hij zich vooral, vrij autodidactisch, in het creëren via computer. Maar hij wou kunstenaar worden en werd aangenomen in een posthogeschoolvorming die daartoe opportune kansen biedt: het HISK, Hoger Instituut voor Schone Kunsten, toen nog in een Antwerpse kazerne. Daar kreeg hij volop de mogelijkheid om vrij te experimenteren. Zo bijvoorbeeld door schimmels kunstwerken te laten worden, o.a. *Mouldy Installation* (1997-99), duizend potjes die elk op hun wijze veranderen of *Mouldy Mattresses* (1998), twee beschimmelde matrassen. Het is inderdaad vanuit een dynamische visie op kunst (ze mag niet verstenen tot een vorm, ze moet steeds in beweging zijn), boeiend om een fris landschapje te schilderen met schimmelende verf dat nadien verwordt tot een industrielandschap.

In zijn zoektocht naar een eigen inbreng in de kunstwereld heeft ook het toeval een rol gespeeld. Besloten om even te pauzeren met het gebruik van reuk in zijn plastisch werk, borg hij zijn preparaten op in potjes en flesjes. Door het gisten gingen sommige stukspringen. Geplaatst in een oude waterloze aquarium konden deze explosies een eigen leven gaan leiden, nu nog steeds als museumstuk in het SMAK.

De ook in het HISK opgezette installatie *Rainworm* (1998) verwijst eveneens naar zijn nieuwsgierigheid tijdens zijn jeugd. Dat wanneer men een regenworm in twee snijdt, men er twee heeft leek hem als kind bijna een mirakel. Zijn *Rainworm* is gemaakt uit blauw geruite of gebloemde regenschermen die op de grond liggen in slangengangzigzag. Hier ziet men ook de lijn die van zijn oeuvre te trekken valt naar het surrealisme: het beeldspel tussen regenworm/regenscherm. Een ander mooi stukje surrealisme is zijn in opbouw zijnde WC-pot vervaardigd uit zijn eigen darmprestaties. Ambachtelijk gezien geen sinecure als men weet hoe onvoorspelbaar een drol kan krimpen als hij opdroogt, maar het is wel een levenswerk.

In dezelfde geest moet men ook zijn liefde voor vis begrijpen en dan bij voorkeur rotte. Als eindwerk in het HISK maakte hij een installatie met een idyllisch eilandje, zeeblauw geschilderde vloer overhangen door visnetten waarin echte vissen een tijdje hun geuren ten beste mochten geven: *Blue Skies* (1999). Of voordien in Watou plande hij rietstengels in een vervallen schuurtje – steeds een mooie omgeving voor installaties – en voegde er geuren aan toe. Wie de moed had om door de rottende visgeur te lopen, werd beloond met een frisse citroengeur, maar men moest de weg ook nog terug: *Reedland* (1998). De 'vis' speelt in de olfactorische theorievorming ook een zeer bijzondere rol. Zonder enige schroom wordt er een visgeur aan *L'origine du monde* toegekend. Deskundigen, vermoedelijk eerder in de mythologie dan in de biologie, zien de oorzaak van de verwantschap met de geur van de intieme delen van de vrouw en deze van de (verse) vis in het vermeende feit dat alle levende wezens uit de zee zouden stammen.

Na zijn HISK-periode heeft Peter de Cupere wel een druk artistiek leven geleid. Het ene multimediaproject volgt het andere op. Boeiend aan dit werk is ook dat hij tot een trend behoort van jonge kunstenaars, die een andere houding aannemen ten opzichte van de relatie kunst versus wetenschap. Daar waar een vorige generatie, zeg maar bv. Panamarenko, met een soort pseudo-wetenschap speelden als vorm van poëzie, wordt nu de wetenschap ernstig genomen. De Cupere weet ook wetenschappelijk wat geuren zijn.

Hij is een echte computerdeskundige. Elk project wordt bestudeerd. Zo bijvoorbeeld was het gieten van beelden in gesmolten geursteentjes (paradichlorobenzenol) geen sinecure. Hij maakt van een boomstam *The Right Tree* (2002), met duizend kg van dat materiaal, 320 cm hoog en 60 cm doorsnee, een uitverkoren pispaal in het bos van Sonsbeek. De knipoog naar de *Fontein*/urinoir van Marcel Duchamp is duidelijk. Eerder had hij, wankelend op de grenslijn van het blasfemische, er een Witte Madonna in gemaakt, die zoals het hoort op een hoekje van een huis stond, tijdens de *Over The Edges* tentoonstelling te Gent, van curator Jan Hoet. Het is boeiend om zien hoe een perfect afgegoten beeld langzaamaan verdwijnt en vormen aanneemt die men bij zeer oude beelden vindt, verweerd en versleten door langdurig ritueel gebruik. De titel is dan ook *Model for Disappearing Art* (2000). Het is ook eigen aan de wijze van maatschappijkritiek van de jaren negentig om de interpretatie open te laten aan de toeschouwer. Het kan de constatering zijn dat de godsdienst vandaag aan belang inboet, maar dit feit bejubelen of betreuren is niet de taak van de kunstenaar. Men kan ook verwijzen naar het verder verdwijnen van het onderscheid. Kunst en leven lopen steeds meer in elkaar over. Maar een ding is zeker als de Madonna verdwenen is, doordat de geursteen verdampt – plassen zou hier ongepast zijn en over de grens van de godslastering – is ze verdwenen, wat van haar verschijning niet altijd kan gezegd worden.

Ik zou nog verder de andere multimediale experimenten kunnen beschrijven. Zijn *Cigarette Bacon Smoke Painting* (1999) verwijst naar het roken en het verbranden van vlees. Het werk speelt in op het feit dat roken de gezondheid kan schaden, maar ook de hypocriete houding van de overheid die vrij ongezellige boodschappen in doodsberichtstijl op een genotsmiddel laat drukken. De Cupere draait de boodschappen om: *Please Smoke*. Een ware aanklacht aan oorlogsmisdaden kon men ziende ruiken in zijn tentoonstelling *The Smell of War* (Poperinge, 2015), waar de eerste gasaanvallen van WOI herdacht werden.

Nu eens als kritiek dan weer als utopie, gidst Peter de Cupere ons snuivend door de wereld, de ogen open, met het verzoek onze snavel niet te houden. Wie met geur werkt, vindt in zeep uiteraard een goede drager en inderdaad de Cupere heeft zeepschilderijen gemaakt die elk op hun eigen manier om zeep gaan: het lot van alles en iedereen.

Willem Elias

RUTH RENDERS

FASTEN YOUR NOSTRILS

Een verkenning van het esthetisch potentieel van geur in het werk van Peter de Cupere

Ontroering. Een juister woord vind ik niet om accuraat mijn eerste ontmoeting te beschrijven met het werk van Peter de Cupere. Het moet ergens in 1997 geweest zijn, toen ik bij het betreden van zijn atelier in het Hoger Instituut voor Schone Kunsten in het voormalig militair hospitaal in Antwerpen bevangen werd door een weeë, aantrekkelijke zoete geur die ik enkel kon associëren met verval en fermentatieprocessen. Voor zover mijn gezichtsveld reikte, bevonden zich restanten van voedsel, schimmelformaties, gedroogde tabaksbladen en kruiden. Mijn behoedzame wandeling door de ruimte voelde als een ware ontdekkingstocht: de vloer dik bezaaid met een enorme hoeveelheid gedroogde tabaksbladeren, twee gebruikte en beschimmelde matrassen pronkend aan een muur als waren het schilderijen van uitzonderlijke picturale kwaliteit, en her en der potjes en schaaltjes met maaltijdresten. Midden in de ruimte stond een werkje opgesteld met als titel *Fleur d'Anus*. Een grillige grijze structuur met trekken van een archetypische bloemvorm 'groeide' doorheen het zitvlak van een oranje krukje, zich lavend aan de feces van de kunstenaar in een glazen bokaal onder het krukje. De sfeer in de ruimte werd al snel bepaald door een mengeling van kinderlijke aantrekking, fascinatie en aversie die we allemaal in meer of mindere mate leken te delen, ook Jan Hoet, die zich enthousiast een pad baande doorheen de gedroogde tabaksbladeren langs aluminiumbakjes met rotte vis en andere etensresten. Schoonheid en ranzigheid gingen hand in hand in deze wonderlijke installatie. De toon was gezet.

Hoewel het gebruik van organische materialen en vergankelijke voedingsproducten geen volstrekt nieuw fenomeen was binnen de kunstgeschiedenis – kunstenaars als Joseph Beuys en Jan Fabre werkten al met vet, boter en andere organische materialen als bloed in een aantal van hun werken – werden esthetische en olfactorische eigenschappen van geuren en geurende materialen, hun emotionele impact op de mens en de impliciete artistieke mogelijkheden hieraan verbonden niet eerder zo grondig onderzocht als door deze jonge kunstenaar.

Enkele maanden later nam Peter de Cupere deel aan een groepstentoonstelling in het poëziedorpje Watou bij Poperinge, West-Vlaanderen. De tentoonstelling werd gecureerd door Jan Hoet, directeur van het toen pas geopende S.M.A.K. in Gent. Bij het betreden van de binnenplaats van een pittoreske boerderij die als één van de locaties dienst deed voor de presentatie van kunstwerken, werden bezoekers onweerstaanbaar aangetrokken door een idyllisch ogend rietlandschap in een charmante open koeienstal. Terwijl ze nietsvermoedend deze ruimte betraden, kregen ze meteen af te rekenen met een onverwachte olfactorische uppercut: een overweldigende stank van rotte vis overspoelde dit vredige, idyllische landschapje en onderwierp de bezoeker aan een extreme beproeving. Achteraf vertelde Peter me over een belangrijk detail in het werk dat ik had gemist terwijl ik bijna kokhalzend weer naar buiten stormde: de dapperen die hun neusvleugels durfden open te houden tot aan het einde van het rietveldje werden beloond met de frisse geur van citroen, een loutering voor de meest veerkrachtige neuzen.

Als een schilder die zijn kleurenpalet samenstelt, verzamelde Peter de Cupere tijdens de eerste jaren van artistieke activiteit een palet van diverse organische en anorganische materialen en de bijhorende processen van verval, alsook de diverse geuren die bij deze processen ontstonden. Parallel aan zijn experimenten met geuren inherent aanwezig in materialen, onderzocht hij ook de mogelijkheden en de beschikbaarheid van synthetische geuren en aroma's, waarvoor hij samenwerkingen opstartte met enkele firma's die aroma's ontwikkelen op industriële schaal. In zijn eerste eigen atelier, een oud schoolgebouw in het commerciële hart van Antwerpen, transformeerde Peter één van de ruimten tot een droomachtige, surreële wereld. De ruimte was volledig bedekt met watten waarmee ook de meubeltjes en de vloer volledig bedekt waren, en een weldadige geur van babypoeder streelde je neusepitheel bij het betreden ervan. Deze kamer in zijn atelier kreeg de titel *Soft world, in honour of my mother*.

Afgeleiden van deze installatie werden ondermeer getoond in Louvain-La-Neuve en in een tentoonstelling in Le Lieu Unique in Nantes, Frankrijk. De installatie kreeg daar de titel *Soft World, tv-room, relax-room* (2000) en was een rechthoekige box volledig bedekt met watten aan binnen- en buitenzijde. Er was slechts een smalle, vertikale wattige opening waar de bezoeker zich met enige moeite doorheen kon wringen om binnen in de ruimte te geraken. De associatie met de baarmoederlijke ervaring of het 'back to the womb' gevoel die door heel wat bezoekers werd gemaakt was uiteraard niet uit de lucht gegrepen. Terwijl de bezoekers zich met veel moeite een weg baanden door de twee wattige vertikale vleugels die de opening waren, riep het vleugje babypoedergeur meteen herinneringen op aan hun vroege kindertijd. Eens binnen, waar een wattig tafeltje en een televisie met daarop beelden van een vrolijk ronddartelende man in een wattenkostuum te zien waren, kon de bezoeker zich neerleggen in een enorme wattenmassa van meer dan een meter hoog, en zich overgeven aan een weldadig gevoel van veiligheid en ongecompliceerde vreugde.

Het werk illustreert Peter de Cuperes meesterlijke talent om onderdrukte of vergeten ervaringen te doen herleven door middel van kunstwerken die door sommige bezoekers ervaren worden als reminiscentiesessies – elementen gericht op het oproepen van door ons geheugen 'verloren' herinneringen zoals die binnen de cultureel erfgoedsector vaak worden georganiseerd. Een specifieke geur of een combinatie van geuren kan – al dan niet in combinatie met andere zintuiglijke elementen – specifieke herinneringen weer tot leven roepen, herinneringen waarvan we het bestaan volledig vergeten waren tot net voor het moment dat we de geur waarnemen.

Peter de Cupere toont ons met zijn werk de nog weinig gekende mogelijkheden van geur als artistiek medium en het ruiken als een esthetische gewaarwording, evenwaardig aan het zien en horen. Net als vroege experimentele fotografen en filmmakers benadrukt hij de artistieke mogelijkheden van zijn medium door de specifieke eigenschappen ervan te benadrukken. De kunstenaar bedient zich daarbij van alle mogelijke andere media en technologieën die hij ter beschikking heeft. De voorbije twintig jaar ontwikkelde hij zo een indrukwekkend oeuvre met sculpturen, installaties, performances, films, interactieve virtuele presentaties, websites en zelfs games *(Olfacio)*, waarin geur steeds de hoofdrol speelt. Hij doet dit met een lichtheid die niet toevallig refereert aan het absurdisme en de institutionele kritiek van de dadaïsten, en ook de vaak erotiserende humor van de surrealisten is nooit veraf. De relatie tussen geuren en erotiek is echter ook in de wereld van parfums steeds hecht geweest.

Odeur d'une poule excitée, een parfumflesje met als lichaam een leeggeblazen eierschaal, is zo'n werkje, klein van omvang, maar rijk aan conceptuele inhoud en kunsthistorische verwijzingen. Het parfumflesje bevat een parfum gemaakt van de uitwerpselen van de kip die het ei legde. In 1921 maakte Marcel Duchamp het werkje *Belle Haleine, Eau de Voilette*, een parfumflesje met daarop een portret van een dame genaamd *Rrose Sélavy*. Duchamp stond in werkelijkheid zelf model voor het portret, gefotografeerd door Man Ray, en de naam *Rrose Sélavy* staat voor "Eros, c'est la vie". *Odeur d'une poule excitée* – één van de Cuperes eerste werken met eieren en eierschalen, een knipoog aan Marcel Broodthaers – is exemplarisch voor de humor en het kunsthistorisch bewustzijn die als een rode draad door zijn verdere oeuvre lopen. Peter de Cupere zette zijn artistieke experimenten met eieren verder. Zijn *Egg Paintings* (meerdere werken van 1998 tot 2000) zijn driedimensionale 'schilderijen' gemaakt van uitgedroogde rauwe eieren ontdaan van hun schaal. In dezelfde periode maakte hij het werk *Eggs* (1998-1999), een eiermandje gevuld met eieren omhuld met aaneengenaaide stukken kippenhuid. *Untitled* (1998-1999) bestaat uit een reeks opeengestapelde glazen bokaaltjes die elk een rauw ei bevatten van een verschillende vogelsoort, waarover zepen gegoten werden met aantrekkelijke fruitgeuren als perzik en aardbei. Net als in *Egg Paintings* en *Eggs* is het werk het resultaat van experimenten met veranderingsprocessen van eieren. Aan de basis van het werk *Untitled* (1998-1999) lag de vraag in welke mate de lekker ruikende zepen en de indringende stank van de rottende eieren zich zouden assimileren in de ene of andere richting. Andere werken met zeep waaronder *Soap Bullets* (1996), *Clean Soap Flowerpot* (1997) en *Soap Cities* (2001-2004) belichten de discrepantie tussen onze associaties van zeep met reinheid en aantrekkelijkheid en de ongezonde, vervuilende aspecten ervan. Onder het laagje humoristische glazuur op het werk van de Cupere bevinden zich vaak subtiele maatschappij- en kunstkritische noten.

Met het werk *My Fresh Feet* (1998-2003) organiseerde de Cupere een krachtmeting tussen zijn eigen lichaamsgeuren en stukken zeep. Een lederen koffertje met daarin een paar schoenen met stukken zeep erin nam de jonge kunstenaar regelmatig mee, verwisselde dan zijn schoenen voor het paar met de stukken zeep erin en activeerde zo een *battle* tussen de zeepgeur en de zweetgeur van zijn voeten. De verwijzing naar de opwaardering van lichaamseigen geuren komt ook voor in *Pipifleur* (2001-2002), een bedpan van waaruit een bloem als een megafoon annex geurversterker reikt tot aan de neus om aldus de eigen plaspartij ook olfactorisch te beleven. Het motief van de bloem komt ook terug in andere voorbeelden, zoals de poëtische *Medical Flower*: een in een medisch verband gewikkelde langstelige bloem die groeit uit een stapel medische encyclopedieën, het kopje hangend aan een draadje ter ondersteuning. Of de prachtige zwarte bloemen die met hun kopje over de rand van een brug hingen in het kasteelpark van Poeke, terwijl ze uit hun kelk de geur verspreidden van de vissen in de vijver waaruit ze groeiden.

Veel van de reeds besproken werken illustreren het belang van experiment voor Peter de Cupere, die verval beschouwt als inherent aan het werk. Het is een proces dat niet dient voorkomen te worden, noch gestimuleerd. In dit verband is Peter de Cupere voorzichtig in zijn woordkeuze: zelden zal hij veranderlijke processen in zijn werk omschrijven als verval, eerder als transformatie. Noch de materialen, noch de geuren, verdwijnen immers. Ze transformeren eerder naar een andere toestand. Deze transformatie vormt op zich een bron van esthetische beleving. De geur en het uitzicht van het organische materiaal verandert in sommige van zijn werken aanzienlijk, een fenomeen waarvan de kunstenaar eveneens de artistieke mogelijkheden verkent. De Cuperes experimenten met schimmels zijn exemplarisch voor dit proces. Tien tafels met daarop 1.000 nauwkeurig geordende petrischaaltjes met verschillende kweekbodems vormen samen het werk *Mouldy Installation* (1997-1999). Samen vormen de diverse soorten schimmels die op de kweekbodems groeien een gevarieerd kleurenpalet met een duffe, maar ook vertrouwde en zelfs aantrekkelijke geur. In het werk *Evolution Painting*, een schilderij dat werd geschilderd met mengsels van gemixte voedingsmiddelen, werkt hij verder op de visuele mogelijkheden van schimmelprocessen. In een time-lapse video is te zien hoe het oorspronkelijke schilderij van een natuurlijk landschap doorheen de tijd – terwijl de organische transformaties in werking treden – langzaam evolueert naar een grauw industrieel ogend landschap.

The Right Tree (2002) is een poëtisch en vrolijk werk, waarin de Cupere de kwaliteiten benut van een materiaal met een specifieke en herkenbare geur. Het werk loodst als een wolf in schaapsvacht een synthetisch product binnen in een natuurlijke omgeving – een prachtig park in Arnhem, waar het deel uitmaakte van de tentoonstelling Sonsbeek IX. De bezoekers aan de tentoonstelling werden uitgenodigd om te urineren tegen het werk, een spierwitte boomstam in het park – desgewenst met plastuit voor de dames. De stam geurde als een schoon urinoir, en leek gemaakt van spierwit marmer of albast. De stam bleek volledig gegoten uit het bij verhitting uiterst giftige paradichloorbenzeen waaruit de desinfecterende blokjes in urinoirs worden gemaakt. Voor dit huzarenwerk had de Cupere meerdere dagen beschermd met een gasmasker en een huidbeschermend kostuum wc-blokjes gesmolten en in de moule gegoten. Onder de stam werd een verborgen bassin voorzien om de vervuilende vloeistof op te vangen. Het spanningsveld tussen natuur en cultuur door de verplaatsing van geuren naar een andere context, is een manier waarop Peter de Cupere onze aandacht vestigt op de diepgewortelde en vaak onbewuste associaties die we maken bij geuren, en op onze intuïtieve en/of aangeleerde reacties erop.

Het is duidelijk dat Peter de Cupere doorheen zijn werk elk denkbaar aspect van het ruiken verkend. Sommige van zijn werken verwijzen naar geur als concept, in andere werken maakt geur inherent deel uit van het materiaal dat wordt gebruikt. Nog een manier waarop hij geur in zijn werk brengt is door het gebruik van toegevoegde geuren (essences, zelfgemaakte geuren, aroma's uit de voedingsindustrie) waarbij hij graag onze conventies rond geuren uitdaagt, of spanningsvelden creëert tussen visuele en olfactorische elementen in een werk. Een voor sommigen schokkend voorbeeld van deze artistieke strategie is *Cigarette Bacon Smoke Painting* (1999), een 'schilderij' dat vanuit een dichter standpunt een compositie blijkt te zijn van duizenden opgerookte sigarettenpeuken. Terwijl je als toeschouwer, gefascineerd door het materiaal een stap dichter zet naar het werk toe, word je getrakteerd op een overweldigend intense geur van gerookt vlees – een combinatie van een materiaal en een geur die associaties uitlokt tussen het roken van sigaretten en de daaruit resulterende verbrande longen.

Door de directe impact van geuren op onze emotionele huishouding kunnen deze onverwacht heftige en onvoorspelbare reacties opwekken. Bovendien is geur vaak een waarschuwingssysteem dat een vluchtreflex in gang zet wanneer we ons bevinden in gevaarlijke situaties. Een tentoonstelling in de St. Lukas Stichting in Brussel in 2003 met als titel *The Collector's House* genereerde een onverwacht felle reactie. De tentoonstelling was een ludiek opgevatte totaalinstallatie die een denkbeeldig huis voorstelde van een gepassioneerd kunstverzamelaar waarin elk element kunst was. In de eetkamer stond een tafeltje waarop 130 blokjes fel ruikende Hervé-kaas uitgestald waren; in een andere ruimte, de badkamer, stond een badkuip gevuld met rode wijn die elke 30 seconden omhoog gezogen werd en via de douchekop weer naar beneden sproeide; in de 'slaapkamer' stond een metalen bed waarin een oude gebruikte matras werd afgekookt tot soep (*Hot Mattress*, 2003), gekruid met oregano en basilicum, en het toilet was opvouwbaar en verplaatsbaar in een reiskoffertje; zelfs tot in de garage toe bestond alles uit kunst: daar stond het werk *Earth Car* (2002), een auto volledig bekleed met aarde en een graszode op het dak waarin grasparkietjes hun nest hadden gemaakt. Doorheen de tentoonstelling waren korte humoristische films te zien waarop een acteur illustreerde hoe de imaginaire kunstverzamelaar 'overleefde' tussen zijn allesoverheersende kunstcollectie. Nadat de gezondheidsinspectie een klacht had ontvangen van personeel dat in het gebouw werkte wegens de aanwezigheid van 'gevaarlijke' geuren, werd opdracht gegeven tot de verwijdering van de kaastafel en de matras. De Cupere merkte op dat vreemd genoeg het wijnbad – dat het meeste risico inhield om ongezonde stoffen te ontwikkelen – mocht blijven staan. Uiteindelijk werd besloten dat één kaasblokje mocht blijven staan, en als een compromis voor de onschadelijke matras die verwijderd moest worden, sneed de kunstenaar de matras in stukken en trok de 'soep' op conservenblikken die ondersteund door een humoristische reclamefilm te koop werden aangeboden als kunsteditie.

Op een speelse manier en door middel van vaak verrassende tegenstellingen wordt de toeschouwer uitgedaagd om de sociaal en intuïtief bepaalde vooringenomenheid ten opzichte van geuren los te laten. De Cuperes bloemensculpturen verwijzen naar de eenvoudige en universeel gekende sensatie van het opsnuiven van de geur van een bloem, maar de archetypische bloemenvormen en diverse geuren worden dooreengeschud en herschikt in nieuwe, vaak bevreemdende entiteiten. De *Flowers* – waarvan de vormen vaak een vermoeden van organische mutilaties opwekken – verspreiden geuren die je niet meteen zou verwachten uit de kelk van een bloem. Sinds 2002 ontstond een reeks bloemen gebaseerd op de zogenaamde alambics. Een alambic is een koperen vat dat tot het begin van de 20ste eeuw gebruikt werd bij de productie van parfums. Vormelijk zou je de *Alambfleurics* zoals de naam reeds aangeeft kunnen omschrijven als een kruising tussen een bloem en een vat, zoals bijvoorbeeld het werk *Alambfleuric Pois Feromoon 1* (2002). De alambfleurics suggereren een proces van geurproductie binnenin hun verdikte steelholte, die via hun kelk wordt vrijgegeven aan de lucht. Deze alambfleurics verspreiden echter geen gewone geuren maar geurloze feromonen. Door gebruik te maken van feromonen in deze en in enkele andere werken, vestigt de kunstenaar onze aandacht op het belang van de als geurloos beschouwde lokstoffen die deels verantwoordelijk zijn voor de fysieke aantrekkingskracht tussen mensen. De suggestie van mogelijke manipulatie van de aantrekkingskracht tussen mensen kan gelezen worden als een verlies van onze binding met natuurlijke processen en de groeiende invloed van wetenschappelijke en technologische evoluties op het menselijke bestaan, waarvan we ons vaak niet een bewust zijn.

Hoewel geur als niet-traditioneel kunstmateriaal nu en dan op weerstand en kritiek stuit, is het ondertussen als artistiek medium aanvaard in de meeste musea en galeries. Dat neemt echter niet weg dat het ruiken als esthetische beleving ook onder de *believers* in geur als artistiek medium vragen oproept over de mogelijkheden en beperkingen ervan. In hun essay *The Aesthetics of Smelly Art* bundelen kunstcritici Larry Shiner en Yulia Kriskovets de theoretische aspecten van olfactorische kunst ter verdediging tegen het traditionele scepticisme ten opzichte van geur, waarbij hun interesse vooral uitgaat naar het begrijpen van de aard en de beperkingen van geur als kunst: "Our concern (...) is less with whether one can classify olfactory works as 'art' (...) than with understanding their nature and limitations as artworks." (Shiner, L. & Kriskovets, Y. 2007: 277). Ze bespreken een aantal mogelijke uitdagingen voor kunstenaars die het medium geur als artistiek medium willen gebruiken. Eén van de uitdagingen van geur als bron voor esthetische ervaringen vinden ze in het feit dat geuren vluchtig en tijdelijk zijn, en dat kunstwerken op basis van geuren er zich daarom minder toe zouden lenen dan visuele of auditieve werken om een geconcentreerde en herhaalbare aandacht op te wekken. Maar, vervolgen ze, net als muziek heeft geur een bepaalde duur en kan daarom in principe op dezelfde manier herbeleefd worden. Dit is echter slechts gedeeltelijk waar. Geuren worden in de wereld van parfums inderdaad ook opgedeeld in tonen – grondtonen, middentonen en hoge tonen – maar hun eigenschappen in tijd en ruimte verschillen, wat verregaande gevolgen heeft voor de creatie van esthetische ervaringen met geuren. Een klank beweegt zich sneller door de ruimte en is daardoor ook makkelijker af te bakenen in de tijd. De creatie van een opeenvolging van verschillende geurtonen binnen een korte tijdspanne naar analogie met een muziekstuk zou een olfactorische kakafonie doen ontstaan. Net dit soort vragen rond de medium-specifieke eigenschappen van geur zijn de drijfveer voor Peter de Cupere in zijn onderzoek naar de esthetische toepassingsmogelijkheden van het medium.

In een aantal werken onderzoekt hij de artistieke mogelijkheden van geur *an sich*. Een voorbeeld hiervan is *Smell Labyrinth* (2002) dat hij maakte in het kasteelpark van Poeke: een enorm doolhof waarvan de wanden bestonden uit neutrale witte lakens. Om de weg te vinden doorheen het labyrint konden de bezoekers enkel steunen op olfactorische informatie. Dit bleek een bijzonder moeilijke opdracht voor veel mensen. Vijf jaar later, in 2007 vulde de reusachtige installatie *Air Polluter* de grote zaal in de Brakke Grond in Amsterdam. Het werk bestond uit een groot aantal glazen maatbekers met vloeibare geurstoffen opgesteld in een cirkel en verbonden door middel van buisjes waardoor de geurdamp naar een centrale koepel kon gezogen worden om daar afgetapt te worden in een ballon. Die met geurdampen gevulde ballon kon je als bezoeker dichtknopen en meenemen. Elke maatbeker was gevuld met een 'aangename' of een 'onaangename' geur, die door de bezoeker door een druk op een knop in een controlekamer kon geactiveerd of gedeactiveerd worden. Ondertussen konden andere bezoekers echter met knopjes naast de maatbekers zelf de selectie weer wijzigen volgens hun eigen voorkeuren en vice versa. Bijgevolg had niemand van de bezoekers volledige controle over de samenstelling van de geurmix in zijn of haar ballon. Het werk is een metafoor voor de subjectiviteit van 'aangename' en 'onaangename' geuren, en de willekeur waarmee in het dagelijks leven ongevraagd diverse geuren ongecontroleerd ons geurepitheel bereiken.

De belangrijkste moeilijkheid bij de creatie van kunst waarin geuren een belangrijke rol spelen, blijft volgens Shiner en Kriskovets het gegeven dat geuren moeilijk systematisch geordend kunnen worden om er complexe werken mee te maken zoals met verschillende kleuren verf of muziektonen en -klanken. Ze merken op dat het probleem veroorzaakt wordt door een zintuiglijke beperking, namelijk: "the relatively low fatigue level for smelling compared with that of seeing and hearing so that the stimulus must be repeated or intensified or the nose given a rest." (Shiner, L. & Kriskovets, Y. 2007: 275). Als voorbeeld van een werk dat wel geslaagd is in het benaderen van de verfijnde esthetische nuance van een muziekstuk verwijzen de auteurs naar het werk *Olfactiano* van Peter de Cupere. Deze 'geurpiano' bestaat uit 26 toetsen die elk een andere geur activeren die in de richting van de toeschouwers wordt geblazen. Een extra toets voorziet de instroom van verse lucht in de ruimte, waarmee het obstakel van duratie en vermenging of opstapeling van verschillende geuren wordt opgelost. De geuren zijn opgedeeld volgens basistonen, middentonen en hoge tonen, een opdeling die een rol speelt bij de compositie van geursonates, of zoals de Cupere ze ook wel noemt: "tijdsparfums, parfums gecreëerd doorheen de tijd". In 2004 gaf de kunstenaar zijn eerste (stille) geurconcert in de Beursschouwburg in Brussel, getiteld *Geursonate voor Brussel*. Met zijn olfactiano's, een collectie geurinstrumenten die hij doorheen de jaren heeft ontwikkeld, evoceert Peter de Cupere met geuren rechtstreeks de associatieve reacties van het publiek. Deze geursalvo's wekken bij de toeschouwer meestal visuele associaties of mentale beelden op. Peter de Cupere gaf ook geurconcerten voor blinde toeschouwers die zoals verwacht veel beter in staat waren om de diverse opeenvolgende en gecombineerde geuren te onderscheiden en de identificeren, wat er op wijst dat ruiken een vaardigheid is die door oefening kan worden verfijnd en ontwikkeld.

De beperkte ontwikkeling van ons reukvermogen heeft volgens de Cupere te maken met het feit dat we bij jonge kinderen wanneer ze hun zintuigen ontwikkelen eerst het zicht en het gehoor stimuleren, en in mindere mate ook de tast en smaak. Geur krijgt in dit proces minder aandacht, pas in een latere fase en vooral vanuit een negatieve benadering. We leren immers intense geuren uit te sluiten. Het resultaat van deze beperkte aandacht voor de ontwikkeling van onze olfactorische vaardigheden heeft volgens de kunstenaar tot gevolg dat we slechts een gelimiteerd aantal geuren binnen een korte tijdspanne kunnen verdragen. Hier situeert zich de motivatie voor wat Peter de Cupere tracht te realiseren via zijn werk: de mogelijkheden van het ruiken aantonen door onze olfactorische vaardigheden op te tillen tot een hoger niveau en onze capaciteit te vergroten in het onderscheiden van verschillende geuren. Een belangrijke motivatie daarbij is om het zintuigelijke genot dat hij zelf beleeft – in het bijzonder het genot dat hij beleeft via zijn neus – te delen met anderen.

Terwijl olfactorische kunst nog in haar kinderschoenen staat, en de meeste kunstenaars slechts sporadisch gebruik maken van geuren in hun werk, heeft Peter de Cupere een indrukwekkend oeuvre ontwikkeld op basis van geuren. Zijn werk zet aan tot een herpositionering van onze perceptie van geur en de sociaal en cultureel bepaalde conventies rond zintuigelijke beleving. Ook een aantal andere hedendaagse kunstenaars maakten reeds werken met geuren, zoals bijvoorbeeld Angela Elsworth (*Actual Odor*, 1998) of Ernesto Neto (*Wonderland*, 2010), hoewel deze werken met geur unicums zijn binnen hun artistieke praktijken. Steeds meer kunstenaars lijken echter de weg te vinden naar geur als artistiek medium, en het staat buiten kijf dat Peter de Cupere met zijn doorgedreven artistieke toepassingen van geuren een sterke bijdrage leverde aan deze evolutie. Of, zoals Shiner en Kriskovets het zo mooi formuleerden in hun essay: "Peter de Cupere heeft een artistieke identiteit gecreëerd die een kruising is tussen een kunstenaar en een olfactorische chemicus die wel eens een model zou kunnen worden voor olfactorische kunstenaars in de toekomst". (Shiner, L. & Kriskovets, Y. 2007: 274).

Ruth Renders, Antwerpen (2008-2016)

PETER DE CUPERE

WHEN SCENT MAKES SEEING, WHEN SEEING MAKES SCENTS

Olfactory Memory
"A woman can be ugly at day time and wonderful at night time." (Guerlain)

HET ZINTUIG ALS CONTEXTDRAGER

Men zou over geur zelf kunnen zeggen dat ze ook context geeft aan haar eigen geurprofiel omdat ze steeds verbonden is met de afkomst van de geur zelf. Met geurprofiel bedoelen we de samenstelling van de geur en waar deze naar verwijst. Zo zal de geur van zweet je doen denken aan een intensieve inspanning of een lichamelijke reactie op iets. Dit op zich kan reeds een olfactorisch kunstwerk zijn wanneer het verbonden is aan een bepaalde situatie, gegeven en/of thema en hierbij meer is dan louter een illustratie te zijn. Het moet minimum als doel hebben de boodschap te versterken of nog beter de boodschap over te brengen. Men zou hier van een letterlijke en of perceptuele geurvertaling van een bepaald gegeven kunnen spreken. De betekenis die deze geurvertaling t.o.v. de situatie/thema van de tentoonstelling met zich meebrengt, kan zo de context van het werk zijn. Zo zal bv. het aanbrengen van dezelfde zweetgeur in een fototentoonstelling over jeugdvoetbalclubs anders ervaren worden dan het toevoegen van zweetgeur in een fototentoonstelling waarbij kinderarbeid in vraag wordt gesteld. Dito met een tentoonstelling over passie t.o.v. een tentoonstelling over worstelen. Zweet gelinkt aan passie draagt iets erotisch in zich, terwijl zweet gelinkt aan worstelaars eerder een plakkerige en minder aangename zweetgeur oproept en dit aldus ook zo olfactorisch ervaren wordt.
Een extremer voorbeeld met zweetgeur zou bv. deze zijn in relatie tot foto's van zieke mensen met extreme letsels. Hier zal de zweetgeur eerder als iets ziekelijks ervaren worden en nog onaangenamer. Zo kan een zelfde nagemaakte zweetgeur anders ervaren worden t.o.v. verschillende beelden. Belangrijk hierbij is dat de werken niet samen worden ervaren met de zweetgeur, maar ieder apart en best, zoals aangehaald, in een verschillende tentoonstelling. Het spreekt voor zich dat niet iedere zweetgeur hetzelfde is, maar vermits geur subjectief vertaald wordt en de geur gelinkt wordt aan een onderwerp waarbij het een link heeft, zal de toeschouwer er vanuit gaan dat de toegevoegde geur behoort tot het getoonde onderwerp. Dit geldt meer voor onaangename geuren dan voor aangename geuren. Bij onaangename geuren heeft men sneller de neiging de neusgaten te willen afsluiten en minder olfactief analytisch de geur te ervaren.
De context van de getoonde beelden geeft dus steeds een andere beleving, ervaring aan de gelinkte geur, maar dit kan ook omgekeerd voorkomen. Men kan hier dus spreken van synesthesie. De invloeden van zintuigen t.o.v. elkaar. En het zijn juist deze wisselwerkingen tussen de zintuigen die maken dat er veel manieren zijn om context te creëren. In de voorbeelden met het zweet geeft het beeld context aan de geur en versterkt de geur het beeld in haar context.

SYNESTHESIE

De wisselwerking tussen de zintuigen om context te creëren geeft meer mogelijkheden dan alleen te focussen op één zintuig zoals het zien. Het kijken naar een beeld wordt in onze hersenen steeds vertaald terwijl geuren het geheugen, emoties en lichamelijke reacties beïnvloeden. Geuren werken sterk op onze herinnering en zijn dan ook voornamelijk subjectief. Geurherinneringen bepalen zo onrechtstreeks mee de ervaring en zo mogelijk ook een gedeelte van de context van een werk. De relatie tussen het zien en het ruiken wordt een wisselwerking waarbij het ervaren van het werk dankzij de eigen geurherinnering juist persoonlijker wordt. M.a.w. het kunstwerk zal niet alleen visueel cognitief betekenis geven, maar ook emotioneel olfactorisch impact hebben. Het spreekt voor zich dat een beeld ook een emotionele reactie kan oproepen, maar door de toevoeging van een geur zal deze ofwel verstrekt worden of juist anders ervaren worden. Dit laatste kan zowel in een positieve als in een negatieve zin en aldus de kijker tot nadenken zetten.
Daarnaast zijn er uiteraard de waarschuwende geurfuncties om ons te behoeden voor gevaar o.a. bij het ruiken van rook, rottingsprocessen en slecht voedsel. Ook ons libido en aangetrokken voelen tot iemand wordt voor een groot deel bepaald door de geur.
De context die geur geeft of via de geur wordt versterkt, wordt mede bepaald door eigen ervaringen met deze geur. Niet alle geuren worden hetzelfde ervaren door een toeschouwer. De eigen geurherinnering bepaalt mee hoe de toeschouwer een geur ervaart. Met geurherinnering bedoelen we het herinneren, lokaliseren van een geur in een eerder ervaren van deze geur in een bepaalde situatie of context. We hebben het hier dan nog niet over de culturele en maatschappelijke identiteit van een geur, want iedere cultuur en zelfs iedere nationaliteit heeft voor sommige geuren een andere betekenis. We focussen hier op de ervaring van de toeschouwer zelf.

THE SCENT READER, GEUREN ANDERS ERVAREN

In het werk *The Scent Reader* wordt het duidelijk dat een geur meerdere contexten kan oproepen naargelang wie de geur waarneemt. *The Scent Reader* bestaat uit zes witte tafels met ieder twee geurmodules. Deze staan in een witte ruimte. Bezoekers kunnen de geuren via de geurmodules ruiken. Op iedere tafel ligt een boek waarin men kan neerschrijven welke herinnering de desbetreffende geur oproept of waaraan dit hen doet denken. Men mag de geur zelf niet vermelden. Men kan de herinnering van voorgaande bezoekers lezen in relatie tot de geur die erbij hoort. Het resultaat is een mix van verschillende ervaringen, herinneringen, referenties naar één en dezelfde geur. Iedere geur krijgt zo meerdere contexten toegemeten. Het werk zet aan tot nadenken over onze geurbewustheid, maar ook over onze eigen levenservaringen en herinneringen. Ondanks het feit dat de meeste bezoekers toch de geur zelf willen raden, schreven velen hun emoties en herinneringen aan de geuren neer. Het omschrijven van een geur zonder de geur zelf te vermelden is niet evident. Dit is geen wetenschappelijk onderzoek maar een artistiek onderzoek om te kijken hoe geuren bij een kunstminnend publiek ervaren worden en context geven. Daarnaast was het de bedoeling om uit deze geuromschrijvingen een aantal nieuwe titels te creëren voor een nieuwe reeks onzichtbare geurschilderijen waarbij geur weer context geeft aan een op het eerste zicht nietszeggende titel. In totaal werden er meer dan 9.000 omschrijvingen gegeven. Er werden duidelijk verschillende contexten aan iedere geur apart gegeven. In volgende voorbeelden is het duidelijk dat er een groot verschil in contextgeving is.

Bij de geur van colasnoepjes werden o.a. volgende omschrijvingen neergeschreven:
- bezoek bij de dokter (werd meerdere keren aangehaald)
- oude zolderkamer
- ouderwetse vrouwen
- de lekkerste wildschotels van moeder
- openen van een zakje vruchtenthee met veel suiker
- goede kerkgeur
- onverbeterlijke snoepjesgeur
- ...

Bij de geur van gras vermelden bezoekers:
- mijn eerste kus
- chemische appelgeur
- als kind spelen in de wei achter het ouderlijk huis
- in de tent tijdens de zomervakantie
- verse lakens 40 jaar geleden
- figuren in de wolken zoeken
- de binnenkant van een appelschil
- bananenmilkshake drinken bij het studeren (de omschrijving van bananengeur kwam meerdere keren voor)
- fietstocht als het net geregend heeft
- spinazie smoothie
- warme zomerdag als kind in het park
- teveel liefde om te dragen
- kerkhof
- feestje
- rozentuin na de regen
- vers gesneden sla
- ...

Bij de geur van champignons:
- de kachel in de keuken van mijn moeder die selderblaadjes en peterselie droogt
- 10 jaar oud, ik speel met vriendjes
- oud winkeltje
- beschimmelde broek
- wandelen in het bos
- beginnende niesbui
- zuur gevoel van een zweterige zomerdag
- hooizolder
- herinnering op het punt te vervagen
- de voorraadkast in ons vroegere huis
- kippenblokjes
- zwoele zomeravonden op de verkeerde plek
- nare lucht, doet mij denken aan een plek waar een misdaad begaan is
- natte tentdoek
- natte sportkleren vergeten uit je tas te halen
- schimmel
- labo plantkunde
- stank
- onze voorraadkast
- ...

Volgende geuren werden beschreven: colasnoepjes, champignon, lavendel, cederhout, steranijs, pepermunt, curry, gerookte zalm, thym, rozen en aardbei.

Voor de bezoekers was de interactie met wat andere bezoekers hebben neergeschreven een extra dimensie. Als kunstenaar is dit bestand met geurbeschrijving niet alleen een manier om te ervaren hoe geur verschillende contexten geeft en terugspeelt op de herinnering, het is ook een middel om tot nieuwe titels te komen voor het werk *Invisible Scent Paintings*.

INVISIBLE (SCENT) PAINTINGS, BETEKENIS GEVEN AAN TITELS

De *Invisible (Scent) Paintings* zijn zoals de titel het zegt geurschilderijen die men niet ziet. Het werk werd getoond in Marta Museum in Herford (DE). De tentoonstellingsruimtes van het museum, ontworpen door Frank Gehry, leken volledig leeg te zijn. In de lege ruimte kreeg men een grondplan mee waarop enkel de titels en de afmetingen van het werk vermeld werden en de locatie waar de desbetreffende *Invisible Scent Paintings* aangebracht waren. Via scratch & sniff werden geuren als schilderijen op de muren aangebracht. De bezoeker diende eerst de titel te lezen, daarna over de muur te wrijven en aan hun vingers of muur te ruiken. Door de geur kreeg de titel van het werk een betekenis. Zo las men de titel *Stop Being Annoying*. Een op zich niet veel verklarende titel tenzij je aan een bepaalde persoon zou denken. Door over de muur te wrijven rook men de geur van citronella. Citronella, een geur die gebruikt wordt om muggen weg te jagen, is een gekende geur. Omwille van het beoogde gebruik van de geur wordt het ook internationaal gemakkelijk gelinkt met verjagen van muggen. Door de geur bij de titel *Stop Being Annoying* te gebruiken, verwijst de titel zo onrechtstreeks naar het vervelende gezoem en steken van muggen. Een andere titel was *Her Smile is a Hidden Perfume Bottle* waarbij men de geur van pepermunt kon waarnemen.

Op zich zijn deze combinaties tussen zinnen en geuren geen groot dravende kunstwerken, toch is de beleving en het vaststellen op zich dat een zin een andere betekenis krijgt door het toevoegen van een geur een extra dimensie die de toeschouwer doet nadenken over de functie en mogelijkheden van geur.

In de tentoonstelling waren er 7 *Invisible Scent Paintings*. Eén ervan was een eerbetoon aan het schilderij *Who's Afraid of Red, Yellow and Blue I* van Barnett Newman van 1966 en droeg dezelfde titel. Drie Scratch & Sniff geuren waren aangebracht volgens de kleurindeling van dit schilderij. De afmetingen van 122 cm x 190 cm werden behouden, maar het werk werd op zijn kant uitgevoerd, i.p.v. vertikaal werd het horizontaal naar geur vertaald. De keuze van de geuren is even mysterieus als de kleurcompositie van het origineel werk. De geuren waren babypoeder, oranjebloesem en pepermunt. Op zich zijn deze geuren geen vertaling volgens de kleuren van het schilderij. Het zou bv. logischer geweest zijn om aardbei als geur voor het rode vlak te nemen, maar door juist voor een synthetische geur van babypoeder te kiezen, werd er meer nagedacht over het doel van het werk. De reden hiervoor was om de toeschouwer mee te voeren in het toenmalig onbegrip voor het kunstwerk.

Als voorbeeld van hoe een geuromschrijving uit het werk *The Scent Reader* evolueert naar een titel in het werk *Invisible Scent Paintings* kan men bij de omschrijving voor een toeschouwer bij de geur gras de zin 'Figuren in de wolken zoeken' als titel van een werk gebruiken. De kijker zal niet aan het idee denken in het gras te liggen wanneer hij de eerste keer deze titel leest, maar eenmaal hij de grasgeur heeft geroken die via scratch & sniff op de muur is aangebracht, zal hij eerst denken aan vredig in het gras te liggen en dan pas de figuren in de wolken te zoeken. Het eerder cognitief lijkend werk verandert hierdoor naar een poëtische weerslag. Een ander voorbeeld welke niet bij vorige geuromschrijvingen zat is de geur van aardbeien gecombineerd met de zin 'Mijn eerste kus'. Dit kan verwijzen naar een heerlijke kus op lippen met lippenstift met aardbeiensmaak, maar moest de geur nu knoflook geweest zijn, is de herinnering olfactief niet zo een leuke, laat staan wanneer deze de geur van bloed zou hebben!

We hebben het gehad over subjectiviteit van de geur. Hoe zit het met culturele geurgewoontes. Als je geur als medium gebruikt kan het geurprofiel van een bepaalde geur anders zijn volgens de locatie waar de geur gebruikt wordt. Zo verschilt bv. de geur van babypoeder in Zwitserland met de geur die men in België kent. Dit is als kunstenaar belangrijk om te weten. Samengestelde geuren zoals babypoedergeur zijn niet steeds hetzelfde. Dit komt omdat ze al decennia bestaan en in iedere cultuur door de jaren heen aangepast zijn of juist door het namaken een ander leven zijn gaan leiden. Dit kan bij het tonen van een werk dus anders overkomen bij de bezoeker. De keuze van de juiste geursamenstelling is dan ook belangrijk om de geloofwaardigheid van de bezoeker te strelen. Maar niet alleen samengestelde geuren die cultureel bepaald zijn kunnen verschillen, een geur kan ook verschillen naargelang de situatie/locatie waarin deze zich bevindt. Zo ruikt de luchtverontreiniging niet overal hetzelfde. Naargelang de stad kunnen er grote verschillen zijn tussen wat de lucht verontreinigt en hoeveel de lucht effectief is verontreinigd.

SMOKE CLOUD, GEUR ALS CONTEXT

Smoke Cloud is een grote wolk gemaakt van intens witte synthetische katoen. Ze wordt hoog in de tentoonstellingsruimte opgehangen. Bezoekers kunnen via een trapladder tot de wolk komen en hun hoofd in de opening van de wolk steken. Het werk heeft veel aantrekkingskracht en de meeste bezoekers willen er dan ook mee op de foto. Wie steekt niet graag zijn/haar hoofd eens in de wolken! Eénmaal je hoofd in *Smoke Cloud* wil je er niet lang blijven. In de wolk is de geur van luchtverontreiniging aangebracht. De geur verschilt voor iedere tentoonstelling waar de wolk getoond wordt. Zo rook de wolk in een tentoonstelling in Havana veel intenser dan de wolk in een tentoonstelling in Nederland. Naargelang de locatie wordt de geurintensiteit van de luchtverontreinigingsgeur aangepast. Ook de samenstelling verschilt. Zo zijn de uitlaatgassen van auto's in Nederland meer gefilterd, dito voor fabrieken. In Havana zorgen de mooie oude Amerikaanse oldtimers voor een niet te harden intense geur van luchtverontreiniging.

Mensen klimatiseren aan een geur. We zijn ons meestal niet bewust hoe een omgevingsgeur ruikt omdat we er in leven. Pas als we even uit onze omgeving zijn weggeweest, ervaren we hoe het echt ruikt. Het is net zoals een parfum dat je pas op je huid hebt aangebracht. In het begin ruik je de geur maar na een tijdje klimatiseert je neus aan de geur en moet je al geconcentreerd aan je huid gaan ruiken om deze waar te nemen. Toch zal deze niet zo intens lijken te ruiken en is de verleiding groot om snel nog even wat geur bij te verstuiven. Dit is net zo voor de luchtverontreiniging. We weten dat ze er is, we kunnen ze ruiken, maar vinden dat ze niet te intens ruikt, dus zal het wel niet erg zijn. Wanneer men met de geur van de stad geconfronteerd wordt in een andere setting waar je het niet verwacht, komt men soms pas tot het besef dat het erger gesteld is met de verontreiniging dan verwacht. *Smoke Cloud* is zo een andere setting. Door de geur van de luchtverontreiniging van de stad in een museale context te brengen en dan nog in een helder magisch witte zachte onschuldige wolk, is het contrast nog groter. Maar spijtig dat niet iedere inwoner naar kunst gaat kijken. De geur geeft hier context aan het werk. Zonder de geur zou de wolk een mooie maagdelijke wolk zijn. De esthetische ervaring van het mooie visuele plaatje verdwijnt naar de achtergrond.

THE SMELL OF A STRANGER, GEUR ALS STATEMENT

De titel doet je eerder denken aan de geur van een vreemdeling, iemand die je niet kent, maar het werk gaat over gentechnologie, de natuur, lichamelijkheid, politiek, invasie, vervuiling, geweld, leven en dood en nog veel meer. De titel werd doelbewust gekozen daar we wel dingen weten over deze items, maar niet in die mate dat we ze echt kennen. Ze trekken aan, maar ze stoten ook af. *The Smell of a Stranger* is samengesteld uit 9 modules. Iedere module is 90 cm x 90 cm x 200 cm h en bevat een inheemse plant. Het werk werd voor de eerste keer getoond in de Biënnale van Havana (CU). Iedere plant was *scent engineered* met een andere geur. Geuren die verwijzen naar bovenstaande aangehaalde items. Zo was er de geur van bloed als referentie naar het leven, de geur van de dood, de geur van buskruit als referentie naar geweld, de geur van angstzweet, de geur van vagina en de geur van sperma als referentie naar lichamelijkheid, sexualiteit en voortplanting, de geur van Amerikaanse nieuwe dollars als referentie naar de onderhandelingen tussen Cuba en Amerika en de synthetische geur van geraniums.

De geuren werden afgestemd op het soort plant dat werd gekozen. Zo rook de plant *epiphytic bromeliad* naar Amerikaanse nieuwe dollars. Wetende dat deze plant een epifyt is kan men snel de link maken tussen de inbreng van Amerika in Cuba. Een epifyt is een organisme dat op een levende plant groeit zonder hieraan voedsel te onttrekken. Een politiek statement is hier niet ver te zoeken, maar de manier van interpretatie laat voldoende vrijheid om in discours te kunnen gaan en zich af te vragen of niet beter een parasitaire plant was gekozen! Zo kan men dit doen voor iedere van deze *scent engineered* planten. Belangrijk hierbij is dat de geuren ook realistisch zijn en identiek zijn nagemaakt.

Neem bij dit werk de geurverandering weg en de context valt weg. De gecreëerde context zelf is hier een statement om over na te denken. Geur geeft hier dus betekenis aan het werk. Daarnaast wordt geur-engineering ook in vraag gesteld. Een nog vrij onbekende technologie die in haar kinderschoenen staat maar waar *The Smell of a Stranger* de toeschouwer laat nadenken over de opportuniteiten en haar gevaren.

GEUR IN DISCOURS

In de *Scent City Walk* in Palermo (IT) werden op 30 locaties verschillende geuren aangebracht in relatie tot de plaats om zo bezoekers te laten nadenken over die locatie of over de context die het werk met zich meebracht. In een straat waar er een concentratie was van juweelwinkels, werd op een muur waar het verboden was iets aan te plakken, een 5 euro biljet en een oud 5.000 lire biljet gekleefd. Het oude lire biljet kreeg de geur van nieuw geld en het 5 euro biljet de geur van oud geld. Door het wisselen van de geur van twee objecten kan men een statement maken en inspelen op hedendaagse maatschappelijke gevoeligheden. Met de komst van de euro heeft men alles duurder gemaakt. Vele inwoners willen terug naar een nationale munteenheid. Als kunstenaar wil je gewoon een discours opwekken door subtiel een statement te maken.

Zo zal het vervangen van wijwater door de geur van bloed, synthetisch nagemaakt en even doorzichtig als water, de kerkganger zijn intrede en het maken van een kruisje met het vervangen wijwater onverwachts een andere input geven en misschien doen nadenken over het vele bloedvergieten die godsdiensten doorheen de geschiedenis met zich hebben meegebracht. Maar zo zal een wijwatervat gemaakt uit vitamine C juist een tegenoverliggende gedachte opwekken, alsof godsdienst hierbij juist genezing kan brengen.

De locatie kan dus ook bepalend zijn voor de keuze van de geuren. In de *Scent City Trail* van Palermo werden zo goedkope kleurrijke onderbroekjes van vrouwen en mannen opgehangen aan de omheining van het bekende *Fontana Pretoria*, onder de Sicilianen gekend als *Fountain of Shame*. Op de onderbroekjes werd ofwel langs de voorkant of achterkant de geur van sperma of vagina aangebracht. Dit werk leidde tot veel hilarische reacties bij de bezoekers die het waagden hun neus in de het ondergoed te stoppen.

DEFLOWERING

Met het werk *Deflowering* wordt op een subtiele manier de gelijkheid van de vrouw nagestreefd en historisch (en voor sommige religies nog steeds) een klacht geuit tegen het niet mogen hebben van (eigen) sexuele verlangens als vrouw.
Deflowering bestaat uit een klein madonnabeeldje gemaakt uit ijs dat langzaam smelt. De bezoeker moet ongeveer een uur tot anderhalf uur wachten vooraleer de magie begint. Na deze tijd komt de geur van vaginaal vocht vrij. Het werk veroorzaakte veel commotie en werd wereldwijd op sociale media immens geliked en geshared; er werd uitgebreid over geschreven, maar ook soms als smaad ervaren. Hoe een klein beeldje van 23 cm hoog zoveel commotie kon veroorzaken lag allemaal verborgen in de geur. De geur was niet zomaar de geur van

vaginaal vocht, maar de mix van vaginageur van 49 vrouwen van verschillende nationaliteiten en rassen. Via een samenwerking aan een onderzoeksproject en het ondertekenen van een geheimhoudingscontract werd er zo 1,7 ml van het vrouwelijk vochtconcentraat verkregen om dit werk te kunnen realiseren. Wetende dat dergelijk 'geurconcentraat' niet evident te verkrijgen is, want we spreken hier niet van nagemaakte geur, wel van de echte essence. 1,7 ml mag weinig lijken, de geur was des te hemels. Voor één afname was er maximum 0,5 ml nodig om resultaat te hebben.

Als reactie op eigen werk en als dank aan de meer dan duizend mails van enthousiaste vrouwen werd het werk *The Paintbrush of Gustave Courbet* gerealiseerd. Een schilderspenseel gemaakt uit schaamhaar waarmee met de geur van vagina op een blanco canvas in een gestileerde vorm 'V' een vagina werd geschilderd. V kan men hier ook zien als het tonen van het vrijheidssymbool dat men kan maken met de middenvinger en wijsvinger. De vrijheid van het vrouw zijn.

DEAD BODY BULLETS

Negen glazen kogels bevatten elk een hoeveelheid geurconcentraat van de universele geur van dode lichamen. De hoeveelheid geurextract wordt bepaald volgens de leeftijd, geslacht, grootte en gewicht. Zo zal een volwassene na distillatie van zijn of haar lichaam meer geurconcentraat opleveren dan het distillaat van een kind of pasgeborene. Als men een mensenlichaam zou distilleren na de dood, dan zou de hoeveelheid geurextract op zich niet zoveel zijn. Hoe groter en hoe dikker het lichaam, hoe meer geurextract. De geur is deze van een pas gestorven persoon en niet van een persoon in verre ontbinding. Hier bepaalt niet alleen de geur zelf de context, maar ook hoeveel geur aanwezig is in de glazen kogels. Het werk zet de toeschouwer aan tot nadenken over de nutteloosheid van het doden.

BESLUIT

Geur als statement, geur als een reactie op een maatschappelijke situatie kan soms meer aanzetten tot nadenken en reflecteren, maar ook de toeschouwer laten overgaan tot een discussiemoment. Een olfactorisch kunstwerk moet dus meer zijn dan louter een geur toevoegen. Er moet betekenis in zitten. Deze betekenis kan in de geur zelf zitten, maar ook in relatie tot een gegeven iets. Het is meestal de wisselwerking die juist een diepere context brengt. Beelden in relatie tot geuren en vice versa kunnen op een andere manier aanzetten tot reflectie dan louter één zintuig. De sterkte van geur t.o.v. de andere zintuigen is juist dat het geheugen, emoties en lichamelijke reacties kan beïnvloeden door opgedane ervaring en zo de toeschouwer nog meer betrokken en cognitief aanzet tot nadenken over de context van het werk.

In het *Olfactory Art Manifest* wordt een opdeling gemaakt volgens *ismen*. De werken die hier besproken zijn vallen vooral onder het *Olfactionisme* daar er steeds een 'Fact' is en de toeschouwer aangezet wordt tot 'Action' om iets te doen. Deze actie is reflectie, nadenken, in discours gaan. Geur is betekenis, geur is context wanneer het de juiste link heeft met het onderwerp en/of de titel. Geur kan zo bijdragen om betekenis te geven aan het werk of zelf de betekenisdrager zijn. Geur gebruiken als concept van het kunstwerk biedt vele toekomstmogelijkheden. Het is aan de kunstenaar en curator om hierop in te spelen en aan de toeschouwer om hun neus te openen.

CARO VERBEEK

"VERFIJNT DE NEUSGATEN!" EEN MANIFESTATIE VAN EEN NIEUW GEURBEWUSTZIJN

"Wij zijn de reuk vergeten. Wij moeten onze neusgaten verfijnen".

Deze woorden werden omstreeks 1916 – precies een eeuw geleden – neergepend door de relatief onbekende Italiaanse kunstenaar Ennio Valentinelli in zijn postuum gepubliceerde manifest *Arte degli Odori* (de Kunst van Geuren). De Futurist had waarschijnlijk niet kunnen vermoeden dat zijn idee om geur tot kunstmedium te bombarderen een voorspellend karakter zou hebben. Al zou het een echte Futurist vast niet verbazen.

In 2014 voegt Peter de Cupere een nieuwe dimensie toe aan zijn geurperformances, geurconcerten, geursculpturen, geurschilderijen en geurinstallaties: het geurmanifest. Het manifest was vanaf het begin van de twintigste eeuw voor kunstenaars het medium bij uitstek om een statement te maken over de unieke, revolutionaire kwaliteiten van hun beweging. Via het gedrukte pamflet stelden kunstenaars tot voorbij de eigen landsgrenzen hun publiek op de hoogte van hun wereldverbeterende kunstpraktijken. Vooral de Futuristen stonden bekend om het uitdragen van hun gemeenschappelijke ideeën middels het papieren massamedium. Zo bestendigden zij in 1909 met hun *Manifesto del Futurismo* hun bestaan als groep. De zintuigen werden – vooral na de Eerste Wereldoorlog – voor hen een grote bron van inspiratie om tot vernieuwende kunst te komen. Pas na het uiten van hun grootste woorden, losten zij hun beloftes in de praktijk (gedeeltelijk) in.

De Cupere, die wel vaker afwijkt van de norm, doet het net andersom. Na minstens 20 jaar aan geurpraktijken, zet hij zijn theorieën erover op papier in zijn *Olfactory Art Manifest*. Hij doet dat met een kunsthistorisch bewustzijn en schatplichtigheid aan het Futurisme; zijn betoog verschijnt een eeuw (plus een jaar) na *La Pittura dei Suoni, Rumori, Odori (The Painting of Sounds, Noises, Smells)*, het allereerste manifest over geur en kunst, geschreven door Carlo Carrà in 1913. In de tekst van de Cupere vinden we dan ook expliciete en impliciete verwijzingen naar zijn voorganger. Ook toont de Belg zich de belichaming van zijn eigen theorie. Want niets dat de duizendpoot erin benoemt, heeft hij niet al eens zelf uitgevoerd.

Het *Olfactisme*, zoals de Cupere de nieuwe stroming heeft gedoopt, betreft "smell as a medium that gives context and/or can be the concept of the work". Hierin toont zich meteen het eerste onderscheid met Carrà. Voor de Italiaanse kunstenaar was geur (net als geluid) slechts een inspiratiebron om uiteindelijk tot een visueel object te komen.

Het 'Olfactisme' is grofweg op te delen in *Olfactionism* en *Olfactorism*. In de eerste categorie liggen zowel 'actie' als 'fact' (feit) besloten. Geur moet als feit een context scheppen om de toeschouwer (dus eigenlijk 'toeruiker') tot actie en reactie te bewegen. Een goed geurkunstwerk verliest zonder zijn aromatische toevoeging aan betekenis. Zou dat niet het geval zijn, dan is de geur slechts garnering. Een goed voorbeeld hiervan is zijn werk *Smoke Cloud* (2014). De toeschouwer als toeruiker klimt op een trap om met zijn of haar hoofd letterlijk in de wolken te geraken. Daar aangekomen neemt die echter geen spreekwoordelijke rozengeur waar, maar de verstikkende lucht van uitlaatgassen en vervuiling. Het verstandelijke en afstandelijke lezen van krantenberichten vanuit onze comfortabele stoel, heeft een geheel andere impact dan een lijfelijke ervaring. De Cupere drukt ons letterlijk met de neus op de feiten zodat niemand er meer omheen kan: dit veroorzaken wij met onze levensstijl. En het zal ons uiteindelijk het ademen verhinderen als we die niet veranderen.

Waar geur vooral een essentieel element is in het *Olfactionism* neemt de reuk in het *Olfactorism* een centrale plek in. In zijn eigen woorden betreft dit concept waar het woord 'factor' en 'actor' in voorkomen "... the creation of smell consciousness of the state in which the spectator finds him/herself by the use of nothing but odors ...". Zo kan een schijnbaar lege ruimte, een olfactief kunstwerk herbergen dat volledig onzichtbaar zijn werk doet. De connectie tussen de reuk en het geheugen, en dus de associaties en emoties die een geur kunnen oproepen, speelt daarbij volgens de Cupere een belangrijke rol. Wie kent niet dat gevoel overvallen te worden door een levendige jeugdherinnering na het inademen van een bekende geur zodra hij ergens binnenstapt? Het geurgeheugen (ook wel Proustiaans geheugen genoemd) is ongekend krachtig. Zelfs bij dementerenden verdwijnt het effect ervan niet. Het is onmogelijk om daarbij niet aan de Cupere's *Smelloflowers* (2007) te denken. In verzorgingstehuis Den Ooiman in Doetinchem plaatste hij gekleurde bloemvormige geurverspreiders. Niet alleen stelden de specifieke luchten de ouderen in staat hun eigen kamer te vinden in een complex waarbij alle gangen en deuren op elkaar lijken, ook riepen de aroma's vroege en levendige jeugdherinneringen op. Dit kan heel geruststellend zijn voor mensen die zich vaak niet eens meer bewust zijn van hun identiteit.

Ook somt de kunstenaar op wat *Olfactisme* niet is onder de term *Olfactourism*. Tenzij er een kunstzinnige context of concept aan ten grondslag ligt, horen aromatherapie, geur- en parfumworkshops, aromajockey-uitvoeringen, technologische gadgets, reclames, parfums die niet voldoen aan het *Olfactorisme* en geurillustraties hier niet bij. Dat de Cupere deze kaders schept heeft te maken met de tot verwarring leidende toeëigening van het label *Olfactory Art* door verschillende disciplines, zoals de parfumerie en de aromatherapie. Het gebrek aan eenduidigheid heeft minder te maken met de al dan niet aanwezige kwaliteit van het eindproduct, dan met het gebrek aan een heldere definiëring. Ook de statusverhogende werking van het stempel speelt mee. Kunst met de hoofdletter 'K' wordt vaak gelijk gesteld aan vaardigheid, vernuft, kwaliteit, originaliteit, auteurschap en het uitsluiten van een commercieel belang. Vele parfumeurs herkennen zichzelf in deze traditionele opvattingen en proberen daarmee het publiek te overtuigen van de systematische onderschatting van hun beroep. En dit is begrijpelijk. Hoe vaak worden klassieke parfumcomposities zoals *Chypre* van Coty (1917), of *Chanel N°5* (1921) niet afgedaan als 'luchtje'? Zou men een schilderij van Picasso ooit een 'plaatje' noemen?

Maar hoewel er geen sluitende definitie van kunst bestaat, zijn in de 20ste en 21ste eeuw binnen het kunstdiscours ook andere principes gaan gelden, zoals het stellen van kritische vragen, engagement en een conceptuele inslag. Deze waarden zijn binnen de kunst minstens even belangrijk, zo niet belangrijker dan ambachtelijkheid en het strelen van het oog, dan wel de tong of de neus. Wellicht dat het er Valentinelli in *Arte degli Odori* daarom veel aan gelegen lag zich duidelijk te onderscheiden van parfumeurs. Hij deed dat door ook de andere kant van de dichotomie van geuren te betrekken, namelijk door stank te includeren. "De complete olfactieve lyriek van de natuur schuilt niet alleen in het welriekende, het huist ook in stank, in het onwelriekende", stelde hij. Ook de Cupere en andere geurkunstenaars kunnen er regelmatig op 'betrapt' worden geuren uit de taboesfeer te verspreiden. Zaad-, zweet (cfr. *Sweat*, 2010, *Life is one sweat study case*, 2015), urine en fecale uitwasemingen zijn hem niet vreemd. Toch vindt men lichaamsidentieke stoffen ook wel in de ondertonen, of basisnoten van parfums. Olfactieve kunst onderscheidt zich van parfum door de specifieke context waarin die zich beweegt en de maatschappelijke vragen die worden gesteld. Een cosmetisch parfum zou hoogstens tot de toegepaste kunst gerekend kunnen worden.

Het is in historisch opzicht overigens interessant om op te merken dat de term *Olfactory Art* al in de negentiende eeuw voor het eerst werd gemunt door de parfumeur en chemicus Septimus Piesse. In zijn traktaat *De kunst van Parfumerie* uit 1855 omschrijft hij hoe parfum een esthetische rol zou kunnen spelen in geurconcerten. Ook komt hij met verklaringen voor synesthetische ervaringen voor de kleur- en toonassociaties die geurstoffen kunnen oproepen. Piesse noemt zelfs de mogelijkheid van een *odofoon*. Tot slot benoemt hij de lyrische vervoering en universele waarden waar parfum een uiting van kan zijn. We moeten ons ook realiseren dat de term 'esthetiek' in de toen nog heersende Kantiaanse betekenis niet sloeg op het individuele smaakoordeel, maar op algemeen geldende waarden die een kunstwerk zouden kunnen manifesteren (en die dus bij iedereen hetzelfde effect zou moeten hebben). Omdat geur bij iedereen andere associaties oproept kan het alleen al om die reden geen onderdeel van de esthetiek zijn, zo redeneerde hij. Daar komt nog bij dat geur geen kennis zou kunnen verschaffen over externe objecten. Deze denkbeelden zijn natuurlijk niet meer van kracht in het huidige kunstdiscours en de Cupere wil ons met zijn manifest fijntjes wijzen op de reikwijdte en potentie van geur als medium in de handen van de kunstenaar.

Ook de Futuristen waren overigens helder over hun afbakeningen. Al vertoont hun agressieve pose overeenkomsten met het territoriale gedrag van mannelijke gorilla's. Vooral de Fransen moesten het ontgelden. Zo hadden de Impressionisten misschien wel op slappe wijze 'gepoogd' om geuren en geluiden te schilderen maar faalden zij hierin als een musicus die geluiden maakt die enkel "werden opgevangen door het trommelvlies van dovemansoren". Zelf hoefden zij daarentegen volgens Carrà slechts "in een kamer met karakteristieke geuren, zoals bloemen en petroleum, te worden opgesloten om – middels een obscuur proces – aan hun geest de meest plastische beelden te doen ontspruiten". *Synesthesie* of de vertaling van het ene zintuig naar het andere, lag ten grondslag aan talloze andere Futuristische manifesten. In relatie tot geur komt het een enkele andere keer voor.

Tien jaar na Carrà, schreef collega Futurist Fedele Azari in 1924 het misschien nog wel meer tot de verbeelding sprekende *La Flora Futurista ed Equivalenti Plastici di Odori Artifciali* ('De Futuristische Flora en Plastische Equivalenten van Kunstmatige Geuren'). Daarin schrijft Azari dat het maar eens afgelopen moest zijn met de zwakke onschuldige bloemenluchten en misselijkmakende pastelkleuren. Het was tijd voor acute, allesdoordringende geuren en felle schreeuwende kleuren. Alleen artificiële geuren zouden de imperfecte natuur kunnen sublimeren en kunnen voldoen aan hun nieuwe honger voor uitgesproken vormen en beelden. De kunstenaar zag met name de parfums van François Coty als zeer geschikte equivalenten van de Futuristische vormentaal. De zware poederige, niet naar bloemen ruikende luchten gaven uiting aan moderniteit en hun afkeer van de bourgeoisie.

Voor de Cupere, die af en toe ook een beroep doet op het markante verschijnsel, is synesthesie weliswaar interessant, maar valt het niet zozeer onder het Olfactisme. Het directe appel op de neus is voor hem essentieel. Hoewel er veel overeenkomsten zijn met zijn historische voorbeelden, verschilt hij op een punt fundamenteel van de Futuristen. De Belgische kunstenaar zou zijn naam geen eer aandoen wanneer hij niet toch een aromatische dimensie aan zijn schrijven zou hebben toegevoegd. Hij ondertekende het manifest met inkt bestaande uit een distillaat van zijn eigen lichaamsgeuren die hij gedurende twee jaar verzamelde. Dit biografische parfum is als het zwarte vierkant waarmee Malevich op een gegeven moment zijn schilderijen begon te signeren, vanuit vereenzelviging met zijn werk. De Cupere voegt de daad bij het woord en geeft context en betekenis door geur als medium in te zetten. Zijn manifest spreekt niet alleen van olfactieve kunst, maar is het ook. Het is ten slotte aan het publiek om met hun nieuw verkregen geurbewustzijn, niet alleen hun kennis, maar ook hun neusgaten te verfijnen.

Caro Verbeek
Geurhistoricus, Vrije Universiteit Amsterdam

PETER DE CUPERE

THE ART OF SMELLING

The Art Of Smelling, Olfactory Art Research was de titel van de solotentoonstelling in Enschede. Aan de hand van werken uit de tentoonstelling wordt uitgelegd vanwaar Peter de Cupere zijn werken hun oorsprong vinden. In deze tentoonstelling moet de bezoeker, zoals bij vele werken van Peter de Cupere, actief deelnemen. Ze gaan o.a. zelf op onderzoek hoe geur in relatie tot het zien kan verschillen en een meerwaarde kan betekenen.

Als we algemeen het 'zien' als uitgangspunt nemen, ontdekken we dat geuren meer boodschap kunnen geven dan louter het 'zicht' alleen. Bij het zien gebruiken we slechts vier verschillende receptoren: rood, groen en blauwe kegeltjes plus staafjes (voor het licht). Elke kleur kan dus in kaart worden gebracht in drie dimensies met een andere waarde voor de transparantie. Het toewijzen van een geur in een dimensionele kaart zou bij wijze van spreken een ontzettend grote dimensionale ruimte vereisen. Dit is een fundamenteel probleem van geurherkenning, en aldus ook om te spreken van een vastgelegde geurherkenning. Om dit beter te duiden werd in de tentoonstelling een werk van 2001, *Touch & Smell the Colours of this World* [1], anders verwerkt in het nieuwe werk *Scratch, Sniff and Imagine the Colours of this World.* De vraag; "Kan de toeschouwer een eigen context geven aan een bepaalde combinatie van een geur met kleur?" is bij dit werk voor de kunstenaar meer primordiaal dan de vraag: "Welke context geeft een geur in combinatie met een kleur?".

Waarom werkt geur subjectief en is het moeilijk om te weten of een bepaalde context bij een werk ook zo wordt ervaren als die beoogde context? Kan een toeschouwer geur als leidraad herkennen om zo de boodschap van het werk te herkennen?

Het verband tussen geur en herinnering wordt opgeslagen in de orbitofrontale cortex. Geur wordt zo bijna altijd in het langetermijngeheugen opgeslagen. Daarom kunnen we bepaalde emoties voelen als we alleen maar een geur ruiken. Geur is, naast primaire functies, zodoende een element wat herinnering oproept. Dat kan een gebeurtenis zijn, maar ook een stemming of een gevoel uit je jeugd.

HET 'PROUSTEFFECT'

De geurherinnering wordt ook het Prousteffect [2] genoemd, ontleent aan de naam van de Franse schrijver Marcel Proust.
Het gegeven 'herinnering' speelt een belangrijke rol. Vermits een persoonlijke herinnering subjectief is, is het ook moeilijk om concreet te zeggen dat een bepaalde geur een bepaalde context zou geven met de uitzondering van een bepaalde 'herinnering als context' op zichzelf. Het werk *Sniff and Imagine the Colours of this World* is hiervan een mooi voorbeeld. De geur-kleurcombinaties geven voor verscheidene toeschouwers verschillende 'contexten'. Het discours dat ontstaat tussen bezoekers onderling over hoe een geur wordt ervaren maakt ook inhoudelijk onderdeel uit van het werk. De meeste contexten refereerden naar hun eigen herinnering die men kreeg bij de combinatie van de geur met de bepaalde kleur. Indien men de geur niet direct herkende, werd er eerst de kleur als uitgangspunt genomen om te bedenken welke geur bij deze kleur zou passen. De geuren waren zo gekozen dat ze ofwel op de herinnering konden verder gaan ofwel op basis van primaire functies.

Deze primaire functies zijn uiteraard niet te onderschatten en vormen ook de basis van het ontstaan van geur. Geur heeft ook een waarschuwingsgraad.

Concreet kan men de functie van het ruiken opdelen in respectievelijk:
- Primaire geur als waarschuwing: denken we maar aan het herkennen van brandlucht, rook, giftig en bedorven voedsel. Bij sommige dieren is deze functie nog extremer. Ze ruiken hun vijanden nog voor dat zij ze zien.
- Geur als genot: het ervaren van geur is direct verbonden met de emotionele centra in de hersenen (limbisch systeem). Hierdoor is de geursensatie die we als plezierig kunnen ervaren heel direct. Het wordt aldus ook intuïtief gestimuleerd. Geur is belangrijk voor het libido. Om van sex optimaal te kunnen genieten nemen we onbewust feromonen waar, hormonale stoffen die ons libido aanwakkeren.
- Geur en smaak: het herkennen en kunnen genieten van voedsel. We hebben maar vier smaakpupillen (met umami erbij vijf, namelijk hartige smaak), dus geur is belangrijk om goed te kunnen genieten bij het eten en drinken, maar zoals eerder aangehaald ook om bedorven of slecht voedsel te herkennen en te weren.
- Geur als spoor: een functie die bij ons verloren is gegaan, maar bij dieren nog sterk aanwezig is. Via de geur een spoor volgen of een weg (terug)vinden.

GEUR ALS HERINNERING

Hoe we een bepaalde geur als een genot of waarschuwing ervaren zal onze manier van herinneren bepalen en aldus ook in onze toekomst laten ervaren hoe op een herinnerde geur gereageerd zal worden. Toch primeert 'geur als waarschuwing' boven andere geurwaarnemingen en kan men er vanuit gaan dat we deze ook sneller herkennen als iets negatiefs. (Niet altijd, de geur van de rook van een barbecue wordt eerder als iets positiefs ervaren op basis van de geurherinnering aan een eerdere barbecue en/of aan de gezelligheid die er bij hoort).

De geur van rook en brandlucht heeft zo een herkenbare waarschuwende geur. Deze geuren worden veel gebruikt in installaties waarbij ze samen met het visuele beeld vragen over bv. luchtverontreiniging opwerpen. In de tentoonstelling *The Art of Smelling* kon men zo voor de eerste keer het werk *Smoke Cloud* zien en olfactief ervaren. Het werk ging later op rondreis doorheen Latijns-Amerika (Havana, Buenos Aires & Rio de Janeiro) in de tentoonstelling *The Importance of Being...*, een rondreizende tentoonstelling met 40 Belgische kunstenaars, georganiseerd door Bruno Devos en met curator Sara Alonso Gómez.

In Enschede werd echter de geur van luchtverontreiniging in *Smoke Cloud* gecombineerd met de geur van buskruit omdat in Enschede er sterk de herinnering aan de explosie van een vuurwerkfabriek[3] heerst.

Milieu en maatschappij en meer bepaald de problemen die men kan vaststellen door toedoen van de mensheid vormen een belangrijke context van Peter de Cupere zijn werk. De perceptie van hoe mensen met het geurzintuig omgaan is hierbij belangrijk. De herinnering vormt hierbij een belangrijk gegeven maar ook de manier en het waarnemen van geur op zich. Het olfactief ervaren van milieuproblemen hangt sterk af van hoe men een geur waarneemt en hoe goed men zelf bewust is van geurherkenning. De toeschouwer moet zich aldus bewust zijn van zijn eigen mogelijkheden en ervaringen met het ruiken. De mondiale toeschouwer heeft te weinig kennis van zijn eigen geurcapaciteit. Hij klimatiseert ook snel aan een geur[4]. M.a.w. hij wordt dus ook te snel gewoon aan de geur van luchtverontreiniging en ervaart hierdoor o.a. ook olfactief te weinig de milieuproblemen. Zolang deze de huiselijke sfeer niet storen kijkt hij ook niet verder in de toekomst en is strikt genomen alleen gefocust op zijn directe omringende wereld. Hij neemt daarbij bewust deel aan de verontreiniging van de maatschappij door eigen luxe niet aan te passen aan meer milieubewuste mogelijkheden.

Via zijn geurinstallaties wil Peter de Cupere de toeschouwer laten nadenken over milieubewust zijn door mogelijke eindresultaten te tonen. Deze eindresultaten kunnen dan installaties zijn zoals *Smoke Cloud* of *Olfactory Tree*. *Olfactory Tree* laat in de buik (bulb) van de boom een identieke boom zien op een schaal van 1/10. Deze kleine boom is echter niet zo natuurlijk bruin en groen, maar volledig zwart en donkergrijs en ruikt verbrand. De binnenkant staat schel in contrast met de buitenkant. Net zoals in de maatschappij wordt er pas nagedacht wanneer men de schade vaststelt en niet eerder.

De *Olfactory Tree* is een Droste-effect, want de kleine boom herhaalt zich in de grote boom en zo zal er zich in de kleine boom wederom een andere kleine boom bevinden die waarschijnlijk helemaal opgebrand en vergaan is. Het is niet aangenaam om de verbrande lucht te ervaren, maar zoals we van voyeurisme houden zullen we toch in de boom kijken en onze neus even ophalen.

Zowel *Smoke Cloud* als *Olfactory Tree* verwijzen naar de CO2 uitstoot. De klimaatverandering is een niet te onderschatten probleem en krijgt gelukkig de laatste jaren meer aandacht. Maar het is ook een proces dat naarmate er meer CO2 wordt uitgestoten en de wereld opwarmt, deze fenomenen ook de hoeveelheid water doen toenemen. In reactie op al die veranderingen stoten planten meer geurende chemicaliën af, genaamd 'biogene vluchtige organische stoffen' (BVOS). BVOS beschermen de plant tegen plagen en zorgen ervoor dat de wereld intenser gaat ruiken. Uit onderzoek blijkt dat planten hun verhoogde uitstoot van BVOS al gestart zijn en dat de wereld dus al geuriger wordt! "De toename is exponentieel. Het kan de afgelopen jaren al met tien procent gestegen zijn en zal in de volgende decennia bij een opwarming met twee of drie graden Celsius met circa dertig à veertig procent verder toenemen[5]."

In de tentoonstelling *The Art Of Smelling, Olfactory Art Research* komt naast de context van milieuverontreiniging (cfr. *Smoke Cloud, Olfactory Tree*) en de afhankelijkheid van de toeschouwer van zijn eigen geurherinnering, ook het aspect geurherkenning en geurwaarachtigheid aan bod. Om de toeschouwer bewust te maken van deze aspecten is er het *Smell Lab*. Dit onderzoekslabo mag dan wel geen wetenschappelijk uiterlijk hebben, toch ervaart de bezoeker zich even als onderzoeker, zijnde eerder een kunstige onderzoeker. De toeschouwer wordt hier in de rol van onderzoekende kunstenaar gepamperd. Tevens wordt men speels teruggeworpen in de tijd. Als een nieuwsgierig kind gaat men op onderzoek uit. Bij het binnenkomen dient men zich eerst aan te kleden met de nodige 'hygiënische' labokledij. Daarna kan men eerst zijn eigen geurbewustzijn testen aan de hand van twee kleine 'smell devices'.

Verder kan men vier verschillende planten ontdekken die via 'Genetic Olfactorisation' (GO) zijn gemodificeerd (GOM) [6]. Via genetische olfactorisatie hebben de planten een andere geur dan hun originele geur verkregen. GOM biedt veel toepassingen. Zo zou men de geur van zweet kunnen veranderen in de geur van rozen of een roos naar chocolade of aardbei laten ruiken. Momenteel is de beleving beperkt tot het denkbeeldig vermogen dat de kunstenaar ons hier laat. Het idee van manipuleren van planten is iets waarmee hij al van bij het begin van zijn oeuvre bezig was. De vraag of mogelijke nieuwe plantensoorten de wereld kunnen verderhelpen is dan ook steeds wederkerig. Deze vraagstelling sluit ook aan bij de context van milieuproblemen om via de natuur zelf mogelijke oplossingen aan te bieden.

Als mens is de kunstenaar geen voorstander van toepassingen van gentechnologie op planten en zeker niet op gewassen die we zelf eten, maar we kunnen dit uiteindelijk niet tegenhouden. De wereld evolueert snel. De wereldpopulatie neemt exponentieel toe [7] en dit heeft ook haar uitwerking op het energieverbruik [8]. Er is dan ook geen zekerheid dat men de CO2 uitstoot effectief voldoende zal kunnen verminderen om de klimaatsverandering in de nabije toekomst tegen te houden. Zoektochten naar energie en voeding zullen gentechnologie alleen maar meer vrijheid bezorgen.

Waar economie op wereldgebied belangrijk wordt, worden steeds toegevingen bewerkstelligd. We kunnen hier schrik voor hebben, maar ook de positieve kant ervan benadrukken en de eventuele negatieve gevolgen duiden. Zo wil Peter de Cupere ook met zijn werk mogelijke positieve ontwikkelingen aantonen. Concepten waarbij vertrokken wordt vanuit de mogelijke gevolgen van de klimaatverandering, die de toeschouwer doet nadenken over zijn toekomst. Vermits geur sterk op de herinnering werkt, zal men later misschien onbewust zijn werk herinneren en onbewust alleen voor de positieve output van nieuwe technologieën kiezen. Zijn werk mag niet louter in deze tijd gezien worden, maar dankzij de sterkte van het olfactief geheugen kan het ons aan toekomstgerichte oplossingen laten herinneren. Door de jaren heen werden al verschillende werken rond gentechnologie gecreëerd. Voorbeelden hiervan zijn de *Alambfleurics* en de *Brewery Flowers*.

Alambfleurics zijn gengemodificeerde bloemen. Zij hebben de vorm van een alambic [9]. Overdag wordt de 'bulb' van de bloem door de zon verhit. In de bulb verdampt de essence van de bloem en deze koelt 's avonds af in de spiraalstengel van de bloem om zo zijn geurextract af te scheiden in de bloemkelk. Voordeel is dat men de bloemen niet meer moet plukken en niet meer vroeg moet opstaan. Men kan nu 's avonds de geurstof aftappen en bij mogelijke plantages kan men dit doen via automatische opvangbakjes. Daar de bloem blijft groeien en groter wordt, verkrijgt men met de jaren ook een betere en veel grotere geurstofproductie.

Brewery Flowers zijn bloemen die via genmodificatie omgebouwd zijn tot een heus fabriek op zich. De planten worden heel groot en hebben iedere dag een immense productie. Er dienen geen vervuilende fabrieken meer gemaakt te worden daar deze *Brewery Flowers* zelf de fabriek zijn en volledig ecologisch werken. Met *Brewery Flowers* kan men o.a. bieren creëren, maar ook andere dranken. Het enige dat extra toegevoegd dient te worden is water en eventueel koolzuurgas, maar deze laatste kan ook op een natuurlijke manier gewonnen worden.

Alambfleurics en *Brewery Flowers* lijken op zich wel fantasievolle bloemen, maar met de snelle evolutie van technologieën bieden ze mogelijke toekomstperspectieven. Zo heeft de kunstenaar met testen via entingen (geen gentechnologie) reeds de vorm van de alambfleuric benadert, maar deze testen bleven niet lang bestaan en schimmelden snel.

In het *Smell Lab* in de tentoonstelling *The Art Of Smelling, Olfactory Art Reserach* worden vier niet alledaagse levende planten getoond waarvan de geur gemodificeerd werd. Dit lijkt alleszins zo voor de toeschouwer. De vier planten staan afgeschermd met een plastiek folie. Via een buissysteem verbonden met trechters kunnen de bezoekers de planten ruiken. Deze ruiken aldus anders dan ze visueel eruit zien of zouden ruiken. De toeschouwer gelooft ook, of wil geloven, dat deze planten effectief anders ruiken dan ze origineel zouden ruiken. De waarachtigheid is hierbij van groot belang. Deze waarachtigheid wordt ook gecreëerd doordat zij zelf mede als onderzoeker zijn 'gedecoreerd'. De toeschouwer voelt zich ook onderzoeker doordat hij labokledij aan heeft. Om het onderzoekend karakter te benadrukken moeten ze ook ruiken via een sprietje dat ze zelf hebben aangebracht aan een papieren mondmasker. Het sprietje moeten ze per plant in de trechter steken en zo snuffelend de geur opsnuiven. De toeschouwer die buiten het labo staat, kan alles doorheen de doorzichtige plastiek meevolgen. Heel de setting creëert het gevoel van een wetenschappelijk onderzoek, terwijl het eerder een onderzoek is naar het zelf leren beter ruiken en zich bewust worden van eigen geurperceptie. Dat de planten via GOM (Genetic Olfactory Manipulation) van geur zijn veranderd, mag voor sommigen ongeloofwaardig klinken, maar door het zelf te ervaren wordt er wel nagedacht of dit effectief wel mogelijk is of kan zijn. De twijfel is hier winnaar. Bij veel van zijn werken speelt de creatie van waarachtigheid een belangrijke rol om de kijker bewust te maken en/of te doen nadenken over de maatschappij, milieu en zijn eigen (geur)grenzen.

Ondanks dat de kunstenaar al meer dan 20 jaar de bloem in relatie tot nieuwe door hemzelf uitgevonden gentechnologieën afweegt ten voordele van een mooiere maatschappij, blijkt het de laatste jaren uit wetenschappelijk onderzoek een niet ver van mijn bed show te zijn. Via 'scent engineering' [10] is het mogelijk om bepaalde bloemsoorten anders te laten ruiken, net zoals men ze ook een andere kleur [11] kan geven. *Scent engineering* bij planten en bloemen is nog steeds niet volledig op punt gesteld, maar men mag er vanuit gaan dat in de toekomst meerdere planten anders zullen ruiken en dito ook anders kunnen smaken. In 2015 realiseerde de kunstenaar het werk *The Smell Of A Stranger* in de XII Biënnale van Havana. Hier werd *scent engineering* tot het uiterste doorgedreven.

De geuraanpassing van een bloem kan ook mogelijke voordelen hebben voor het voortbestaan van bv. de bijen. Zo kan men de geur van de bloem sterker maken, zodat bijen de planten beter terugvinden in de luchtverontreinigde wereld. Een mooie referentie hierbij zijn de werken rond *Pollinators*. *Pollinators* zijn bijen die een geurmasker dragen. Men kan dit ruikmasker ook op verschillende manieren interpreteren. Zo kan het masker een mini-gasmasker zijn om de ongezonde lucht uit te zuiveren zodat bijen langer leven, maar kan het masker ook juist een masker zijn om beter te kunnen ruiken. Als het ware een soort van actief ruikend en filterend masker dat de bijen naar de juiste bloemen en planten leidt. Maar evengoed zouden de pollinators eerder mini-drones kunnen zijn die via geurdetectie hun functie als 'bevruchters' van bloemen en planten tot doel hebben. Wetende dat het woord 'drone' afgeleid is van de Engelse benaming van een mannelijke bij, is dit nog niet zo een ver afliggende gedachte.

Naast de vier 'GOM Plants' zijn er nog vijf andere onbestaande planten. Twee van hen, *Pep & Straw*, zitten in een aparte plastieken cel. Pep & Straw behoren tot dezelfde plantensoort. Ze zijn verkregen door CVGO ('Creative Visualisation Genetic Olfactorisation'). Bij aanraking kan er een toxische reactie ontstaan met je huid, maar hun geuren zijn duidelijk herkenbaar als pepermunt en aardbei. De twee planten ontstonden per toeval door het toepassen van een verkeerde VGM ('Visual Genetic Modification') String. De kunstenaar was niet onder de indruk van zijn gecreëerde planten maar door toepassing van GOM kregen ze voor hem een meerwaarde. Door hun vorm en geur doopte hij ze Pep & Straw verwijzend naar de geuren Peppermint en Strawberry. Men dient wederom het rietje in de trechter te steken om de geuren waar te nemen. Dit zijn zelf gecreëerde planten waarbij gespeeld wordt met het verhaal achter het genetisch manipuleren. Of de planten echt bestaan, laat hij graag in het midden. Dit kan hij zichzelf gunnen dankzij zijn creatieve vrijheid als kunstenaar. Bij deze planten is het idee van 'Genetic Olfactory Modification of Manipulation' verder doorgedreven. Door twee onbestaande planten te creëren en hen door GOM te behandelen krijgen ze een bestaansrecht. Hier speelt ook weer de waarachtigheid een rol. De waarachtigheid werd nog verder doorgedreven met de drie resterende planten waarbij de toeschouwers eerst via hun rietje aan hun mondmasker aan de planten dienen te ruiken om een idee te krijgen wat voor soort planten het zijn. De kunstenaar noemt hen 'VBS Plants', afkorting van 'Visualisation By Smell'.

VBS gaat nog een stap verder dan GOM. Bij VBS moet de toeschouwer zelf een beeld scheppen van wat voor soort plant of bloem men ruikt. De 'VBS Plants' lijken op zich zonder geurtoevoeging helemaal niet op planten. Maar door de toevoeging van geur en de context waarin ze getoond worden, ervaart men ze wel als planten. Van origine zijn de *VBS Plants* gevonden objecten, vormen of afvalmateriaal waarvan de vorm intrigeerde. Wel te verstaan dat de keuze van de objecten aanspraken met het idee ze als plant voor te stellen en waarbij ze elk een specifieke geur zouden krijgen. Hier wordt de toeschouwer dus helemaal bedot naar waarachtigheid toe, maar door de context blijft het idee overeind. Men kan hierbij aan toekomstsituaties denken waarbij door de technologische vooruitgang en misvorming van natuurelementen door de vervuiling, mogelijke doomscenarios ontstaan. Nochtans is dit niet de eerste aanleiding voor het maken van dit werk. De naam VBS, 'Visualisation By Smell', zegt al waarover het gaat. Een beeld scheppen via geur. 'The sense of smell' wordt hier uitgedaagd. Net zoals bij het werk *Scratch, Sniff and Imagine the Colours of this World*, moet de kijker eerst ruiker zijn en via de combinatie van de geur met het object, de vorm en de kleur een eigen beeld scheppen.

'Visualisation By Smell' is een uitdaging voor de toeschouwer om zijn eigen geurgrenzen te verleggen. Niet alleen stil te staan bij het raden welke geur het is, maar verder te gaan op zijn instinctieve reactie gevormd door herinnering en vaststelling van wat de geur in combinatie met het zicht ervaart. De context van VBS ligt hem juist in de eigen perceptie, eigen kunnen en eigen vertaling en wordt mede ook bepaald door de opgedane kennis. Het cognitieve gaat hier een dialoog aan met het subjectieve. Om het werk te begrijpen dient men te redeneren. Sommigen zullen het niet eens doorhebben dat de getoonde 'VBS Plants' puur gevonden objecten zijn waar betekenis aan werd gegeven d.m.v. geur. En wie het doorheeft zal hopelijk voldoende kennis in zich dragen om meer te zien dan louter het object of de geur, maar zal een synthese maken van beiden. Tevens benadrukt het werk de context van mijn kunst waar milieuproblemen door vervuiling naar toe kunnen leiden.

De tentoongestelde GOM en VBS planten en bloemen passen perfect in de betekenis die het concept *Flower* voor de kunstenaar heeft.
Een *Flower* is meer dan alleen een bloem. Het is een hoorn naar de maatschappij, een uitlaat en een schreeuw. *Flowers* als metafoor geeft zoveel meer betekenis aan het begrip bloem. Geen ideaal van schoonheid, maar betekenisdrager. Een *Flower* geeft een boodschap.
Ze doet de toeschouwer nadenken en de 'schoonheid' van de maatschappij in vraag stellen. Men moet het begrip *Flower* niet als een puur esthetisch gegeven zien, maar een betekenisdrager.

Op het einde van het *Smell Lab* gaat de toeschouwer zelf aan de slag met het vullen van een rood reageerbuisje met zelf gekozen kruiden en vloeistof. Deze hangt hij daarna in de laatste gang tussen de reageerbuisjes van vorige bezoekers. De geur in de gang is interactief omdat deze steeds een mix zal zijn van de verschillende geursamenstellingen. De bezoeker maakt dus mee deel uit van hoe de geur in de gang met de reageerbuisjes zal evolueren.

Op het gelijkvloers van de tentoonstelling bevinden zich verder nog een fotoserie van de 'smell devices' *Breath Odor* en *Stereo Sound Odor* en *Mono Sound Odor* die verwijzen naar de eerste proeven die men moet doen in het smell lab. Daarnaast staat het werk *Heaven*.

Heaven lijkt op een doodskist waarop een grasmat ligt. In de grasmat is er een gat. Wanneer men op de buik op de grasmat gaat liggen en met de neus in het gat duikt, ruikt men de geur van *Heaven*. Wanneer we aan het woord 'heaven' denken, denken veel mensen aan de metafoor van 'naar de hemel gaan wanneer ze dood gaan'. *Heaven* is hierop een subtiele persiflage waarbij logisch bekeken het een concrete vaststelling is. Mensen worden nu éénmaal begraven of uitgestrooid wanneer men dood is en gaan dus naar de aarde. De geur van de aarde ruikt niet hemels, maar naargelang de locatie waar je begraven wordt naar een warme zwamachtige ondergrond. In de installatie is de geur van champignons overheersend. De toeschouwer kijkt ook niet naar de hemel wanneer men op het gras gaat liggen om de neus in de grond te steken. Bij het werk *Heaven* start of stopt de tentoonstelling. Het is het tegenovergestelde van *Smoke Cloud* maar toch staan ze gelijk op het vlak van kritiek over het menselijk acteren. *Heaven* kan ook gezien worden als het resultaat van *Smoke Cloud*, nl. de dood. En hiermee relativeert het werk ook het menselijk bestaan. De tentoonstelling *The Art Of Smelling* is dus eigenlijk een soort van levensloop waarbij de toeschouwer verschillende stadia doorloopt. Zo wordt men met *Cocoon* teruggeworpen in de tijd door het ruiken van babypoeder en start men eigenlijk zijn eigen leven opnieuw. Via het *Smell Lab* ontdekt men zichzelf en moet men stilstaan bij de waarheid en waarachtigheid. Het *Smell Lab* bepaalt eigenlijk in hoeverre men open zal staan om het andere te ontdekken en zichzelf in vraag te stellen. De *Olfactory Tree* is een verwijzing hoe we de wereld kapot maken door de natuur niet waardig te nemen en *Smoke Cloud* is de *Heaven* die sommigen onder ons voor ogen hebben, maar geconfrontreerd worden met de geur van luchtverontreiniging en buskruit. Of hoe de hemel en de hel dicht bij elkaar liggen, zonder daar expliciet naar te willen verwijzen. Voor een geoefend kijker of lezer zal het duidelijk zijn dat deze tentoonstelling ook over meer kan gaan dan alleen de context van klimaatsveranderingen, milieuproblemen en de maatschappij, maar ook een onderliggende tussen de regels leesbare terechtwijzing van religie.
In de tentoonstelling werd er ook een kleine *Scent Space* getoond waar men in een verdonkerde kleine ruimte over kurkuma moest lopen. Kurkuma is een Indiase geelwortel en geeft de typische geur aan currypoeders, maar wordt ook gebruikt als kleurstof en geneesmiddel [12 13]. Als specerij heeft kurkuma helende werkingen [14], maar vooral de geur blijft lang in je neusepitheel hangen.

Scent Spaces komen in verschillende versies voor in zijn werk. Zo zijn *Smoke Room* met zijn meer dan 750.000 gebruikte sigarettenpeukjes en *Smile Room* waarin een badkamer volledig met tandpasta is bedekt ook *Scent Spaces*. In *Scent Spaces* ervaart de toeschouwer met heel zijn lichaam de bevangenis van geur. In de tentoonstelling vind je *Cocoon* terug. Een ruimte helemaal met watten bekleedt. Zowel binnenin als aan de buitenkant isoleren synthetische witte watten de ruimte. Cocoon werkt op de herinnering. De babypoedergeur die aanwezig is in de kamer werpt je terug in de tijd dat je nog maar pas op de wereld kwam [15]. De installatie is een herwerking van verschillende eerder gemaakte wattenruimtes die destijds de titel kregen *My Soft World, In Honour Of My Mother* [16]. Op die manier is de tentoonstelling ook een herinnering op zich geworden aan eerder gemaakte geurinstallaties. Even tijd voor jezelf nemen, we doen het te weinig in de gehaaste wereld van technologieën waarin we leven. *Cocoon* is een vlucht en nog meer een mentale vlucht. Je wordt via de zachtheid van de watten en de geïsoleerdheid van de ruimte terug naar jezelf geworpen.

Naast *Cocoon* hangen er 7 foto's uit een eerder gedane performance [17] samen met het wattenpak [18] waarmee de performance werd gedaan. De foto's tonen de éénzaamheid waarmee de kunstenaar af te rekenen heeft. Hoe zedig de wattenruimte ook mag lijken, erin proberen te leven is niet zo aangenaam dan er maar tijdelijk in vertoeven zoals de bezoeker het betaamt.

Op zich zou deze tentoonstelling af zijn geweest, ware het niet dat er ook een gedeelte op de eerste verdieping plaats vond. De werken op de eerste verdieping sluiten ook aan bij de verhaallijn van de tentoonstelling. Via de *Odor Telescope* kan men een roos vanop afstand ruiken. De roos staat opgesteld op het terras van de bovenste verdieping in het tegenoverliggende Twente Museum. Wanneer men door de telescoop kijkt, ziet en ruikt men de roos van op afstand.

In de video *Paris, Mon Amour* [19] wordt, na een wandeltocht doorheen Parijs, een roze wolk bevrijdt uit een oude valies. De wolk bleek te ontstaan door het oppompen van de valies met daarin een blendmix van rozenblaadjes.

Het is duidelijk dat *Odor Telescope* en de video *Paris, Mon Amour* de roos als onderwerp gemeenschappelijk hebben. Tevens is er een link naar *Smoke Cloud*, alleen zou de wolk in de video *Paris, Mon Amour* veel aangenamer en meer poëtisch ruiken. De *Odor Telescope* die stiekem een rode roos in het oog houdt, is even poëtisch en geeft tegelijkertijd ook een gevoel van voyeurisme. Naast de *Odor Telescope* vinden we nog een aantal tekeningen terug die het idee achter dit werk illustreren. De *Odor Telescope* werd al eerder getoond in de tentoonstelling *Kortrijk Vlaandert* [20].

In een aanpalende ruimte hangen drie *Cigarette Paintings* en een klein tafeltje met stoeltje bekleed met gebruikte sigaretten. De geur is een mix van asfaltgeur, gerookt vleesaroma en de geur van uitlaatgassen. Samen geven ze de bezoeker het idee dat ze de gebruikte sigaretten zelf ruiken. De geur van de originele gebruikte sigaretten werd dus verwijderd en vervangen door de toegevoegde rookgeuren. Het totaal is eigenlijk een aparte geurinstallatie naast de tentoonstelling maar heeft ook linken met het andere werk. Zo is er de rookverwijzing en ook door de geur van gerookt vlees een hint naar het verbranden van je eigen longen. Tevens is het kleine tafeltje en stoeltje bekleed met sigarettenpeukjes en staande in een massa op de grond liggende peuken een symbolische kwinkslag naar de 'onschuldige' jeugd. Een jeugd waar menig kind voor een keuze kwam te staan of je stoer mee zou doen met het roken van een sigaret of niet. En dit is wat we de dag van vandaag nog steeds hebben. Een keuze maken. En keuzes dienen we te maken voor het behoud van onze natuur. Of beter gezegd het verbeteren van onze natuur.

Uit ervaring en reacties uit eerdere tentoonstellingen is geweten dat de meeste mensen eerder het werk appreciëren omdat ze zoveel sigarettenpeukjes samen zien tot één werk. Ze kijken meestal op van de hoeveelheid sigarettenpeukjes die erbij komt kijken, wat aanzet om dieper over het werk na te denken. Dit heb je veel in kunst en vind je ook terug bij andere kunstvormen. Zo is men soms meer verwonderd over de techniciteit die een kunstenaar bij een schilderij kan opbrengen om het werk te maken, maar kijkt men te weinig naar waarom de kunstenaar dit werk heeft geschilderd. Maar er is natuurlijk ook de esthetische appreciatie van een werk. Dit is uiteraard niet verkeerd. Door de juiste esthetiek te gebruiken, kun je namelijk ook de boodschap beter overbrengen.

Bij de werken van duizenden sigarettenpeukjes heb je ook nog de geur die de toeschouwer rechtstreeks aanvalt. Nog voor dat hij een concreet oordeel kan scheppen over het werk, zal hij door de geur al een onbewust vooroordeel hebben gecreëerd [21]. Dit vooroordeel wordt daarna in vraag gesteld doordat men er verder gaat over nadenken. Doordat de geur geen 100% sigarettengeur is, maar een mix van verschillende andere naar rook verwijzende geuren, is het vooroordeel over roken dubbel en geeft dit aan de toeschouwer de mogelijkheid het werk, zonder dat hij er zich van bewust is, te herkaderen.

Voetnoten

1 Tentoonstelling:"Silhouettes 'n' Shadows", Fundament Foundation, Tilburg, Netherlands, 01.09.2001 – 28.10.2001

2 In zijn boek 'A la recherche du temps perdu' beleeft de hoofdpersoon een intens gevoel van vreugde dat hij niet thuis kan brengen, nadat hij een cakeje, een madeleine, in de lindebloesemthee sopt en opeet. Dit cakeje gesopt in de lindebloesemthee doet hem denken aan zijn gelukkige jeugd.

3 Op 13 mei 2000 werd Nederland opgeschrikt door de explosie van de vuurwerkfabriek S.E. Fireworks in Enschede. Naast het verschrikkelijke feit dat er door de exploderende fabriek (die midden in de woonwijk Roombeek stond) 23 doden vielen, werd de hele woonwijk (van ongeveer 40 ha groot) weggeblazen. http://mens-en-samenleving.infonu.nl/diversen/17939-enschede-roombeek-na-de-vuurwerkramp.html

4 Pamela Dalton, Psychophysical and Behavioral Characteristics of Olfactory Adaptation Chem. Senses (2000) 25 (4): 487-492 doi:10.1093/chemse/25.4.487 http://chemse.oxfordjournals.org/content/25/4/487.abstract

5 BVOCs and global change, BVOC emissions in a changing world: an increasingly fragrant world? Josep Peñuelas, Michael Staudt, Trends in plant science doi:10.1016/j.tplants.2009.12.005 (volume 15 issue 3 pp.133 - 144)

6 GOM Genetic Olfactory Modification, term welke regelmatig terugkomt in de werken van Peter de Cupere

7 Jason Bremner, Ashley Frost, Carl Haub, Mark Mather, Karin Ringheim, and Eric Zuehlke, Population Reference Bureau, www.prb.org, Vol. 65, No. 2, july 2010, world population highlights: key findings from prb's 2010 world population data sheet. http://www.prb.org/pdf10/65.2highlights.pdf

8 International Energy Agency, World Energy Outlook 2013, How will global energy markets evolve to 2035? http://www.worldenergyoutlook.org/media/weowebsite/factsheets/weo2013_factsheets.pdf

9 De alambic (alambiek) behoort tot de oudste chemische apparaten en wordt al sinds Alexander de Grote (400 v. Chr.) gebruikt voor distillatie. Tegenwoordig wordt de alambic nog gebruikt in oude drankstokerijen of traditionele parfumbedrijven (cfr. Grasse). De oorsprong van de naam is niet geheel duidelijk maar mogelijk is het afgeleid van 'al inbiq', wat in het Arabisch 'in het vat' betekent. In de loop der tijd is de naam dan verbasterd van het Latijnse 'alembicus', het Franse 'alambic' en het oud-hollandse 'alembijk' tot het huidige 'alambic'.

10 Eran Pichersky and Natalia Dudareva, Scent engineering: toward the goal of controlling how flowers smell. http://labs.mcdb.lsa.umich.edu/labs/pichersky/references/Scentengineering.pdf

11 Tanaka, Y.; Brugliera, F.; Chandler, S. Recent Progress of Flower Colour Modification by Biotechnology. Int. J. Mol. Sci. 2009, 10, 5350-5369, http://www.mdpi.com/1422-0067/10/12/5350

12 Bharat B. Aggarwal, Anushree Kumar, Manoj S. Aggarwal, and Shishir Shishodia, Curcumin Derived from Turmeric (Curcuma longa): a Spice for All Seasons, © 2005 by CRC Press LLC, http://diyhpl.us/~bryan/papers2/longevity/Curcumin_A_Spice_For_All_Seasons.pdf

13 Mishra S, Palanivelu K. The effect of curcumin (turmeric) on Alzheimer's disease: An overview. Ann Indian Acad Neurol [serial online] 2008 [cited 2014 Jan 4];11:13-9. Available from: http://www.annalsofian.org/text.asp?2008/11/1/13/40220

14 B. Sasikumar, Genetic resources of Curcuma: diversity, characterization and utilization, Plant Genetic Resources: Characterization and Utilization, Volume 3, Issue 02, augustus 2005, pp 230 – 251 http://journals.cambridge.org/action/displayAbstract?fromPage=online&aid=685284 Published online: 12 februari 2007

15 Betekenissen van bepaalde geuren kunnen verschillen naargelang de cultuur. Wanneer ik het over geuren hebben die bij een bepaalde cultuur thuis horen, heb ik het steeds over de Westerse wereld, tenzij anders vermeld.

16 'My Soft World in Honour of My Mother' werd voor de eerste keer getoond in de 3° Biennale d'Art Contemporain de Louvain-La-Neuve", 13 mei tot 12 juni, 2000 in Louvain-La Neuve.

17 Olfactory Performance: 'The Soft Man, His Table And His Chair', 2000, 7 z/w photographs, 50 cm h x 70 cm b, Ed. of 3, 2 e.a, voor de eerste keer getoond in de solo tentoonstelling in Tim Van Laere Gallery, Antwerpen, 14 september tot 21 october, 2000.

18 Cotton Suit, made of 4000 natural cotton balls, voor de eerste keer getoond in de 3° Biennale d'Art Contemporain de Louvain-La-Neuve", 13 mei tot 12 juni, 2000 in Louvain-La Neuve

19 'Paris, Mon Amour', video, kleur, 7 min., http://vimeo.com/3137978
Voor de eerste keer getoond in de groepstentoonstelling: "Hit you with a flower", Tim Van Laere Gallery - Antwerp, Belgium, July - August, 2005, Atelier Van Lieshout, Jim Butler, Victoria Civera, Sergio De Beukelaer, Peter de Cupere, Bojan Fajfric, Nicolas Provost, Edward Lipski, Maryam Najd, Peter Rogiers, Thomas Schütte, Serse, Su-mei Tse, Juan Uslé, Franz West

20 Kortrijk Vlaandert, curator Hilde Van Canneyt, Kortrijk, BE, 04.07.2013 – 18.08.2013

21 Geur speelt in op de herinneringen, (tenzij men de geur nooit eerder heeft waargenomen), Harth R.: Brein en Geest, Hoe het brein de geest creëert, Bodoni, Baarn, 1995

HSUAN HSU

DE GEUR VAN RISICO

Vanaf de jaren 1990 produceerde Peter de Cupere een opmerkelijke verzameling olfactorische kunstwerken die experimenteren met de geur van zweet, genitaliën, snoep, tandpasta, urine, afval, vervuiling, gras, kardemom, pepermunt en andere stoffen. Volgens critici Larry Shiner en Yulia Kriskovets, creëerde de Cupere "een artistieke identiteit die een kruising is tussen kunstenaar en olfactorisch chemicus en in de toekomst model kan staan voor andere olfactorische kunstenaars". [1] In zijn werken komen tal van geurgerelateerde thema's aan bod, maar onlangs stelde de Cupere in Havana twee werken tentoon die aantonen dat olfactorische kunst ook een onderwerp als milieuverontreiniging kan behandelen.

In tegenstelling tot een visuele voorstelling van vervuiling en verontreiniging geeft de olfactorische kunst zowel materieel als representatief gestalte aan milieurisico's. Geur werd al lang uitgesloten van de esthetiek (omdat hij Kantiaanse waarden zoals autonomie en belangeloosheid bedreigt) en museumtentoonstellingen (omdat geur vluchtig is, moeilijk te bevatten en een bedreiging vormt voor zowel bezoekers als nabije kunstwerken). De geurwaarneming werd gemarginaliseerd omdat ze de mogelijk onhandelbare, bovenlichamelijke aard van alle materie openbaart. Stacy Alaimo beschrijft het als "de materiële verbindingen tussen de menselijke lichamelijkheid en de bovenmenselijke wereld". [2] Toch zorgden net de eigenschappen die geur ooit marginaliseerden ervoor dat het vanaf de jaren 1960 een intrigerend medium werd voor experimentele kunstenaars. Kunstenaars en critici voelen zich niet alleen tot geur aangetrokken omwille van zijn meeslepende kwaliteiten, maar ook omdat geur herinneringen kan oproepen en inwerkt op het limbisch systeem van de hersenen. [2] Volgens antropoloog Mark Graham vertoont geur een opvallende verwantschap met de postmoderne esthetische waarden. Zicht werd beschreven als het modernistische zintuig bij uitstek (Levin 1993). Zicht onderscheidt, verdeelt en ordent de wereld in elkaar uitsluitende categorieën. Geur werd daarentegen benoemd als postmodernistisch (Classen, Howes en Synnott 1994: 203-5). Het is het zintuig dat categorieën doet samensmelten en grenzen overstijgt. Het is moeilijk te lokaliseren, moeilijk te bevatten en heeft een veranderend en vergankelijk karakter. [3]

Aangezien lucht een vergankelijke, beweeglijke en bovenlichamelijke aard heeft, kan ze niet functioneren als een 'zuiver' esthetisch medium. Om te worden waargenomen, moeten geuren worden toegevoegd die communiceren met ons lichaam en de omgeving op manieren die we niet altijd onder controle hebben. Lucht kan een medium zijn voor verontreiniging maar ook voor gewaarwording. Bovendien zijn luchtdeeltjes, die met onze lichamen en geesten kunnen interageren, niet altijd waarneembaar en wordt hun bedwelmende vermogen niet volledig begrepen. Voor zover de overdracht gepaard gaat met dergelijke onzekere bovenlichamelijke uitwisselingen, overstijgt geur het ideaal van zuiverheid dat zowel de visuele waarneming als conventionele milieuwaarden beheerst.

De olfactorische kunst biedt een krachtig medium voor esthetische experimenten met toxinen in de lucht. Antropoloog Timothy Choy stelt in zijn baanbrekende discours over de luchtvervuiling in Hongkong dat lucht functioneert als een heuristiek die tal van atmosferische ervaringen kan omvatten. De abstractie van lucht kan niet worden gebaseerd op de vergelijking van eenheden of een gemeenschappelijk domein waarbinnen specifieke kenmerken moeten worden geordend, maar gebeurt door de samenvoeging van materialiteiten die niet tot elkaar kunnen worden herleid (bijvoorbeeld adem, vocht, SARS, deeltjes, enzovoort). Nadenken over de materialiteit van lucht en de menselijke verstrengelingsdichtheid met betrekking tot lucht, betekent ook aandacht besteden aan de stollende en smeltende grenzen tussen mensen, regio's en gebeurtenissen.[4]

Lucht vestigt de aandacht op onze materiële interacties met verschillende atmosferische stoffen. Daarnaast belichaamt lucht de vaak over het hoofd geziene stroom van levende materialen tussen gedifferentieerde ruimten en geografische schaalniveaus. Lucht is voor Choy dus een belangrijk element om een theorie te vormen over sociale relaties en gevoelens in materiële termen. "Nadenken over lucht, dat wil zeggen, lucht niet beschouwen als het tegenovergestelde van vastheid, kan een manier bieden om na te denken over relaties en bewegingen tussen plaatsen, mensen, dingen, schalen; een manier om de gebruikelijke valkuilen van particulariteit en universaliteit te voorkomen."

Door de nadruk te leggen op de vluchtige positie van Cuba in het mondiale geopolitieke systeem, illustreren de recente werken van de Cupere hoe olfactorische kunst op een viscerale manier de omgevingsverschillen kan overbrengen die worden gepropageerd door geografisch ongelijke ontwikkeling. *Smoke Cloud* (2014), dat te zien was tijdens de tentoonstelling *The Importance of Being*... van 2015 in Havana, [5] bestaat uit een ladder onder een witte wolk die aan het plafond van de galerij hangt. De bezoekers stappen één voor één op de ladder, steken hun hoofd in de wolk en ruiken de geur van luchtvervuiling. De installatie interageert met de bezoekers, zowel visueel (door anderen het ongerijmde schouwspel te bieden van een lichaam met zijn hoofd in een wolk) als bovenlichamelijk (door de ruiker de geur van luchtvervuiling te laten opsnuiven). De uitdrukking 'met het hoofd in de wolken' verwijst doorgaans naar de neiging tot fantasie of idealisme. De smogwolk van de Cupere dompelt de bezoekers onder in de materialiteit van lucht: via chemische of psychosomatische kanalen kan de geur van smog de stemming of gezondheid van een bezoeker fysiek beïnvloeden. De resulterende wrijving tussen de visuele en olfactorische dimensies van *Smoke Cloud* – beschouwing vs. inademing van smog, beklimming vs. intoxicatie, zichtbare schoonheid vs. onzichtbare schade – verstoort de visuele orde van de kunstgalerij. De hoofden van de bezoekers verdwijnen een voor een in de wolk. Voor degene die op de ladder staat, verdwijnt de galerijruimte terwijl de geur van smog komt opzetten. Volgens de Cupere is de beslissing om de wolk te vullen met de geur van luchtvervuiling deels geïnspireerd op de slechte luchtkwaliteit van Havana, meer bepaald "de krachtige geur van benzine die de oude Chevy's en Buicks uitbraken". [6] De vervuilde lucht van *Smoke Cloud* verwijst niet alleen naar de luchtvervuiling in de Cubaanse steden, maar ook naar de oorsprong ervan die in de handelsembargo's uit de periode van de Koude Oorlog ligt.

The Smell of a Stranger (2015), de bijdrage van de Cupere aan de twaalfde Biënnale van Havana, werd buiten tentoongesteld aan het Hoger Instituut voor Technologie en Toegepaste Wetenschappen aan de Universiteit van Havana. Door de vermenging van geurengineering, bio-engineering en het ethos van speculatieve fictie, creëert *The Smell of a Stranger* een waarschuwende allegorie over bio-engineering en over 'het zich openstellen' van Cuba voor de Amerikaanse handel en diplomatie. Op basis van geuren geleverd door International Flavors & Fragrances, kon de Cupere negen inheemse Cubaanse bloemen en planten genetisch modificeren. Hoewel de resultaten lijken op natuurlijke exemplaren, verspreidt de flora van de Cupere een aantal niet te rijmen geuren, zoals "nieuwe Amerikaanse dollars, bloed, sperma, vagina, lijk, buskruit, zweet (de geur van angst), luchtvervuiling en geraniums". [7] Door de schoonheid van de lokale planten te laten contrasteren met geuren die doen denken aan sekstoerisme, arbeidsuitbuiting, militair geweld, vervuiling, industriële voedselproductie (de kunstenaar wilde de geuren van hamburgers en frietjes toevoegen, maar ze werden weggelaten om technische redenen [8]) en de dood, suggereert de Cupere dat het openstellen van de handel en diplomatie tussen de VS en Cuba onder de regering Obama verwoestende gevolgen kan hebben voor de bevolking en het milieu van Cuba. Volgens de kunstenaar "baant de westerse cultuur zich langzaam een weg [in Cuba] en zal de hoofdstad automatisch volgen. Cuba heeft een schat aan natuur en cultuur die kan worden gebruikt met slechte bedoelingen". [9] De postnatuurlijke toestand van genetisch gemanipuleerde bloemen verwijst in bredere zin naar de kwetsbaarheid van het Cubaanse milieu voor kapitalistische invallen. *The Smell of a Stranger* ontkracht de verwachting dat bloemen en planten verfrissende, 'natuurlijke' geuren afgeven. De ruiker blijft verward, zelfs walgend achter door de viscerale of onnatuurlijke geuren. Verschillende ruikers kunnen de geur van sperma, zweet, geld en voedsel fysiek opwindend of weerzinwekkend vinden. De geur van luchtvervuiling kan, net zoals bij *Smoke Cloud*, letterlijk giftig zijn voor milieugevoelige bezoekers. Dergelijke fysieke reacties brengen visceraal over hoe de omgeving die we creëren ons lichaam, geest en gevoel beïnvloedt aan de hand van bovenlichamelijke uitwisselingen. Door het werk buiten op te stellen onderstreept de kunstenaar de visuele continuïteit van de planten met de natuurlijke omgeving van Cuba. Daarnaast omzeilt hij de praktische problemen waarmee curatoren in een overdekte galerij worden geconfronteerd, zoals ongewenste blootstelling en geurvermenging.

De titel van de installatie verwijst naar de culturele specificiteit van geur of de manier waarop onze perceptie van aantrekkelijke en afstotende geuren varieert over de culturele grenzen heen. [10] Geur mag dan al culturele en sociale grenzen afbakenen, *The Smell of a Stranger* roept het idee op van een ethische ontmoeting met de 'Andere', een multicultureel scenario waarin Cubanen en buitenlanders elkaar beter kunnen leren kennen. In plaats van de belofte van multiculturele reukzin in te lossen, confronteert de Cupere de bezoeker met een heel ander soort 'vreemdeling': postnatuurlijke planten die menselijke geuren verspreiden. Heel wat van deze geuren zijn noch Cubanen noch Amerikanen 'vreemd': sperma, geld, lijken, buskruit, luchtvervuiling. Hun vreemdheid ligt echter in de juxtapositie ten opzichte van elkaar en de schijnbaar 'natuurlijke' planten van de installatie. Hoewel de geuren van Amerikaans en Belgisch voedsel kunnen worden beschouwd als een "grappige verwijzing naar onze westerse cultuur met de geur van hamburgers" [11], krijgt de verwijzing naar hamburgers en friet een donkere connotatie wanneer ze wordt gecombineerd met de geur van geld en dode lichamen. Hamburgers en frietjes mogen dan al symbool staan voor de Amerikaanse en Belgische cultuur, [12] het zijn ook voedingsmiddelen die een bovenlichamelijk effect hebben op het menselijk lichaam wanneer je ze eet of ruikt. Industrieel geproduceerd fastfood is een instrument van ongezonde voeding en obesitas. Lauren Berlant noemt het een 'langzame dood' [13] op wereldschaal: het verbruik van hamburgers kan worden vergeleken met een uitwisseling van geld voor vroegtijdige overlijdens in ongelijk ontwikkelde gebieden. Of ze nu worden overgebracht via fastfood, sekstoerisme, kapitalistische uitbuiting of militarisering, [14] ongelijke ontwikkeling en economisch imperialisme dreigen nieuwe gezondheidsrisico's met zich mee te brengen voor de Cubaanse mens en andere levensvormen. De 'vreemdeling' is hier niet de Amerikaanse cultuur, maar het soort plaats dat Cuba dreigt te worden. Het concept 'langzaam geweld' van Rob Nixon verwijst naar een wijdverspreide vorm van milieugeweld waarvan de 'temporele dispersie' uitdagingen inhoudt voor de vertegenwoordiging en het politiek engagement. Het idee verduidelijkt waar het bij de dystopische geuren van de Cupere om gaat: omdat het jaren kan duren voor de gezondheidseffecten van fastfood, militarisering en ongebreideld kapitalisme zichtbaar worden, gebruikt de Cupere een speculatieve – maar tegelijk materiële en visceraal bovenlichamelijke – vorm van tijdelijke condensatie als een middel om uitdrukking te geven aan toekomstige bedreigingen. [15] *The Smell of a Stranger* creëert daarmee een krachtige allegorie die waarschuwt voor de grimmige kansen die door de geïntensiveerde neoliberalisering van de Cubaanse economie ontstaan. De kwetsbaarheid van Cuba voor ongelijke transnationale stromen van verlangen, risico en uitbuiting wordt op deze manier proleptisch gedramatiseerd. Net als in het magisch realisme registreren de genetisch gemanipuleerde Cubaanse planten van de Cupere de ontwrichtende effecten van transnationale contacten en kapitaalverkeer op de lokale realiteit.

De meer dan realistische aspecten van *The Smell of a Stranger* bestaan echter daadwerkelijk als materiële producten van de genetica, biotechnologie en geurwetenschap. De olfactorische kunstwerken van de Cupere zijn een uitdaging voor de typische ijle lucht van westerse musea, die erop gericht zijn kunstvoorwerpen duidelijk zichtbaar voor te stellen. Ze bedwelmen de lichamen van de toeschouwers/toeruikers tot in hun diepste wezen en doen de milieuproblemen op geografische schaal ver buiten de 'witte kubussen' van klimaatgeregelde galerijen treden. Ze tonen aan dat de olfactorische esthetiek over het vermogen beschikt om de hedendaagse kruisingen te onderscheiden tussen milieurisico's, ongelijke regio's en de transformatieve mentale, emotionele en fysieke effecten van lucht op gedifferentieerde lichamen en bevolkingen.

Hsuan Hsu

Voetnoten

Dit essay is een aangepaste versie van een artikel dat oorspronkelijk werd gepubliceerd in Resilience: A Journal of the Environmental Humanities. Met dank aan University of Nebraska Press voor de toestemming om de gebruikte fragmenten te mogen herdrukken.

1 Larry Shiner en Yulia Kriskovets, "The Aesthetics of Smelly Art", Journal of Aesthetics and Art Criticism 65:3 (zomer 2007), 274.

2 Stacy Alaimo, Bodily Natures: Science, Environment, and the Material Self (Bloomington, Indiana, 2010), 2.

3 Mark Graham, "Queer Smells: Fragrances of Late Capitalism or Scents of Subversion?" in The Smell Culture Reader, ed. Jim Drobnick (Oxford: Berg, 2006), 305.

4 Timothy Choy, "Air's Substantiations" in ed. Kaushik Sunder Rajan, Lively Capital: Biotechnologies, Ethics, and Governance in Global Markets (Durham: Duke University Press, 2012) 128.

5 Nog voor de tentoonstelling in Havana was Smoke Cloud voor het eerst te zien op 'The Art of Smelling, an Olfactory Art Research' (2014), een solotentoonstelling van de Cupere in Nederland. De kunstenaar merkte echter op dat het werk is geïnspireerd op de geur van luchtvervuiling in Havana (zie n° 6 hieronder).

6 Sam Steverlynck, "A Major Exhibition of Belgian Art Opens in Havana", http://www.havana-live.com/news/2015/02/23/a-major-exhibition-of-belgian-art-opens-in-havana.html (geraadpleegd op 1 sep. 2015).

7 Peter de Cupere, persoonlijke communicatie met de auteur, 20 maart 2016.

8 Op basis van de eerste interviews werd in gepubliceerde verslagen over de tentoonstelling vermeld dat de Cupere "de geur van sperma, zweet, lijken, geld, buskruit, luchtvervuiling, hamburgers en friet" zou gebruiken. De geuren van hamburger en Belgische frieten (waarbij de laatste geur ook een verwijzing was naar het land van herkomst van de kunstenaar) werden uiteindelijk weggelaten om technische redenen (Katherine Brooks, "Artist 'Scent Engineers' Plants to Smell Like Dead Bodies, Sperm, and Air Pollution", Huffington Post [13 mei 2015], http://www.huffingtonpost.com/2015/05/13/peter-de-cupere-scent_n_7274034.html [geraadpleegd op 1 sep. 2015], Peter de Cupere, persoonlijke communicatie met de auteur, 20 maart 2016).

9 Geciteerd in Brooks, "Artist 'Scent Engineers' Plants".

10 Zie bijvoorbeeld Gale Largey en Rod Watson, "The Sociology of Odors" in The Smell Culture Reader, ed. Drobnick, 29-40, Martin F. Manalansan IV, "Immigrant Lives and the Politics of Olfaction in the Global City" in The Smell Culture Reader 41-52 en Alan Hyde, "Offensive Bodies" in The Smell Culture Reader, 53-58.

11 Sara Alonso Gómez, "Exhibition 'The Smell of a Stranger' by Peter de Cupere" (23 mei 2015), https://www.facebook.com/events/1595498134023675 (geraadpleegd op 1 sep. 2015).

12 De Cupere legt uit dat Belgische frieten verwijzen naar zijn eigen medeplichtigheid als Belg en Europeaan, zodat "de Amerikaanse eetcultuur niet als enige schuldige wordt aangewezen. Mensen moeten eerst kijken wat ze zelf verkeerd doen voor ze anderen de schuld geven. De wereld is niet van mij alleen, maar van ons. Het is jammer dat ik deze twee geuren niet kon gebruiken." (Peter de Cupere, persoonlijke communicatie met de auteur, 20 maart 2016)

13 Lauren Berlant, "Slow Death (Sovereignty, Obesity, Lateral Agency)", Critical Inquiry 33 (zomer 2007), 754-80.

14 De geur van buskruit symboliseert hier verschillende stukken die eerder in 2015 door de Cupere naast kogels en legerhelmen werden geplaatst en gecombineerd met de geur van lijken en bloed in de tentoonstelling 'The Smell of War', waar hij naast curator ook deelnemend kunstenaar was.

15 Rob Nixon, Slow Violence and the Environmentalism of the Poor (Cambridge: Harvard University Press, 2011), 3.

PETER DE CUPERE

NEUZEN EN BINNENNEUZEN

Stel je voor dat mensen een neus op hun gezicht hadden die naar binnen was gericht. Geen uitwendige neus dus, maar een inwendige. Een exacte kopie van een echte neus, maar gewoon naar binnen. Een neus die als het ware als een mal zou kunnen dienen voor een andere neus. Hoe zou je dan ademen en ruiken? Waar zouden de olfactorische zenuwen liggen? Hoe zou er een verbinding met het limbische systeem worden gemaakt?

En hoe zouden we seks hebben? Je zou immers veel dichter bij je partner kunnen komen als de ene een inwendige neus had en de andere een uitwendige. Hoe geweldig zou het niet zijn als de ene neus in de andere paste. Elkaar 'neuzen' zou een heerlijk onderdeel van de intimiteit zijn. Maar wie zou een uitwendige en wie een inwendige neus hebben? Zouden we ze binnenneuzen en buitenneuzen noemen of inwendige en uitwendige neuzen? Zou een binnenneus zo goed kunnen ruiken als een buitenneus of omgekeerd? Zouden de neusgaten elkaar en de binnenkant van de neus ruiken? Zouden ze op elkaar ademen? Welke mens zou welke neus hebben? Kunnen we deze neuzen vergelijken met een penis en vagina? Zou een vrouw een binnenneus hebben en een man een buitenneus of omgekeerd of gemengd? Zou een binnenneus zacht en soepel zijn als een vagina en zou een buitenneus hard als een penis kunnen worden? Wat zou het zalig zijn als de ene in de andere paste. Zouden de neusharen worden gewaxt? Zouden er wipneuzen zijn, haakneuzen, stompe neuzen, grote en kleine neuzen? En wat met bloedneuzen, verstopte neuzen en loopneuzen? Zou gezichtsneuken realiteit worden?

ANNELIES NAGELS

EENS WAS IK EEN MENS (2016)

In *La Passion de Jeanne d'Arc* – een Franse stomme film uit 1928 – zien we hoe actrice Maria Falconetti kaal geknipt wordt in de scène waarin ze als Jeanne d'Arc klaar gemaakt wordt voor de executie. Het verhaal deed destijds de ronde dat de hele filmcrew toekeek hoe Falconetti kaal geknipt werd en in tranen uitbarstte. Dat het knippen van haren grote emoties kan losmaken hoeft niet te verbazen.

Laurent Philippon wijdt in zijn boek over haar één hoofdstuk aan 'los haar'. Haar heeft een relatie met ons dierlijk verleden. Wanneer we het temmen met borstels, kammen, spelden, poeders en oliën benadrukken we onze evolutie weg van het primitieve en richting beschaving. Maar wanneer we het los laten hangen, bevrijden we onszelf en keren we terug naar onze natuurlijke staat. Daardoor vallen er ook remmingen weg. Vele eeuwen lang en in verschillende maatschappijen, werd het los dragen van haar voorbehouden voor intieme momenten. In sommige culturen is het überhaupt tonen van haar enkel toegelaten in intieme kring. Ook bij een man kan lang haar kracht en mannelijkheid symboliseren. Denk maar aan de figuur van Samson in het oude testament.

Als je haar afgeschoren wordt, kan dat gedwongen of vrijwillig zijn. Bij het vrijwillig kaalscheren gaat het vaak om het begin van een nieuwe levensfase. Het is zwaar beladen met symboliek. Monniken die in het klooster treden, pelgrims bij een bedevaart, maar ook het kaalscheren als teken dat je als jongere tot een subcultuur wilt behoren. In zijn werk *Eens was ik een mens* focust Peter de Cupere de aandacht op het onvrijwillig kaalgeschoren of geknipt worden. Twee erg uiteenlopende situaties linkt hij aan elkaar. Aan de ene kant toont hij getuigenissen van kankerpatiënten. Het verlies van haar is een gekende bijwerking van chemotherapie. Aan de andere kant toont hij getuigenissen van overlevenden van het vernietigingskamp Auschwitz. Daar werden mensen bij aankomst kaal geschoren onder het mom van hygiëne, maar het was duidelijk een vorm van vernedering.
In zijn interviews met de kankerpatiënten en de Auschwitz-overlevenden gaat Peter de Cupere in op hun geurervaringen. Bij de kankerpatiënten gaat dit over het verlies aan reukvermogen, of het veranderen ervan. Sommige geuren worden sterker waargenomen. Andere niet meer. Bij de Auschwitz-overlevenden focust de kunstenaar op hoe geur een herinnering kan uitlokken. De connectie tussen haar en geur zit immers in de traumatische ervaring die samenhangt met het verlies van haar. Zoals blijkt uit een onderzoek aan de Universiteit van Utrecht, zorgt geur soms voor terugkeer van aangeleerde angstassociaties.
Het menselijk reukorgaan maakt – anatomisch gezien – deel uit van de hypothalamus. Op die plek in de hersenen wordt geur verwerkt. De hypothalamus speelt een cruciale rol bij onbewust en instinctief gedrag, denk maar aan het reguleren van emoties als angst en de lichamelijke reactie daarop. Tegelijk is deze hersenzone betrokken bij geheugenverwerking. Er zijn dus belangrijke verbanden tussen de wijze waarop angst aangeleerd wordt en de wijze waarop geurinformatie wordt verwerkt. Tussen het geheugen en geur kan dan ook een sterke relatie bestaan, resistent tegen uitdoving. Dit geldt nog meer wanneer een geur aanwezig is bij heftige emotionele gebeurtenissen. Geur kan als een sleutel dienen voor een herinnering waarmee een emotie gepaard gaat. Dit hoeft geen geur te zijn die bewust wordt waargenomen. Het kan ook gaan om een onbekende of neutrale geur. Het Amerikaanse leger heeft zogenaamde 'oefendorpen' om hun soldaten in een realistische situatie te laten oefenen. Bij een voorbereidend bezoek aan deze dorpen gaven oorlogsveteranen aan dat zonder de typische penetrerende geur die voortkwam uit een combinatie van lijken, wapenkruid en open riolen er geen sprake kon zijn van een correcte weerspiegeling van wat zij in Irak hadden beleefd. Geur werd door hen als essentieel ervaren.

De geur van de concentratiekampen is uiteraard lang vervlogen. Maar naast stapels koffers, kleren, schoenen en brillen kan je in Auschwitz tot vandaag nog steeds de bergen haar zien liggen. Afgeknipte vlechten, paardenstaarten, los haar. In de ruimtes waar deze 'collecties' nog steeds te bezichtigen zijn, hangt een zeer specifieke geur. En na een bezoek aan Auschwitz, blijft deze geur de bezoeker ongetwijfeld sterk bij.

Met de titel van het werk – *Eens was ik een mens* – verwijst Peter de Cupere naar het boek dat Primo Levi schreef in 1947 over zijn tijd in het concentratiekamp Auschwitz. Het onvrijwillig verlies van haar gaat gepaard met een gevoel van verlies van identiteit. Het hoofdpersonage uit dit boek vertelt over het kampleven en over hoe de ontmenselijking steeds maar verder gaat. Op een schijnbaar objectieve wijze doet Levi verslag van alle kleine dagelijkse gebeurtenissen. Maar tussen de lijnen door hangt er een constante spanning.

Uit zijn collectie van ca. 21.000 menselijke paardenstaarten toont de kunstenaar in dit werk een kleine selectie. De staarten krijgen een eigen geur mee. Een menselijke geur, die verbonden is met een welbepaalde menselijke identiteit. Hiermee wil Peter de Cupere al die verloren identiteiten weer in ere herstellen. De menselijkheid terug naar voren brengen en laten zegevieren.

PETER DE CUPERE

TER NAGEDACHTENIS VAN CAFLO YROT (1874-1970, UA)

De Oekraïense kunstenaar Caflo Yrot was dokter, tolk en leraar. In zijn vrije tijd maakte hij kunstwerken waarbij hoofdzakelijk geur als medium en het idee van geur centraal stonden. Hij kwam echter nooit naar buiten met zijn werken. Begin april 2014 nam Caflo's zoon contact op met Peter de Cupere om hem te laten kennismaken met de werken van zijn vader.

Men moet het werk van Caflo Yrot in zijn tijdsgeest plaatsen. Kunst was eind 1800, begin 1900 niet zo extreem vooruitstrevend in Oekraïne. Caflo Yrot was hierop een uitzondering.

Le parfum de sang (Het parfum van bloed) – Als dokter was Caflo Yrot sterk geïnteresseerd in het lichaam en de geuren van het menselijk lichaam. Hij was van mening dat bloed het meest persoonlijke parfum was. Bloed heeft nochtans een vrij metaalachtige geur. Voor Caflo was bloed het parfum van het leven. Zonder bloed kunnen we niet leven, maar we kunnen ons eigen levensparfum niet ruiken omdat het in ons lichaam zit. Om de geur te kunnen waarnemen, kwam hij op het idee om een parfumpomp te verbinden aan een naald. Door in je lichaam te prikken en het bloed over je huid te verspreiden, kon je je eigen levensparfum ruiken. Een absurd idee, maar heel gedurfd voor zijn tijd. En als dokter wist hij waarschijnlijk wel wat hij deed.

Tabac à Priser Rouge (Tabak om te snuiven, rood) – Zijn *Tabac à Priser Rouge* bestond uit verschillende thema's. Hij maakte een reeks briefkaarten van apotheken waarbij hij telkens een rode bal op een fles aanbracht. De rode bal kan worden beschouwd als de neus van een clown, zoals bij andere van zijn werken. Een andere reeks bestond uit afbeeldingen van openbare gebouwen met een rode bal op. Hij hing zijn werken altijd ondersteboven. Dat was geen louter esthetische beslissing. Voor Caflo Yrot betekende het dat men zijn werk anders moest lezen, met andere woorden in omgekeerde zin. De neus van de clown moet hier dus niet worden geïnterpreteerd als iets vrolijks, maar heeft eerder een pijnlijke betekenis. Het was zijn manier om te reageren op bepaalde situaties. Een prachtig voorbeeld hiervan is zijn reeks met postzegels van Hitler. Hij was een fervent tegenstander van Hitler en wilde hem bespotten door een rode neus op hem te plakken en de postzegel ondersteboven te hangen. Caflo Yrot plaatste ook graag kleine opmerkingen bij zijn objecten, net als in tijdschriften of boeken. Zo schreef hij de namen van bloemen en planten op de technische tekeningen van kogels.

Meer informatie over het werk van Caflo Yrot is te vinden op de website www.theolfactory.org, in de publicatie van *The Smell of War* (www.thesmellofwar.be) en binnenkort op de website www.cafloyrot.com.

PETER DE CUPERE

TO CONCEPTUALISE AN IMAGE
A Visual Journey

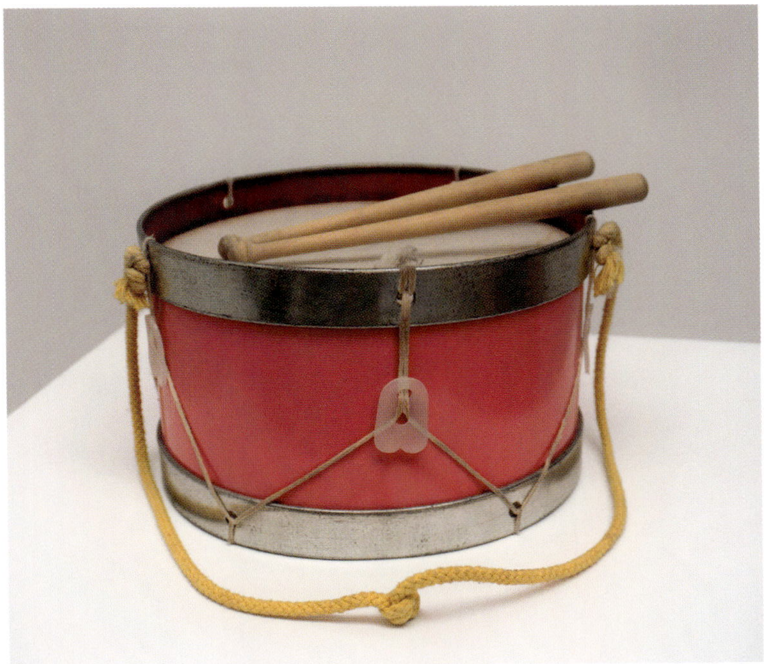

 Smell Drum, 1974

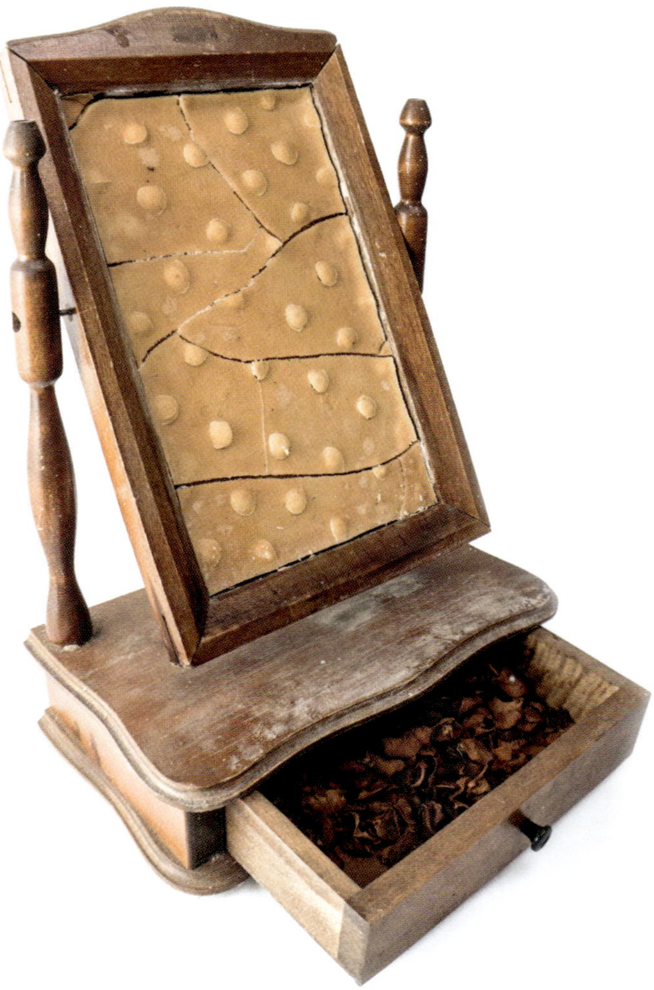

Broken Soap Mirror, 1998

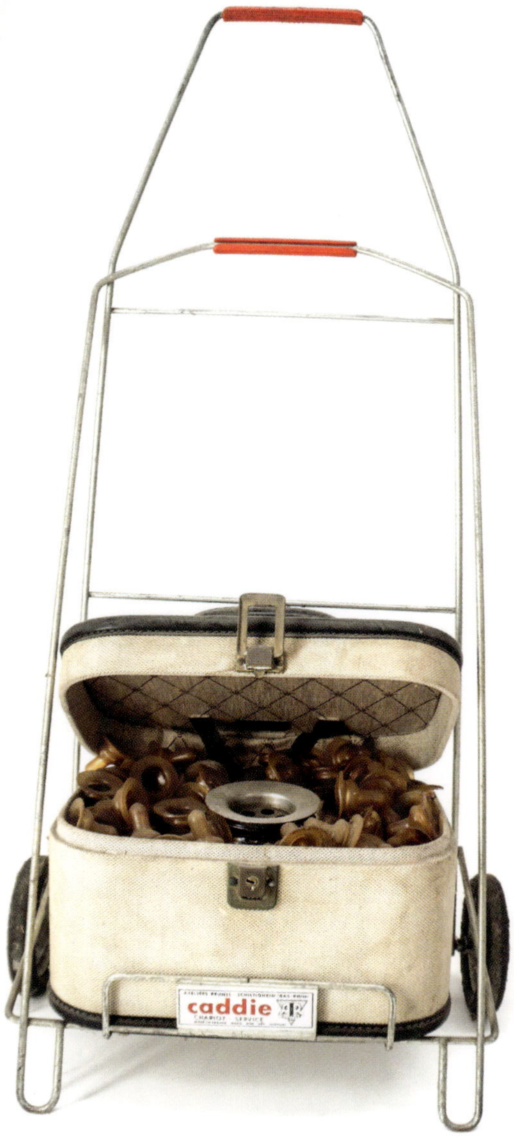

 Beauty of Birth, 1997

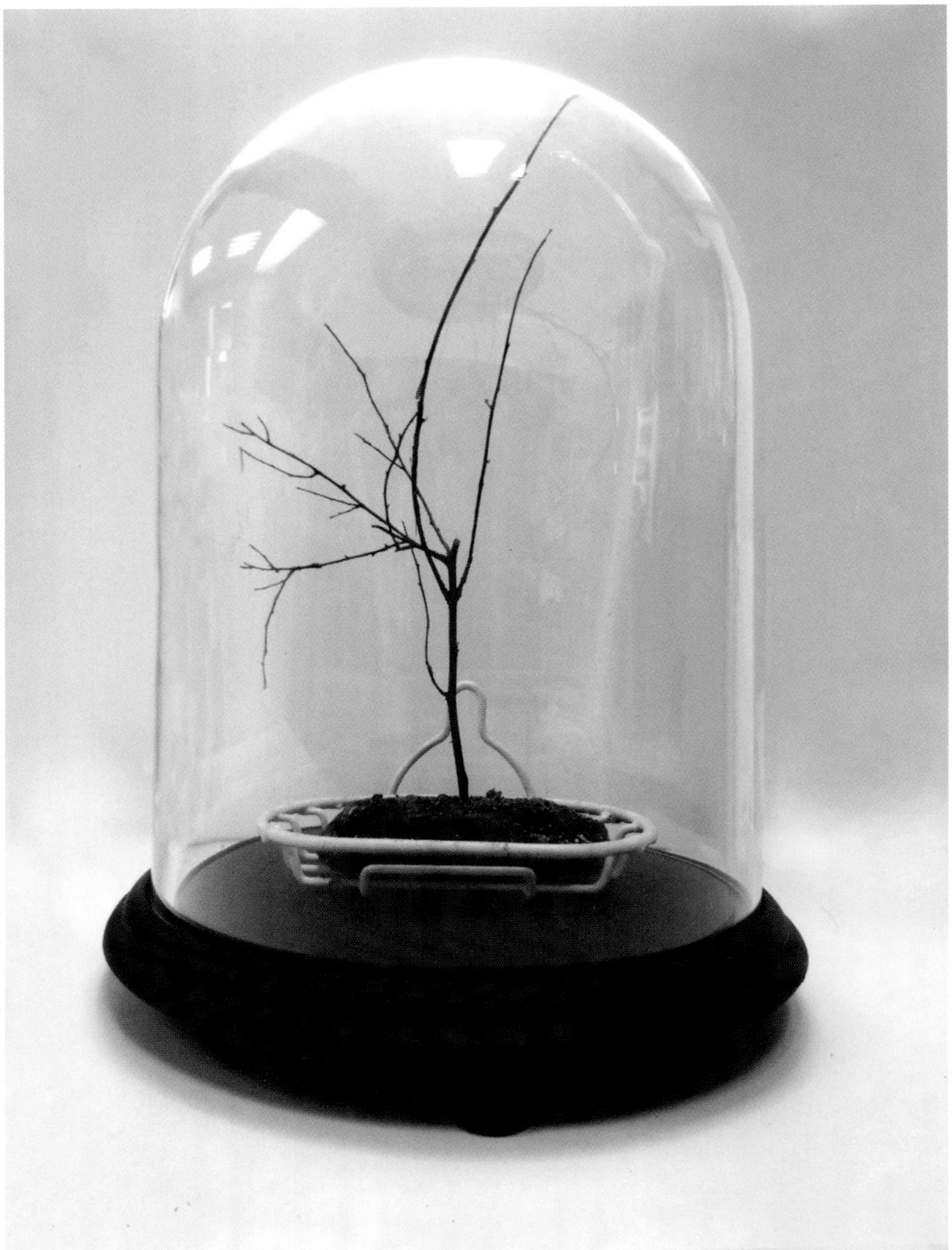

Earth Soap, 2002

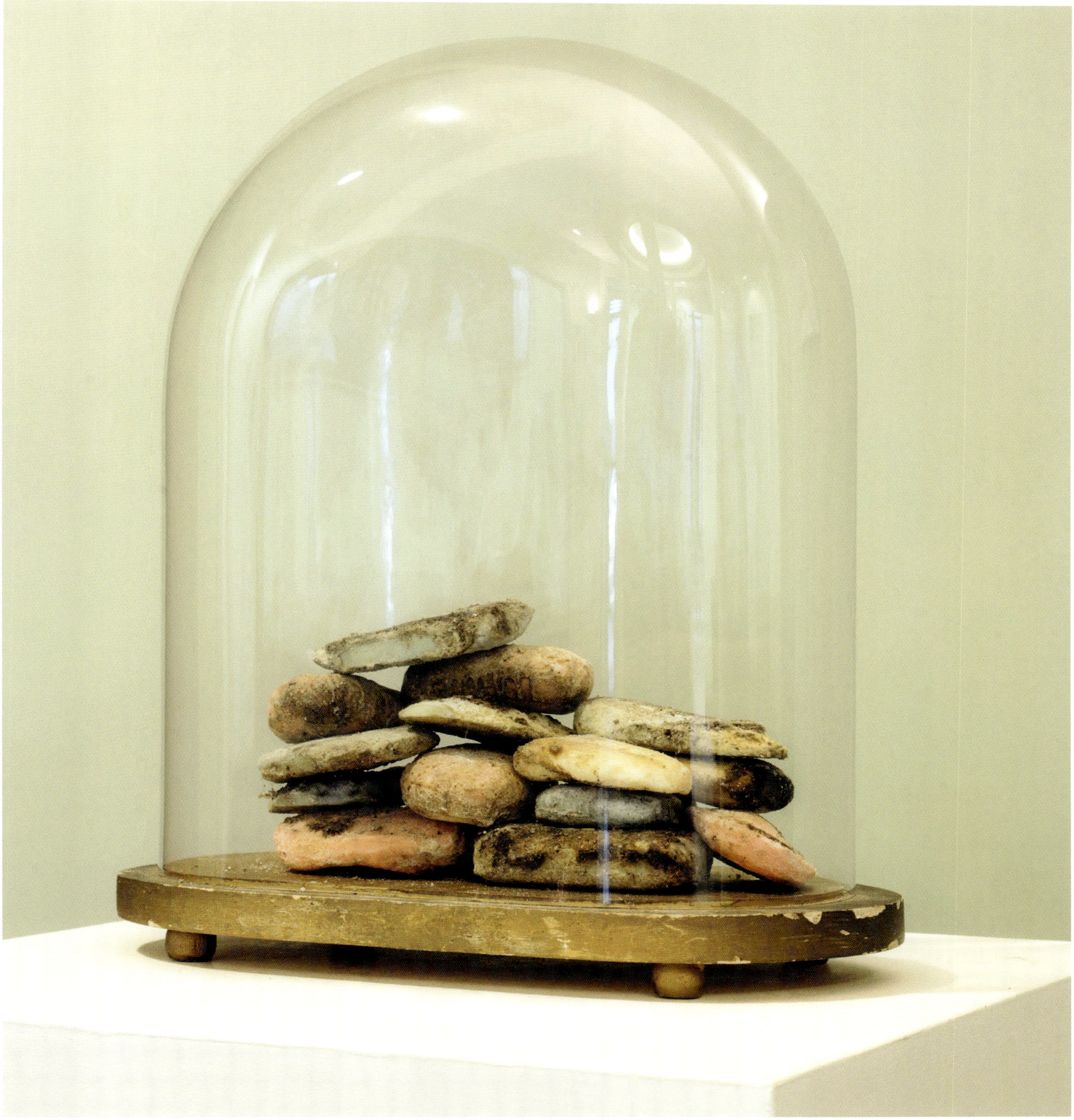

 Future Garbage 2, 1996-1998

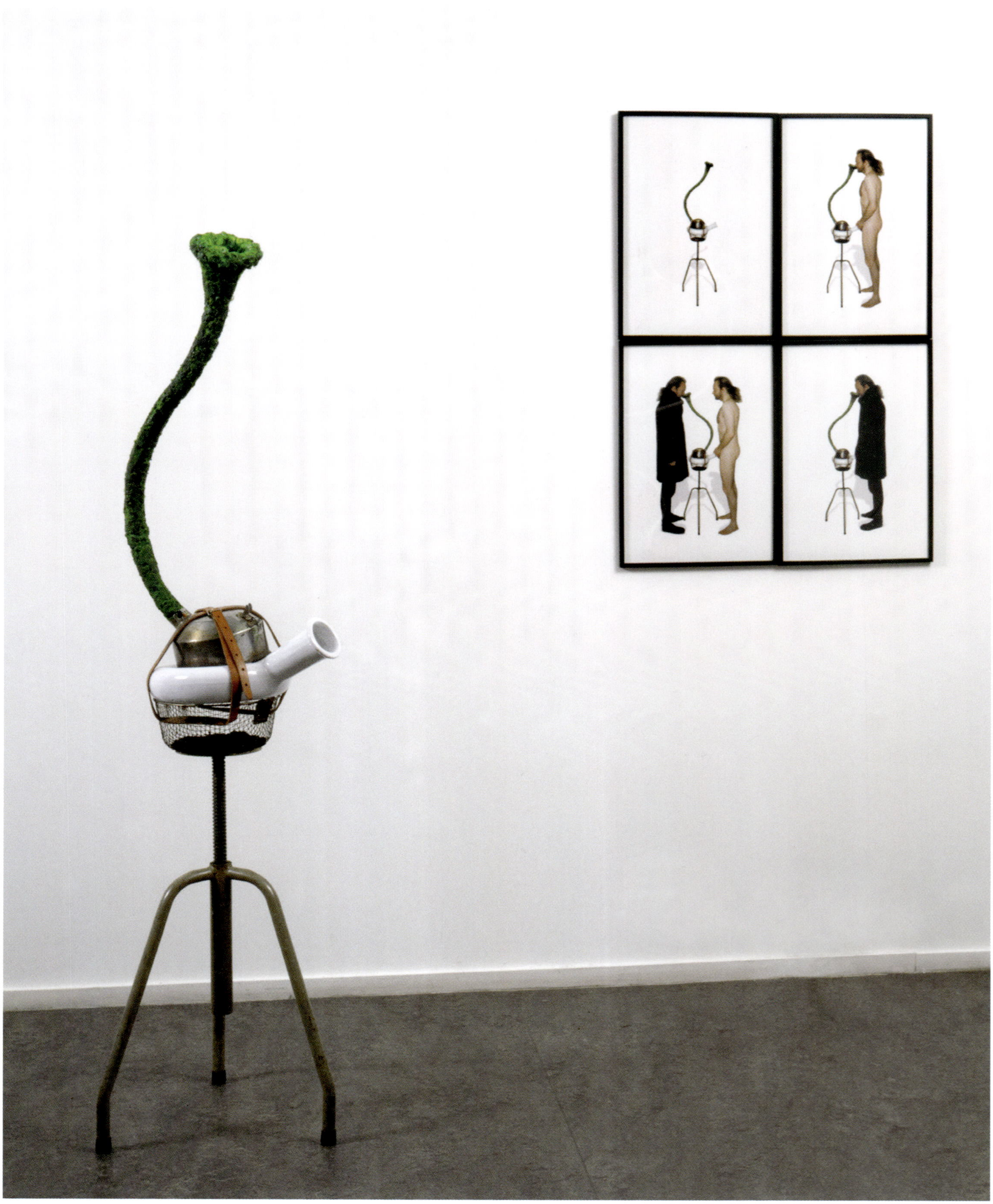

Pipifleur, 2001-2002

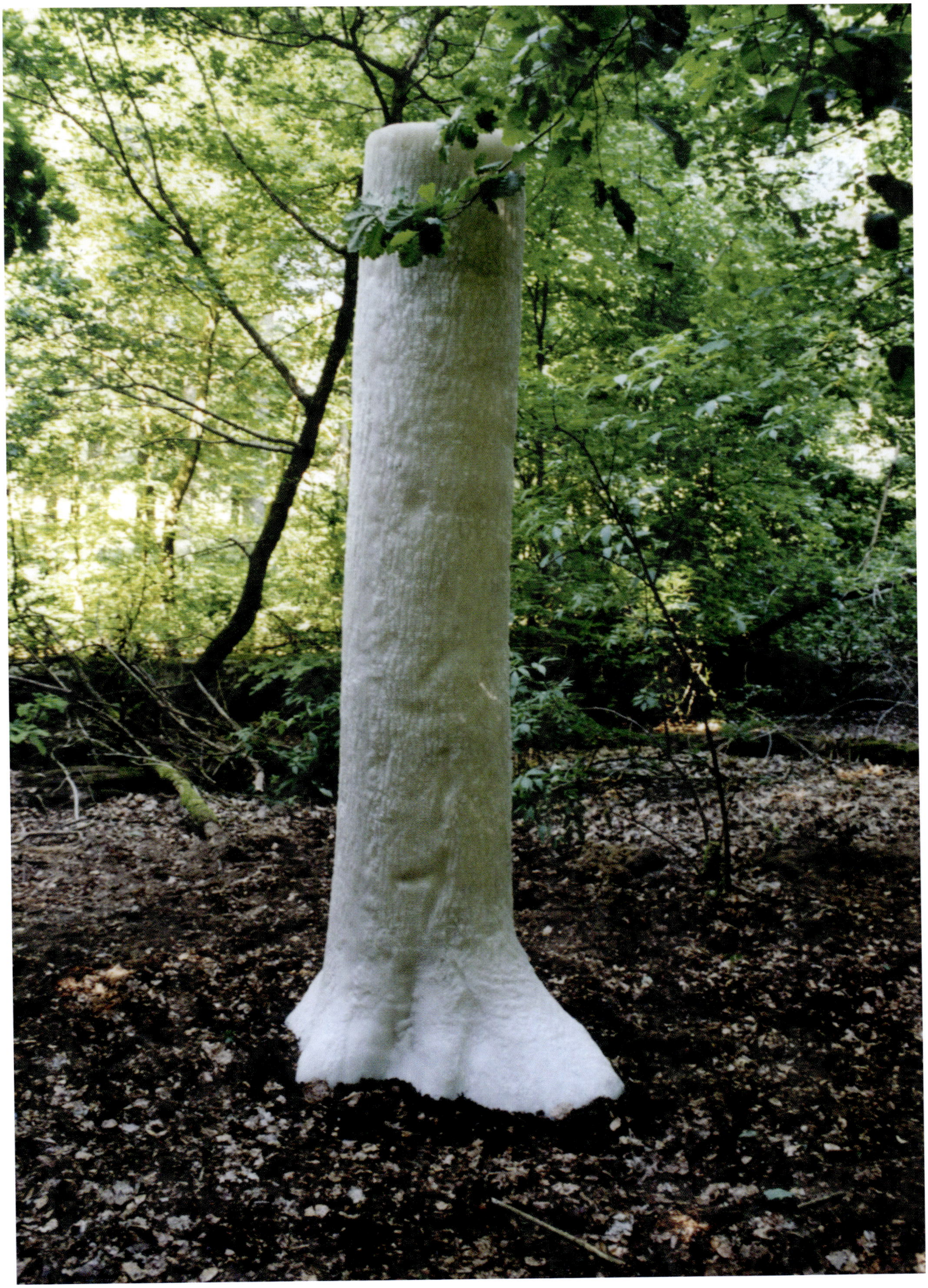

The Right Tree, 2001

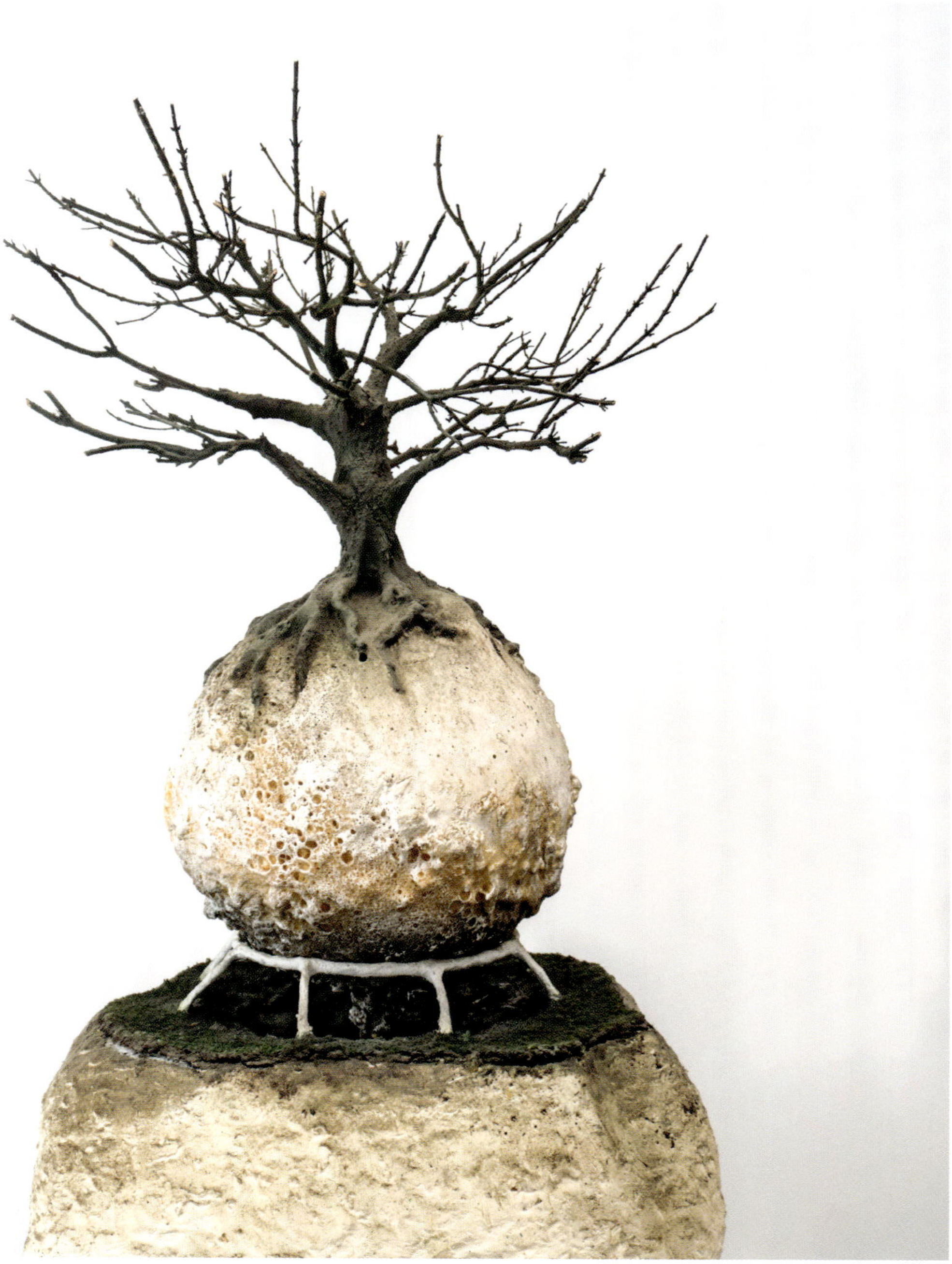

Peppertreeduplicateballs PTDB-Treevirus, 2008

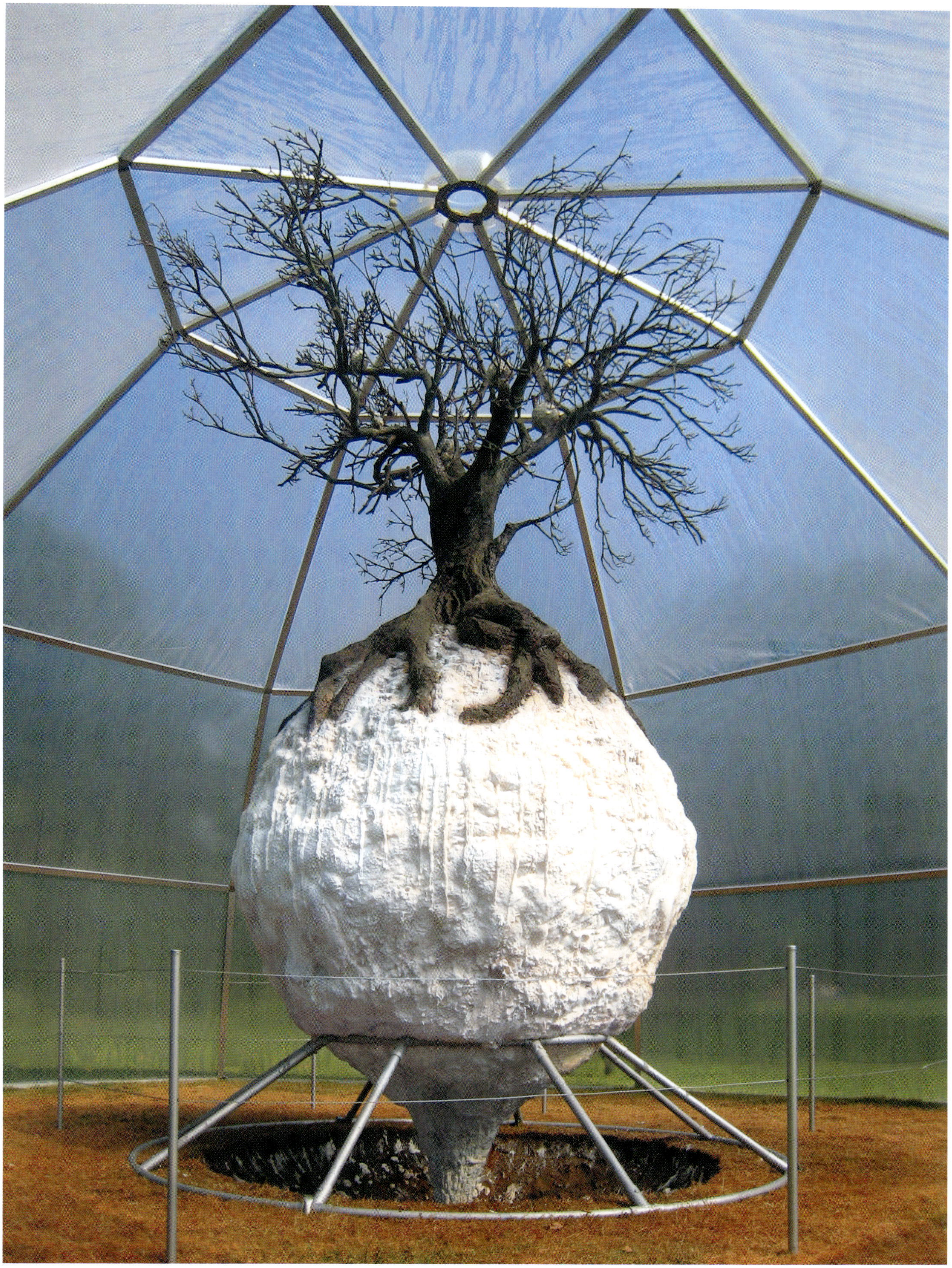

Peppertreeduplicateballs PTDB-Treevirus, 2008

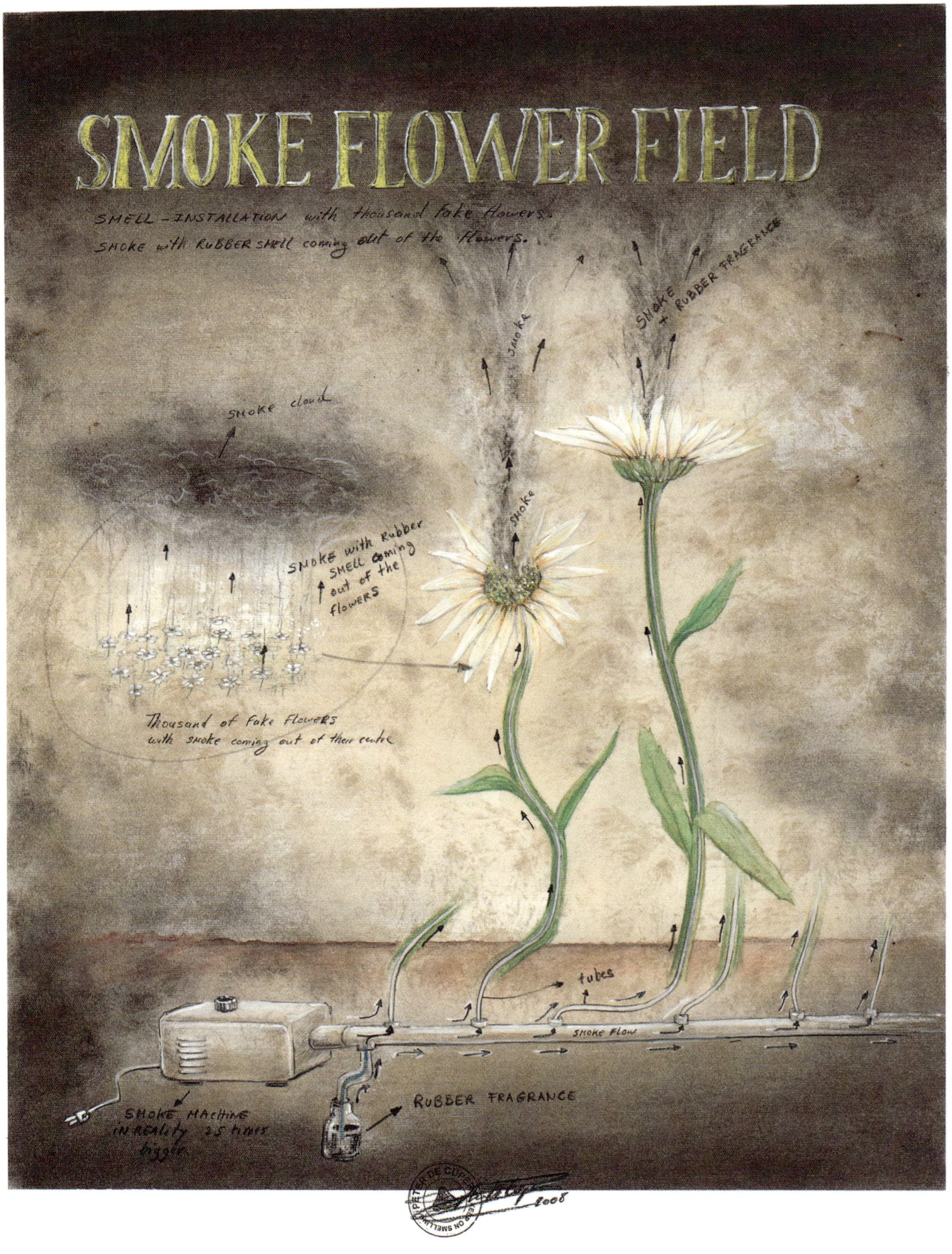

Smoke Flower Field, 2008

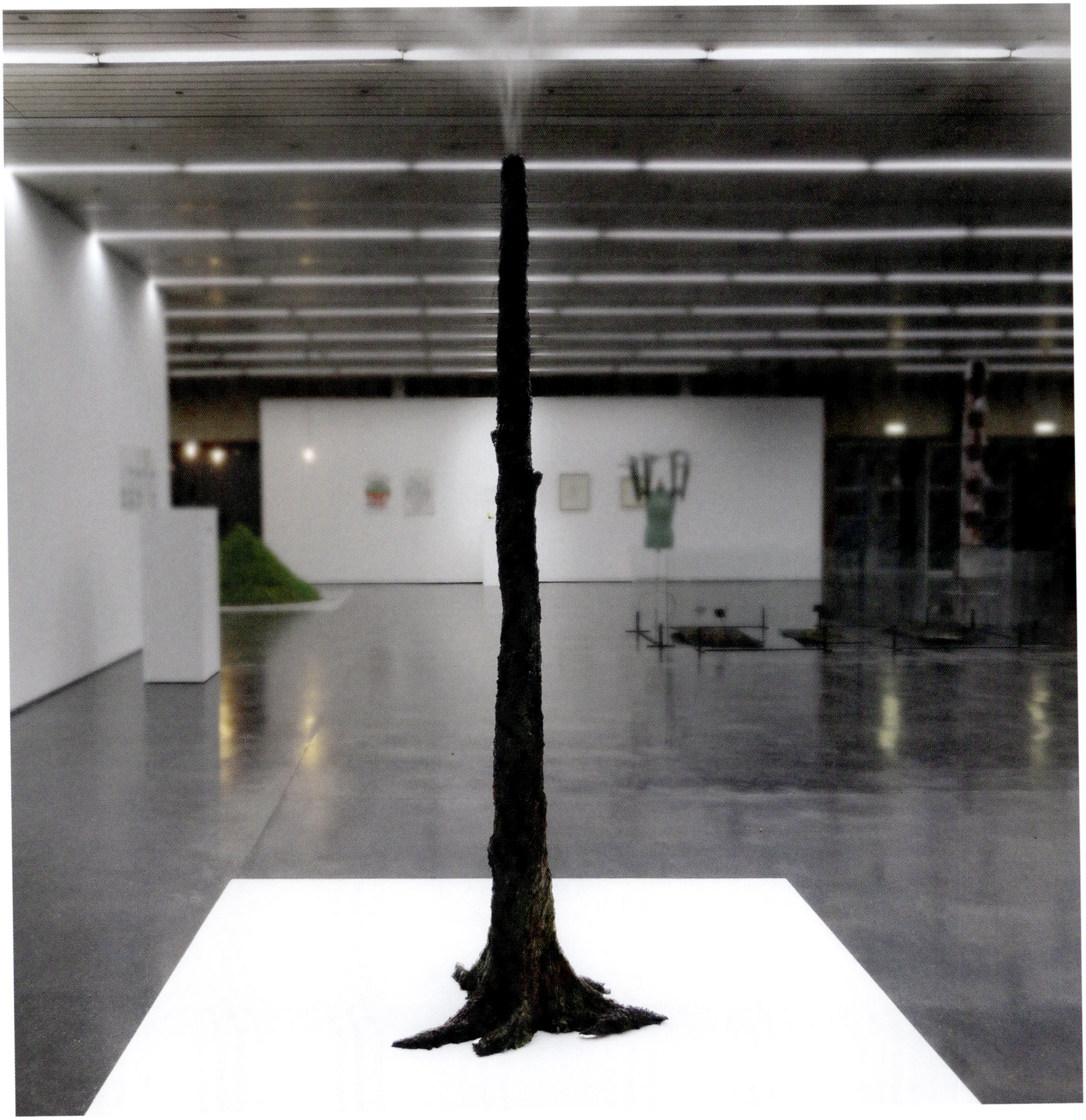

 Factory Tree, 2015

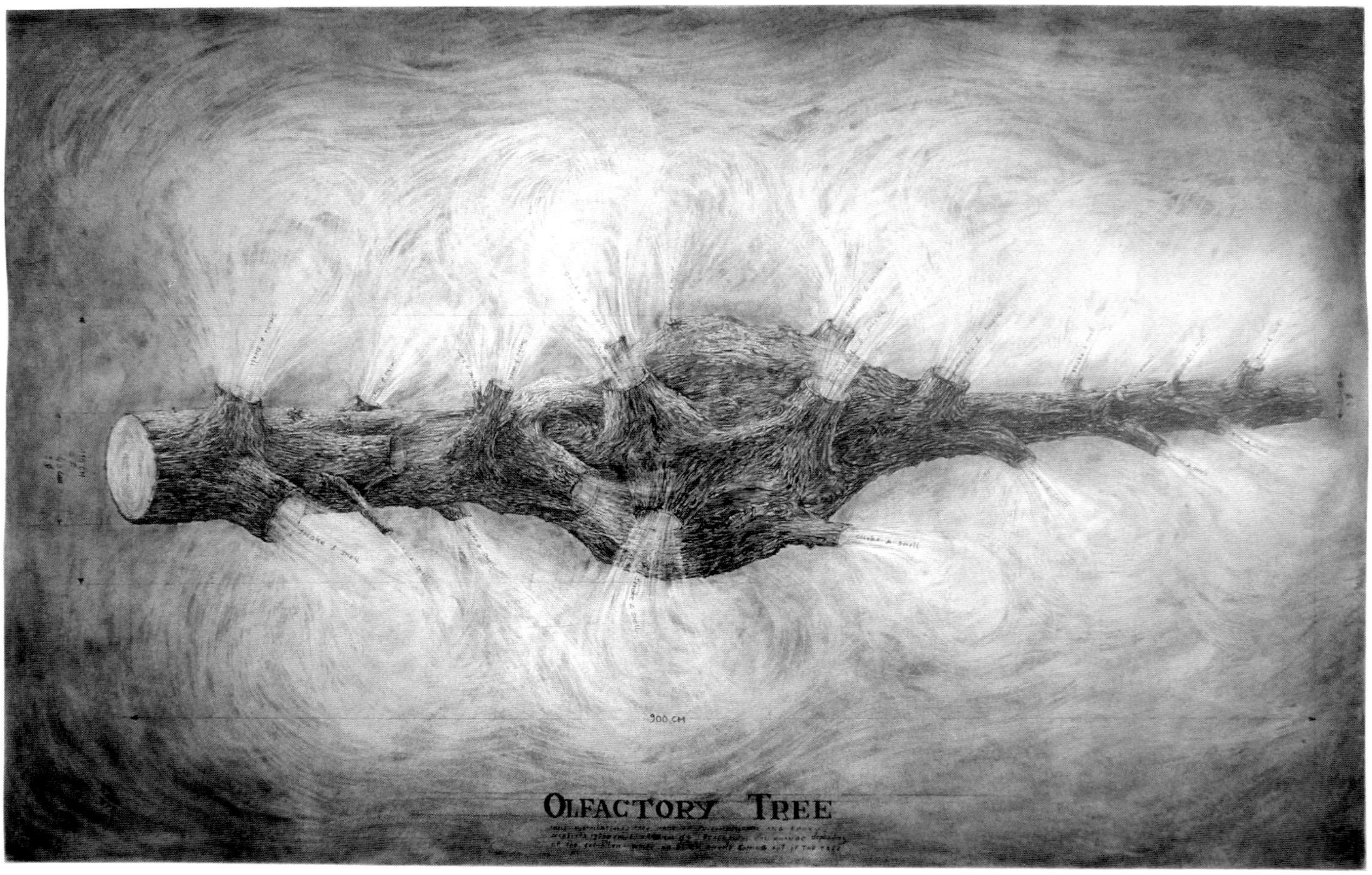

Drawing Olfactory Tree, 2010

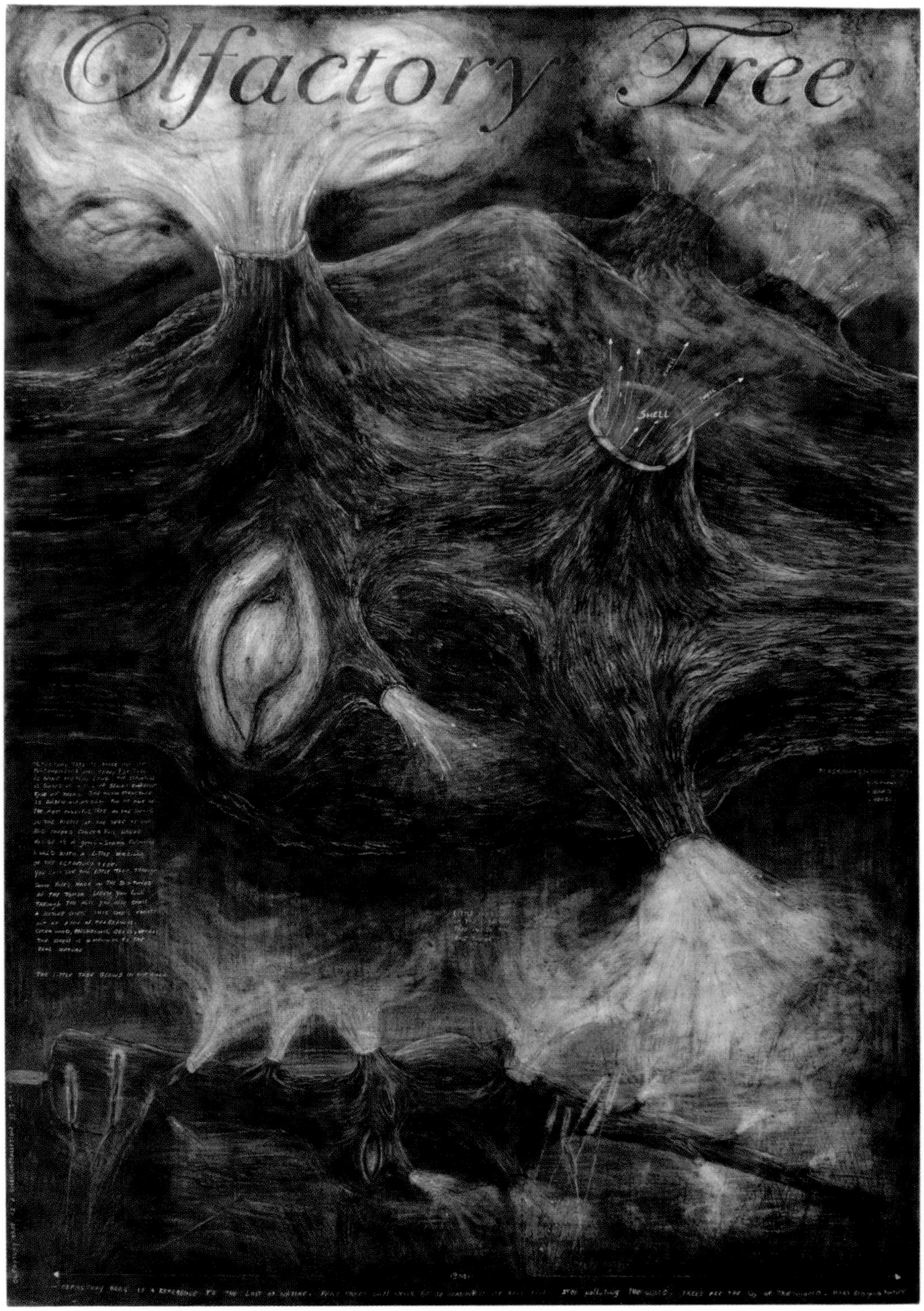

Drawing Olfactory Tree, 2010

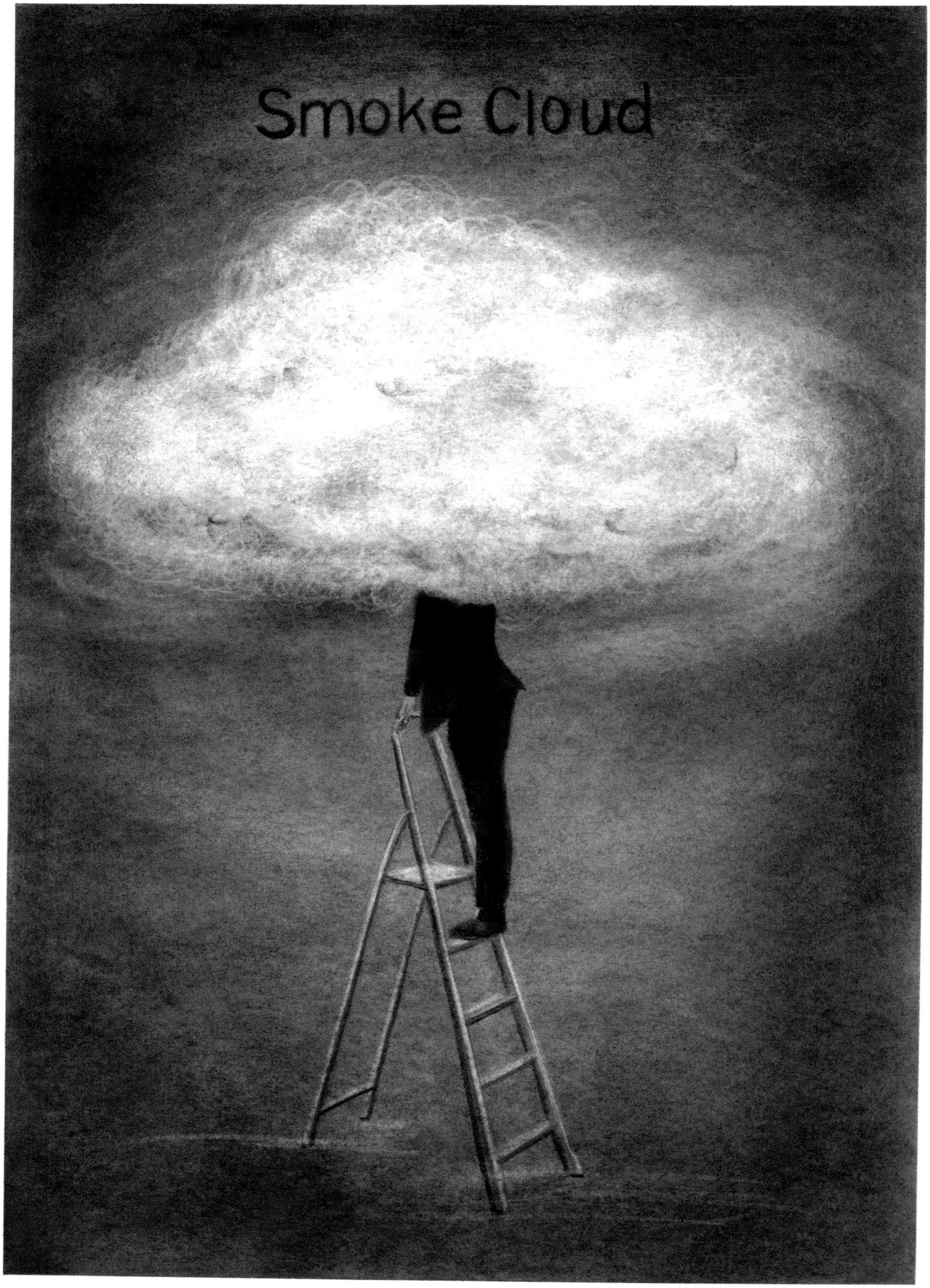

SCRATCH & SNIFF THE SMOKE CLOUD

Edition Scratch & Sniff the Smoke Cloud, 2016

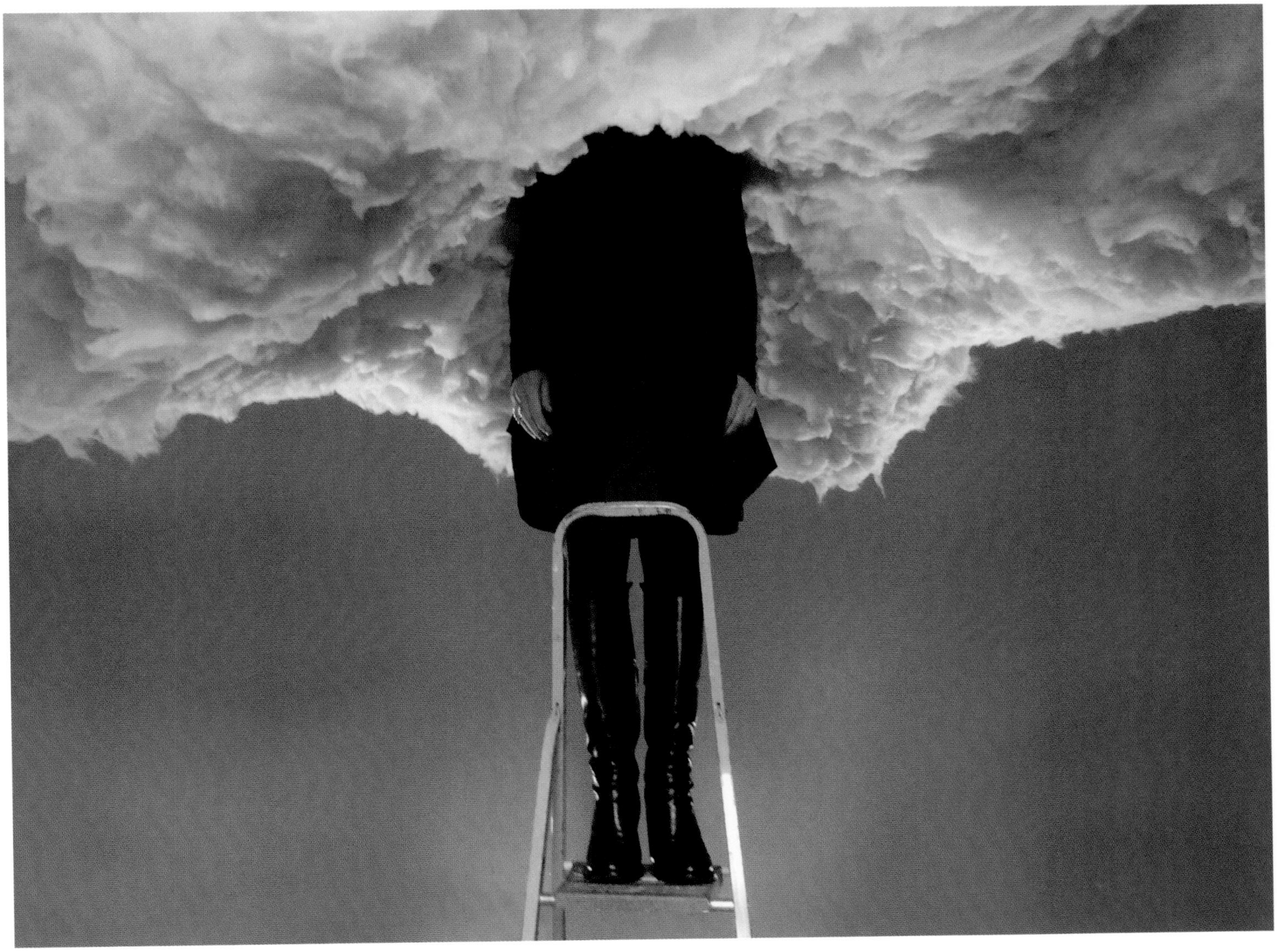

Smoke Cloud, 2013

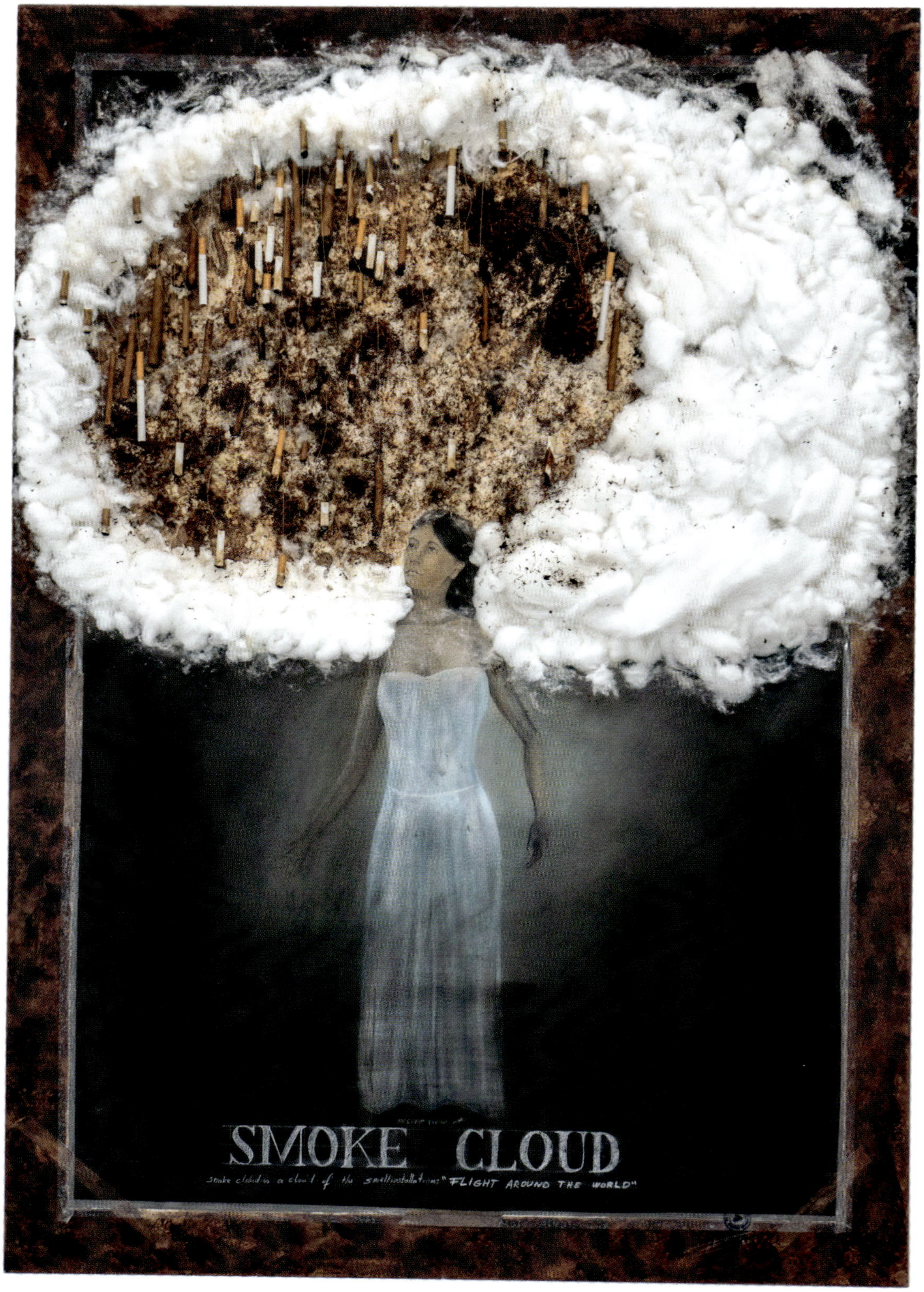

Smoke Cloud, 2001

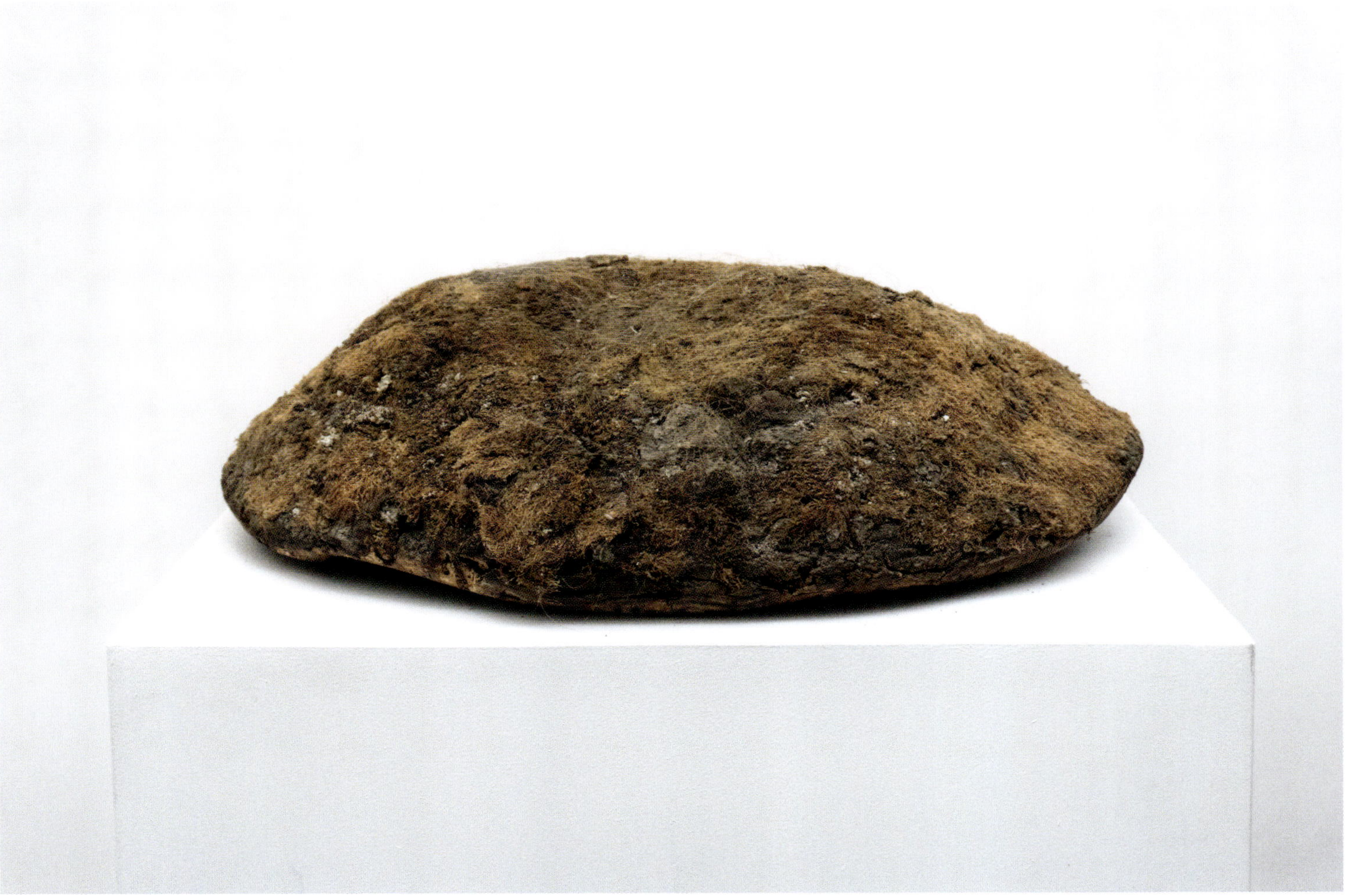

 Nature Pillow, 2001

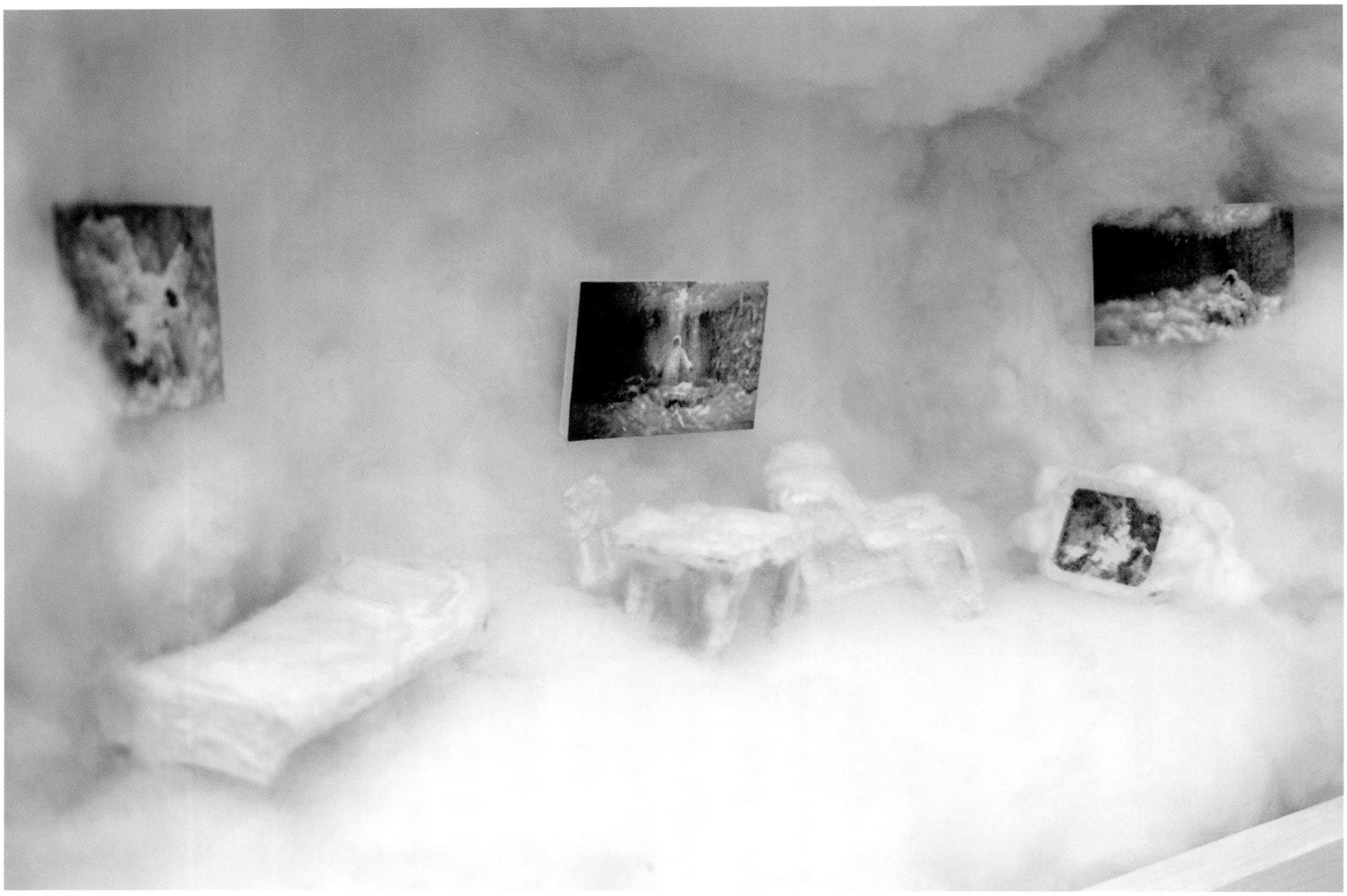

▲ Model Soft World (detail), 2000

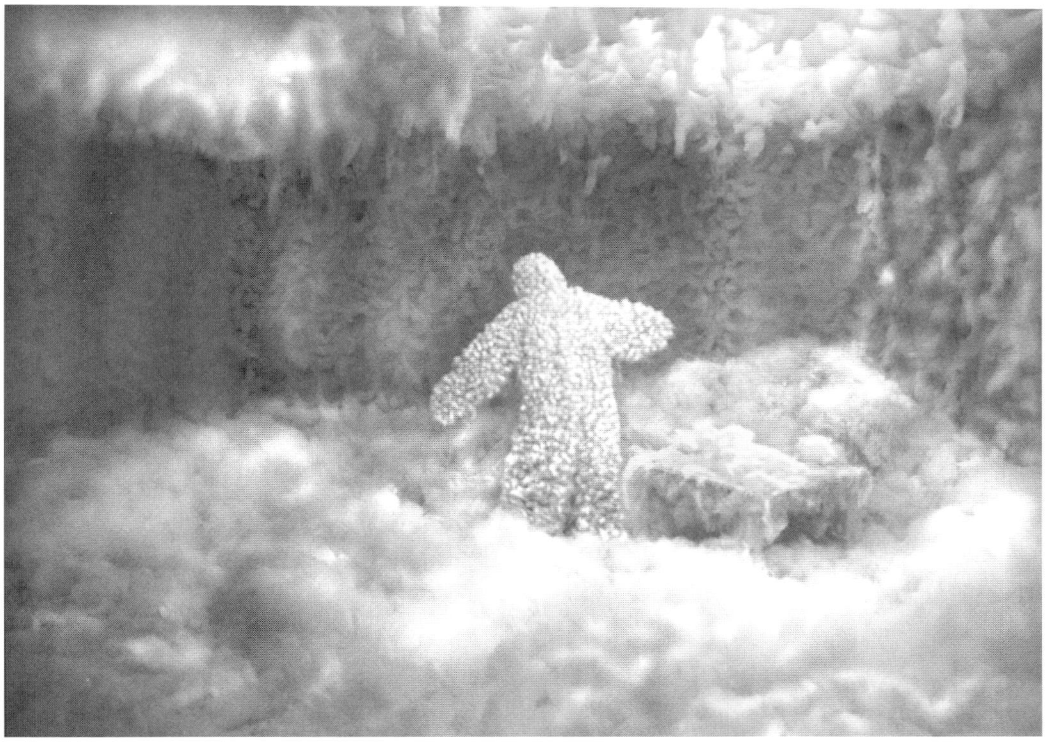

Photograph The Soft Man, His Table And His Chair, 2000

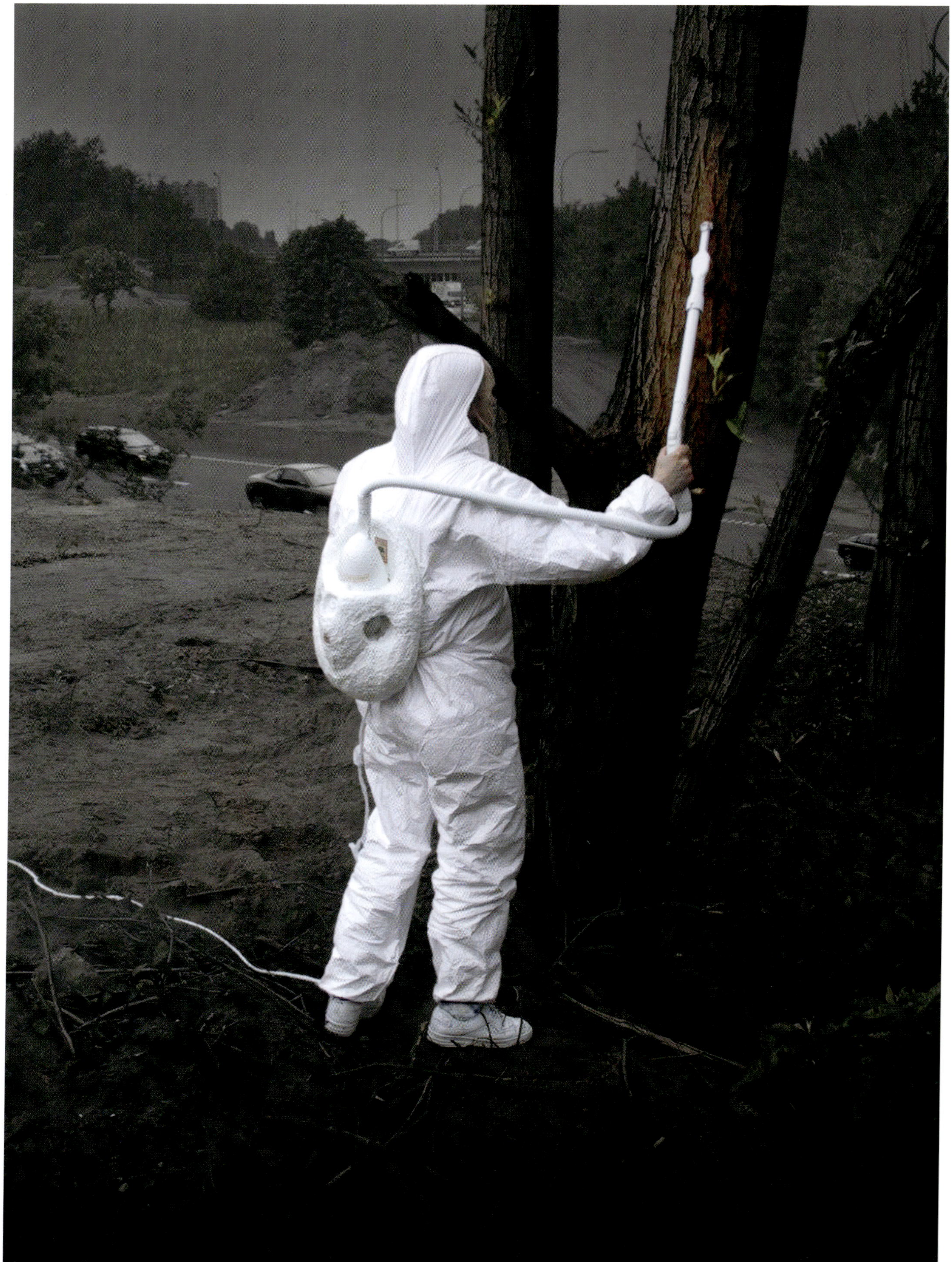

Photograph Nature Cleaner, 2004

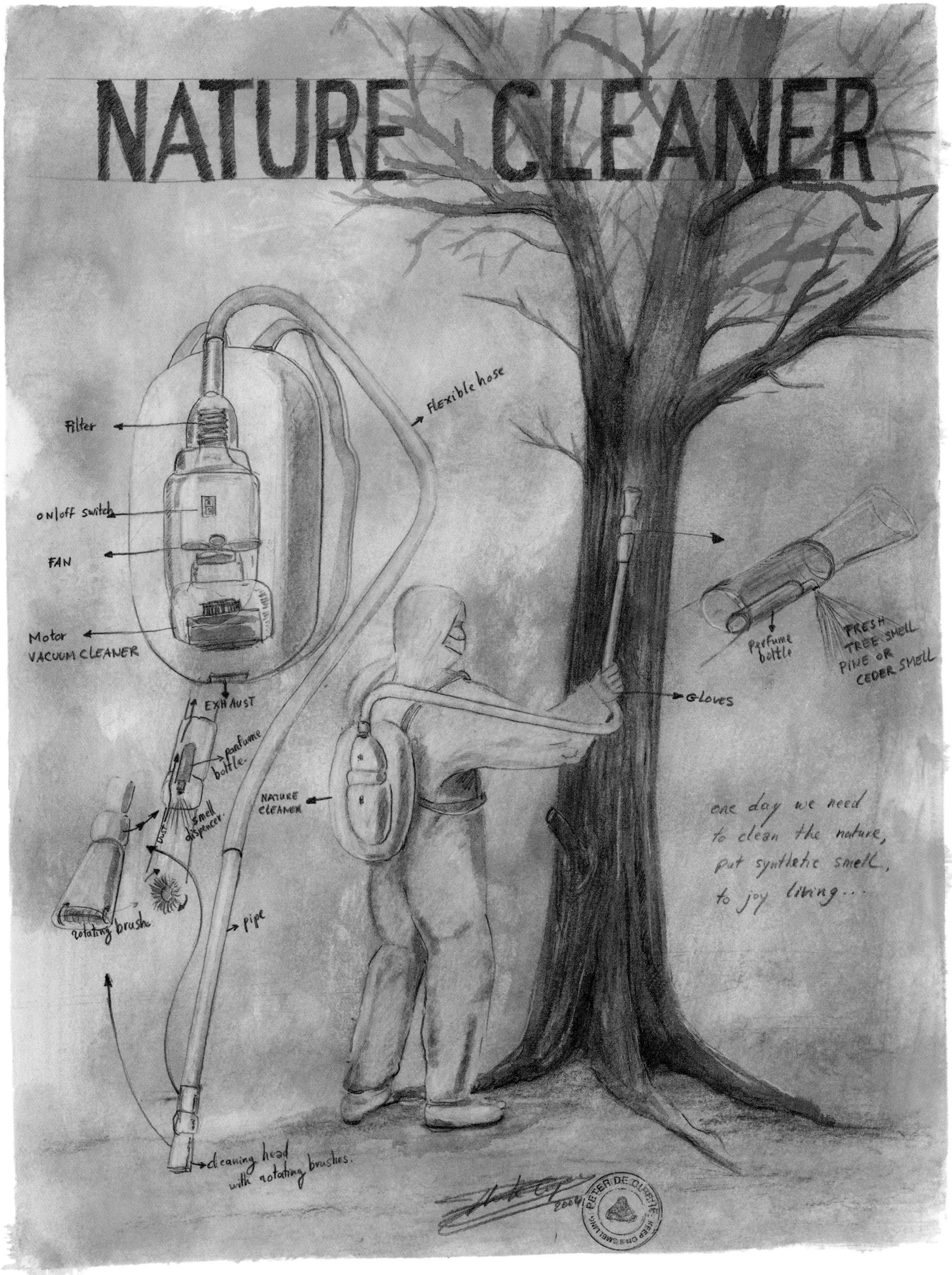

 Drawing Nature Cleaner, 2004

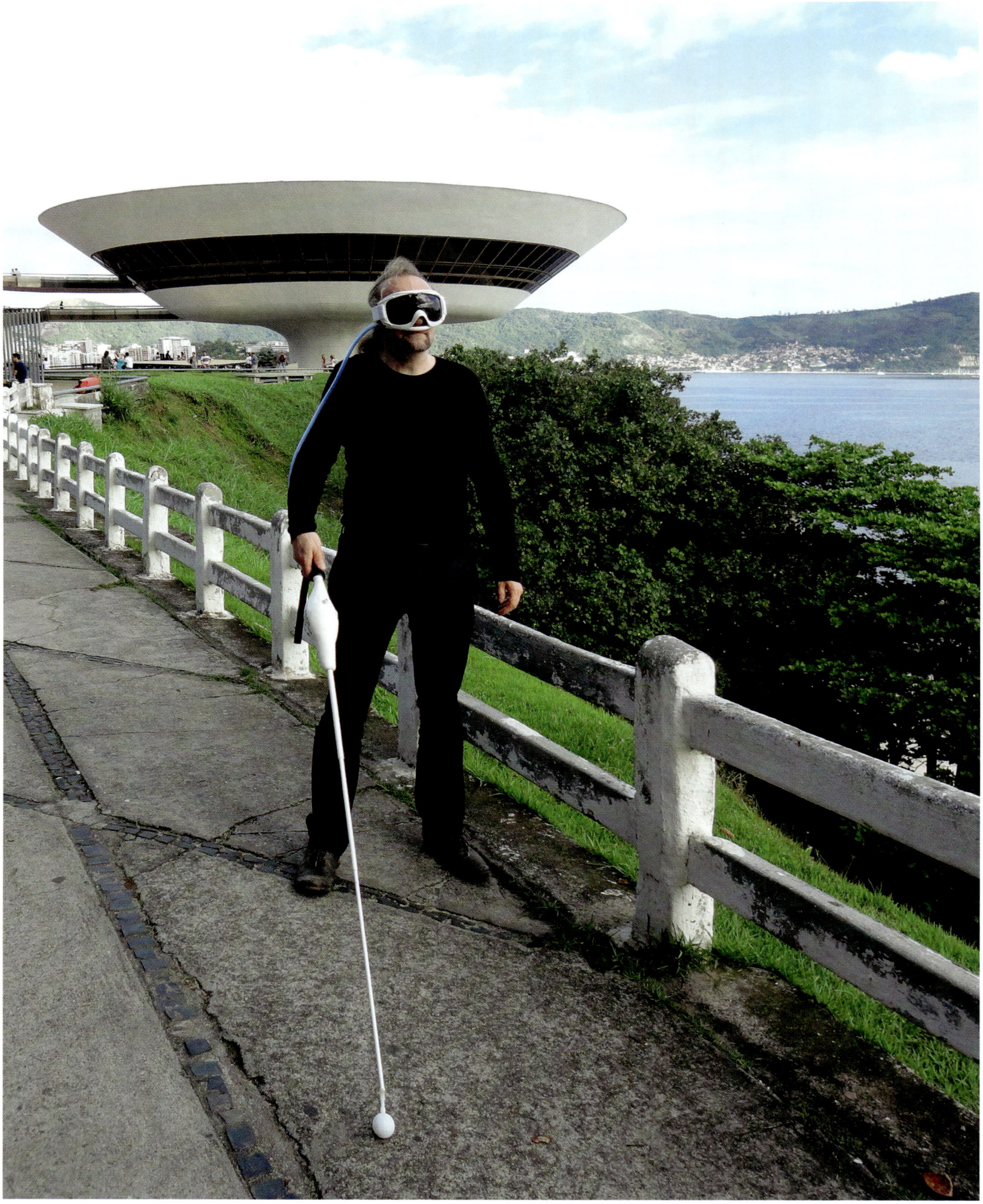

The Blind Smell Stick, 2012

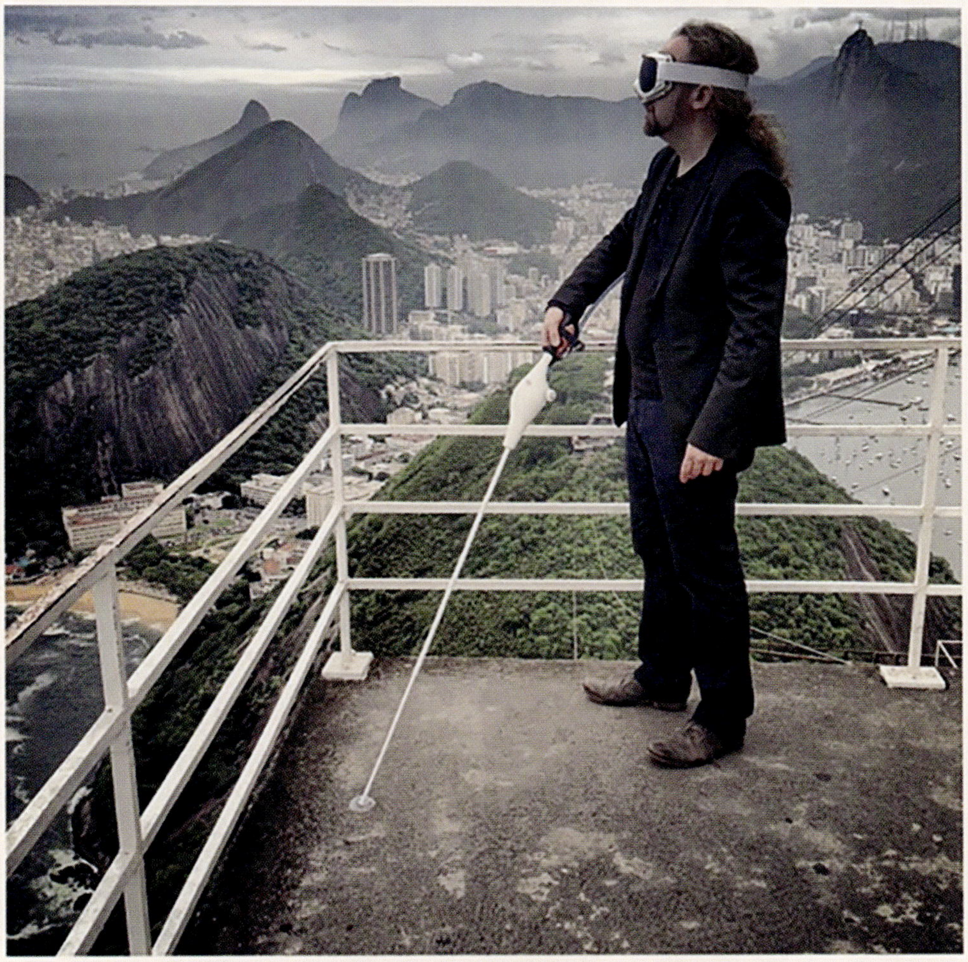

 The Blind Smell Stick, 2012

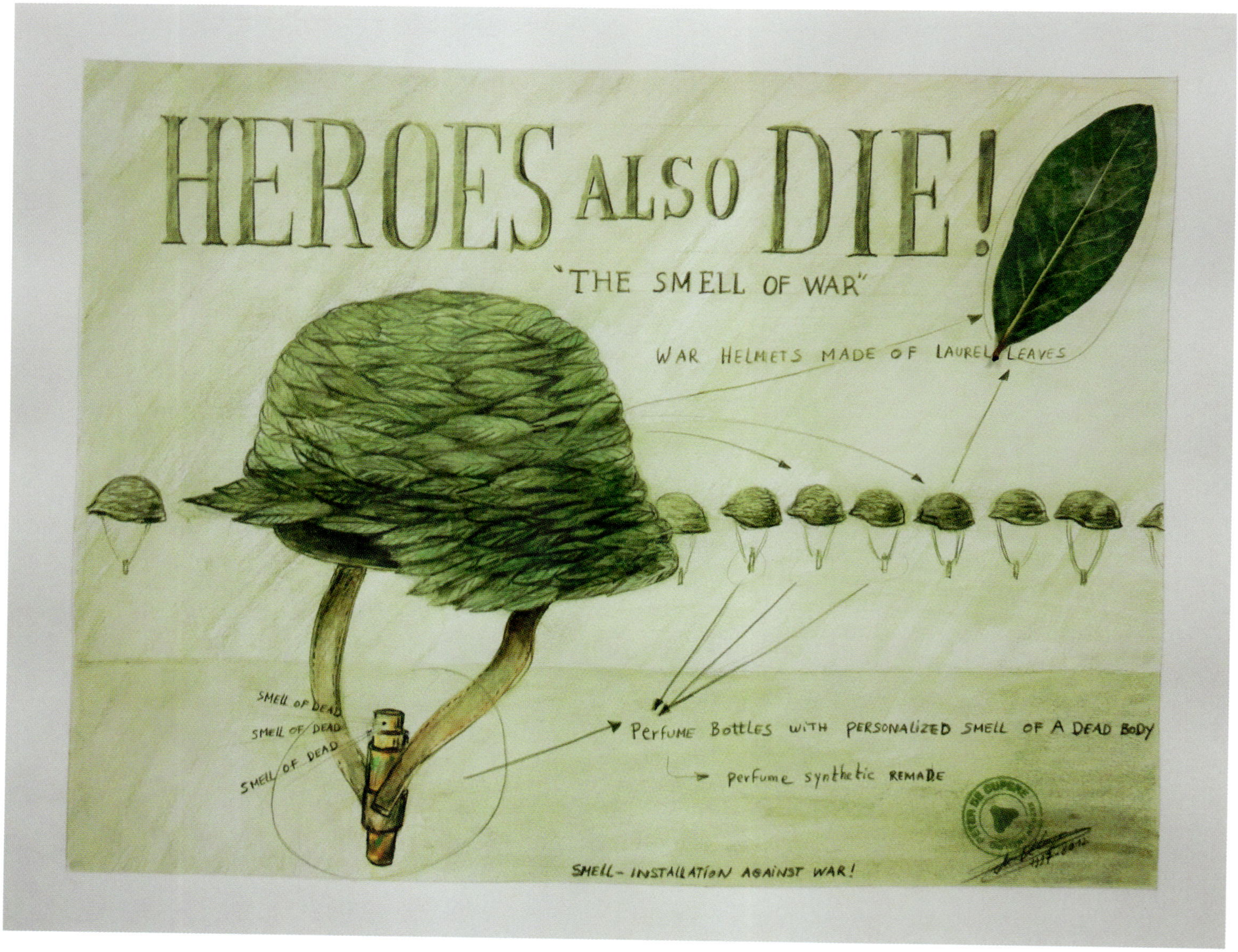

Drawing Heroes Also Die, 1997 - 2012

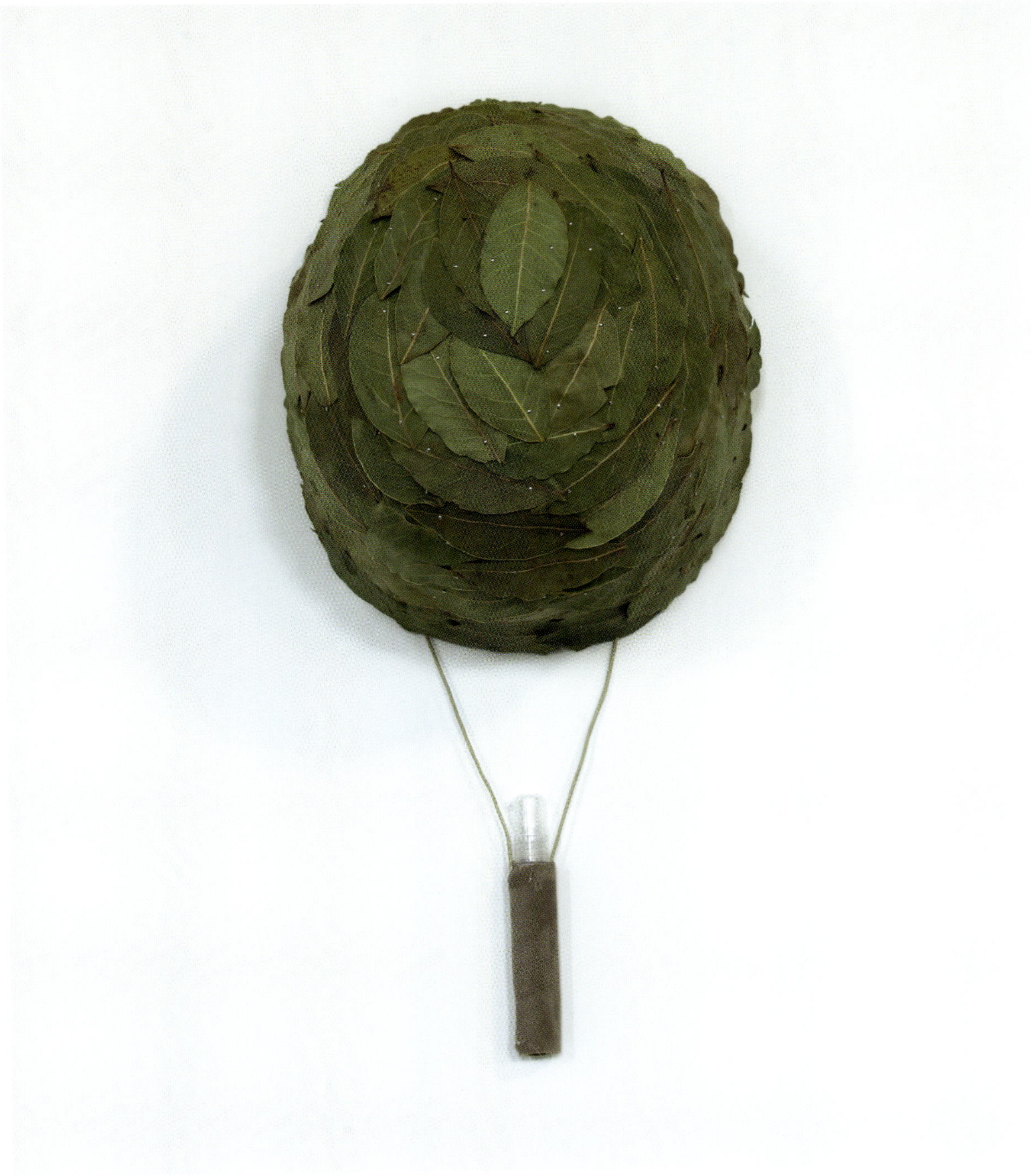

Heroes Also Die, 2015

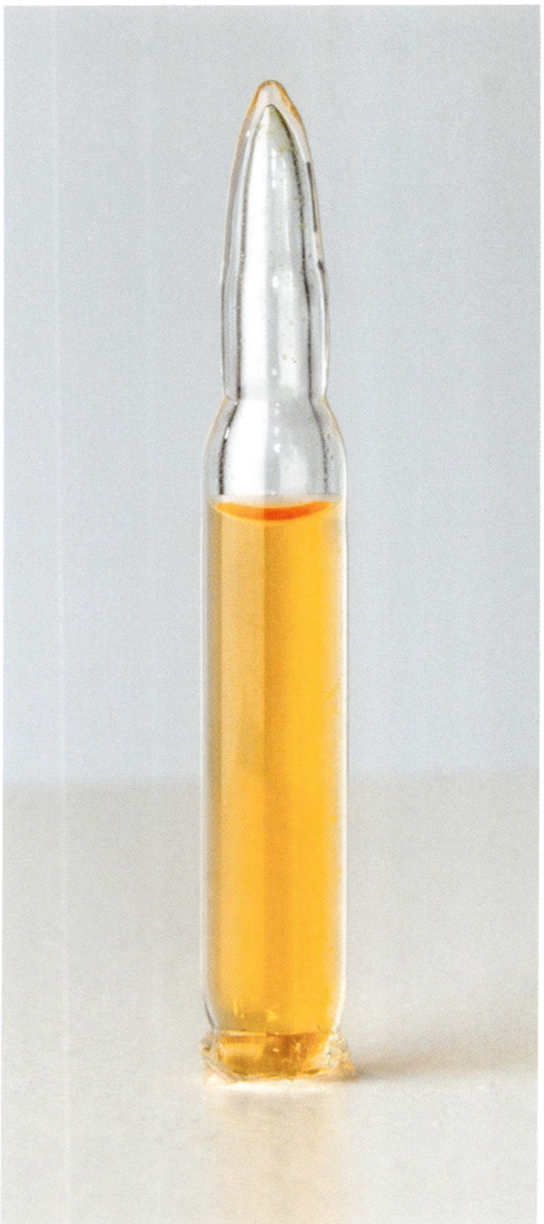

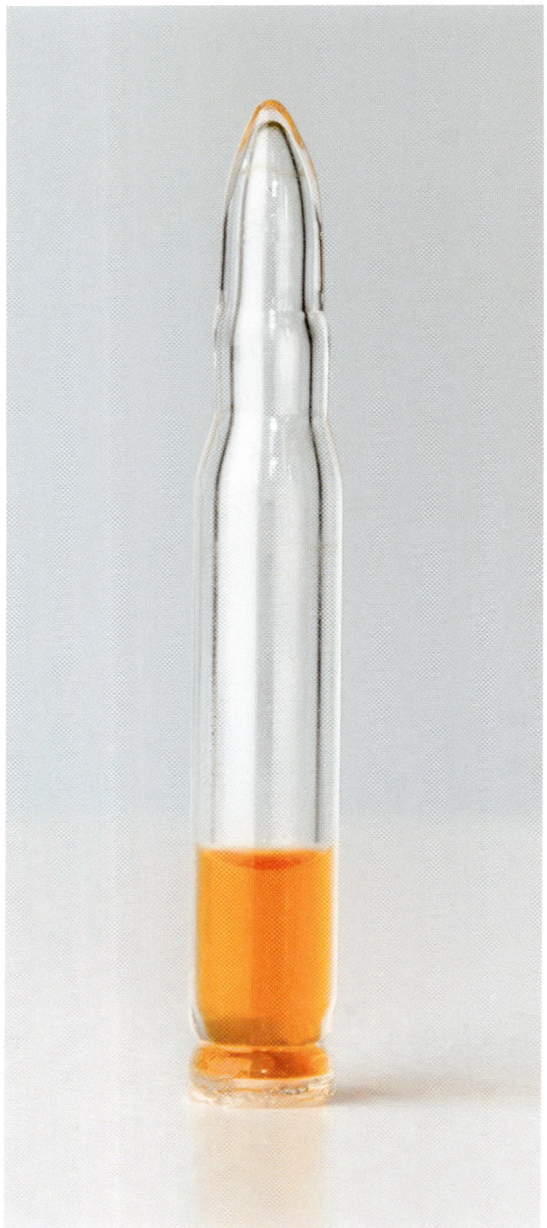

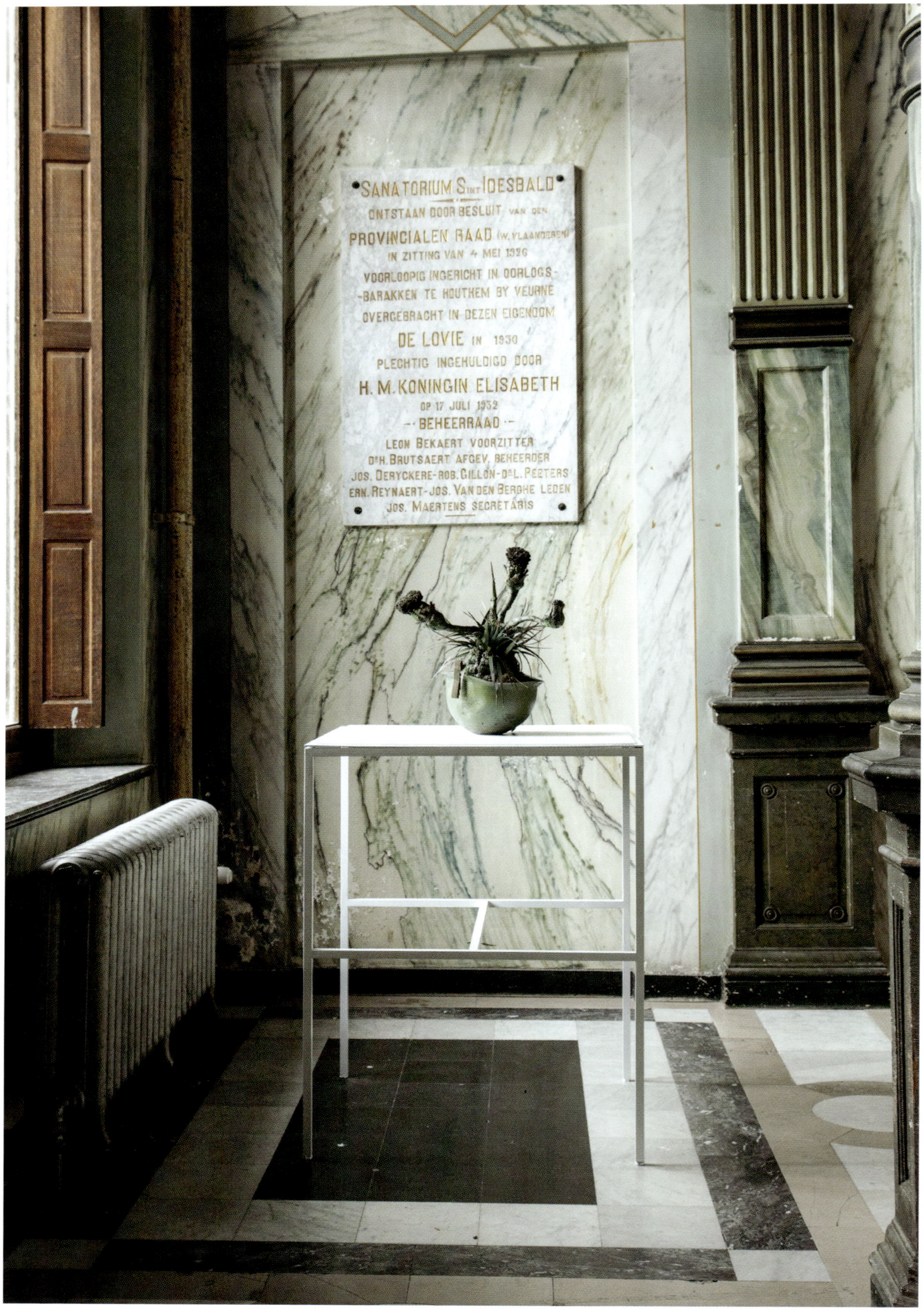

War Flower, 2014

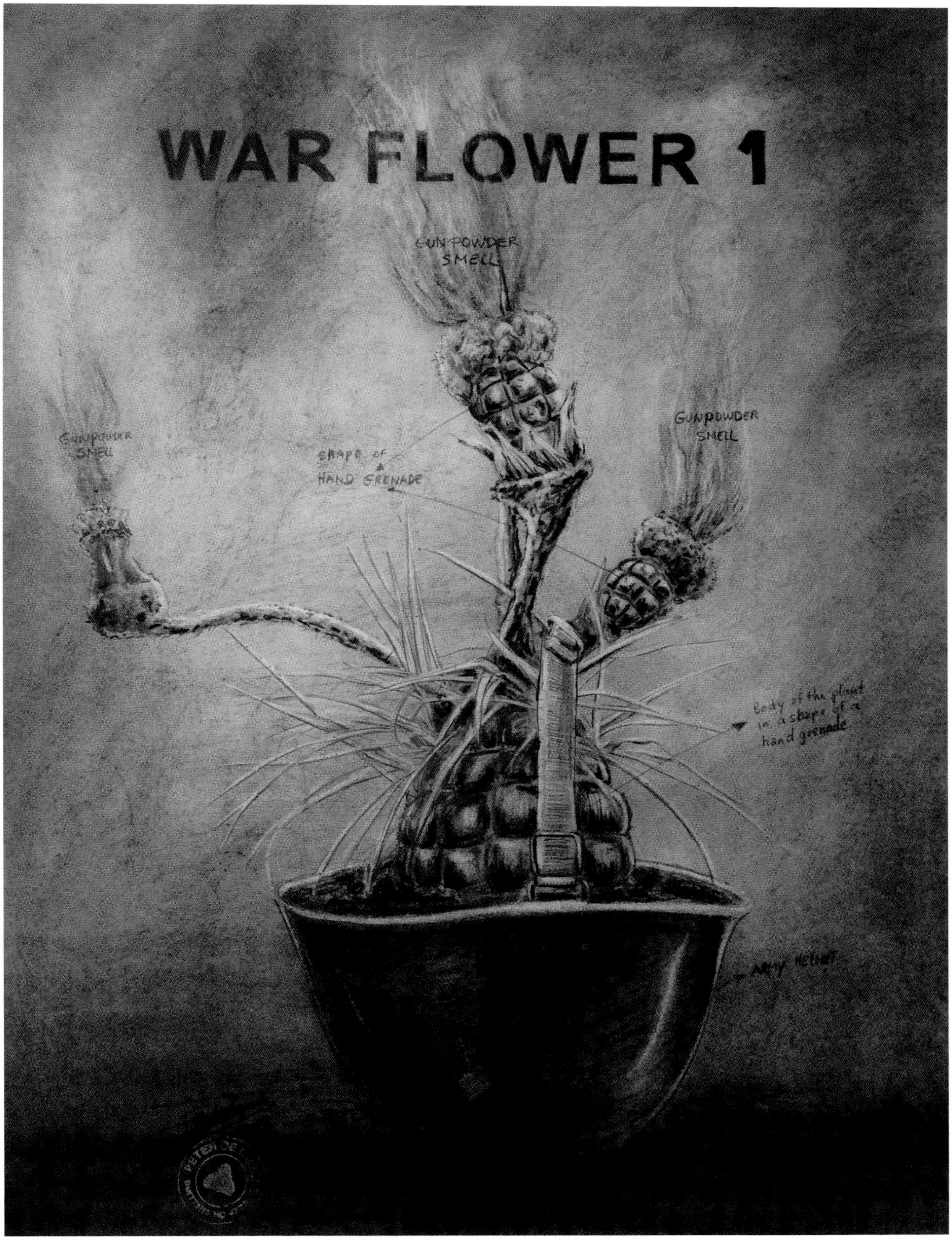

 Drawing War Flower, 2014

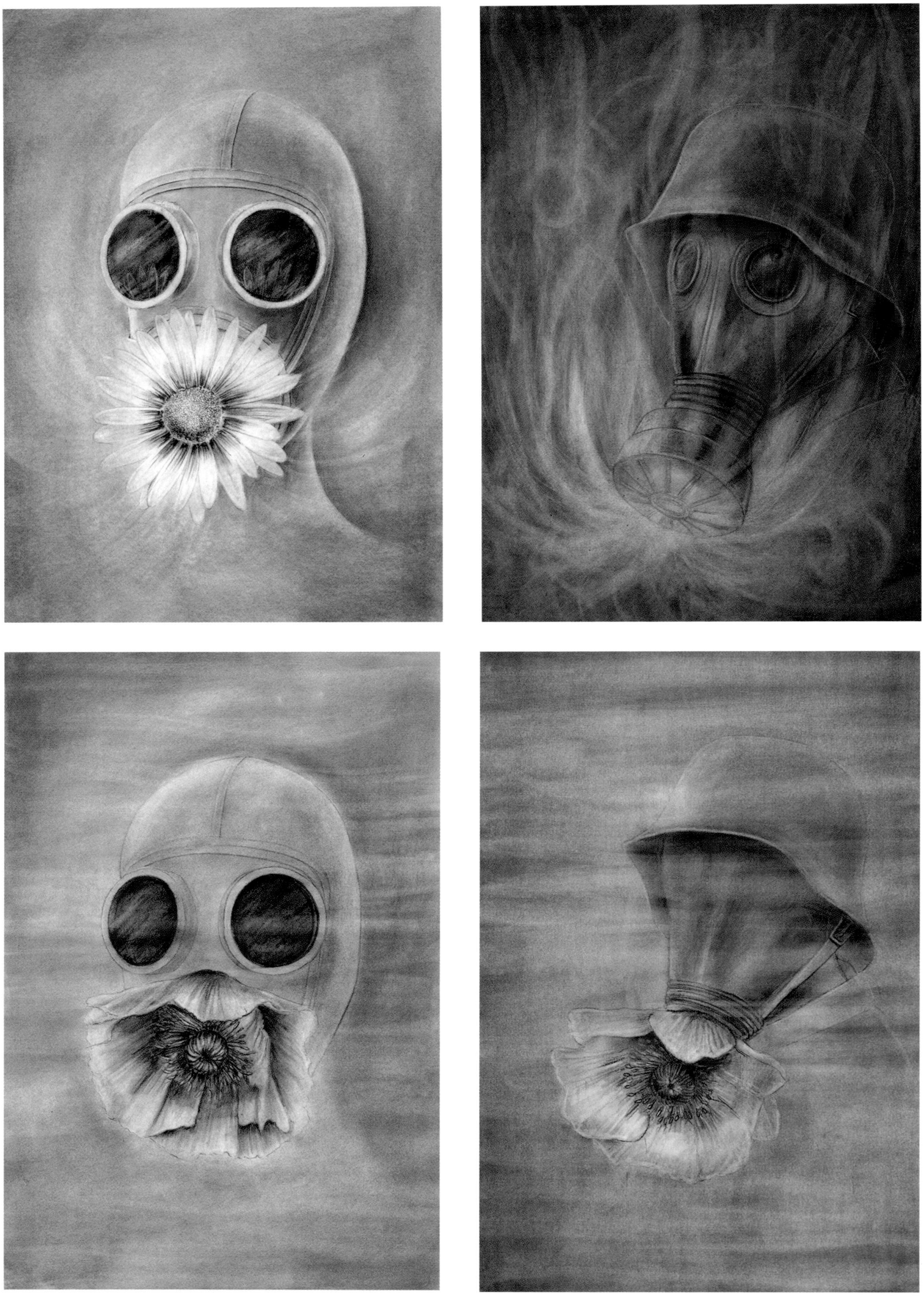

Drawings Flower Masks, 2015

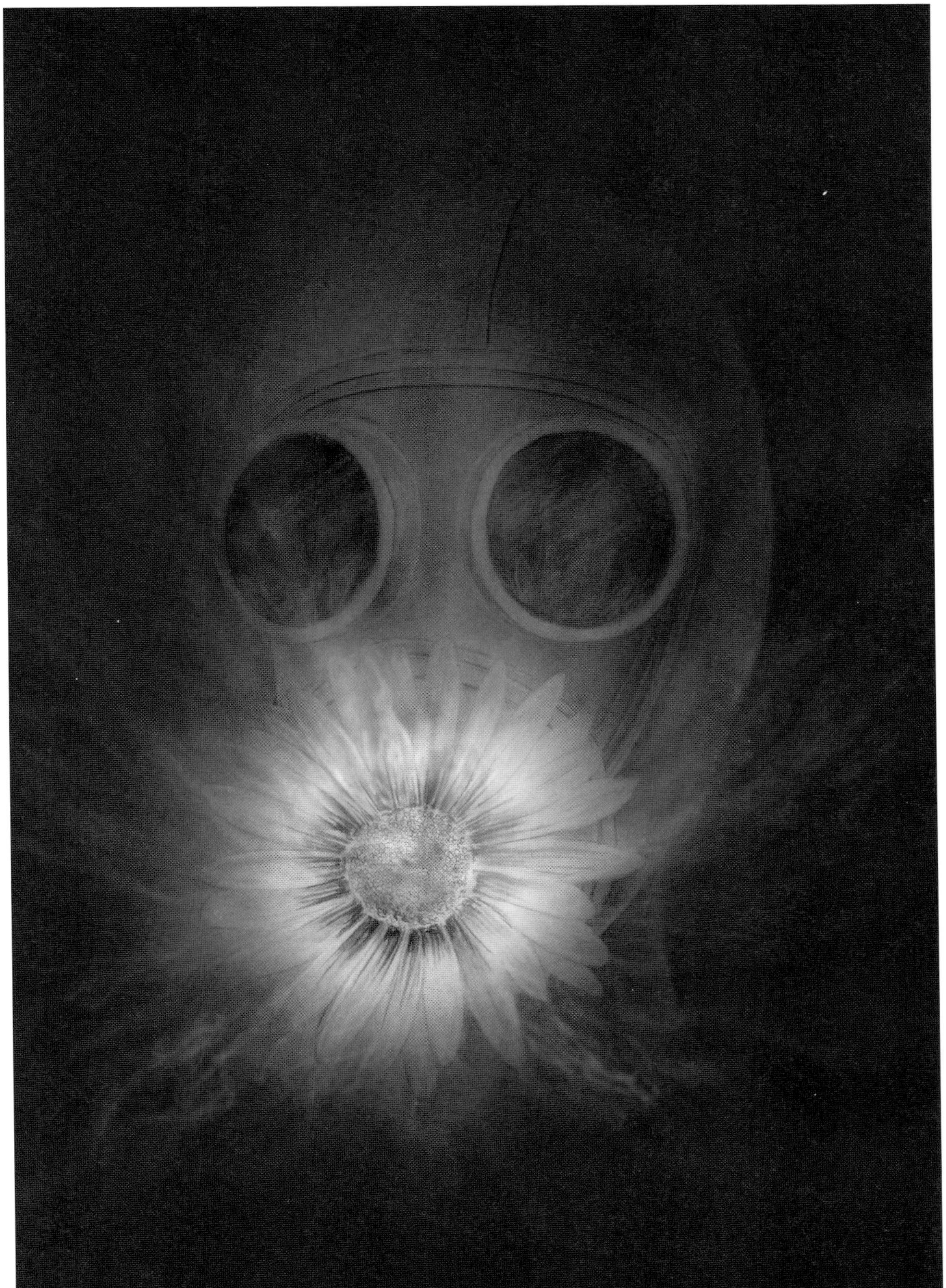

 Drawing Flower Mask, The Smell of War, 2015

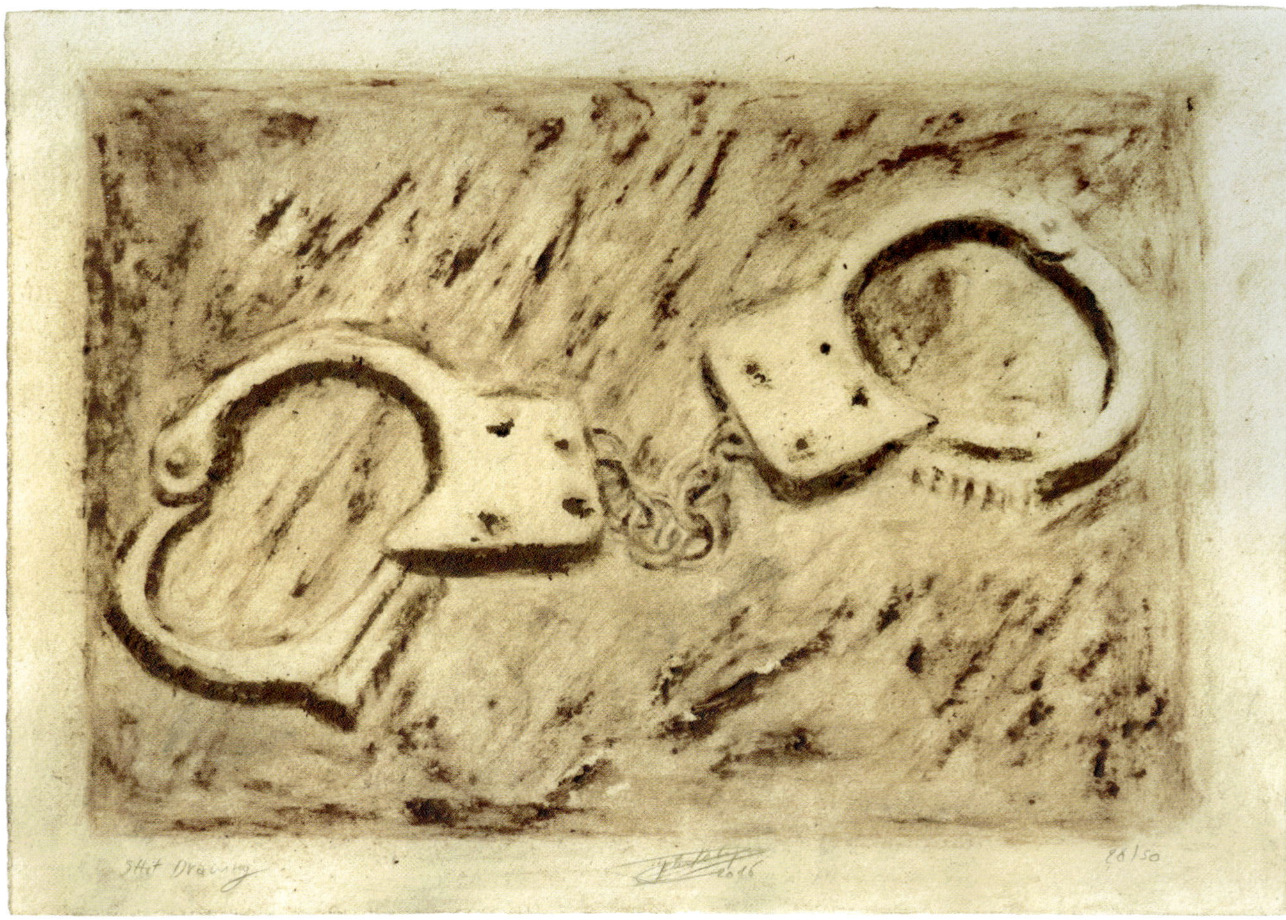
Shit Drawing
2016

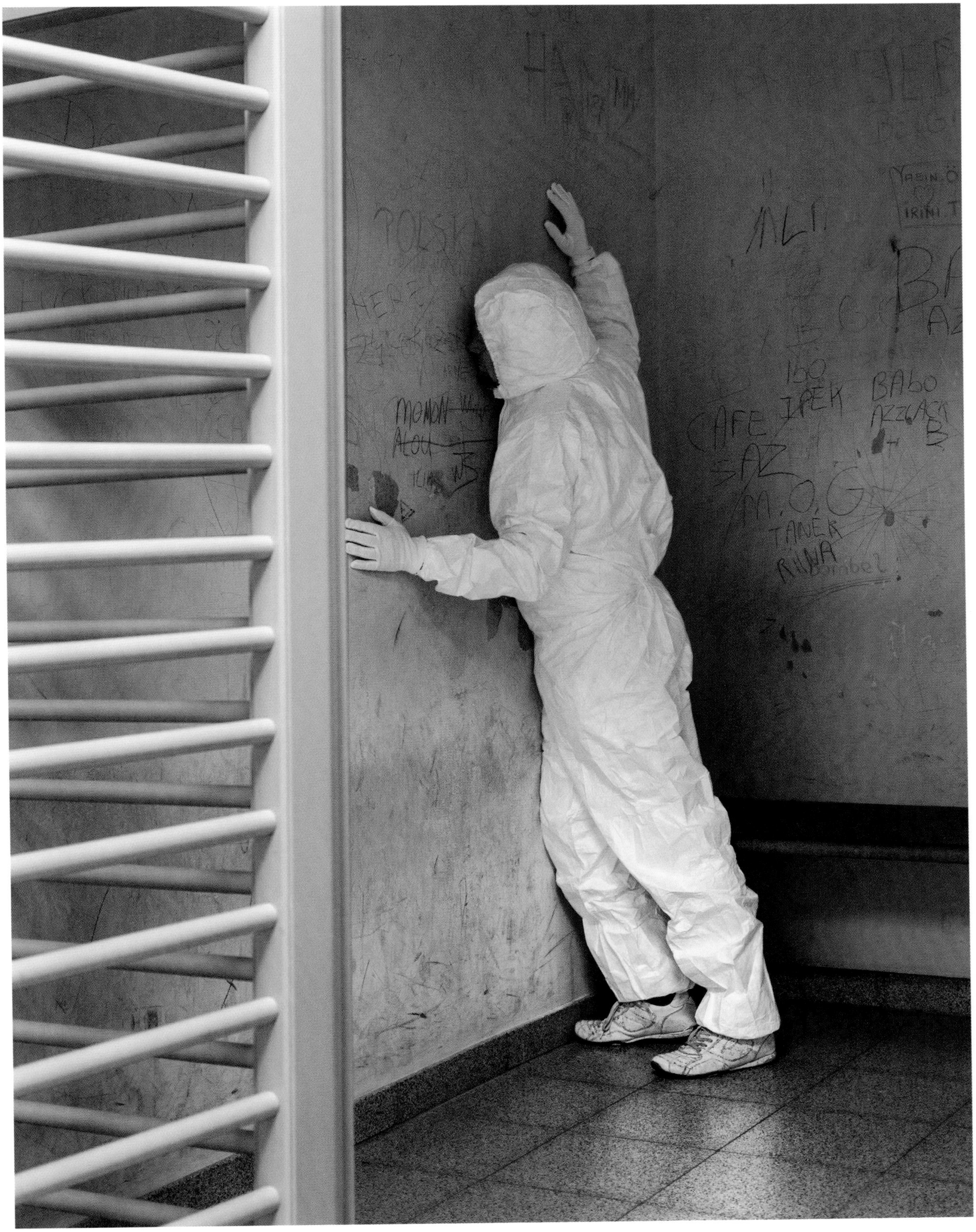

Photograph from Performance Sniff Your Jail, 2016

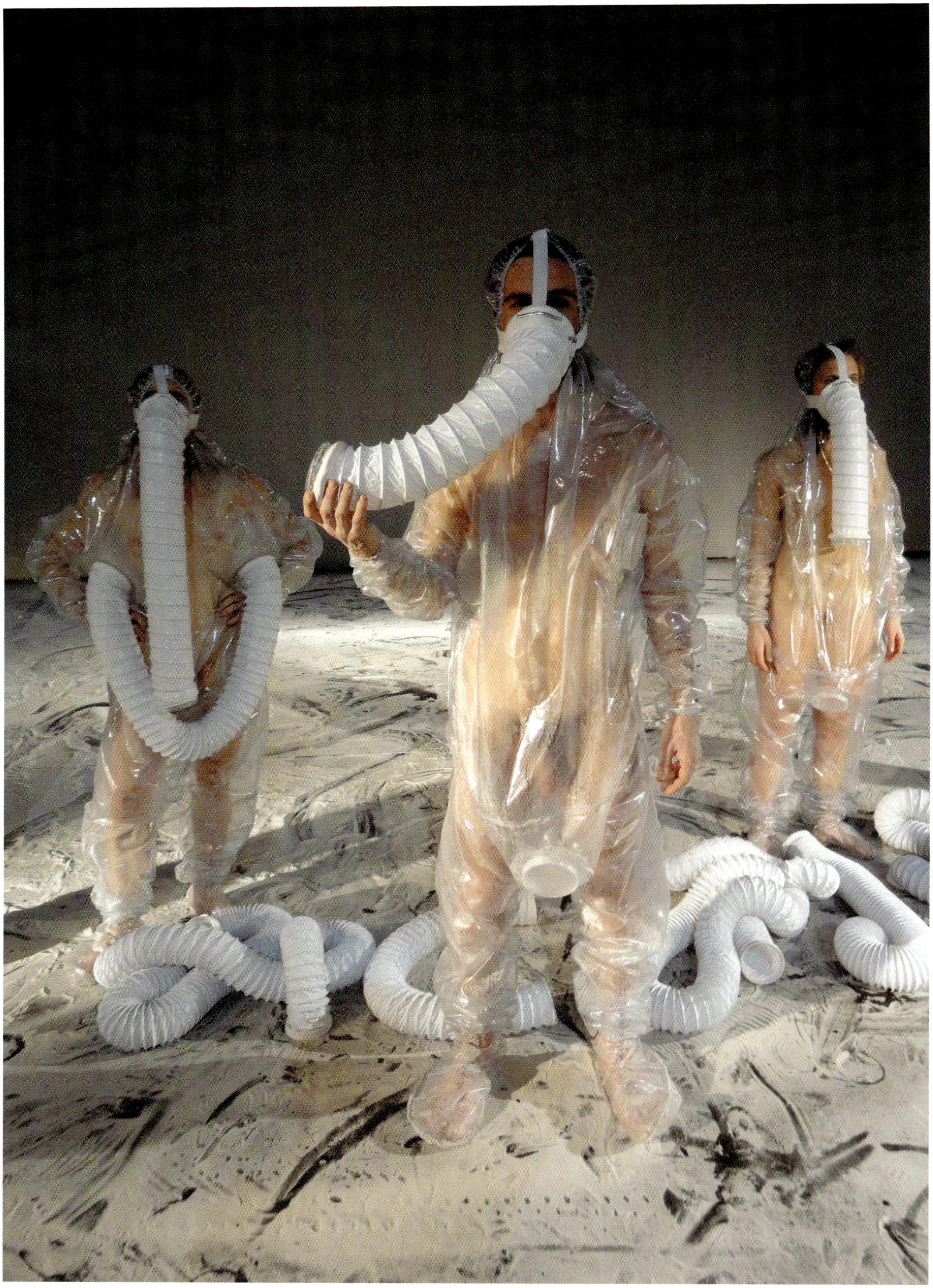

Sweat, 2010

Touch & Smell the Colours of this World, 2001

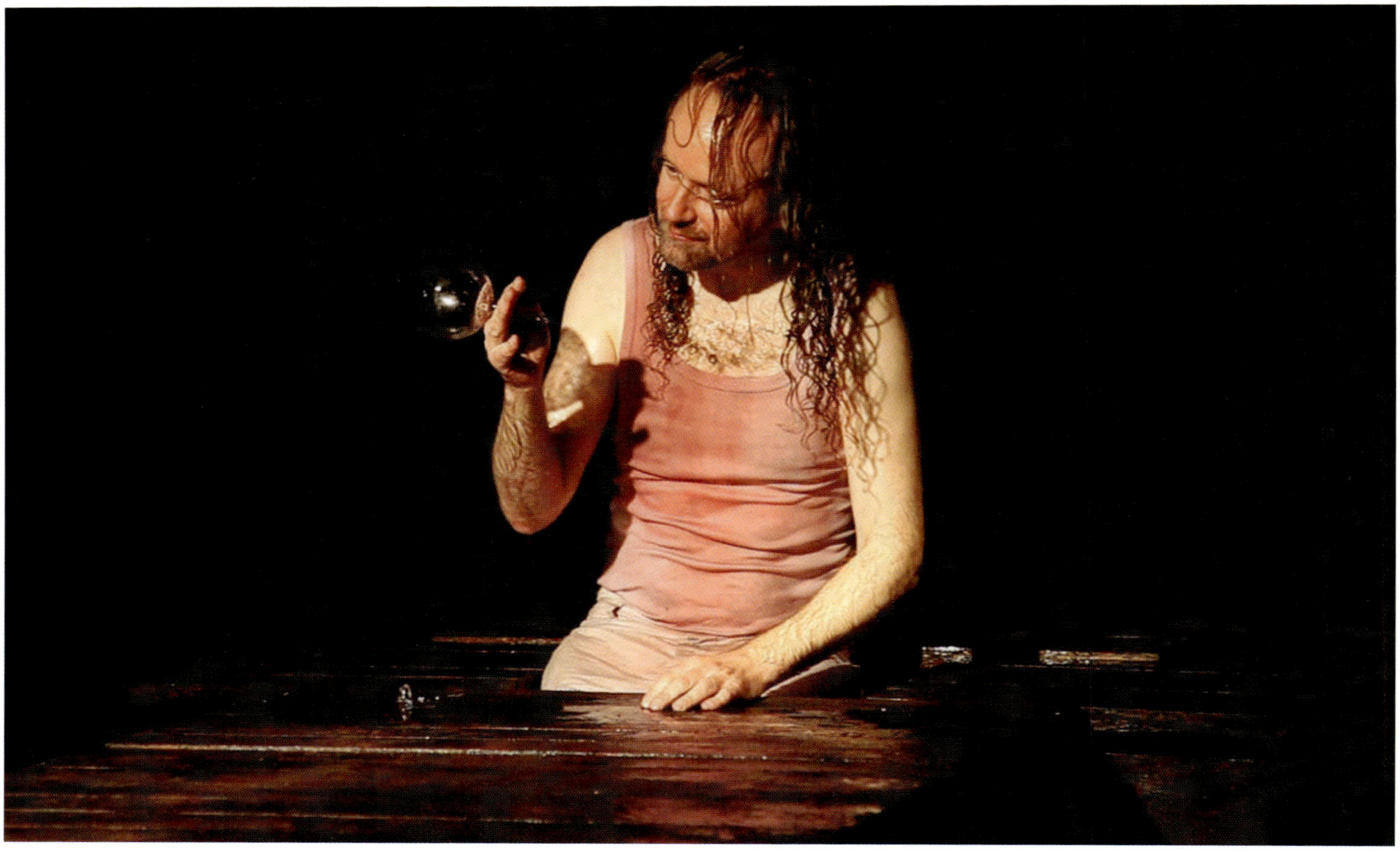

Video Drunken, 2013

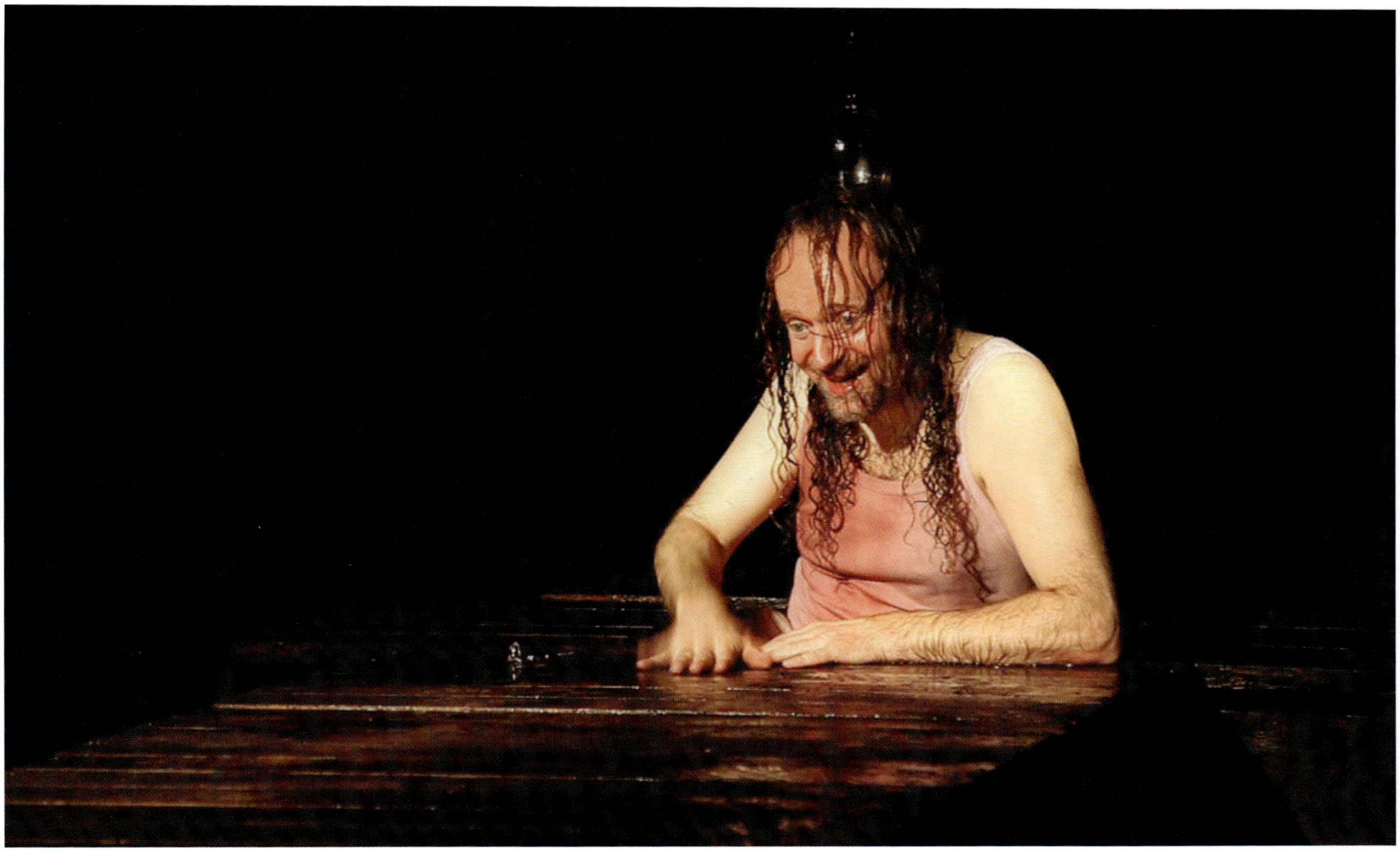

 Video Drunken, 2013

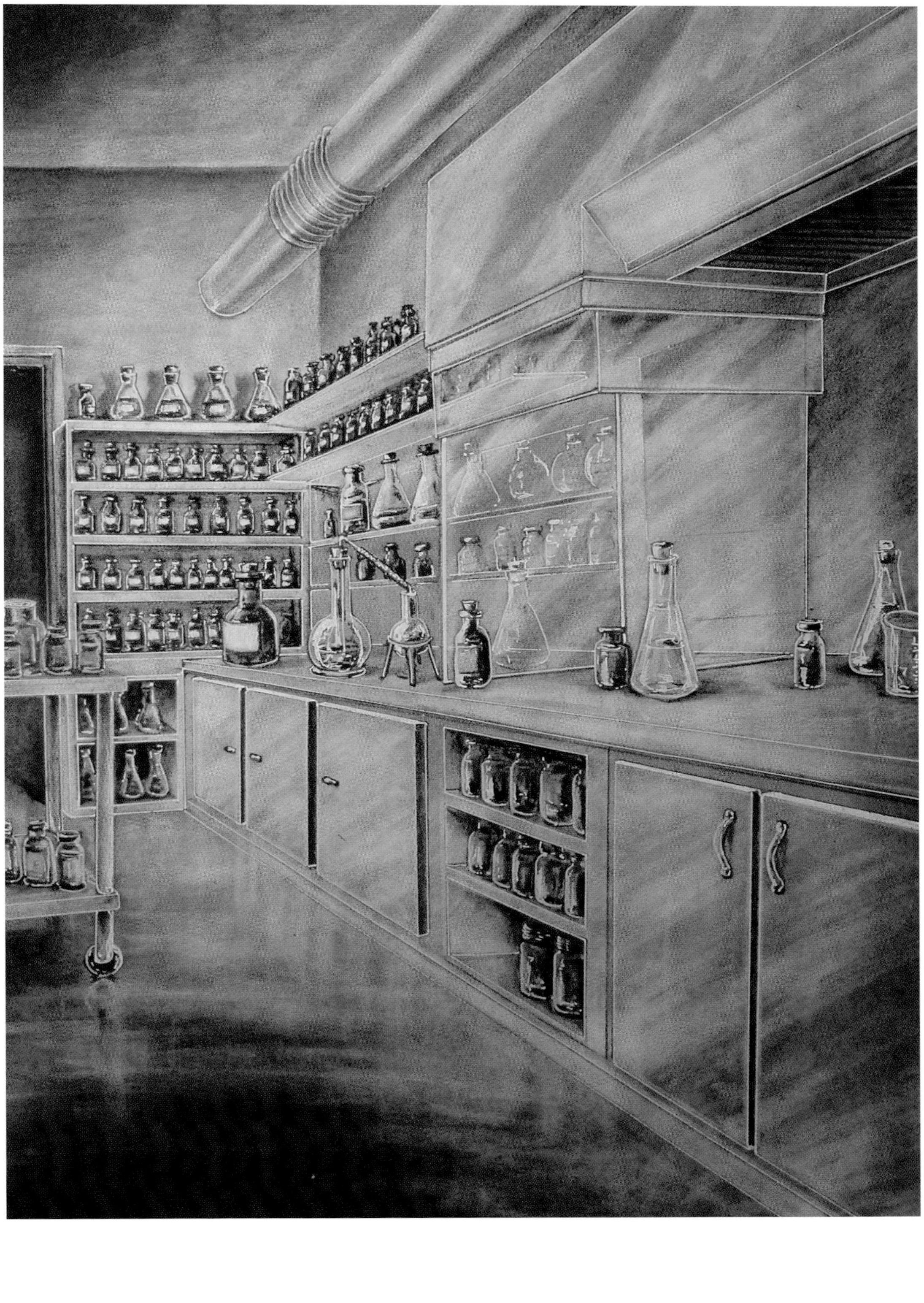

 Drawing Miniature Lab, 2012

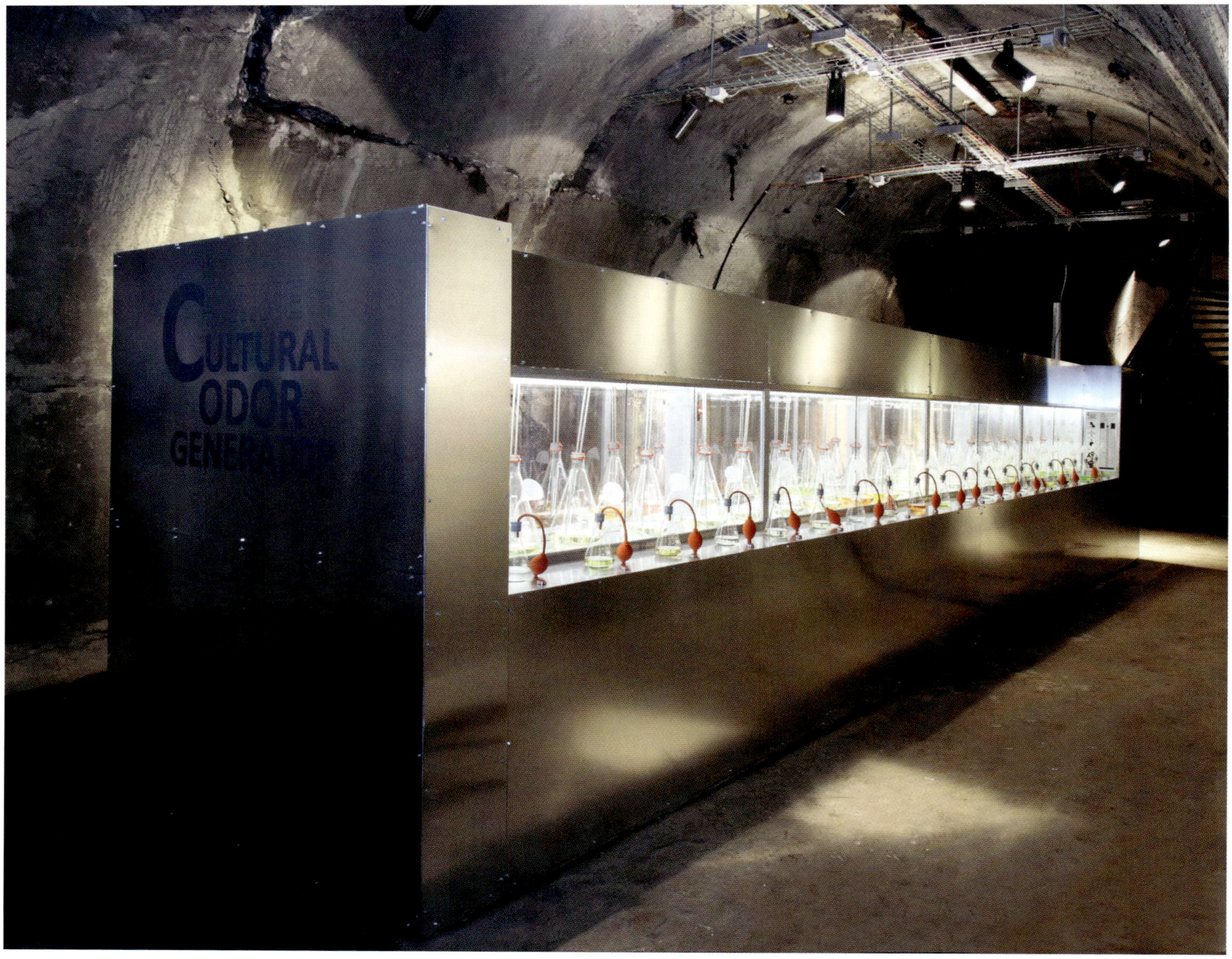

Cultural Odor Generator, 2012

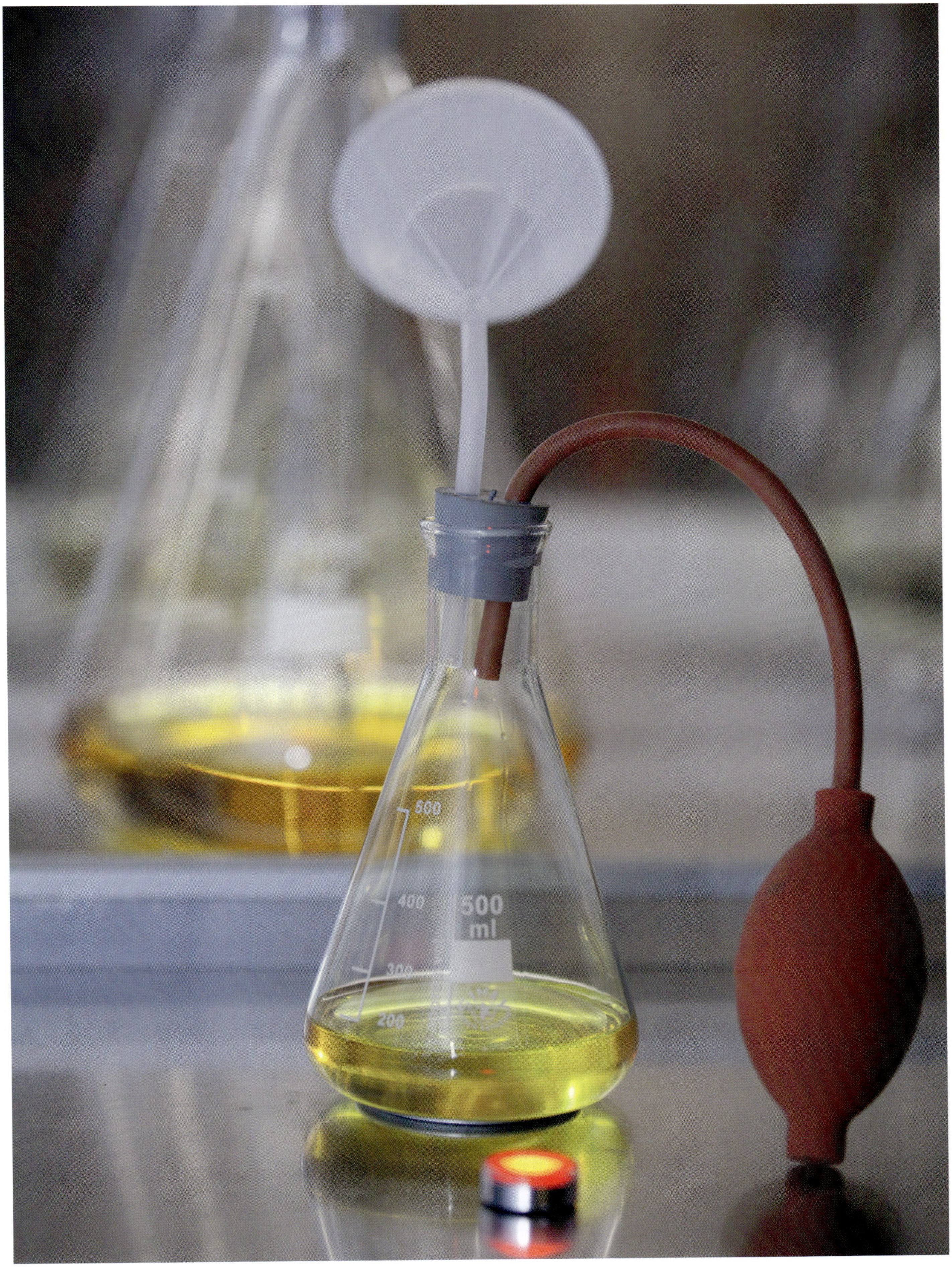

 Cultural Odor Generator, 2012

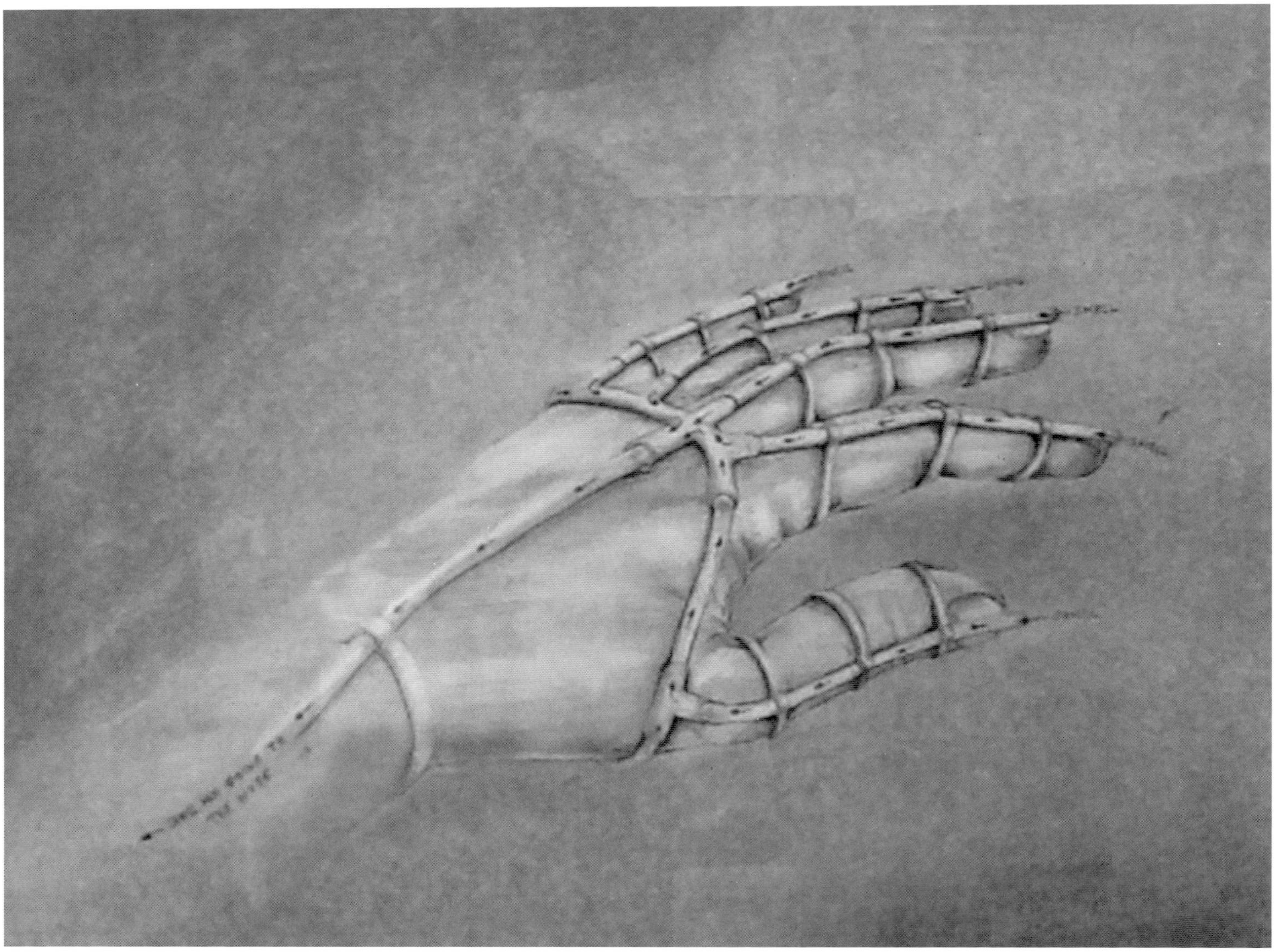

Drawing Blind Smell Touch, 2012

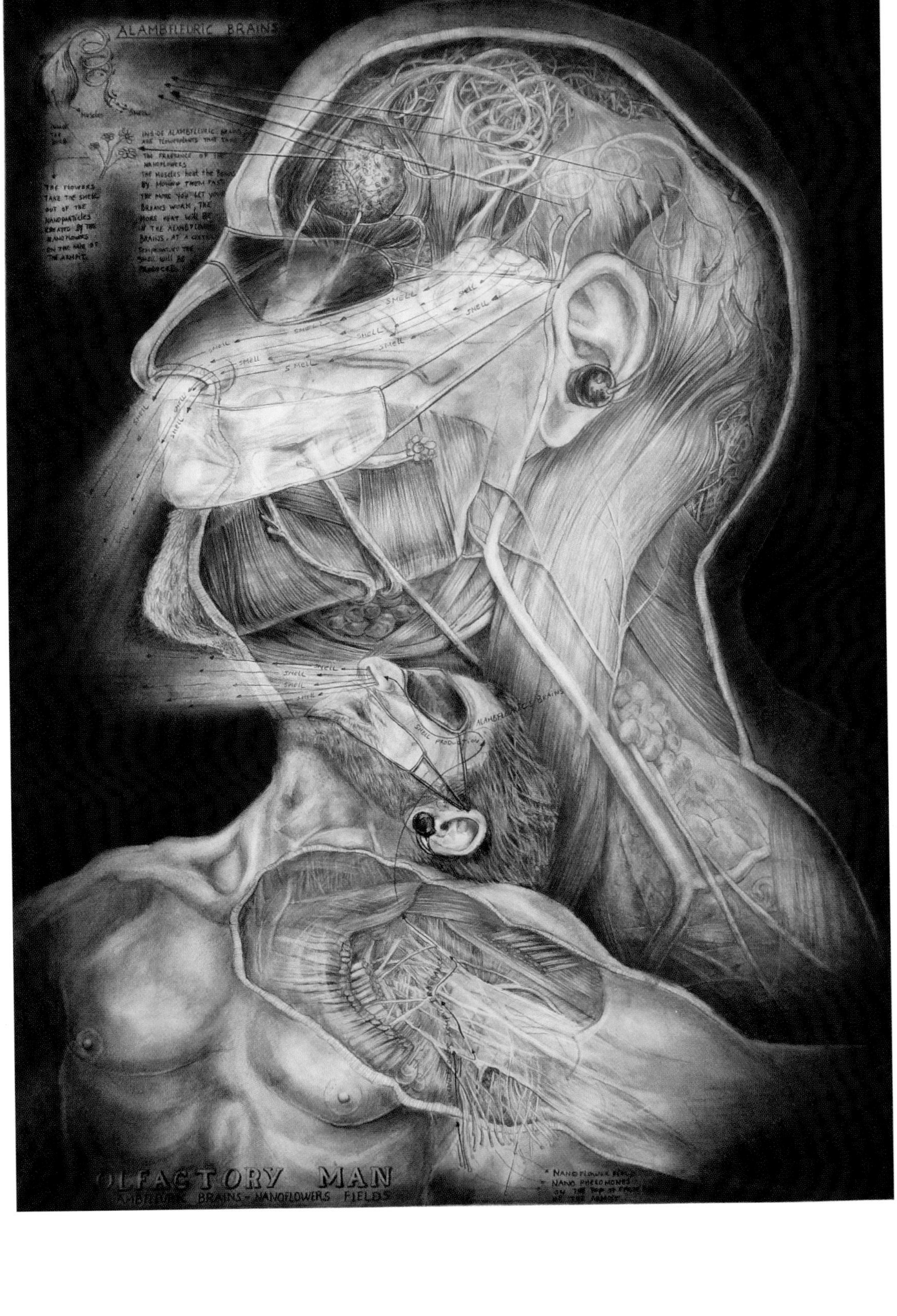

Drawing Olfactory Man, 2010

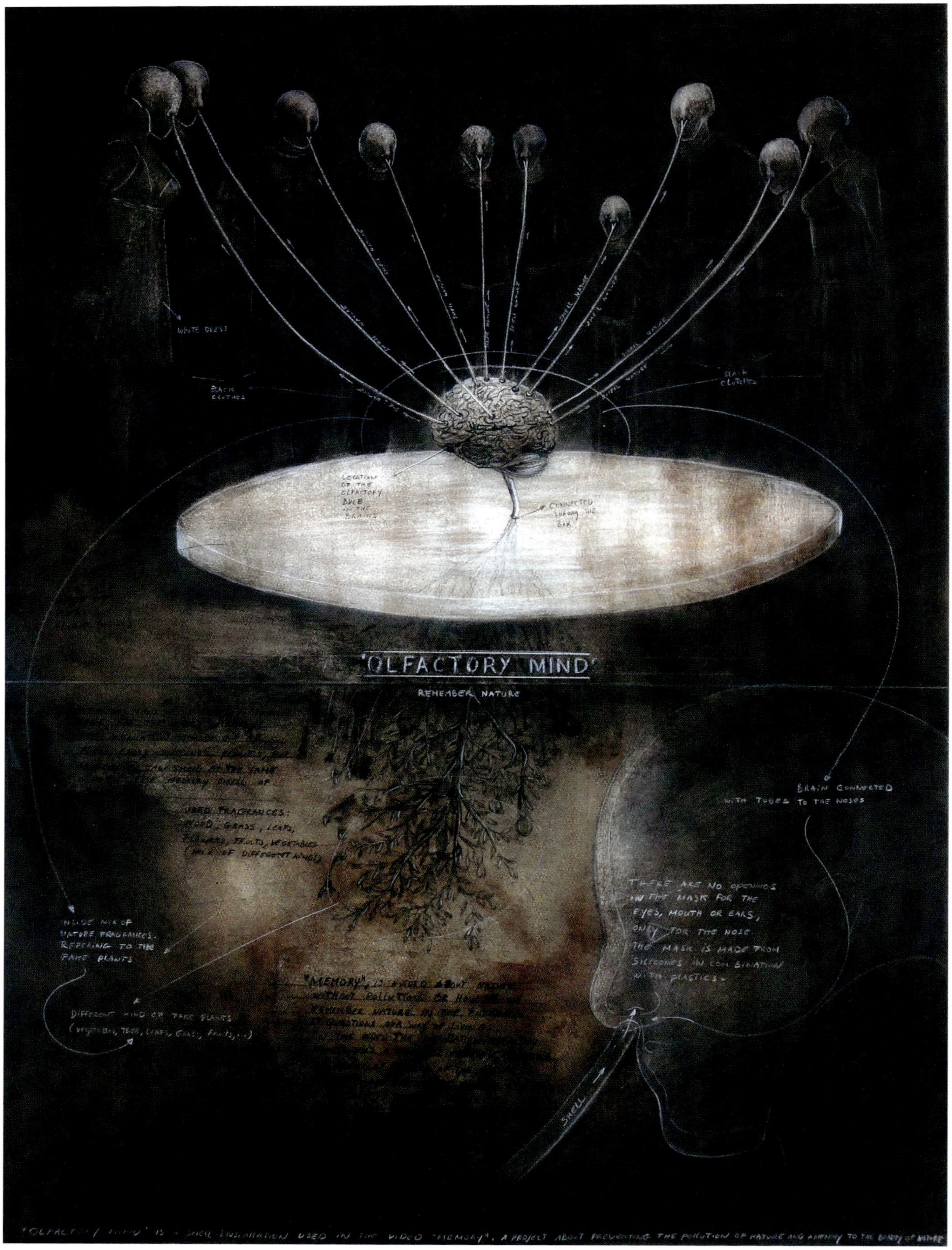

Drawing Olfactory Mind, 2011

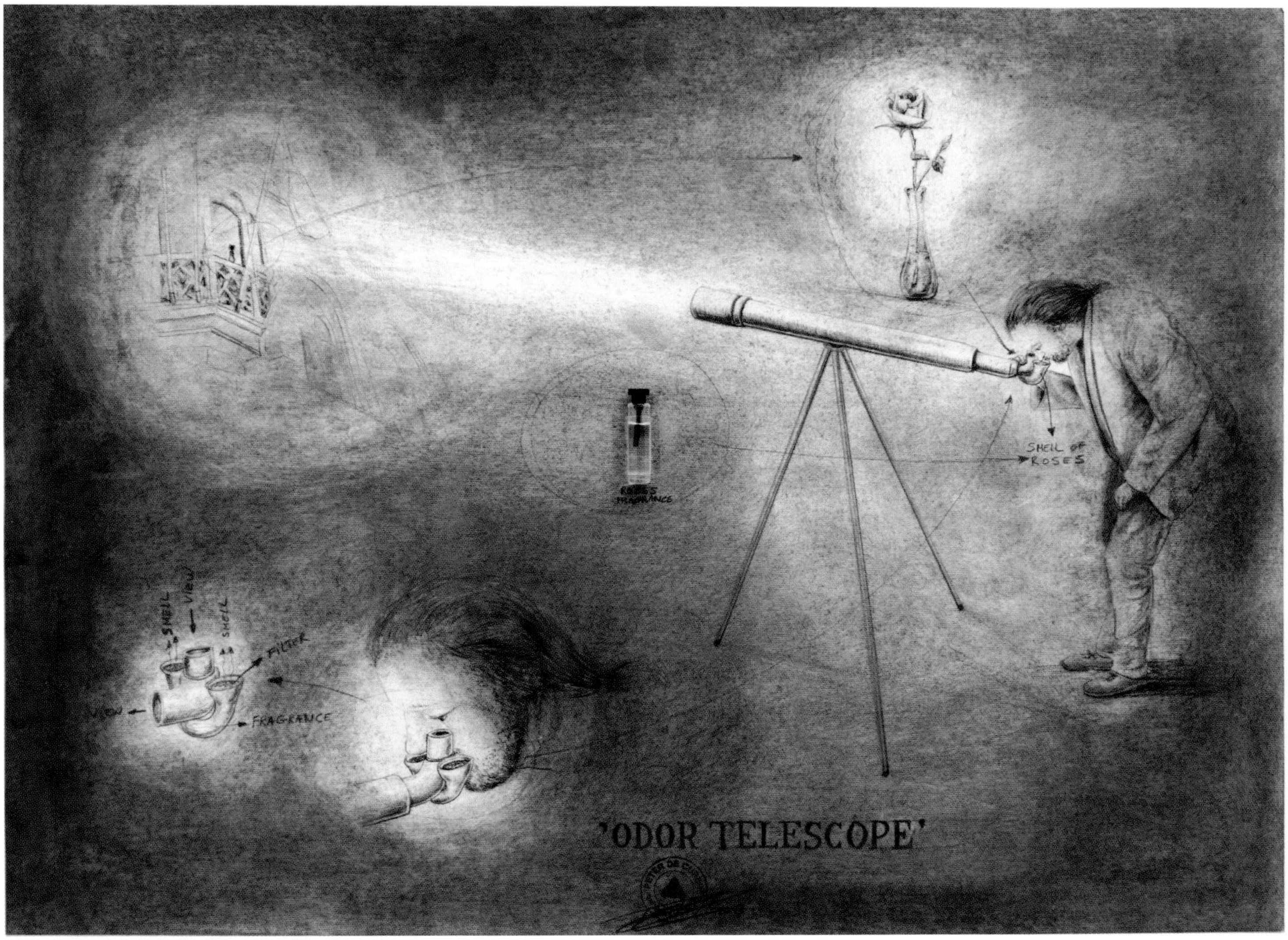

 Odor Telescope, 2013

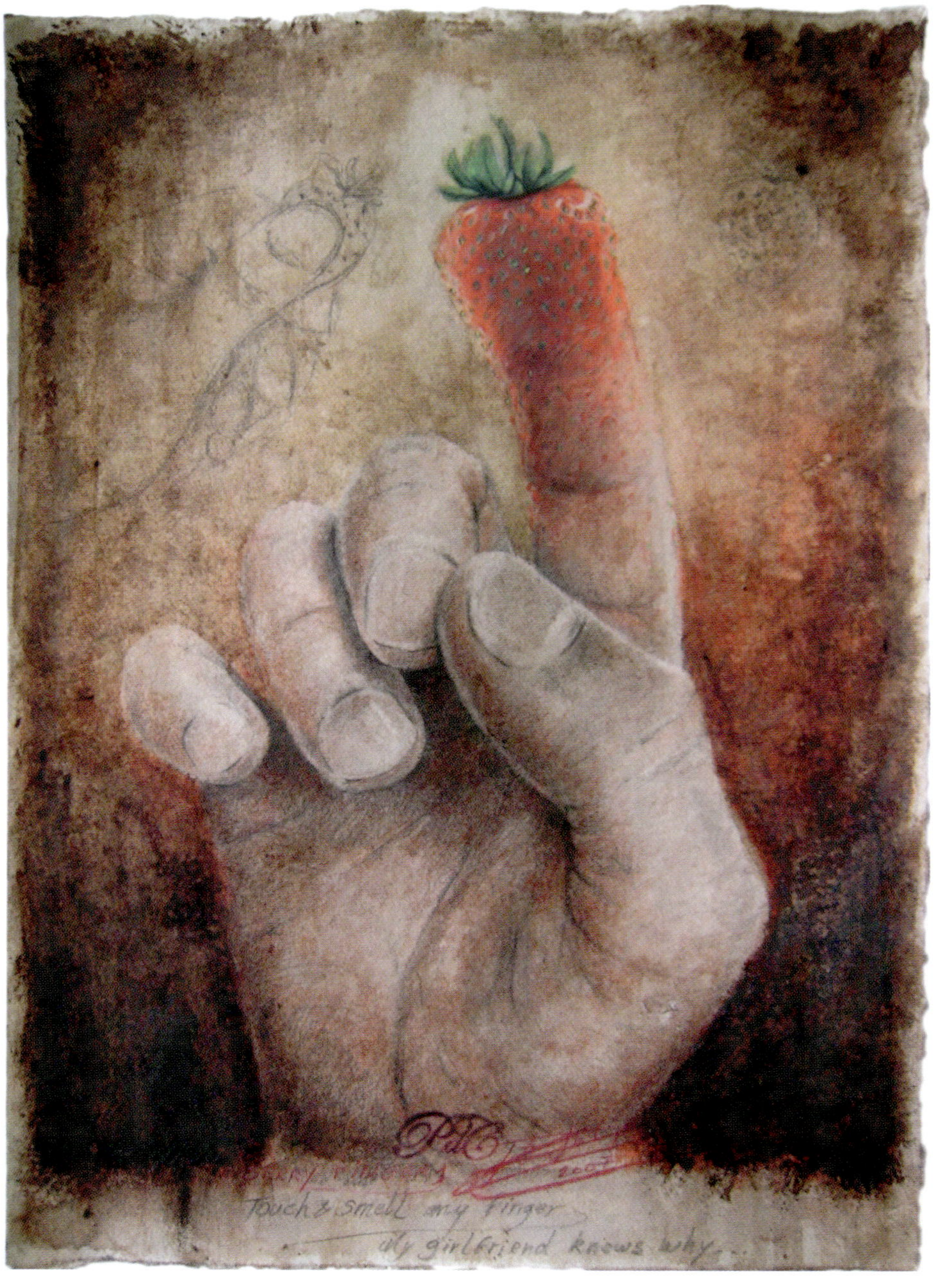

Touch & Smell My Finger, My Girlfriend Knows Why, 2007

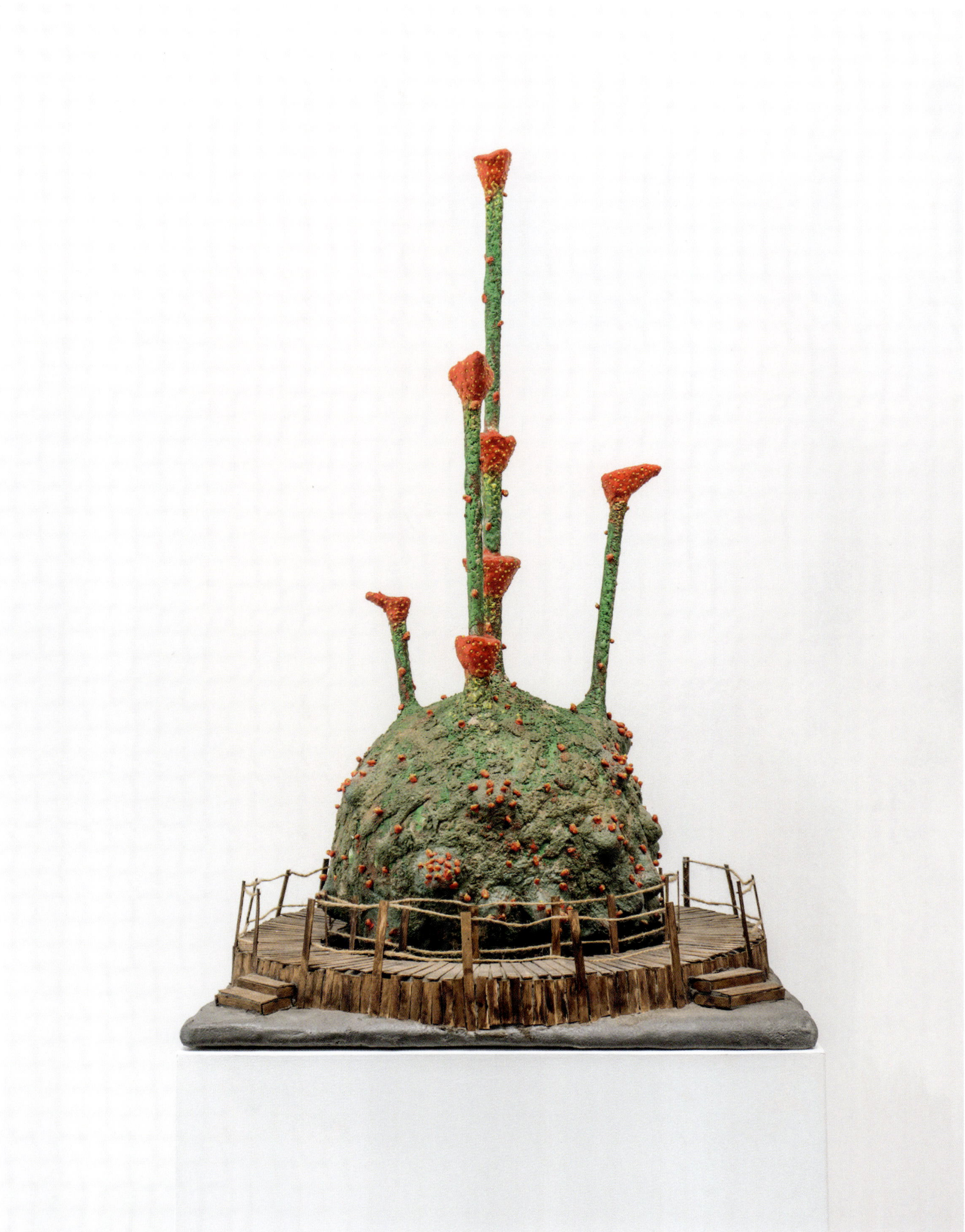

Model Flower Fragum Cardamomi, 2011

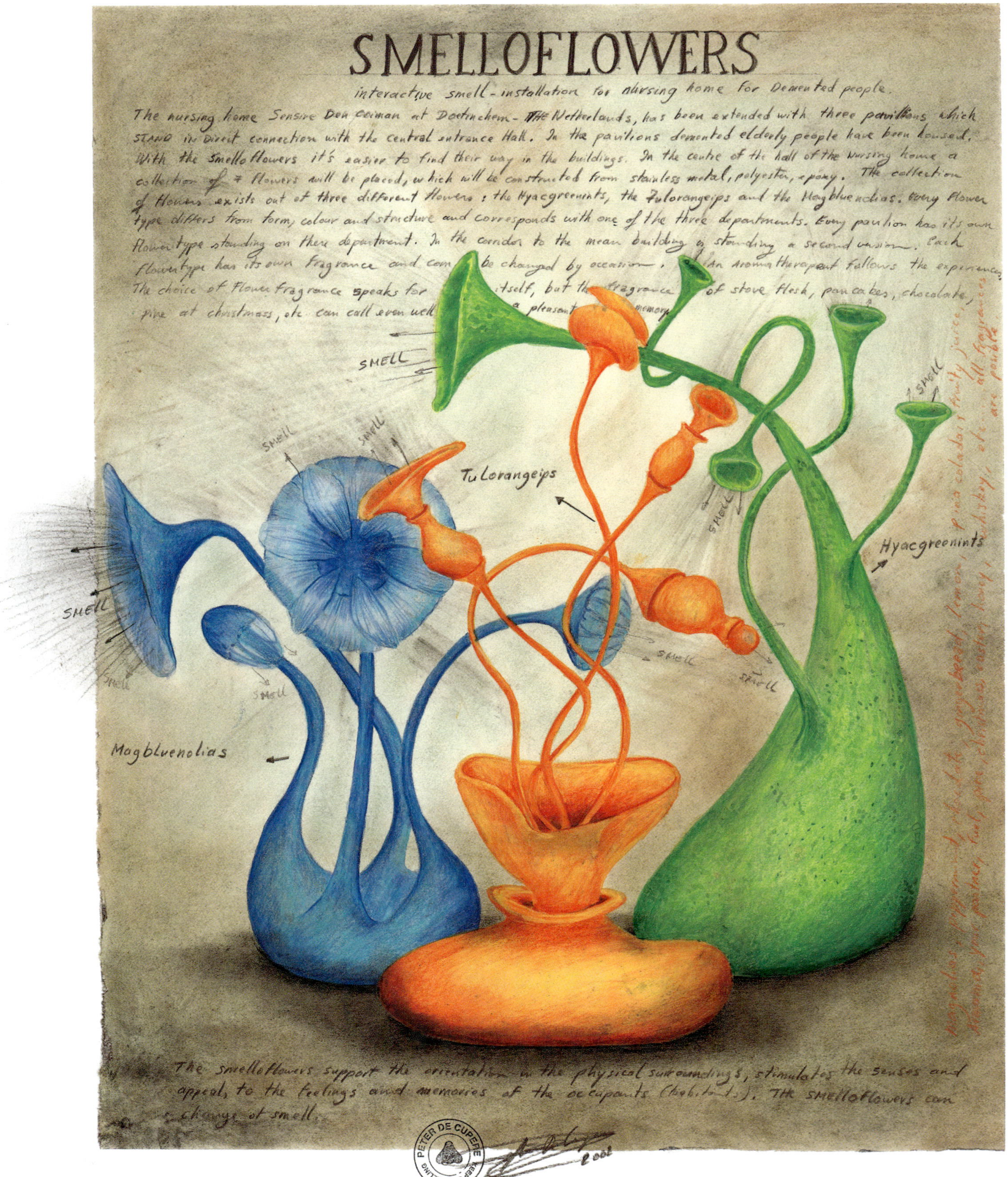

Smelloflowers, 2002

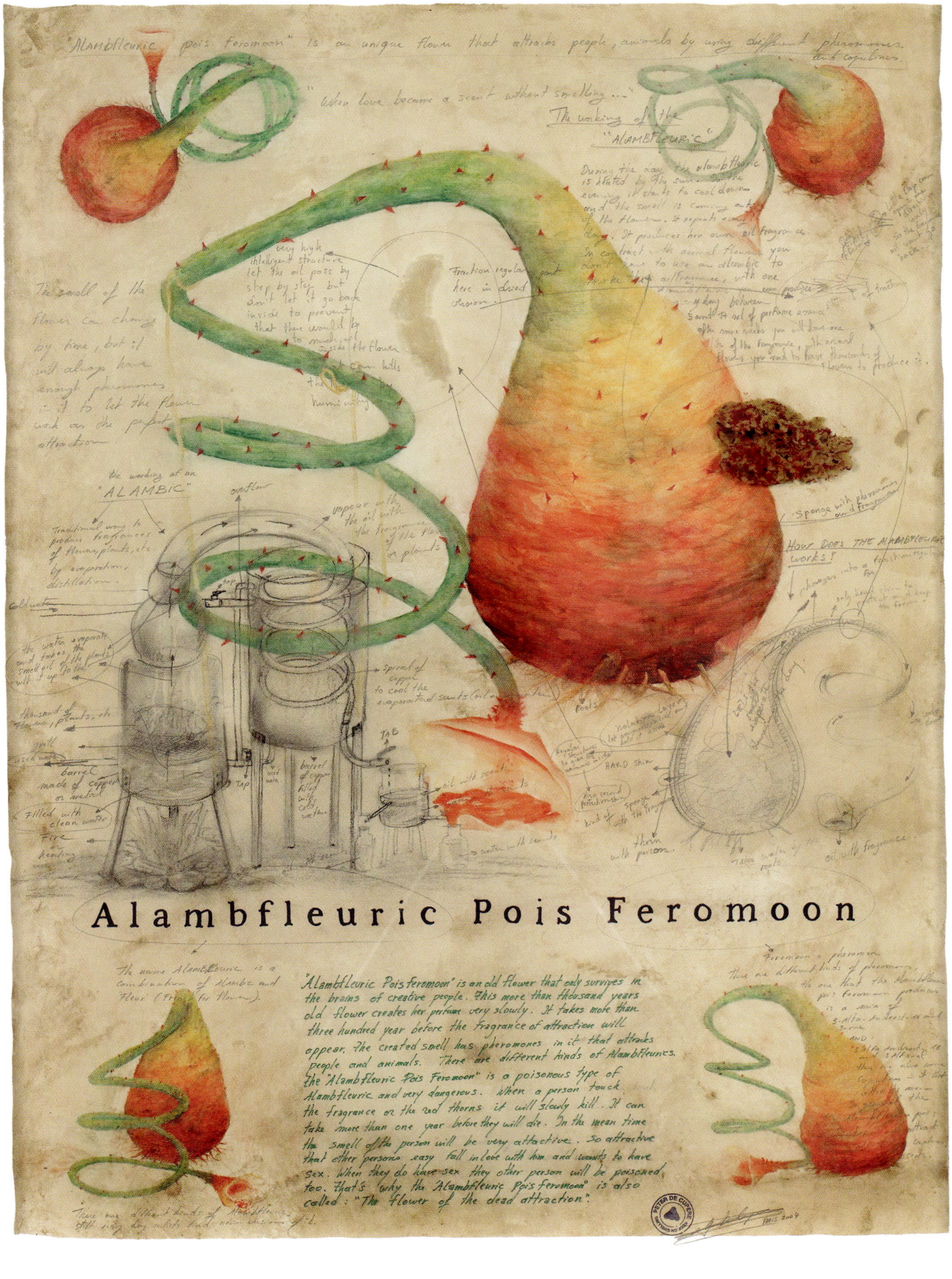

 Drawing Alambfleuric Pois Feromoon, 2004

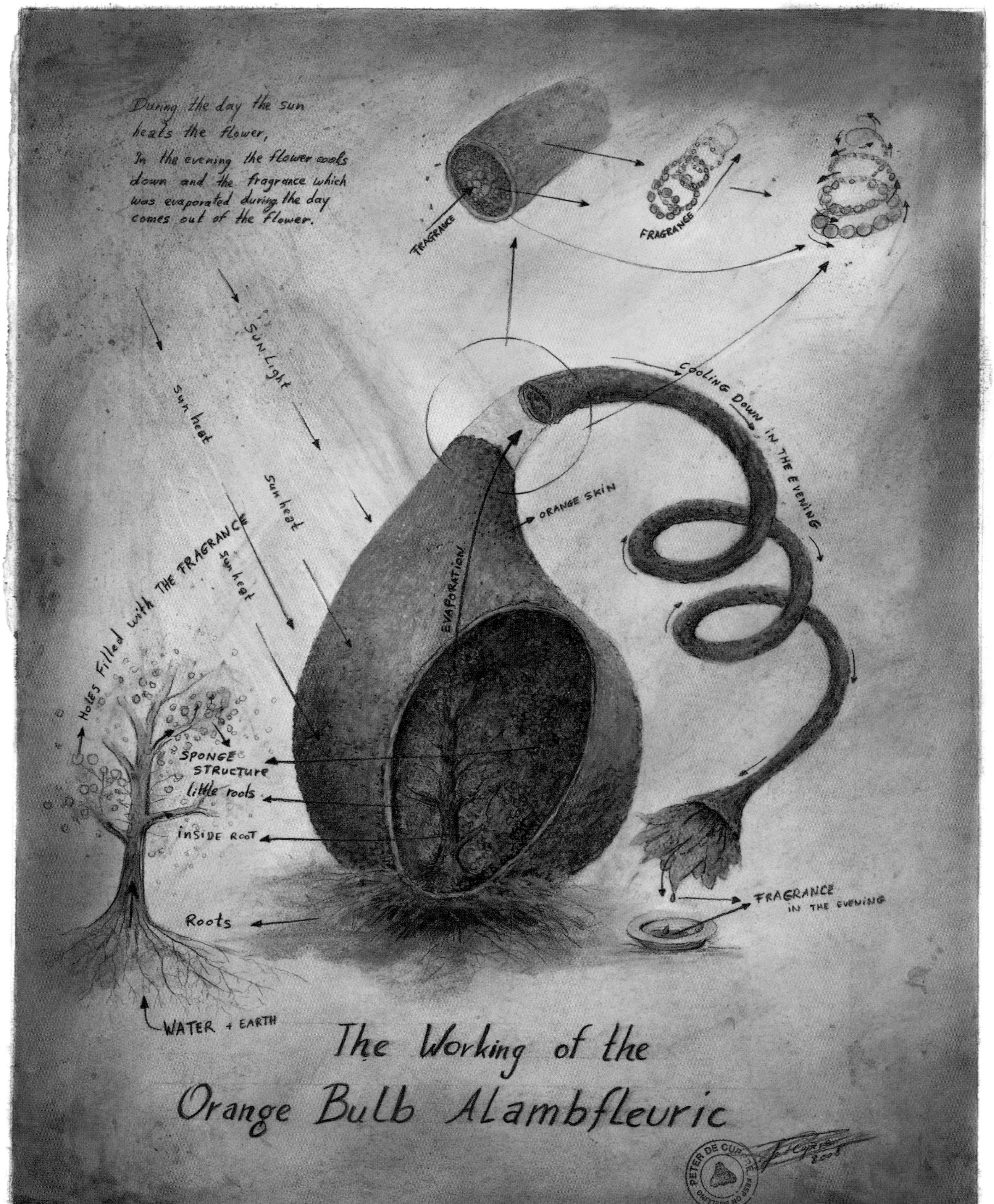

Drawing Orange Bulb Alambfleuric, 2008

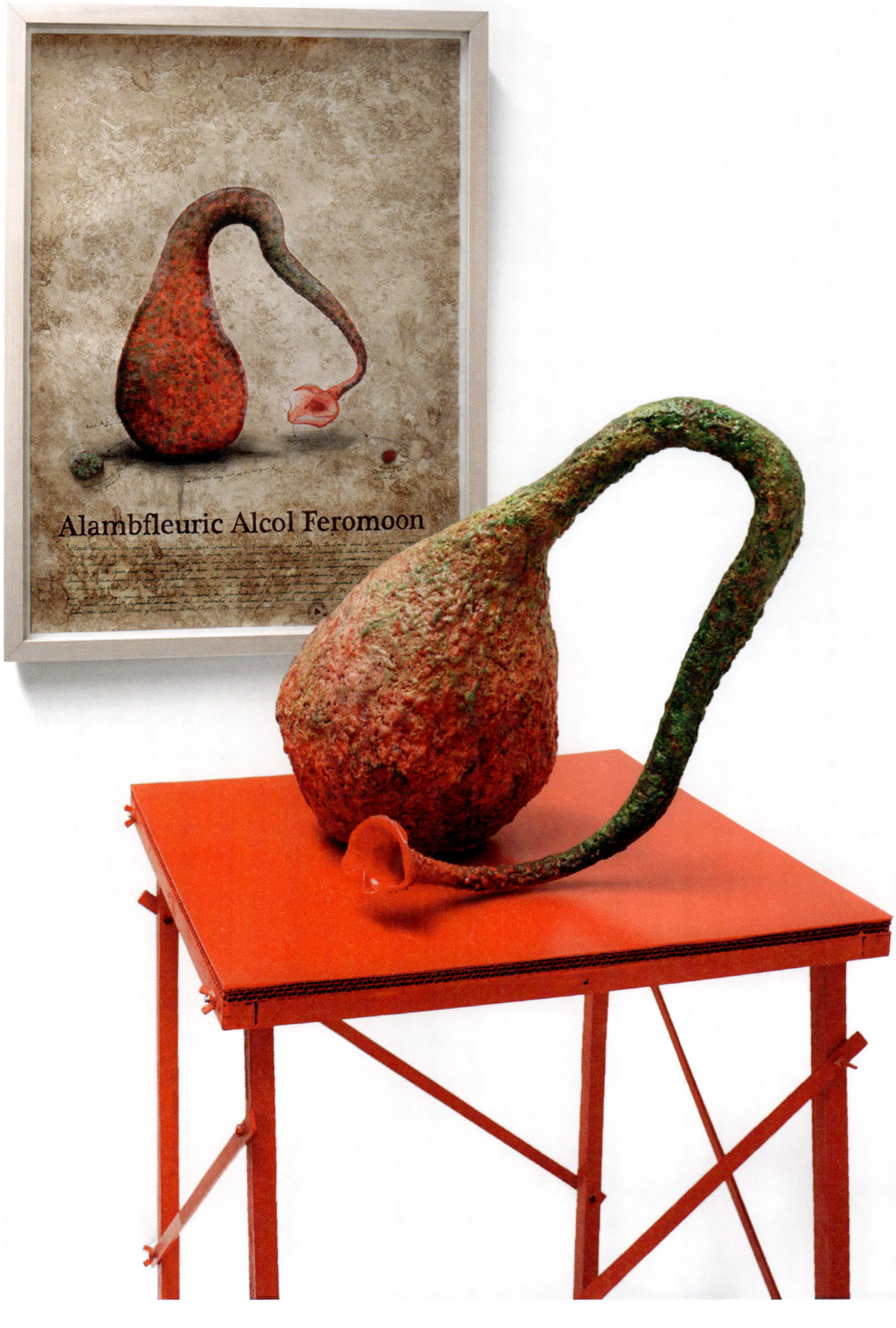

 Drawing & Sculpture Alambfleuric Alcol Feromoon, 2005

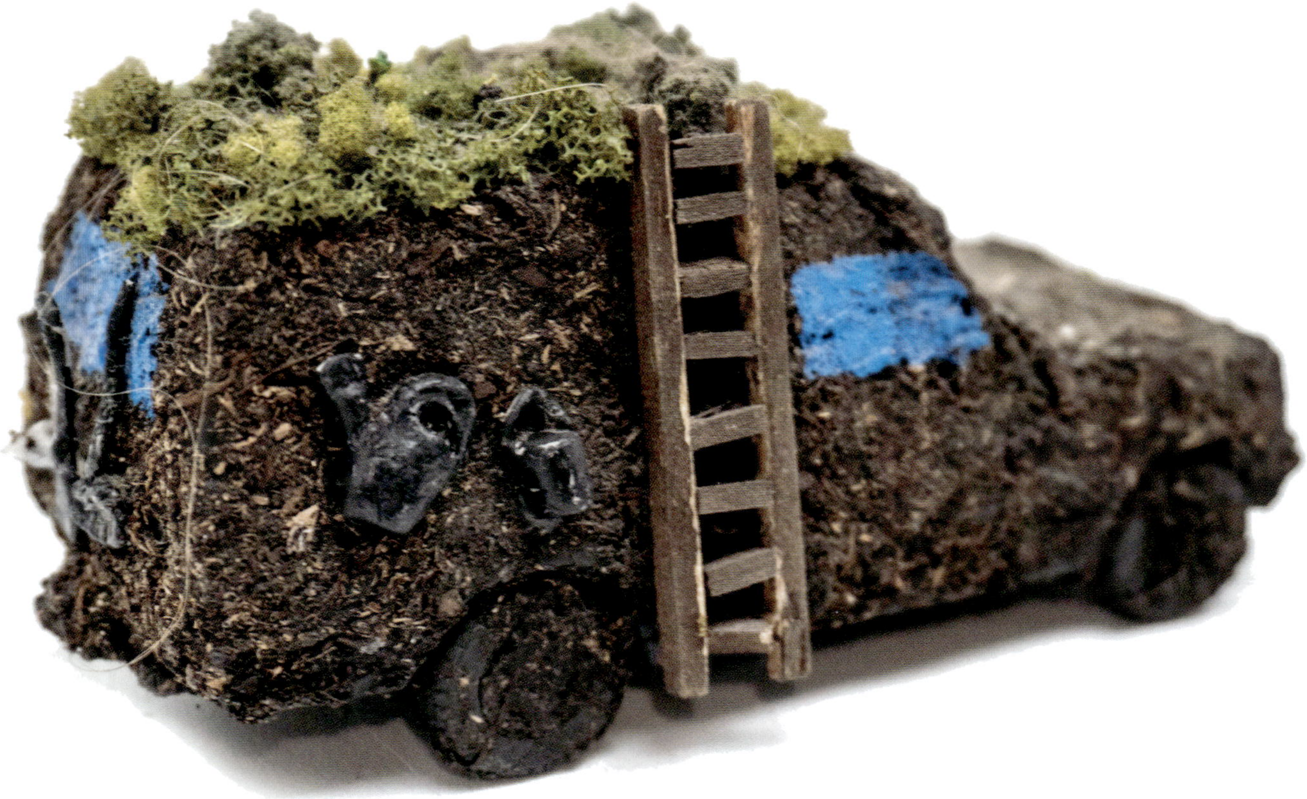

Model Earth Car, 2002

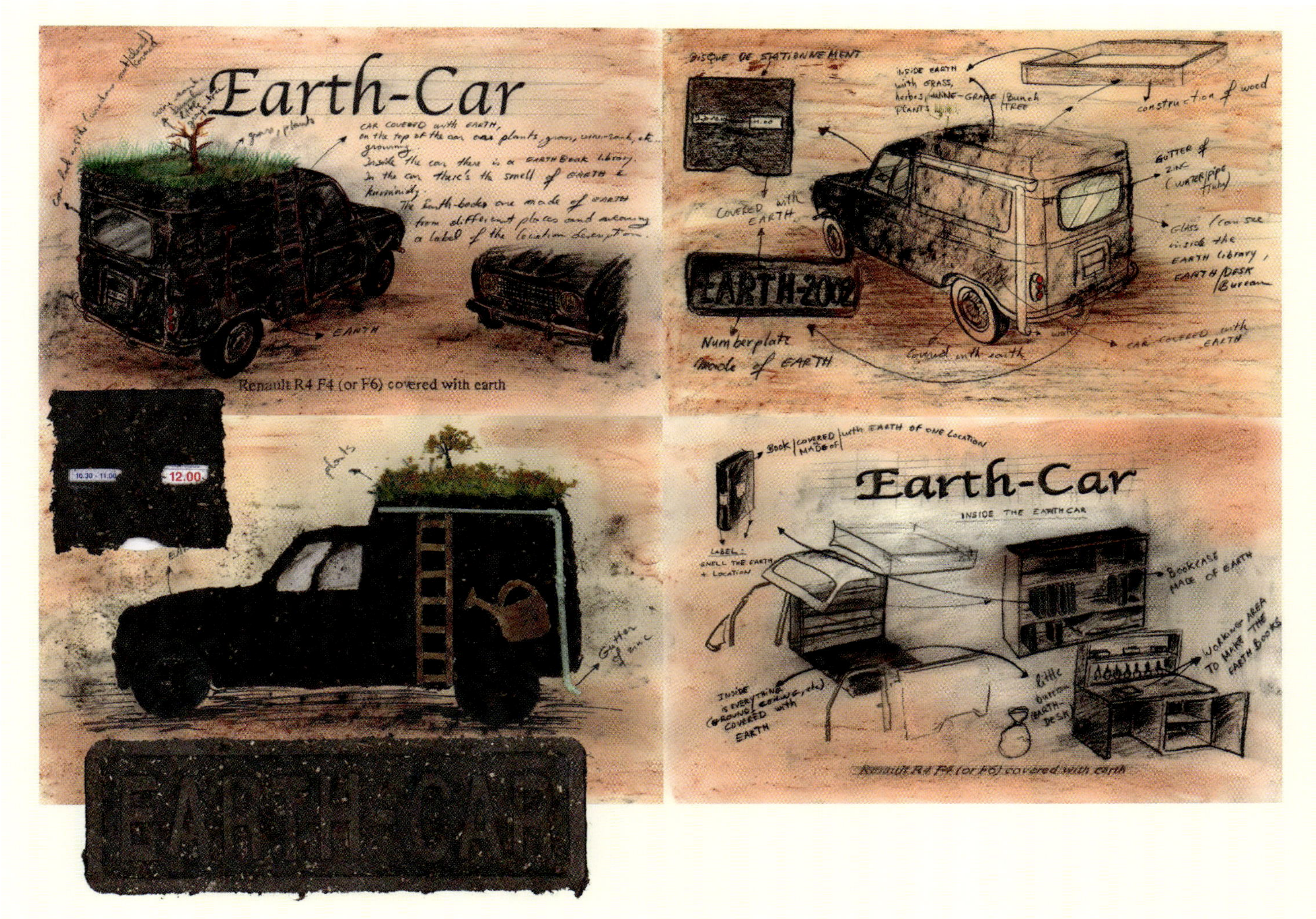

Drawing Earth Car, 2002

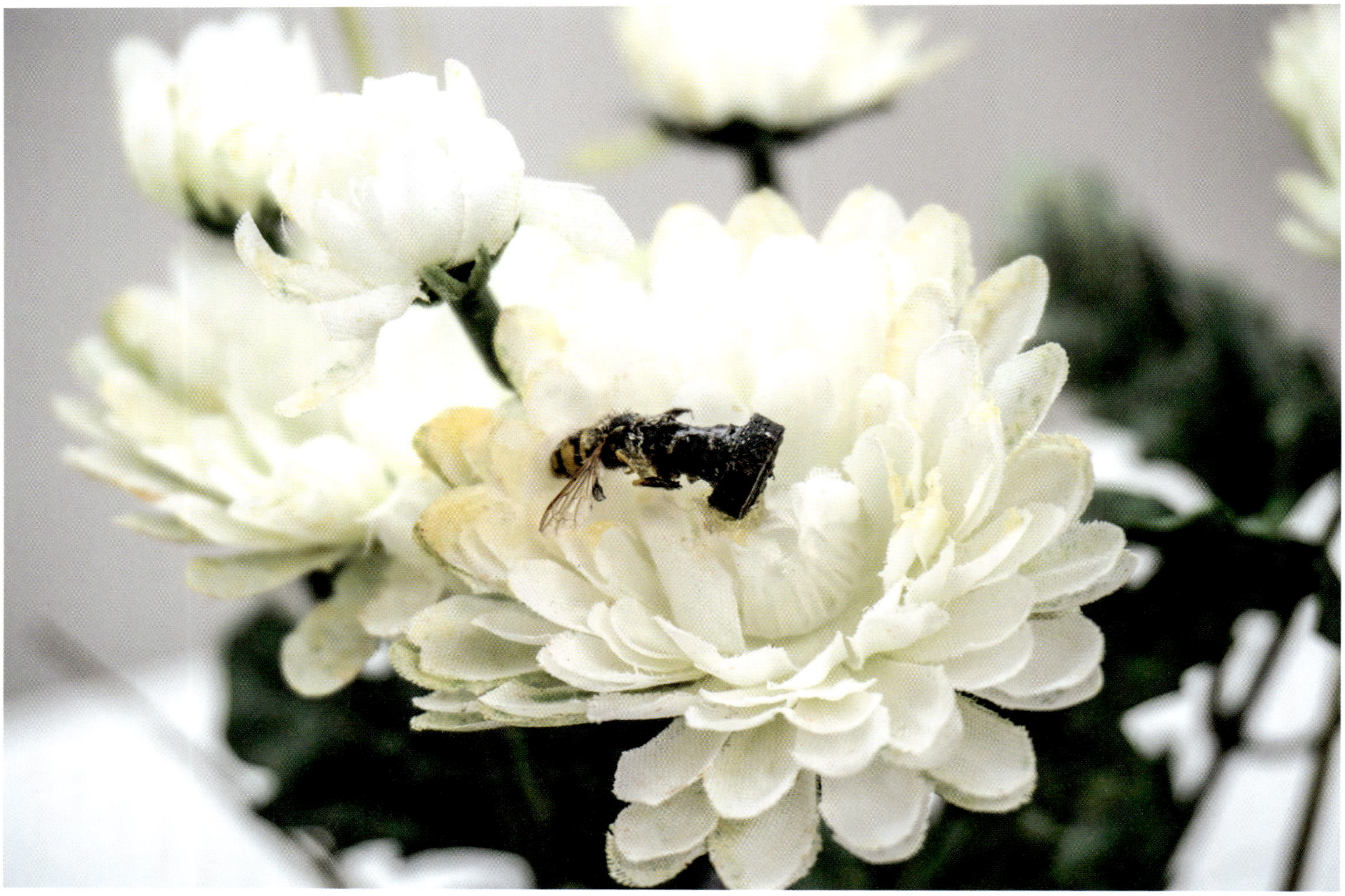

Pollinator, 2014

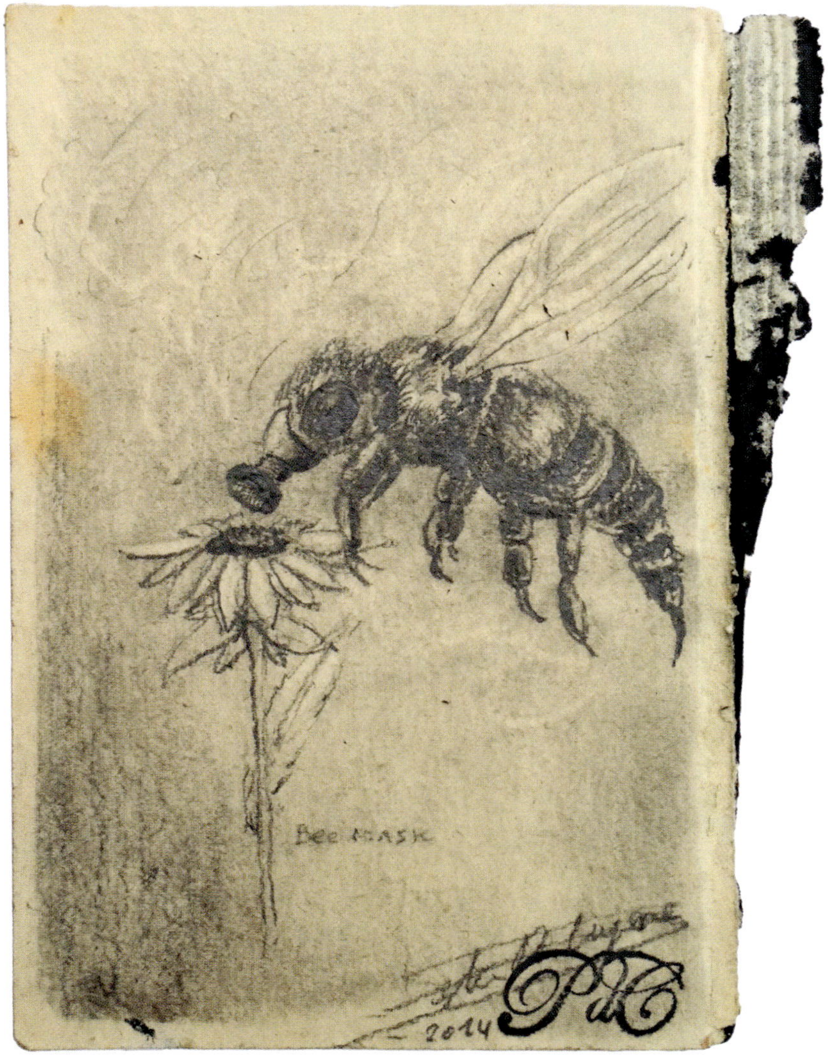

 Drawing Pollinator, 2014

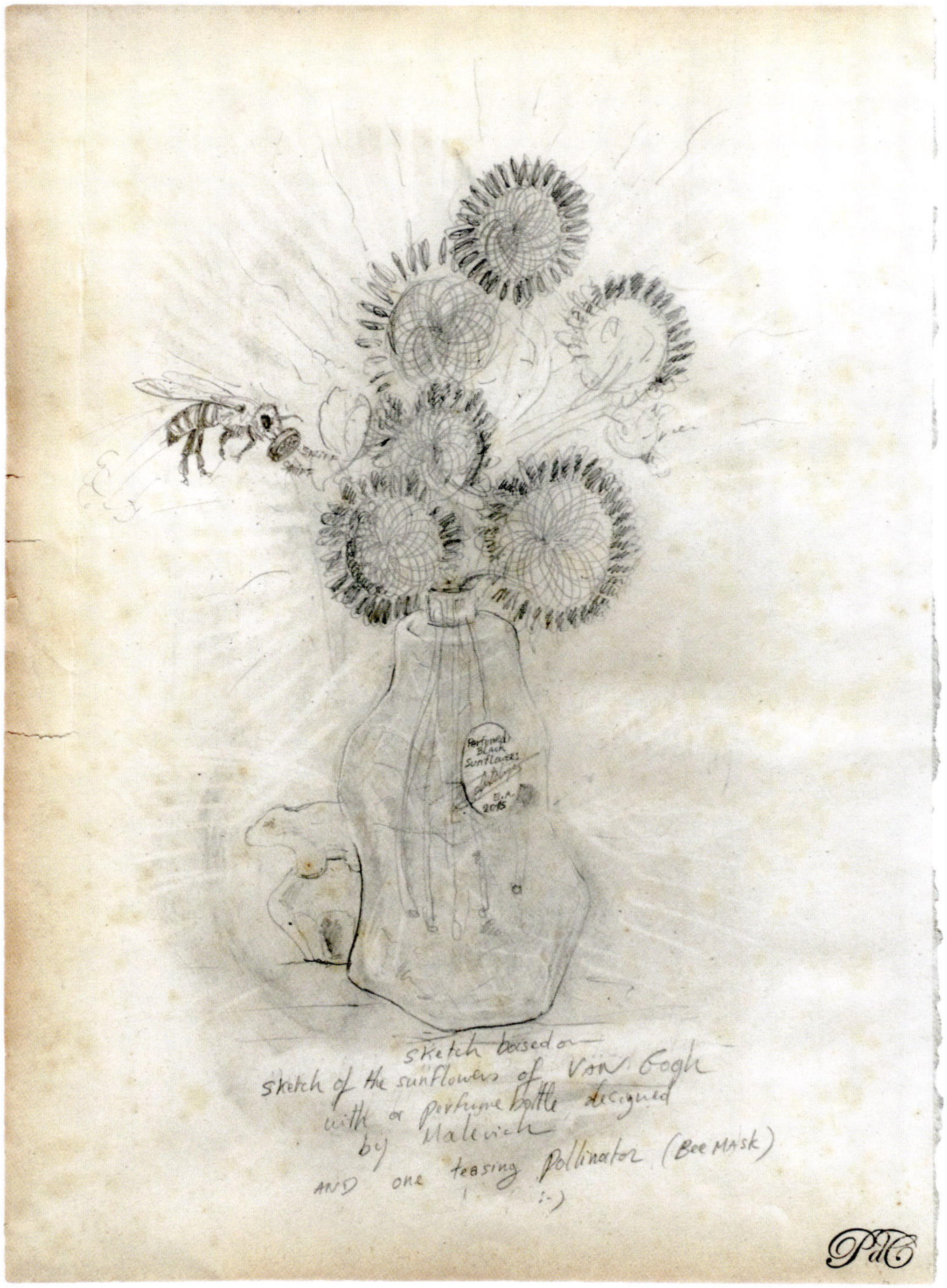

213 Perfumed Black Sunflowers, 2015

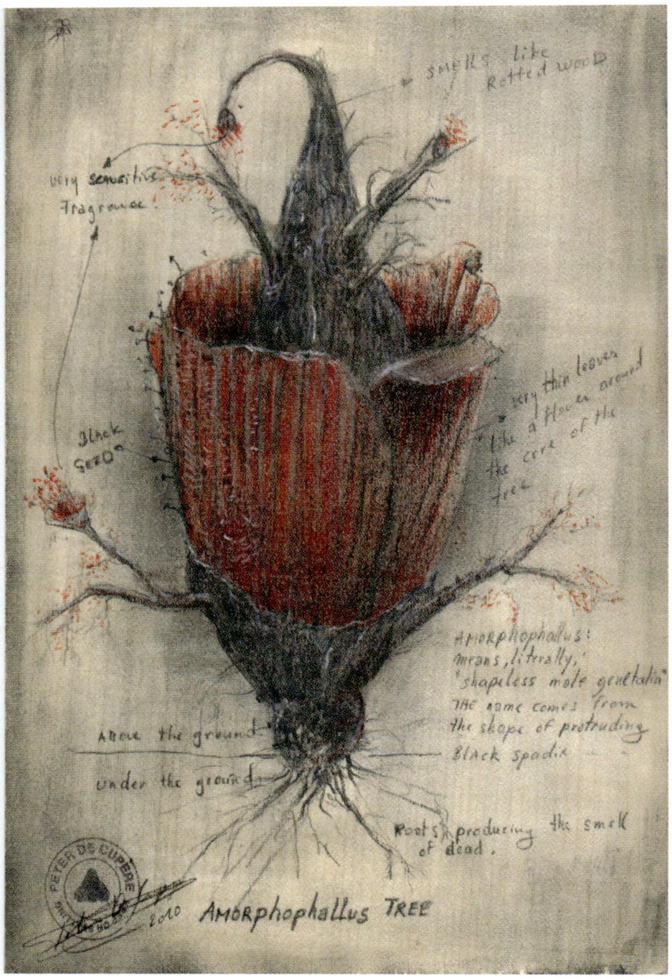
smells like
Rotted wood
very sensitive
Fragrance!
very thin leaves
like a flower around
the core of the
tree
Black
seeds
Amorphophallus:
means, literally,
"shapeless male genitalia"
the name comes from
the shape of protruding
Black spadix
Above the ground
under the ground
Roots producing the smell
of dead.
PETER DE CUPERE
2010
Amorphophallus TREE

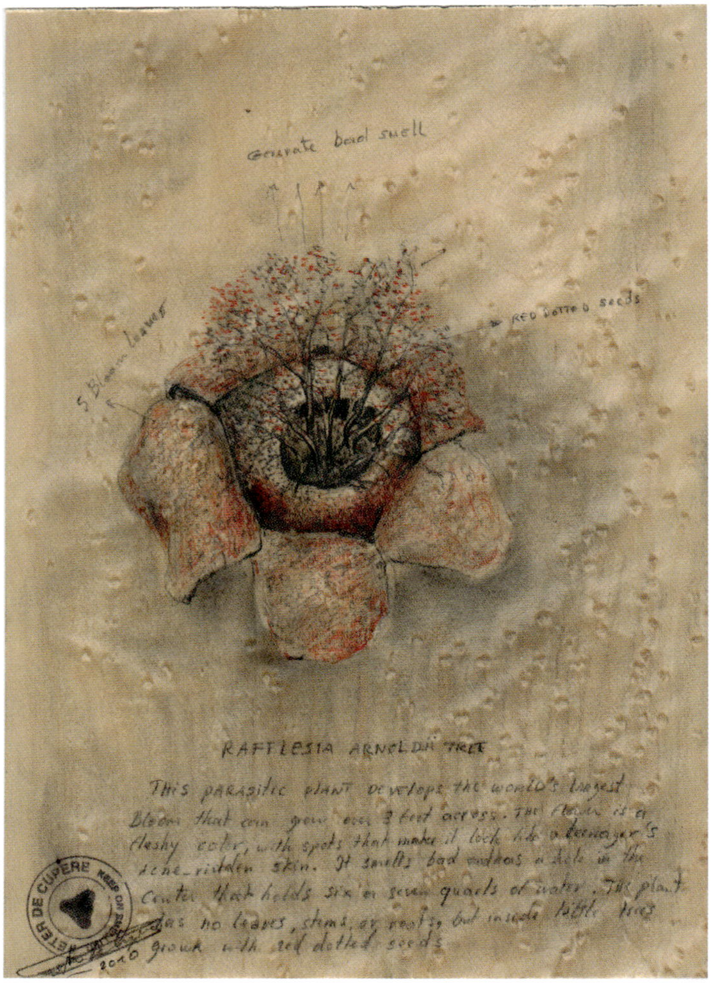
Generate bad smell
Red dotted seeds
5 Bloom leaves
RAFFLESIA ARNOLDII TREE
This parasitic plant develops the world's largest
Bloom that can grow over 3 feet across.
PETER DE CUPERE
2010

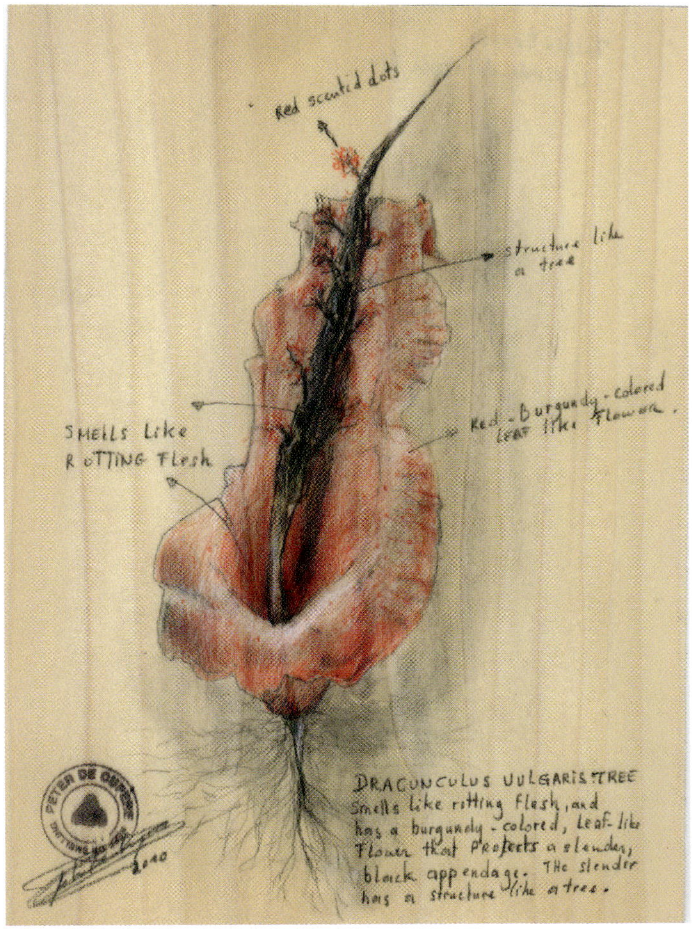

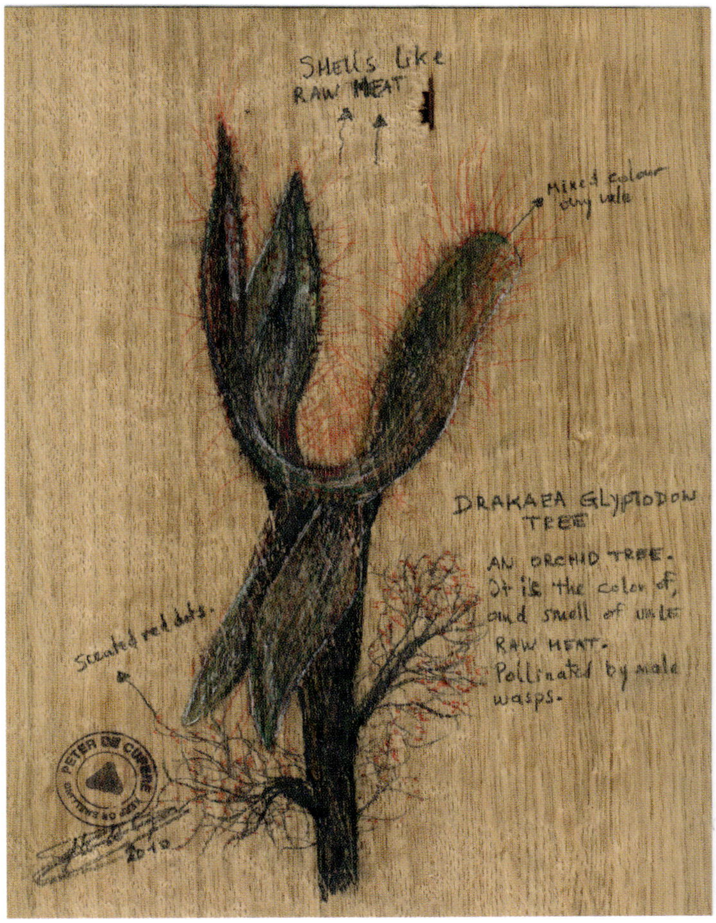

Drawings Flowers on wood veneer, 2010

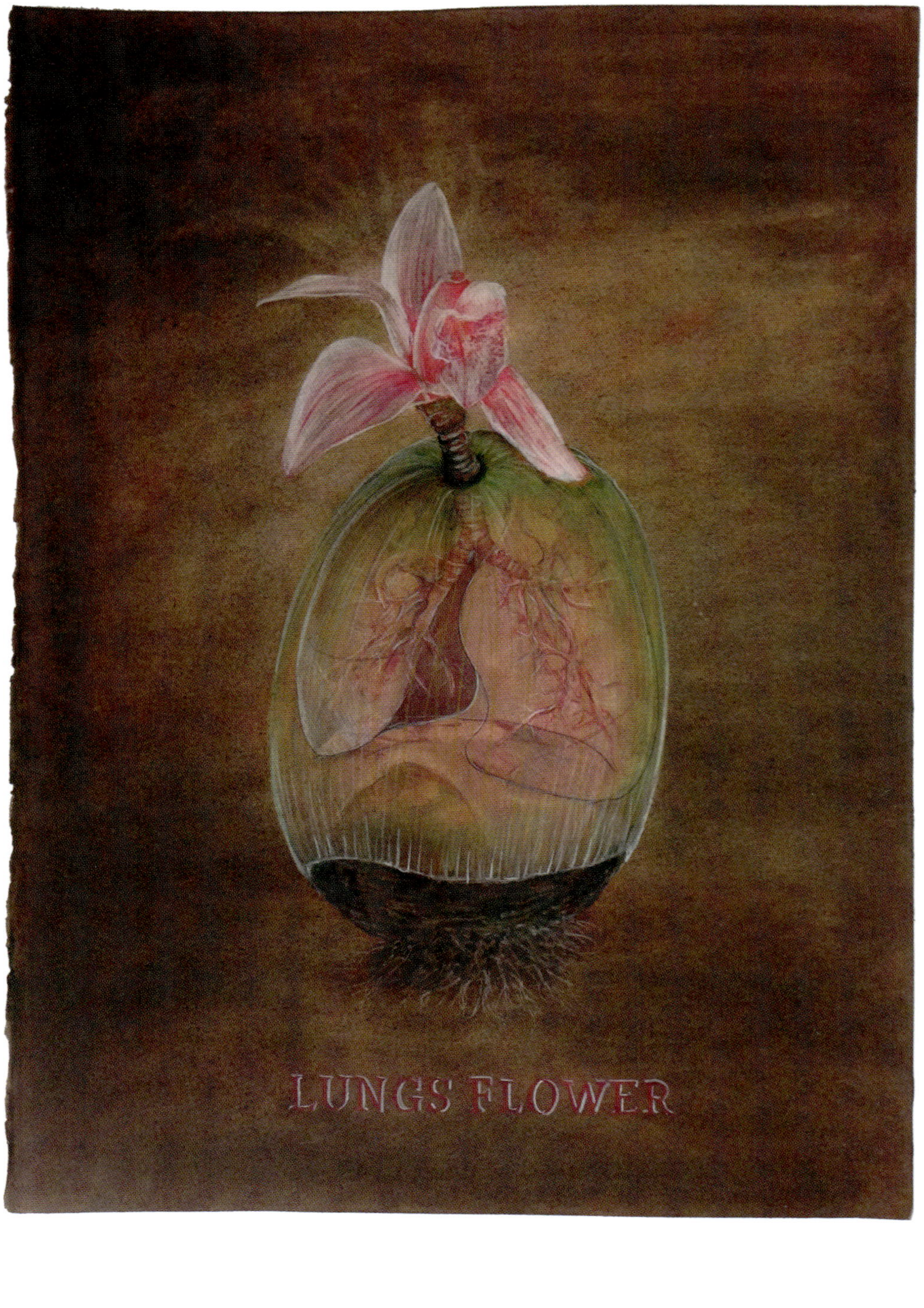

Lungs Flower, 2013

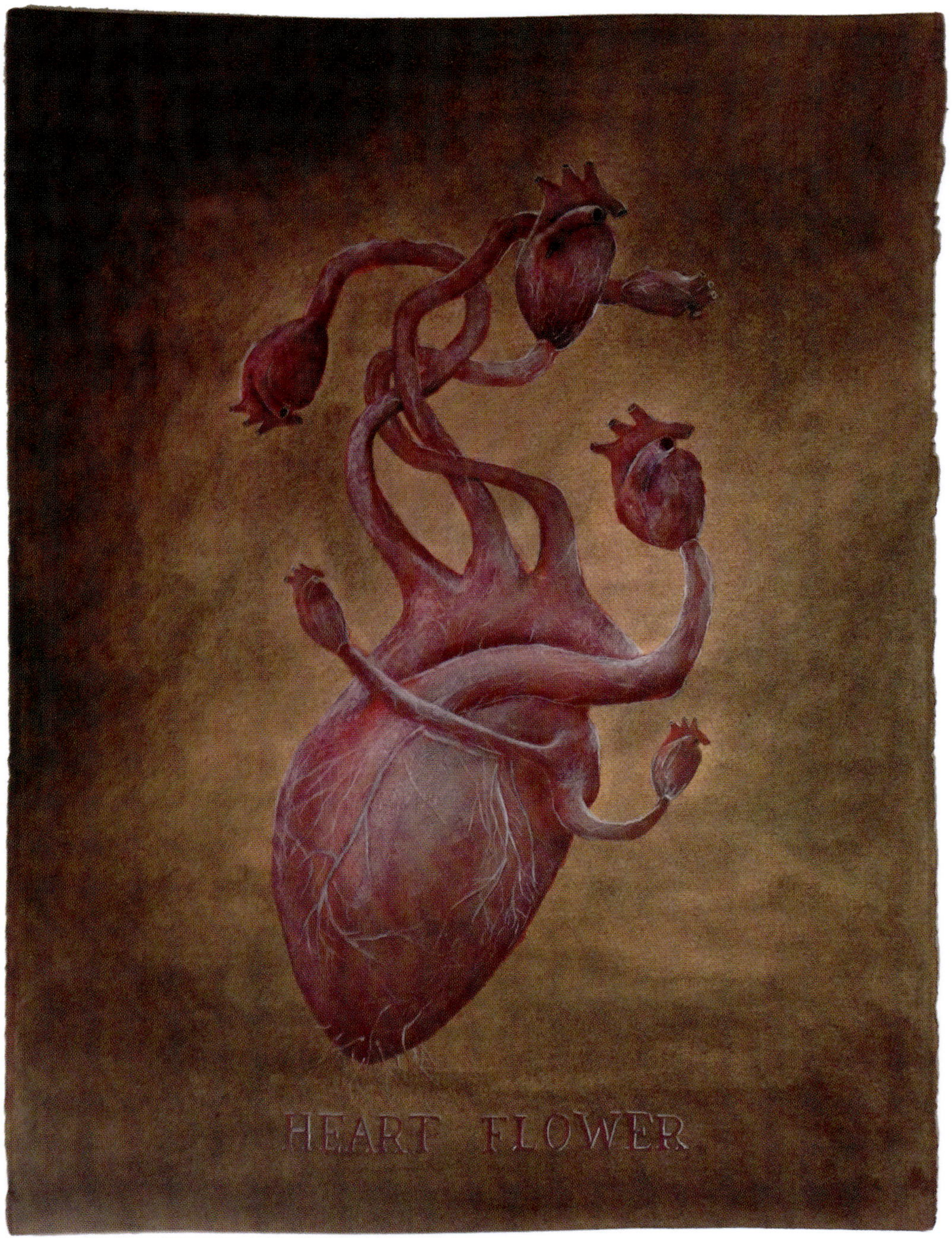

 Heart Flower, 2013

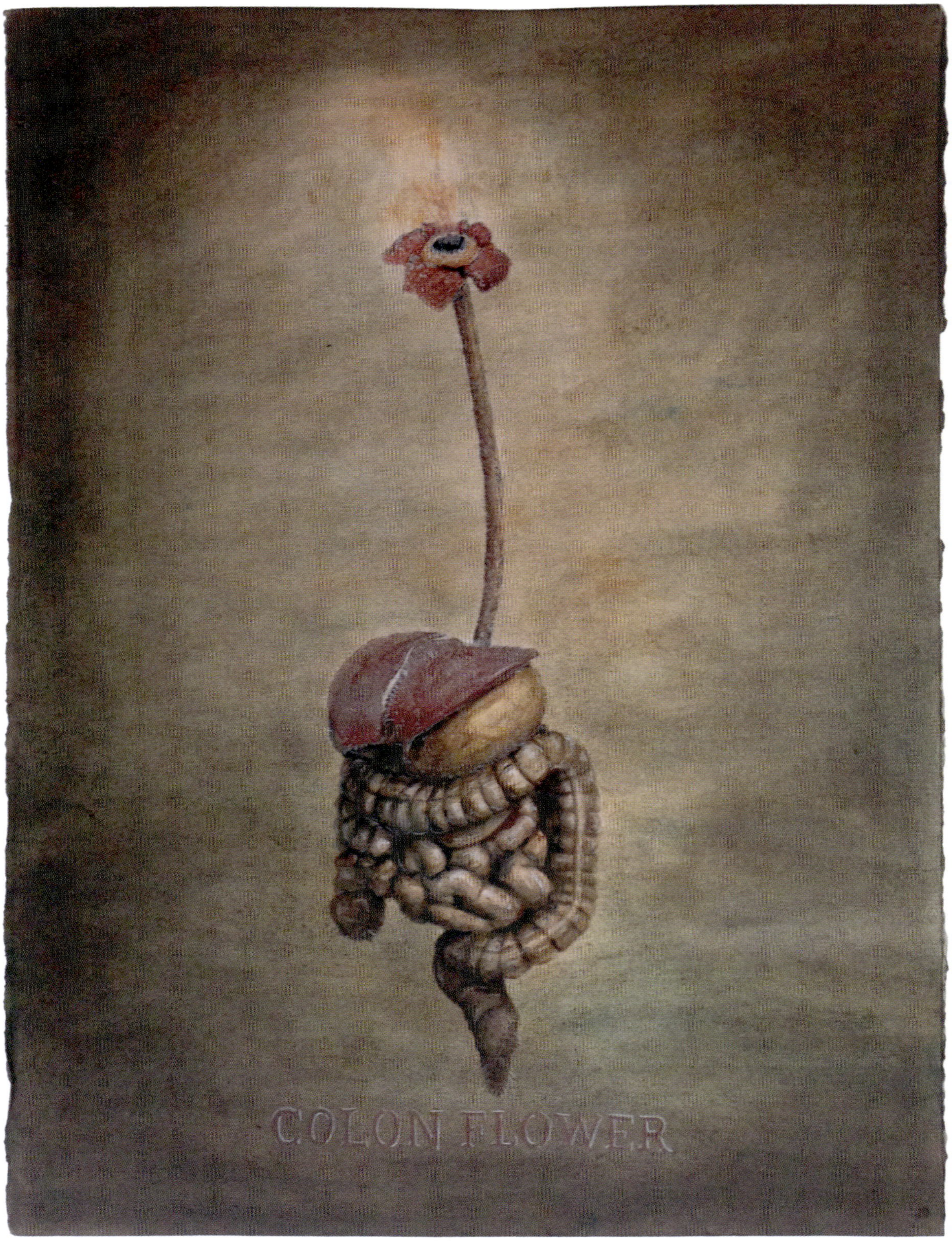

Colon Flower, 2013

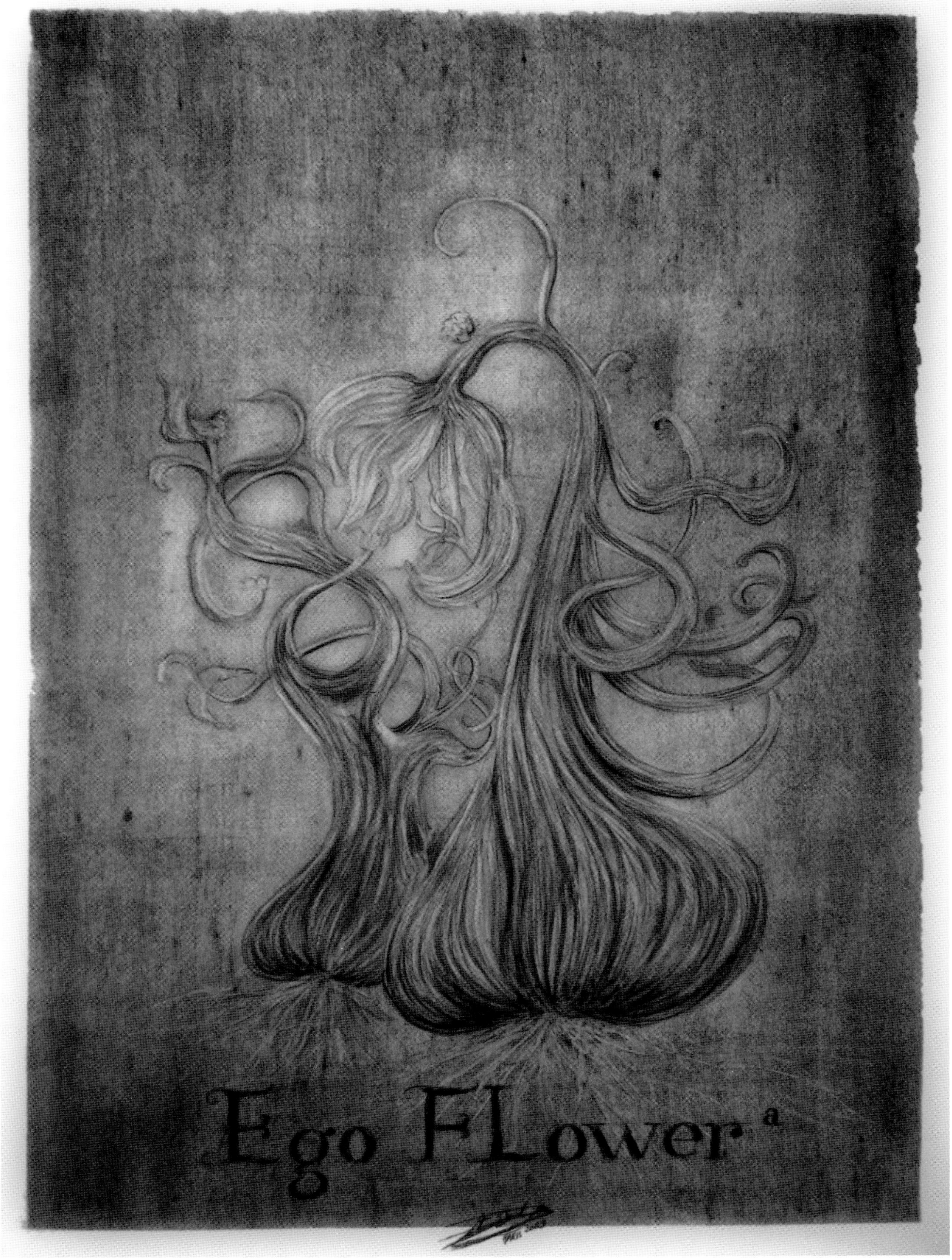

219 Ego Flower, 2005

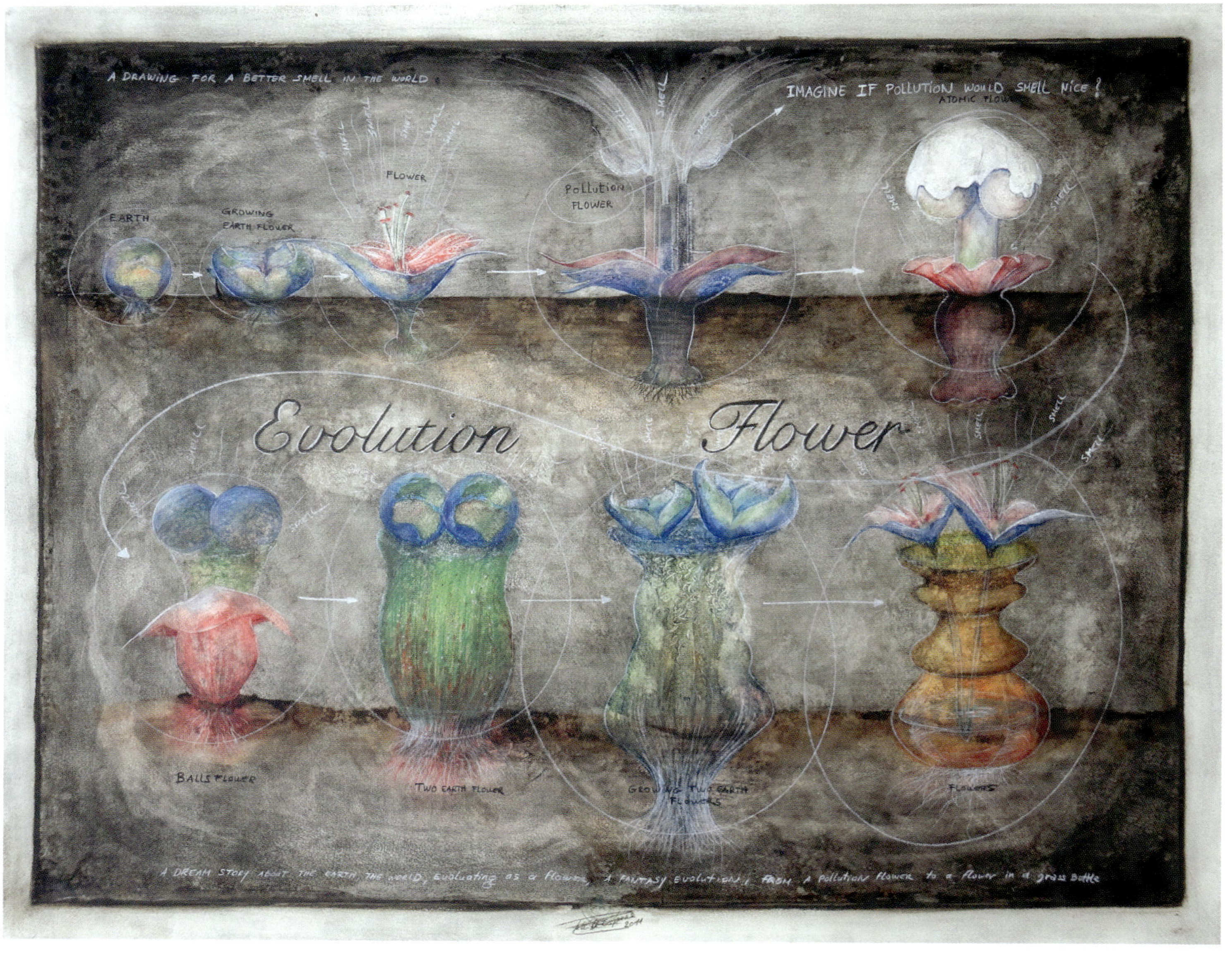

Evolution Flower, 2011

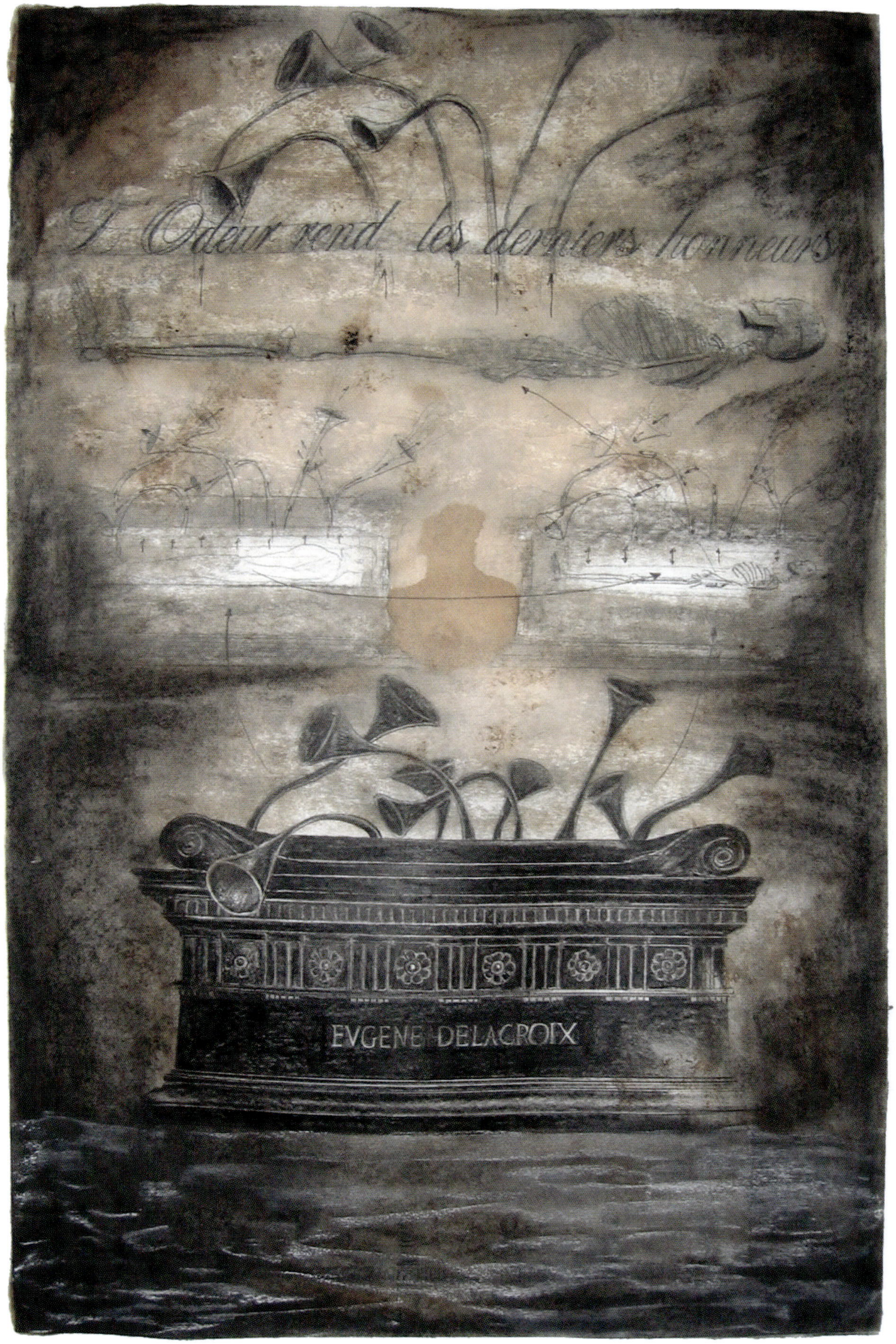

 Drawing l'Odeur Rend Les Derniers Honneurs, 2005

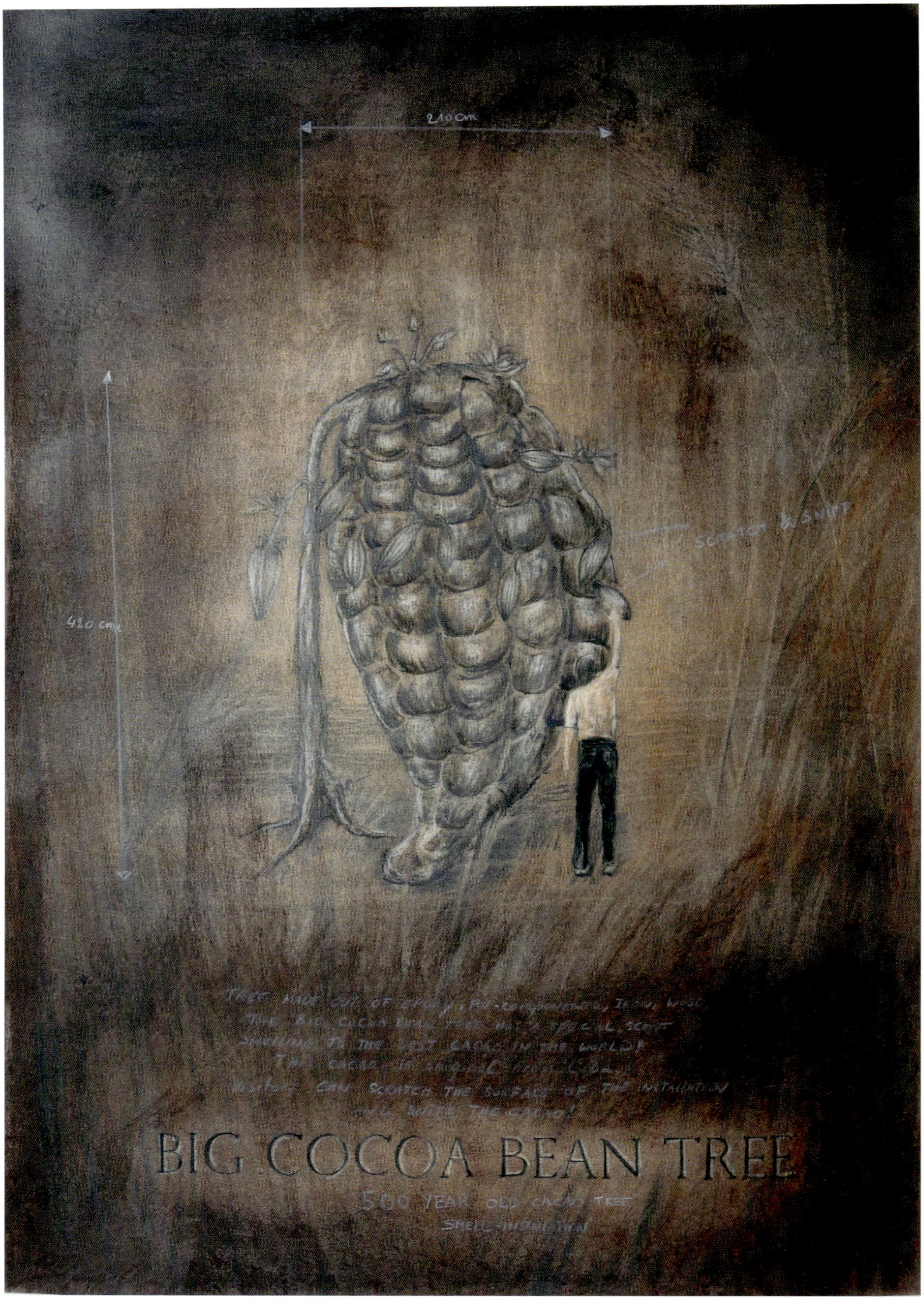

Big Cocoa Bean Tree, 2011

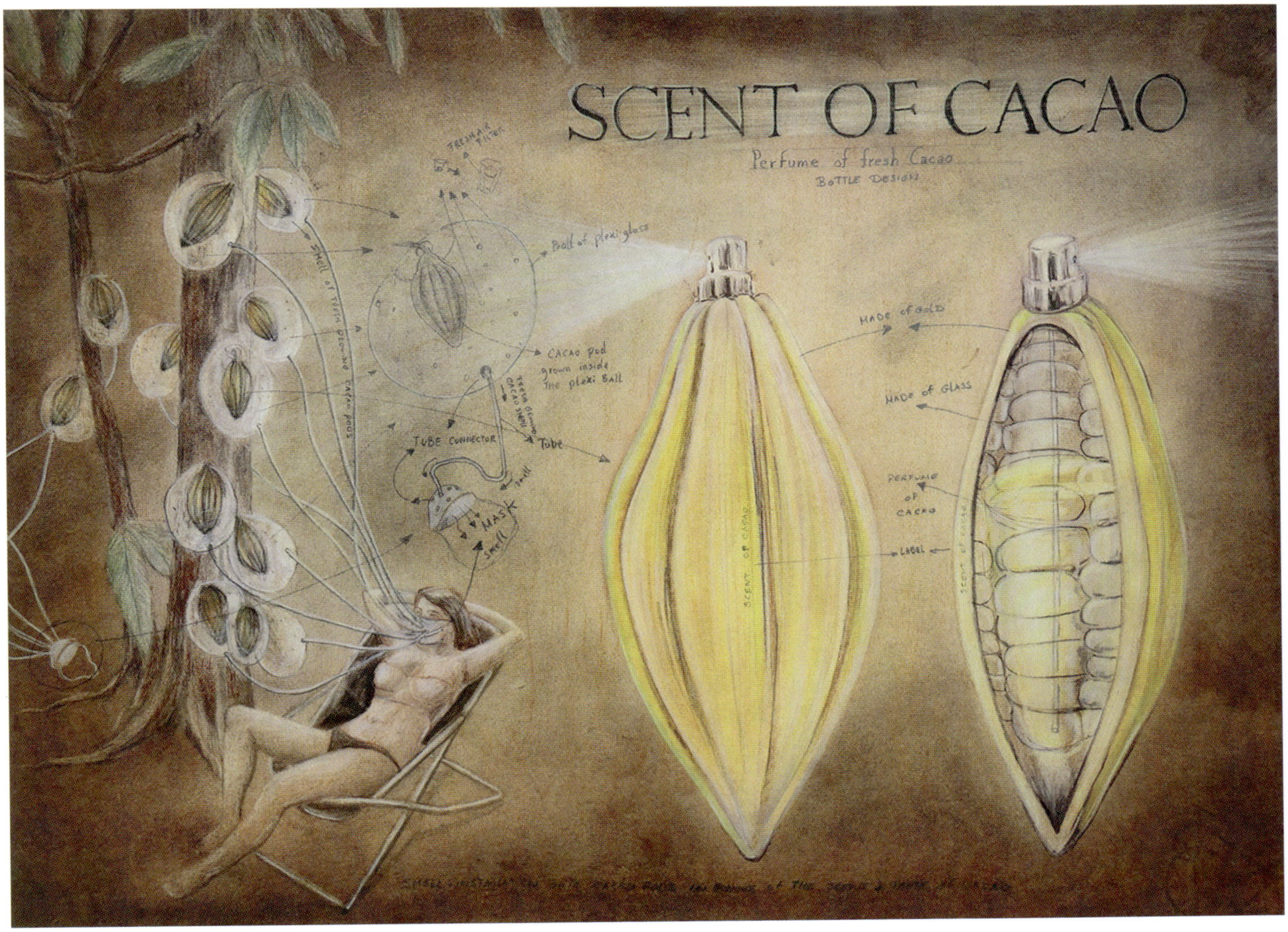

 Drawing Scent Of Cacao, 2011

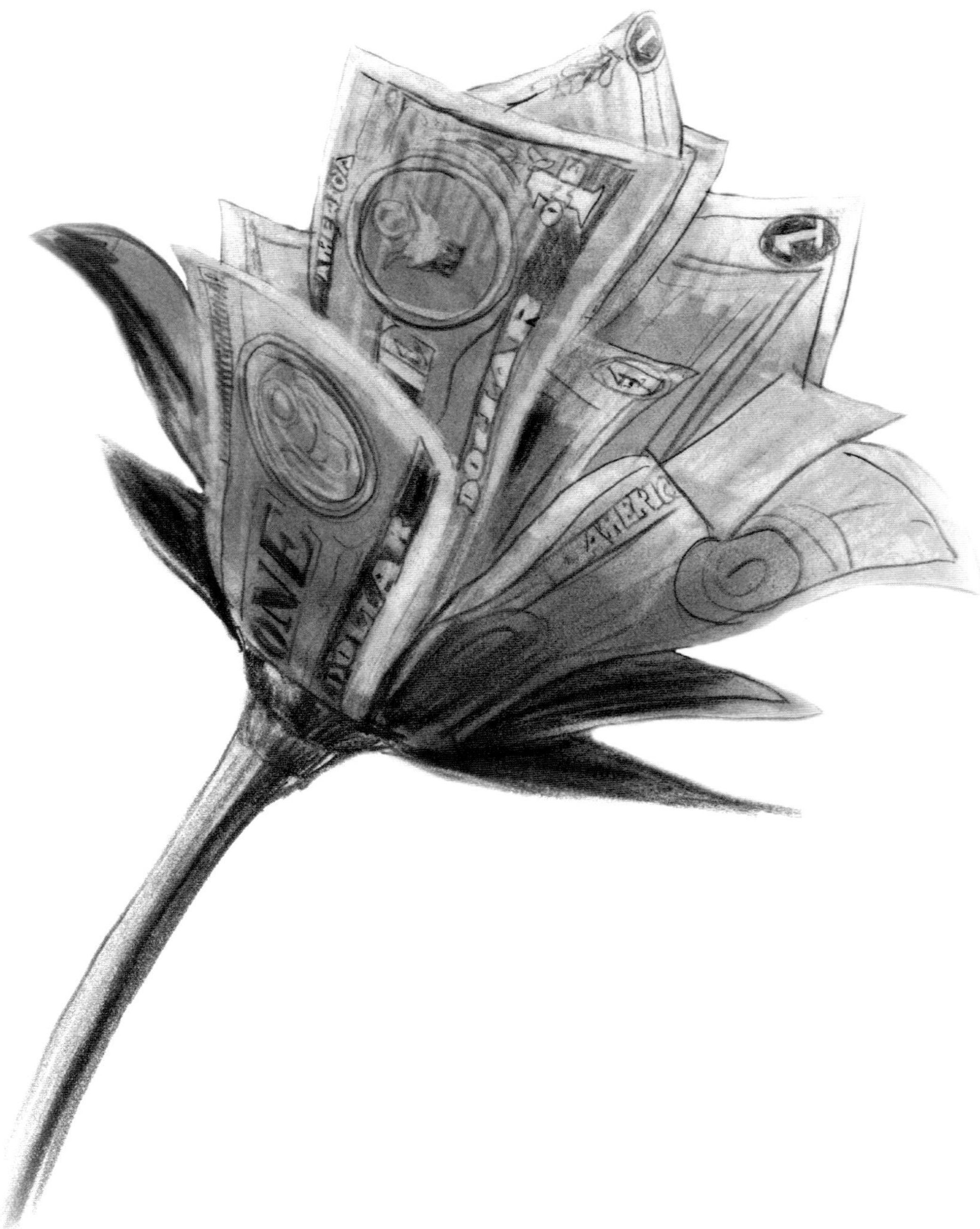

Drawing The Smell Of A Stranger, Smell of Money, 2015

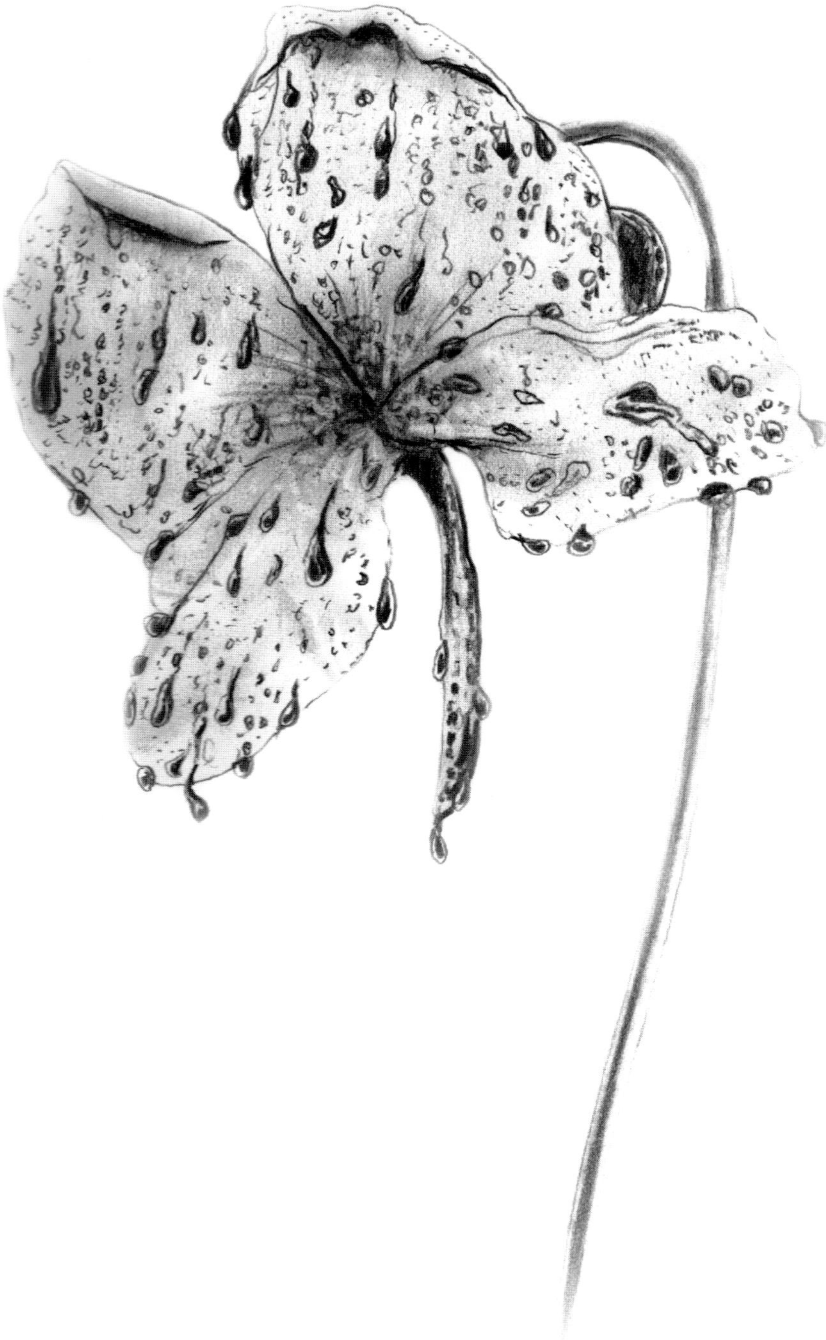

Drawing The Smell Of A Stranger, Smell of Sweat, 2015

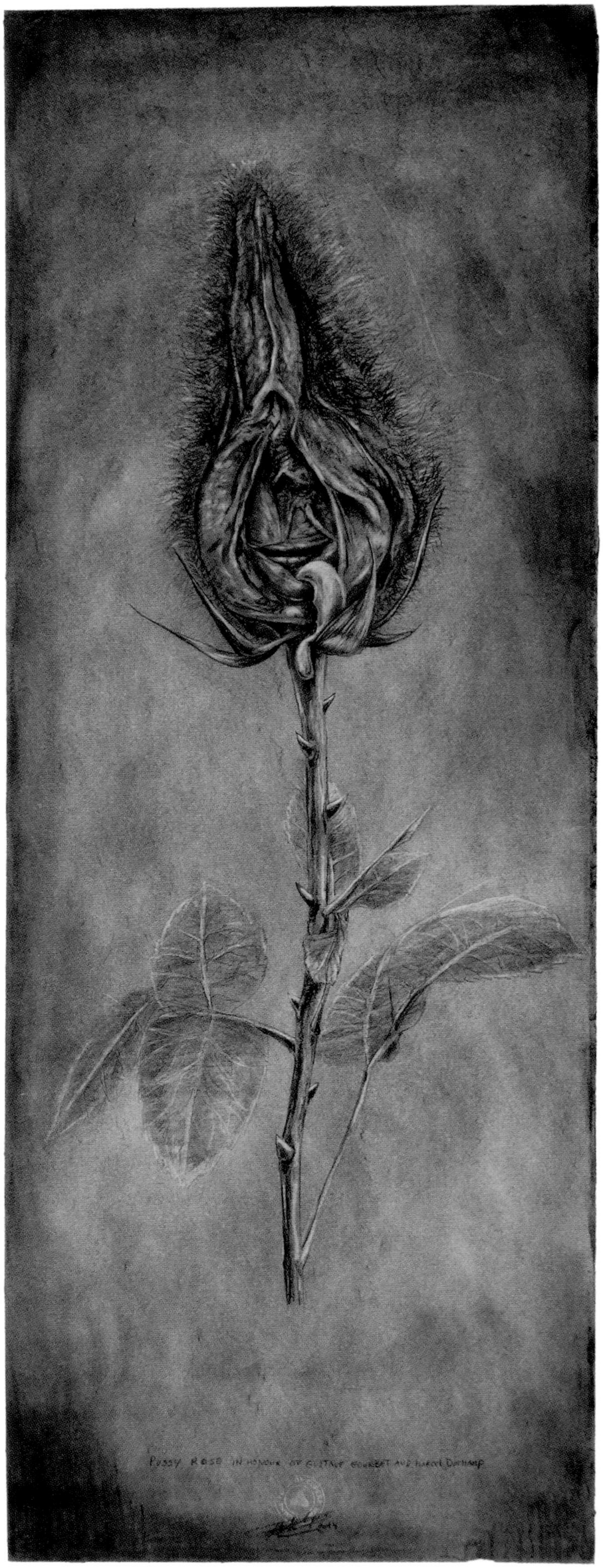

Pussy Rose In Honour Of Gustave Courbet And Marcel Duchamp, 2014

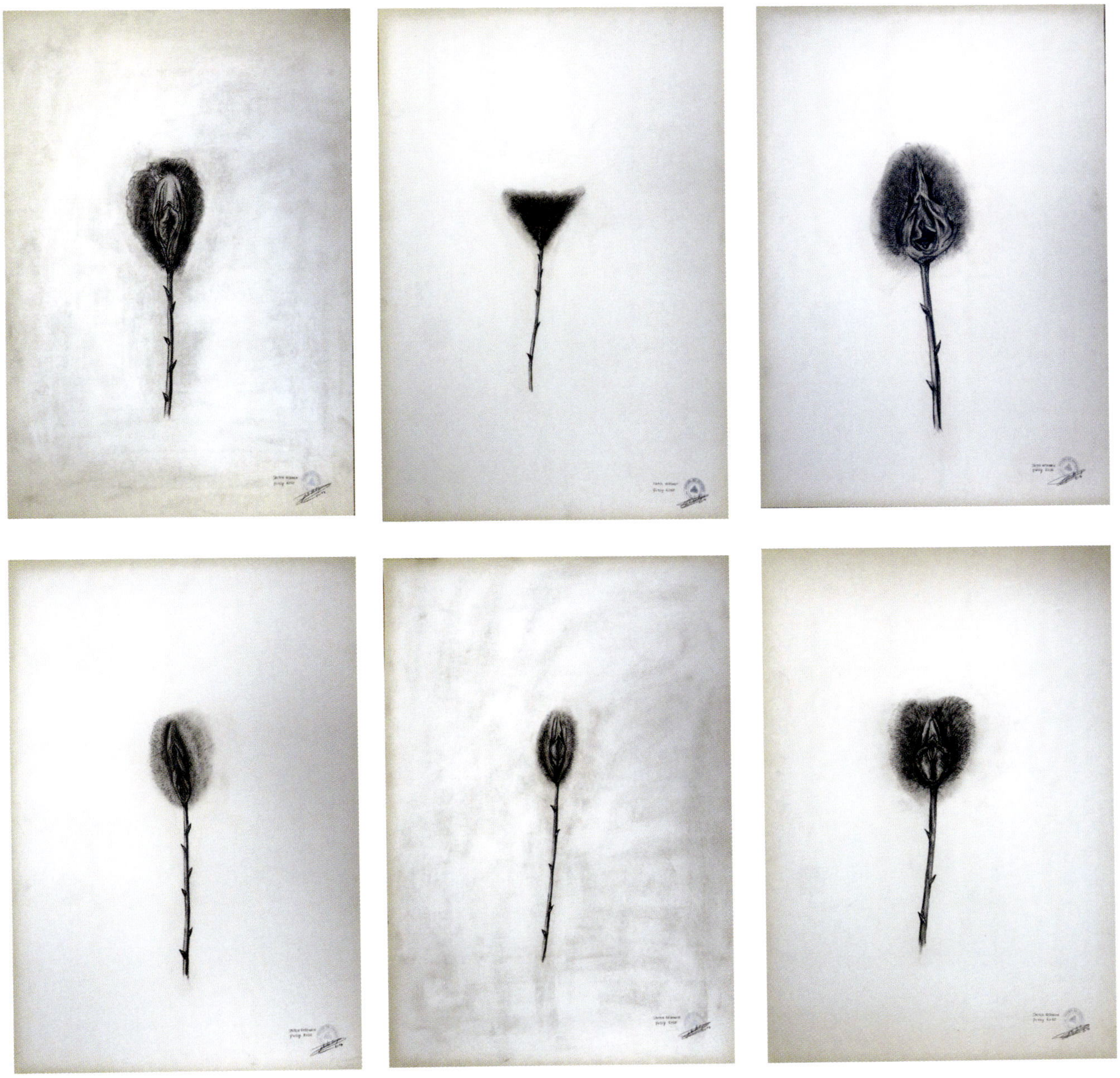

 Pussy Roses, 2014

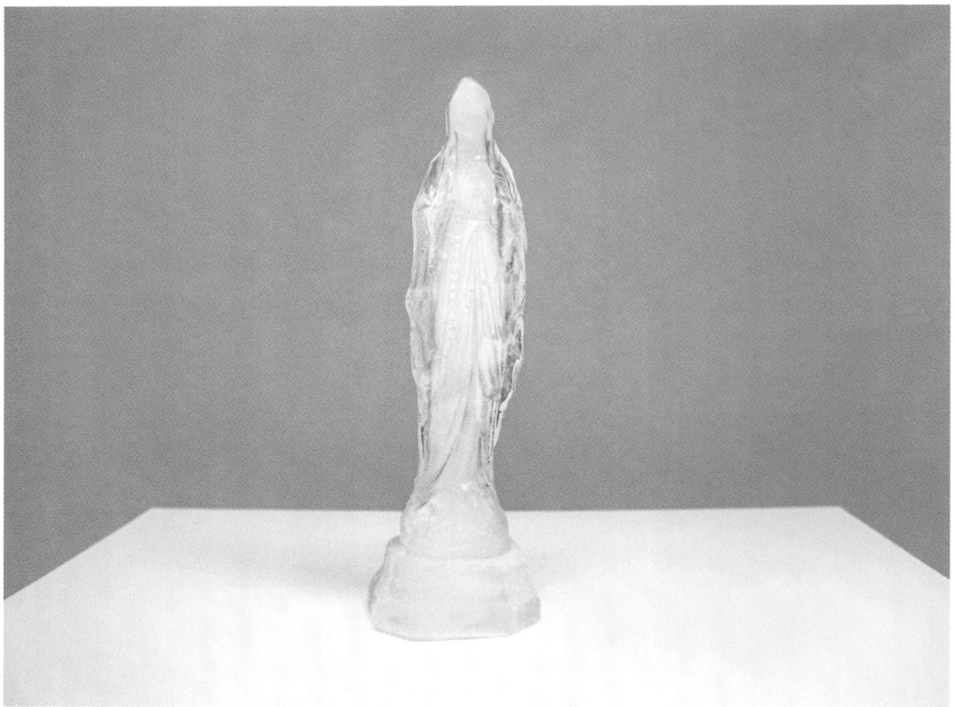

Deflowering, 2014

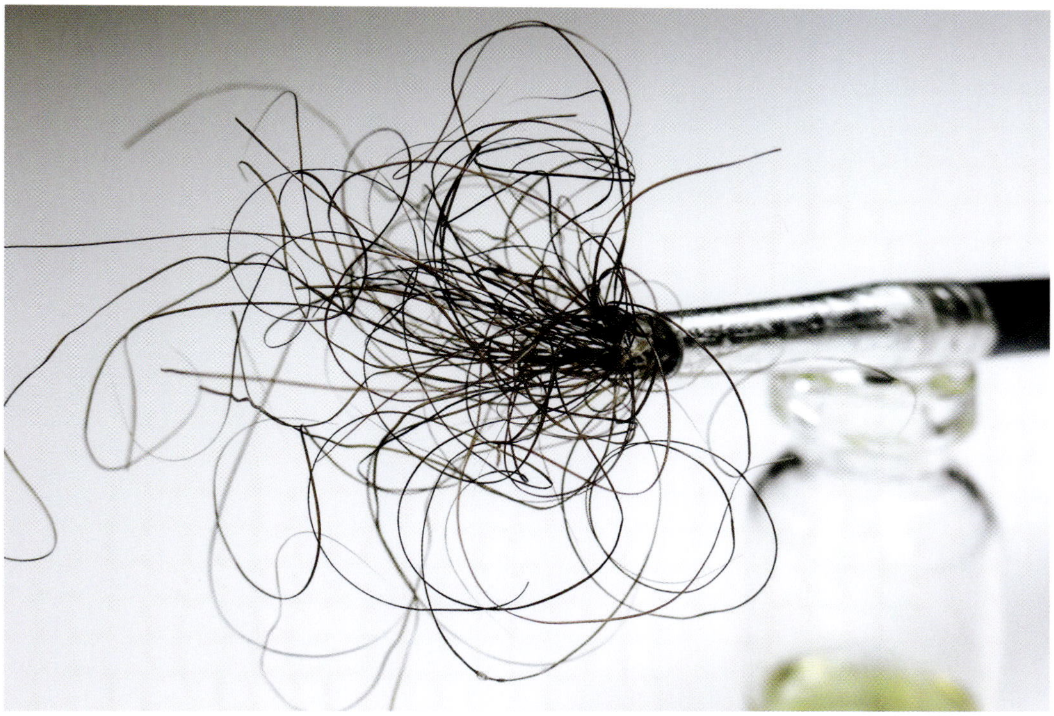

 The Paintbrush of Gustave Courbet, 2014

Out of the series Sweat Drawing, 2003-2014

 Jardins De Bagatelle Guerlain I, 2002

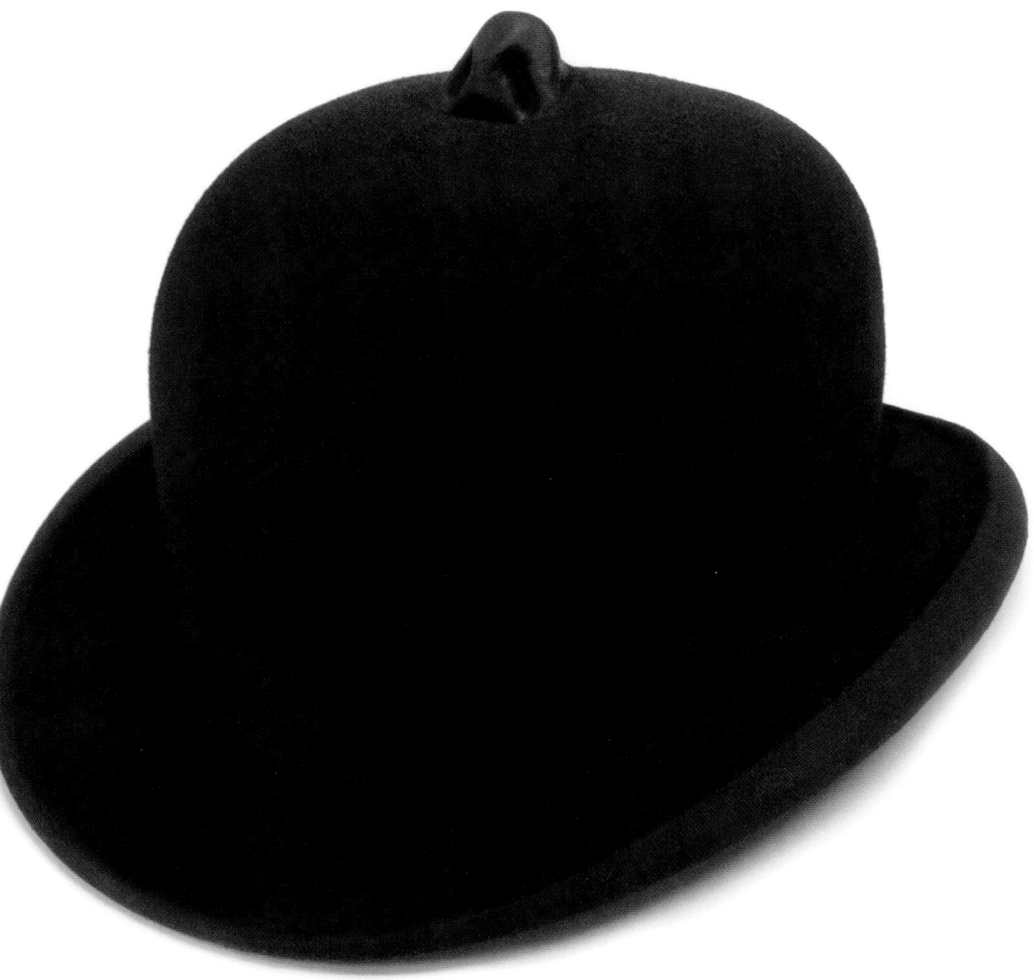

The Man With His Nose On His Hat Smelling Air Pollution, 2015-2016

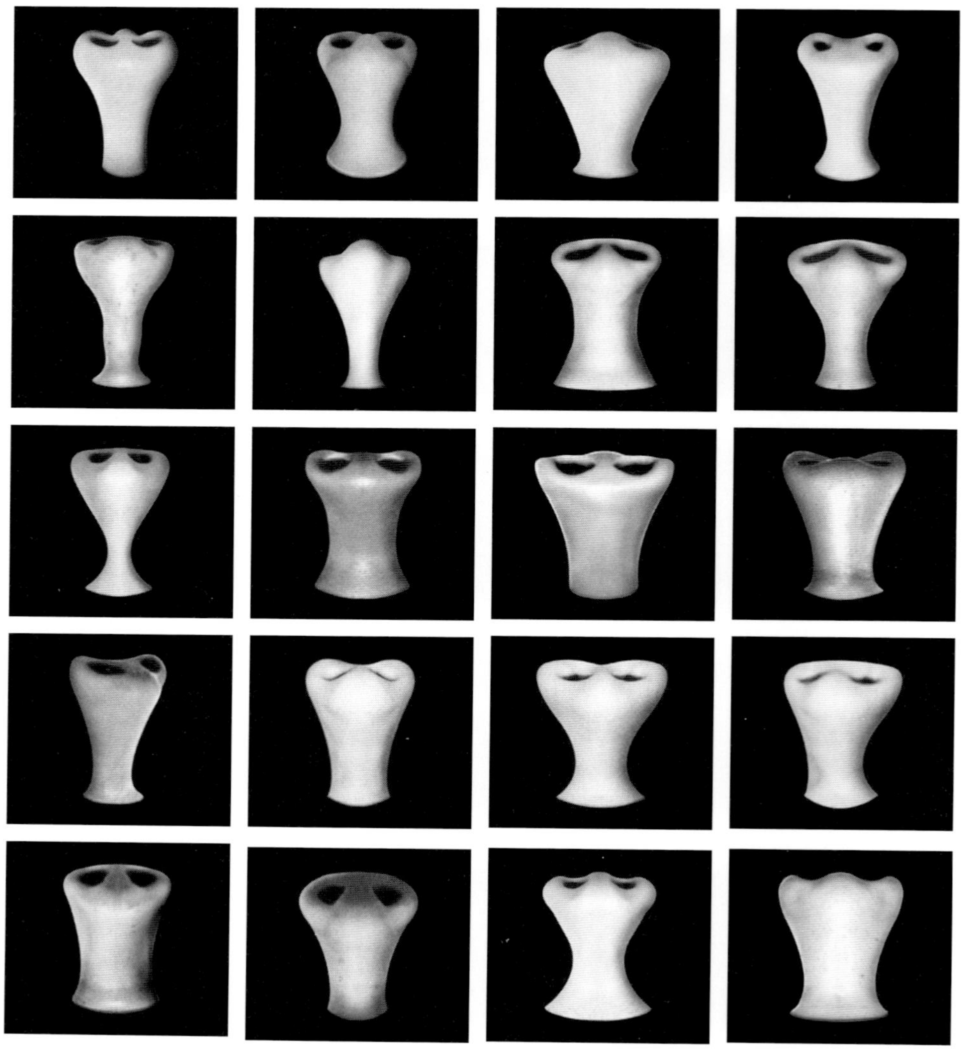

Nose Vases, 1995-1996

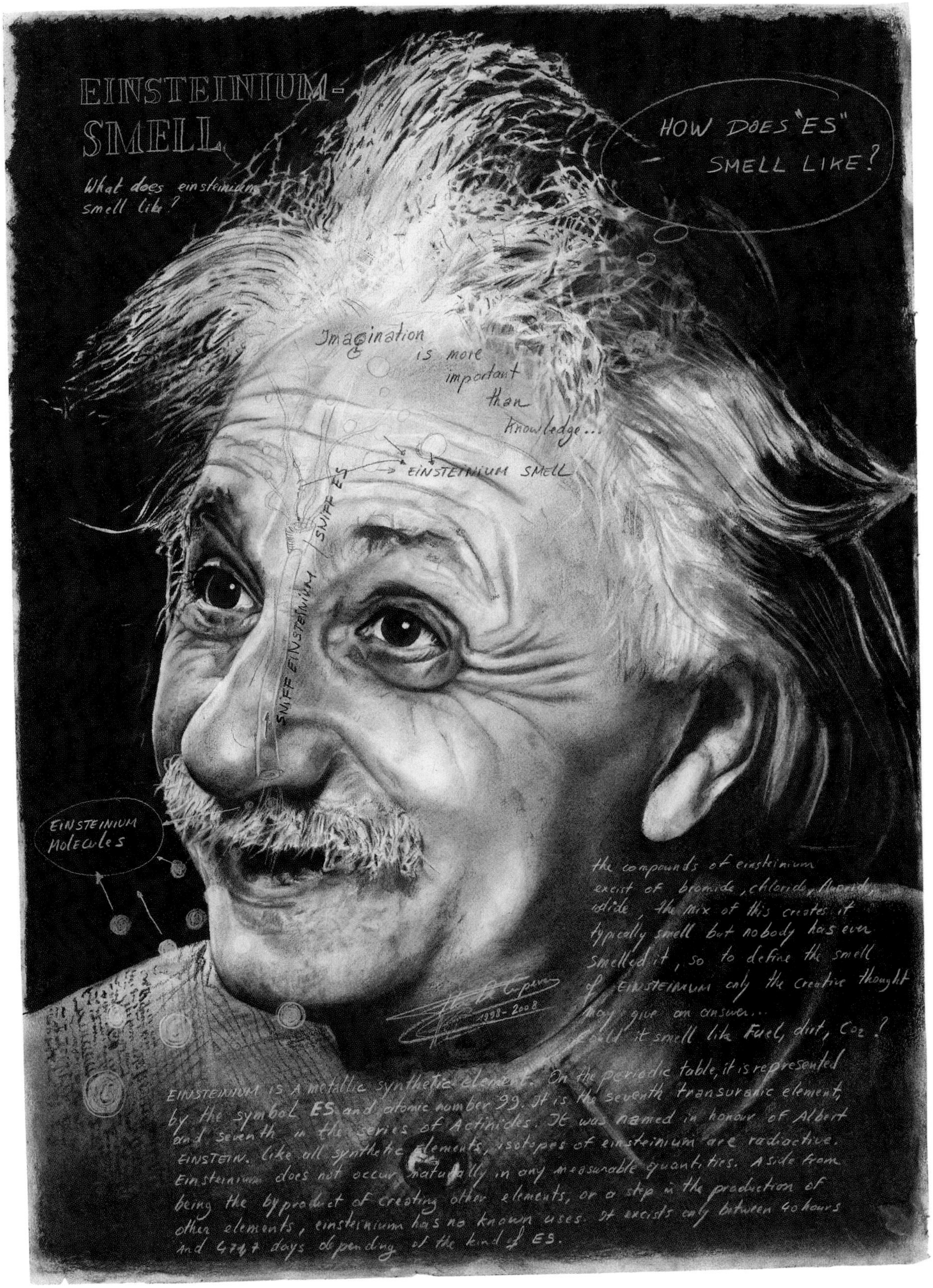

 Einsteinium Smell, 1998-2008

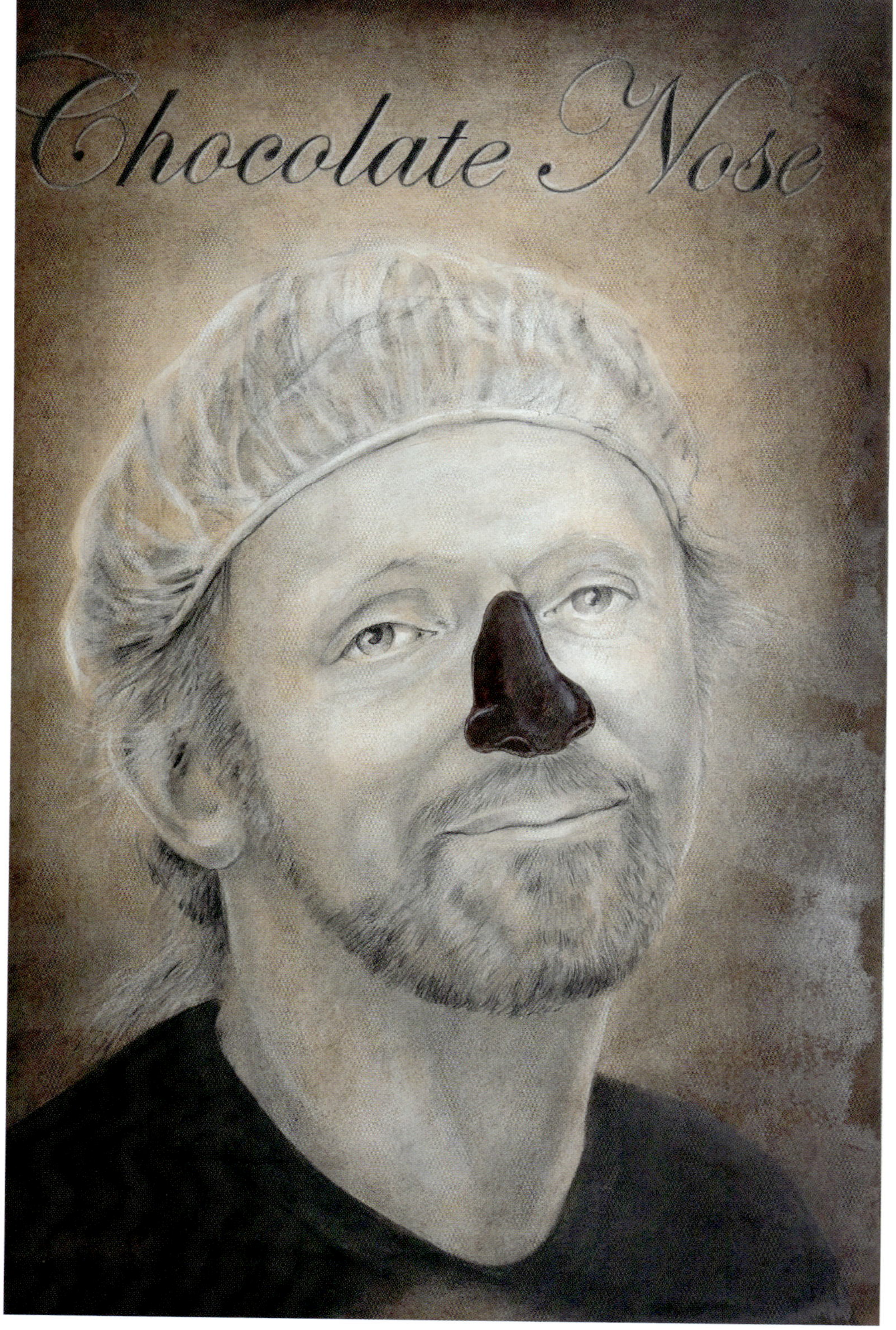

Drawing Chocolate Nose 2, 2011

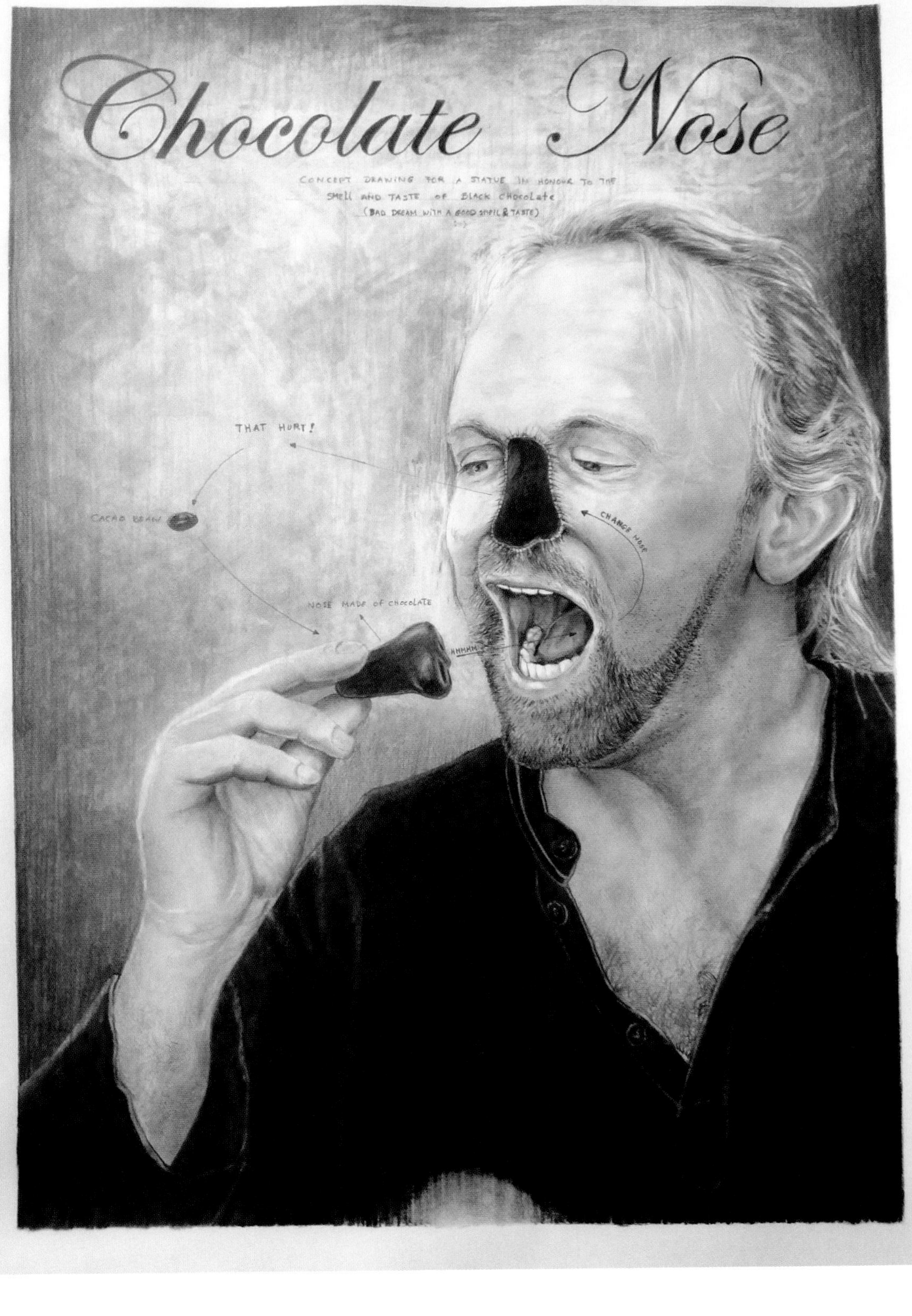

 Drawing Chocolate Nose 1, 2011

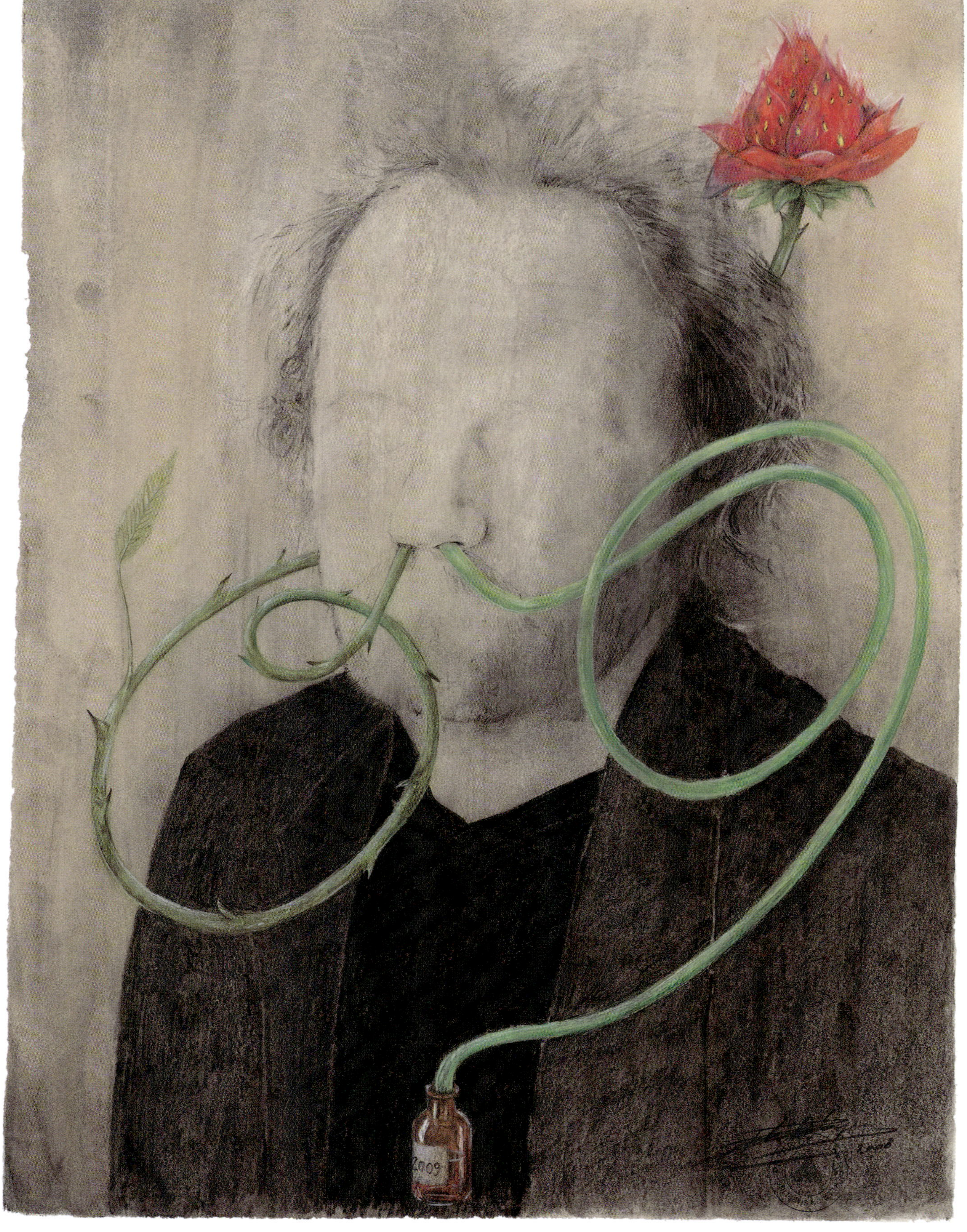

Self-Portrait 09, 2009

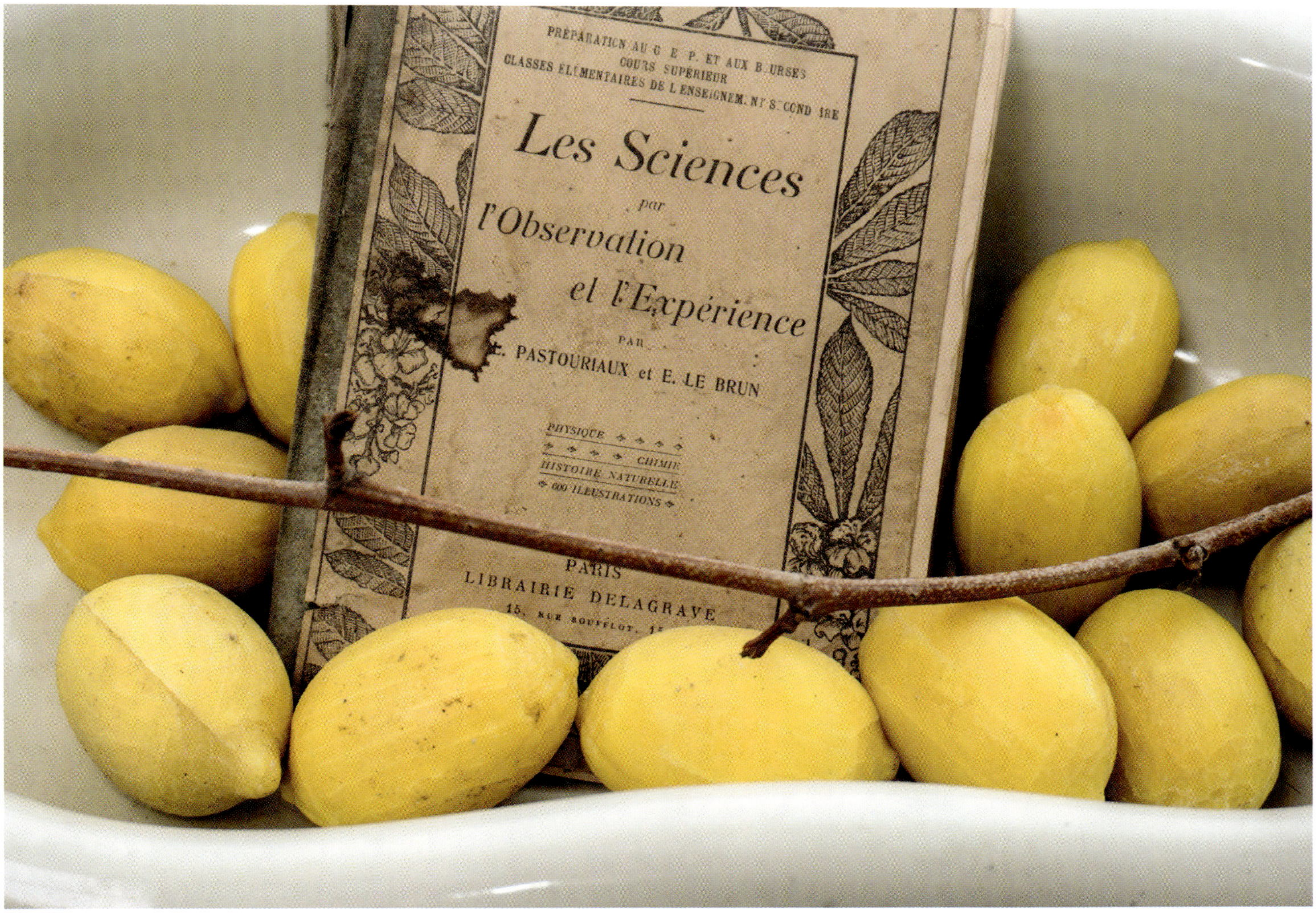

Les Sciences par l'Observation et l'Expérience (detail), 2000

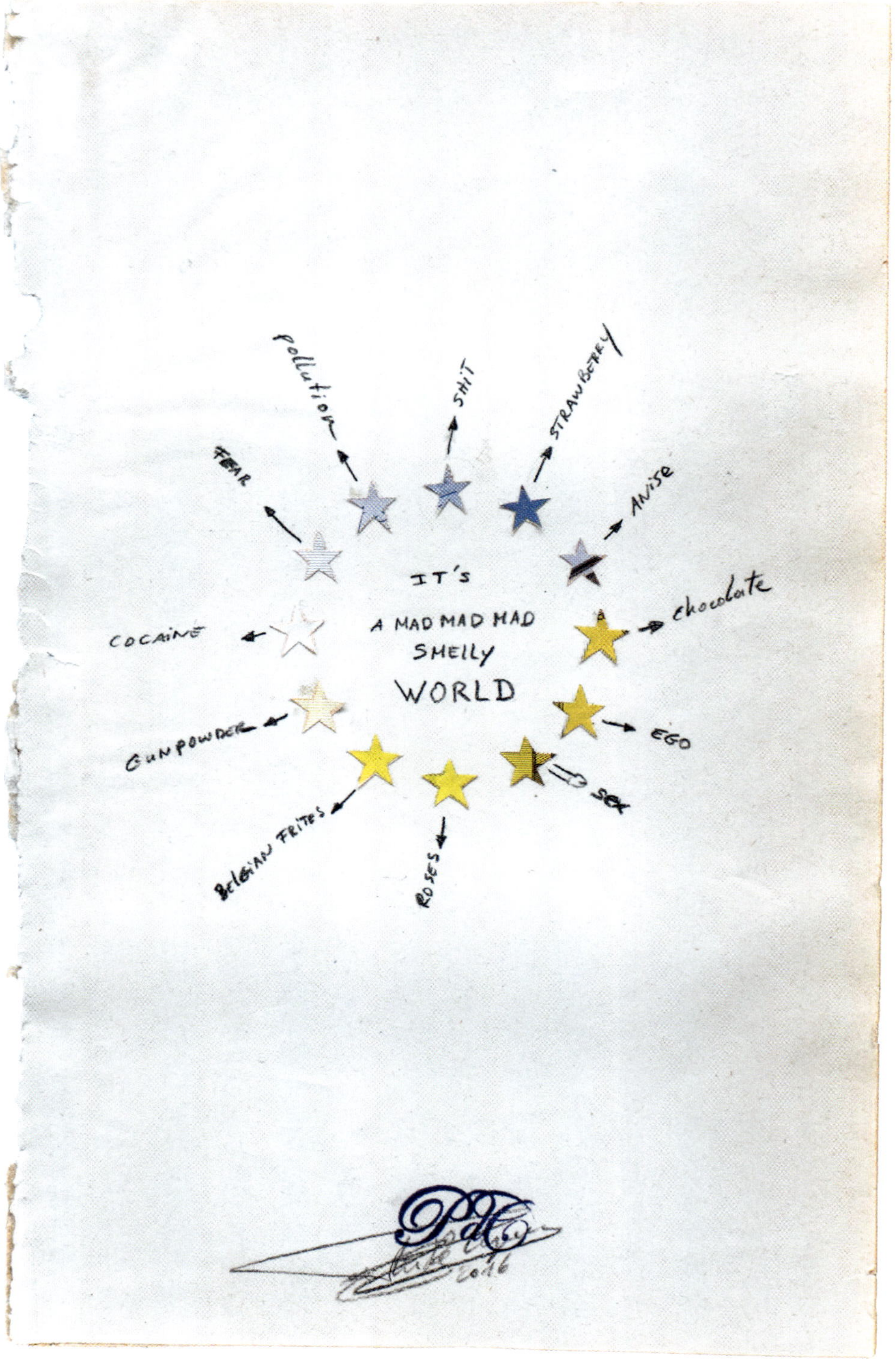

It's A Mad Mad Mad Smelly World, 2016

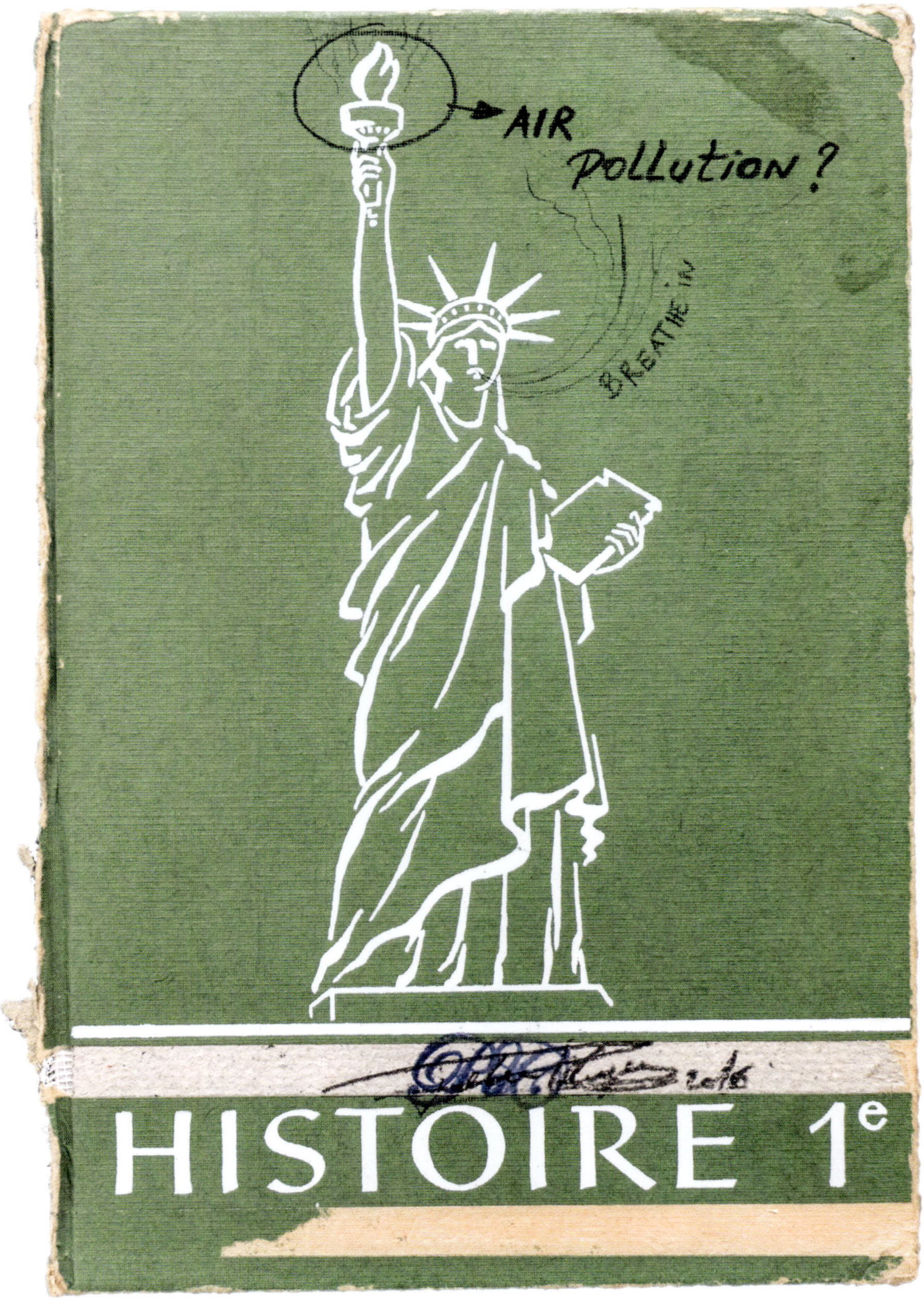

 Histoire 1, 2016

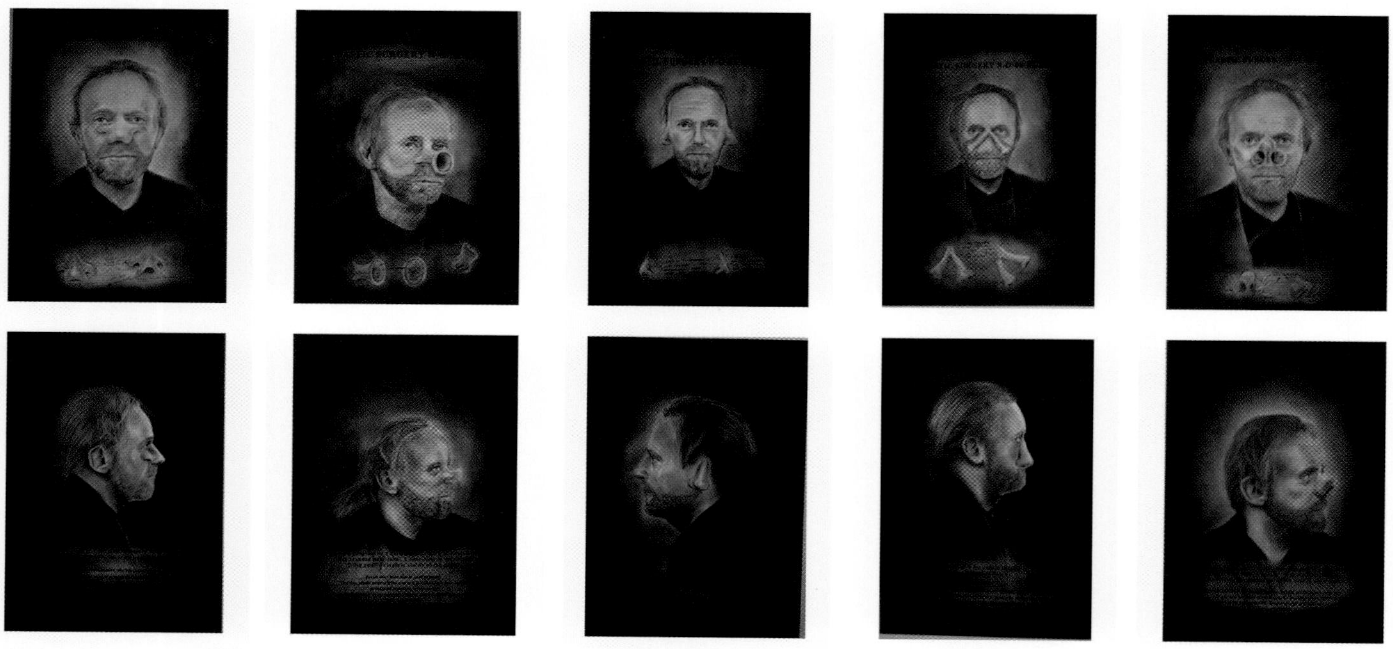

Nose-X's, 2004

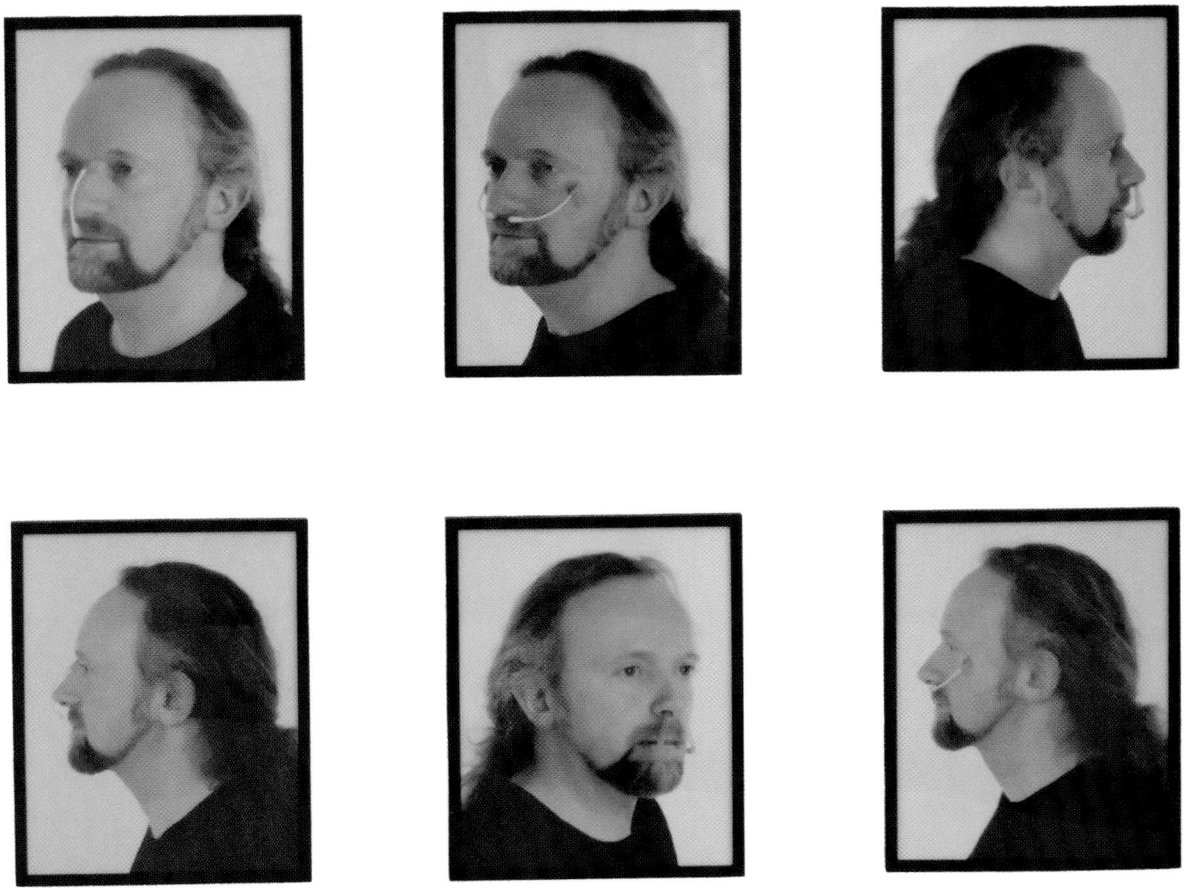

Photographs Smell Devices, 2013

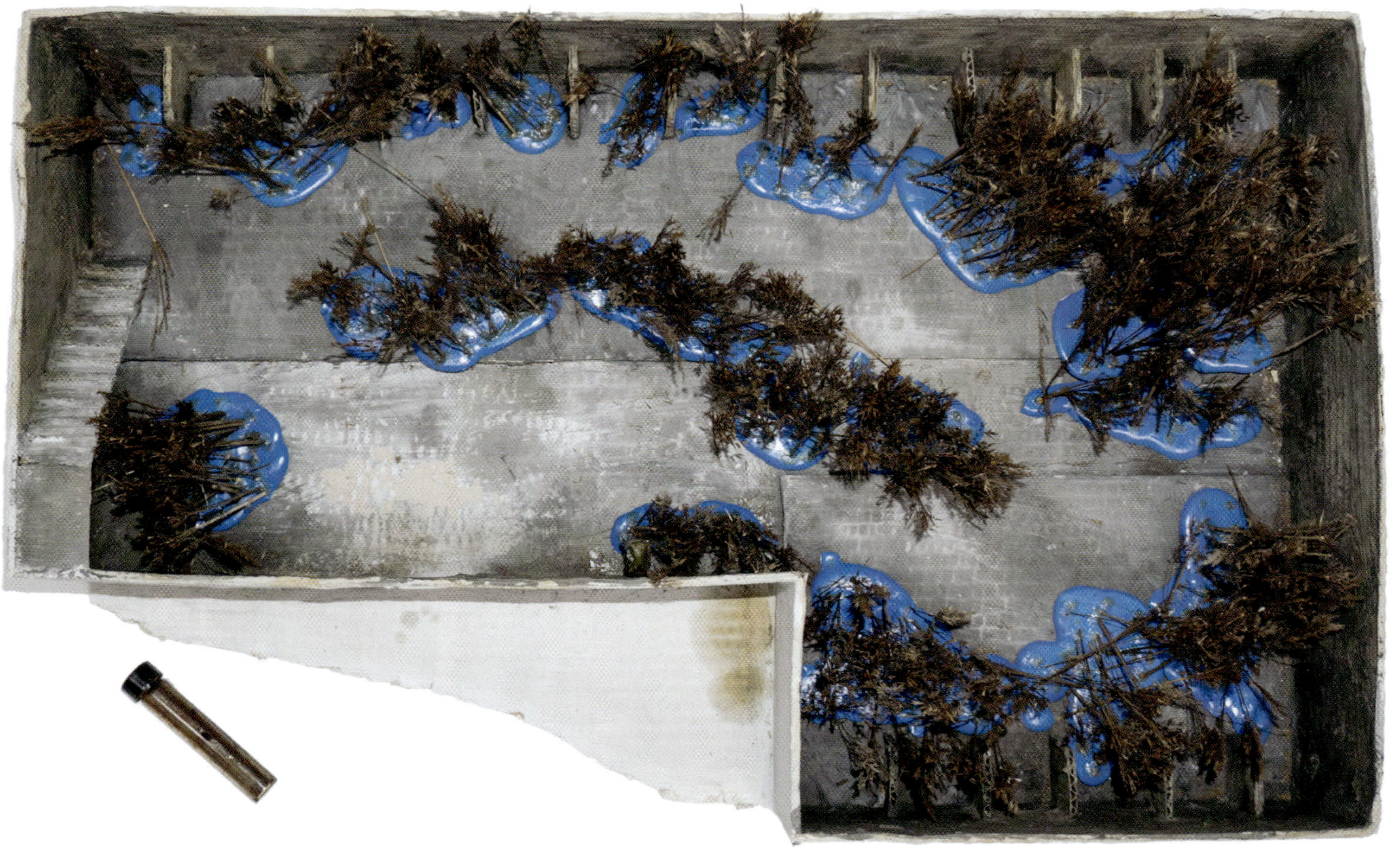

Model Reed Land, 1998

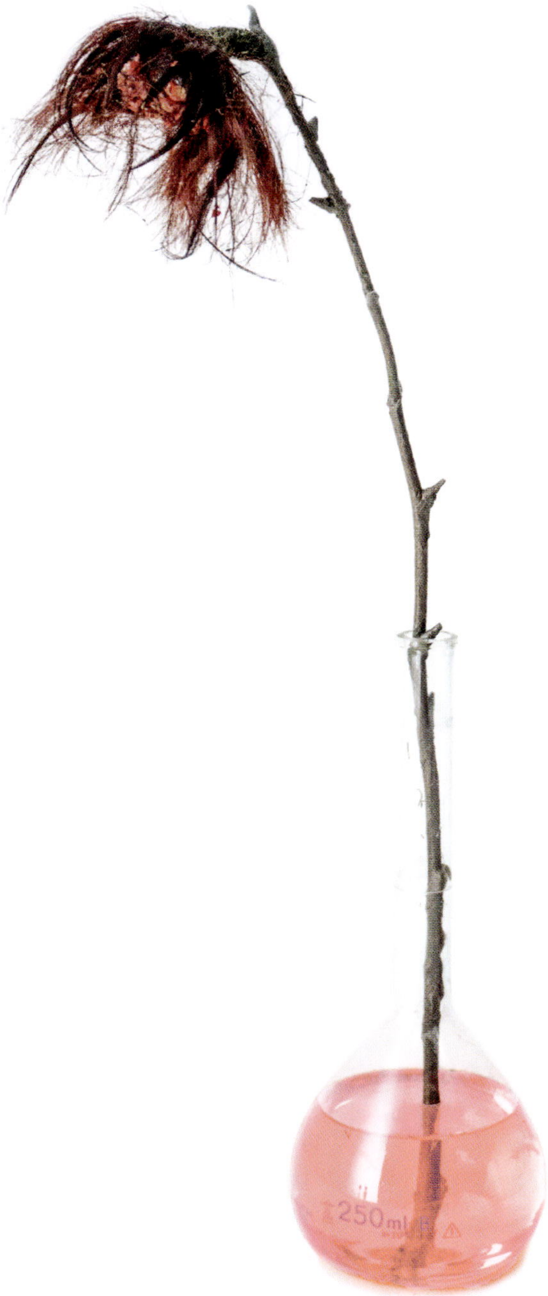

Hair Rose, 2016

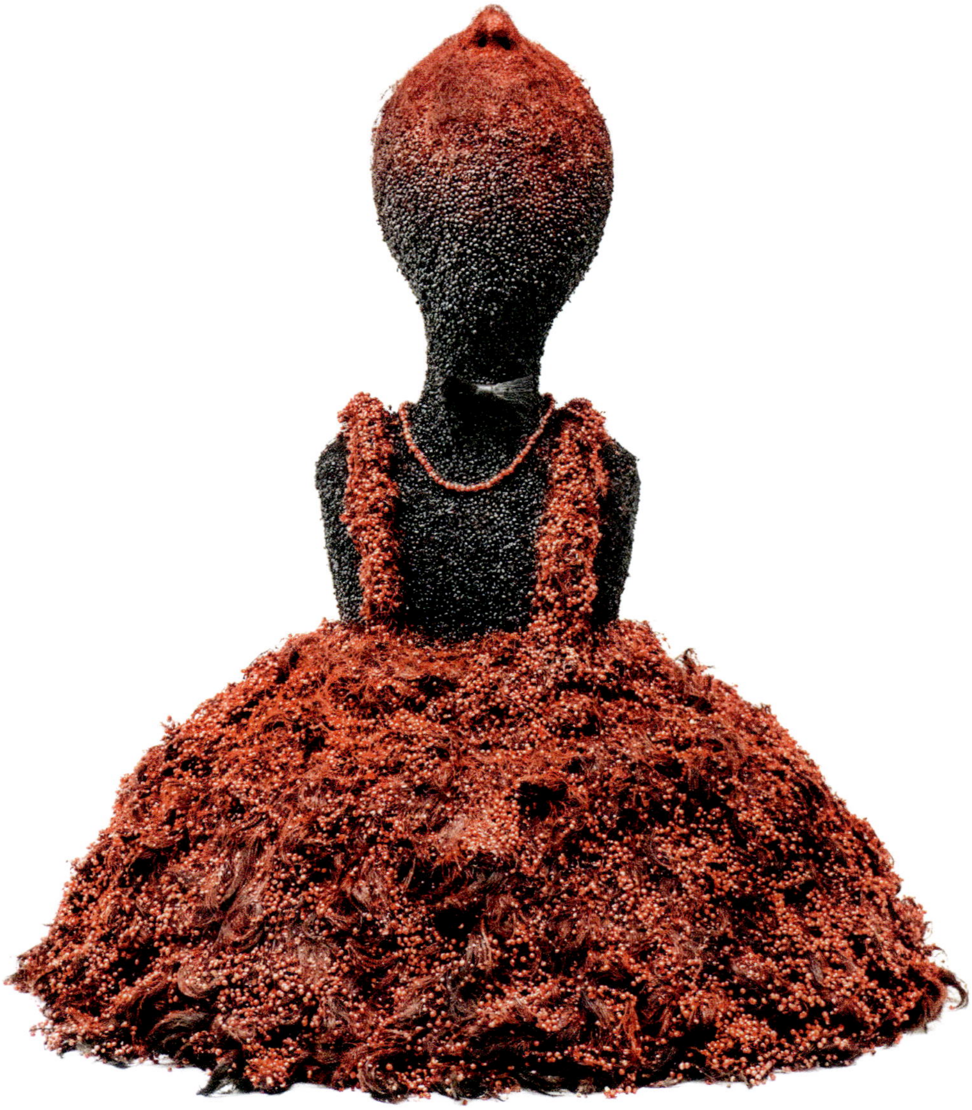

Madame Poivre Rose I, 2016

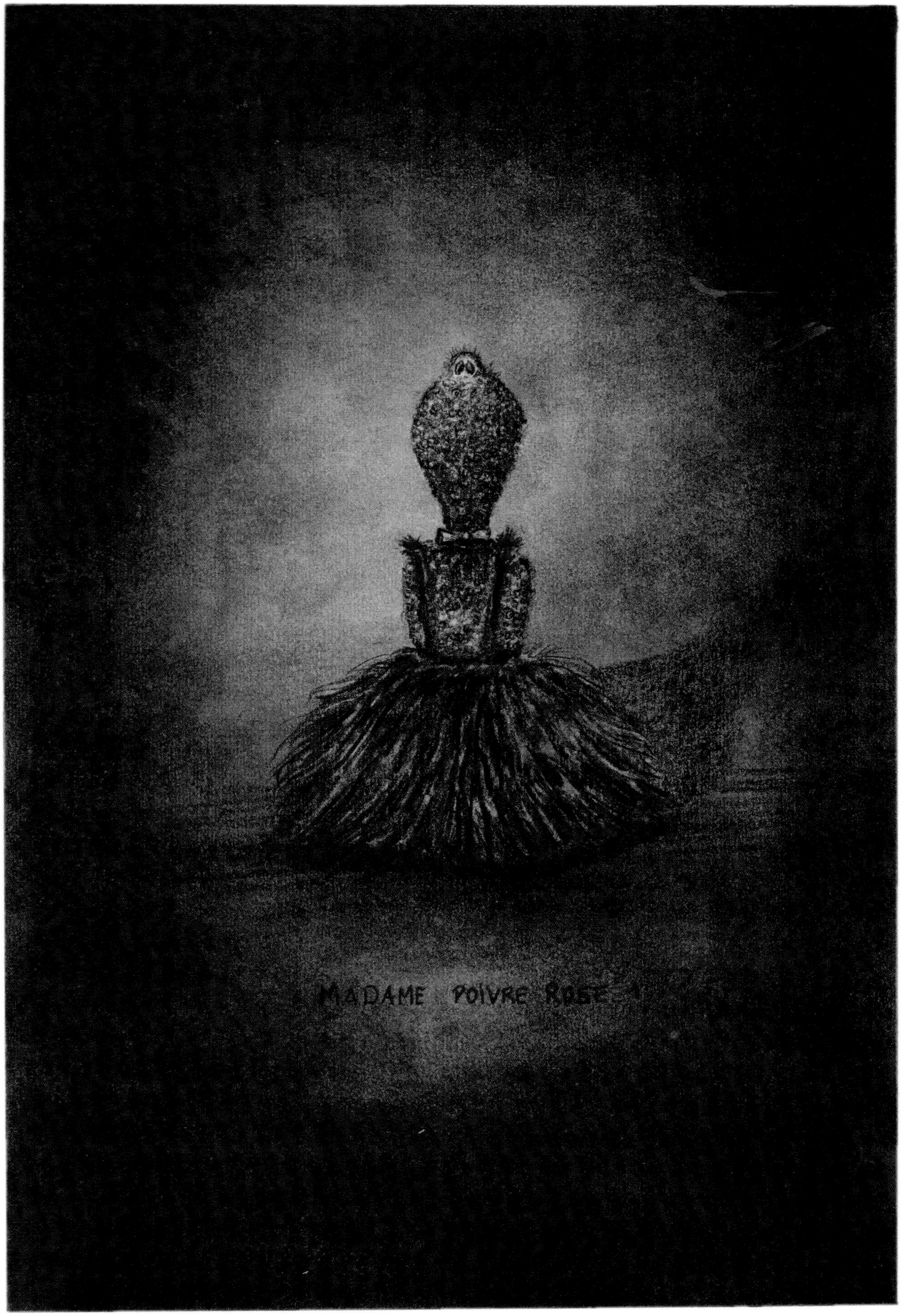

 Drawing Madame Poivre Rose I, 2016

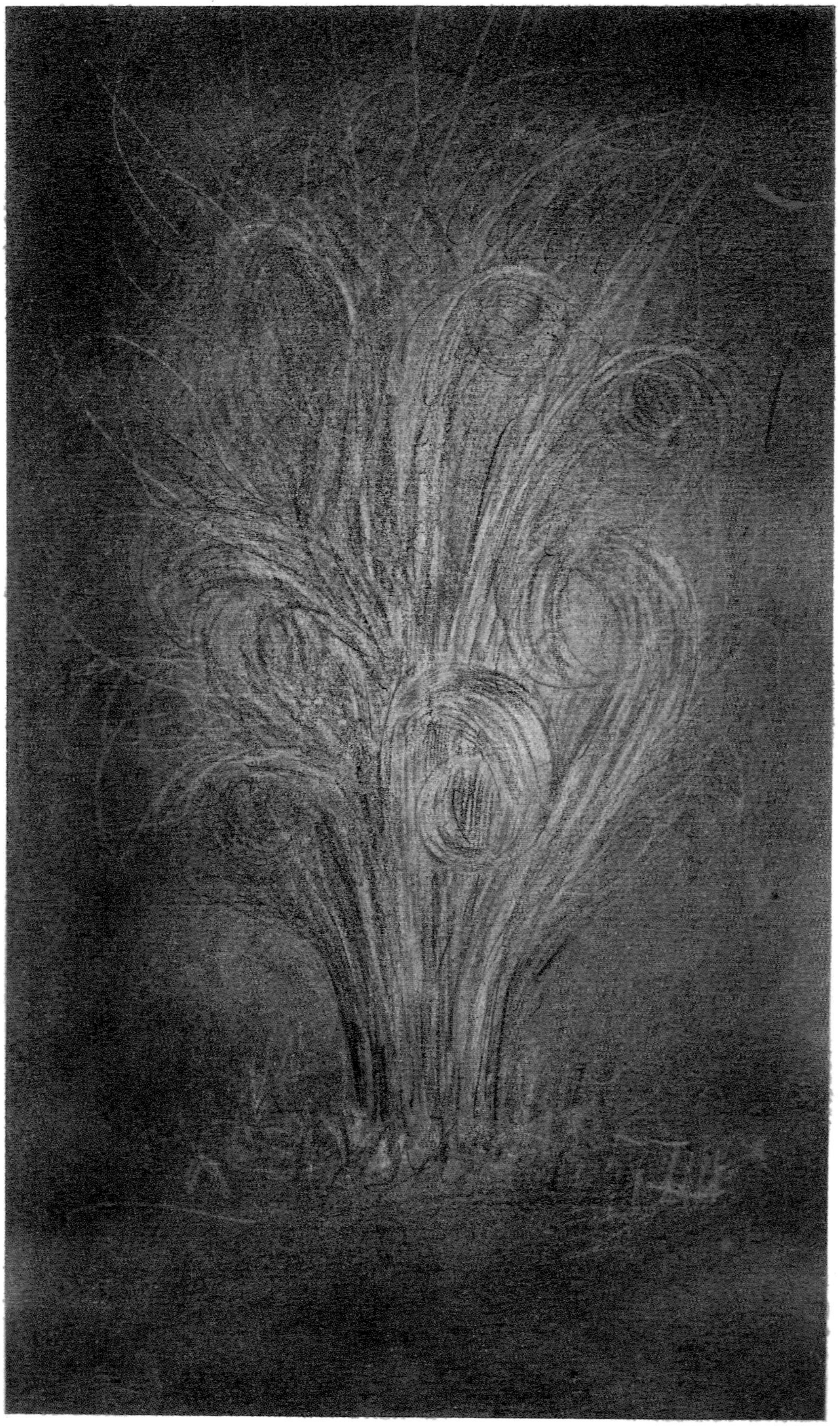

Hair Flower, 2016

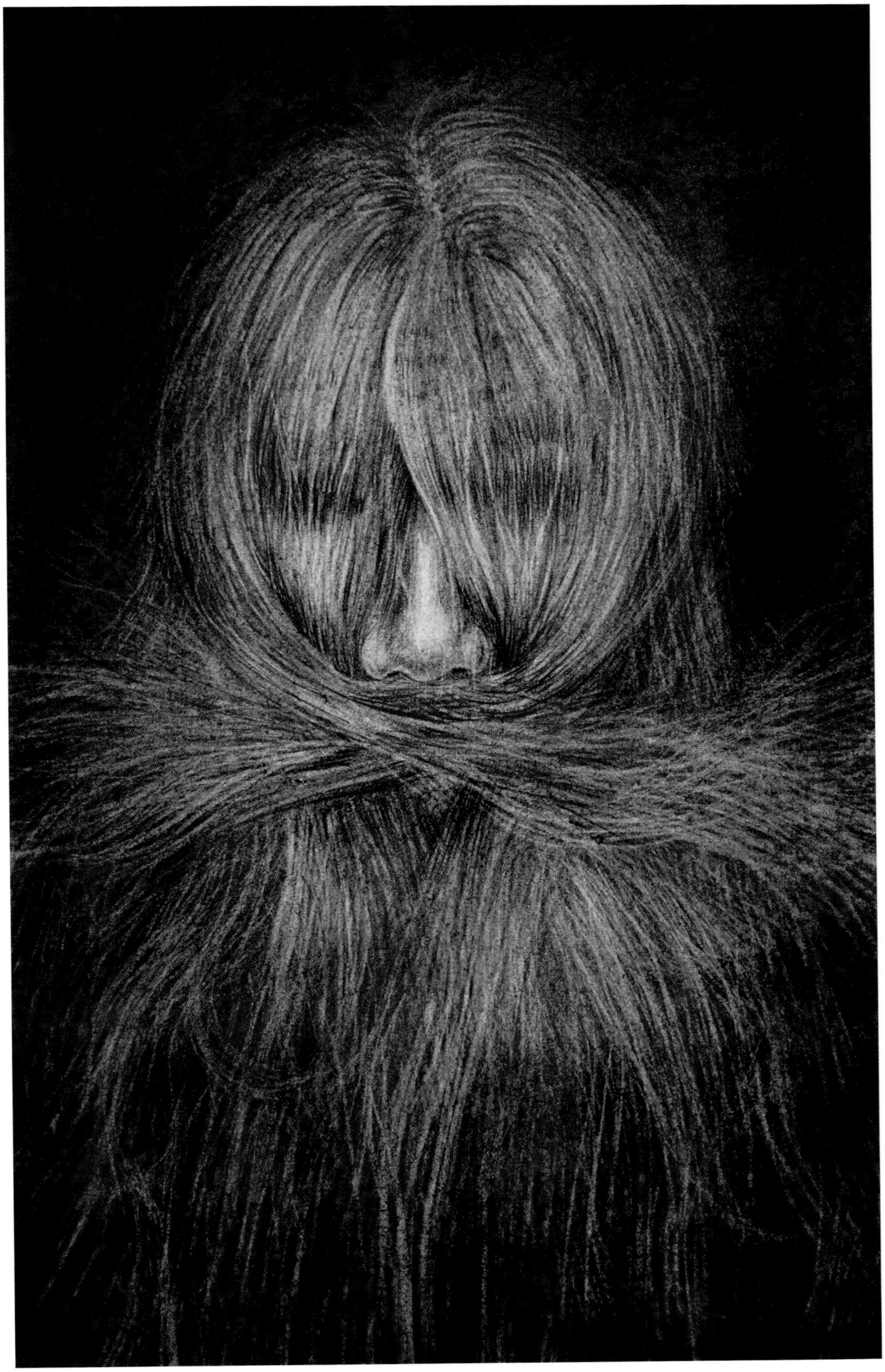

 Hair Self-portrait, 2016

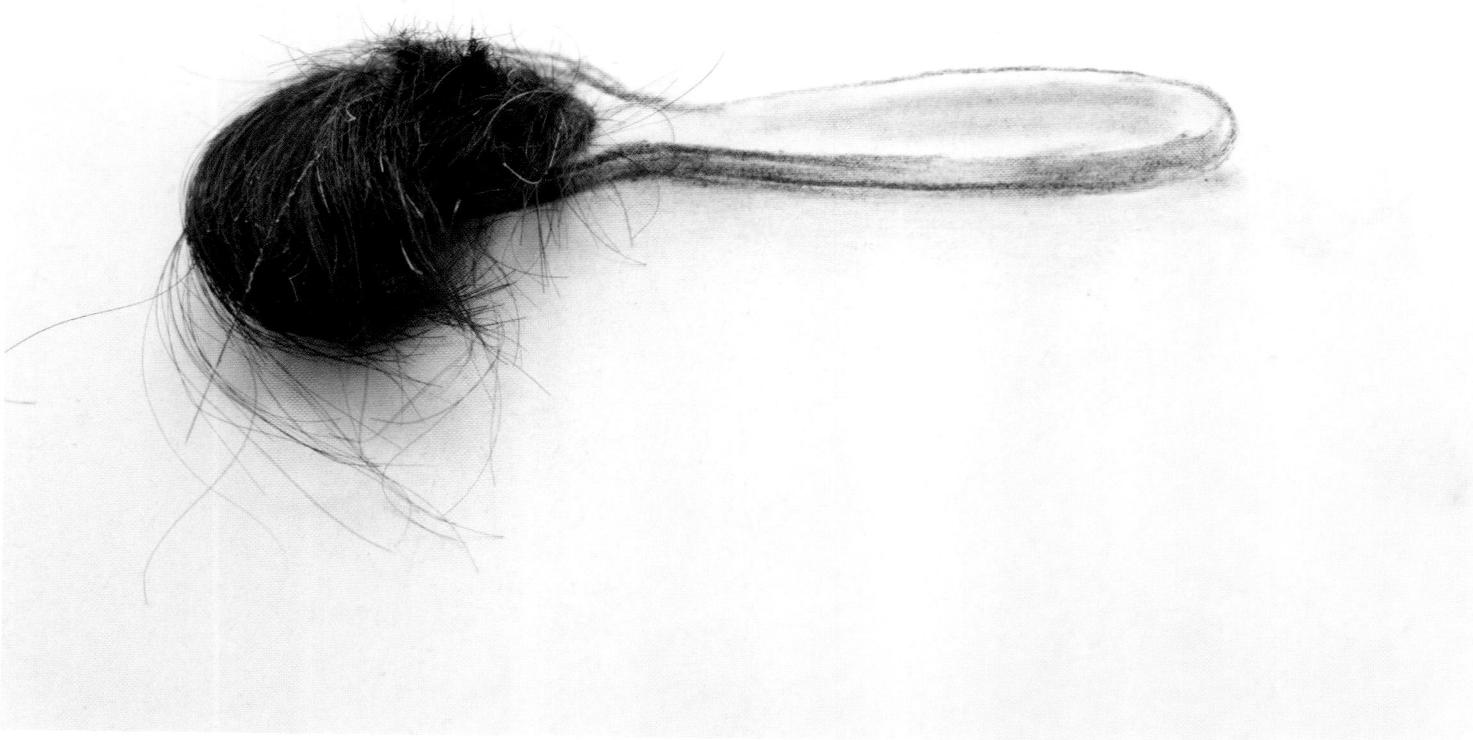

Soft Memory, Ungaro pour Homme III, detail, 2016

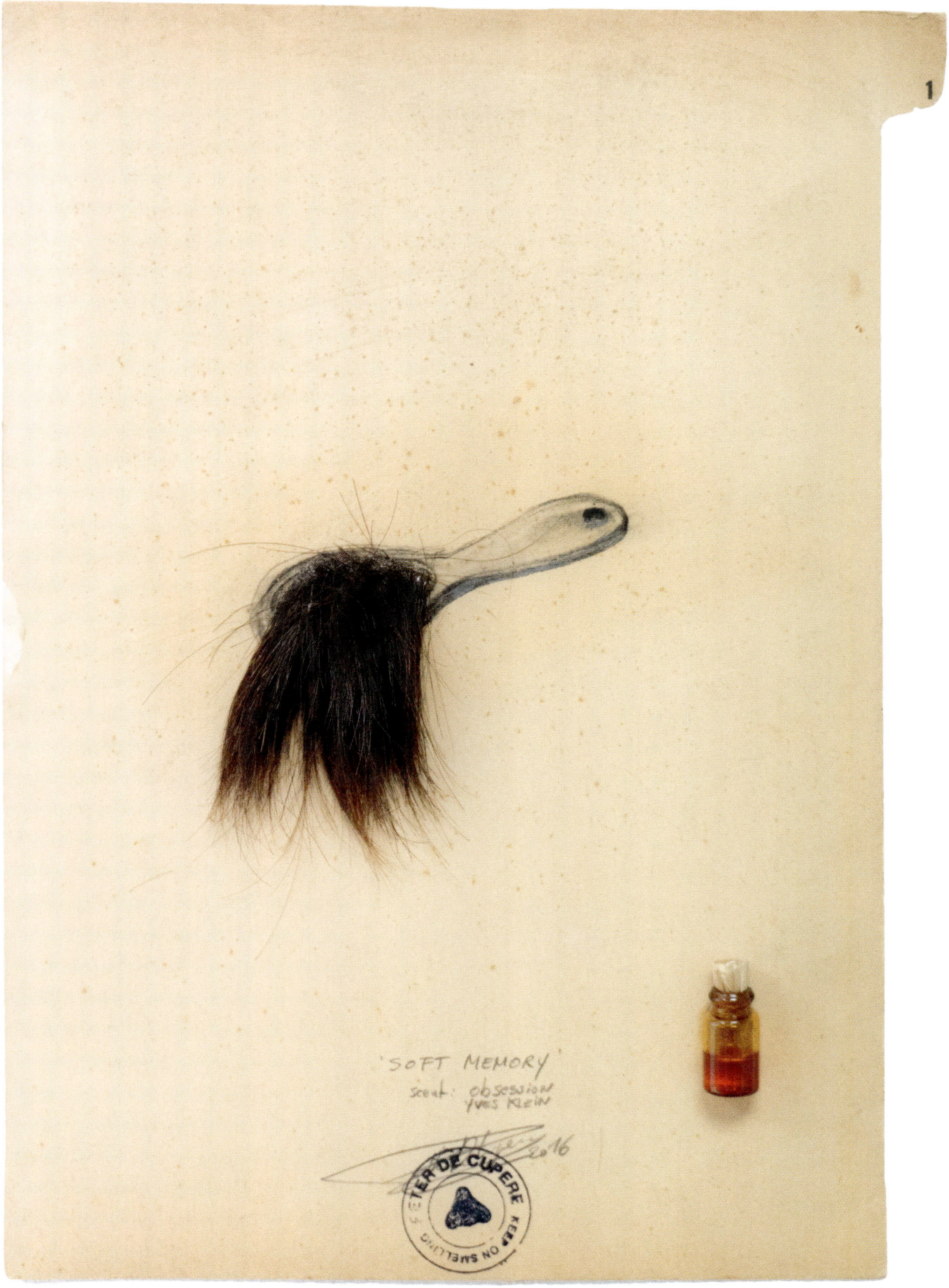

 Soft Memory, Obsession, Calvin Klein, 22 x 30,5 cm, 2016

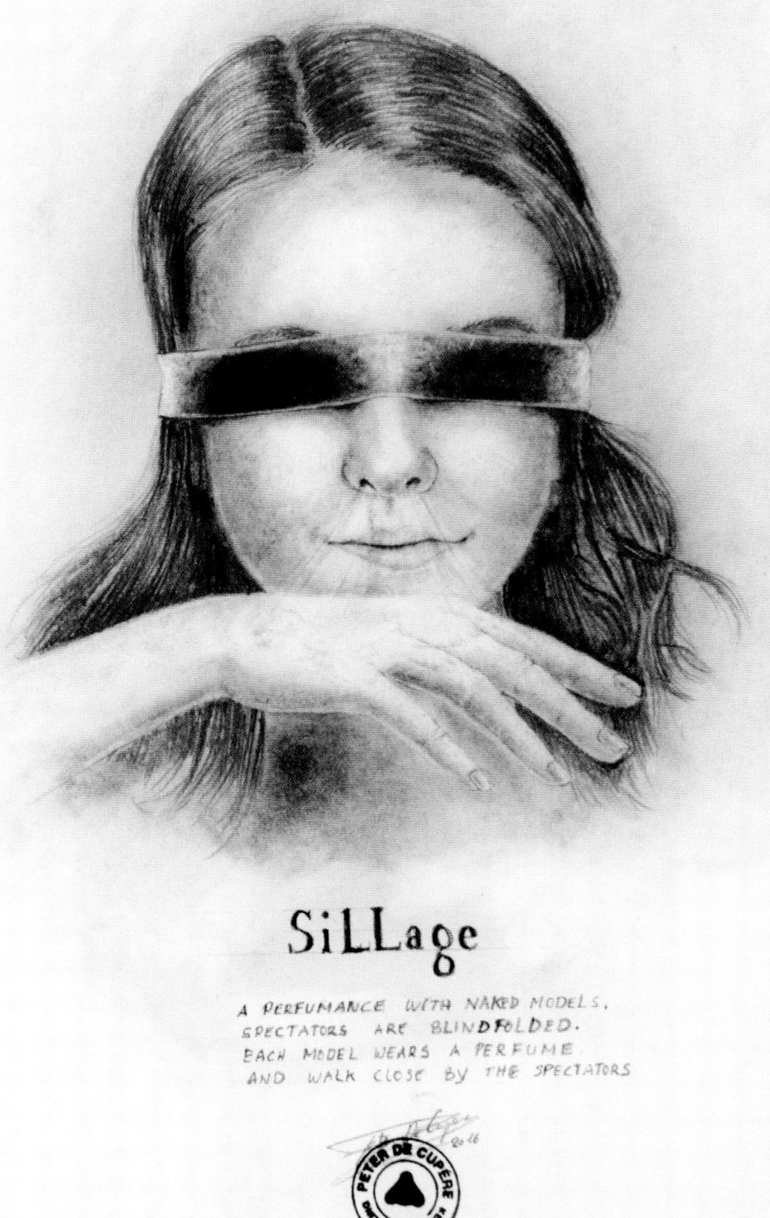

 Drawing Sillage, 2016

PETER DE CUPERE

TWENTY YEARS OLFACTORY ART
Een overzicht van kunstwerken

PETER DE CUPERE

CULTURE & SOCIETY
Maatschappij & Cultuur

EL AROMA DE UN DESCONOCIDO

THE SMELL OF A STRANGER

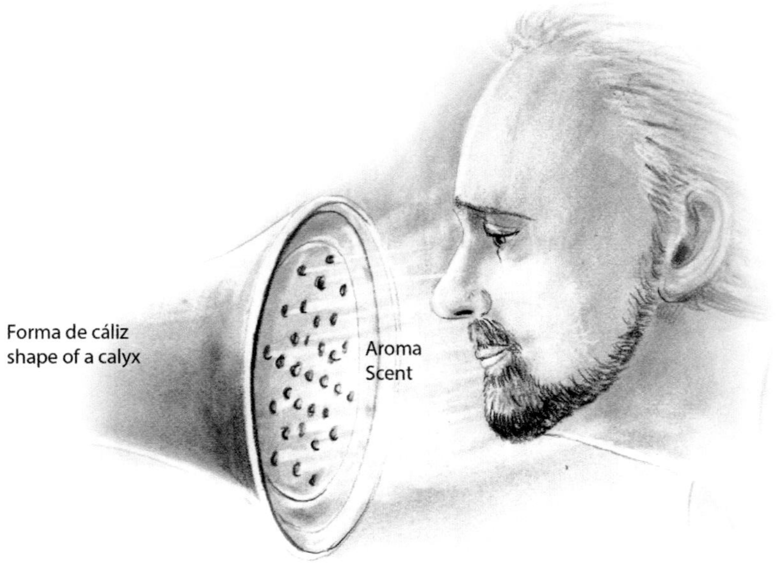

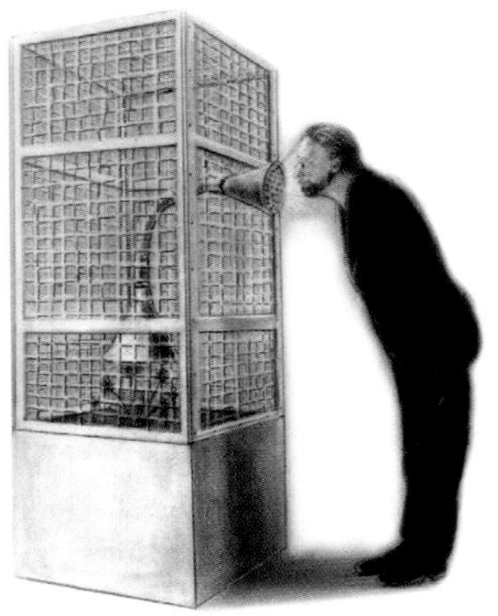

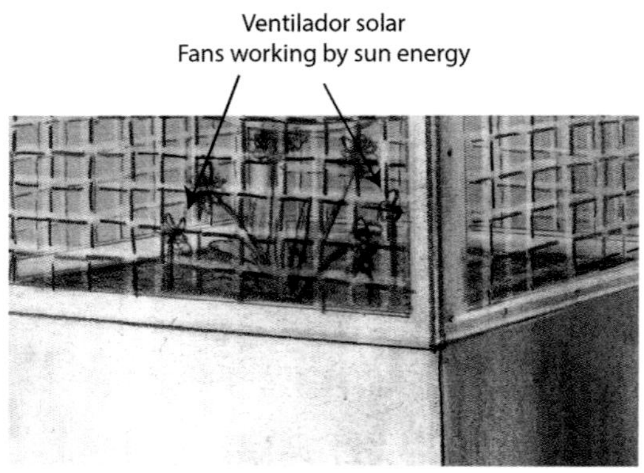

Artista: Peter de Cupere (BE,1970)
Título: El aroma de un desconocido
Planta de aroma obtenido ingenierilmente
Aroma: **Geranios**
! Acerque su nariz al embudo

Artist: Peter de Cupere (BE,1970)
Title: The smell of a stranger
Scent engineered plant
Scent: **Gerariums**
! Smell by putting your nose to the funnel

Agradecimientos especiales al director del Centro Wifredo Lam, organizador de la Bienal de La Habana, Jorge Fernández; a la curadora del proyecto "El aroma de un desconocido", Sara Alonso Gómez; a Bruno Devos, por su coordinación y apoyo; a la Embajada del Reino de Bélgica en Cuba; a IFF y su equipo de investigación Meabh Mc Curtin; a Gregoire Hausson, Christian Alori dirigido por Bernardo Fleming.

Special thanks to the director of Wifredo Lam Art Center and organisator of the Biennial of Havana Jorge Fernández; to curator of the project "The Smell of a stranger", Sara Alonso Gómez, to Bruno Devos' for his coordination and support, to the Belgian embassy in Cuba, to IFF and their scent research team perfumers Meabh Mc Curtin, Gregoire Hausson, Christian Alori led by Bernardo Fleming.

IFF International Flavors & Fragrances Inc. The Olfactory Flanders State of the Art www.peterdecupere.net

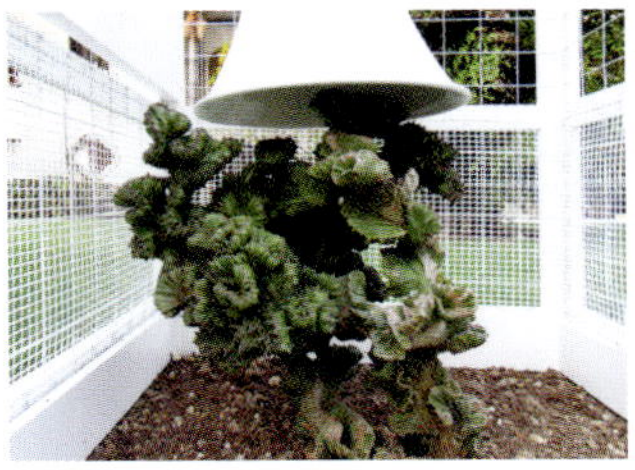
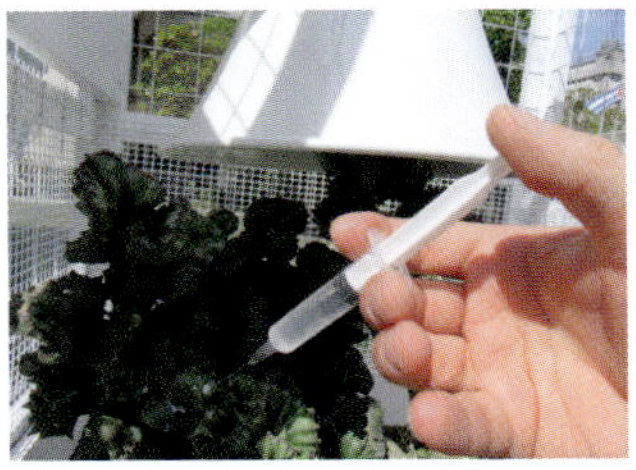
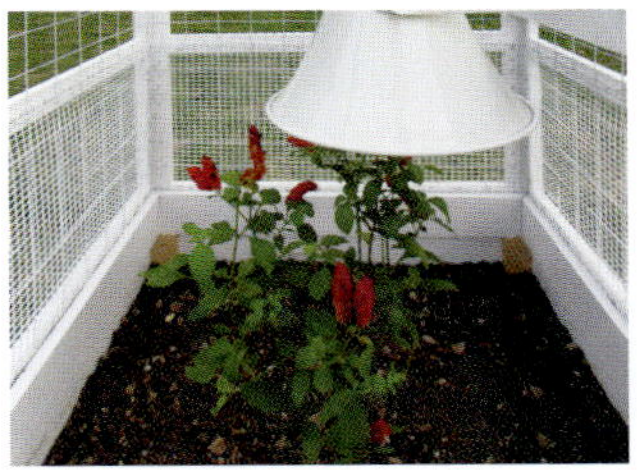
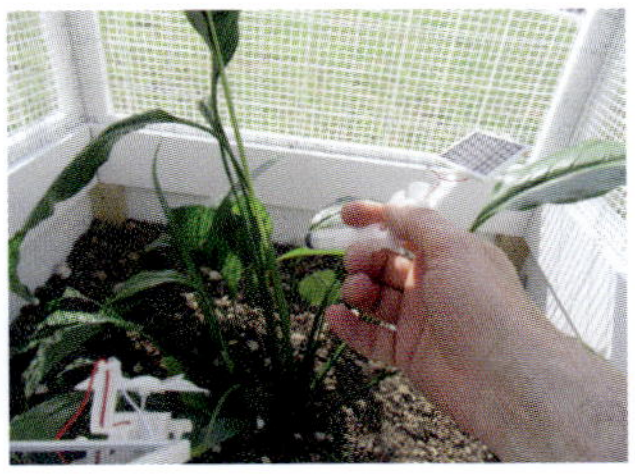
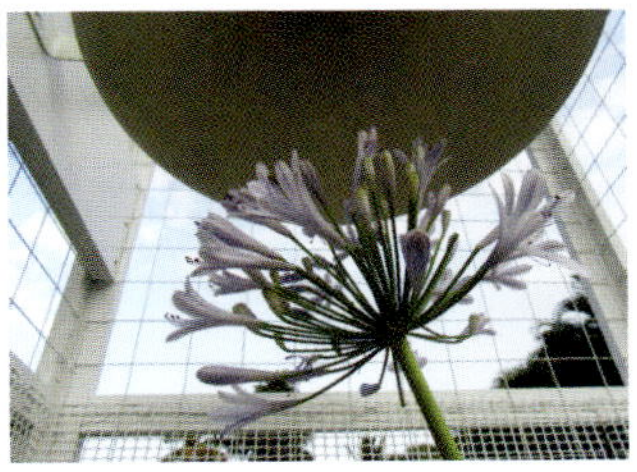
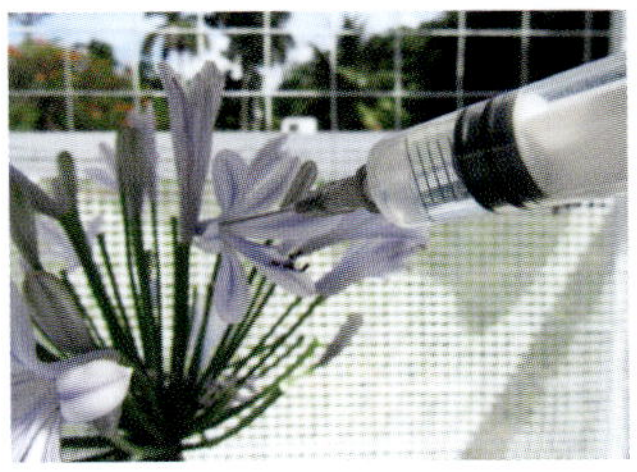
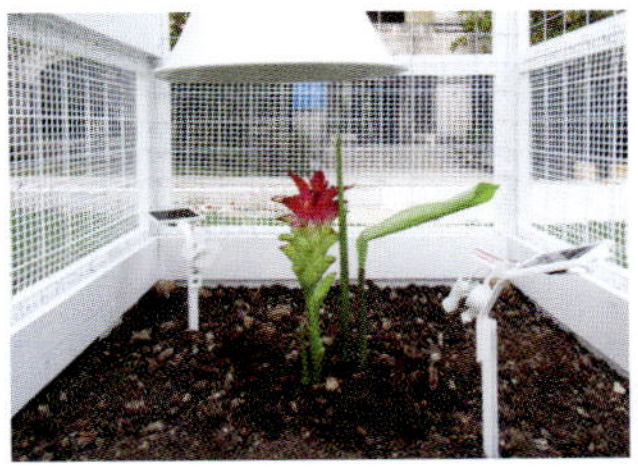
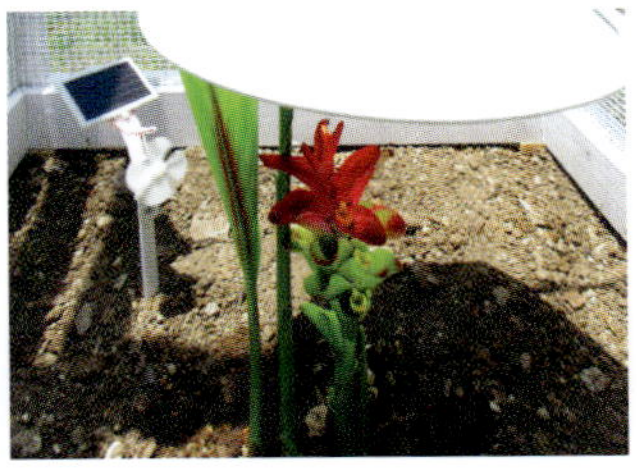
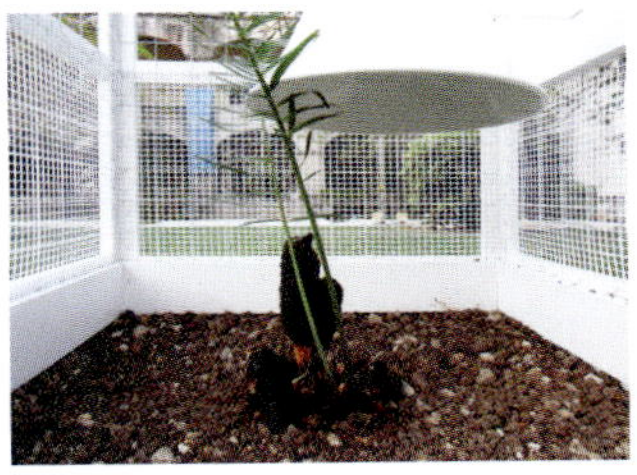
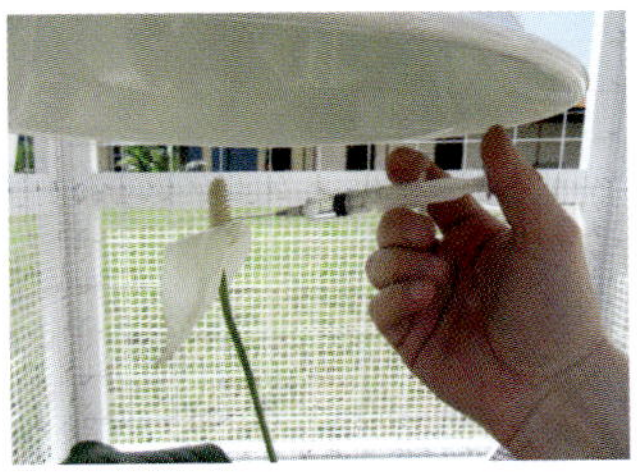
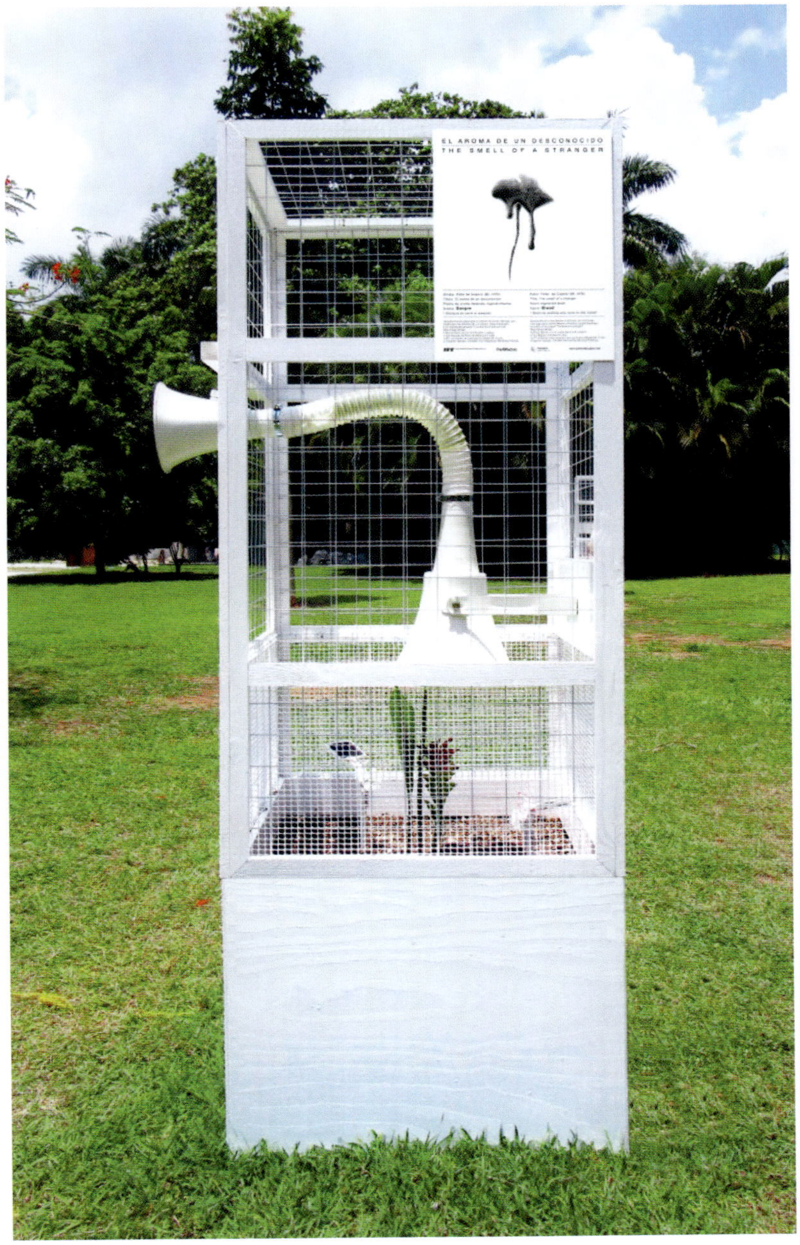

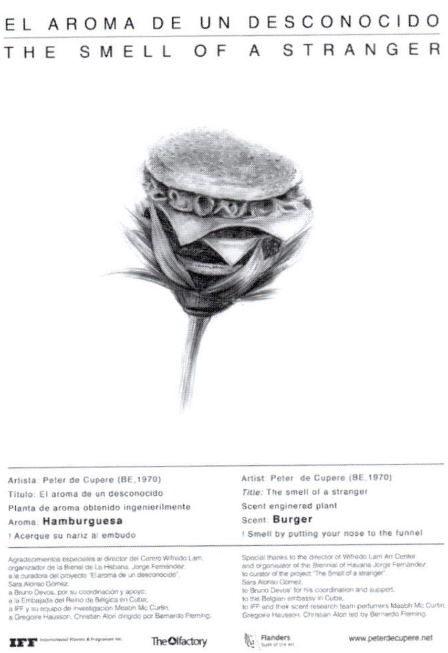

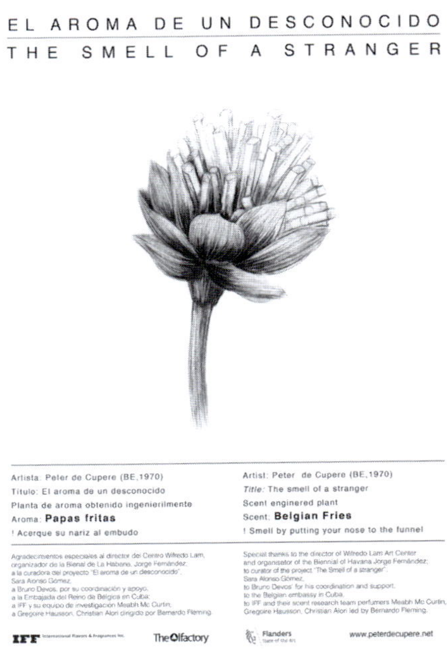

The Smell of A Stranger

Through 'Scent Engineering' the artist changes the scent of 9 local Cuban plants and flowers. Scents: scent of vagina, sperm, sweat, dead bodies, money, gun powder, air pollution, blood & geranium.

Supported by the Flemish Government, Ecoflor & Bruno Devos, director at Stockmans Printing, www.stockmans.be.
Fragrances supported by IFF Research lab, Bernardo Fleming and his team of expert fragrance designers (olfactive design): Meabh Mc Curtin, Gregoire Hausson, Christian Alori, www.iff.com.

Door 'scent engineering' heeft de kunstenaar de geur van 9 inheemse planten en bloemen aangepast.
Geuren: vagina, sperma, overleden persoon, geld, buskruit, luchtverontreiniging, bloed & geranium.

Met de steun van het Ministerie van de Vlaamse Gemeenschap, Ecoflor & Bruno Devos, directeur bij Stockmans Uitgeverij.
De geuren werden ontwikkeld in samenwerking met IFF Research lab, Bernardo Fleming met een team van geurexperten en -designers: Meabh Mc Curtin, Gregoire Hausson, Christian Alori, www.iff.com.

XII Bienal de La Habana, curator Jorge Fernández, co-curator, Sara Alonso Gómez, Havana, CU, 22.05.2015-22.06.2015

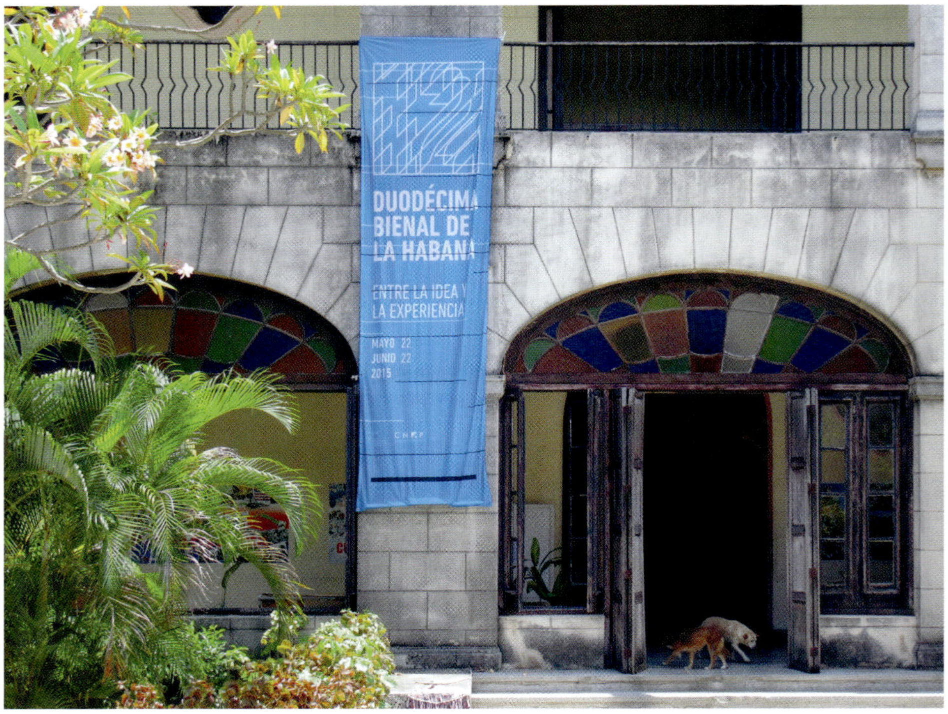

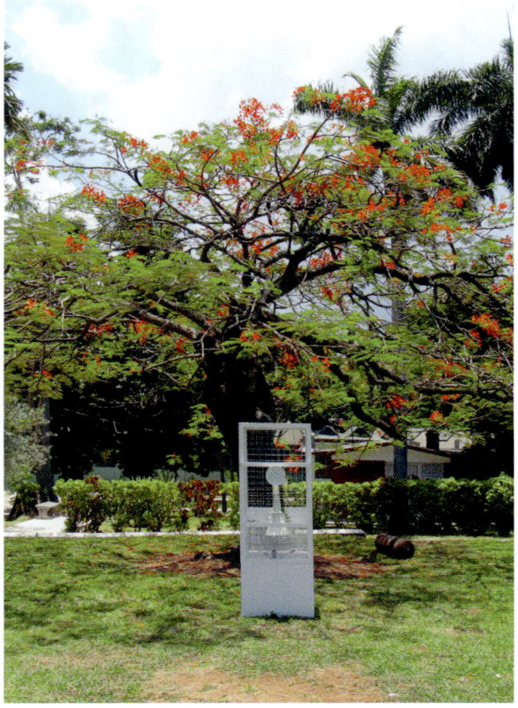

The Smell of A Stranger

XII Bienal de La Habana, curator Jorge Fernández, co-curator, Sara Alonso Gómez, Havana, CU, 22.05.2015-22.06.2015

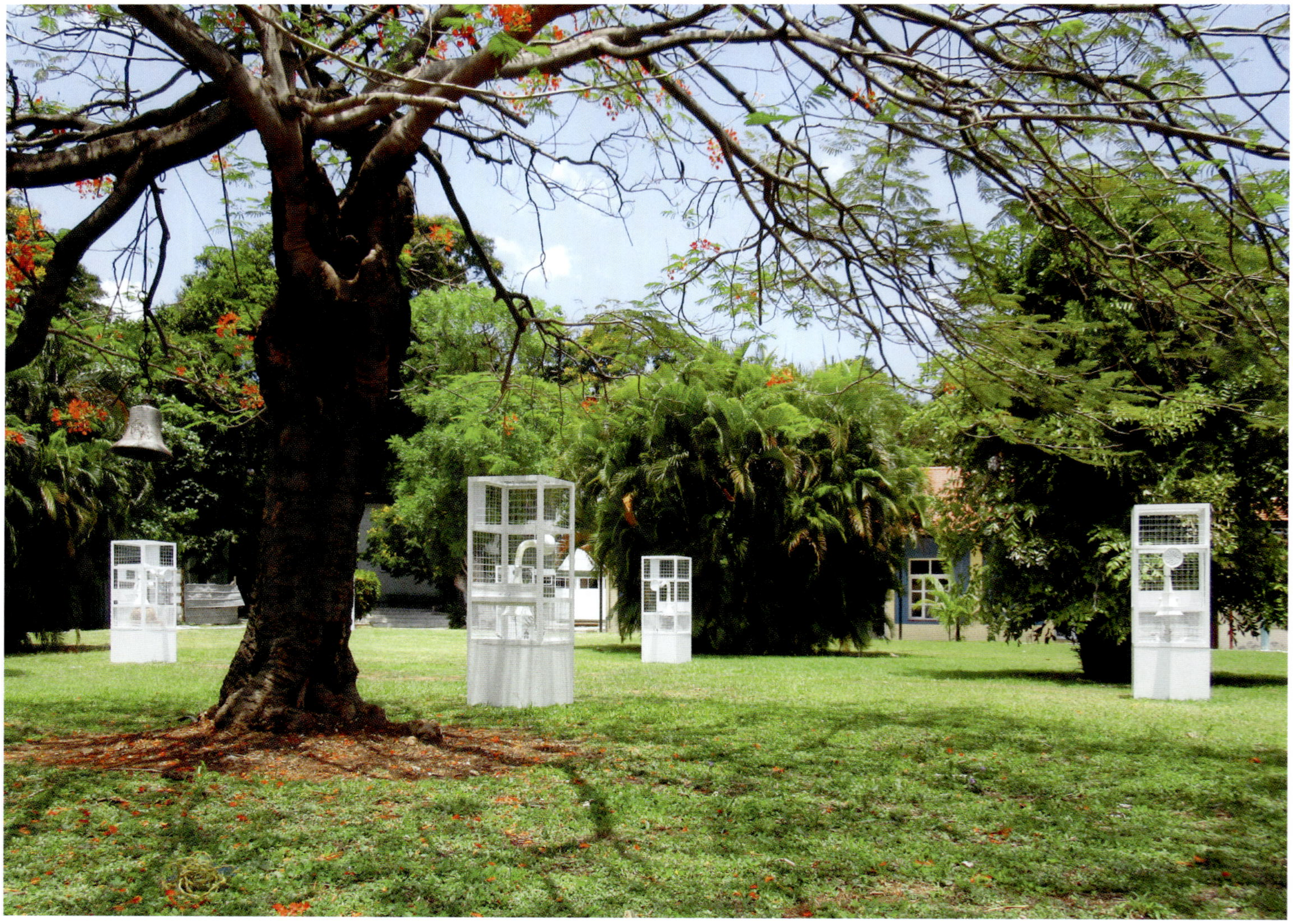

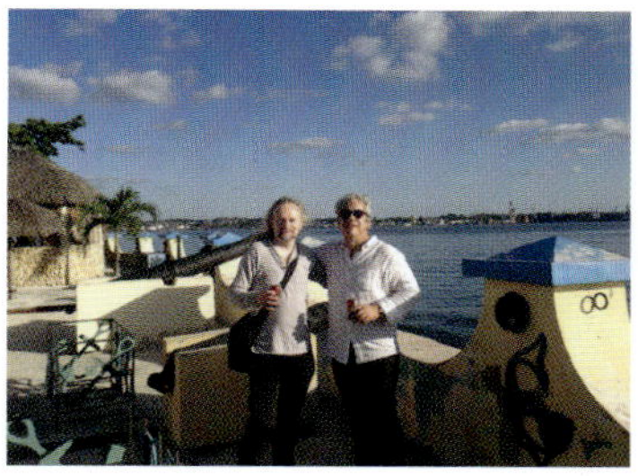
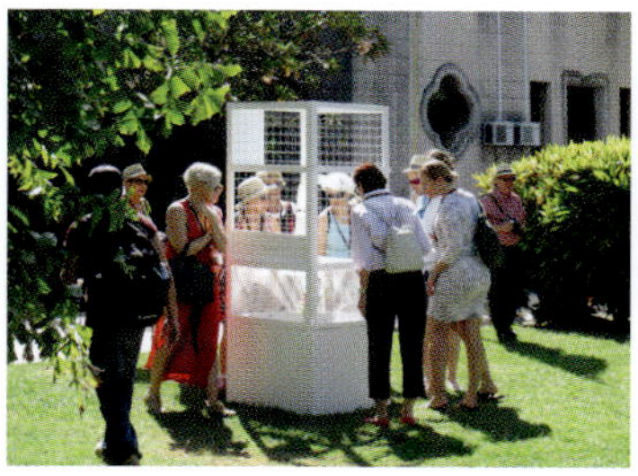
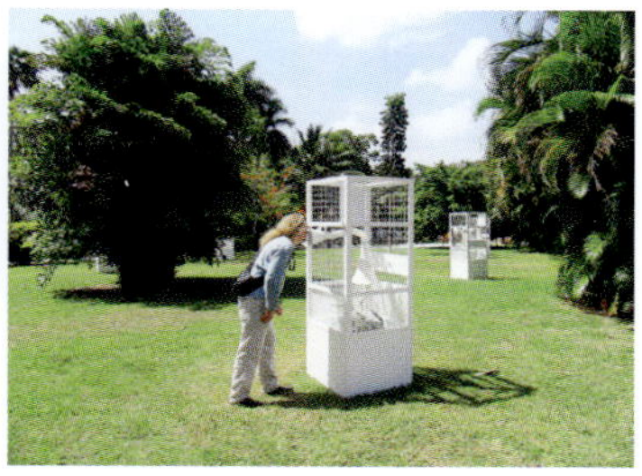
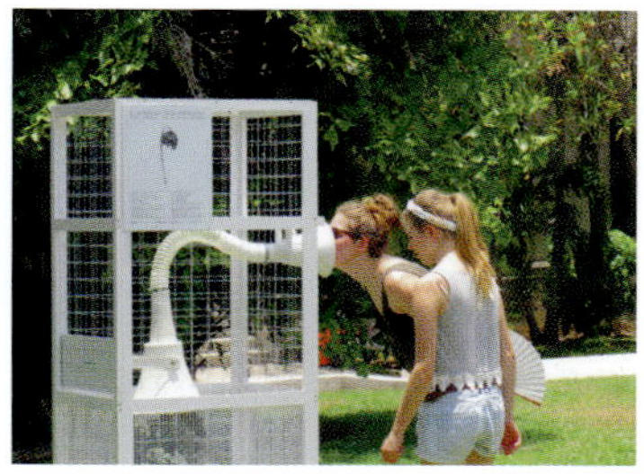
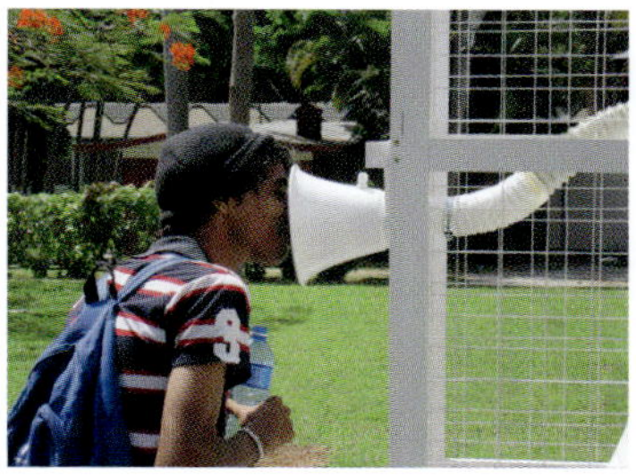
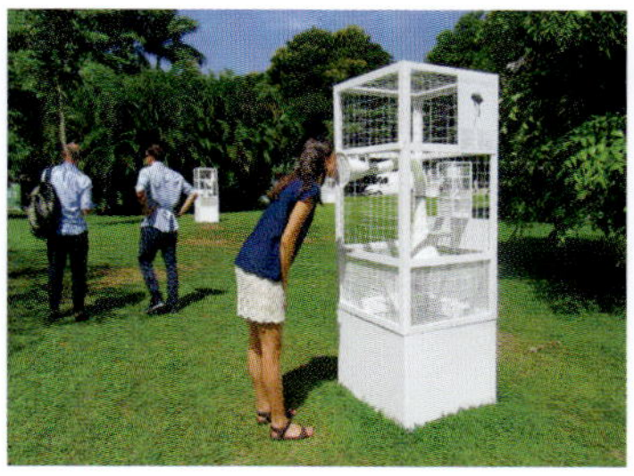
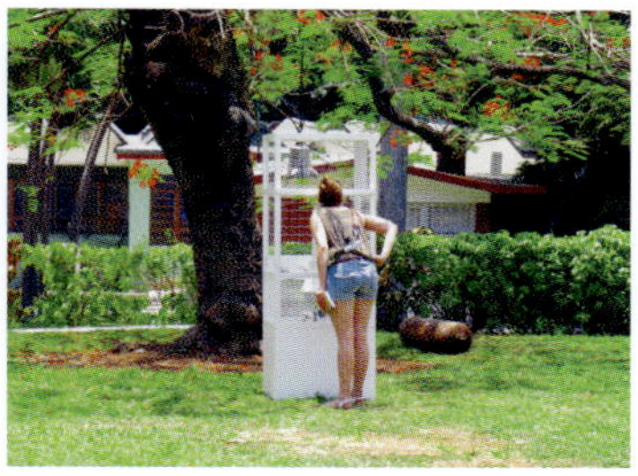
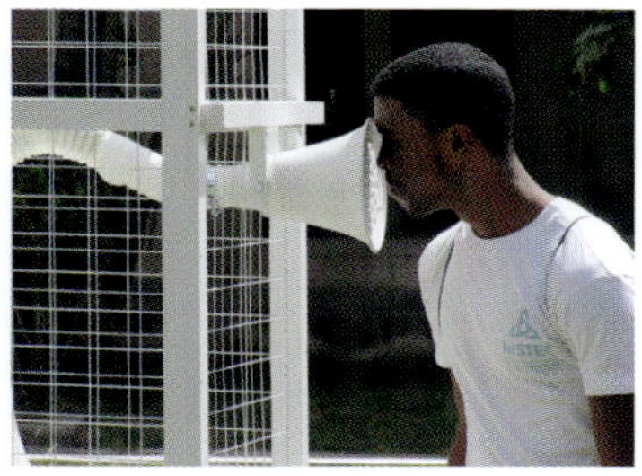
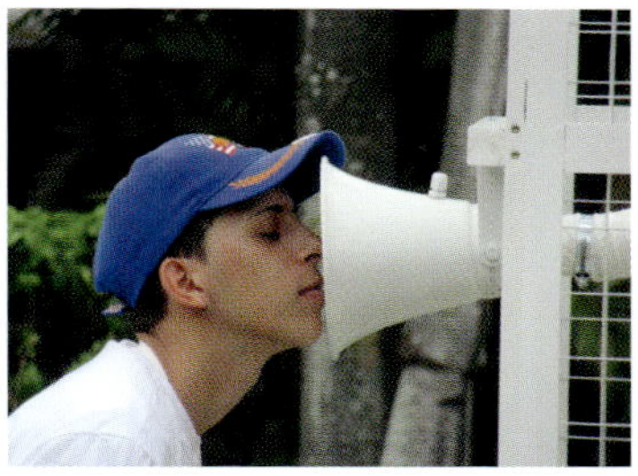
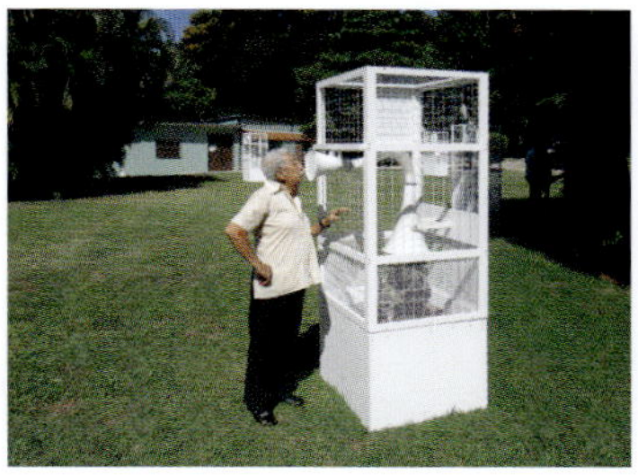
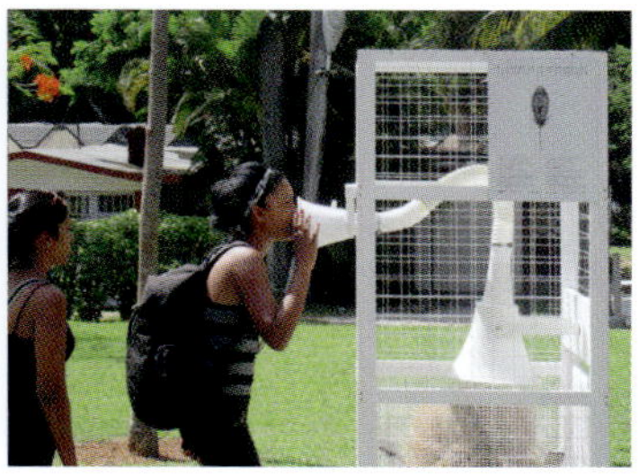
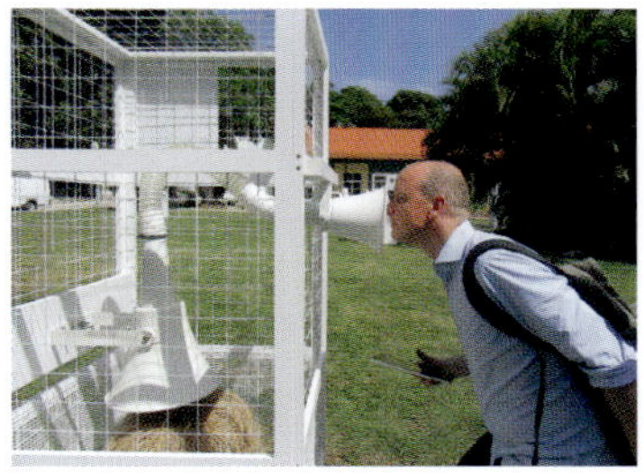
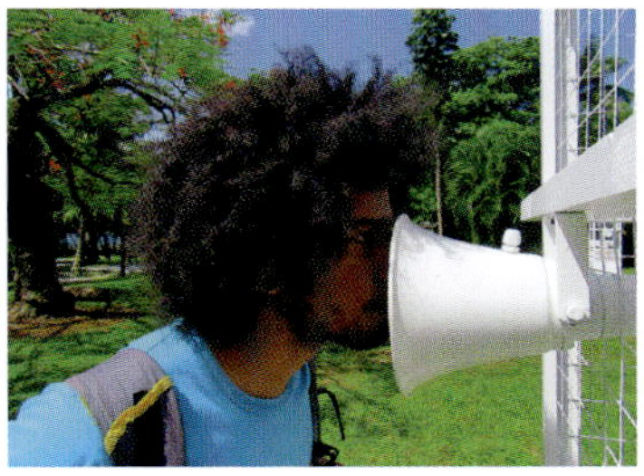
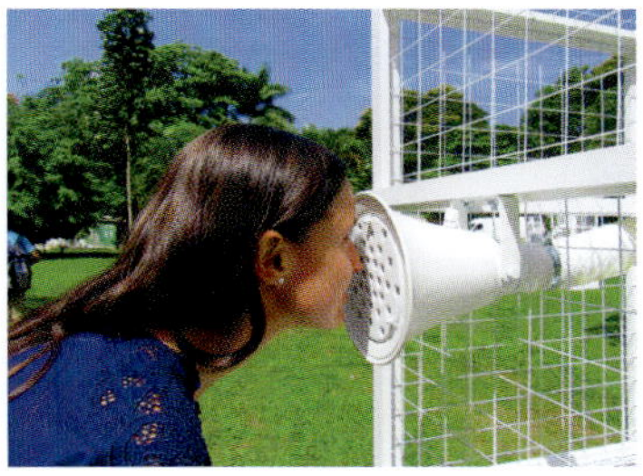
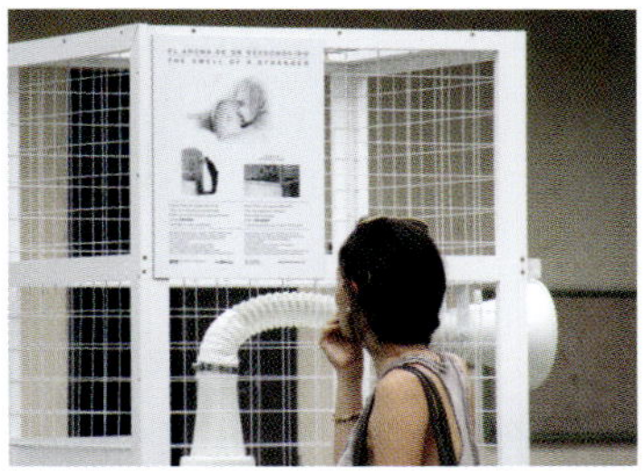
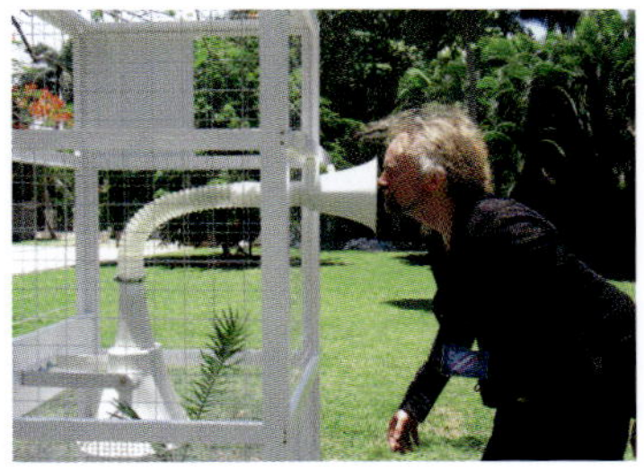
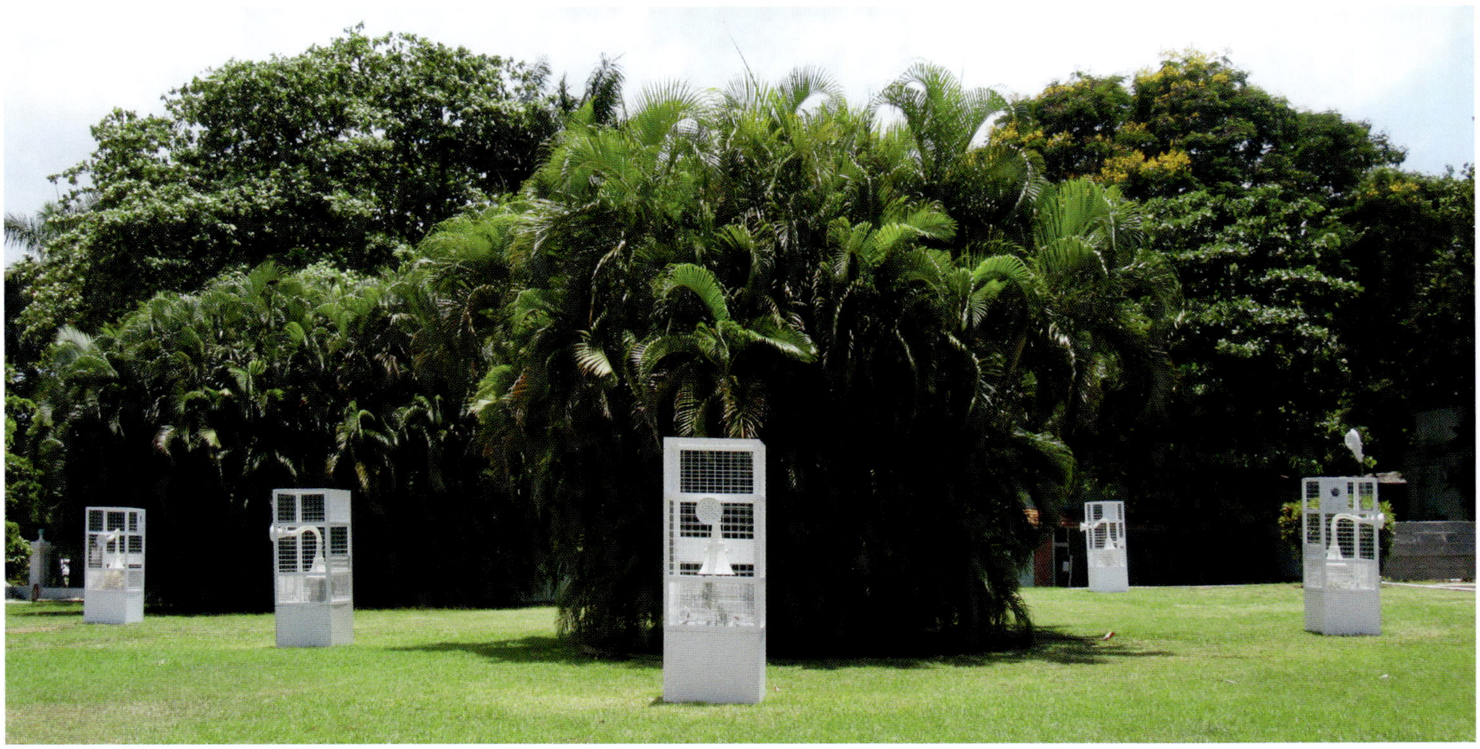

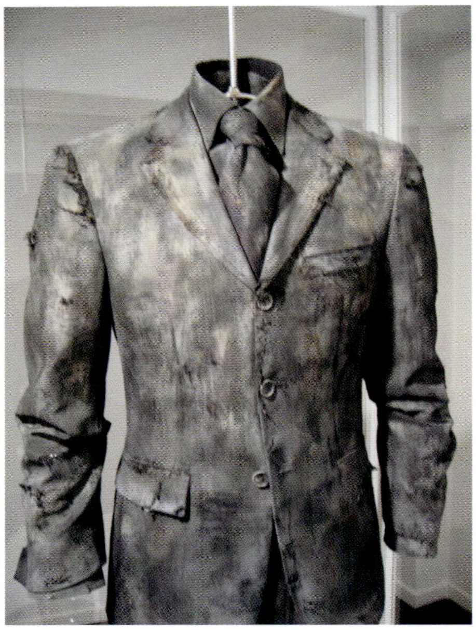

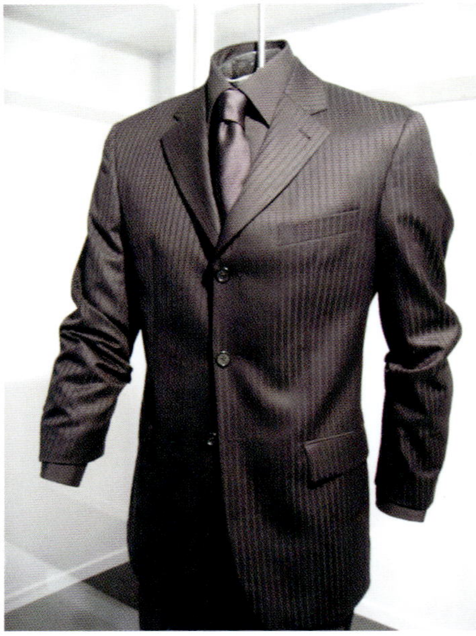

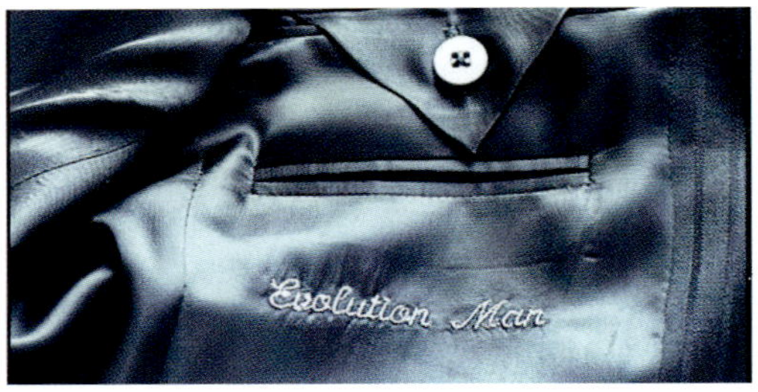

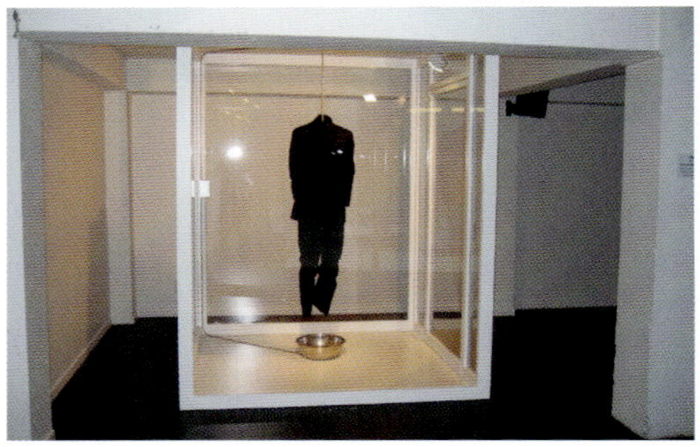

Evolution Man

Two identical men's suits hang in two separate rooms. One of the suits is new, the other worn and faded and damaged with time. Perfume drips from both suits into a cone-shaped bowl. Visitors pass through a door to enter the small plexiglass rooms and smell the perfume. The new suit has an exaggerated smell of a delicious perfume, while the old suit has a dryer smell, and yet one can detect undertones of perfume in it. It seems as though the perfume symbolizes the sweat in the suit. Just as every individual has a distinctive body odour, so too does this suit. The allusion to the evolution of the suit is not only visual, it is also supported through the olfactory sense by using the appropriate perfume. The difference between the two perfumes was that the new suit smelled of fresh cranberries and the used and worn suit of dried cranberries. A subtlety that for Peter de Cupere was the starting point for having these perfumes made in this way.

Peter de Cupere refers to the personality of every individual in the world. There are allusions to class differences between wealth and poverty. But over and above that, the work shows the quality and beauty of a fabric through the passage of time. That the suits were made of exceptionally high quality fabric is clear from the perfection of the tailoring. He decided not to use a standard brand, but the high quality label 'Scabal', a Belgian fashion label with a long-standing tradition. Peter de Cupere worked closely with Christophe Laudamiel to produce the exceptional perfumes used. (Christophe Laudamiel was still working as a perfumer at IFF at the time, before launching his own perfume brand, Dreamair). The installation is accompanied by a video in which we see a man in the changing suit. His body is still, with only his head and arms able to move. He looks at his own suit and sees it grow old and then new following the rhythm of his own breathing.

At the opening, the Belgian musician Stijn Meuris performed a poem he had written and that was added to the exhibition.

Twee dezelfde herenkostuums hangen op in twee aparte ruimtes. Het éne kostuum is nieuw, het andere verouderd en door de tijd verbleekt en aangetast. Uit de twee kostuums druppelt er parfum in een conische schaal. De bezoeker kan via een deur de kleine plexiglazen ruimtes betreden en de geur ervaren. Het nieuwe pak ruikt overdreven naar een heerlijk parfum, het oude bewerkte kostuum heeft een drogere geur, maar toch herkent men de ondertoon van het andere parfum erin. Het lijkt alsof het parfum hier symbool staat voor het zweet van het kostuum. Zoals iedereen een persoonlijke lijfgeur heeft, zo heeft dit kostuum zijn eigen typische geur. De verwijzing naar de evolutie van het kostuum is niet alleen visueel duidelijk, maar wordt olfactief ondersteund door het aangepaste parfum. Het verschil tussen de twee parfums was dat het nieuwe kostuum naar verse cranberries rook en het gebruikte versleten kostuum naar gedroogde cranberries. Een subtiliteit die voor Peter de Cupere het uitgangspunt was om deze parfums zo te laten creëren.

Peter de Cupere verwijst naar de persoonlijkheid van iedere mens in de wereld. Er zijn verwijzingen naar de verschillen in klasse tussen armoede en rijkdom. Maar buiten dit alles wordt ook de fijnheid en mooiheid van een stof door het tijdskarakter getoond.
Dat de kostuums van uitzonderlijke kwaliteitsstof zijn gemaakt komt uitdrukkelijk naar voor in de perfectie waarmee het kostuum is afgewerkt. Er werd niet voor een standaardmerk gekozen, maar voor het kwaliteitslabel 'Scabal', een Belgisch kledingmerk met traditie. Peter de Cupere werkte nauw samen met Christophe Laudamiel om deze uitzonderlijke parfums samen te stellen. (Christophe Laudamiel werkte op dat moment nog als parfumeur bij IFF en startte later met zijn eigen geurbedrijf Dreamair). De installatie wordt begeleid met een video waarin men een man in het veranderlijke herenkostuum ziet. Zijn lichaam staat stil, alleen zijn hoofd en armen kunnen bewegen. Hij kijkt naar zijn eigen kostuum en ziet het kostuum op het ritme van zijn ademhaling verouderen en terug verjongen.

Op de opening droeg de Belgische muzikant Stijn Meuris een door hem geschreven gedicht voor welke toegevoegd werd aan de tentoonstelling.

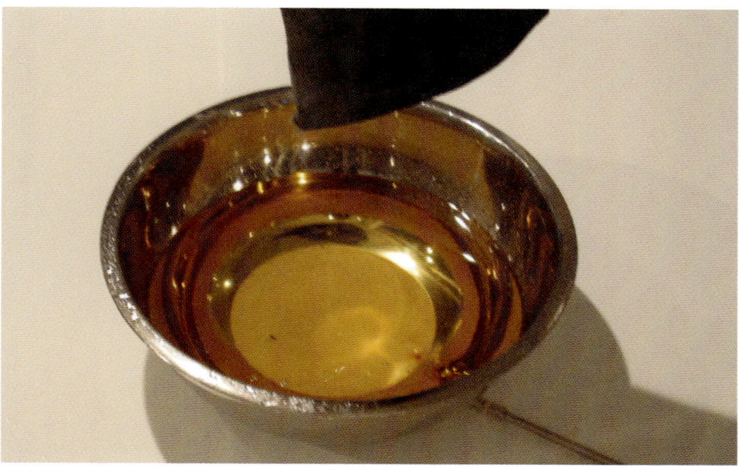

Mariages, MOMU, Fashion Museum,
curator Lieve Van Gorp, Antwerp, BE
17.09.2004-12.12.2004

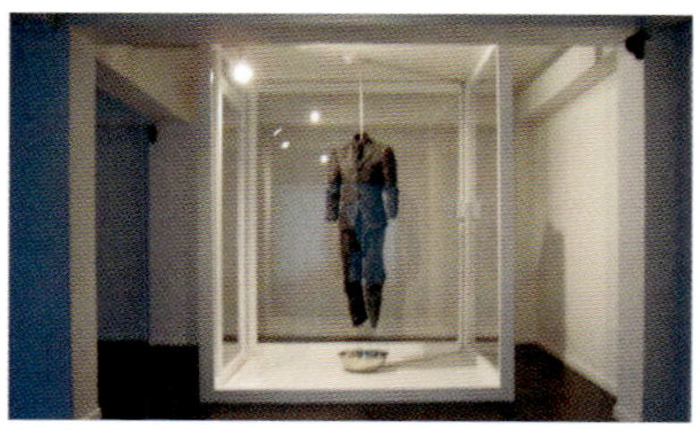

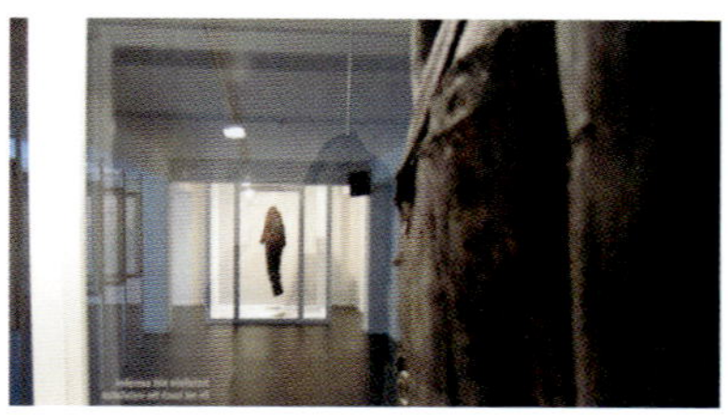

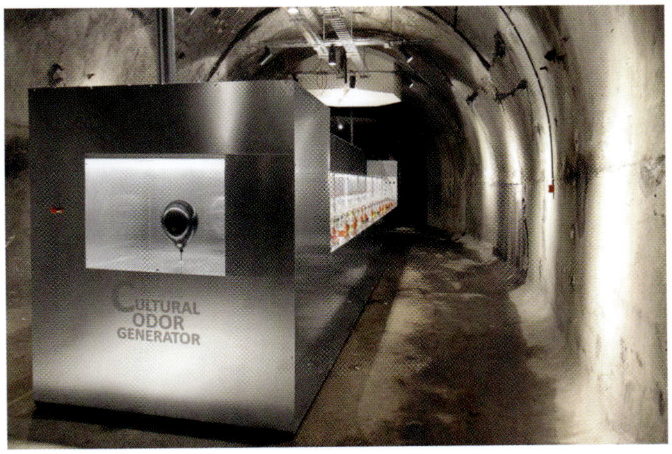

Cultural Odor Generator, 2010

Smell installation, 900 cm x 170 cm x 200 cm with 40 different smells

Based on the nationalities living in the city of Genk, 40 smells were selected that are directly or indirectly linked to the history of the city. The smells were chosen mainly on the basis of cultural, behavioural and eating patterns and smells that relate to the coal mine.

The odour installation was programmed in such a way that the end result of the selection of smells always depended on the previous visitors.
Just as we are faced with unexpected smell situations in our society, the Cultural Odour Generator provides you with some surprises.

Geurinstallatie, 200 cm x 900 cm x 170 cm met 40 verschillende geuren

Op basis van de aanwezige nationaliteiten wonend in de stad Genk werden 40 geuren geselecteerd die rechtstreeks of onrechtstreeks aansluiten bij de geschiedenis van de stad Genk.
De geuren zijn hoofdzakelijk gekozen op basis van culturele gedrags- en eetpatronen en geuren die in relatie staan met de steenkoolmijn.

De geurinstallatie is zo geprogrammeerd dat het eindresultaat van de geurselectie steeds afhankelijk is van voorgaande bezoekers.
Net zoals wij in de maatschappij geconfronteerd worden met onverwachte geursituaties, laat Cultural Odor Generator je op dezelfde wijze verrassen.

Green Light District, Buda Fabriek, curator Christophe De Jaeger, Kortrijk, BE, 08.11.2014-08.02.2015
Cultural Odor Generator, C-Mine, Genk, BE, April 2012-April 2014

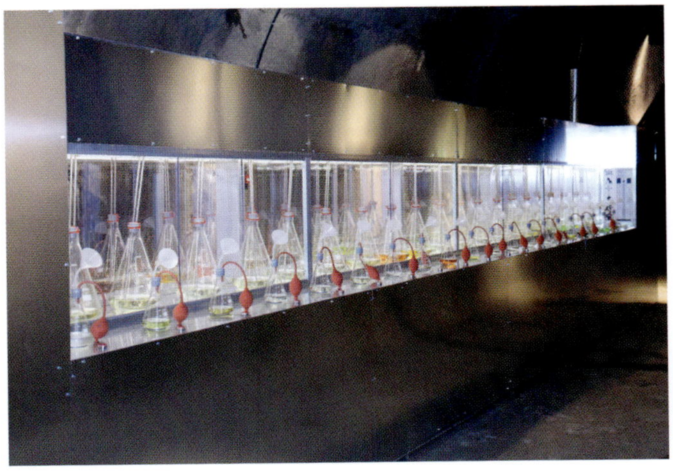

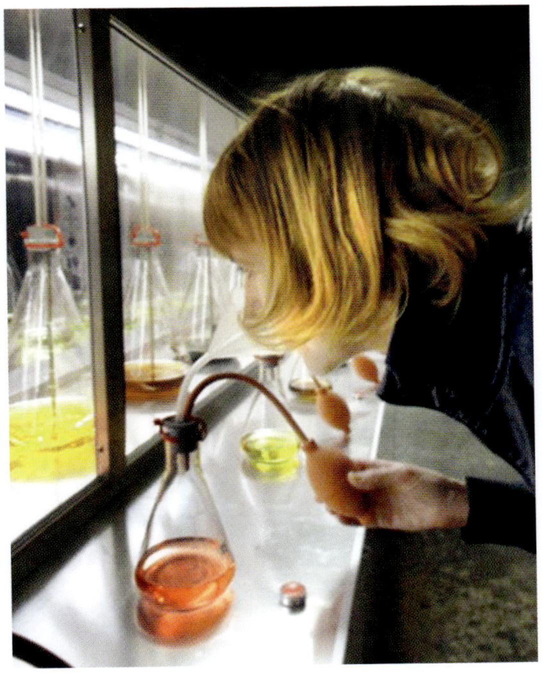

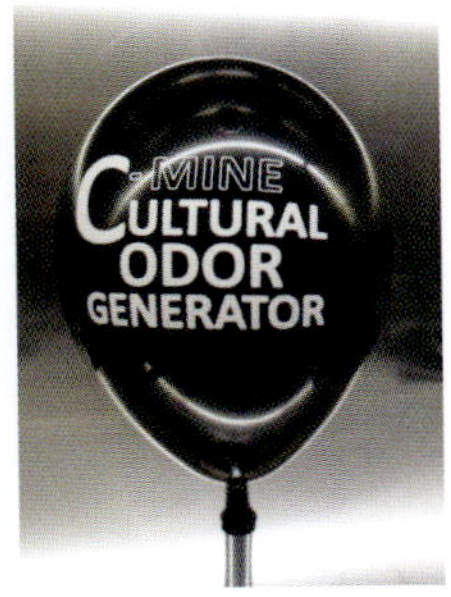

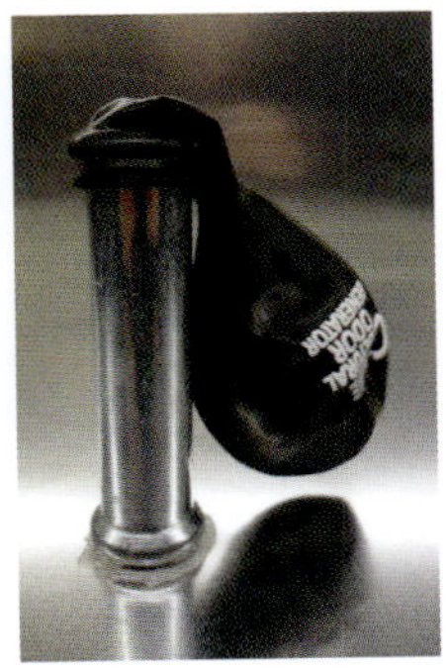

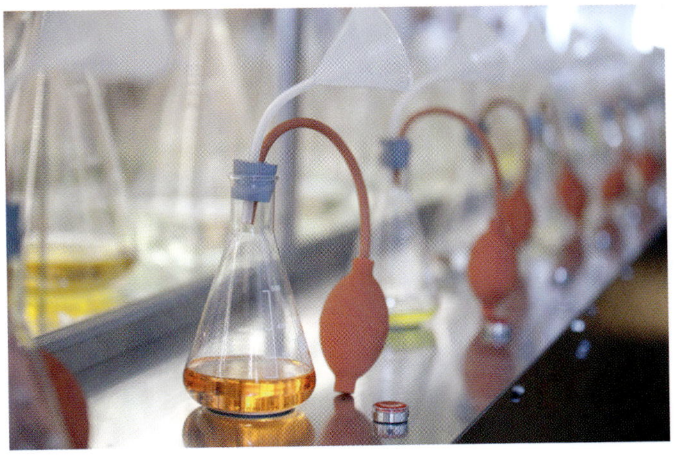

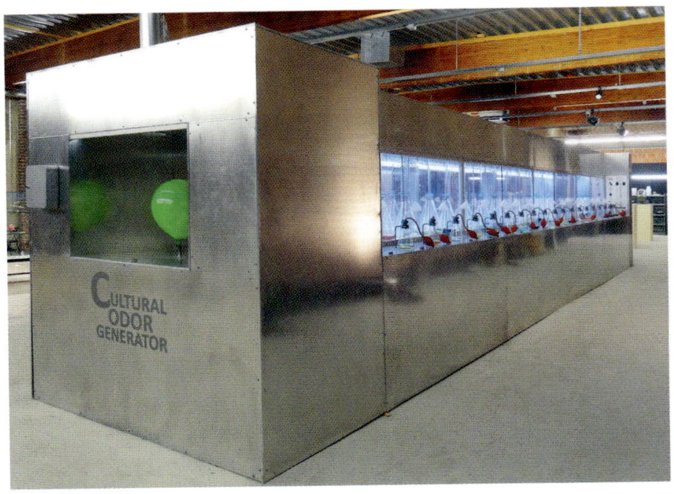

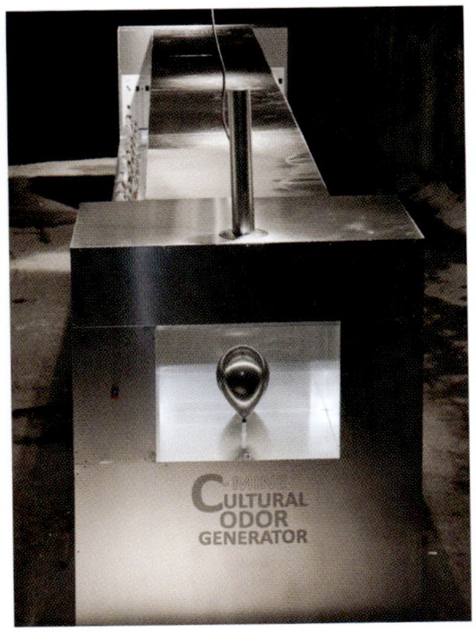

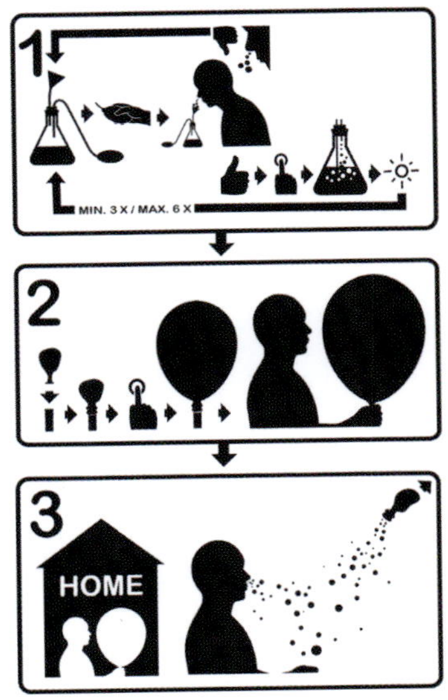

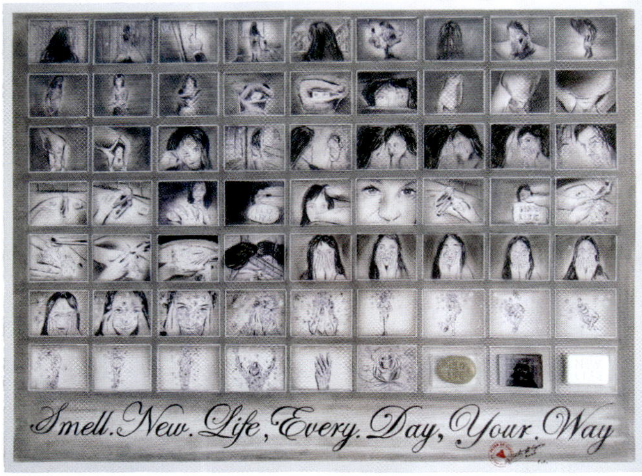

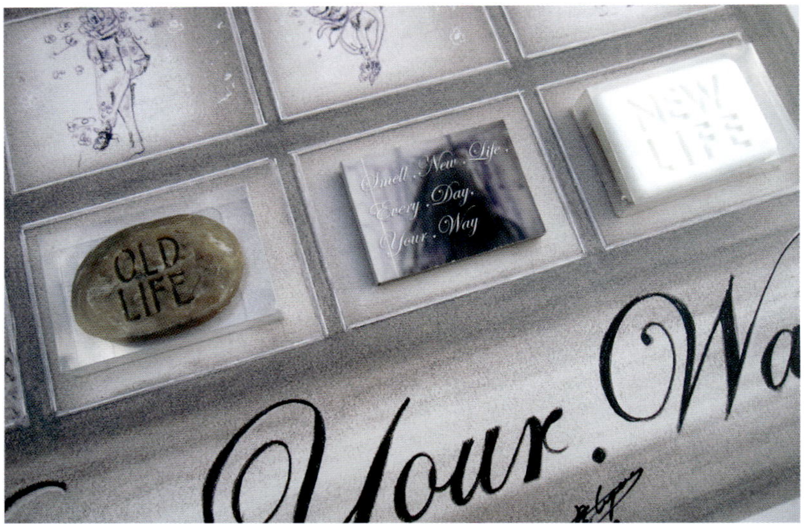

Smell New Life, Every Day Your Way, 2010

Edition of 100, 3 A.P. - 58 cm x 78,5 cm

Two small hotel soaps. A brownish soap with the name 'Old Life' engraved on it smells less pleasant than the lighter, white soap with the name 'New Life', which smells lovely and fresh. A booklet in which all the small drawings are reproduced accompanies the edition. The edition was created to support the hotel project in Oostmalle carried out by Kina vzw, a non-profit organisation. They offer free hotel rooms for three days to people who have ended up on the street due to unforeseen circumstances, such as a fire or eviction due to rent arrears or domestic disputes. People in such situations can spend three days in the hotel free of charge, during which they are provided with further assistance in looking for solutions. There is a copy of this work in each of the rooms, and the two pieces of soap are placed in the bathroom next to the sink, together with the booklet.
The different soap smells encourage them to think about their future and give them hope for a fresh start. A better life.

Twee kleine hotelzepen. Een bruin uitziende zeep met de naam *Old Life* erin gegraveerd ruikt minder aangenaam dan de heldere witte zeep met de naam *New Life* welke heerlijk en fris ruikt. Bij de editie hoort ook een klein boekje waarin de kleine tekeningen gedrukt staan. De editie werd gemaakt ter ondersteuning van het hotelproject in Oostmalle van Kina vzw. een non-profit organisatie. Zij bieden gratis, gedurende drie dagen, een hotelkamer aan aan mensen die op straat komen te staan door niet gewilde omstandigheden. Bijvoorbeeld bij brand of uitzetting wegens wanbetaling of huiselijke ruzies. Deze mensen kunnen dan drie dagen gratis verblijven in het hotel waar men hen tijdens deze drie dagen verder helpt met het zoeken naar oplossingen. De editie hangt op iedere hotelkamer en in de badkamer liggen bij het lavabo de twee stukjes zeep samen met het miniboekje. De verschillende geuren van de zeepjes laten hen nadenken over hun toekomst en geven hen hoop op een nieuwe start, een beter leven.

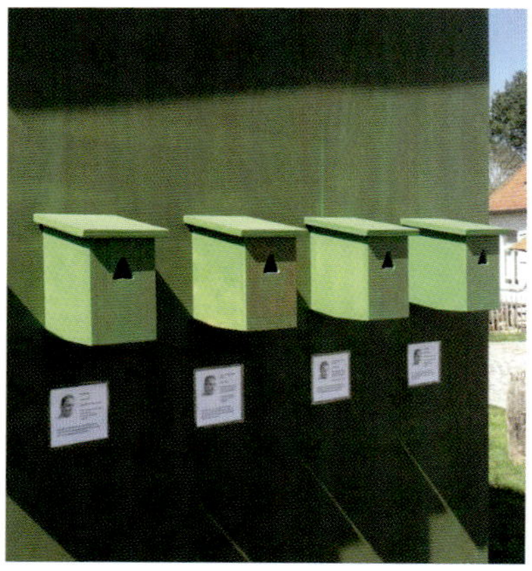

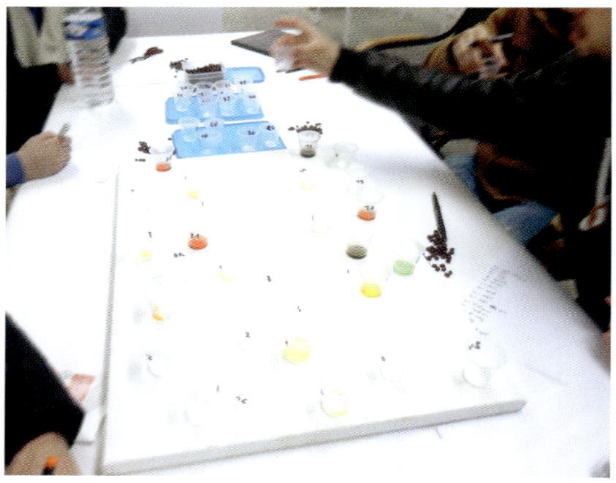

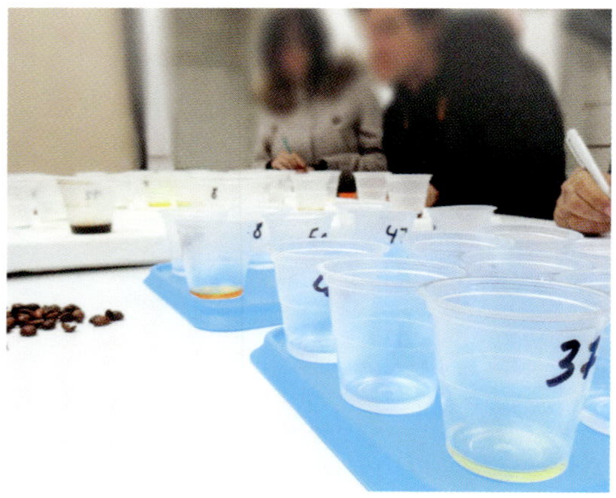

Nose Houses, 2014

Nose Houses are bird houses in which the opening is in the shape of a nose. You can stick your nose in it to smell the scents in the bird house. The smells placed in the bird houses vary depending on the project.
In the project 'Vreemde Vogels' [Strange Birds], 10 Nose Houses were placed on the largest bird house (Guinness Book of World Records) in the world. Smells were applied to the Nose Houses that referred to a positive and negative memory of five refugees. Along with their story, this allowed their recollections to be shared with others.

Nose Houses zijn vogelkastjes waar de opening de vorm van een neus heeft. Men kan hier de neus insteken om de geur aanwezig in het vogelkastje te ruiken. De geuren die aangebracht worden in de vogelkastjes verschillen naargelang het project.
In het project 'Vreemde Vogels' werden 10 *Nose Houses* op het grootste vogelhuis (Guinness Book of World Records) ter wereld aangebracht. In de *Nose Houses* waren geuren aangebracht die verwezen naar een positieve en negatieve herinnering van 5 vluchtelingen. Samen met hun verhaal konden zo hun herinneringen aan anderen verteld worden.

Vreemde Vogels, Fintele, org. Regionaal Landschap IJzer & Polder, Lo-Reninge, BE 13.05-30.08.2016

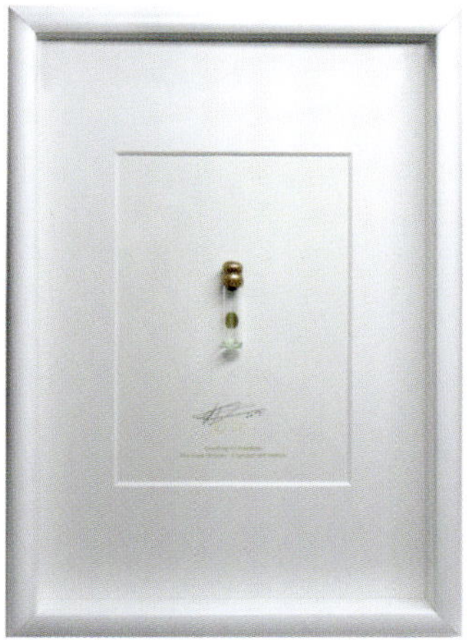

Golden Edition, 2016

21 cm x 29,7 cm

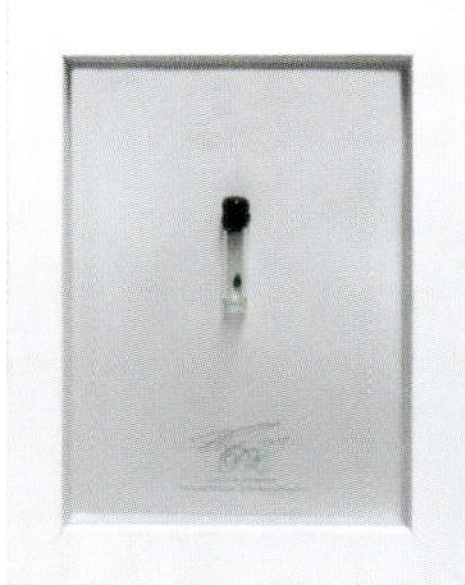

Green Edition, 2016

14,8 cm x 21 cm

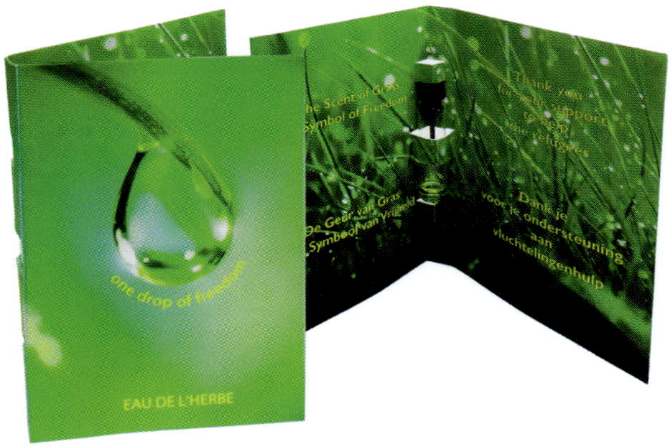

One Drop of Freedom, 2016

More economical versions of One Drop of Freedom were on sale, such as a (fake) Gold or Green variety with a framed droplet of the scent of grass.

Als goedkopere versies kon men een (fake) Gouden of Groene editie van een 'met een druppeltje grasgeur' ingekaderd *One Drop Of Freedom* kopen.

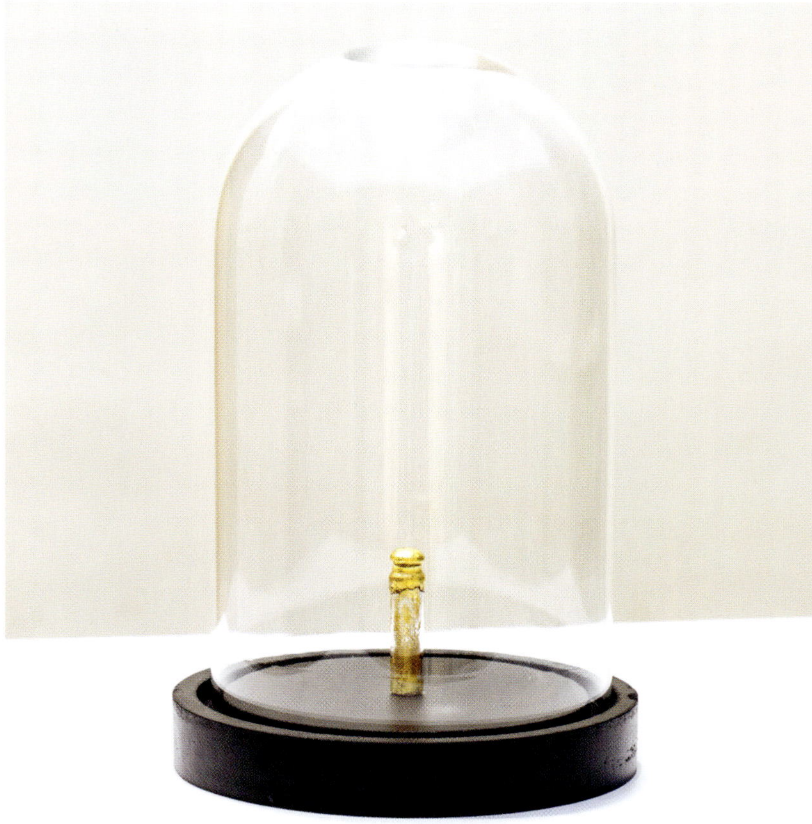

One Drop of Freedom 24K, 2016

4,5 cm x 0,5 cm Ø
Glass dome / Stolp: 21,5 cm x 14 cm Ø
2 editions

Sealed aroma vial / Afgesloten ampul met aroma

A 24K gold leaf plated aromatic flacon containing a droplet of the scent of grass.
The One Drop of Freedom 24K version is the most expensive scent in the world. As a strong symbol to support refugee aid organisations 1,000 euro was paid for this version of the one droplet of the scent of grass. Two copies of the 24K gold leaf version were made, one remains the property of the artist.

24K bladgoud bekleed aromaflesje met een druppeltje grasgeur. 'One Drop of Freedom 24K' versie is de duurste geur ter wereld. Symbolisch werd ter ondersteuning van vluchtelingenhulporganisaties in Vlaanderen 1.000 euro voor 1 druppeltje grasgeur in deze versie betaald. De 24K bladgoud versie werd op 2 exemplaren gemaakt waarvan 1 exemplaar voor de kunstenaar zelf.

Concept One Drop of Freedom, 2016

One droplet of the subtle scent of freshly mown grass in a bottle of perfume. You can smell the grass and enjoy it, but it demands time to catch the tiny droplet. It seeps out very slowly, sticking to the glass on its way to freedom. The saying goes that the grass is always greener on the other side (of the world...). The aroma of grass engenders an image of fatigue and then lying down on the ground after a long flight over water.
Numerous donation opportunities were presented.
Refugee Aid Flanders and the Limburg Platform for Refugees gratefully received support, thanks to the kind donations of art enthusiasts and the selfless cooperation of Peter de Cupere, along with many other volunteers of the PXL-MAD School of Arts including lecturers Dirk Kenis and Griet Moors.

Eén druppeltje subtiele geur van pas afgemaaid gras in een parfumflesje. Je kunt het gras ruiken en ervan genieten, maar het vraagt tijd om het druppeltje op te vangen. Traag sijpelt het eruit, plakkend aan de glaswand op zoek naar vrijheid. Het gras is groener langs de andere kant van de wereld, zegt men...
De geur van gras vleit uitgeput neer op de grond na een vlucht over het water.
Er werden verschillende donatiemogelijkheden aangeboden.
Met de donatie van kunstliefhebbers en met de belangeloze medewerking van Peter de Cupere en vele andere vrijwilligers van de PXL-MAD School of Arts, docenten Dirk Kenis en Griet Moors, werden zo Vluchtelingenhulp Vlaanderen en het Limburgs Platform Voor Vluchtelingen extra ondersteund.

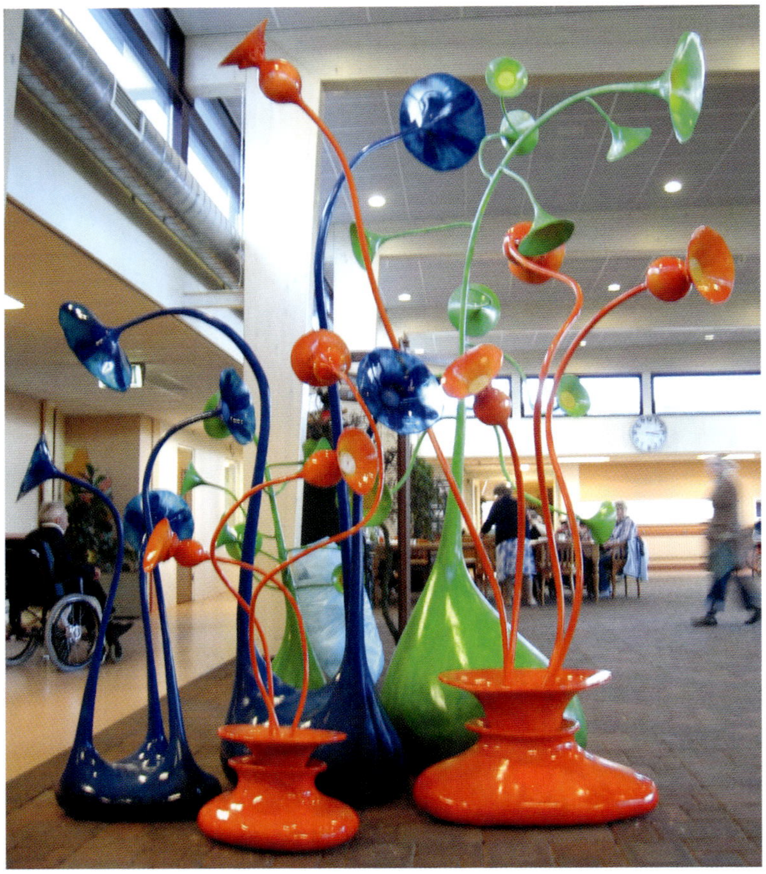

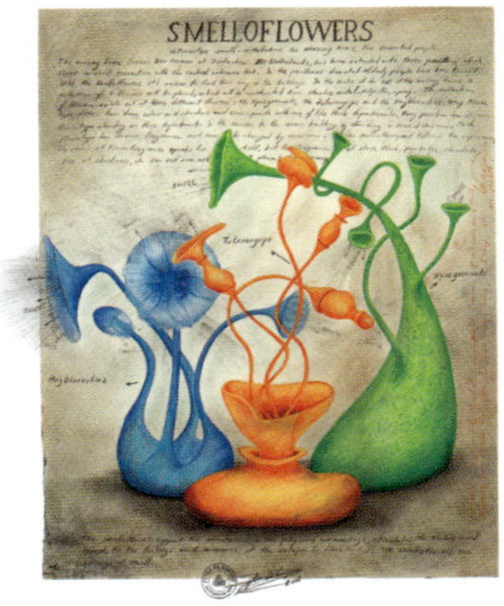

Drawing Smelloflowers

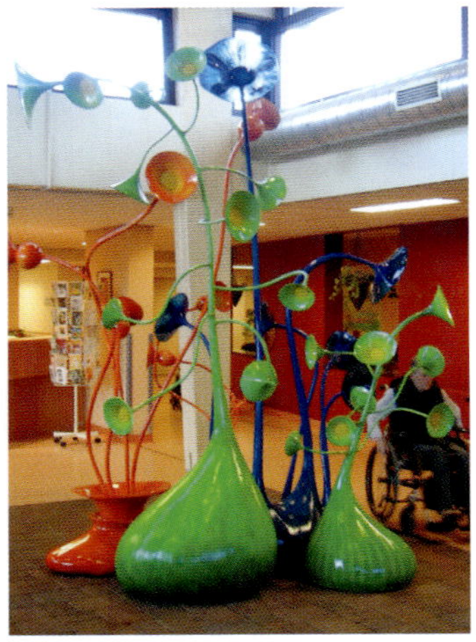

Smelloflowers, 2004-2005

An artwork integrated into the Sensire Den Ooiman nursing home in Doetinchem. The 3 pavilions house elderly patients suffering from dementia. They can find their way back to their homes without realising it, via the scent that is adjusted for each residential group.

Kunstintegratie in verpleeghuis Sensire Den Ooiman te Doetinchem, NL. In de drie paviljoens zijn demente bejaarden gehuisvest. Ze vinden onbewust hun weg terug naar hun verblijfplaats via de geur welke per bewonersgroep wordt aangepast.

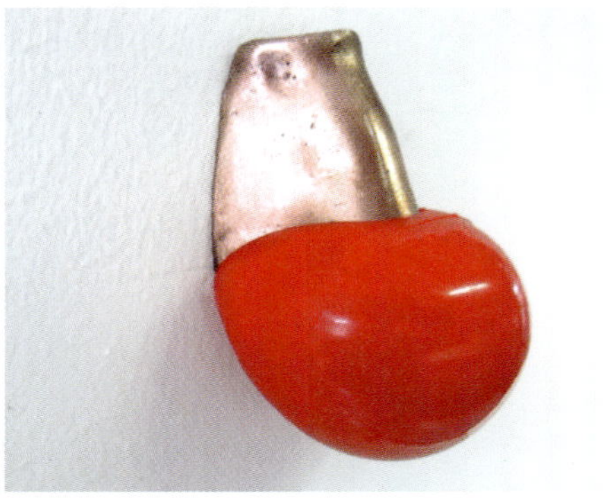

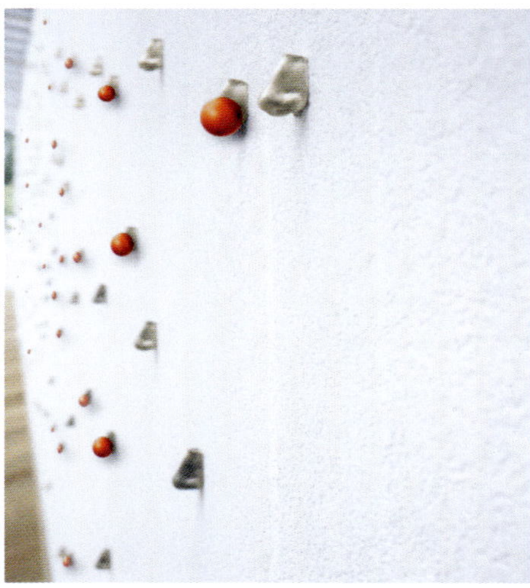

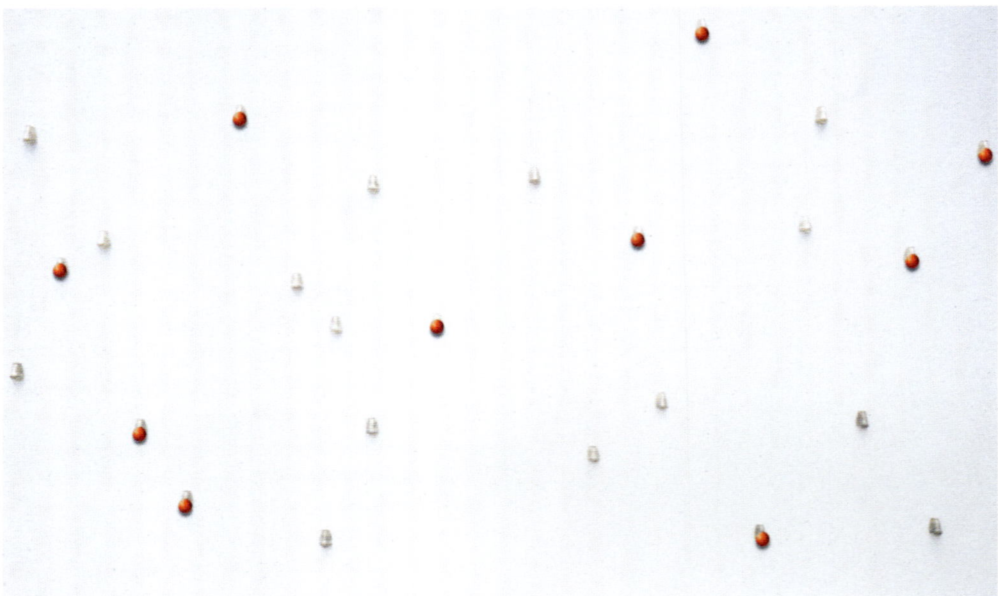

Little Noses, Little Noses and Little Noses, 1999

±300 cm x 2000 cm

333 noses of bronze (real size of the nose of the artist), red plastic clown noses for the visitors.
By entrance of the child clinic you have the smell of strawberry.

333 neuzen in brons (ware grootte van de neus van de kunstenaar), rode plastieken clownneuzen voor bezoekers.
Bij de ingang van het kinderziekenhuis word je omgeven door de geur van aardbei.

Art integration in a public building: Child Clinic Free University Brussels, Jette, BE
Noses, Noses & Noses, Art integration, Children's clinic
Free University Brussels, BE, inauguration 07.05.1999

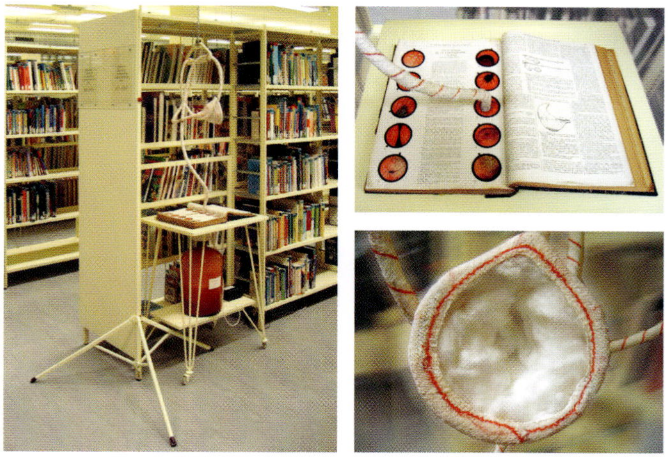

Medical Flower 2 Gastroscopy, 2005

Mixed smell media

A flower made with traditional stretch bandage and medical cotton wool from an old medical publication on gastroscopy. An oxygen concentrator and a ventilation system are used to spread the smell of Dettol (disinfectant used to clean the floor and furniture in hospitals). The disinfectant smells so strong that visitors need to take a step back to view the artwork).

Uit een oude medische publicatie over gastroscopie komt er een bloem, gemaakt uit klassiek rekverband en klinische katoenen watten. Door middel van een oxi-derivator en beluchtingssysteem wordt er geur van dettol verspreidt (ontsmettingsproduct gebruikt in klinieken om de grond en meubilair te zuiveren). Het ontsmettend product is zo sterk olfactief aanwezig dat enige afstand tot het werk genoodzaakt is.

The scent of information and paper, Culturama 2005,
Stadsbibliotheek Henry Van de Velde, Leuven, BE, 17.02.2005-19.02.2005

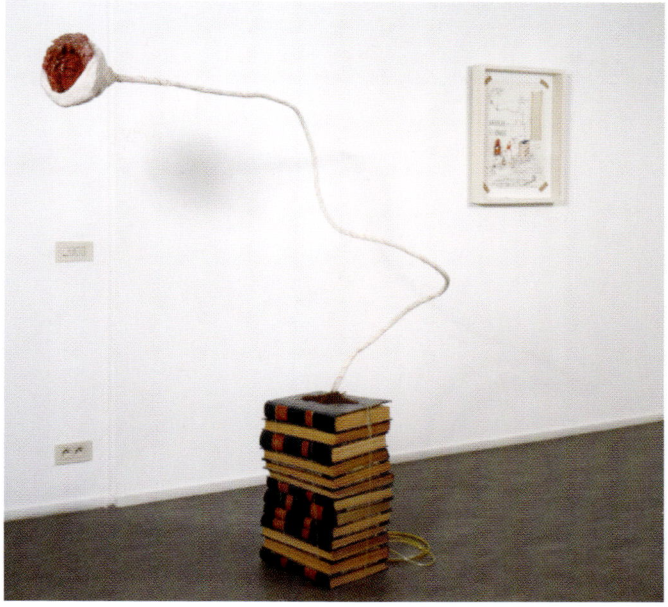

Medical Flower 1, 2002

Smell of mercurochrome, ether or pus, medical press journals, medical bandage, smell-activator

De geur van mercurochrome, ether en etter, medische tijdschriften, medisch verband en geuractivator

Peter de Cupere, Smellcom Happening, Smell Kiss Performance, rockconcert
Admiral Freebee, Van Laere Contemporary Art, Antwerp, BE, 14.09-21.10.2000

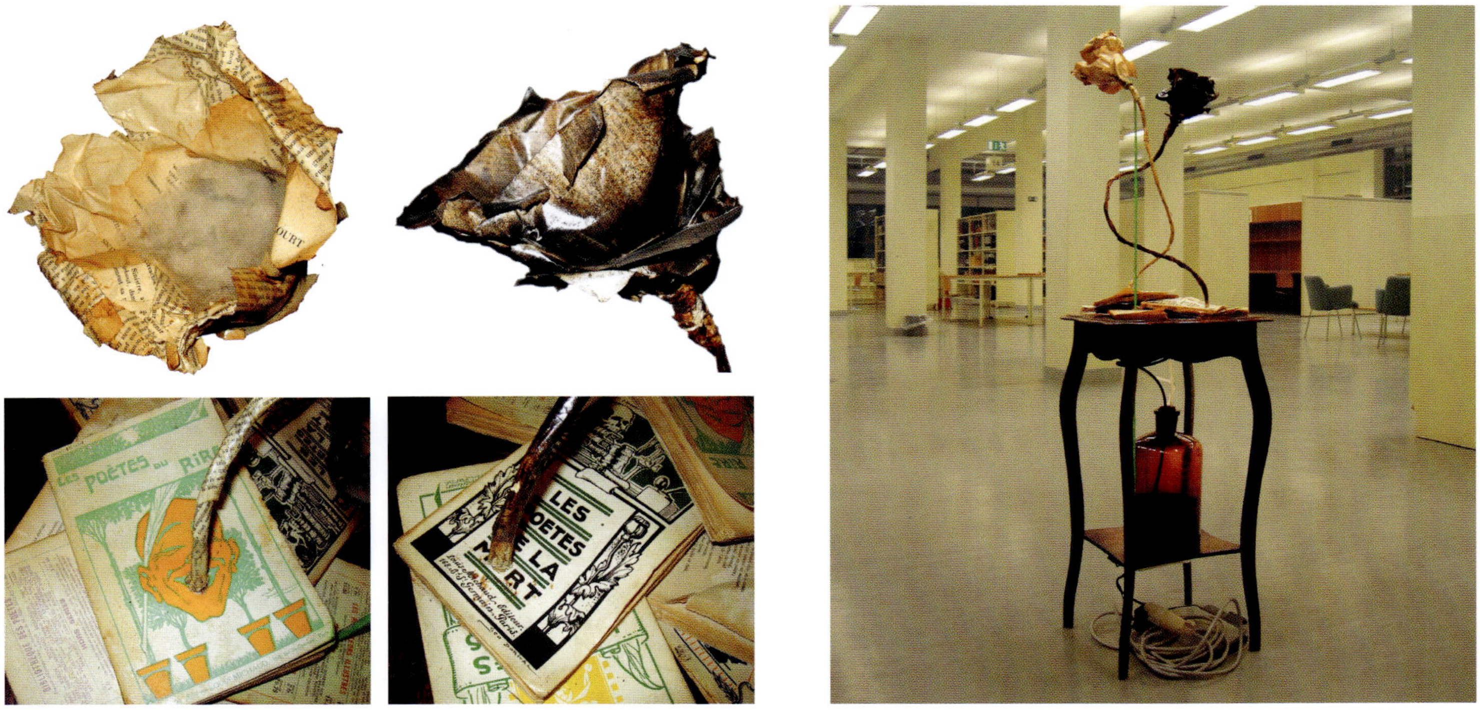

Les Fleurs Des Poètes, 2003

137 cm x 39 cm x 39 cm

Olfactory sound installation. Flowers made of two poem books, scent of eucalyptus, sounds of laughter and crying.

Olfactorische geluidsinstallatie. Bloemen gemaakt van 2 gedichtenboeken, de geur van eucalyptus, geluiden van lachen en schreeuwen.

The scent of information and paper, Culturama 2005, Stadsbibliotheek Henry Van de Velde, Leuven, BE, 17.02.2005-19.02.2005

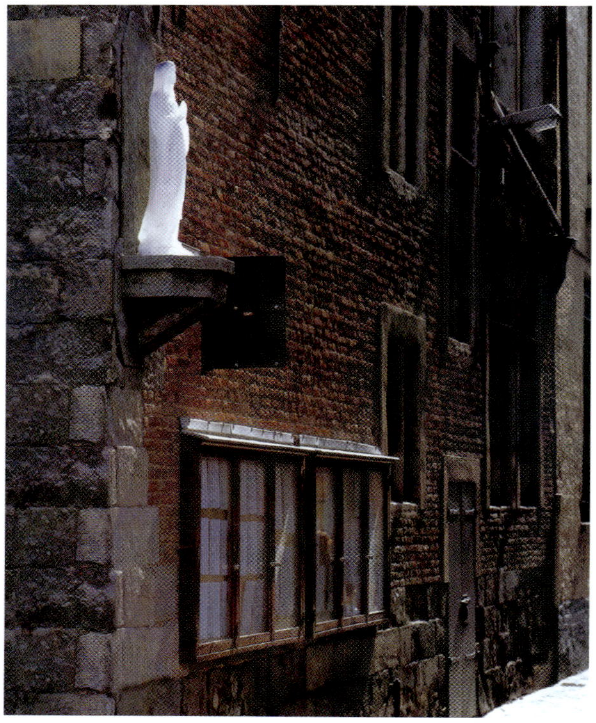
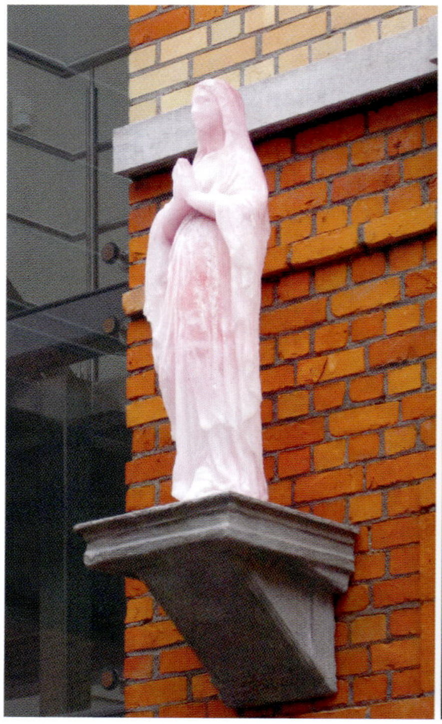
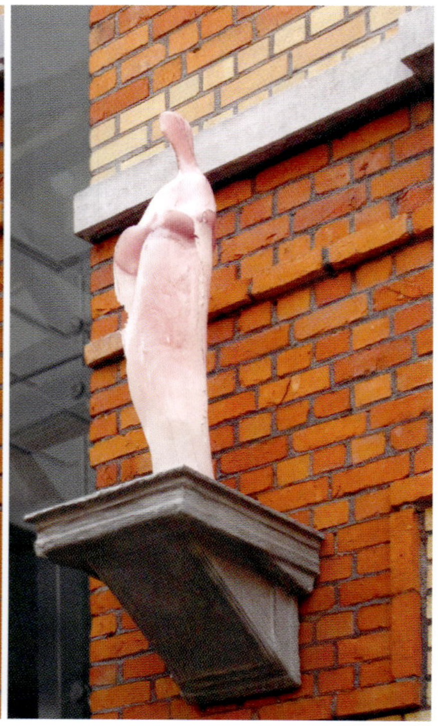

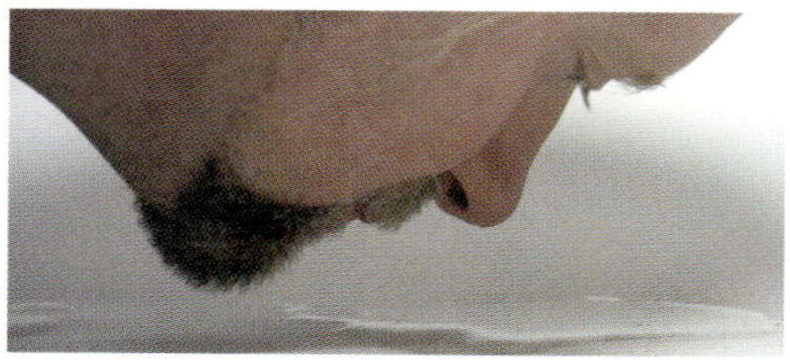
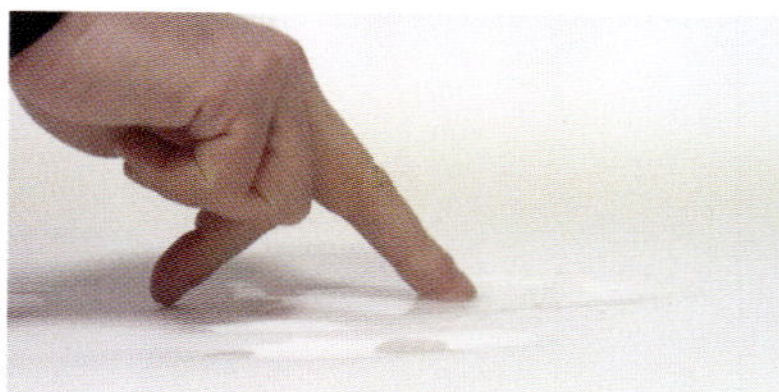
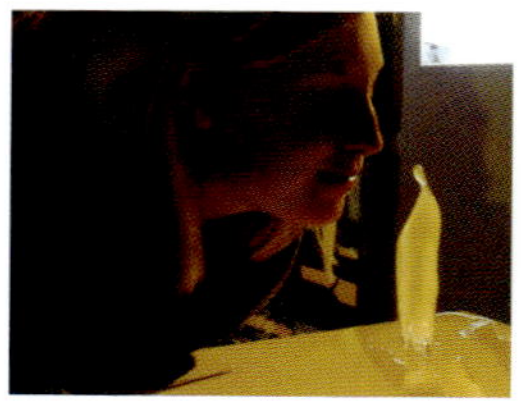
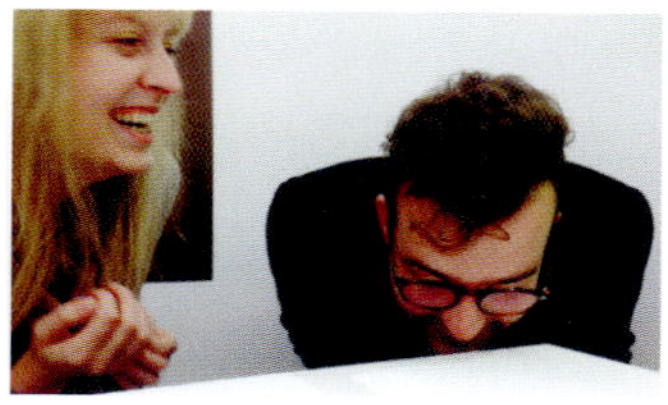

Deflowering, 2014

23 cm x 6,5 cm x 6,5 cm

'Deflowering of Madonna' is a new olfactory artwork by Peter de Cupere.
During one hour, a statue made of frozen holy water melts. In the statue is a spot with real vaginal scent! When the Madonna melts, the vaginal scent starts to mix with the holy water. In the room, you start smelling the beauty of woman. When you touch the melted liquid, the original vaginal scent stays on your finger for a long time.
The smell of the pussy is real vaginal scent conserved as an odorous substance and prepared by a professional lab. The smell is produced by movement and sweating in the female intimate area. The scent is a mix of different women of different origins, and is a tribute to the freedom of being a free woman, exploring your sexual desires.
After ±1 hour the vaginal scent will appear in the air. After melting, visitors are allowed to touch the melted Madonna and enjoy her scent of passion.

Deflowering of Madonna is een nieuw olfactorisch werk van Peter de Cupere.
Na ongeveer een uur blootgesteld te zijn, smelt een standbeeldje van een madonnafiguur, gemaakt uit bevroren heilig water. In het beeldje bevindt zich een concentraat met echte geur van vaginale afscheiding. Wanneer de Madonna smelt, mixt het concentraat met het heilige water. In de ruimte begin je de geur van de schoonheid van de vrouw op te nemen. Wanneer je het vocht aanraakt, blijft de originele vaginale geur lang nawerken op je vinger en maak je symbolisch deel uit van de sexuele passies van de vrouw. Deze geur is samengesteld in samenwerking met een professioneel labo, die door de beweging en zweetafscheiding van de intieme geslachtsdelen van de vrouw afname hebben kunnen doen om de gevormde geur samen te stellen. De geur is een mix van verschillende vrouwen van verschillende origine.
Het werk is een ode aan de vrijheid van de vrouw die haar sexuele verlangens kan blootgeven.

Bad Moon Festival, Kievitsnest, curator Jan Van Woensel, Antwerp, BE, 30.11.2014
The Olfactory, 33 olfactory art exhibitions in 7 weeks, Hasselt, Antwerp, Brussels, Ghent, BE, 15.09.2014-30.10.2014

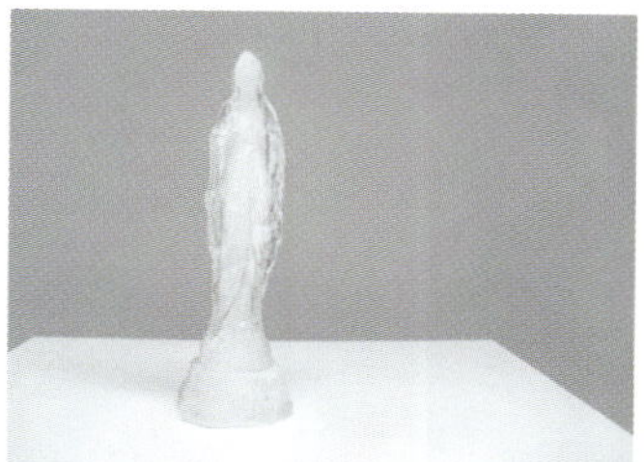
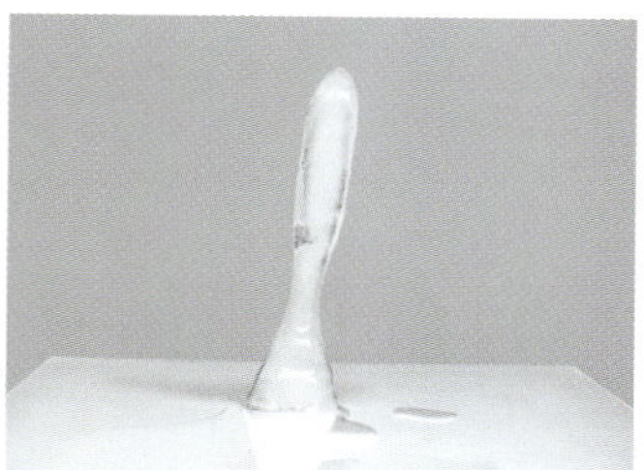
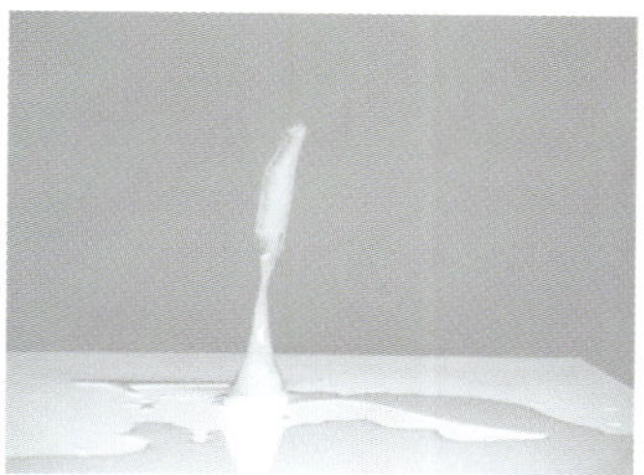

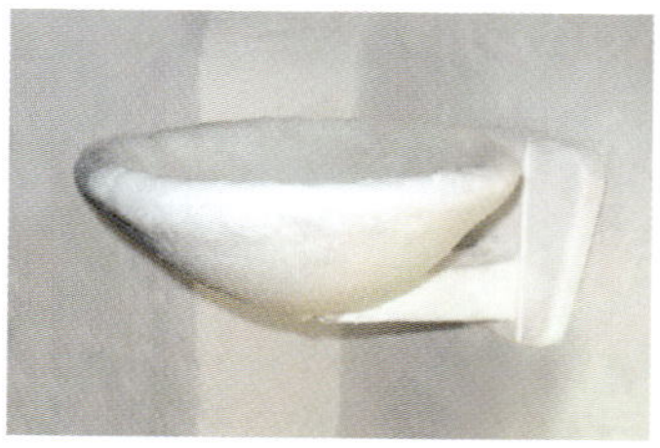
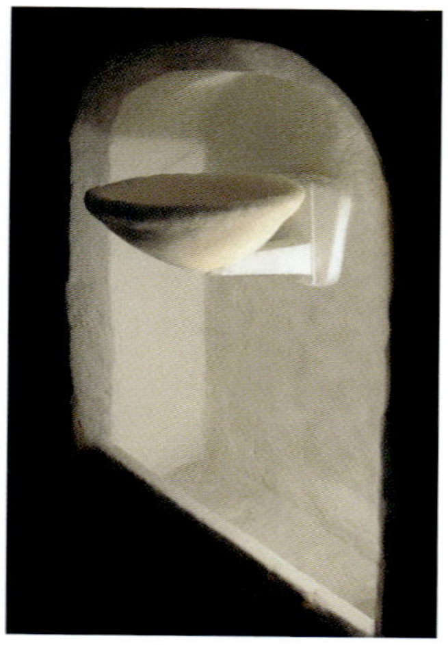

Holy Vitamin, 2007

Holy water font made of pure vitamin C

Wijwatervat gemaakt uit pure vitamine C

Smell the Castle, Castle Beauvoorde,
curator Annemie Morisse, Beauvoorde, BE
15.07.2007-30.08.2007

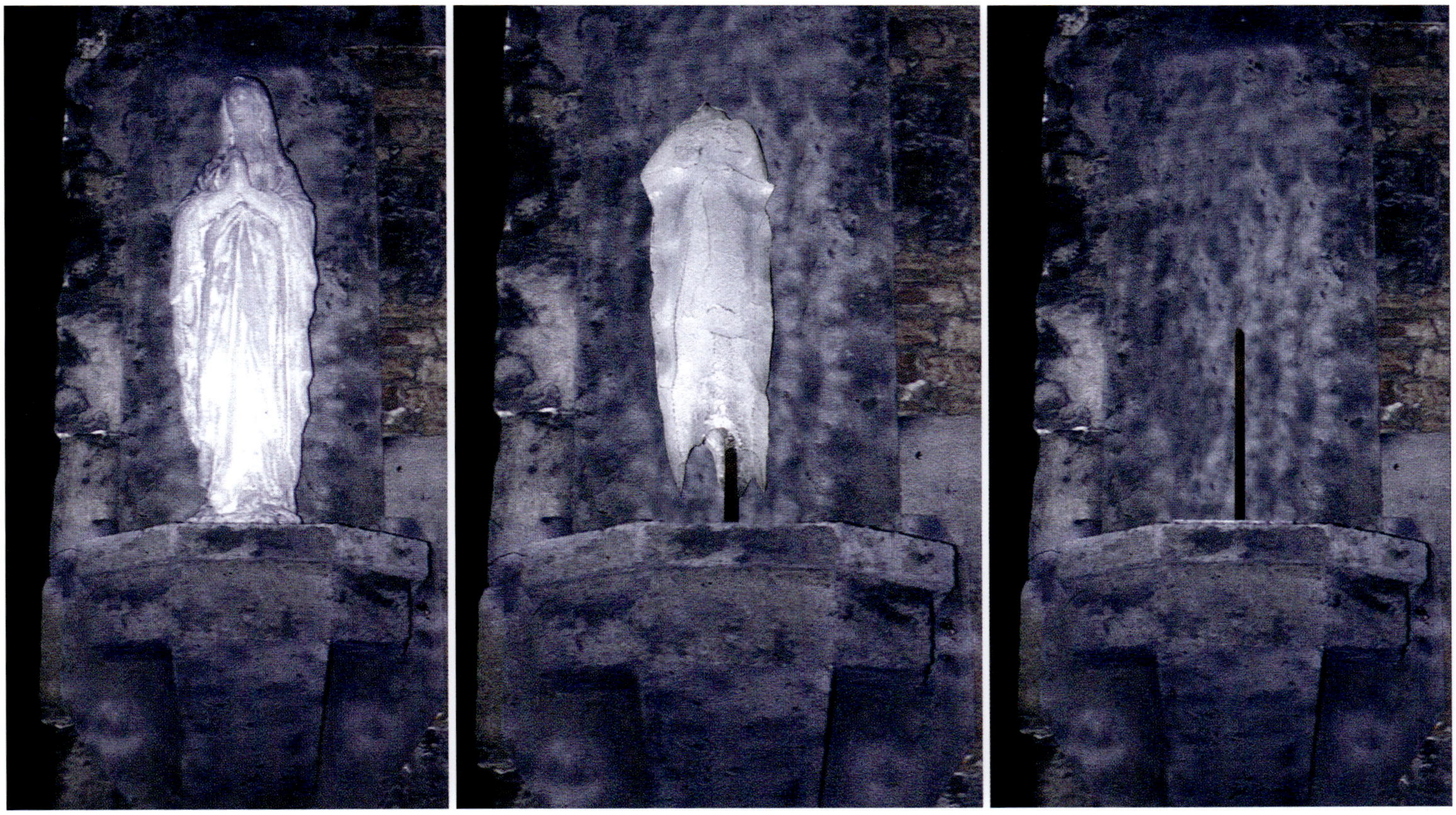

Model for Disappearing Art, 2000

Weight: ±35 kg, 100 cm

White Madonna statue made of para-dichlorobenzene (urinal blocks).
Disappears in one month upon contact with the air.

Wit madonnabeeldje gevormd uit paradichlorobenzeen (urinoirblokjes).
Verdwijnt binnen circa 1 maand na contact met lucht.

Het Zelfde en het Andere, organisatie Unie Vrijzinnige Verenigingen, Zebrastraat, curator Willem Elias, Ghent, BE, 27.09.2009-25.10.2009 (Pink Version)
Leere & Vision, Museum Marta Herford, curator Maïté Vissault, Herford, DE, 26.05.2006-07.07.2006 (White Version)
Tussen kunst en kitsch, Culture Center De Breughel, curator Martine Geerts Gerkenberg-Bree, BE, 19.09.2002-21.09.2002 (Blue Version)
Over The Edges, S.M.A.K., curator Jan Hoet, co-curator Giacinto Di Pietrantonio, Ghent, BE, 01.04-30.06.2000

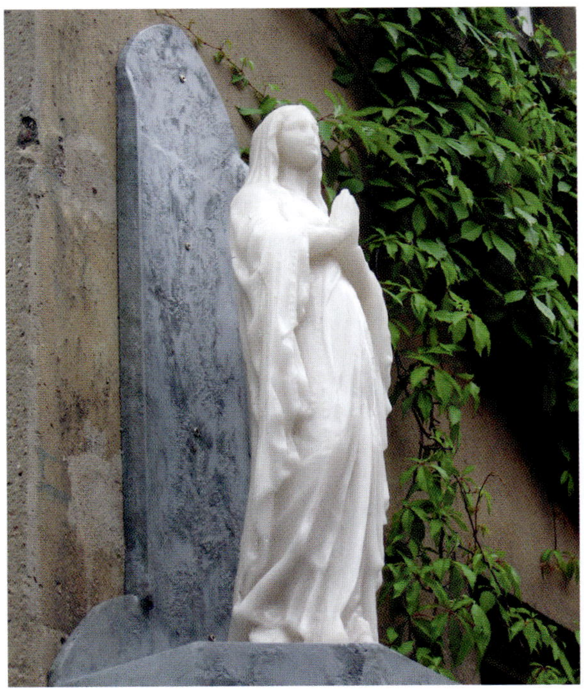

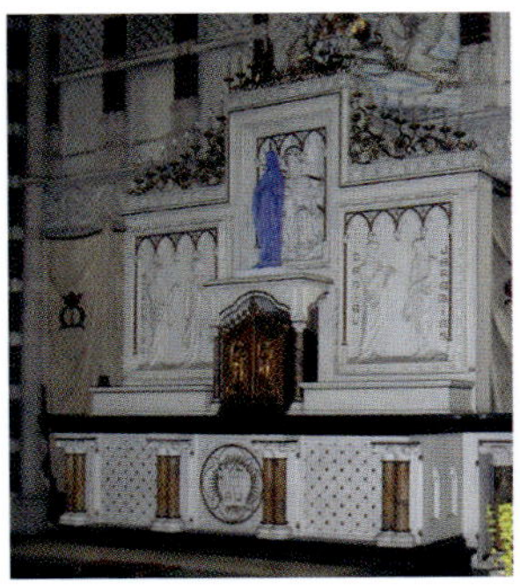

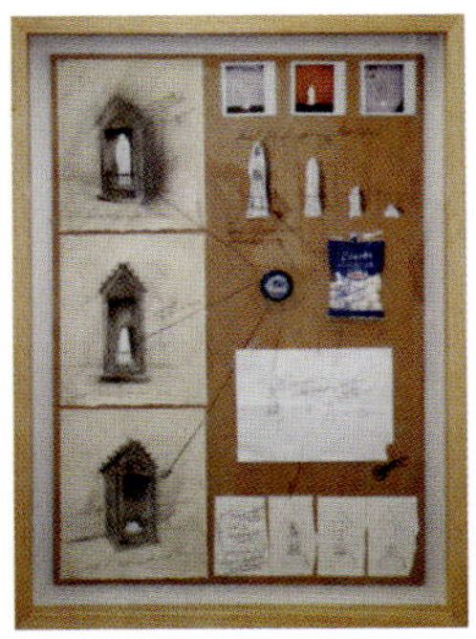

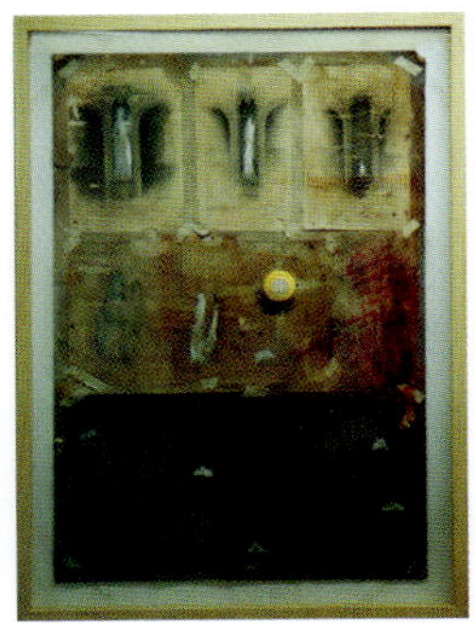

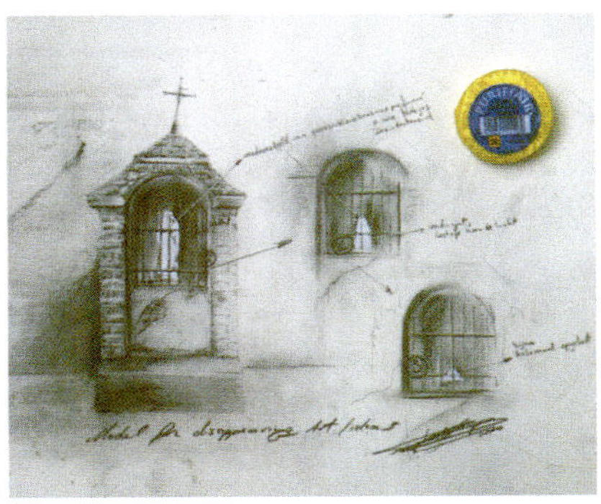

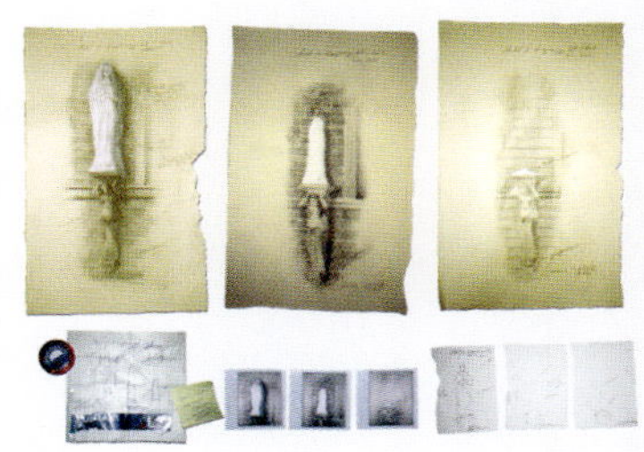

Drawings Model for Disappearing Art, 2000

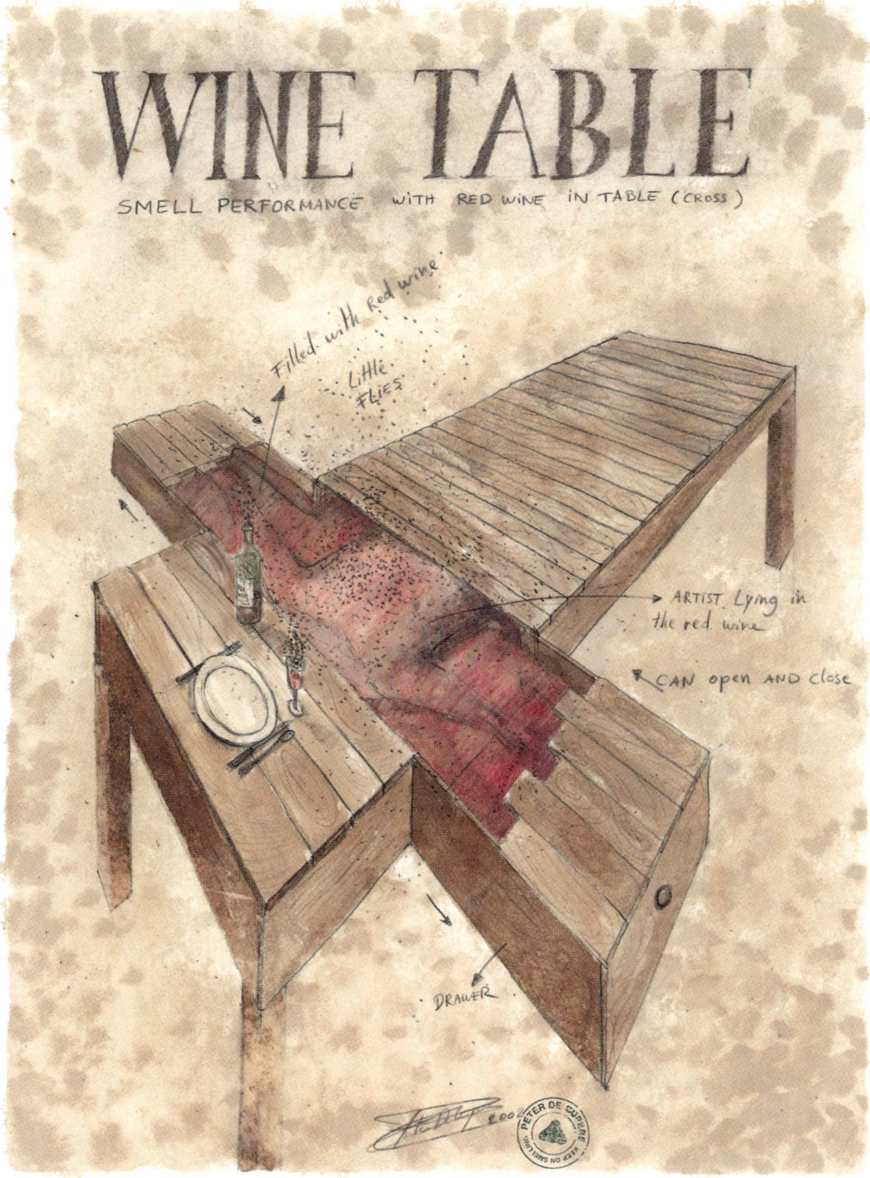

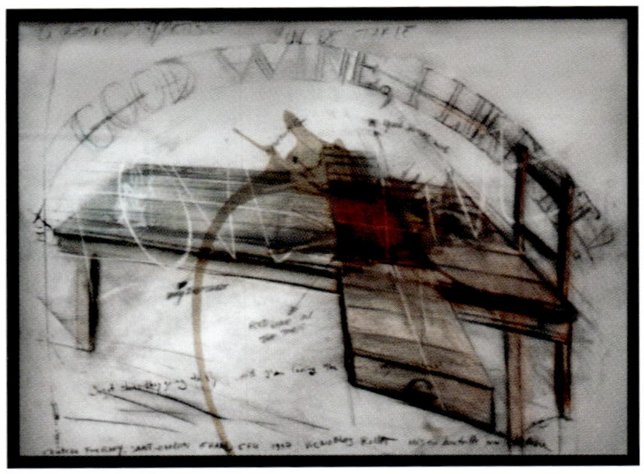

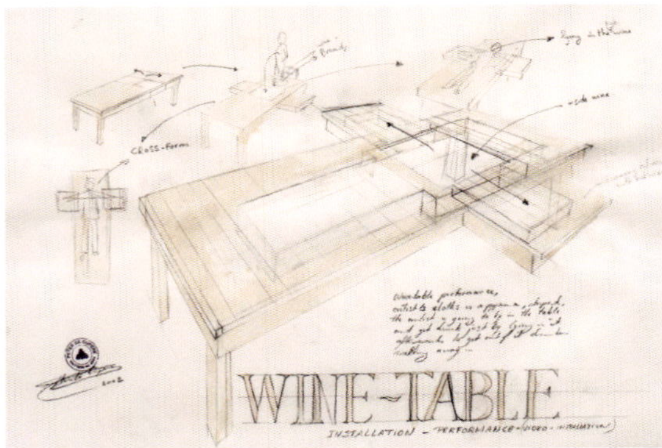

Drawing Wine Table, 2002

Watercolour, coloured pencils and bistre
Framed 62.7 cm x 50 cm

Aquarel, kleurpotloden en bister
Ingekaderd 62,7 cm x 50 cm

Model Drunken, 2013

Wood, epoxy, metal, dried red wine.

Hout, epoxy, metaal, opgedroogde rode wijn.

Table / Tafel 36.5 cm 120 cm x 67 cm
Chair / Stoel 36.5 cm x 21 cm x 20 cm
Plexiglass box 59 cm 173 cm x 103 cm

Sniff Your Jail, org. Balie Tongeren, curators Paul Morrens, Johan Smets, Justice Palace Tongeren, BE, 14.05.2016-19.06.2016

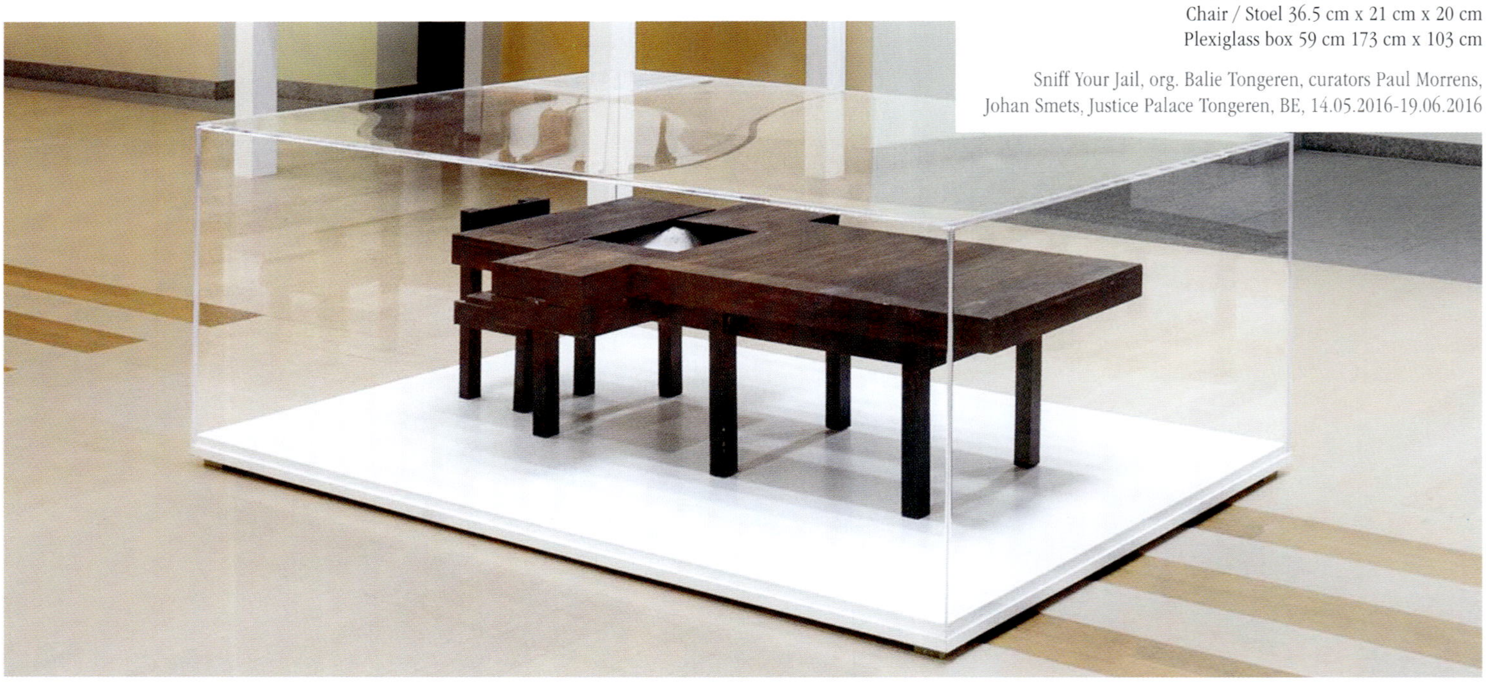

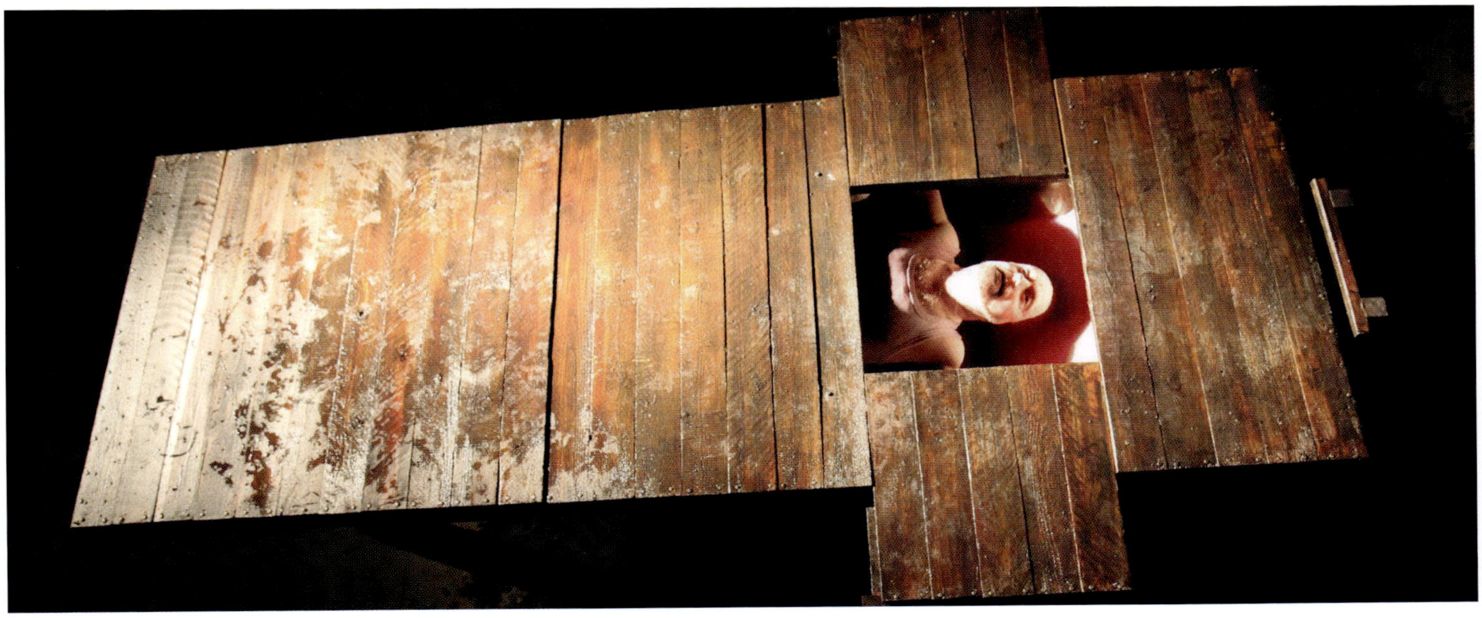

Drunken, 2013

Video HD, 12 min. 31 sec.

Drunken is based on the drawing Wine Table from 2002. In the performance 'Drunken' one sees the artist as a loner sitting at a table. After drinking the red wine, he opens two drawers of the table. The latter are positioned opposite one another and as such create the shape of a 'cross' together with the table. By opening the drawers one sees that a part of the surface of the table also opens up and a space filled with red wine becomes visible. He fills his glass again from this sea of red wine, drinks and crawls into the table, laying himself down in the wine. Waiting on a state of complete drunkenness, not just orally, but physically sucking up the red alcohol into his body. Afterwards he crawls back out of the table and lets his behaviour and stature be determined by the influence of his being drunk. The artist finishes back at the table where he started.

With this, the artist wants to research into behavioural changes. The latter can vary from very cheerful to melancholy or plain aggressiveness. Alcohol subdues the nerve cells which put a brake on the behaviour. It brings the person in a happy state of mind, but it can also have a negative effect on others. The behaviour that the artist shows due to his drunkenness give waddling, stumbling dimensions which coincide with falling and tumbling. Some might see this as neurological symptoms or show references to mentally and/or physically reactions. A link to some extreme psychiatric cases is not farfetched if one should not know that the cause is alcohol.

Furthermore questioning religion: 'the table in the symbol of the cross'. The artist comes down stumbling from the cross, infatuated by the alcohol of the red wine. Whether the artist wants to question religion, he leaves it up to the imaginary perception of the spectator. But before going outside of the olfactory video installation, take another deep breath and let the scent of alcohol and red wine, lead you your own way.

Drunken is bebaseerd op de tekening *Wine Table* van 2002. In de performance Drunken ziet men de kunstenaar eenzaam aan een tafel en na het drinken van een glas rode wijn, opent hij twee schuiven. De twee schuiven die tegenover elkaar gemonteerd zijn in de tafel, vormen in open toestand een kruis. Door het openen van de lades gaat een deel van de oppervlakte open en merkt men dat de tafel gevuld is met rode wijn. De eenzame kunstenaar vult keer op keer zijn glas uit deze rode zee van wijn, kruipt op de tafel, duikt in de tafel en laveert zich uitgebreid aan de wijn tot hij compleet dronken is. Deze status bereikt hij niet alleen door het drinken van de wijn, maar eveneens door volledige absorptie van de wijn in het lichaam. Hierna kruipt hij terug uit de constructie en zijn onvoorspelbaar gedrag wordt vanaf nu gestuurd door zijn dronken toestand. Hij eindigt terug aan de tafel zoals de performance begonnen is.

Deze performance kadert in het onderzoek van Peter de Cupere naar gedragsveranderingen die evolueren van opgewekt naar melancholisch en zelfs leiden naar agressief gedrag, door de invloed van alcohol op het zenuwstelsel. Dit gedrag kan ook negatieve effecten hebben op andere mensen. In parallel heeft het gedrag dat de kunstenaar toont door zijn staat van dronkenschap invloed op zijn fysiek gedrag dat evolueert naar waggelen, struikelen en zelfs vallen. Men kan deze bewegingen interpreteren als neurologische symptomen met mentale of fysieke gevolgen. Zelfs een link naar extreem psychiatrisch gedrag is niet ver gezocht indien men niet zou weten dat alcohol aan de basis ligt van zijn toestand.

De kunstenaar stelt misschien met de compositie van de tafel als kruis en de manier waarop hij afstapt van de tafel - dit kruis - onder invloed van de alcohol van de rode wijn, religie in vraag. De toeschouwer moet hier zelf over oordelen. Alvorens u deze olfactorische video-installatie verlaat, neem dan gerust nog eens diep adem en laat de geur en nevel van alcohol en rode wijn tot u komen zodat u uw weg verder kan zetten.

Sniff Your Jail, org. Balie Tongeren, curators Paul Morrens, Johan Smets, Justice Palace Tongeren, BE, 14.05.2016-19.06.2016
Blood, Artisit, Alden-Biesen, curator Joannes Késenne, Lut Maris, BE, 04.06.2014-30.08.2014
Middle Gate, curator Jan Hoet, Geel, BE, 29.09.2013-19.01.2014

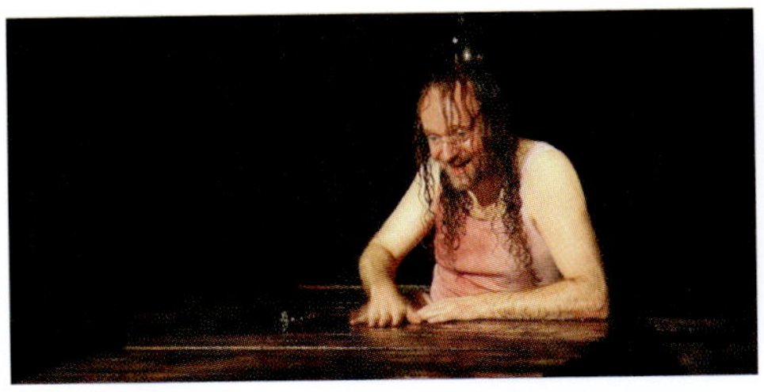
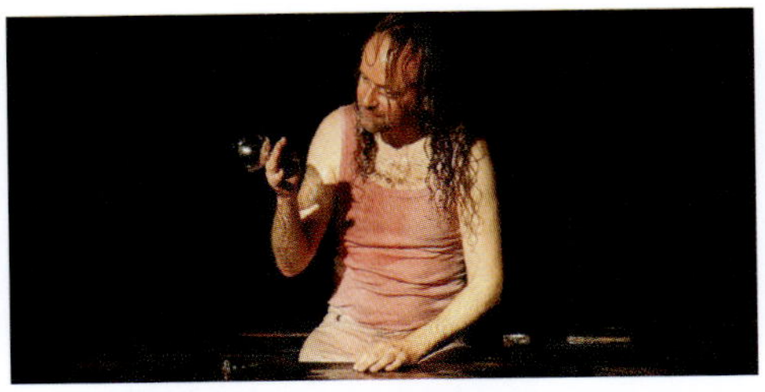
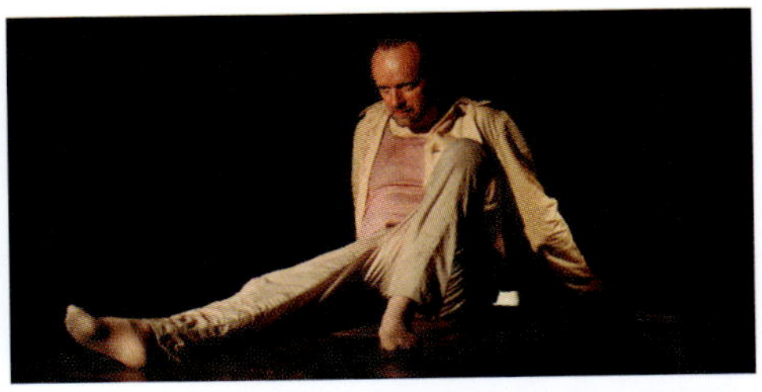
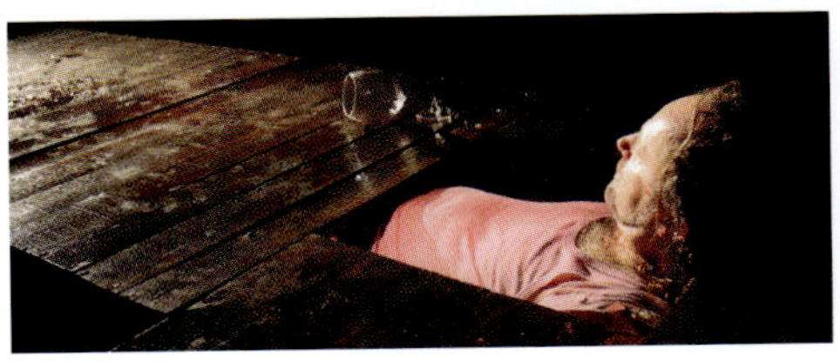
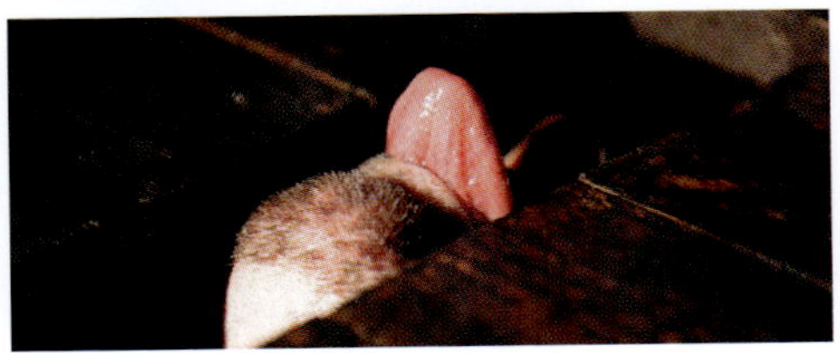
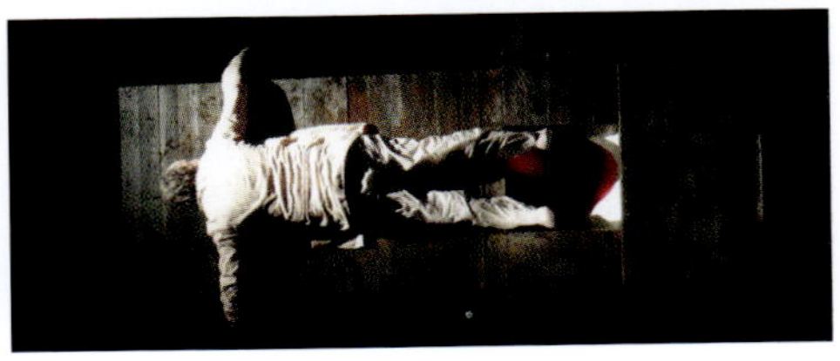

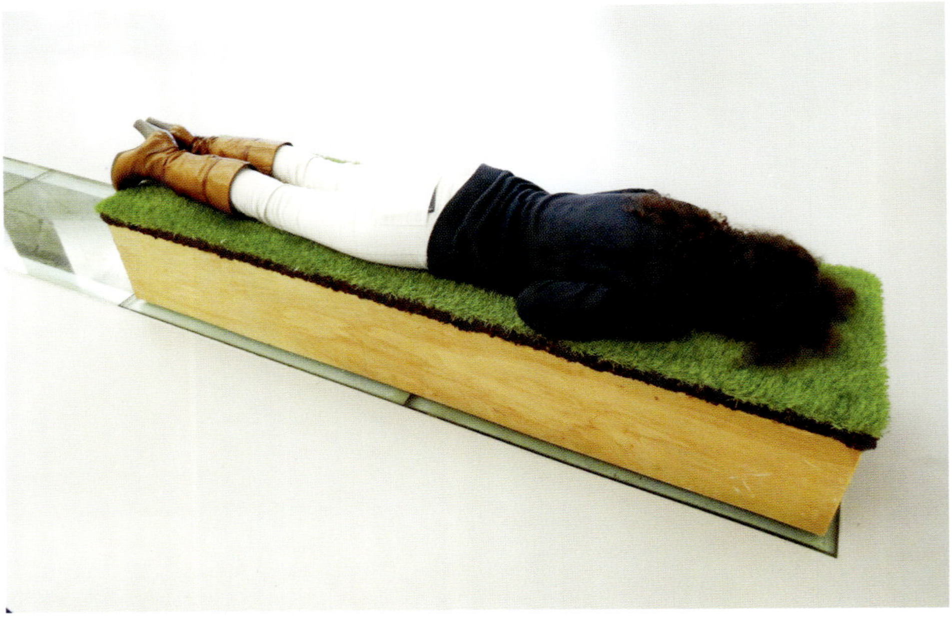

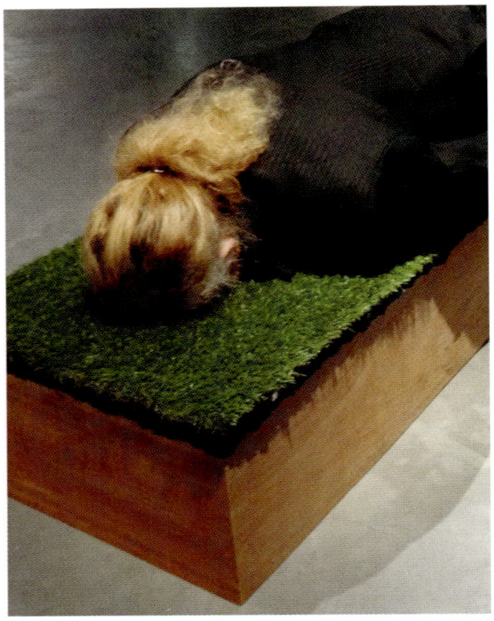

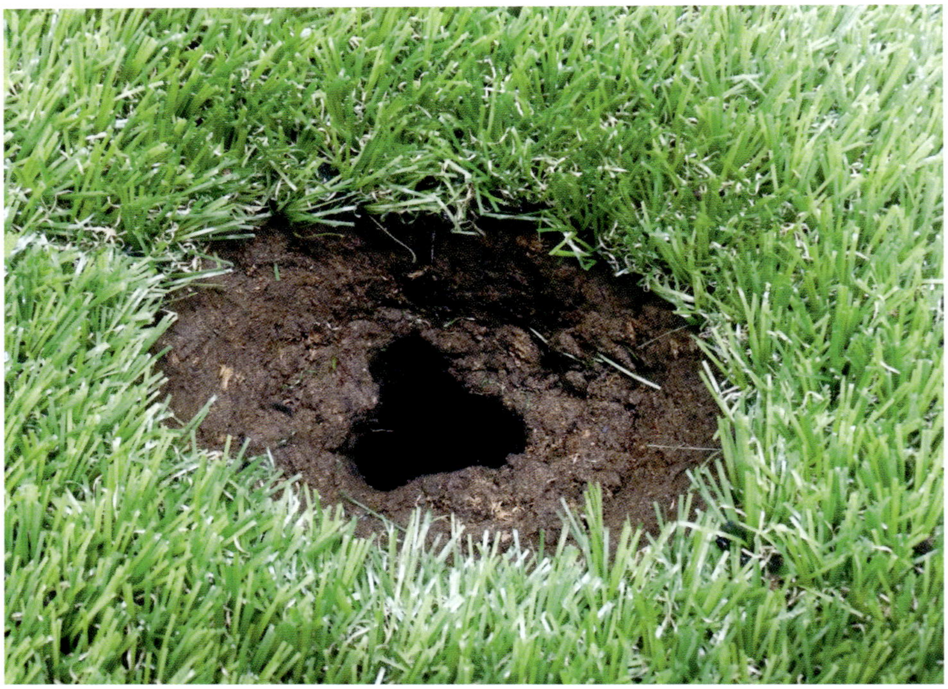

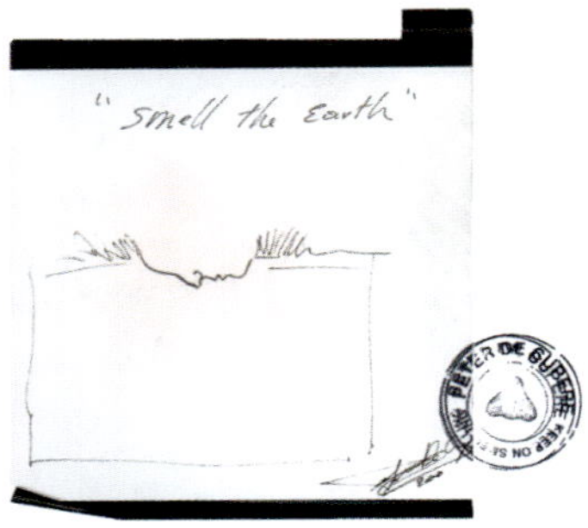

Smell The Earth, 2000

Sketch

Heaven, 2013

35 cm x 195 cm x 51,5 cm

Artificial grass, wood, earth, glue, the scent of earth in combination with the scent of mushroom

Kunstgras, hout, aarde, lijm, de geur van aarde in combinatie met de geur van paddenstoelen

The Art of Smelling, Olfactory Art Research, Art Center Rozendaal 21, curator Yasmijn Jarram, Enschede, NL 01.12.2013-02.03.2014
Urban Explorers Festival, Scent City Trail, Dordrechts Museum, Dordrecht, NL, 11.05.2013-12.05.2013

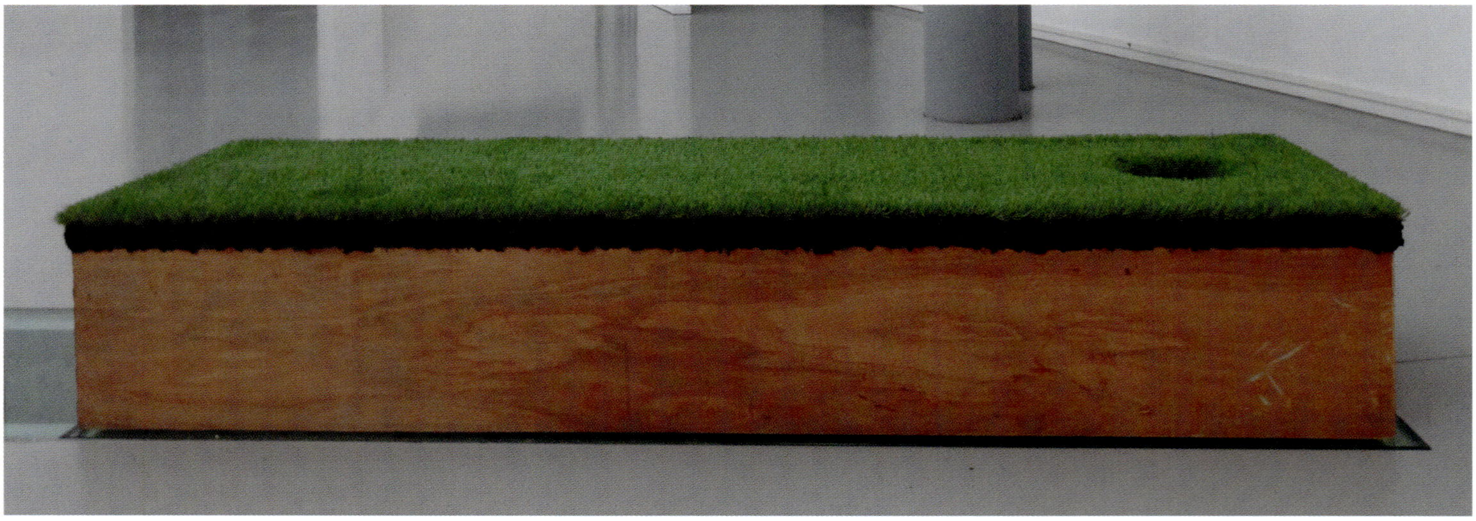

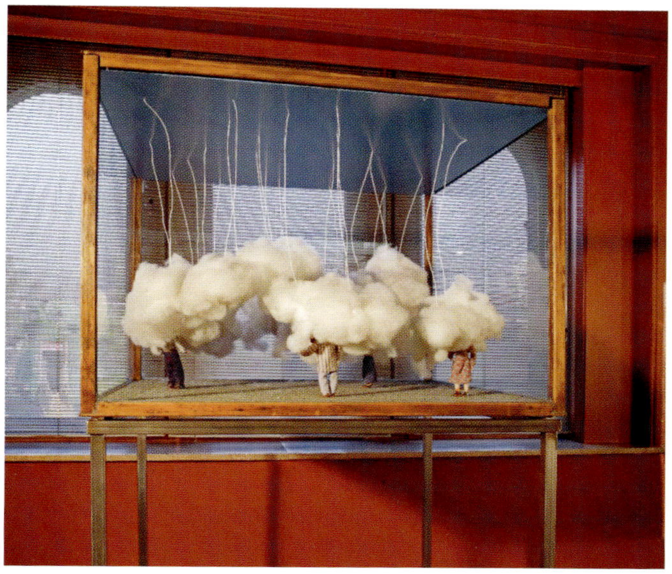

Flight Around The World, Model, 1999-2000

Model for installation / Maquette

Cutting Edge, confrontation Dieter Appelt-Peter de Cupere, curator Bart De Baere, Van Laere Contemporary Art, ARCO Artfair Madrid, ES, 13-19.02.2001

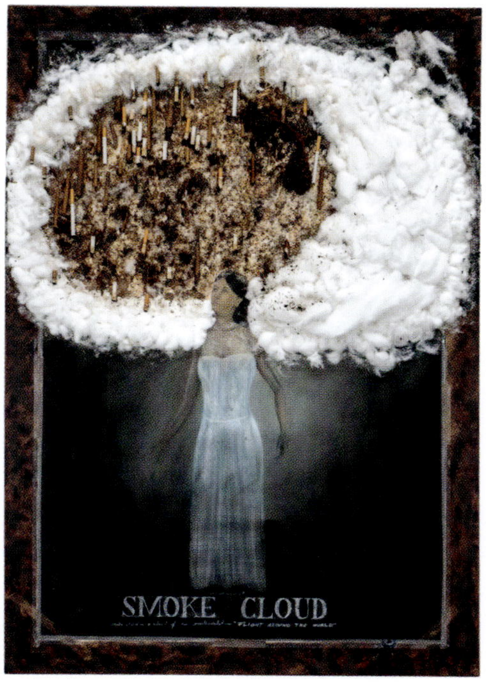

Flight Around The World, Smoke Cloud, 2000-2001

150 cm x 110 cm

Pastel, graphite, cotton, used cigarettes and cigars, tape

Pastelverf, grafiet, katoen, gebruikte sigaretten en sigaren, tape

Cutting Edge, confrontation Dieter Appelt-Peter de Cupere, curator Bart De Baere, Van Laere Contemporary Art, ARCO Artfair Madrid, ES, 13-19.02.2001

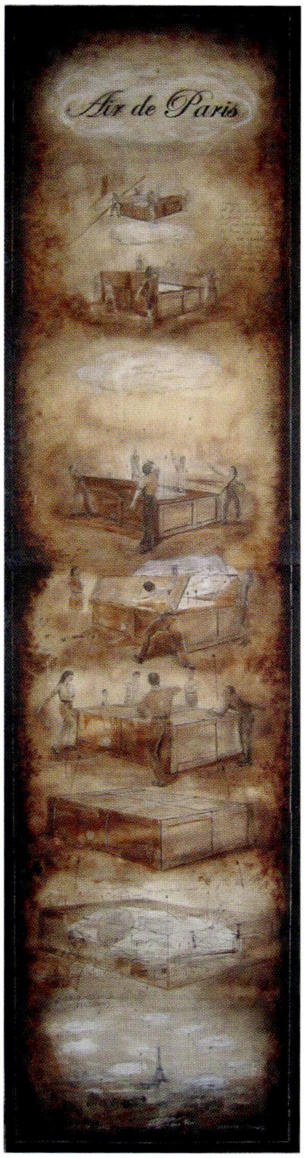

Air De Paris, 2005

Drawing of cloud installation

Voorbereidende tekening van de installatie

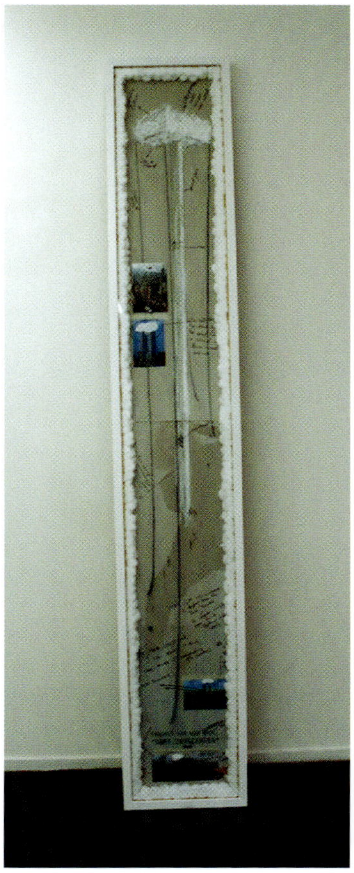

Project For N.Y., 2000

190 cm x 30 cm x 10 cm

Peter de Cupere, Smellcom Happening, Smell Kiss Performance, rockconcert Admiral Freebee, Van Laere Contemporary Art, Antwerp, BE, 14.09-21.10.2000

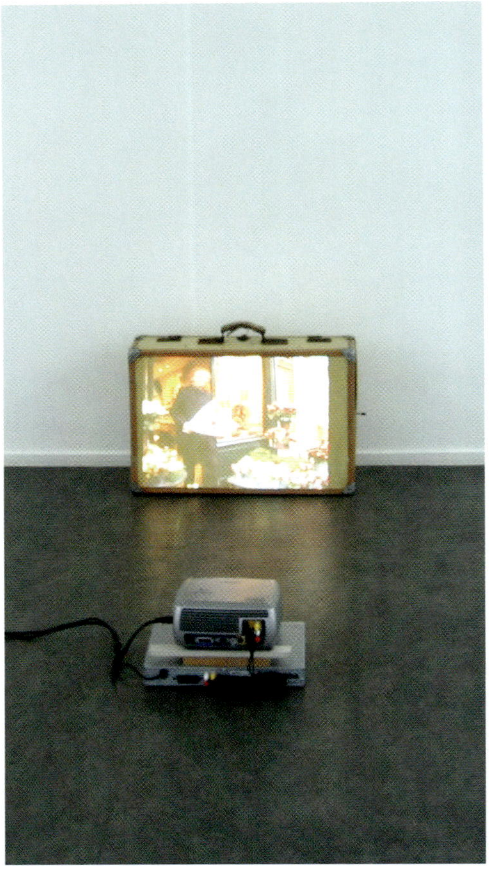

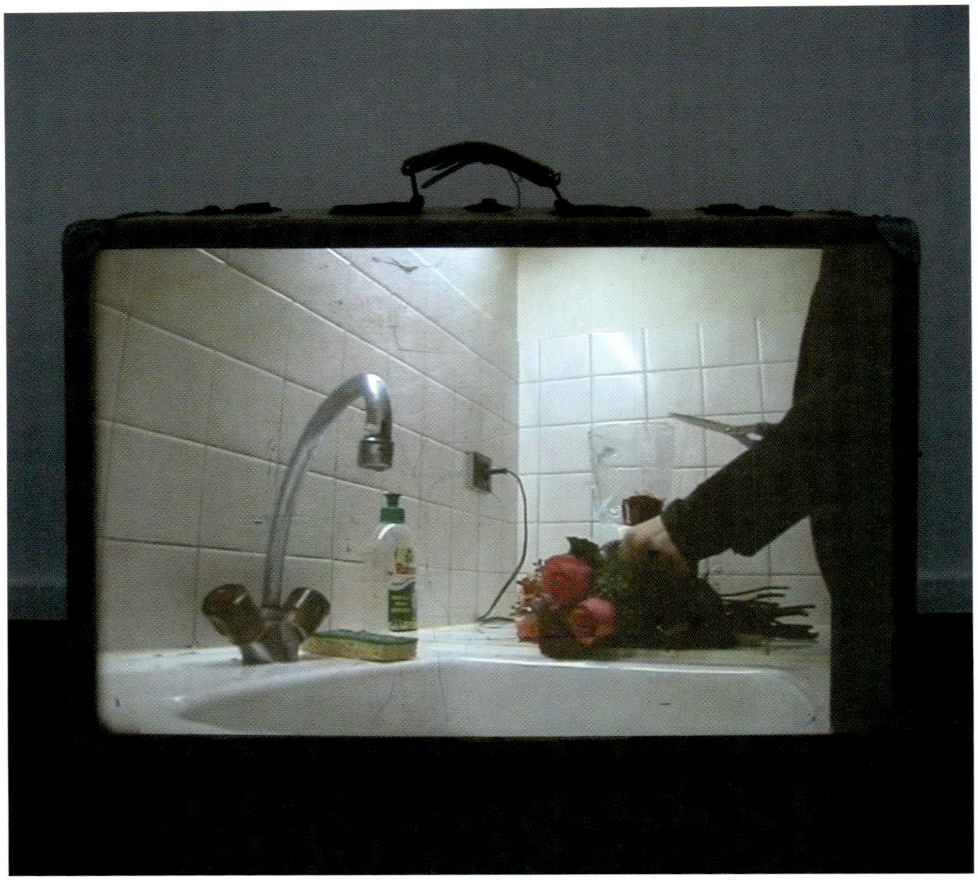

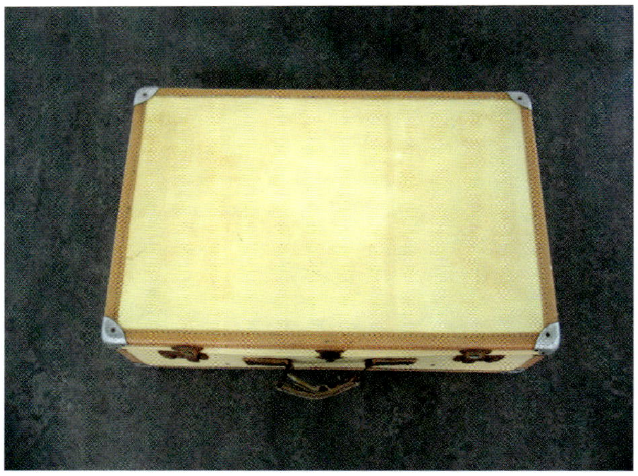

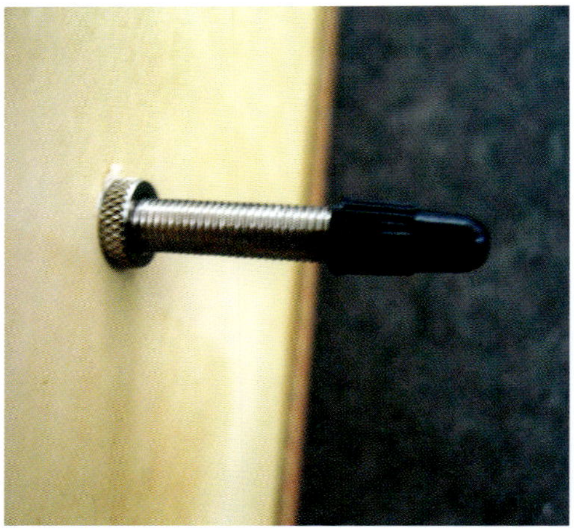

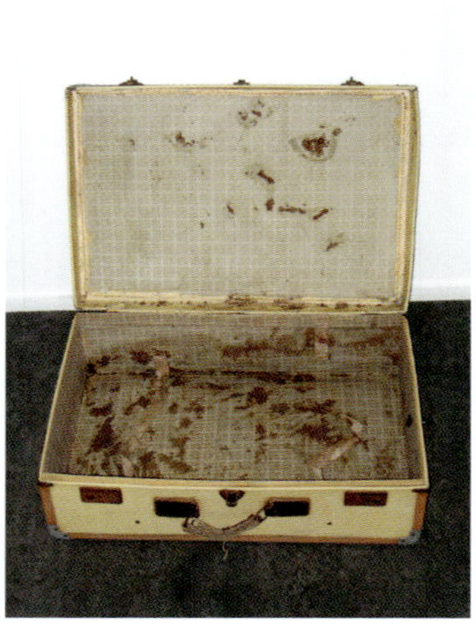

Paris, Mon Amour, 2005

In this video, Peter de Cupere takes us with him through the streets of Paris.
The video begins in a flower shop and ends on the Pont des Arts.
During filming, the artist had problems with the security guards at the Louvre who thought he wanted to blow up a suitcase – which he did, in the end, though not in the way one might have expected!

At the end of the video, a pink cloud escaped from the suitcase.
During the video, the smell of roses can be detected.
It can be shown by projecting it on the suitcase itself or in an exhibition space, where the smell of roses fills the room.

Peter de Cupere neemt ons in deze video, gefilmd in Parijs, mee doorheen de stad.
De video begint in een bloemenwinkel en eindigt op Pont des Arts. Tijdens de opnames kreeg de kunstenaar problemen met de veiligheidsdiensten van het Louvre omdat men dacht dat hij een valies wou opblazen, wat hij uiteindelijk ook deed, al was het niet zoals men het verwacht zou hebben!

Uit de valies komt op het einde van de video een roze wolk.
Tijdens de video wordt de geur van rozen waargenomen.
De video kan gepresenteerd worden via projectie op de valies zelf of in een tentoonstellingsruimte waarbij de geur van rozen de ruimte vult.

Lupercalia, Theater Tinnenpot, Vermeylenfonds, curator Willem Elias, Gent, BE, 15.02.2014
Air Polluter, De Brakke Grond, curator Fleurie Kloostra, Amsterdam, NL, 09.06.2007-15.07.2007
Peter de Cupere, Sergio De Beukelaer & Maryam Najd, Van Laere Contemporary Art, Antwerp, BE, 26.01.2006-11.03.2006

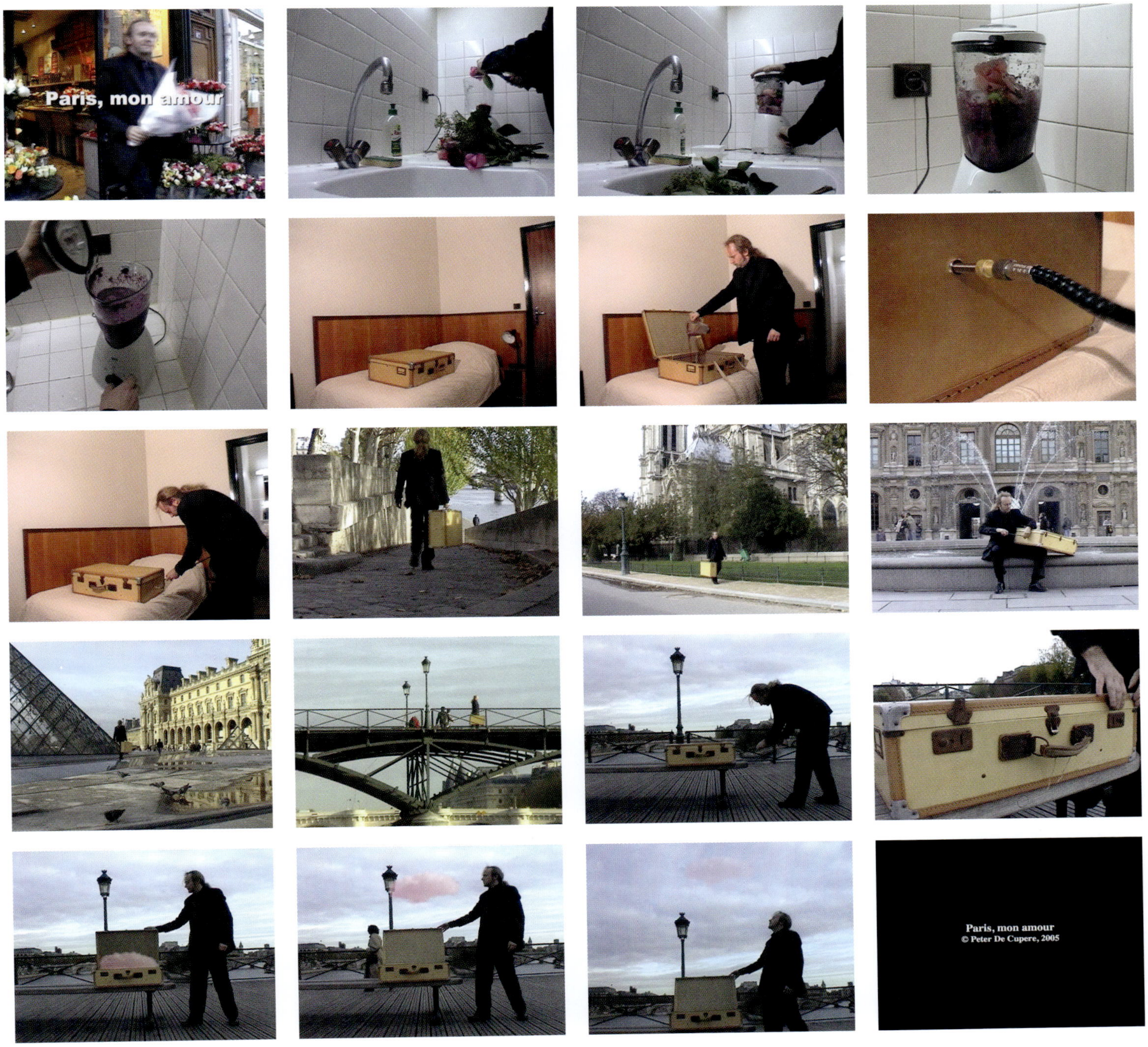
Paris, mon amour
Paris, mon amour
© Peter De Cupere, 2005

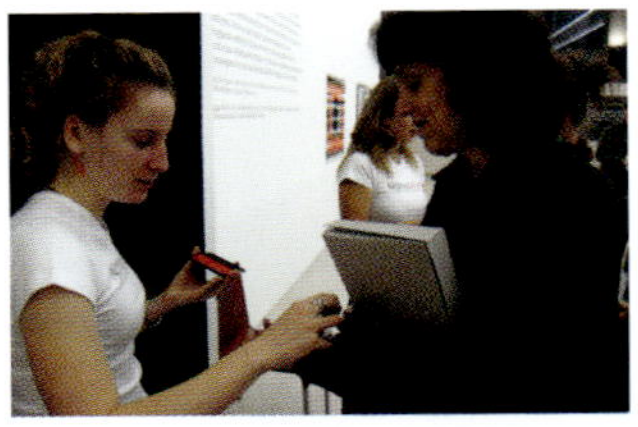

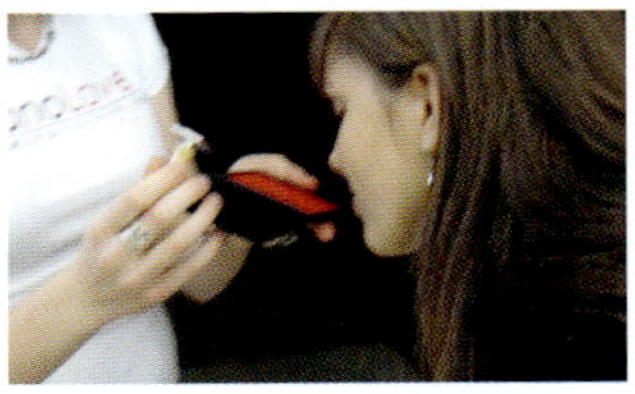

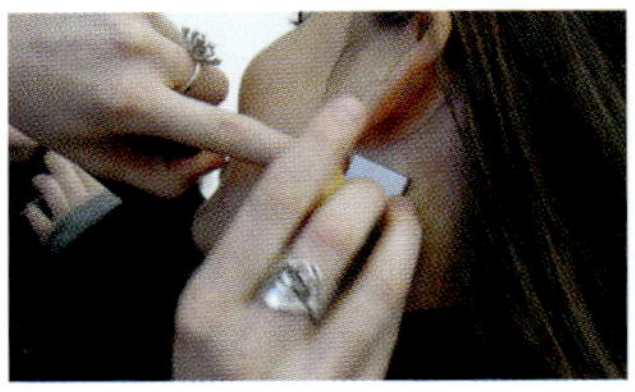

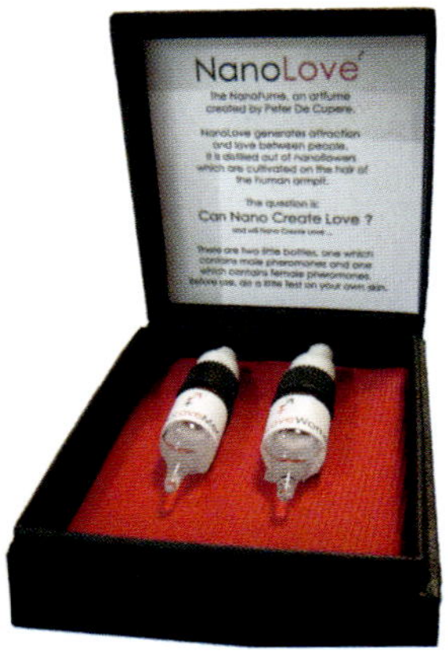

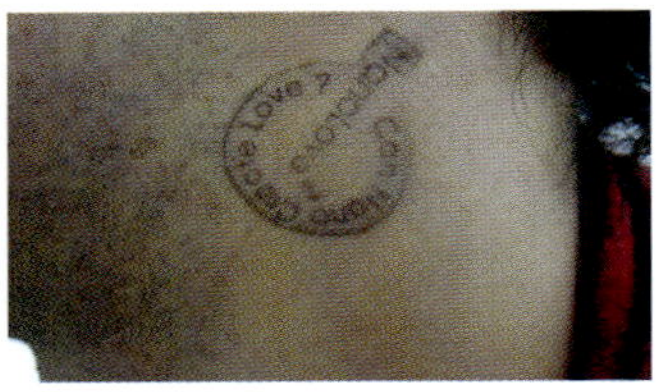

NanoLove, 2007

NanoLove is distilled out of nanoflowers which are cultivated on the hair of the human armpit. NanoLove is a nanofume (perfume on nano scale!). It is scentless and created with pheromones.

NanoLove is gedistilleerd uit nanobloemen die gecultiveerd worden met okselhaar. NanoLove is een nanoparfum (parfum op nanoformaat). Geurloos en gecreëerd met feromonen.

NANO NU, Flemish Parliament, org. M HKA & Viwta, curator Edwin Carels, Brussels, BE, 09-10.11.2007

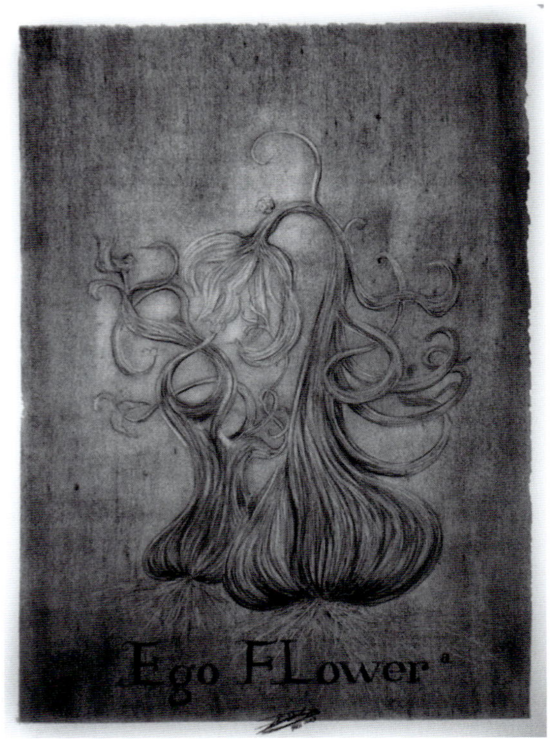

Ego Flower, 2005

65 cm x 45 cm

Graphite, charcoal

Grafiet, houtskool

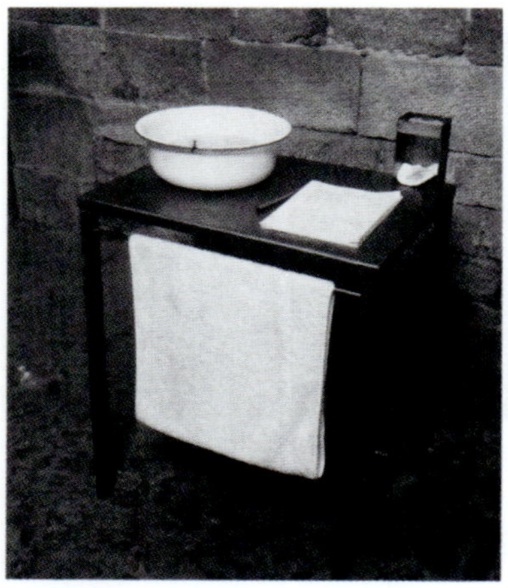

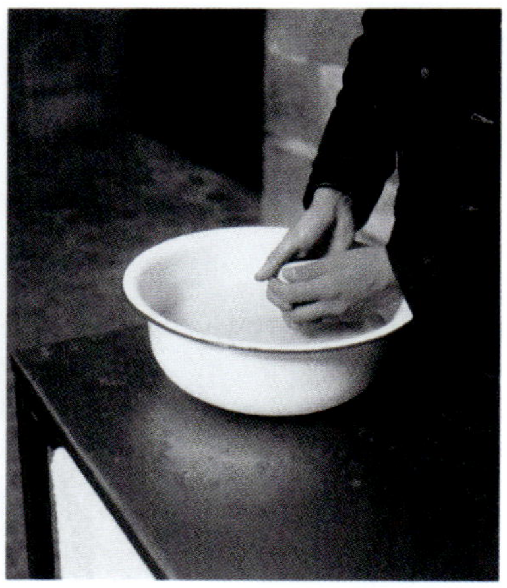

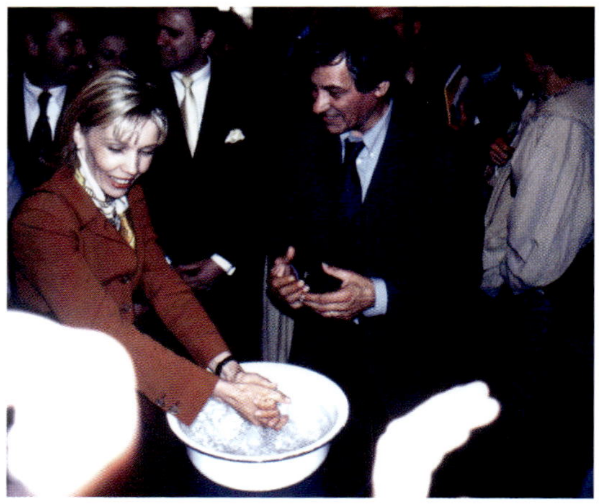

Curator Jan Hoet with/met Doris Schröder-Köpf
Preview Expo 3 Räume-3 Flüsse, Hann. Münden, 2000

Innocent, 1996

Visitors wash their hands using the same soap and in the same water as their predecessors and dry their hands with the same towel. After that, they write their first and last name on a sheet. After the end of the exhibition, the remaining water is poured into a bottle and the names of the visitors are listed on it as ingredients.

Only the names of the visitors who provided both first and last names and a signature appear among the ingredients.

Bezoekers wassen hun handen met dezelfde zeep in het gebruikte water van hun voorgangers en drogen hun handen af met dezelfde handdoek. Daarna schrijven ze hun voornaam en familienaam op een blad. Na afloop van de tentoonstelling wordt het resterende water in een fles gedaan en komen de namen als ingrediënten op de fles te staan.

Alleen de namen waarvan zowel de voornaam, familienaam en handtekening vermeld staan, maken deel uit van de ingrediënten van dit werk.

Sniff Your Jail, org. Balie Tongeren, curators Paul Morrens, Johan Smets, Justice Palace Tongeren, BE, 14.05.2016-19.06.2016
3 Räumen, 3 Flüsse, curator Jan Hoet, Hann. Münden, DE, 10.06-30.09.2000
Tentoonstellingszaal Academie Leuven, 1996

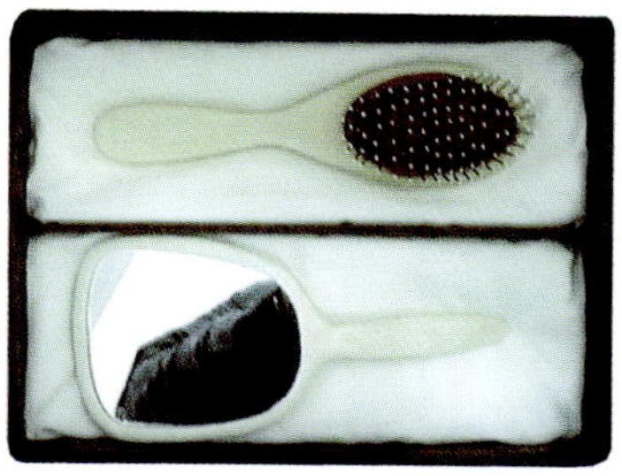

Smell Objects, 1996-1997

Mirror and brush made of soap, strawberry smell, reactive product

Spiegel and borstel gemaakt van zeep, aarbeigeur en reactief product.

Peter de Cupere, Black Beauty smell happening, Van Laere Contemporary Art, Openingsspeech Jan Hoet and rockconcert Admiral Freebee, Antwerp, 03.06-07.07.1999

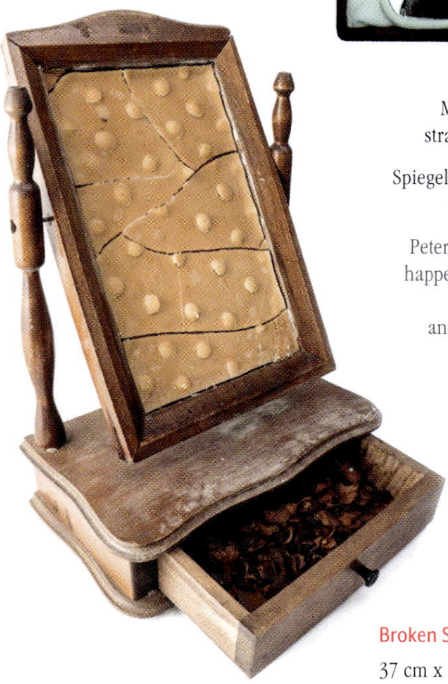

Broken Soap Mirror, 1998

37 cm x 24,5 cm x 14,5 cm

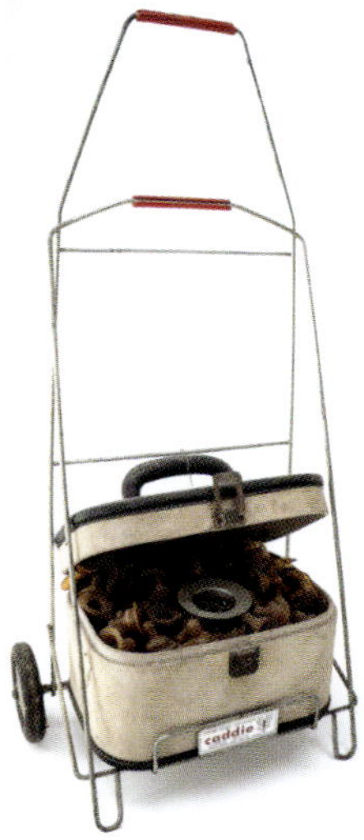

Beauty of Birth, 1997

87,5 cm x 43 cm x 26 cm

Scent: Baby powder

Beauty of Birth consists of a vanity case on a trolley. The case is filled with babies' dummies. Between the dummies you can spot an outlet radiating the fragrance of baby powder. The beauty of birth is an emblem for carrying around the beauty of your own birth which remains with you throughout your life. Or in other words: a load to carry for life. You need to kneel if you wish to catch the scent; a symbolic act of reverence by which you acknowledge the beauty.

Geur: Babypoeder

Beauty of Birth bestaat uit een beautycase welke gedragen wordt door een caddy. De beautycase is gevuld met fopspenen. Tussen de fopspenen ziet men een afvoer waar de geur van babypoeder uit komt. Beauty of Birth staat symbool voor het levenslang meedragen van de schoonheid van je geboorte, m.a.w. een levenslange zware last om te dragen. Wil je de geur ruiken, moet je neerknielen. Een symbolische eerbiedwaardige actie om de schoonheid ervan waar te nemen.

Peter de Cupere, Black Beauty smell happening, Van Laere Contemporary Art, Openingsspeech Jan Hoet and rockconcert Admiral Freebee, Antwerp, BE 03.06-07.07.1999

Black Beauty Perfume, 1998-1999

People in black cat suits with holes cut in them have these openings sprayed black. They then ask the visitors: 'Smell me' or 'Smell my black spot'. The perfume looks dry, but by touching the skin with their nose when sniffing, the visitors will receive a little black spot on the end of their noses.

De huid van personen die een 'cat suit' met gaten dragen, zijn zwartgespoten op de plekken waar de gaten zich bevinden. Aan de bezoekers wordt gevraagd 'Ruik aan me' of 'Ruik even aan mijn zwart plekje'. Het parfum lijkt droog, maar bij het aanraken van de zwart gespoten huid met de neus, zal er een zwart vlekje op de neus van de curieuze ruiker tevoorschijn komen.

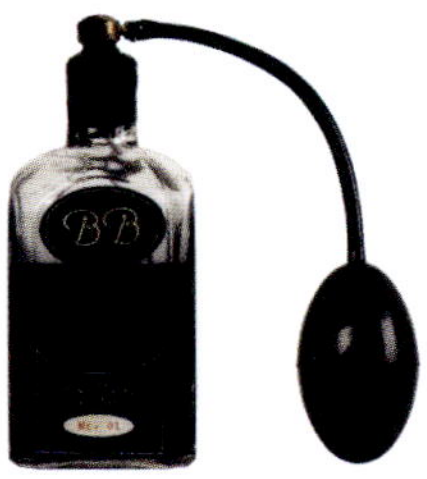

Flirt, Smart Project Spaces, Amsterdam, curators Thomas Peutz, Una Henry, NL, 16.02-31.03.2002
Peter de Cupere, Black Beauty smell happening, Van Laere Contemporary Art, Openingsspeech Jan Hoet and rockconcert Admiral Freebee, Antwerp, BE, 03.06-07.07.1999

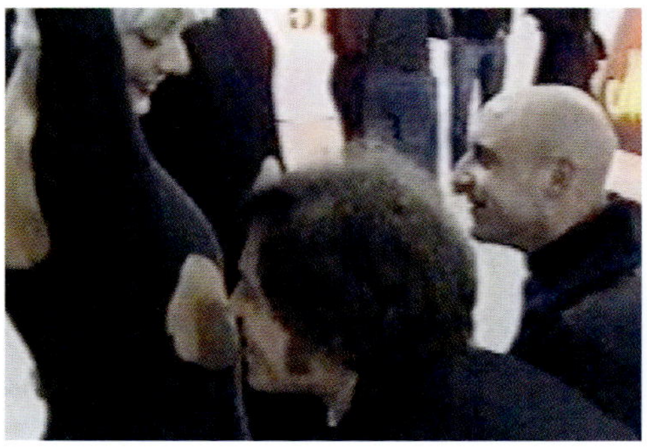

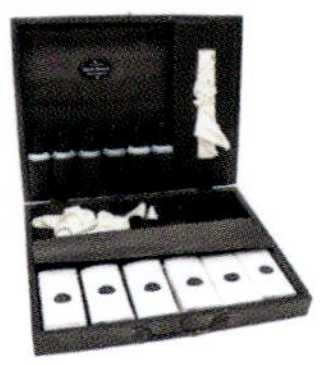

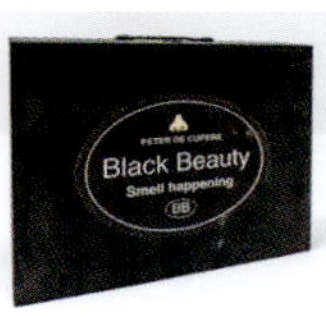

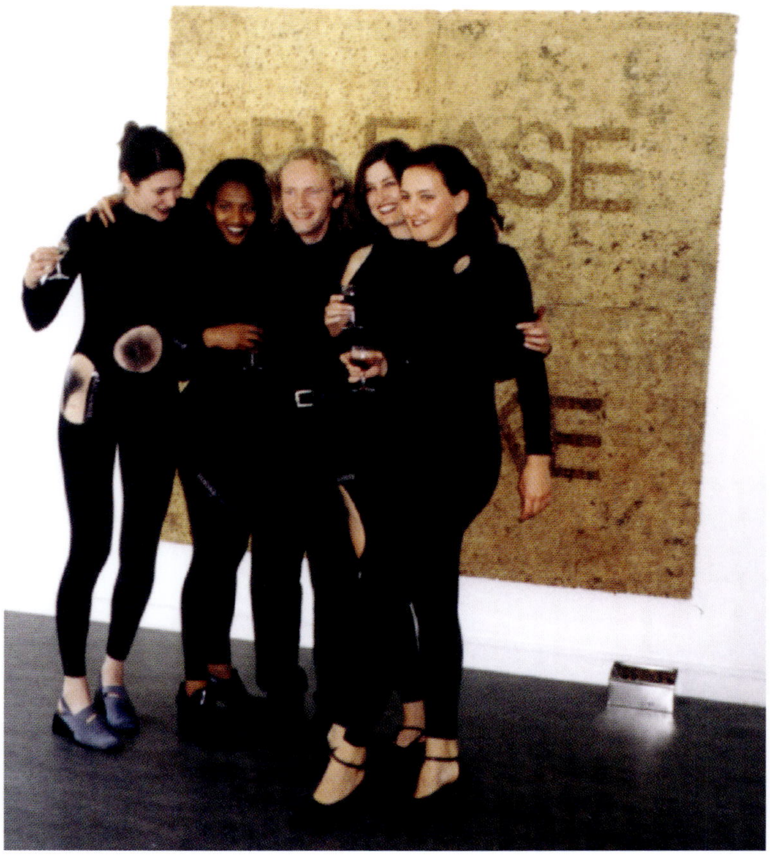

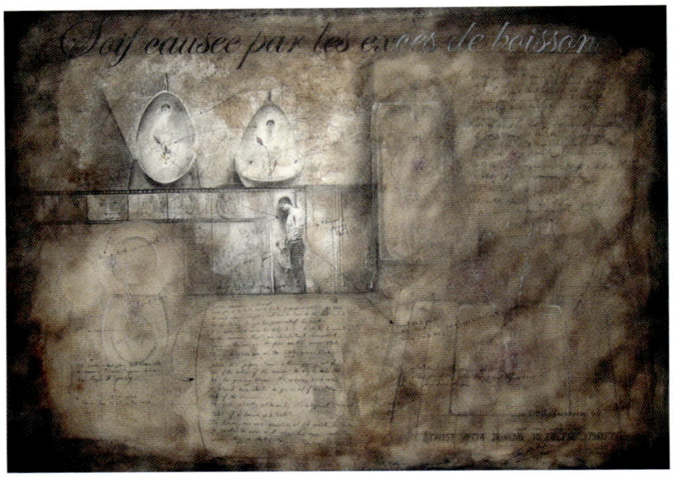

Soif causée par les excès de boisson, 2005

Concept drawing for a new performance with alcohol

Concepttekening van een nieuwe performance met alcohol

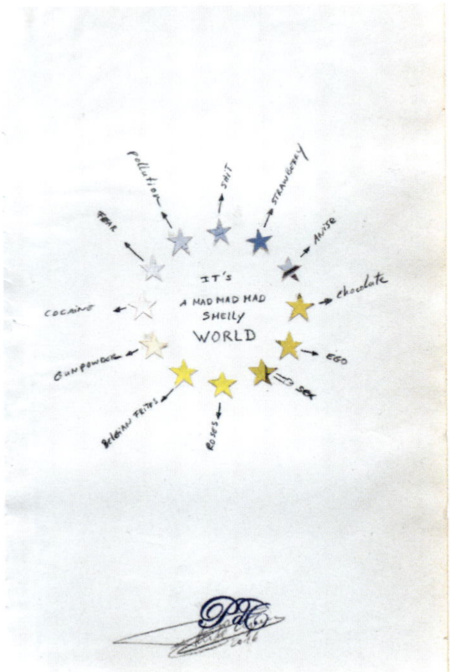

It's A Mad Mad Mad Smelly World, 2016

24,5 cm x 15,5 cm

Drawing, pencil, stars cut out of 50 euro

Tekening met sterren uitgekapt uit een briefje van 50 euro

Sniff Your Jail, org. Balie Tongeren, curators Paul Morrens, Johan Smets, Justice Palace Tongeren, BE, 14.05.2016-19.06.2016

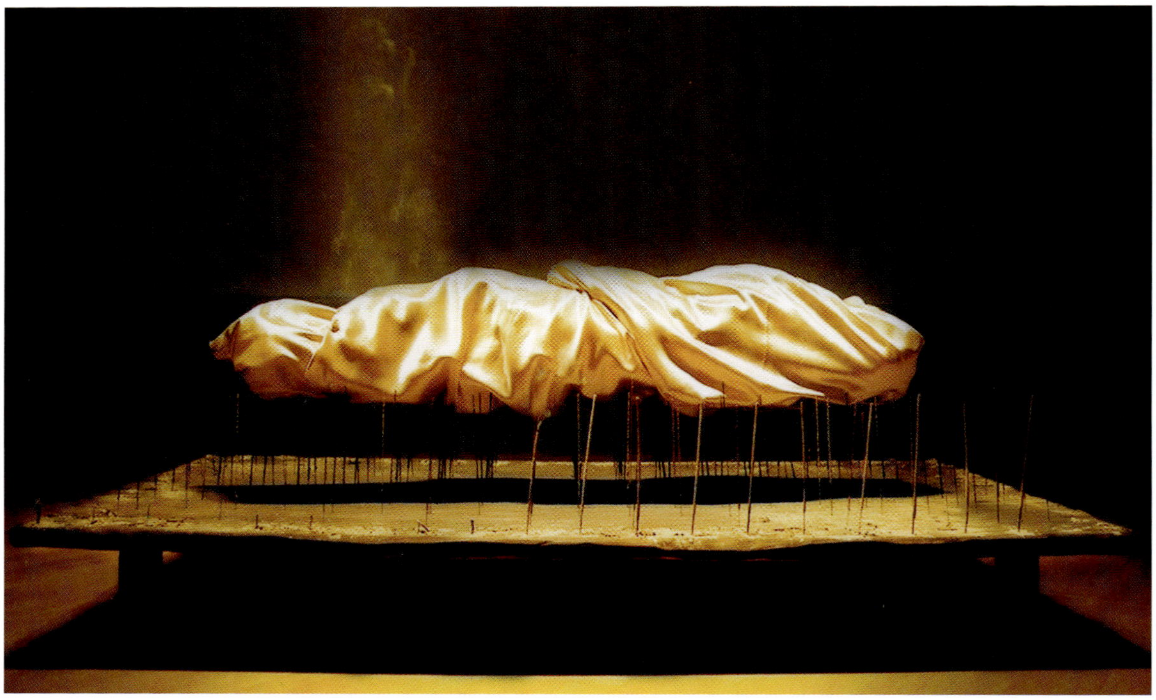

Lady On Incense, 2000

Size: 240 cm x 110 cm x 60 cm

Materials: incense, wood, doll, shiny fabric, iron, cotton
Exhibition Incense in the Museum of Fine Arts in Ghent. Bed made out of incense sticks. On the sticks rests a female figure. One stick was burned continuously. The exhibition was focused on Fernand Khnopff's piece 'Incense'. During the inauguration of the expo on a Sunday morning some of the original sticks were replaced by the soft drug cannabis.

Materiaal: wierook, hout, speelgoedpop, blinkende stof, ijzer, katoen
Tentoonstelling Wierook in het Museum van Schone Kunsten, Gent. Bed gemaakt van wierookstokjes. Op de wierookstokjes rust een vrouwelijke figuur. Continu werd er één wierookstokje verbrand. De tentoonstelling stond in het teken van de aankoop van het werk 'Wierook' van Fernand Khnopff. Tijdens de plechtige opening op een zondagochtend waren een paar wierookstokjes per ongeluk vervangen door cannabisstokjes.

Methamorphosis, vzw Phidias, curator Christa Vevey, Barcelona, ES, Februari-April, 2002
In honour of Fernand Khnopff, Museum of Fine Arts Ghent, Ghent, BE, 15.10-30.11.2000

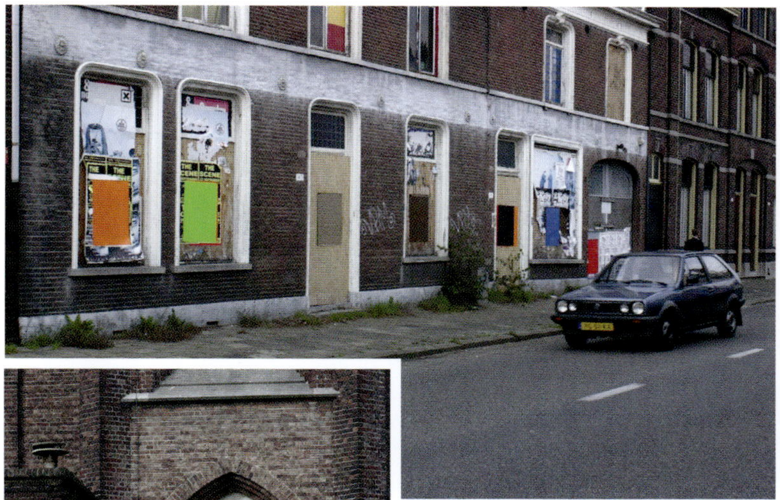

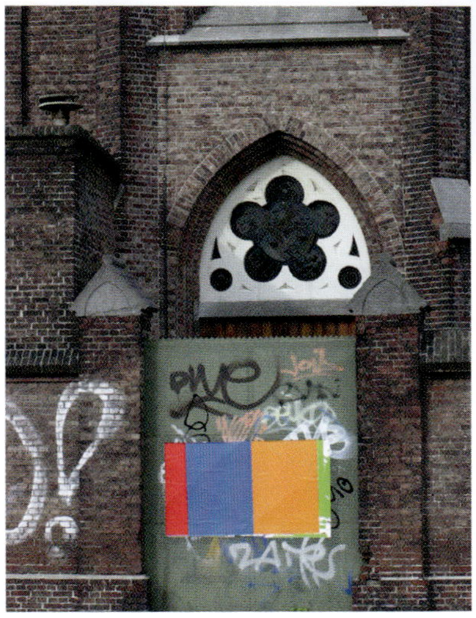

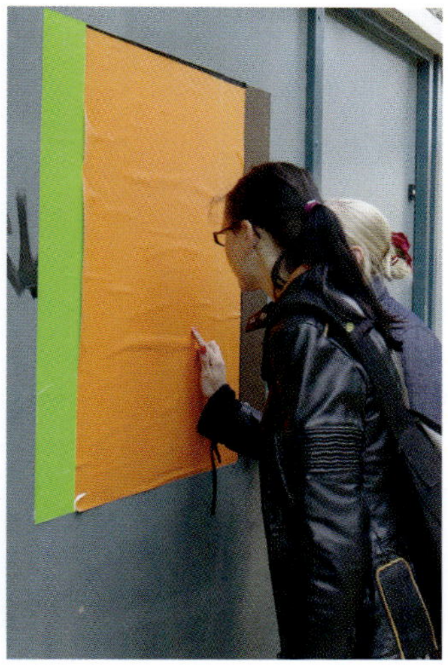

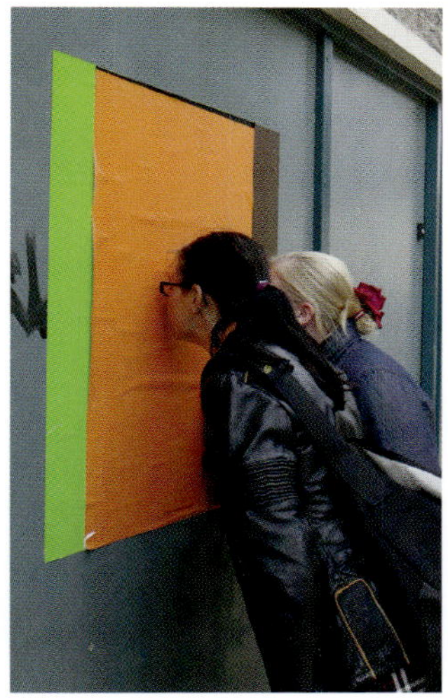

Touch & Smell The Colours Of This World, 2001

Different posters with different smells are hanging on different locations in the city. To smell the scents visitors must rub the colour. On the bottom of the poster is printed the text:
"Touch & smell the colours of this world".
Scents: rubberband, tabac, grass, whiskey, fuel, anchovy, mokka (as concept it can also be other fragrances)

Verschillende posters met verschillende geuren hangen op verschillende plaatsen in de stad. Om de geuren te ruiken moeten bezoekers op het kleurvlak wrijven. Onderaan de posters is het volgende gedrukt:
"Touch & smell the colours of this world".
Geur: rubber, tabac, gras, whisky, benzine, ansjovis, mokka (in het concept kunnen ook andere geuren gebruikt worden)

Silhouettes 'n' Shadows, Fundament Foundation, Tilburg, NL, 01.09-28.10.2001

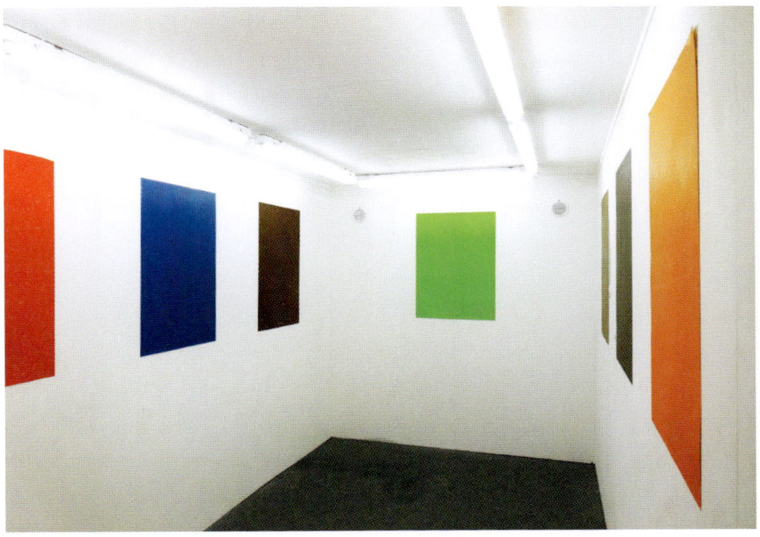

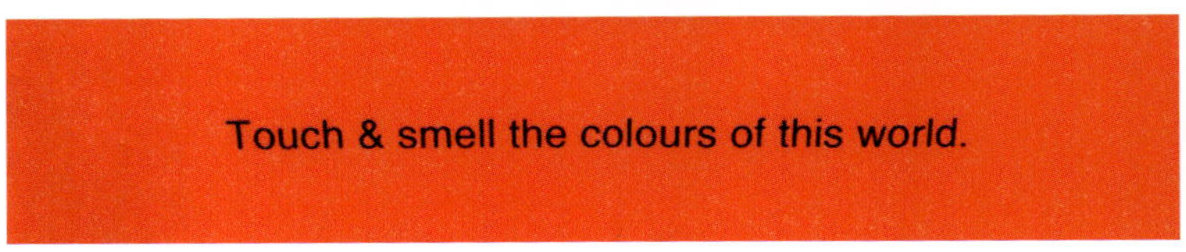

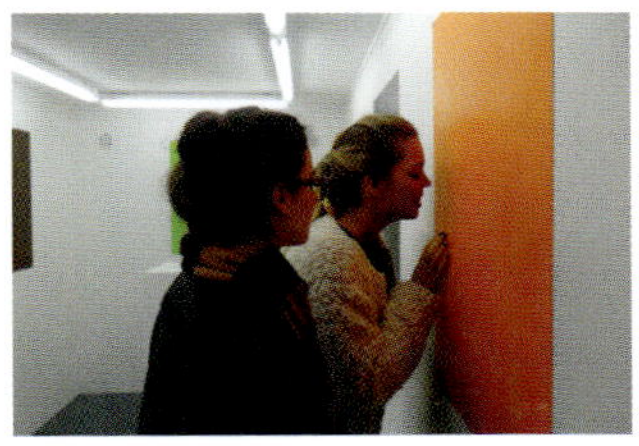

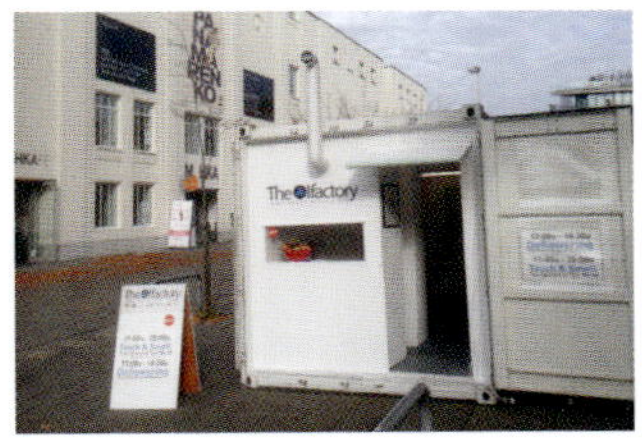

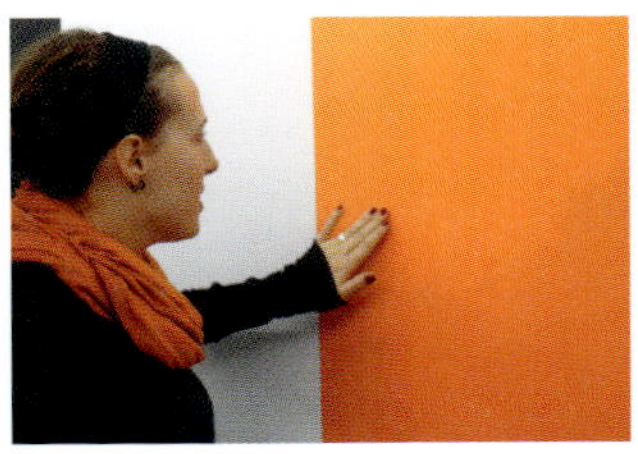

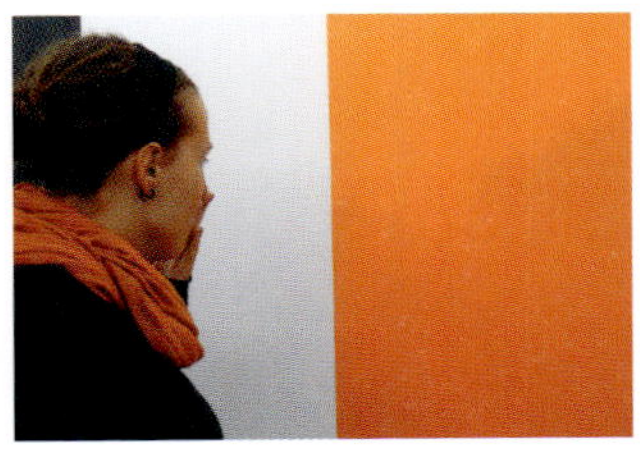

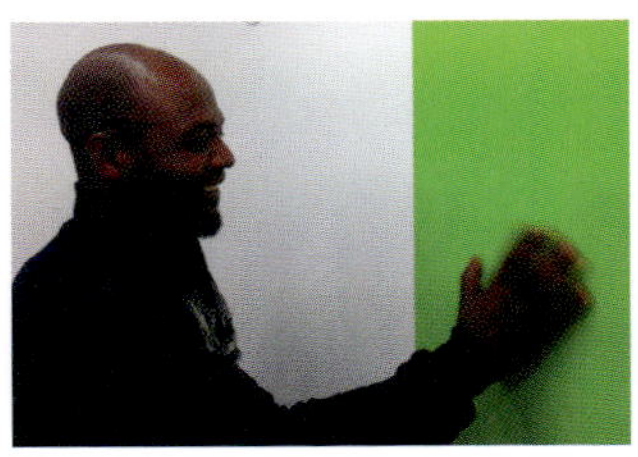

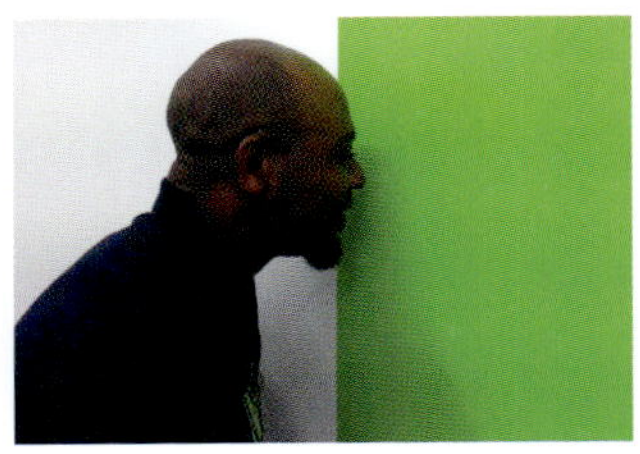

Touch & Smell The Colours Of This World, 2014

Remake of the 2001 version.

Herziene versie van de originele versie van 2001.

Touch & Smell The Colours of This World, The Olfactory, Antwerp, 24.10.2014

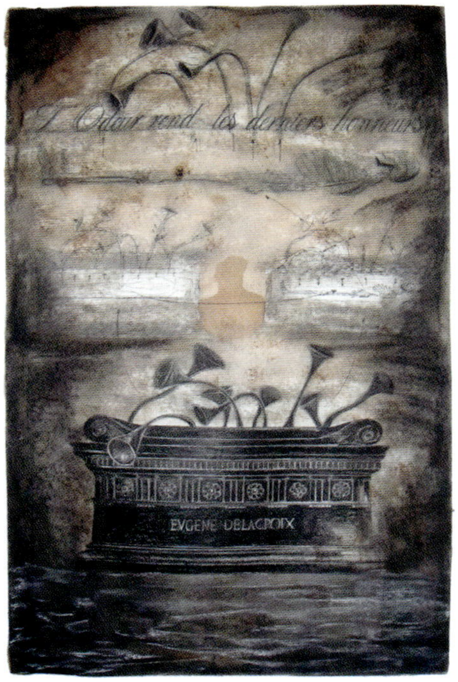

L'odeur Rend Les Derniers Honneurs, 2005

Drawing / Tekening

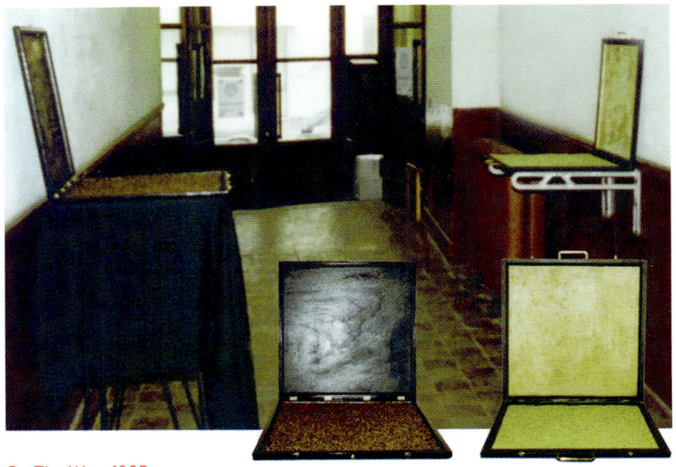

On The Way, 1995

Two narrow, black wooden suitcases. One of the cases is standing on a base with wheels, over which a black cloth has been draped. The suitcase is covered in black artificial leather and filled with cloves. The second case stands on a luggage carrier and is lacquered in black. The suitcase is filled with thyme and other green herbs. The two works are presented facing each other. Visitors have to open the suitcases and close them again after they have smelled the scent.

Twee zwarte houten smalle koffers. Eén valies staat op een onderstel met wieltjes waar een zwart doek is op aangebracht. De koffer is bekleed met zwart nepleder en gevuld met kruidnagels. De tweede koffer staat op een bagagerek en is zwart gelakt.
De koffer is gevuld met thijm en andere groene kruiden. De werken worden tegenover elkaar gepresenteerd. De bezoekers moeten zelf de koffers openen en terug sluiten nadat ze de geuren hebben geroken.

Final Year Students Fine Arts, Sint-Lukas Brussel, Moving Art Studio, Brussels, BE
14-28.06.1996

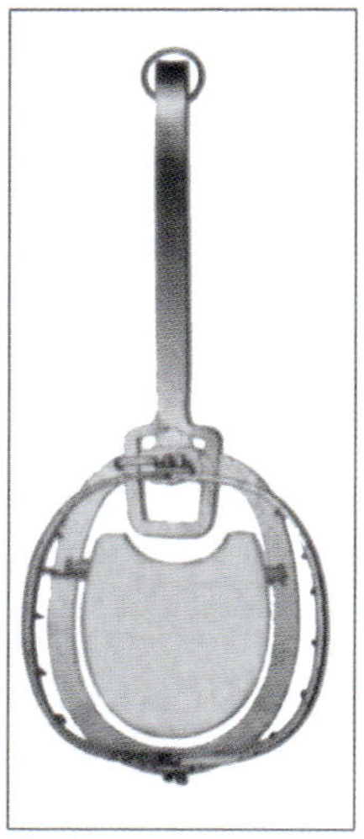

Before smelling

Your last smell, 1995-1996
Artist: Peter de Cupere
Materials: Fox Trap, iron plate covered with soap.

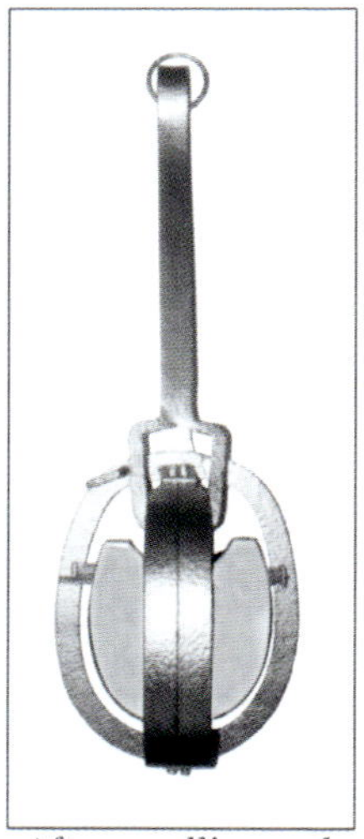

After smelling and touching the soap with the nose

Spring 98, Jong Talent in Antwerpen, Koningin Fabiolazaal, Antwerpen, BE
10.04-03.05.1998
Last year students Fine Arts Sint-Lukas Brussel, Moving Art Studio, Brussels, BE
14-28.06.1996

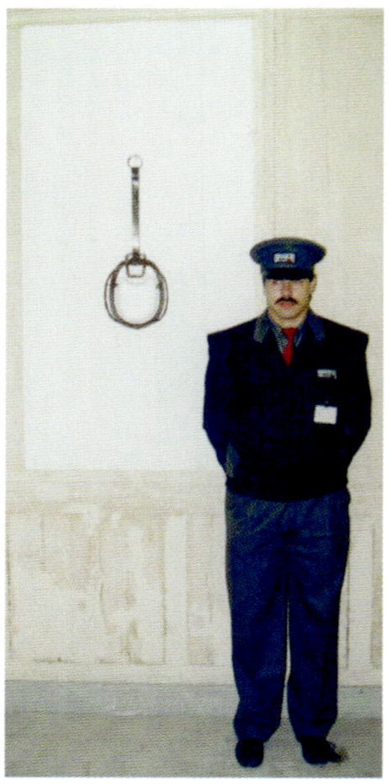

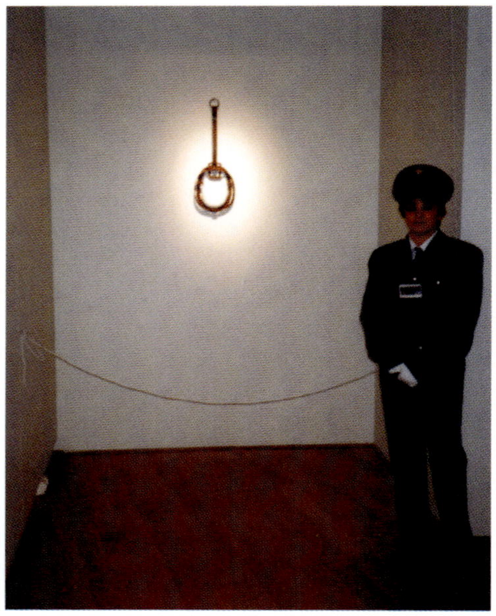

Your Last Smell, 1995-1996

An almost scent-free layer of soap was applied to a set fox trap. If anyone wishes to smell the soap and touches their nose to it, that will be the last scent they smell. Generally, you take your last breath when you die, but in this work you would die from the last breath you take. When the work was exhibited, a guard was placed next to the work for safety reasons, or the work was placed in a Plexiglas box.
The work was part of a final project at the Sint-Lukas art school in Brussels.
For safety purposes, extra security was provided.

Een bijna geurloos zeepvlak werd aangebracht op een opgespannen vossenklem. Van zodra men aan de zeep wil ruiken en de zeep aanraakt met de neus ruikt men zijn laatste geur. Normaal ademt men zijn laatste adem uit als men sterft, bij dit werk ademt men zijn laatste adem in bij het heengaan. Bij het tentoonstellen van het werk stond er voor de veiligheid steeds een bewaker of werd het werk achter een plexibox tentoongesteld.
Het werk maakte onderdeel uit van het afstudeerproject in de Sint-Lukas Hogeschool in Brussel. Voor de veiligheid werd er een extra beveiliging aangebracht.

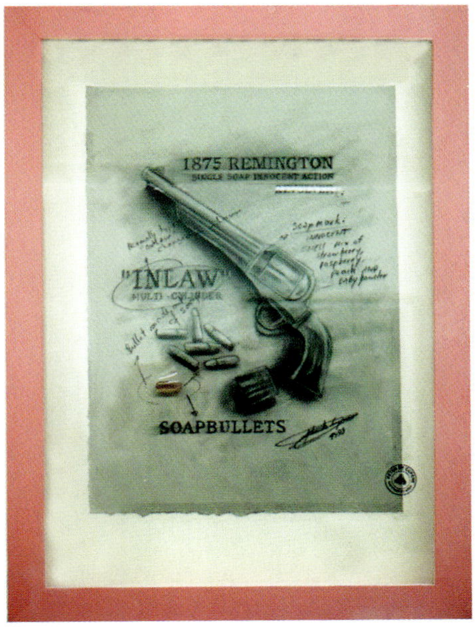

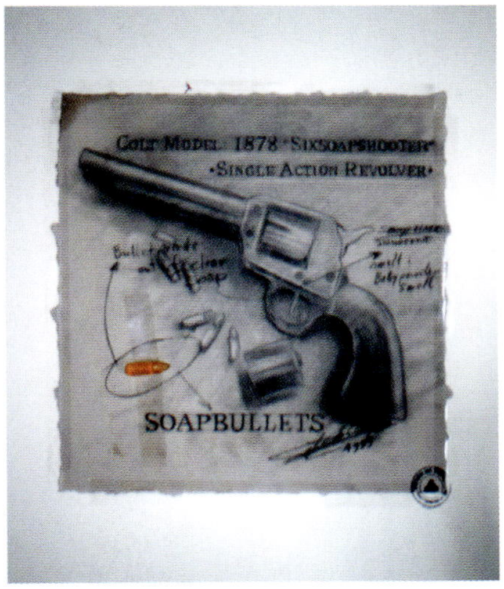

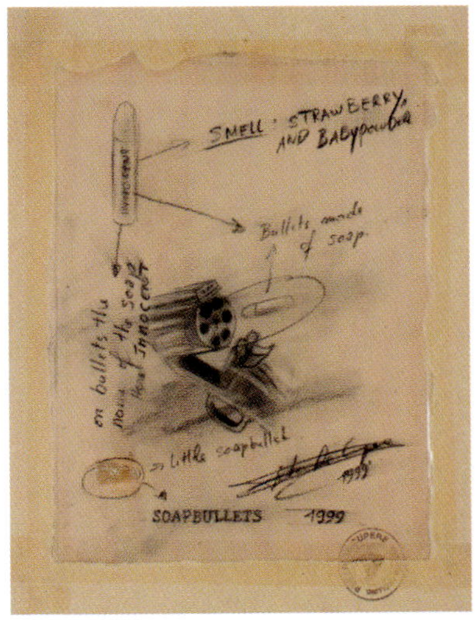

Drawings Soap Bullets, 1999-2000

Peter de Cupere, Smellcom Happening, Smell Kiss Performance, rockconcert Admiral Freebee, Van Laere Contemporary Art, Antwerp, BE 14.09-21.10.2000

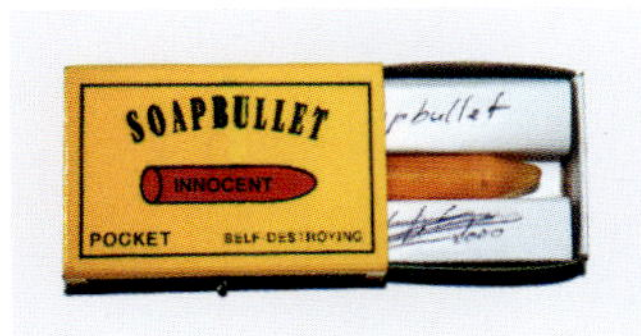

Innocent Soap Bullet, 2000

A bullet made of soap.

Kogel gemaakt uit zeep.

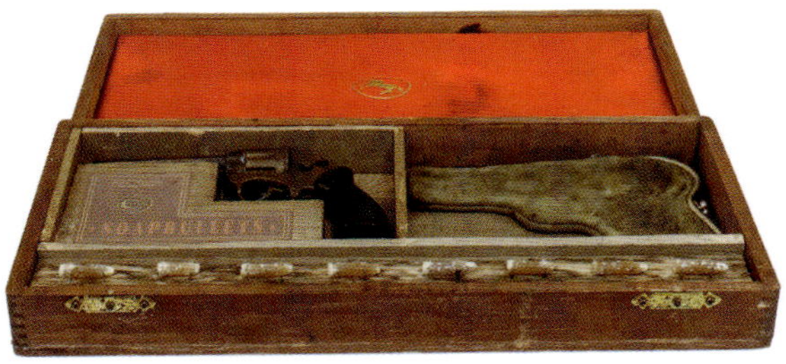

Self-Destroying Soap Bullets (Colt), 1999

Strawberry-scented soap bullets.

Kogeltjes gemaakt van zeep met aardbeiengeur

Sniff Your Jail, org. Balie Tongeren, curators Paul Morrens, Johan Smets, Justice Palace Tongeren, BE, 14.05.2016-19.06.2016
Peter de Cupere, Smellcom Happening, Smell Kiss Performance, rockconcert Admiral Freebee, Van Laere Contemporary Art, Antwerp, BE, 14.09-21.10.2000

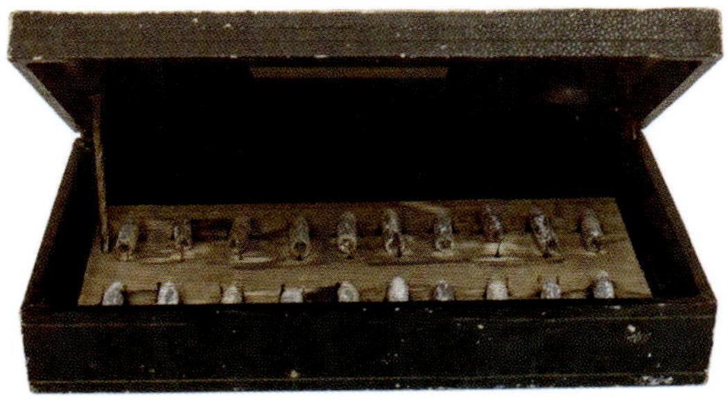

Self-Destroying Soap Bullets for Henry Deringer, 2000

Strawberry-scented soap bullets.

Kogeltjes gemaakt van zeep met aardbeiengeur

Sniff Your Jail, org. Balie Tongeren, curators Paul Morrens, Johan Smets, Justice Palace Tongeren, BE, 14.05.2016-19.06.2016
Peter de Cupere, Smellcom Happening, Smell Kiss Performance, rockconcert Admiral Freebee, Van Laere Contemporary Art, Antwerp, BE, 14.09-21.10.2000

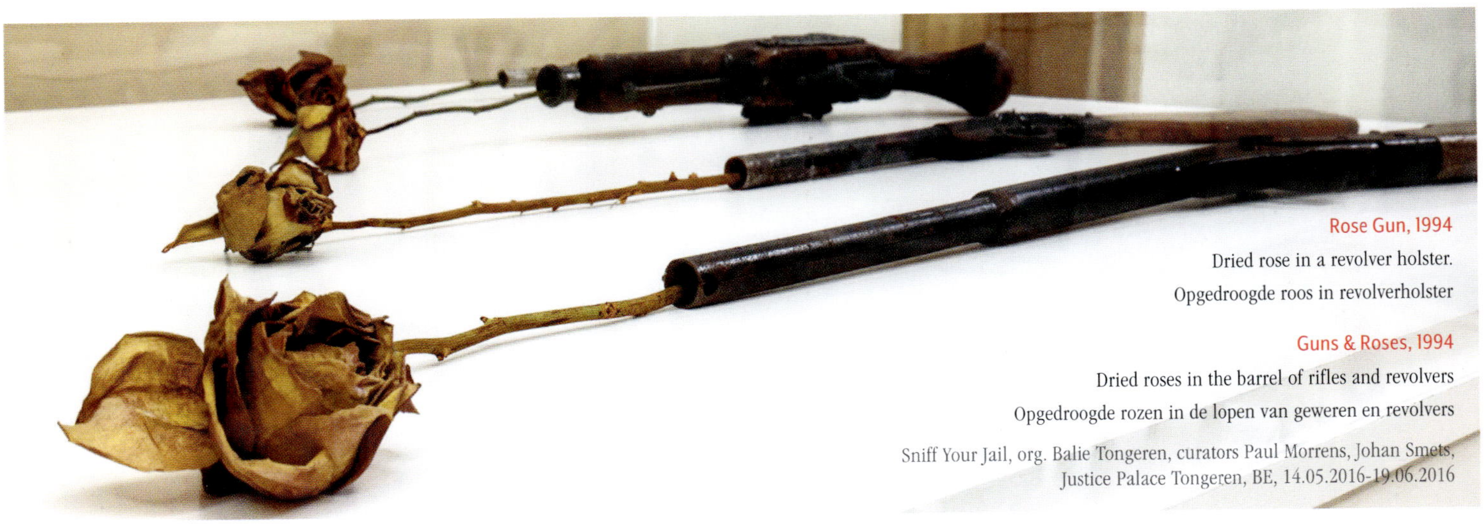

Rose Gun, 1994

Dried rose in a revolver holster.

Opgedroogde roos in revolverholster

Guns & Roses, 1994

Dried roses in the barrel of rifles and revolvers

Opgedroogde rozen in de lopen van geweren en revolvers

Sniff Your Jail, org. Balie Tongeren, curators Paul Morrens, Johan Smets, Justice Palace Tongeren, BE, 14.05.2016-19.06.2016

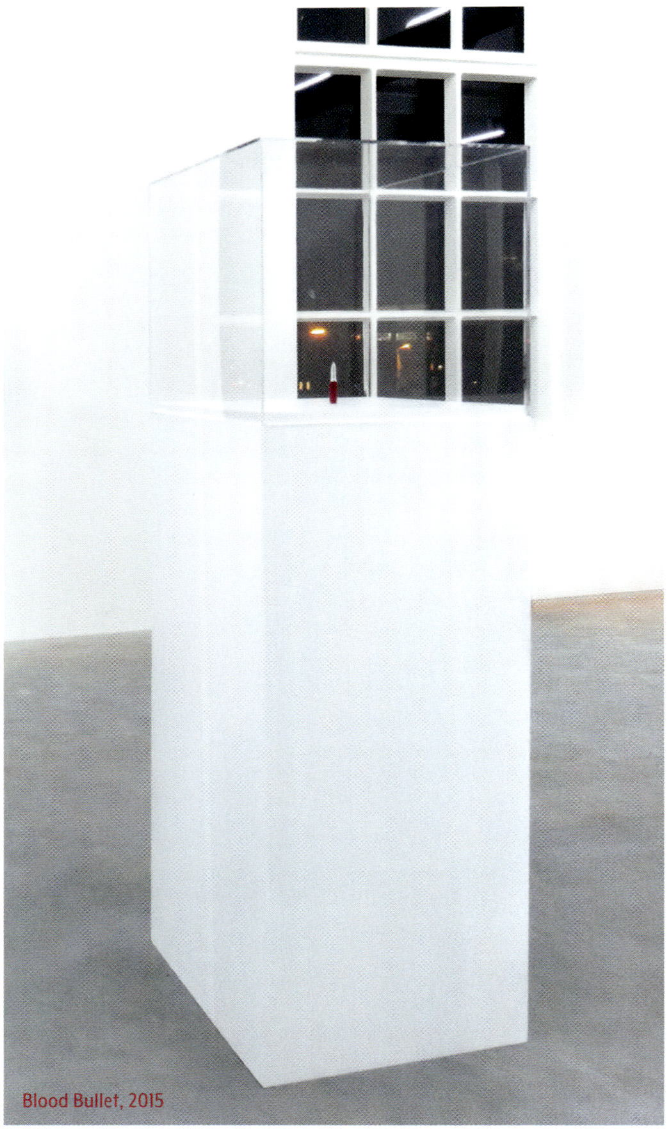

Blood Bullet, 2015

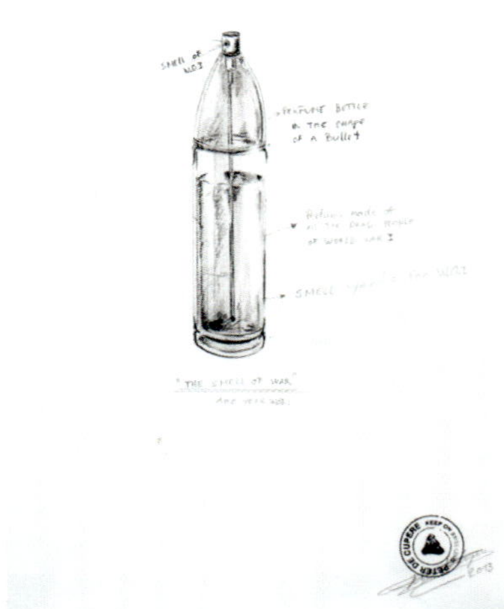

Perfume Bullet, 2013

Drawing / Tekening

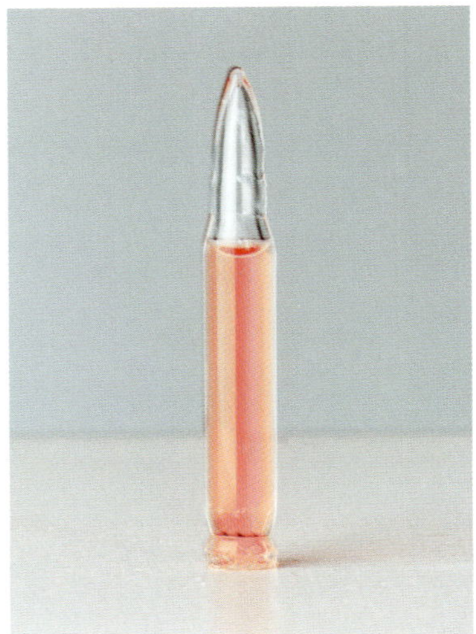

Love Bullet, 2015

Pheromones coloured in a glass bullet

Roosgekleurde feromonen in een glazen kogel

Dead Body Bullets, 2015 / Blood Bullet, 2015,
Black Oil Bullet, 2015 / Black Money Bullet, 2015

Artificial smells in glass bullets.
The smell of blood, the smell of death and the smell of American dollars were developed by IFF perfumers Meabh Mc Curtin, Gregoire Hausson, Christian Alori and Bernardo Fleming.

Nagemaakte geuren in glazen kogels.
De geur van bloed, de geur van de dood en de geur van Amerikaanse dollars werden ontwikkeld door IFF parfumeurs Meabh Mc Curtin, Gregoire Hausson, Christian Alori en Bernardo Fleming.

Sniff Your Jail, org. Balie Tongeren, curators Paul Morrens, Johan Smets, Justice Palace Tongeren, BE 14.05.2016-19.06.2016
Schone Kunsten, Cacaofabriek, curator Ageeth Boermans, Helmond, NL, 20.12.2015-24.01.2016
De Negende Maand, Munthuis Tongeren, org. Stad Tongeren, BE, 05.09.2015-27.09.2015
The Smell of War, 100 years WW1, Castle De Lovie, curator Peter de Cupere, Poperinge, BE, 30.04.2015-31.08.2015

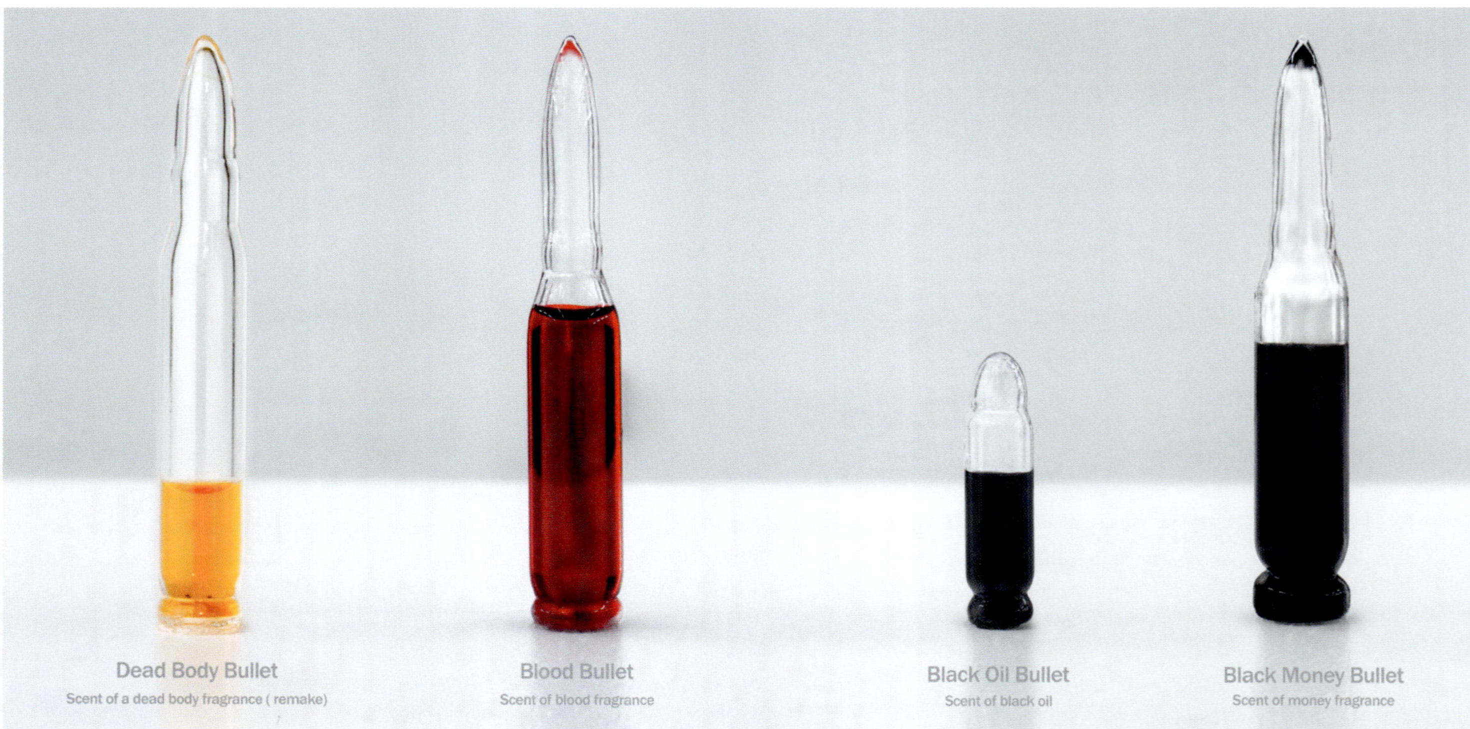

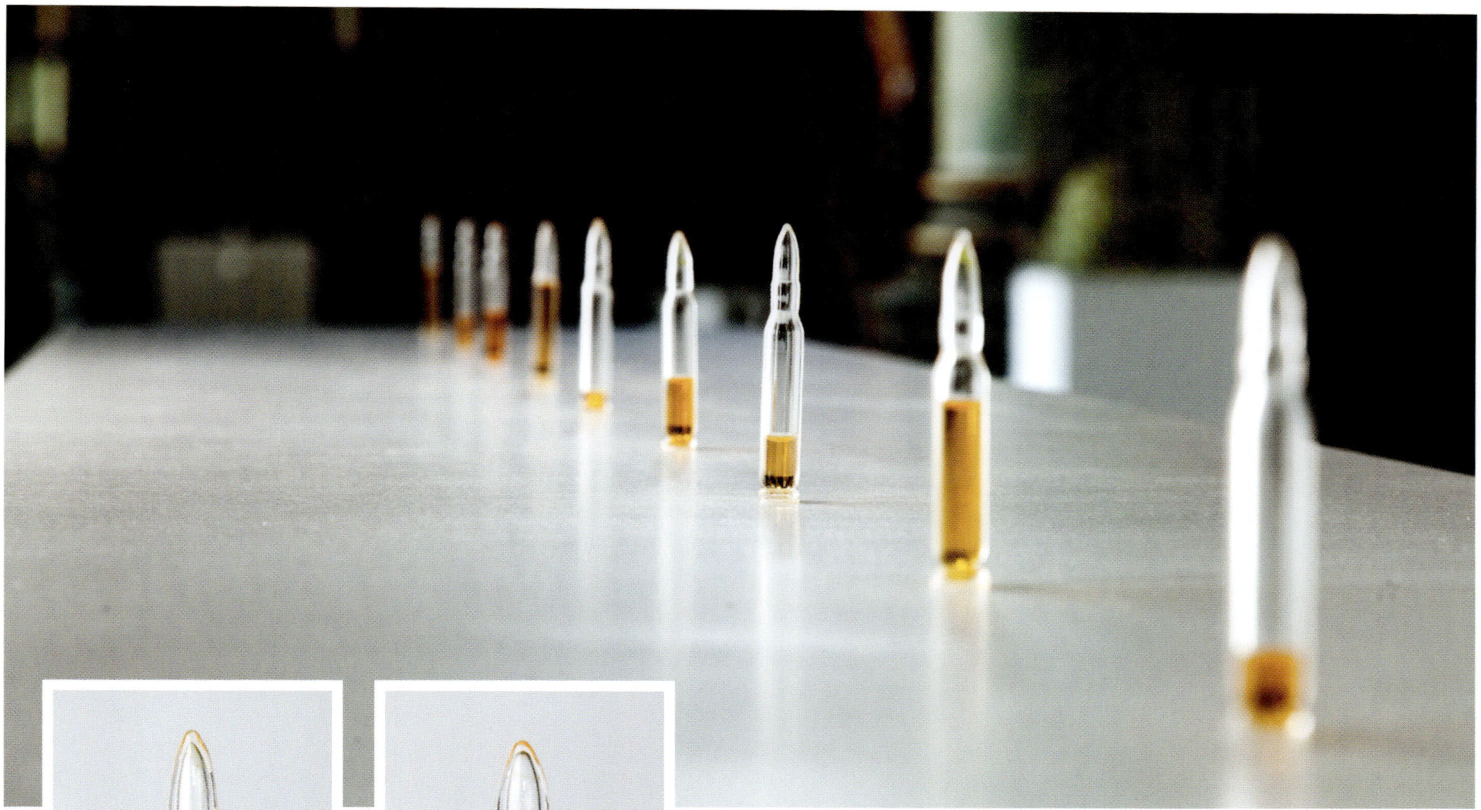

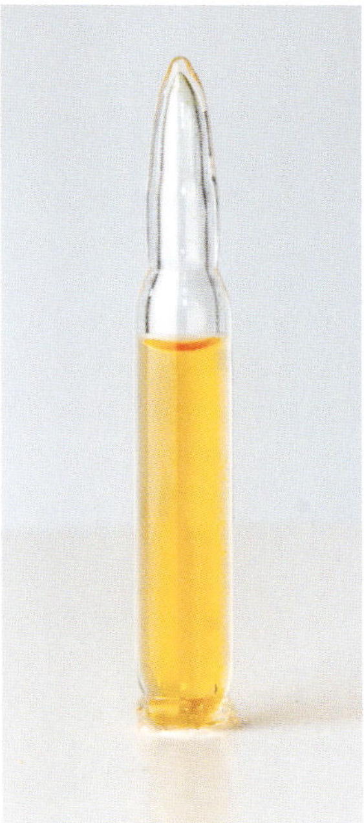

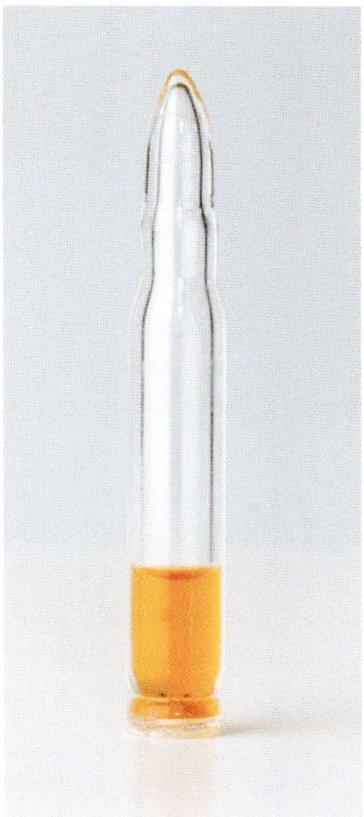

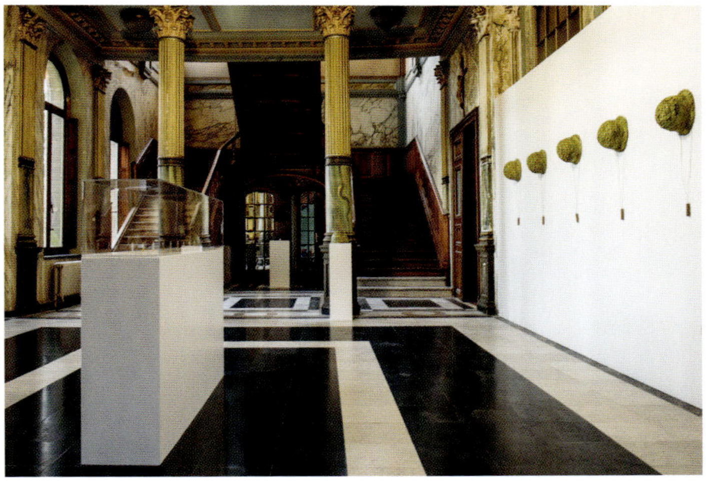

Dead Body Bullets, 2015

Scent: dead bodies

Dead Body Bullets is a concept from the year 2000. 15 years later, the artist realized this concept for the exhibition 'The Smell of War' (2015). Nine glass bullets each contain an amount of scent concentrate. The scent is a universal scent of dead bodies.

The amount of scent extract is defined by the age, gender, size and weight of the body at the time of death. Thus an adult, after distillation of his or her body, will produce more scent concentrate than that of a child or a newborn. If a human body were distilled after death, the volume of scent extract would not be very much. The larger and fatter the body, the more scent extract it produces.

To make the scent of a dead person as natural as possible, the artist sought the help of IFF perfumers Meabh Mc Curtin, Gregoire Hausson, Christian Alori and Bernardo Fleming. The scent is that of a person who has just died and not a person in a further state of decomposition. The scent of death is clearly present. The scent therefore questions the killing.

Geur van dode lichamen

Dead Body Bullets is een concept van het jaar 2000. Vijftien jaar later is dit concept gerealiseerd in het kader van de tentoonstelling *The Smell of War*. Negen glazen kogelhulsen bevatten elk een kleine hoeveelheid geurconcentraat. Deze geur is de universele geur van het lichaam van een overleden persoon. De hoeveelheid geurextract houdt rekening met leeftijd, geslacht, lengte en gewicht op het tijdstip van overlijden. Dit betekent dat het geurconcentraat van een volwassene, na distillatie van zijn of haar lichaam, een groter geurconcentraat voortbrengt dan dit van een kind of pasgeborene. In realiteit zou deze distillatie van geurextract slechts heel beperkt zijn en rekening houden met de grootte en vetgehalte van het corps. Om de geur van een dode persoon zo accuraat mogelijk na te bootsen, kreeg Peter de Cupere hulp van IFF en haar geurspecialisten Meabh Mc Curtin, Gregoire Hausson, Christian Alori en Bernardo Fleming. Uiteindelijk hebben zij een geur nagebootst van een pas overleden persoon en niet de confronterende geur van een lichaam in een verdere staat van ontbinding. De geur van de dood is aldus expliciet aanwezig en wekt serieuze vragen op over het doden van mensen.

Sniff Your Jail, org. Balie Tongeren, curators Paul Morrens, Johan Smets, Justice Palace Tongeren, BE, 14.05.2016-19.06.2016
Schone Kunsten, Cacaofabriek, curator Ageeth Boermans, Helmond, NL, 20.12.2015-24.01.2016
De Negende Maand, Munthuis Tongeren, org. Stad Tongeren, BE, 05.09.2015-27.09.2015
The Smell of War, 100 years WW1, Castle De Lovie, curator Peter de Cupere, Poperinge, BE, 30.04.2015-31.08.2015

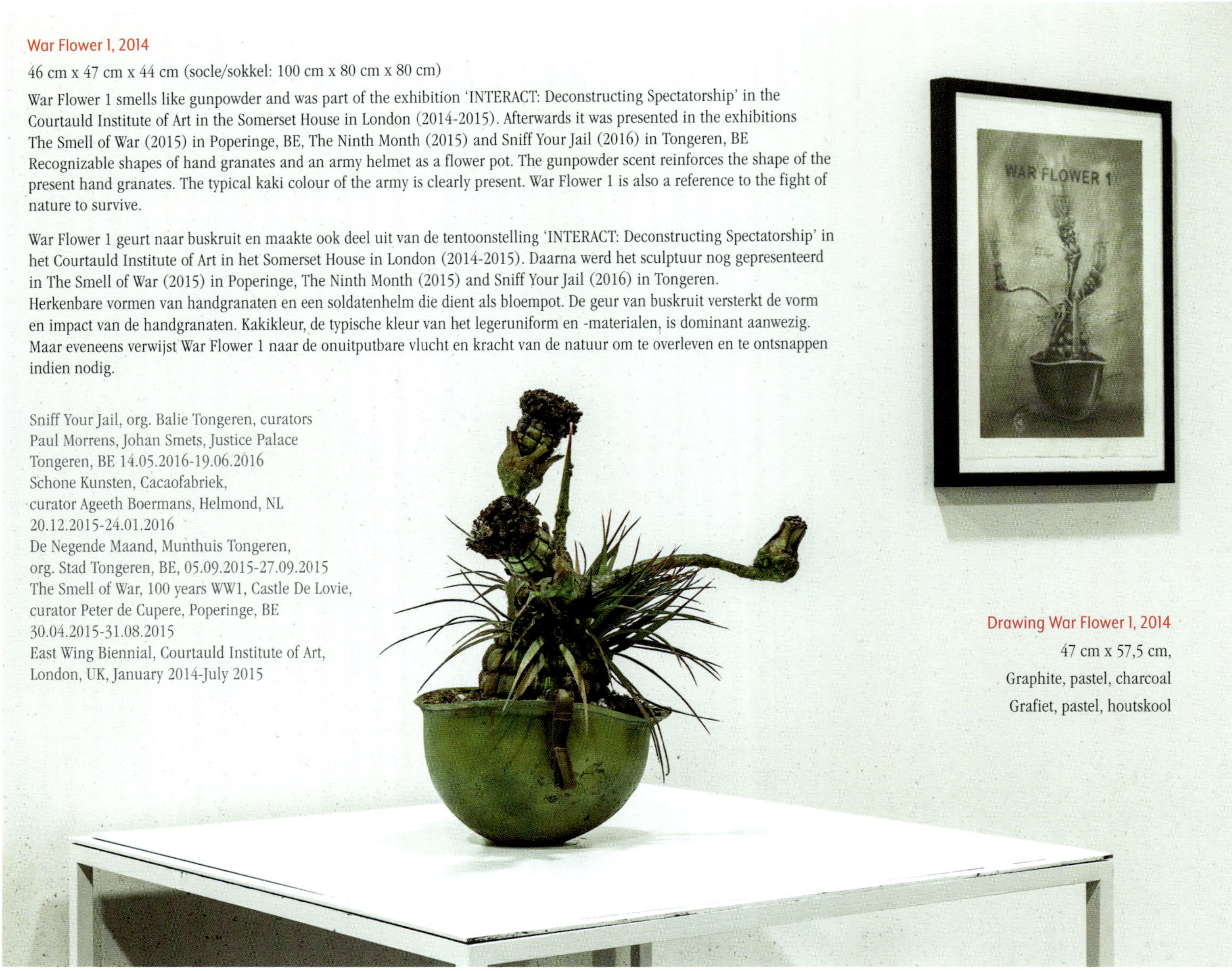

War Flower 1, 2014

46 cm x 47 cm x 44 cm (socle/sokkel: 100 cm x 80 cm x 80 cm)

War Flower 1 smells like gunpowder and was part of the exhibition 'INTERACT: Deconstructing Spectatorship' in the Courtauld Institute of Art in the Somerset House in London (2014-2015). Afterwards it was presented in the exhibitions The Smell of War (2015) in Poperinge, BE, The Ninth Month (2015) and Sniff Your Jail (2016) in Tongeren, BE Recognizable shapes of hand granates and an army helmet as a flower pot. The gunpowder scent reinforces the shape of the present hand granates. The typical kaki colour of the army is clearly present. War Flower 1 is also a reference to the fight of nature to survive.

War Flower 1 geurt naar buskruit en maakte ook deel uit van de tentoonstelling 'INTERACT: Deconstructing Spectatorship' in het Courtauld Institute of Art in het Somerset House in London (2014-2015). Daarna werd het sculptuur nog gepresenteerd in The Smell of War (2015) in Poperinge, The Ninth Month (2015) and Sniff Your Jail (2016) in Tongeren.
Herkenbare vormen van handgranaten en een soldatenhelm die dient als bloempot. De geur van buskruit versterkt de vorm en impact van de handgranaten. Kakikleur, de typische kleur van het legeruniform en -materialen, is dominant aanwezig. Maar eveneens verwijst War Flower 1 naar de onuitputbare vlucht en kracht van de natuur om te overleven en te ontsnappen indien nodig.

Sniff Your Jail, org. Balie Tongeren, curators Paul Morrens, Johan Smets, Justice Palace Tongeren, BE 14.05.2016-19.06.2016
Schone Kunsten, Cacaofabriek, curator Ageeth Boermans, Helmond, NL 20.12.2015-24.01.2016
De Negende Maand, Munthuis Tongeren, org. Stad Tongeren, BE, 05.09.2015-27.09.2015
The Smell of War, 100 years WW1, Castle De Lovie, curator Peter de Cupere, Poperinge, BE 30.04.2015-31.08.2015
East Wing Biennial, Courtauld Institute of Art, London, UK, January 2014-July 2015

Drawing War Flower 1, 2014
47 cm x 57,5 cm,
Graphite, pastel, charcoal
Grafiet, pastel, houtskool

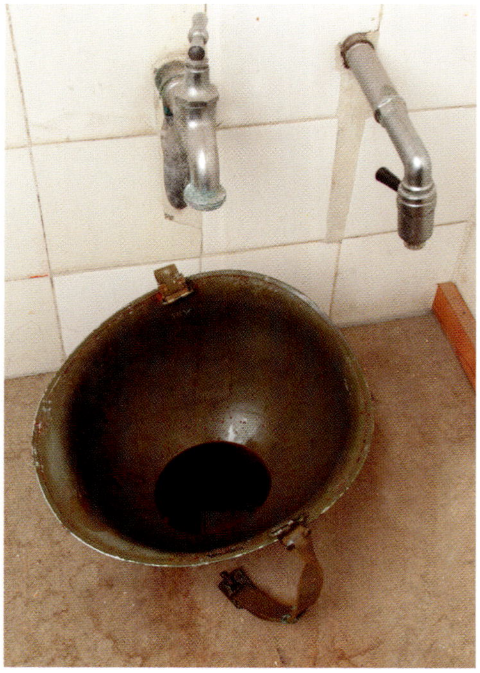

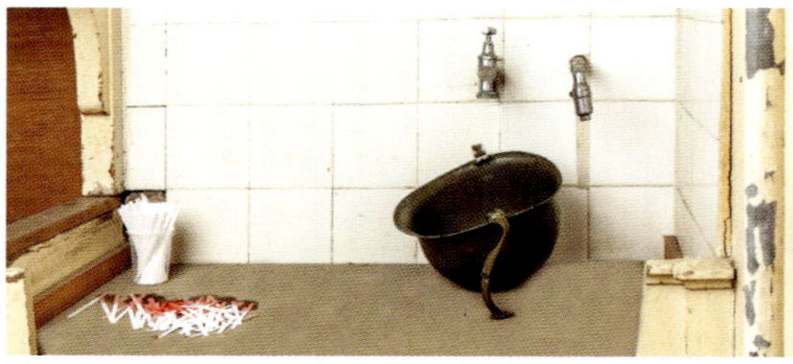

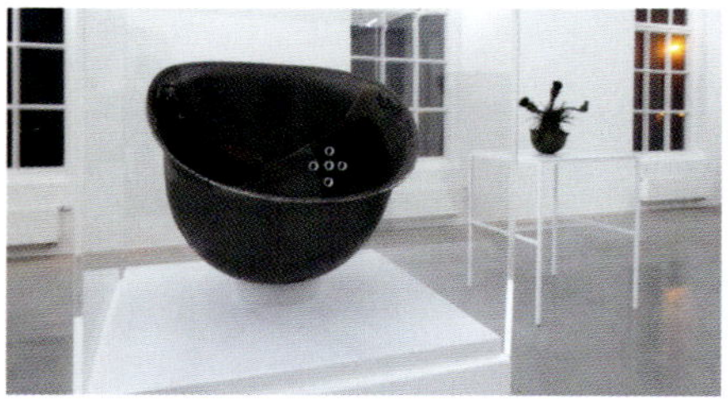

Blood Drop Monument

From a closet, blood drips unexpectedly. This is caught in an army helmet. The blood, nevertheless, is not real but a red dye. Blood drips from a tap into the army helmet. To experience the scent of blood, you have to try and catch a drop of scented blood in your hands or drip a paper strip into the blood to smell it. For the realization of the scent, Peter de Cupere sought help with the IFF perfumers Meabh Mc Curtin, Gregoire Hausson, Christian Alori and Bernardo Fleming. They succeeded to reproduce the scent of fresh blood.

Bloed lekt uit een kraan, onverwacht en at random. Het bloed wordt opgevangen in een helm. Het is geen echt bloed maar een verfstof. Om de geurervaring van het bloed te maximaliseren moet je trachten een bloeddruppel te capteren in je hand of op een papieren strip om eraan te ruiken. Voor het aanmaken van de geur zocht Peter de Cupere steun bij IFF en haar parfumeurs Meabh Mc Curtin, Gregoire Hausson, Christian Alori en Bernardo Fleming. Zij slaagden erin de geur van vers bloed te simuleren.

Schone Kunsten, Cacaofabriek, curator Ageeth Boermans, Helmond, NL, 20.12.2015-24.01.2016
De Negende Maand, Munthuis Tongeren, org. Stad Tongeren, BE, 05.09.2015-27.09.2015
The Smell of War, 100 years WW1, Castle De Lovie, curator Peter de Cupere, Poperinge, BE, 30.04.2015-31.08.2015

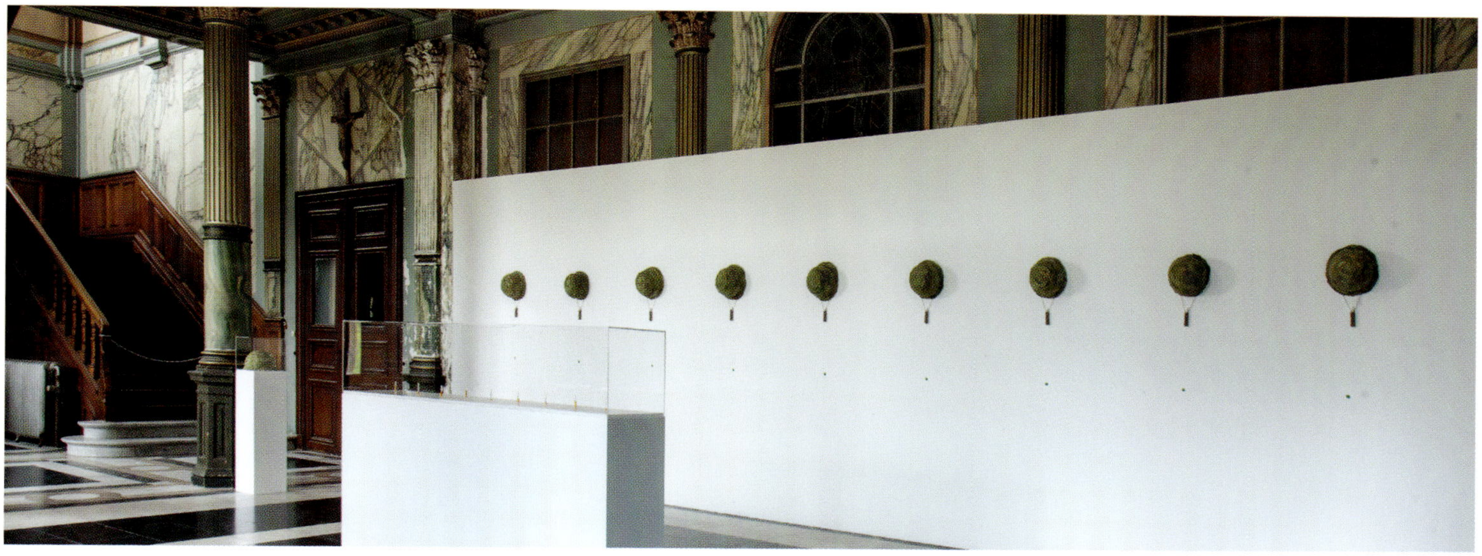

Heroes Also Die, 2015

9 helmets made of laurel leafs, under each helmet hangs a perfume bottle filled with the smell of a dead person. Visitors could smell each dead body perfume through a little smell device in the wall. Each perfume was unique and represented the personality of the dead person. In front of the helmets the work *Dead Body Bullets*.

Negen helmen met laurier hangen aan de muur, in stilte. Onder de helm hangt een parfumflesje, gevuld met een geur van een dode persoon. Elke bezoeker kan aldus de parfumgeur van een dood lichaam ervaren dankzij een klein geurapparaatje in de muur. Elk parfum was uniek en vertegenwoordigde de personaliteit van de overledene. Voor deze installatie was het werk Dead Body Bullets gepresenteerd.

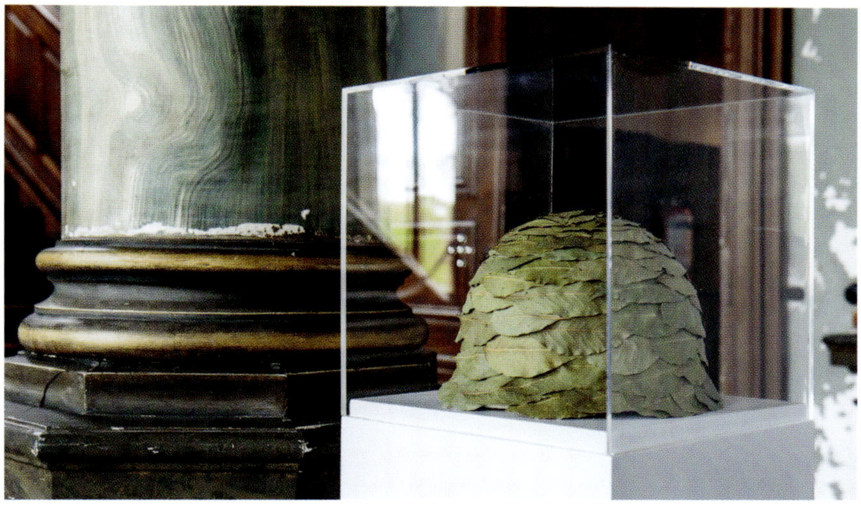

Drawing Heroes Also Die, 1997-2012

Aquarel

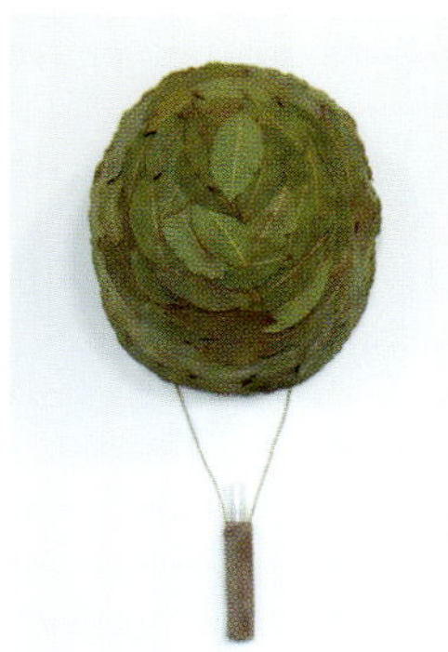

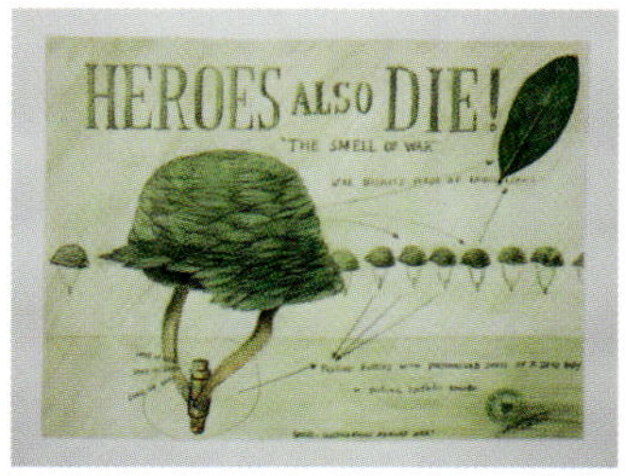

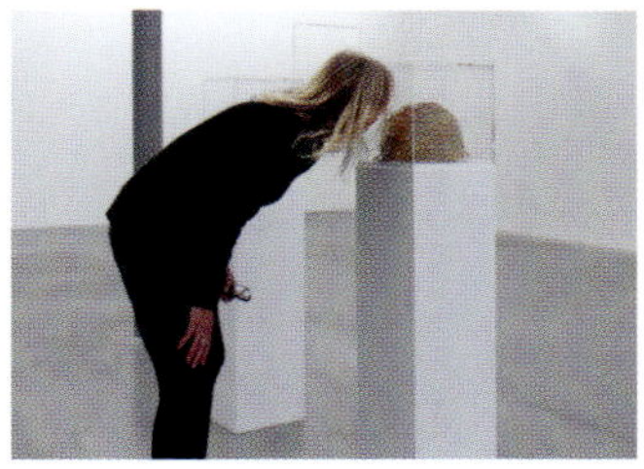

Heroes Also Die (1997-2015)

The work 'Heroes also die' was partially the occasion which led to the exhibition The Smell of War. Artist Peter de Cupere already came up with the concept of this work in 1997. The work exists out of army helmets made from laurel leaves. One helmet is presented separately. In this one, the scent of laurel can be detected very well.

In Classical History, laurel was a sign of victory. Conquerors were dressed with a wreath of victory, made of laurel leaves. The term laureate is a remainder of this symbolism. A certain number of expressions is based on laurel,'such as 'resting on its laurels', 'being honored', and 'harvest laurels'.

However, heroes also die: nine helmets with laurel leaves hang at the wall. Under the helmet hangs a perfume bottle. It was the intention to foresee a different scent of death for each of the perfume bottles. The visitor could squirt his most favorite death scent on him or herself and thus mentally revive a dead (hero) by carrying his or her scent. Eventually the artist decided to put the scent module underneath the work so that one can smell the scents.
The scents were composed by the IFF perfumers Meabh Mc Curtin, Gregoire Hausson, Christian Alori and Bernardo Fleming. Every scent of death has a personal touch and is a reference to the individual, the character of the hero concerned. It is to the spectator him/herself to fill this in, since scents have very strong personal experiences.

Heroes also die lag deels aan de basis van de expo *The Smell of War*. Het idee en concept van de thematiek lag sinds 1997 in de schuif van de kunstenaar. Het kunstwerk bestaat uit soldatenhelmen die gemaakt zijn uit laurierbladen. Één helm wordt alleenstaand gepresenteerd in de opstelling. Deze laatste helm heeft een uitgesproken lauriergeur.

In de klassieke geschiedenis, stond laurier symbool voor 'de overwinning'. Succesvolle veroveraars of winnaars van veldslagen werden gedecoreerd met een lauwerkrans gemaakt uit laurierbladen. In onze huidige woordenschat refereert de term laureaat naar deze symboliek. Ook verschillende uitdrukkingen verwijzen naar de lauwerkrans zoals 'op zijn lauweren rusten', 'gelauwerd zijn' of 'lauweren oogsten'.

Helaas, 'Heroes also die'. Negen helmen met laurier hangen aan de muur, in stilte. Onder de helm hangt een parfumflesje. De bedoeling is om elk parfumflesje met een verschillende geur van de dood te vullen. Elke bezoeker kan aldus zijn of haar favoriete doodsgeur aanbrengen op zijn of haar lichaam en op die manier de dode persoon laten herleven dankzij zijn geur. Uiteindelijk besliste de kunstenaar om de bezoekers de mogelijkheid te geven onder elke helm te ruiken aan de geur van elke overleden persoon. De geuren werden samengesteld door IFF en haar parfumeurs Meabh Mc Curtin, Gregoire Hausson, Christian Alori en Bernardo Fleming. Elke doodsgeur heeft een persoonlijke touch en verwijst naar de persoonlijkheid achter de overleden held. De bezoeker kan zelf interpreteren op basis van geuren en herinneringen hoe men deze persoonlijkheid invult. Je eigen persoonlijke ervaring zal dit proces sturen.

Schone Kunsten, Cacaofabriek, curator Ageeth Boermans, Helmond, NL, 20.12.2015-24.01.2016
De Negende Maand, Munthuis Tongeren, org. Stad Tongeren, BE, 05.09.2015-27.09.2015
The Smell of War, 100 years WW1, Castle De Lovie, curator Peter de Cupere, Poperinge, BE, 30.04.2015-31.08.2015

The Smell Of War

In 2015, Peter de Cupere was invited by Annemie Morisse of the city of Poperinge, Belgium, to put on an exhibition to mark the 100th anniversary of the first gas attacks. He served as curator for the exhibition 'The Smell of War'.

Smells work powerfully on olfactory memory. Smells can elicit a particular response from visitors, either consciously or unconsciously. It is the perfect way to awaken a recollection of the First World War via the senses.

What does war smell like? Visitors could experience the smells of fear, triumph, death, mud and gunpowder, among others, in 'The Smell of War' exhibition. Smells are the most direct way to evoke the senses that tell the story of war. Peter de Cupere selected 21 internationally renowned artists to give that story a context. 11 of the invited artists work with smell.

Participating artists: Alex Schweder (US), Caflo Yrot (UA), Camilla Maurer (DE), Christophe Laudamiel (FR), Clara Ursitti (UK), Dr Elena Bodnar (UA), Gayil Nalls (US), John Bijnens (BE), Lisa Kirk (US), Maki Ueda (JP), Mattia Casalegno (IT), Nancy Slangen (BE), Nathan Vincent (US), Oswaldo Maciá (CO), Peter de Cupere (BE), Philippe Vandenberg (BE), Priyanka Choudhary (IN), Sue Corke (UK), Hagen Betzwieser (DE), George Grosz (DE) and Otto Dix (DE).

For more information, please visit www.thesmellofwar.be

In 2015 werd Peter de Cupere door Annemie Morisse van de Stad Poperinge uitgenodigd om een tentoonstelling te maken omtrent het 100-jarig bestaan van de eerste gasaanvallen. Als curator realiseerde hij zo de tentoonstelling *The Smell of War*. Geur werkt sterk op olfactorische herinneringen. Via geur kan men bij bezoekers bewust of onbewust een bepaalde reactie opwekken. Het is de perfecte manier om ook gevoelsmatig een herinnering aan de Eerste Wereldoorlog op te roepen. Hoe ruikt een oorlog? Bezoekers konden o.a. de geur van angst, triomf, dood, modder en buskruit in de tentoonstelling 'The Smell of War' ervaren. Geuren zijn de meest directe manier om het zintuiglijke verhaal van de oorlog op te roepen.

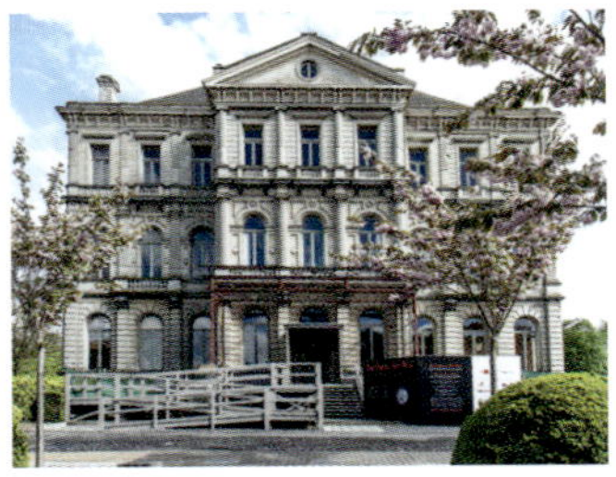

The Exhibition Location Castle De Lovie, Poperinge, BE

Peter de Cupere selecteerde 21 internationale kunstenaars om context aan dit verhaal te geven. 11 van de uitgenodigde kunstenaars werken met geur. Deelnemende kunstenaars: Alex Schweder (US), Caflo Yrot (UA), Camilla Maurer (DE), Christophe Laudamiel (FR), Clara Ursitti (UK), Dr. Elena Bodnar (UA), Gayil Nalls (US), John Bijnens (BE), Lisa Kirk (US), Maki Ueda (JP), Mattia Casalegno (IT), Nancy Slangen (BE), Nathan Vincent (US), Oswaldo Maciá (CO), Peter de Cupere (BE), Philippe Vandenberg (BE), Priyanka Choudhary (IN), Sue Corke (UK), Hagen Betzwieser (DE), George Grosz (DE) en Otto Dix (DE).

Meer info op www.thesmellofwar.be

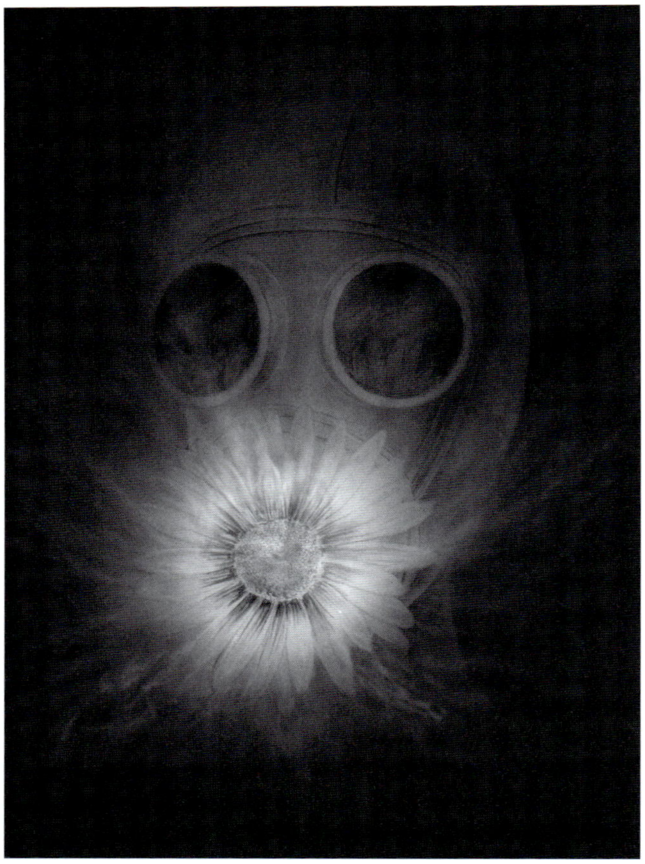

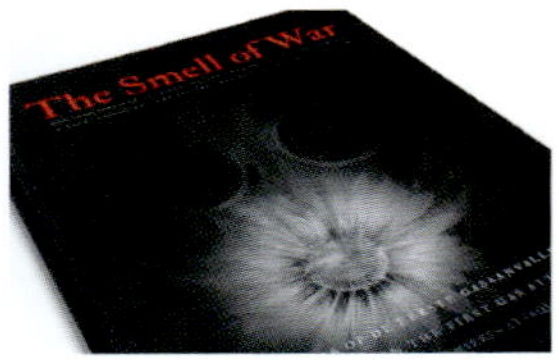

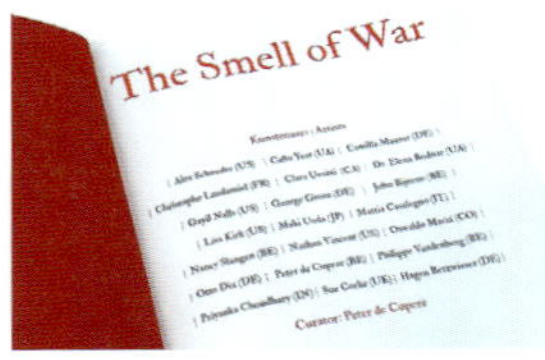

Publication
The Smell Of War, 2015

Printed by Stockmans Printing
112 pag.

The Flower Mask, 2015

84 x 118,9 cm

Dibond print behind plexi / Dibond druk achter plexi, edition of 7 + 3 A.P.

Artist and curator Peter de Cupere realized a set of drawings in which masks with flower feature as the starting point. Based on these drawings, he made a video. In the video we see 49 pupils from the free primary school De Kastanje (The Chestnut), from Krombeke and Proven. They each have a gas mask and they come to a performance of the artist. Every gas mask has a flower as a filter.

Kunstenaar en curator Peter de Cupere realiseerde een aantal tekeningen waarin maskers met bloemen de hoofdrol spelen. Gebaseerd op deze tekeningen heeft hij een video gemaakt. In de video zien we 49 leerlingen van de Vrije Basisschool De Kastanje van de gemeentes Krombeke en Proven. Deze dragen allemaal een gasmasker en zijn toeschouwer bij de performance van de kunstenaar. Elk gasmasker heeft een bloem als filter.

Sniff Your Jail, org. Balie Tongeren, curators Paul Morrens, Johan Smets, Justice Palace Tongeren, BE 14.05.2016-19.06.2016
Schone Kunsten, Cacaofabriek, curator Ageeth Boermans, Helmond, NL, 20.12.2015-24.01.2016
De Negende Maand, Munthuis Tongeren, org. Stad Tongeren, BE, 05.09.2015-27.09.2015
The Smell of War, 100 years WW1, Castle De Lovie, curator Peter de Cupere, Poperinge, BE 30.04.2015-31.08.2015
East Wing Biennial, Courtauld Institute of Art, London,UK, January 2014-July 2015

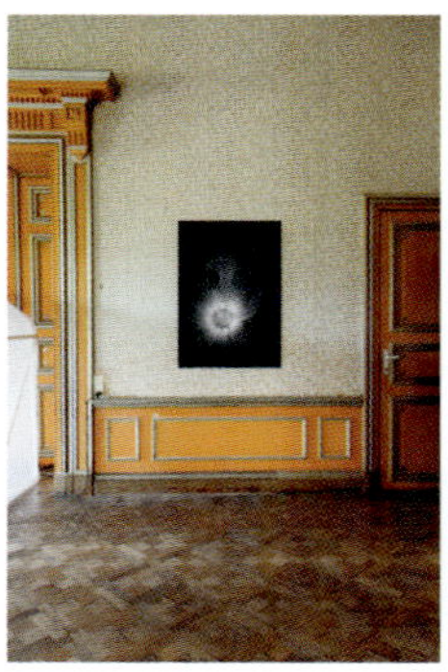
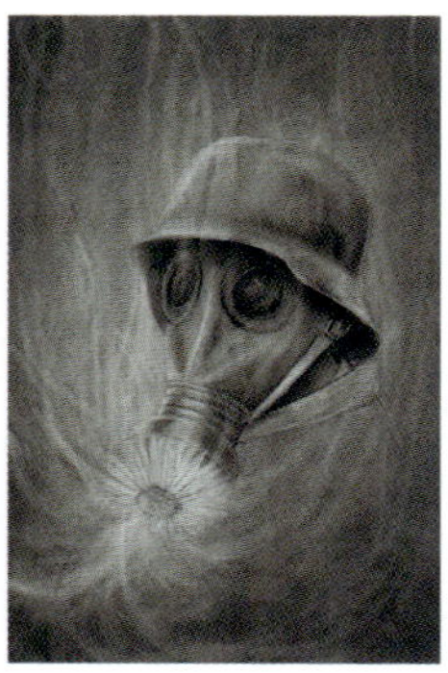
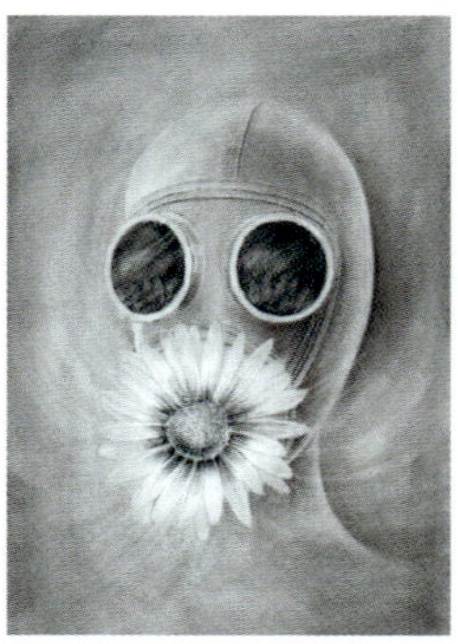
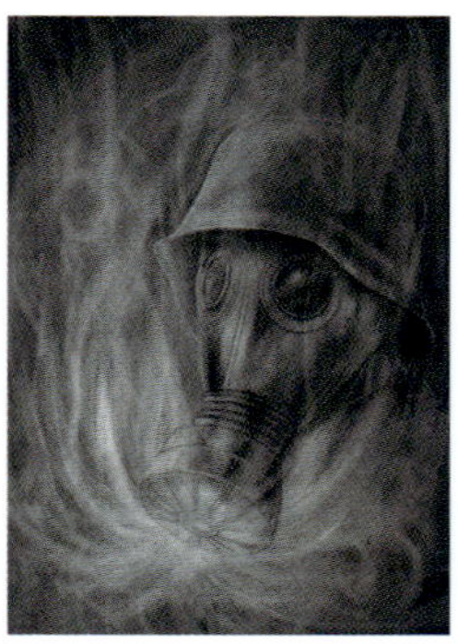
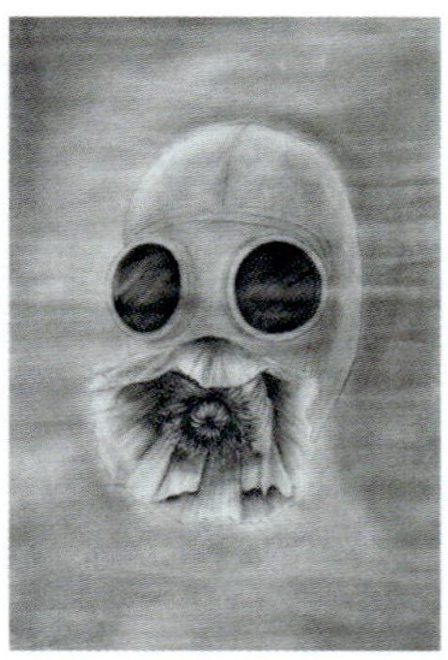
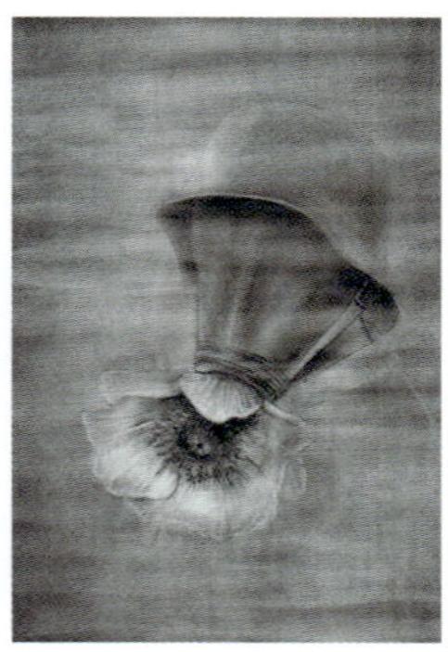

Drawing Flower Masks, 2015

59,5 cm x 42 cm, Charcoal, graphite / Houtskool, grafiet

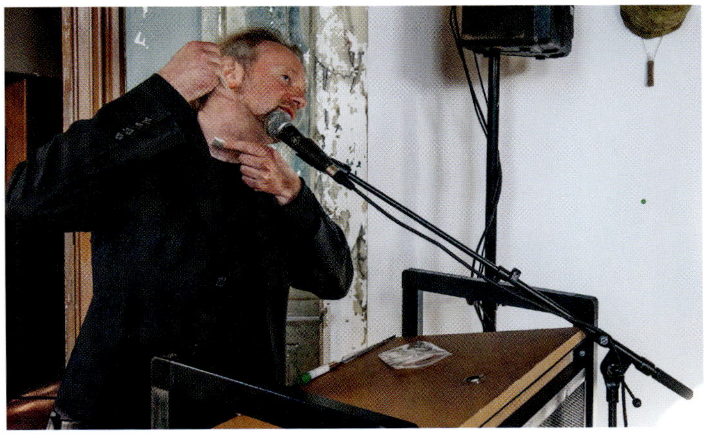

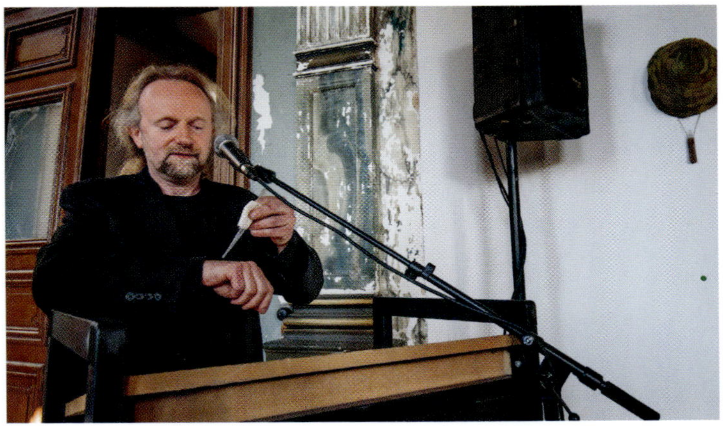

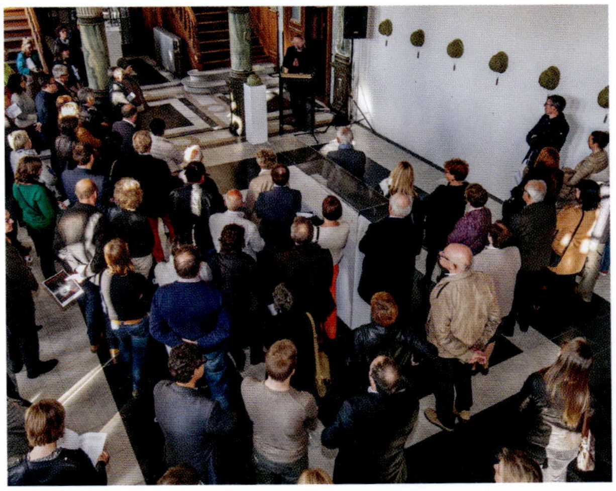

Perfumance Dead Alive And An Honour To Life, 2015

At the opening, after his opening speech, Peter de Cupere sprayed himself with perfume with an artificial scent of death, and secondly with an artificial smell of blood. The smell of death was intended symbolically to give the dead a presence and bring them back to life in people's memory. The smell of blood was a symbolic reference to the smell of life. The latter was also in part a tribute to Caflo Yrot, who in 1899 perfumed himself with his own blood in order to make a statement as a doctor.
The smells used by Peter de Cupere for his perfumance at the event were developed by IFF perfumers Meabh Mc Curtin, Gregoire Hausson, Christian Alori and Bernardo Fleming.

Op de opening parfumeerde Peter de Cupere zich na zijn openinsgsspeech met een nagemaakte geur van de dood en als tweede een nagemaakte geur van bloed. De geur van de dood om symbolisch zo de doden weer recht te laten staan, tot leven te brengen en tot het herinnering te brengen. De geur van bloed als symbolische verwijzing naar de geur van het leven. Deze laatste was ook deels een eerbetoon aan Caflo Yrot die zich in 1899 zelf parfumeerde met zijn eigen bloed om als dokter een statement te maken.
De geuren die Peter de Cupere gebruikte voor zijn speech perfumance waren ontwikkeld door IFF parfumeurs Meabh Mc Curtin, Gregoire Hausson, Christian Alori en Bernardo Fleming.

The Smell of War, 100 years WW1, Castle De Lovie, curator Peter de Cupere, Poperinge, BE
30.04.2015-31.08.2015

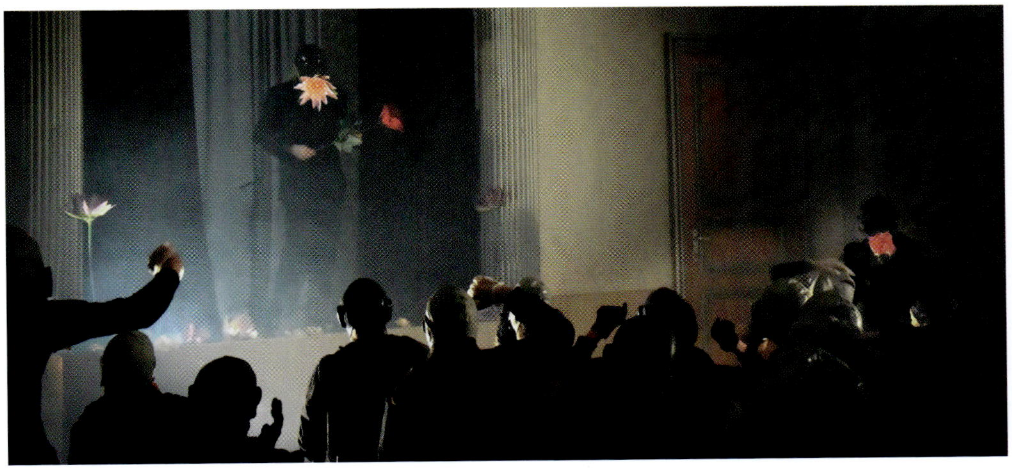

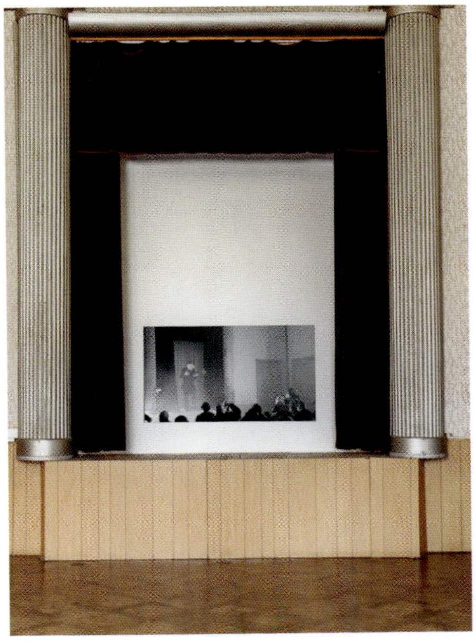

The Flower Mask, 2015

Black & White Video, HD, 7 min. 14 sec.

Sniff Your Jail, org. Balie Tongeren, curators Paul Morrens, Johan Smets, Justice Palace Tongeren, BE, 14.05.2016-19.06.2016
The Smell of War, 100 years WW1, Castle De Lovie, curator Peter de Cupere, Poperinge, BE, 30.04.2015-31.08.2015

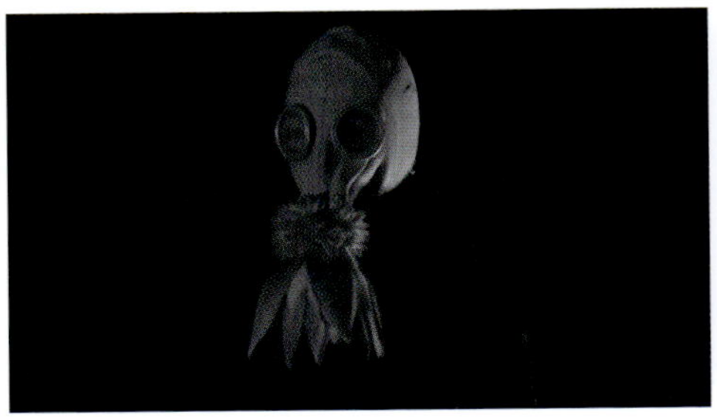

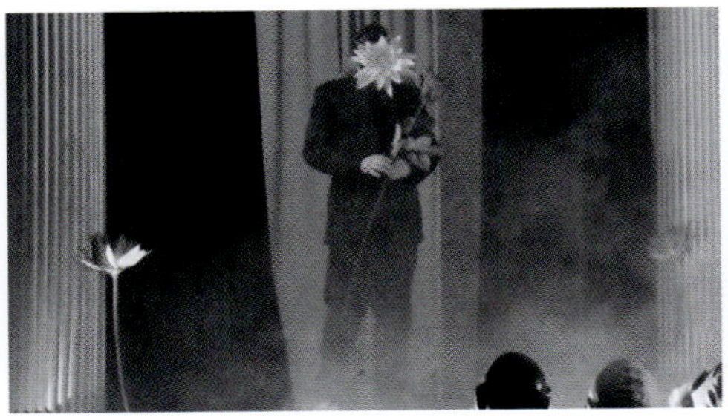

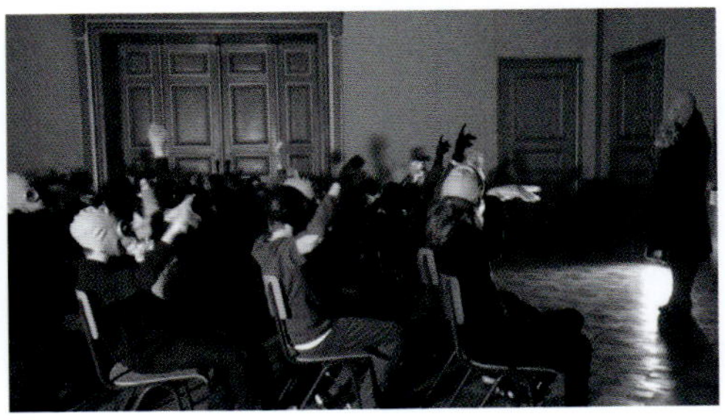

Screenshots of the video The Flower Mask

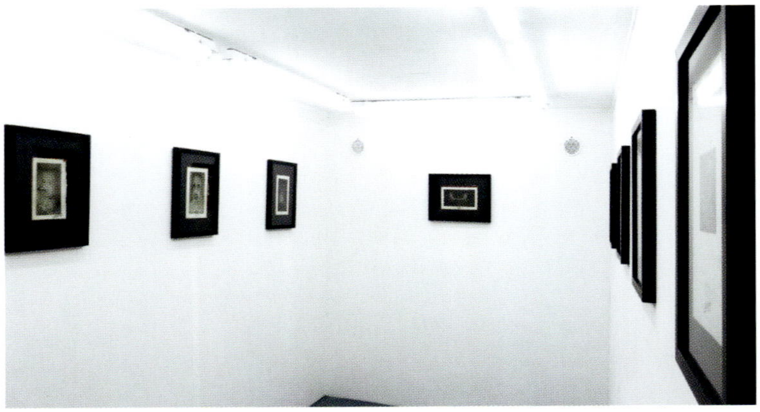
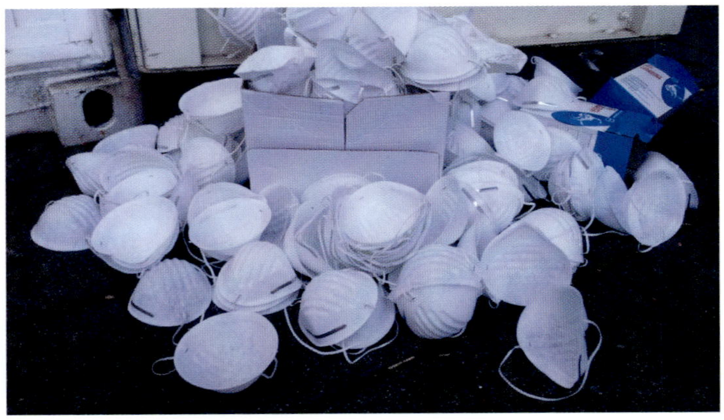
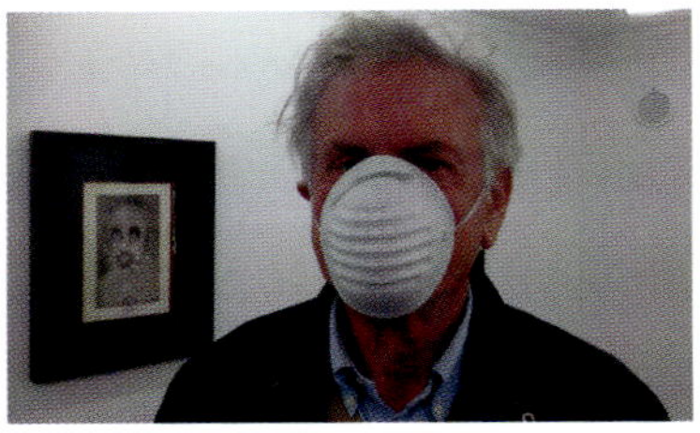
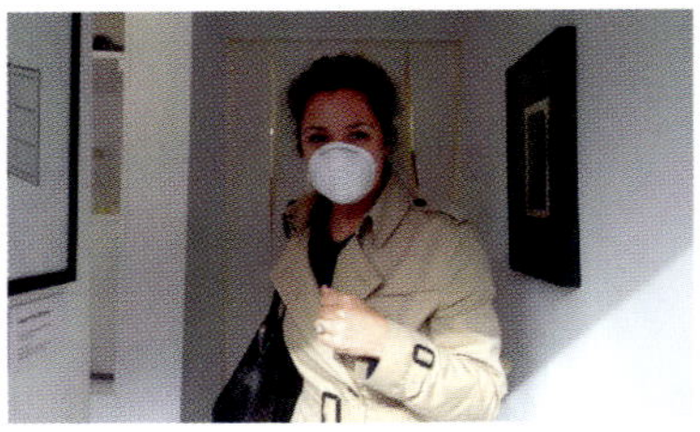
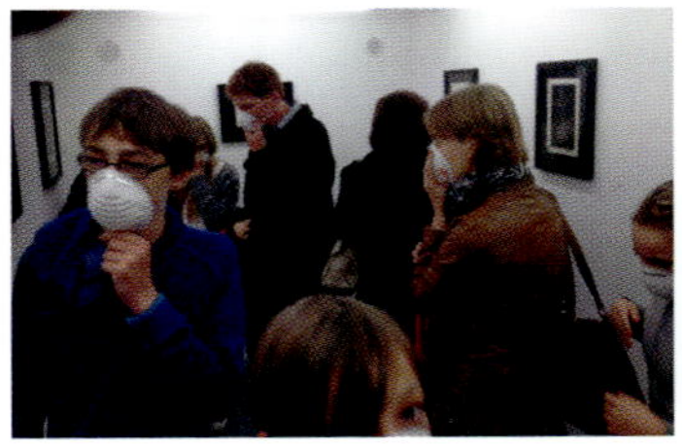
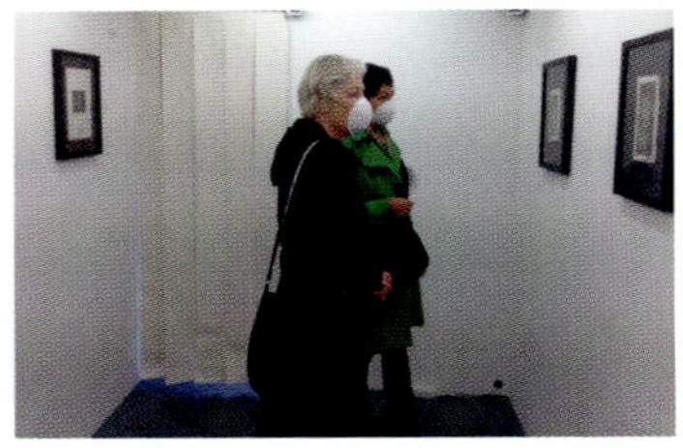

'The Smell Of War - Prelude'

'The Smell Of War - Prelude' shows a series of drawings about war mask concepts. It is a reflection on the first gas attacks in Belgium about one hundred years ago. This exhibition was a prelude to the exhibition 'The Smell of War' in Poperinge in 2015. In The Olfactory people needed to wear a simple white mask. The exhibition room was scents intensive!

Germany's first attempt with chemical weapons in mass occurred in 1915 at the second battle of Ypres in Belgium. Different types of gas were used during the war. When you first encounter mustard gas, you may not even know anything about the effect on you. The best way to detect mustard gas is through smell. Soldiers exposed to mustard gas only noticed a funny smell and had a hard time to recognise this as a gas attack. Even under heavy doses, however, their noses adapted to the smell quickly, giving them the impression that the gas had dissipated. Have you ever noticed you can't smell something, be it good or bad, after you've been sniffing it for a few minutes? The same principle applies during a mustard gas attack. Mustard gas, in particular, has a rather nice aroma. Gas victims from World War I recalled a sweet and spicy scent that reminded them of lilacs, garlic, horseradish, onions, or—you guessed it—mustard. In general, 'blister agents' such as mustard gas smell pretty good. Another blister agent developed around the time of the First World War, lewisite, smells intensely of geraniums. A blister agent called phosgene oxime has an unpleasant, irritating smell—but with hints of freshly mown hay. The related diphosgene smells like anise.

So in the exhibition 'The Smell of War - Prelude' visitors had to deal with an intensive odour. This odour could be a reference to a gas attack, but can also be the smell of sweat from people in danger! At the entrance visitors got a fresh white mask to wear. They didn't had to wear it, but it made probably their visit more pleasant!

Het eerste massaal gebruik van chemische wapens door Duitsland in 1915 had plaats tijdens de tweede slag om Ieper in België. Verschillende types gas werden tijdens de Eerste Wereldoorlog aangewend. De eerste maal dat je geconfronteerd wordt met mosterdgas heb je geen idee van de effecten van dit oorlogswapen. De beste manier om het gebruik van mosterdgas te ontdekken is via het ruiken. Soldaten, regelmatig blootgesteld aan het gas, merkten enkel een ietwat speciale geur op en hadden geen idee van het feit dat ze onder vuur lagen met deze techniek. Later werd het gas zelfs bij zwaardere gasaanvallen minder snel opgemerkt, doordat er een gewoontegevoel ontstond in de neus ten aanzien van het gas. Deze ervaring van geurverlies maken we zelf ook mee, zelfs bij uitgesproken positieve of negatieve geuren waar je regelmatig of gedurende enkele minuten achter elkaar aan wordt blootgesteld. Mostergas heeft eigenlijk een aangenaam aroma en slachtoffers van de gasaanvallen verwezen in hun geurbeschrijving naar een zoete en kruidige geur, zoals bv. lila, look, radijs, ajuin of mosterd. Dit betekent dat dergelijke oorlogsgassen relatief aangenaam ruiken. Een ander gas dat in deze periode ontwikkeld werd, lewisiet, geurt naar geraniums. Fosfeengas heeft anderzijds een onaangename en irriterende geur maar wel met flarden vers gemaaid hooi. Difosgeen ruikt dan weer naar anijs.

Tijdens het bezoek aan de expo *The Smell of War - Prelude* werden bezoekers blootgesteld aan een intense geur. Deze geur had een dubbele betekenis, enerzijds refererend naar een gasaanval, maar ook naar angstzweet van mensen in levensgevaar. Aan de ingang ontvingen bezoekers een wit masker om te dragen. Niemand was verplicht om dit masker te dragen maar het had wel tot doelstelling je geurtechnisch te beschermen tijdens het bezoek van de expo.

The Olfactory, Antwerp, BE, 25-26.10.2014

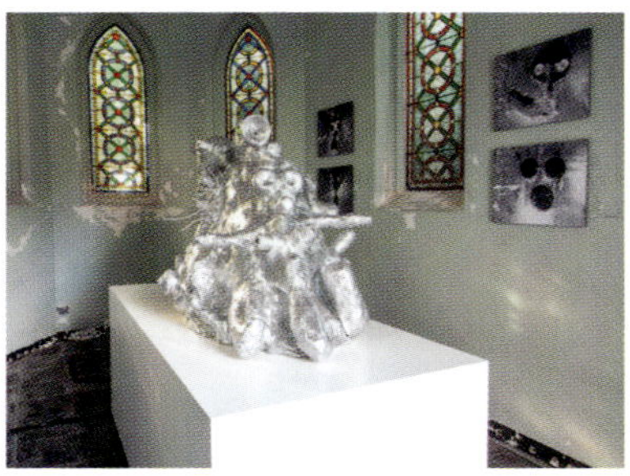

Sculpture of Gas Masks, 2015

Installation, card board, several materials, epoxy, aluminum, chrome

This sculpture is presented in the small chapel, an outside location opposite the castle.
The installation is the result of several workshops at De Lovie. These took place in April 2015. The artist Peter de Cupere introduced his scent concept to a number of inhabitants of De Lovie. They smelled, felt the gas masks and watched other artists going about creatively with gas masks.

Then the inhabitants, together with their supervisors went to work. With all sorts of materials, gas masks were created.
In a second phase, the creations received an epoxy layer. Eventually all the gas masks were brought together into a piece of art foreseen of a layer of aluminum and chrome. The inhabitants could pick the scent. It became intermittently a scent of lemon and a scent of sweat.

Installatie bestaande uit karton, diverse materialen, epoxy, aluminium en chroom

Deze sculptuur wordt gepresenteerd in de kleine kapel, recht tegenover het kasteel. Het sculptuur werd gemaakt gedurende verschillende workshops in april 2015 in Kasteel De Lovie. Peter de Cupere introduceerde zijn geurconcepten aan een aantal bewoners van deze site. Ze geurden en voelden aan de gasmaskers, en keken toe hoe andere kunstenaars creatief omgingen met deze maskers.

Inwoners en hun begeleiders startten hun opdracht en met allerhande materialen werden de gasmaskers gemaakt. In een tweede fase kregen deze een epoxylaag. Alle maskers werden samengebracht om één kunstwerk te maken, voorzien van een laag aluminium en chroom. De geur werd gekozen door de inwoners en twee geuren werden uiteindelijk gebruikt: de geur van citroenen en een zweetgeur.

The Smell of War, 100 years WW1, Castle De Lovie, curator Peter de Cupere, Poperinge, BE, 30.04.2015-31.08.2015

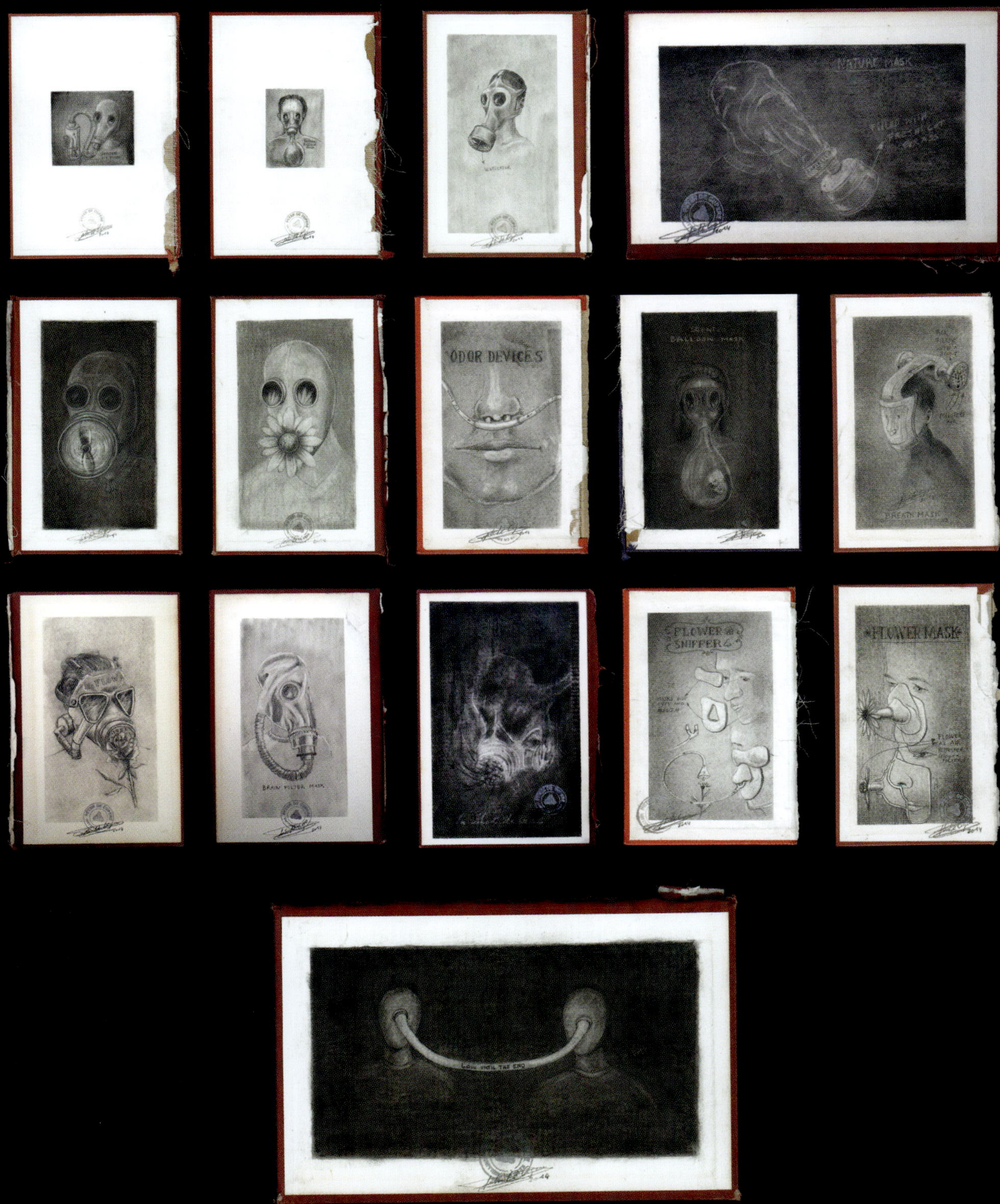

Gas Masks, 2014

Various gas mask drawings on book covers, various sizes

Diverse tekeningen met gasmaskers op covers van boeken

Sniff Your Jail, org. Balie Tongeren, curators Paul Morrens, Johan Smets, Justice Palace Tongeren, BE, 14.05.2016-19.06.2016

De Negende Maand, Munthuis Tongeren, org. stad Tongeren, BE, 05.09.2015-27.09.2015

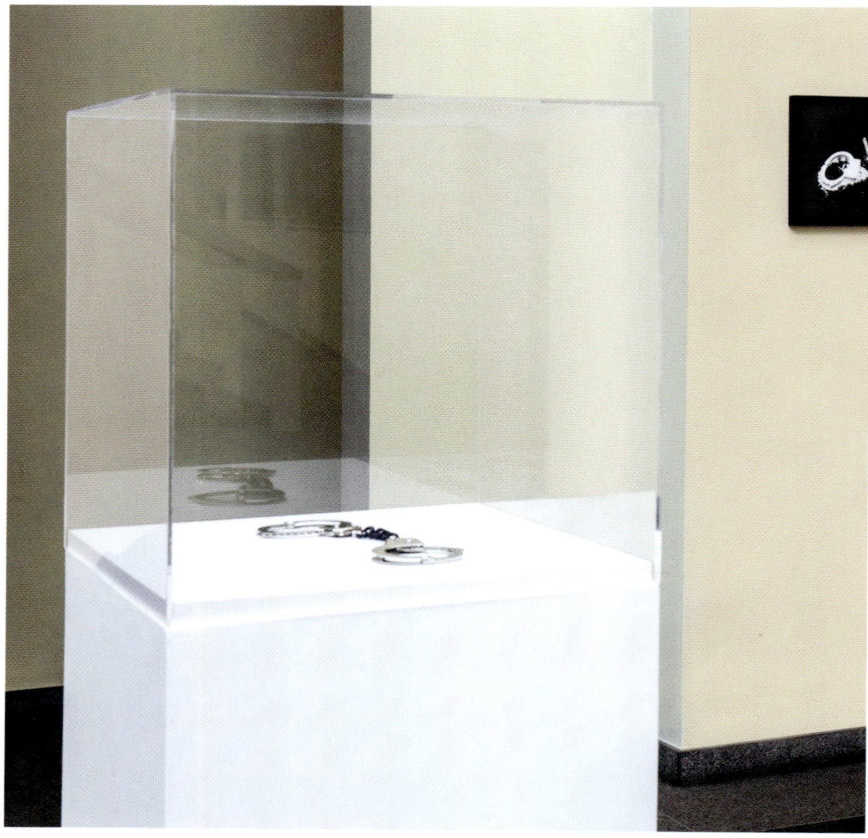

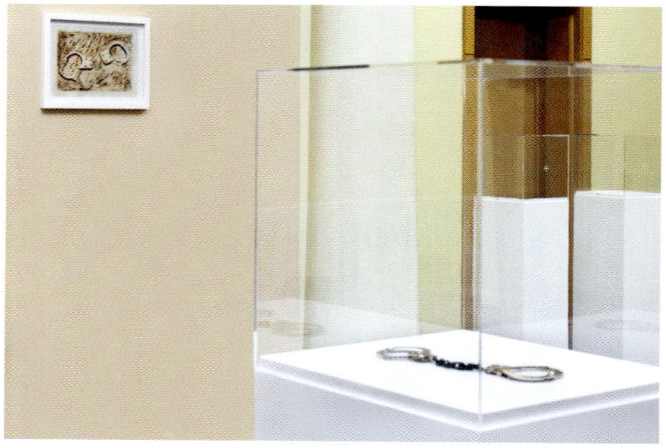

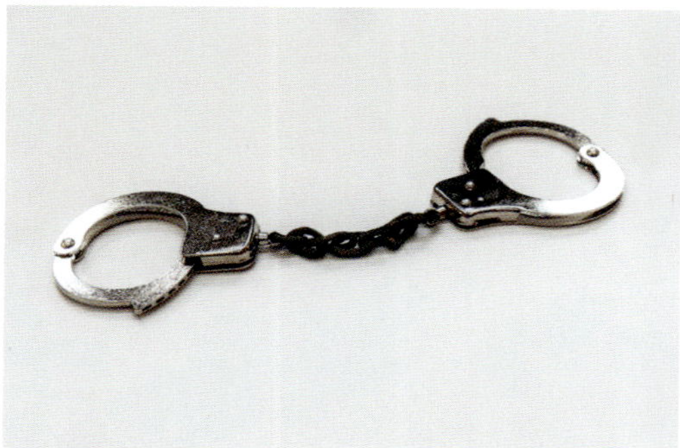

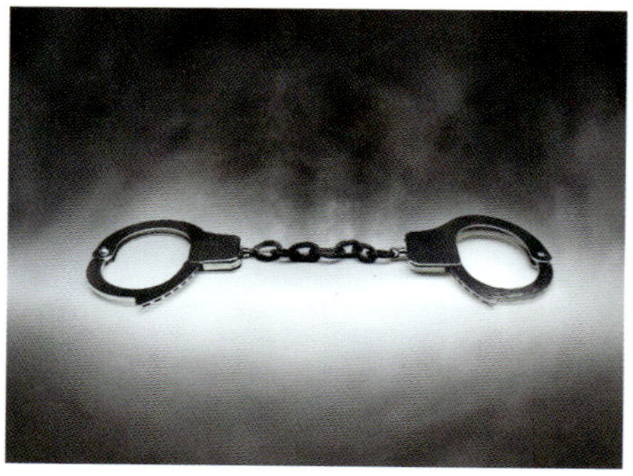

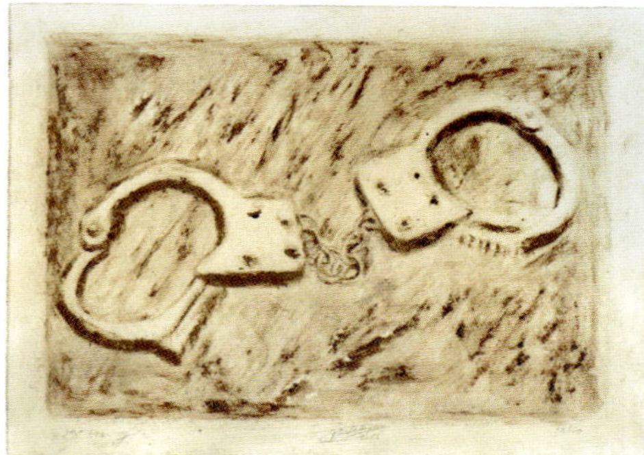

Smoke Your Jail, 2016

Sculpture made of hash and metal handcuffs.

Sculptuur gemaakt uit hasj en metalen handboeien.

Sniff Your Jail, org. Balie Tongeren, curators Paul Morrens, Johan Smets, Justice Palace Tongeren, BE, 14.05.2016-19.06.2016

Smoke Your Jail, 2016

Art print on 240 gram matt paper, 30 cm x 40 cm
Print run: 50 copies, 3 A.P.

Kunstprint op 240 gram mat papier, 30 cm x 40 cm
Oplage van de editie: 50 exemplaren, 3 A.P.

Sniff Your Jail, org. Balie Tongeren, curators Paul Morrens, Johan Smets, Justice Palace Tongeren, BE 14.05.2016-19.06.2016

Shit Drawing, 2016

The original drawing was made with hash and vodka, scanned in, and offered as a limited edition print.
Art print on 240 gram matt paper, 30 cm x 40 cm
Print run: 50 copies, 3 A.P.

De originele tekening werd met hasj en vodka getekend, ingescand en als editie aangeboden.
Kunstprint op 240 gram mat papier, 30 cm x 40 cm.
Oplage van de editie: 50 exemplaren, 3 A.P.

Sniff Your Jail, org. Balie Tongeren, curators Paul Morrens, Johan Smets, Justice Palace Tongeren, BE 14.05.2016-19.06.2016

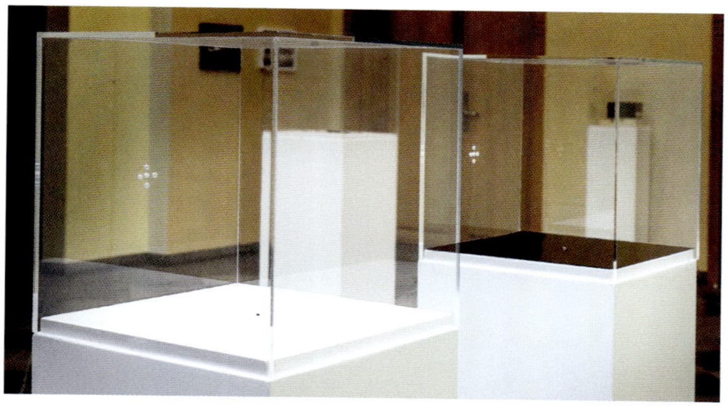

Shit Snot, 2016

Object under plexiglass box on a base

Object onder plexibox op sokkel

Sniff Your Jail, org. Balie Tongeren, curators Paul Morrens, Johan Smets, Justice Palace Tongeren, BE, 14.05.2016-19.06.2016

White Snot, 2016

Object under plexiglass box on a base

Object onder plexibox op sokkel

Sniff Your Jail, org. Balie Tongeren, curators Paul Morrens, Johan Smets, Justice Palace Tongeren, BE, 14.05.2016-19.06.2016

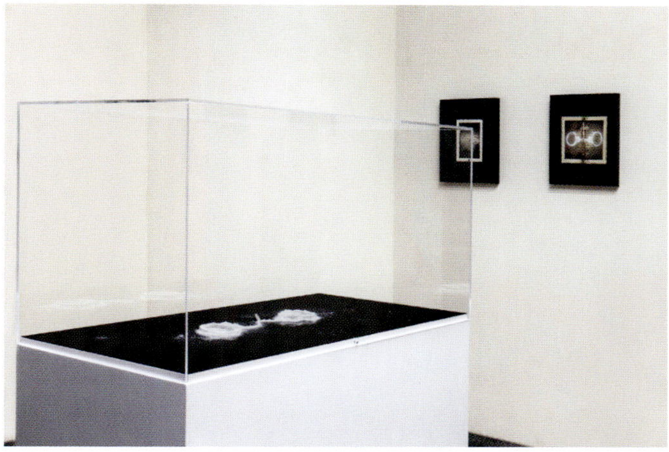

Sniff Your Jail, 2016

Sculpture / Sculptuur

Sniff Your Jail, org. Balie Tongeren, curators Paul Morrens, Johan Smets, Justice Palace Tongeren, BE, 14.05.2016-19.06.2016

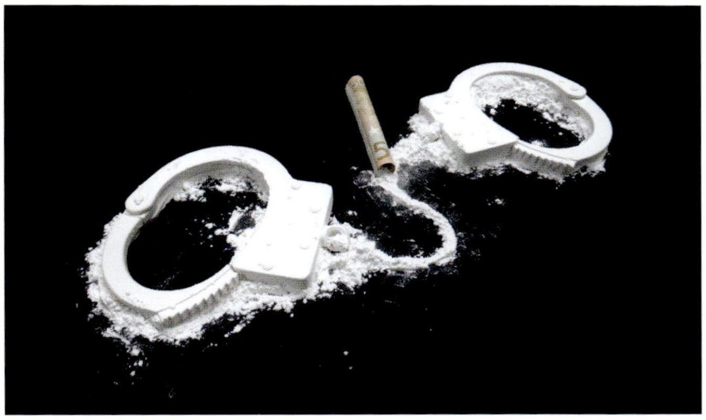

Sniff Your Jail, 2016

Art print on 240 gram matt paper, 30 cm x 40 cm
Print run: 50 copies, 3 A.P.

Kunstprint op 240 gram mat papier, 30 cm x 40 cm
Oplage van de editie: 50 exemplaren, 3 A.P.

Sniff Your Jail, org. Balie Tongeren, curators Paul Morrens, Johan Smets, Justice Palace Tongeren, BE, 14.05.2016-19.06.2016

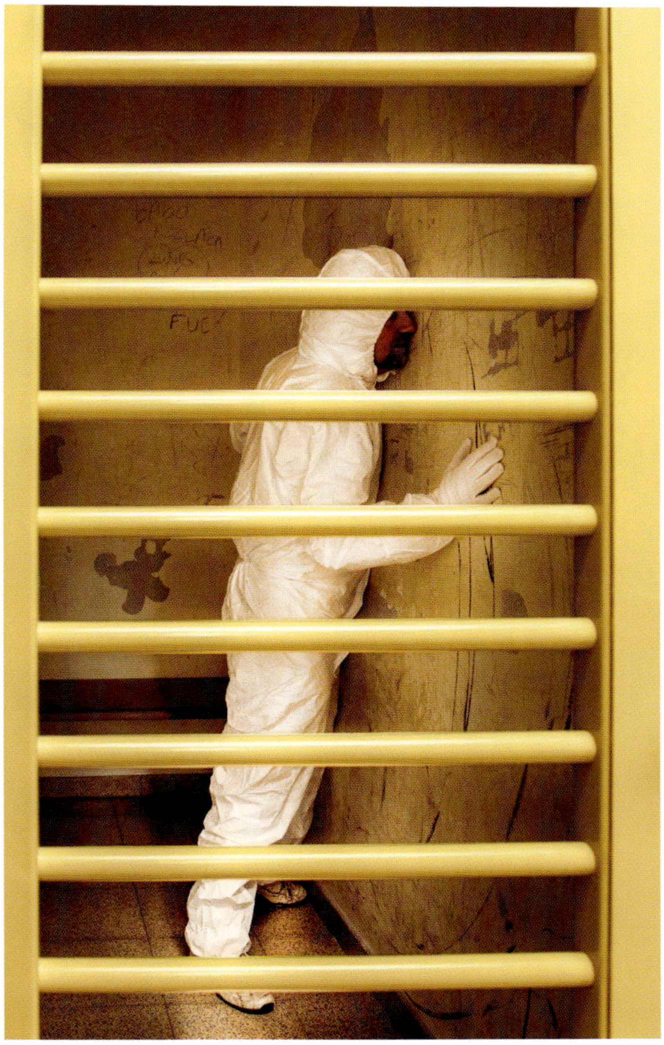

Sniff Your Jail, 2015

Smell-It-Yourself Performance. Sniff the walls and find the smells!
In every jail cell, a different smell is applied to a particular spot which can be discovered only by sniffing the walls and then trying to identify the smell.

Smell-It-Yourself Performance. Ruik aan de muren en zoek de geuren!
In iedere gevangeniscel werd er telkens een andere geur op een bepaalde plaats aangebracht die je alleen maar kunt ontdekken door de muren te besnuffelen en daarna de geur proberen te herkennen.

Sniff Your Jail, org. Balie Tongeren, curators Paul Morrens, Johan Smets, Justice Palace Tongeren, BE, 14.05.2016-19.06.2016

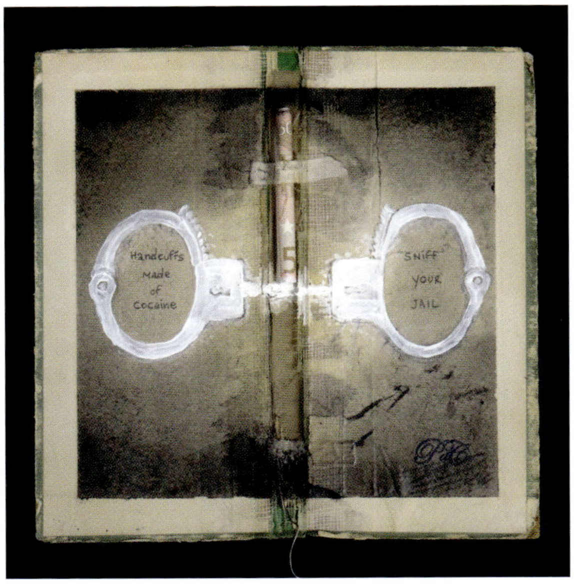

Sniff Your Jail, 2016

Drawing / Tekening

Sniff Your Jail, org. Balie Tongeren, curators Paul Morrens, Johan Smets, Justice Palace Tongeren, BE
14.05.2016-19.06.2016

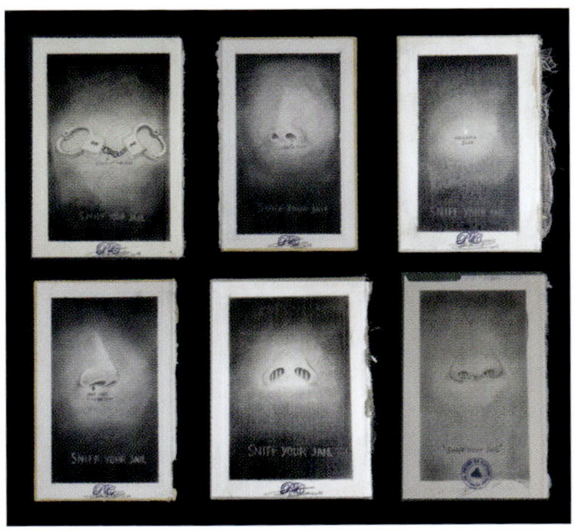

Sniff Your Jail Drawings, 2014

Different drawings on book covers

Diverse tekeningen op covers van boeken

Sniff Your Jail, org. Balie Tongeren, curators Paul Morrens, Johan Smets, Justice Palace Tongeren, BE
14.05.2016-19.06.2016

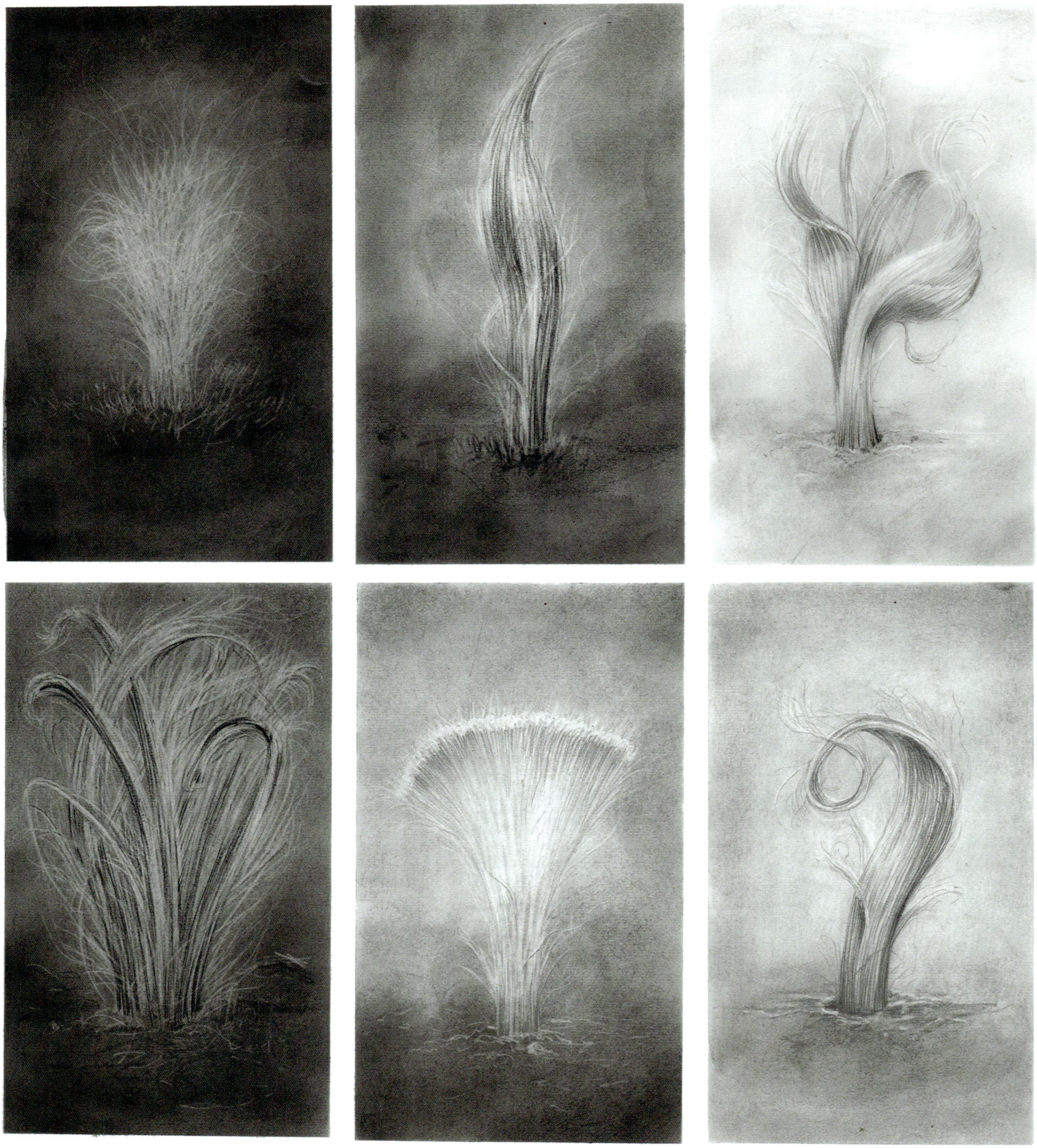

Drawings Hair Flowers, 2016

30 cm x 40 cm

Eens was ik een mens (Is This Mankind), De Warande, curator Annelies Nagels, Turnhout, BE, 10.09.2016-22.01.2017

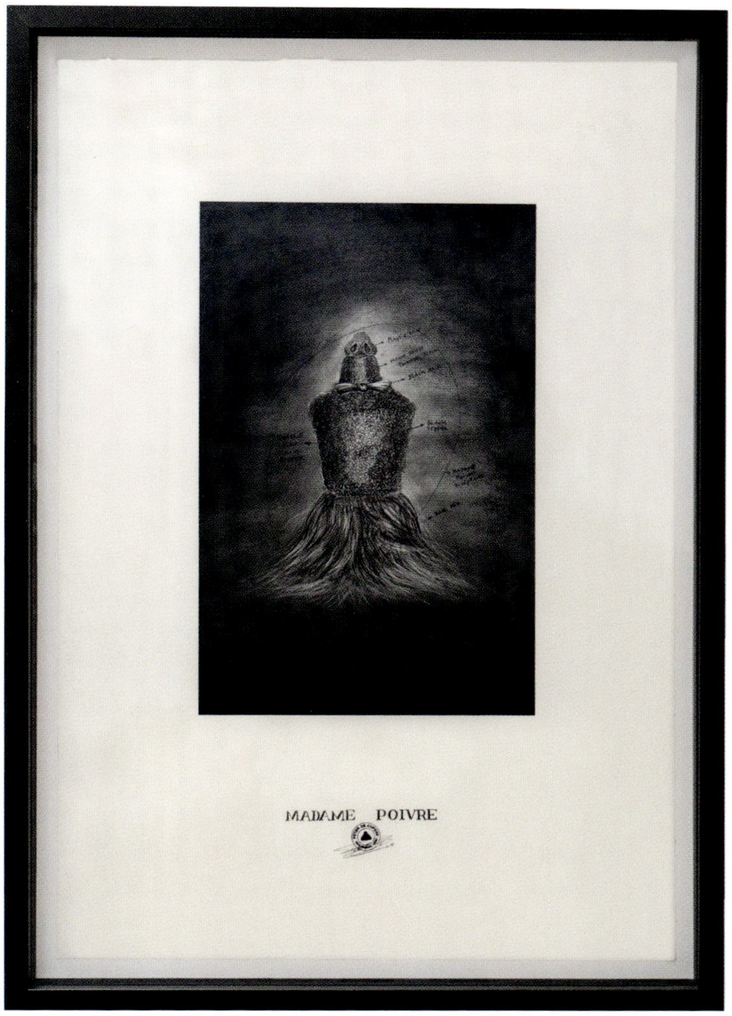

Madame Poivre I, 2016

104 cm x 74 cm

Graphite, charcoal, pencil / Grafiet, houtskool, potlood

Unidentical Twins, Rotary Izegem, curator Gery Van Tendeloo, Kortrijk, BE, 08.09-06.10.2016

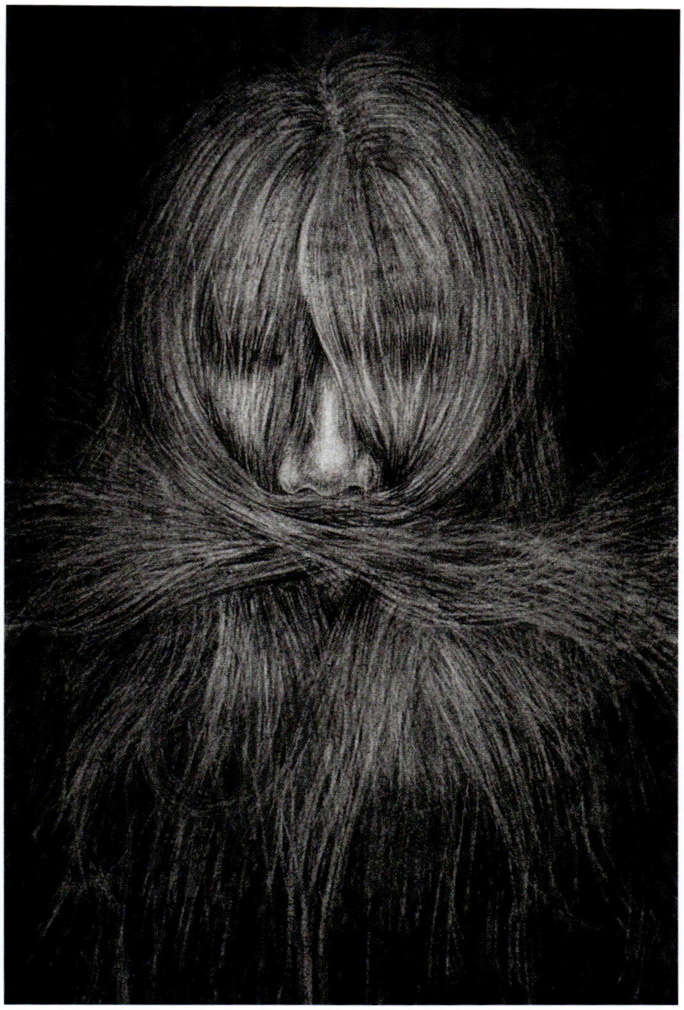

Is this Mankind, 2016

53,5 cm x 34,5 cm

Graphite, charcoal, pencil, pastel / Grafiet houtskool, potlood, pastel

Eens was ik een mens (Is This Mankind), De Warande, curator Annelies Nagels, Turnhout, BE 10.09.2016-22.01.2017

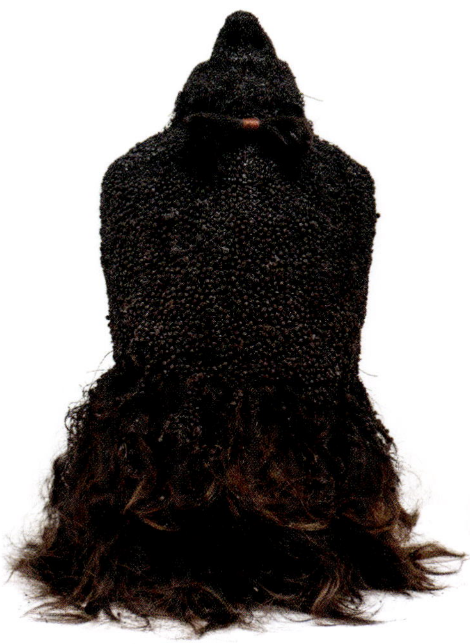

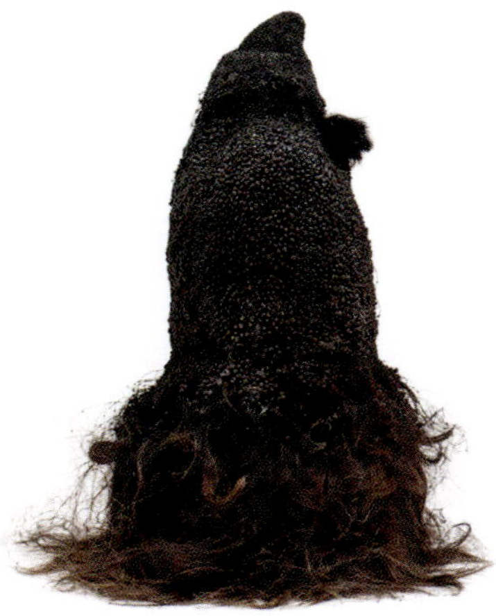

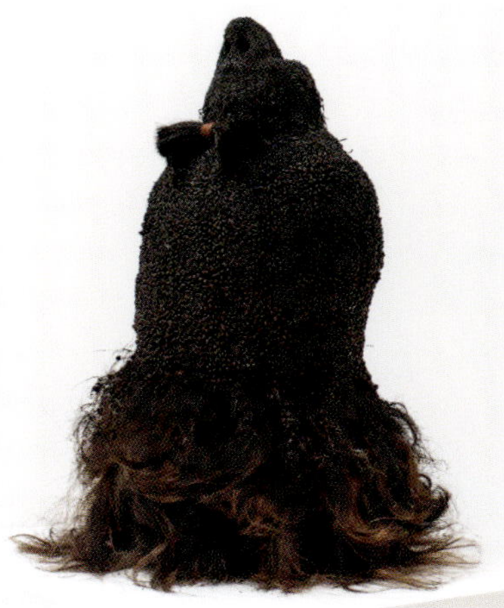

Madame Poivre I, 2016

46 cm x 30 cm x 30 cm

Material: mannequin, hair, black peppercorns, poppy seeds, plastic, paint, glue.
Scent: Strawberry or Madame Rochas Eau de Parfum, Guerlain

Materiaal: pasvorm, haar, zwarte peperbolletjes, maanzaad, plastiek, verf, lijm.
Geur: Aardbei of Madame Rochas Eau de Parfum

Unidentical Twins, Rotary Izegem, curator Gery Van Tendeloo, Kortrijk, BE, 08.09-06.10.2016

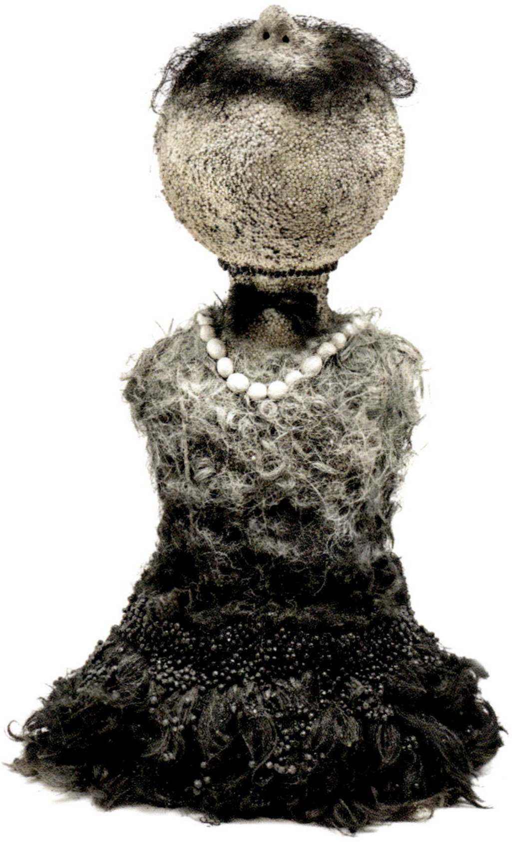

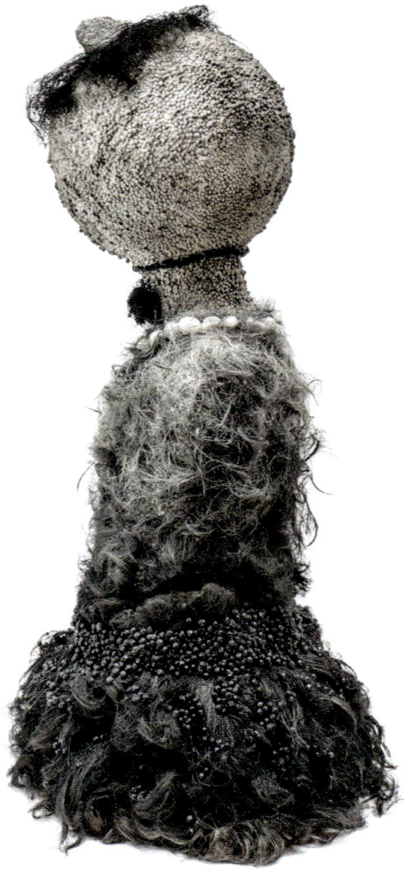

Mme Poivre Blanc, 2016

83 cm x 50 cm x 40 cm
Plexibox: 100 cm x 60 cm x 60 cm

Hair, dressmaker form, nutmeg, white peppercorn, dried juniper, poppy seed, paint. Presented in plexibox with extra holes for smelling
Scent: babypowder, almond, Chanel N° 5 perfume depending on her mood.

Haar, pasvorm, muskaatnoten, witte peperbolletjes, gedroogde jeneverbes, maanzaad, verf. Gepresenteerd onder plexibox met geurgaten
Geur: babypoeder, amandelen of Chanel N° 5 afhankelijk van haar humeur.

Eens was ik een mens (Is This Mankind), De Warande, curator Annelies Nagels, Turnhout, BE, 10.09.2016-22.01.2017

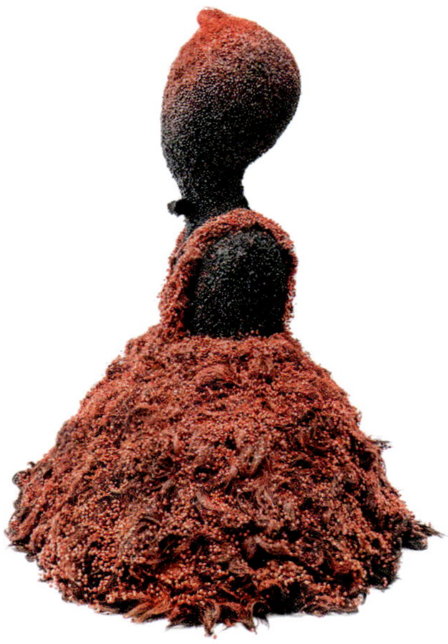

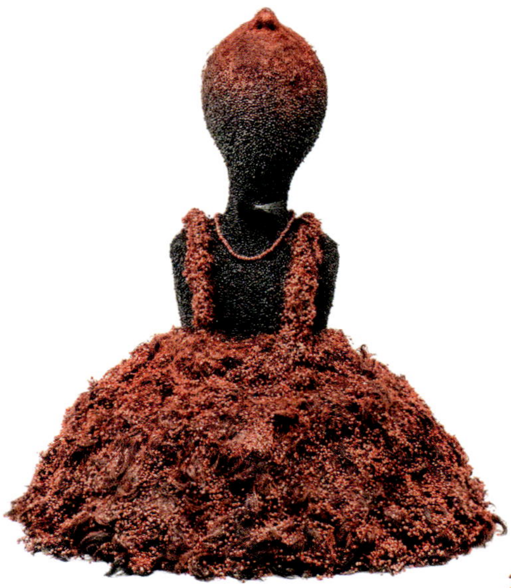

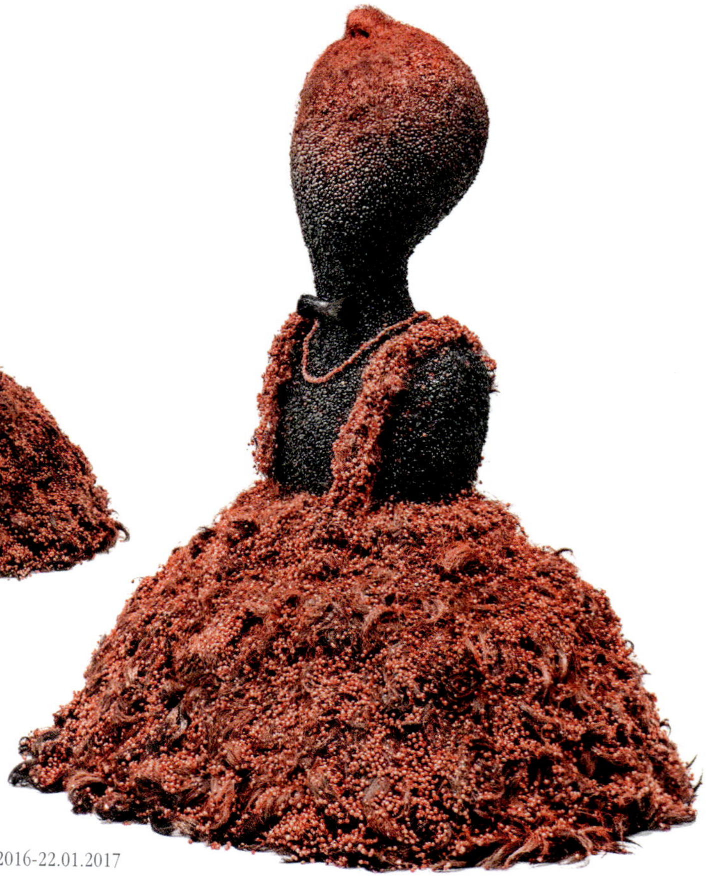

Madame Poivre Rose, 2016

95 cm x 85 cm x 70 cm
Plexibox: 100 cm x 100 cm x 100 cm

Hair, dressmaker form, rose peppercorn, paint. Presented in plexibox with extra holes for smelling
Scent: roses, strawberry or Opium perfume depending on her mood.

Haar, pasvorm, rose peperbolletjes, verf. Gepresenteerd onder plexibox met geurgaten.
Geur: rozen, aardbeien of Opium parfum afhankelijk van haar humeur.

Eens was ik een mens (Is This Mankind), De Warande, curator Annelies Nagels, Turnhout, BE, 10.09.2016-22.01.2017

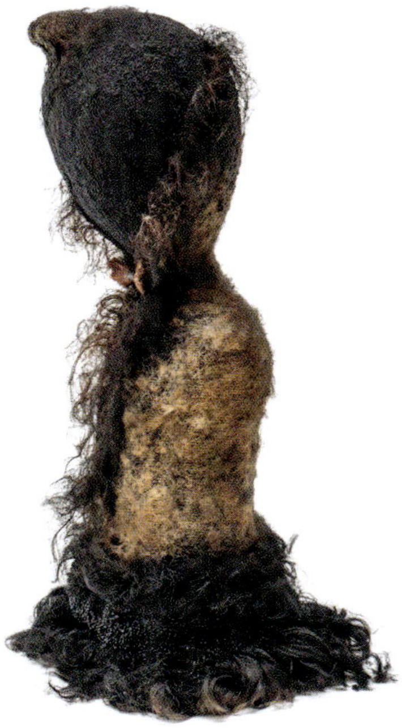
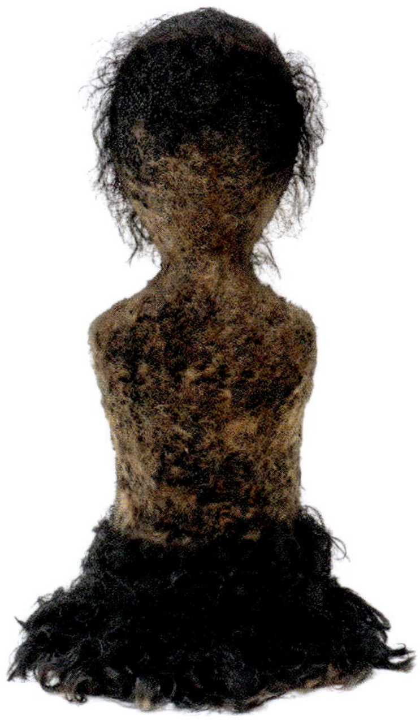
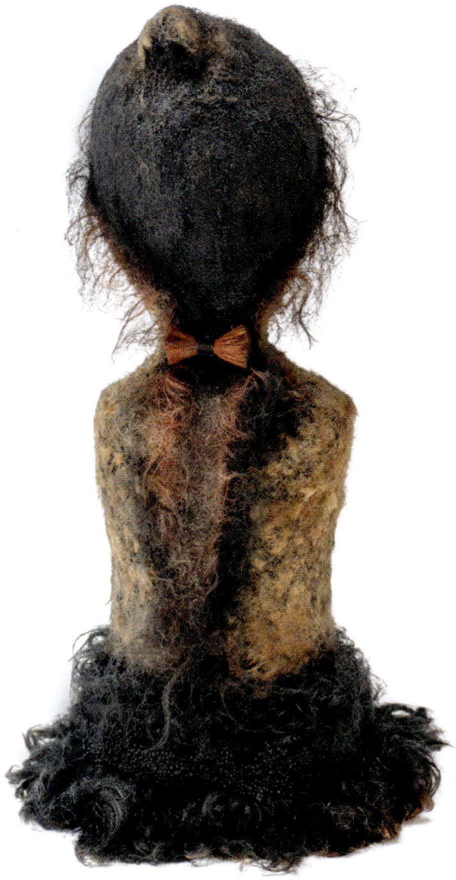

Monsieur Poivre II, 2016

87 cm x 42 cm x 37 cm
Plexibox: 100 cm x 60 cm x 60 cm

Hair, dressmaker form, black peppercorn, poppy seed, paint. Presented in plexibox with extra holes for smelling
Scent: cedarwood or Evolution perfume depending on his mood.

Haar, pasvorm, zwarte peperbolletjes, maanzaad, verf. Gepresenteerd onder plexibox met geurgaten.
Geur: cederhout of parfum Evolution Man afhankelijk van zijn humeur.

Eens was ik een mens (Is This Mankind), De Warande, curator Annelies Nagels, Turnhout, BE, 10.09.2016-22.01.2017

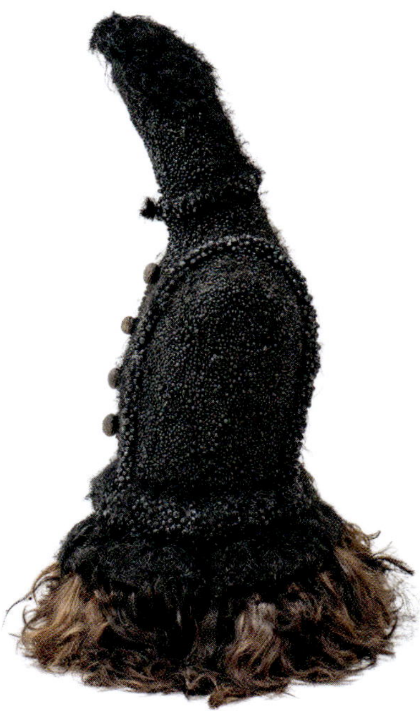
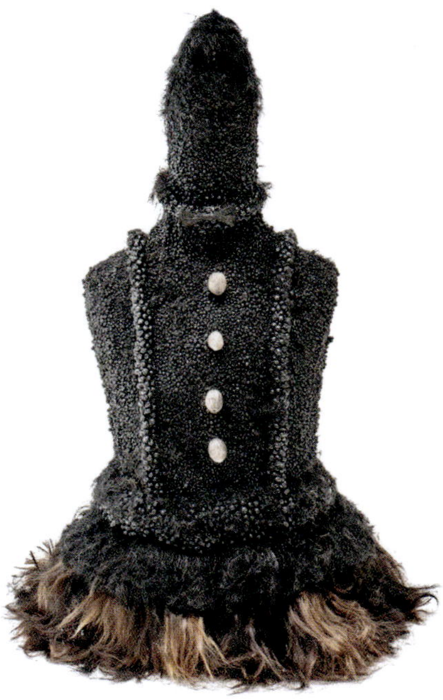
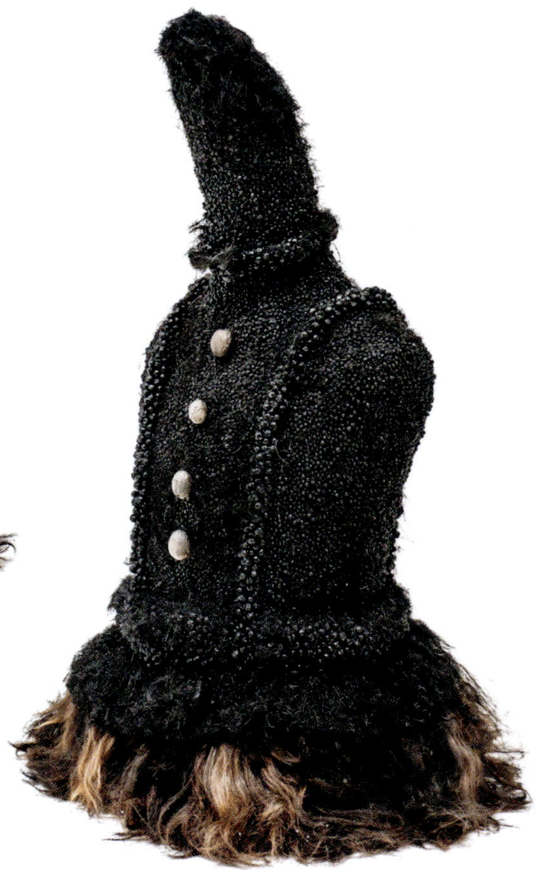

Monsieur Poivre I, 2016

87 cm x 42 cm x 37 cm
Plexibox: 100 cm x 60 cm x 60 cm

Hair, dressmaker form, black peppercorn, poppy seed, paint. Presented in plexibox with extra holes for smelling.
Scent: cedarwood, mushroom or female perfume depending on his mood.

Haar, pasvorm, zwarte peperbolletjes, maanzaad, verf. Gepresenteerd onder plexibox met geurgaten.
Geur: cederhout, paddenstoelen of een vrouwenparfum naargelang zijn humeur.

Eens was ik een mens (Is This Mankind), De Warande, curator Annelies Nagels, Turnhout, BE, 10.09.2016-22.01.2017

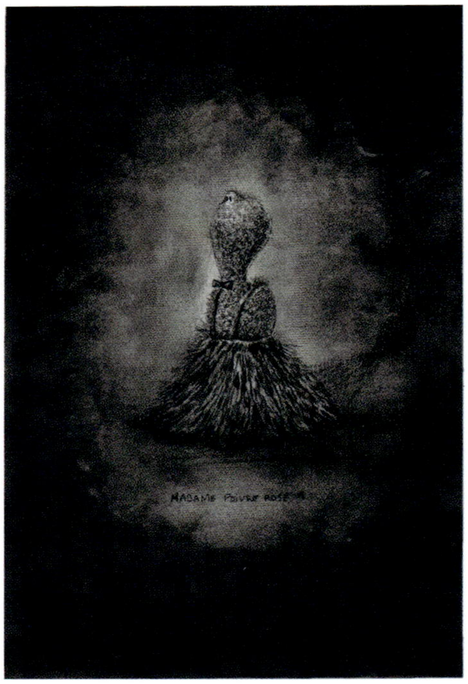

Drawing Madame Poivre Rose I, 2016

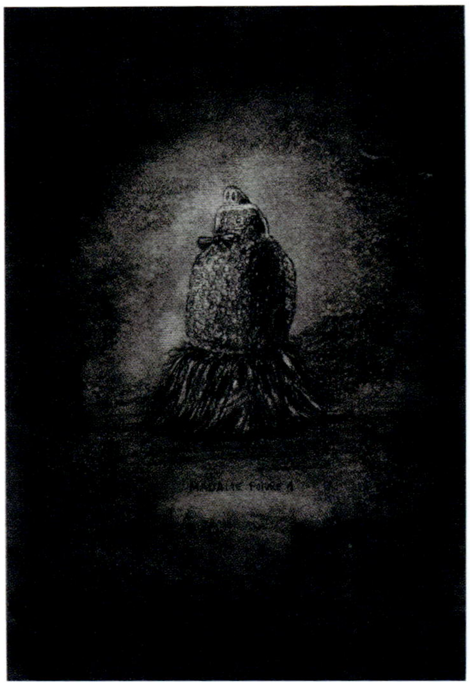

Drawing Madame Poivre I, 2016

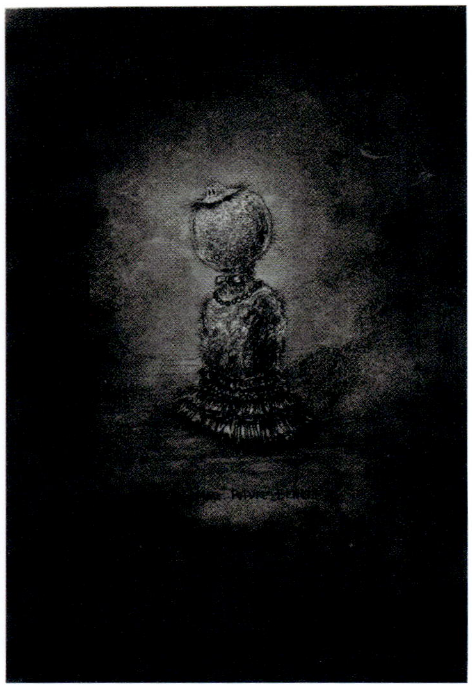

Drawing Mme Poivre Blanc I, 2016

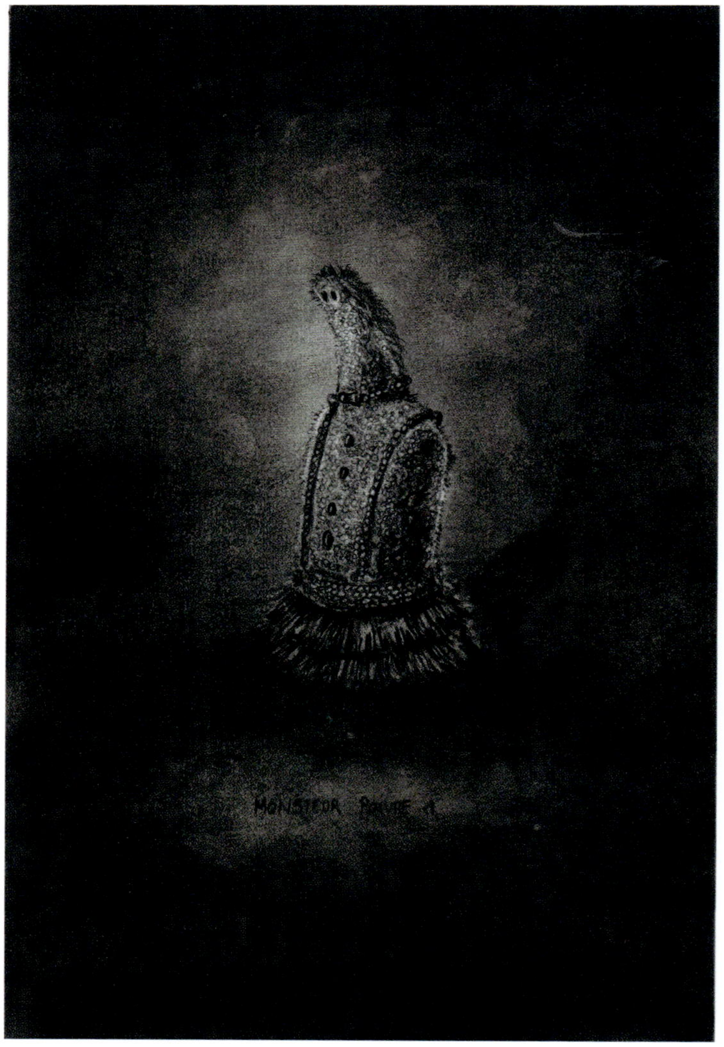

Drawing Monsieur Poivre I, 2016

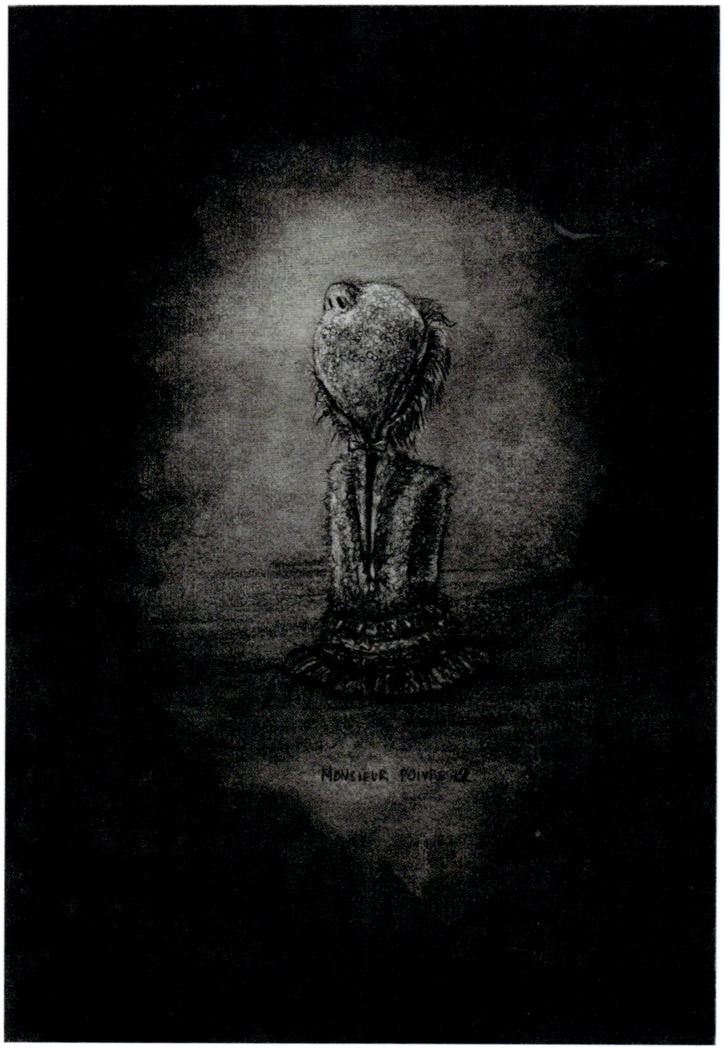

Drawing Monsieur Poivre II, 2016

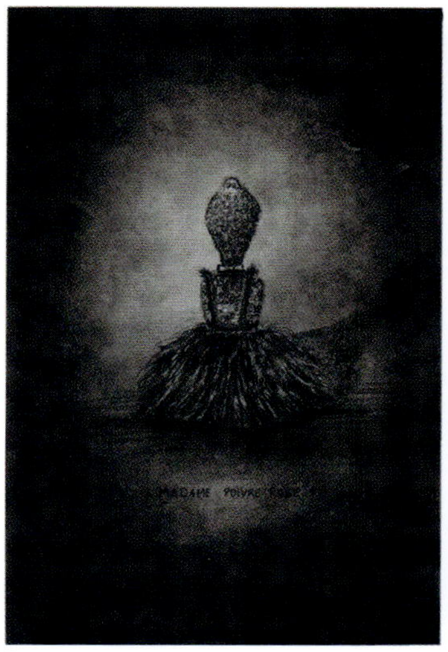
1

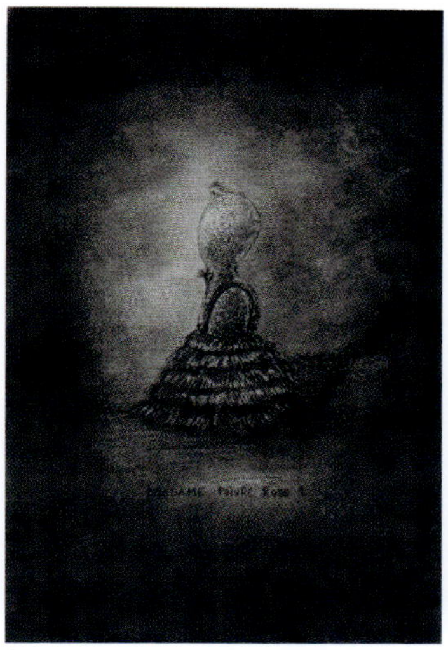
2

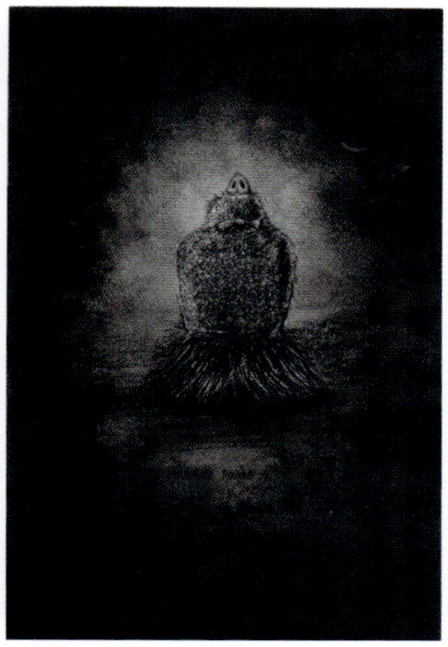
3

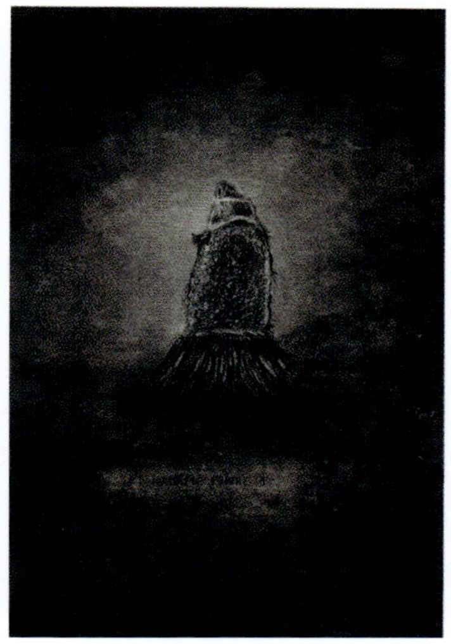
4

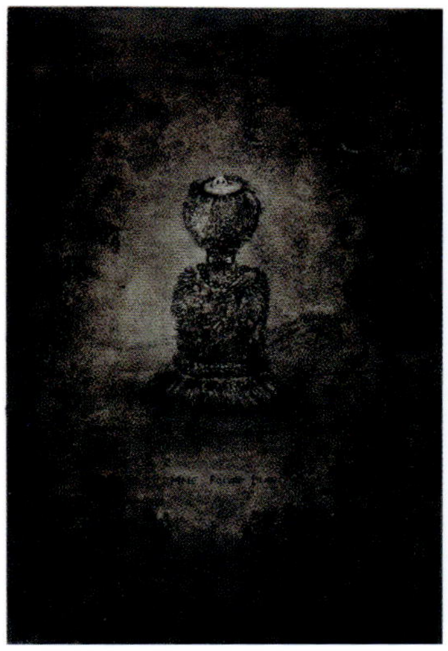
5

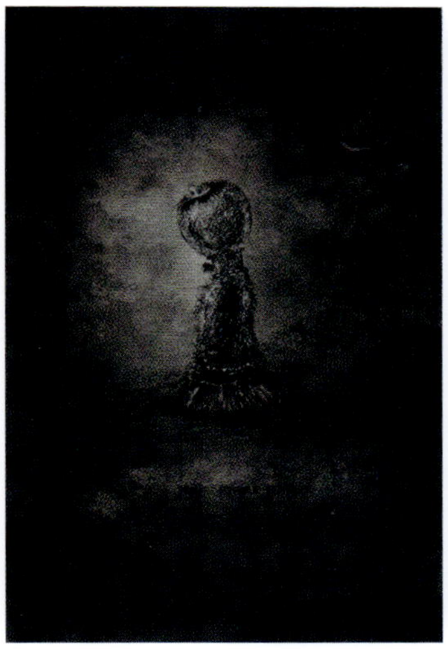
6

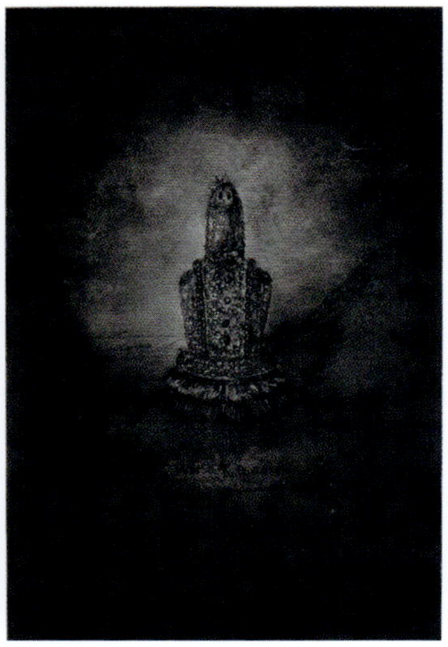
7

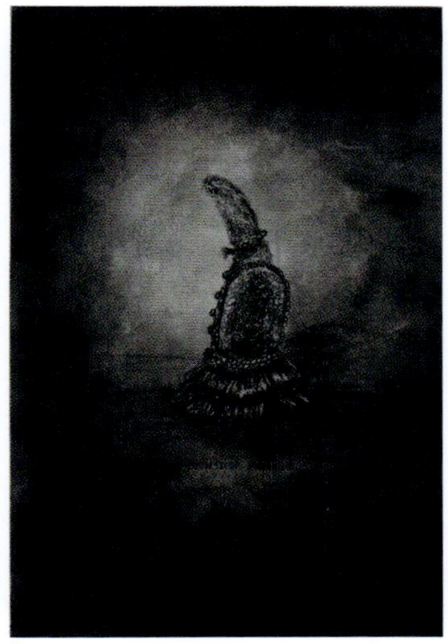
8

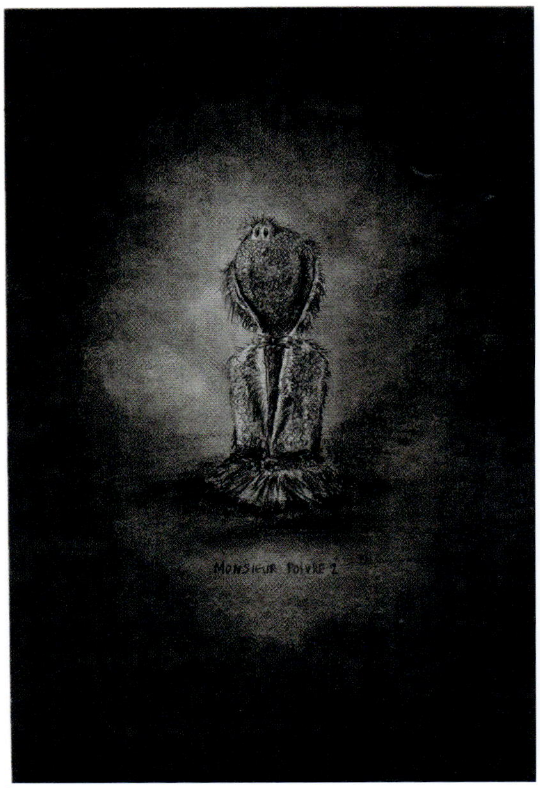

9

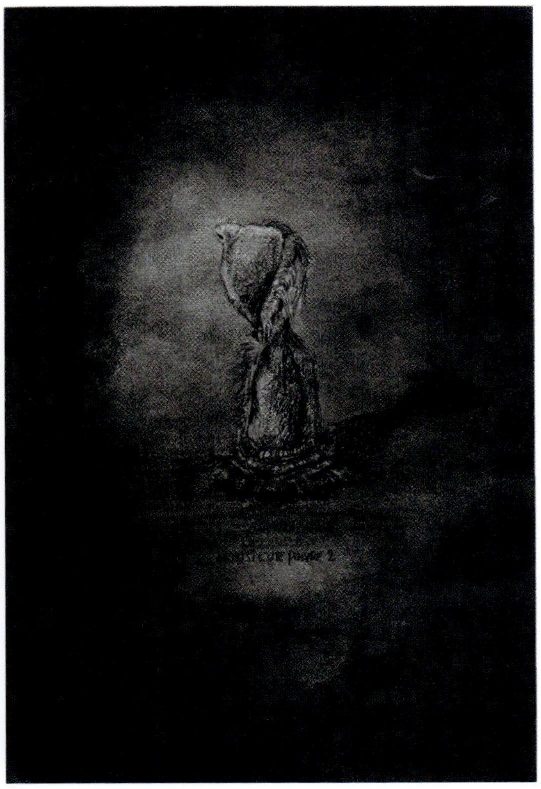
10

1-2

Drawing Madame Poivre Rose I, 2016

3-4

Drawing Madame Poivre I, 2016

5-6

Drawing Mme Poivre Blanc I, 2016

7-8

Drawing Monsieur Poivre I, 2016

9-10

Drawing Monsieur Poivre II, 2016

Eens was ik een mens (Is This Mankind), De Warande, curator Annelies Nagels, Turnhout, BE, 10.09.2016-22.01.2017

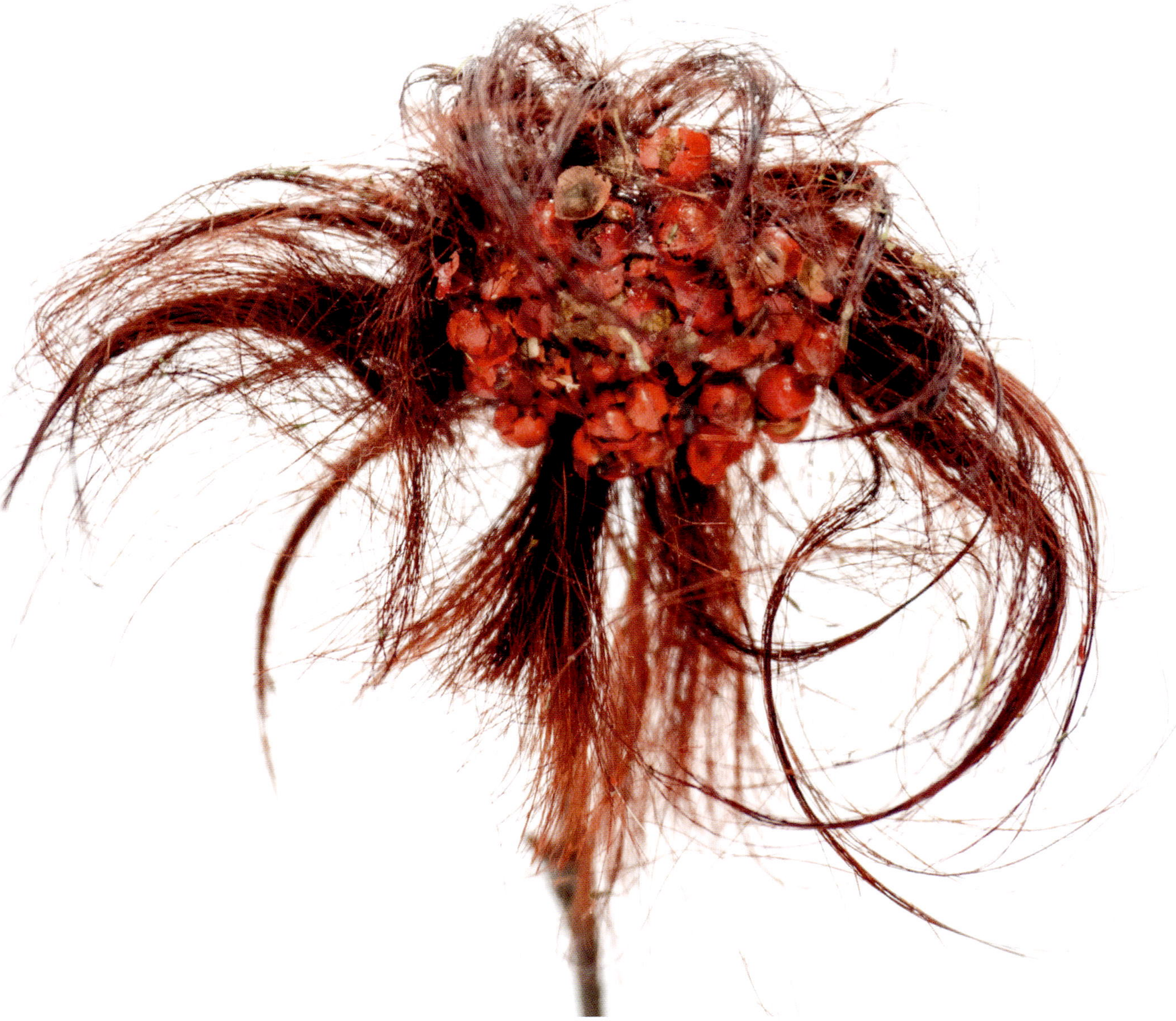

Hair Rose 1 detail, 2016

Stalk of roses, epoxy, hair, rose peppercorn, dill, paint, scent of roses

Rozensteel, epoxy, haar, roze peperbolletjes, dille, verf, rozengeur

Eens was ik een mens (Is This Mankind), De Warande, curator Annelies Nagels, Turnhout, BE, 10.09.2016-22.01.2017

Selection of a series of 31 Soft Memory Drawings

Eens was ik een mens (Is This Mankind), De Warande,
curator Annelies Nagels, Turnhout, BE
10.09.2016-22.01.2017

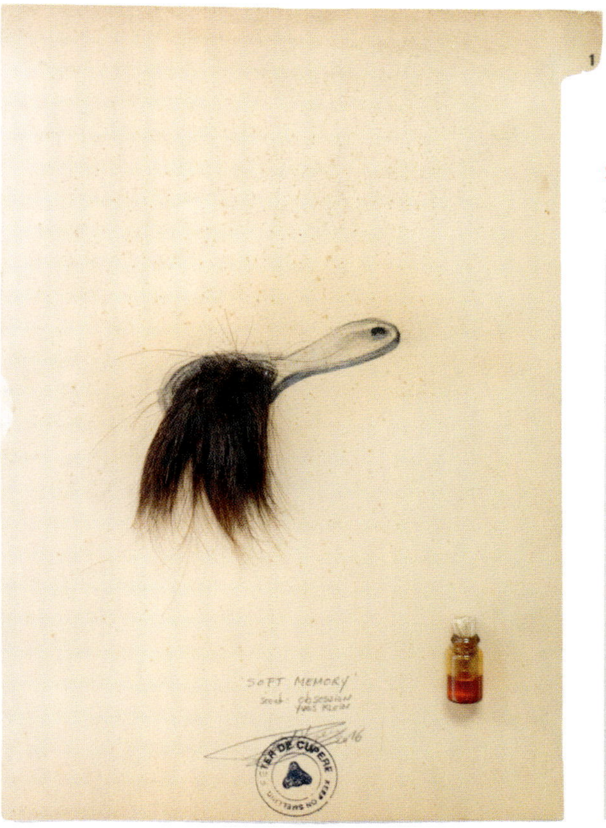

Soft Memory, Obsession, Calvin Klein, 2016

22 cm x 30,5 cm

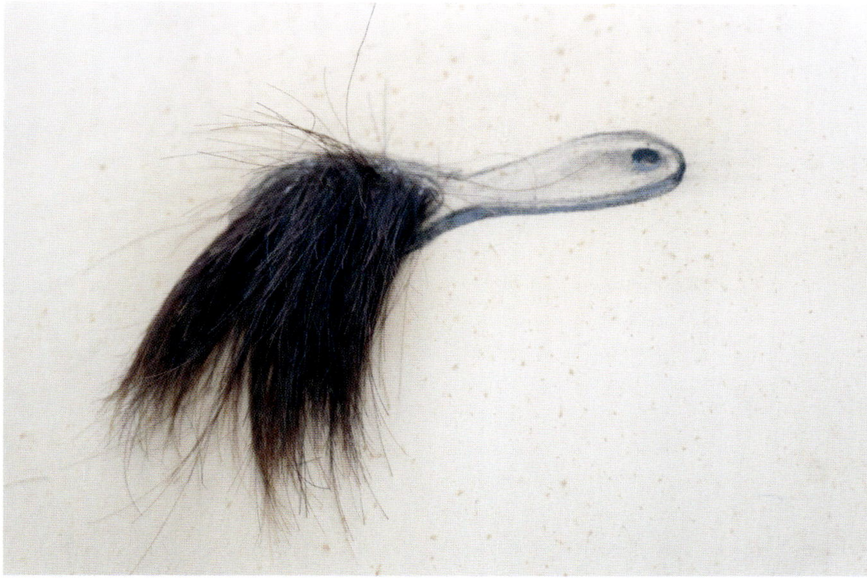

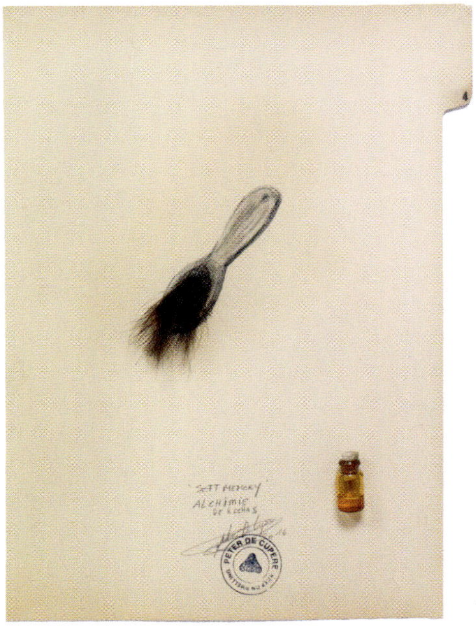

Soft Memory, Alchemie de Rochas, 2016

22 cm x 30,5 cm

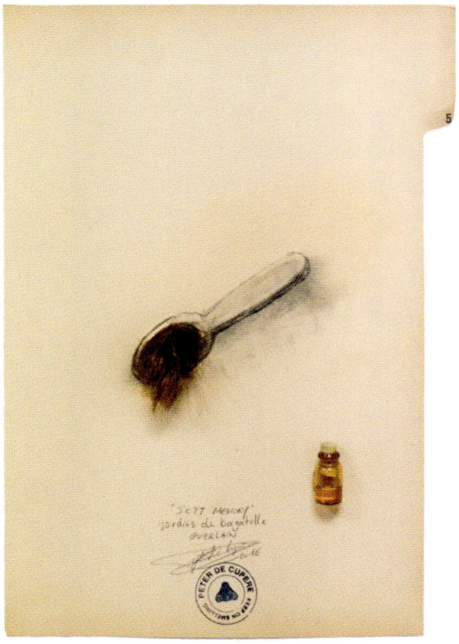

Soft Memory, Jardins de Bagatelle, Geurlain, 2016

22 cm x 30,5 cm

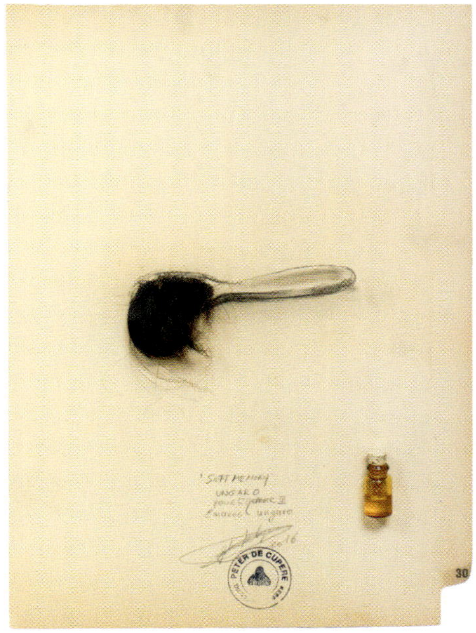

Soft Memory, Ungara pour Homme III, Emanuel Ungaro, 2016

22 cm x 30,5 cm

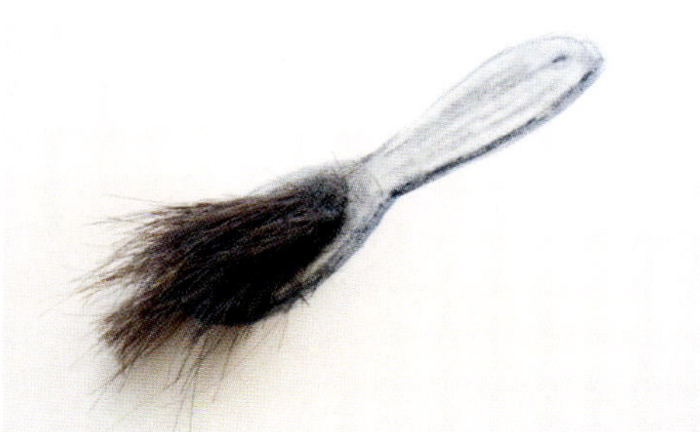

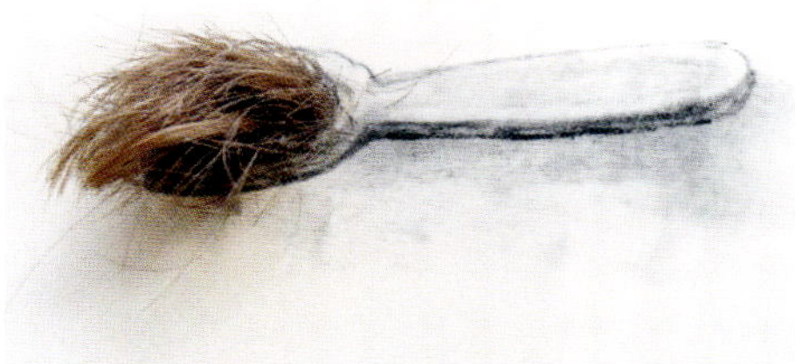

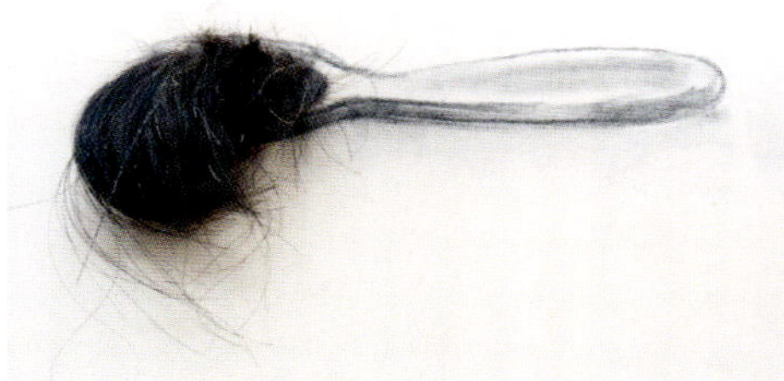

PETER DE CUPERE

ECOLOGY & SUSTAINABILITY
Duurzaamheid & Ecologie

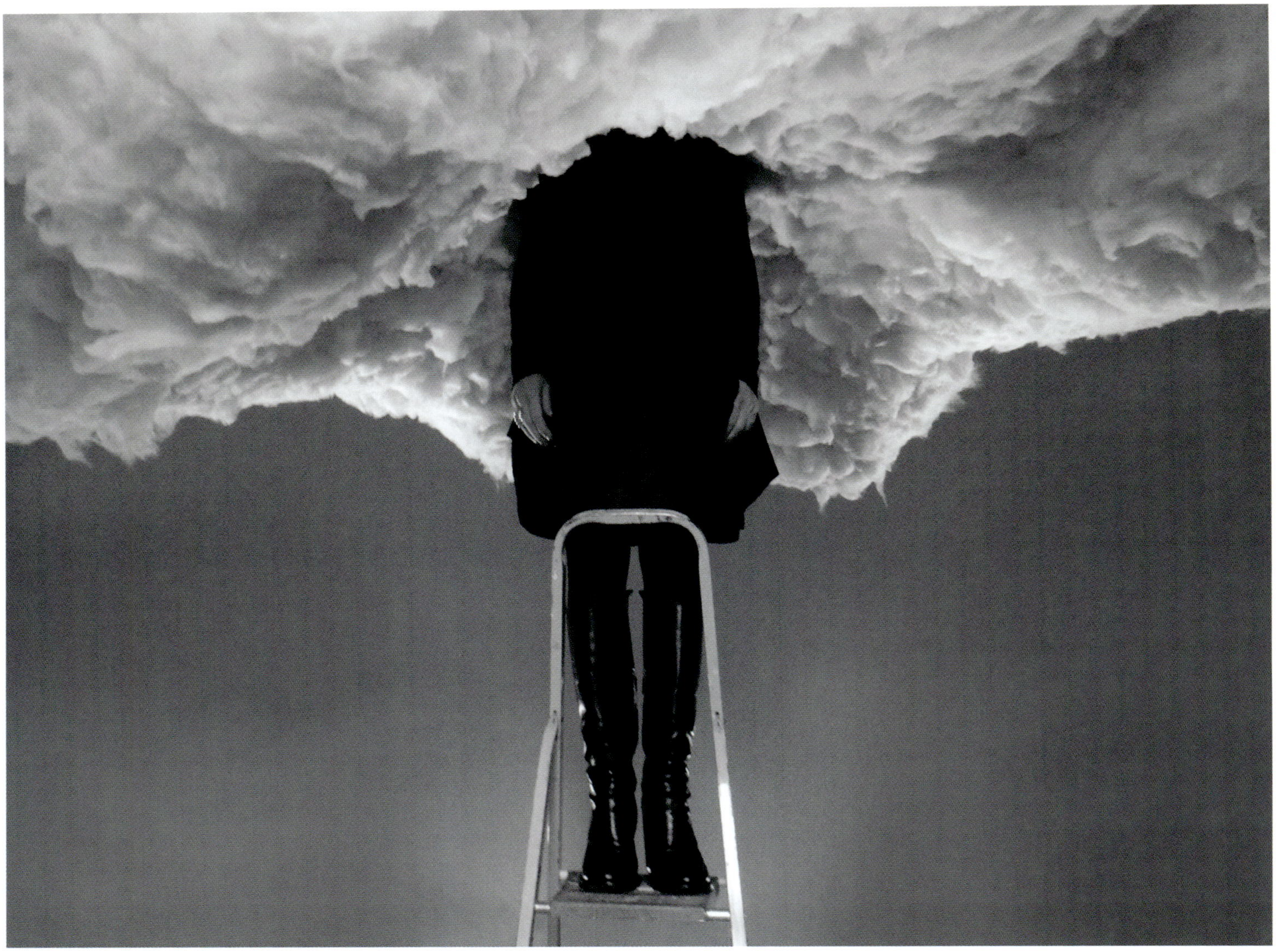

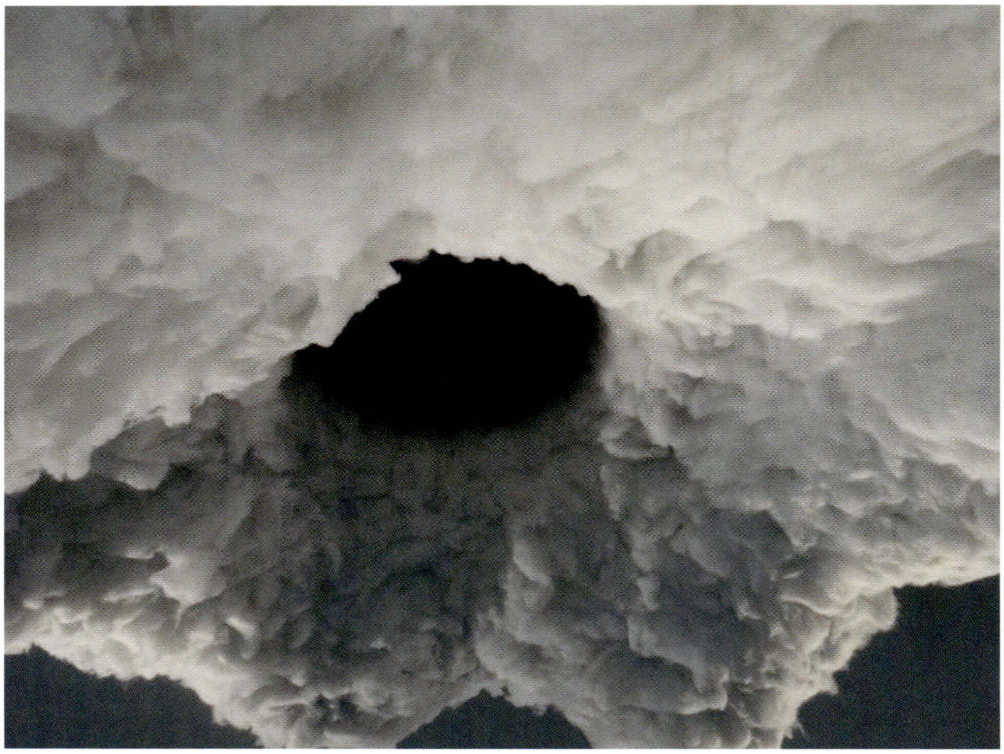

Smoke Cloud, 2013

Synthetic white cotton, polyester, epoxy, wood, metal, ladder, theater cables. Smell of air pollution and smoke.

Synthetische witte watten, polyester, epoxy, hout, metaal, ladder, beveiligingskabels. Geur van luchtverontreiniging of rook.

The Importance of Being..., Museu de Arte Moderna, curator Sara Alonso Gómez, organized by Bruno Devos, Rio de Janeiro, BR, 16.12.2015-28.02.2016
The Importance of Being, Museo de Arte Contemporáneo, curator Sara Alonso Gómez, organized by Bruno Devos, Buenos Aires, AR, 17.07.2015-04.10.2015
The Importance of Being, Museo Nacional de Bellas Artes, curator Sara Alonso Gómez, organized by Bruno Devos, Havana, CU, 13.02.2015-26.04.2015
The Art of Smelling, Olfactory Art Research, Art Center Rozendaal 21, curator Yasmijn Jarram, Enschede, NL 01.12.2013-02.03.2014

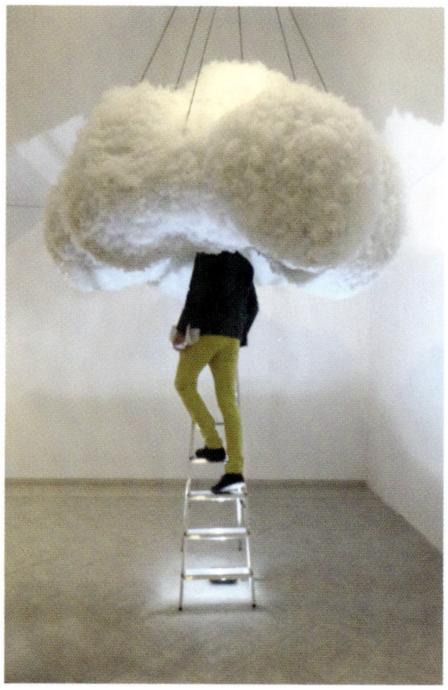

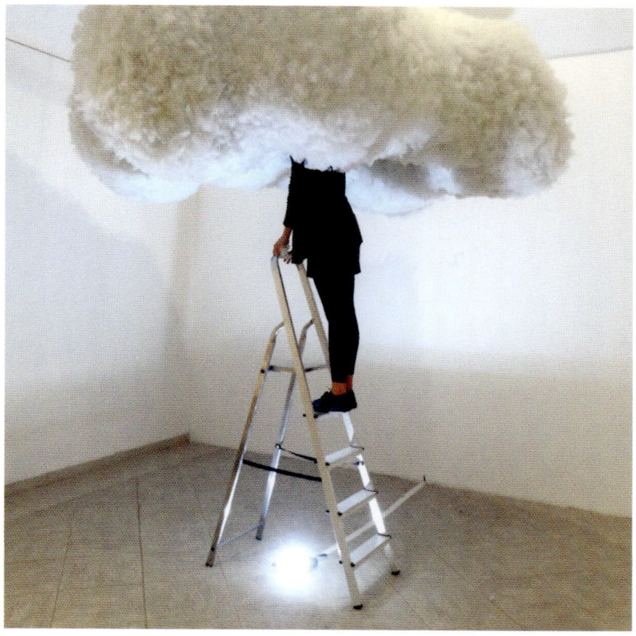

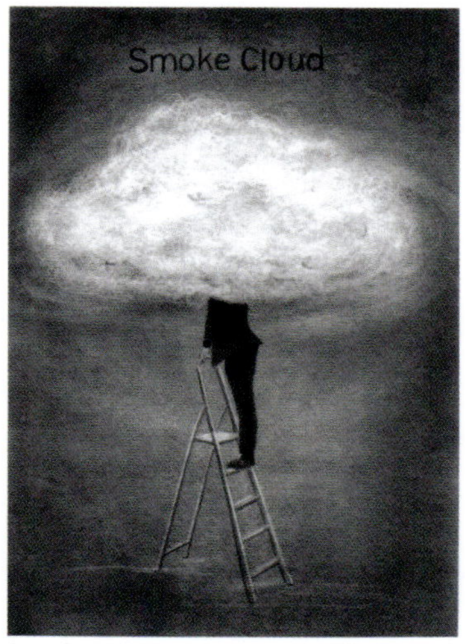

Smoke Cloud Edition, 2015

23,5 cm x 30,3 cm

Edition for the exhibition
The Importance of Being...

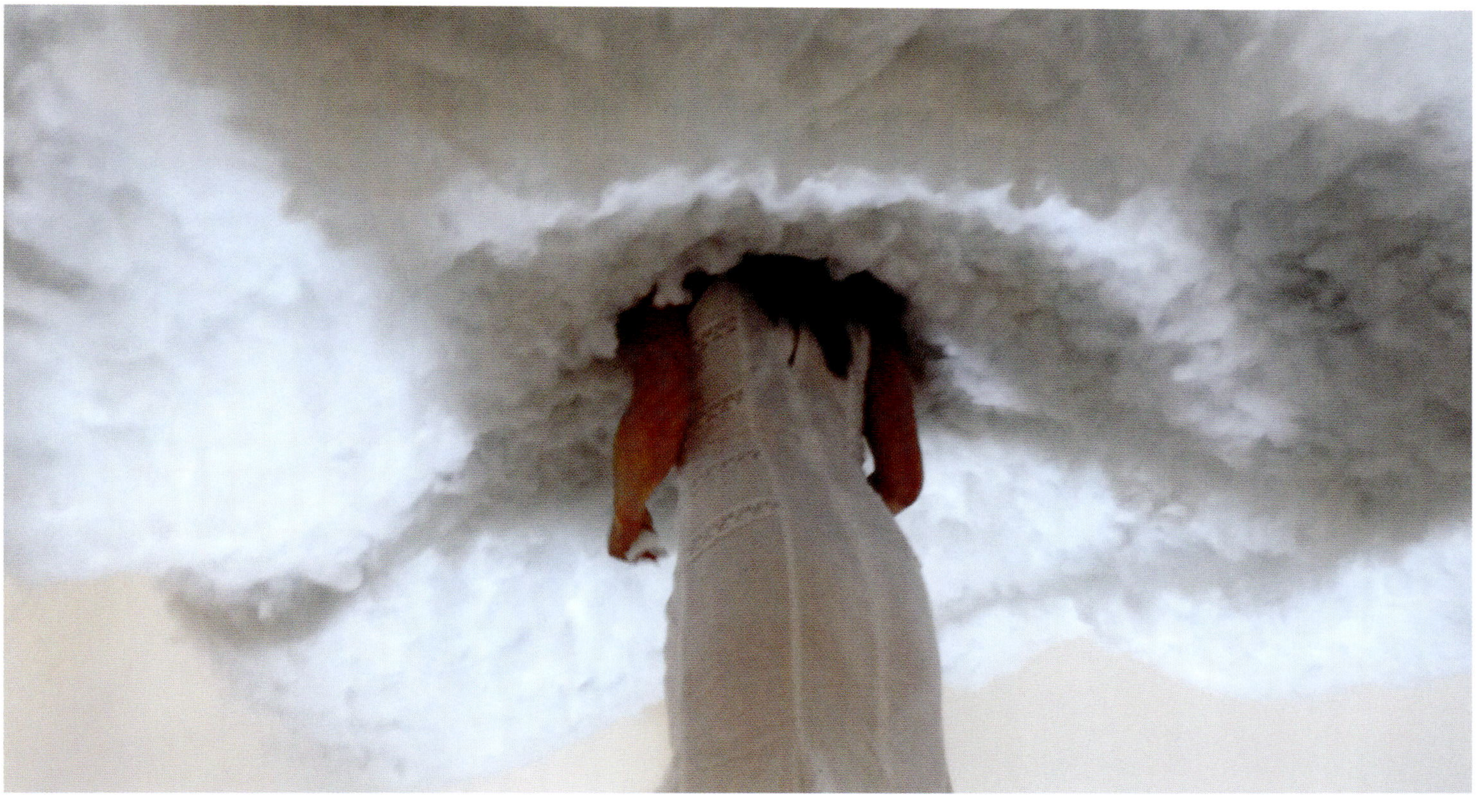

Drawings Smoke Cloud, 2015

40 cm x 30 cm

Graphite, charcoal, pencil

Grafiet, houtskool, potlood

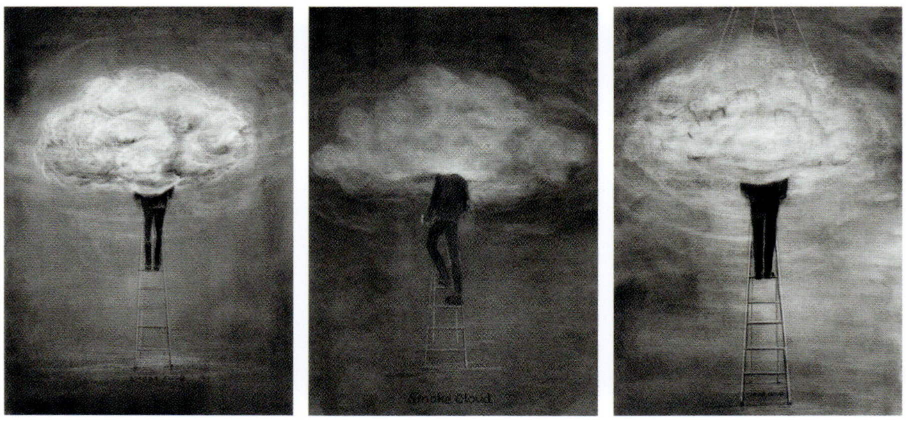

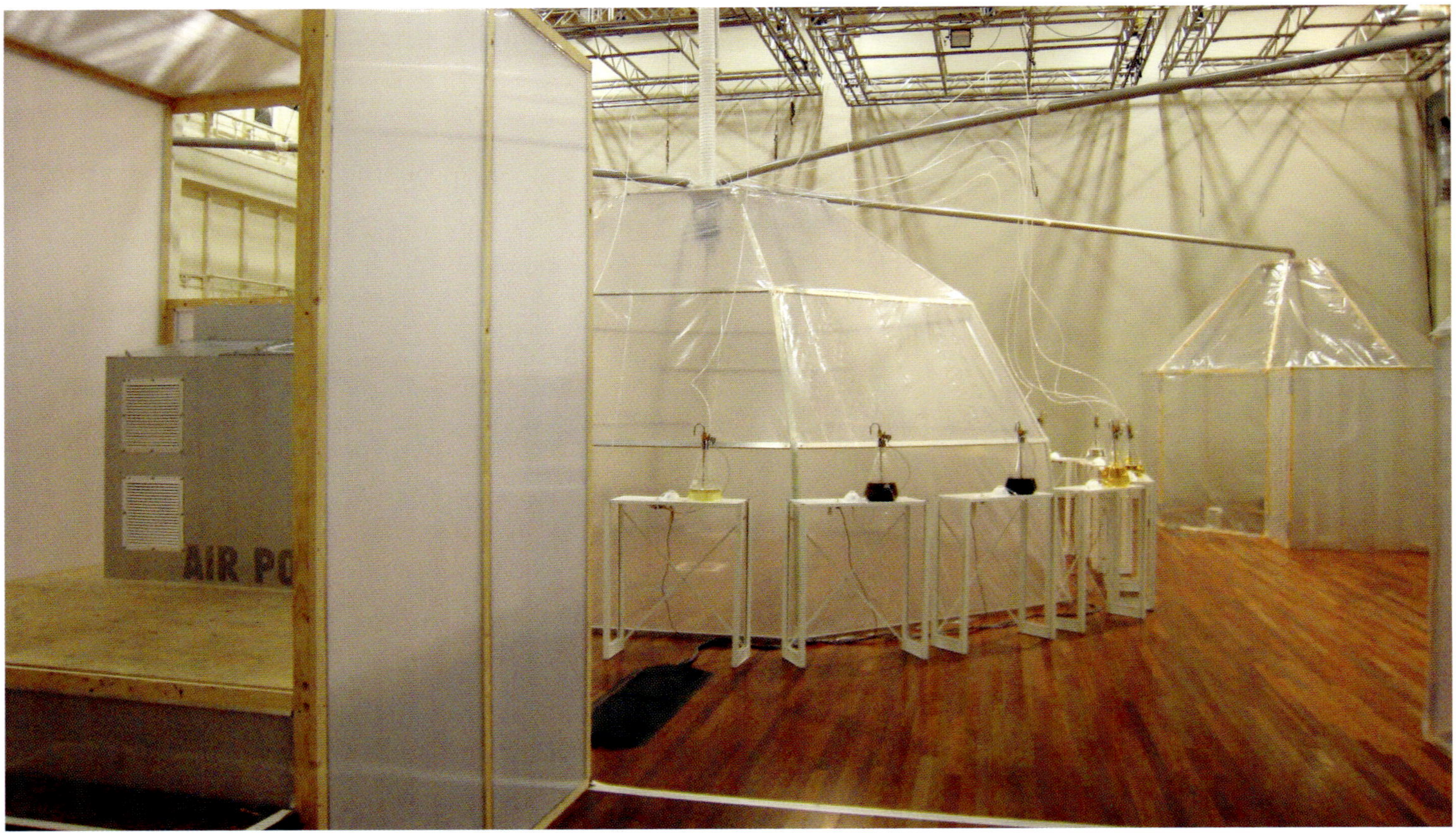

Air Polluter, 2007

Air Polluter is an interactive smell installation on a surface of 20 by 20 metres. Via a control panel at the beginning of the installation, one can activate both good and bad smells. These can later be changed within the installation itself.

When you enter the exhibition, you are given a balloon that can be filled with the combined smells at the end of the smell installation. Since other visitors can activate or deactivate smells as well, the visitor has only limited control over the final result. In addition to the control room and the large hemisphere where people can fill their balloon with the mix of scents, there are four more biospheres connected to the large hemisphere via Air Floating Tubes. Around the large hemisphere stand the Smell Distributors.

They give off the selected smells. They are large Erlenmeyer flasks of 5 litres, filled with scent from which the smells are pushed via a smell activator along a centrally controlled magnetic valve and aereator towards the Air Floating Tubes. The visitor can smell each scent at its Smell Distributor. Here the visitor also has the possibility of activating or deactivating a smell.

In Biosphere I the visitors themselves are responsible for deciding whether or not the watercress receives sufficient water. They can add cotton wads along wire in the air and plant fresh watercress. The cress grows very quickly on cotton wads. A few days later, the cress is fully grown and ready to eat. If the watercress does not receive sufficient water, or if it is left to dry out, it begins to smell bad.

In Biosphere II there is a racing bike. The temperature in this biosphere is higher. If the visitor rides intensively on the racing bike, the smell of his or her sweat mingles with the rest of the smell combination.

In Biosphere III a car exhaust pipe is set up and connected to a smoke machine. Visitors can decide how much smoke should be generated.

In Bioshere IV there is a plastic greenhouse to which fertiliser pellets have been added. The greenhouses can be opened and closed to determine how much they will be aerated in order to mix the unpleasant smell with the rest of the smell combination.

The interaction of the visitor and the smell experience is very important. By being able to determine the extent to which the air will be contaminated, visitors may stop and think about air pollution in general, and in particular the problem of foul smells.

Air Polluter is een interactieve geurinstallatie op een oppervlakte van 20 bij 20 meter. Via een controlepaneel bij het begin van de installatie kan men zowel goede als slechte geuren activeren. In de installatie zelf kan men nog wijzigingen aanbrengen.

Bij het binnenkomen van de tentoonstelling krijgt men een ballon die gevuld kan worden met de samengestelde geuren bij het eindpunt van de geurinstallatie. Daar andere bezoekers ook de mogelijkheid hebben om geuren te activeren of te deactiveren heeft de bezoeker slechts een beperkte controle over het uiteindelijke resultaat.

Naast de controleruimte en de grote hemisfeer waar men de ballon met de geurmix kan vullen, zijn er nog vier biosferen welke met de grote hemisfeer verbonden zijn via Air Floating Tubes. Rond de grote hemisfeer staan de Smell Distributors. Zij leveren de geselecteerde geuren. Het zijn grote Erlenmeyers van 5 L gevuld met geurstof waarbij de geur via een geuractivator, een centraal gestuurd magnetisch ventiel en beluchting naar de Air Floating Tubes wordt geleid. De bezoeker kan bij iedere Smell Distributor de desbetreffende geur ruiken. Hier heeft de bezoeker ook de mogelijkheid om een geur te activeren of terug te deactiveren.

In Biosphere I neemt de bezoeker zelf verantwoordelijkheid of de tuinkers (cresson) voldoende water krijgt of niet. Op draden in de lucht kan men zelf watten aanbrengen en nieuwe tuinkers planten. Tuinkers groeit snel op watten. Na een paar dagen is tuinkers al volgroeid en geschikt voor consumptie. Wanneer men tuinkers niet voldoende water geeft of laat uitdrogen begint deze onaangenaam te ruiken.

In Biosphere II staat een koersfiets. Biosphere II is extra verwarmd. Door intens op de koersfiets te rijden kan zo de zweetgeur van de bezoeker mee opgenomen worden in de geurcompositie.

In Biosphere III staat een uitlaatpijp van een auto opgesteld verbonden met een rookmachine. Men kan hier bepalen hoeveel rook er wordt gecreëerd.

In Bioshere IV is een opstelling van plastieken kweekserres waarin mestkorrels werden aangebracht. De kweekserres kunnen open en dicht gezet worden om te bepalen in hoeverre ze belucht worden om de onaangename geur ervan mee op te nemen in de geurcompositie.

De interactie van de bezoeker en de geurbeleving zijn heel belangrijk. Door de bezoeker mee te laten bepalen hoe de lucht verontreinigd zal worden, staat men waarschijnlijk meer stil bij het probleem van luchtverontreiniging en meer bepaald bij het aspect van geurhinder.

Air Polluter, De Brakke Grond, curator Fleurie Kloostra, Amsterdam, NL, 09.06-15.07.2007

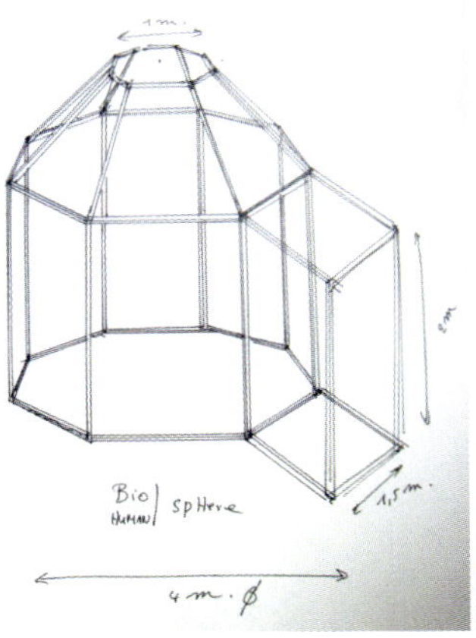

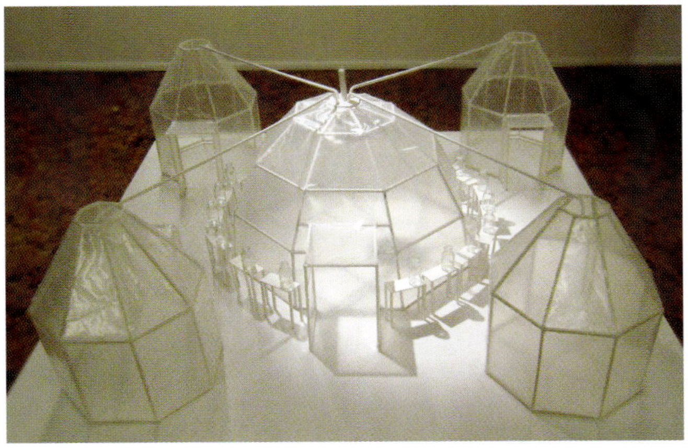

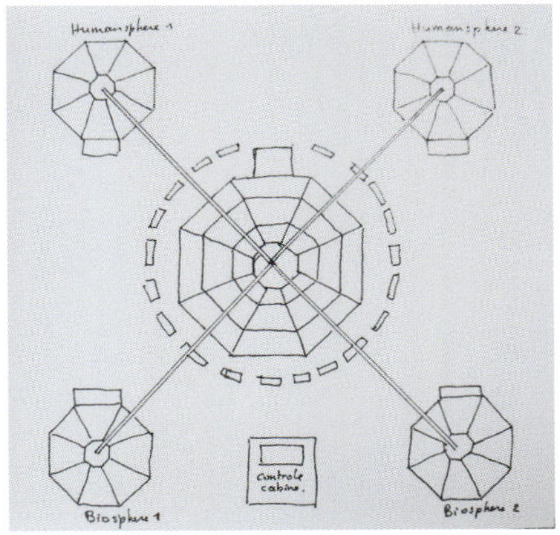

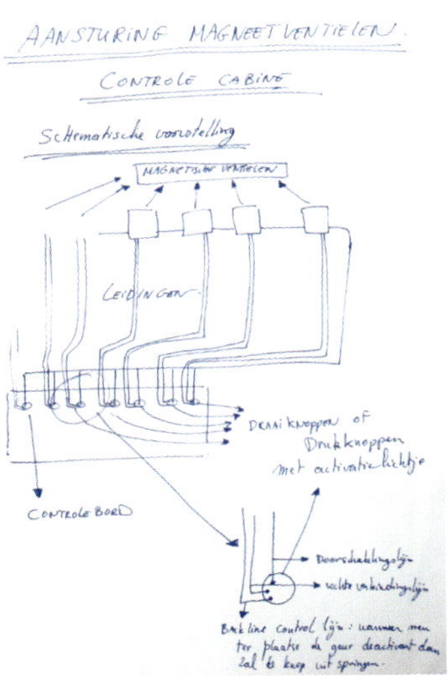

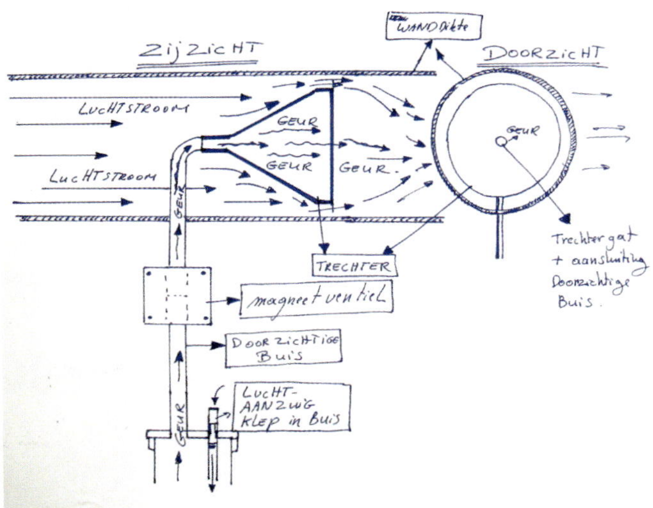

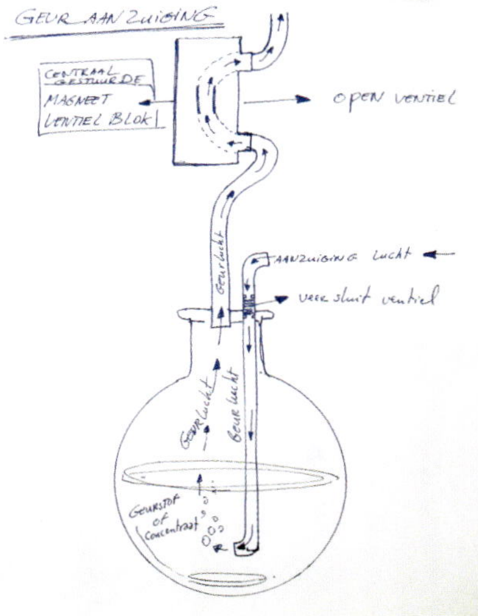

Concept Sketches & Model of Air Polluter, 2007

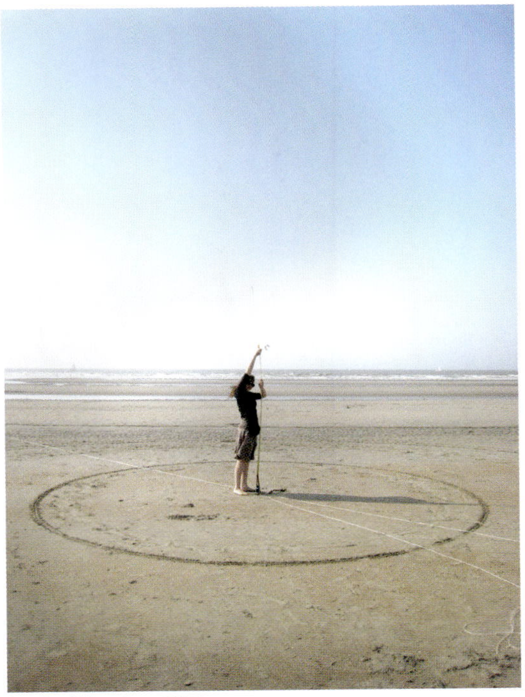

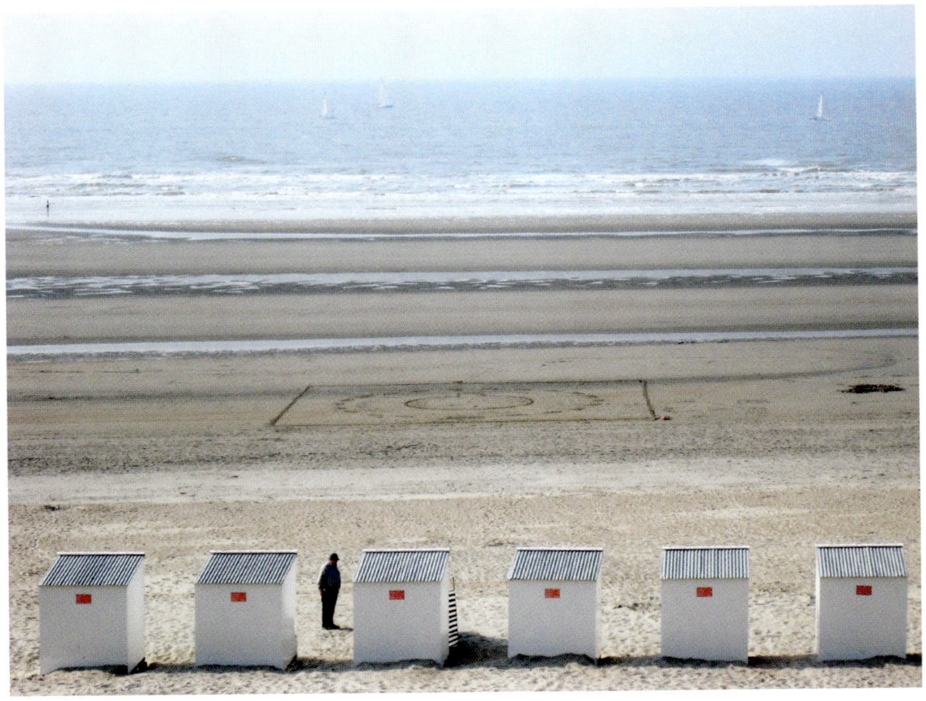

Sea Sand Drawings, 2007

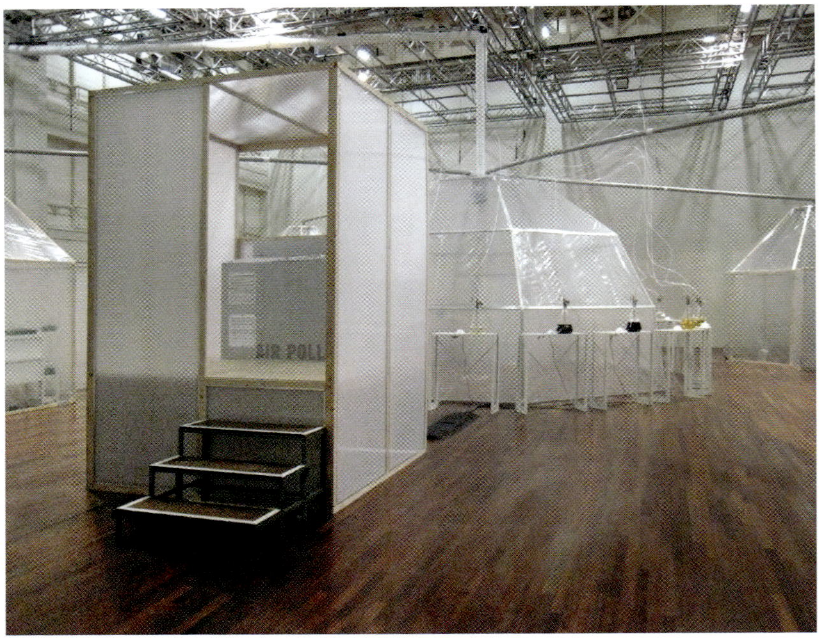

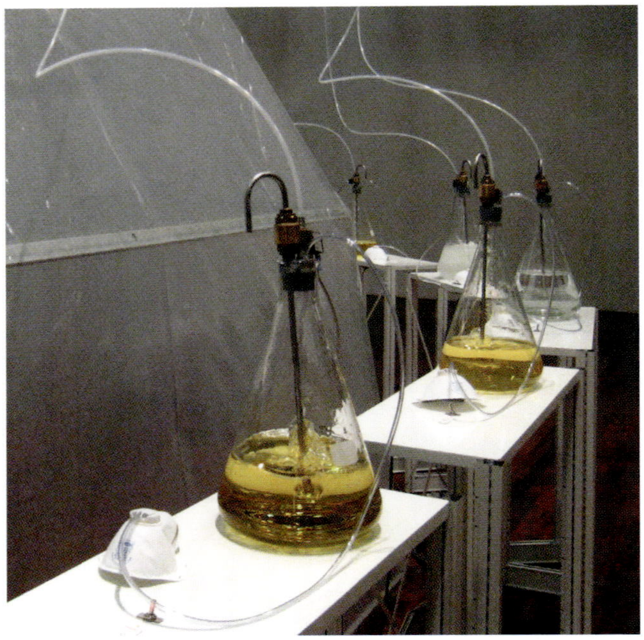

Smell Distributors

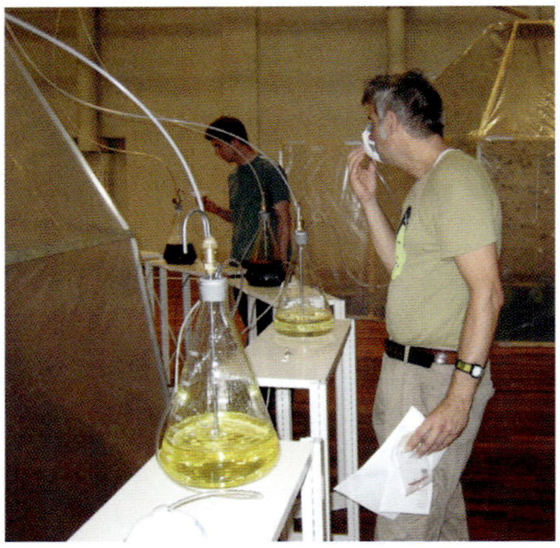

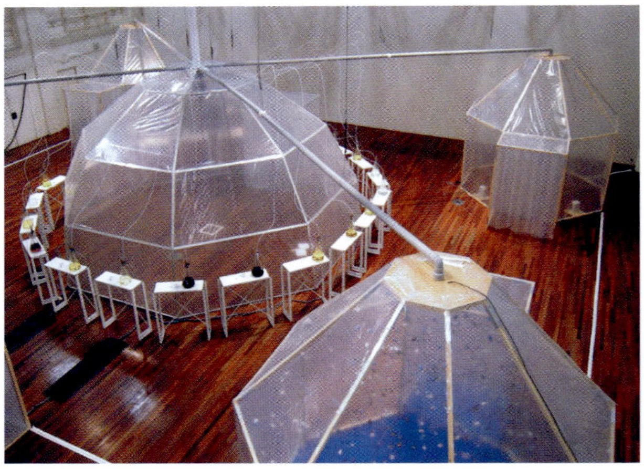

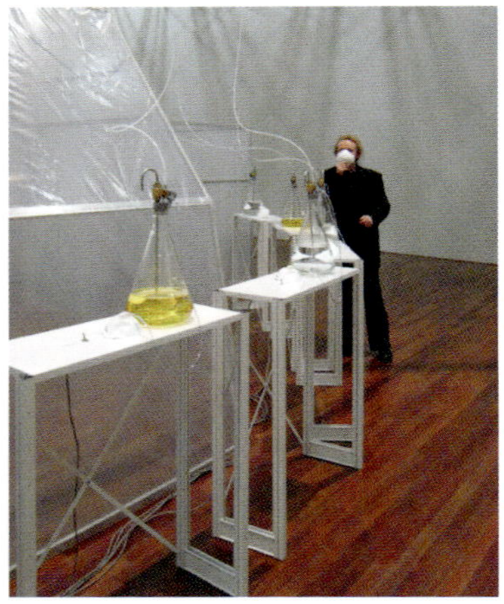

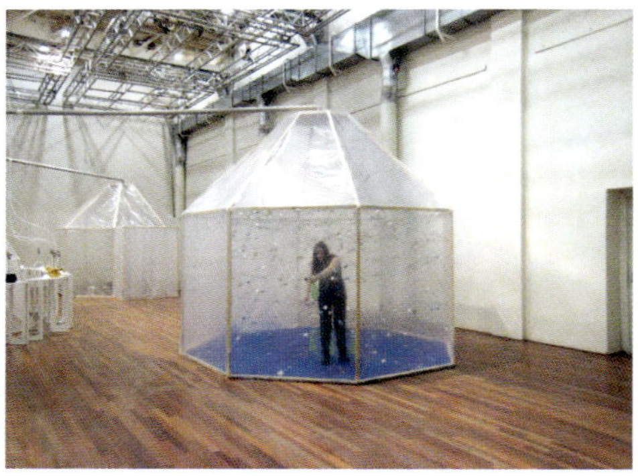

Biosphere I

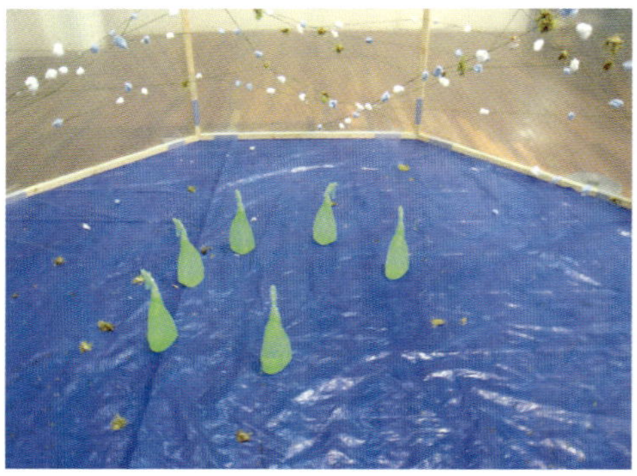

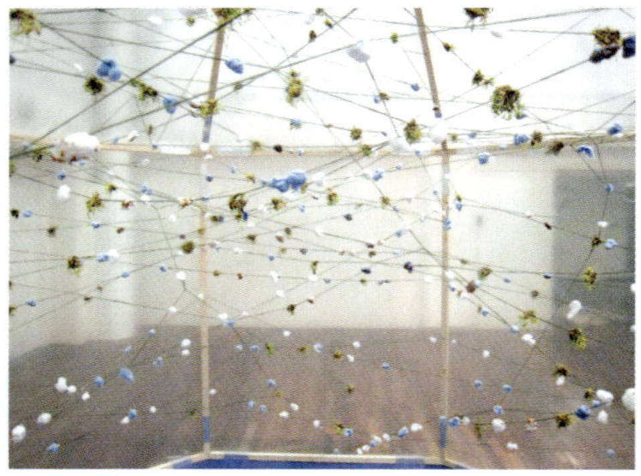

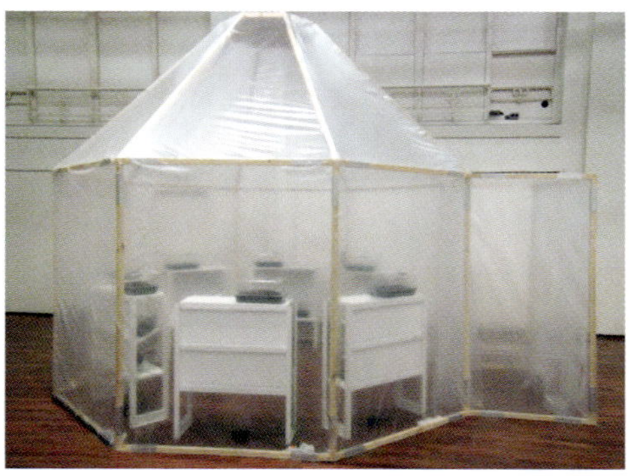

Biosphere IV

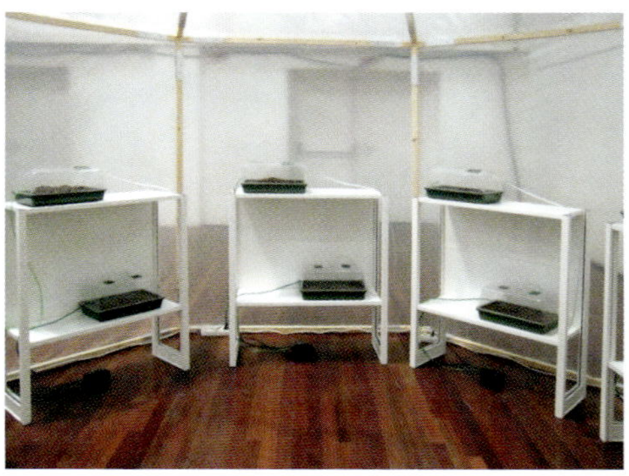

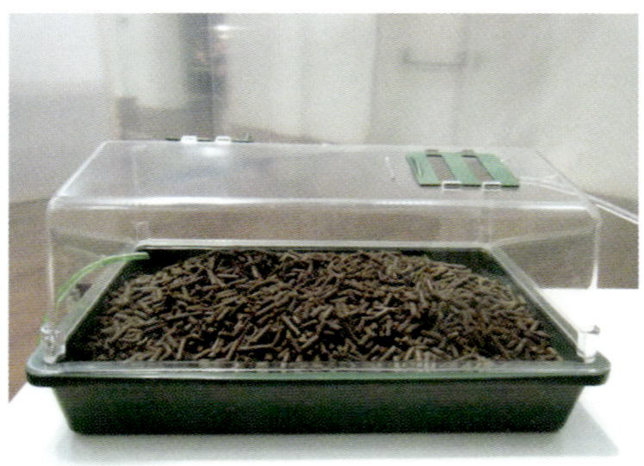

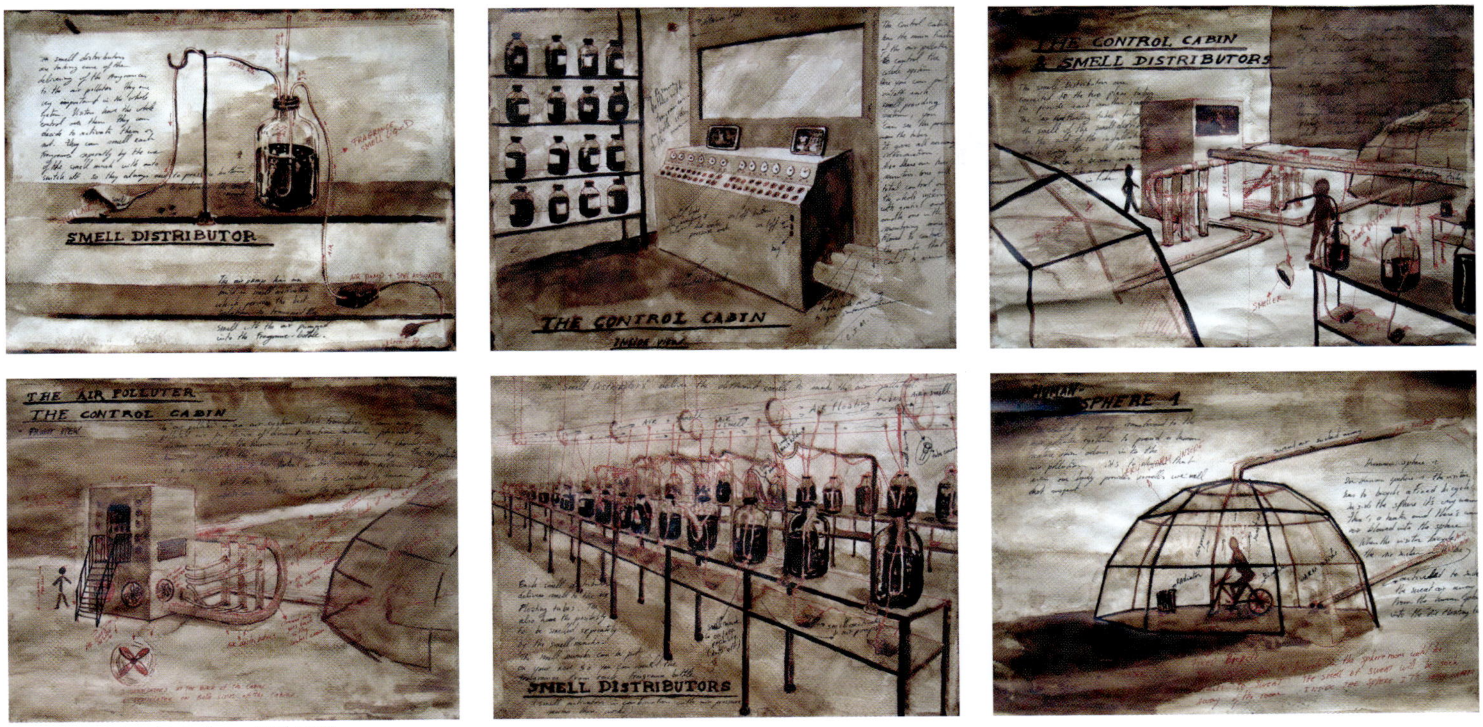

Concept Drawings Air Polluter, 2006-2007

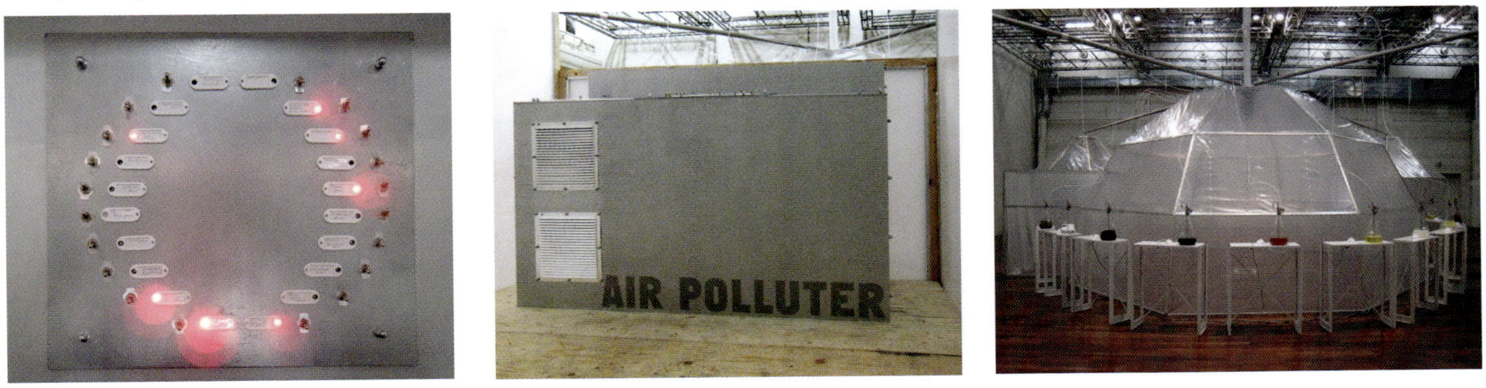

Control Cabin

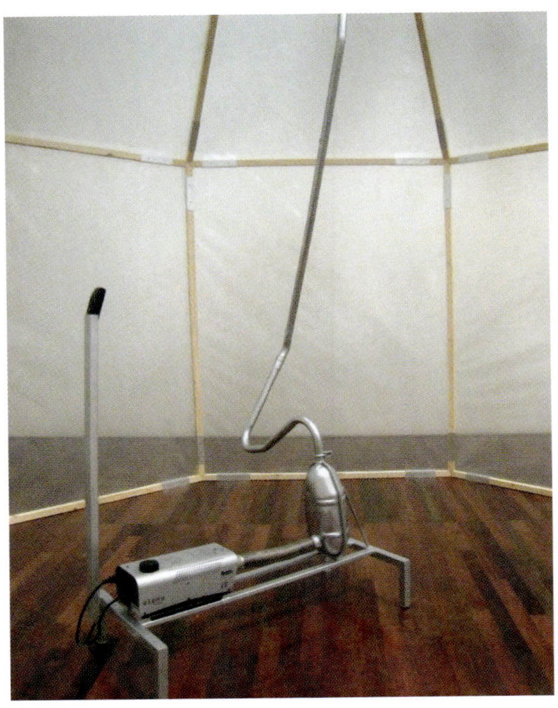

Biosphere III

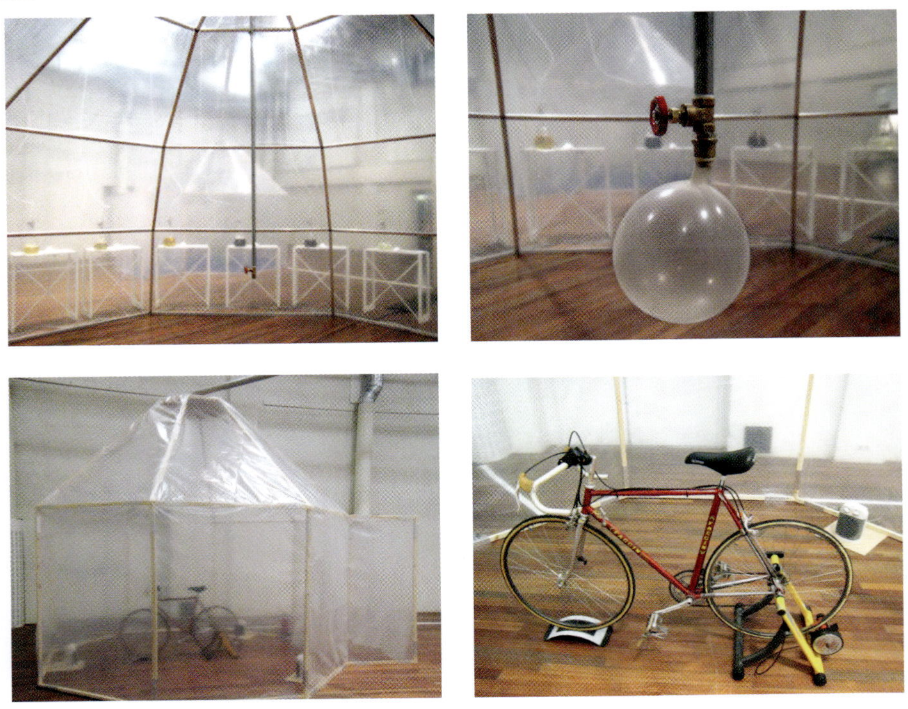

Biosphere II

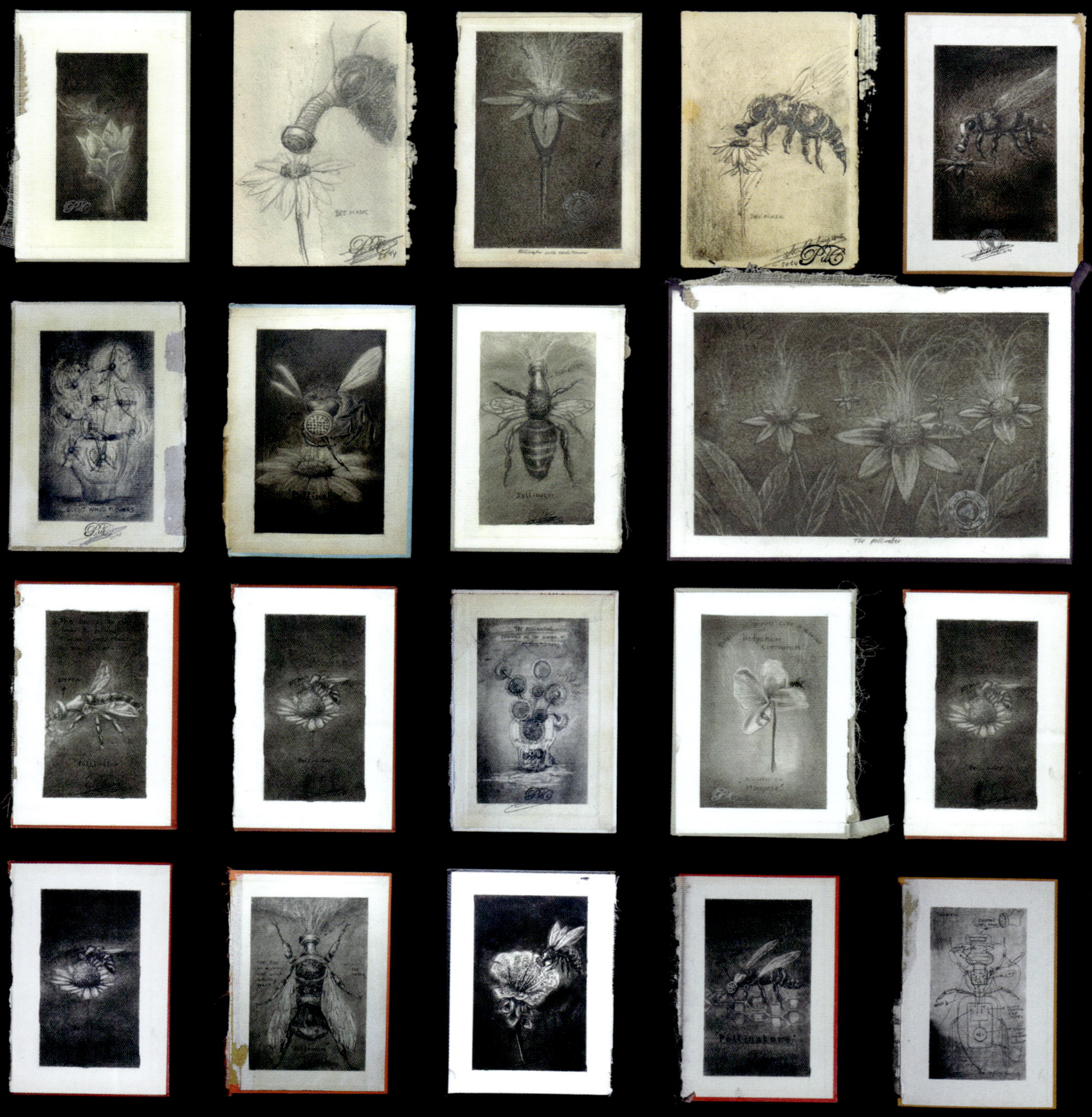

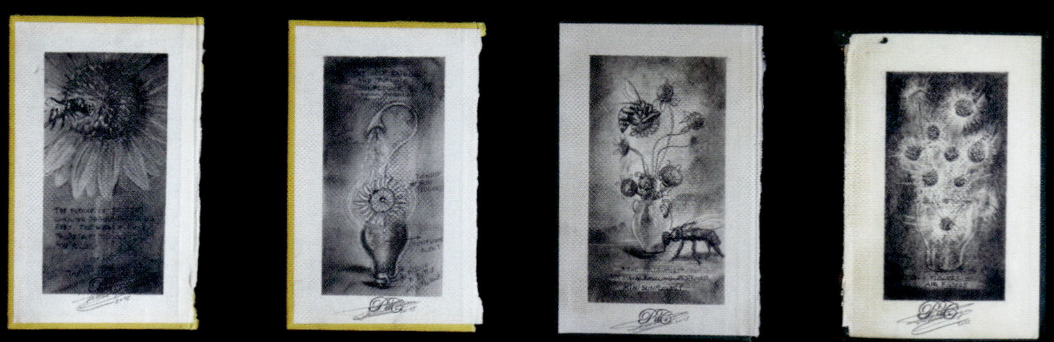

Drawings The Pollinator 2014

Various drawings on the covers of old books, depicting bees with a gas mask. Various sizes

Verschillende tekeningen op covers van oude boeken waarbij bijen met een gasmasker worden afgebeeld. Variabele afmetingen

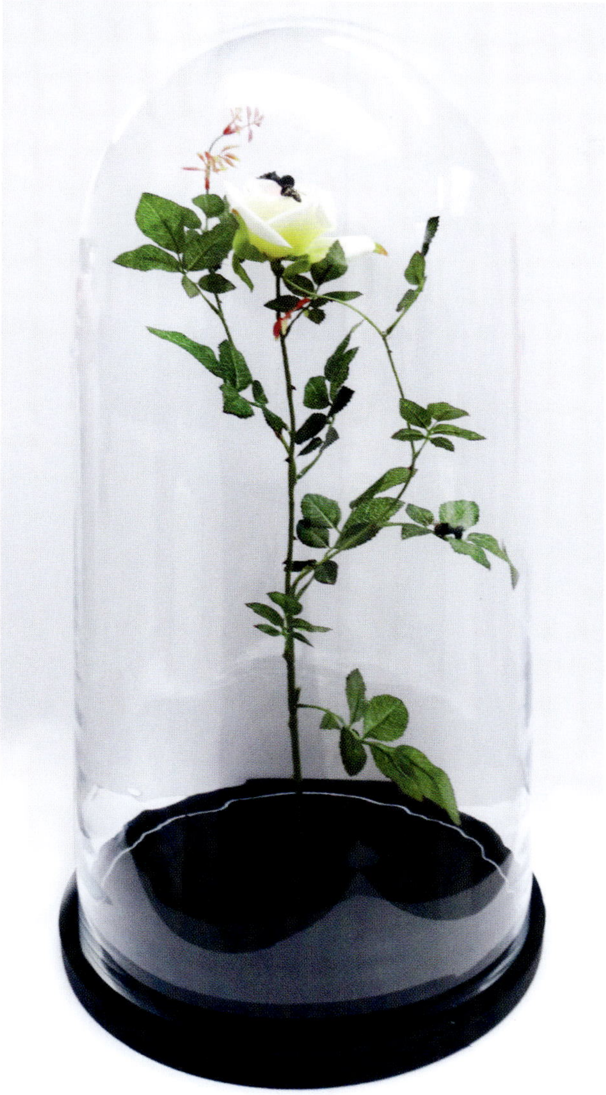

Pollinators

Pollinators are bees wearing a gas mask. You can interpret this mask in different ways. It may be a miniature gas mask to purify the polluted air and thus extend bees' life, or it may be a mask intended precisely to enhance the olfactory sense. A sort of active smelling and filtering mask that leads the bees to the right flowers and plants. But the pollinators may even be computer-operated mini-drones that are intended to serve as 'pollinators' of flowers and plants via a smell detector. Given that the word 'drone' is derived from the term for a male bee, it may not be too far-fetched an idea. Various versions of this work have been realized.

Pollinators zijn bijen met een geurmasker. Men kan dit ruikmasker ook op verschillende manieren interpreteren. Zo kan het masker een mini-gasmasker zijn om de ongezonde lucht uit te zuiveren zodat bijen langer leven, maar kan het masker ook juist een masker zijn om beter te kunnen ruiken. Als het ware een soort van actief ruikend en filterend masker dat de bijen naar de juisten bloemen en planten leidt. Maar evengoed zouden de pollinators eerder computergestuurde mini-drones kunnen zijn die via geurdetectie hun functie als 'bevruchters' van bloemen en planten tot doel hebben. Wetende dat het woord 'drone' afgeleid is van de Engelse benaming van een mannelijke bij, is dit nog niet zo'n ver afliggende gedachte. Er werden verschillende versies van dit werk uitgewerkt.

De Negende Maand, Munthuis Tongeren, org. Stad Tongeren, BE, 05.09.2015-27.09.2015
Green Light District, Buda Fabriek, curator Christophe De Jaeger, Kortrijk, BE, 08.11.2014-08.02.2015

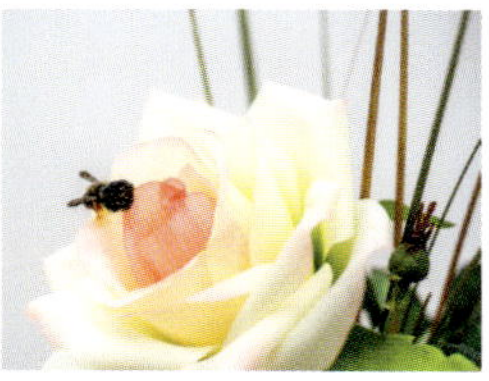

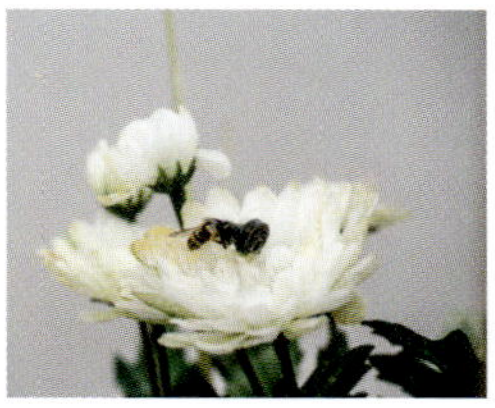

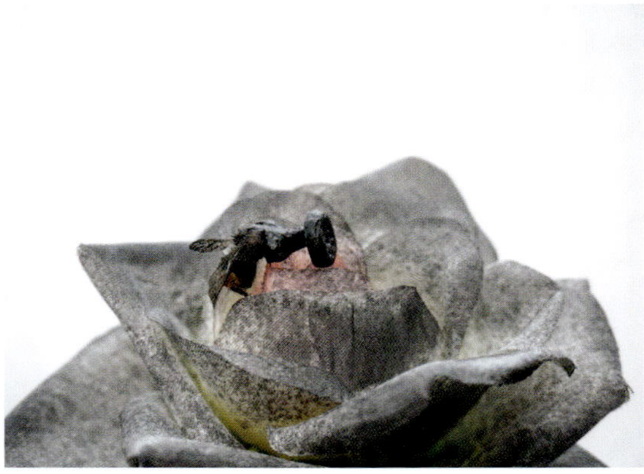

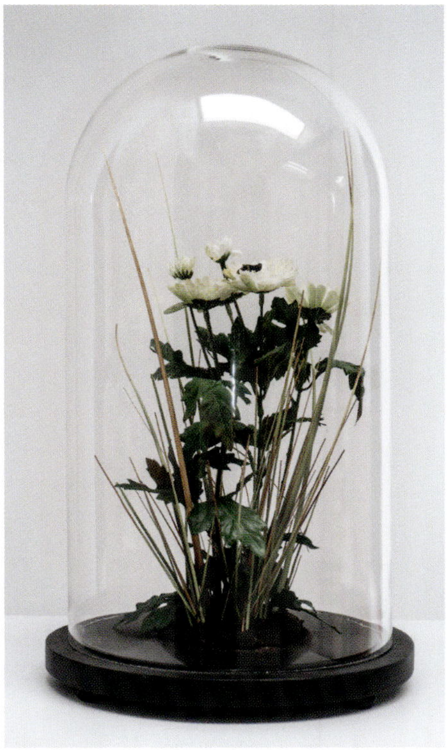

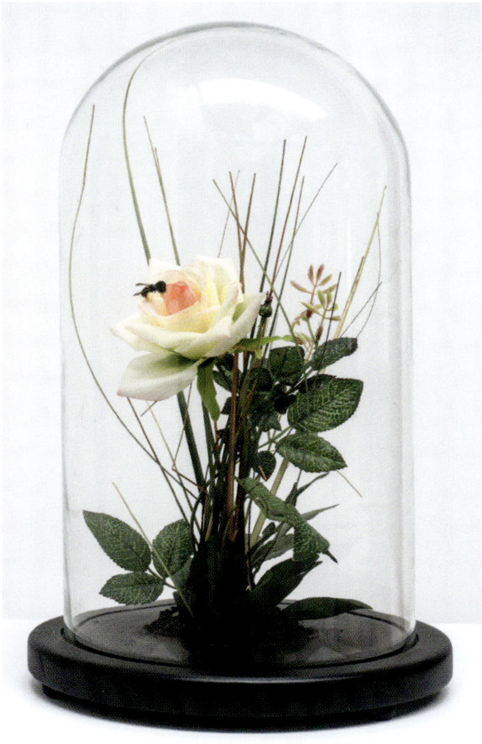

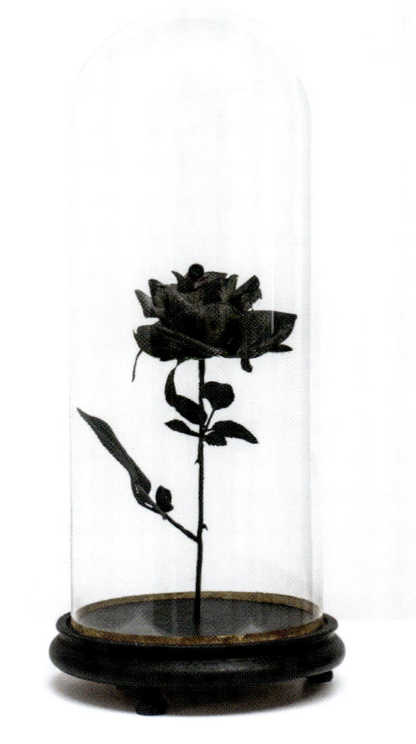

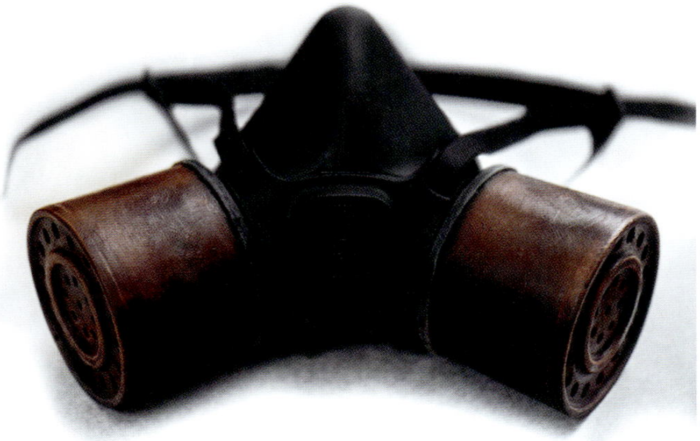

Cocoa Air Mask, 2015

The mask symbolizes breathing in more pleasant air. Air pollution makes our air unhealthy and unpleasant. Cocoa Air Mask lets you experience the air and the scent of Cocoa 5 Senses in a different way. The artist Peter de Cupere and chocolatier Patrick Mertens created the Cocoa Air Mask, an air purifying mask with filters made of chocolate. The smell of Cocoa 5 Senses is applied to the filter.

Het masker staat symbool om een aangenamere lucht in te ademen. Luchtverontreiniging maakt onze lucht ongezond en onaangenaam. *Cocoa Air Mask* laat je de lucht dankzij de geur van Cocoa 5 Senses op een andere manier beleven. Kunstenaar Peter de Cupere en Chocolatier Patrick Mertens creëerden de *Cocoa Air Mask*. Een luchtzuiveringsmasker waarvan de filters gemaakt zijn uit chocolade. In de filters is de geur van Cocoa 5 Senses aangebracht.

Una Grande Abbuffata, World Expo Milan, Belgian Pavilion, org. Gluon, curator Christophe De Jaeger, Milan, IT, 19/20-09-2015

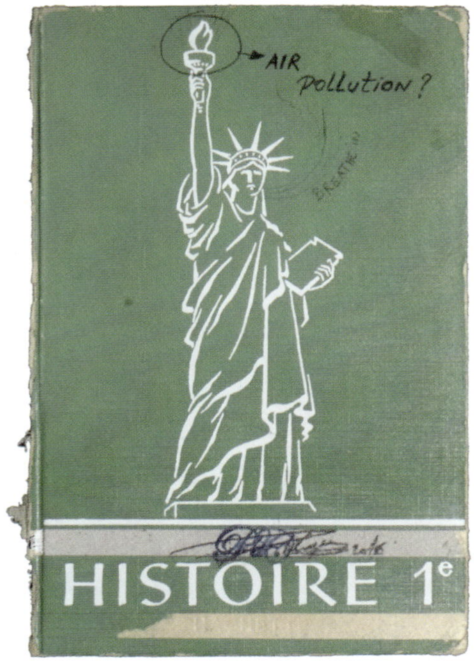

Histoire 1, 2016

30 cm x 20 cm

Sniff Your Jail, org. Balie Tongeren, curators Paul Morrens, Johan Smets, Justice Palace Tongeren, BE, 14.05.2016

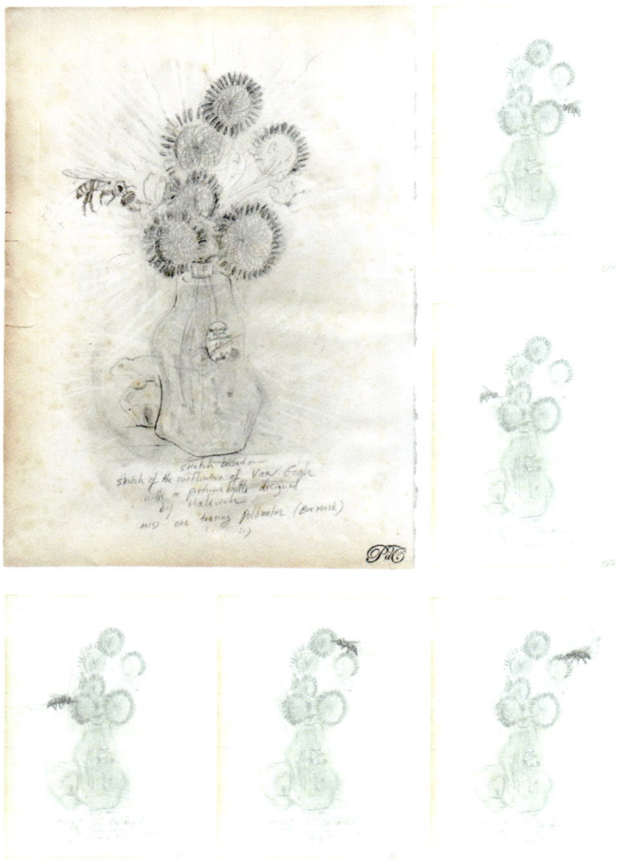

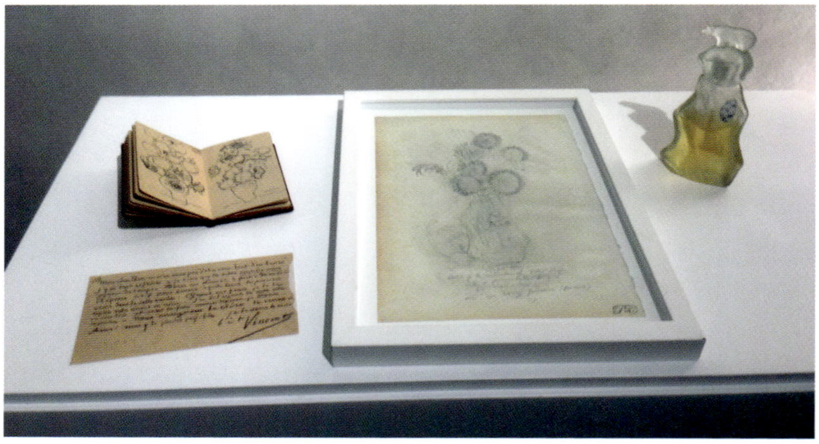

Perfumed Black Sunflowers, 2015

40 cm x 30 cm

Limited edition in 45 copies, 3 A.P.
Sketch of sunflowers in a perfume bottle designed by Kazimir Malevich. A different pollinator has been drawn on each print, making each copy an original. The edition was exhibited with Van Gogh's sketch for the Sunflowers and the perfume bottle designed by Malevich.

Editie op 45 exemplaren, 3 A.P.
Schets van zonnebloemen in een parfumfles ontworpen door Kazimir Malevich. Op iedere editie is een andere pollinator getekend wat iedere editie origineel maakt. De editie werd tentoongesteld met de schets van de zonnebloemen van Van Gogh en het ontworpen parfumflesje van Malevich.

Van Gogh & Malevich versus Next Door, Living Tomorrow, curator Barbara Dietrich, Vilvoorde, BE 27.11.2015-30.06.2015

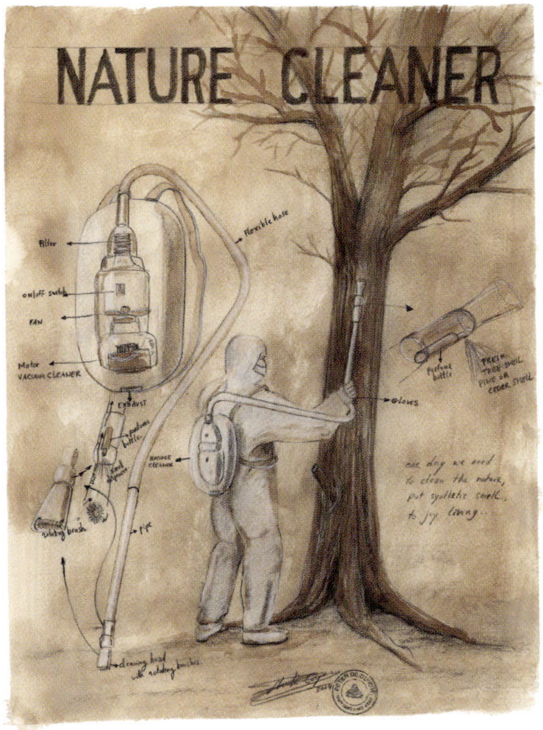

Drawing Nature Cleaner, 2004

62,5 cm x 50,5 cm

Bister, aquarel, grafiet

Garbage City, Van Laere Contemporary Art, Antwerp, BE, 20.05.2004-03.07.2004

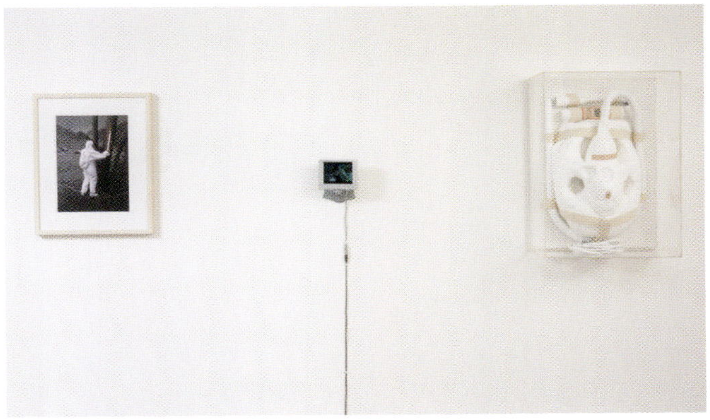

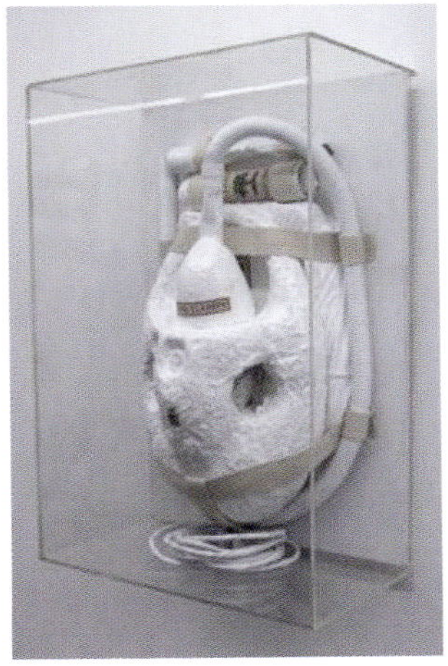

Nature Cleaner, 2004

Video where the artist cleans trees with a vacuum cleaner and puts underarm deodorant on the cleaned trees. After that, the tree is labelled with a ticket. In the background, cars are passing by on the highway.

Video waarin de kunstenaar bomen schoonmaakt met een stofzuiger en de opgekuiste boomstammen bestuift met deodorant. Na deze operatie wordt de boom geregistreerd met een label. In de achtergrond hoort men het geluid van auto's op een nabijgelegen snelweg.

Object + video + photo/foto
Photo/foto + video: edition of 5 + 1 A.P.

Garbage City, Van Laere Contemporary Art, Antwerp, BE, 20.05.2004-03.07.2004

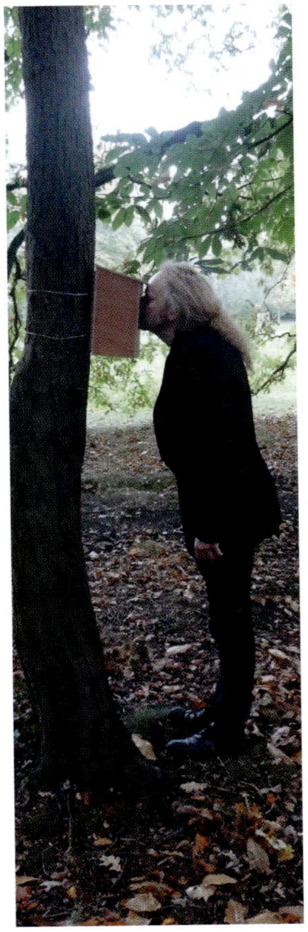

Nose Houses, 2014

Nose Houses are bird houses in which the opening is in the shape of a nose. You can stick your nose in it to smell the scents in the bird house. The smells placed in the bird houses vary depending on the project.
At the Van de Sokkel (2014) exhibition, there were plant smells combined with scents that evoked air pollution. After the exhibition, the empty Nose Houses were suspended higher up in the trees so that birds could nest in them over the winter.
In the project 'Vreemde Vogels' [Strange Birds], 10 Nose Houses were placed on the largest bird house (Guinness Book of World Records) in the world. Smells were applied to the Nose Houses that referred to a positive and negative memory of five refugees. Along with their story, this allowed their recollections to be shared with others.

Nose Houses zijn vogelkastjes waar de opening de vorm van een neus heeft. Men kan hier de neus insteken om de geur, aanwezig in het vogelkastje, te ruiken. De geuren die aangebracht worden in de vogelkastjes verschillen naargelang het project.
In de tentoonstelling Van de Sokkel (2014) werden plantengeuren gecombineerd met geuren die verwijzen naar luchtvervuiling. Na de tentoonstelling werden de leeggemaakte *Nose Hoses* hoger in de bomen gehangen zodat vogels hier hun nest voor de winter konden maken.
In het project 'Vreemde Vogels' werden 10 *Nose Houses* op het grootste vogelhuis (Guinness Book of World Records) ter wereld aangebracht. In de *Nose Houses* waren geuren aangebracht die verwezen naar een positieve en negatieve herinnering van 5 vluchtelingen. Samen met hun verhaal konden zo hun herinneringen met andere mensen gedeeld worden.

Van de Sokkel, Hof De Bist, CC Ekeren, curators Johan Pas, Christine Clinckx, Kris Van Dessel, Ekeren, BE
25.10.2014-26.10.2014

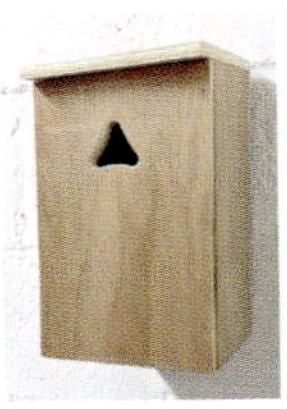

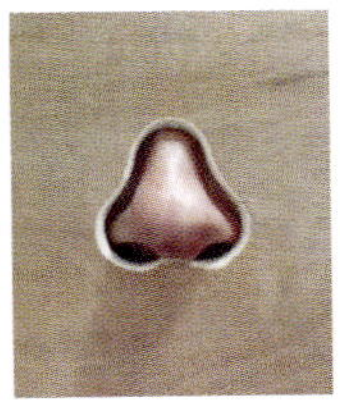

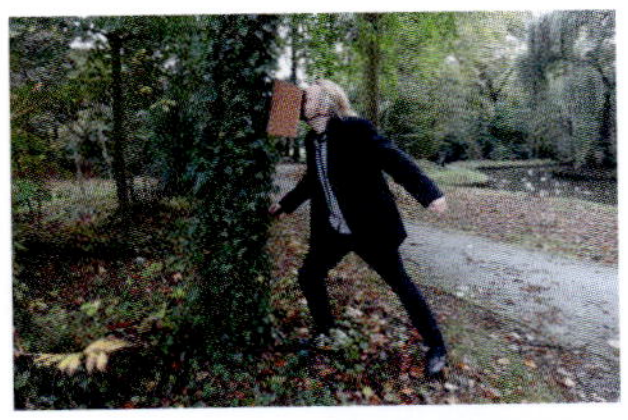

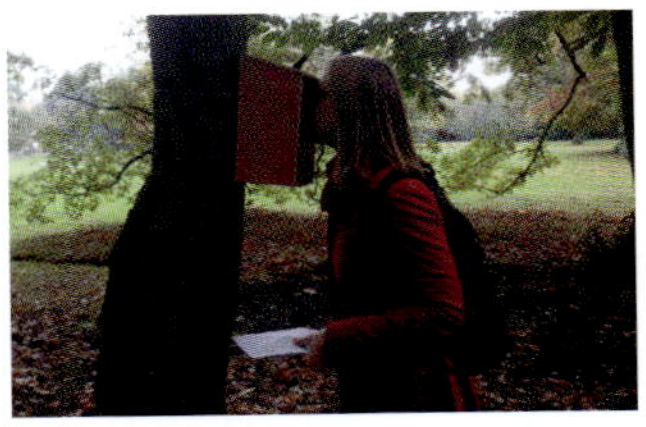

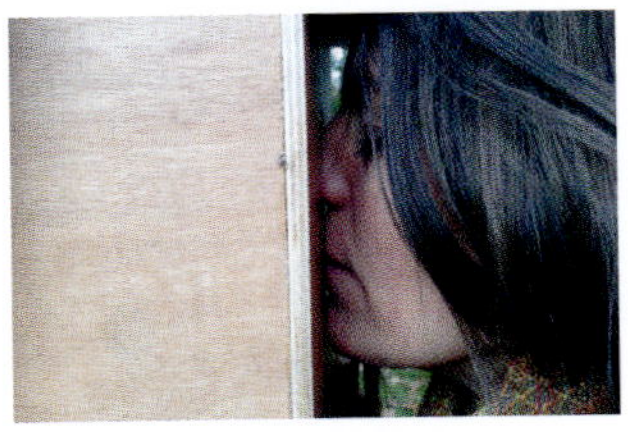

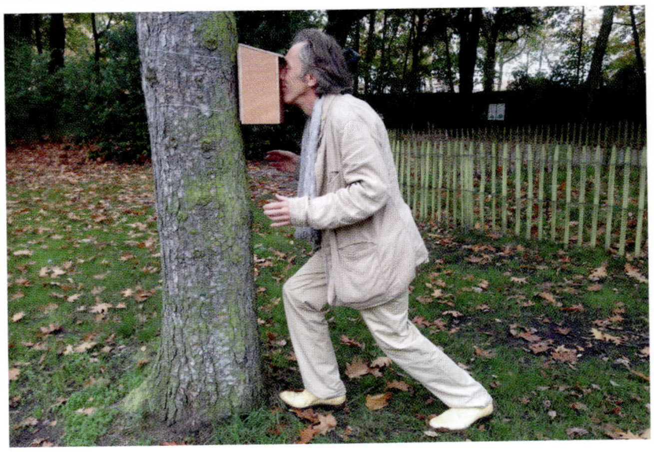

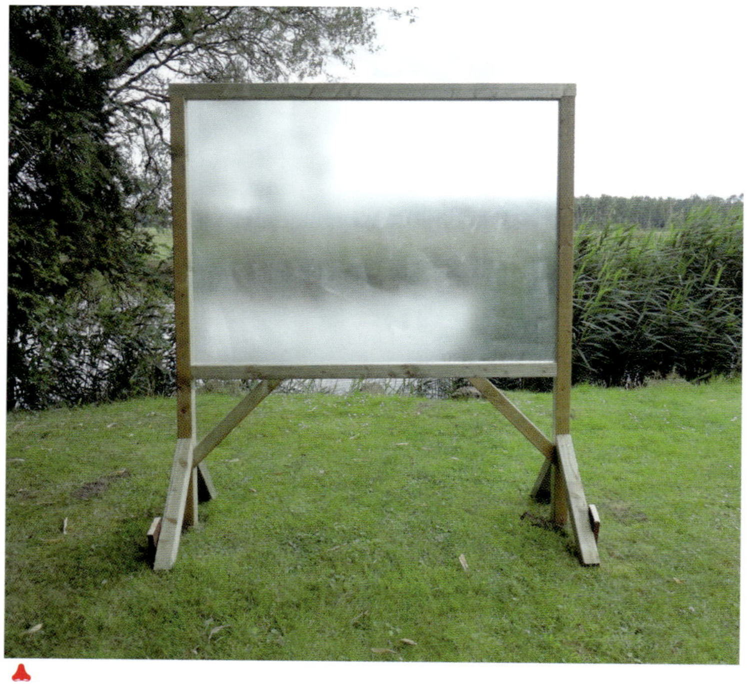

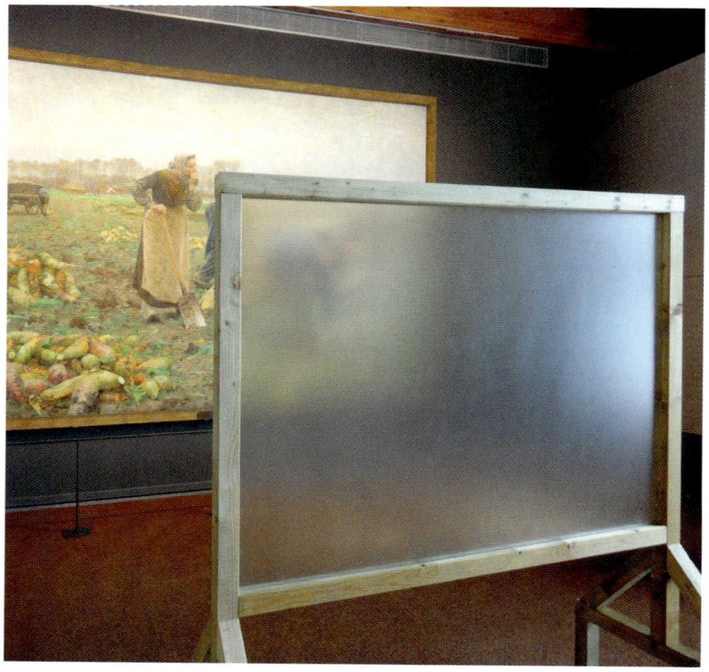

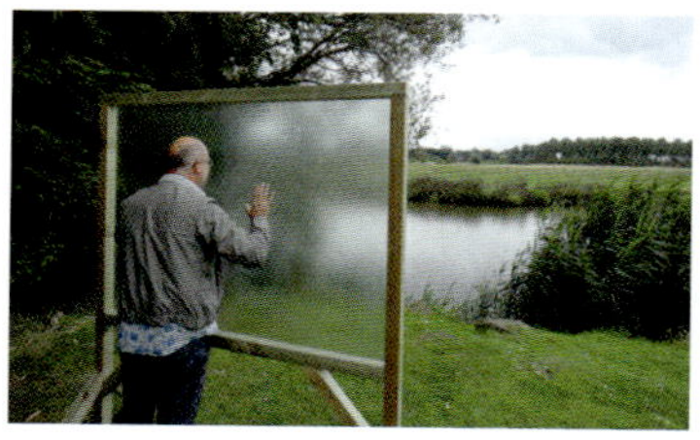

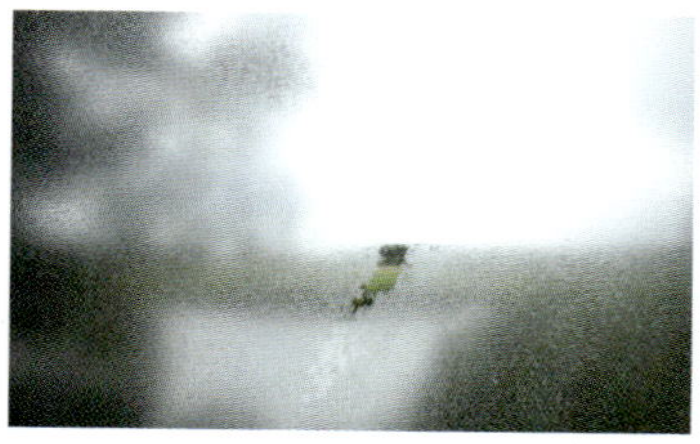

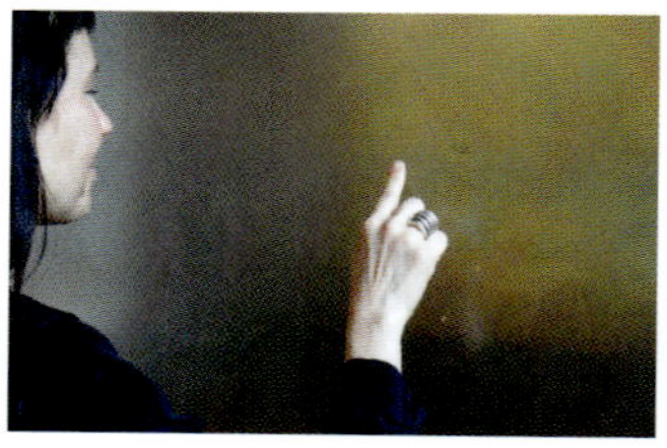

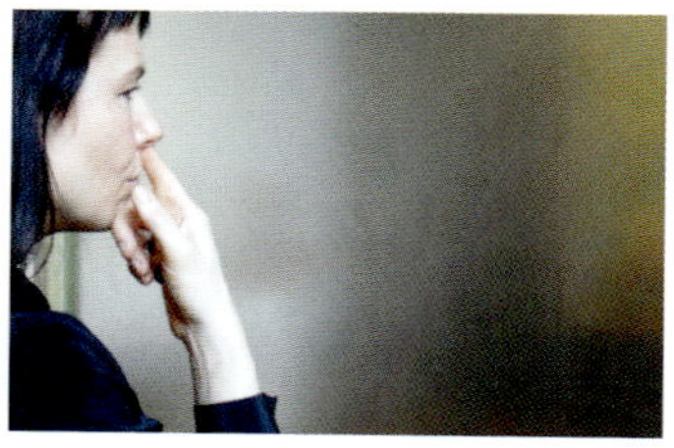

Scratch & Sniff Nature

Rub the glass with your finger and then smell your finger to smell the scent.

In the museum in Deinze, Belgium, the artist engaged in a scent dialogue with the painting 'Bietenoogst' [Beet Harvest] by Emile Claus. The smell of the cultivated soil was different in the past than it is today. The influence of pollution, to which fertilizers also contribute, changes the structure and composition of the soil and therefore also its smell.

Citizens of the world, and especially urban dwellers, do not have a clear image of what nature really smells like, and thus do not readily notice changes in smell. It is only when someone is personally confronted with unpleasant smells that the issue of smell pollution gains attention.

Peter de Cupere offered the viewer the opportunity to reflect on the 'Beet Harvest'. An artist such as Emile Claus knew perfectly how to use touches of colour and light to create a certain mood in which the viewer feels almost a part of the painting. Every time the artist saw the work, he could smell the scent of the soil. Hence the idea, in honour of Emile Claus' painting, of putting in an interactive smell installation to enable the viewer to have the same experience as that of the artist. The work is ephemeral. The more one rubs it in order to perceive the smell, the more visible the painting becomes but the less perceptible the smell, as it is gradually rubbed away. In the process, visitors leave fingerprints and smudges on the glass, and through the actions of the visitors you end up with a different painting. The visitor's finger becomes the paintbrush in this case.

Scratch & Sniff Nature takes you back in time. It is a reminder of and a reference to history and causes you to stop and think about smells in our society, with all its unpleasant odours and pollution. For what does nature really smell like?

A second Scratch & Sniff Nature installation was placed along the Leie River. People looked up at the meadow on the other bank. By rubbing on the glass, visitors could smell the scent of grass from the other side of the river.

Wrijf met je vinger over het glas en ruik aan je vinger om de geur waar te nemen.

In het museum in Deinze ging de kunstenaar een geurdialoog aan met het schilderij 'Bietenoogst' van Emile Claus. De geur van bewerkte grond van vroeger rook anders dan de geur van nu. Onder invloed van milieuverontreiniging waar o.a. meststoffen deel van uitmaken, verandert de grond van samenstelling en structuur, dus ook van geur.

De mondiale burger en meer bepaald de stadsmens heeft niet echt een beeld van hoe de natuur echt ruikt en staat dan ook niet snel stil bij geurverandering. Het is pas wanneer je zelf geconfronteerd wordt met geurhinder dat geurverontreiniging aandacht krijgt.

Peter de Cupere laat de toeschouwer stilstaan bij het schilderij 'Bietenoogst'. Een kunstenaar als Emile Claus wist perfect met kleurtoets en lichtgebruik een bepaalde sfeer op te wekken waar je als toeschouwer bijna als het ware deelneemt aan het schilderij. Iedere keer als de kunstenaar het schilderij zag, rook hij de aardegrond. Dit was ook de aanleiding om ter ere van Emile Claus' schilderij een interactieve geurinstallatie te plaatsen om de bezoeker dezelfde ervaring mee te geven welke de kunstenaar ervaren heeft. Het werk is efemeer. Hoe meer men wrijft om de geur waar te nemen, hoe zichtbaarder het schilderij weer wordt, maar hoe minder de geur waarneembaar zal worden omdat deze juist weggewreven wordt. Tevens laten de bezoekers zo vingerprints en vegen achter op het glas en krijgt men een ander schilderij door toedoen van de kijker. De vinger van de bezoeker wordt hier mede het penseel.

Scratch & Sniff Nature werpt je terug in de tijd. Het is herinnering en verwijzing naar de geschiedenis en het laat je nadenken over onze maatschappelijke geursituatie onder invloed van al de geurhinder en geurvervuiling. Want hoe ruikt de natuur echt?

Een tweede *Scratch & Sniff Nature*-installatie werd langs de rivier de Leie geplaatst. Men keek uit op het grasveld van de tegenover liggende oever. Als men op het glas wreef, rook men hier de grasgeur van de andere zijde van de rivier.

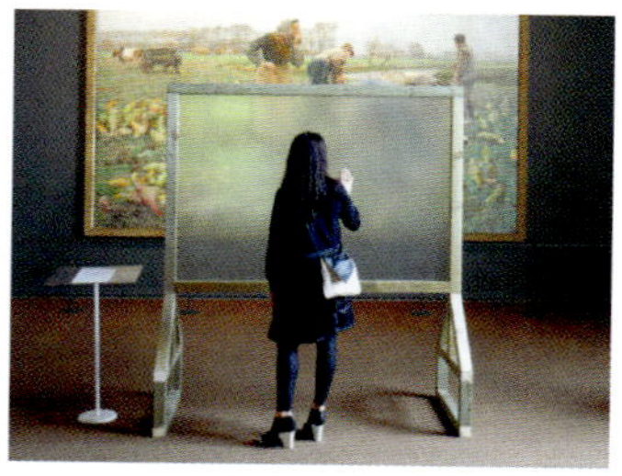

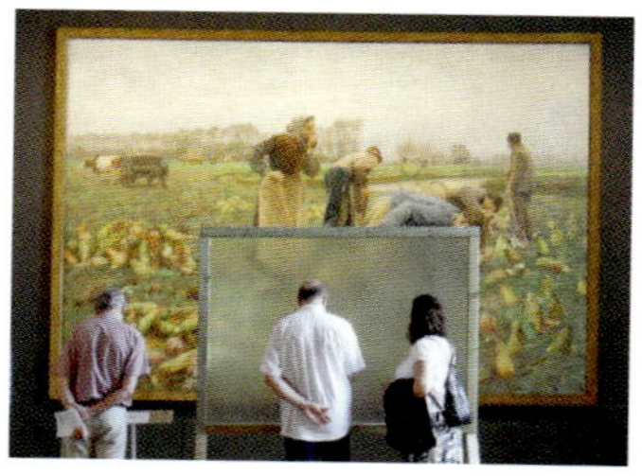

Efemeer, Museum van Deinze & de Leiestreek, curator William Ploegaert, Deinze, BE 01.07.2012-07.10.2012

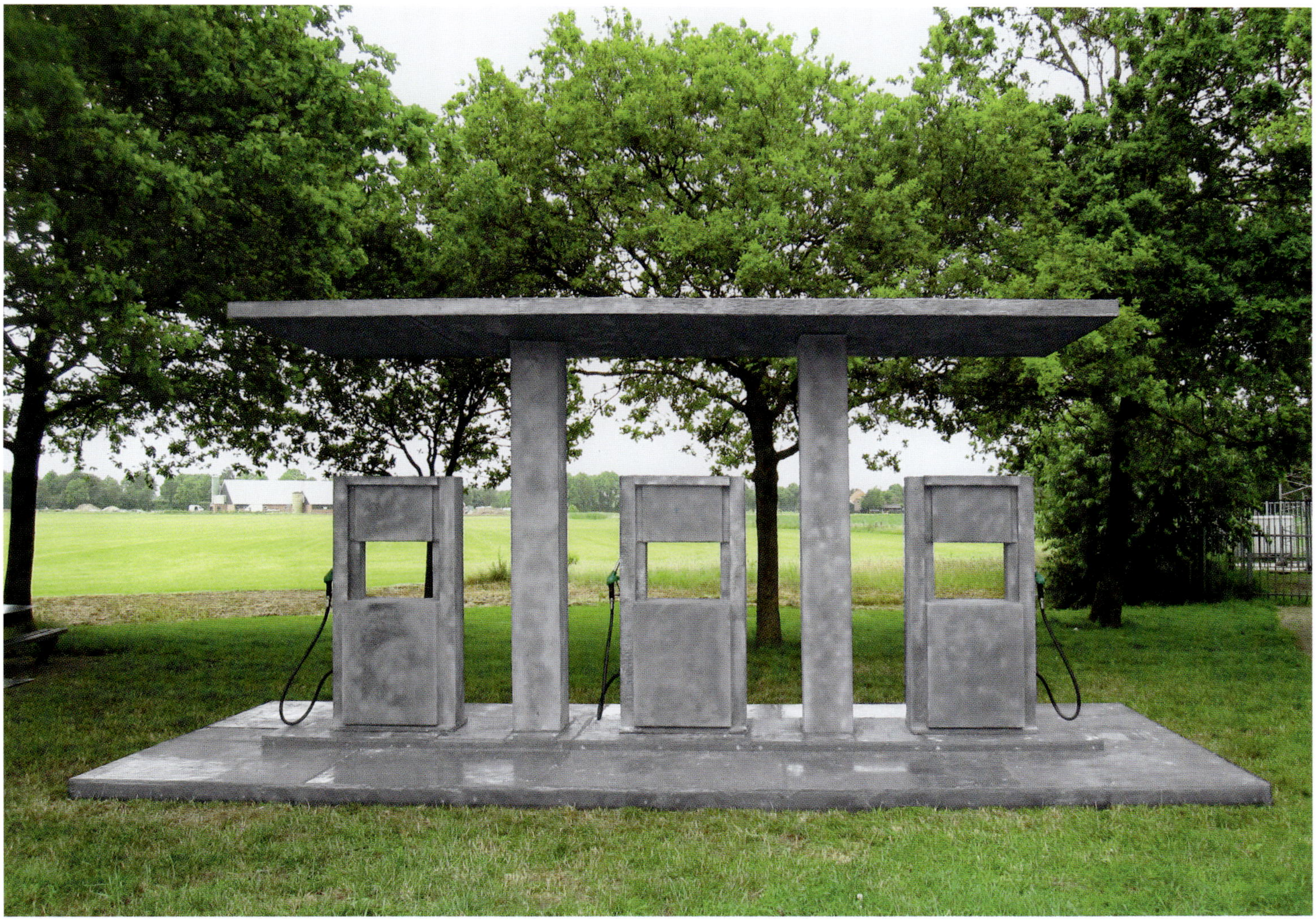

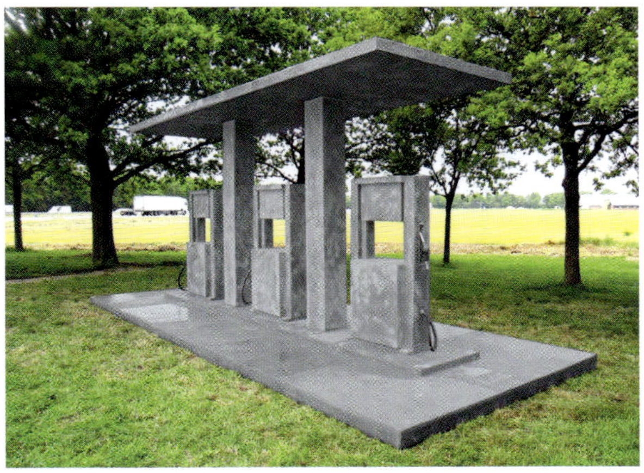

Scentedo[2]

Service station made of imitation concrete (epoxy); visitors can fill up on the scents.
Smells: grass scent, lavender, bubble-gum, liquorice and the smell of exhaust fumes.
Gas station installed at an official parking stop at the A1 highway in Deventer (NL).
Visible and accessible from the highway.

Tankstation gemaakt uit namaakbeton (epoxy), bezoekers kunnen geur tanken,
Geuren: grasgeur, lavendel, bubbelgum, dropgeur of de geur van uitlaatgassen.
Het tankstation stond eerst opgesteld op een parking langs de A1 autosnelweg in Deventer
zodat deze ook vanaf de autosnelweg bereikbaar en zichtbaar was.

'Everyone curator', Izegem, org. Verbeke Foundation, 20.12.2009-20.12.2010
'IAMA1', organisatie Kunstenlab Deventer, NL, Aktuele Kunst Hengelo (AkkuH) and Kunstvereniging Diepenheim, curator Koen Bril, 06.06.2009-01.09.2009

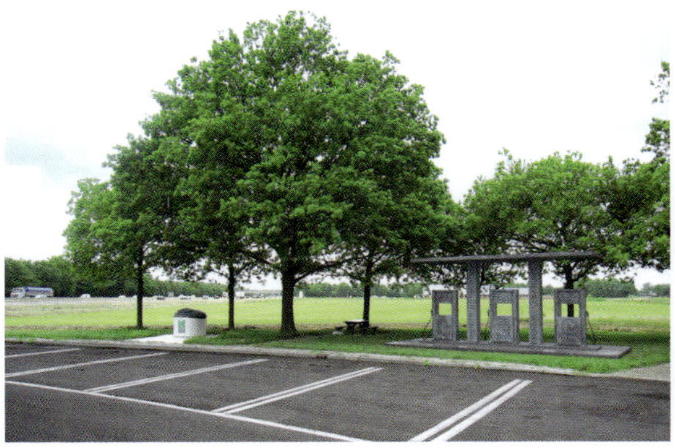

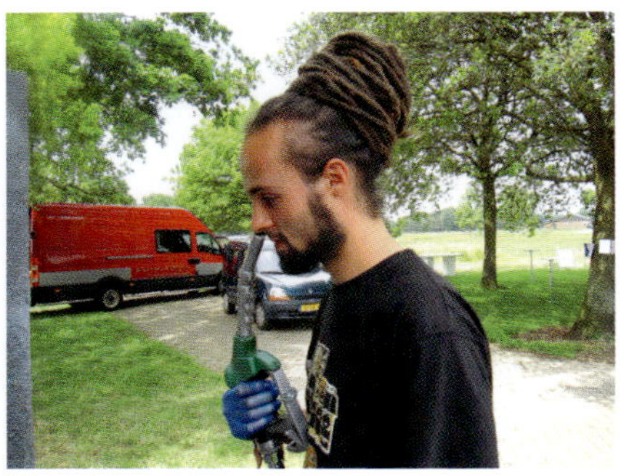

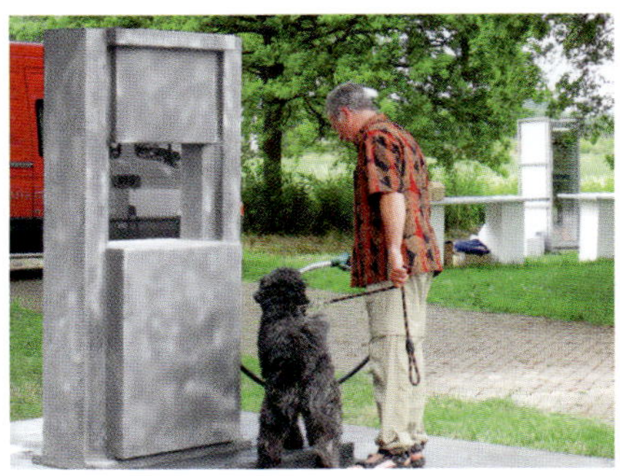

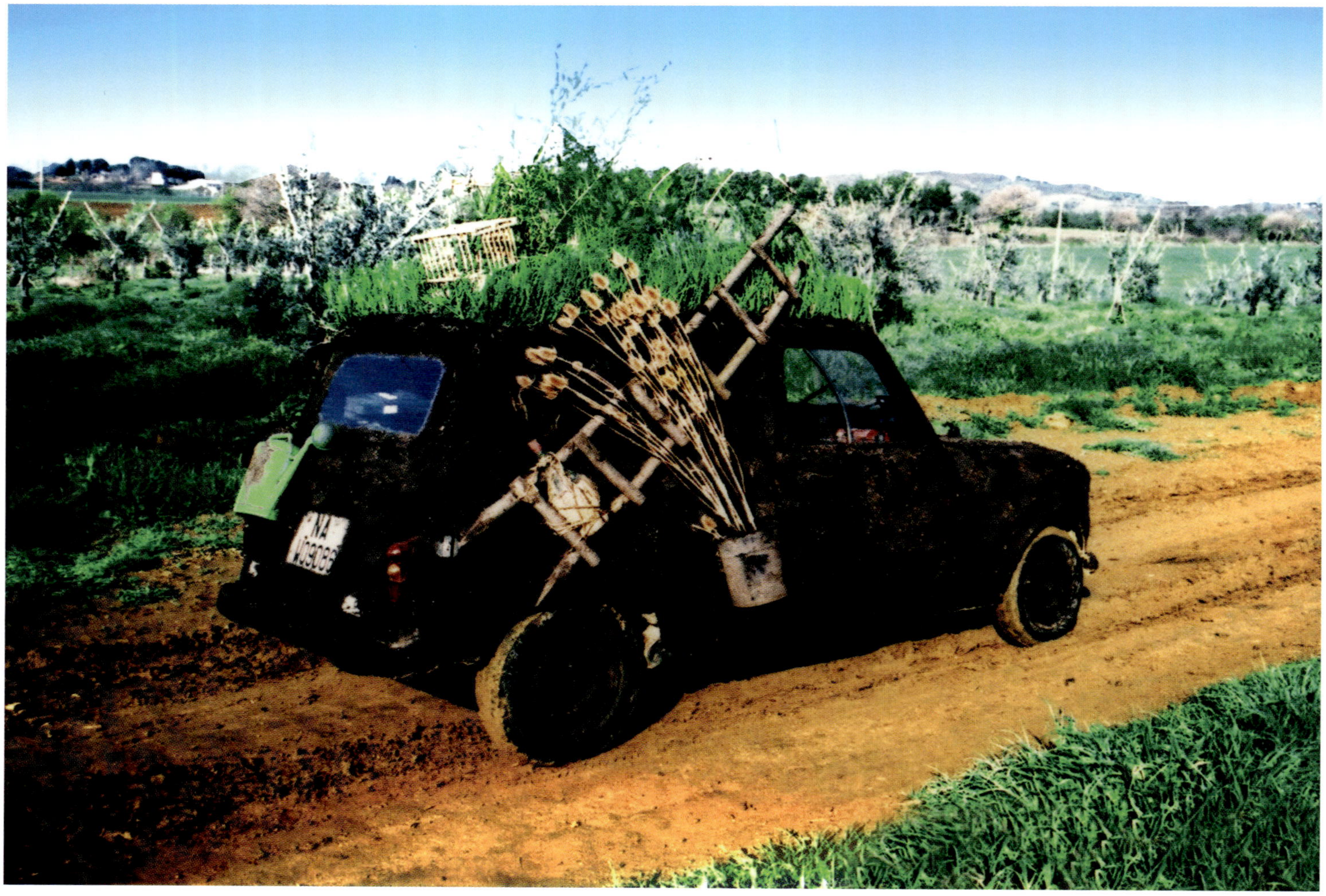

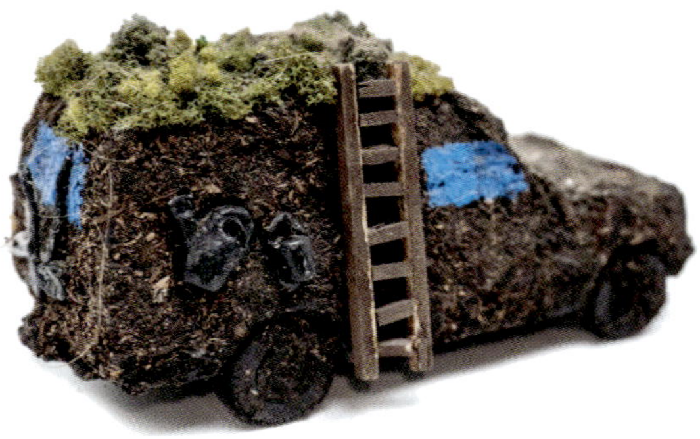

Model Earth Car, 2001

Earth Car, 2002

Car covered in- and outside with Earth and fake plants, different smells like thym, anis, pine, olives, grapes; depending on the exhibition also with birds and video. Inside the Earth Car are books made of earth with the text 'Smell the Earth'

Auto zowel aan de binnen- en de buitenzijde met aarde en kunstplanten met verschillende geuren zoals tijm, anijs, den, olijven en druiven. Afhankelijk van de locatie van de presentatie eventueel met vogels en video. Binnenin de auto bevinden zich boeken, gemaakt uit aarde en met de tekst 'Smell the Earth' op de cover.

Vormidable, Vlaamse Hedendaagse Beeldhouwkunst, Museum Beelden aan Zee, Lange Voorhout, Den Haag, NL, 20.05.2015-30.08.2015
Green Summer, Verbeke Foundation, Kemzeke, BE, 29.05.2010-31.10.2010
Artificial Nature, Verbeke Foundation, Kemzeke, BE, 23.05.2009-15.11.2009
Dis-moi +, MAMAC, Musée d'Art Moderne et d'Art Contemporain, org. Les Brasseurs, Liège, BE 21.04.2006-04.06.2006
Mo(NU)ment@Bornem, Monumental vzw, curator Ruth Renders, Bornem, BE, 09.05.2004-28.08.2004
The Collector's House, St.-Lucas Stichting, curator Filip Luyckx, Brussels, 17.01.2003-22.03.2003
Overbruggen, Brugge Culture City 2002, curator Johan Pas, NICC Brugge, BE, 12.09-17.11.2002
Quattro Vendi, curator Letitzia Ragglia, Manciano, IT, 16.03-20.06.2002

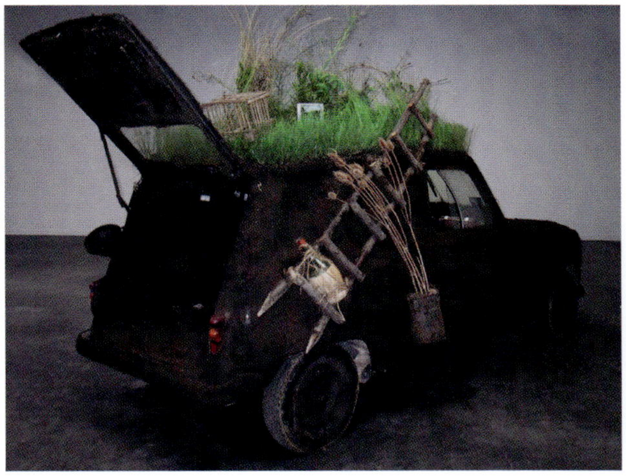

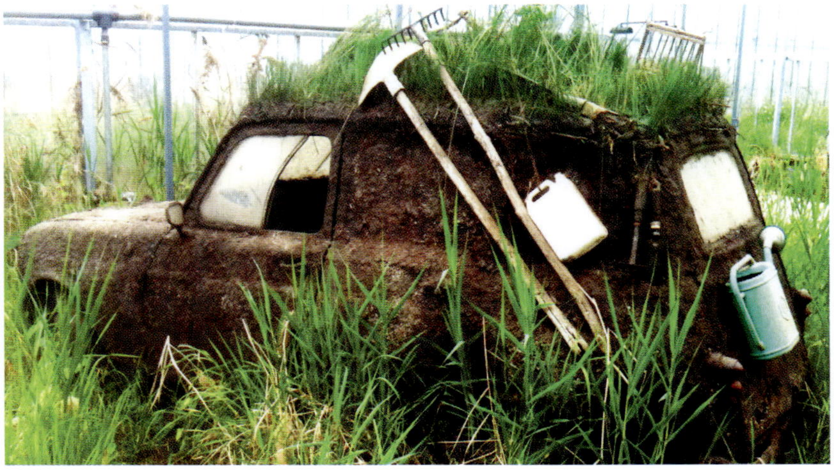

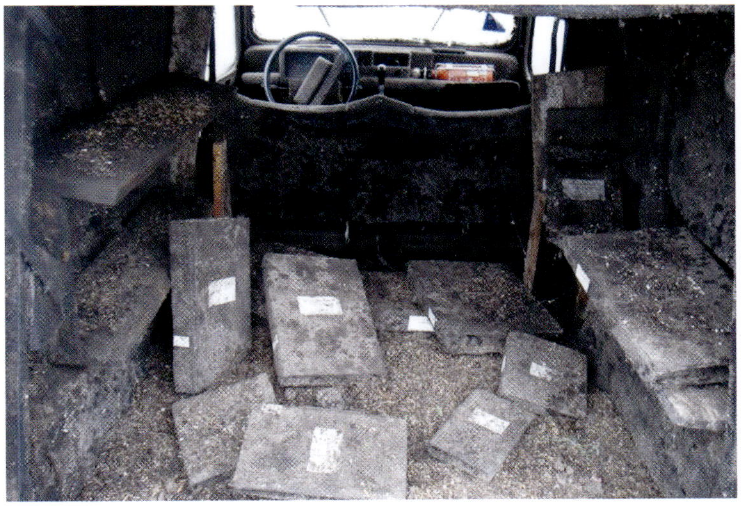

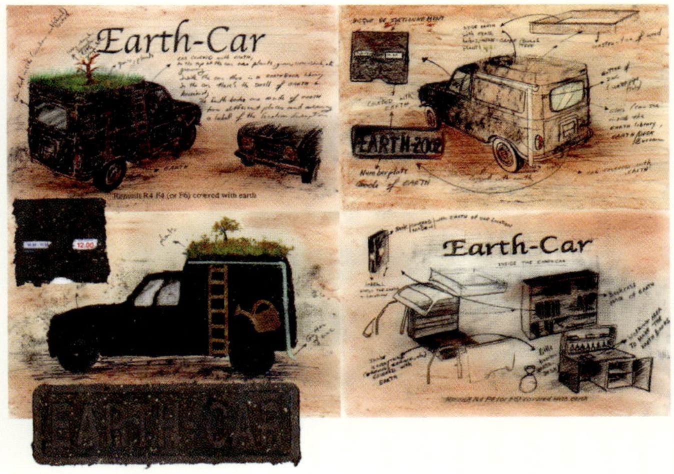

Drawing Earth Car, 2001

70 cm x 110 cm

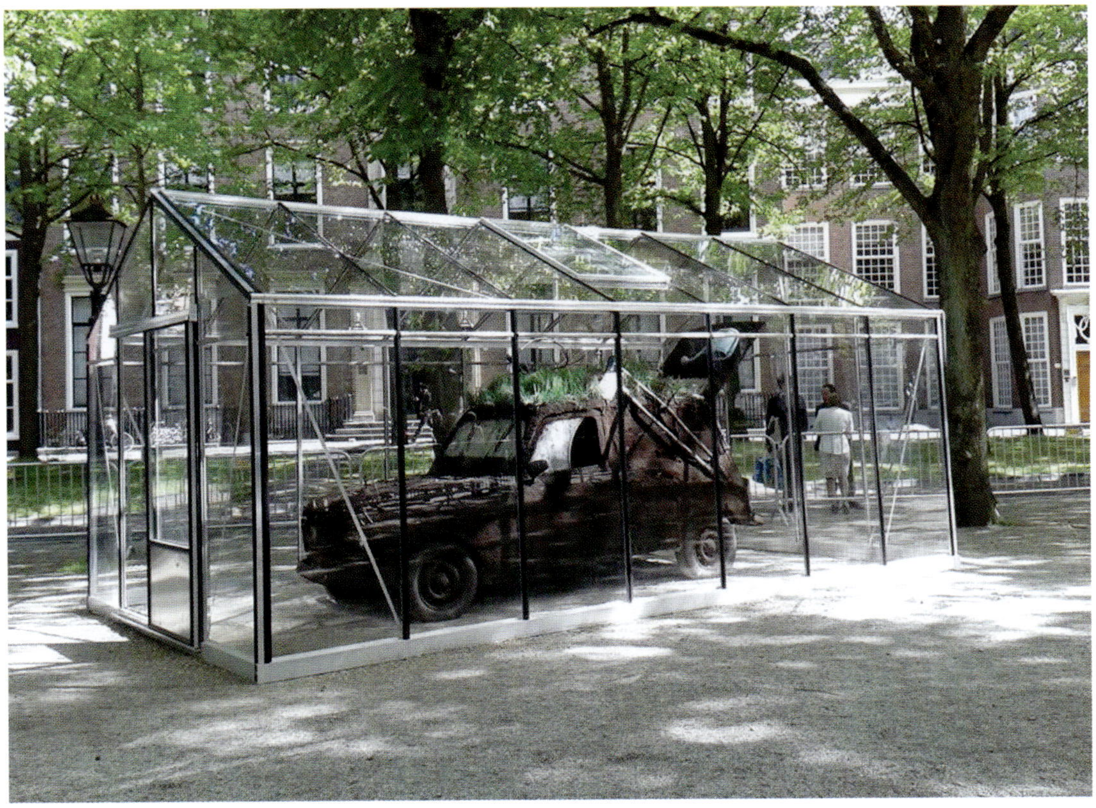

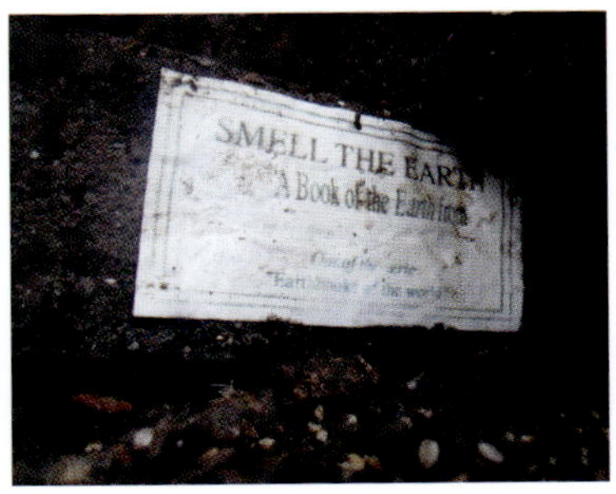

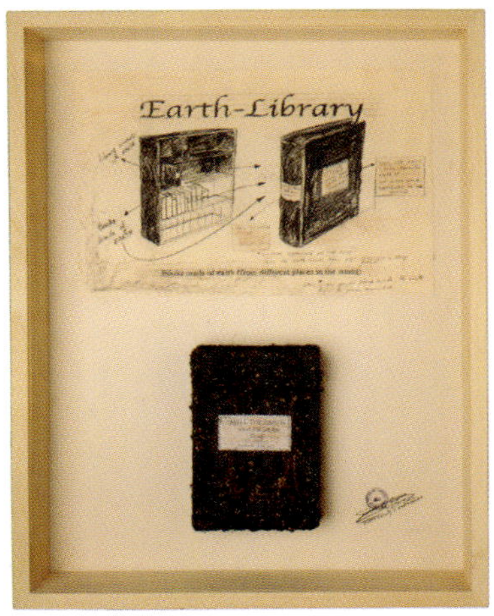

Drawing Earth Library, 2000-2001

Garbage City Holiday Park

'Garbage City' is a mock mini-city made from waste materials where you as a visitor can stay just like in a holiday park. The concept is simple: You rent a 'Garbage House' for a certain period and stay there. Furthermore, during this period you make other Garbage Houses together with your co-residents, which can then be let to other people. In this way 'Garbage City' grows into a larger community. It is a way of spending your holiday in a creative way while also becoming more conscious of the mountain of waste and its effects on society. Each Garbage House gets its own added smell, so that direct references to specific products disappear. This distinctive smell is lightly present in the rubbish house built, in order to act on one's state of mind. In the exhibition you can find out for yourself what such a Garbage House would look like.
In 'Garbage City Holiday Park', Peter de Cupere makes a number of reflections on the pollution of our communities and its effect on our environment. These are not critical arguments, but more poetic reflections on the phenomenon of pollution.
A deep respect for the environment and thus primarily for the smells of nature is interspersed throughout the work. Even though the smell substances are made by the artist in such a way as to be identical to nature, the question remains as to how much you as a visitor experience a certain smell as natural. Given the absence of natural references within the four walls of the exhibition space, you are easily influenced by preconceptions.

'Garbage City' is een geconstrueerde mini-stad gemaakt uit afval waar je als bezoeker kunt verblijven net zoals in een vakantiepark. Het concept is eenvoudig. Je huurt een 'Garbage House' voor een bepaalde periode en je verblijft daar. Tijdens je verblijf, bouw je andere Garbage Houses samen met je huisgenoten, die op hun beurt verder zullen verhuurd worden aan toekomstige bezoekers. Op die manier groeit 'Garbage City' in een grotere community. Het is een mogelijkheid om je vakantie door te brengen op een creatieve manier waarbij je geconfronteerd wordt met de bergen afval die we dagelijks produceren en een invloed hebben op onze gemeenschap. Elk Garbage House krijgt haar eigen toegevoegde geur zodat directe referenties naar gebruikte materialen verdwijnen. Deze uitgesproken geur is subtiel aanwezig in het afvalhuis zodat je constant bewust bent van de situatie. In de tentoonstelling kan je ervaren hoe zo een Garbage House eruit zou zien.
In 'Garbage City Holiday Park', maakt Peter de Cupere op heel duidelijke manier reflecties over de vervuiling en haar effecten op het milieu. Zijn bijdrage op het fenomeen van vervuiling gebeurt meer op een poëtische manier dan met tal van kritische argumenten.
In zijn werk vindt men steeds een diep respect voor het milieu waarbij geuren uit de natuur constant doorheen zijn werk vloeien. Alhoewel de geursubstanties die de kunstenaar maakt identiek zijn aan de originele en natuurlijke geuren, blijft de vraag in hoeverre de bezoeker deze geuren ook als natuurlijke geuren ervaart. Door het verdwijnen van de natuur of directe referenties naar de natuur binnen de ruimte van een tentoonstelling, wordt je snel beïnvloed door bestaande vooroordelen.

The Sented Brick, The Olfactory, Hasselt, BE, 13.10.2014
Green Summer, Verbeke Foundation, Kemzeke, BE 29.05.2010-31.10.2010
Peter de Cupere, Hans Op de Beeck, Koen van den Broek, Sergio De Beuckelaer, curator Paul Morrens, Justice Court Antwerpen, Antwerp, BE, 21.11.2002-28.11.2002
Garbage City, Van Laere Contemporary Art, Antwerp, BE 20.05.2004-03.07.2004

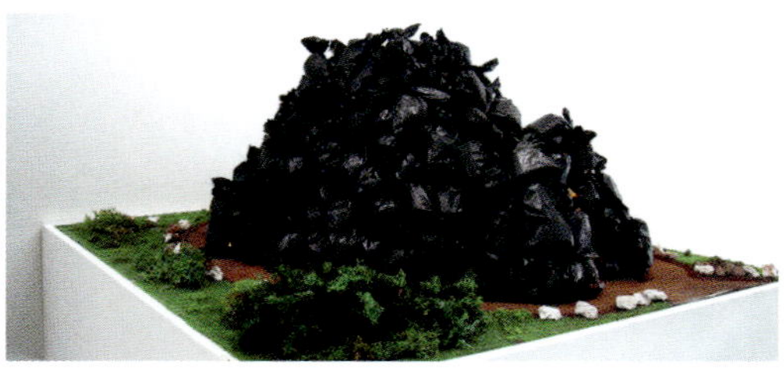

Model Black Garbage Iglo, 2004

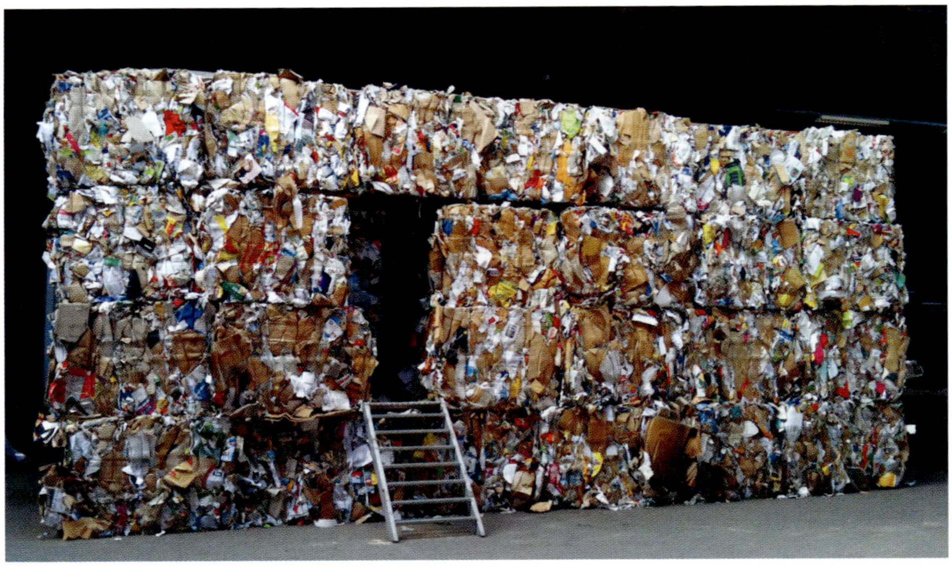

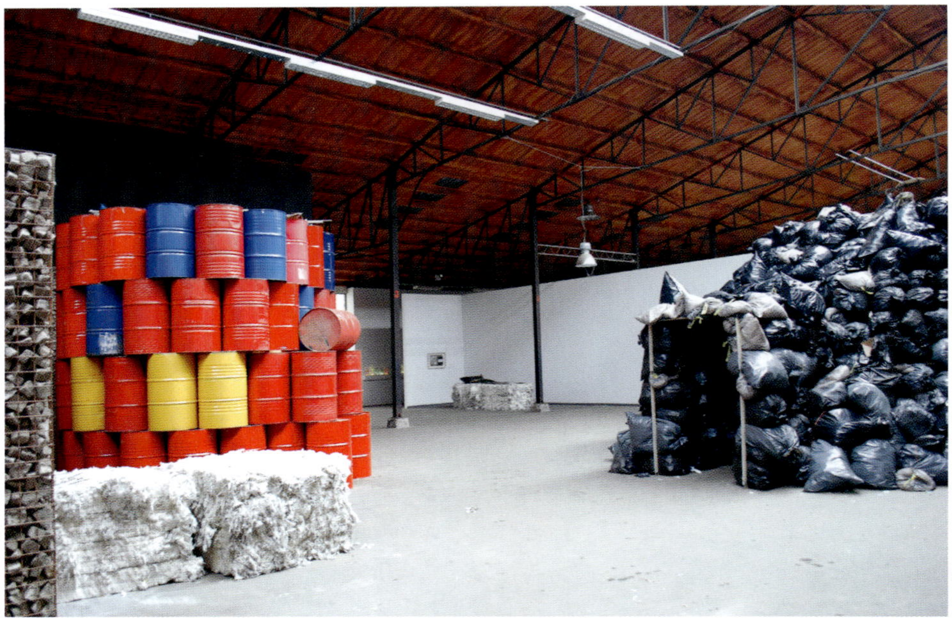

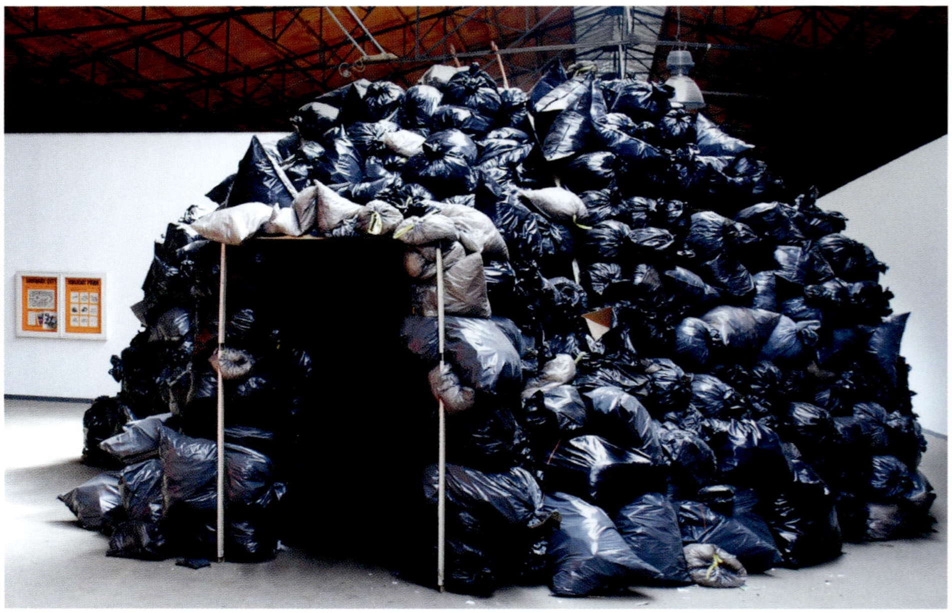

Black Garbage Iglo, 2010

Green Summer, Verbeke Foundation, Kemzeke, BE, 29.05.2010-31.10.2010

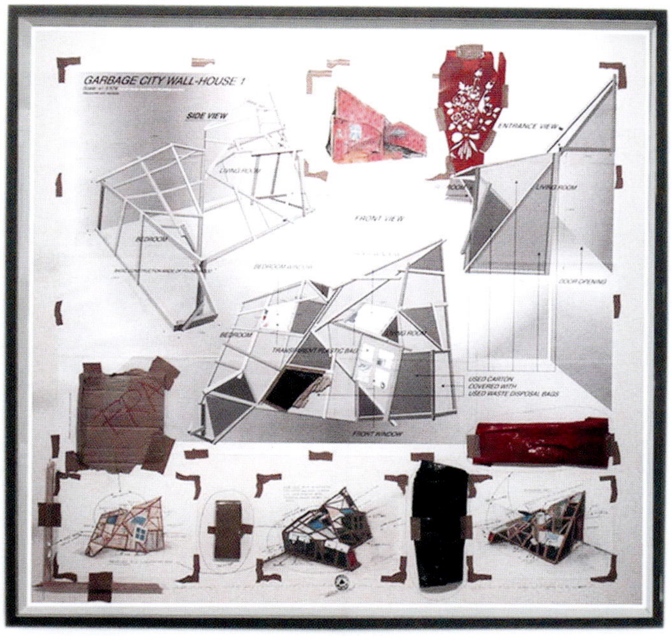

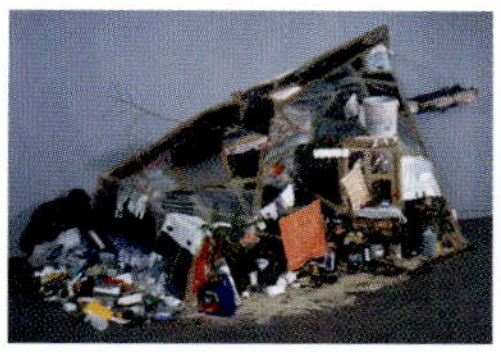

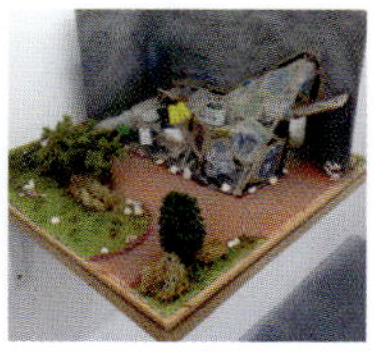

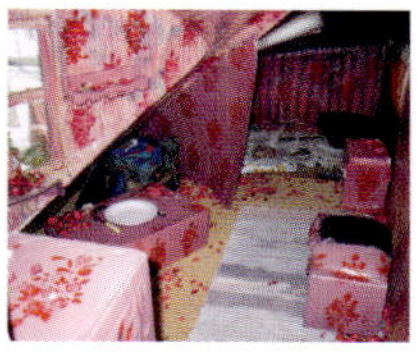

Garbage City Wall House 1, Installation, Technical Drawing & Model, 2004

Garbage City, Van Laere Contemporary Art, Antwerp, BE, 20.05.2004-03.07.2004

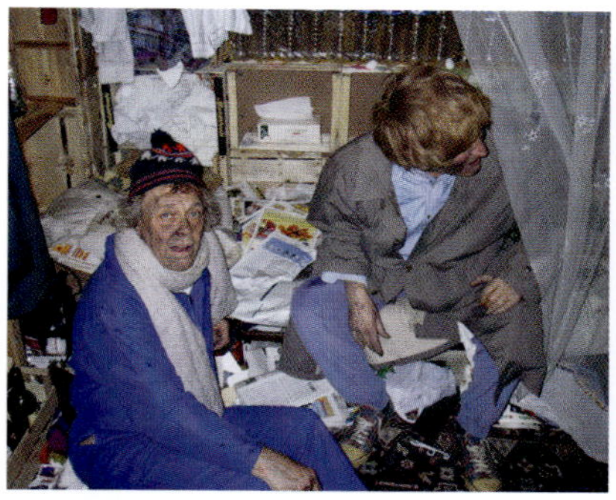

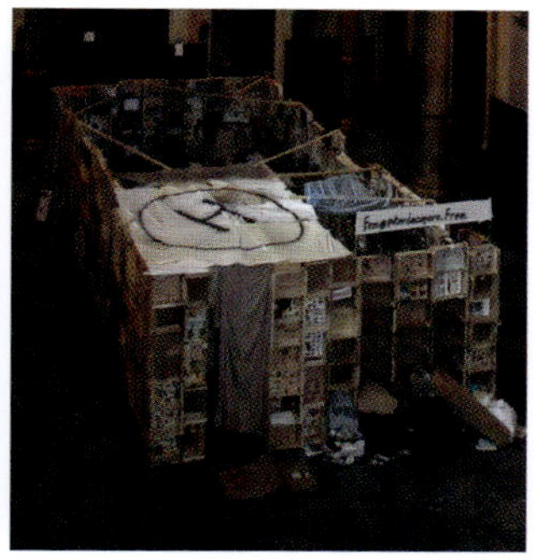

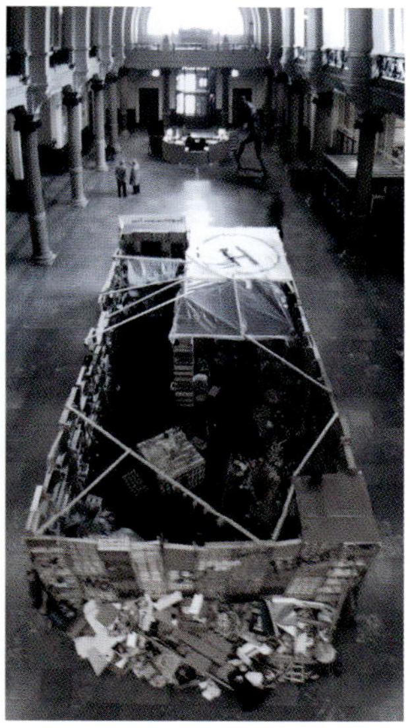

Crate House, 2003

Smell installation about poverty, garbage and freedom. Made of garbage and fruit crates
±500 cm x 1000 cm x 300 cm

Peter de Cupere, Hans Op de Beeck, Koen Van den Broek, Sergio De Beuckelaer, curator Paul Morrens, Justice Court Antwerpen, Antwerp, BE, 21.11.2002-28.11.2002

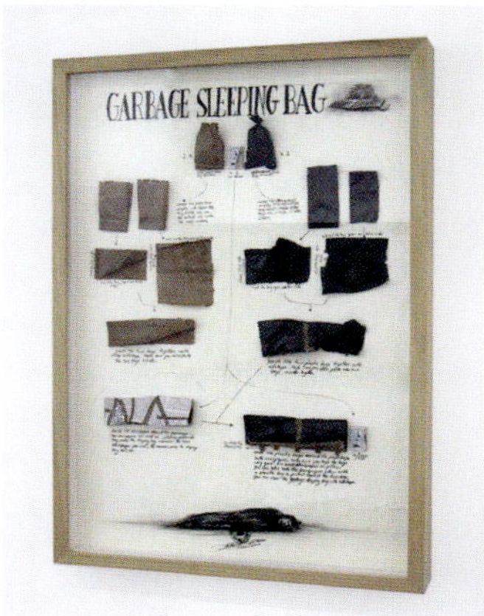

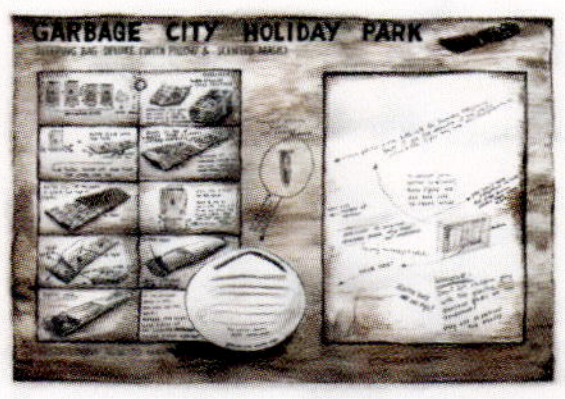

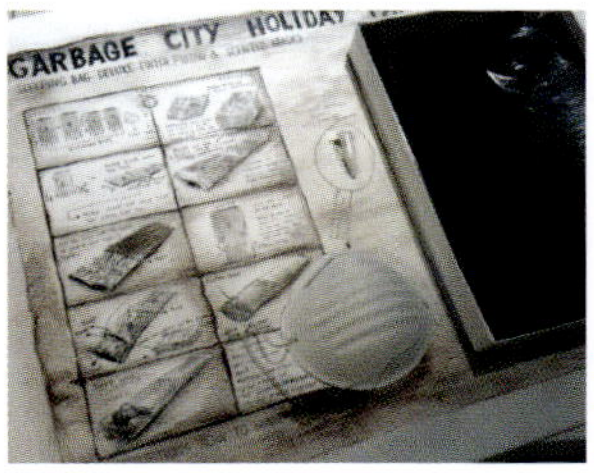

Edition Garbage Sleeping Bag, 2004

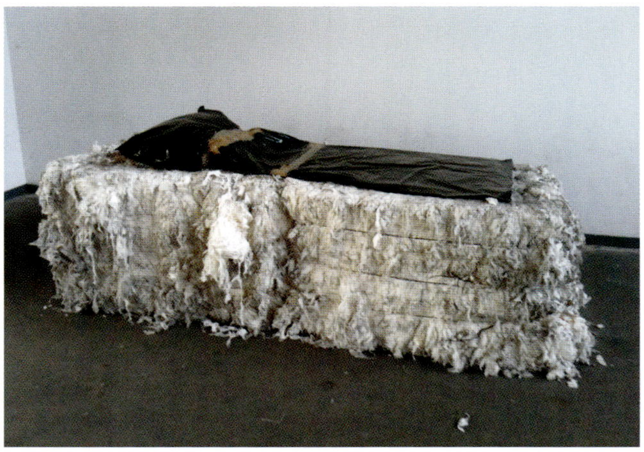

Green Summer, Verbeke Foundation, Kemzeke, BE, 29.05.2010-31.10.2010

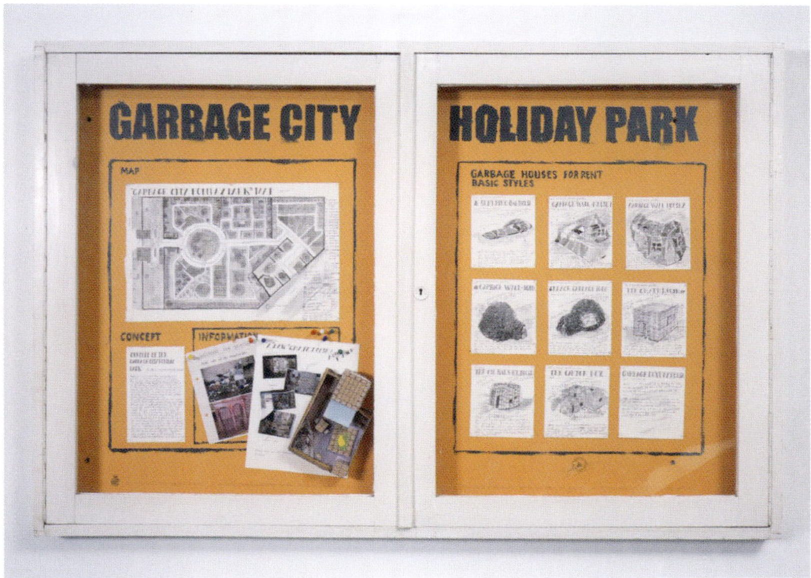

Concept Drawings Garbage City Holiday Park, 2004

100 cm x 149,5 cm x 6,5 cm

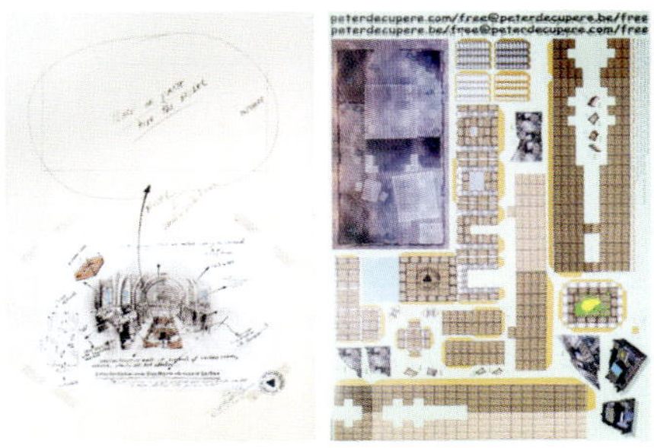

Edition Garbage City Holiday Park, 2010

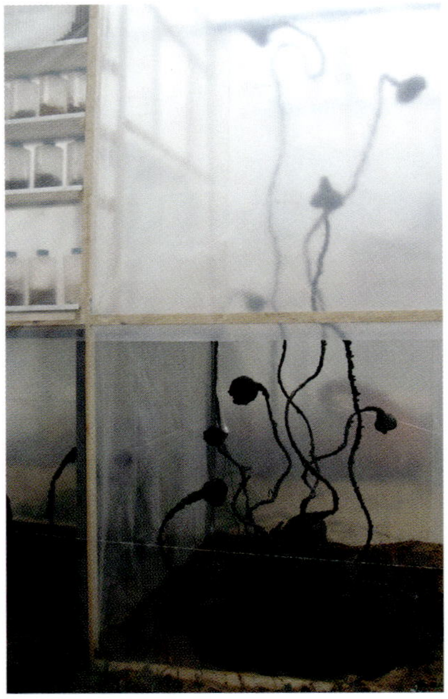

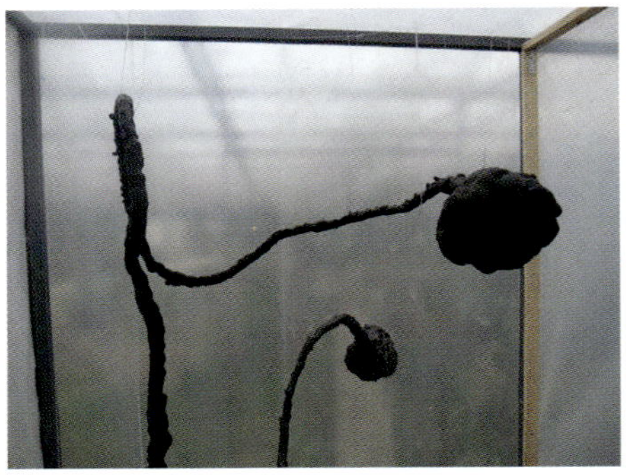

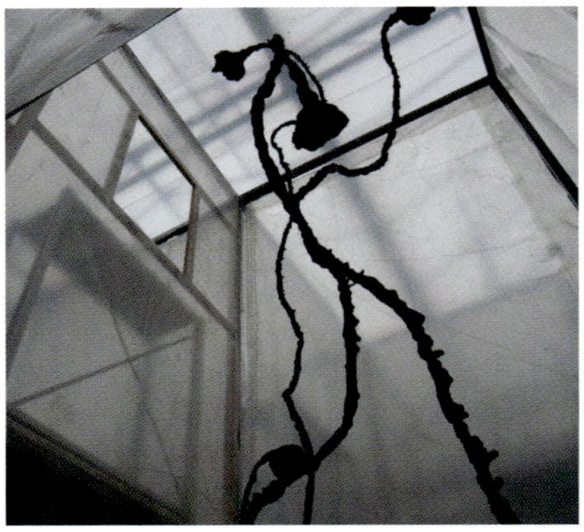

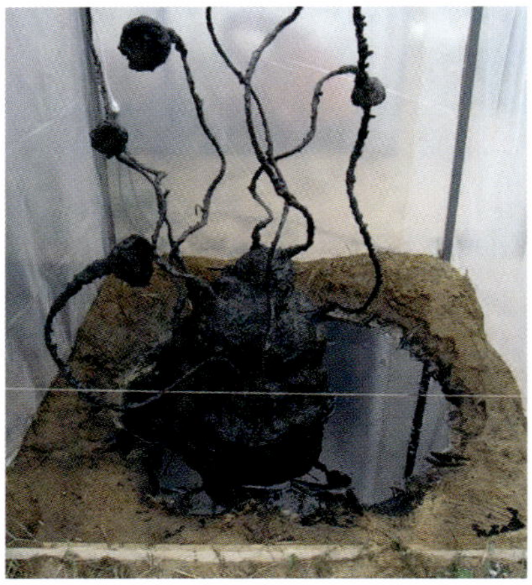

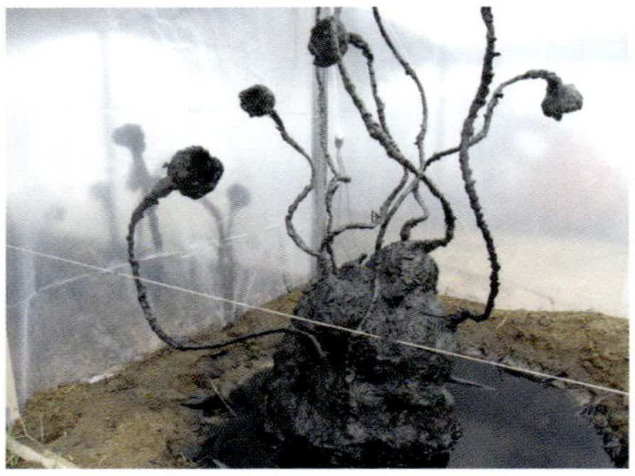

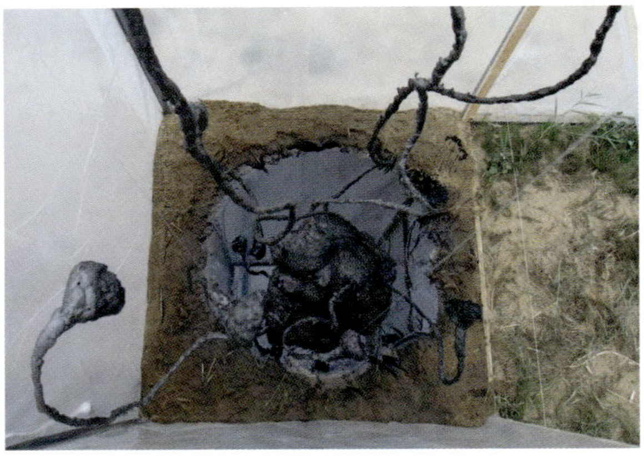

Black Oil Flower, 2009

Black Oil Flower, flowers turning polluted air into black crude oil.
Scent: polluted air & oil.

Black Oil Flower, bloemen die vervuilde lucht omzetten naar zwarte olie.
Ze ruiken naar vervuilde lucht en olie.

Artificial Nature, Verbeke Foundation, Kemzeke, BE, 23.05.2009-15.11.2009

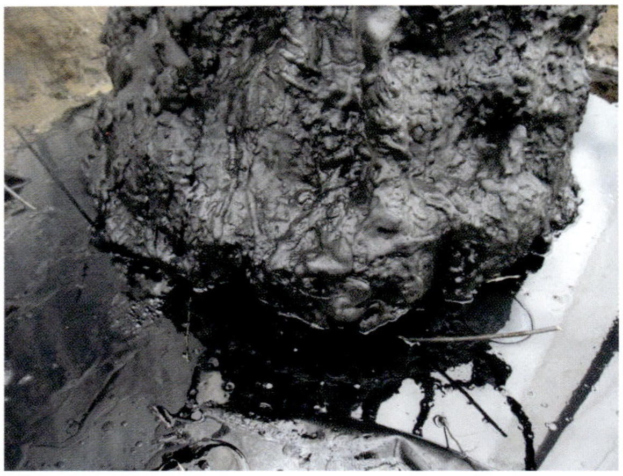

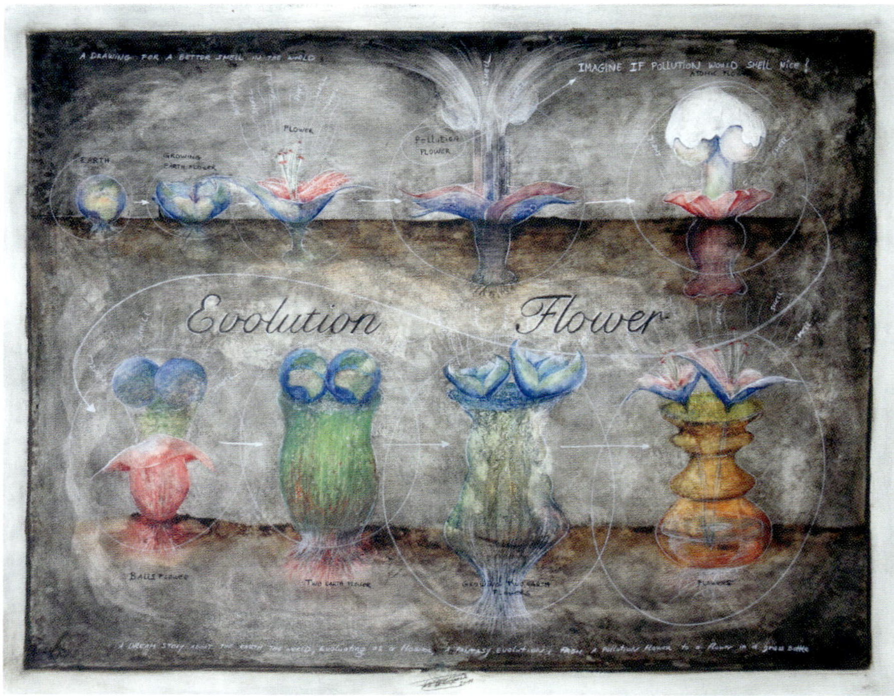

Evolution Flower, 2011

Mixed media
70 cm x 91 cm

Un Autre Monde, J.J. Grandville, Félicien Rops Museum,
curator Ronny Van De Velde, Namur, BE,25.06.2011-11.09.2011

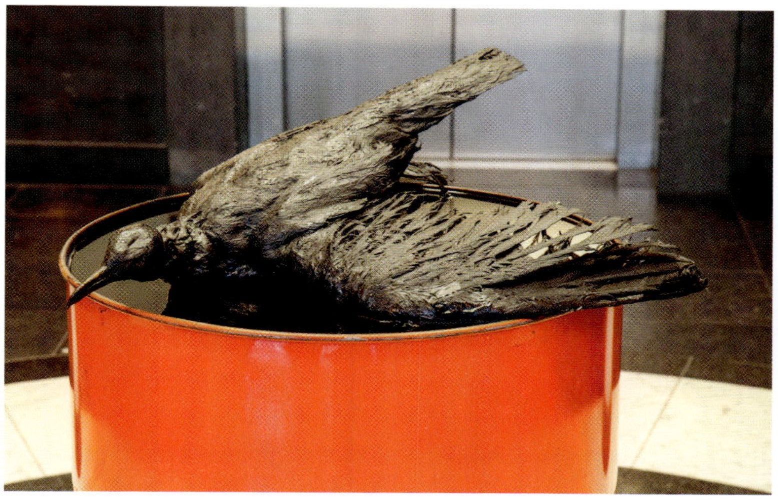

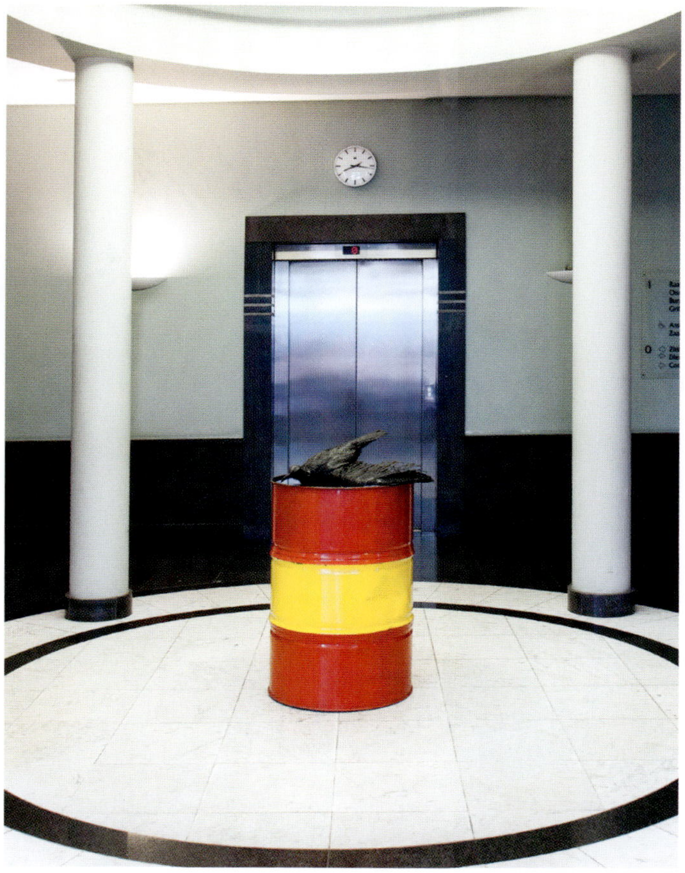

Oil Bird, 2004

H 110 cm x W 80 cm (Bird) x 57 cm

Seagull covered in oil, lying in black waste oil in a metal barrel.

Met olie vervuilde opgezette zeemeeuw, liggend op vervuilde zwarte olie in een metalen ton.

Sniff Your Jail, org. Balie Tongeren, curators Paul Morrens, Johan Smets,
Justice Palace Tongeren, BE, 14.05.2016-19.06.2015
Garbage City, Tim Van Laere Gallery, Antwerp, BE, 20.05.2004-03.07.2004

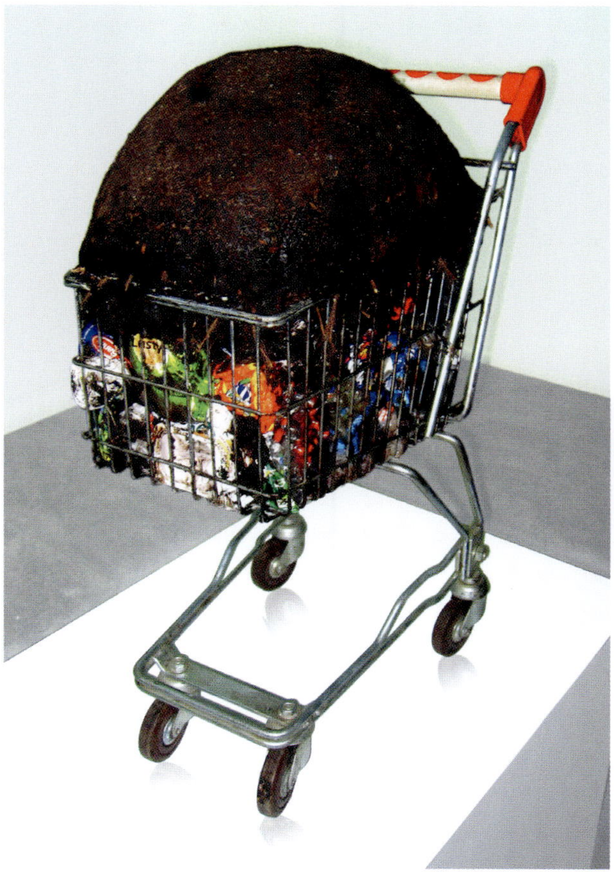

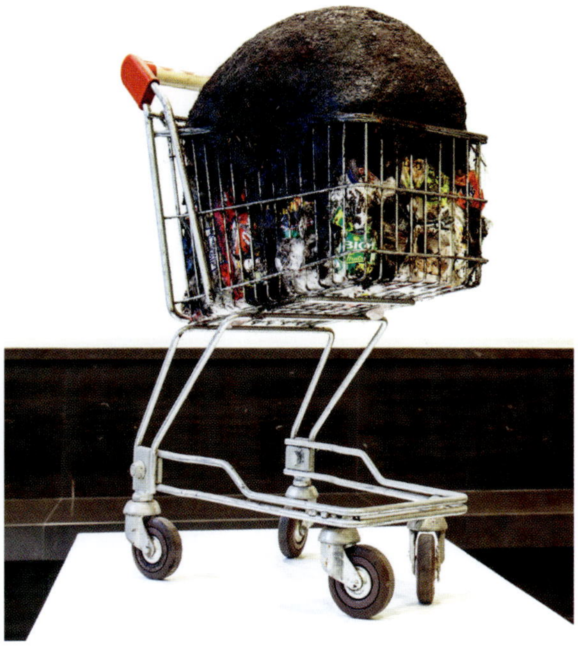

Pregnancy of the World, 2005

Mini-shopping cart with rubbish left from the items purchased, covered with a pregnant belly made of earth.

Mini-winkelkar met restafval van aangekochte goederen bedekt met een zwangere buik gemaakt uit aarde.

Sniff Your Jail, org. Balie Tongeren, curators Paul Morrens, Johan Smets,
Justice Palace Tongeren, BE, 14.05.2016-19.06.2015
ARCO, Art fair Madrid, Van Laere Contemporary Art, Madrid, ES, 08.02.2006-13.02.2006

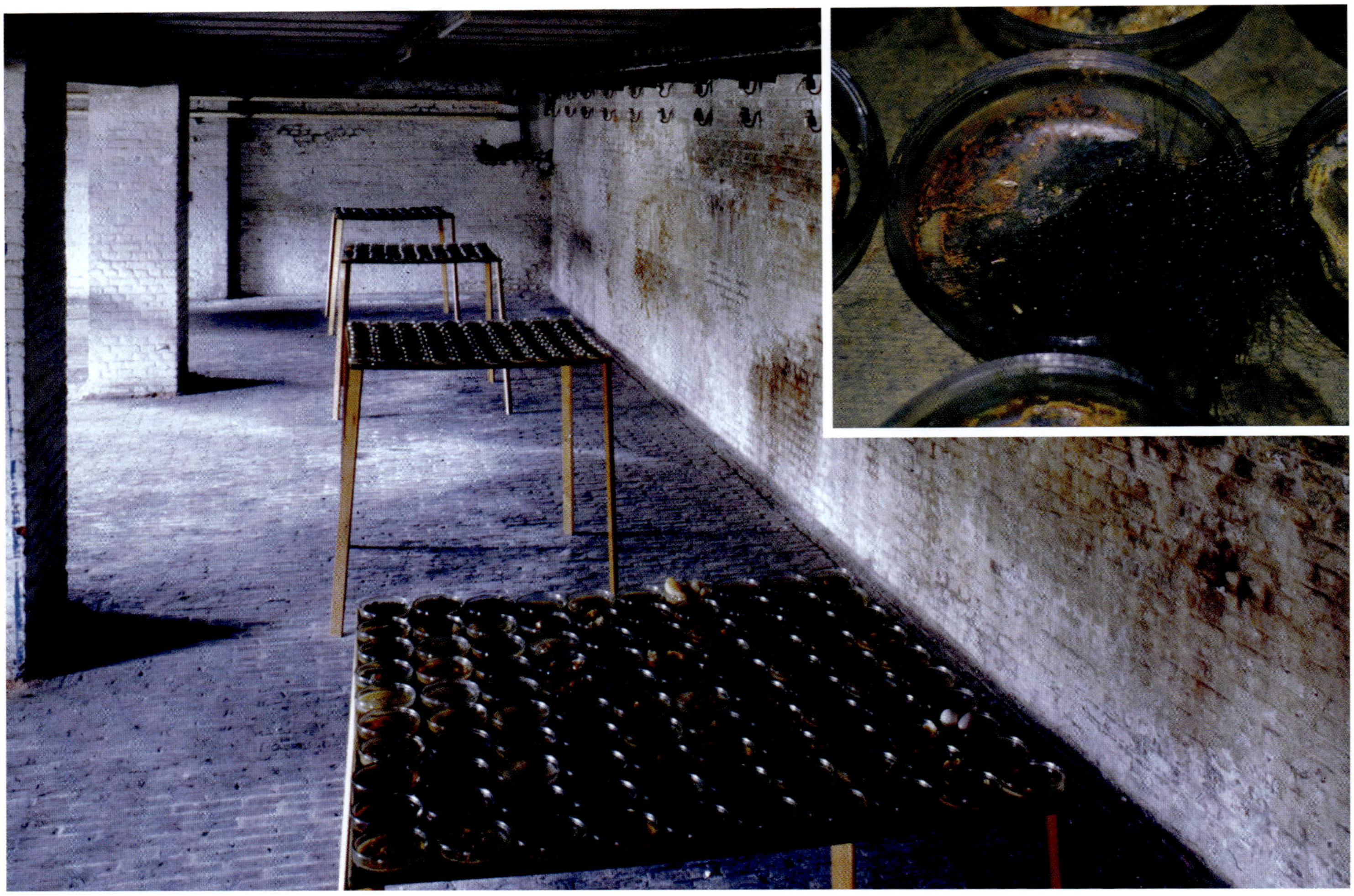

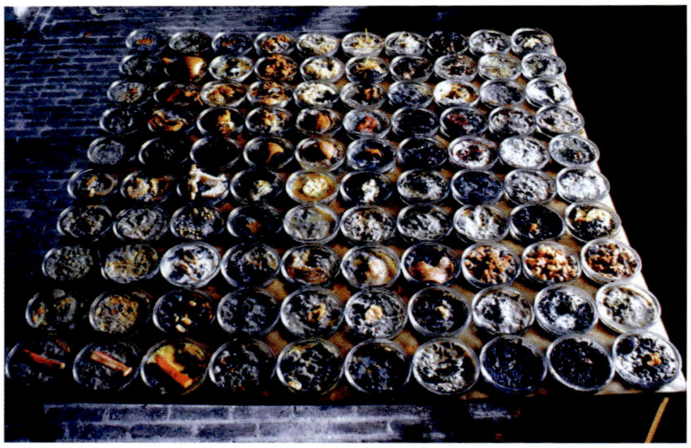

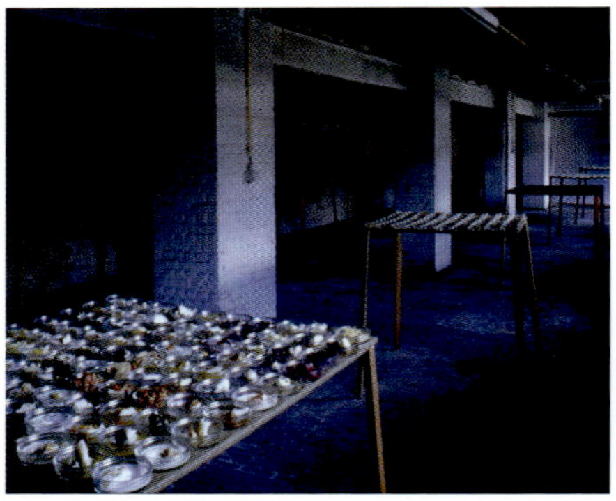

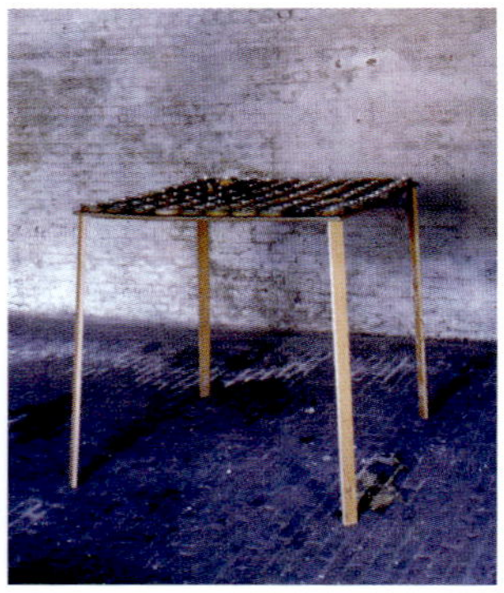

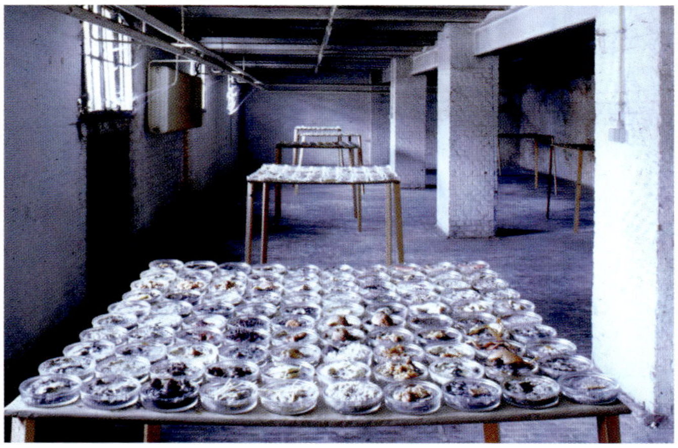

Mouldy Installation, 1997-1999

1,000 pots with different mouldy food organised in a group of 100 per table, placed on 10 tables in the space. The mould activators are water, milk and orange juice.
Dimensions of the space vary. Tables: H 100 cm x W 100 cm x D 100 cm

Installed work in the cellars of the HISK, Hoger Instituut voor Schone Kunsten (Higher Institute of Fine Arts)

1,000 glass bowls with various types of mould. Artistic research into how fungi change in both colour and smell, from which a work-in-progress painting was produced using basic ingredients, such as vegetables, fruit, etc. Title of painting: Evolution Painting.

In situ werk in de kelders van het HISK, Hoger Instituut voor Schone Kunsten.
1.000 glazen schalen met verschillende soorten schimmels. Artistiek onderzoek naar hoe schimmels van kleur en geur veranderen om daarna met de basisingrediënten, groenten & fruit, een veranderlijk schilderij te maken met als titel *Evolution Painting*.

Akademie der Künsten, Exhibited 3 tables on invitation by Dieter Appelt, Berlin, DE, 03-04.2002

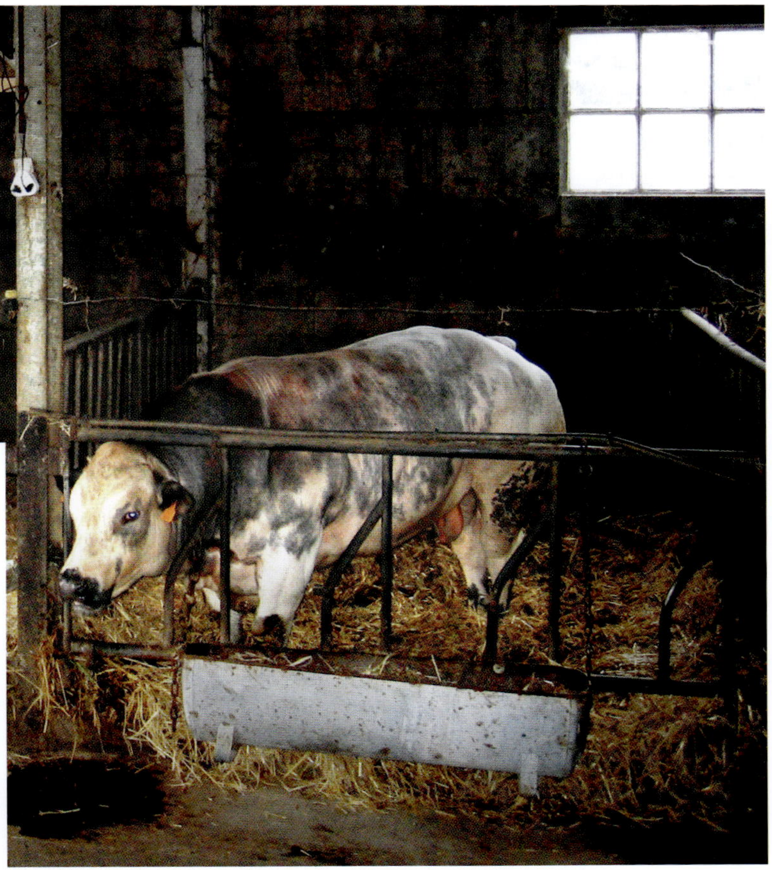

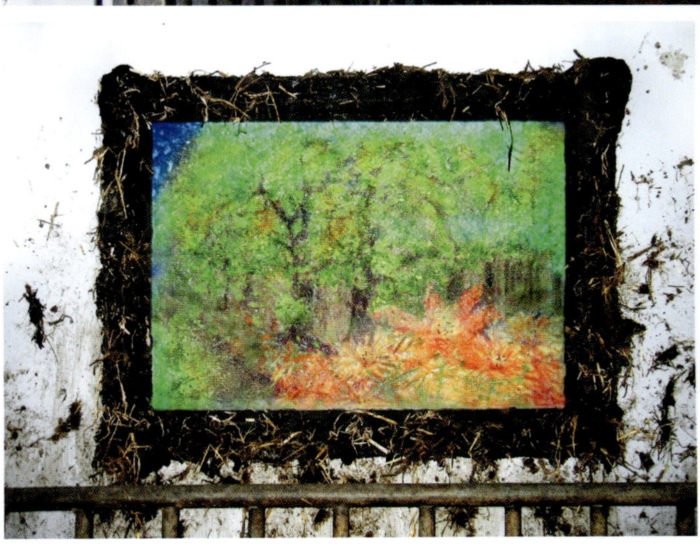

Evolution Painting in the exhibition Déjeuner sur l'herbe,

Evolution Painting, 1997-2005

Video 720 x 576, full colour, 3 min., 2005

From the work titled 'Mouldy Installation', one can deduce which vegetables and fruit in what conditions produce a particular grey colour after they grow mouldy. This way, two differently coloured vegetables can end up being of almost the same colour, or two or more vegetables with the same colour may end up looking completely different after becoming mouldy. It is with this fact as its starting point that 'Evolution Painting' was made.

Vegetables and fruit were mixed separately or in combinations in a blender. The shakes were used to make this painting. Once the kitschy landscape was painted, the work was stored in a home-made climate box. For the next 23 days, a photo was taken every few minutes. After 23 days in the climate box, the photos were linked together like an animated film that makes it possible to observe the evolution of the work clearly on video. The once kitschy but delightful, natural smelling landscape was turned, by the mould, into a filthy-looking industrial scene. The trees became smokestacks, the foliage turned into polluting clouds of smoke.

Uit het werk Mouldy Installation werd experimenteel afgeleid welke groenten en fruit onder welke omstandigheden een bepaalde grauwe kleur kregen nadat ze beschimmelen. Zo kunnen twee verschillend gekleurde groenten als eindresultaat praktisch dezelfde kleur verkrijgen of kunnen twee of meerdere groenten met dezelfde kleur juist na het beschimmelen er van kleur totaal verschillend uitzien. Vertrekkende vanuit dit gegeven werd *Evolution Painting* gemaakt. Groenten en fruit werden afzonderlijk of in combinaties gemixt in een blender. De shakes dienden als verf om het schilderij te maken. Eens het kitscherige natuurlandschap was geschilderd, werd het werk in een zelf gemaakte klimaatbox opgeslagen. Met een fototoestel werd gedurende 23 dagen om de paar minuten een foto genomen. Na 23 dagen in de klimaatbox werden de foto's als een animatiefilm achter elkaar geplaatst en kon men zo de evolutie van het werk duidelijk waarnemen op video. Het eens kitscherige lekker natuurlijk ruikend landschap ging al schimmelend over in een vervuilend uitziende industrie en industrieel landschap. De bomen werden schoorstenen, het loof werd een vervuilende rookwolk.

Déjeuner sur l'herbe, curator Stef Van Bellingen, Vlaamse Ardennen, BE, 25.06.2006-30.07.2006
De Gustibus, Broel Museum, curators Lieven Van Den Abeele, Veerle Van Durme & Anne Petre, ING Kortrijk, BE, 14.02.2007-29.04.2007

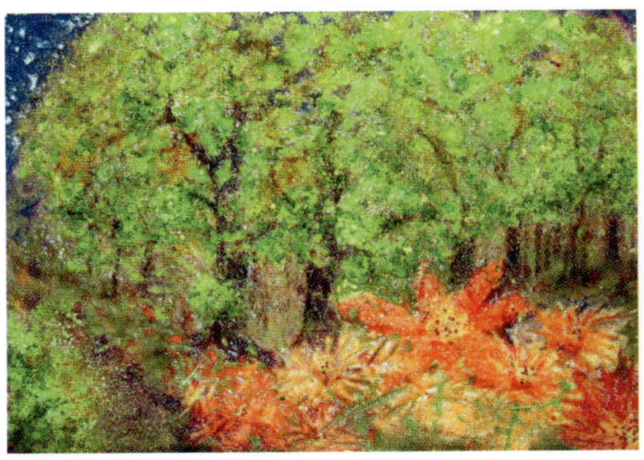

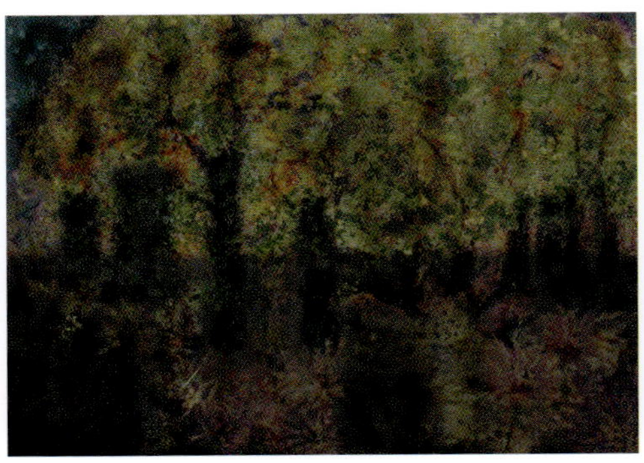

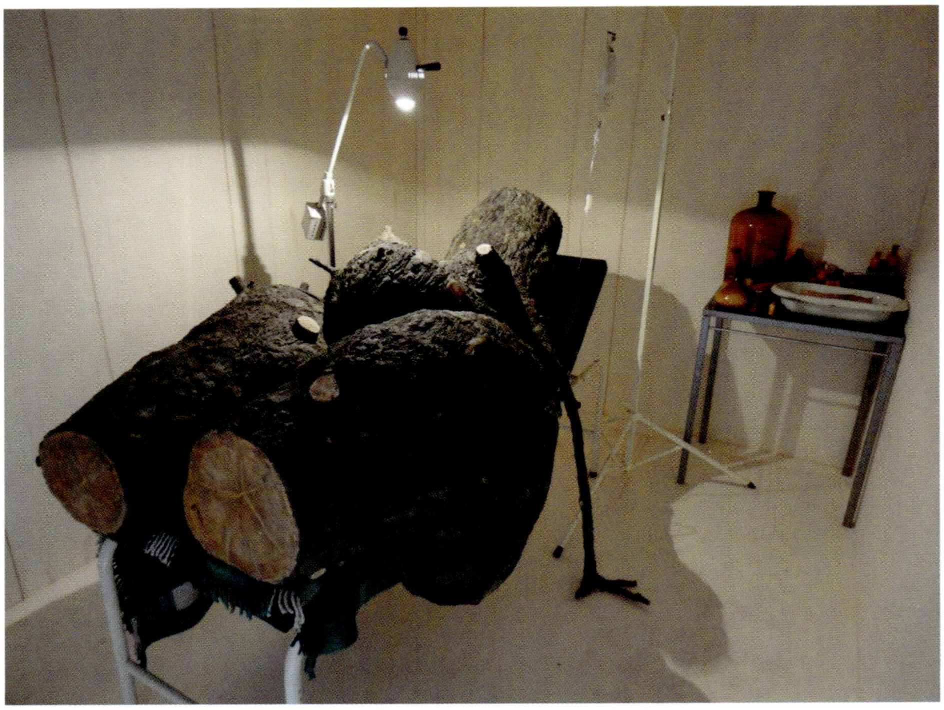

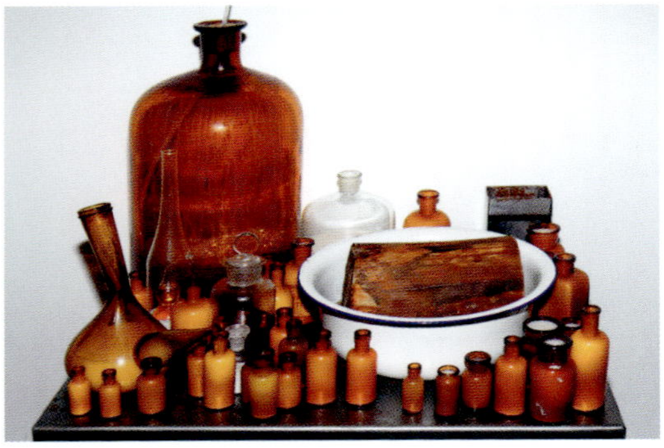

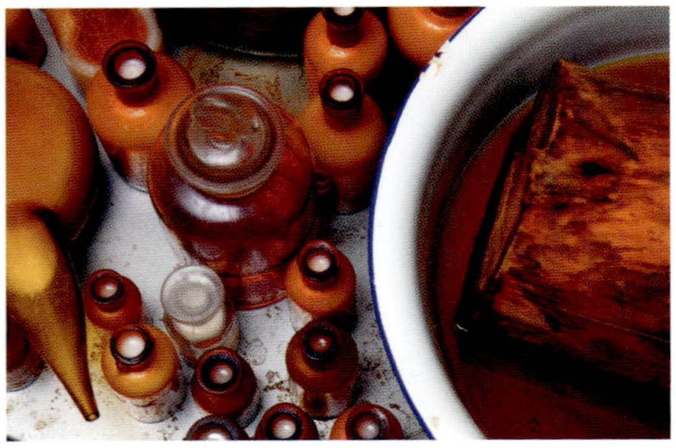

Sick Tree, 2010 in the exhibition Crossover, Brussels

Sick Trees, 2010

Epoxy, wood, glass, iron, smell of Dettol

Epoxy, hout, glas, ijzer, geur van Dettol

Crossover, The Royal Flemish Academy of Science and Arts, curator Sven Vanderstichelen, Brussels, BE, 11.12.2010-30.01.2011
Artist Project, Art Brussels, Artexis, curators Karen Renders & Nele Verhaeren, Brussels, BE, 22.04.2010-25.04.2010

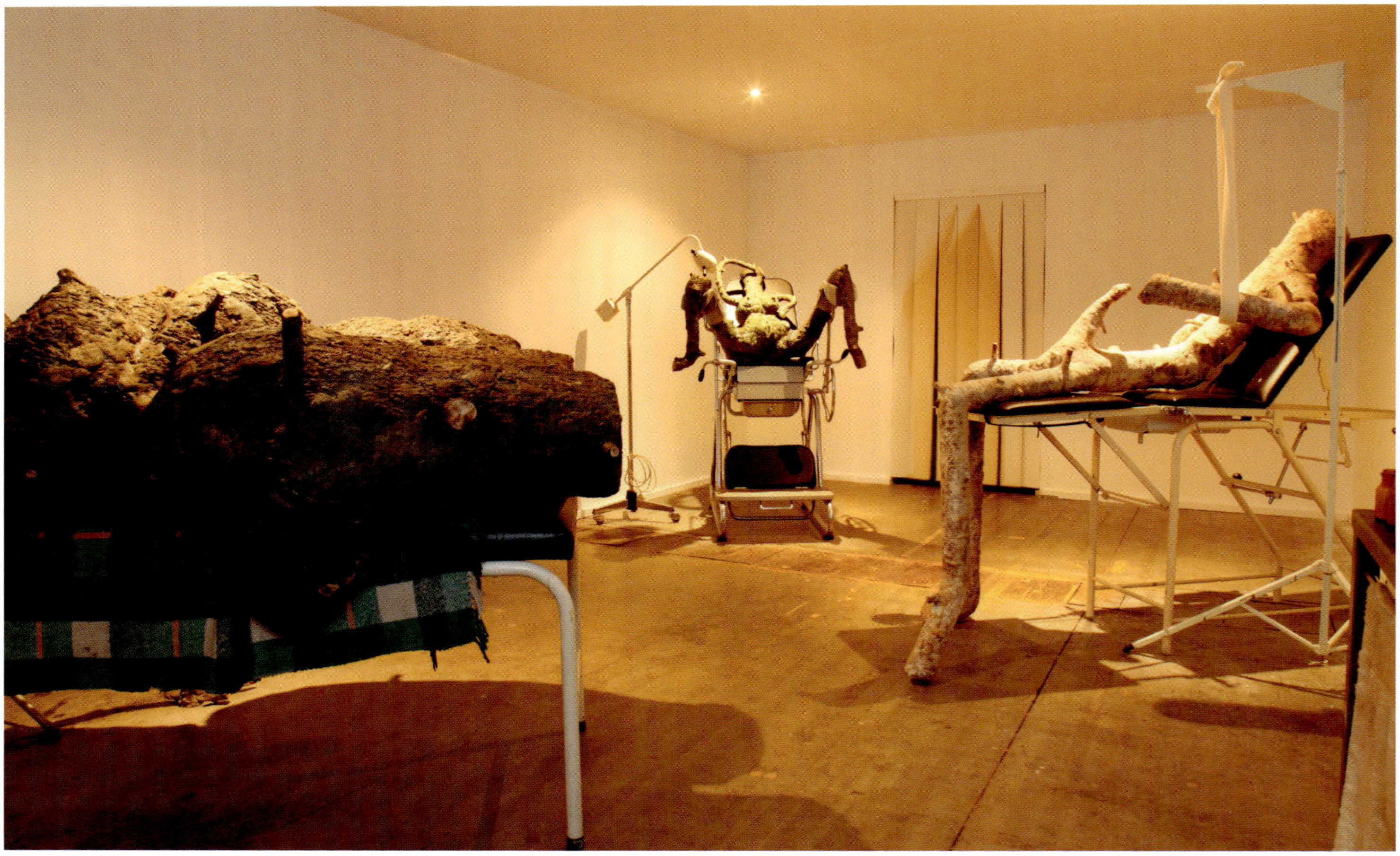

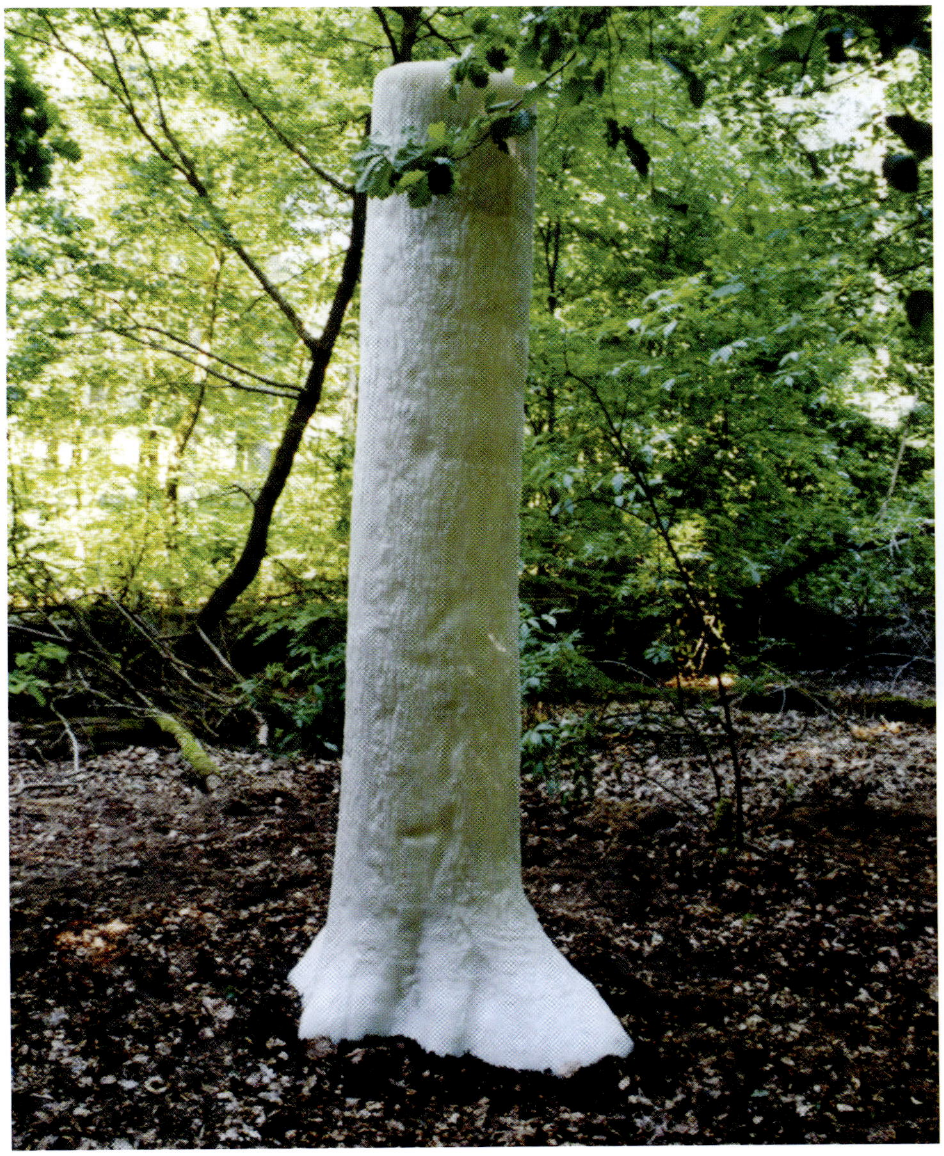

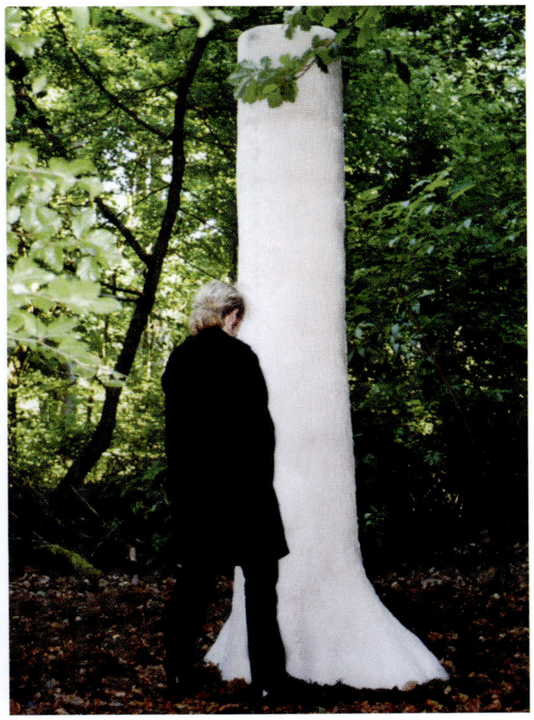

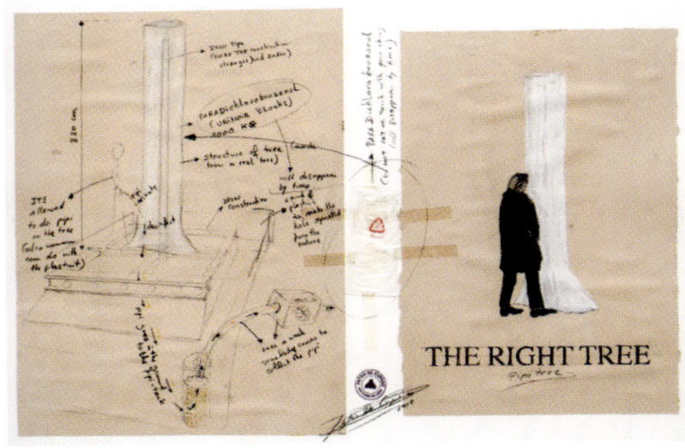

Drawing The Right Tree, 2001

54 cm x 76 cm

The Right Tree, 2002

H 300 cm x Ø 60 cm

Tree made of materials from disinfectant toilet blocks, para-dichlorobenzene. Visitors could urinate against the tree. Women were provided with urination devices. The urine was captured in an underground reservoir. The tree sublimated very gradually.

Boomstam gemaakt met desinfecterende wc-blokjes uit paradichloorbenzeen.Bezoekers kunnen urineren tegen de stam. Voor vrouwen is er een plastuit voorzien. De urine wordt opgevangen dankzij een ondergronds reservoir. De boom lost zelf heel traag op.

Sonsbeek 9, curator Jan Hoet, Arnhem, NL, 03.06-23.09.2001

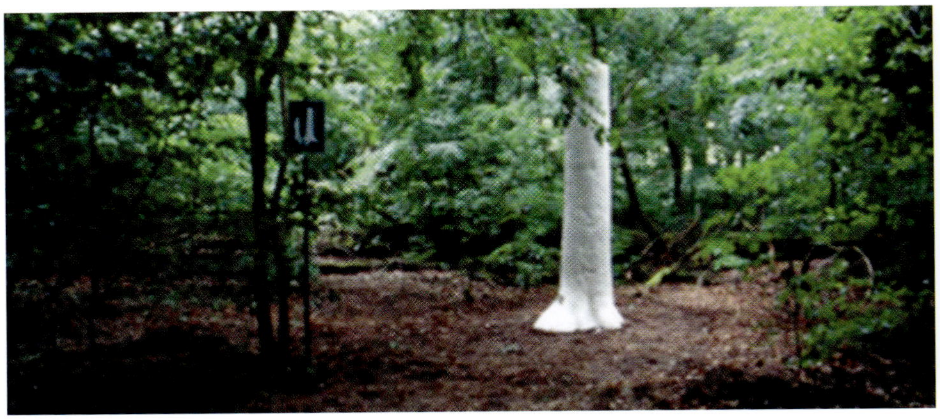

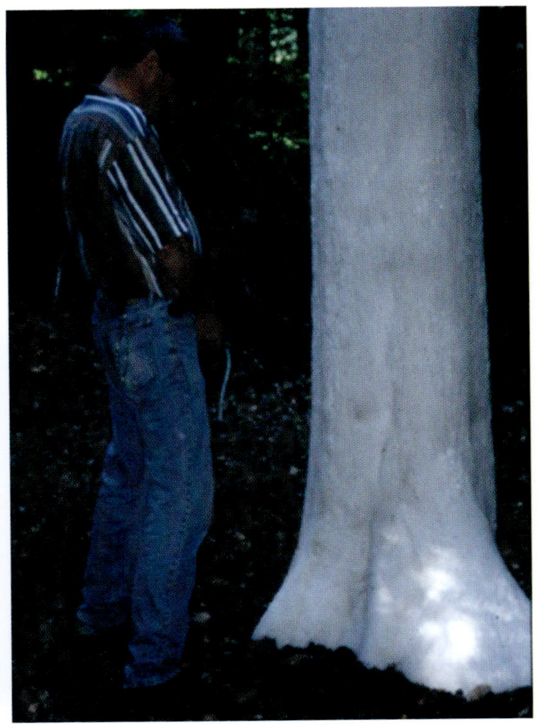

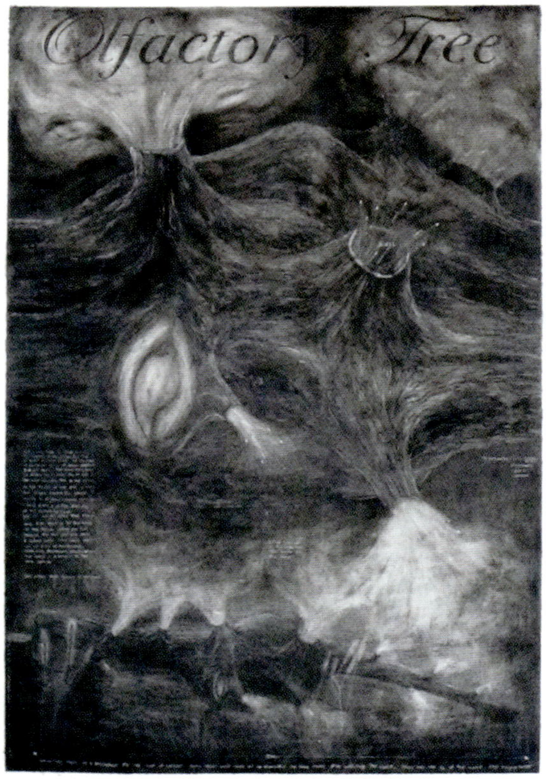

Drawing Olfactory Tree, 2010

192,5 cm x 134 cm

Drawing on canvas

Tekening op doek

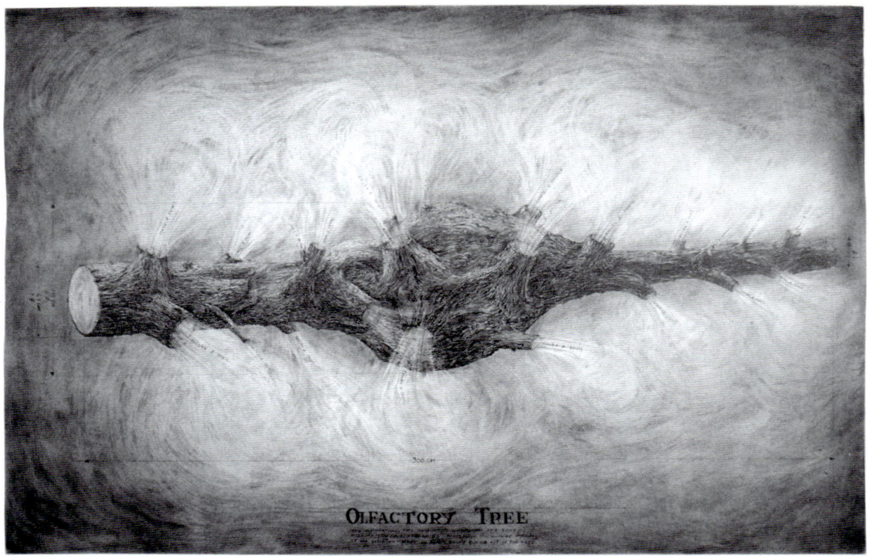

Olfactory Tree Drawings, 2010

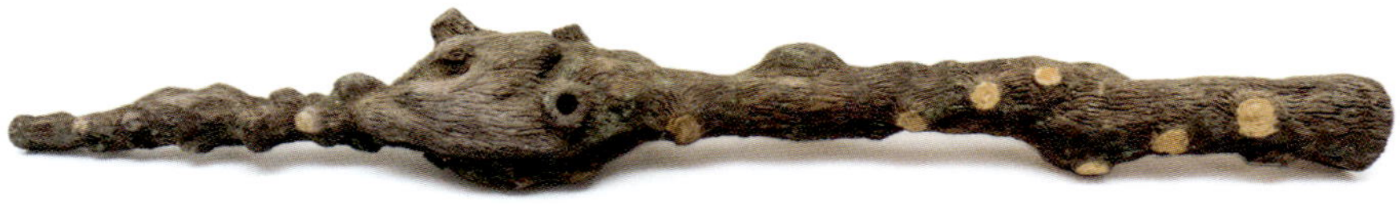

Olfactory Tree Model, 2010

Epoxy, 94 cm x 12,5 cm x 9 cm

Olfactory Tree, Pocketroom, curator Wim Waumans, Antwerpen, BE, 12.09.2010-31.10.2010

Olfactory Tree

Tree made of epoxy, L 900 cm
Smell in the tree: burned scent

Boom gemaakt uit epoxy, 900 cm
Geur in de boom: verbrande geur

Solo-Tentoonstellingen:
The Art of Smelling, Olfactory Art Research, Art Center Rozendaal 21, Yasmijn Jarram, Enschede, NL, 01.12.2013-02.03.2014
Olfactory Tree, Pocketroom, curator Wim Waumans-Antwerpen, BE 12.09.2010-31.10.2010

Groepstentoonstellingen:
Aandacht, Aandacht (Attention, Attention), C-Mine, curator Annelies Nagels, Genk, BE, 15.09.2015-15.11.2015
Aandacht, Aandacht (Attention, Attention), Warande, curator Annelies Nagels, Turnhout, BE, 25.03.2015-24.05.2015

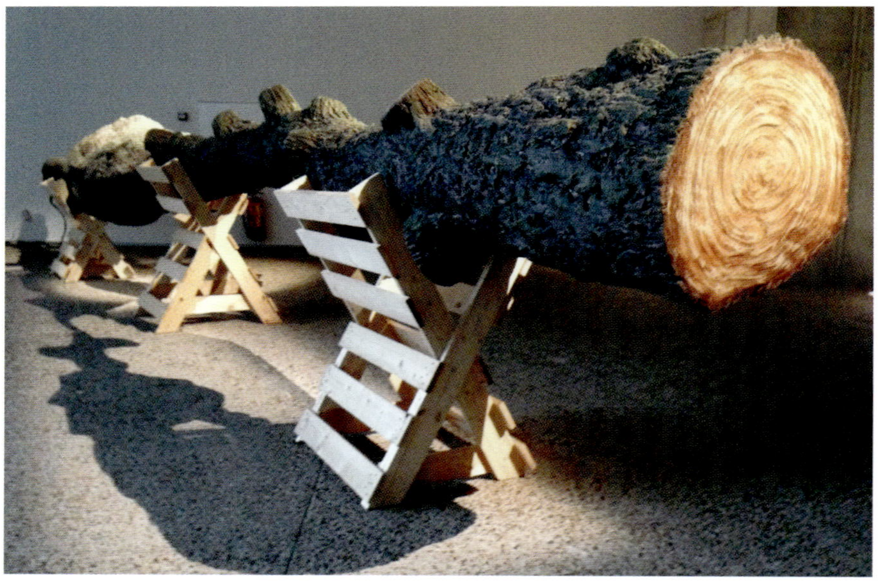

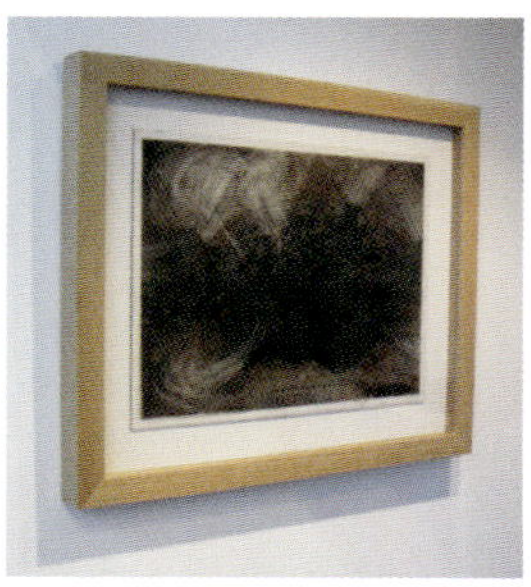

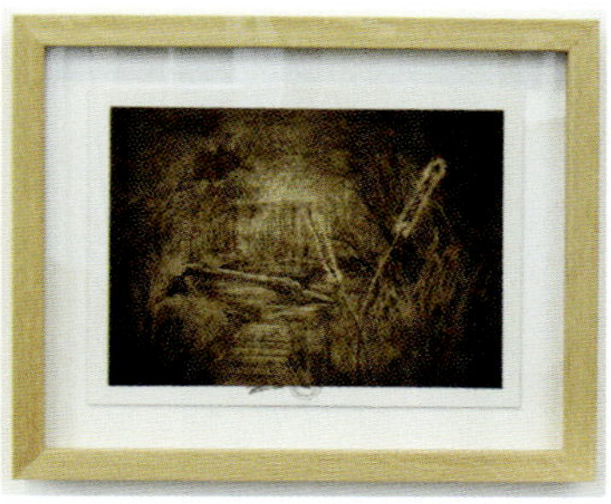

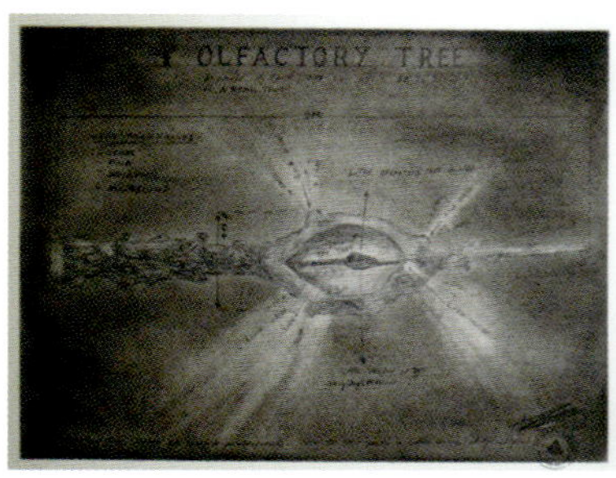

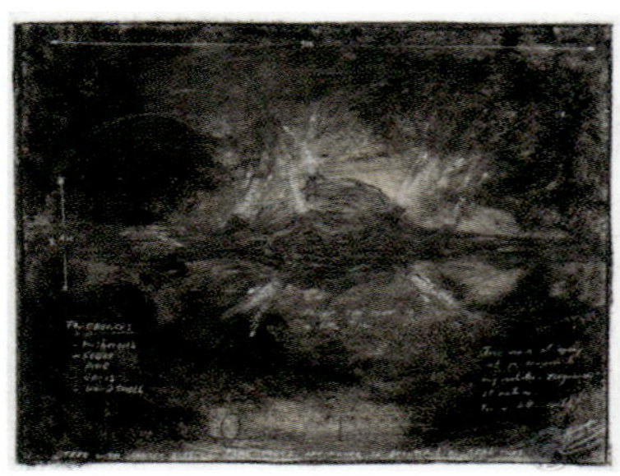

Olfactory Tree Drawings, 2010

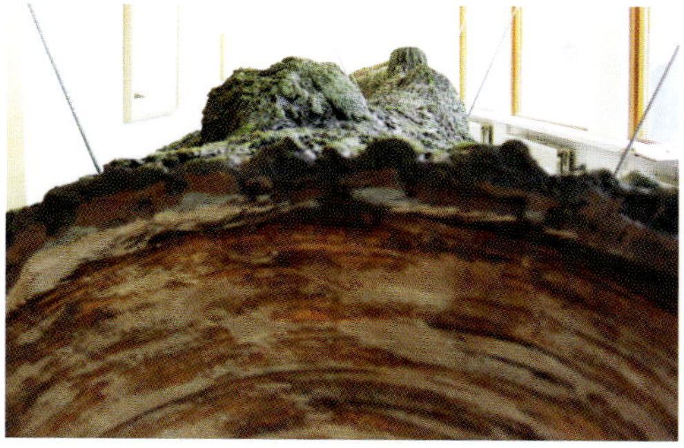
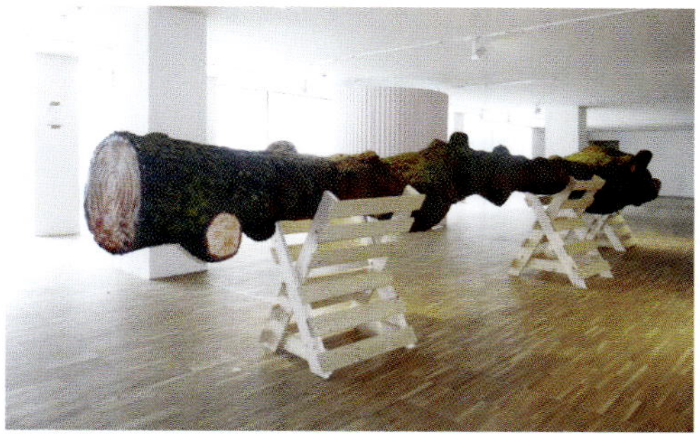
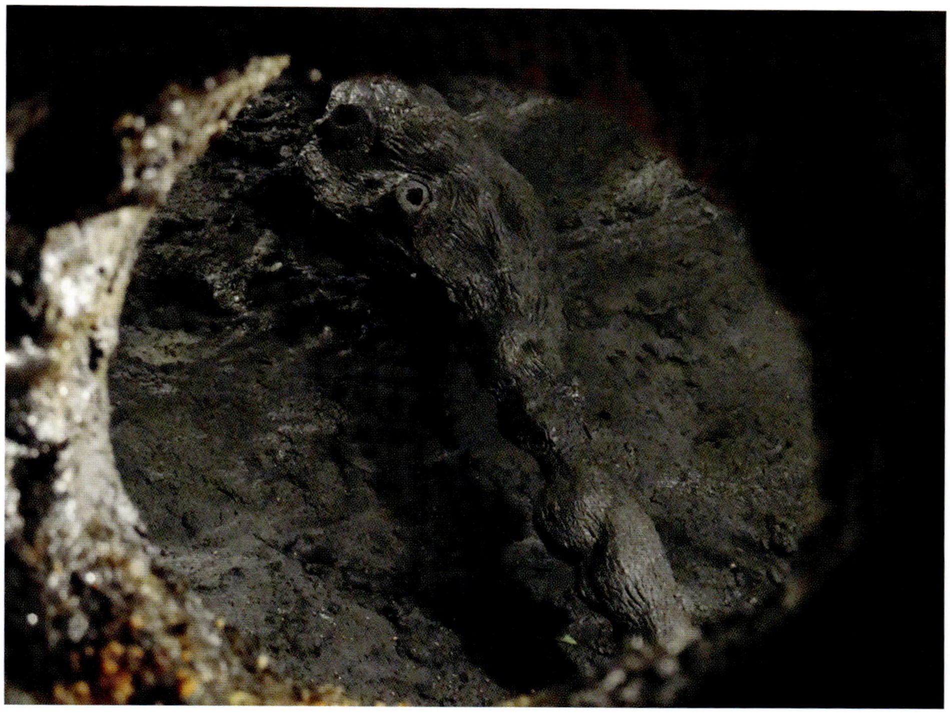
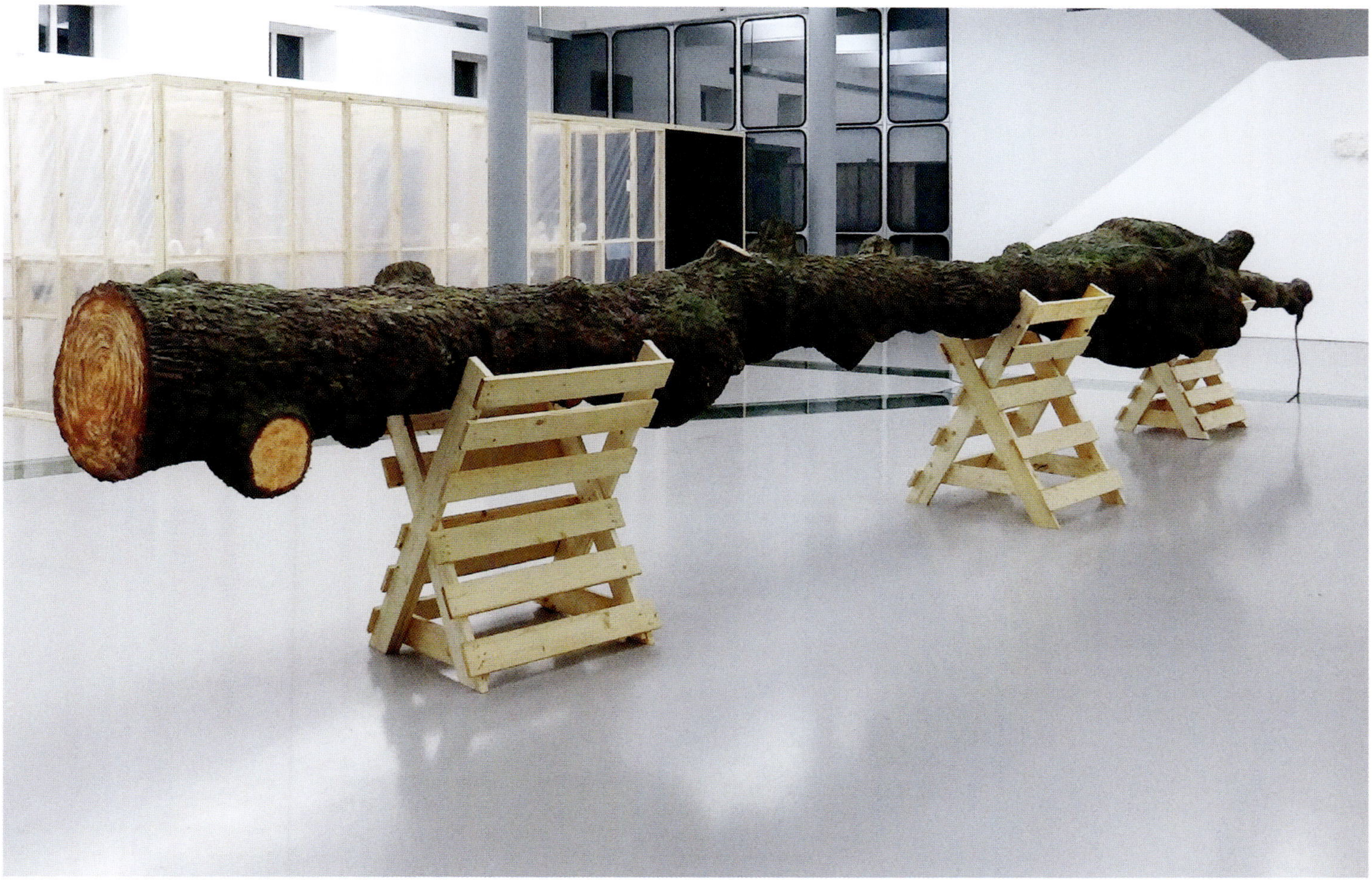

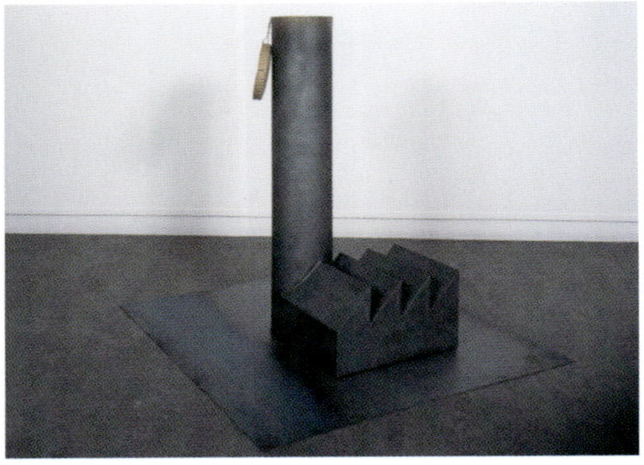

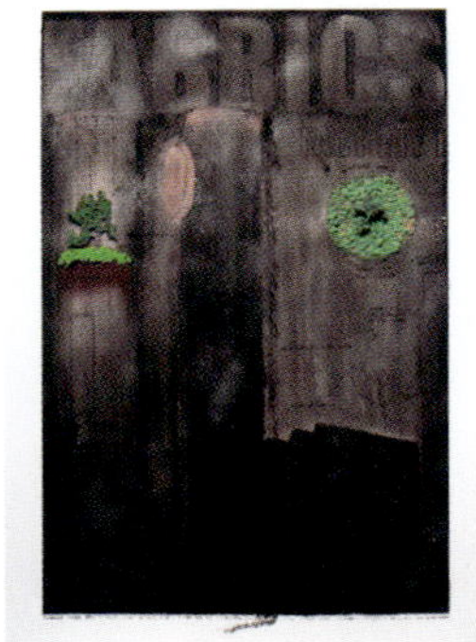

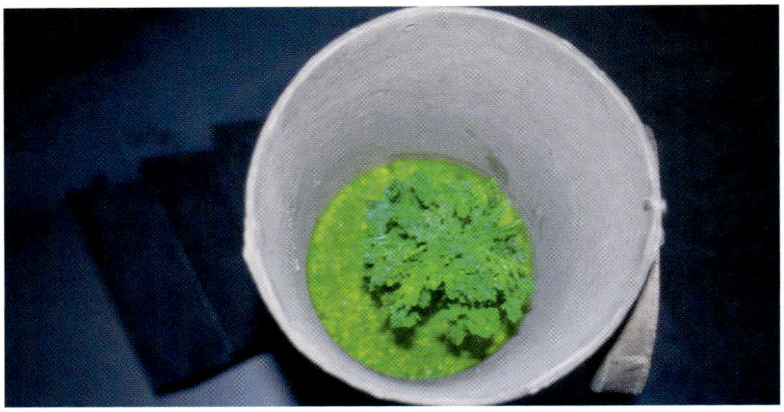

Fabrics I, 2004

H 97 cm x W 42 cm x D 40 cm

Factory made of carton, painted iron, metal plate, model tree and grass, smell of pine.

Fabriek gemaakt van karton, beschilderd ijzer, maquette met boom en gras, met de geur van den.

Garbage City, Van Laere Contemporary Art, Antwerp, BE, 20.05.2004-03.07.2004

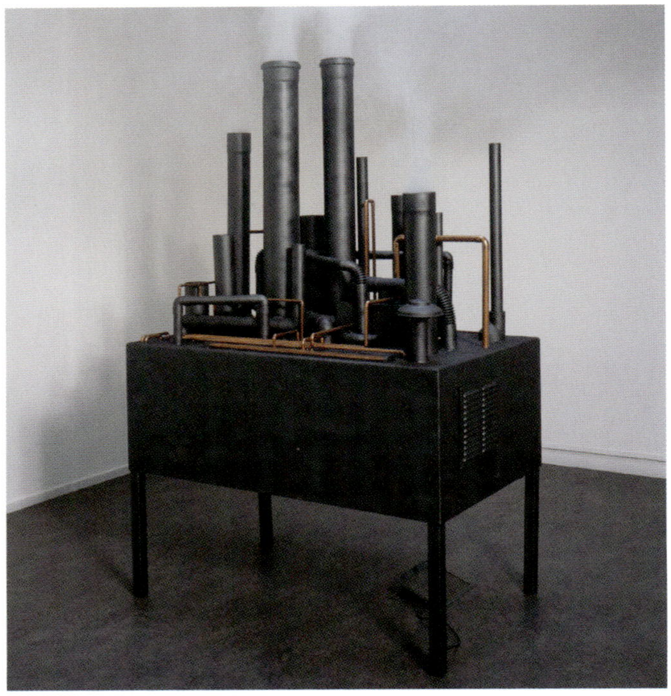

Fabrics III, 2004

H 190 cm x W 122 cm x D 81 cm

Factory made of iron, copper and plastic, painted iron, smoke machinery, smell of pine. Out of the fabrics comes smoke with pine smell. The visitor can decide by himself how long the factory will smoke.

Fabriek gemaakt van ijzer, koper en plastiek, geschilderd ijzer, stoomuitrusting, met de geur van den. Uitstoot van rook uit de schoorsteen met dennengeur. De bezoeker kan zelf beslissen hoelang de fabriek stoomt.

Garbage City, Van Laere Contemporary Art, Antwerp, BE, 20.05.2004-03.07.2004

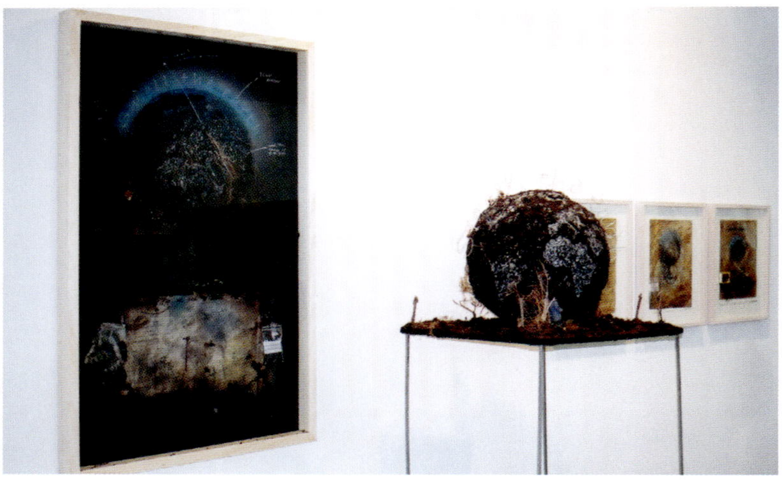

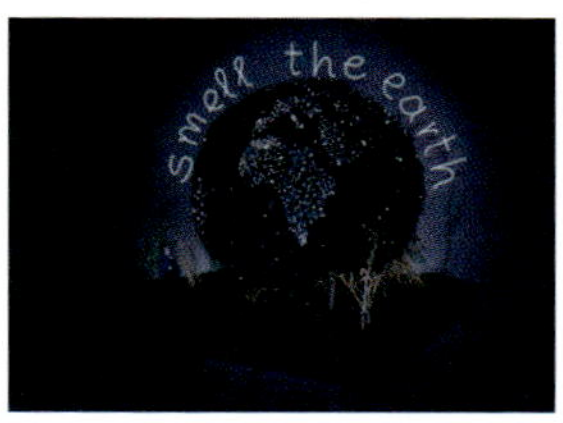

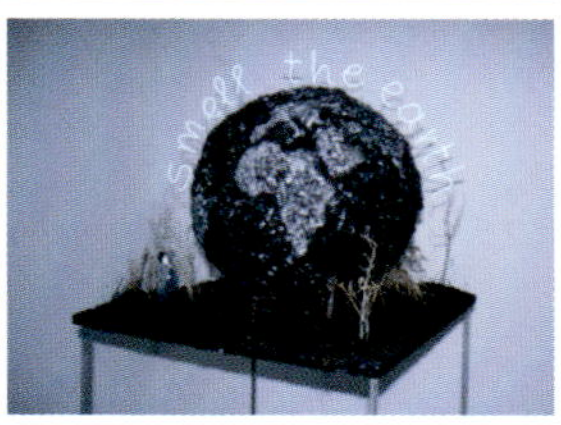

Smell The Earth, 2000

Earth, glue, fluorescent paint, metal, wood, etc. Text lights up in the dark. Concept for big globe with 10,000 real glow-worms.

Aarde, lijm, fluorescerende verf, metaal, hout, etc. De tekst licht op in het donker. Concept voor een grote aardbol met 10.000 echte glimwormen.

Metamorphosis, Peter de Cupere, Berlinde De Bruyckere, Peter Buggenhout, Johan Tahon, Galleria d'Arte Moderna, curator Christa Vyvey, San Gimignano, IT, Dec.-Jan.2000-2001
Smell the Castle, Castle Beauvoorde, curator Annemie Morisse, Beauvoorde, BE, 15.07.2007-30.08.2007

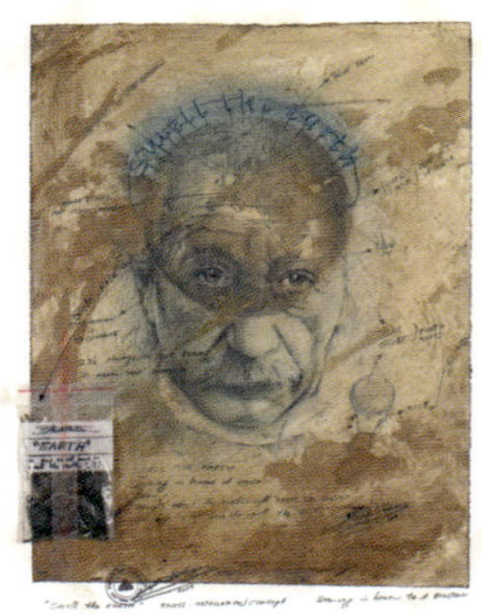

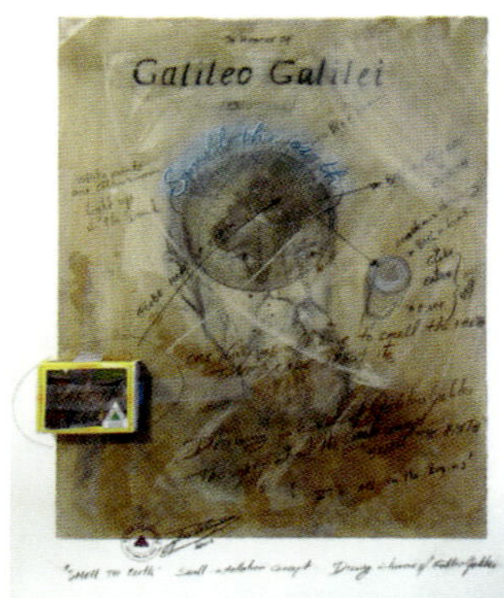

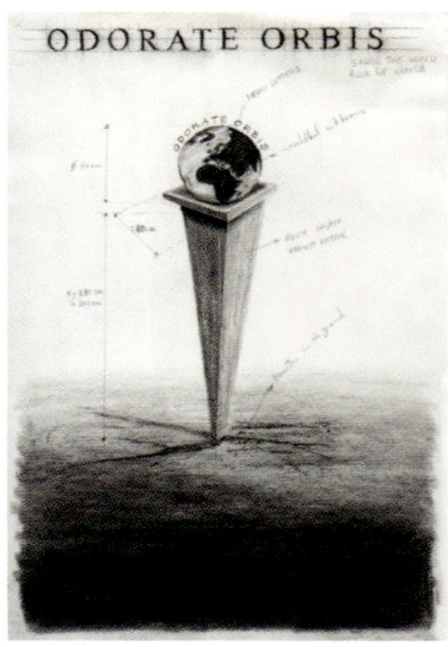

Drawing Odorate Orbis

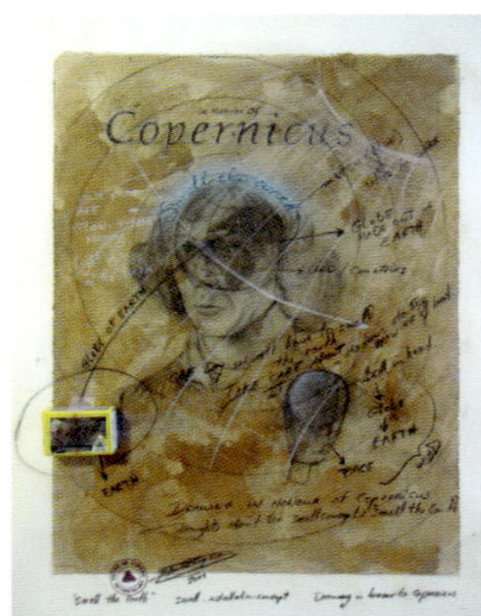

Smell the earth, 2001

Different drawings

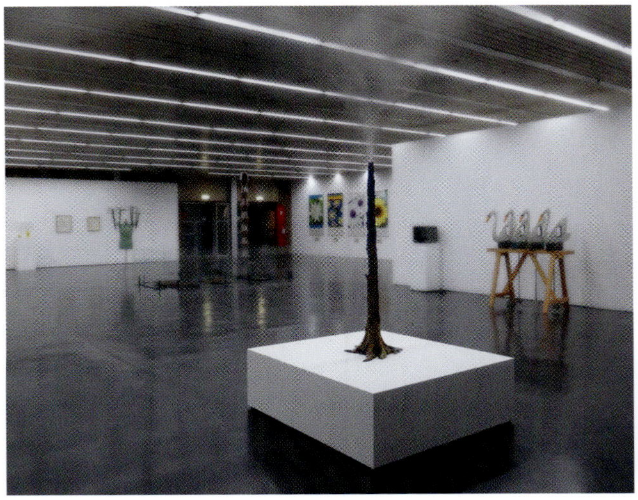

Factory Tree, 2015

135 cm x 42 cm x 42 cm (without base)
Coloured epoxy, aluminium, smoke machine
Scratch & sniff on the tree trunk; smell of acrid smoke
Smoke from the tree trunk: synthetic apple scent

135 cm x 42 cm x 42 cm (zonder sokkel)
Ingekleurde epoxy, aluminium, rookmachine
Scratch & sniff op de boomstam: verbrande rookgeur
Rook uit boomstam: synthetische appelgeur

Art Eco, CC Strombeek, Strombeek-Grimbergen, curator Luk Lambrecht, BE, 09.01.2015-12.02.2015

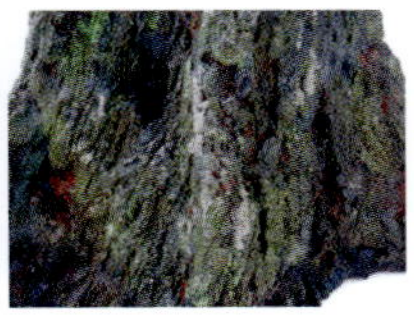

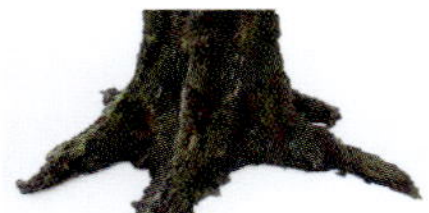

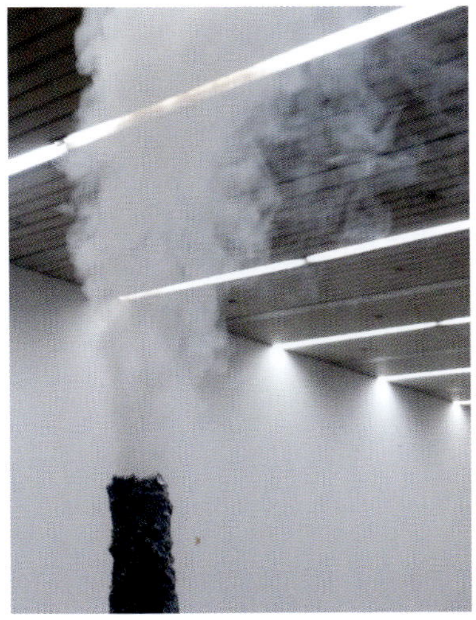

Factory Tree by Peter de Cupere

How bad would air pollution be if trees polluted the air and factories purified it?

It is a hypothetical question to which the answer will presumably remain negative, just as the result of our current climate conditions is a response to our past deeds. There is no action without a reaction. That is a law of physics written by nature and it forms the basis of our existence.

The strength of Factory Tree lies in the simplicity of reversing the relationship of humans to nature. By having a tree serve as a chimney–and no longer as an air purifying lung–the artist challenges the viewer to think about a typical 'What if' question. What if nature was the polluter, rather than humans?

The visual representation of the question helps viewers understand the question better and inspires them to think about our climate conditions.

The visualisation of Factory Tree presents an answer that is experienced as all the more meaningful thanks to the use of scent as signifier. If viewers rub the tree and smell their fingers, they will get a burning smell which becomes more intense near the top of the tree. The smell of smoke can be regarded as air pollution, yet the artist has made the actual smoke coming from the tree smell of apples.

The decision to use a synthetic apple scent is also a deliberate one to illustrate the typical way people camouflage their mistakes. The tree trunk is in fact not an apple tree trunk. Peter de Cupere is playing on items that are not immediately recognizable and that can symbolize what human beings produce. Thus Factory Tree is not only a statement calling into question how we handle nature and how as humans we are responsible for our own pollution. Factory Tree also questions the growing bio-technology and genetic technology industries, as a result of which plants will no longer be what they were, but will be modified and adapted to humanity's race for profit.

The eternal quest for gain. When ECO-ART becomes ECOnomy Art. But it is time to stop limiting ourselves to looking at nature–we have to learn again to smell it in order to understand where we are heading!

Hoe erg zou de luchtvervuiling zijn moesten bomen de lucht vervuilen en fabrieken de lucht zuiveren?
Het is een hypothetische vraag waarop het antwoord waarschijnlijk even negatief zou blijven zoals het resultaat van onze huidige klimaatomstandigheden een antwoord is op onze gedane daden. Actie komt nooit zonder reactie. Het is een fysische wet geschreven door de natuur en het vormt een basis voor ons bestaan.
De sterkte van *Factory Tree* ligt in de éénvoud van het omkeren van de mens-natuur relatie. Door een boom als schoorsteen te laten functioneren en niet meer als luchtzuiverende long, laat de kunstenaar de toeschouwer nadenken over een typische 'What if question'. Wat als de natuur zou vervuilen i.p.v. de mens?
De visuele representatie van de vraagstelling doet de toeschouwer de vraag beter begrijpen en zet ook aan tot nadenken over onze klimaatomstandigheden.
In de visualisatie van *Factory Tree* ligt ook het antwoord welke des te meer wordt ervaren door het gebruik van de geur als betekenisdrager. Als men over de boom wrijft en aan de vingers ruikt zal men een verbrande lucht ruiken welke naar de top van de boom toe intenser wordt. De geur van rook kan men als luchtvervuiling zien, nochtans laat de kunstenaar de effectieve rook die uit de boom komt geuren naar appelen. De keuze om een synthetische appelgeur te gebruiken is ook doelbewust om het typische verbloemen van de mens zijn fouten te illustreren. Tevens is de stam van de boom niet de stam van een appelboom. Peter de Cupere speelt hier met niet direct herkenbare items die symbool kunnen staan voor wat de mens produceert. Zo is *Factory Tree* niet alleen een statement over het in vraag stellen van hoe we met de natuur omgaan en hoe we als mens verantwoordelijk zijn voor onze eigen vervuiling en toekomst . *Factory Tree* bevraagt ook de toenemende biotechnologie, gentechnologie waarbij in de toekomst planten niet meer zullen zijn zoals ze waren, maar eerder een aangepast bestaansrecht zullen hebben uit winstbejag van de mensheid.
Een eeuwige zucht naar voordeel. Wanneer ECO-ART, ECOnomy Art wordt. Maar het is tijd dat we stoppen met alleen naar natuur te zien, we moeten onze natuur ook weer leren ruiken om te begrijpen waar we naartoe gaan!

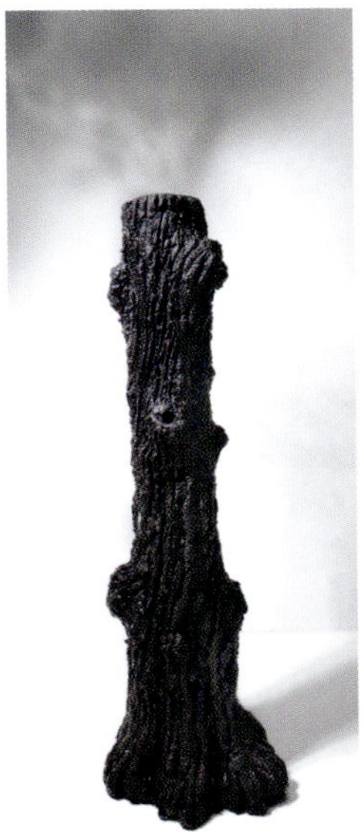

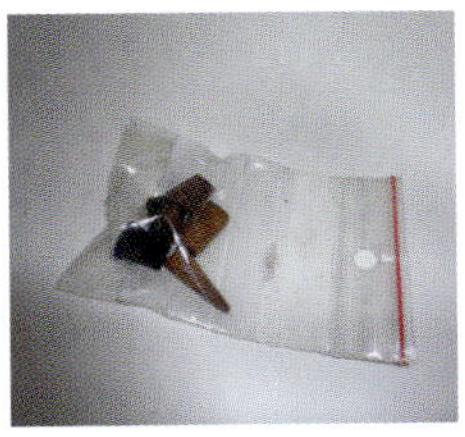

Edition Smoke Tree, 2012

25 cm x 8,5 cm x 7,5 cm
Edition of 50, 3 A.P. for 10 years Z33 Art Centre, Hasselt, BE
curated by Jan Boelen

Made of painted zellaan, smoke scratch and sniff, incense charcoals. While scratching the tree, a burned smell escapes. The incense charcoals on top of the tree can be burned and let the tree smoke.

Gemaakt van beschilderd zellaan, geur en wrijf met rookgeur en wierookblokjes. Als men over het boompje wrijft ruikt men een verbrande lucht. Men kan wierookkoontjes in de top van de boom laten verkolen en zo het boompje laten roken.

10 Years Z33, Z33 Art Center, curator Jan Boelen, Hasselt, BE 10-11.11.2012

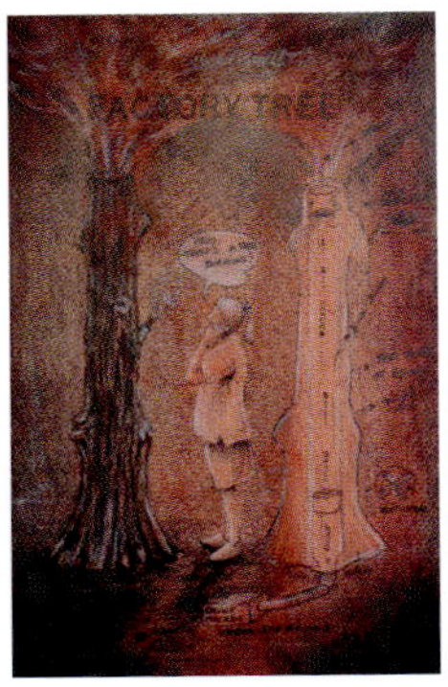

Factory tree, 2012

29,7 cm x 21 cm

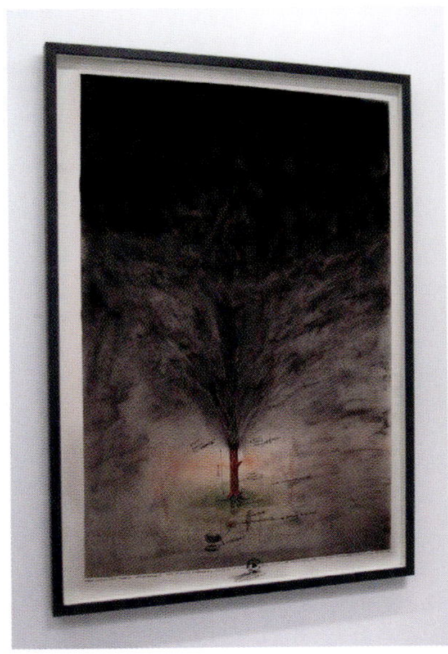

Fabrics 2, Nature Factory 1, 2004

103 cm x 72 cm

Garbage City, Van Laere Contemporary Art, Antwerp, BE, 20.05.2004-03.07.2004

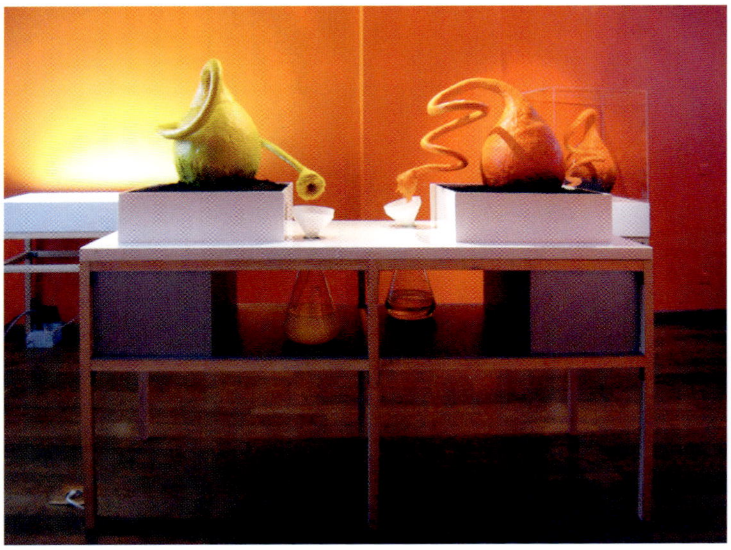

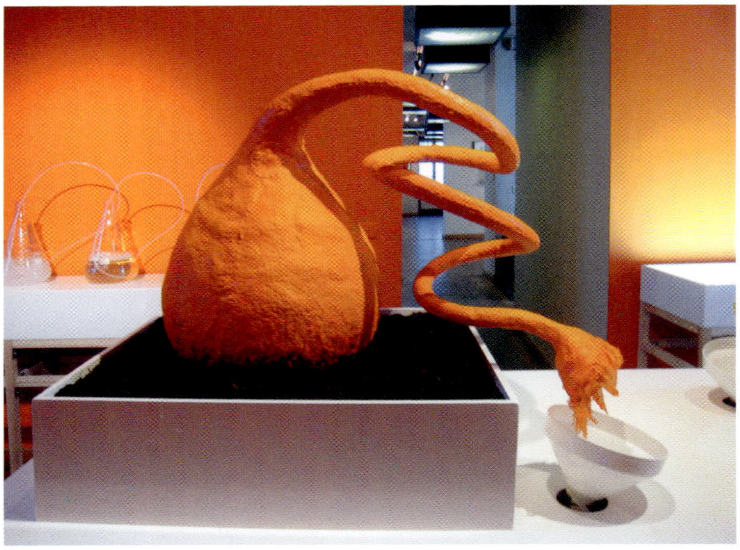

The Orange Bulb, 2008

Various alambfleurics, the skin of which can be softly pressed down, giving off a smell of orange or lemon. Scent drips from the sculptures.
At the exhibition Olfactology Lab, The Orange Bulb in the National Gin Museum in Hasselt (2008), the first organic experiments were exhibited in which one could see the early stages of the flowers. The work was later shown at the 'Artificial Nature' exhibition at de Verbeke Foundation, (Kemzeke, BE, 2009), where a larger version was also displayed.

Diverse alambfleurics waarbij de huid zacht indrukbaar is en een geur van appelsien of citroen afgeeft. Uit de sculpturen druppelt de geurstof.
In de tentoonstelling Olfactology Lab, The Orange Bulb in het Nationaal Jenevermuseum in Hasselt (2008) werden ook de eerste bio-experimenten tentoongesteld waarbij men mogelijke beginstadiums van de bloemen kon zien. Het werk werd later tentoongesteld in de tentoonstelling Artificial Nature in de Verbeke Foundation, (Kemzeke, BE, 2009) waar tevens ook een grotere versie werd getoond.

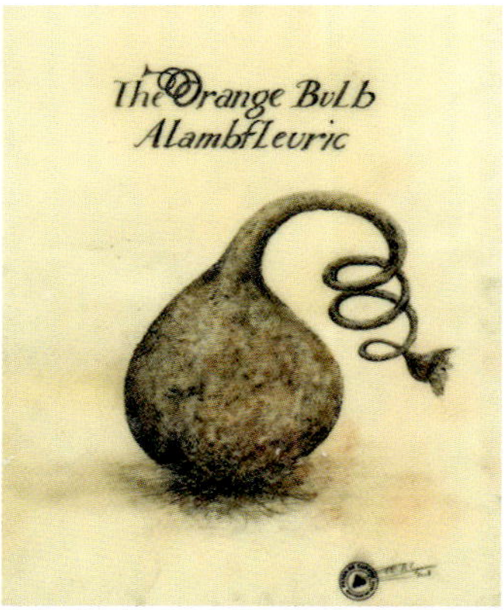

Artificial Nature, Verbeke Foundation, Kemzeke, BE
23.05.2009-15.11.2009
Olfactology Lab, The Orange Bulb Alambfleurics,
Nationaal Jenevermuseum,
curator Davy Jacobs, Hasselt, BE, 26.04.2008-31.08.2008

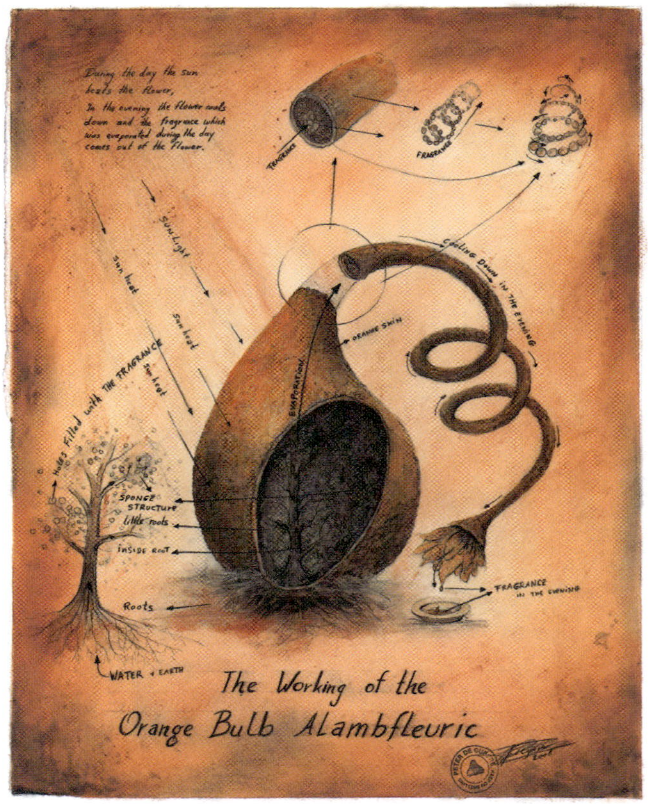

Drawing The Working of the Orange Bulb Alambfleuric, 2008

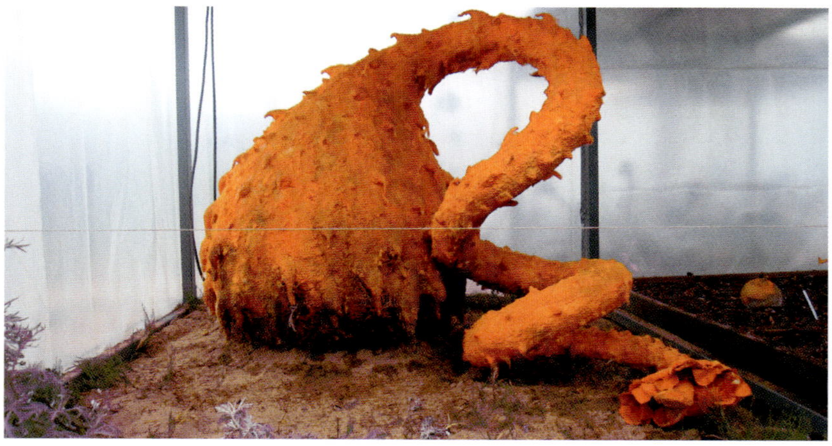

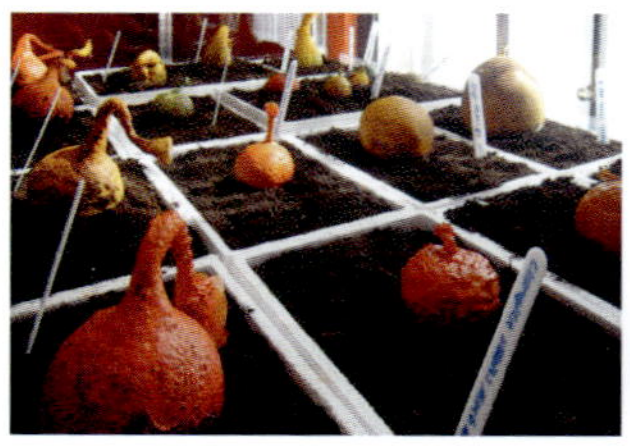

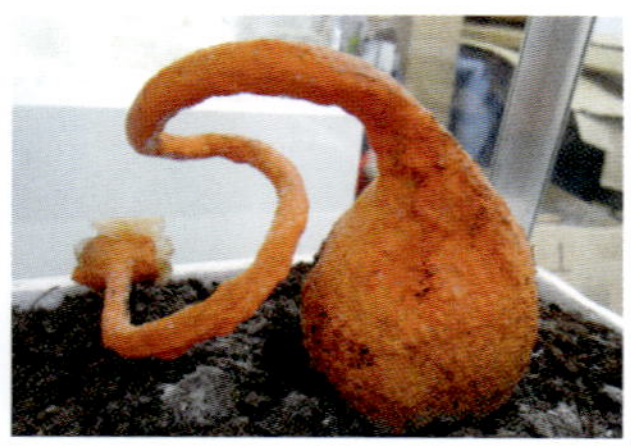

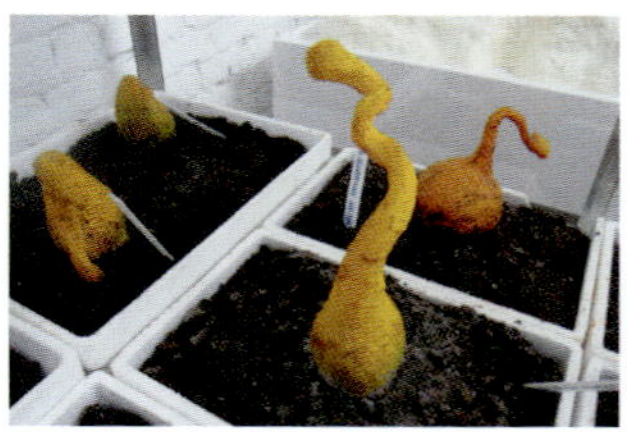

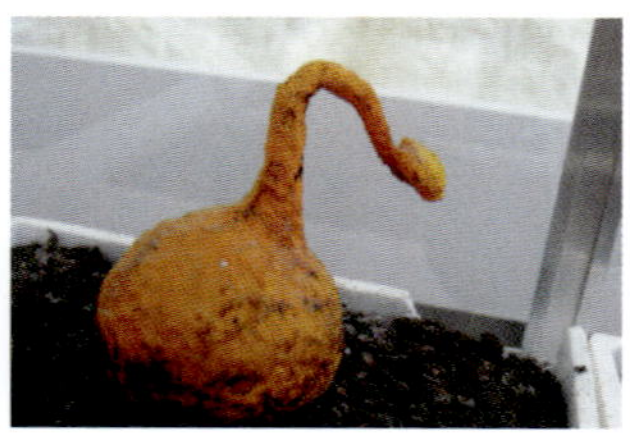

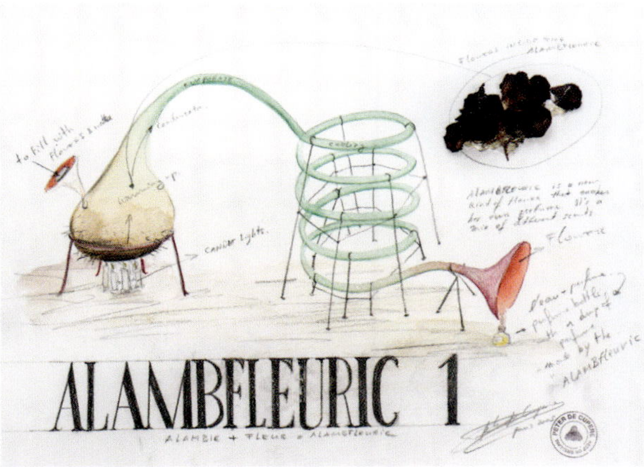

Drawing Alambfleuric 1, 2004

31,5 cm x 42 cm

Alambfleurics are genetically modified flowers shaped like alembics. During the daytime, the 'bulb' is heated by sunlight and the flower essence in the bulb evaporates.
In the evening, it diffuses into the spiral stem to ultimately secrete its aroma in the calyx .
The advantage is that there is no need to get up early to pick flowers anymore.
You can easily extract the scent in the evening and in plantations this can even be done automatically, in small containers.
The flower keeps growing bigger and bigger, so as the years go by, the quality and quantity of the scent improves.

Alambfleurics zijn gengemodificeerde bloemen. Zij hebben de vorm van een alambic. Overdag wordt de 'bulb' van de bloem door de zon verhit. In de bulb verdampt de essence van de bloem en deze koelt 's avonds af in de spiraalstengel van de bloem om zo zijn geurextract af te scheiden in de bloemkelk. Voordeel is dat men de bloemen niet meer moet plukken en niet meer vroeg moet opstaan. Men kan nu 's avonds de geurstof aftappen en bij mogelijke plantages kan men dit doen via automatische opvangbakjes. Daar de bloem blijft groeien en groter wordt, verkrijgt men met de jaren ook een betere en veel grotere geurstofproductie.

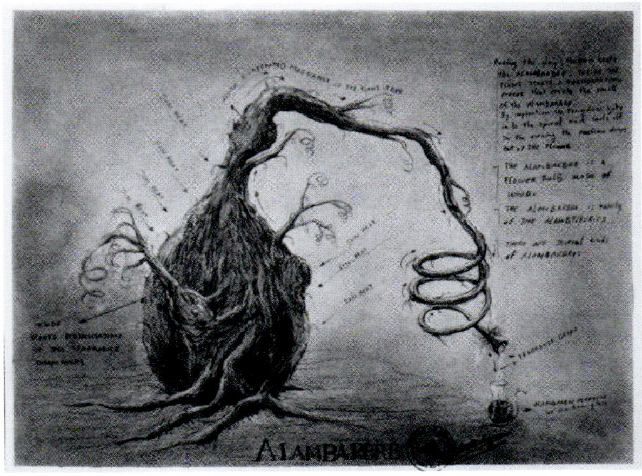

Drawing Alambarbre, 2010

Alambfleuric Alcol Feromoon, 2005

Drawing: 94.5 cm x 73.5 cm, Watercolour, graphite and coloured pencils
Scent Sculpture: 145 cm x 65 cm x 65 cm
Wood, paint, plastic, PU components, PU glue and filler. Scent of pheromones or mixed with a scent you can choose yourself.

Tekening: 94,5 cm x 73,5 cm, aquarel, grafiet en kleurpotloden
Geursculptuur: 145 cm x 65 cm x 65 cm
Hout, verf, plastiek, PU-componenten, PU-lijm en vulsel. Geur van feromonen of gemixt met een zelf te kiezen geur.

Smell the Castle, Castle Beauvoorde, curator Annemie Morisse, Beauvoorde, BE, 15.07.2007-30.08.2007
Peter de Cupere, Sergio De Beukelaer & Maryam Najd, Van Laere Contemporary Art, Antwerp, BE 26.01.2006-11.03.2006

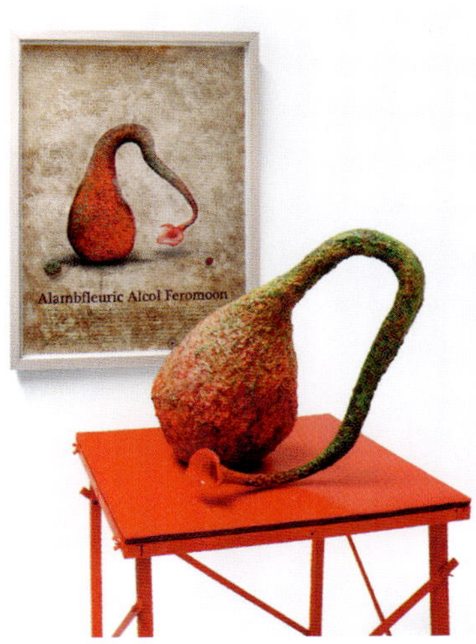

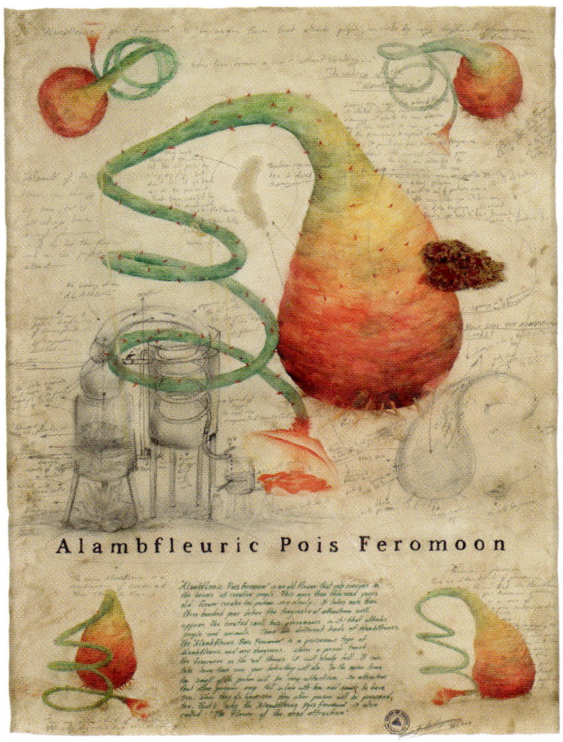

Drawing Alambfleuric Pois Feromoon, 2004

94,5 cm x 73,5 cm

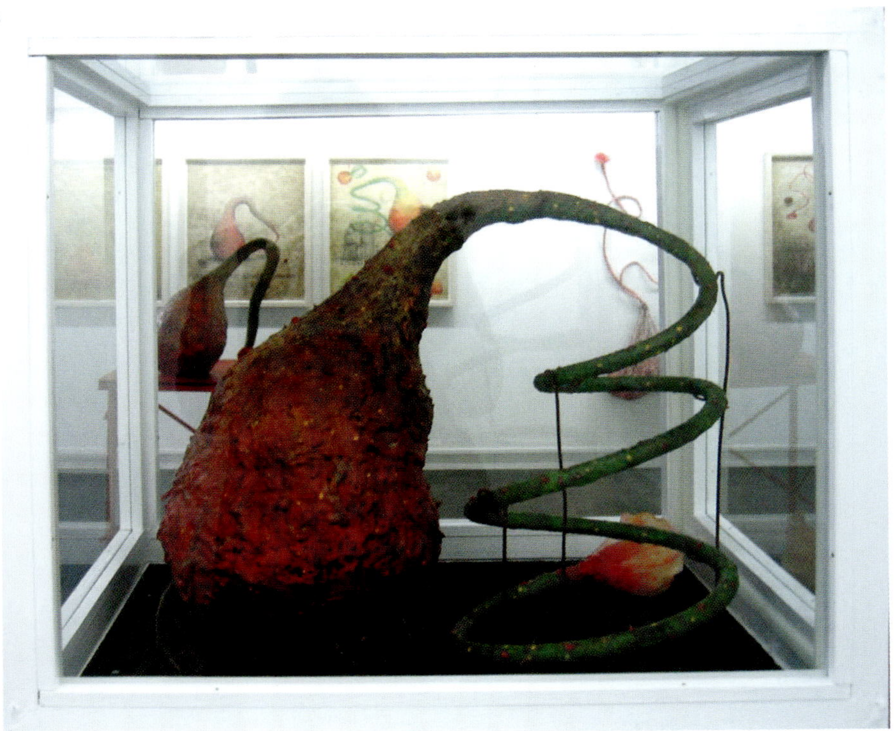

Alambfleuric Pois Feromoon, 2005

Scent Sculpture

Peter de Cupere, Sergio De Beukelaer & Maryam Najd, Van Laere Contemporary Art, Antwerp, BE, 26.01-11.03.2006

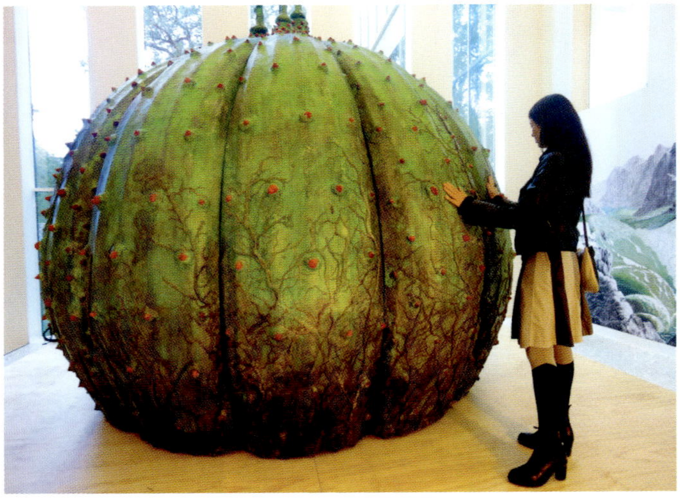

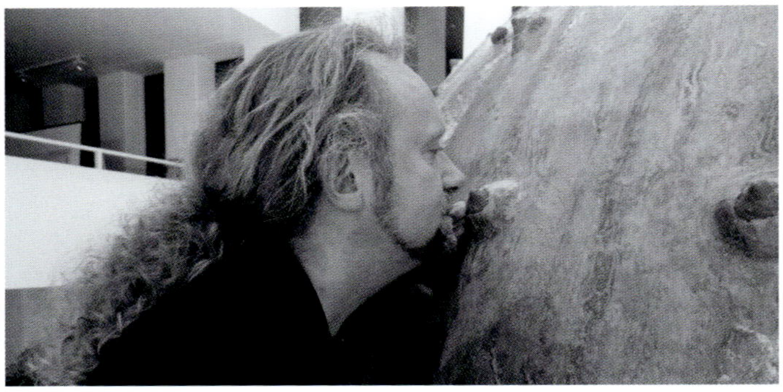

Fragum Cardamomi, 2012

900 cm x 320 cm Ø
Sculpture made of epoxy, aluminium, scratch & sniff
Smell: strawberry and cardamon fragrance in scratch & sniff form.
Fragum Cardamomi is the first scratch & sniff sculpture in the world. Visitors can discover the smells of the work by rubbing it and then smelling their fingers.

Sculptuur gemaakt uit epoxy, aluminium, scratch & sniff
Geur: aardbei en cardamon geur in scratch & sniff vorm
Fragum Cardamomi is de eerste Scratch & Sniff sculptuur in de wereld. Bezoekers kunnen de geuren van de sculptuur ontdekken door er op te wrijven en aan hun vingers te ruiken.

Nature Now, CBK Drenthe, De Nieuwe Kolk, curator Toos Arends, Assen, NL
24.09.2012-08.01.2013
Creativity World Forum, Ethias Arena Hasselt, BE, curator Nora Weytens,
16-17.11.2012
Foto © smart-pictures.be

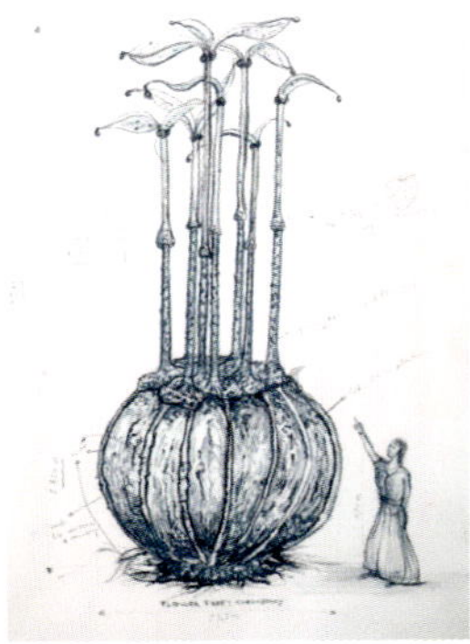

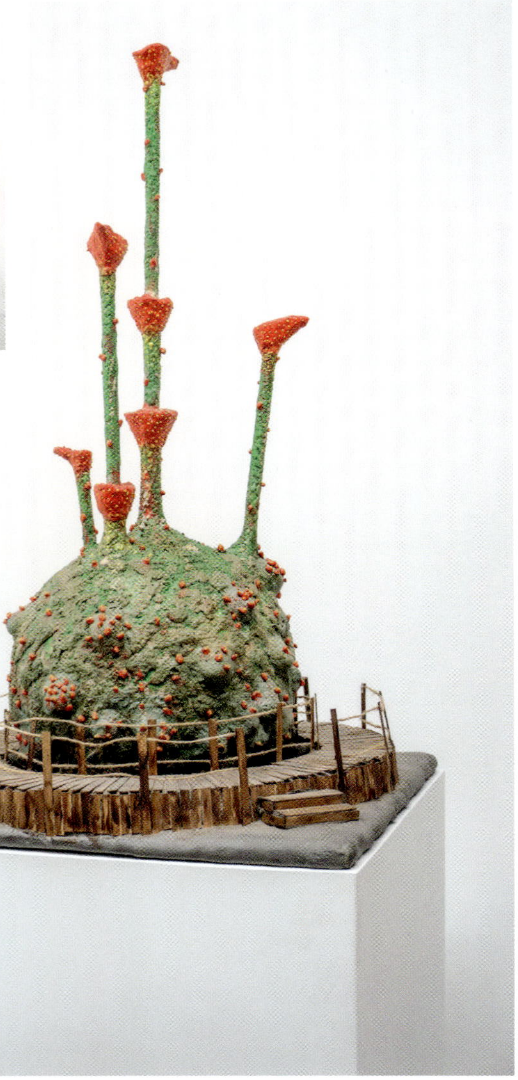

Model Fragum Cardamomi Flower, 2012

73 cm x 44,5 cm x 44,5 cm

Epoxy, wood, scratch & sniff strawberry

Epoxy, hout, scratch & sniff aardbei geurstof

Vormidable, Vlaamse Hedendaagse Beeldhouwkunst, Museum Beelden aan Zee, Lange Voorhout, curator Stef van Bellingen, Den Haag, NL, 20.05.2015-30.08.2015
Creativity World Forum, Ethias Arena Hasselt, curator Nora Weytens, 16-17.11.2012
Foto © smart-pictures.be

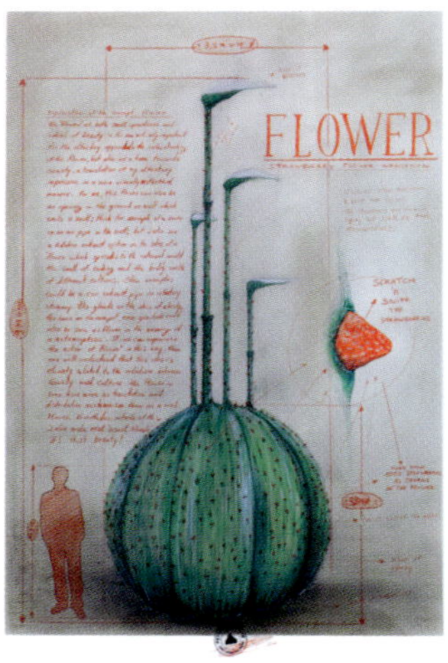

Flower Fragum Cardamomi, 2012

Drawing / Tekening 67 cm x 47 cm
Framed / Ingekaderd 82 cm h x 61,5 cm

Nature Now, CBK Drenthe, De Nieuwe Kolk, curator Toos Arends, Assen, NL, 24.09.2012-08.01.2013

Flower Fragum Cardamomi, 2011

64 cm x 47.5 cm
Framed / Ingekaderd 82 cm x 61.5 cm

Nature Now, CBK Drenthe, De Nieuwe Kolk, curator Toos Arends, Assen, NL, 24.09.2012-08.01.2013

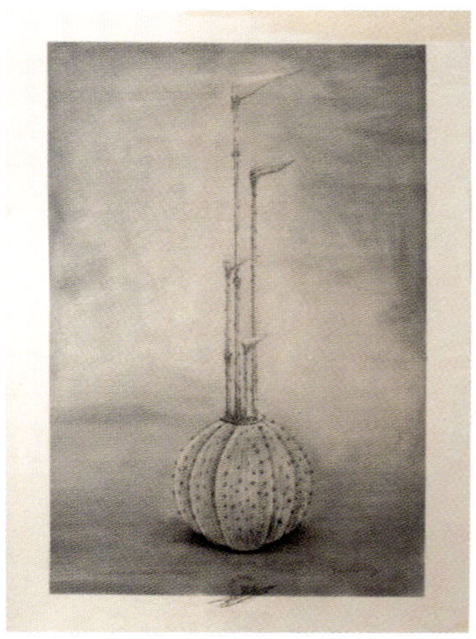

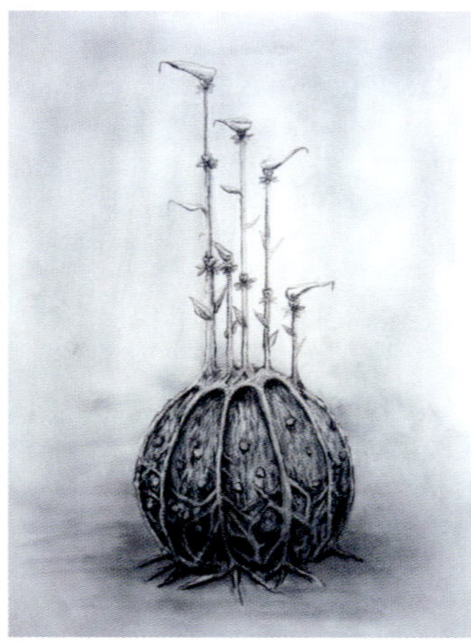

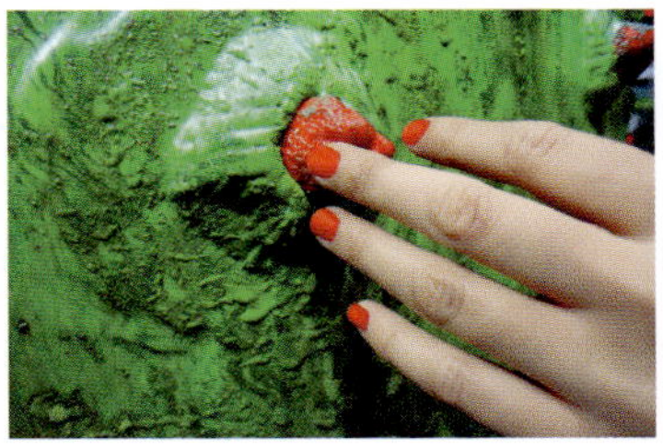
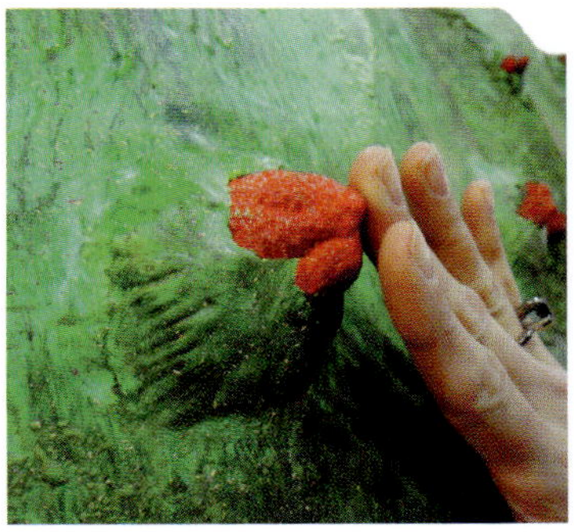
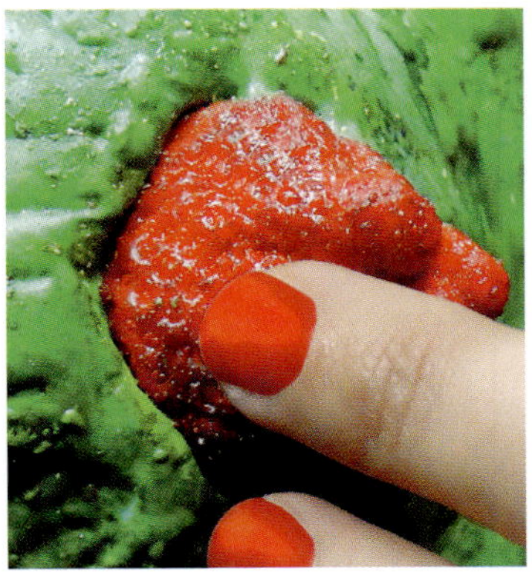
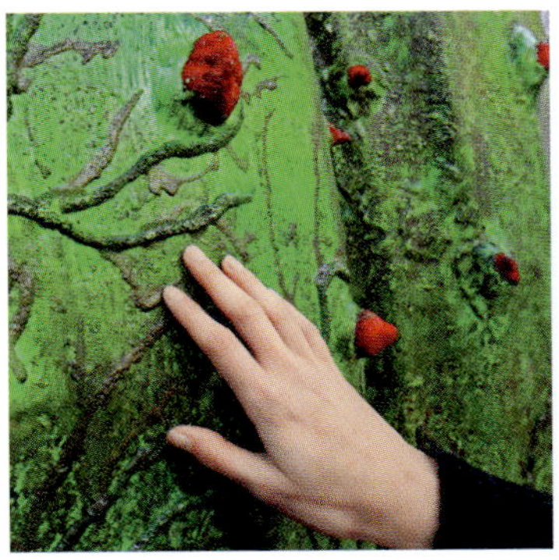
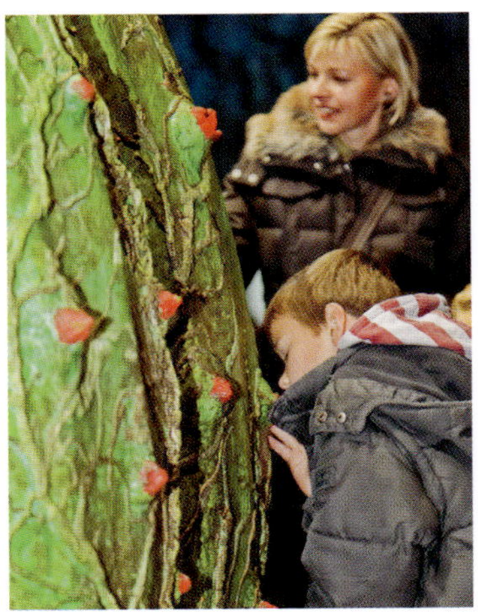
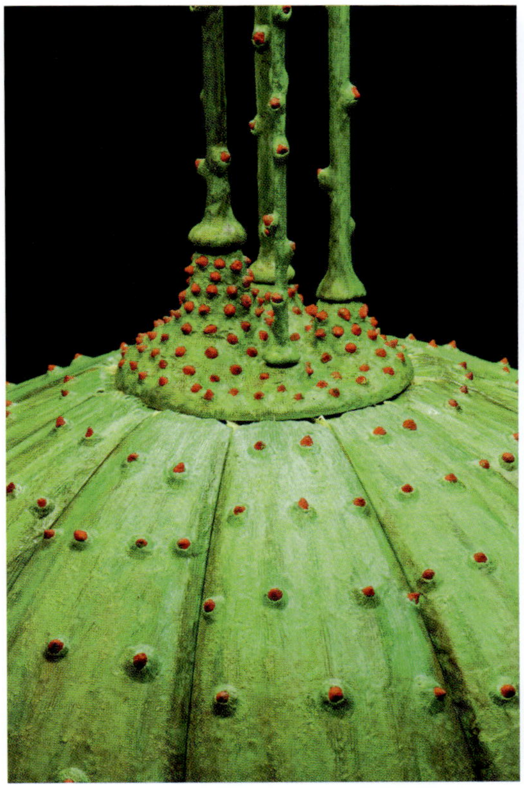
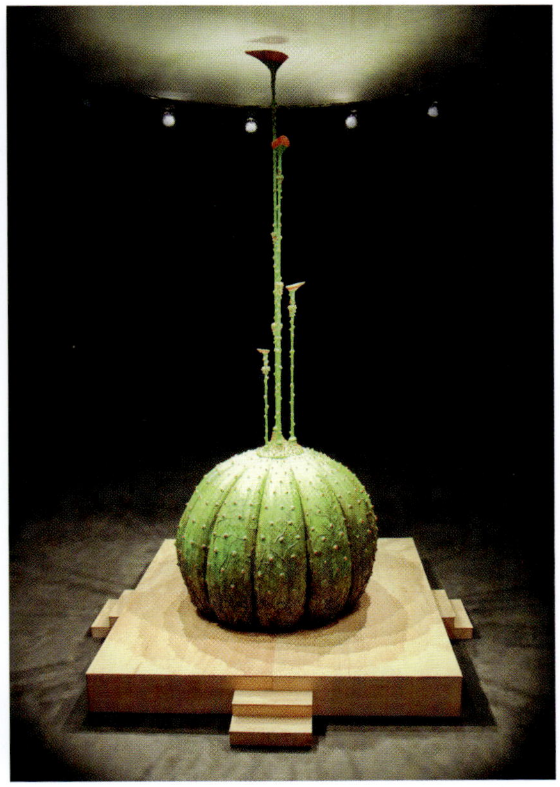
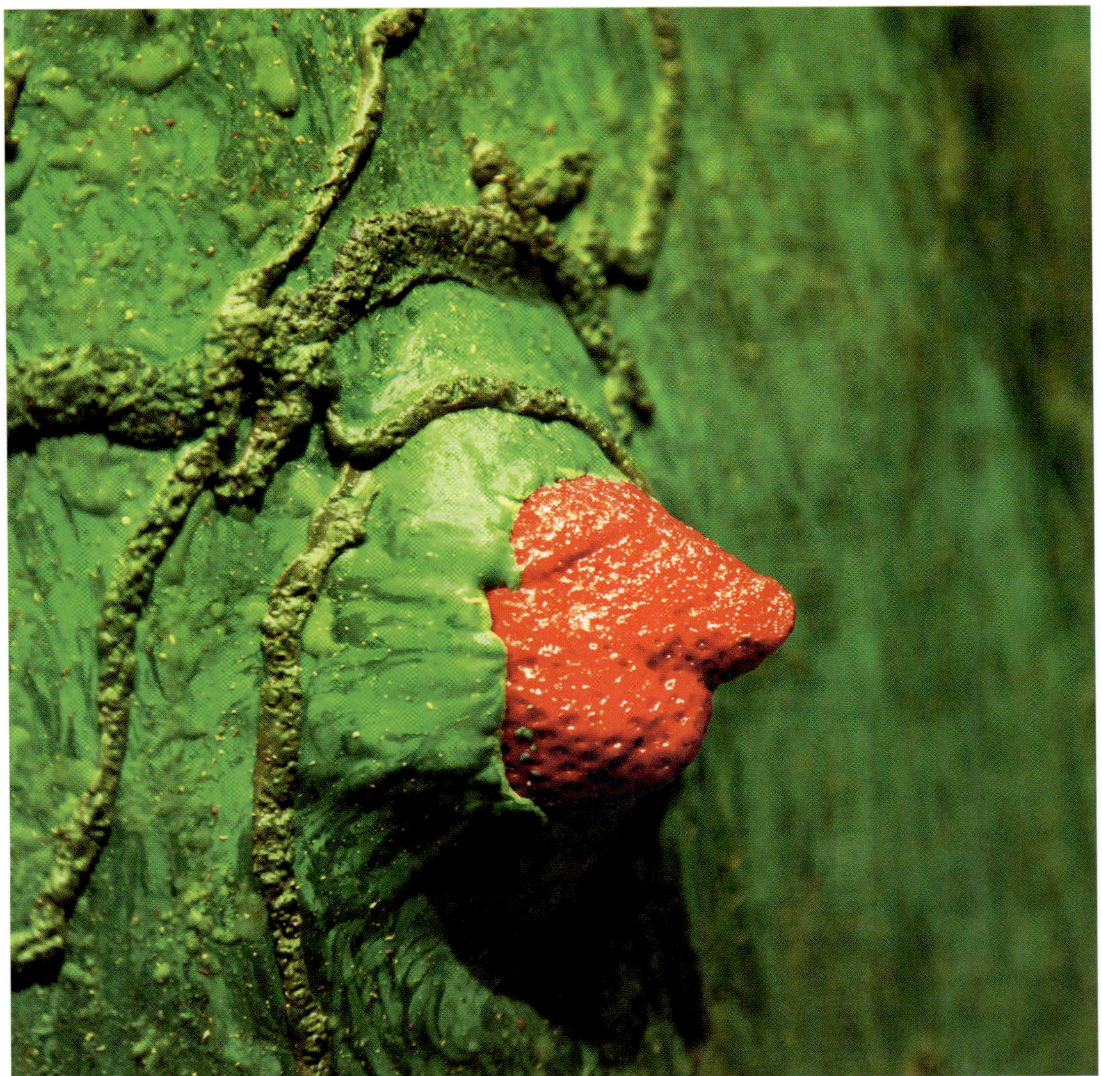

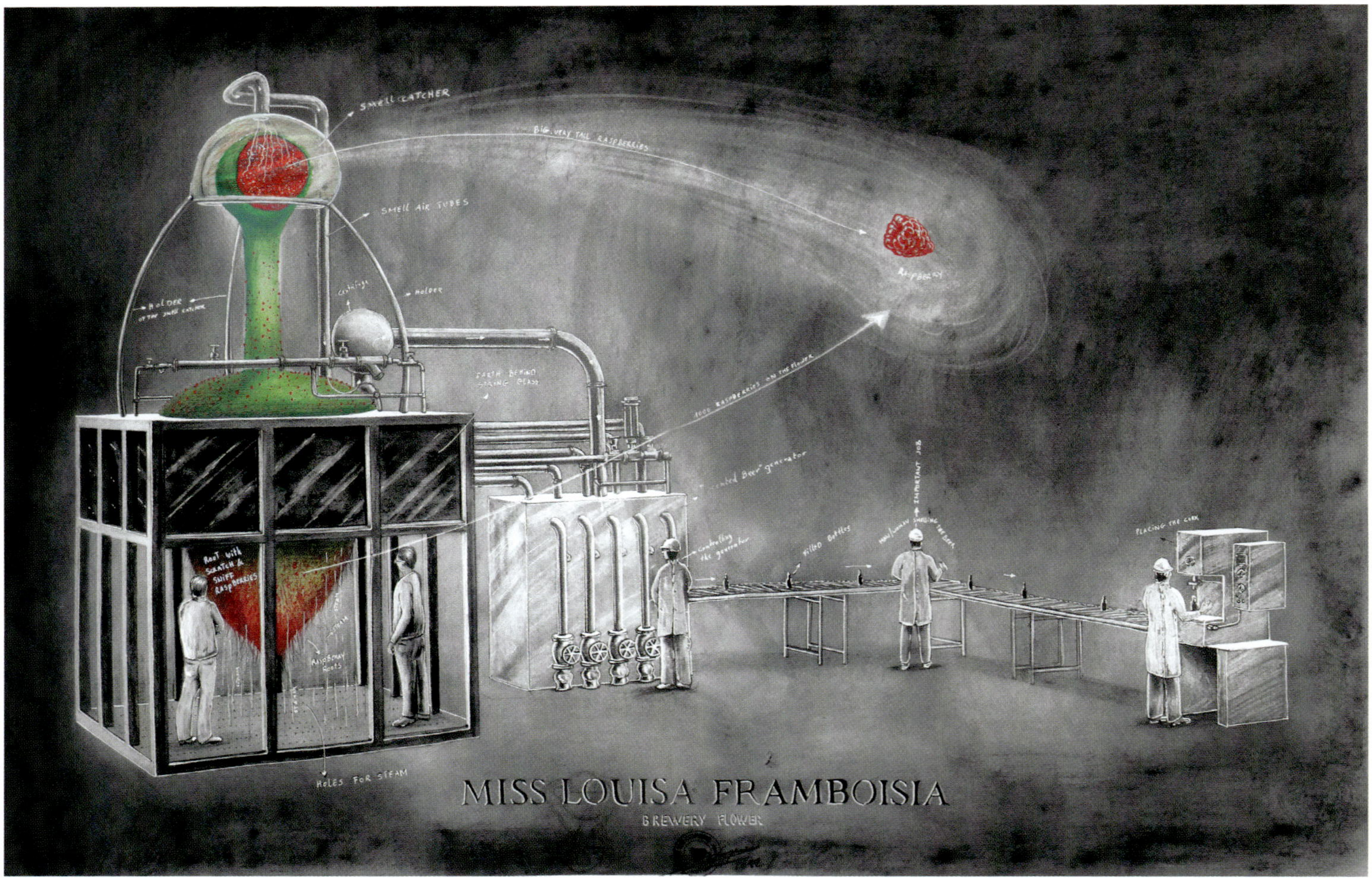

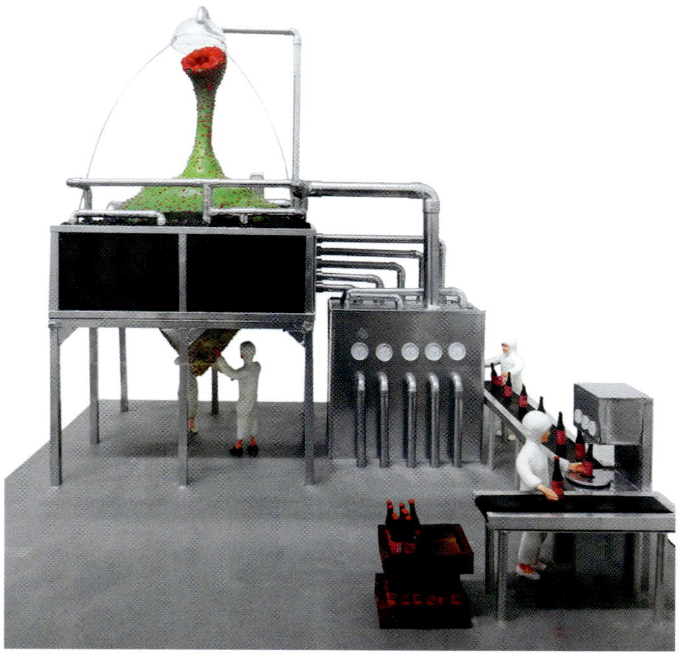

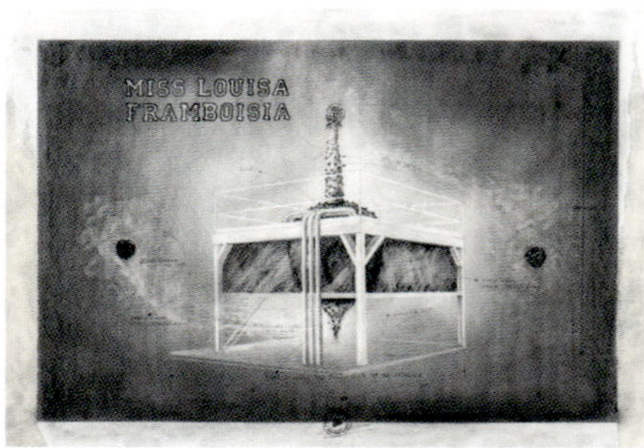

Drawing Miss Louisa Framboisia, 2012

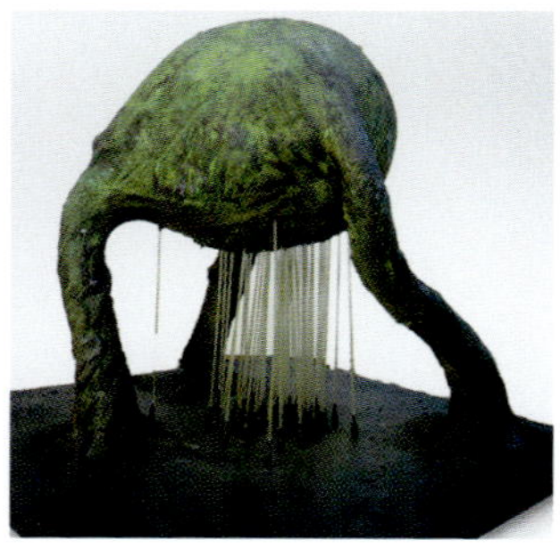

N.G.M. Hop Bulb Model, 2012

Scent Sculpture, epoxy and plastics
Geursculptuur, epoxy en plastiek

Miss Louisa Framboisia model, 2012

Epoxy, wood, plastic aluminium, paper, rubber, etc.
Under plexiglass box on a metal base, 180 cm x 80 cm x 80 cm

Epoxy, hout, plastiek, aluminium, papier, rubber, etc.
Onder plexibox op metalen sokkel, 180 cm x 80 cm x 80 cm

Panamarenko versus Next Door, Living Tomorrow, curator Barbara Dietrich, Vilvoorde, BE 30.01.2015-30.06.2015
Next Door, Living Tomorrow, curator Barbara Dietrich, Vilvoorde, BE, 12.05.2014-31.12.2014
Kanal, Ondernemen is een kunst, Prov. West-Vlaanderen, curators Christa Vyvey, Michel Dewilde, Ingelmunster-Roeselare, BE, 23.06.2012-31.10.2012

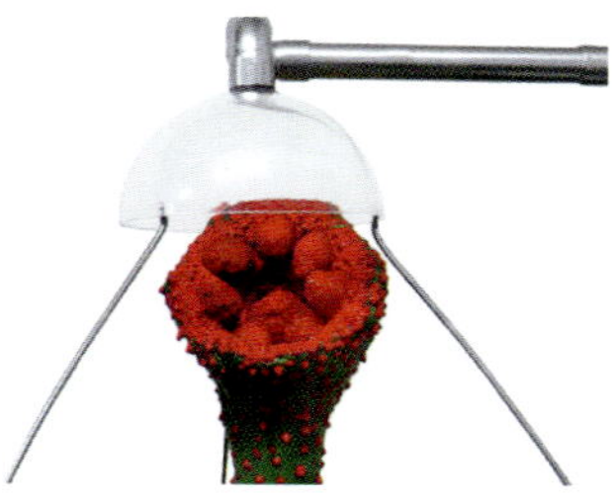
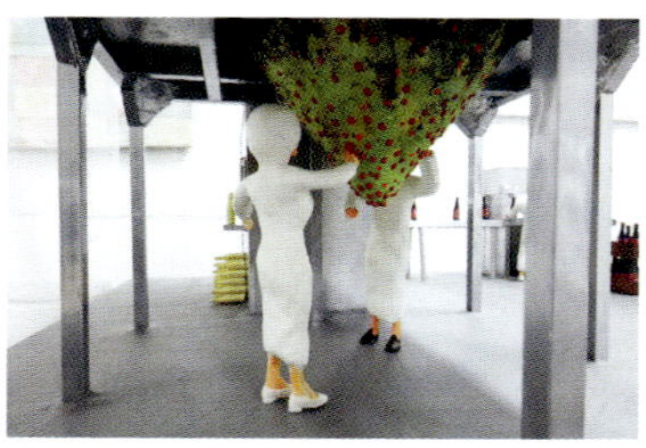
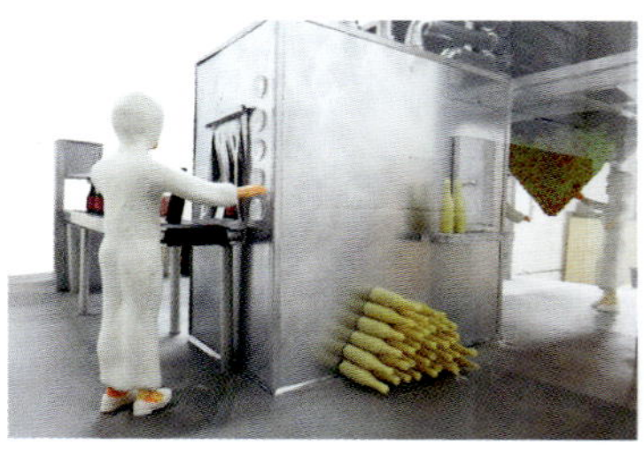
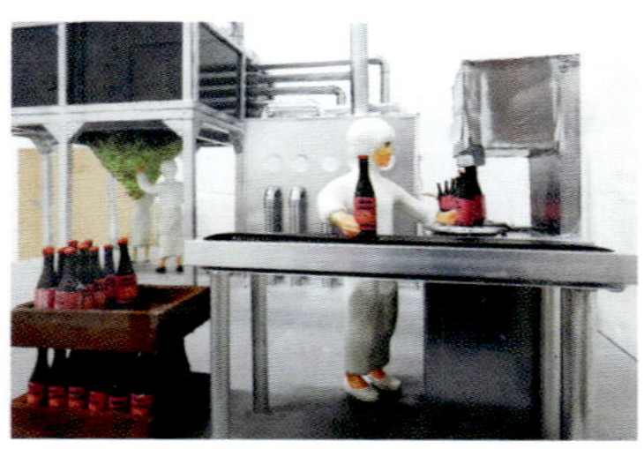

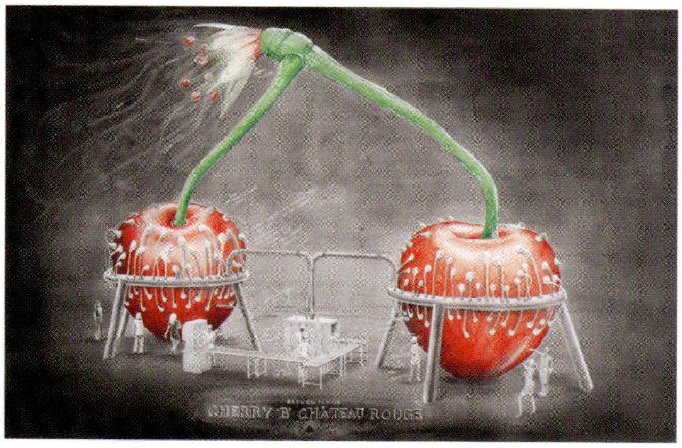

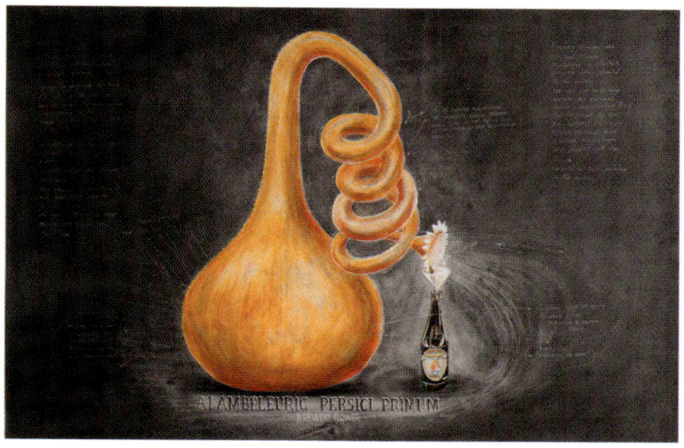

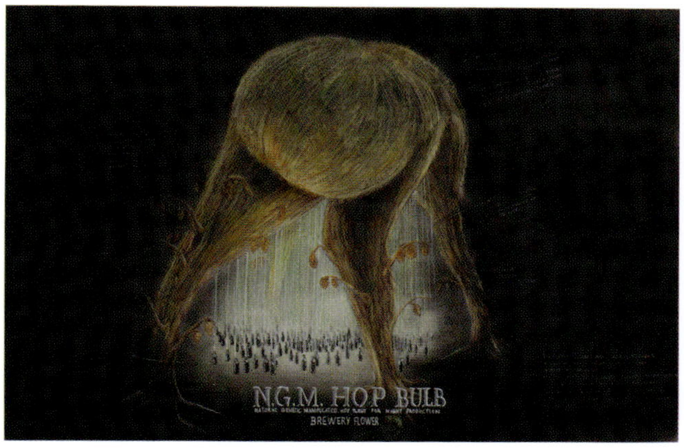

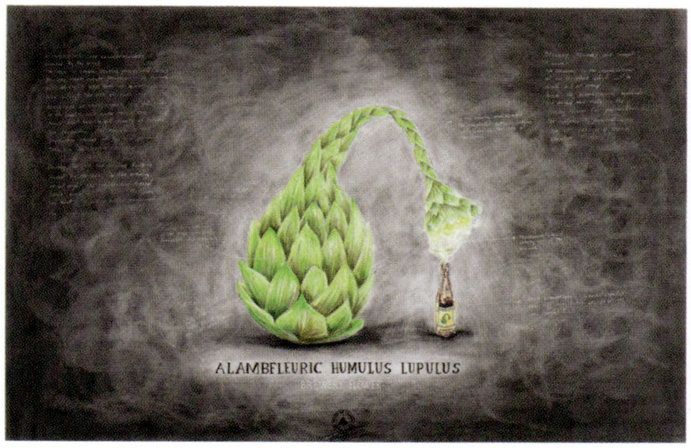

Brewery Flowers, 2012
Different drawings
Diverse tekeningen
Framed / ingekaderd
99 cm x 67 cm

Panamarenko versus Next Door, Living Tomorrow, curator Barbara Dietrich, Vilvoorde, BE 30.01.2015-30.06.2015
Next Door, Living Tomorrow, curator Barbara Dietrich, Vilvoorde, BE 12.05.2014-31.12.2014
Kanal, Ondernemen is een kunst, Prov. West-Vlaanderen, curators Christa Vyvey, Michel Dewilde, Ingelmunster-Roeselare, BE 23.06.2012-31.10.2012

Brewery Flowers

'Brewery Flowers' are plants that produce beer by themselves through internal fermentation.

The idea of seeing flowers as a brewery is a logical step in the work of Peter de Cupere. He has already made several types of flowers for which distillation was the central idea. 'Alambfleurics' are a fine example. During the day, the sun warms the bowl of flowers. Inside, the scent evaporates, and in the evening it cools off in the flower's spiral stem and is collected in the calyx. A small, botanical scent factory, as it were. No need to cut any more flowers, you can simply tap the rich liquid scent in the evening from the flower's calyx. The word 'Alambfleurics' is a compound of the French 'Fleur' and 'Alambic', better known as a distillation system.

The brewery flowers have thus been conceived, but the process itself is a bit more complex, and a pipe construction is added to each flower, referring to the countless pipes and barrels used when brewing beer.

It may seem a utopian proposal, but it is technologically feasible. Once people begin to conceive of plants in such a way that they produce an end-product in themselves, and in large quantities, no one should be surprised that the idea is also beneficial to the environment. That is the context in which Peter de Cupere works as a visual artist: alluding subtly to the problem of the environment and eliciting questions about potential models for the future. Once plants no longer have to be processed but can become biological suppliers of an end-product, the focus is solely on the quality of the substructure, the purity of the rainwater and checking the end-product for taste, smell and safety. There will be no more need to pollute the air by burning gas, oil or other fuel sources. In addition, plants are a more aesthetic experience than our current factories.

Imagine the canal zone with a plantation of large flowers along the canal, with a system of pipes to transport the resulting end-products. In addition to their products, the plants also serve to purify the air, making an additional contribution to nature.

Peter de Cupere's sketches are veritable jewels. As a virtuoso draughtsman from his earliest years, his concept drawings represent a moment of reflection to think further about the possibilities, as well as searching for an aesthetic result to match the concept.

For Peter de Cupere, an artist who works with smells, choosing to make 'Flower' sculptures is a logical step. Flowers, as the producers of delightful scents, have always inspired him with their beauty and smell. But for Peter de Cupere, the concept of a 'Flower' is more than just a plant. It is a metaphor that represents many things. He sees the flower as a funnel towards the outside world.

'Brewery Flowers' zijn planten die zelf bier aanmaken door interne gisting.
Het idee van bloemen te concipiëren als een brouwerij is een logische stap in het werk van Peter de Cupere. Hij realiseerde al verschillende bloemsoorten waarin het idee van distillatie centraal staat. Zo zijn zijn 'Alambfleurics', hiervan een mooi voorbeeld. Overdag verwarmt de zon de bloembol. Binnenin verdampt de geurstof, 's avonds koelt deze af in de spiraalstengel van de bloem en wordt deze opgevangen in de kelk. Als ware het een kleine plantaardige geurfabriek. Men hoeft geen planten meer af te doen, maar kan gewoon 's avonds het rijkelijk vocht aftappen vanuit de bloemkelk. Het woord 'Alambfleurics' is een samenstelling van het Franse 'Fleur' en 'Alambic', beter gekend als distillatiesysteem. Zo zijn de brewery flowers ook geconcipieerd, alleen is het proces iets ingewikkelder en is er bij iedere bloem een buizenconstructie aangebracht refererend naar de talloze buizen en vaten welke gebruikt worden bij het distilleren van bier.

Het lijkt een utopische voorstelling maar technologisch gezien zou het best kunnen bestaan. Van zodra men planten zo kan concipiëren dat ze zelf het eindproduct maken in grote hoeveelheid, zal men er niet verbaasd van zijn dat dit idee ook het milieu ten goede komt. Dit laatste is ook een context waar Peter de Cupere als beeldend kunstenaar rond werkt. De milieuproblematiek op een subtiele manier weergeven en vragen laten oproepen over mogelijke toekomstmodellen. Van zodra planten niet meer verwerkt moeten worden, maar biologisch leveranciers kunnen zijn van een eindproduct, dient men enkel te focussen op de kwaliteit van de ondergrond, zuiverheid van het regenwater en controleren van het eindproduct op smaak, geur en veiligheid. Men dient niet meer de lucht te verontreinigen door verbranding van gassen, mazout of andere brandstoffen. Daarnaast zijn de planten ook een meer esthetische ervaring t.o.v. de momenteel aanwezige fabrieken.

Beeld je de kanaalzone in met langs het kanaal een plantage van grote bloemen waaraan wel een buissysteem verbonden is om het afvoeren van de gecreëerde eindproducten. De planten hebben naast hun productie ook de functie om lucht te zuiveren waardoor dit een extra bijdrage aan de natuur levert.

De ontwerptekeningen van Peter de Cupere zijn echte pareltjes. Als een virtuoos tekenaar, van kleins af aan, zijn de concepttekeningen voor de kunstenaar een reflectiemoment om verder na te denken over de mogelijkheden, maar ook een zoeken naar een esthetisch gegeven dat aansluit bij het concept.

Dat Peter de Cupere als beeldend kunstenaar werkend met geur kiest om 'Flower' sculpturen te maken is een logische stap. Bloemen hebben als producent van heerlijke geuren de kunstenaar steeds geïnspireerd door hun schoonheid en geur. Maar voor Peter de Cupere is het begrip 'Bloem' meer dan gewoon een plant. Het is een metafoor voor veel. Hij ziet de bloem als een trechter naar de buitenwereld toe.

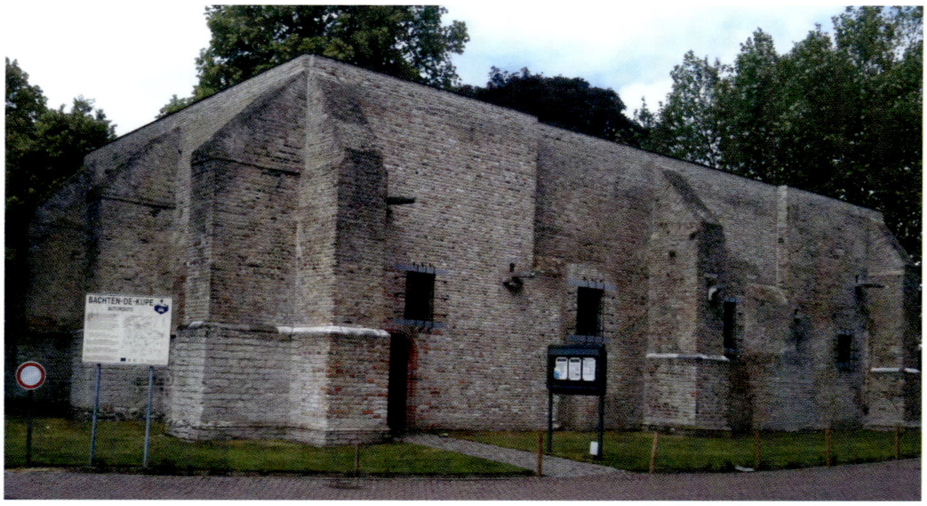
BACHTEN-DE-KUPE
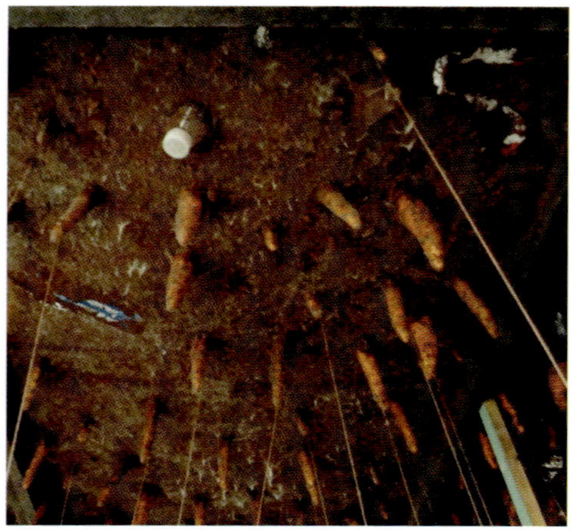
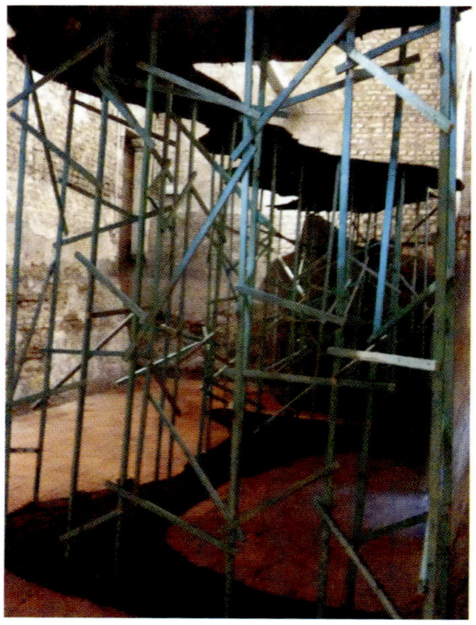
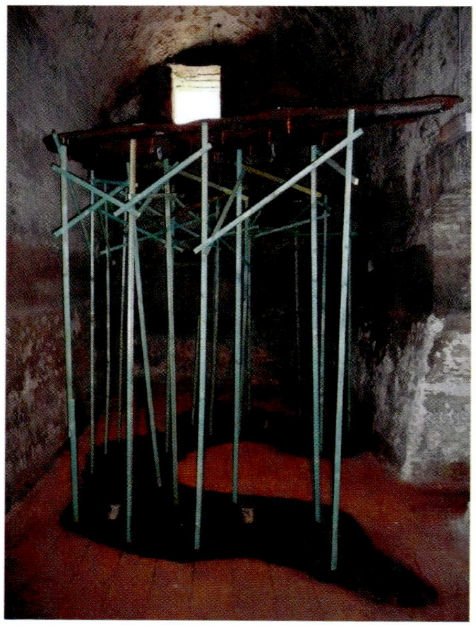
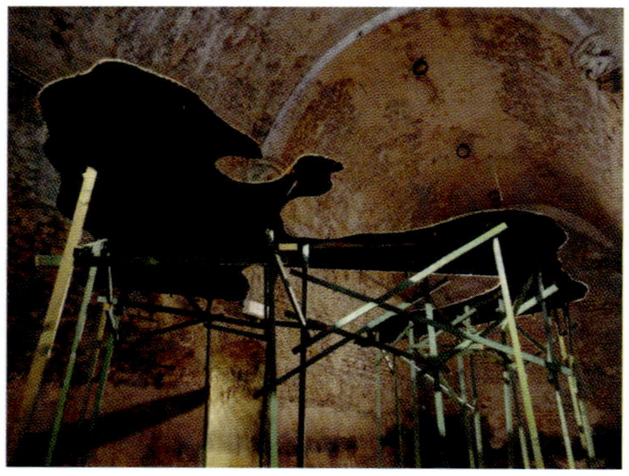
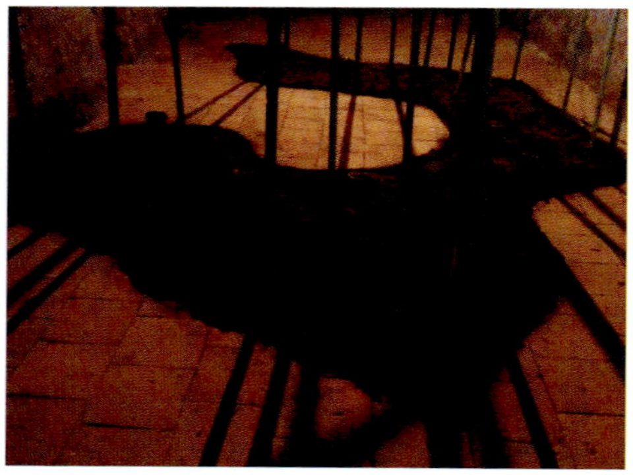
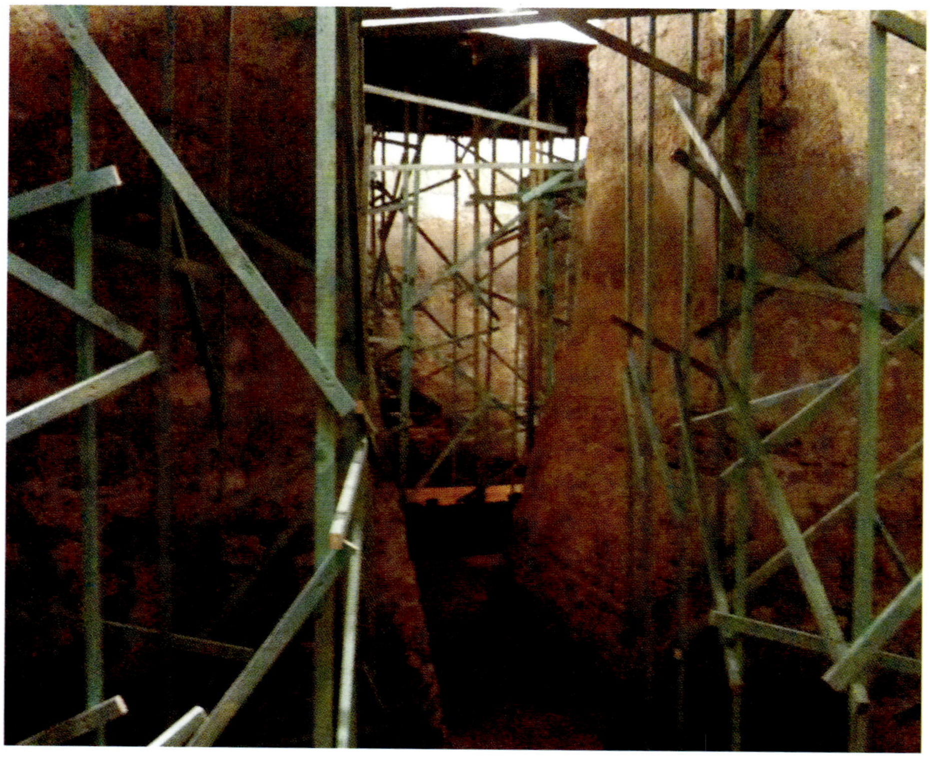
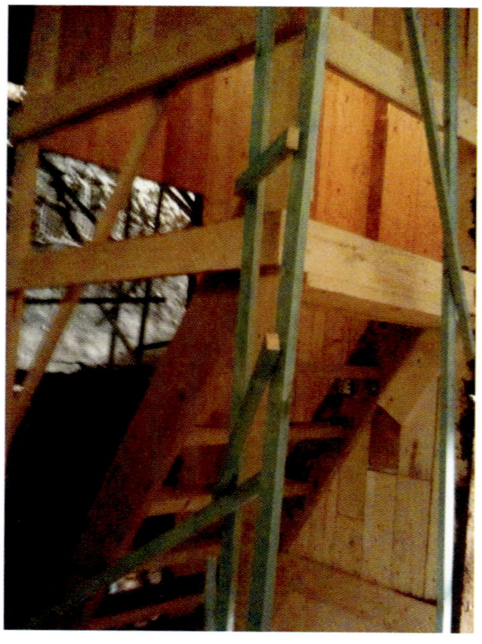

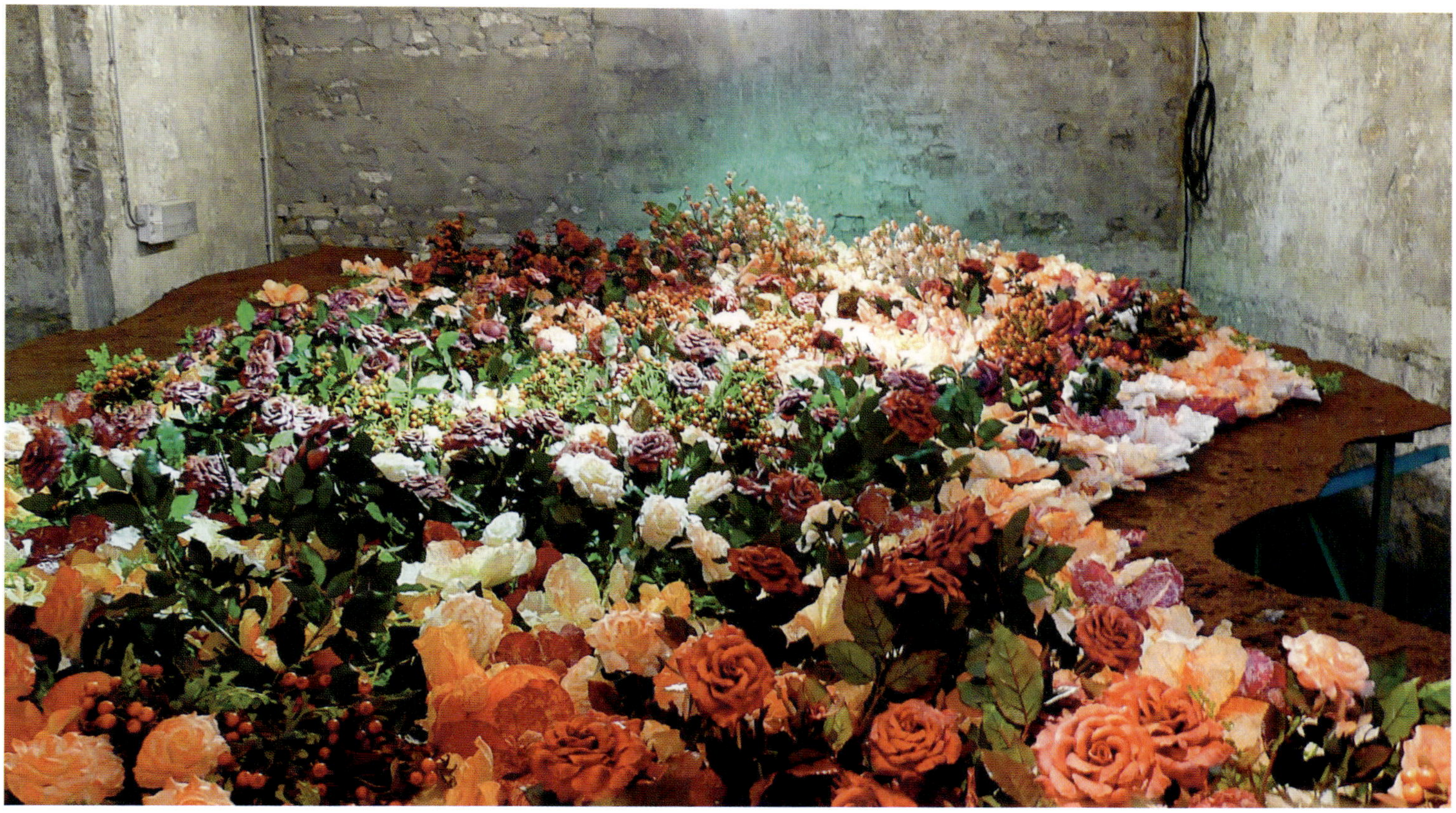

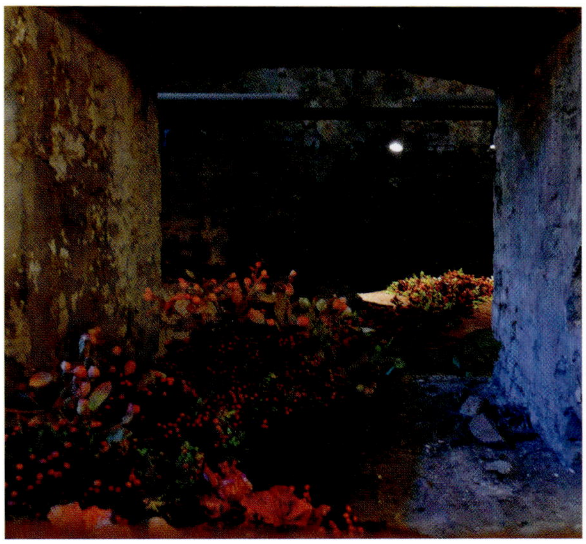

Memory Garden, 2010

430 cm x 2000 cm x 1000 cm

Olfactory installation, wood, earth, 3,000 silk and plastic artificial flowers. Smell of earth, fungus, grass and flower mixture

Visitors wander first through a structure made of wooden slats, seeing earth with roots and rubbish sticking out above them. It smells mouldy, of earth and fungus. A wooden staircase leads to a sort of viewing tower above the structure. Here, the visitor can look out through a narrow crack in the wooden structure onto a field with more than 3,000 artificial flowers. The artificial flowers are normally used in churchyards. Before viewers can see the flowers clearly, they have to get used to the faint light in which they are displayed. The flowers smell of a mix of intense floral scents, combined with a slight smell of grass.

Olfactorische installatie met hout, aarde, 3.000 zijden en plastieken namaakbloemen. Geur van aarde, zwammen, gras en bloemenmix

Bezoekers wandelen eerst tussen een constructie van houten latten en zien boven hen aarde met wortelen en vuilnis uitsteken. Het ruikt er muf, naar aarde en zwammen. Via een houten trap komt men in een soort van uitkijktoren boven de constructie terecht om door een smalle spleet in de houten constructie over een veld met meer dan 3.000 namaakbloemen te kijken. De namaak sierbloemen worden normaal gebruikt op kerkhoven. Voor men de bloemen duidelijk waarneemt moet men eerst wennen aan het felle licht waarin ze getoond worden. De bloemen ruiken naar een mix van intense bloemengeuren gecombineerd met een lichte grasgeur.

Sun-Light, org. Phidias & 5-Art, curator Christa Vyvey, Veurne, BE, 19.06.2010-12.09.2010

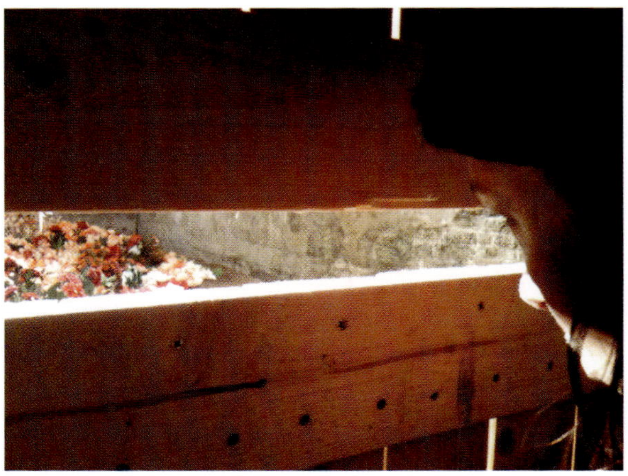

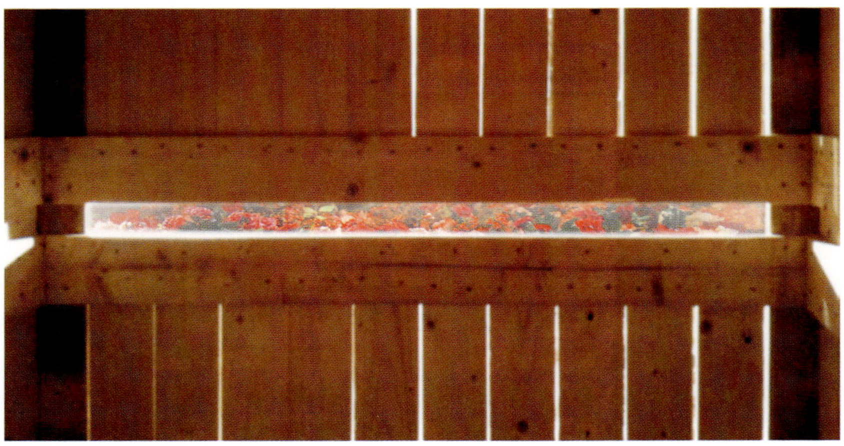

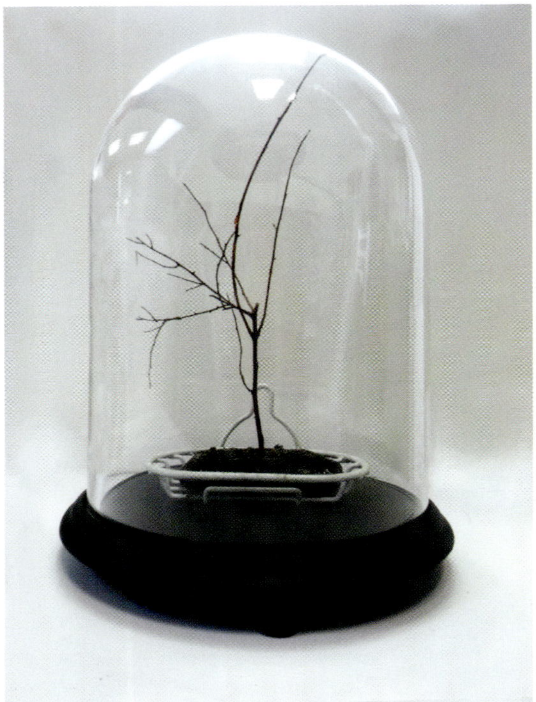

Earth Soap, 2002

32 cm x 24 cm x 24 cm

Soap made of earth and soap, soap dish and branch

Zeep gemaakt uit aarde en zeep, zeephouder en tak

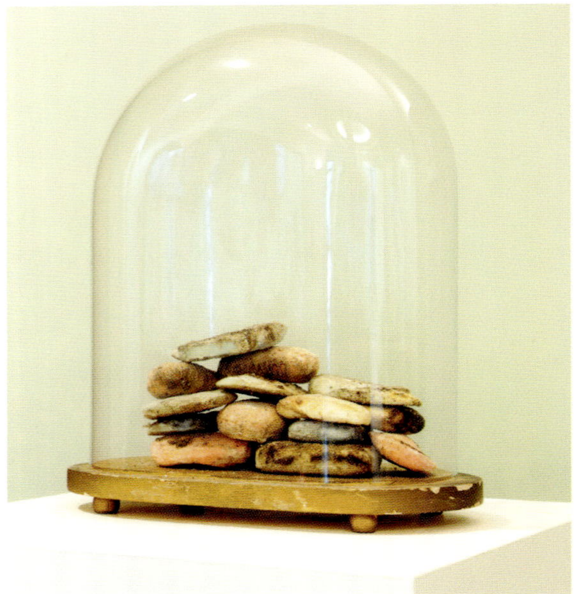

Future Garbage 2, 1996-1998

Burned pieces of soap under oval glass cover on plinth

Verbrande stukken zeep onder glazen ovale stolp op sokkel

Sniff Your Jail, org. Balie Tongeren, curators Paul Morrens, Johan Smets, Justice Palace Tongeren, BE, 14.05.2016-19.06.2015

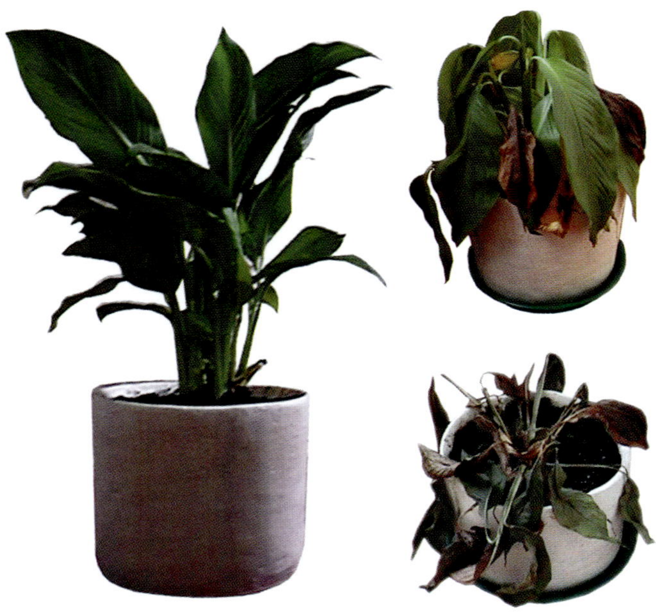

Clean Flowerpot, 1997

Flowerpot made of soap, died plant

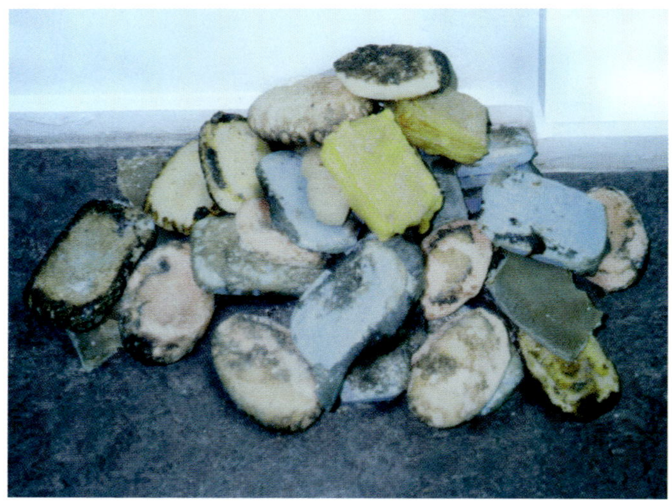

Future Garbage 1, 1996-1998

Burned pieces of soap on the floor in a corner of the room

Verbrande stukken zeep op de grond in een hoek van de ruimte

Garbage City, Van Laere Contemporary Art, Antwerp, BE, 20.05.2004-03.07.2004

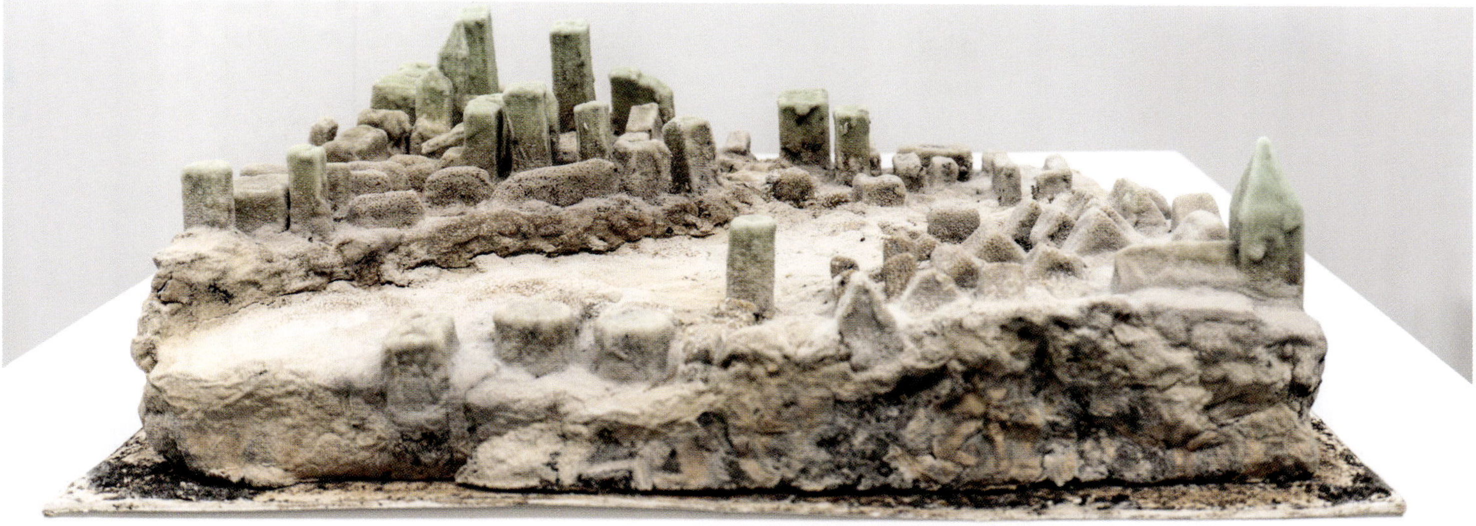

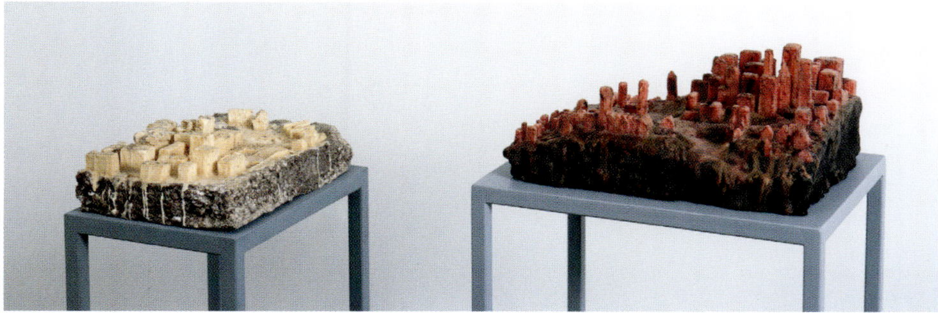

SOAP CITIES, 2001-2004

Small cities made of 50 % soap and 50 % earth, different smells (under plexiglass box on metal plinth)

Kleine steden gemaakt van 50% zeep en 50% aarde, verschillende geuren (onder plexiglazen constructie op metalen drager)

Soap City White: 2001-2002, H 130 cm x W 31 cm x D 22.5 cm
Soap City Red: 2004, H 137 cm x W 37 cm x D 28 cm
Soap City Green, 2003, H 138 cm x 35 cm x 30 cm

Garbage City, Van Laere Contemporary Art, Antwerp, BE
20.05.2004-03.07.2004

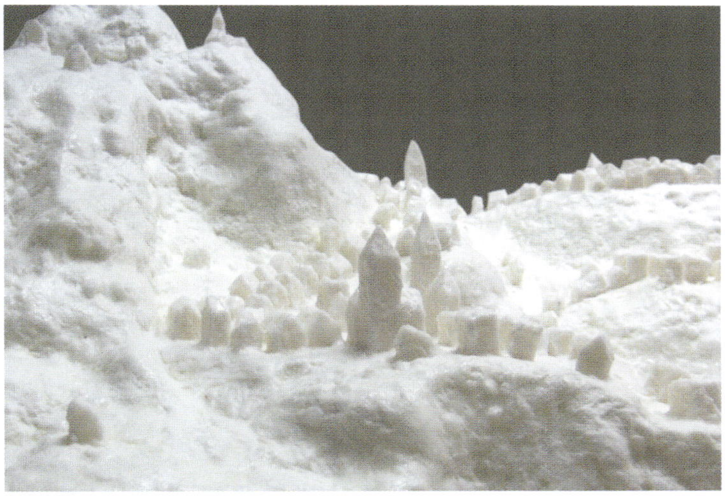

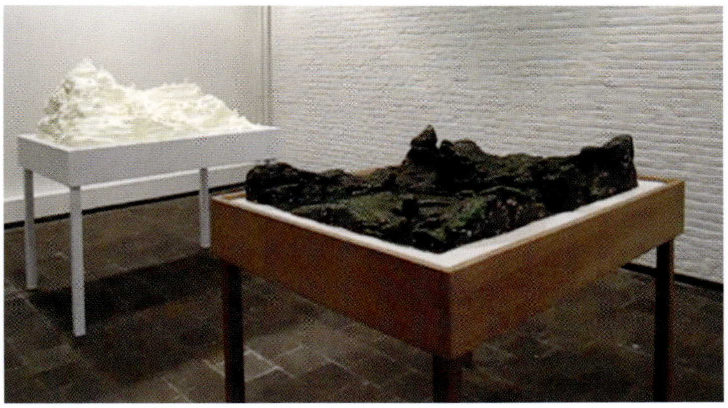

SOAP CITY, 2008

100 % epoxy based soap. The soap smells of peppermint.
Smell and colour change over time. The colours become greyer and the smell becomes musty.

100% zeep op een expoxy basis. De zeep ruikt naar pepermunt. Geur en kleur veranderen doorheen de tijd. De kleuren worden grauwer en de geur wordt muf.

True Love, De Markten, org. Kunst in Huis, Brussels, 14.11.2008-21.12.2008

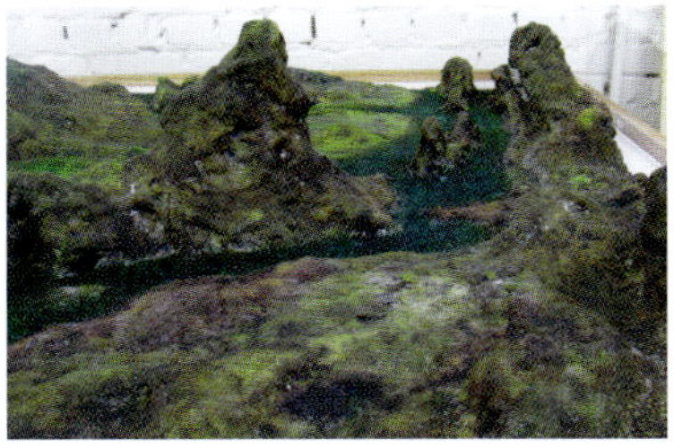

SOAP LANDSCAPE, 2008

50 % earth, 50 % soap scented with a grass smell. Smell and colour change over time. The colours become greyer and the smell becomes musty.

50% aarde, 50% zeep met de geur van gras. Geur en kleur veranderen doorheen de tijd. De kleuren worden grauwer en de geur wordt muf.

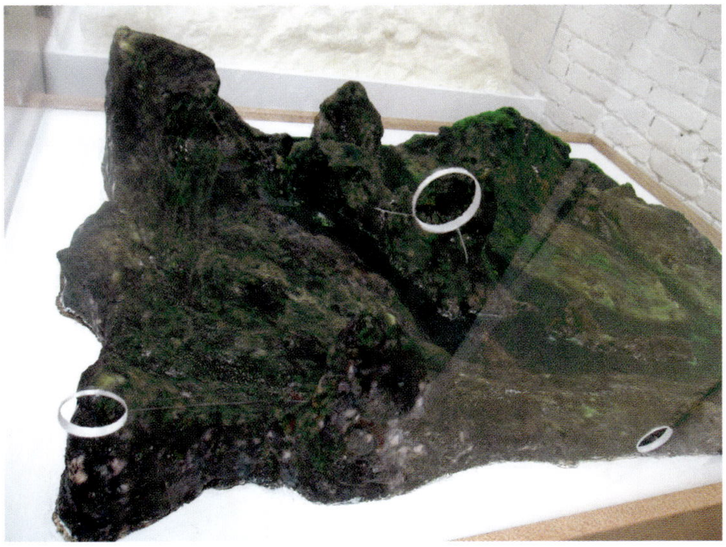

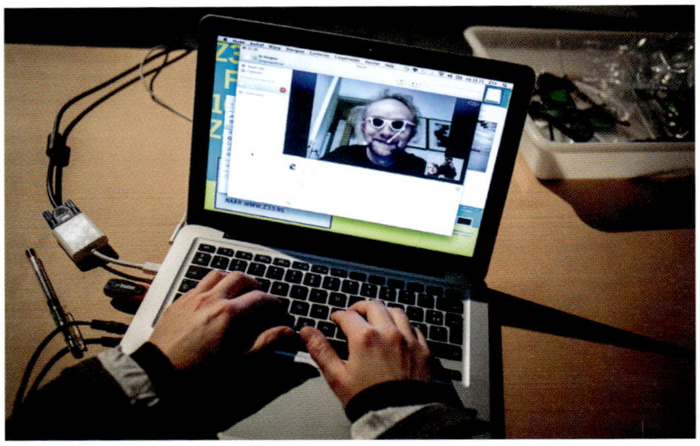

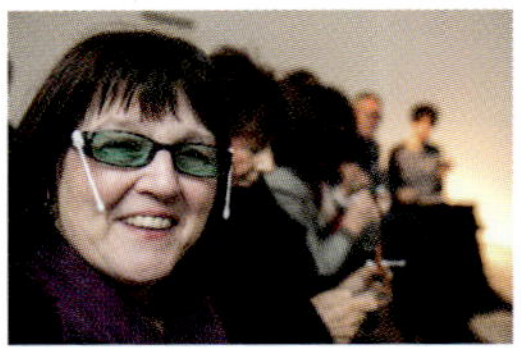

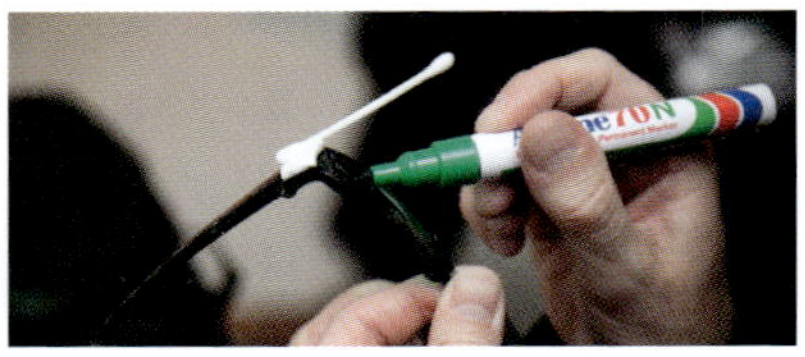

The Grass Is More Green ..., 2010

10 years Z33 Art Centre, Hasselt, Videoconference featuring a performance with the scent of grass. This included a cotton bud perfumed with grass scent, pasted on green translucent sunglasses.

10 jaar Z33, Hasselt, met een videoconferentie en performance met de geur van gras. Tijdens de videoconferentie werd een watje met grasgeur bevestigd aan een zonnebril.

10 Years Z33, Z33 Art Center, curator Jan Boelen, Hasselt, BE, 10-11.11.2012

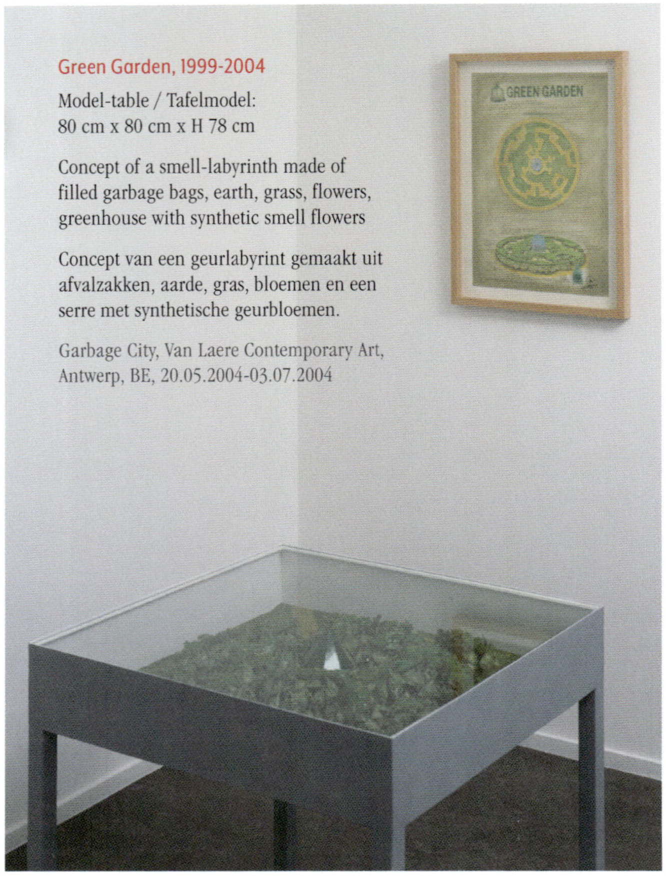

Green Garden, 1999-2004

Model-table / Tafelmodel:
80 cm x 80 cm x H 78 cm

Concept of a smell-labyrinth made of filled garbage bags, earth, grass, flowers, greenhouse with synthetic smell flowers

Concept van een geurlabyrint gemaakt uit afvalzakken, aarde, gras, bloemen en een serre met synthetische geurbloemen.

Garbage City, Van Laere Contemporary Art, Antwerp, BE, 20.05.2004-03.07.2004

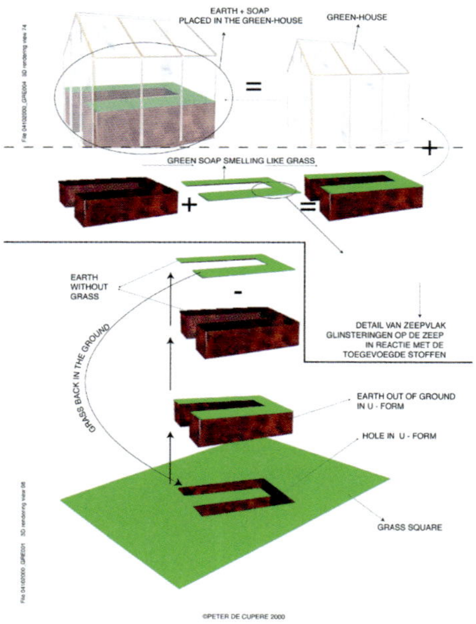

Green Grass

Green Soap, earth, greenhouse, smell of grass, reaction product

Groene soep, aarde, serre, grasgeur en reactief product.

Diasporical Thoughts, Liebaert Projects vzw, Tacktoren, curatoren Jo Coucke en Veerle Van Durme, Kortrijk, BE, 10.10-21.11.2000

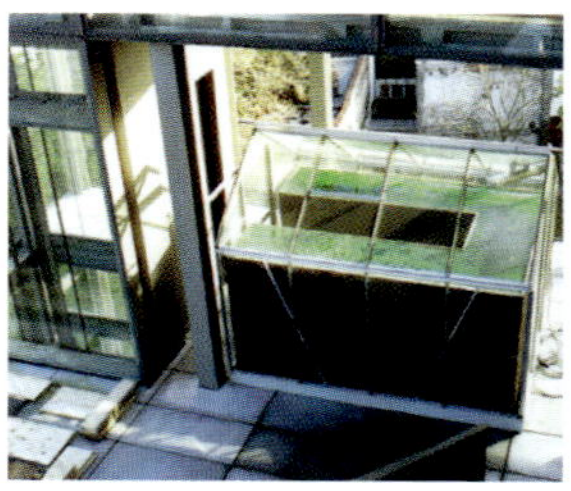

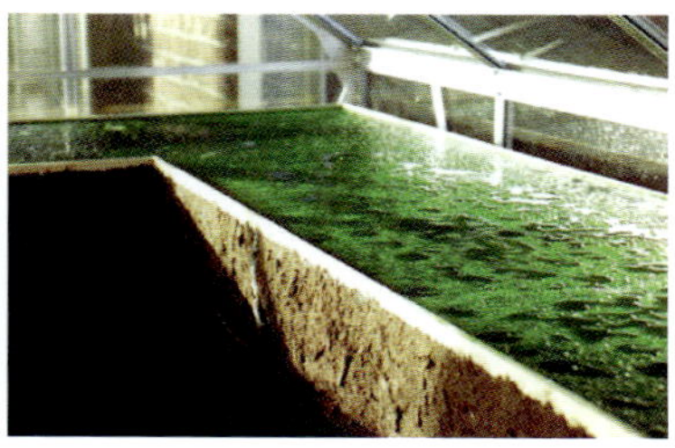

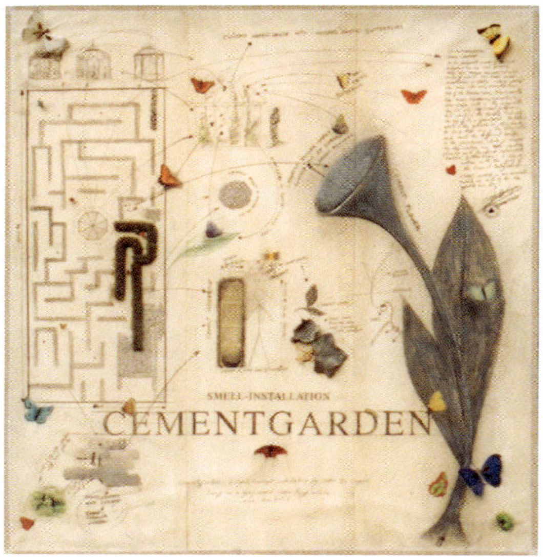

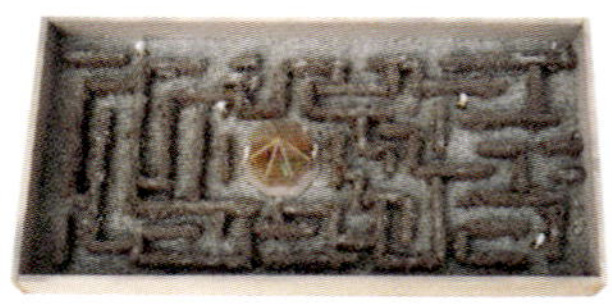

Cement Garden, 2000-2001

Drawing / Tekening: 130 cm x 130 cm
Model: 55 cm x 30 cm x 8 cm

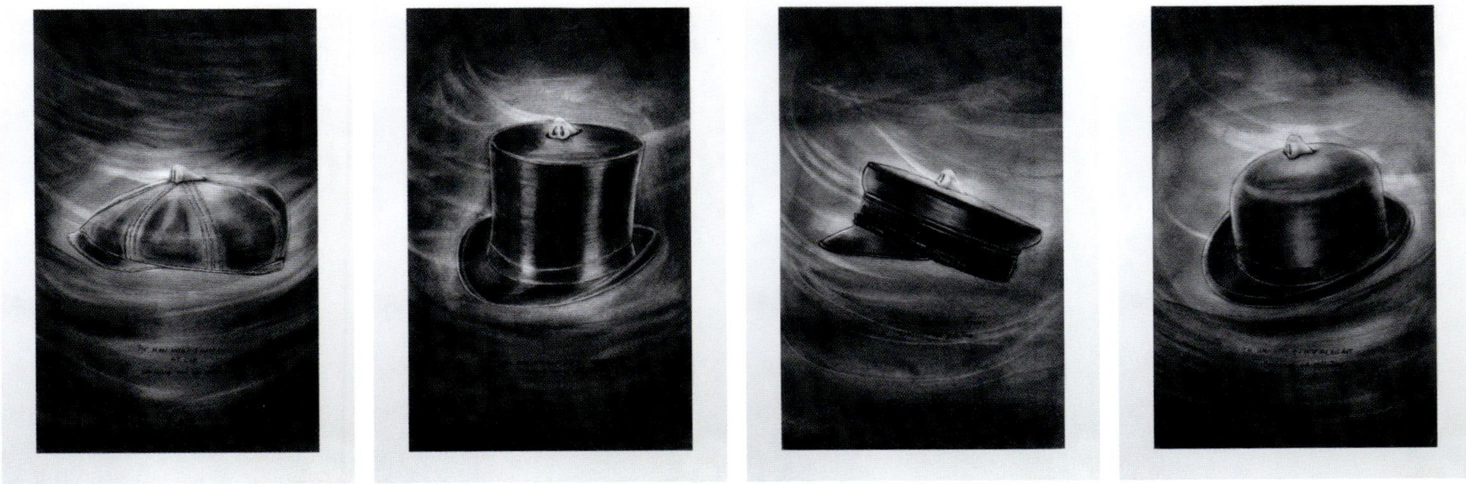

The Man With His Nose On His Hat Smelling Air Pollution, 2015-2016
Drawings, sculpures & photographs
Tekeningen, sculpturen & foto's

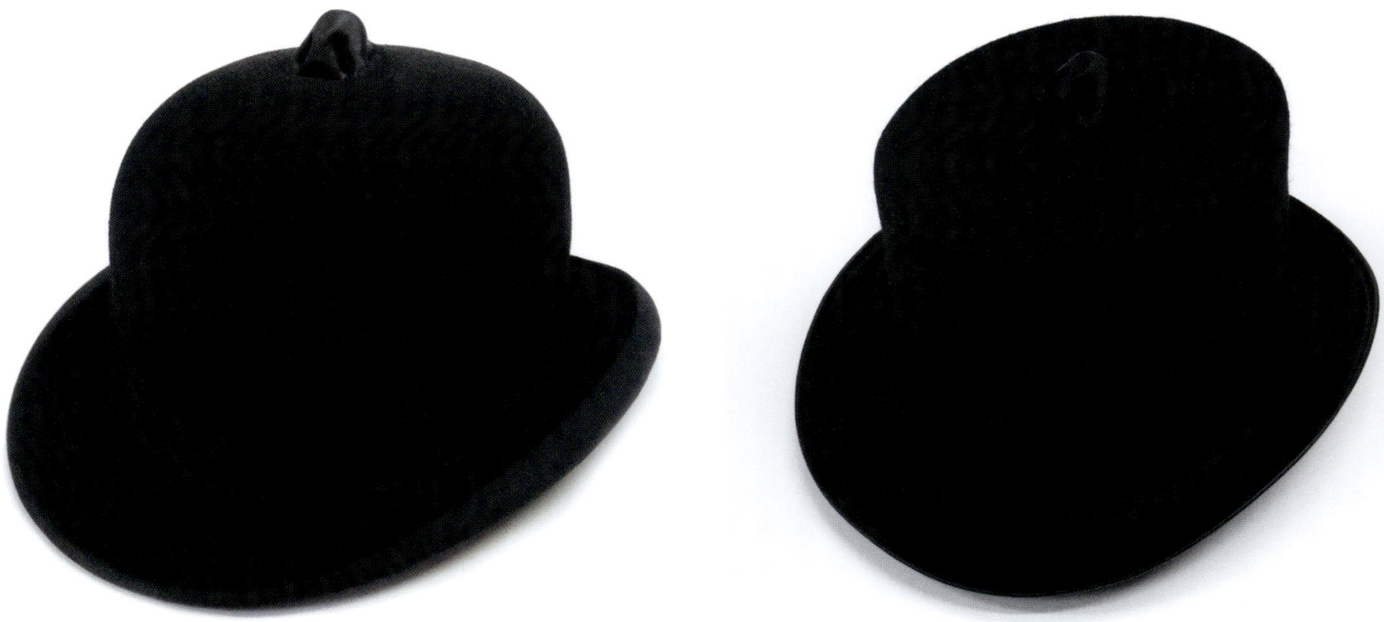

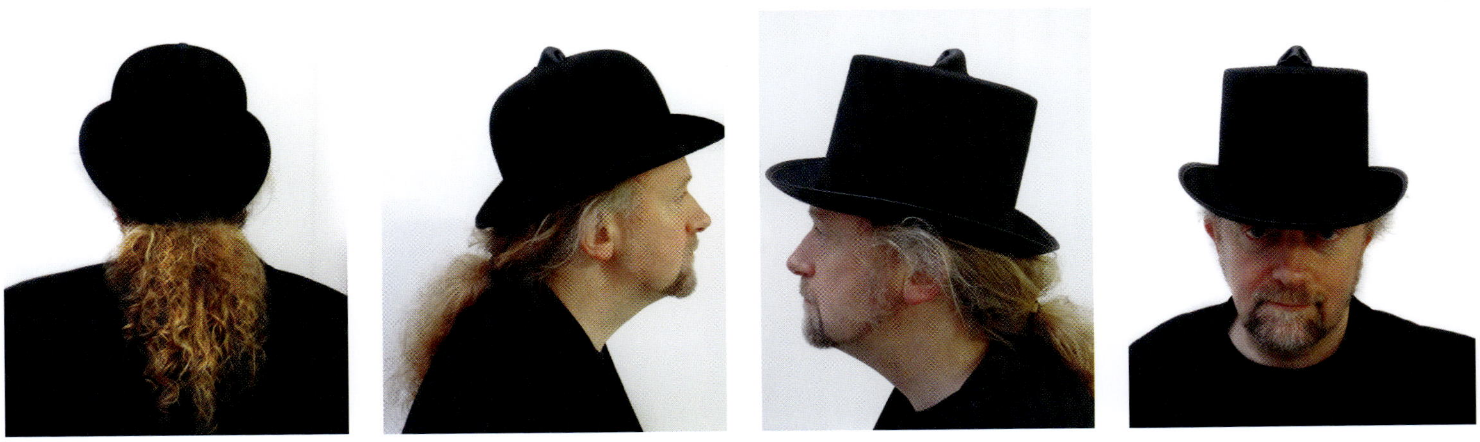

PETER DE CUPERE

TO EXPERIENCE
Ervaringsgeoriënteerd

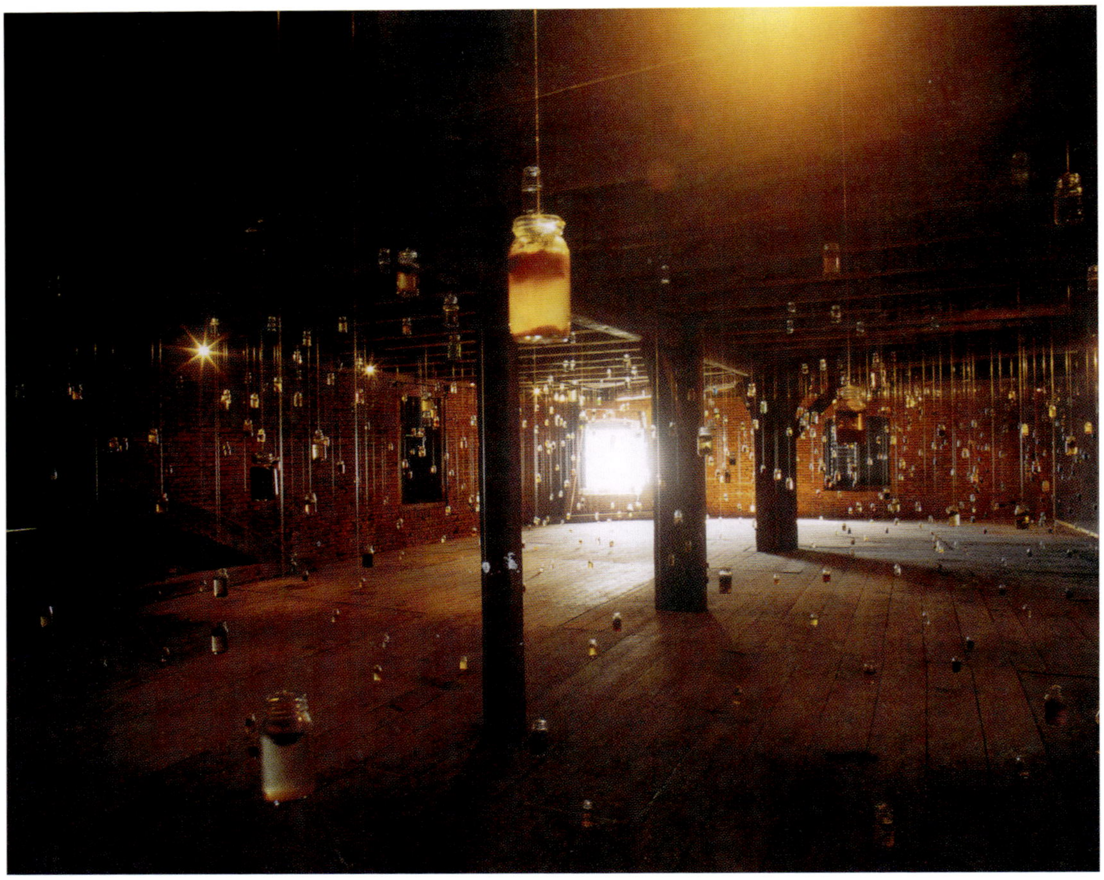

Recycled Raindrops, 2000

1,000 Pots of glass filled with water and rests of food, a little bit of fish smell

1.000 glazen bokalen gevuld met water en voedingsresten, met een lichte visgeur.

3 Raümen, 3 Flüshen, curator Jan Hoet, Hanne-Münden, DE, 10.06-30.09.2000

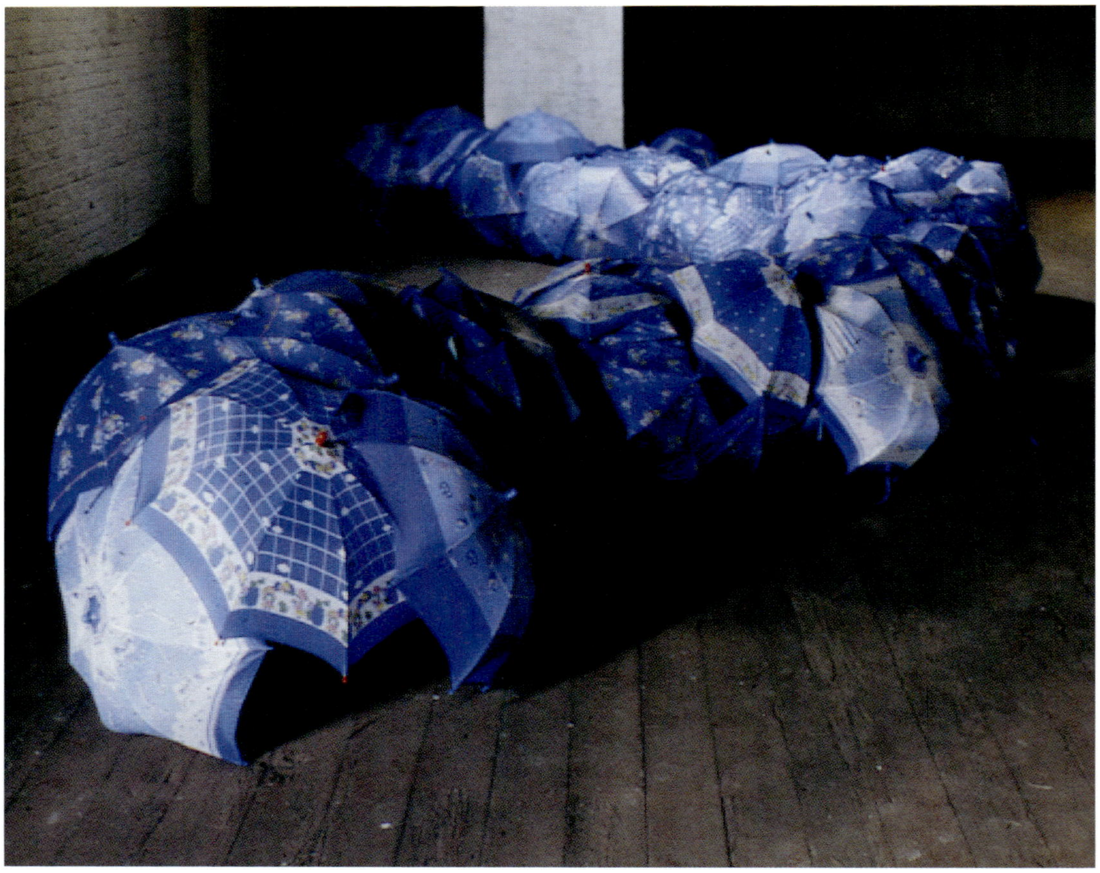

Rain Worm, 1997

Umbrellas in the shape of a rain worm. The scent of each umbrella is different.

Paraplu's in de vorm van een regenworm. De geur van iedere paraplu verschilt.

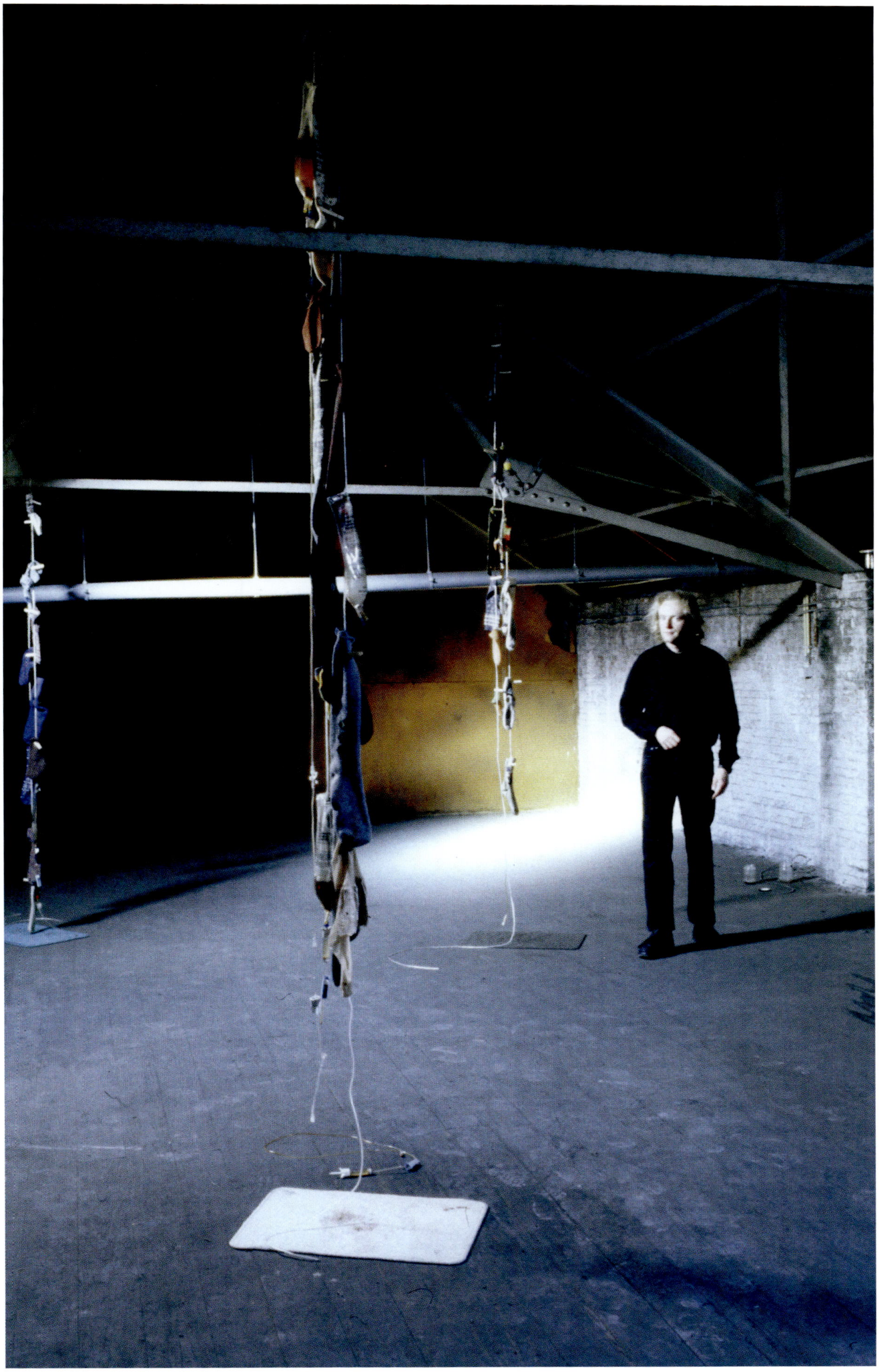

Sick Socks, 1998

99 different socks hanging on the ceiling in combination with medical baxters with the smell of feet perspiration. Dimensions are variable

99 verschillende sokken hangen aan het plafond in combinatie met medische baxters met de geur van zweetvoeten.
Verschillende dimensies.

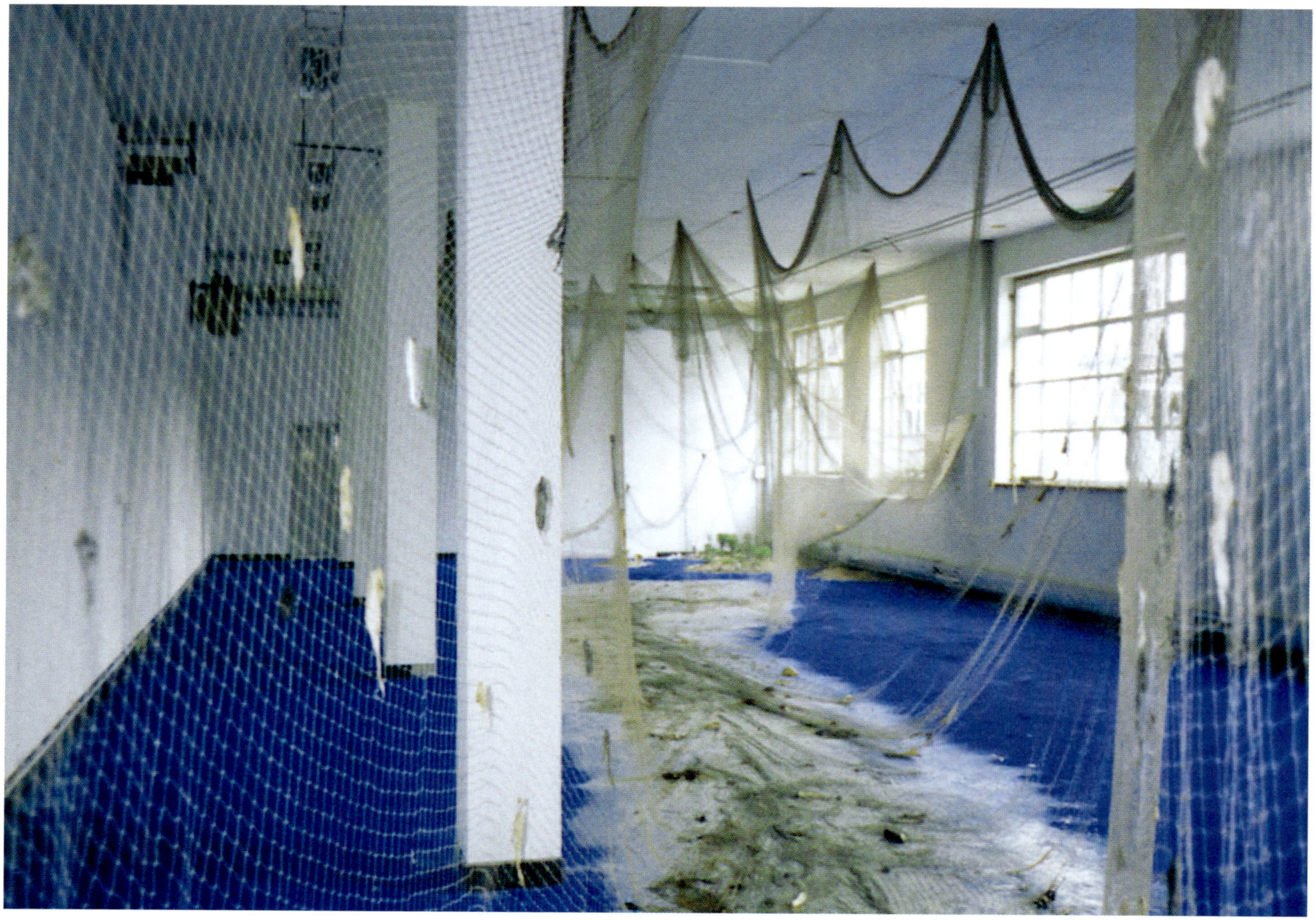

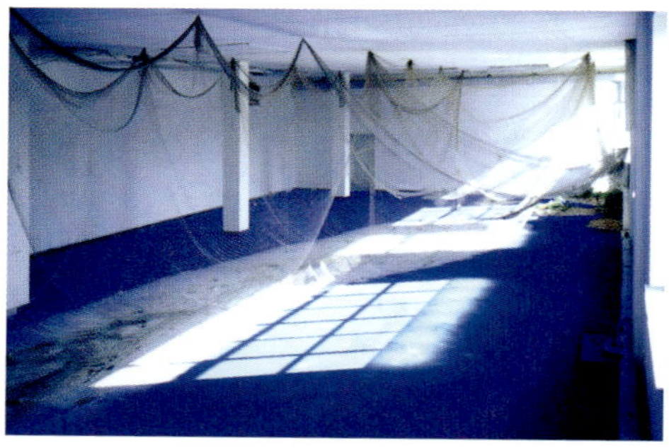

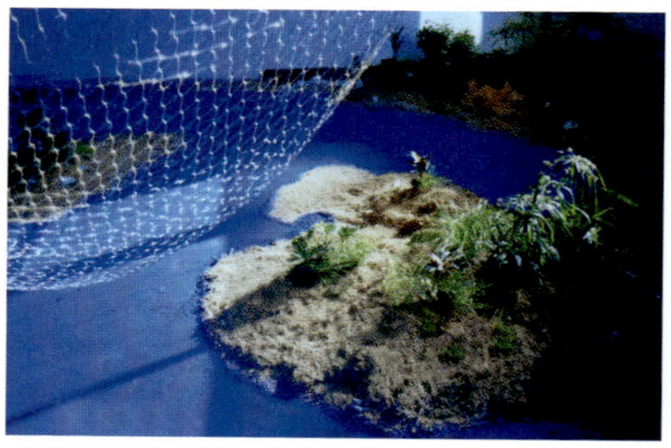

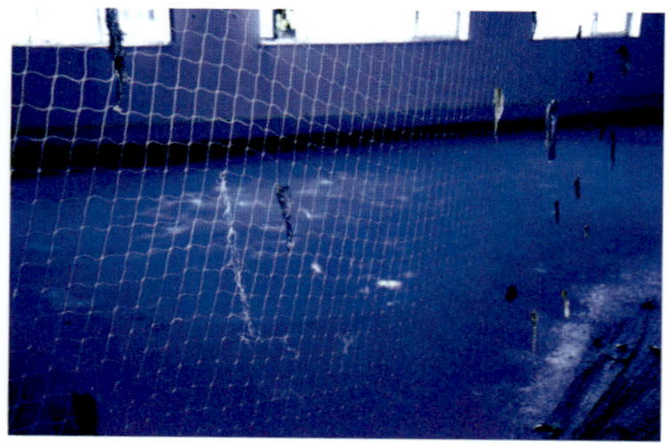

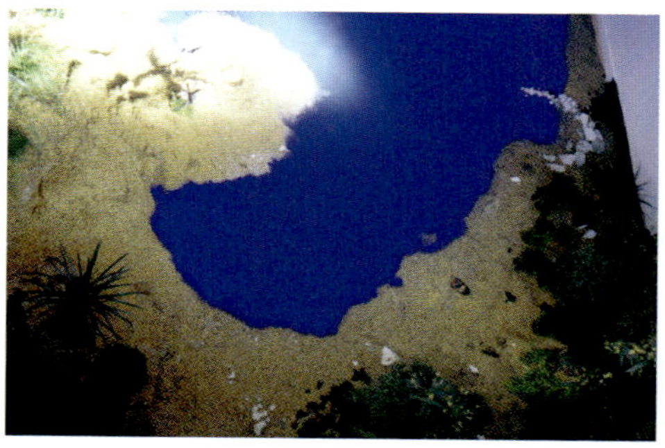

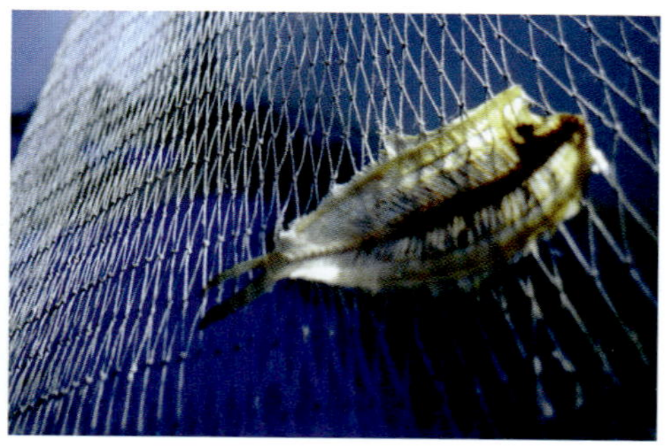

Blue Skies, 1999

±5 m H x 15 m W x 35 m D

1,000 m² fish-net, dried fish and synthetic fish smell. Salsa music, coconut-smell, island made of bird-seed and real miniature plants. 70 kg blue pigment. CD-player.

Een visnet van 1.000 m² met gedroogde vis en synthetische visgeur. Salsa muziek, kokosnoot, een eiland gemaakt van vogelzaden en miniatuurplanten. 70 kg blauw pigment. CD-speler.

Bouillon, HISK Higher Institute for Fine Arts, Flanders, Antwerp, BE, 11.06-20.06.1999

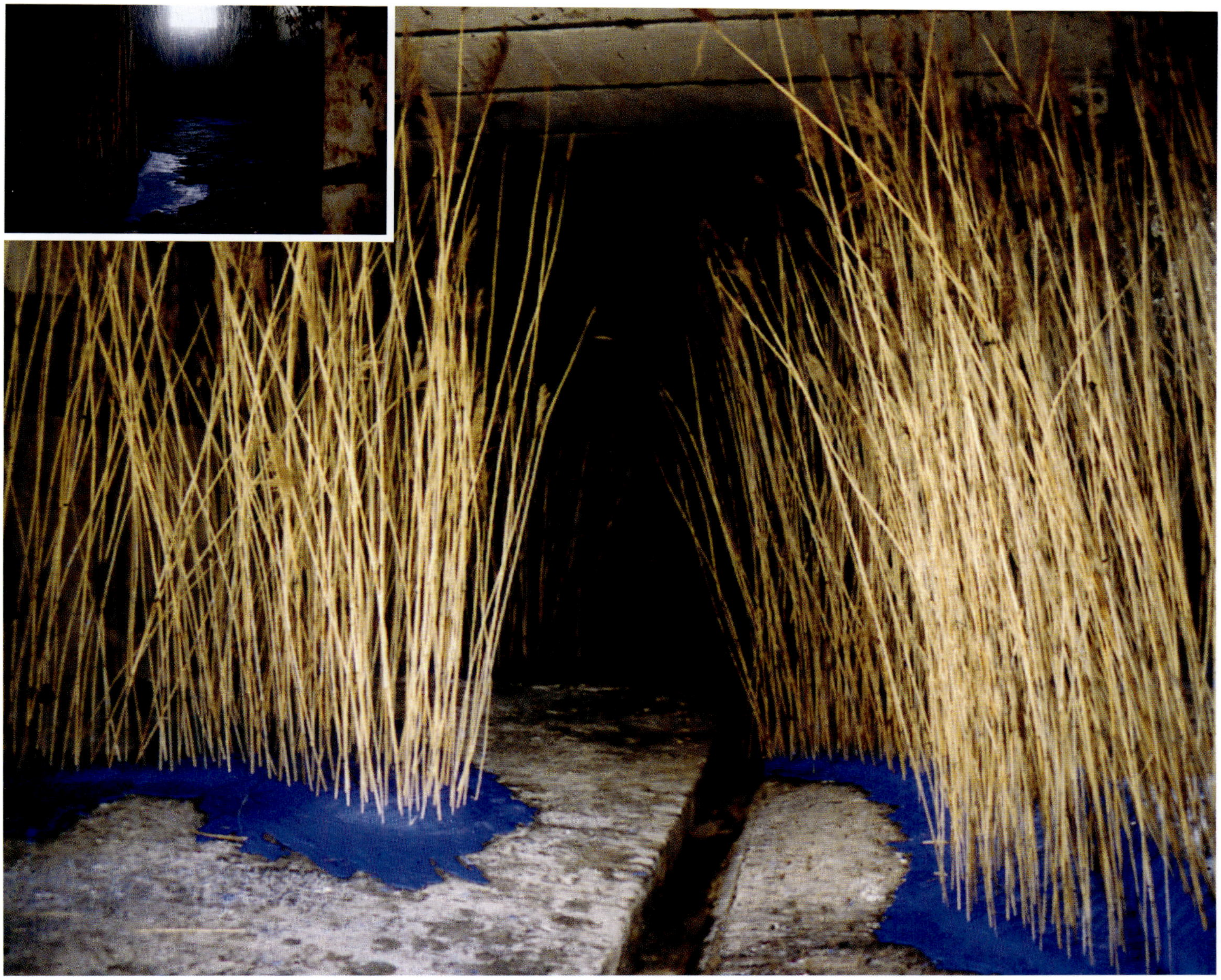

Reed Land, 1998

±240 cm x 600 cm x 1300 cm.

Walkingpath in a reed-land on a blue underground. It smells to rotten fish and lemon.

Wandelpad in een rieten veld met een blauwe ondergrond. Geur van rotte vis en citroen.

Voor het verdwijnt, en daarna (Before it Disappears, and After), curator Jan Hoet, Watou, BE, 29.06-06.09.1999

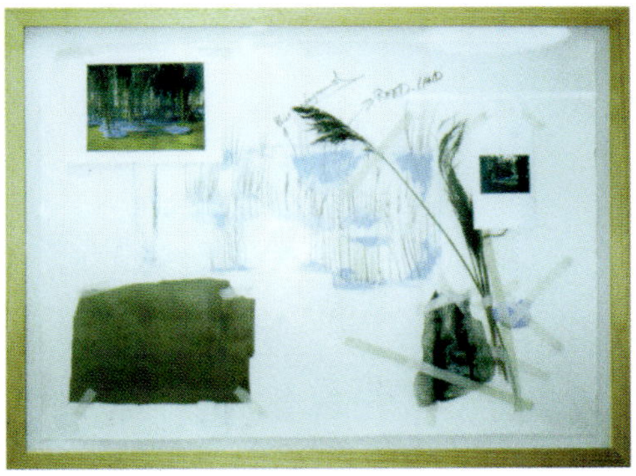

Drawing Reed Land, 1998

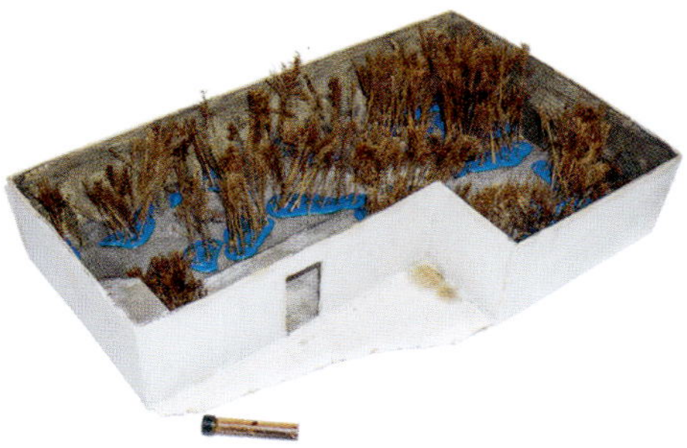

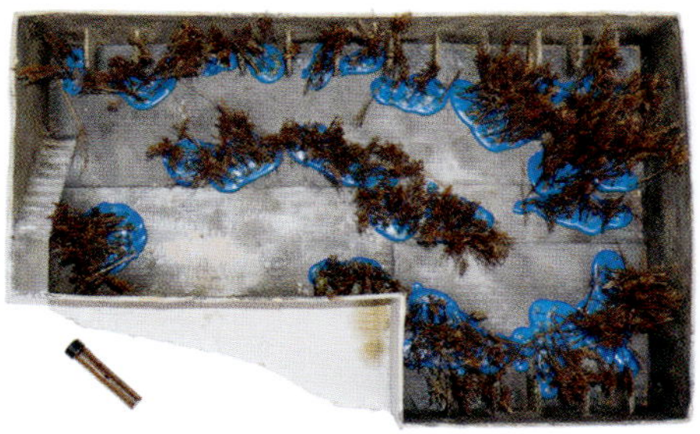

Model Reed Land, 1998

10 cm x 54 cm x 33,5 cm

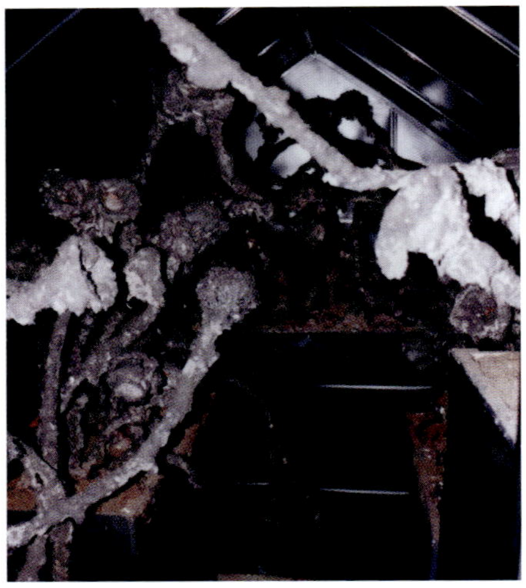

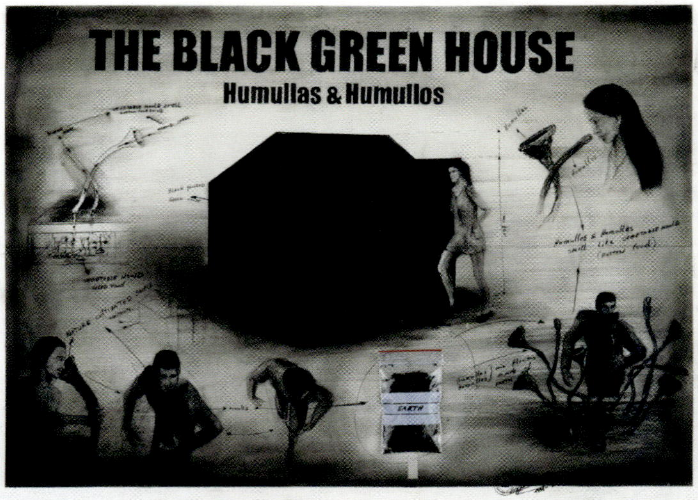

Black Green House, 2000

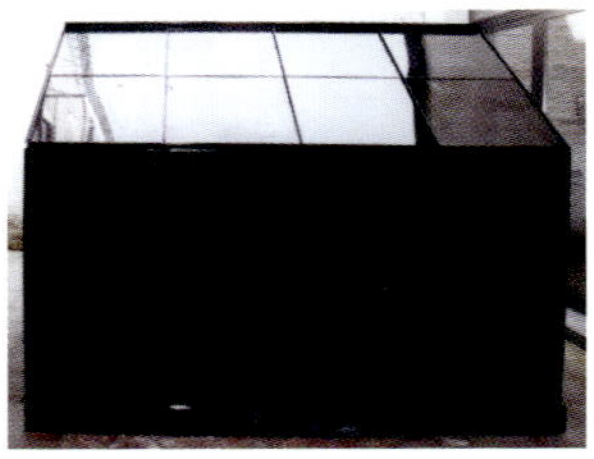

Greenhouse painted black, inside which are Humullas and Humullos; flowers with earthy smells: sweet-peach and pina colada mixed with the scent of humus and mushrooms

Een zwart geschilderde serre, binnenin met Humullas en Humullos. Bloemen met een aardgeur, zoete perzik en een piña coloda met de geur van humus en paddestoelen.

Peter de Cupere, Smellcom Happening, Smell Kiss Performance, rockconcert Admiral Freebee, Van Laere Contemporary Art, Antwerp, BE, 14.09-21.10.2000

Drawing Black Green House, 1998-2000

80 cm x 120 cm

From Memory, Museum Dr. Guislain, Ghent, BE 10.10.2009-02.05.2010
Peter de Cupere, Smellcom Happening, Smell Kiss Performance, rockconcert Admiral Freebee, Van Laere Contemporary Art, Antwerp, BE, 14.09-21.10.2000

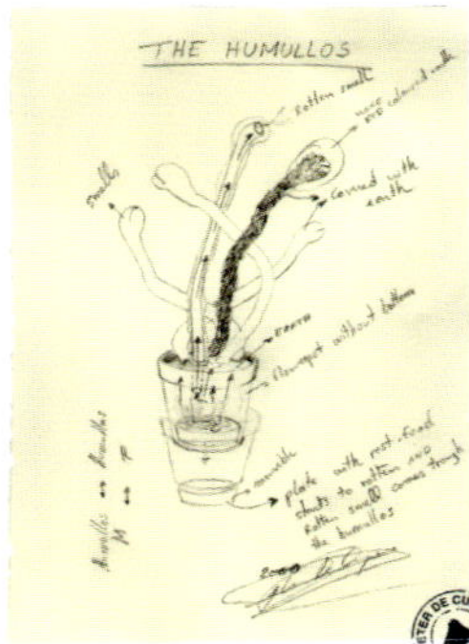

Sketch The Humullos, 2000

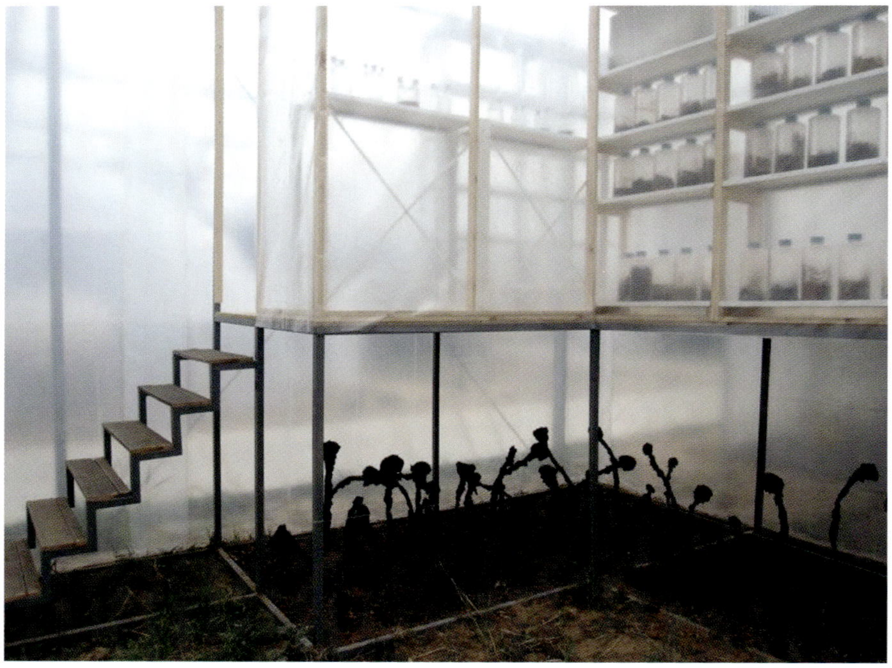

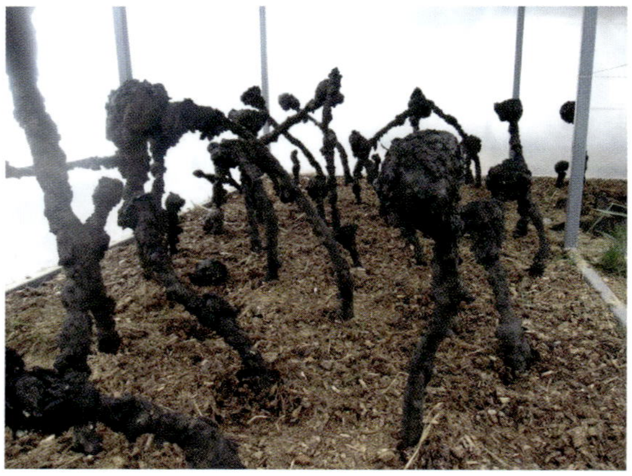

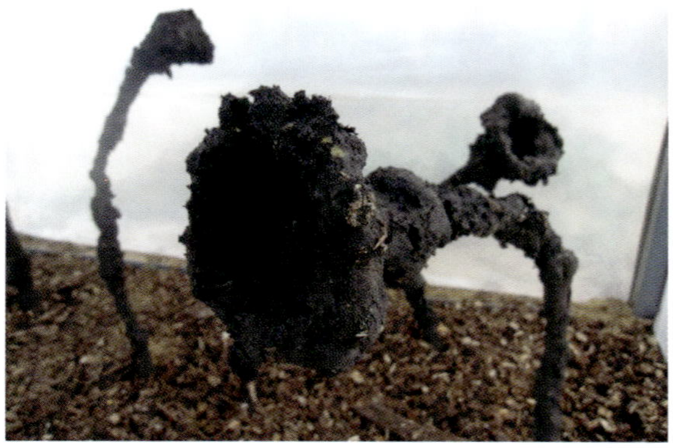

Humullos, 2009

Humullos flowers, made from earth, growing out of the ground with earth smell.
Humullos, bloemen die van aarde zijn en uit de grond groeien. De geur die ze afgeven is die van aarde.
Artificial Nature, Verbeke Foundation, Kemzeke, BE, 23.05.2009-15.11.2009

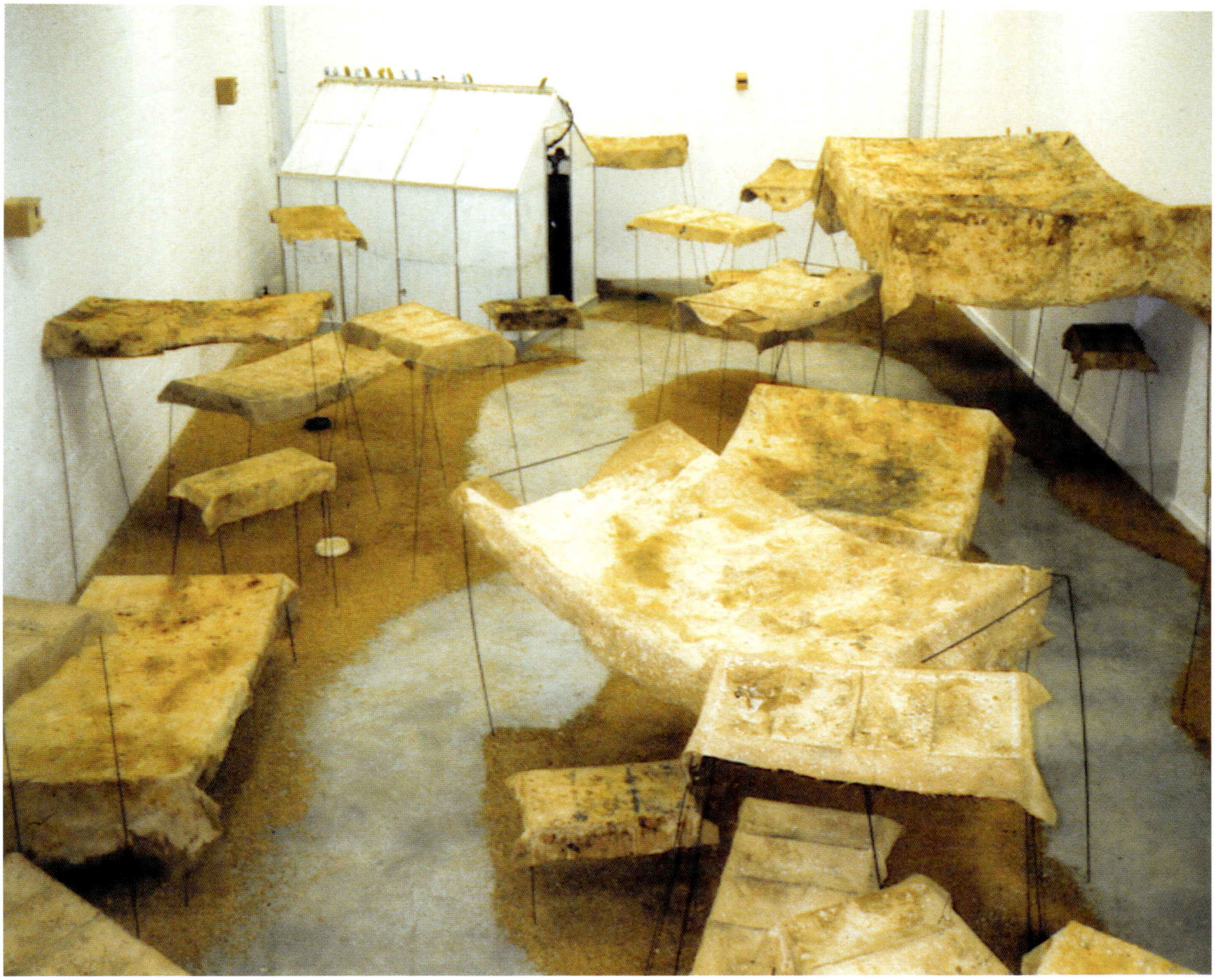

Garden, 1999

450 cm x 750 cm x 1700 cm

100 birds, 15 nesting-boxes, floating plateaus on thin iron bars, dried food, greenhouse with Humullas, 320 kg bird-seed, smells; celery, grass, truffle, green paprika smell, etc.

100 vogels, 15 vogelkastjes, zwevende plateaus op dunne ijzeren constructie, gedroogd eten, serre met Humullas, 320 kg vogelzaad, geur van selder, gras, truffel en groene paprika.

Solo exhibition in the association of the S.M.A.K., Ghent, BE, 07.05-06.06.1999

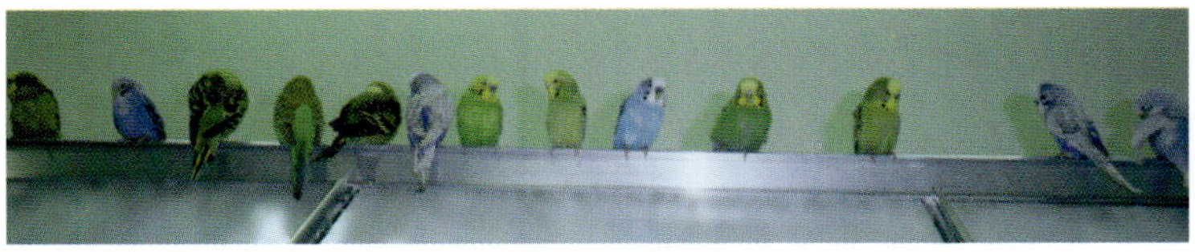

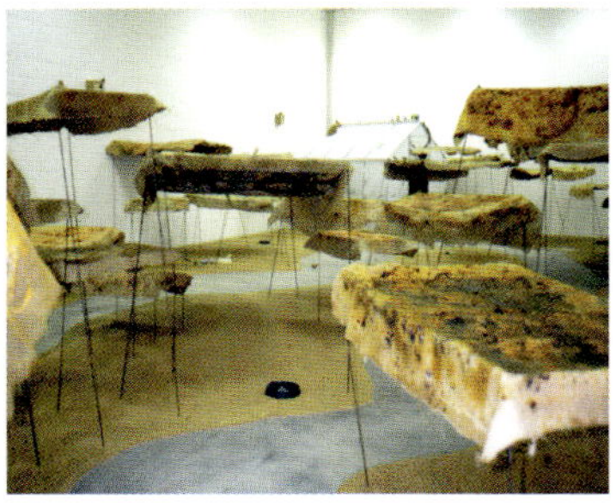

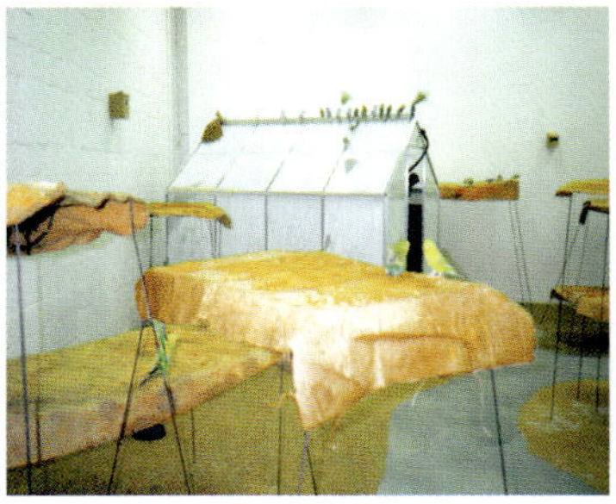

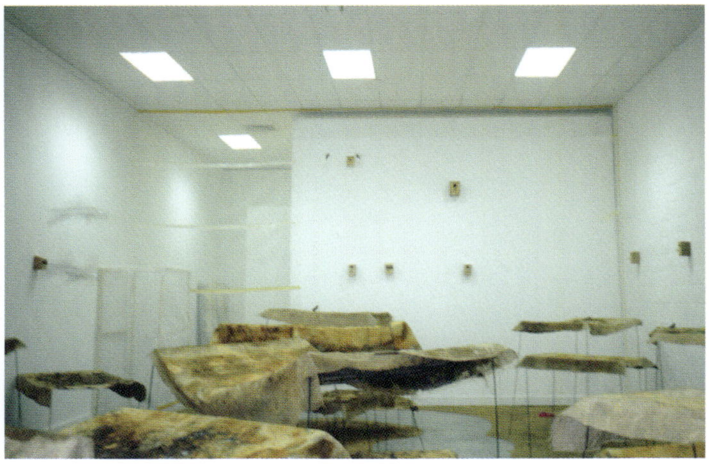

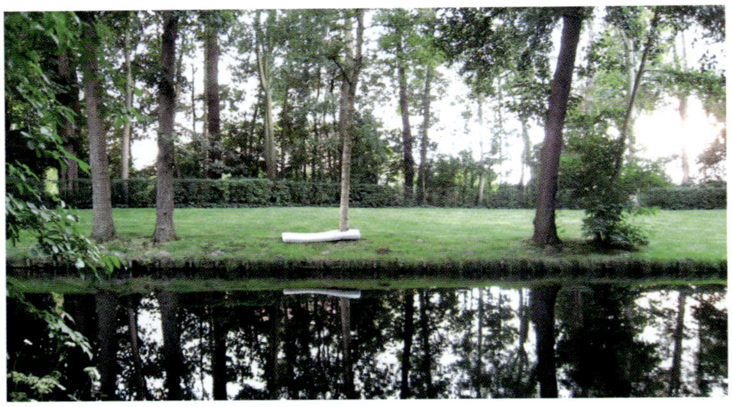

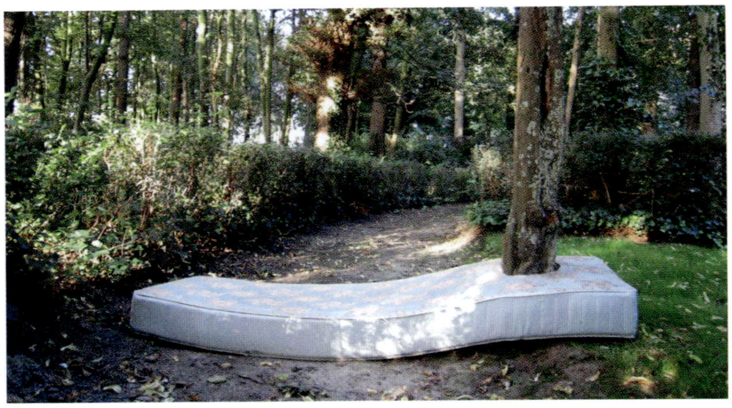

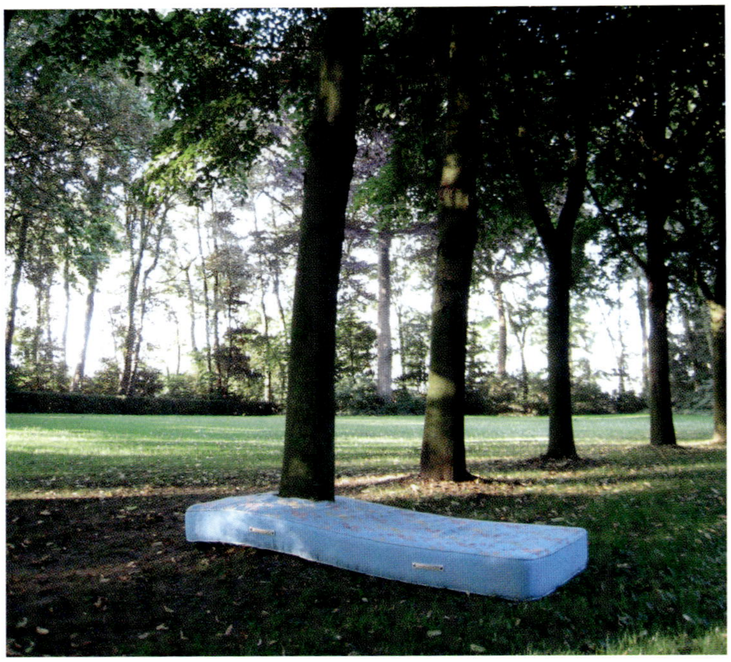

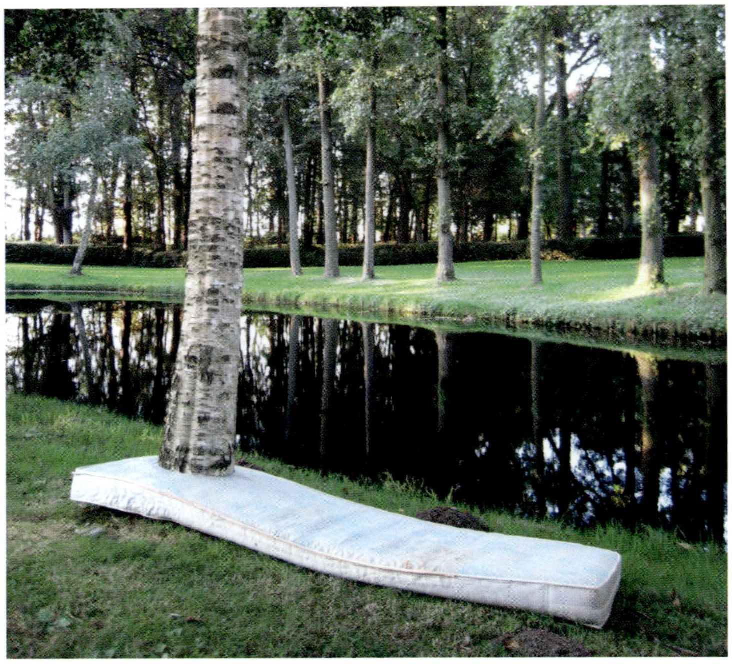

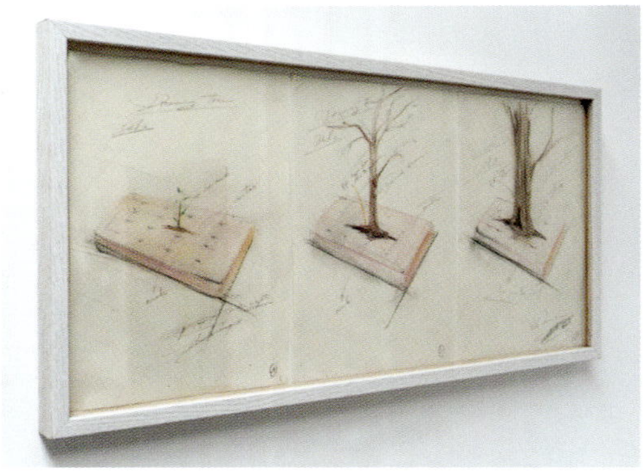

Drawing Dreaming Trees, 2002

3 drawings in frame / Tekeningen - 33,5 cm x 68 cm

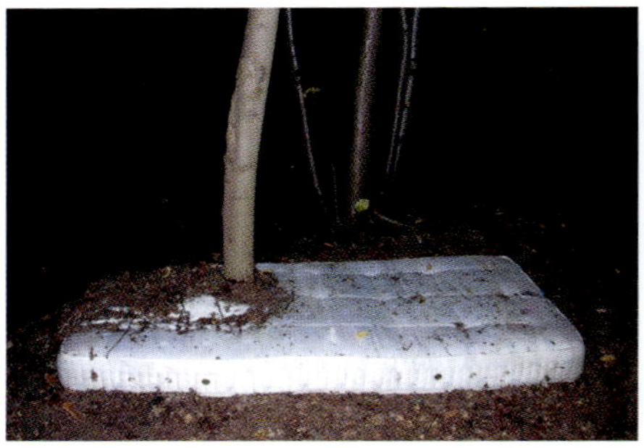

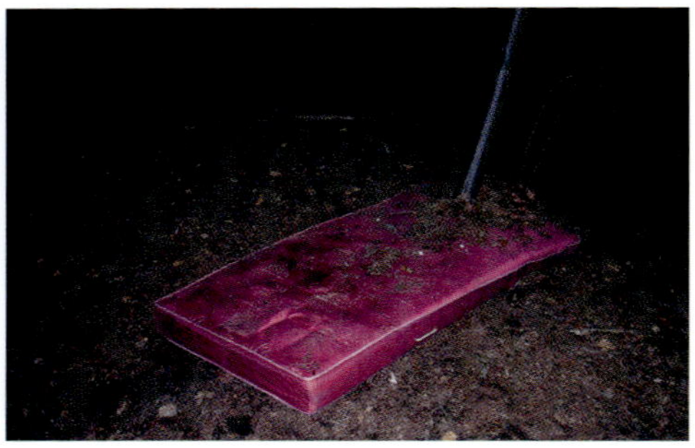

Dreaming Trees, 2002

Trees growing in perfumed mattresses with different smells like anis, cloves and thym

Bomen groeien uit geparfumeerde matrassen met verschillende geuren zoals anijs, kruidnagel en tijm

Smell the Castle, Castle Beauvoorde, curator Annemie Morisse, Beauvoorde, BE, 15.07.2007-30.08.2007

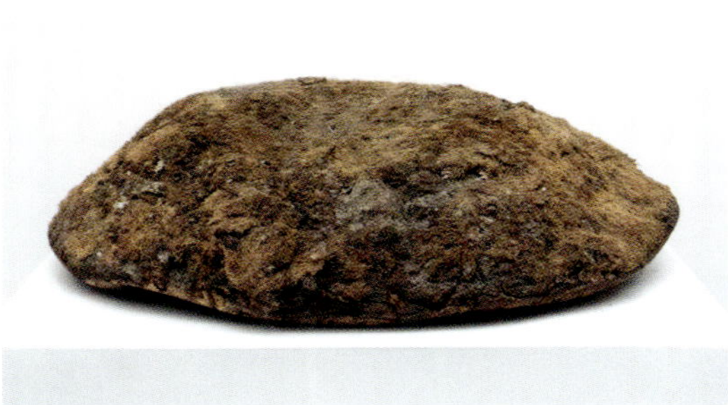

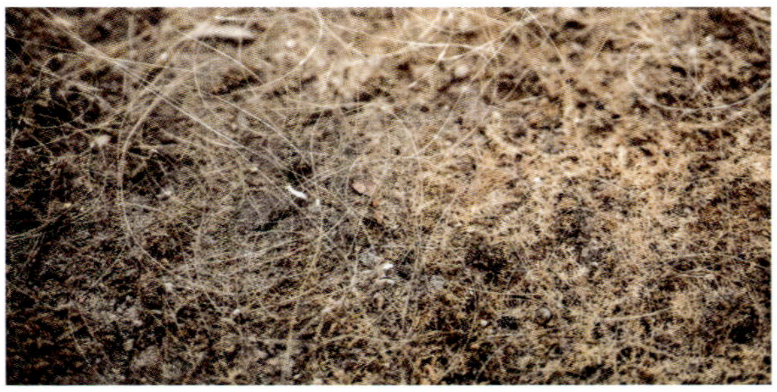

Nature Pillow, 2001

Moss with long human blond hair, thym, paprika and celery smell

Mos gemaakt met lang menselijk haar, tijm-, paprika- en seldergeuren

Living landscape, Museum Groeneveld, NL, 07.10.2008-31.05.2009
Smell the Castle, Castle Beauvoorde, curator Annemie Morisse, Beauvoorde, BE
15.07.2007-30.08.2007

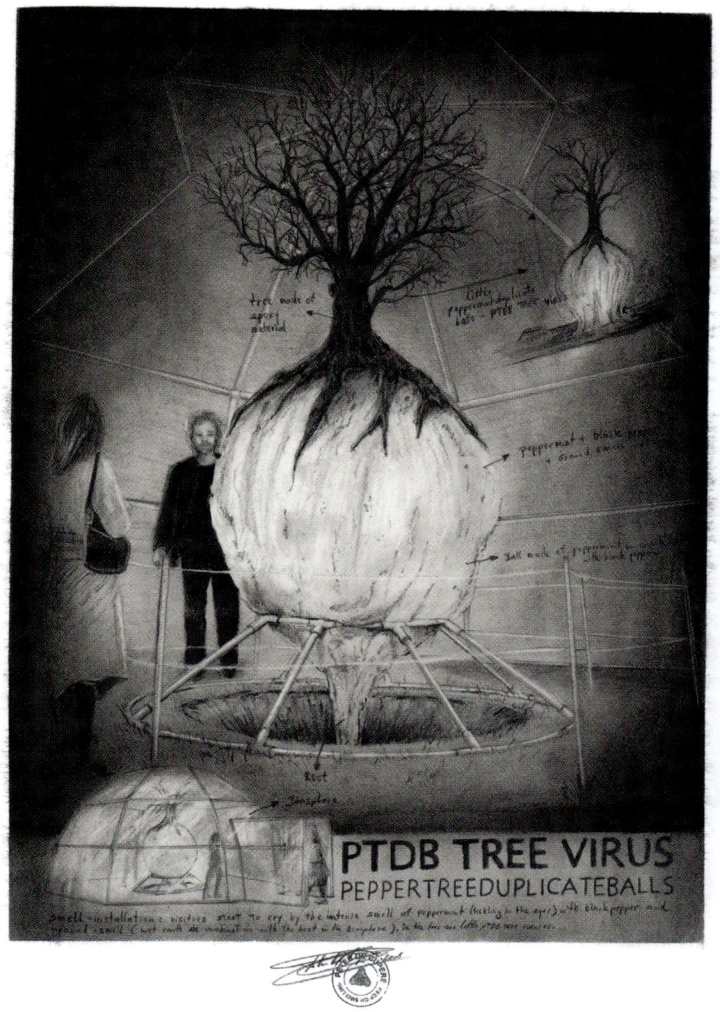

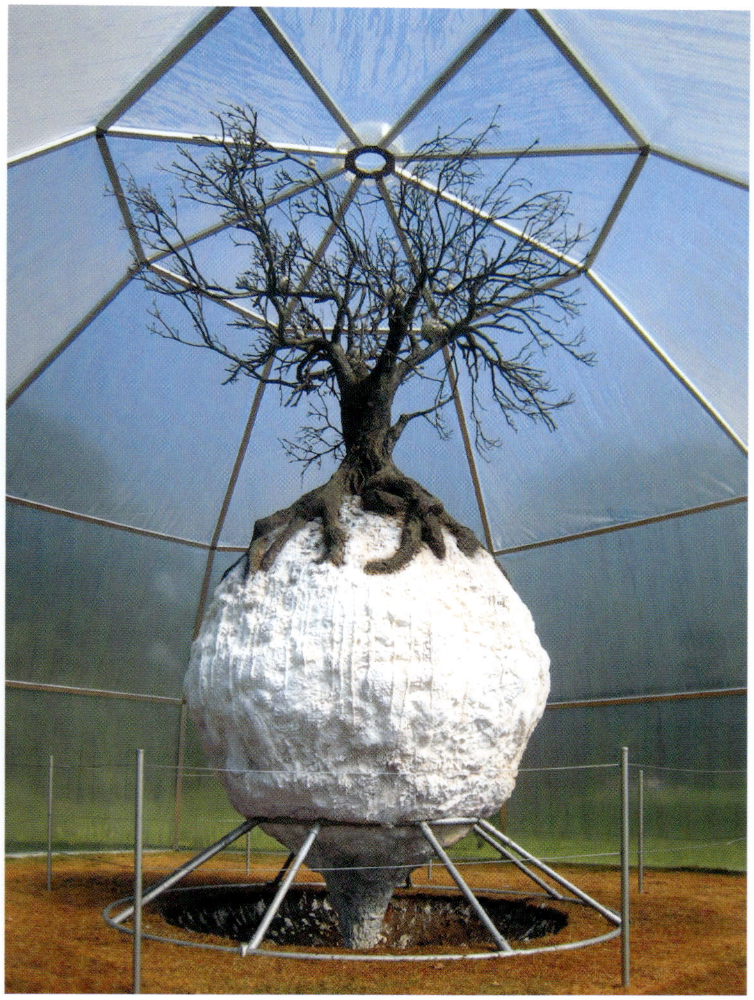

Peppertreeduplicateballs PTDB-Tree Virus, 2008

Olfactory installation / Olfactorische installatie, 400 cm x 700 cm Ø

Peppertreeduplicateballs PTDB-Tree Virus is a smell installation in which the smell of peppermint in combination with black pepper and a smell activator is so strong and intense that visitor's eyes water when viewing the work. It looks like they are crying. The whole installation is constructed in a hemisphere in which the temperature partly determines the intensity of the smell. There are small ptdb-tree viruses in the tree, small white balls with miniature trees on top. The whole concept is based on the idea of mistletoe. This is semi-parasitic and takes nutrients from the tree but can also photosynthesise itself.

Peppertreeduplicateballs PTDB-Tree Virus is een geurinstallatie waarbij de geur van pepermunt in combinatie met zwarte peper en een geuractivator zo intens en sterk aanwezig is, dat de bezoeker tranen in de ogen krijgt bij het aanschouwen van het werk. Heel de installatie is gebouwd in een hemisfeer waarbij de temperatuur mede de geurintensiteit bepaald. In de boom bevinden zich kleine ptdb-tree virusjes, kleine witte bollen met kleine boompjes erop. Heel het concept is gebaseerd op het idee van maretakken. Dit zijn half-parasieten welke voedsel onttrekken aan de boom, maar wel hun eigen fotosynthese houden.

Artificial Nature, Verbeke Foundation, Kemzeke, BE, 23.05.2009-15.11.2009
Exoten, Beelden op de Berg 2008, University Wageningen, org. Urban Aesthetics, curator Kim Knoppers, Wageningen, NL, 07.06.2008-21.09.2008

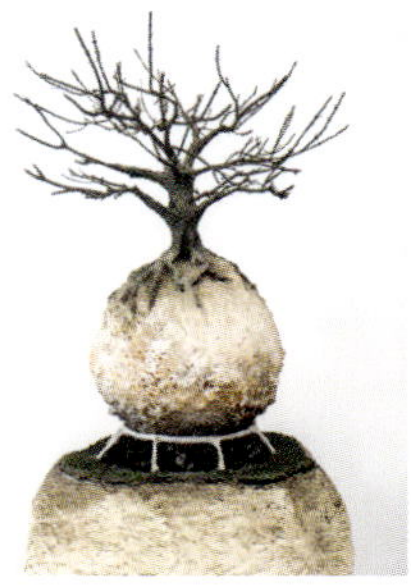

Model Peppertreeduplicateballs PTDB-Tree Virus, 2008

170 cm x 50 cm x 50 cm

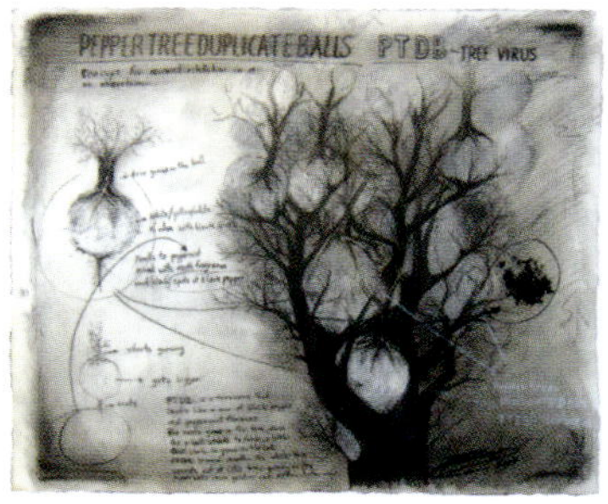

Drawings Peppertreeduplicateballs PTDB-Tree Virus, 2008

Variable dimensions

Verschillende dimensies

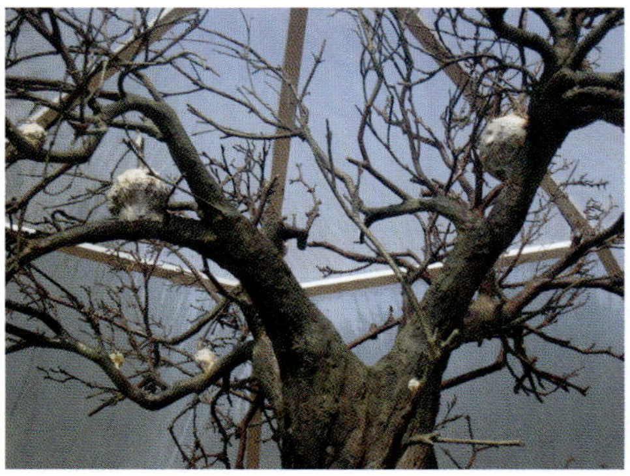

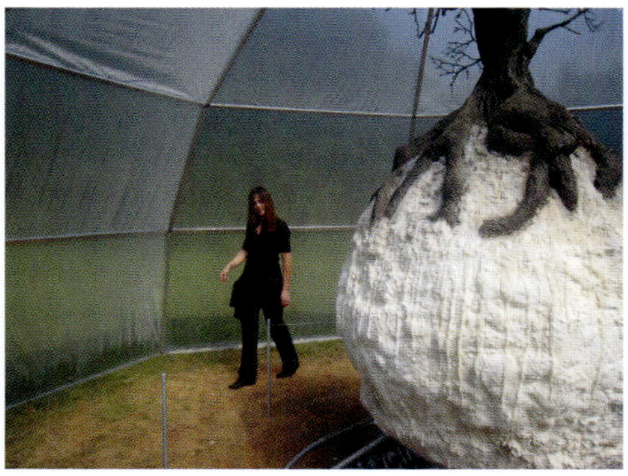

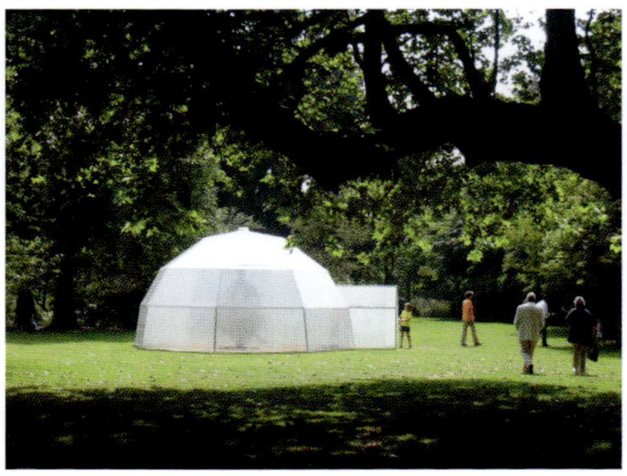

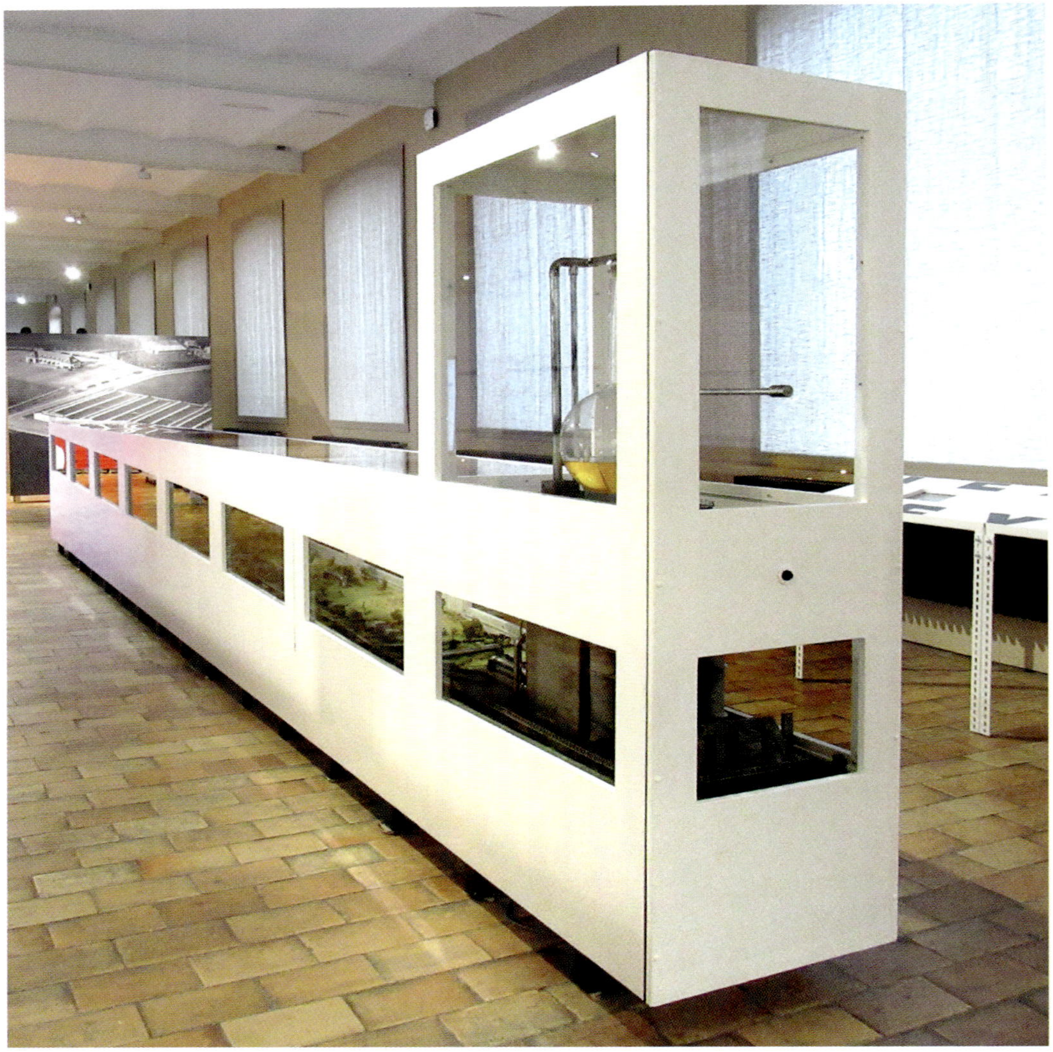

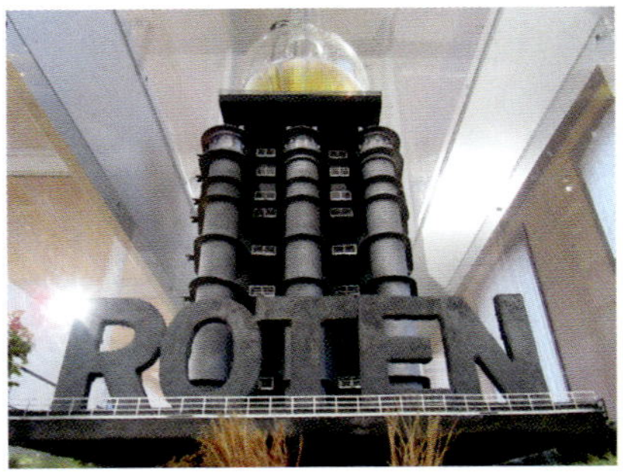

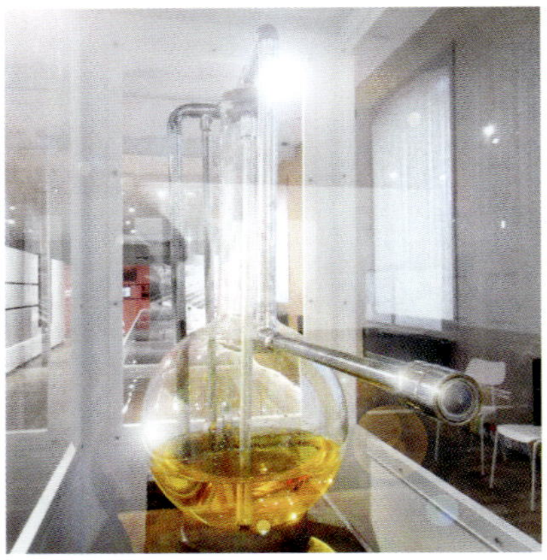

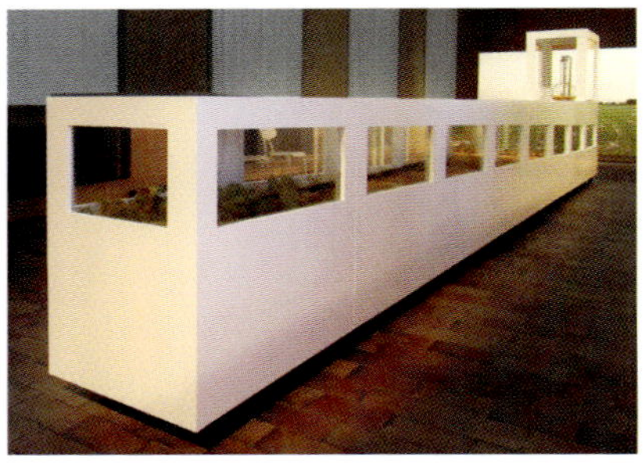

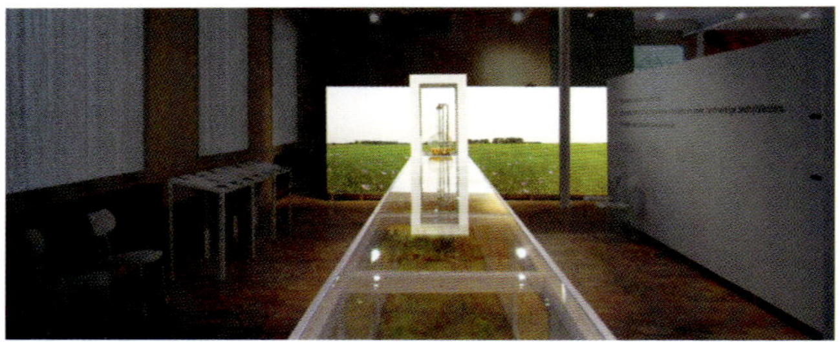

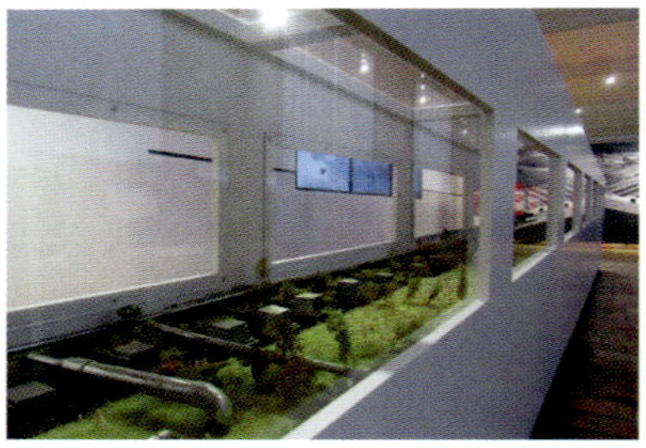

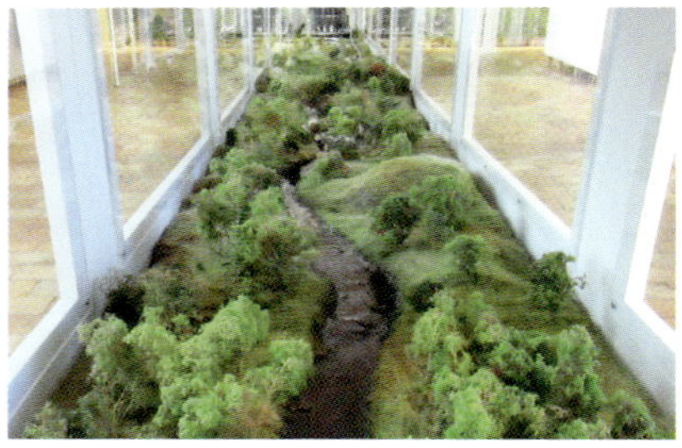

Roten Eau De Leie, 2015

Mixed media, 200 cm x 800 cm x 50 cm

'Roten Eau de Leie' is an artistic integration in the Texture Museum in Kortrijk, Belgium. The installation is 8 m long and introduces the Leie River in full flow. The work consists of a large miniature landscape which the Leie River flows through. Small modules visually capture the smell of the river, in which flax is soaking. The flax is soaked in water in order to separate the fibres from its stem. It is a delicate process that, until 1943, was carried out in large wooden vats–the so-called 'hekkens'–in the Leie. During the soaking, the natural glue or pectin in the flax stalks dissolved and separated from the woody husk. After 1943, the same process was carried out in concrete vats in the flax-growing region.
Peter de Cupere created his own version of this soaking process, and reproduced the specific smell of the soaking flax. The smell is not particularly attractive in itself. The perfume that Peter de Cupere created in his lab, based on samples, descriptions and smell analyses, was presented to a council of experts, or 'smell panel' of former flax workers. They were able to determine whether the artificial smell was a correct reproduction. The artist based his work on the pointers provided by the smell panel in order to optimise the result.
Visitors can experience the smell for themselves. Pushing a button causes the perfume to bubble forth and the smell is released.

'Roten Eau de Leie' is een kunstintegratie in het Texture Museum in Kortrijk.
De installatie is 8 meter lang en stelt de Leie voor met een hoog vervaldebiet. Het bestaat uit een groot miniatuurlandschap waar de rivier de Leie doorheen vloeit. Kleine modules vangen visueel de geur op van de rivier waarin vlas wordt geroot. Roten is het weken van vlas in water om de vlasvezels los te kunnen maken van de vlasstengel. Het is een delicaat proces dat tot 1943 gebeurde in grote houten bakken – de zogenaamde hekkens – in de Leie. Tijdens het roten lost de natuurlijke lijm of pectine in de vlasstengels op zodat ze vrij komen van de houtachtige bast. Na 1943 gebeurde diezelfde bewerking in de betonroterijen in de vlasstreek.
Peter de Cupere creëerde zijn eigen versie van het roten en hermaakte de specifieke geur van roten. Een geur op zich die niet zo lekker ruikt. Het parfum dat Peter de Cupere in zijn labo creëerde op basis van stalen, beschrijvingen en geuranalyses werd voorgelegd aan een raad der wijzen of 'geurpanel' van oud-vlassers. Zij konden beoordelen of die kunstmatige geur een correcte reproductie was. De kunstenaar baseerde zich op de aanwijzingen van het geurpanel om zijn resultaat te optimaliseren. De bezoeker kan nu zelf de geur waarnemen. Door op een knop te drukken begint het parfum te bubbelen en wordt de geur vrijgegeven.

Roten, Eau de Leie, Texture Museum, curator Sylvie De Coster, Kortrijk, BE, Installation in Situ, June 2015

THe Pink Lady, 974+, 2003

974 Pink snails made of polyester, different measures, covered with smell slime in combination with silicones. Smell of mud, peach in combination with coffee and candy smell

974 paarse slakken gemaakt uit polyester in verschillende maten, bedekt met een geurslijm in combinatie met siliconen. De geur van modder en perzik in combinatie met een koffie- en snoepjesgeur.

Tracer, Museum Pam Ename, curator Edith Doove, Ename, BE, 13.09.2003-02.11.2003

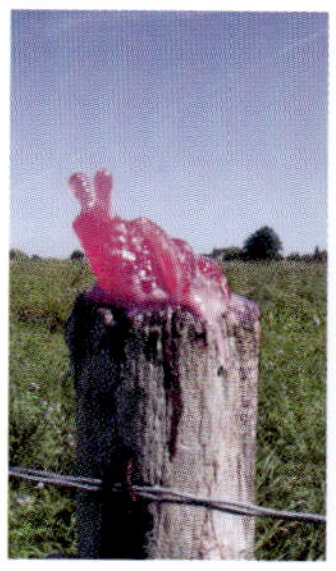

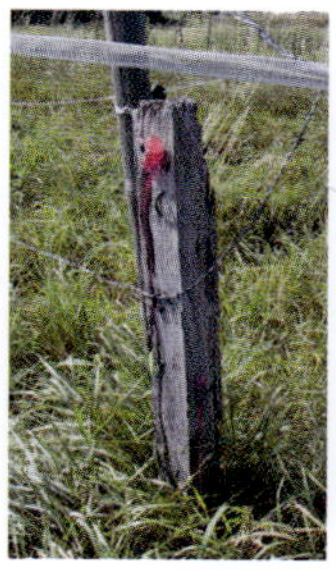

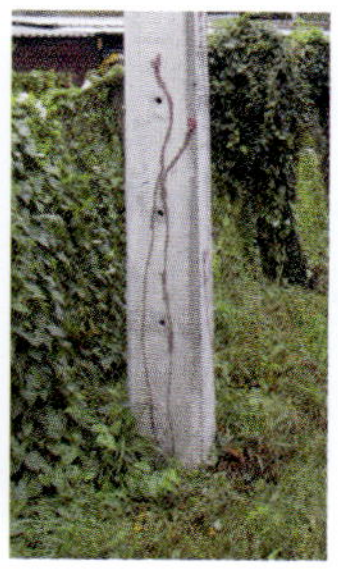

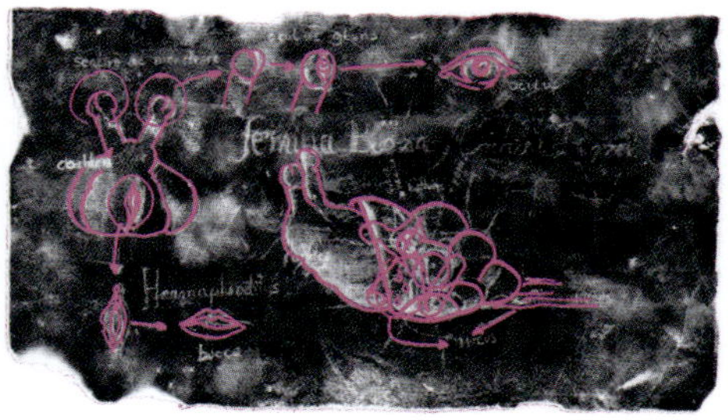

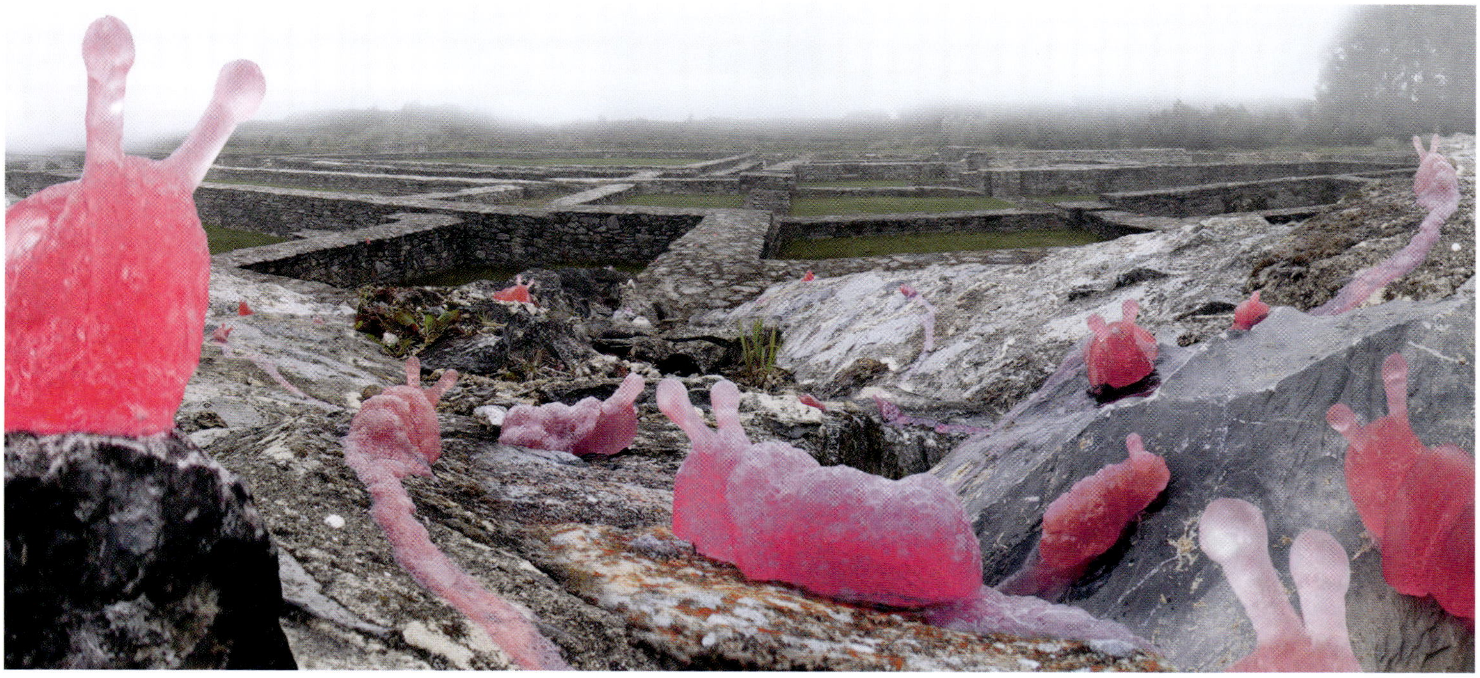

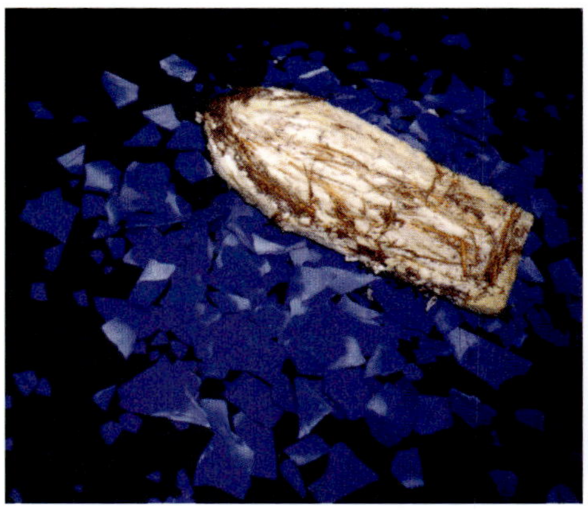

Model For Salt Reed Boat on Lemon Smell, 1998- 1999

Salt, reed, blue painted stones

Zout, riet, blauw geschilderde stenen

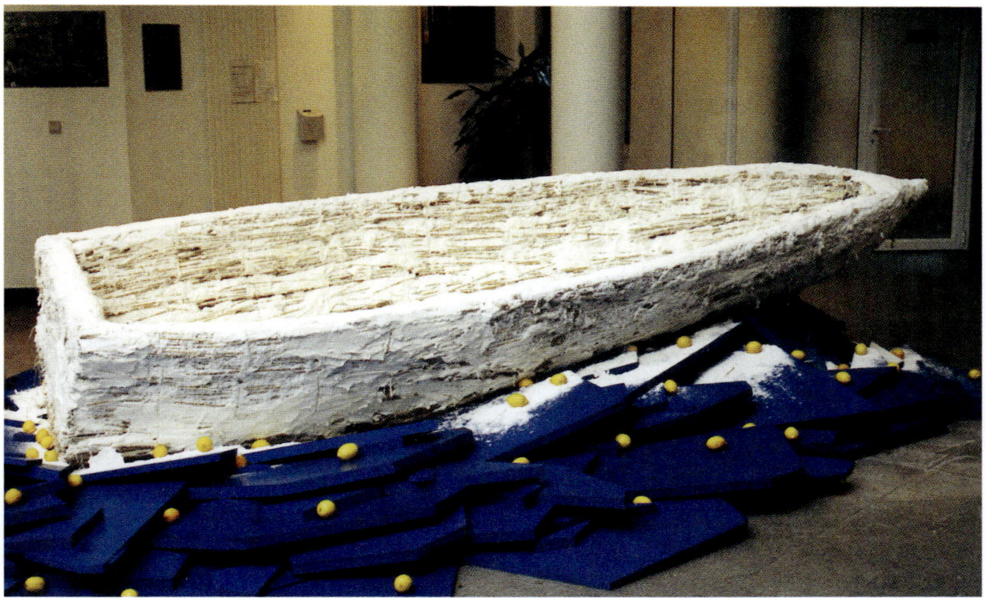

Salt Reed-Boat on Lemon Smell, 1999

±120 cm x 480 cm x 220 cm.

Boat made of reed and salt, lying on blue stones in combination with lemons. In the room is a very intensif smell of lemon. Art-integration in a public building of the Flemish Gouverment

Een boot gemaakt uit riet en zout, gelegen op blauwe stenen in combinatie met citroenen. In de kamer bevindt zich een intense geur van citroen. Kunstintegratie in publieke gebouwen van de Vlaamse Overheid.

Saltreedboat on lemon smell, Artintegration, Ministery of the Flemish Gouverment, Copernicus building Antwerp, BE, 1999

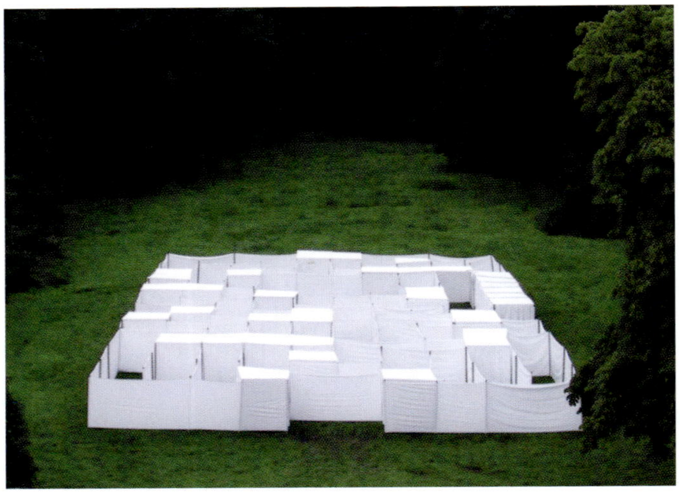

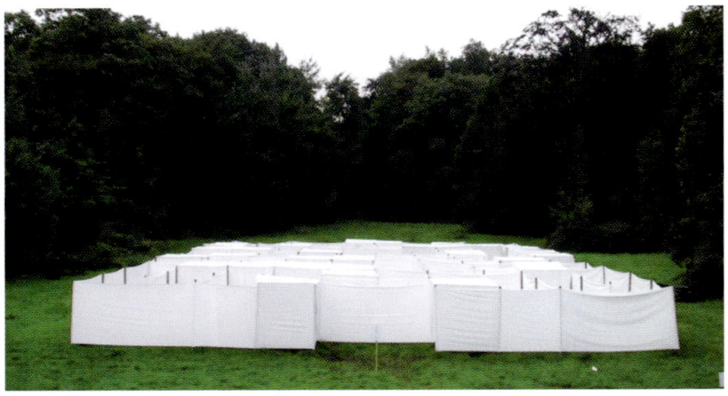

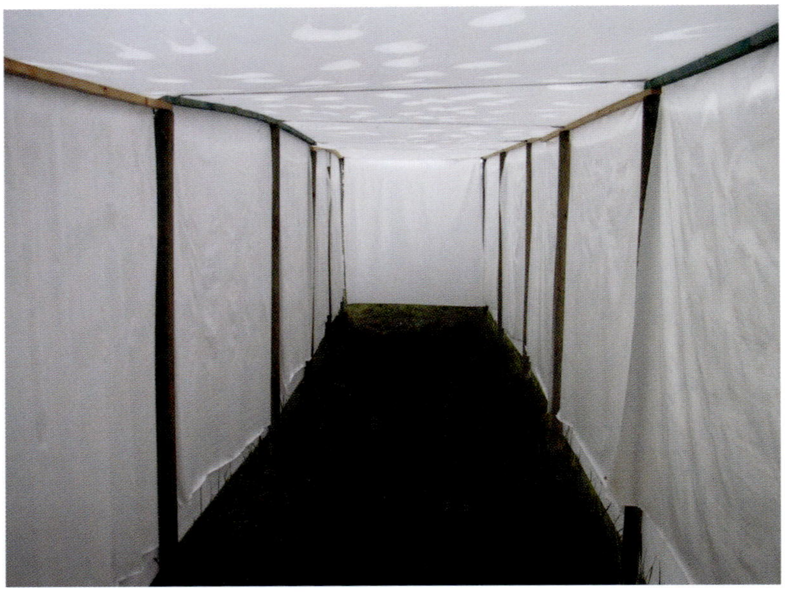

Smell Labyrinth, 2002

Labyrinth (15 m W x 30 m L) with 23 different scents. Some scents come back on different places but with the same form of smellspace.

Labyrint met 23 verschillende geuren. Sommige geuren komen meermaals voor op andere plaatsen maar met hetzelfde geurprofiel.

Smell Castle & Park, Castle of Poeke, curator Christa Vyvey, Helikon vzw, Poeke, BE
18.08-25.08.2002

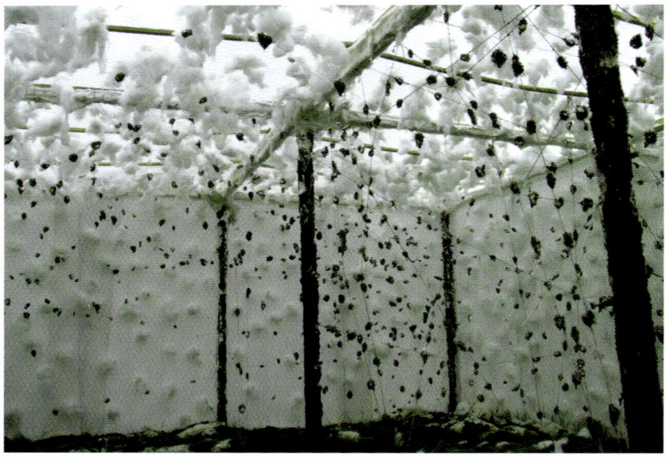

Cresson, 2002

±300 cm x 1500 cm x 1500 cm

Smell-installation, cresson growing on white cottonpads sticked to white rows

Geurinstallatie, waarbij cresson groeit op watten gekleeft op witte doeken

Smell Castle & Park, Castle of Poeke, curator Christa Vyvey, Helikon vzw, Poeke, BE
18.08-25.08.2002

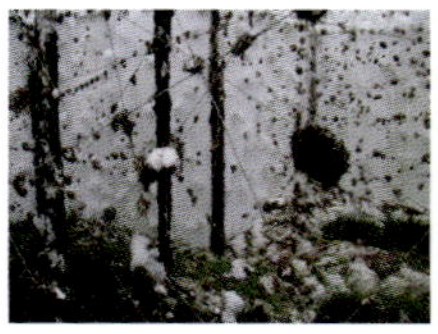

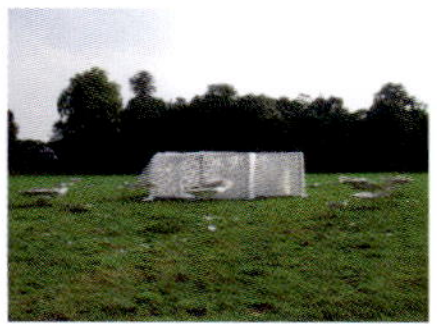

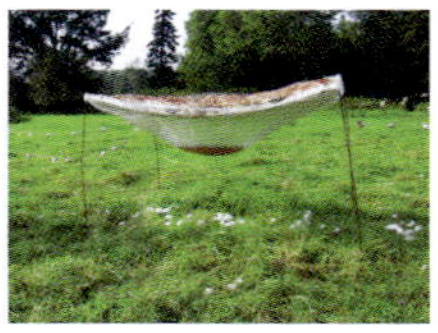

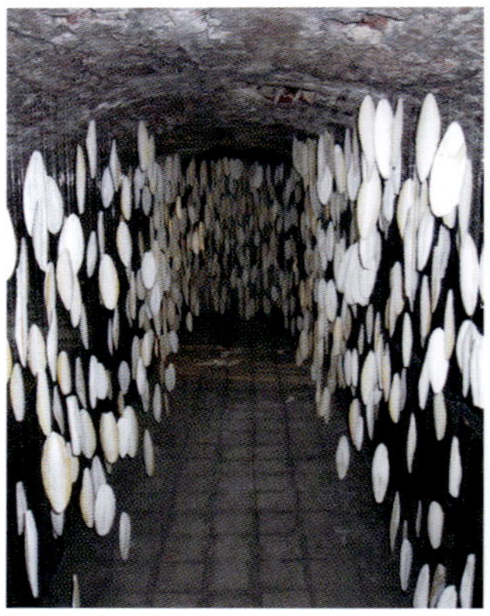

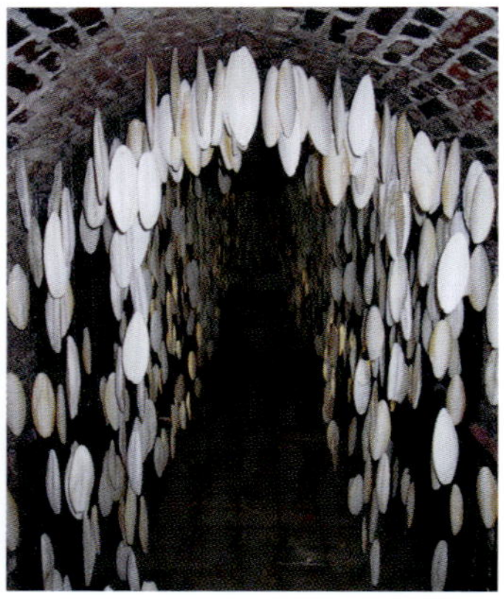

Fish and lemon smell, 2002

1,000 sepia's, fish and lemon smell

1.000 sepia afdrukken, vis- en citroengeur

Smell Castle & Park, Castle of Poeke, curator Christa Vyvey, Helikon vzw, Poeke, BE
18.08-25.08.2002

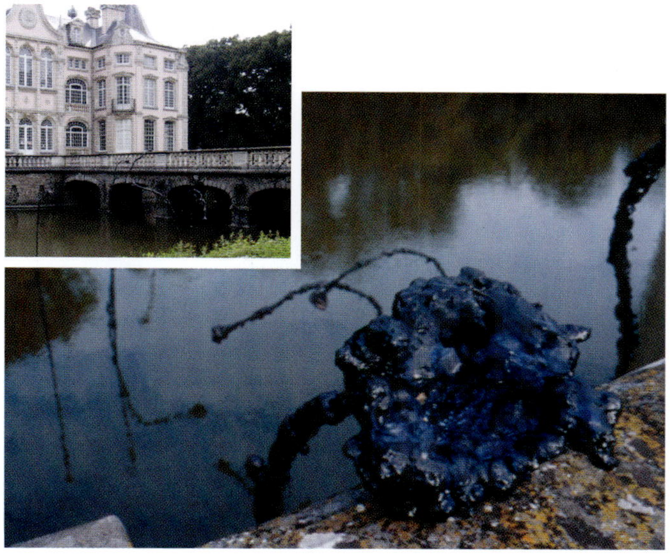

Black Fish Flowers, 2002

50 Black flowers in the water, smelling like fish
Different measures: between 250 cm and 600 cm

50 zwarte bloemen in water met visgeur
Verschillende formaten tussen 250 cm en 600 cm

Smell Castle & Park, Castle of Poeke, curator Christa Vyvey, Helikon vzw, Poeke, BE
18.08-25.08.2002

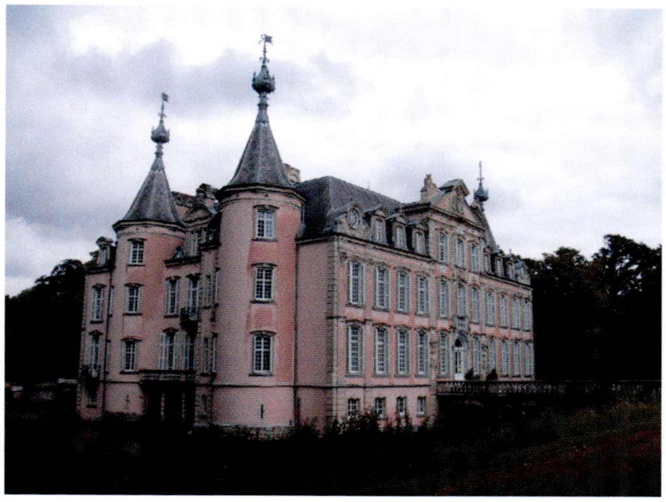

The Rose Castle, 2002

Perfumed pink castle with smell of pink roses

Geparfumeerd roze kasteel met de geur van roze rozen

Smell Castle & Park, Castle of Poeke, curator Christa Vyvey, Helikon vzw, Poeke, BE
18.08-25.08.2002

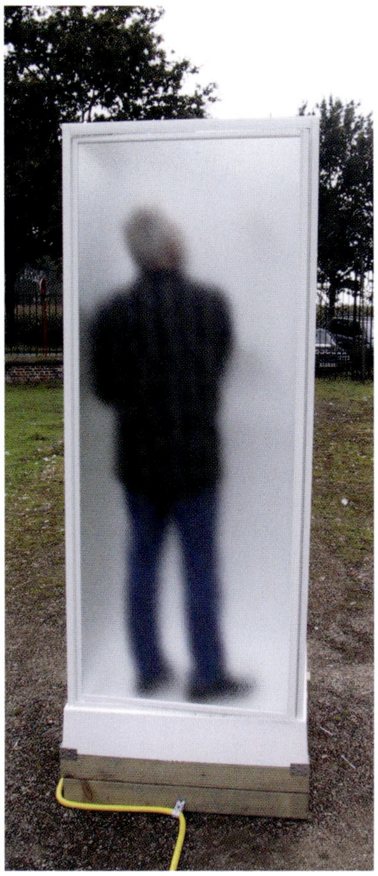

Scent Shower, 2002

Visitor could take a shower of perfumed air with lemon scent.

De bezoeker kon een douche nemen met geparfumeerde lucht met een citroengeur.

Smell Castle & Park, Castle of Poeke, curator Christa Vyvey, Helikon vzw, Poeke, BE
18.08-25.08.2002

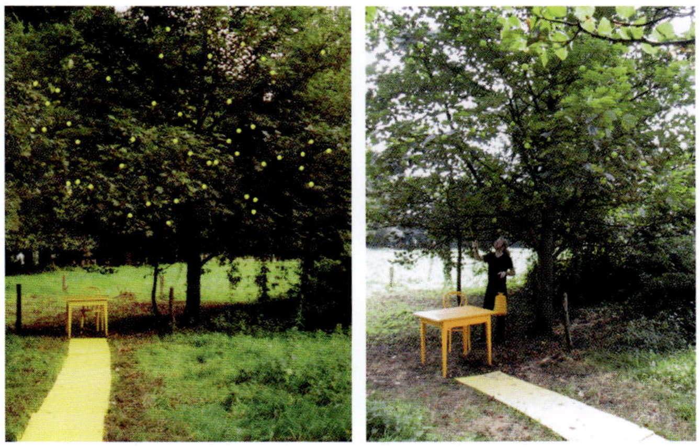

Tennis Lemon Perfumance, 2002

Tree with 300 perfumed tennisballs with lemon smell, yellow table and chair for tennis lemon perfumance.

Boom met 300 geparfumeerde tennisballen met een citroen geur; gele tafel en stoel voor een tennis-citroen 'perfumance'.

Smell Castle & Park, Castle of Poeke, curator Christa Vyvey, Helikon vzw, Poeke, BE
18.08-25.08.2002

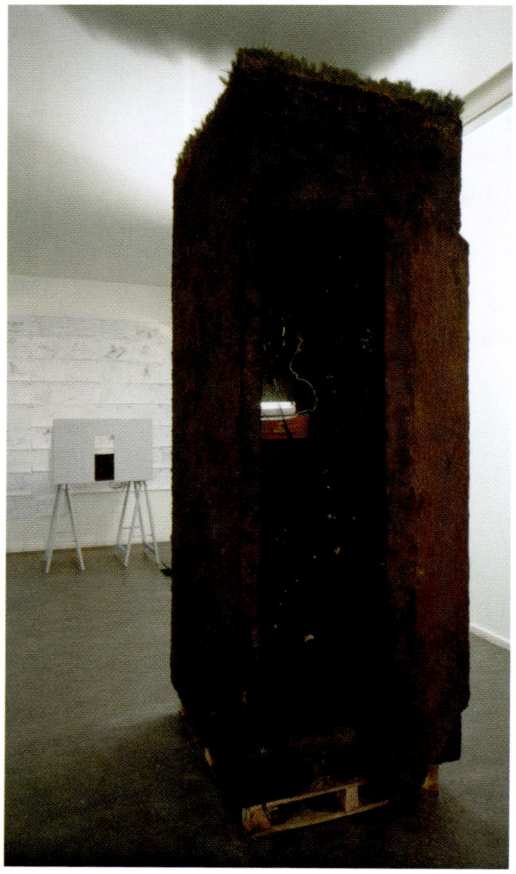

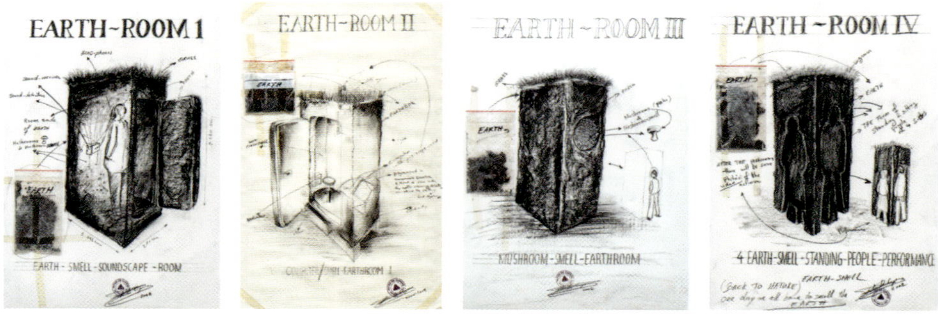

Drawings Earth-Room, 2002

Earth Room, 2002

Sound-smell-installation, fake mushrooms made of epoxy, fake green plants, grass, CD player, neon light.
Smell: mushrooms
Sounds of life from above the ground

Geur-geluidsinstallatie, nep paddestoelen gemaakt uit epoxy, nep groene planten, gras, CD-speler, neonlicht.
Geur van paddestoelen
Omgevingsgeluiden van leven boven de grond

Peter de Cupere, perfume-happening, rockconcert Admiral Freebee, Van Laere Contemporary Art, Antwerp, BE
07.03 -13.04.2002

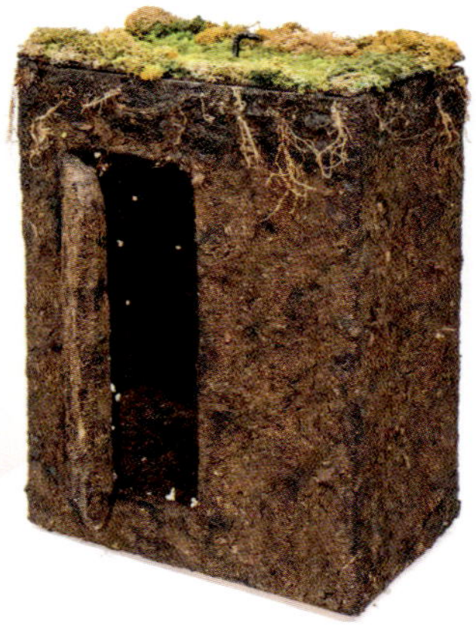

Model Earth Room, 2002

Earth, glue, wood, fake grass, mushroom scent

Aarde, lijm, hout, nepgras, geur van paddestoelen

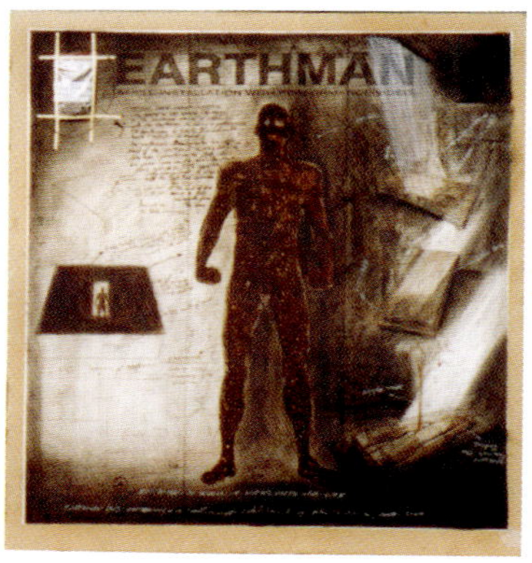

Peter de Cupere, perfume-happening, rockconcert Admiral Freebee, Van Laere Contemporary Art, Antwerp, BE
07.03 -13.04.2002

Drawing & Model Earth Man, 2002

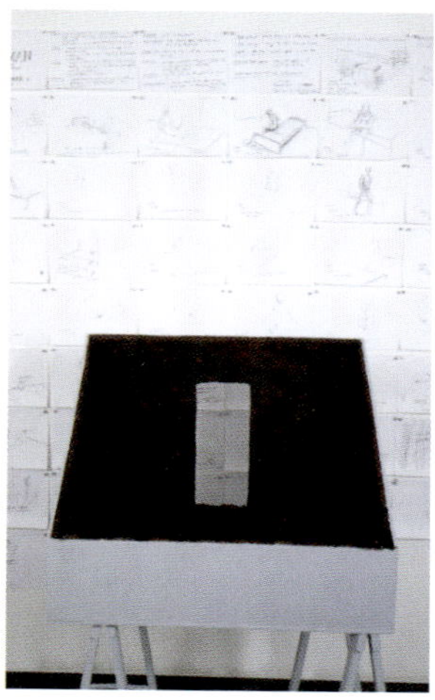

Earth Man, 2002

Video-smell-installation concept, model and storyboard, 2001-2002
Room with bed, table, chair. Room and all furniture totally covered with Earth. Naked man on video also covered with earth.
Presentation of the video: on a monitor covered with earth in the Earthroom shown.
Smell of wet earth and mushrooms.

Concept voor videogeurinstallatie, model en storyboard, 2001-2002
Kamer met bed, tafel, stoel. De ganse kamer en het meubilair zijn bedekt met aarde.
Videopresentatie op een monitor bedekt met aarde in de Earthroom-presentatie.
Geur van vochtige aarde en paddestoelen.

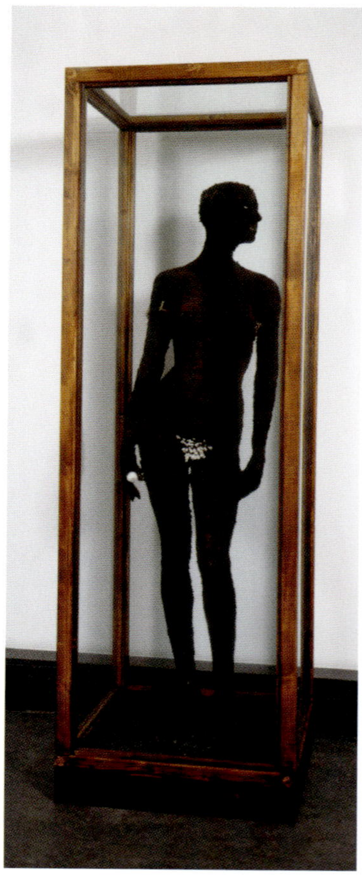

Earth Woman, 2001-2002

Woman made out of earth, pop and fake mushrooms
Scent: mushrooms and earth

Vrouw gemaakt uit aarde, paspop en nep paddestoelen.
Geur van paddestoelen en aarde.

Peter de Cupere, perfume-happening, rockconcert Admiral Freebee, Van Laere Contemporary Art, Antwerp, BE, 07.03 -13.04.2002

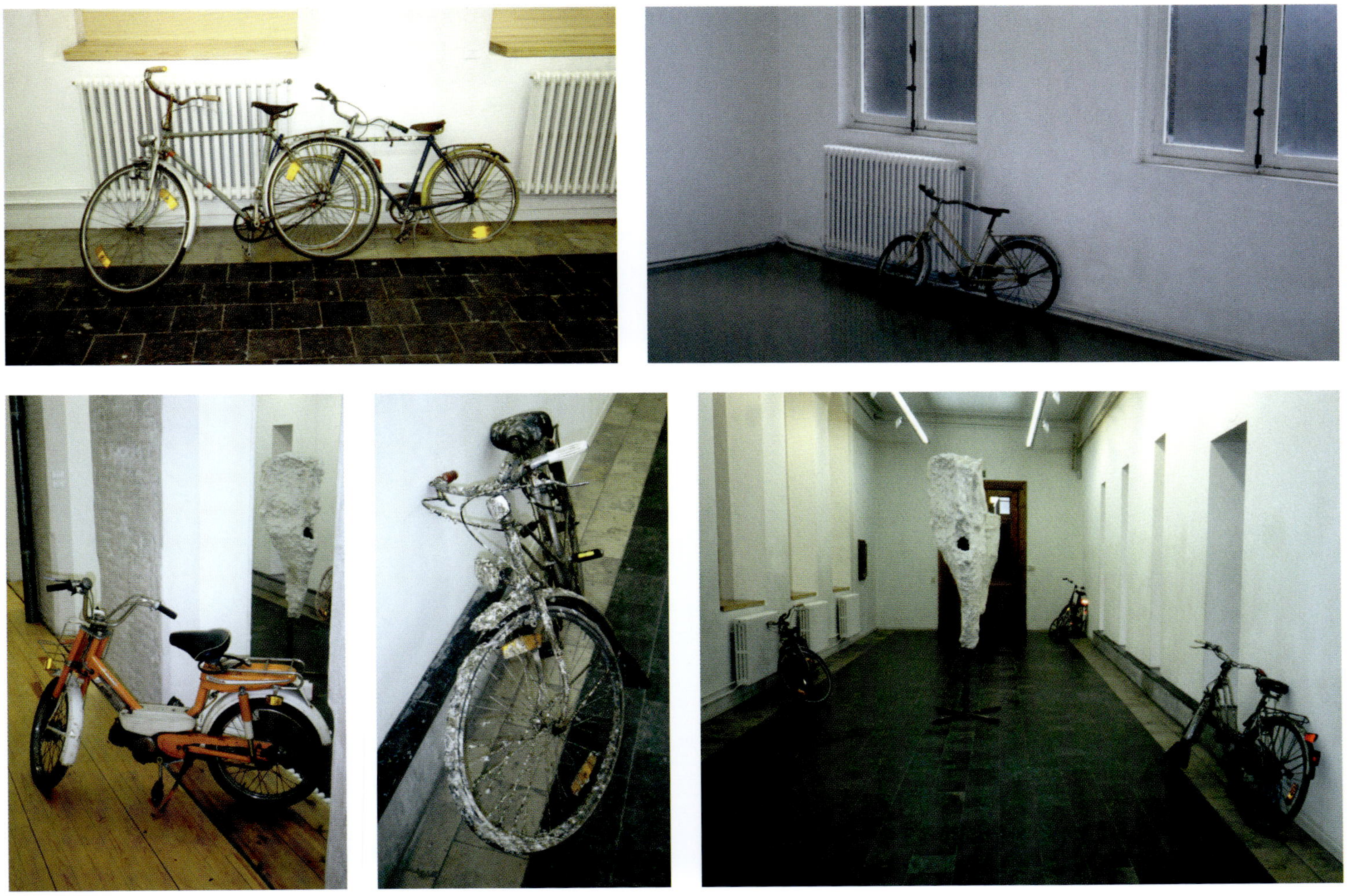

Smell Bikes, 1999

Different bikes are smelling of different smells. Among the smells: strawberry, vanilla, cocoa, orange, cheese flavour, meat flavour, sweat smell, lemon, etc. Variable dimensions

Verschillende fietsen met verschillende geuren, waaronder aardbei, vanille, cacao, appelsien, kaas- en vleesgeur, zweet en citroen. Verschillende formaten.

S.M.A.K. KRACHT, Witte Zaal, org. S.M.A.K., curator Jan Hoet and students, Ghent, BE, 21.01-21.02.1999

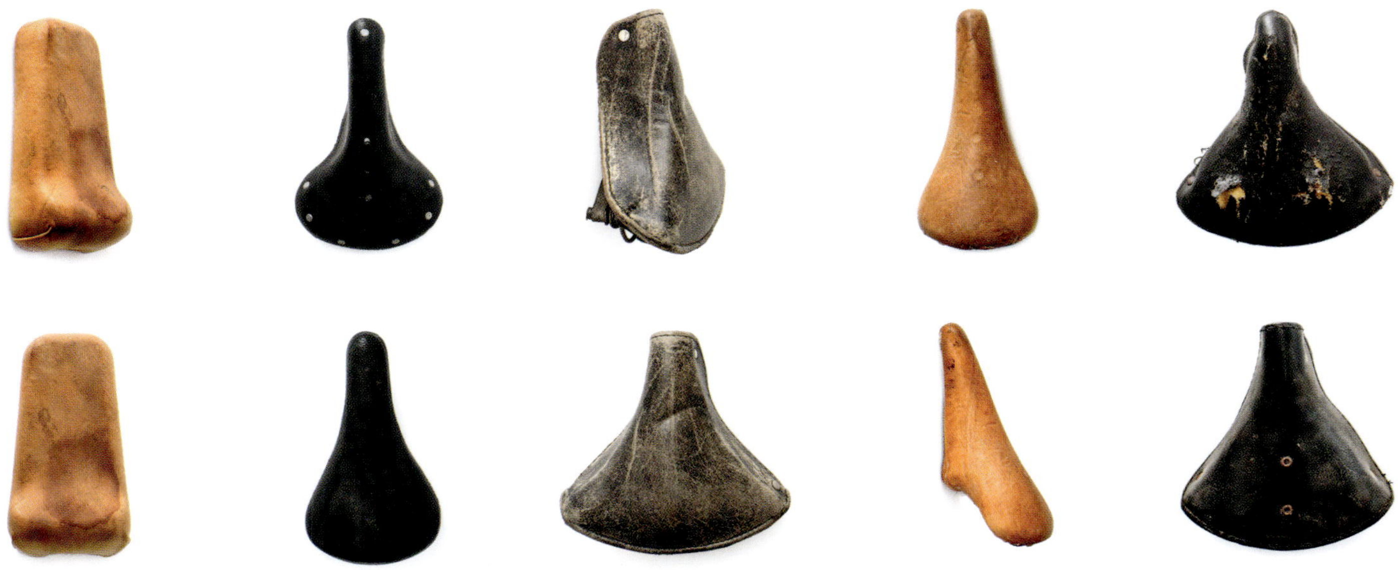

Smell Saddles, 1998-1999

Perfumed bicycle saddles with various scents. The saddles hang with their wide end facing downwards.

Geparfumeerde fietszadels met diverse geuren. De zadels hangen met hun brede kant naar onder.

Peter de Cupere, Black Beauty smell happening, Van Laere Contemporary Art, Openingsspeech Jan Hoet and rockconcert Admiral Freebee, Antwerp, 03.06-07.07.1999

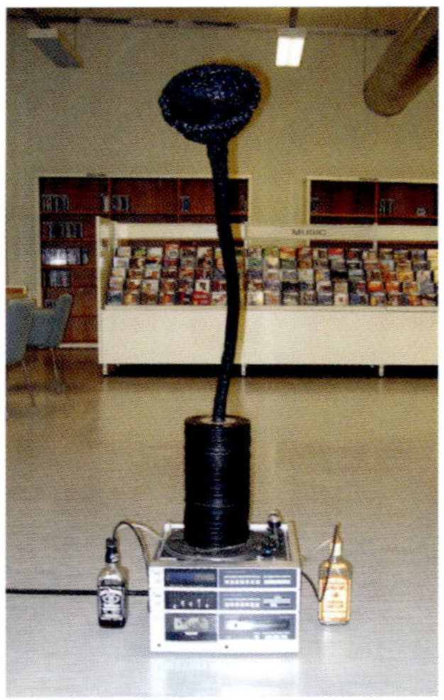

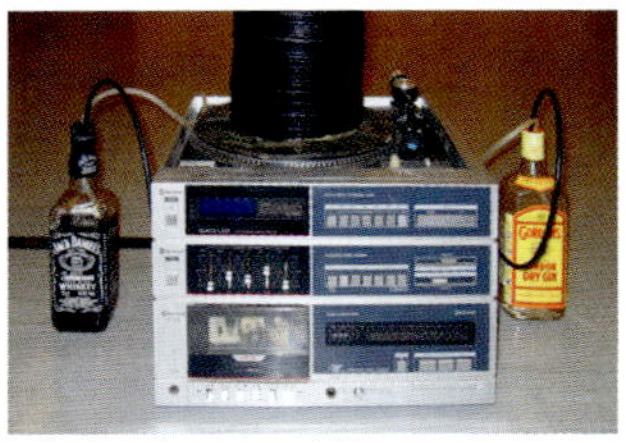

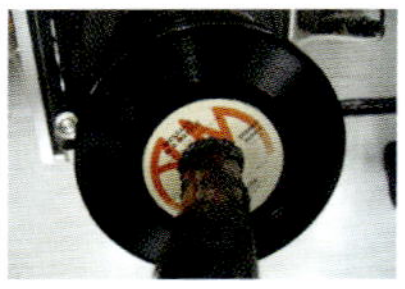

Rock Flower, 2002-2005

Smell of Jack Daniels Whiskey and Gordon Dry Gin, music song 'Message in a bottle' by The Police was playing in loop.

De geur van Jack Daniels Whiskey en Gordon Dry Gin.
De muziekopname 'Message in a bottle' van The Police werd continu afgespeeld.

The scent of information and paper, Culturama 2005, Stadsbibliotheek Henry Van de Velde, Leuven, BE
17.02.2005-19.02.2005

Fleur d'Anus, 1998-1999

Flower with the smell of the shit of the artist,
Plastics, glass, smellactivator, chair, latex, silicone.

Bloem met de geur van de ontlasting van de kunstenaar. Gemaakt met plastiek, glas, geuractivator, stoel, latex en siliconen.

Metamorphosis, Peter de Cupere, Berlinde De Bruyckere, Peter Buggenhout, Johan Tahon, vzw Phidias, curator Christa Vyvey, Rome, IT, 23.03-17.04.2001
Peter de Cupere, Black Beauty smell happening, Van Laere Contemporary Art, Openingsspeech Jan Hoet and rockconcert Admiral Freebee, Antwerp, 03.06-07.07.1999
Peter de Cupere, Vereniging, S.M.A.K., Ghent, 07.05-06.06.1999

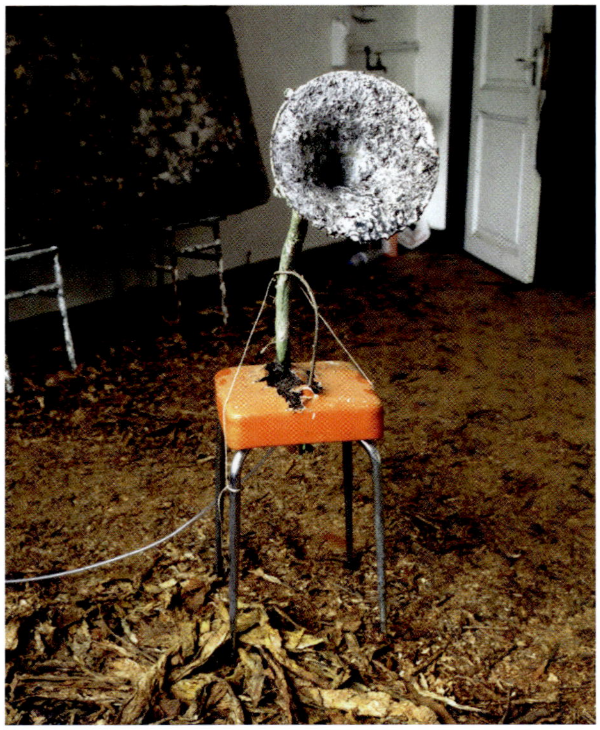

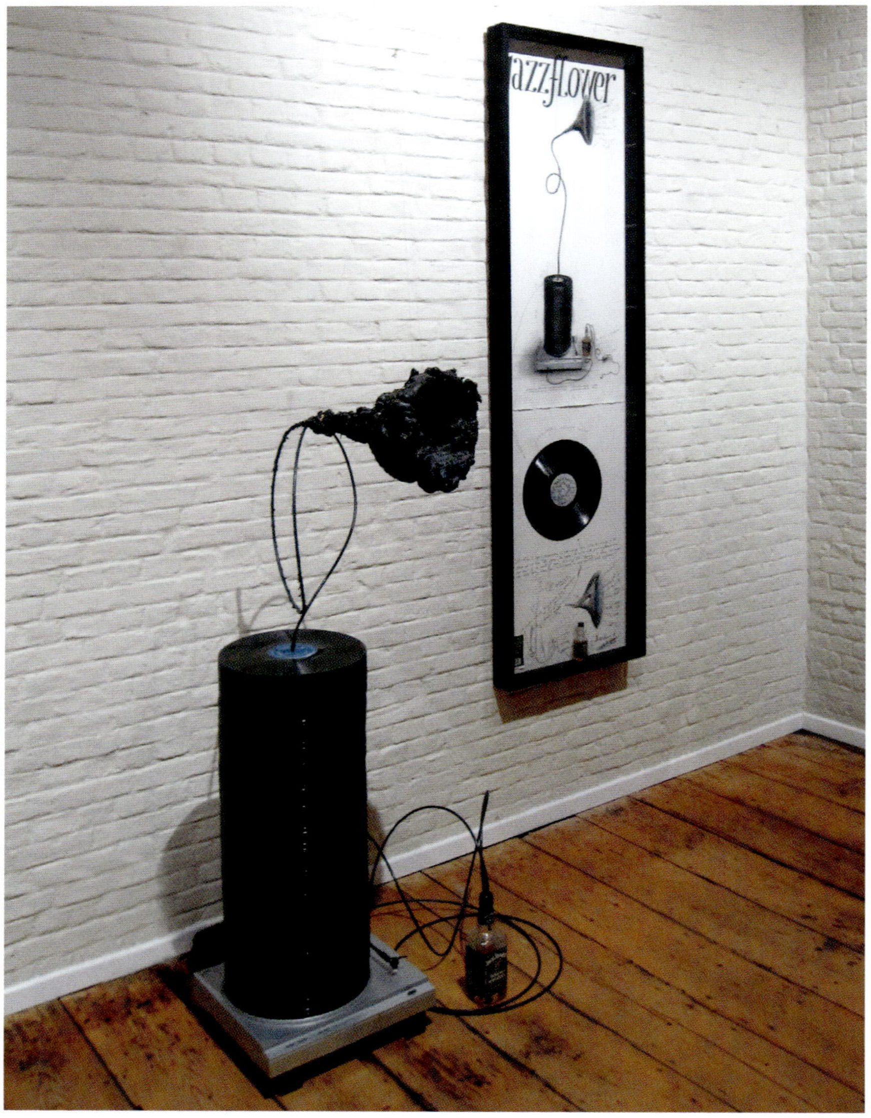

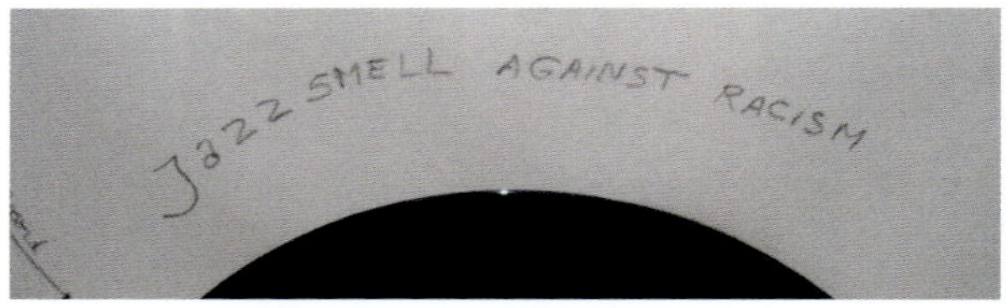

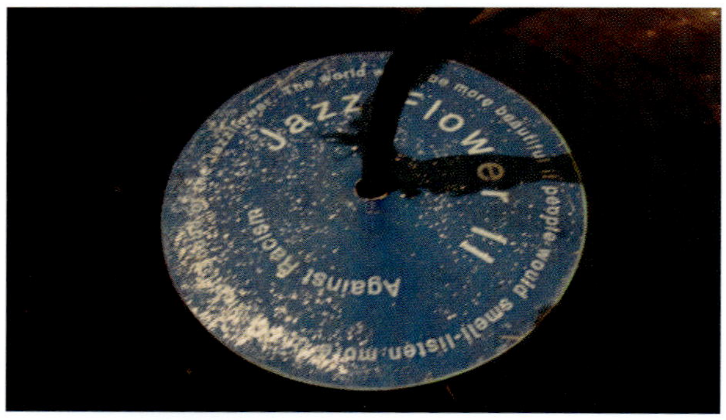

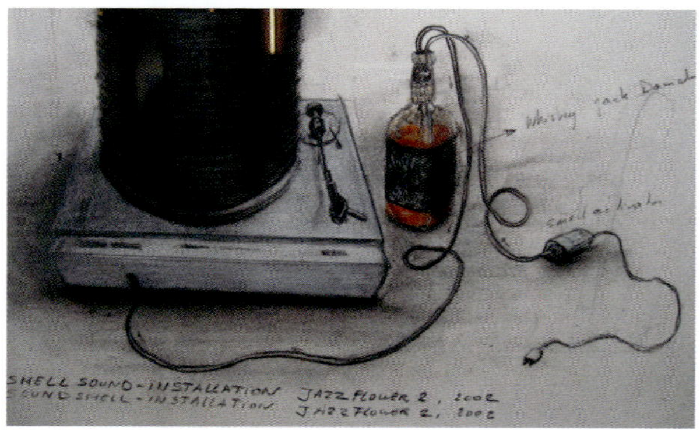

Jazz Flower, 2002

Flower made of ±370 Jazz LP records, whiskey smell (Jack Daniels), CD-player, music: Kind of Blue (Miles Davis), smell-activator

Bloem gemaakt van circa 370 Jazz vinyl platen met de geur van Jack Daniels Whiskey. Geuractivator. CD-speler met muziek van Miles Davis 'Kind of Blue' in loop.

Art Brussels, Van Laere Contemporary Art, 2002

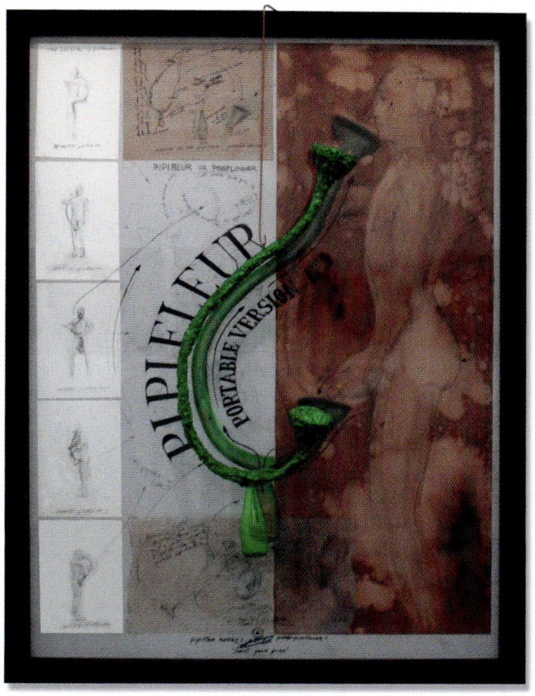

Portable Pipifleur, 2002

170 cm x 120 cm
Object, people can pee in it and smell their own pee.
Drawing: possible situations and versions + explanation of the portable Pipifleur.

Object waar mensen in kunnen urineren en hun eigen urine ruiken. Tekening met mogelijke schetsen van verschillende versies met een uitleg voor de draagbare Pipifleur.

Art Cologne, Van Laere Contemporary Art, 2002

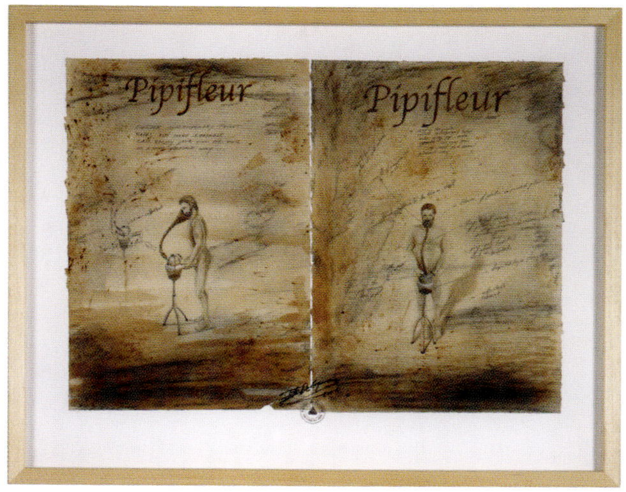

Drawing Pipifleur, 2002

Van Laere Contemporary Art, Antwerp, March-April 2002

Pipifleur, 2001-2002

Object, people can pee in it and smell their own pee or that of others. Photographs: 4 photographs, ed. of 3, 1 A.P.

Object waar mensen in kunnen urineren en hun eigen urine ruiken of de urine van anderen. Foto's: 4 foto's, ed. of 3, 1 A.P.

Art Cologne, Van Laere Contemporary Art
Van Laere Contemporary Art, Antwerp, March-April 2002

Drawing Pipifleur, 2002

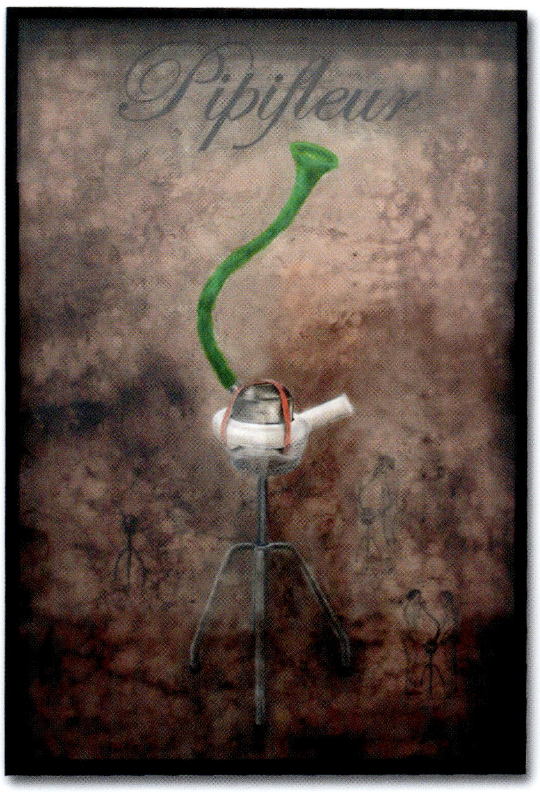

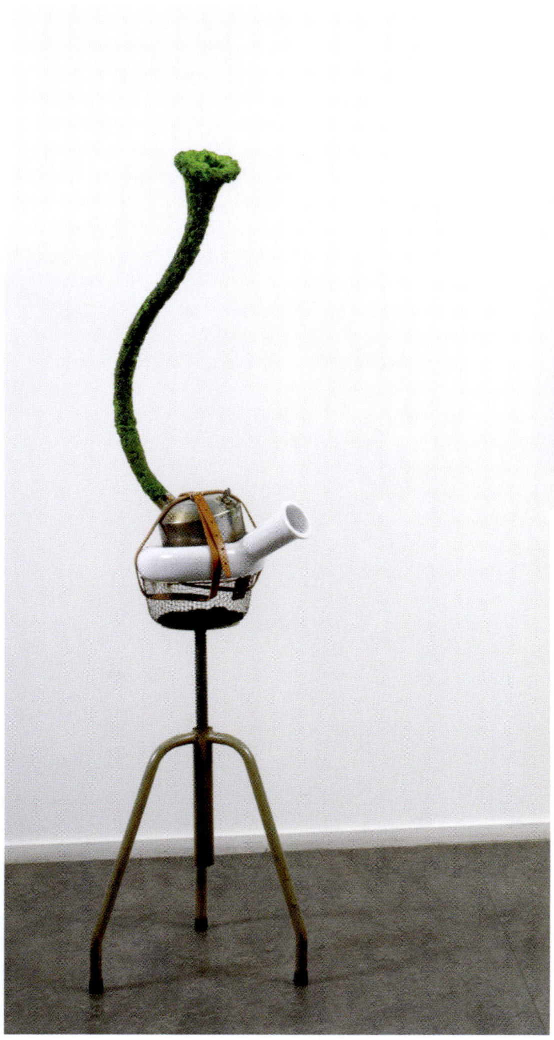

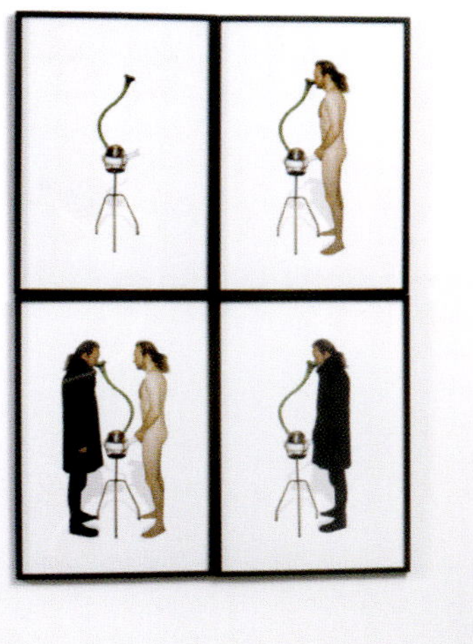

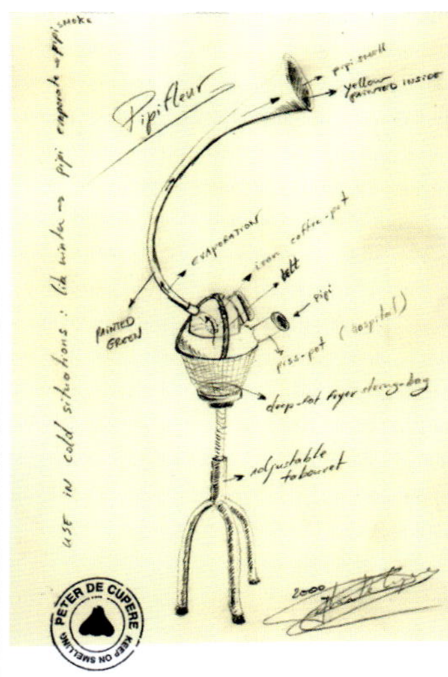

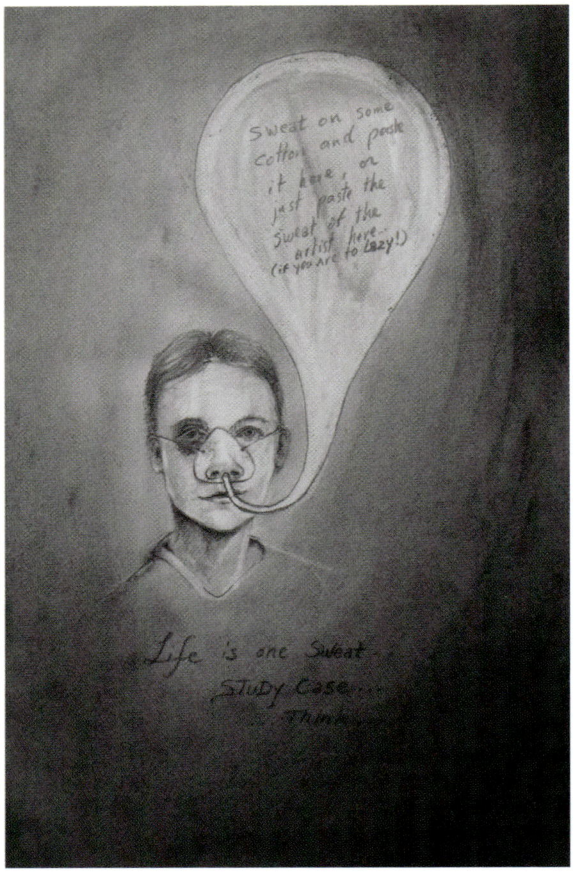

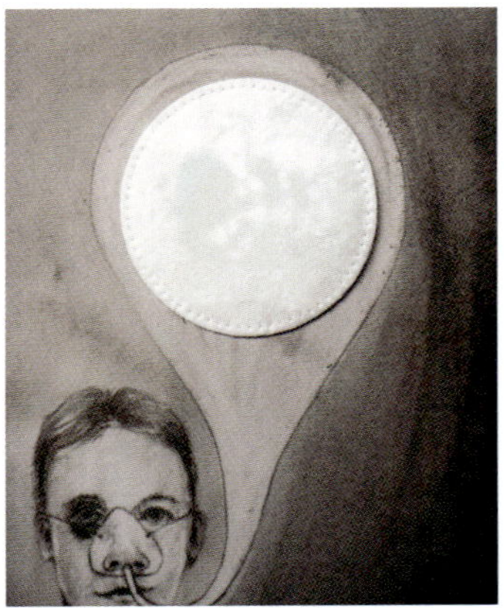

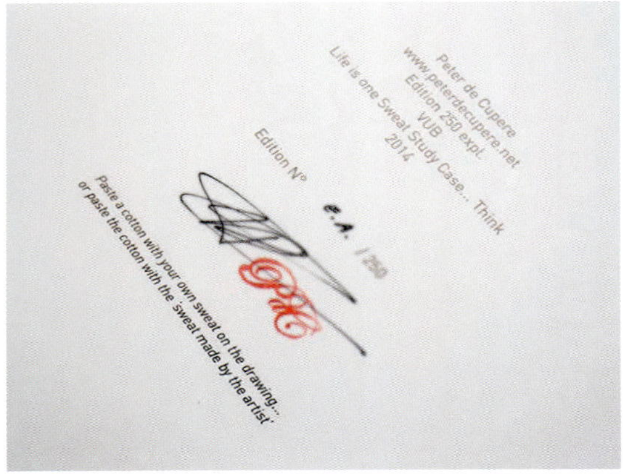

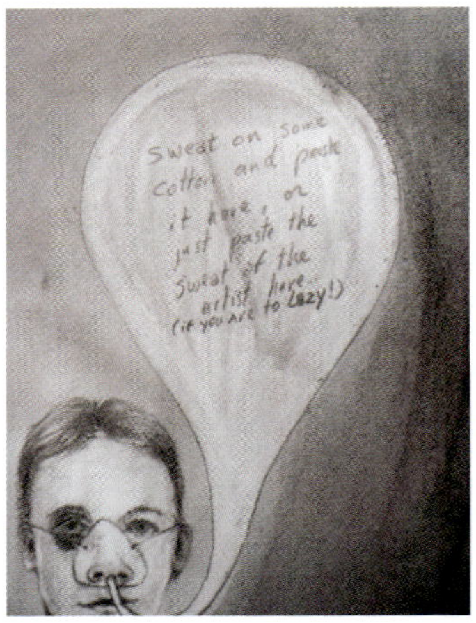

Life Is One Sweat Studycase ... Think ..., 2015

Limited edition in 250 copies in A4 format for the diploma award ceremony for graduates of the Free University of Brussels (VUB). A smell of sweat was applied to a round, white cotton wad.

Editie op 250 exemplaren op A4 formaat voor de diploma-uitreiking van de afgestudeerden aan de VUB. Op een rond wit katoenen watje werd de geur van zweet aangebracht.

Sweat, edition presentation, Free University Brussels (VUB), Brussels, BE
09.01.2015

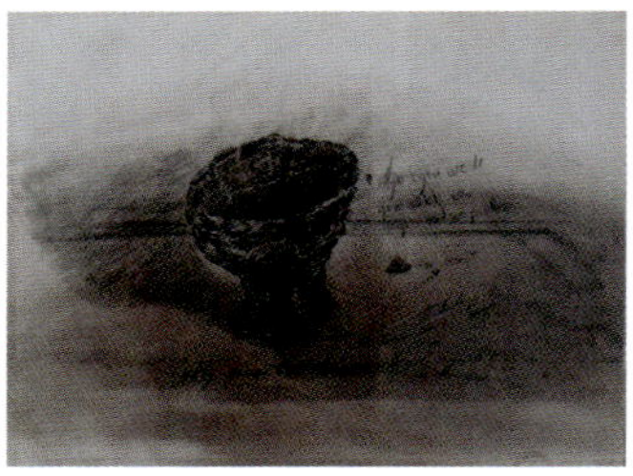

Shit Toilet Drawing, 1998

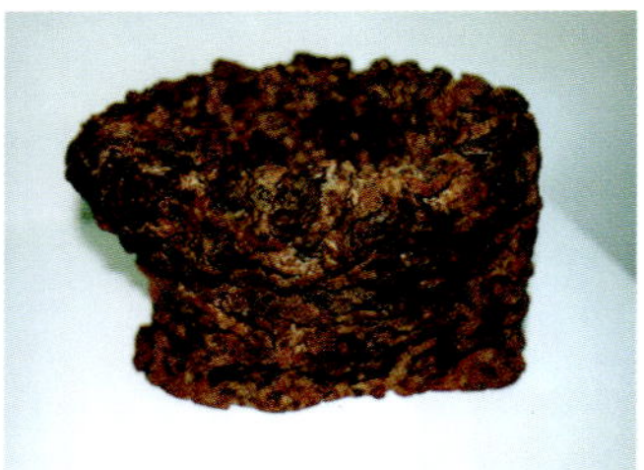

Shit Toilet Model, 1998

Mini toilet made out of chocolate and shit

Mini-wc gemaakt van chocolade en ontlasting

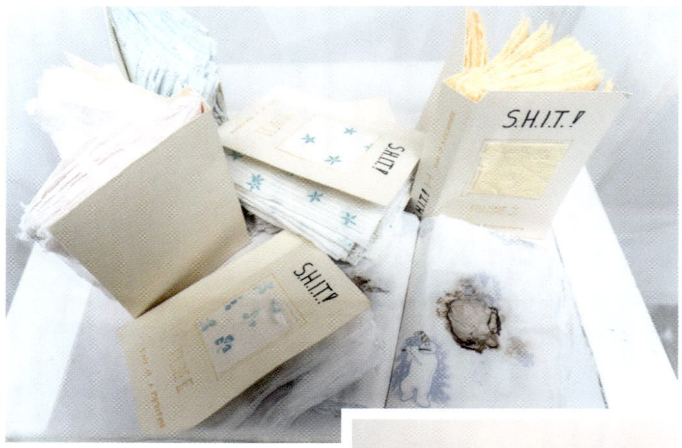

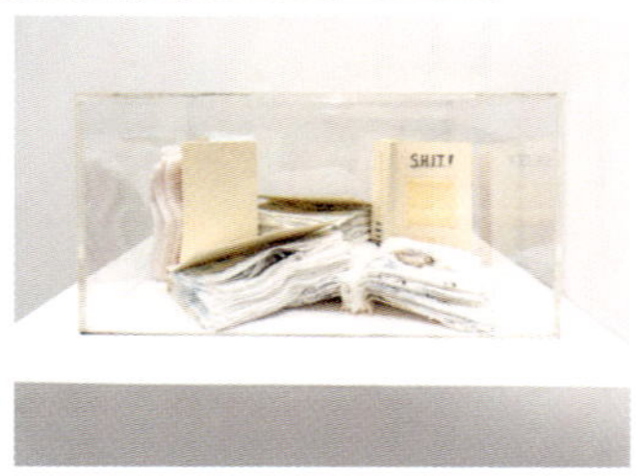

S.H.I.T. Books, 2005

Books made out of toilet paper.

Boeken gemaakt uit gebruikt toiletpapier

The scent of information and paper, Culturama 2005, Stadsbibliotheek Henry Van de Velde, Leuven, BE
17.02.2005-19.02.2005

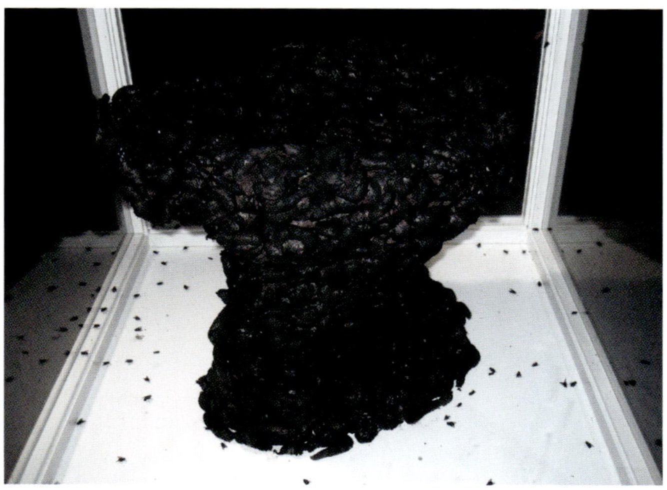

Shit Toilet, 1998-2005

Toilet made of human shit in combination with a conservation glue.

Toilet gemaakt van menselijke uitwerpselen in combinatie met een bewaarlijm.

Play Ground, HISK Higher Institute for Fine Arts, Flanders, Artfair Lineart Ghent, curators Willem Elias, Sven Vanderstichelen, Ghent, BE, 01.12.2005-06.12.2005

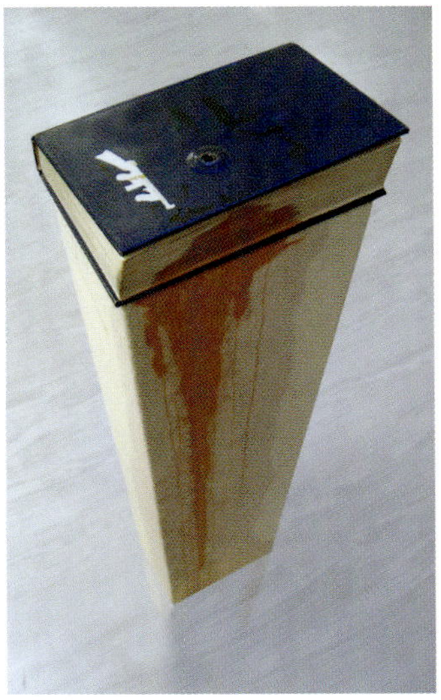

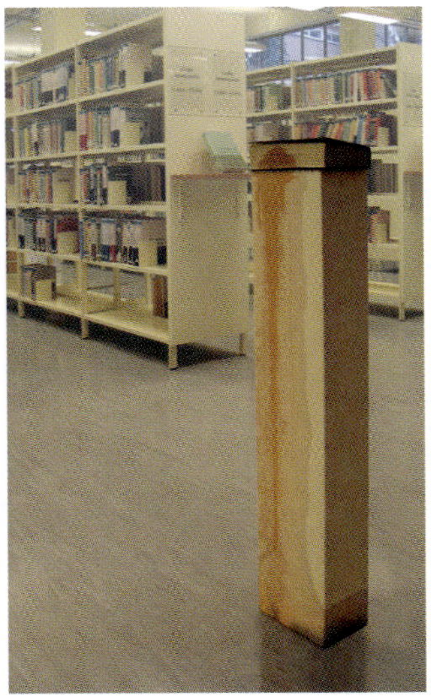

Al Capone, 2005

Mixed smell media

In a book about Al Capone a hole has been shot apparently. A deep brown orange liquid with the smell of smoked meat is dripping out of the book. Every quarter of an hour a loud gunshot sounds in the library.

In een boek over Al Capone lijkt met een revolver een gat geschoten. Uit het boek druppelt een diep bruin-oranje vloeistof met de geur van gerookt vlees. Om het kwartier klinkt er luid een geweerschot doorheen de bibliotheek.

The scent of information and paper, Culturama 2005, Stadsbibliotheek
Henry Van de Velde, Leuven, BE, 17.02.2005-19.02.2005

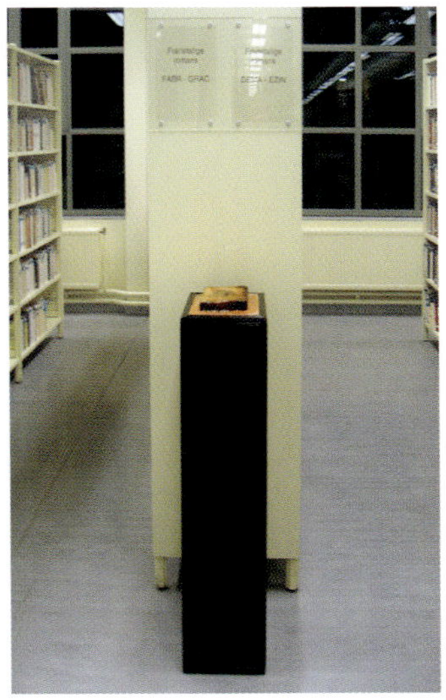

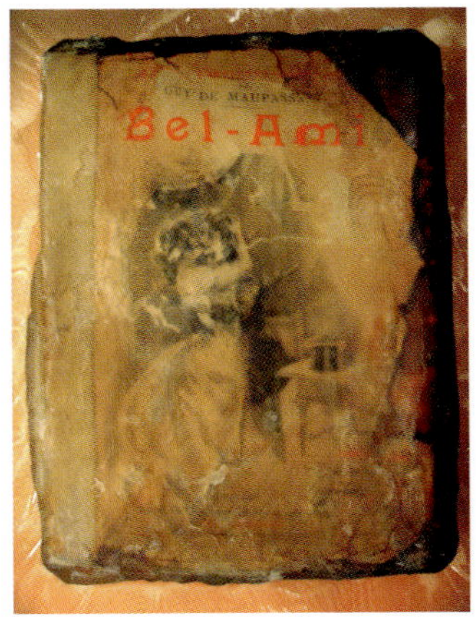

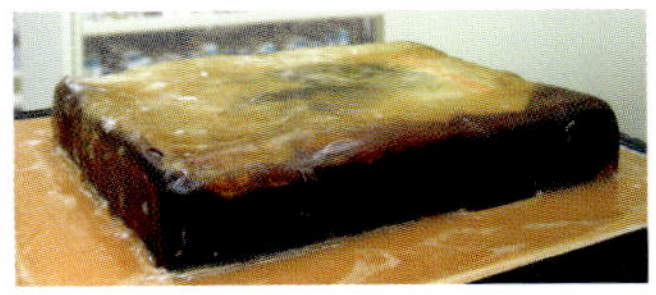

Soap Book, Bel-Ami, 2005

Mixed smell media

An old book publication of Guy de Maupassant, Bel-Ami, of 1901 is extensively covered by soap and smells intensively to French jasmine. The soap conserves the book but reacts and crystallises in time by contact with air. This process makes the book become invisible behind a white gauze.

Een oude publicatie van Guy de Maupassant, Bel-Ami, uit 1901 is in zeep gegoten en ruikt intensief naar Franse jasmijn. De zeep conserveert het boek, maar reageert door de tijd met het contact aan de lucht waardoor er een soort van kristallisatie zal ontstaan en het boek onduidelijker zal worden en verdwijnen achter een witte waas.

The scent of information and paper, Culturama 2005, Stadsbibliotheek
Henry Van de Velde, Leuven, BE, 17.02.2005-19.02.2005

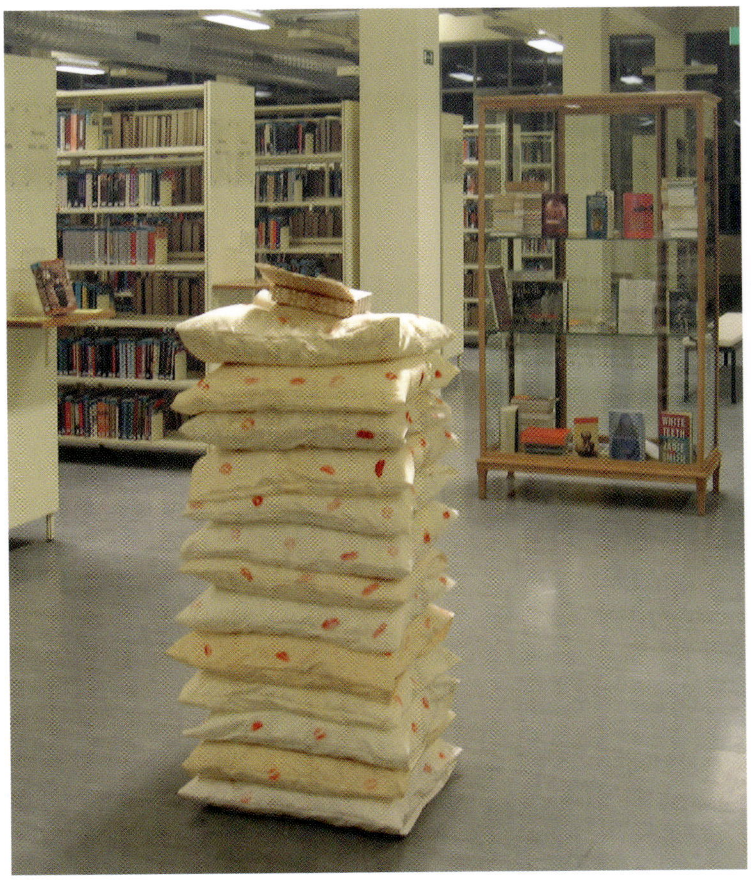

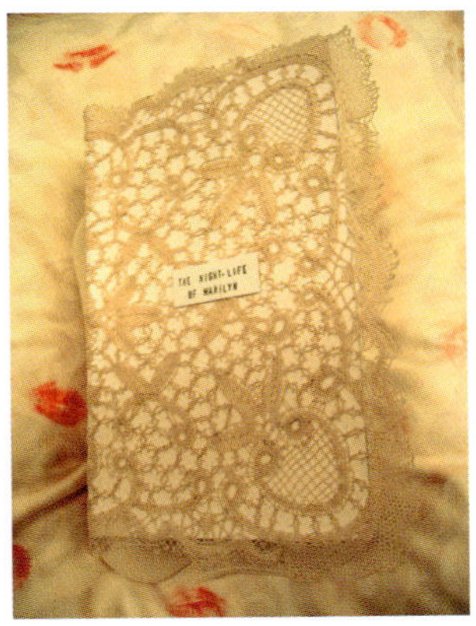

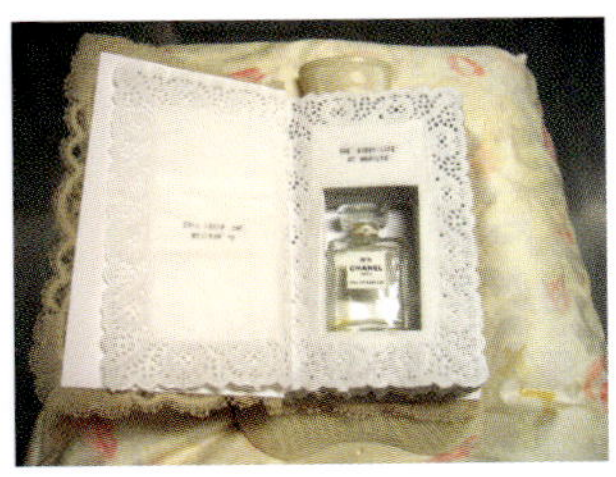

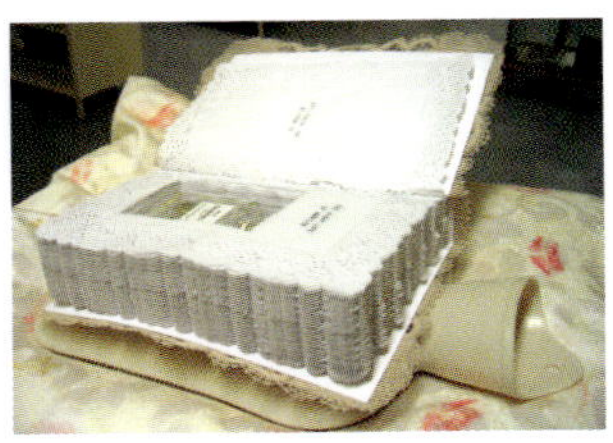

Nightlife Of Marilyn, 2005

Perfume bottle Chanel N° 5 fragrance, book, hot water bag, kisses on pillows

Parfumfles Chanel N° 5, boek, warmwaterkruik, afdruk van kusjes op hoofdkussen

A book made out of lace instead of paper. In the book an empty perfume bottle of Chanel N° 5 is placed. The book lies on a hot jar and a stack of pillows. The pillows are perfumed with Chanel N° 5 and covered with red lipstick prints, a souvenir of imprints by visitors. The installation is created in honour of Marilyn Monroe's quote "I only wear N° 5 when I sleep".

Een boek gemaakt van kanten onderleggers met daarin een lege Chanel N° 5 parfumfles. Het boek ligt op een warme waterkruik en een stapel verschillende kussens. De kussens zijn geparfumeerd met Channel N° 5 en staan vol afdrukken van lippenstift van meerdere bezoekers. Een subtiel eerbetoon aan Marilyn Monroe's uitspraak: "I only wear N° 5 when I sleep".

The scent of information and paper, Culturama 2005, Stadsbibliotheek
Henry Van de Velde, Leuven, BE
17.02.2005-19.02.2005

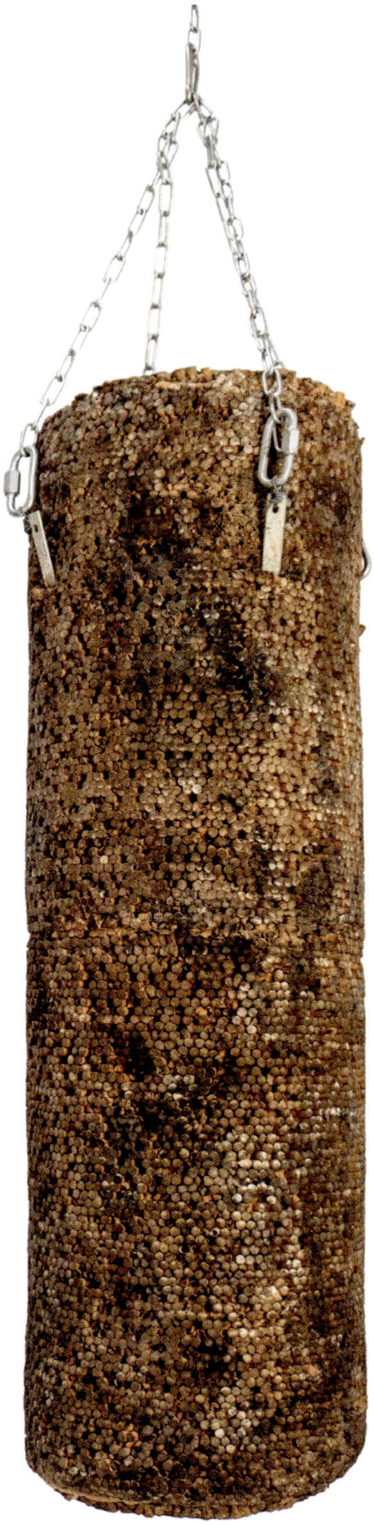

A Smoke Fight, 2001

105 cm x 32 cm Ø

Boxing bag covered with used cigarette butts. During exhibitions the boxing bag smells like smoked meat and is hanging in the middle of an empty gallery space.

Boksbal bekleed met gebruikte sigarettepeuken. Tijdens tentoonstellingen ruikt de boksbal naar gerookt vlees en hangt op in het midden van een lege ruimte.

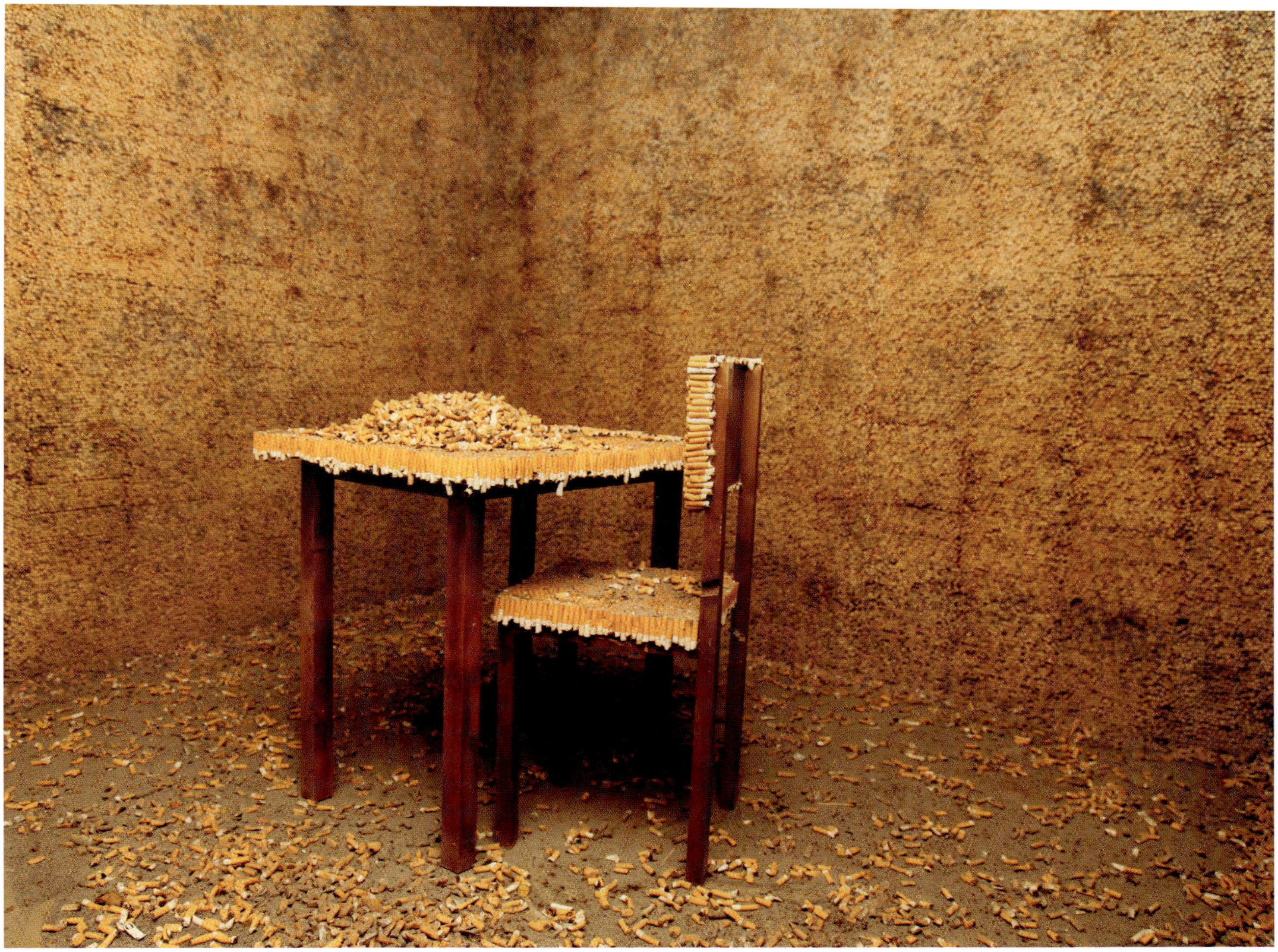

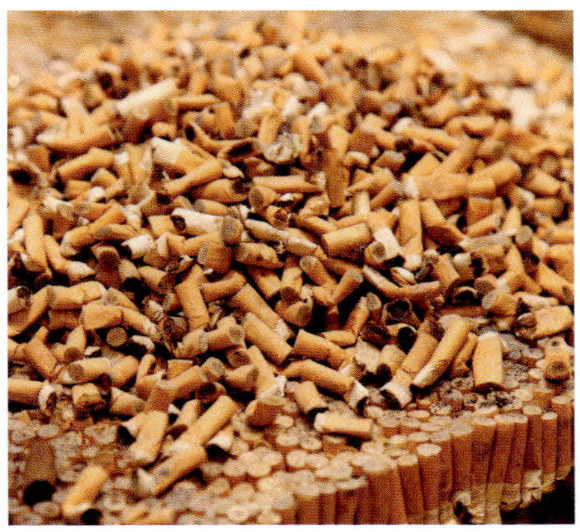

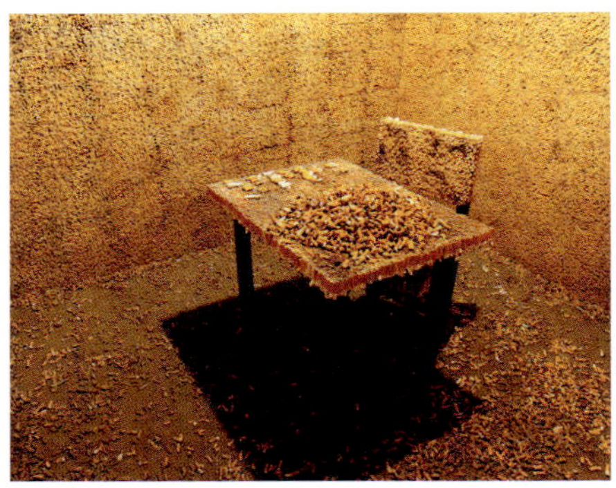

Smoke Room, 2010

750,000 cigarette butts. Smell: smell of smoke

750.000 gebruikte sigarettenpeukjes met rookgeur

There's Something in the Air, curator Caro Verbeek, Villa Rot, Burgrieden-Rot, DE, 22.03.2015-28.07.2015
Festival De Wereld van Witte de With, Rotterdam, NL 09.06.2010-12.09.2010
Artist Project, Art Brussels, org. Artexis, curators Karen Renders & Nele Verhaeren, Brussels, BE 22-26.04.2010

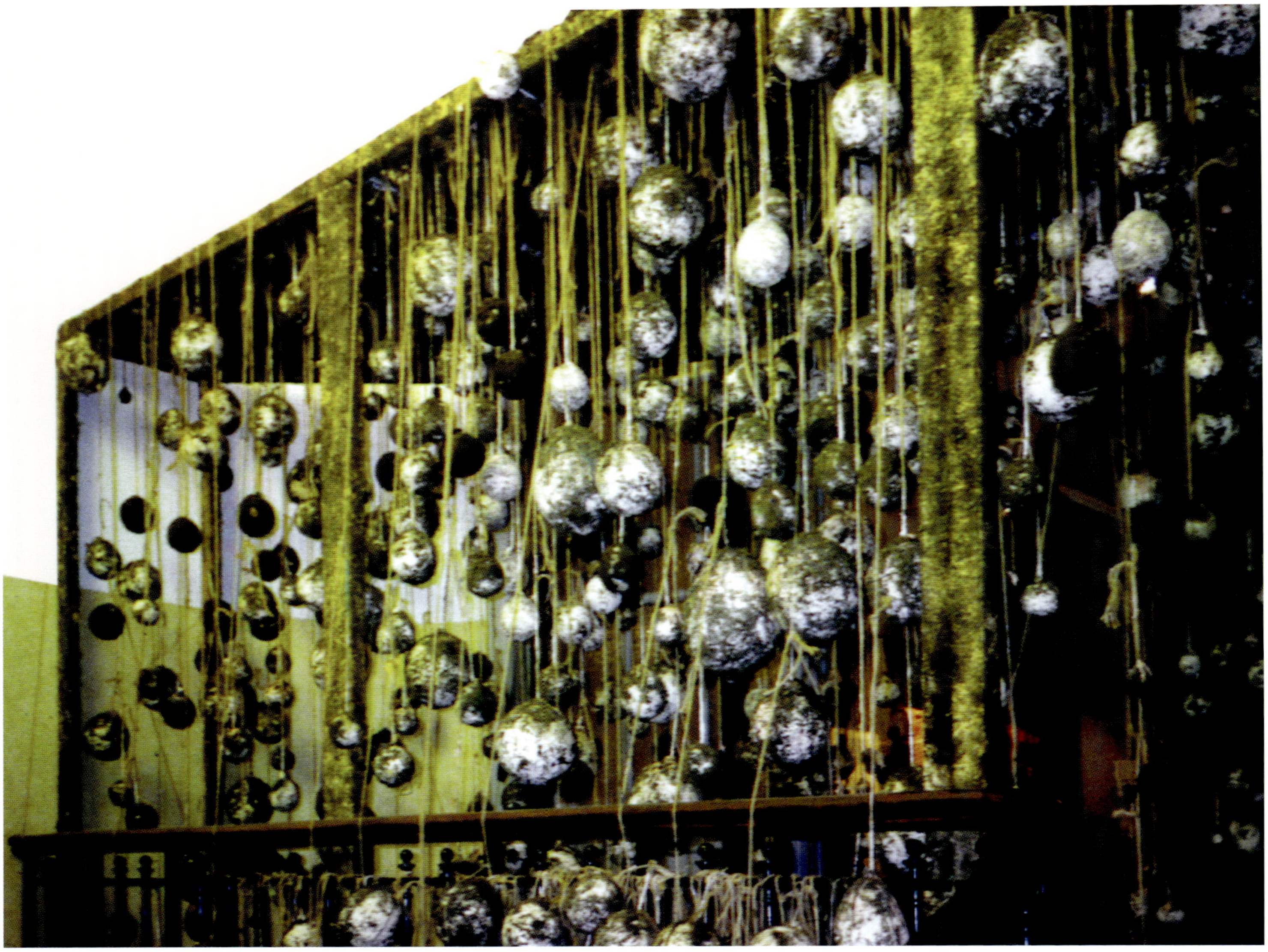

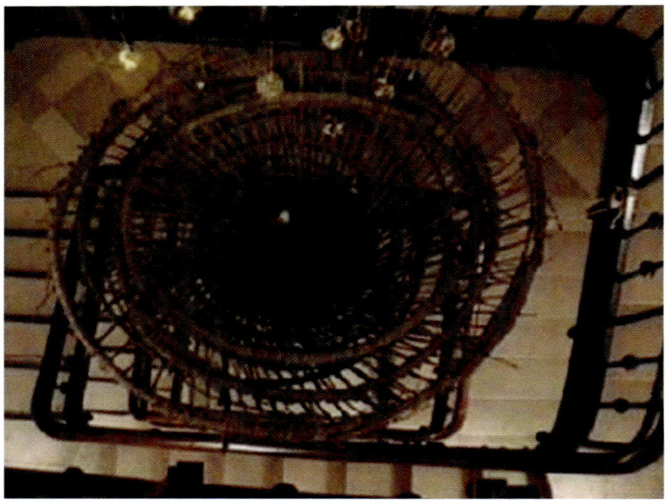

Mentha Piperita, 1998-1999

1,013 peppermint-balls hanging in the staircase. plaster, plaster bandage, formlatex, paint, balloons, rope, wood, 120 kg fine grounded peppermint, 40 kg peppermint flavour. Variable dimensions

1.013 pepermuntbollen hangen in een traphal met plaaster, gipsverband, formlatex, verf, ballonnen, koord, hout, 120 kg gemalen pepermunt, 40 kg pepermuntgeur. Variabele dimensies

Mentha Piperita, Museum of Middle-Africa Tervuren, BE, Okt.1998-Nov.1999

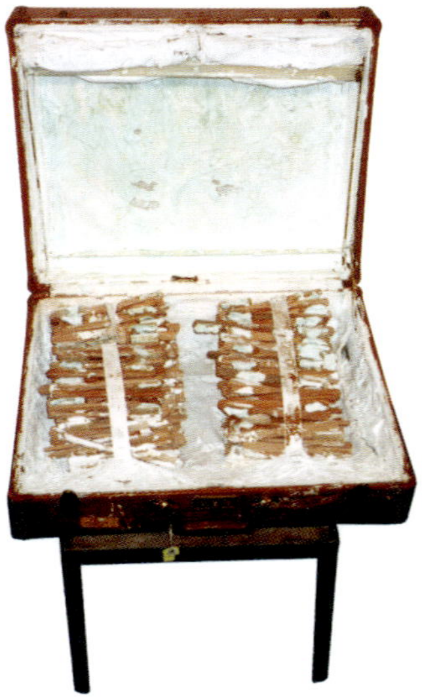

Breath Suitcase, 2001

Toothbrushes, toothpaste, suitcase, eucalyptus-peppermint smell

Tandenborstels, tandpasta, koffer, eucalyptus-pepermuntgeur

The Collector's House, St.-Lucas Stichting, curator Filip Luyckx, Brussels, BE 17.01.2003-22.03.2003

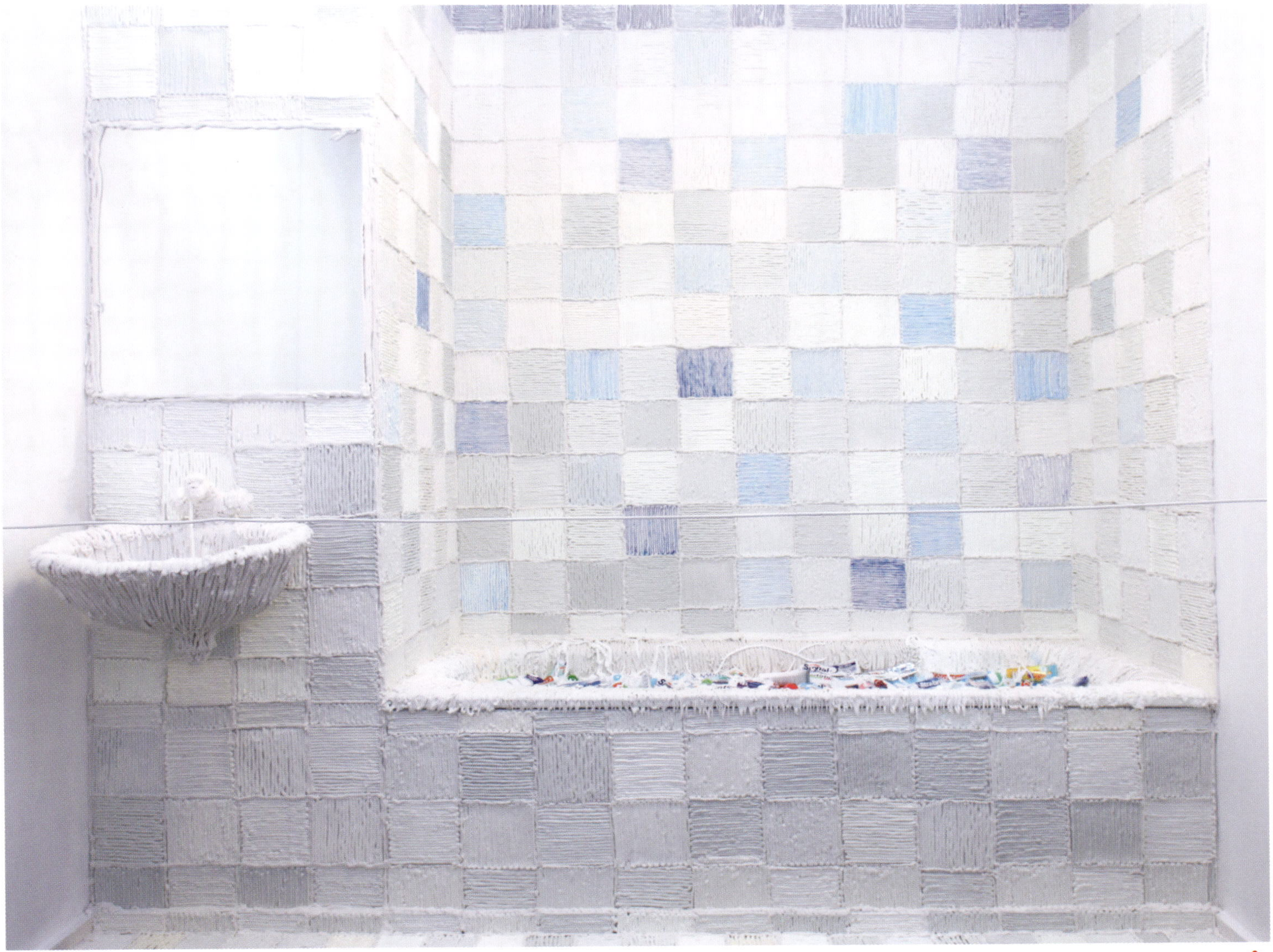

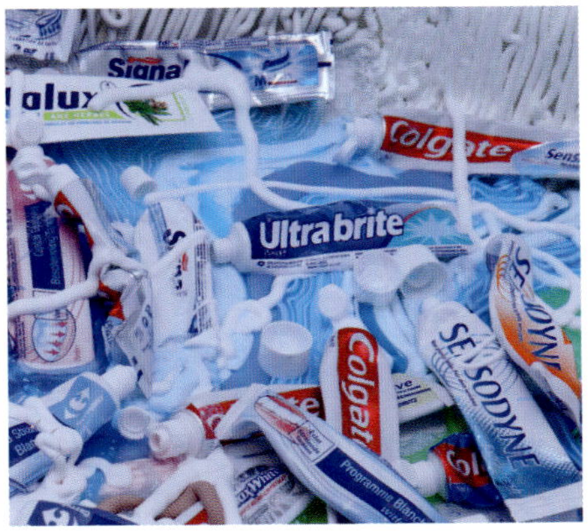

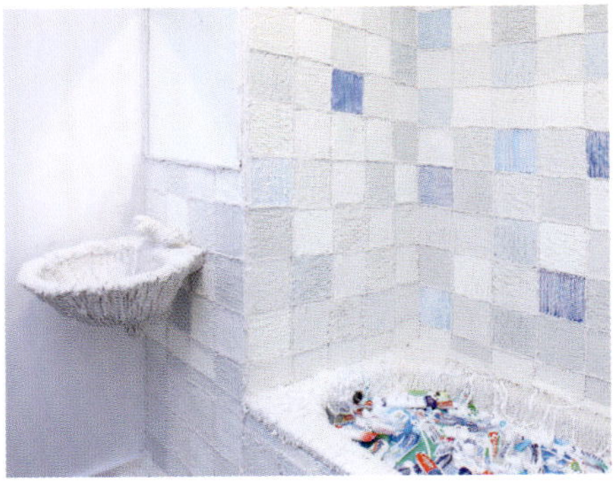

Smile Room, 2010

A room covered with toothpaste
tubes of toothpaste, PU components, smell activator, bathtub, sink, peppermint

Ruimte bekleed met tandpasta
tandpastatubes, PU-componenten, geuractivator, badkuip, lavabo, pepermunt

Festival De Wereld van Witte de With, Rotterdam, NL, 09.06.2010-12.09.2010
Artist Project, Art Brussels, org. Artexis, curators Karen Renders & Nele Verhaeren, Brussels, BE, 22-26.04.2010

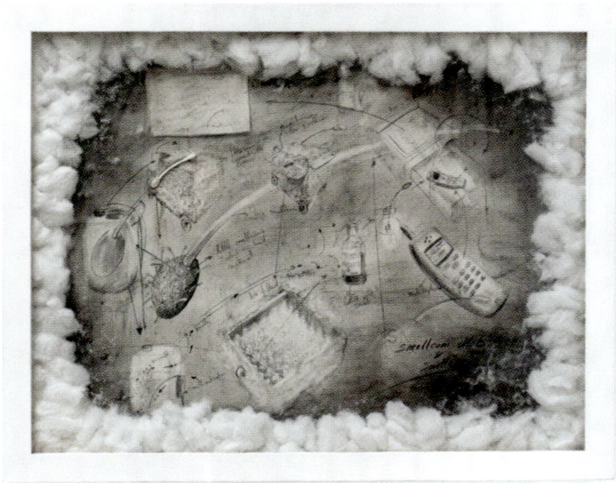

Drawing Smellcom, 1999-2000

58 cm x 74,5 cm

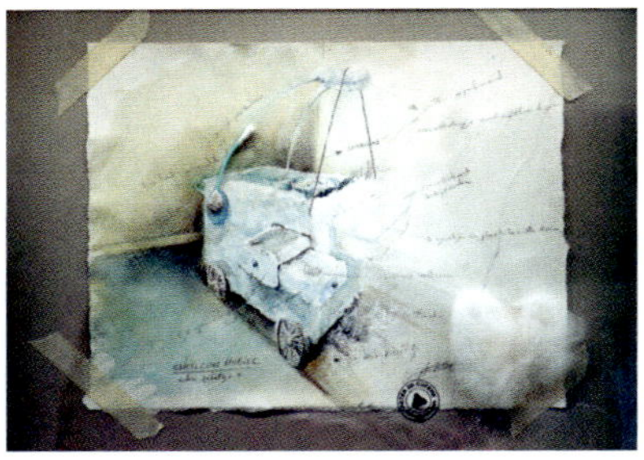

Smellcom Mob 028, 1999-2000

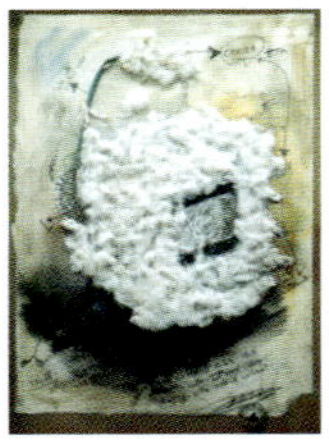

Naked Cotton Woman Performance Mob, 1999-2000

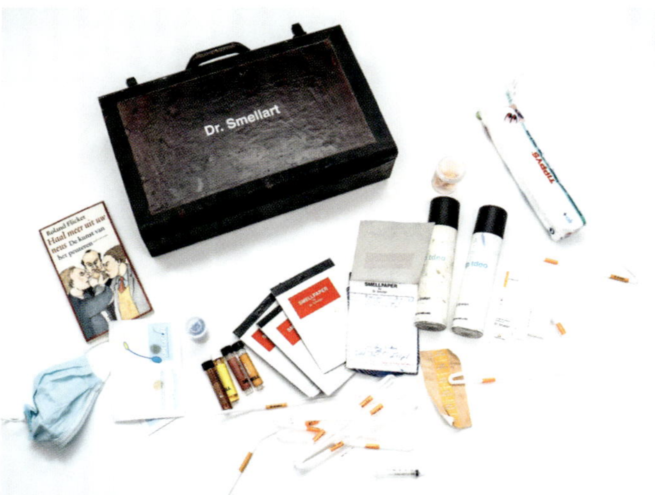

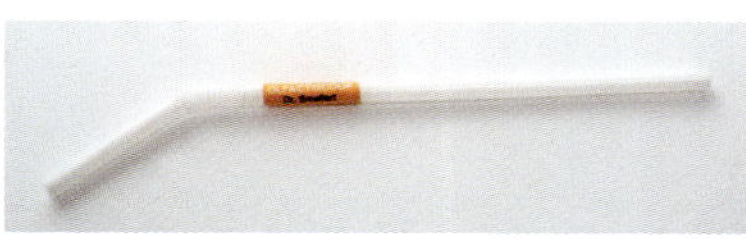

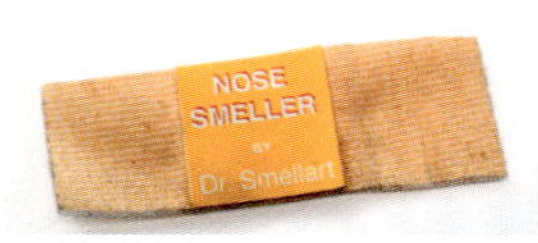

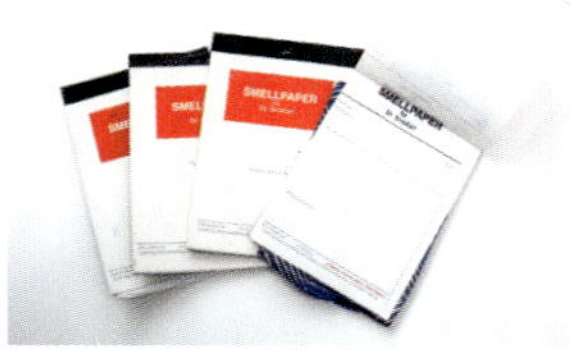

Perfumance Dr. Smellart, 2000

Perfumance 'Dr. Smellart', Over The Edges, S.M.A.K., Ghent, BE, 24.06.2000

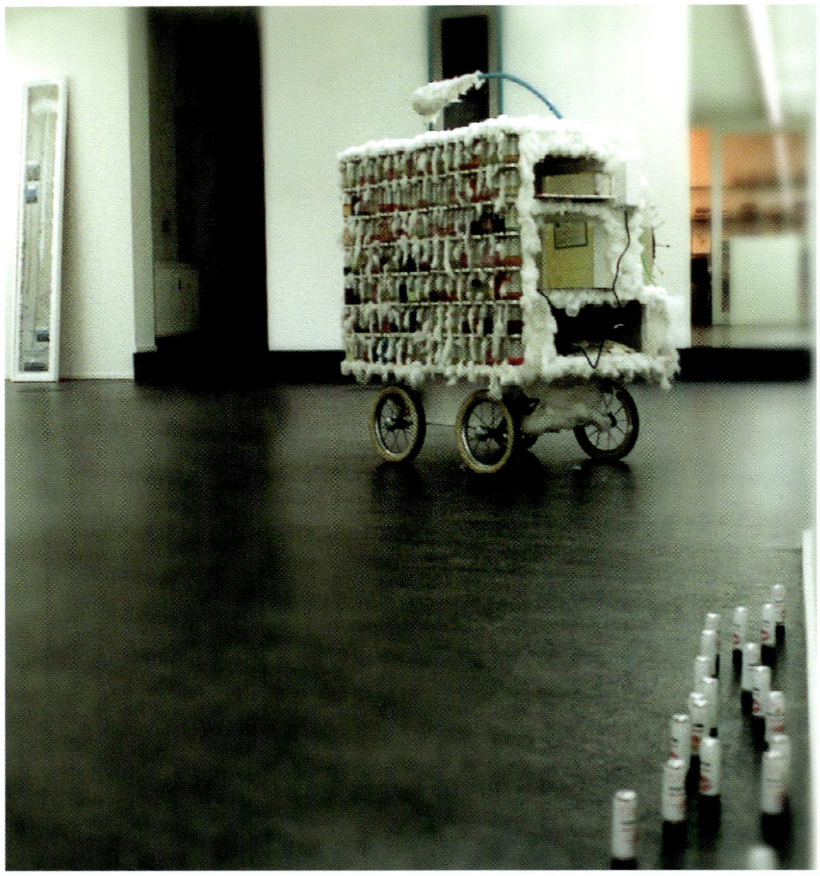

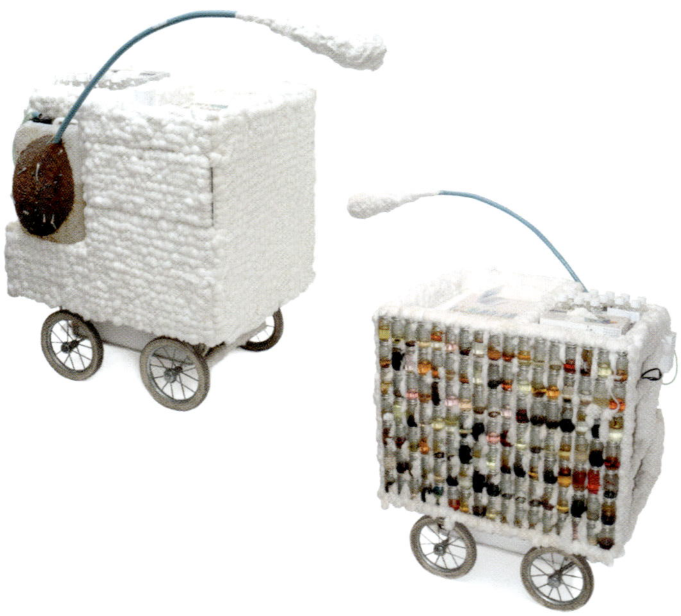

Smellcom Mob, 1999

The Smellcom Mob was made for the occasion of an evening event for Ericsson at the S.M.A.K. in Ghent, Belgium. Visitors were given a Q-tip of which one side was replaced by putty and the other side, which still had the cotton tip, was perfumed. The Smellcom was then stuck on to a mobile phone and so you could phone with a smell. The Smellcom Mob was later exhibited at the Van Laere Contemporary Art gallery in Antwerp in 2000.

De Smellcom Mob werd gerealiseerd naar aanleiding van een nocturne voor Ericsson in het S.M.A.K. te Gent. Bezoekers kregen een oorwattenstaafje waarvan één zijde vervangen was met kleefgum en de andere zijde waar nog katoenen watten zat, werd geparfumeerd. De Smellcom werd dan op een gsm gekleefd zodat men met een geur kon telefoneren. De Smellcom Mob werd achteraf tentoongesteld in Van Laere Contemporary Art in Antwerpen in 2000.

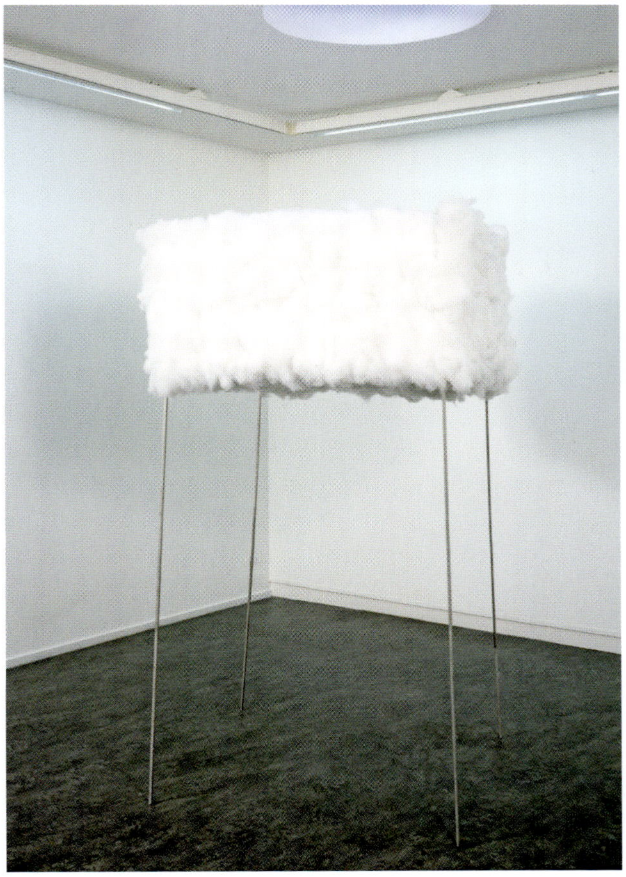

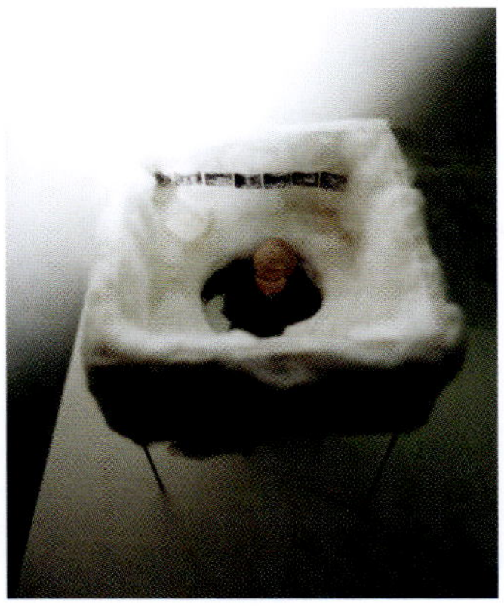

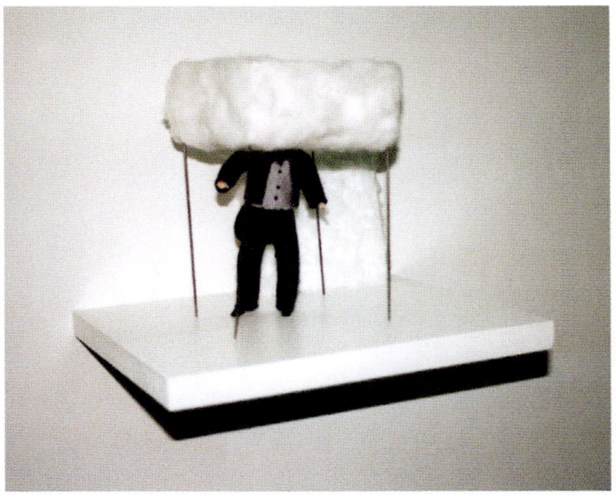

Model Soft Sculpture, 2000

Soft Sculpture, 2000

Visitors can put their head in the sculpture and smell.
Babypowder smell, cotton, inox, wood, little photographs, doll, light (in little TV).

Bezoekers kunnen hun hoofd in de sculptuur brengen en ruiken.
Geur van babypoeder, constructie van katoen, inox, hout, kleine foto's, een pop en een lichtbron in een kleine TV.

Van Laere Contemporary Art, Antwerp, BE, 14.09-21.10.2000

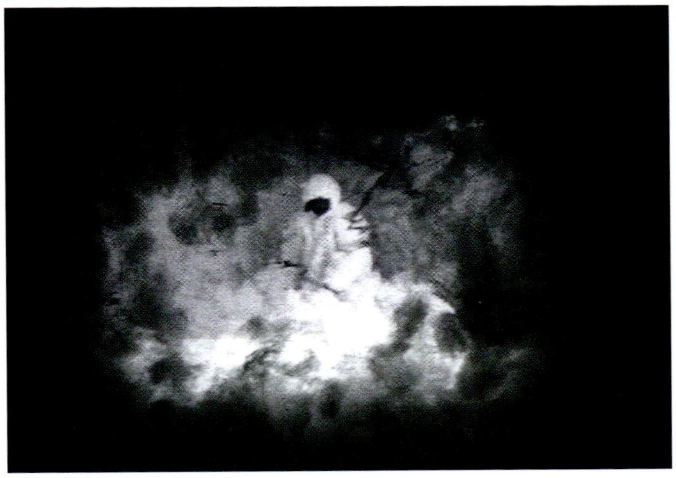

Video The Softman, 2000

A man dressed in a cotton suit playing, eating and sleeping in the cotton room.

Een man gekleed in een wattenpak, speelt, eet en slaapt in de katoenen wattenkamer.

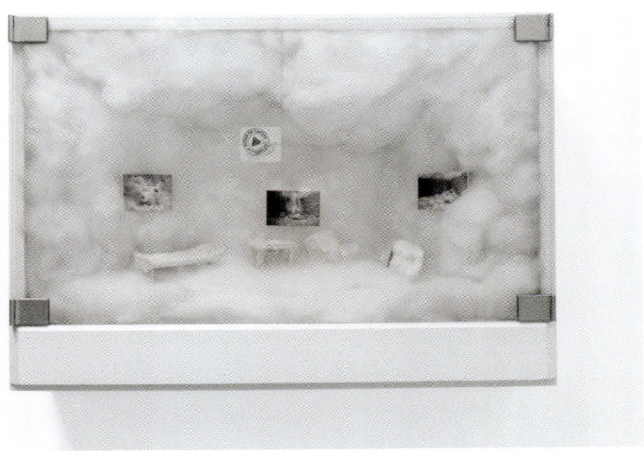

Model Soft World, 2000

43,5 cm x 63,5 cm x 18,8 cm

Cotton, miniprints and balsa wood, smell of baby powder

Watten, mini-prints en balsahout, geur van babypoeder

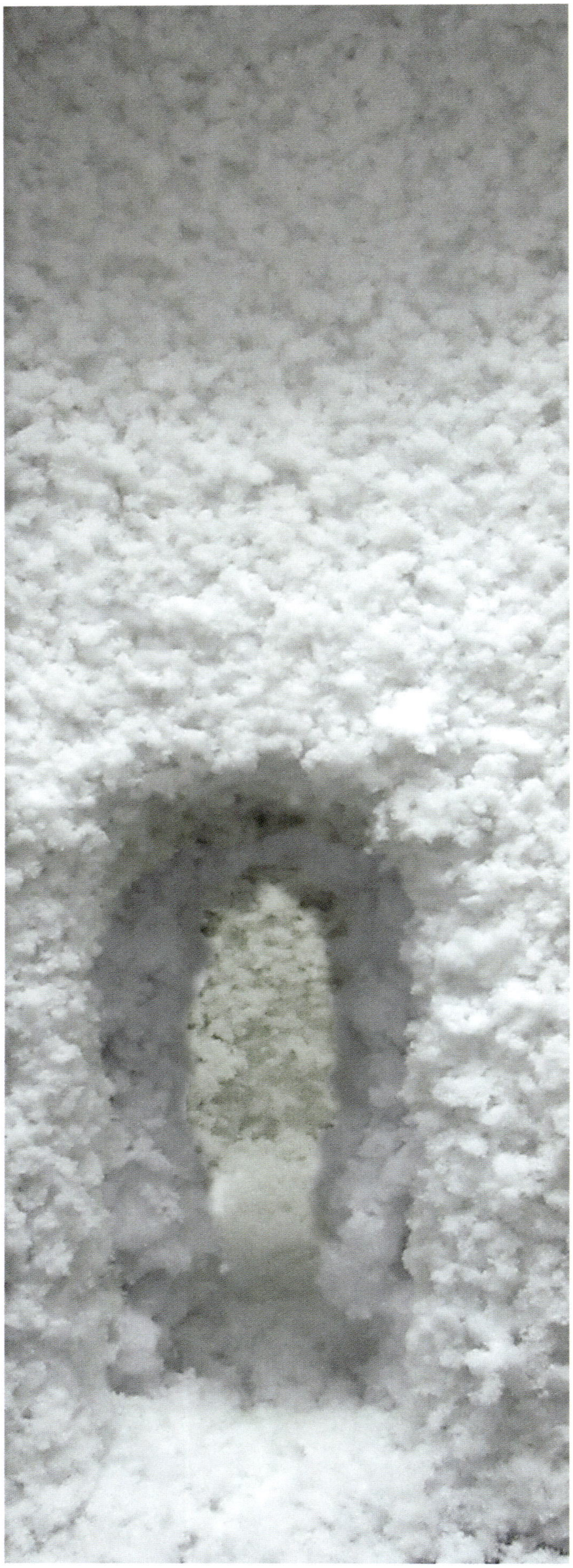

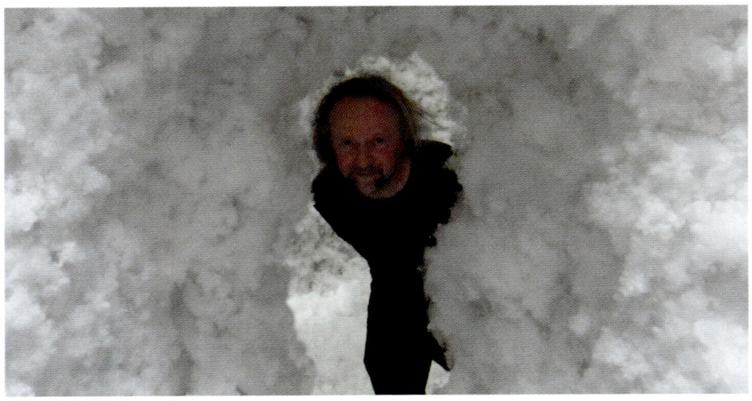

Scented Cloud Space, 2015

Room totally covered with cotton

Een kamer volledig bedekt met katoenen watten.

Jazz Age. The Roaring 20s, Fashion Museum Hasselt, curator Kenneth Ramaekers, Hasselt, BE 12.09.2015-13.03.2016

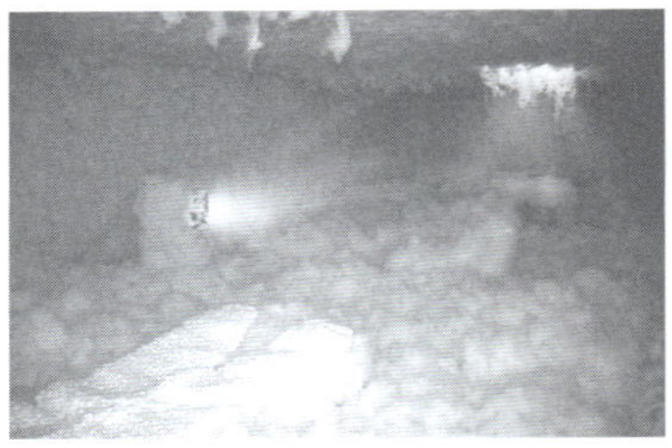

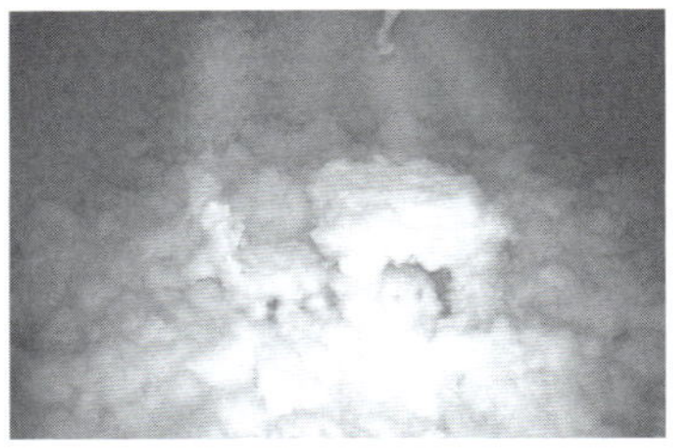

My Soft World In Honour Of My Mother, 2000

Room totally covered with cotton, inclusive all furniture and video-monitor
Materials: cotton, wood, babypowder smell, seat, monitor, video. Size: 60 m²

Een kamer volledig bedekt met katoenen watten, inclusief al het meubilair en de video-installatie. Materialen: geur van babypoeder, zetel, monitor en video. Formaat 60 m²

Biennale d'Art Contemporain, Le Fil Rouge, curator Philippe Braem, Louvain-La-Neuve, BE 13.05-12.06.2000

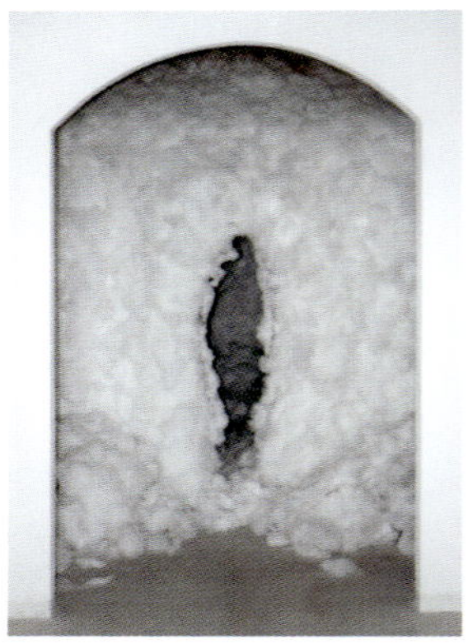

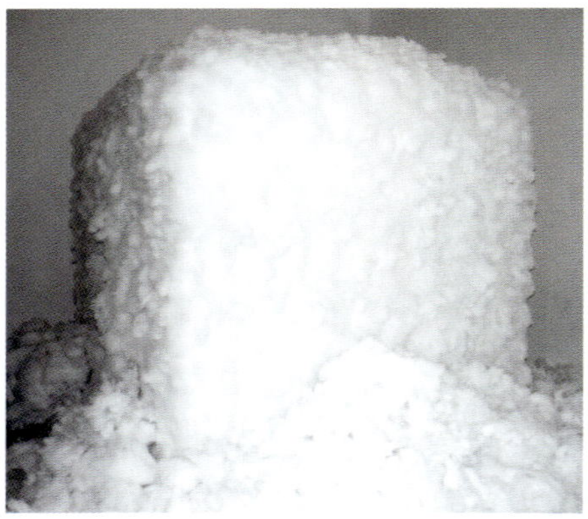

Soft World Writing Room, In Honour Of My Mother, 2000

265 cm x 220 cm x 250 cm

Materials: cotton, wood, baby powder scent, chair, table

Materialen: geur van babypoeder, zetel, tafel, hout en katoenen watten

Metamorphosis, Galleria d'Arte Moderna, curator Christa Vevey, San Gimignano, IT, 03.12.2000-20.02.2001

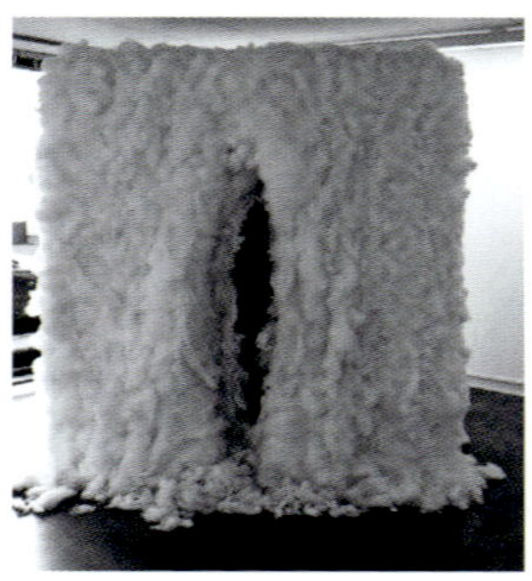

Soft World Writing Room,
In Honour Of My Mother, 2000

Table, 265 cm x 220 cm x 250 cm

Materials: cotton, wood, babypowder smell, chair,

Materialen: geur van babypoeder, zetel, hout en katoenen watten

Van Laere Contemporary Art, Antwerp, BE
14.09-21.10.2000

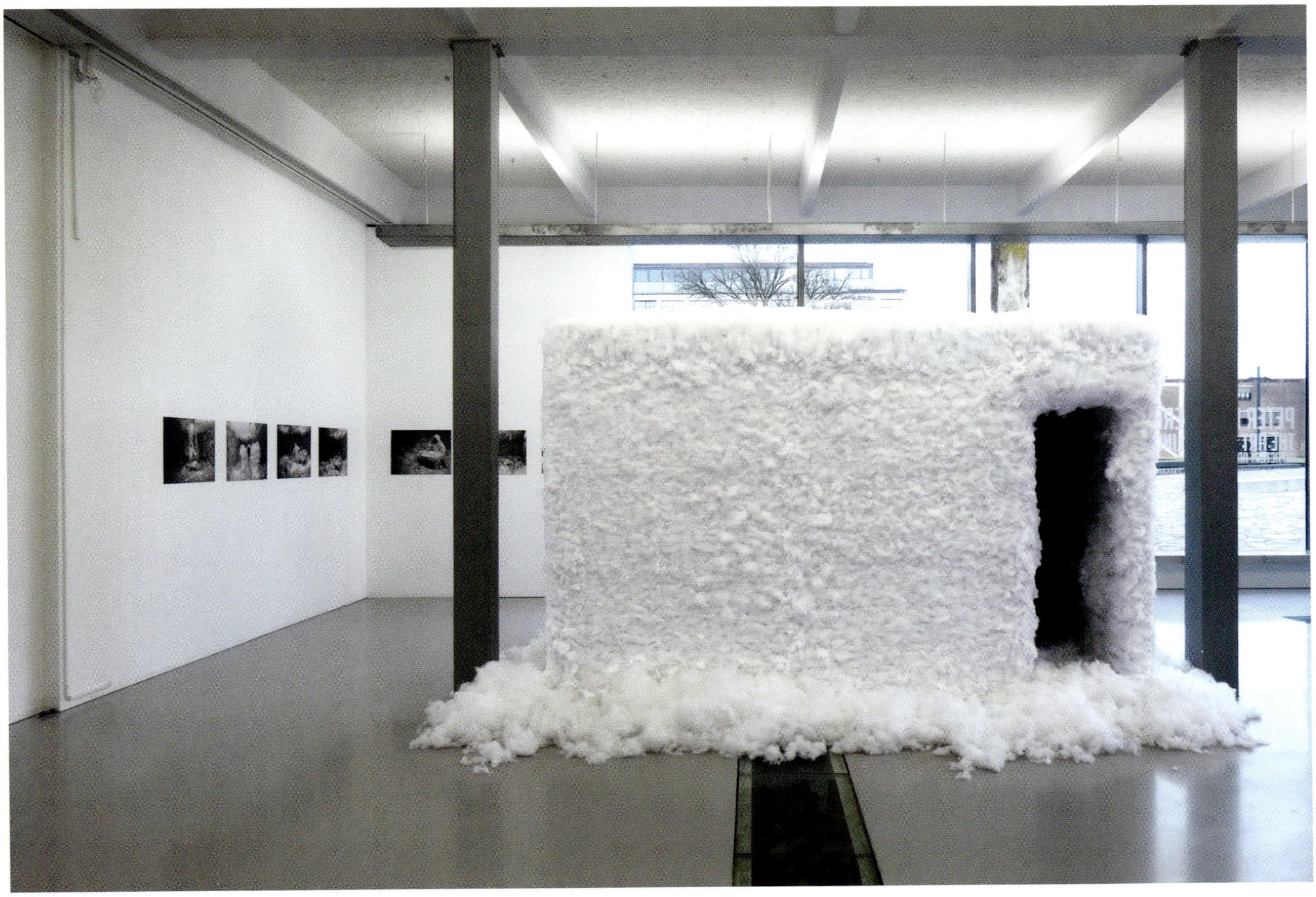

Cocoon, 2013-2014
Soft World installation with the scent of babypowder
Soft World installatie met geur van babypoeder
The Art of Smelling, Olfactory Art Research, Art Center Rozendaal 21, curator Yasmijn Jarram, Enschede, NL, 01.12.2013-02.03.2014

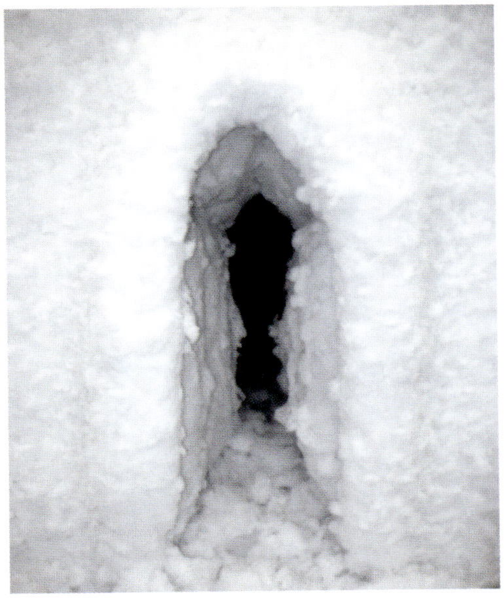

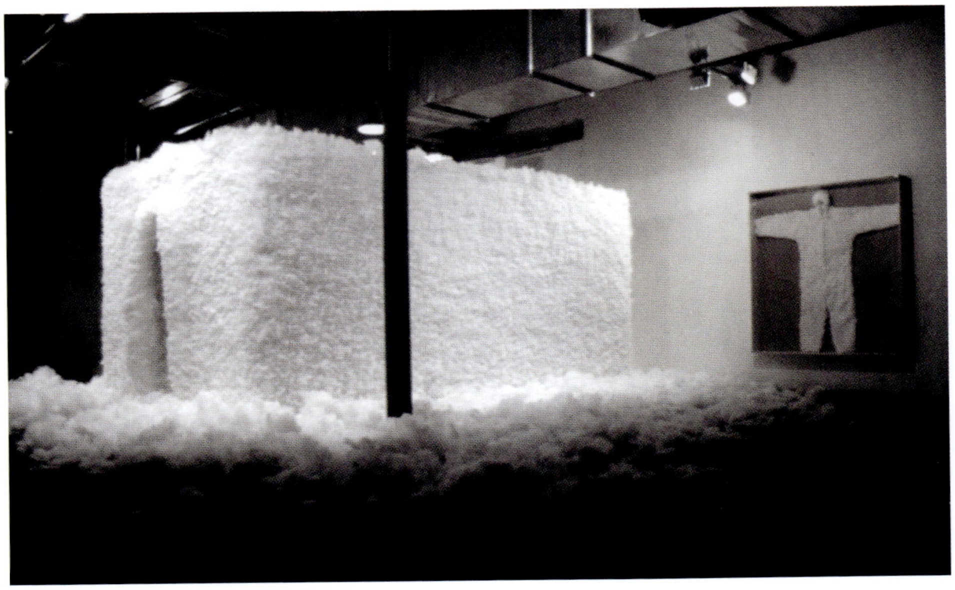

Soft World, TV-Room, In Honour Of My Mother, 2000
Materials: cotton, wood, babypowder smell, seat, TV, video, 265 cm x 220 cm x 250 cm
Materialen: geur van babypoeder, katoenen watten, hout, zetel, TV-monitor en video: formaat 60 m²
Aller Retour, Le Lieu Unique, Nantes, FR, 11.10-21.11.2001

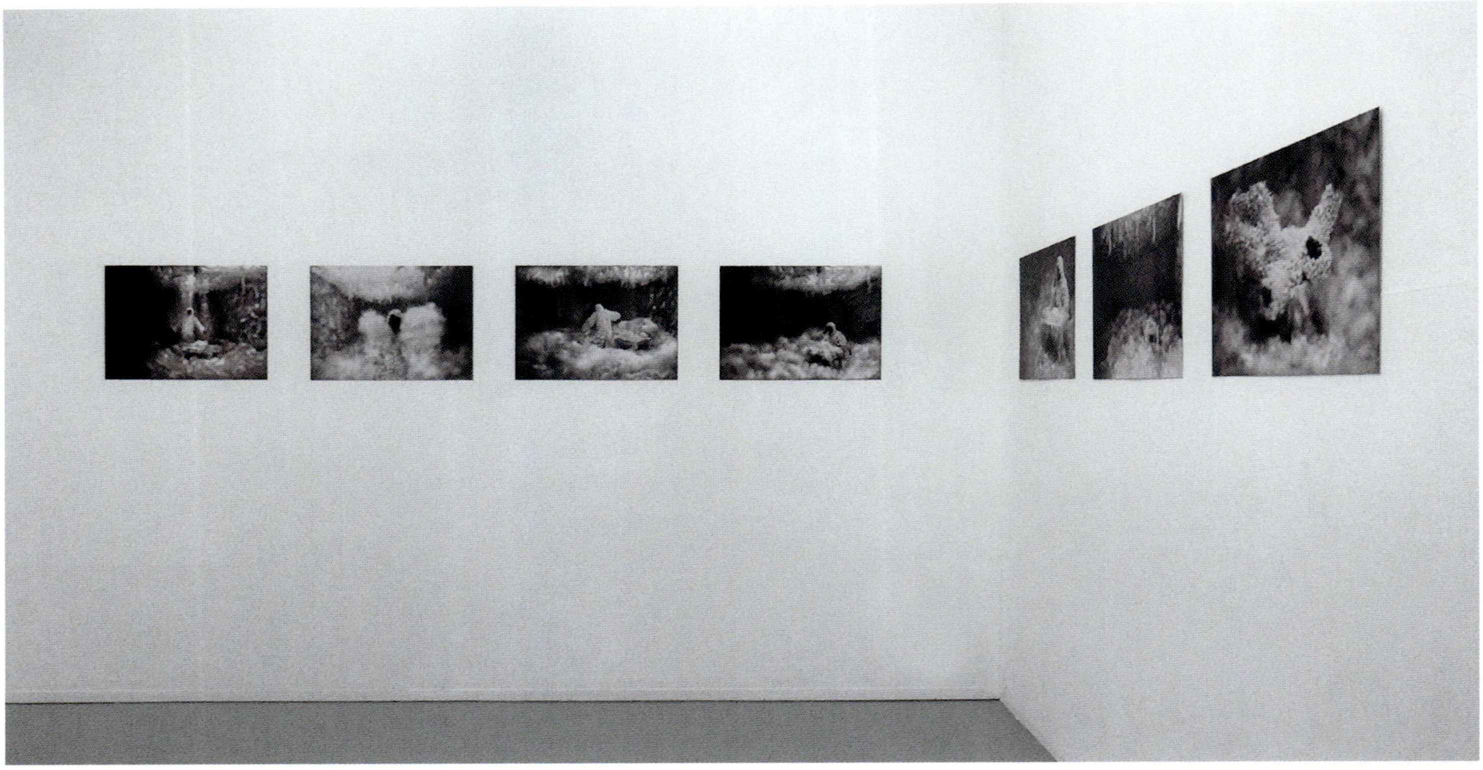

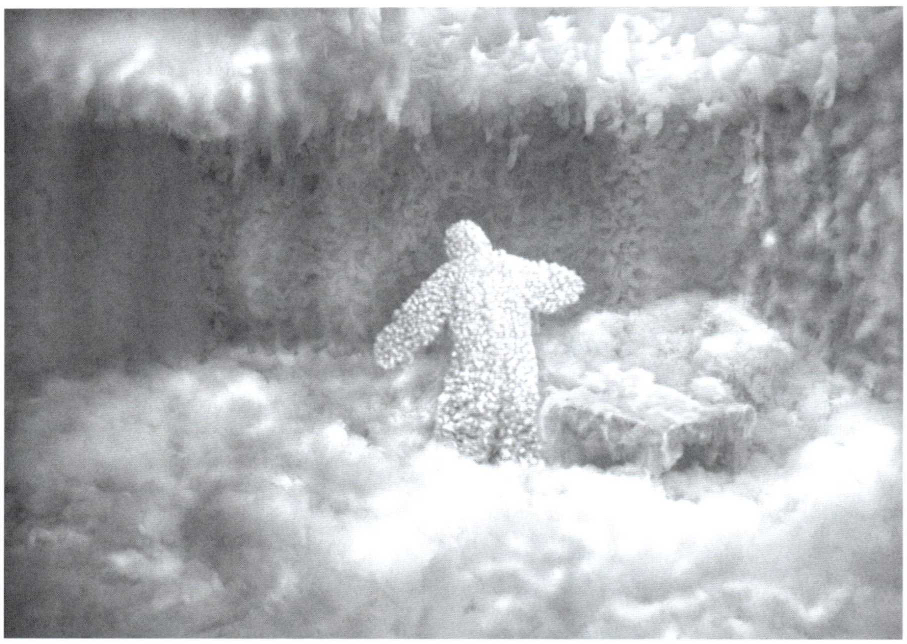

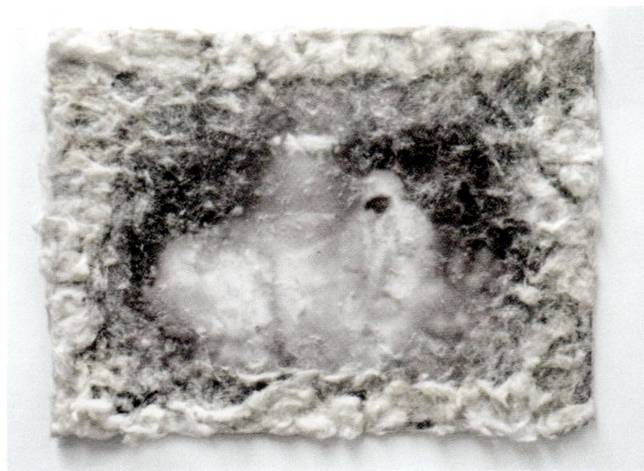

Edition Soft Man, 2000

38 cm x 28 cm

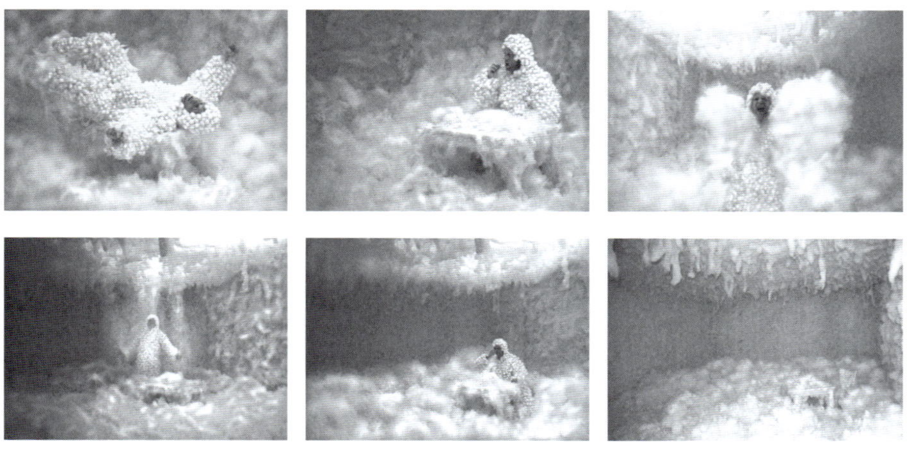

The Soft Man, His Table And His Chair, 2000

70 cm x 50 cm.

7 photographs on aluminium, UV-filter, edition of 3, 2 A.P.

7 foto's op aluminium met UV-filter, editie van 3, 2 A.P.

The Art of Smelling, Olfactory Art Research, Art Center Rozendaal 21, curator Yasmijn Jarram, Enschede, NL, 01.12.2013-02.03.2014
Van Laere Contemporary Art, Antwerp, BE, 14.09-21.10.2000

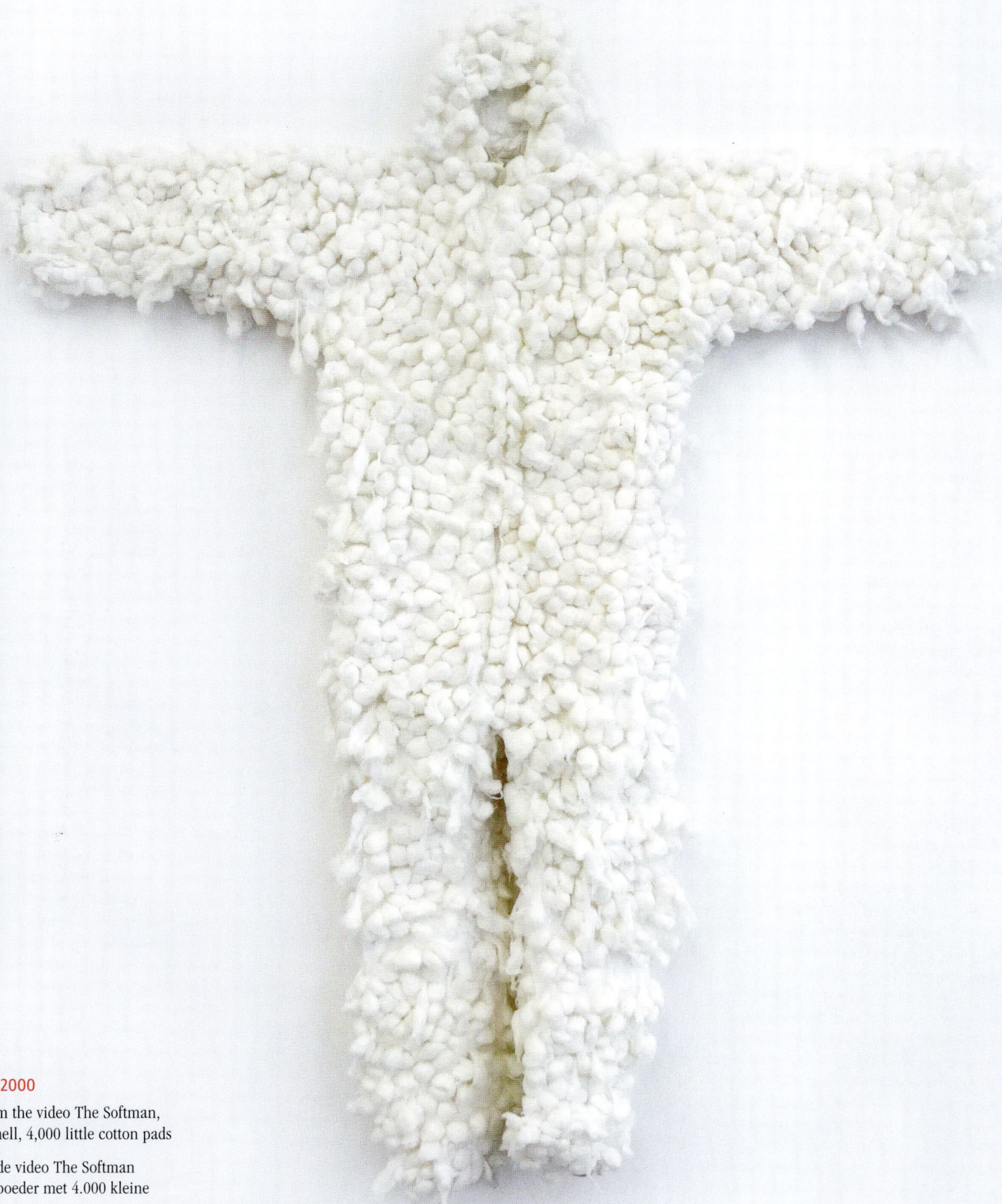

Soft Man Suit, 2000

Cotton suit from the video The Softman, babypowder smell, 4,000 little cotton pads

Wattenpak uit de video The Softman
Geur van babypoeder met 4.000 kleine wattenvlokjes

The Art of Smelling, Olfactory Art Research, Art Center Rozendaal 21, curator Yasmijn Jarram, Enschede, NL, 01.12.2013-02.03.2014
Van Laere Contemporary Art, Antwerp, BE
14.09-21.10.2000

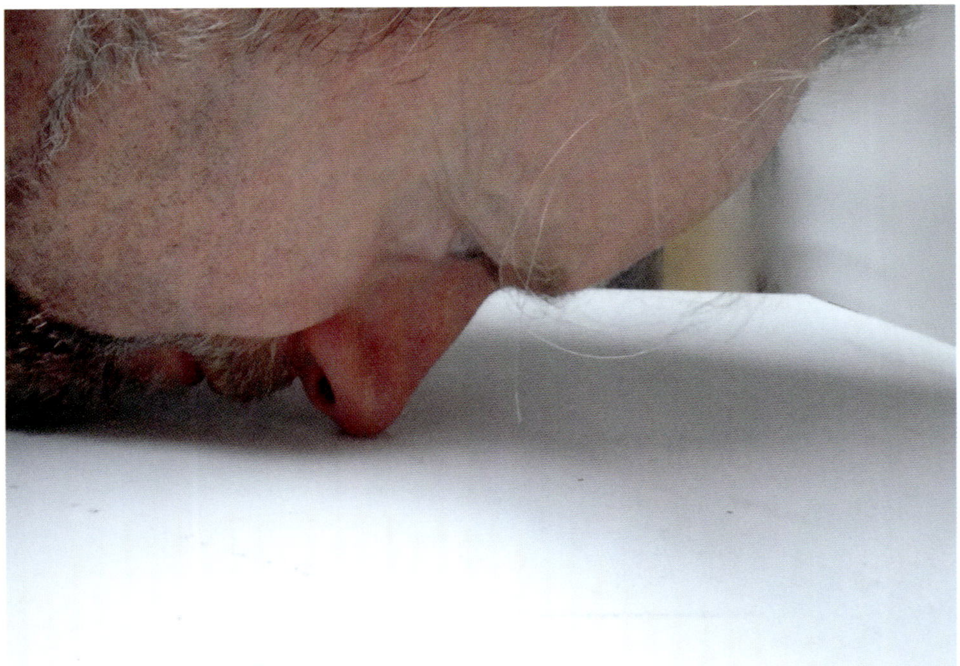

Invisible (Scent) Sculpture, 2015

Different versions with different scents depending of the exhibition.
In the exhibition 'There's something in the air' the scent was created with peppermint and combined with scratch & sniff.

Afhankelijk van de tentoonstelling verschillende versies met verschillende geuren in uitvoering.
In de expo 'There's something in the air' werd de geur gecreëerd met pepermunt in combinatie met kras & wrijf.

There's Something in the Air, Villa Rot, curator Caro Verbeek, Burgrieden-Rot, DE, 22.03.2015-28.07.2015

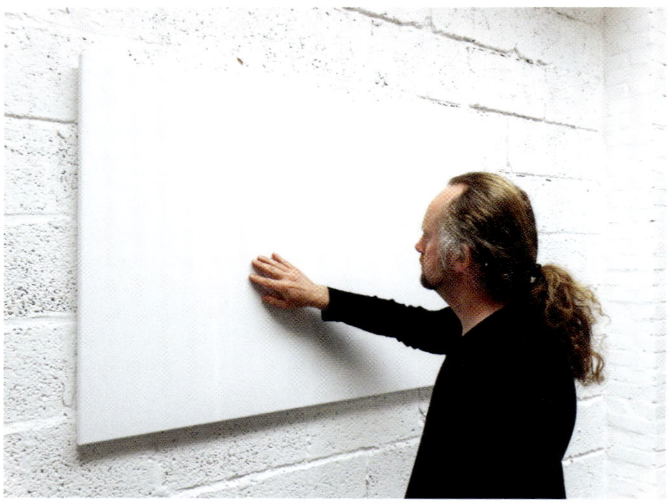

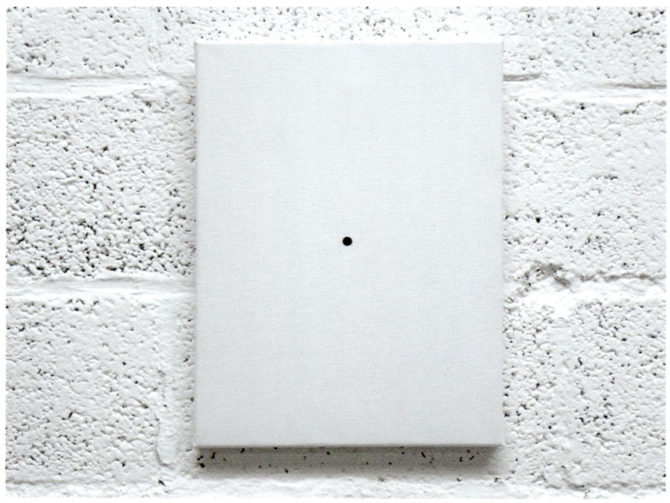

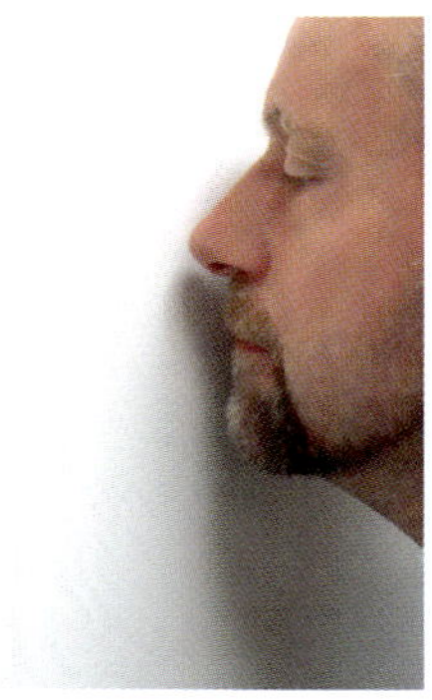

Invisible Scent Paintings, 2014

Different invisible scent paintings with scratch & sniff. Smell depends on the scratch & sniff position.

Verschillende onzichtbare geurschilderijen met scratch & sniff. De geur verschilt naargelang waar je wrijft en ruikt.

Scent Hole(s) Paintings, 2014

In the canvas one or more holes present a smell.

In de canvas zijn één of meerdere gaten aangebracht waardoor een geur waar te nemen is.

Image / Afbeelding:
Scent Wind Hole Painting, 2014

Execution with mini fan to blow the smell through the hole.

Achter de canvas is een mini-ventilator aangebracht die de geur doorheen het gaatje blaast.

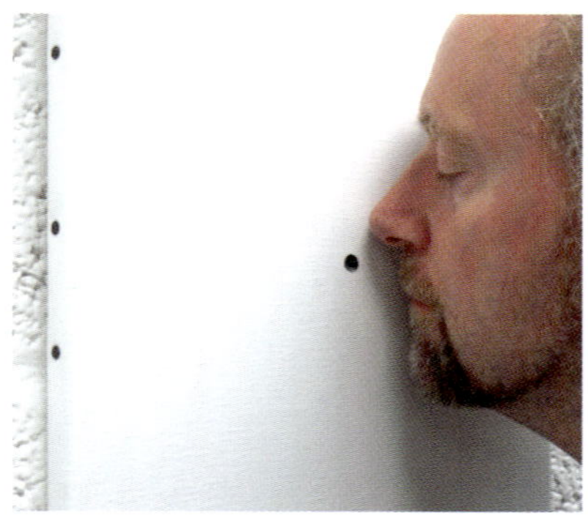

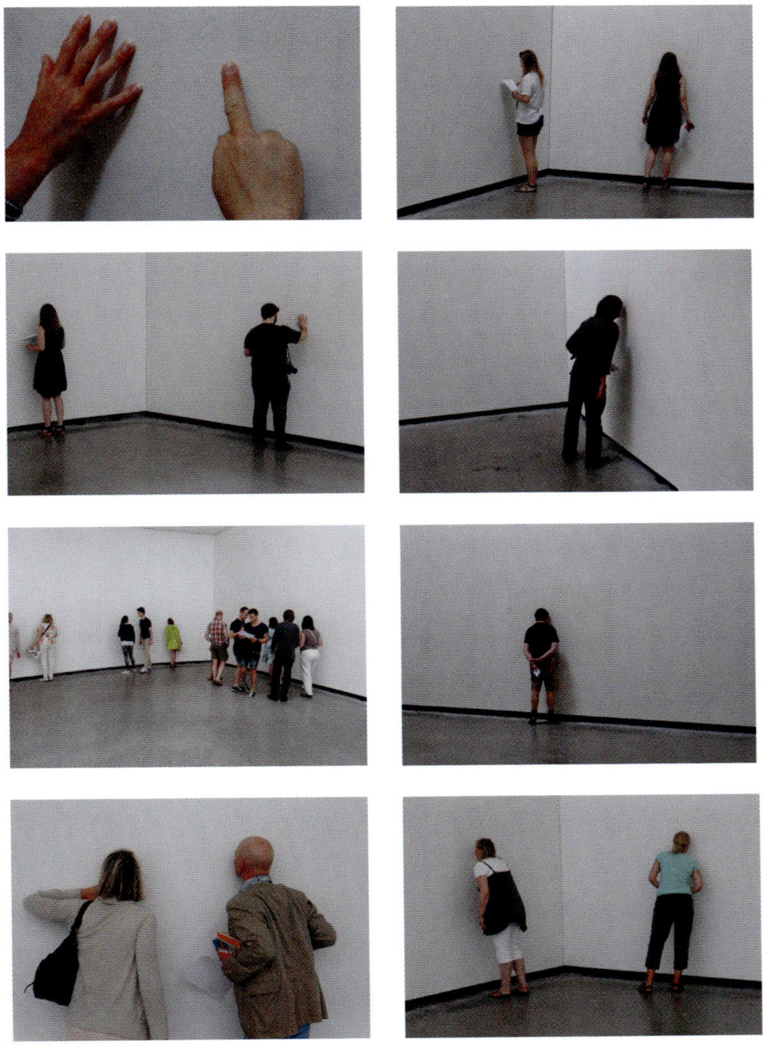

Invisible Scent Paintings, 2014

Scratch & sniff paint on the walls, different titles combined with different smells.

Kras en geur verf op de muren. Verschillende titels van de werken met verschillende geuren.

Invisible Scent Paintings, The Olfactory, Hasselt, Antwerp, 16.09.2014
Marta Museum in Motion, Marta Museum, curator Franziska Brückmann, Herford, DE
08.06.2014-15.06.2014

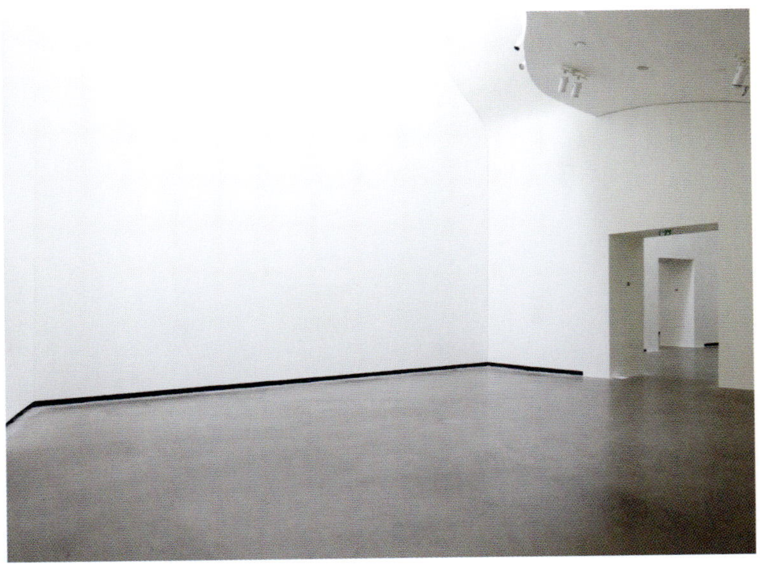

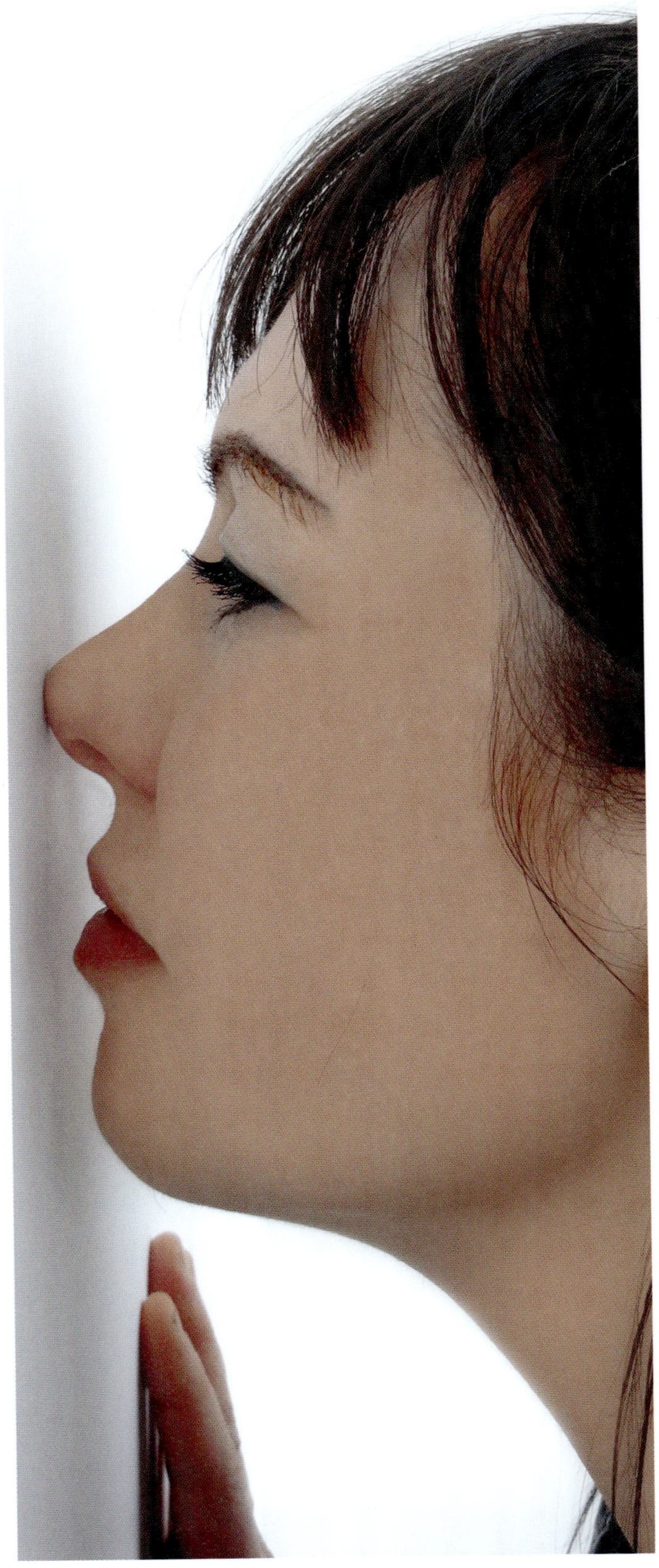

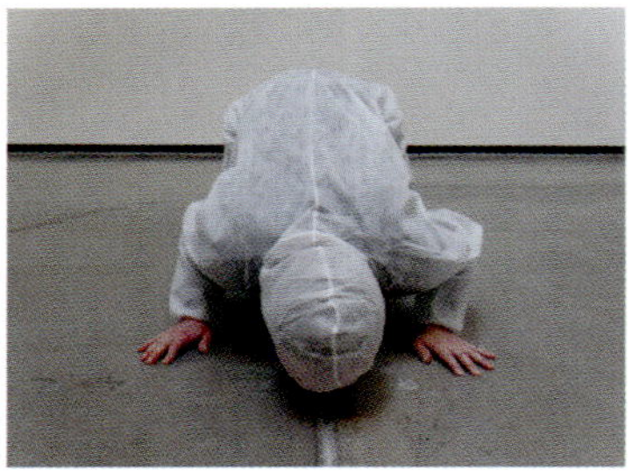

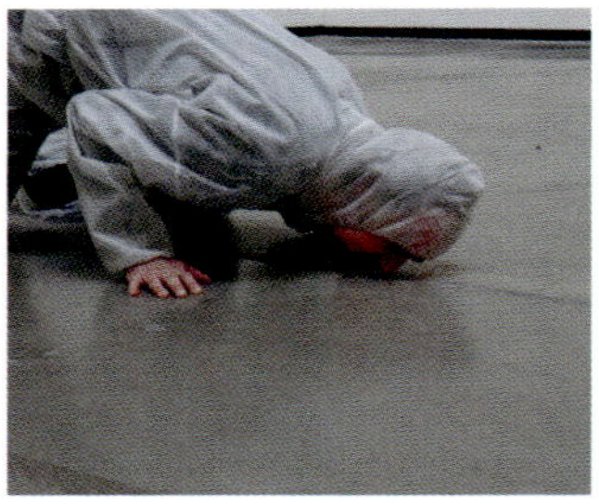

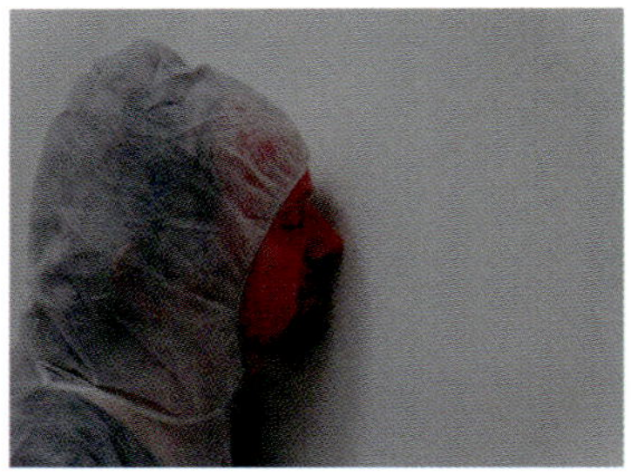

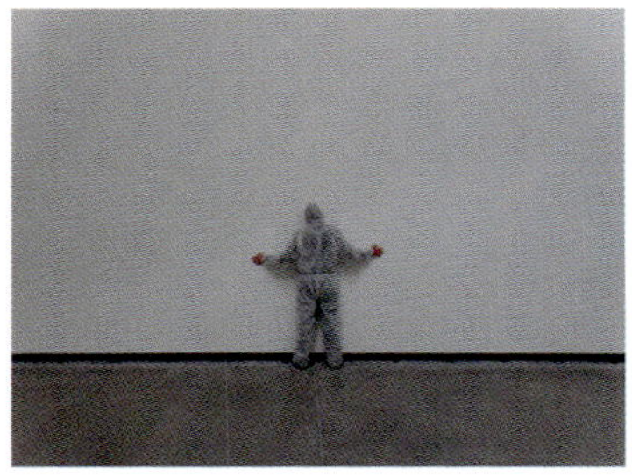

Sniffing The Museum, 2014

Video HD, 3 min.

In the sniffing video performance in the museum Marta in Herford (designed by Frank Gehry) goes peter de Cupere smelling the disappeared artworks. He tries olfactrilly and mentally to imagine what kind of work was present on a location inside the museum. It's also a kind of preparation before exhibiting works to know and understand the location better. He also sniffed around outside of the building.

In de video van de geurperformance in het Marta-museum in Herford (DE), ontworpen door architect Frank Gehry, geurt Peter de Cupere aan de verdwenen of verwijderde kunstwerken. Olfactorisch en mentaal probeert hij zich in te beelden welk kunstwerk op welke plaats in het museum aanwezig was. Tegelijkertijd is het een inlevingsoefening en onderzoek naar de ruimte vooraleer eigen werk te presenteren. De kunstenaar heeft eveneens de buitenzijde van het museum besnuffeld.

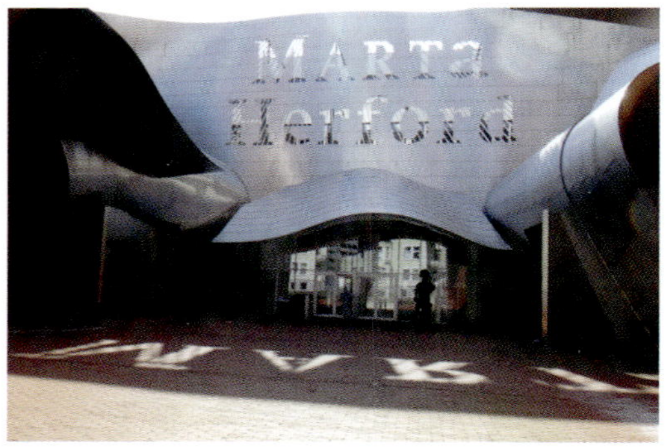

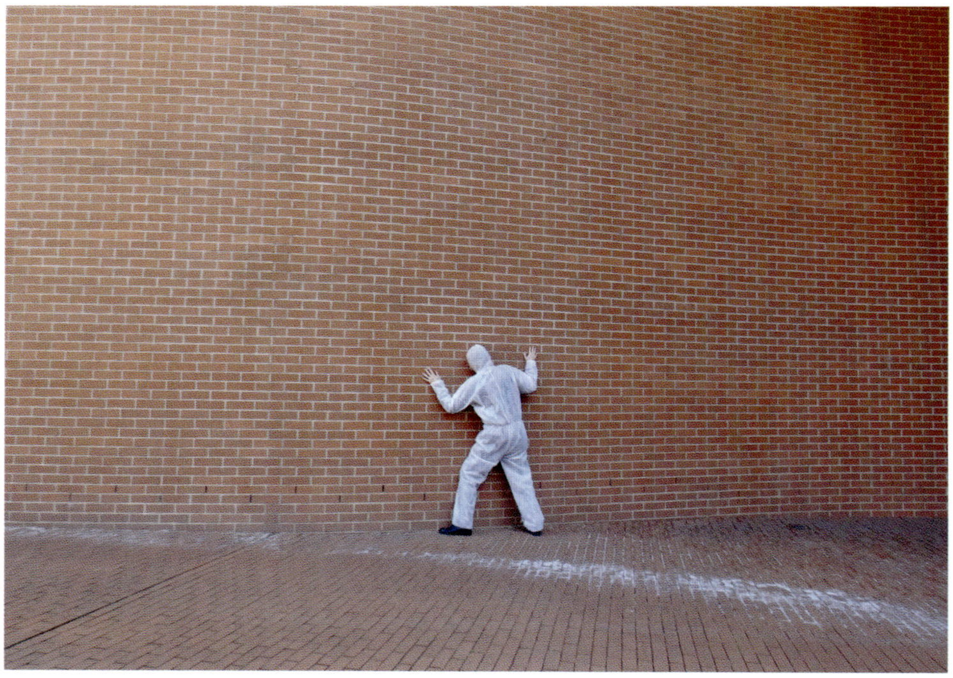

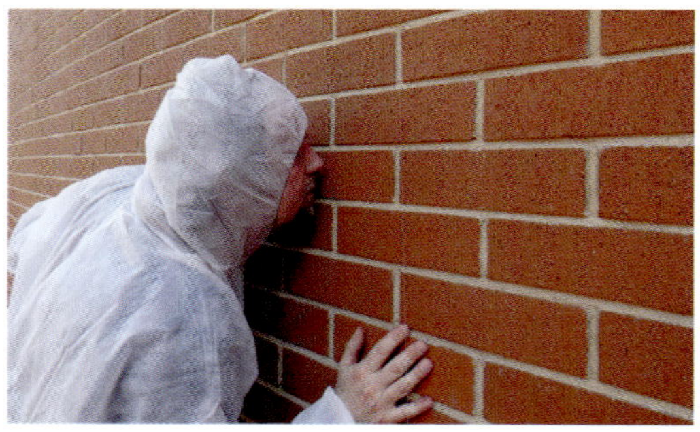

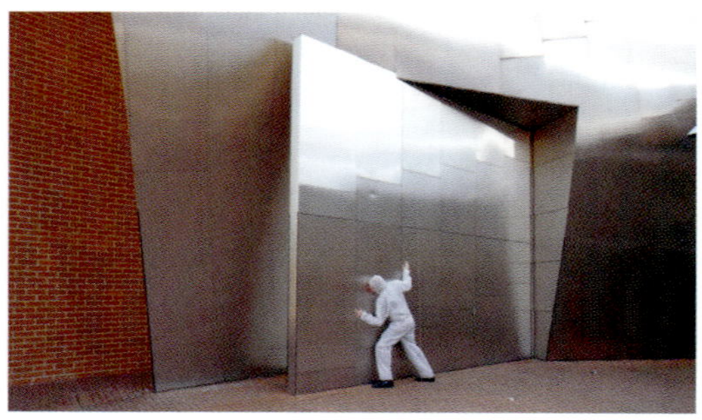

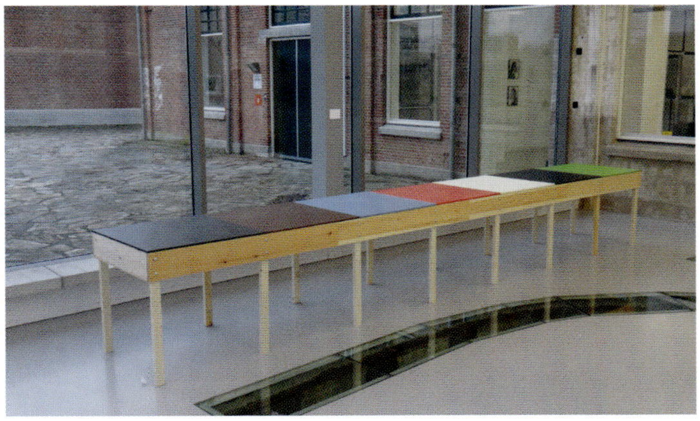
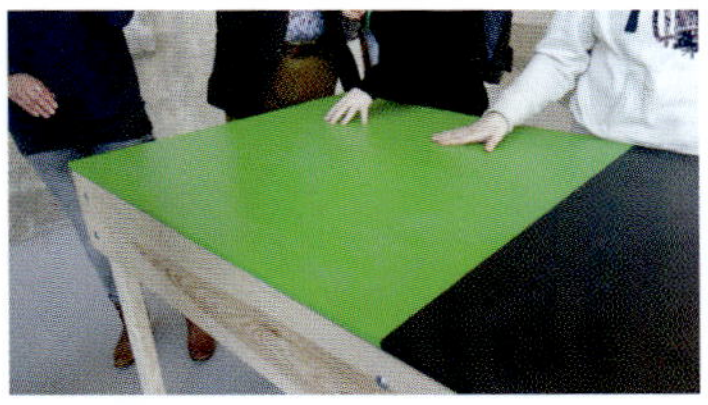
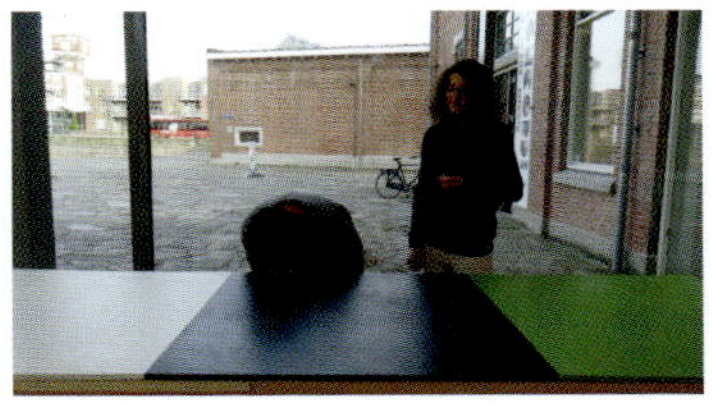
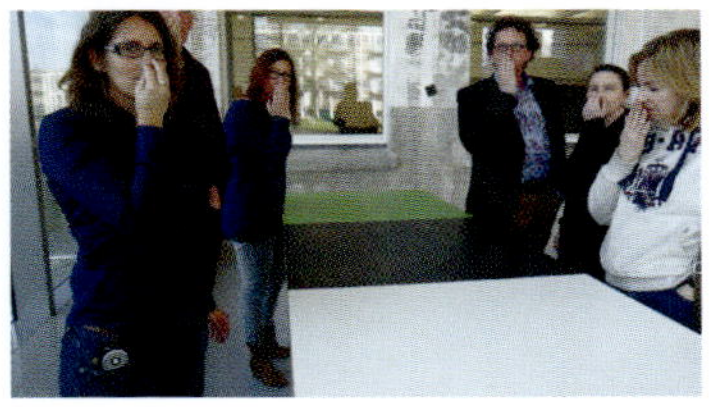

Sniff And Imagine The Colours Of This World, 2014

Installation of different scratch & sniff smells, combined with different colours.

Installatie van verschillende scratch & sniff geuren gecombineerd met verschillende kleuren

The Art of Smelling, Olfactory Art Research, Art Center Rozendaal 21, Yasmijn Jarram, Enschede, NL, 01.12.2013-02.03.2014

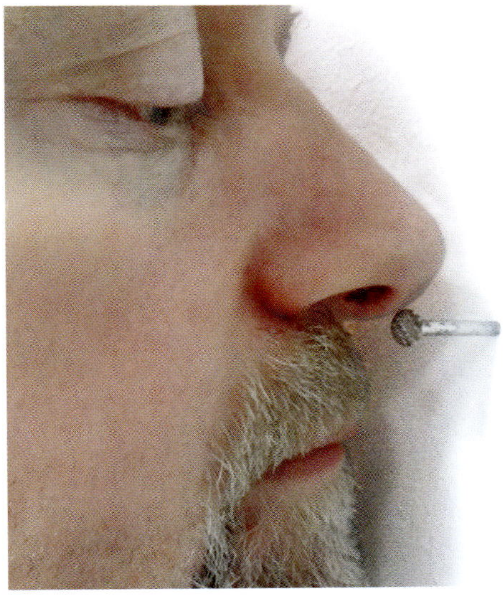
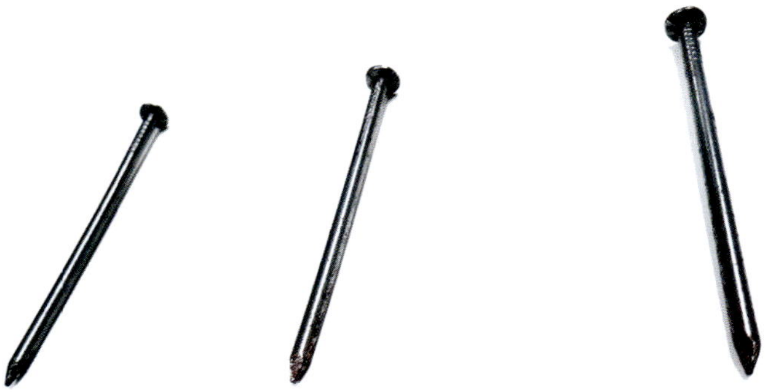

The Evolution Of Painting, 2015

3 iron nails, 3 titles
The nail of the old Painting smells like mushrooms
The nail of the Contemporary Painting smells like turpentine
The nail of the Future Painting smells like gunpowder

3 ijzeren nagels, 3 titels
De nagel met de voorstelling van een oud schilderij ruikt naar paddestoelen.
De nagel met het hedendaags schilderij ruikt naar terpentijn.
De nagel met het toekomstige schilderij geurt naar buskruit.

There's Something in the Air, Villa Rot, curator Caro Verbeek, Burgrieden-Rot, DE, 22.03.2015-28.07.2015

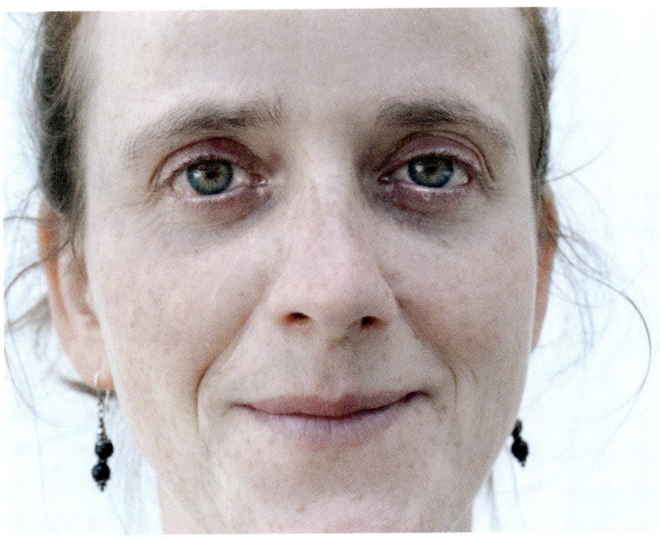
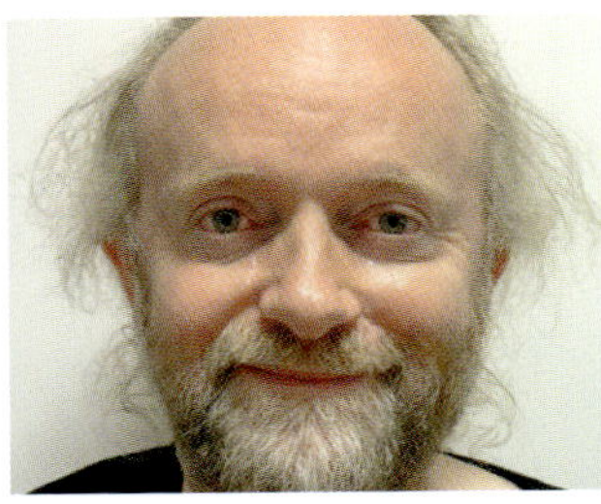
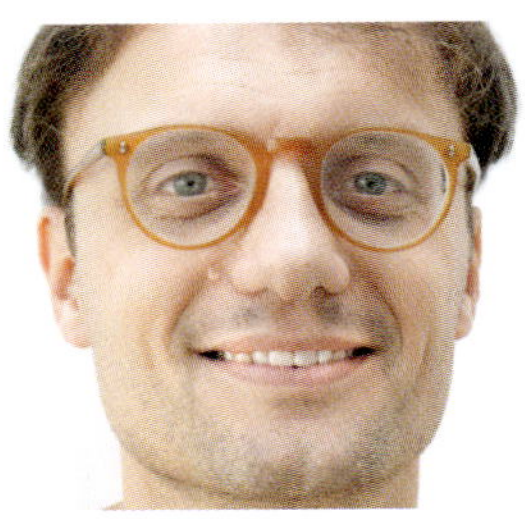

Scented Tears

When entering the empty exhibition space, visitors begin to cry in reaction to the smell. Thus they become part of the installation and witness each other's grief.

Bij het binnenkomen van de lege tentoonstellingsruimte beginnen bezoekers te huilen als reactie op de geur. Ze worden hierdoor zelf onderdeel van de installatie en zien zo elkaars verdriet.

Scented Tears, The Olfactory,, Hasselt, BE, 17.09.2014

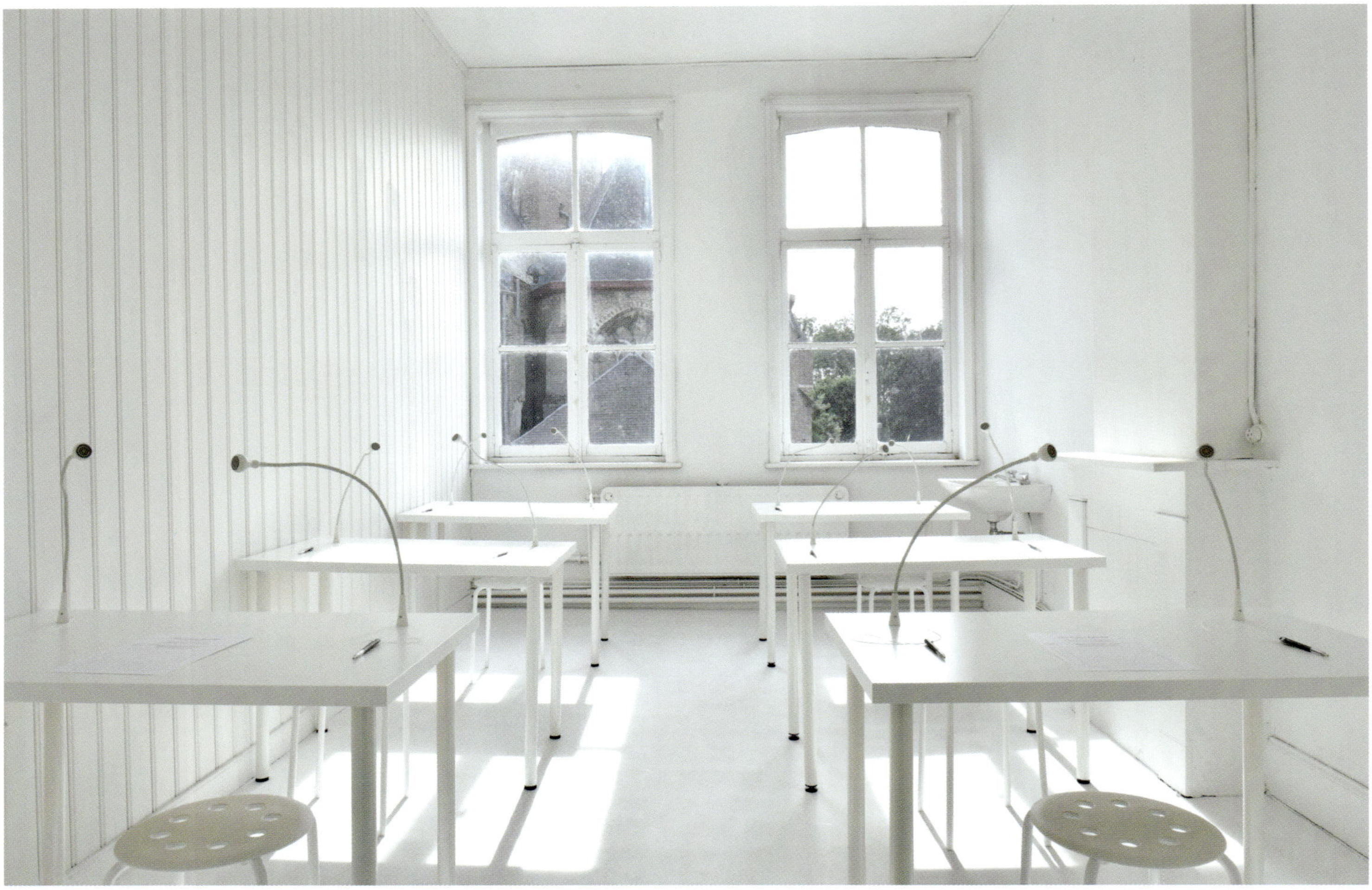

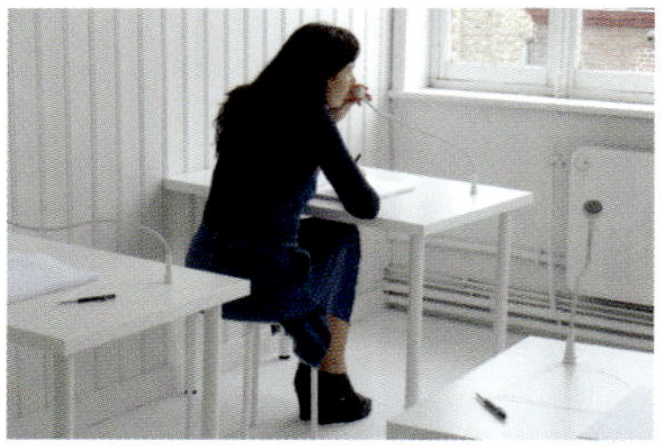

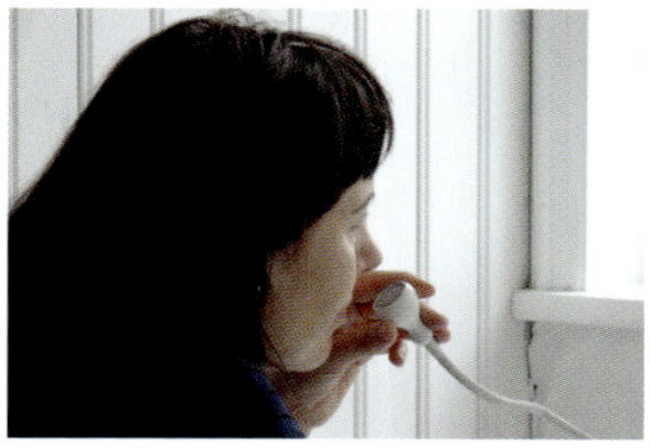

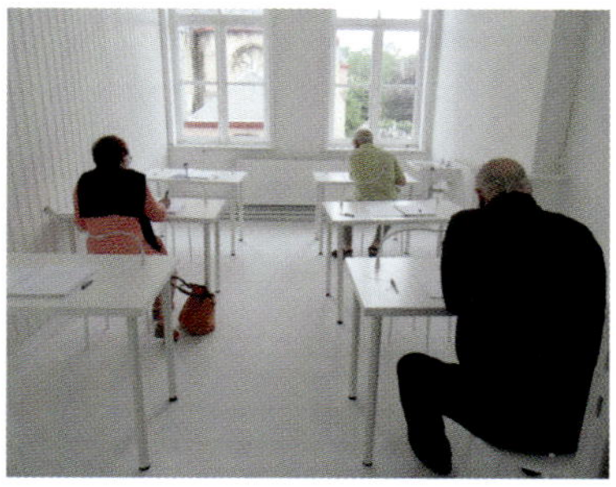

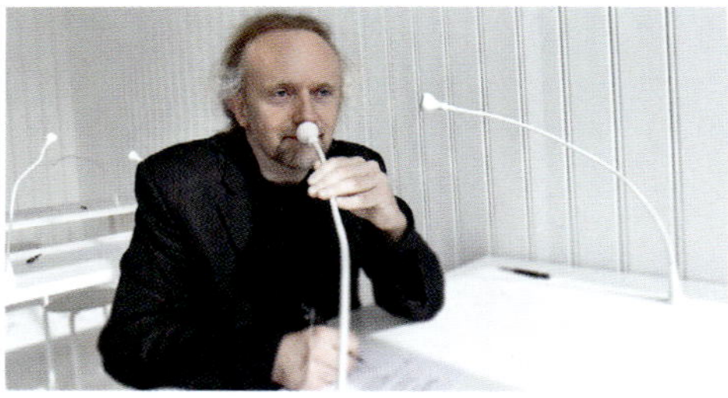

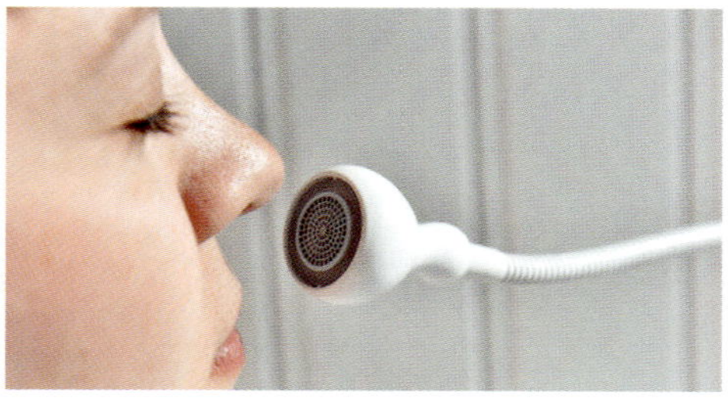

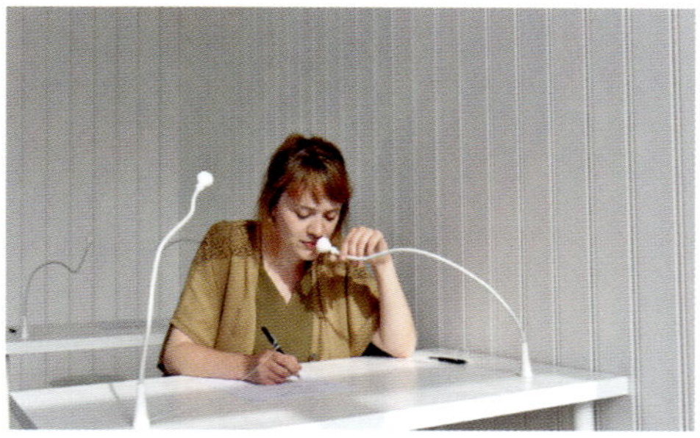

The Scent Reader, 2015

Installation consisting of 6 tables with 2 scent modules each. Visitors are asked to write down their own olfactory experiences and can read the olfactory experiences and memories of other visitors.

Installatie met 6 tafels met telkens 2 geurmodules. Bezoekers schrijven zelf hun geurervaringen op en kunnen de geurervaringen of herinneringen van andere bezoekers lezen.

Manufracture, Images and thoughts that matter, PXL-MAD, Hasselt, BE
24.09.2015-27.10.2015
In the lee of the in-between, Kunstenfestival Watou, curator
Jan Moeyaerts, Watou, BE, 04.07.2015-30.08.2015

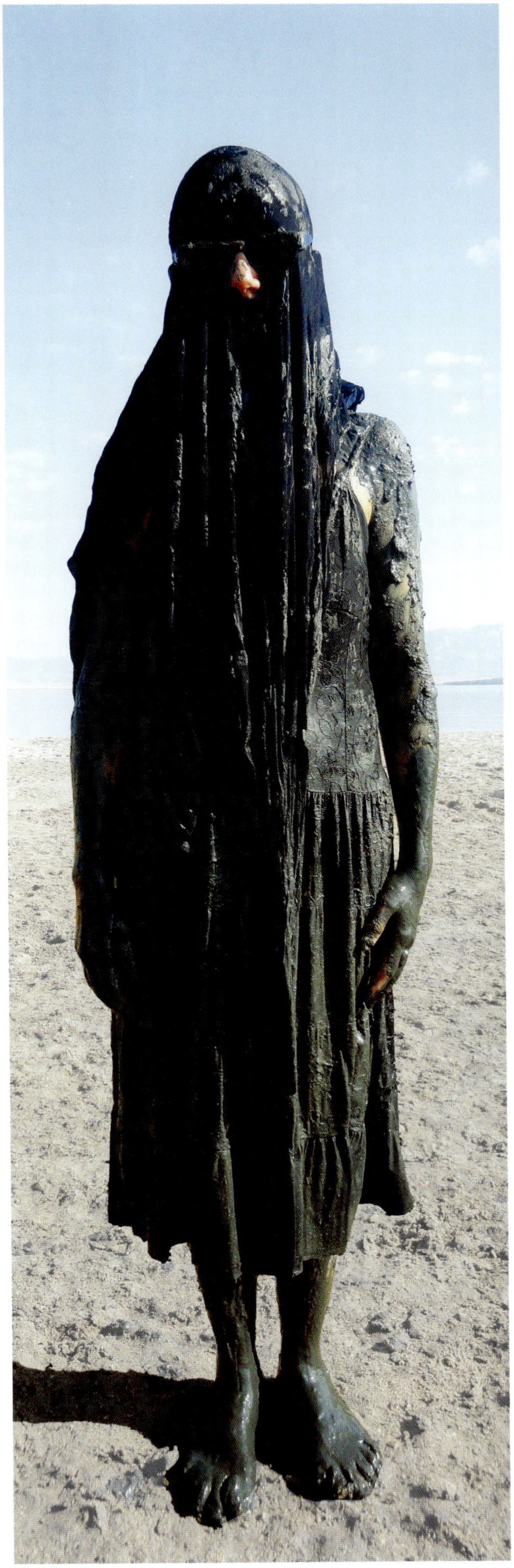

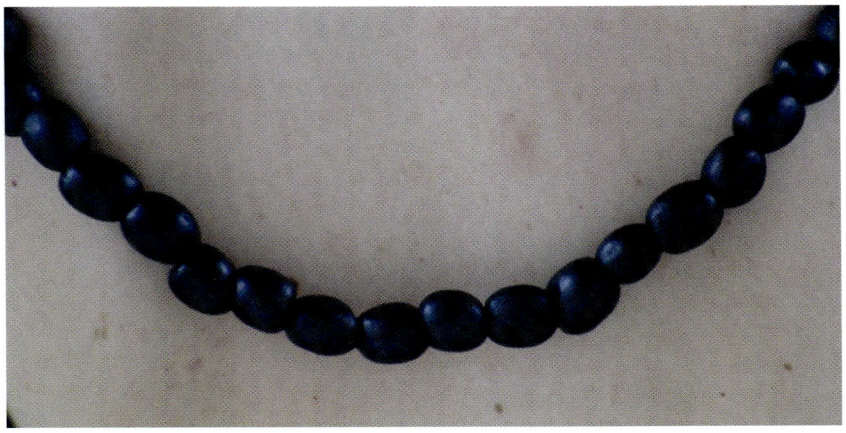

Black Pearls, 2011-...

Black Pearls is a short film in which 5 parallel stories approach black olives from a different angle. The video was shot among other places in Italy, Croatia, France and Belgium. At the time of publication of the book, the short film was still in production. In the drawing Olfactory Mind, you see a design for one of the settings of the short film. The black olive is always used as the starting point. It has a very specific smell. The first shots date from 2011 on the island of Isola Comacina, where the artist spent 3 weeks as artist-in-residence.

Black Pearls is een kortfilm waarbij 5 parallel lopende verhalen zwarte olijven op een andere manier benaderen. De video-opnames werden gedaan in Italië, Kroatië, Frankrijk en België. Bij publicatie van dit boek is de kortfilm nog steeds in productie. In de tekening *Olfactory Mind* zie je een ontwerp van één van de settings van de kortfilm. Als uitgangspunt wordt steeds de zwarte olijf genomen. Deze heeft een heel specifieke geur. De eerste opnames dateren van 2011 op het eiland Isola Comacina waar de kunstenaar 3 weken als artist in residence verbleef.

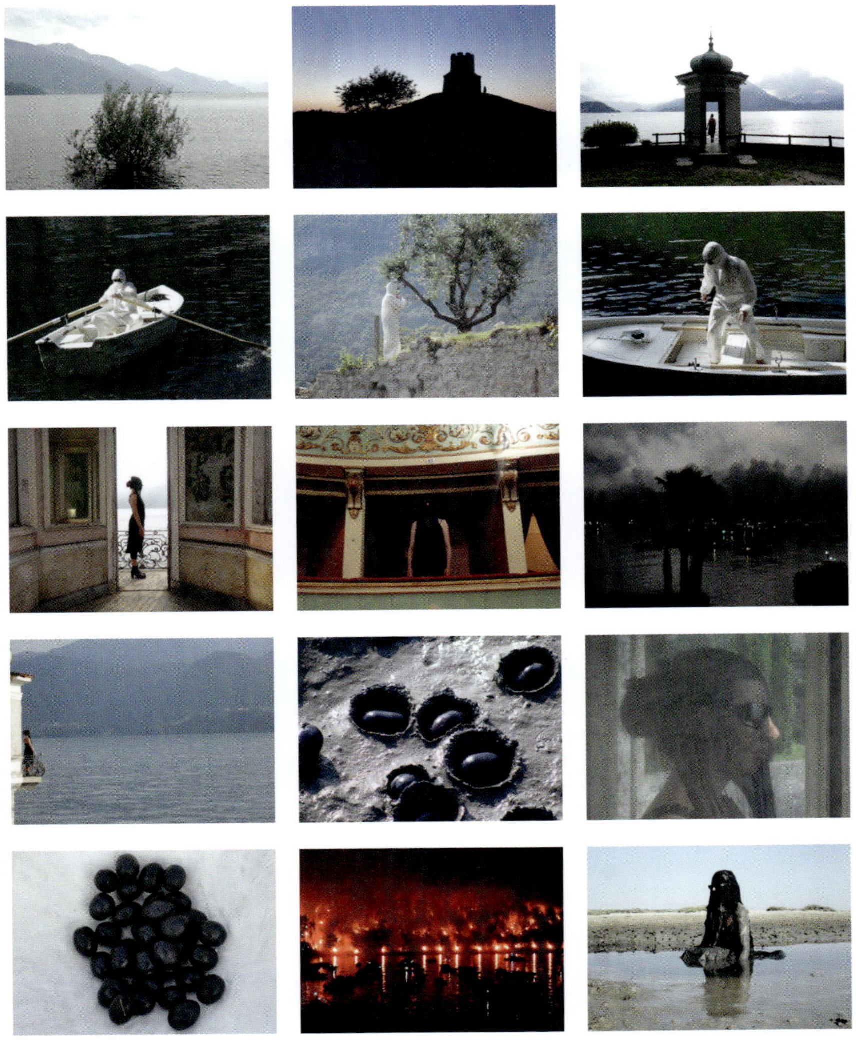

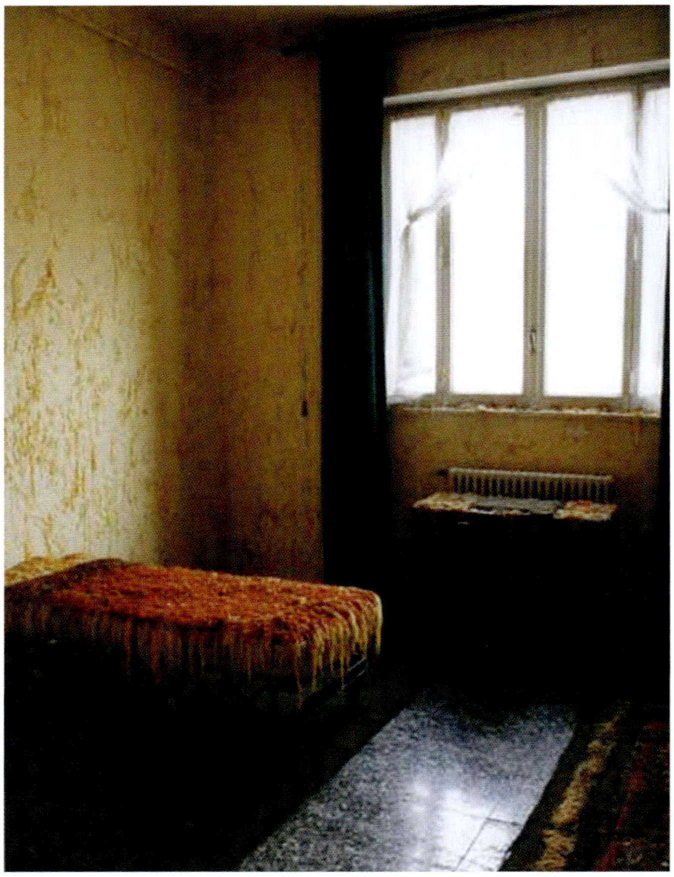

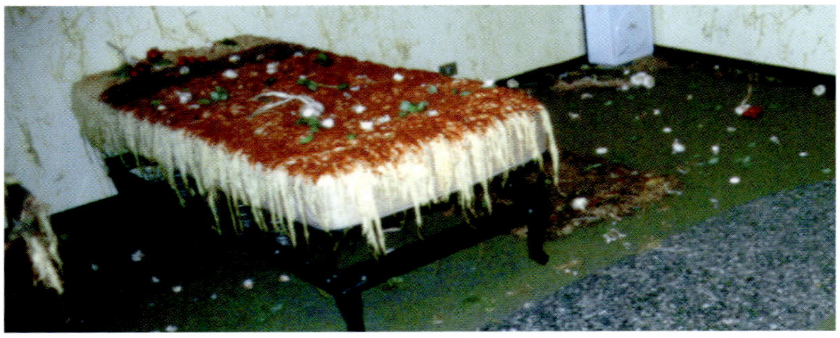

Una Pasta Per Giulietta, 2001

Smell-installation: room covered with spaghetti, different spices, vegetables, Italian love-poem, spaghetti-flowers outside on the balcony.

Geurinstallatie. Kamer bedekt met spaghetti, verschillende kruiden, groenten, een Italiaans liefdesgedicht, spaghettibloemen buiten op het balkon.

Methamorphosis, vzw Phidias, Academia Belgica, curator Christa Vevey, in cooperation with the Belgian Embassy, Rome, IT, 23.03-17.04.2001

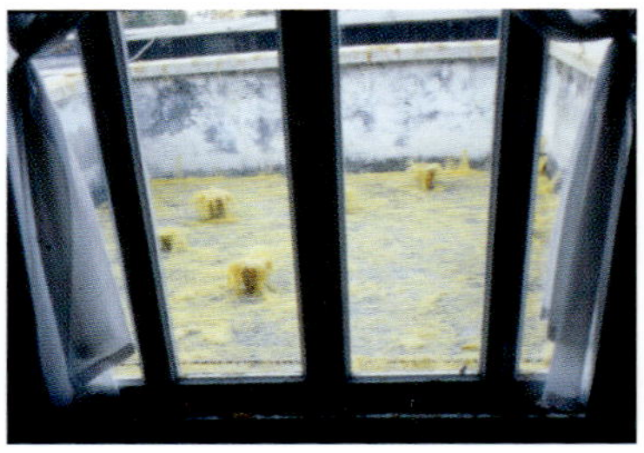

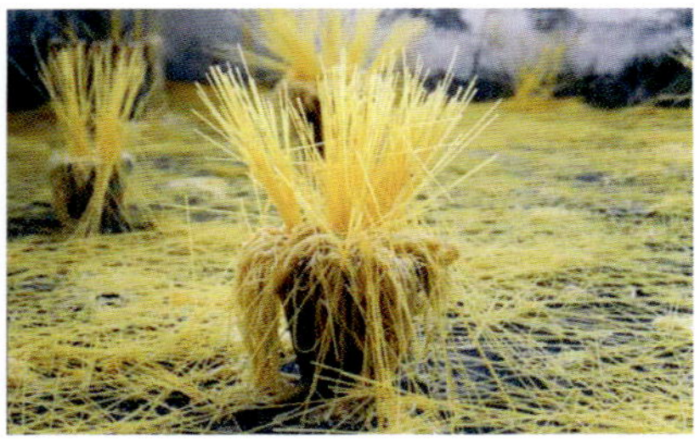

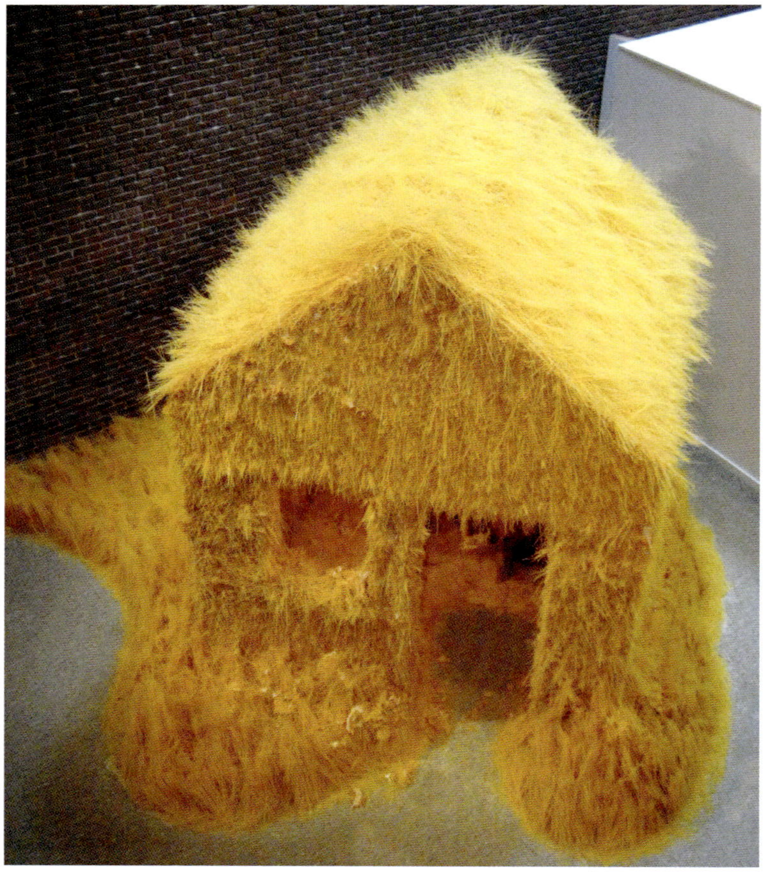

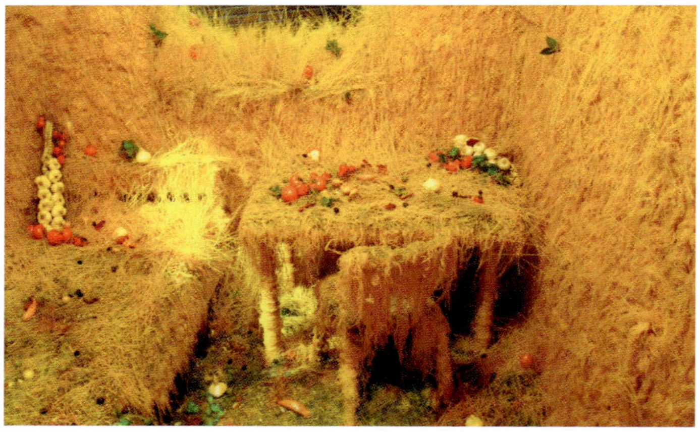

Spaghetti House, 2007

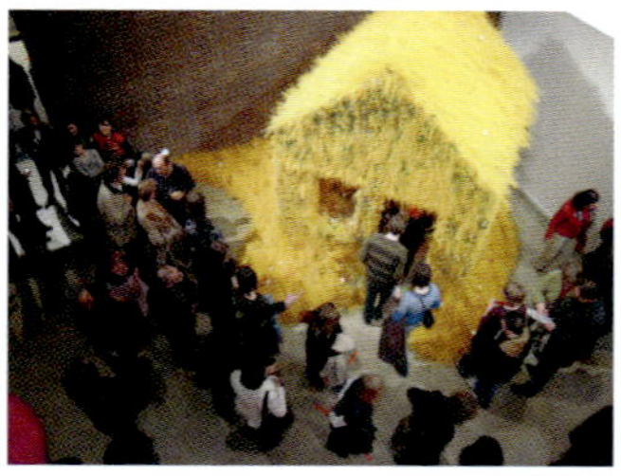

Spaghetti House is made of 700 kg of boiled spaghetti and 200 kg dried spaghetti. It took one week to complete the whole installation. From morning till night 4 people were cooking and pasting the spaghetti. The installation was perfumed with typically Italian fragrances used in food like basilicum, oregano and tomato extracts.

Spaghetti House is samengesteld uit 700 kg gekookte pasta en 200 kg gedroogde pasta. Om de hele constructie te bouwen werd er gedurende één week van 's morgens vroeg tot 's avonds laat pasta gekookt en aangebracht in de constructie. De installatie werd geparfumeerd met een typische Italiaanse culinaire geur gekruid met veel basilicum, oregano en tomatenextracten.

Storm op komst, Warande, Turnhout, BE, 30.03.2007-15.04.2007

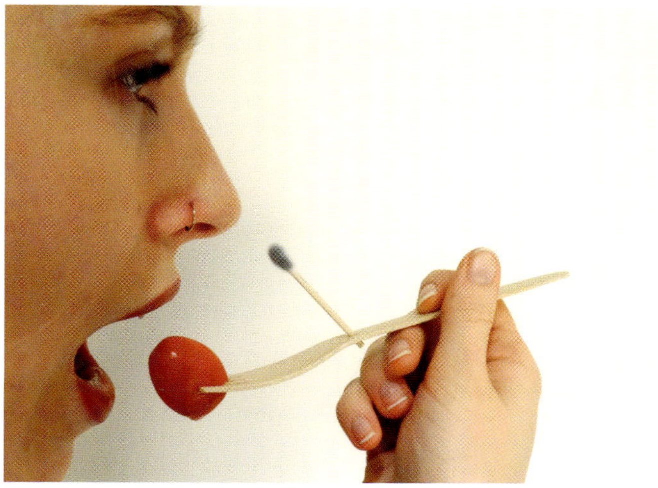

Tasting Air Pollution, 2003

During their meal, visitors are confronted with air pollution.

Tijdens het eten wordt men geconfronteerd met de luchtvervuiling.

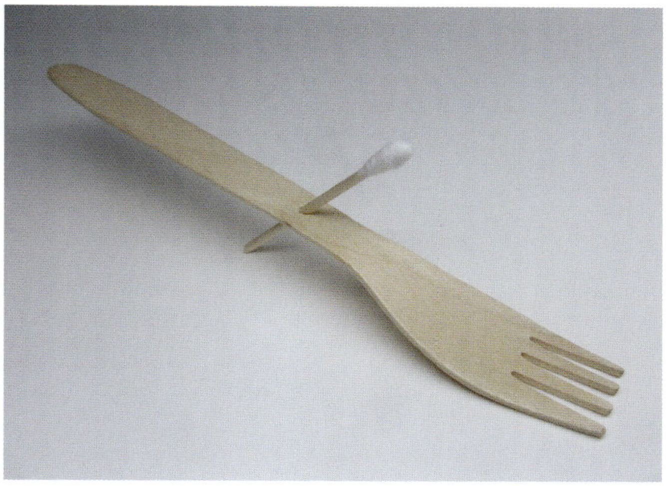

Eating Scents, 2000-2003

Concept involving edible scents, allowing for a radically different culinary experience.

Concept om met geuren te eten. Hierdoor kan men een totaal andere eetbelevenis teweeg brengen.

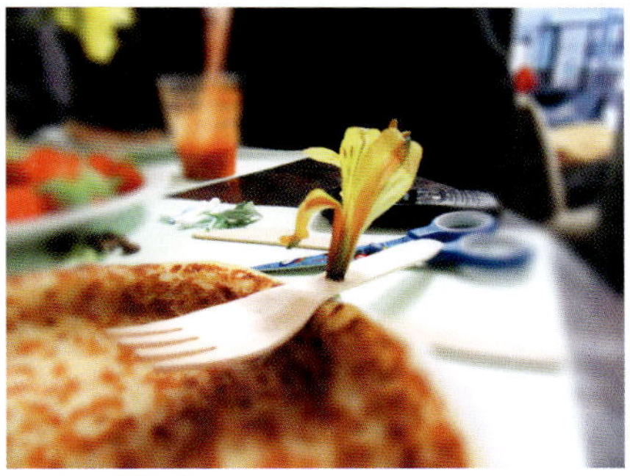

Scent Eating And Drinking, 2000-2015

Over a period of 15 years Peter de Cupere realized different kinds of scent dinners. Somethimes combined with scent drinks. scent dinners give another taste and feeling by what you eat.

Photos Experimental workshop week Sense It Mad! in Turnhout with students of the PXL-Mad School of Arts.

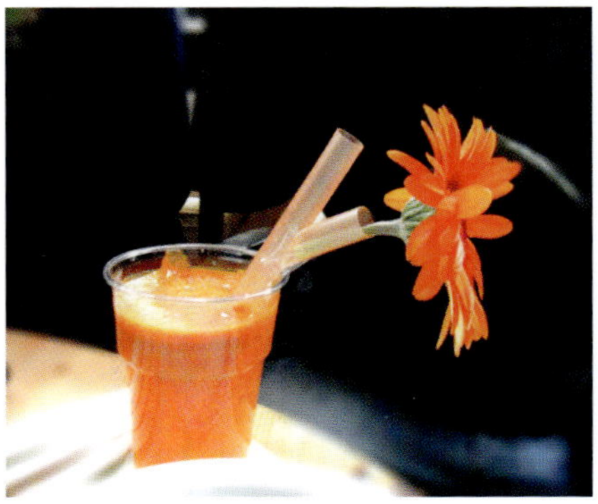

Tijdens de laatste vijftien jaar organiseerde Peter de Cupere diverse geurdiners, soms in combinatie met geurdranken.
Deze geurdiners creëren een nieuwe gevoelservaring op het vlak van proeven van de maaltijd.

Foto's van de experimentele workshop week Sense it Mad! In Turnhout (BE) met studenten van de PXL-Mad School of Arts.

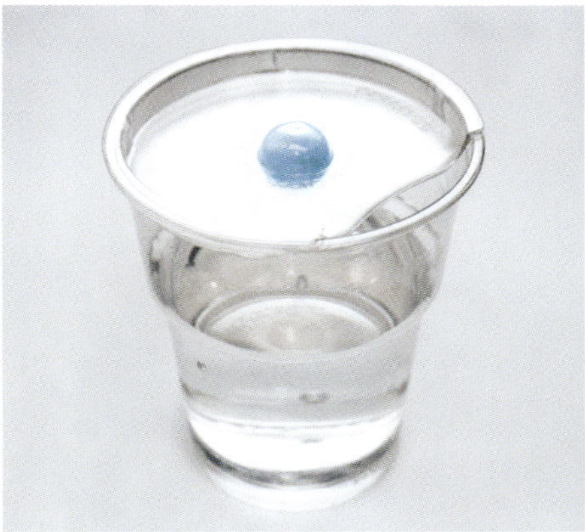

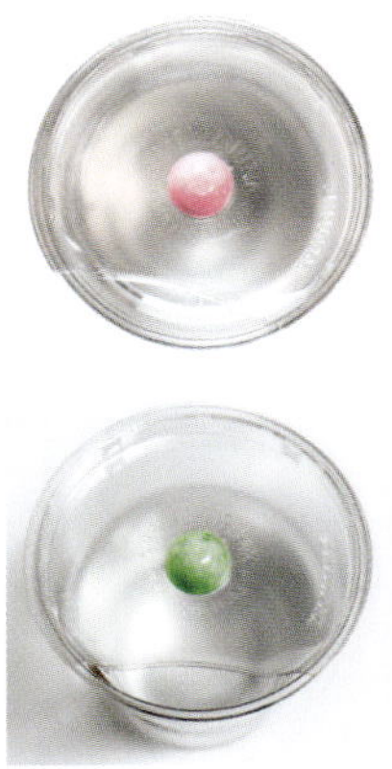

Smelldrinks, 2003

A scent concept invented back in 1996 by Peter de Cupere and realised in 2003 for the 'smell film' Sniff Receptor. On opening night, more than 700 visitors tried out various Smelldrinks.
Via a small scent container, one can experience a smell while drinking water.
The water can be replaced by sparkling water, for example, combined with the scent of Coke or fruit juice. At the opening, the following scents could be tested, among others: the smell of coffee or peppermint with warm water, the smell of Coke, orange, celery, lemon, strawberry, amaretto (sweet almond scent).

Geurconcept, reeds in 1996 uitgevonden door Peter de Cupere en gerealiseerd in 2003 voor de geurfilm *Sniff Receptor*. Tijdens de openingsavond probeerden meer dan 700 bezoekers verschillende Smelldrinks uit.
Via een kleine geurhouder kan men tijdens het drinken van water een extra geurbelevenis hebben. Men kan het water vervangen door bruiswater en dit bv. combineren met de geur van cola of fruitsap. Op de opening kon men o.a. volgende geuren uittesten: de geur van koffie of pepermunt met warm water, de geur van cola, appelsien, selder, citroen, aardbei, amaretto (zoete amandelgeur).

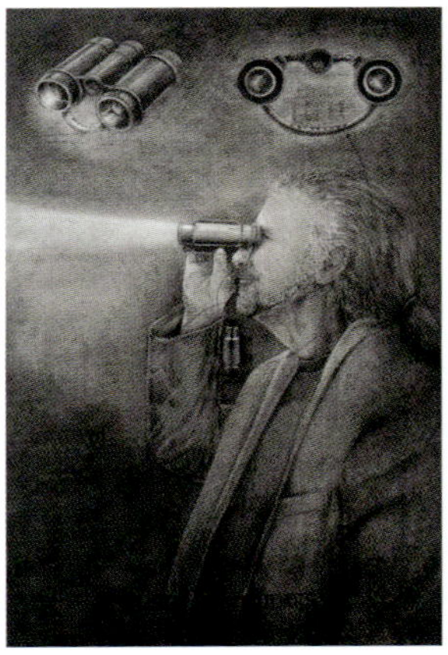

Smell Binocular, 2013

Framed 59,5 cm x 42,5 cm x 7 cm

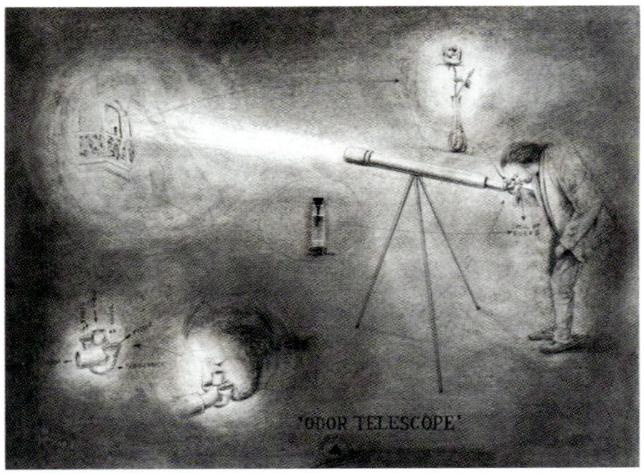

Odor Telescope, 2013

67 cm x 53 cm x 7 cm

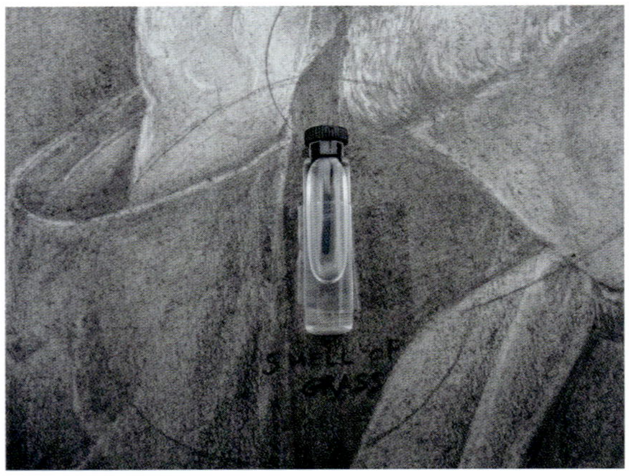

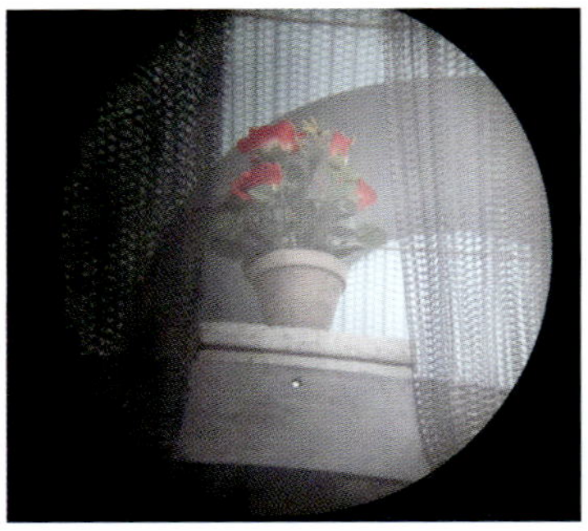

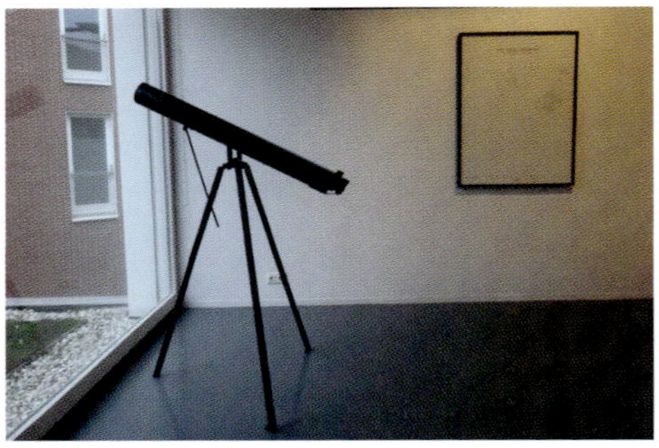

The Art of Smelling, Olfactory Art Research, Art Center Rozendaal 21, Yasmijn Jarram, Enschede, NL 01.12.2013-02.03.2014

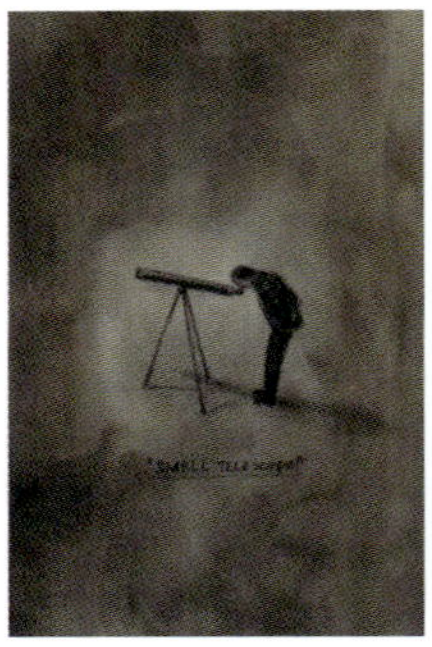

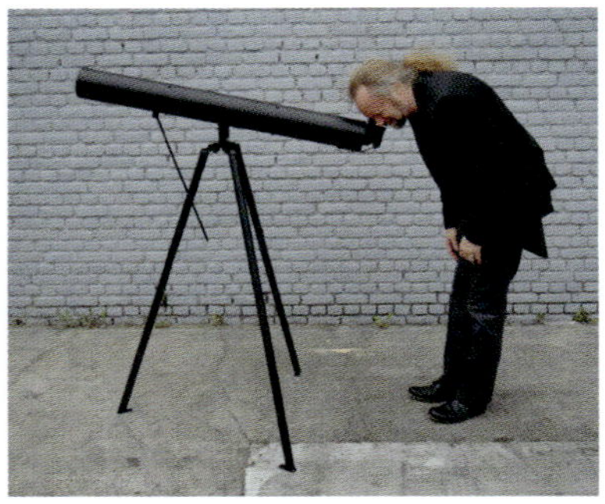

Smell Telescope, 2013

Drawing on wood / Tekening op hout, 30 cm x 20 cm x 3 cm

Odor telescope, 2013

The odour telescope is used to smell objects from a distance. At an exhibit in Kortrijk, Belgium, for example, visitors could smell the gunpowder in a cannon ball from a distance. At the exhibition 'The Art of Smelling, Olfactory Art Research' in Enschede, the Netherlands, people could smell a rose on a balcony on the museum across the street.

Met de odor telescope kan men objecten vanop een afstand ruiken. Zo kon men in een tentoonstelling in Kortrijk het buskruit van een kanonskogel vanop afstand ruiken. In de tentoonstelling The art Of Smelling, Olfactory Art Research in Enschede kon men een roos op een balkon van het tegenoverliggend museum ruiken.

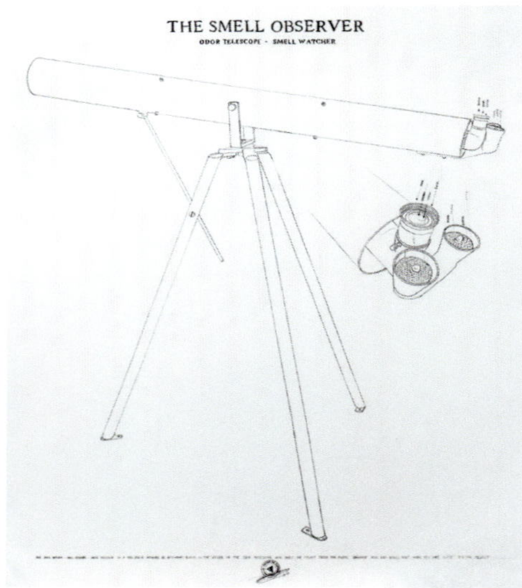

The Smell Observer, 2013

Drawing, 113,5 cm x 87,5 cm

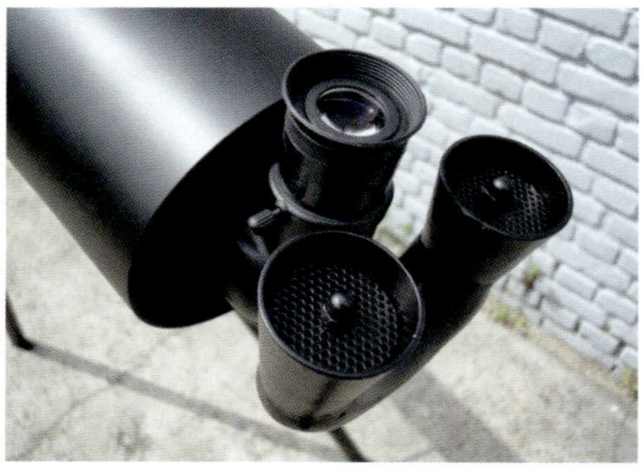

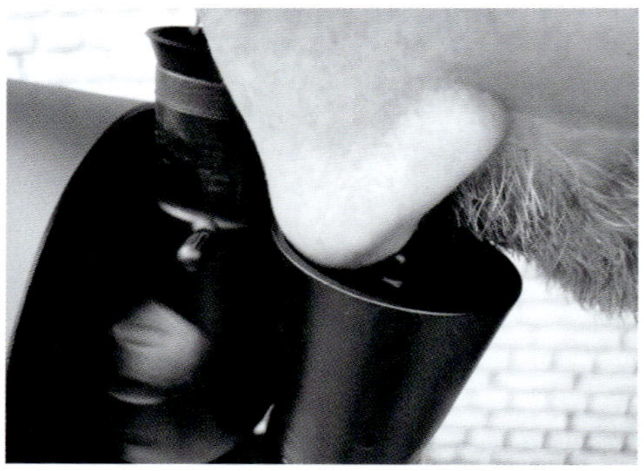

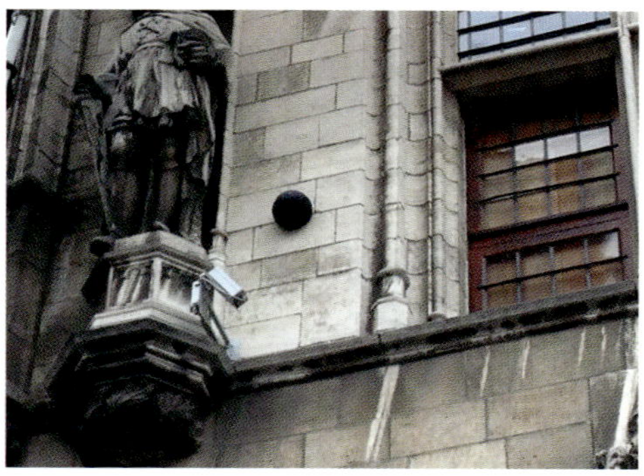

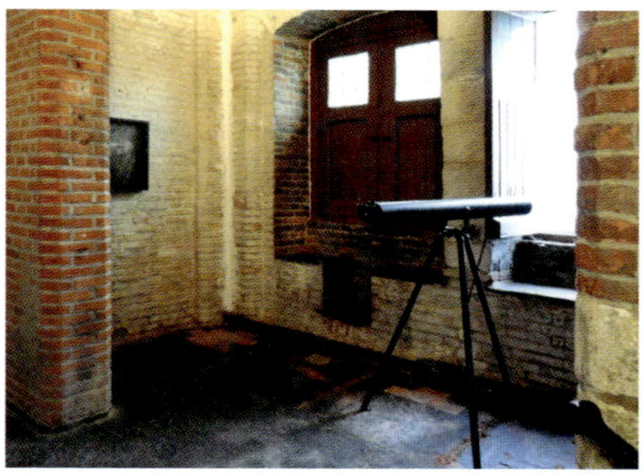

Kortrijk Vlaandert, curator Hilde Van Canneyt, Kortrijk, BE, 04.07.2013-18.08.2013

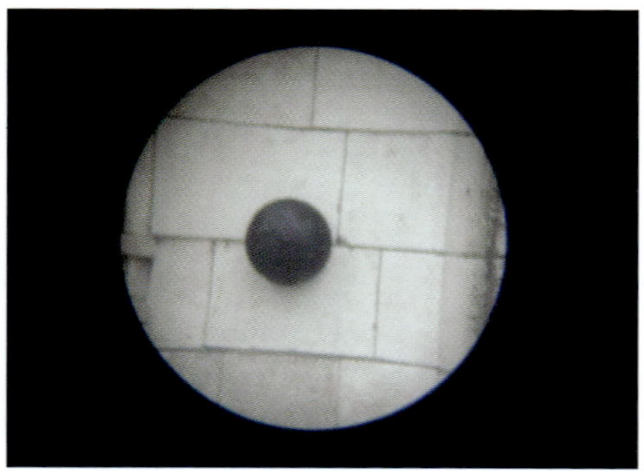

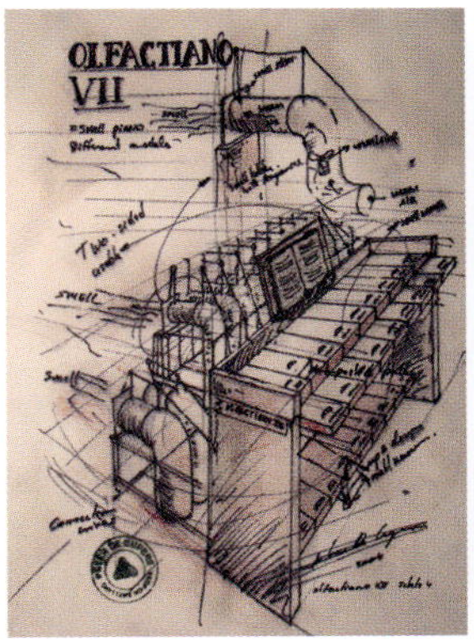

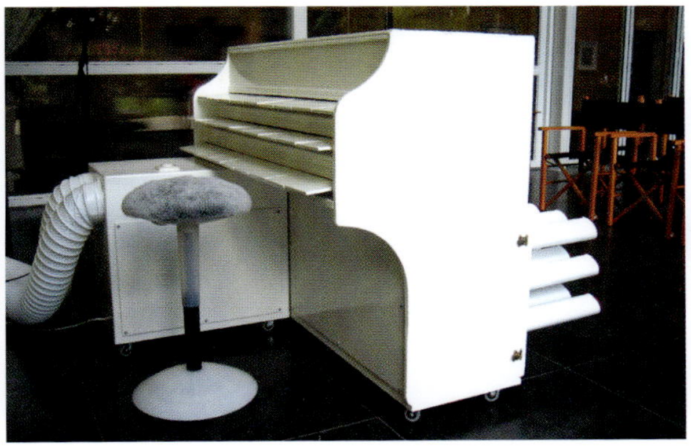
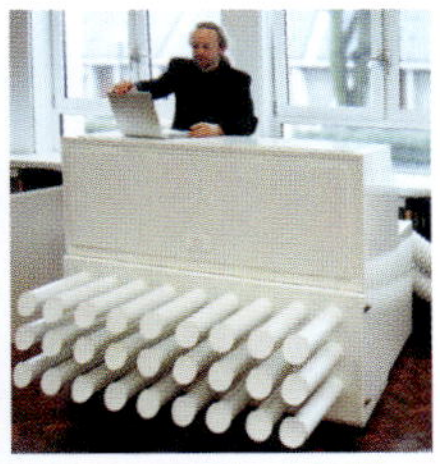
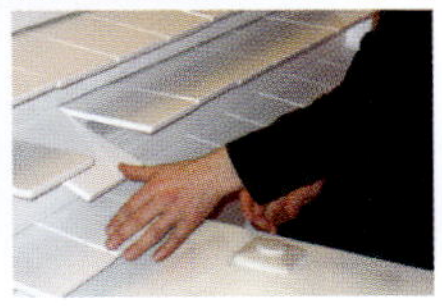
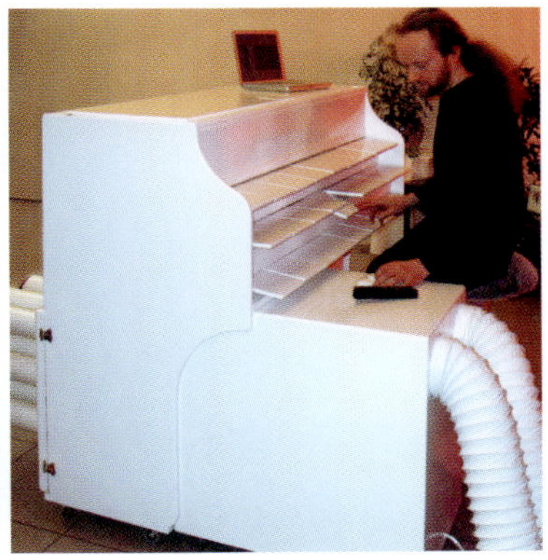

Olfactiano VII, 2004

The Olfactiano works like a mix of a piano and an organ. The 'scent composer' uses the adjustable airpower to create a scent sonata. The keys of the scent piano are subdivided into three layers, just like the three notes in a perfume–base, middle and top notes. The Olfactiano has 27 keys, allowing the user to create more than 4,374 different scent combinations depending on the desired scent intensity. The fragrances can be replaced by other scents depending on the concert. The scent intensity must be adjusted to the venue, the ventilation in the room, the humidity level and the number of participants in the scent concert. Olfactiano VII is the seventh olfaction work created by the artist, but the first one that can play for an audience. The six earlier versions were made for the artist's personal use, to compose concerts and experiment with mixing fragrances to explore their effects in different situations. The artist chose 27 specific scents–or rather, 26 scents and 1 scent divider that is left open to fill the room with fresh air. The idea of using 26 scents is based on his research into the creation of a scent alphabet. So instead of actually reading a book, you could simply close your eyes and focus on the fragrances and the way they mix. You could sniff the sentences and let your imagination do the rest. This would have a lot of benefits, also for people with visual disabilities. The artist has been carrying out research into the creation of a scent alphabet since 1996. Barely a year later, he created his first Olfactiano.

The way people react to a scent concert depends on a lot of factors. Blind people are generally the most excited about it and they can recognise the scents better than anyone else. People who can see sometimes react in a strange way. It always depends on the kind of scent concert the artist has created. The reaction of the audience is mostly based on their own memories of a specific scent. For example, some people might not recognise the smell of leather and can be scared of this fragrance, especially if it is pigskin. The smell of cowhide is less scary for them. Does this say something about the persons in question or how memory works, or how we relate to things in general? There are more reactions, of course, too many to mention. And what with different cultures? People's reaction to certain fragrances is also, in a way, influenced by their origins.

As such, every single concert is surprising. When participating in a scent concert, you will experience first-hand how your deeper senses are given meaning. To sniff around in the dark and listen to or 'read' smells, makes you realise there are still a lot of things to discover through your own body. The artist sees the scent concert as a way to create a perfume through time. As the room fills with the different scents, at a given moment there will be a general scent in the room, which will linger. That's the best sign to stop the concert. Most concerts take between 7 and 15 minutes. This might seem very short, but in these minutes the audience is overwhelmed with fragrances of the best quality. The participants are surprised at how they can smell each scent separately until a certain level is reached. Most of the time, it is achieved after 5 minutes, but depending on the humidity, temperature, size, volume and shape of the room, the concert can last longer. To help him prepare his concerts, the artist developed a dedicated computer programme. Before starting the concerts, he programs certain parameters linked to the measurements of the room, temperature and humidity levels. That allows him to prepare the concert properly. He just needs to check the scent scores on his monitor. The artist has been working on an eighth version for three years, which will have more features and will provide a selection of over 100 different scents!

De Olfactiano functioneert als een mix tussen een piano en een orgel. De geurcompon(ist)ent genereert een aanpasbare luchtdruk om een sonate te creëren. De tonen van de geurpiano zijn opgesplitst in 3 lagen, net zoals de 3 toonaarden in een parfum namelijk lage, midden- en hoge noten. De Olfactiano heeft 27 toetsen waardoor de gebruiker 4.374 verschillende geurcombinaties kan maken, afhankelijk van de gewenste geurintensiteit. De geuren kunnen vervangen worden door andere geuren in functie van het concert. De geurintensiteit moet aangepast worden aan de locatie, waarbij ventilatie, vochtigheid en het aantal toeschouwers een rol spelen.

Olfactiano VII is reeds de zevende geurpiano, maar de eerste die ook daadwerkelijk kan spelen voor een publiek. De vorige zes edities werden gemaakt voor persoonlijk gebruik van de kunstenaar, om concerten te componeren of te experimenteren met verschillende geurmixen en hun effecten binnen verschillende situaties. De kunstenaar koos bewust voor 27 specifieke geuren – of beter gezegd 26 geuren en 1 geurverdeler die functioneert om binnen de ruimte verse lucht te voorzien.

Het idee om 26 geuren te gebruiken is gebaseerd op zijn onderzoek om een geuralfabet te ontwerpen. In plaats van een boek te lezen, kan je eenvoudigweg je ogen sluiten en je concentreren op de geuren en de wijze dat ze met elkaar vermengen. Je kan de geuren ook opsnuiven en in je verbeelding laten werken.

Dit kan een groot voordeel zijn voor mensen met een visuele handicap. Sinds 1996 doet de kunstenaar reeds onderzoek naar dit geuralfabet. Slechts één jaar later ontstond de eerste Olfactiano.

Mensen reageren heel uiteenlopend op een geurconcert. Blinde mensen reageren met het grootste enthoesiasme en zij slagen er ook meestal in geuren beter te herkennen. Mensen die zien, reageren soms heel raar, afhankelijk van de gemaakte keuzes van de kunstenaar. De reacties van mensen variëren voornamelijk naargelang hun persoonlijke herinneringen aan een specifieke geur. Verschillende mensen kunnen de geur van leer niet herkennen of schrikken er soms zelfs van, vooral als het varkensleder is. De geur van koeienleder is minder confronterend. Zegt dit enerzijds iets over het individu of hoe geheugen werkt en hoe we naar de dingen kijken? Er zijn nog tal van andere reacties. En wat gezegd over de invloed binnen verschillende culturen? Mensen reageren heel verschillend en individueel op bepaalde geuren. De reden is dat we sterk worden beïnvloed door onze roots.

Dit betekent dat elk concert weer een verrassing inhoudt voor de toeschouwer. Wanneer je een optreden life meemaakt, ervaar je in een bevoorrechte situatie de waarde van je diepere gevoelens. In het donker ruiken en geuren lezen, doet een mens beseffen dat er nog heel veel zaken te ontdekken zijn, o.a. via het lichaam.

Voor de kunstenaar is een geurconcert een manier om een nieuw parfum te maken doorheen de tijd. Wanneer de ruimte zich vult met de verschillende geuren, zal er na verloop van tijd één geur zijn die overheerst. Dat is het moment om het concert te staken. De meeste concerten duren gemiddeld tussen 7 en 15 minuten. Dit lijkt kort maar eigenlijk wordt het publiek overweldigd door geuren van de beste kwaliteit. Tot men een zeker saturatieniveau bereikt, kan men alle geuren nog vatten en ruiken maar na een vijftal minuten treedt geurgewenning op, die op zijn beurt afhankelijk is van vochtigheid en temperatuur, maar ook van het formaat, volume en vorm van de ruimte.

Om zijn composities te creëren maakt de kunstenaar gebruik van een speciaal ontworpen computerprogramma dat rekening houdt met verschillende parameters zoals de dimensies van de ruimte en temperatuur- en vochtigheidsniveaus. Op zijn monitor controleert de kunstenaar de geurscores. De toekomstige en achtste geurpiano is in constructie en deze nieuwe versie zal Peter de Cupere toelaten om zijn concerten nog beter te beheersen en te kunnen spelen met een selectie van 100 geuren.

Scentconcerts with the Olfactiano through Europe, different locations, BE, 2004-2007
First exhibition and scent concert: 'Cordoba', scent piano and scent concerts, Beursschouwburg, curator Guido Minne, Brussels, BE, 10-21.11.2004
The scents for the first Scent Concerts were sponsored by IFF International.

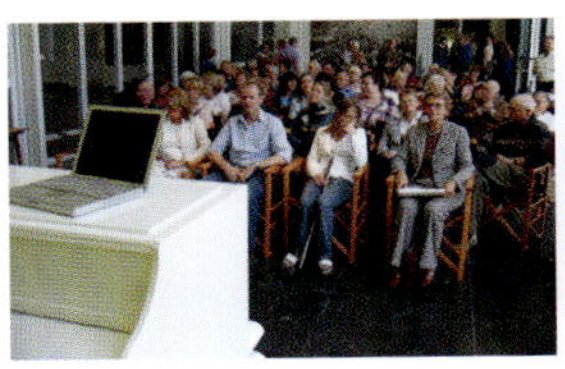
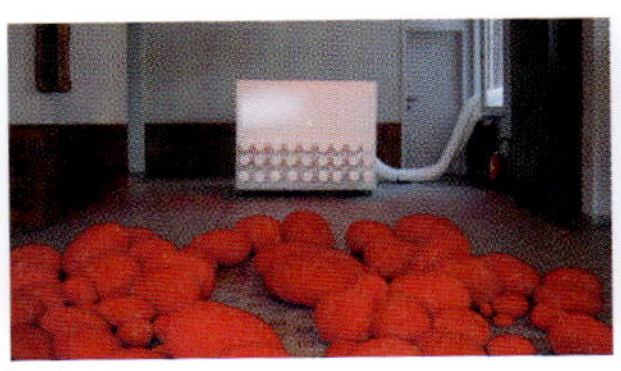
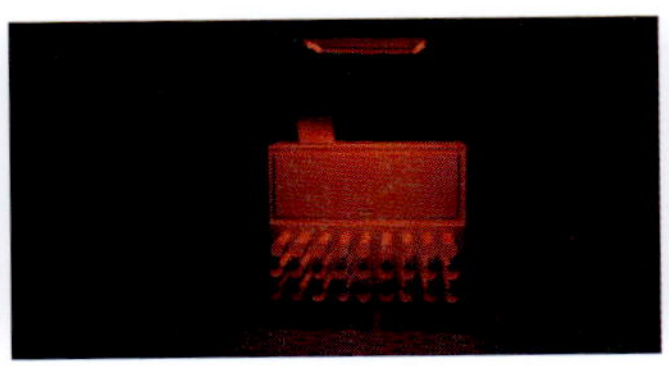
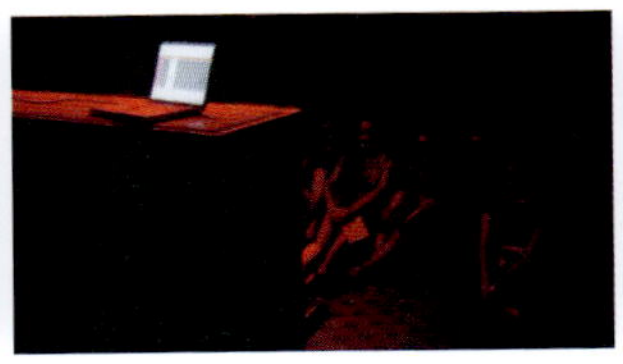
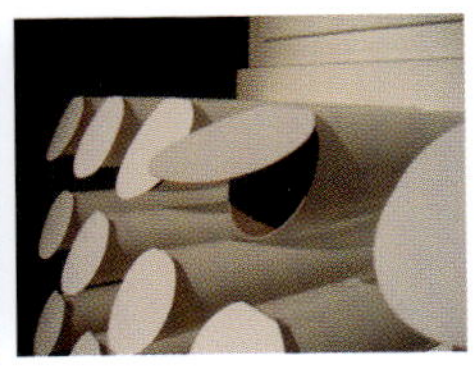

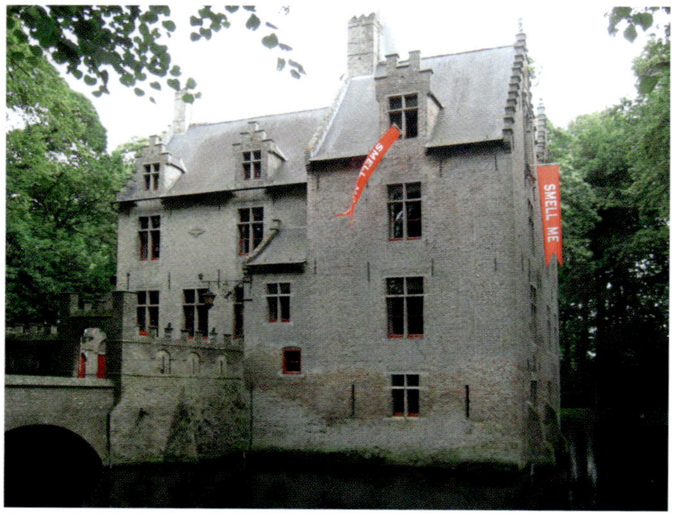

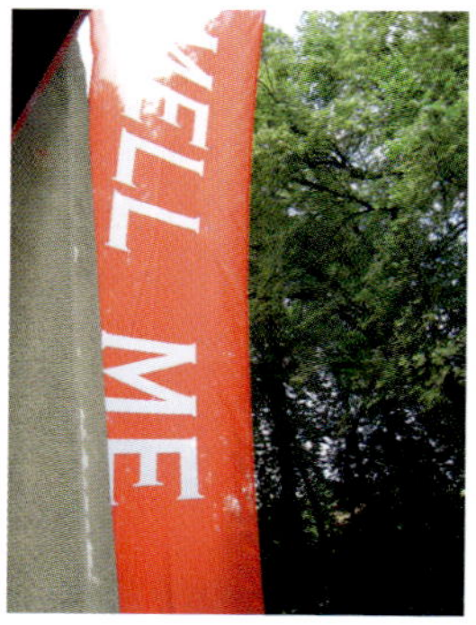

Smell Me, Smell The Castle, 2007

The banners of the castle invited visitors to smell on the walls and furniture in parallel with the artworks in the exhibition.

De vlaggen op het kasteel nodigden sommige bezoekers uit om niet alleen de werken in de tentoonstelling te gaan ruiken maar ook de muren en meubelen.

Smell the Castle, Castle Beauvoorde, curator Annemie Morisse, Beauvoorde, BE
15.07.2007-30.08.2007

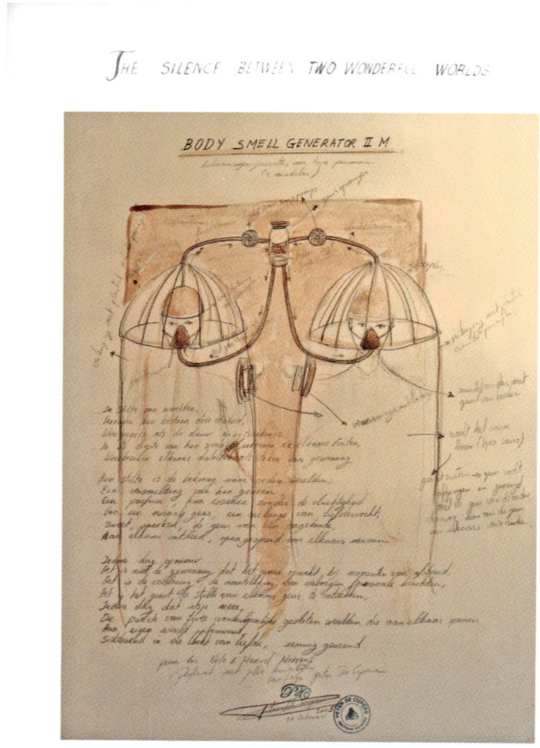

Drawing Body Smell Generator, 2005

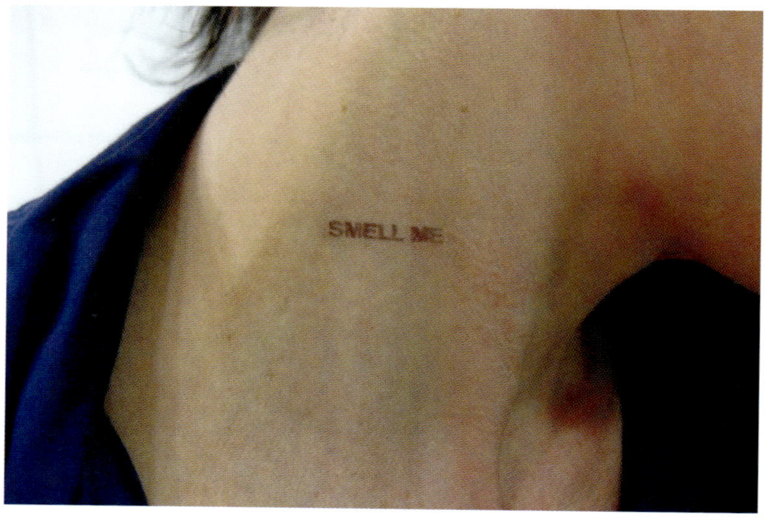

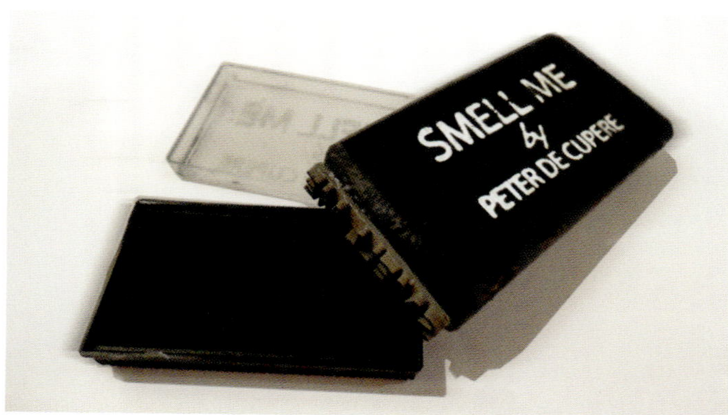

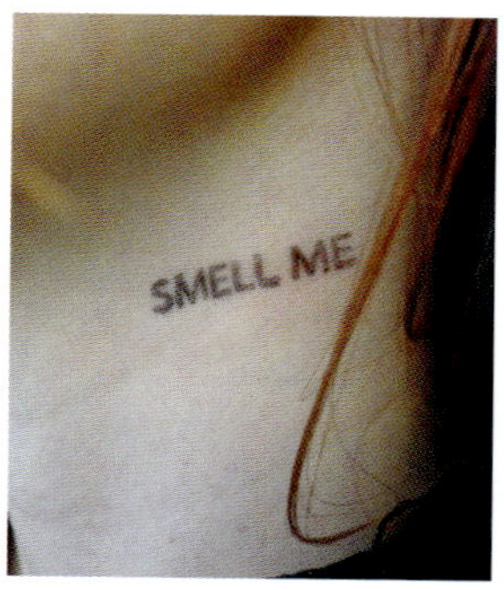

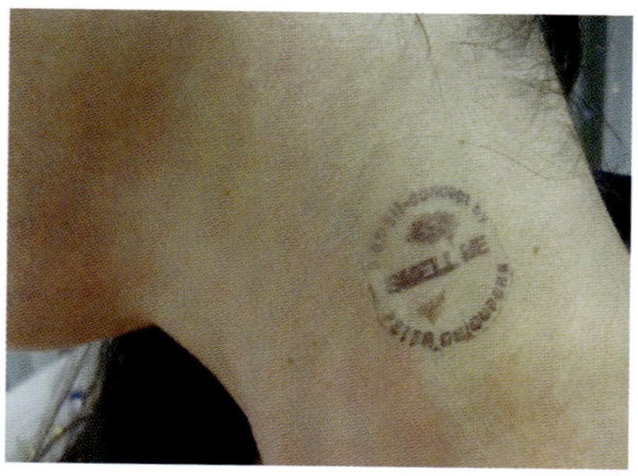

Smell Me Perfume happening

Visitors are given a special scent-stamp, inviting other people to smell you. This interactive play of olfactory attraction or rejection is something every visitor can experience. The 'Smell Me Perfume', which the artist describes as your most personal perfume, has been tested and approved by a willing public at various times during openings, lectures and events since 1998. Discover for yourself the magic of what your own scent does to other people.

Bezoekers krijgen een speciale geurstempel bij de inkom die anderen aanzet aan je te ruiken. Dit interac tief spel van aantrekking en afstoting op olfactorisch gebied zal iedere toeschouwer levendig kunnen ervaren. Dit 'Smell Me Perfume', welke de kunstenaar als je meest persoonlijke parfum omschrijft, werd al verscheidene keren sinds 1998 tijdens openingen, lezingen, evenementen uitgetest en goedgekeurd door een welwillend publiek. Ontdek zelf de magie van je eigen geur op anderen! De Smell Me Happening werd sinds 2000 meer dan 20 keer gedaan tijdens openingen en lezingen.

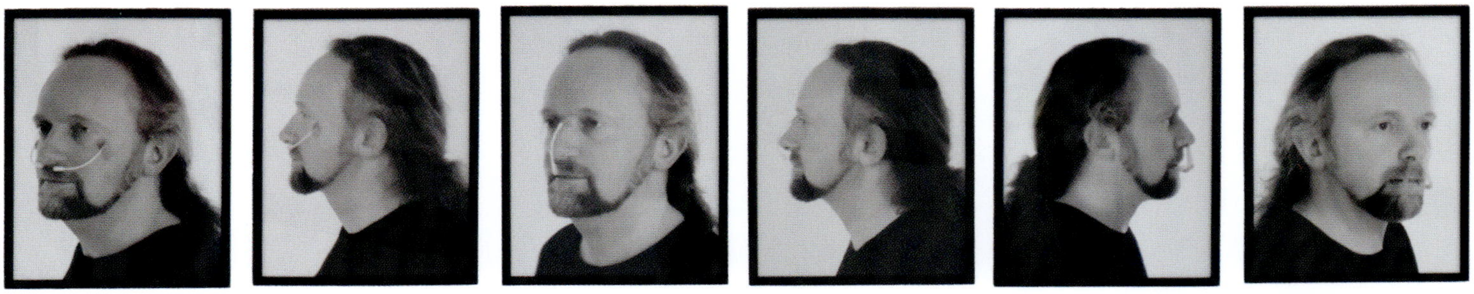

Breath Odor Devices, Stereo Sound Device, Mono Sound Device, 2014

These smell devices allow you to experience something of your own body odours.
They are very simple tools that anyone can make. The Breath Odour Device consists of two cut-off drinking straws.
The longer (both in time and in size of straw) the cut-off part sits in your mouth, the more the smell will change.
To perceive the smell of sound via a Sound Odour Device, you have first to remove some ear wax using a cotton bud and smell it. People will notice a very light smell that is a bit greasy. But if you listen to classical music for two days and then to heavy metal for two days, and eat the same foods and do the same things, you will notice a difference in smell. When the artist presented this work for the first time, people assumed that this clearly offered the first proof that sound also has a smell. That is, heavy metal music smells different, more metallic. This has nothing to do with the name of the music style, but simply the fact that it causes more blood to flow to the ears. The result is that the smell is more metallic, since blood is also perceived as having a metallic odour.

Via deze 'geur devices' kan men sommige van zijn eigen lichaamsgeuren ervaren.
Het zijn éénvoudige tools die men zelf kan maken. De *Breath Odor Device* bestaat uit twee afgeknipte drankspriestjes. Hoe langer (zowel in tijd als in grootte van sprietje) het afgeknipte gedeelte van het drankspriestje in je mond zit, zal de geur veranderen. Om de geur van geluid waar te nemen via een 'Odor Sound Device' moet men eerst met het wattenstaafje wat oorvet weghalen en hieraan ruiken. Men zal een vrij lichte geur opmerken die lichtjes vettig is. Maar als men nu twee dagen naar klassieke muziek luistert en daarna twee dagen naar heavy metal muziek en telkens ook hetzelfde eet, en hetzelfde doet, zal men een geurverschil opmerken. Toen de kunstenaar dit voor de eerste keer presenteerde, ging men er vanuit dat er duidelijk een eerste bewijs was gegeven dat geluid ook een geur heeft.
De heavy metal muziek ruikt nl. anders, meer bepaald meer metaalachtig. Dit heeft niets te maken met de benaming van de muziek maar eerder met het feit dat het harde muziek is en hierdoor meer bloed naar het gehoorte stroomt. Dit brengt met zich mee dat de geur meer metaalachtig wordt vermits bloed ook als een metaalachtige geur wordt ervaren.

Sense of Smell, Symposium, Moti Museum, Breda, NL, 02.12.2014
The Art of Smelling, Olfactory Art Research, Art Center Rozendaal 21, Yasmijn Jarram, Enschede, NL, 01.12.2013-02.03.2014
Kortrijk Vlaandert, curator Hilde Van Canneyt, Kortrijk, BE, 04.07.2013-18.08.2013
Urban Explorers Festival, Scent City Trail, Dordrechts Museum, Dordrecht, NL, 11.05.2013-12.05.2013

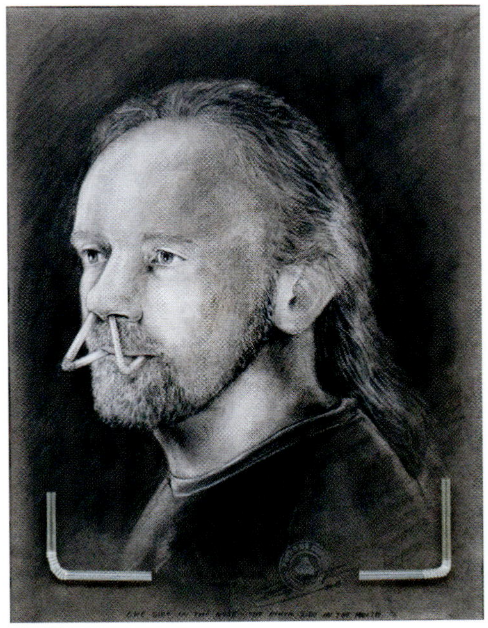

Breath Odor, 2013-2014

Grafiet, houtskool, 2 drankspriestjes,
36,5 cm x 28 cm

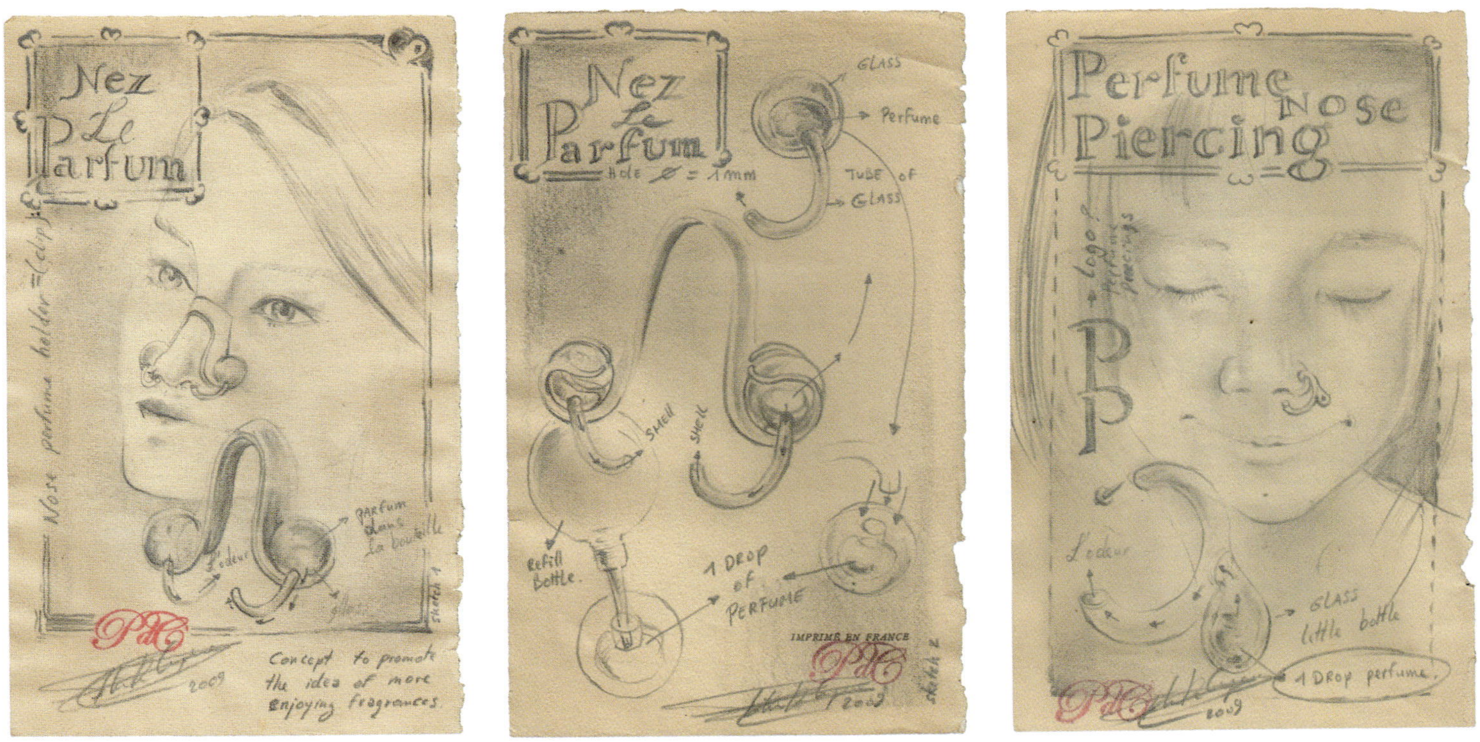

Perfume Jewels, 2009

Different sketches and designs for scent jewels, as an accessory to the nose. / Verschillende ontwerpen voor geurjuwelen, te dragen aan de neus.

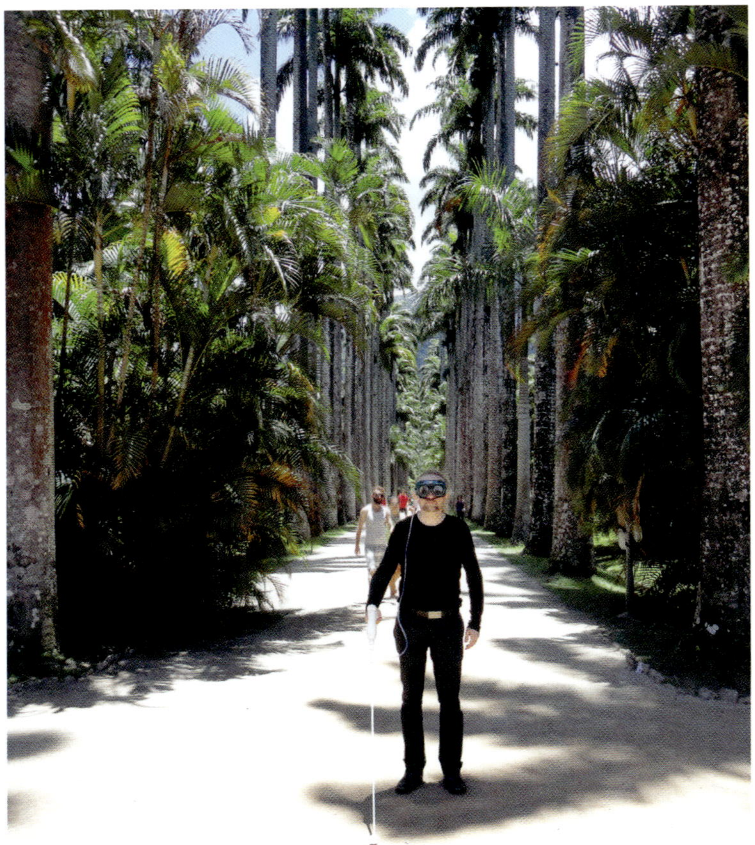

Blind Smell Stick, 2012

Find your way by smelling.

Discover the city and your surroundings simply by smelling.

With a Blind Smell Stick, you 'redesign' your own perception of a given location. By navigating via smells, you experience the city differently. You smell the ground and all the miasmas you encounter along the way. An experienced smeller would be able to find his or her way back by following the scents.

The Blind Smell Stick is an instinctive device. It allows you to refocus on your own instinctive behaviour. Depending on the smell you perceive, you will walk a bit farther or take a different route or take a short break to take in the unexpectedly rich olfactory palette.

If we gave every street a different smell, blind people could determine where they are in the city purely on the basis of the smell. To warn them in advance of an approaching intersection, for example, the smell of smoked meat could be used. When the light turns green, a smell of freshly mown grass could be activated so that they know the crosswalk is free–wide open like a meadow–to cross. We could think up more smell symbols in order to alert the visually impaired and make it more pleasant for them to find their way. But we don't have to perfume the entire street. We can also install a trail of scent that they can follow with the Blind Smell Stick.

The Blind Smell Stick is more than a smell device to help blind people find their way. It can be used in exhibitions to draw visitors' attention to smells in our society. The Blind Smell Stick consists of a number of components that ensure that the smells are drawn quickly and without any dust into the hollow part of the stick and are transported via a pipe to the user's nose. Another device that goes with the Blind Smell Stick is the Blind Smell Touch.

Several prototypes of both the Blind Smell Stick and the Blind Smell Touch have been created. The challenge now is to transport the smell even faster. Both smell devices are in progress and can be followed on the website www.smelldevices.com.

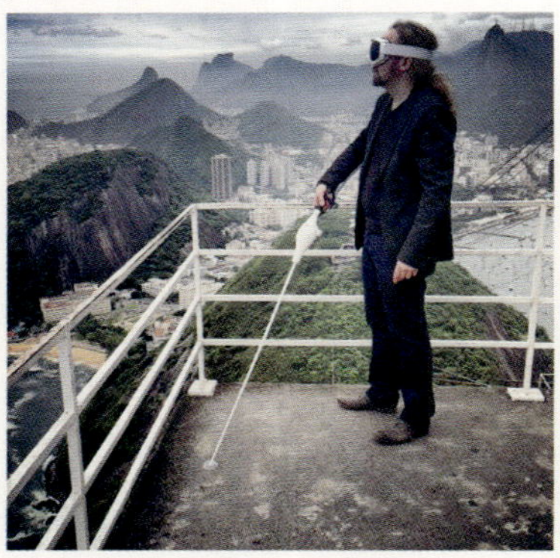

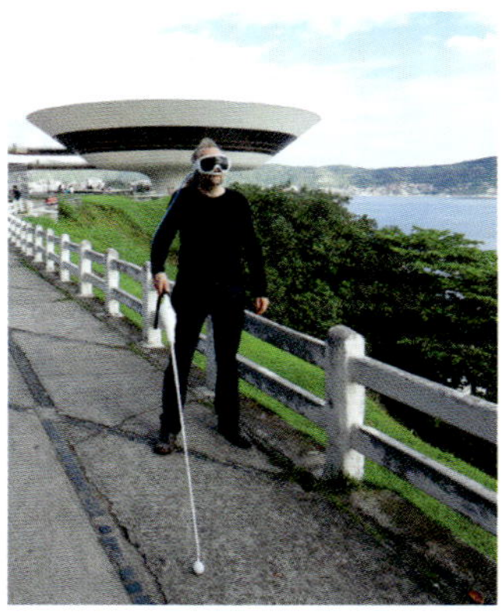

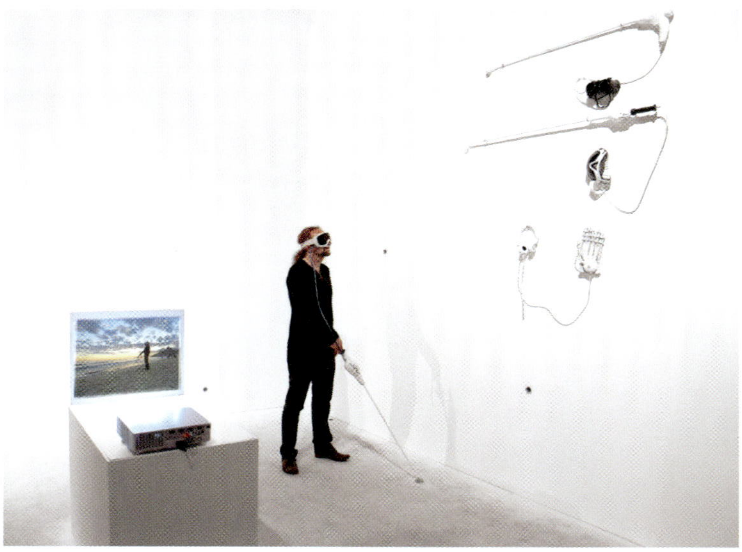

Vind je weg door te ruiken.

Ontdek de stad en je omgeving door gewoon te ruiken.

Met een *Blind Smell Stick* 're-design' je je eigen perceptie van een bepaalde locatie. Door te navigeren via te ruiken, ervaar je de stad op een andere manier. Je ruikt de grond en al de miasmen die zich op je weg bevinden. Een goed geoefend ruiker zou zo zijn weg ook kunnen terugvinden.
De Blind Smell Stick is een instinctief device. Het laat je terug focussen op je eigen instinctief gedrag. Naargelang welke geur je waarneemt, zal je verder wandelen of juist een andere weg inslaan of even verpozen bij het onverwachte rijke olfactorische pallet.

Moesten we iedere straat een geur geven zouden blinden puur op basis van de geur kunnen weten waar ze zich in een stad bevinden. Om hen te waarschuwen voor een kruispunt zou er zo bv. de geur van gerookt vlees gebruikt kunnen worden om hen tijdig in te lichten dat er een kruispunt is. Wanneer een licht op groen springt zou er een geur van een vers gemaaid grasveld even geactiveerd worden, zodat men weet dat het zebrapad vrij en wijds als een grasveld is om over te steken. En zo kunnen we wel meer geurtekenen bedenken om via de geur een blinde te waarschuwen en het hem aangenamer te maken om zijn weg te vinden. Maar we hoeven niet heel de straat te parfumeren. We kunnen ook een geurspoor aanleggen dat ze met een Blind Smell Stick kunnen volgen.

De Blind Smell Stick is meer dan een geurdevice om blinden op weg te helpen. Het kan in tentoonstellingen aangewend worden om bezoekers attenter te maken op geuren in de maatschappij. De Blind Smell Stick bestaat uit een aantal onderdelen die ervoor zorgen dat de geuren snel en zonder stof opgezogen worden in de holte van de stok en zo via een buiskanaal de geur transporteren naar de neus van de gebruiker. Een ander device dat aansluit bij de Blind Smell Stick is de *Blind Smell Touch*.
Zowel de Blind Smell Stick als de Blind Smell Touch zijn in verschillende prototype-versies uitgewerkt. De uitdaging is nu om de geur nog sneller te kunnen transporteren. Beide smell devices zijn in ontwikkeling en kunnen gevolgd worden op de website www.smelldevices.com

Sense of Smell, Symposium, Moti Museum, Breda, NL, 02.12.2014
Blind Smell Stick & Touch, The Olfactory, Ghent, BE, 6-12.11.2014
Creativity World Biennale, Rio De Janeiro, BR, 20.11.2012-25.11.201

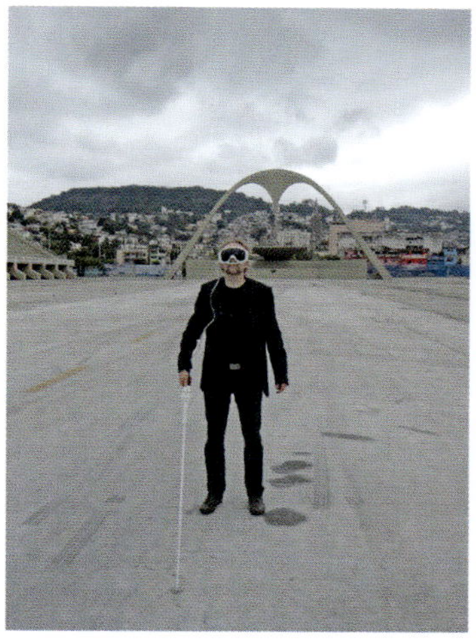

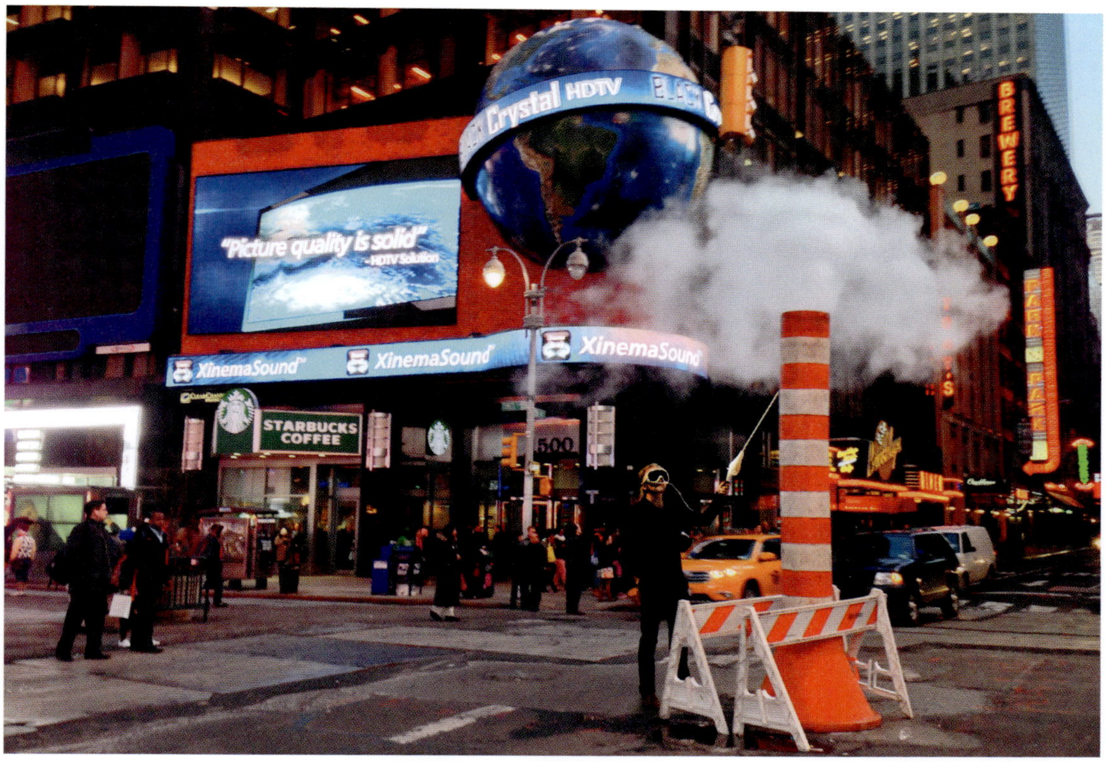

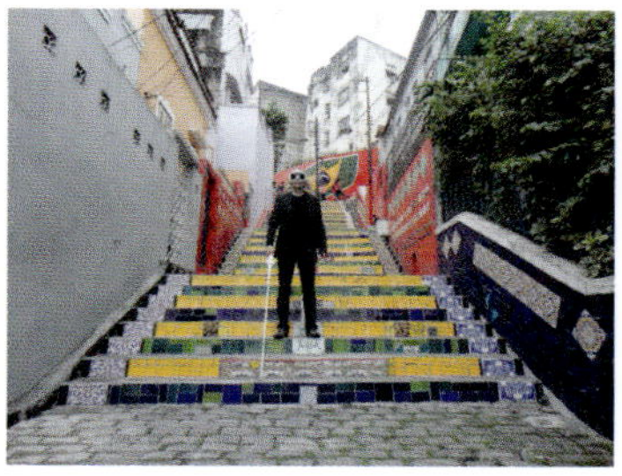

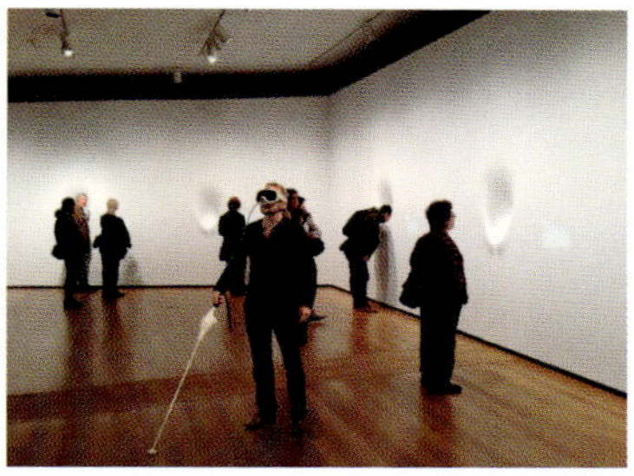

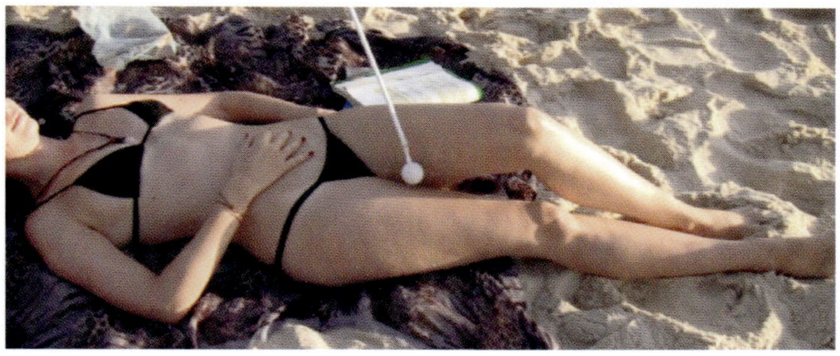

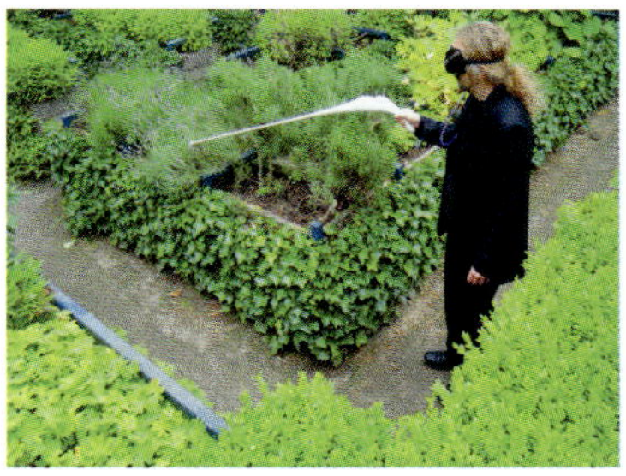

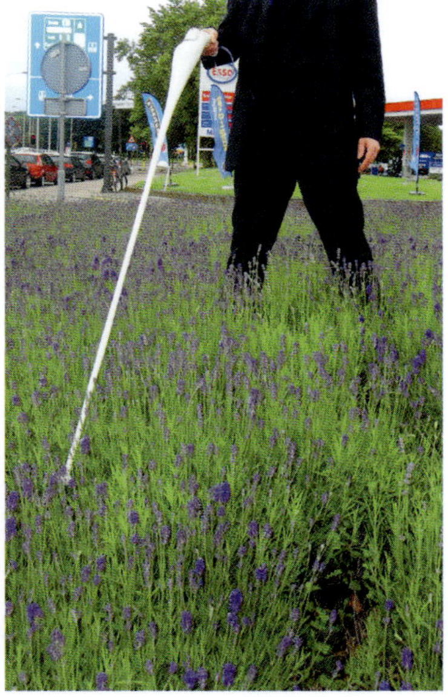

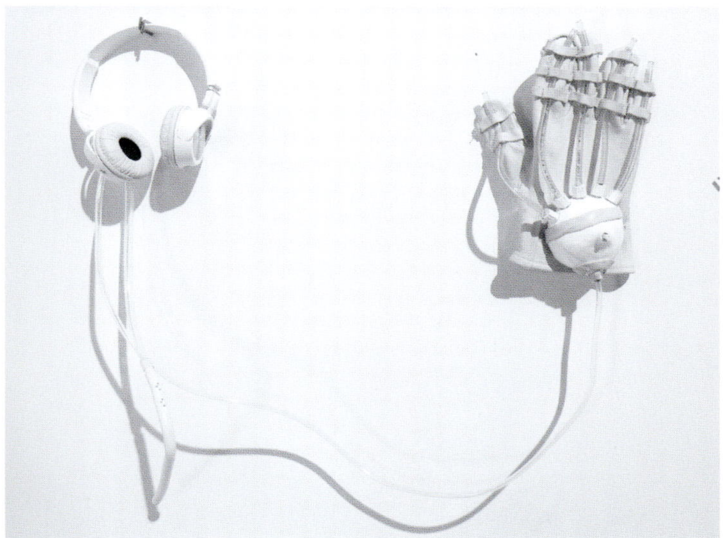

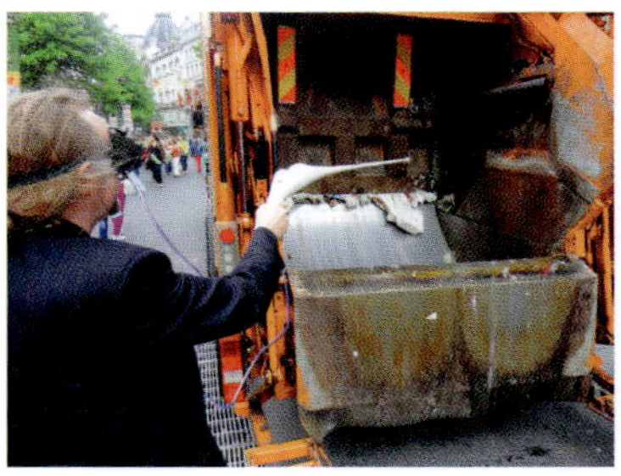

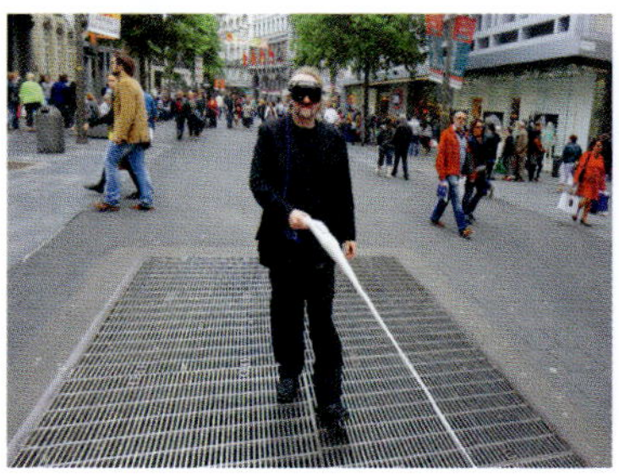

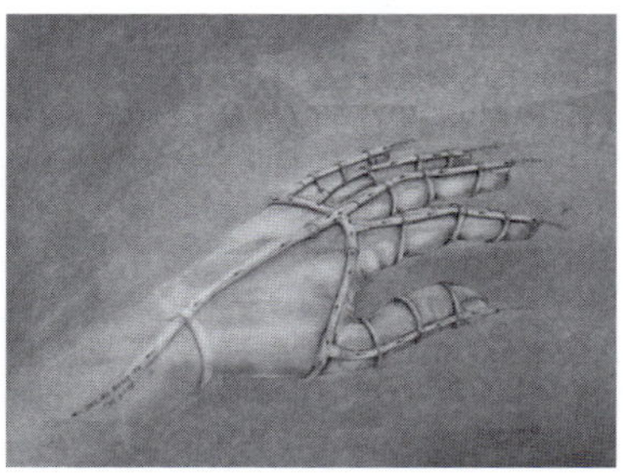

Blind Smell Touch, 2012

The Blind Smell Touch is a glove that allows you to smell objects, food, plants and persons at arm's length.

De Blind Smell Touch is een handschoen waarmee je objecten, voedsel, planten, personen op armafstand kan ruiken.

Sense of Smell, Symposium, Moti Museum, Breda, NL, 02.12.2014
Blind Smell Stick & Touch, The Olfactory, Ghent, BE, 6-12.11.2014
Off Senses/Future Senses, Gemak, The Hague, NL, 01.08.2014-27.09.2014
Creativity World Biennial, Rio de Janeiro, BR, 20.11.2012-25.11.2012

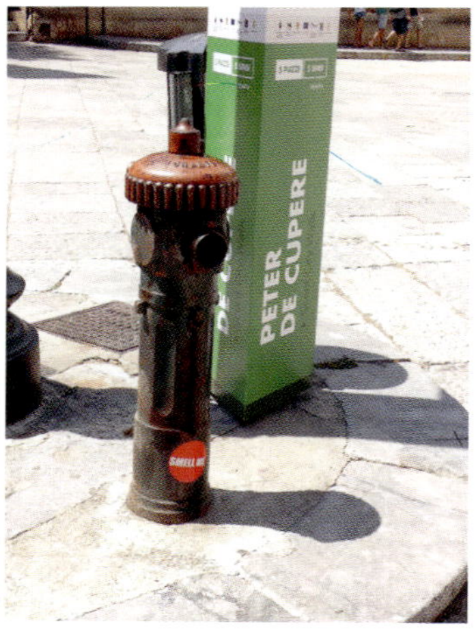

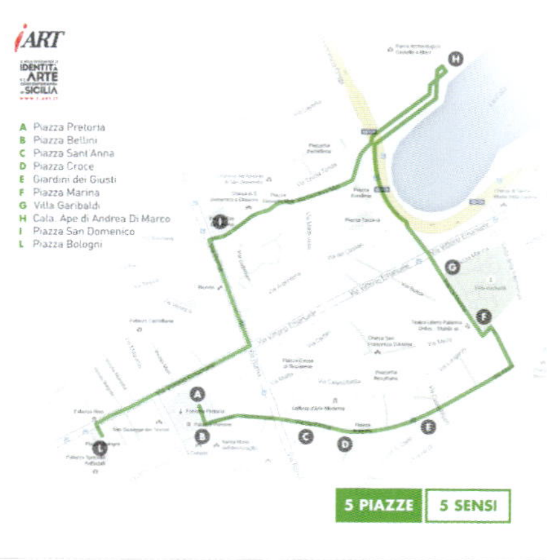

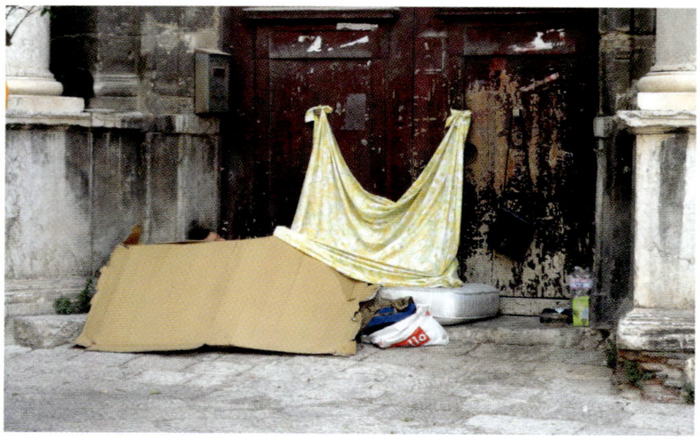

The artist had the permission of a homeless person to perfume his residence with lavender so that he could sleep wonderfully the next couple of nights. As a gift, the homeless person receives a bottle with lavender extract. The contrast of a homeless person's residence with the wonderful smell of lavender gives the visitor a different view on the usually not good smelling situation in which the homeless person lives.

De kunstenaar had de toelating van een dakloze om zijn tijdelijke verblijfplaats te parfumeren met lavendel zodat hij de volgende nachten kon slapen in een aangename geur. Als geschenk ontving de dakloze een fles met lavendelextract. Het contrast van de geïmproviseerde verblijfplaats en de heerlijke geur van lavendel confronteert de bezoeker met de situatie van daklozen.

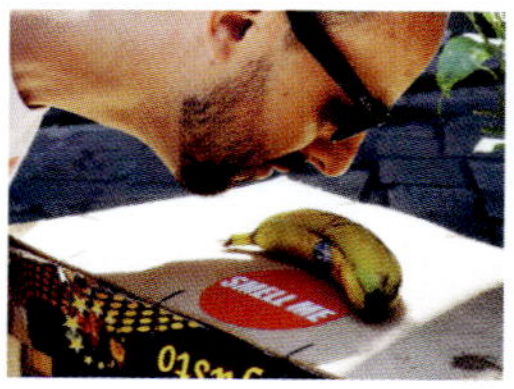

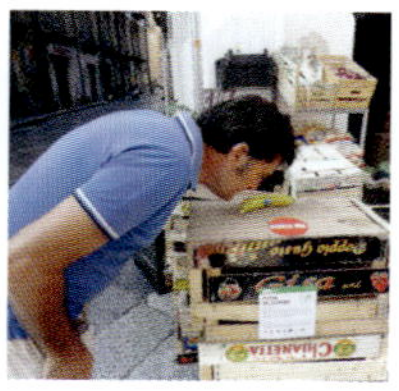

A banana was smelling to vagina scent.
Een banaan met vaginageur.

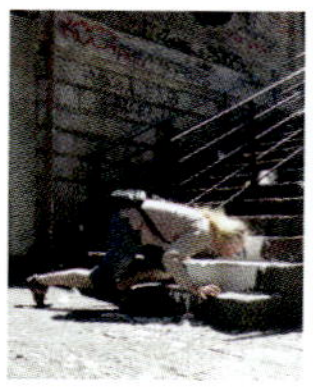

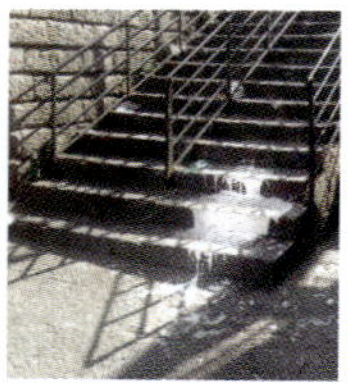

The scent of sperm was added on a white splash of paint. / De geur van sperma in een witte verfvlek.

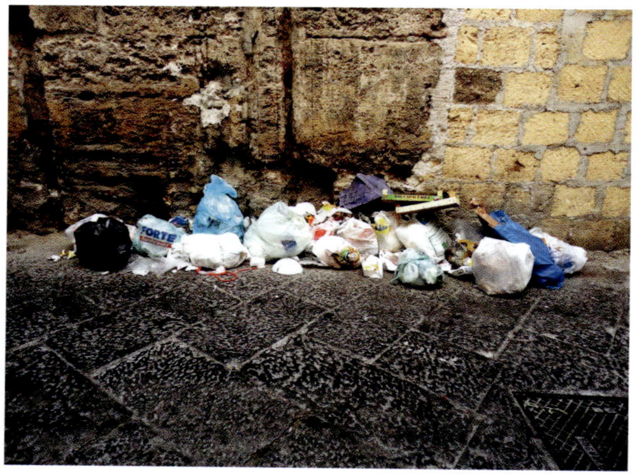

33 smells connect 10 important historical locations of Palermo. On their way, people could experience the scent of garbage bins differently because they were all perfumed with peppermint or the scent of Limoncello, a typical Sicilian alcoholic drink. Sometimes no scent is added and the visitor is confronted with the intense stench which is being reinforced by the sun beams in Palermo where on average it was 32 °C in the shade!

33 geuren verbinden 10 belangrijke en historische plaatsen in Palermo. Onderweg konden de deelnemers de geur van een vuilbak anders ervaren omdat ze allemaal geparfumeerd waren met pepermuntsmaak of de geur van Limoncello, een typische Siciliaanse alcoholische drank. Op bepaalde plekken is geen geur aangebracht. Soms wordt de bezoeker overvallen door een extreme stank, versterkt door de warmte bij een gemiddelde temperatuur van 32°C.

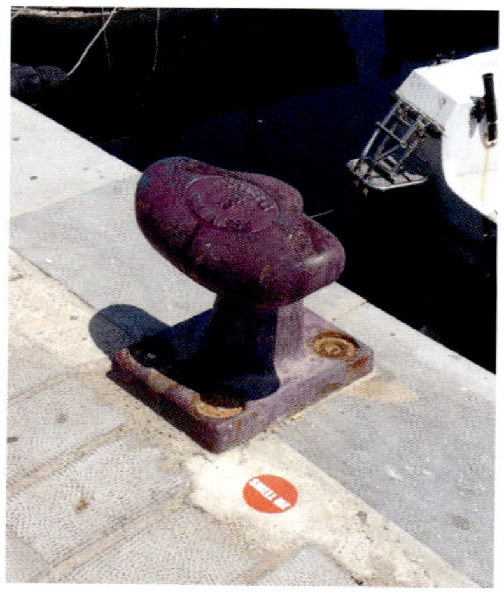

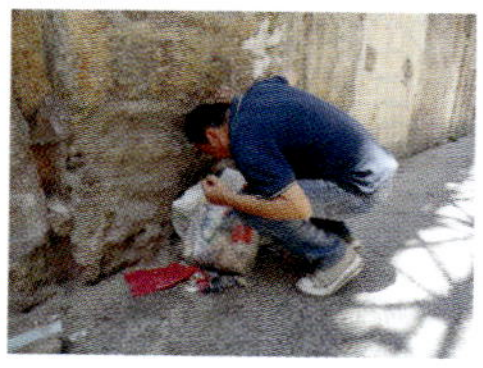

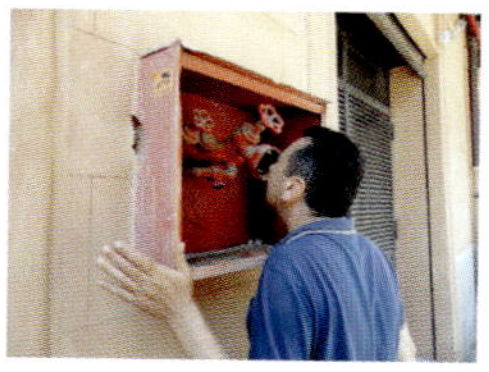

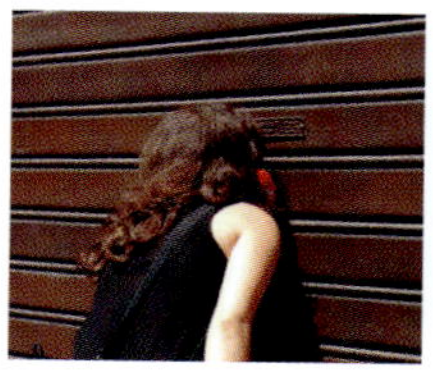

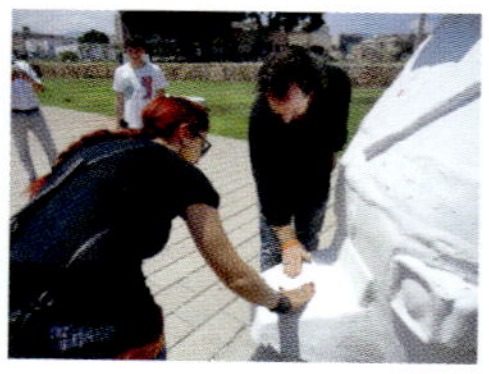

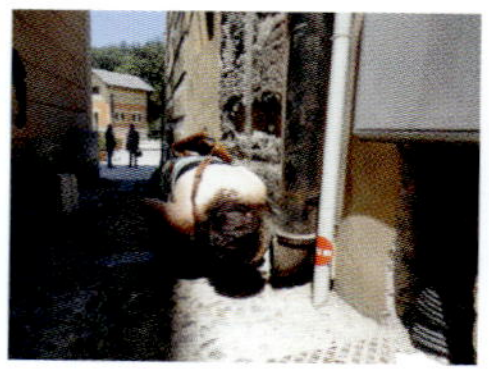

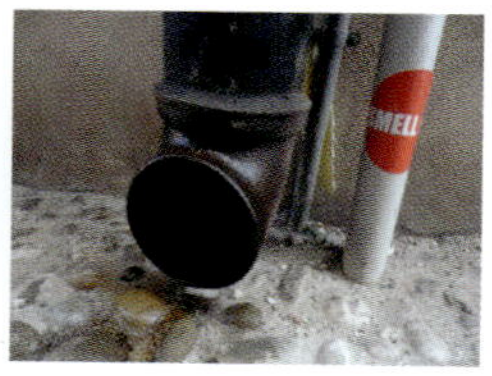

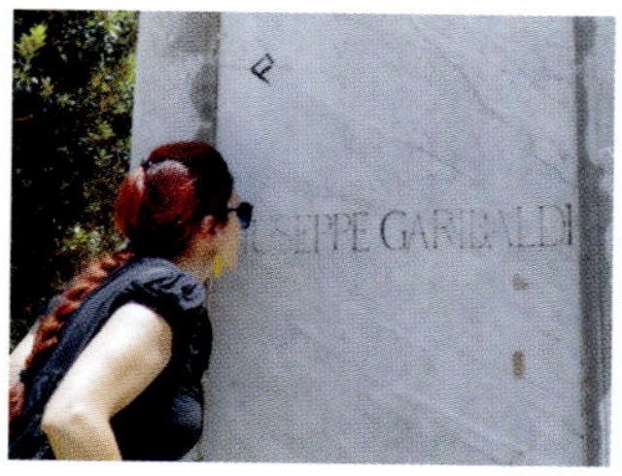

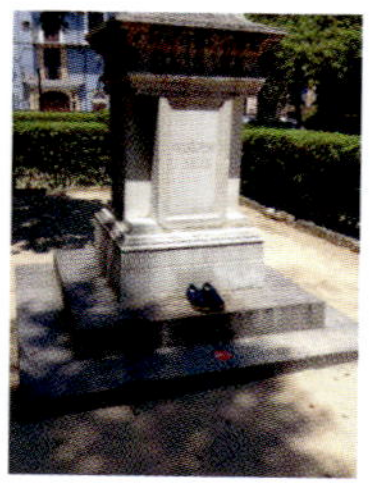

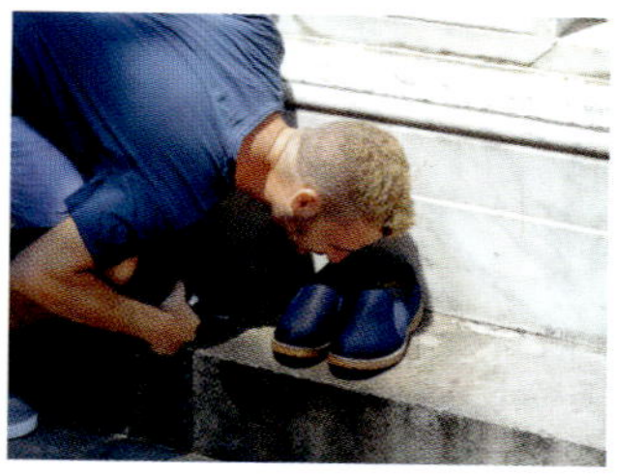

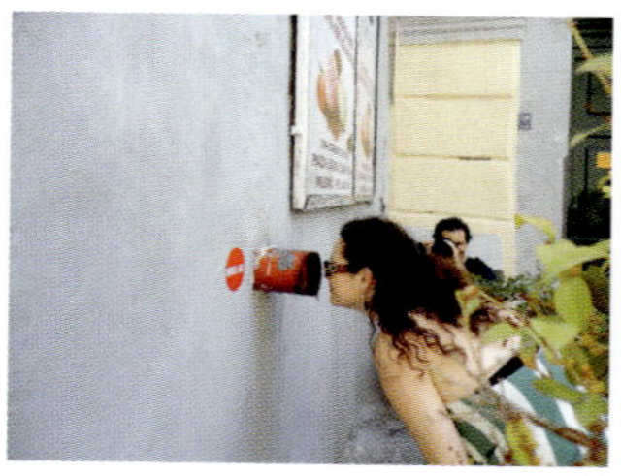

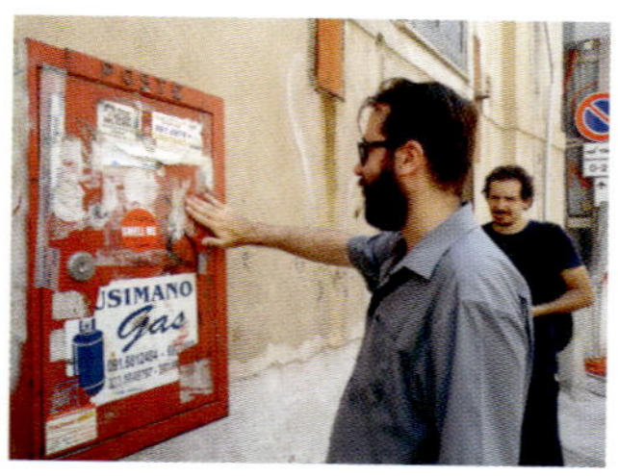

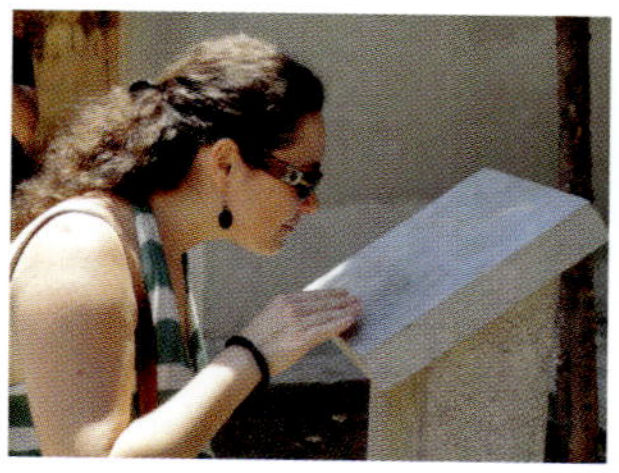

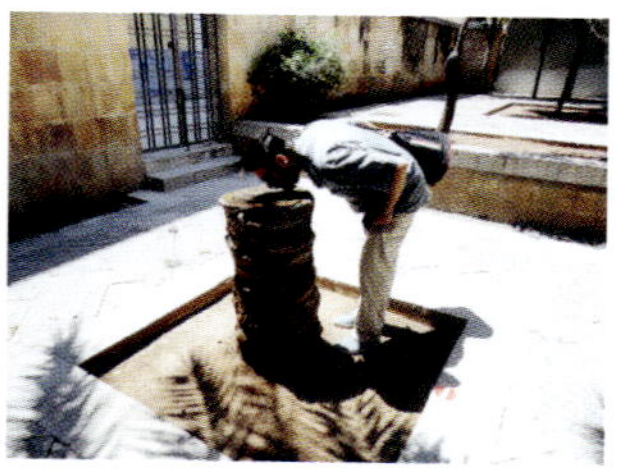

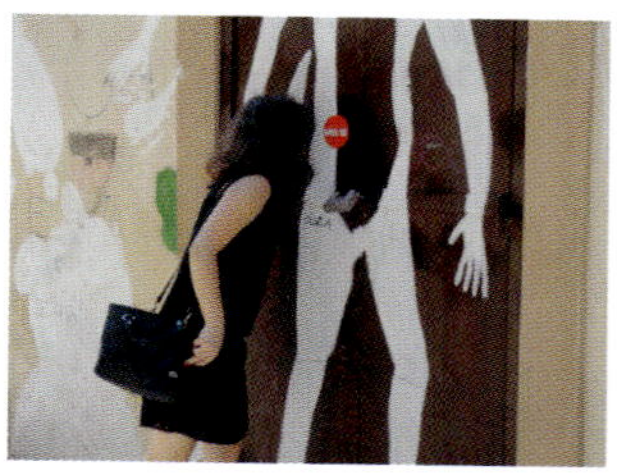

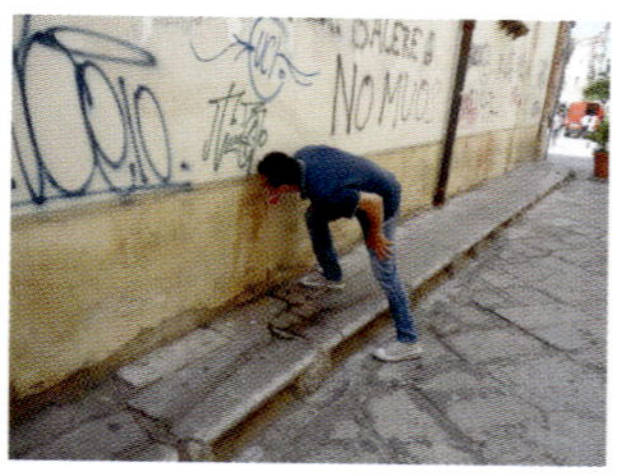

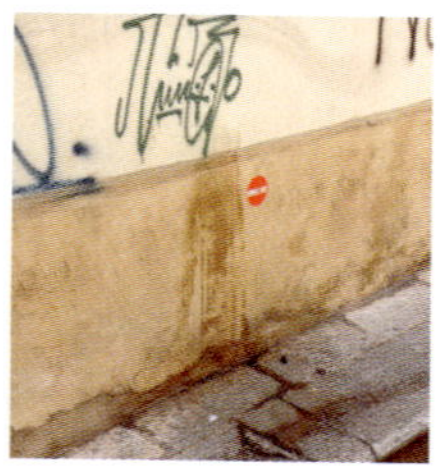

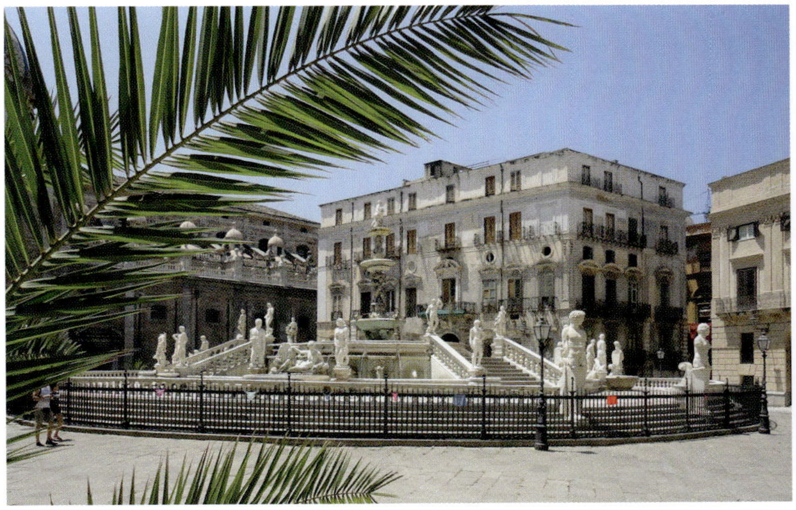

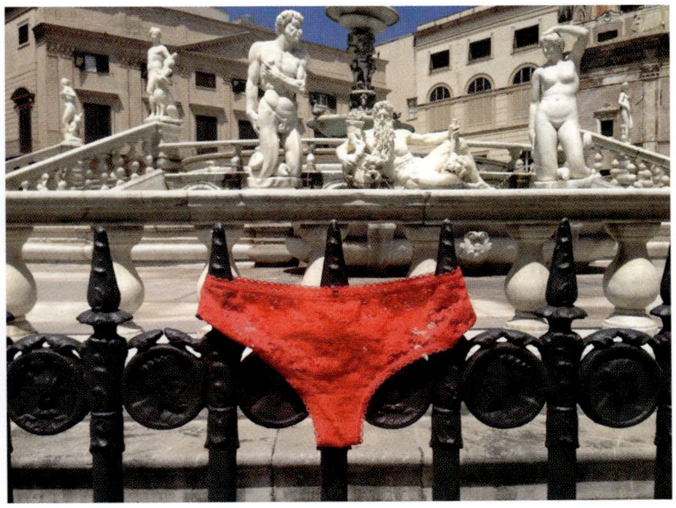

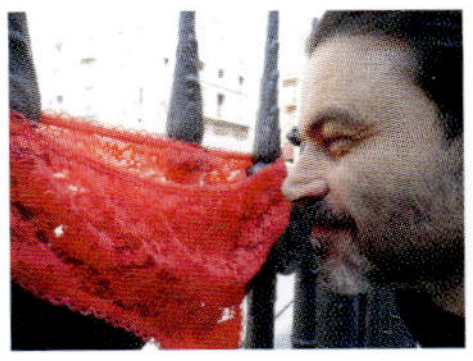

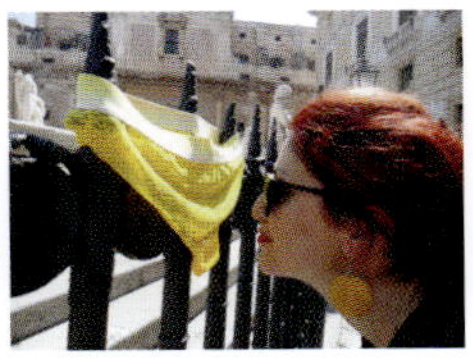

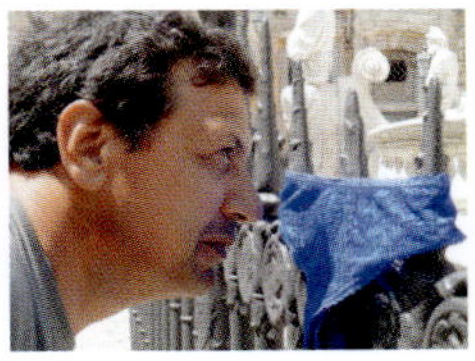

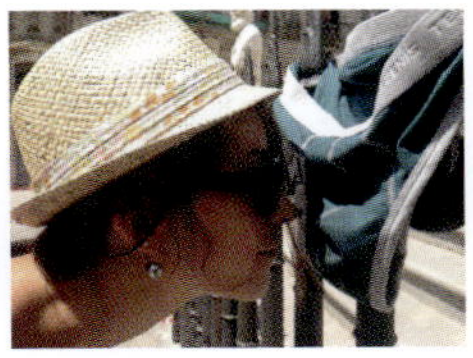

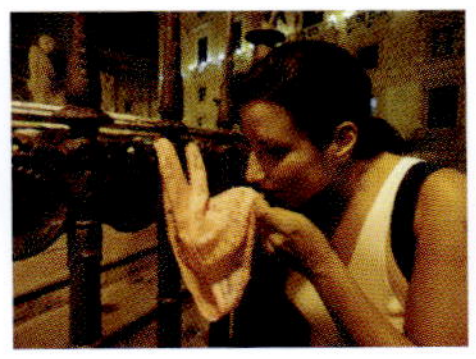

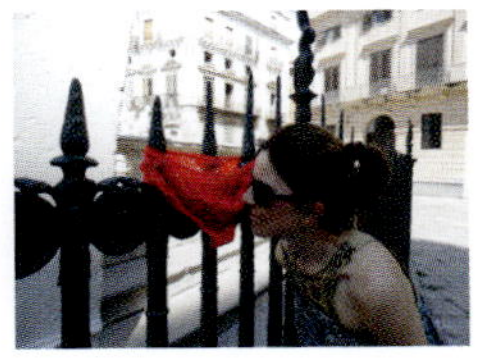

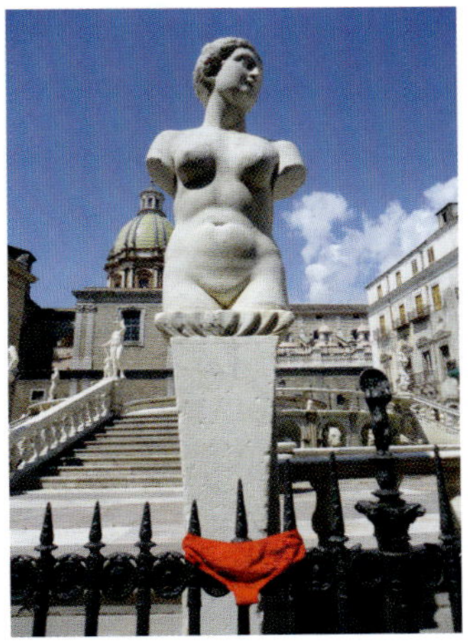

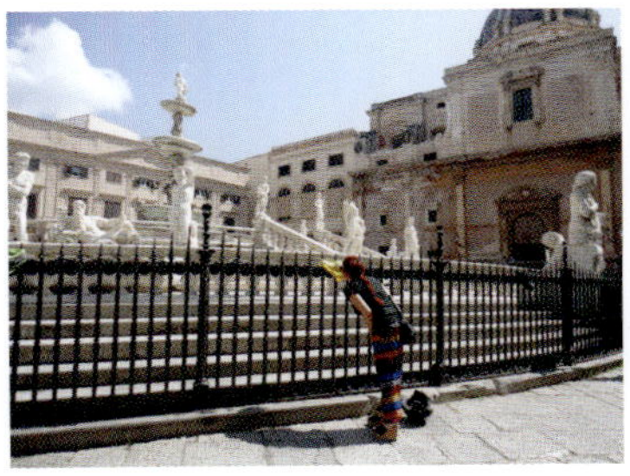

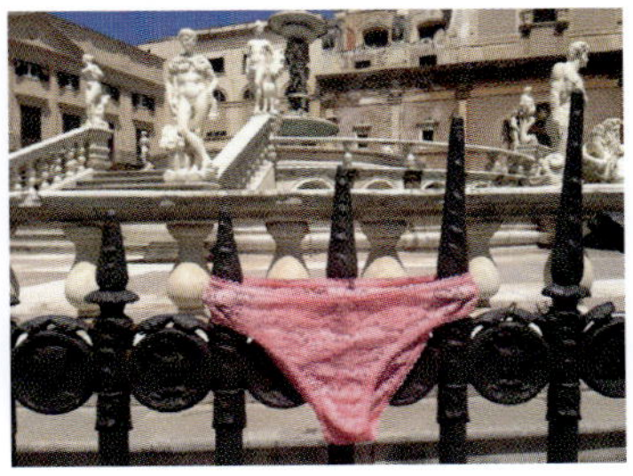

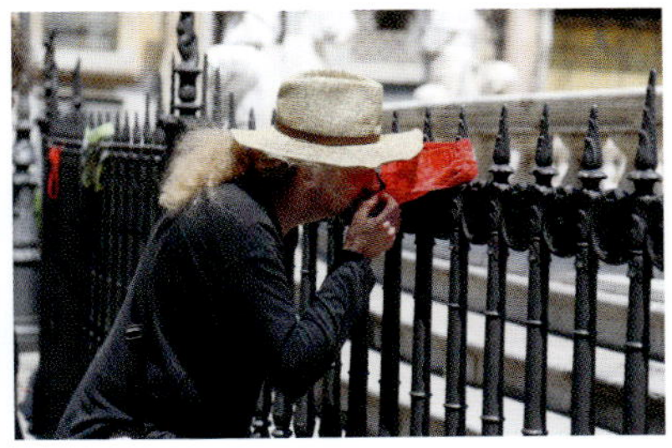

Palermo Scent City Walk, 25th July 2015

33 smells connect 10 important historical locations of Palermo.

33 geuren verbinden 10 historisch belangrijke plekken van Palermo.

5 Piazze, 5 sense, Scent City Walk, org. Associazione Canecapovolto, curator Chiara Canali, Palermo, IT, 25.07.2015

On Piazza Pretoria, also known as square of Shame the artist added male and female underwear in relation to the naked statues and let smell the underwear to sperm and vagina.

Op Piazza Pretoria, gekend als het plein van de Schaamte, hing de kunstenaar zowel ondergoed van mannen en vrouwen in relatie met de naakste standbeelden. Het ondergoed was geparfumeerd met de geur van sprema en vagina.

In the street known for its many jewellery stores the artist taped old Italian money, otherwise known as the previous currency, the Lire, and a new 5 euro bill onto the wall. He perfumed these respectively with the scent of old used money and the scent of new money. The scents were so concentrated that they will create some commotion. The scent of the old Lire partially smelled like anxiety sweat. This is typical for used money which has travelled through many countries and carries years of bacteria and sweat with it. That the scent also smells like anxiety sweat, does not need an explanation because money always brings along a story and after all we are here in Palermo, the old city in previous times known for the maffia and corruption. But maybe the artist had perfumed the new bill of 5 euro with the scent of anxiety sweat and the old Lire with the scent of new money and thus he links this to the current European situation of the Euro, waking up the desire for a national currency to the modal population.

In de straat bekend om zijn vele juweliers kleeft de kunstenaar oud Italiaans geld, namelijk een oud Lirebiljet, en een nieuw briefje van vijf euro op de muur. Hij parfumeert deze respectievelijk met de geur van oud en gebruikt geld en met de geur van nieuw geld. De geuren zijn sterk geconcentreerd zodat ze zeker enige commotie zullen doen opleven. De vraag is hoelang de biljetten zullen blijven hangen? De geur van de oude Lire ruikt deels ook naar angstzweet. Dit is typisch voor frequent gebruikt geld dat door vele handen is aangeraakt en jarenlang bacteriëen en zweet met zich meedraagt. Dat de geur eveneens naar angstzweet ruikt, hoeft geen verdere uitleg want aan geld kleven steeds verhalen en een geschiedenis en we zitten niet voor niets in het Siciliaanse Palermo, gekend om haar historie met de maffia en corruptie. Maar misschien parfumeert de kunstenaar juist het nieuwe vijf eurobiljet met de geur van angstzweet en het oude Lirebriefje met de geur van nieuw geld?
Op die manier legt hij een link naar de huidige Europese monetaire situatie en de psychologische complexiteit van de euro. Het verlangen naar een retour van de oude nationale munten van voor de muntunie leeft sterk bij een deel van de Europese bevolking.

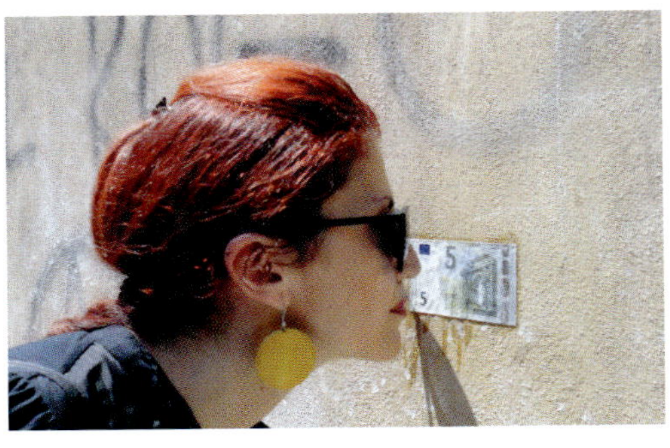

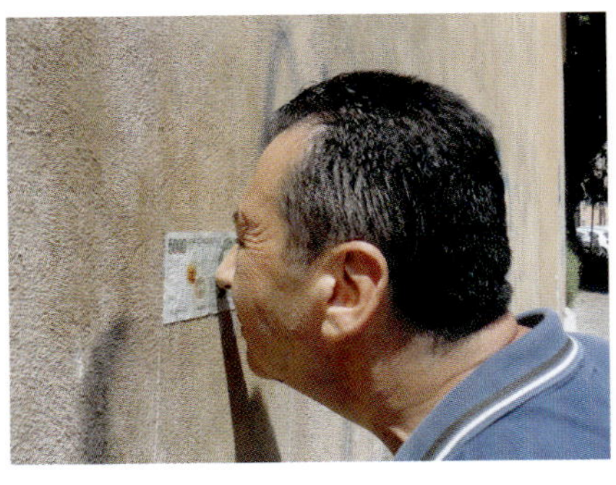

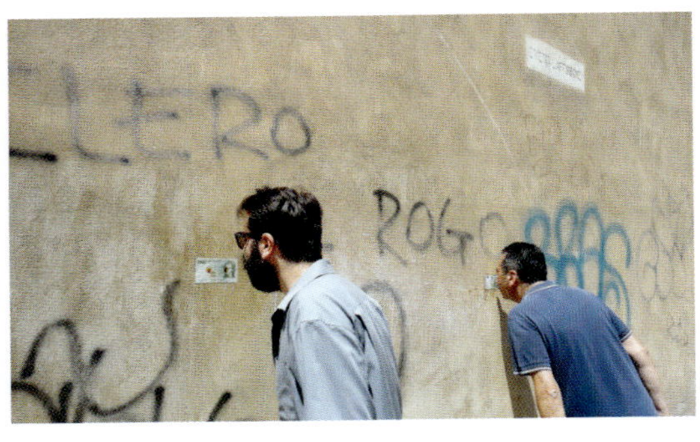

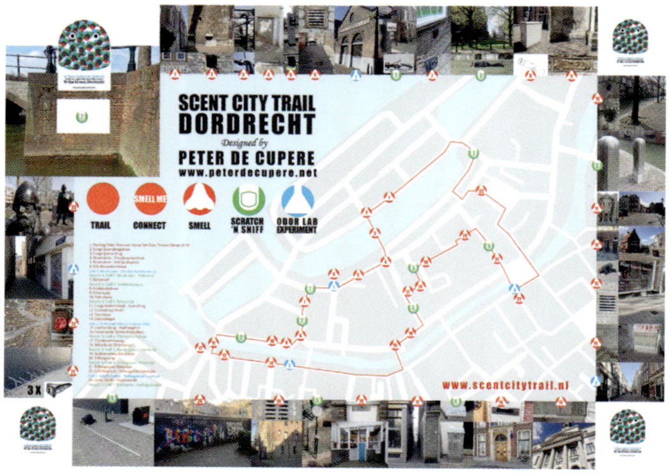

Scent City Trail, 2013

On different places in the city, smells were added to the specific location which could change the context of this spot or create a different experience.

Op diverse plaatsen werden geuren aangebracht die aan de locatie een andere context gaven of de bezoeker op een andere manier de plaats lieten ervaren.

Urban Explorers Festival, Scent City Trail, Dordrechts Museum, Dordrecht, NL, 11.05.2013-12.05.2013

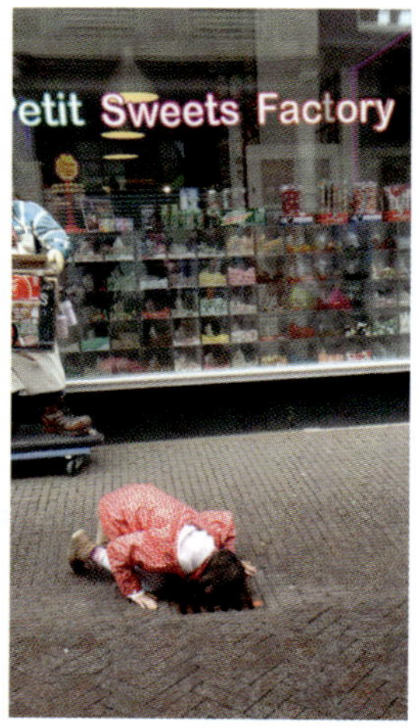

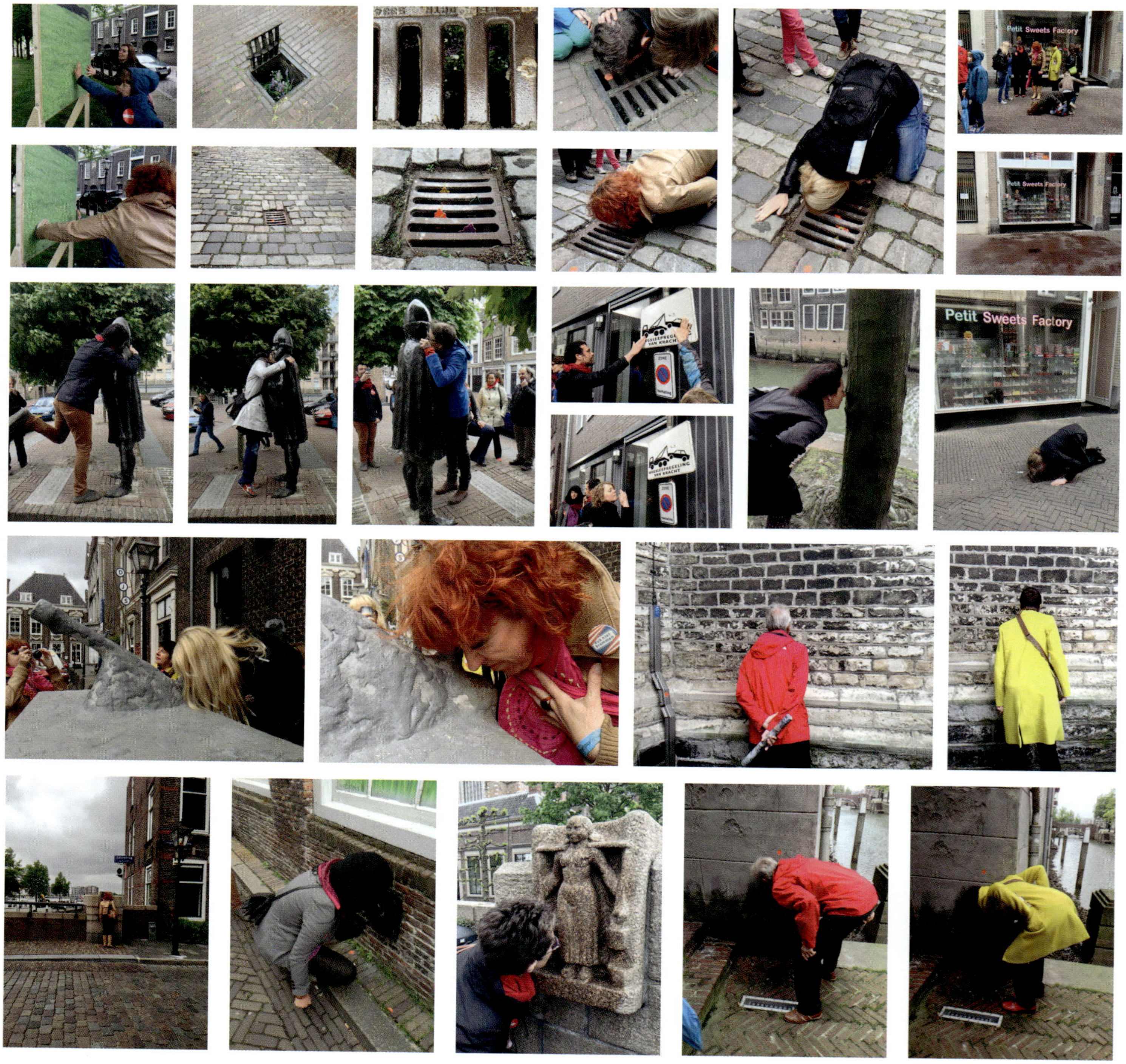

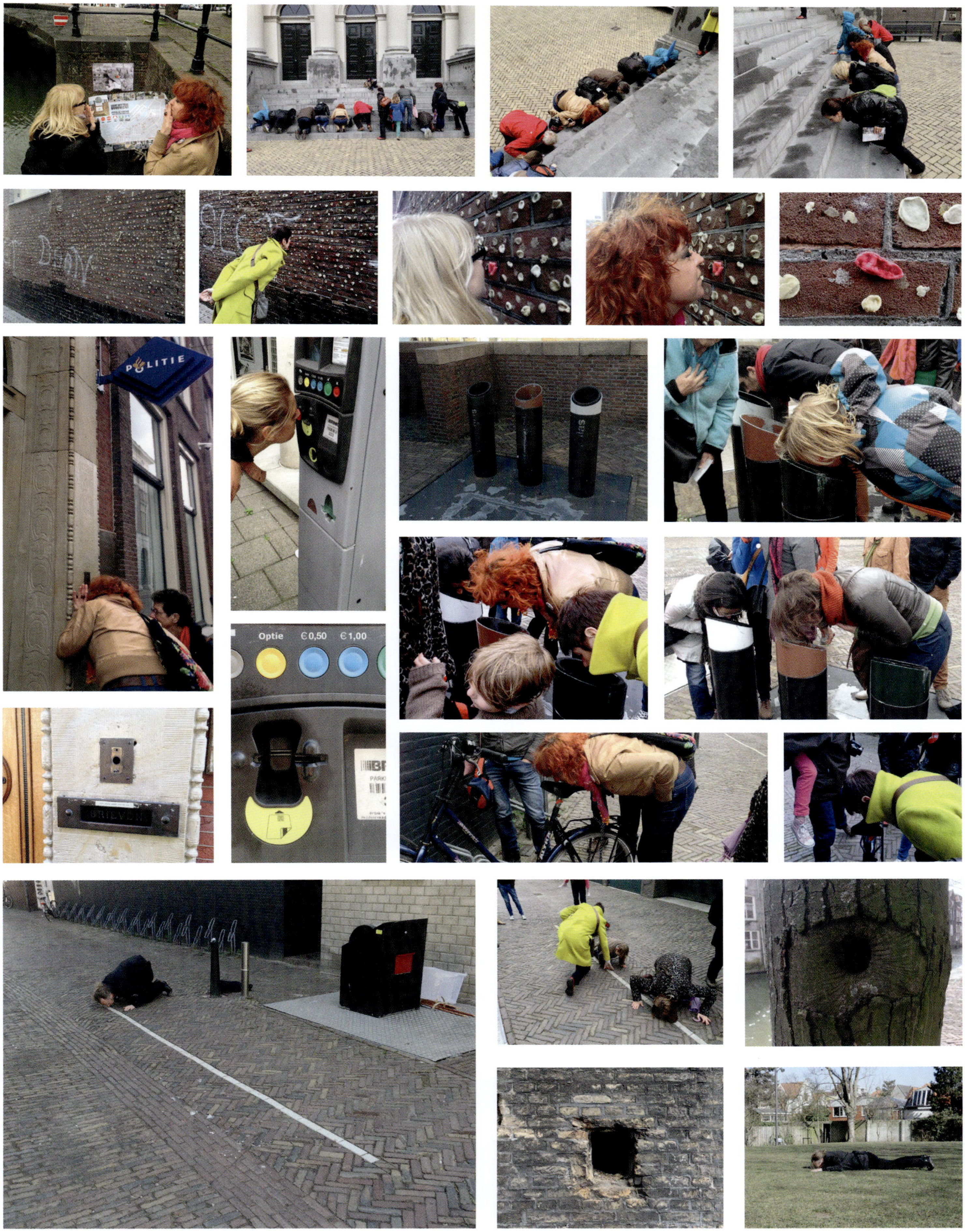
POLITIE
Optie
€0,50
€1,00

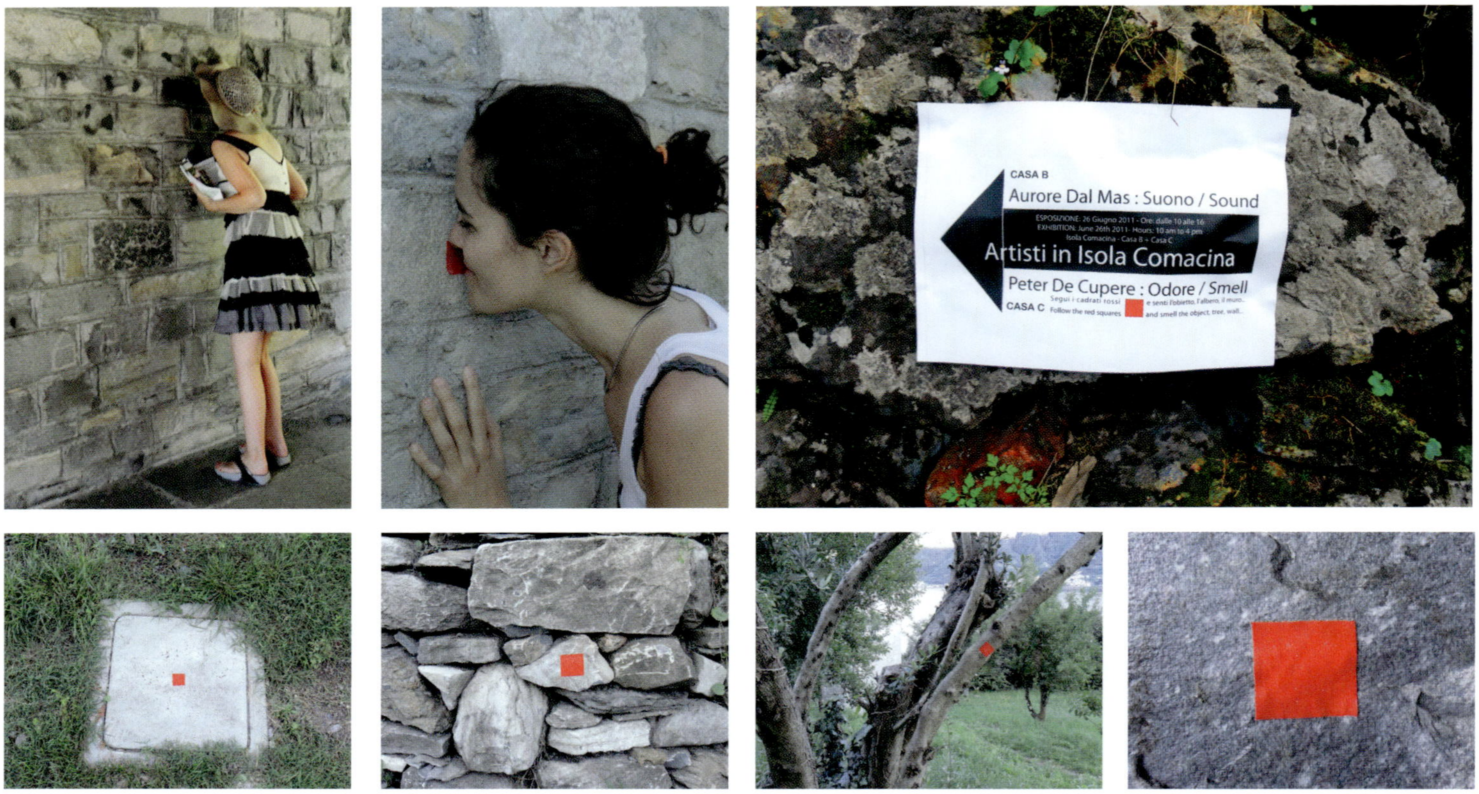

Scented Island, 2011

On different places on the island, smells were added which could change the context and create a different perception of a place.

Op diverse locaties werden geuren aangebracht waardoor de bezoeker een andere perceptie van de locatie kreeg.

Sound & smell interventions, Artisti in Isola Comacina with Aurora Dal Mas, Italy, IT, 26.06.2011

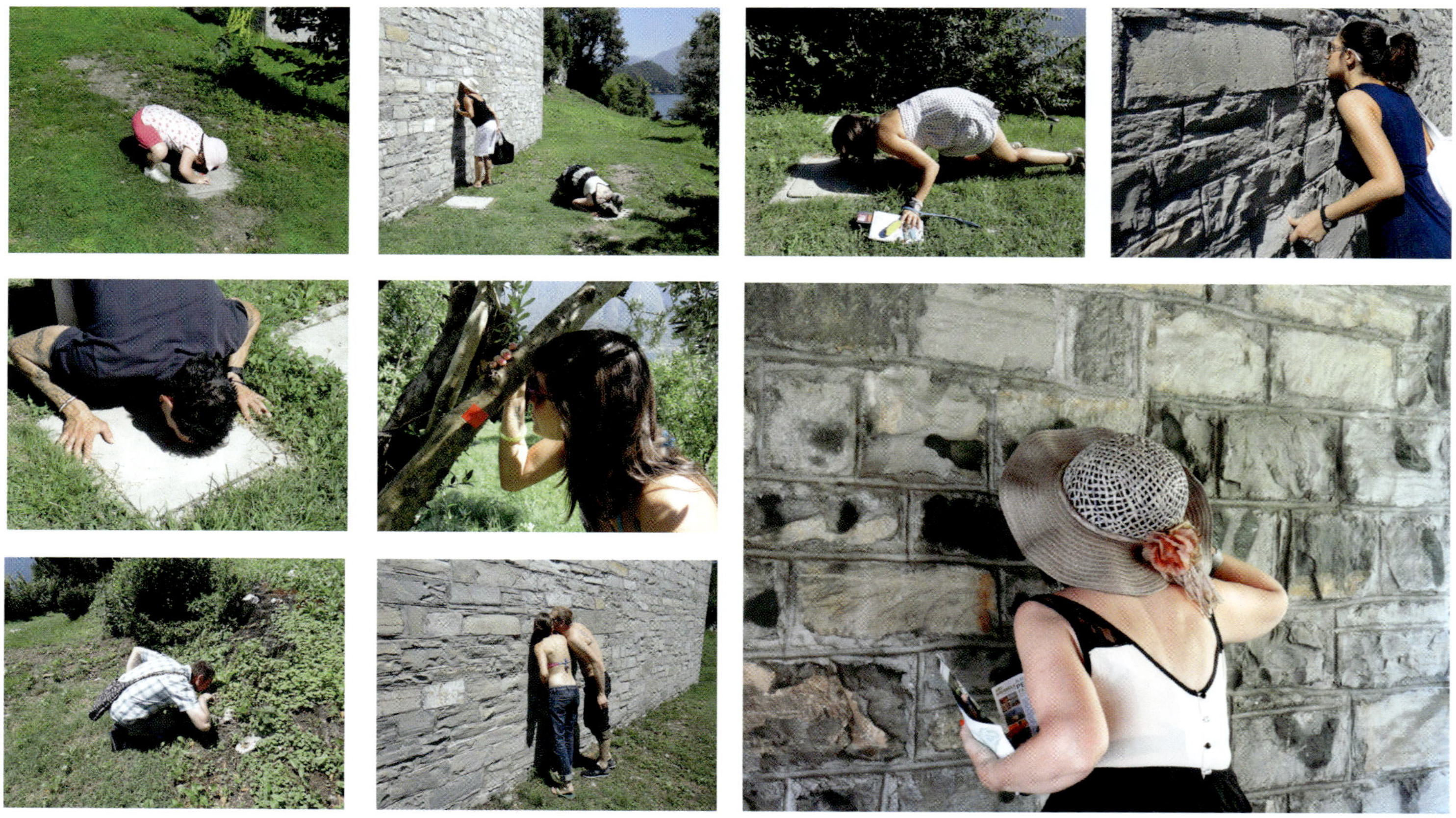

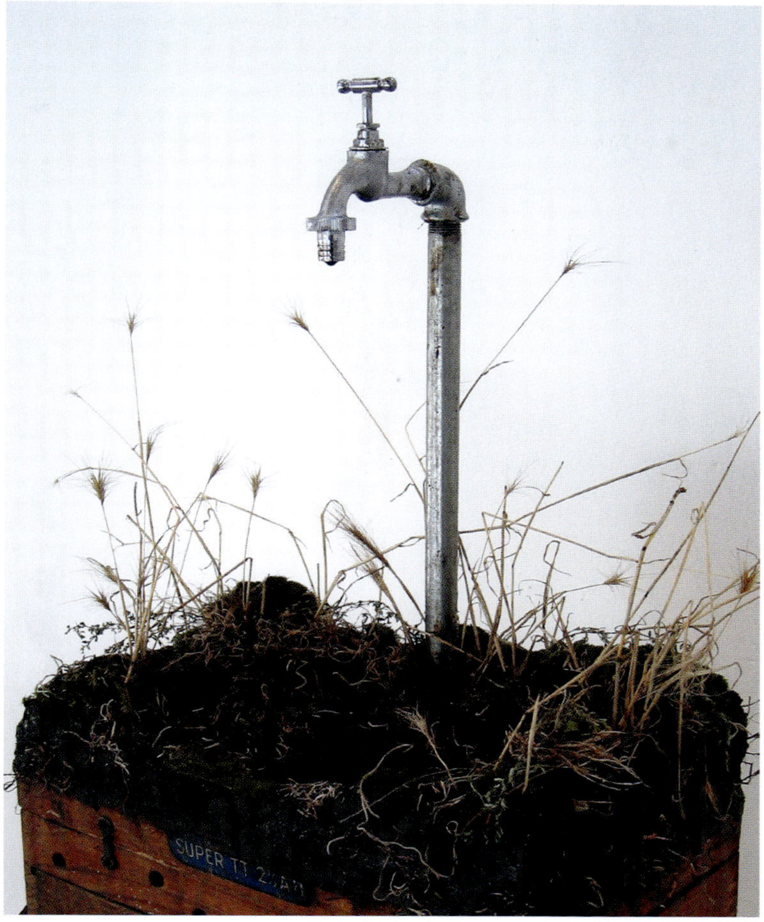

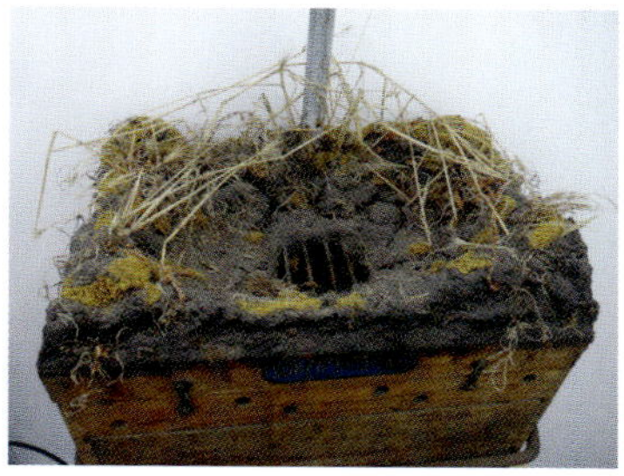

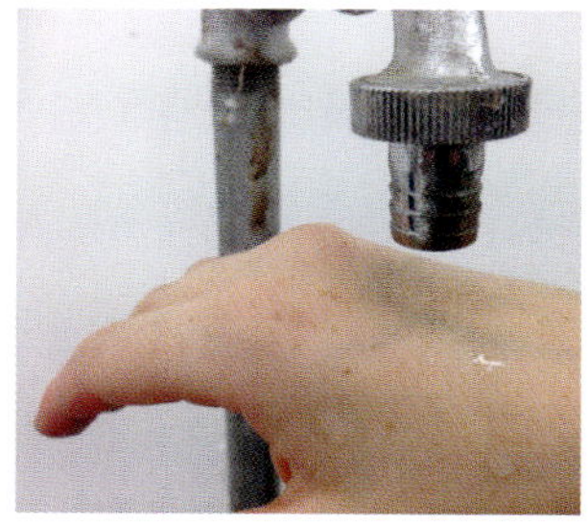

Drop Perfume, 2006

City Perfume Concept. This is the model for a proposition for a city smell as monument. When you hold your hand under the tap a drop of perfume falls.
In the exhibition Dots in 2006 visitors could try out the model of the concept with chocolate fragrance.

In The Olfactory in 2014 people could smell O'Hasselt, a scent for the city of Hasselt. Drop Perfume was realized before in real at the artist home.
Visitors to the artist studio could take a drop of the sweat of the artist while he was working in his studio.

Een concept voor een stadsparfum. Dit is het model met het voorstel om de geur van een stad als monument te plaatsen. Wanneer je je hand onder de kraan houdt, valt er een druppel parfum. In de tentoonstelling Dots in 2006 konden bezoekers het model van dit concept testen met chocoladegeur.

Tijdens The Olfactory in 2014 werden bezoekers geïntroduceerd met de geur O'Hasselt, een geur voor de stad Hasselt. *Drop Perfume* werd origineel in het atelier van de kunstenaar uitgetest. Bezoekers konden een druppel zweet van de kunstenaar opvangen terwijl hij aan het werken was in zijn studio.

Scent as a Monument, The Olfactory, Hasselt, BE, 18.10.2014
Dots, Warp art-project, curator Stef Van Bellingen, Sint-Niklaas, BE
09.09.2006-22.10.2006

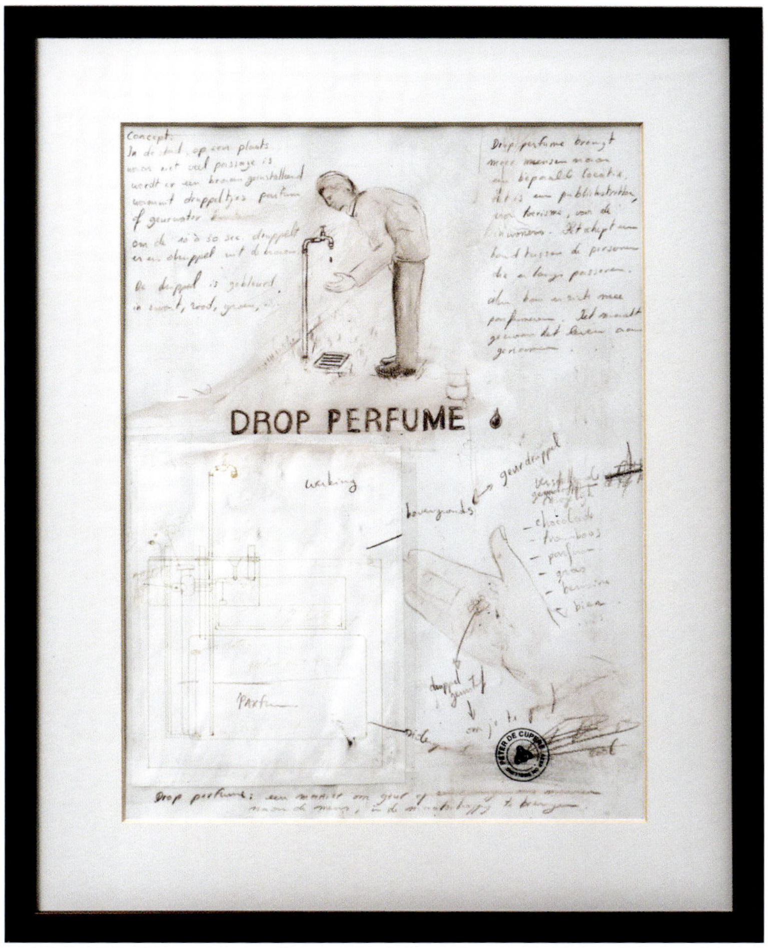

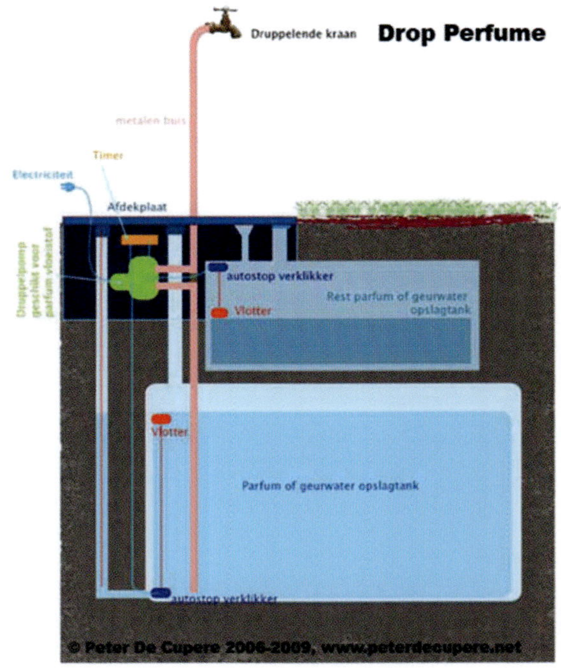

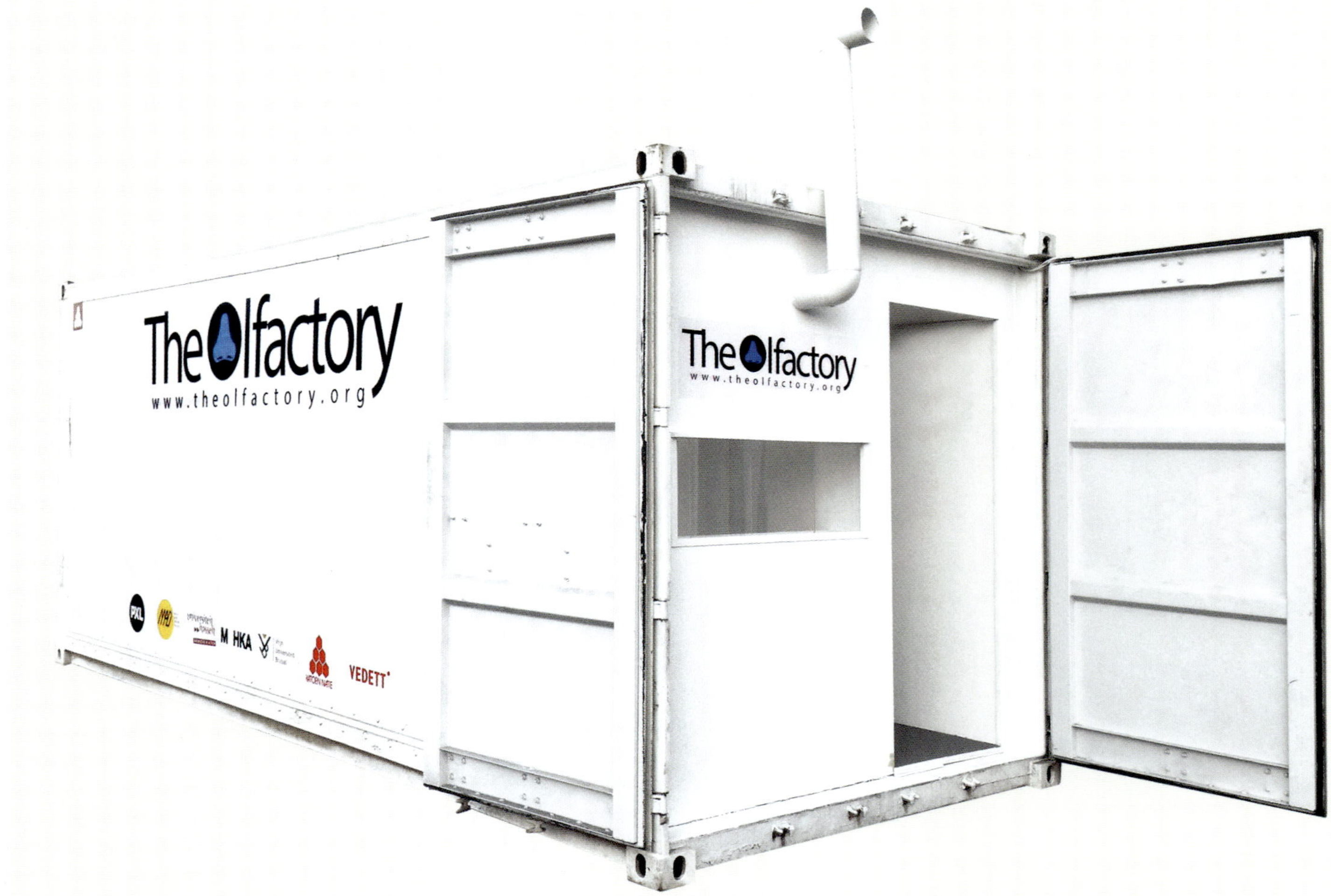

A total of 33 exhibitions were held over a period of 7 weeks, spread across 5 different locations.
Er werden 33 tentoonstellingen in 7 weken tijd gerealiseerd op 5 verschillende locaties.

Edition The Olfactory
100 ex., genummerd en gehandtekend, 40 cm x 50 cm

The Olfactory

The first exhibition was in honour of Andy Warhol.
Every 15 minutes, a different smell was blown into the room.

De eerste tentoonstelling werd opgedragen ter ere van Andy Warhol.
Om de 15 minuten werd er een andere geur in de ruimte geblazen.

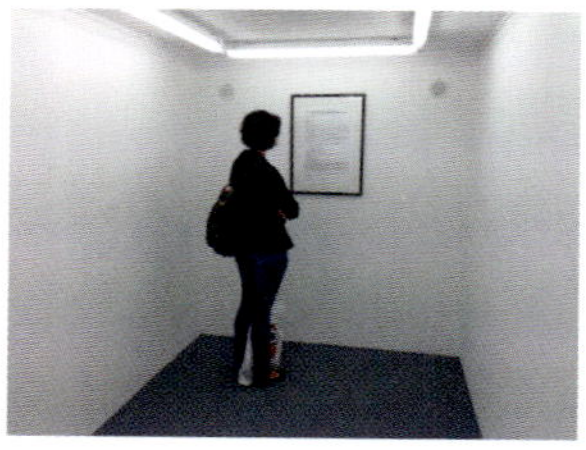

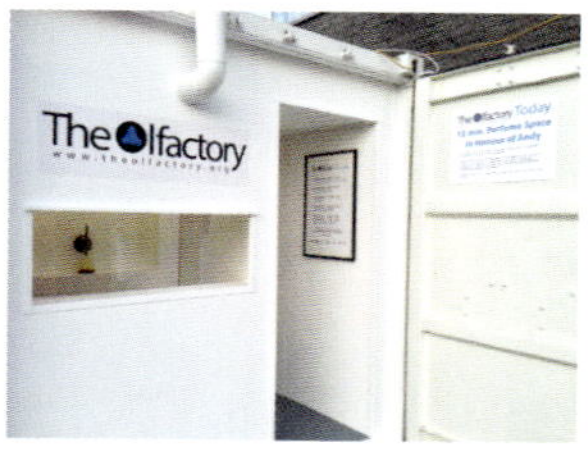

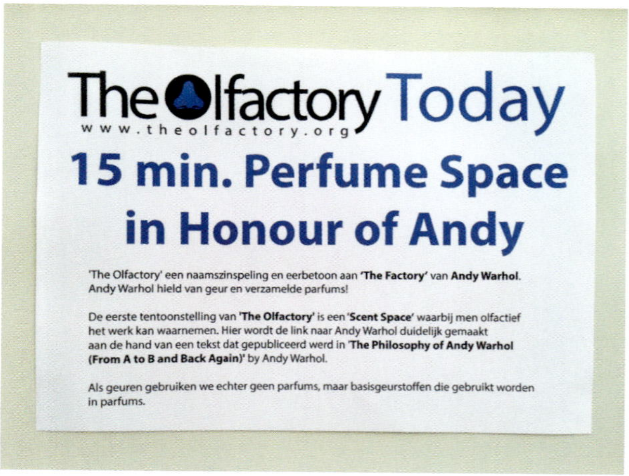

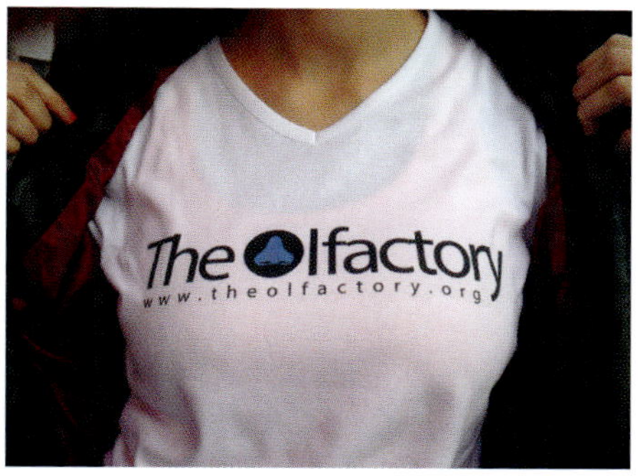

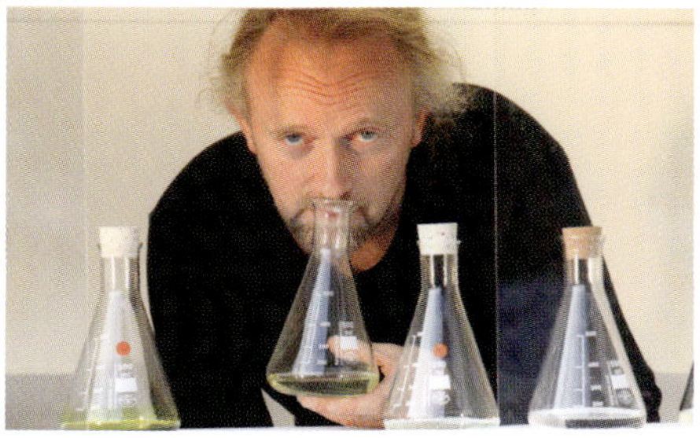

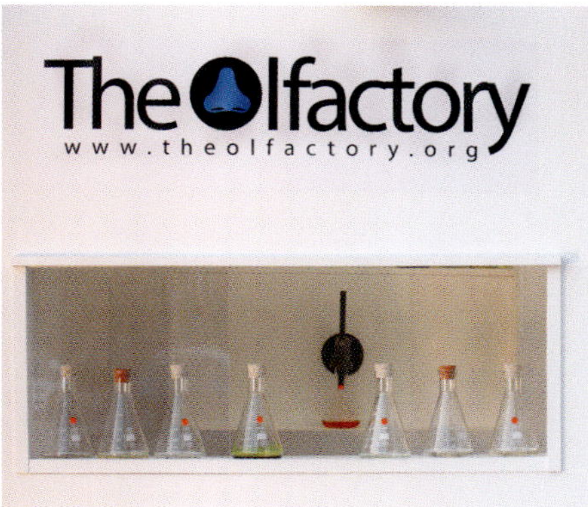

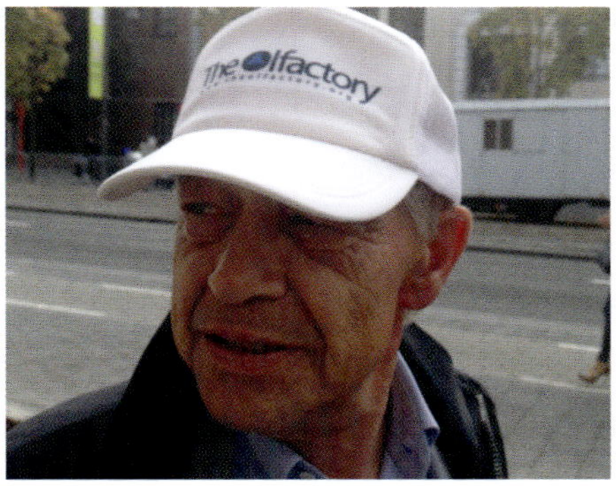

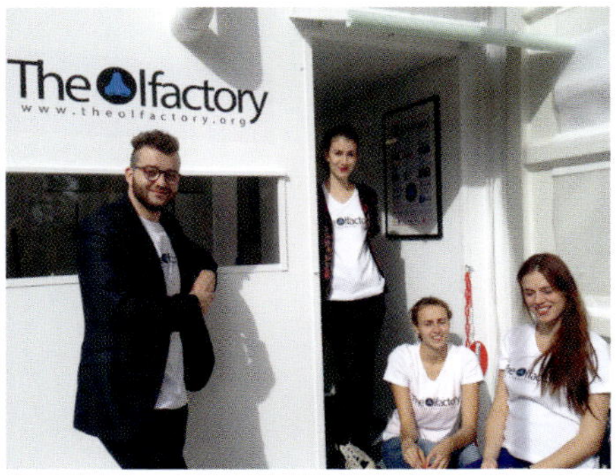

The Olfactory team

On photo: Sarah Reynders, Jorden Boulet, Lien Hillen and Elissa De Groote

The Olfactory

'The Olfactory' was a travelling exhibition concept of artist Peter de Cupere. From mid-September 2014 and at set timepoints, exhibitions are organised in a removable container with each of these exhibitions having scent as a starting point.

> "I switch perfumes all the time. If I've been wearing one perfume for three months, I force myself to give it up, even if I still feel like wearing it, so whenever I smell it again it will always remind me of those three months. I never go back to wearing it again; it becomes part of my permanent smell collection.
>
> ...
>
> Seeing, hearing, touching, tasting are just not as powerful as smelling if you want your whole being to go back for a second to something. Usually I don't want to, but by having smells stopped up in bottles, I can be in control and can only smell the smells I want to, when I want to, to get the memories I'm in the mood to have. Just for a second. The good thing about a smell-memory is that the feeling of being transported stops the instant you stop smelling, so there are no aftereffects. It's a neat way to reminisce...".

But 'The Olfactory' is more than just a 'Scent Space' or smell room. In the container, new olfactory and visual work was exhibited every two days, sometimes even every other day. Peter de Cupere hereby shows own work, but also invited other artists to show their work. Besides this, there are exhibitions which enlighten the use of scent throughout history. Art historically from Duchamp and the manifest of Carlo Carrà 'La Pittura dei suoni, rumori, odori: Manifesto futurista' [The Painting of Sounds, Noises, Smells: Futurist Manifesto]. This is the first manifest in which is referenced to scent. But also how perfume is linked to artists. For instance, Kazimir Malevich designed amongst others a perfume bottle (1908) and other artists were also discussed.

Maybe the most exclusive is the discovery of the Ukrainian artist Caflo Yrot (1874-1970). During his life, he never exhibited his works. Caflo Yrot is his pseudonym, because of political and personal reasons, he never wanted to use his proper name. Peter de Cupere discovered him through his doctoral thesis at the PXL-MAD School of Arts in Hasselt where he is now teaching olfactory art in the Open Lab and where he coordinates and teaches the English Master Art Sense(s) Lab (www.artsenseslab.be). It was the son of Caflo Yrot who contacted Peter de Cupere and brought him into contact with his father's works.

'The Olfactory' is an experimental and interactive concept. The exhibition program was fixed, but was adjusted every week according to the interaction which took place. Same as in 'The Factory' of Andy Warhol, there were unexpected performances and happenings. After the travelling container project Peter de Cupere made from The Olfactory a non-profit organization to promote olfactory art. The first group exhibition he realized was 'The Smell of War' in Castle De Lovie in Poperinge, Belgium. There he showed 21 international artists from which 11 are working with scents. More info about The Olfactory you can find on the website 'www.olfactory.org'.

The Olfactory was a research exhibition for Peter de Cupere's PhD 'When Scent Makes Seeing, When Seeing Makes Scents'.

'The Olfactory' was een reizend tentoonstellingsconcept van beeldend kunstenaar Peter de Cupere. Vanaf midden September 2014 en op geregelde tijdstippen werden in een verplaatsbare container een reeks tentoonstellingen gehouden waarbij geur het uitgangspunt was.

'Olfactory' betekent 'sense of smell'. Olfactory Art is de term die men geeft aan kunstwerken met geur. 'The Olfactory' is ook een creatieve zinspeling en eerbetoon aan 'The Factory' van Andy Warhol. Andy Warhol hield van geur en verzamelde parfums. In de eerste tentoonstelling van de reeks wordt de link naar Andy Warhol duidelijk gemaakt aan de hand van een tekst van hem. Hieronder vind je een extract, gepubliceerd in 'The Philosophy of Andy Warhol (From A to B and Back Again)' van Andy Warhol.

> "I switch perfumes all the time. If I've been wearing one perfume for three months, I force myself to give it up, even if I still feel like wearing it, so whenever I smell it again it will always remind me of those three months. I never go back to wearing it again;
> it becomes part of my permanent smell collection.
>
> ...
>
> Seeing, hearing, touching, tasting are just not as powerful as smelling if you want your whole being to go back for a second to something. Usually I don't want to, but by having smells stopped up in bottles, I can be in control and can only smell the smells
> I want to, when I want to, to get the memories I'm in the mood to have. Just for a second. The good thing about a smell-memory is that the feeling of being transported stops the instant you stop smelling, so there are no aftereffects. It's a neat way to reminisce ...".

Maar 'The Olfactory' was meer dan alleen een 'Scent Space' of geurruimte. In de container werd om de twee, soms zelfs elke dag een nieuw beeldend én olfactief werk getoond. Peter de Cupere toonde hierbij niet alleen eigen werk, maar nodigde ook andere kunstenaars uit om hun werk te delen. Daarnaast waren er tentoonstellingen waarbij geurgebruik doorheen de geschiedenis werd toegelicht. Kunsthistorisch vanaf Duchamp en het manifest van Carlo Carrà 'La Pittura dei suoni, rumori, odori: Manifesto futurista' [The Painting of Sounds, Noises, Smells: Futurist Manifesto]. Dit is het eerste manifest waarin verwezen wordt naar geur. Verder werd getoond hoe parfum linken met verscheidene kunstenaars kan hebben. Zo ontwierp Kazimir Malevich een parfumflesje in 1908. Maar misschien wel het meest exclusieve verhaal was de ontdekking van de Oekraïense kunstenaar Caflo Yrot (1874-1970). Tijdens zijn leven kwam hij nooit naar buiten met zijn kunstwerken. Caflo Yrot is een pseudonym; om politieke en persoonlijke redenen wou hij zijn echte naam niet gebruiken. Peter de Cupere ontdekte hem dankzij zijn doctoraatsonderzoek aan de PXL-Mad School of Arts te Hasselt waar hij nu Olfactory Art doceert in het Open Lab en de Engelstalige Master Art Sense(s) Lab (www.artsenseslab.be). Het was de zoon van Caflo Yrot die Peter de Cupere contacteerde en in contact bracht met het werk van zijn vader.

'The Olfactory' was een experimenteel en interactief concept. Het tentoonstellingsprogramma lag vast, maar werd week na week aangepast volgens de interactie die plaatsvond. Zo waren er net zoals in 'The Factory' van Andy Warhol onverwachte performances en happenings. Meer informtie over The Olfactory is te vinden op www.theolfactory.org.

'The Olfactory' was een onderzoeksproject in het kader van het doctoraat van Peter de Cupere 'When Scent Makes Seeing, When Seeing Makes Scents'.

The Olfactory, 33 olfactory art exhibitions in 7 weeks, Hasselt, Antwerp, Brussels, Ghent, BE, 15.09.2014-30.10.2014

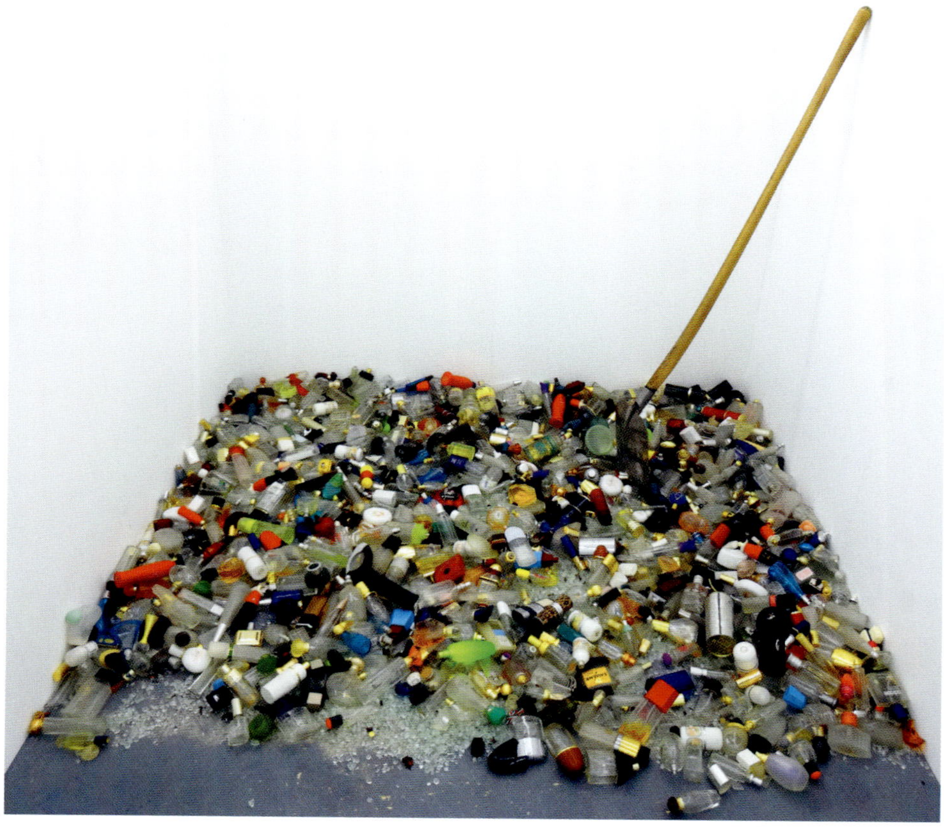

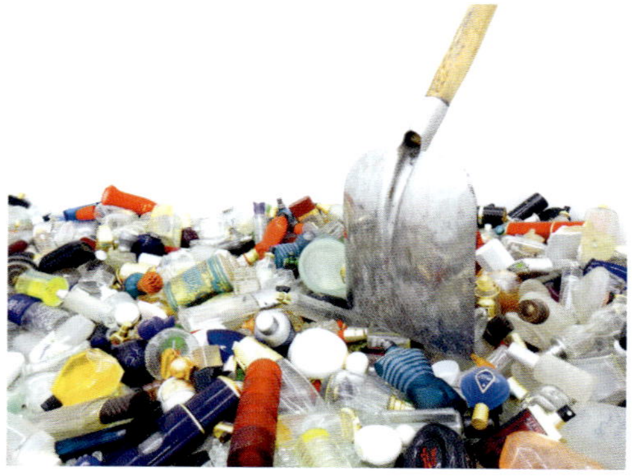

Perfume Desert Storm, 2014

Video HD, 1 min 21 sec.

Video perfumance with 1,000 perfume bottles.
Filmed and shown in The Olfactory

Video perfumance met 1.000 parfumflesjes.
Gerealiseerd en tentoongesteld in The Olfactory

Sound Scent / Scent Sound, The Olfactory, Hasselt, BE
24.09.2014

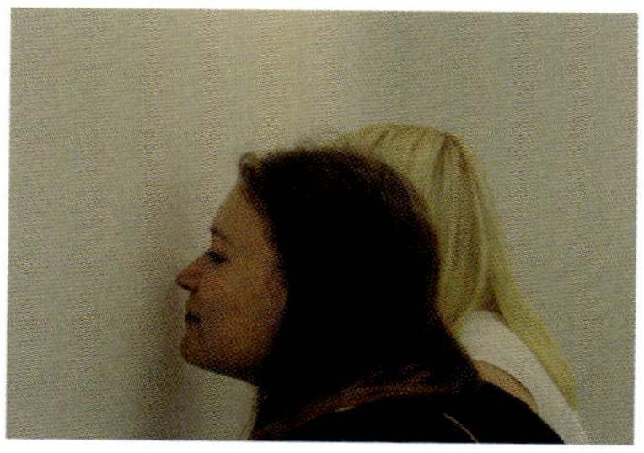

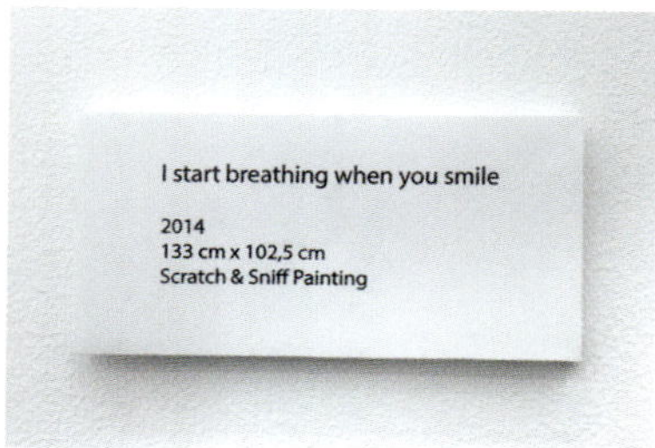

Invisible Scent Paintings, 2014

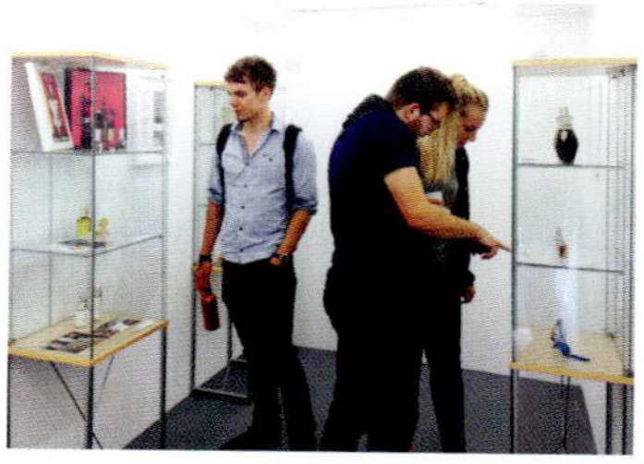

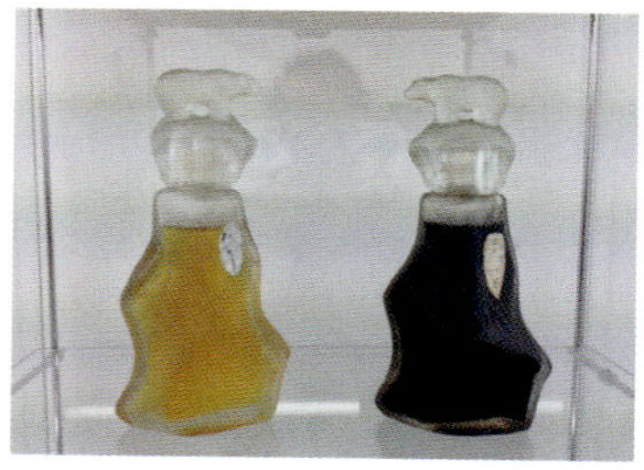

Exhibition Perfume Bottles in Art History

Perfume bottle designed by Kazimir Malevich in 1908 and brought to market in 1911. In 1917, Caflo Yrot replaced the perfume with black, used oil and stuck a label designed by himself on the bottle.

Parfumflesje ontworpen door Kazimir Malevich in 1908 en op de markt gebracht in 1911. Caflo Yrot veranderde in 1917 het parfum door zwarte vervuilde olie en kleefde een eigen ontworpen etiket op het flesje.

Perfume Bottles in Art History, The Olfactory, Hasselt, BE, 19-20.09.2014

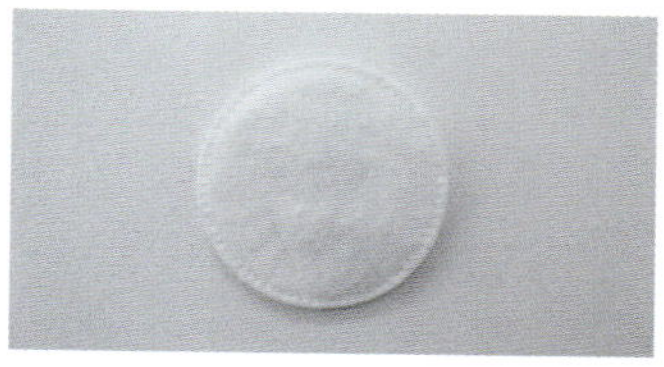

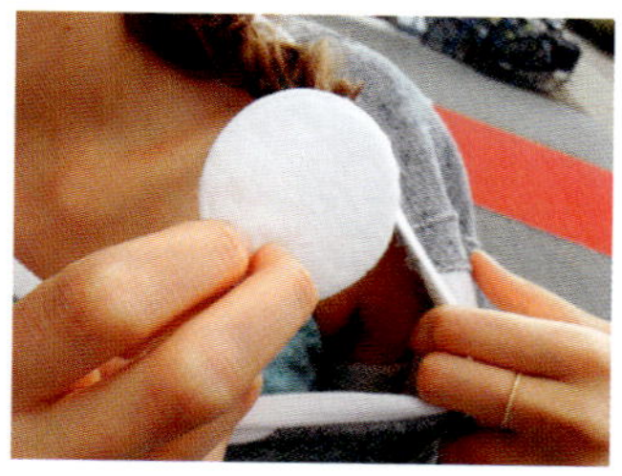

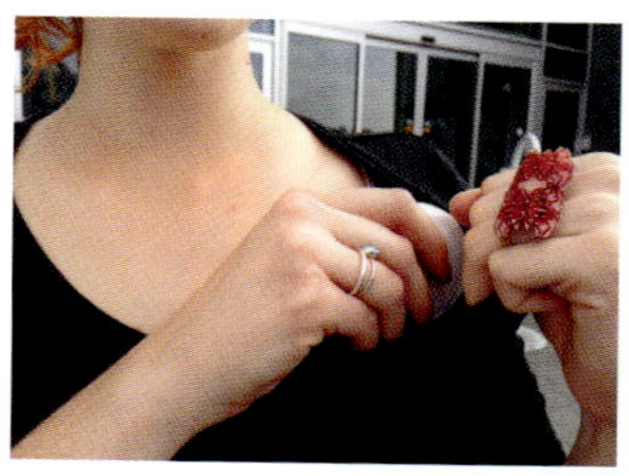

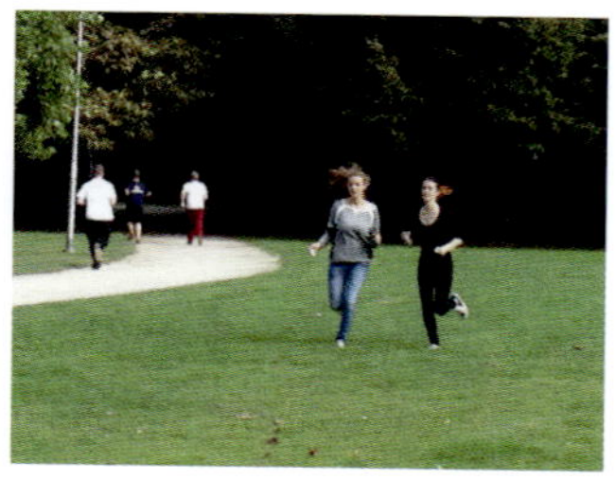

Sweat Sound Installation, 2014

The Olfactory, Hasselt, BE, 26.09.2014

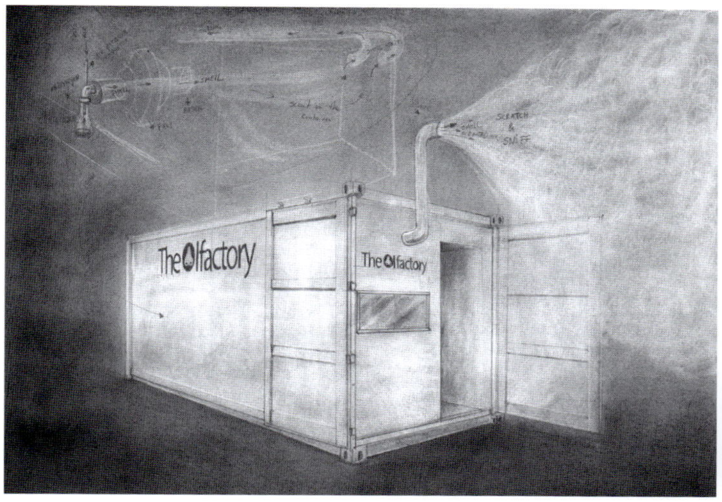

Drawing + Edition The Olfactory, 2014

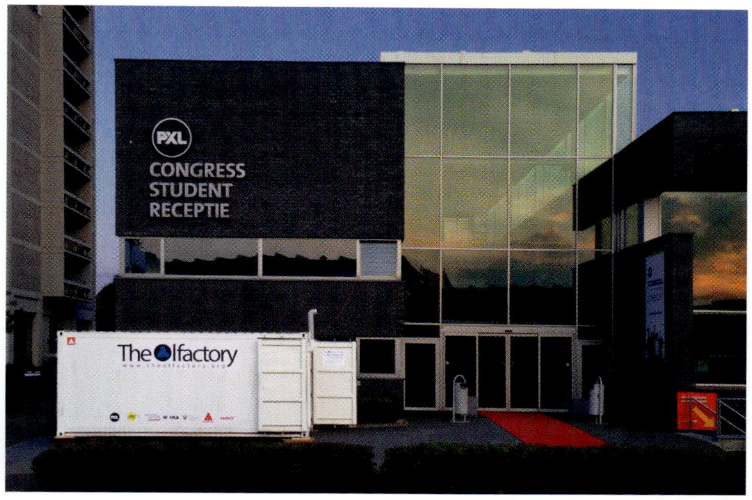

The Olfactory, 2014

Location / Locatie PXL Hogeschool, Hasselt, BE

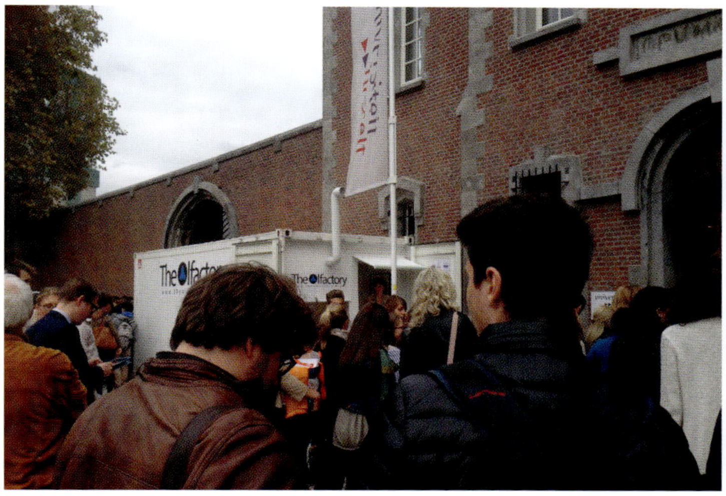

The Olfactory, 2014

Location / Locatie UHasselt, University of Hasselt, BE

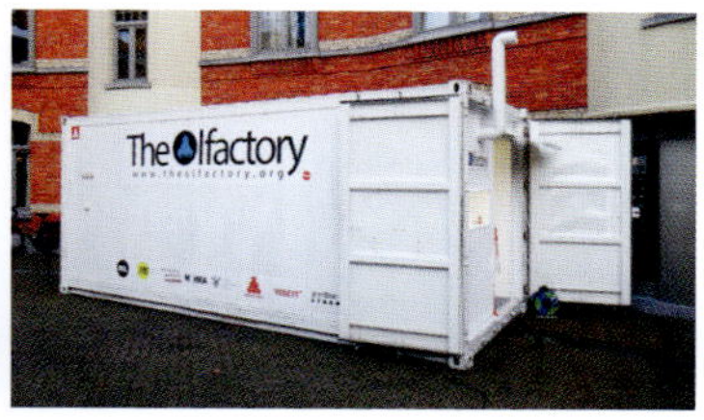

The Olfactory, 2014

Location / Locatie Zebrastraat, Gent, BE

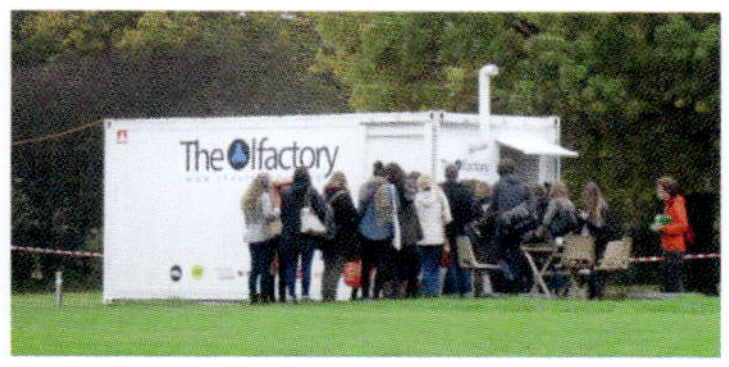

The Olfactory, 2014

Location / Locatie VUB, Brussels, BE

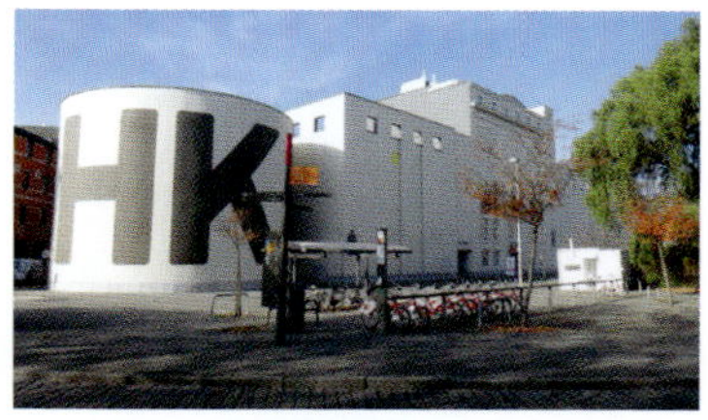

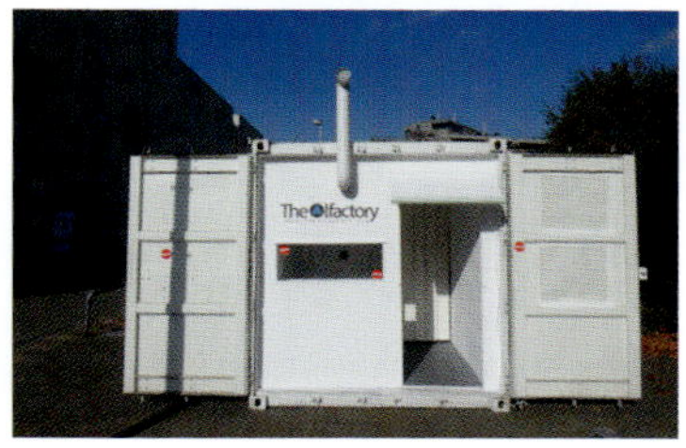

The Olfactory, 2014

Location / Locatie M HKA, Museum of Contemporary Art, Antwerp, BE

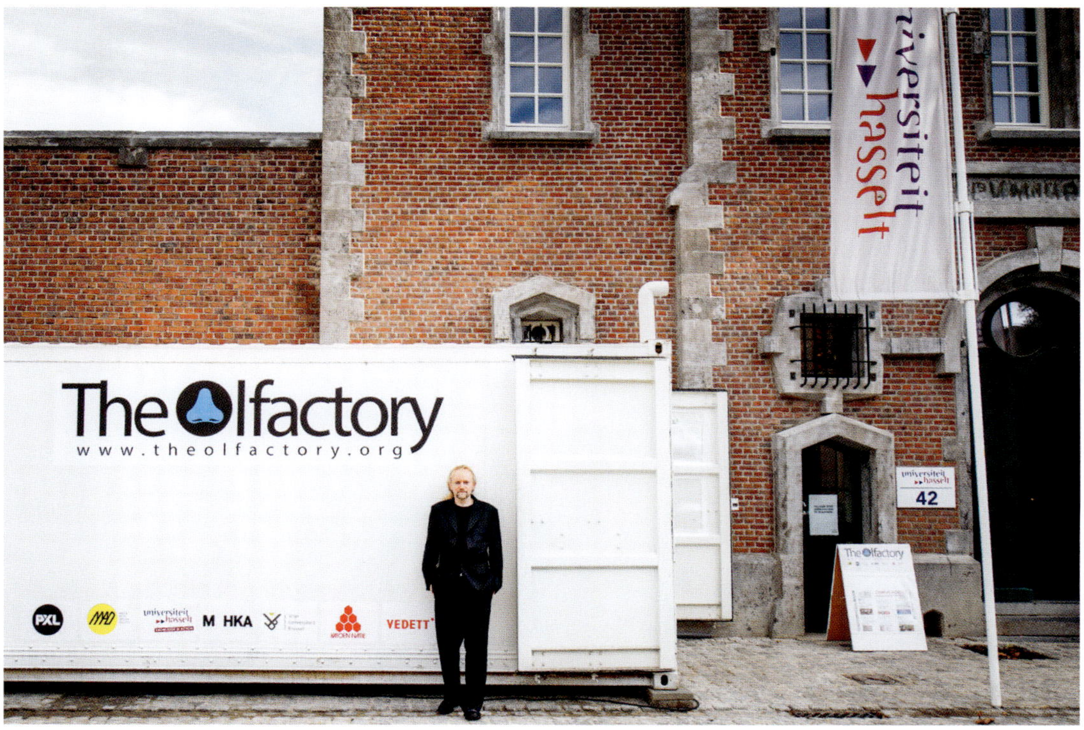

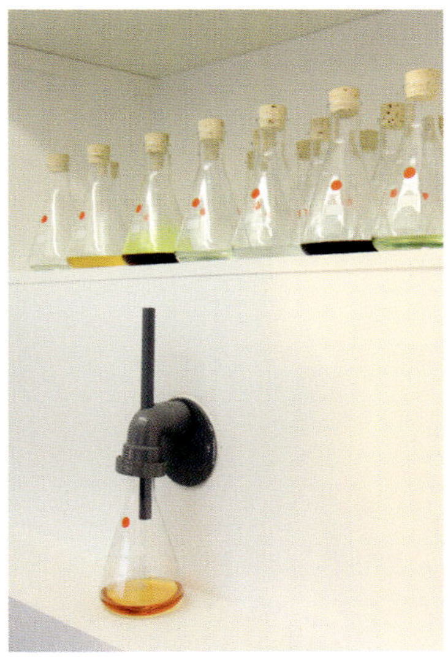

The Scent Distributor

Scents are quickly and easily blown into the space and extracted again when necessary.

Geuren worden op eenvoudige wijze in de ruimte geblazen en terug afgezogen wanneer nodig.

Scented Kiss happening

This ode to Oscar Wilde was held for the first time in 1999 at the Free University of Brussels (VUB) during an exhibition about 'Kisses'. Various scents are applied to the wall or a canvas. Participating visitors at the happening are given a free lipstick with specially designed packaging if they plant one or more kisses on their favourite scent on the wall or canvas.

Deze ode aan Oscar Wilde werd voor de eerste keer in 1999 op de VUB gebracht tijdens een tentoonstelling over 'Kussen'. Op de muur of canvas worden diverse geuren aangebracht. De deelnemende bezoeker aan de happening krijgt een gratis editie van een lipstick met speciaal ontworpen verpakking als men één of meerdere kussen op zijn/haar favoriete geur op de muur of canvas zet. De Scented Kisses Happening werd al meerdere malen herhaald, gelinkt aan verschillende situaties of contexten.

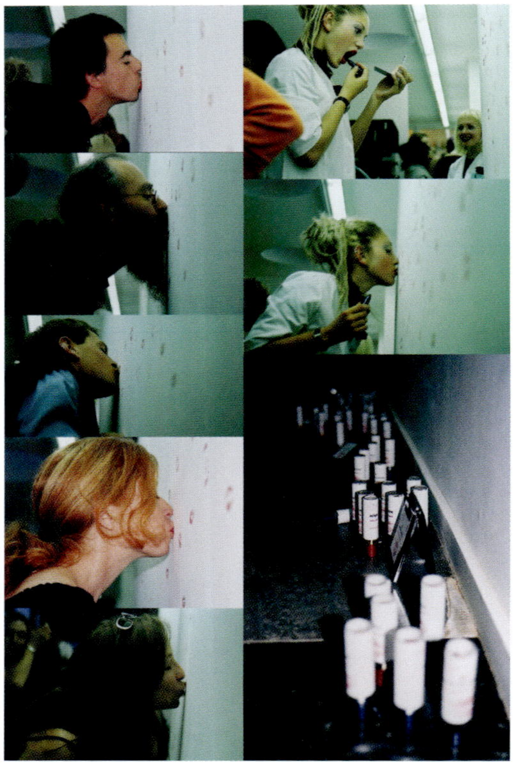

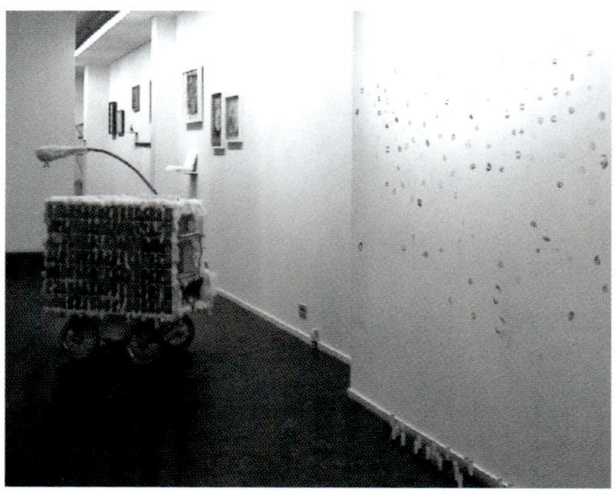

Smell Kiss Happening: Kiss Me, 2000

Wall perfumed with sweet strawberry smell and raspberry smell. Visitors can kiss the perfumed wall.

Een muur geparfumeerd met zoete aardbeien- en frambozengeur. Bezoekers kunnen deze muur kussen.

Peter de Cupere, Smellcom Happening, Smell Kiss Performance, rockconcert Admiral Freebee, Van Laere Contemporary Art, Antwerp, BE, 14.09-21.10.2000
Kussen, Galery' VUB, Free University Brussels, BE, 07-29.10.1999

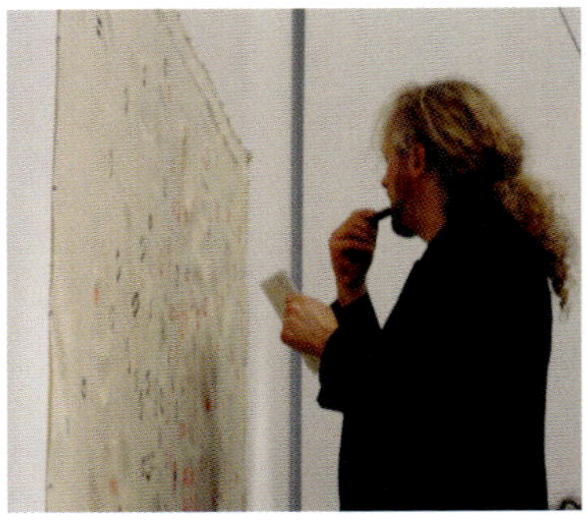

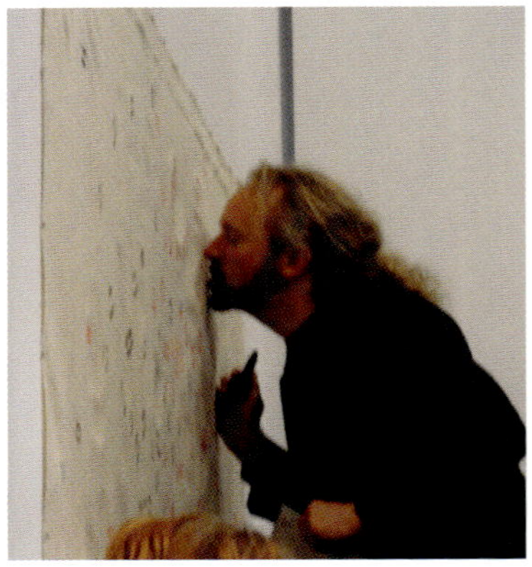

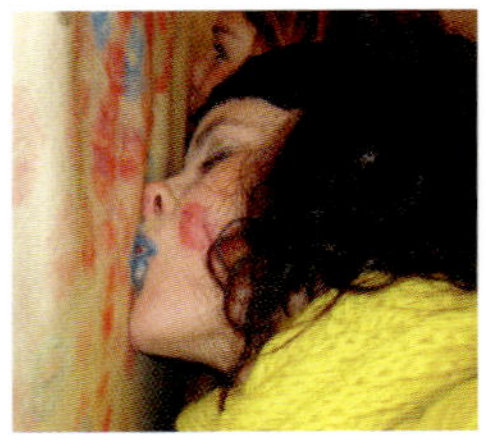

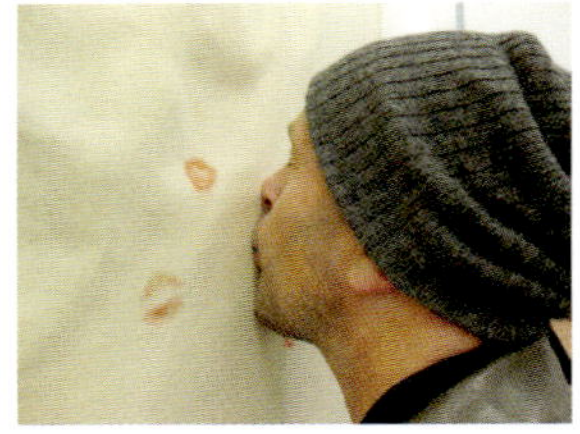

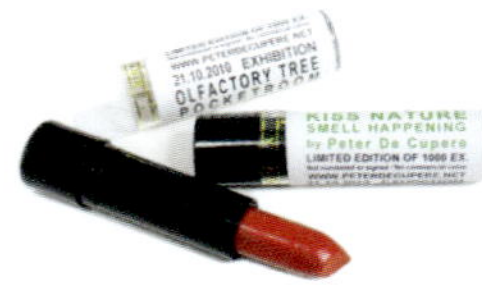

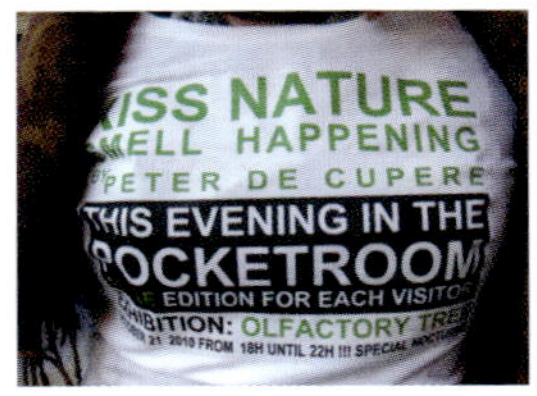

Kiss Nature, Smell Happening, 2010

Wall perfumed with nature fragrances. Visitors got a lipstick edition for free when they kissed the prefered scent on the perfumed canvas with the lipstick.

Een muur geparfumeerd met geuren uit de natuur. Deelnemers ontvingen een editie van een speciale lippenstift wanneer ze hun favoriete geur op het geparfumeerde canvas kusten met de lippenstift.

Olfactory Tree, Pocketroom, curator Wim Waumans, Antwerpen, BE 12.09.2010-31.10.2010
Special Nocturne Kiss Nature Smell Happening, 21.10.2010

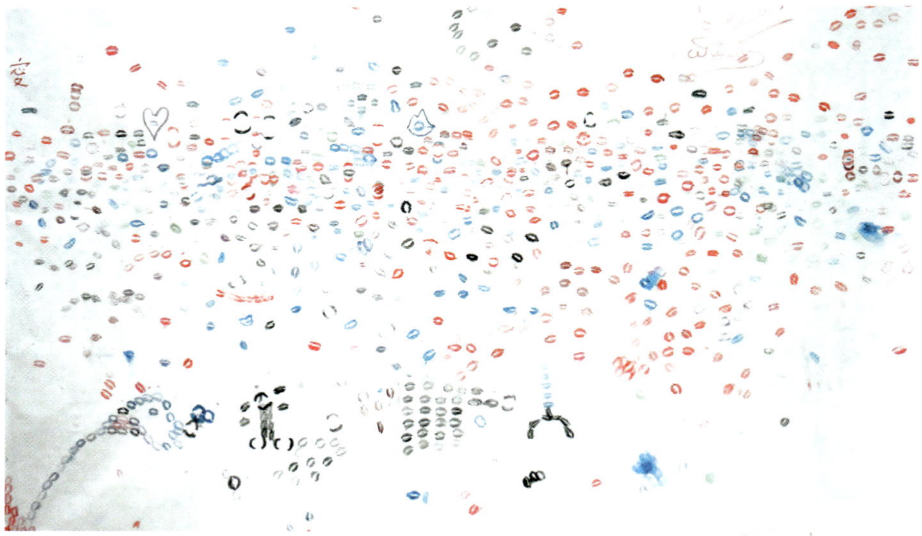

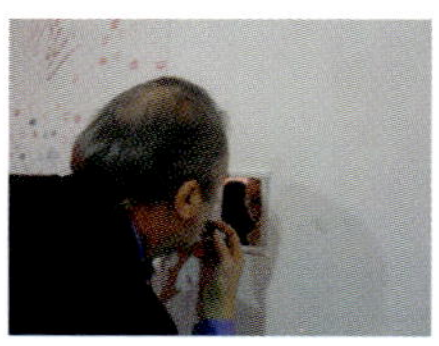

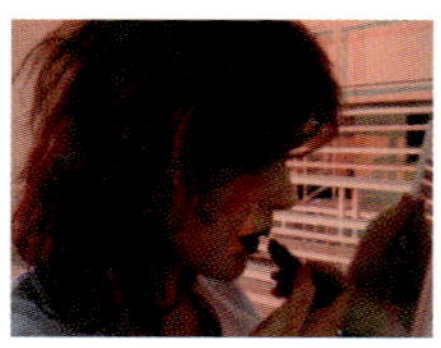

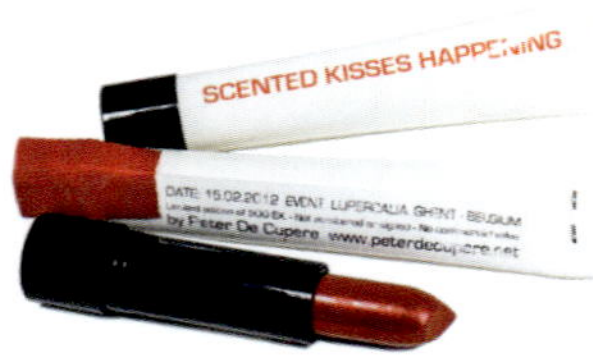

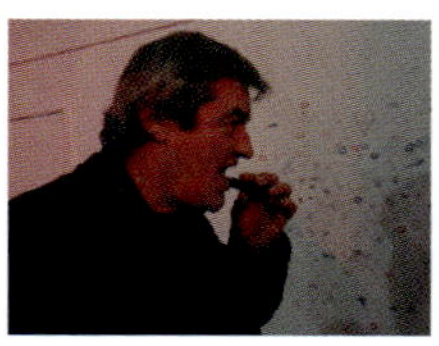

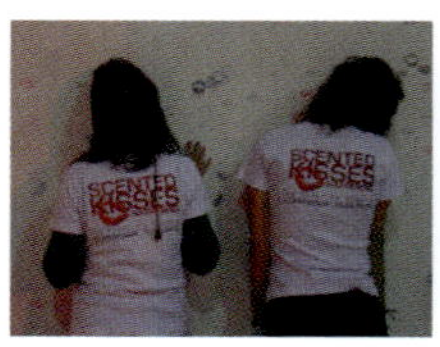

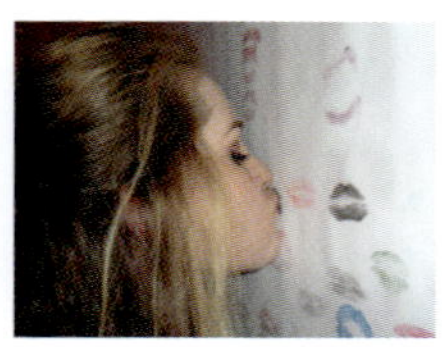

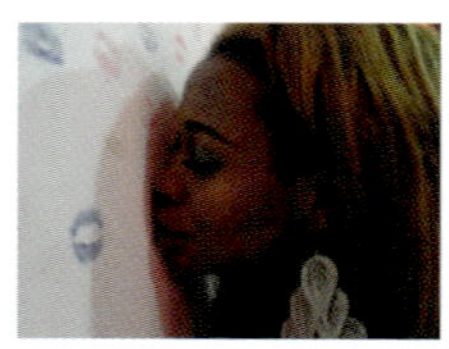

Scented Kisses Happening, 2012

Various erotic scents were applied to a cloth. Visitors to the Lupercalia event would thus visualise their preferred scent without being consciously aware of it.

Op een doek werden verschillende erotische geuren aangebracht. Bezoekers aan het Lupercalia event visualiseerden zo zonder het bewust te weten hun voorkeur voor een bepaalde geur.

Lupercalia, Theatre Tinnenpot, org. Vermeylenfonds, Ghent, BE,15.02.2012

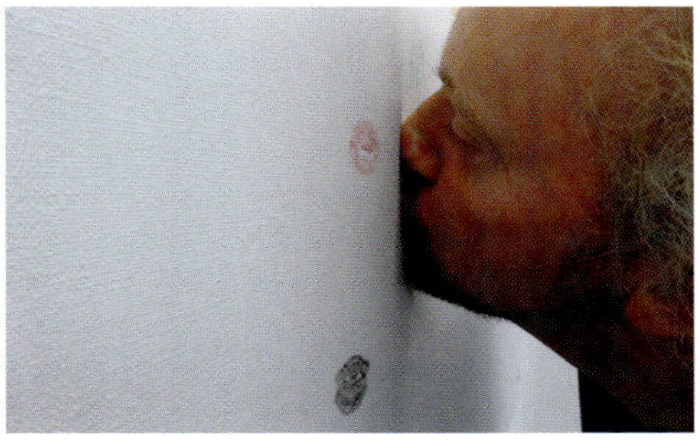

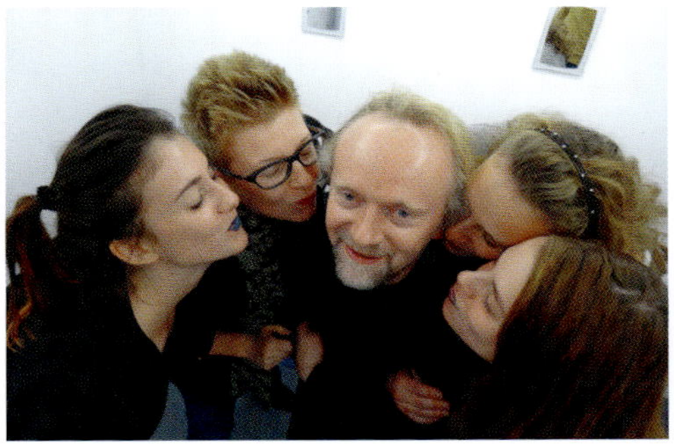

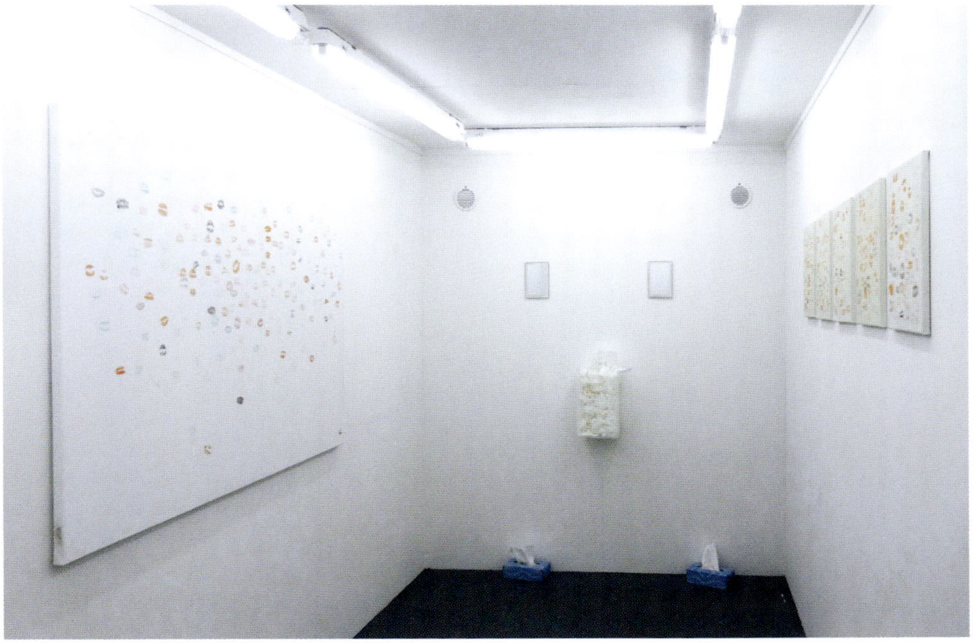

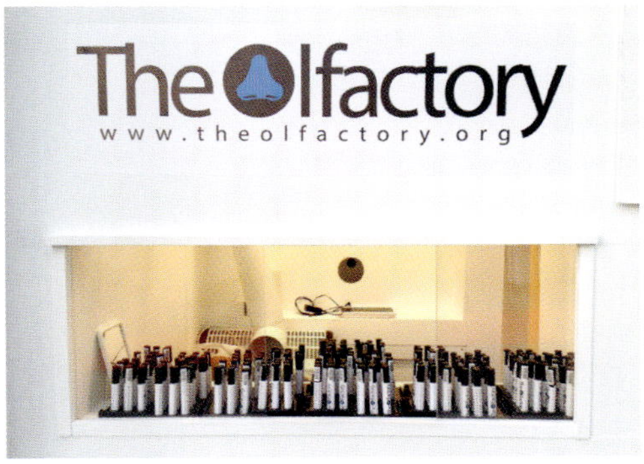

Scented Kisses Happening, 2014

On 23 September 2014, the Scented Kisses Happening was held at The Olfactory. More than 200 students took part in the happening. The scents were applied to canvas. On 5 small painter's canvases, people could smell the scents individually and try them out while kissing. On the large canvas, visitors could go in search of their favourite scent from the smaller canvases. This gave rise to a particular pattern drawn by the kisses on the large canvas based on the personal choices of the participants.

Op 23 september 2014 ging de Scented Kisses Happening in The Olfactory door. Meer dan 200 studenten namen deel aan de happening. De geuren waren aangebracht op canvas. Op 5 kleine schilderdoeken kon men de geuren apart ruiken en al kussend proeven. Op het grote canvas kon men op zoek gaan naar hun favoriete geur van de kleine doeken. Zo ontstond een bepaald patroon en kustekening op het grote doek, gebaseerd op de persoonlijke voorkeuren van de deelnemers.

Scented Kisses, The Olfactory, Hasselt, BE, 23.09.2014

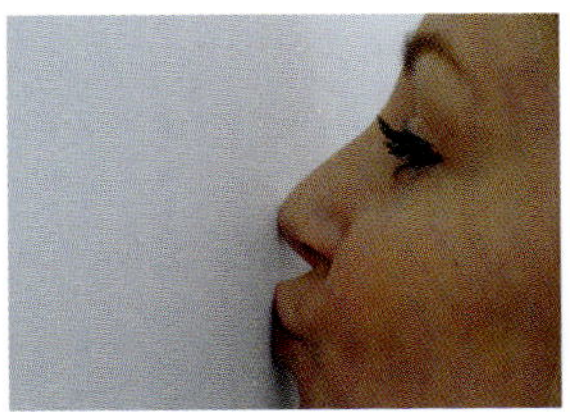

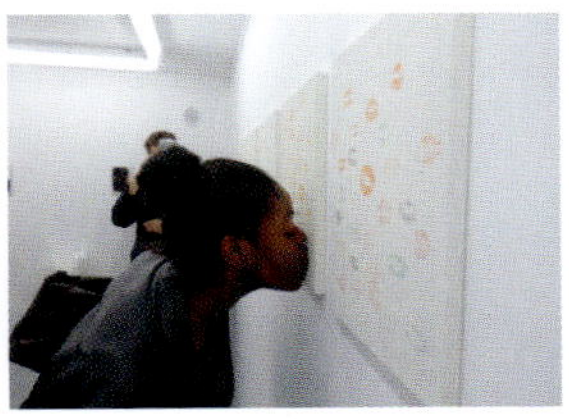

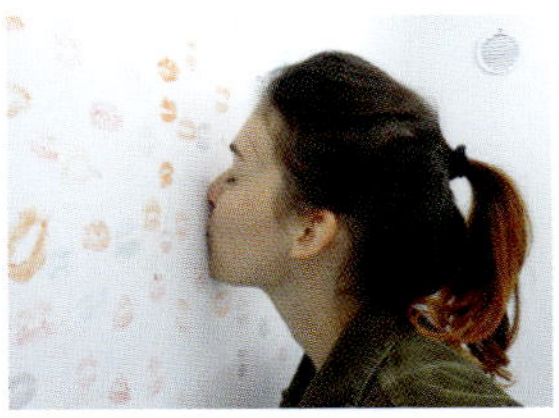

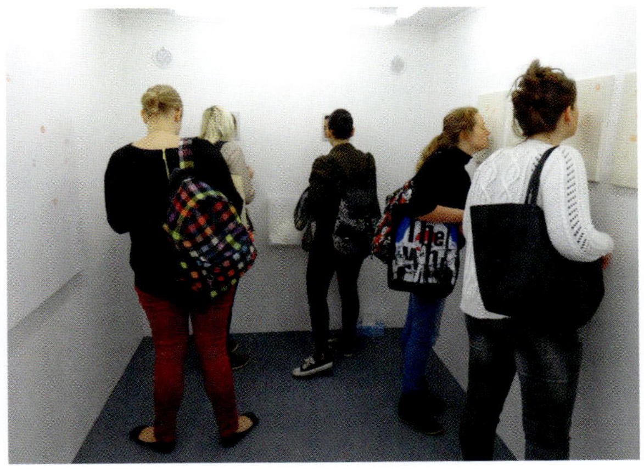

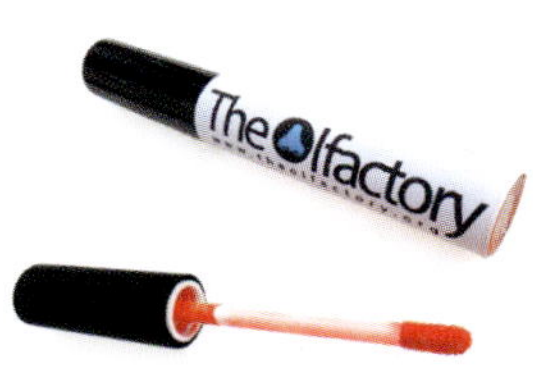

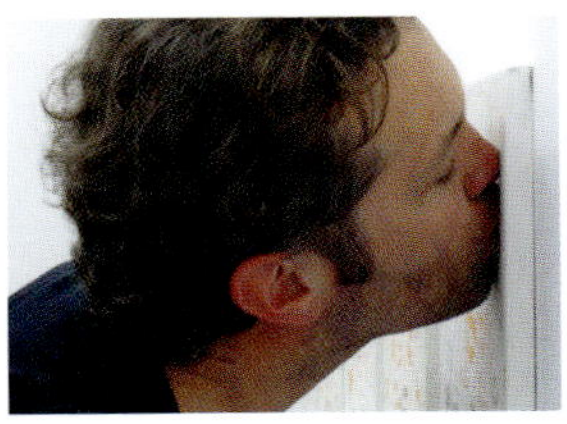

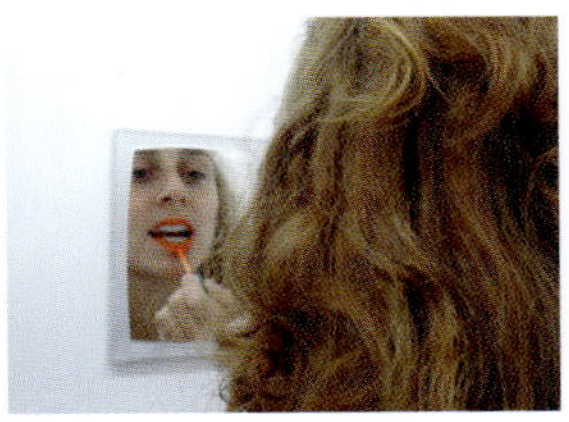

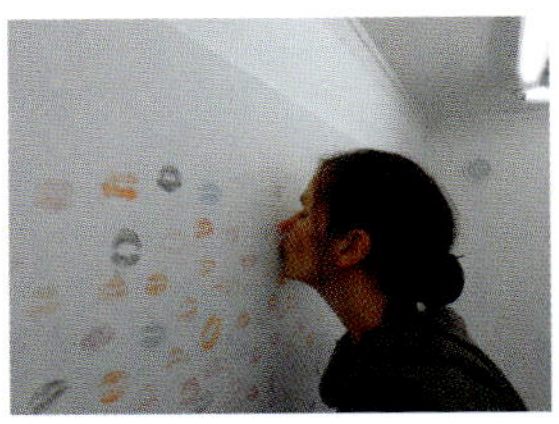

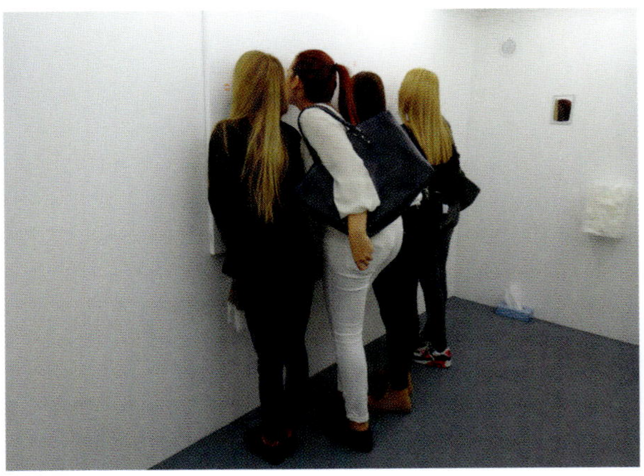

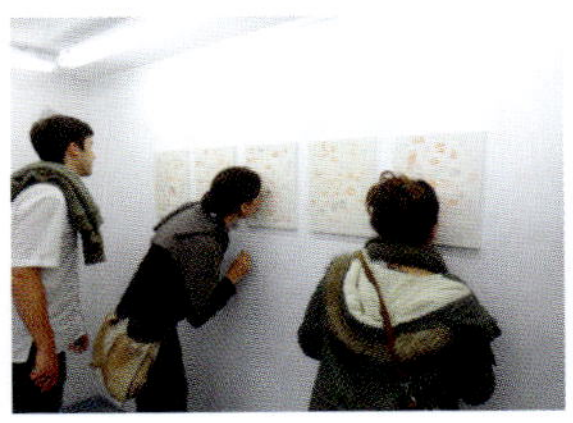

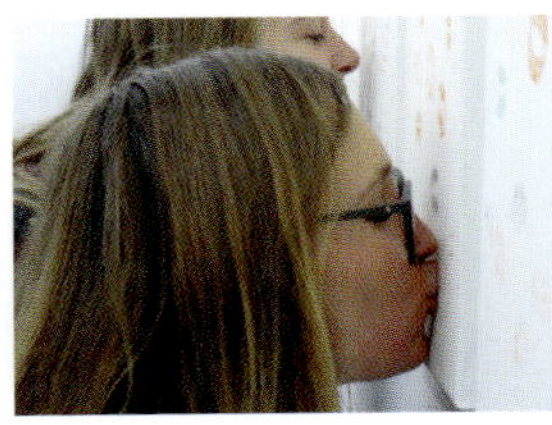

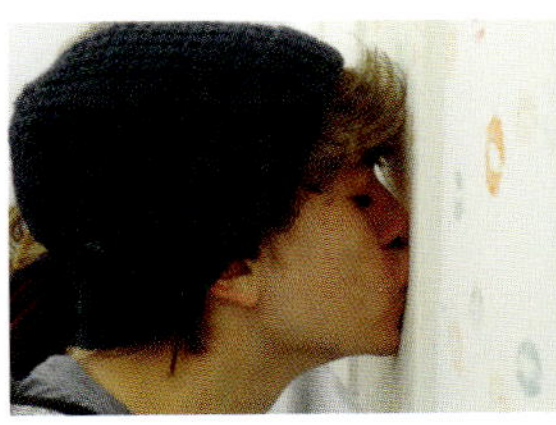

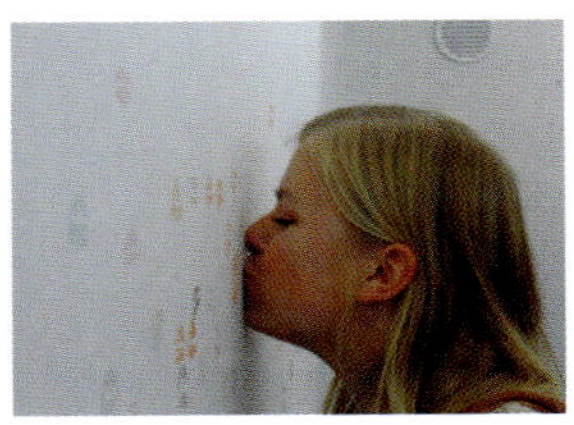

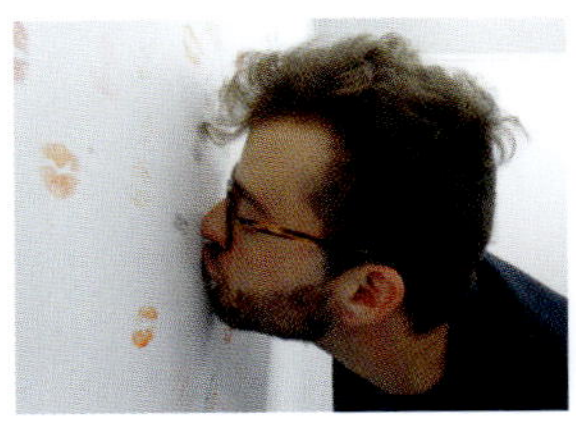

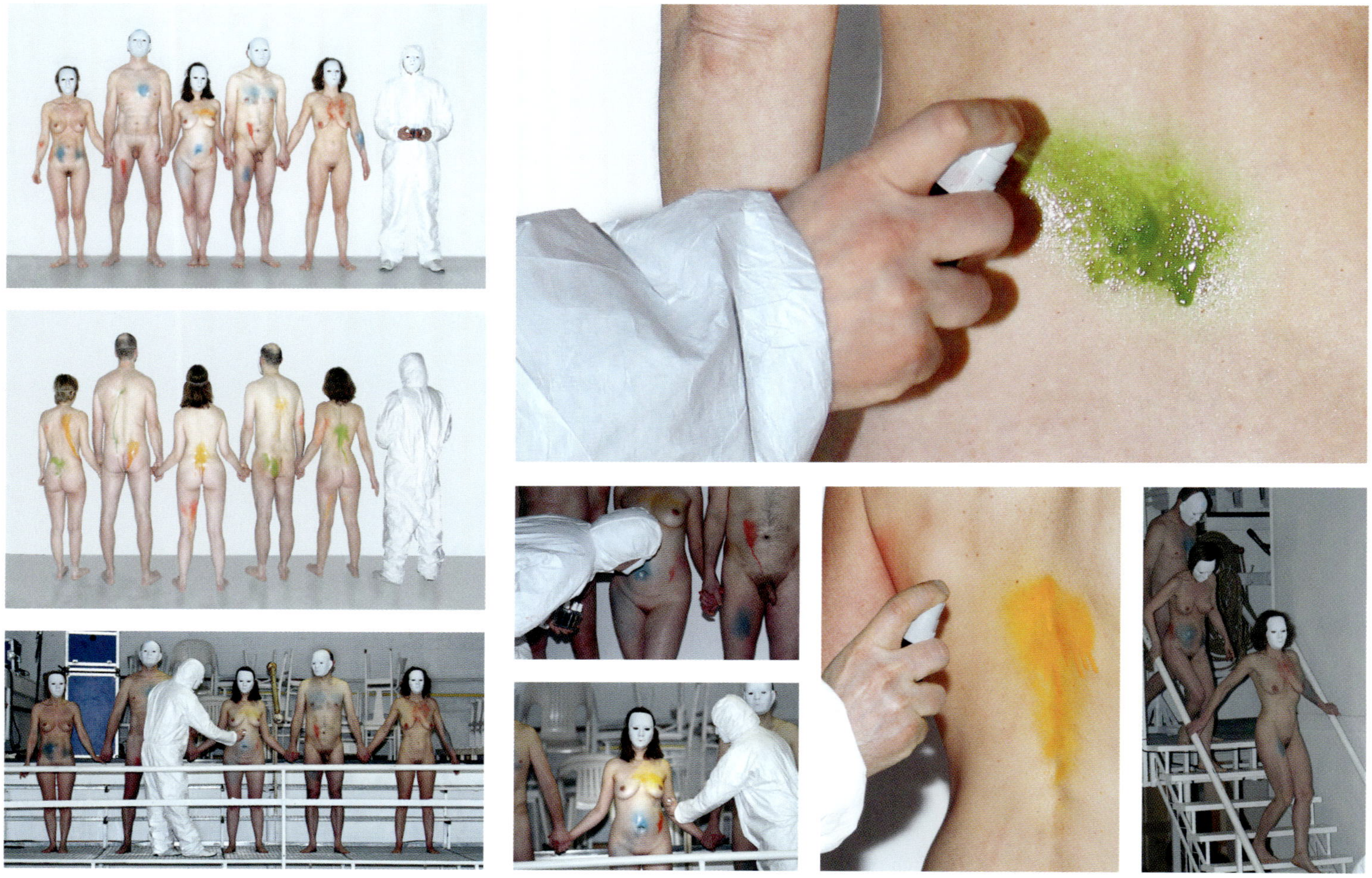

Smell My Colours I, 2014

5 naked people, each wearing a neutral white mask, were sprayed with coloured scents. After the perfumance, they wandered among the public and invited them to smell them.

5 naakte personen met een wit neutraal masker op werden geparfumeerd met gekleurde geuren. Na de perfumance wandelden ze door het publiek en lieten zich aan de aangebrachte geurkleuren op hun lichaam ruiken.

Lupercalia, Theatre Tinnenpot, Vermeylenfonds, curator Willem Elias, Gent, BE, 15.02.2014

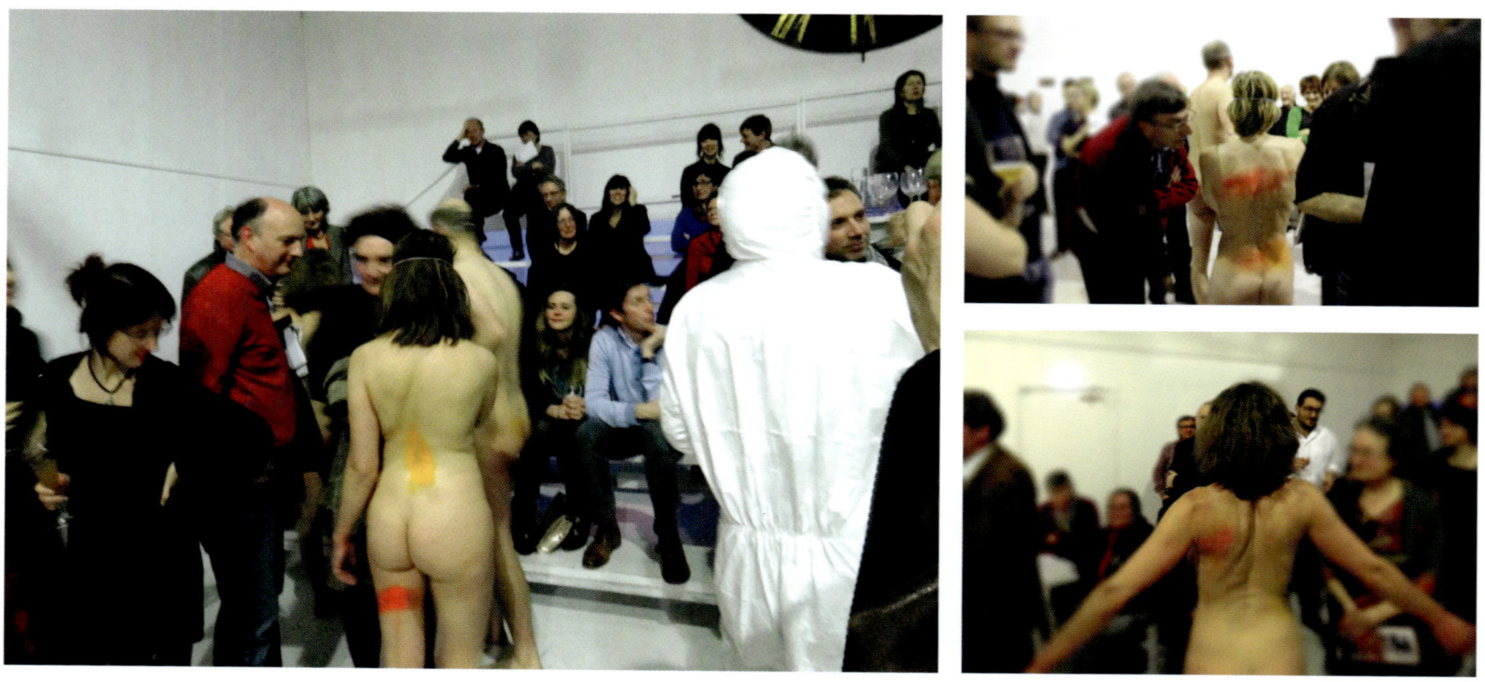

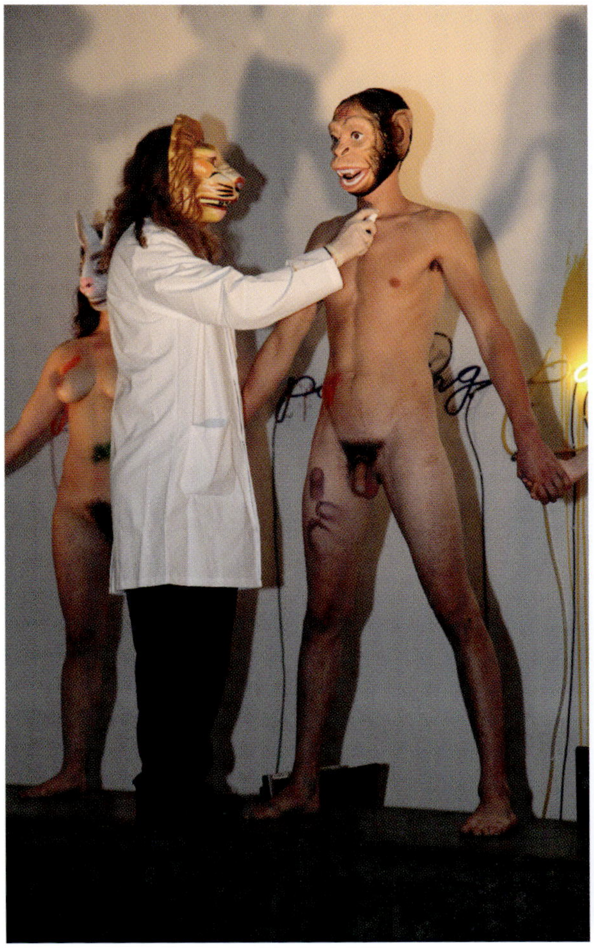

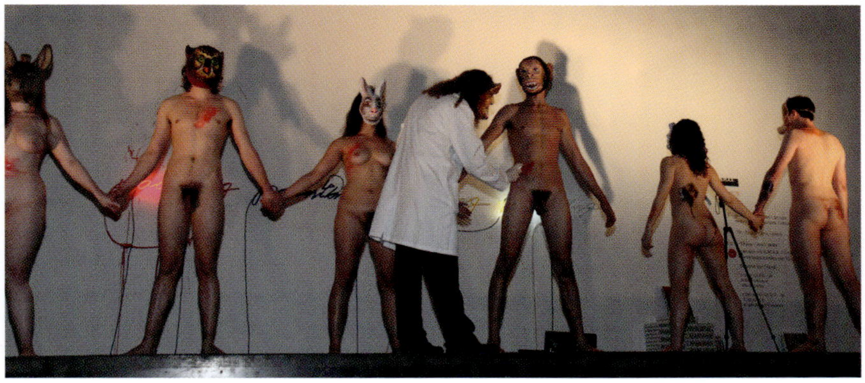

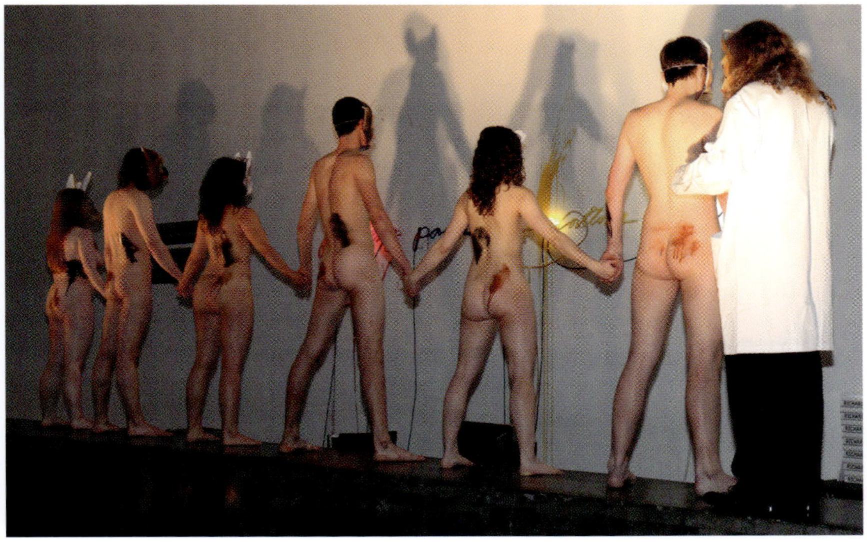

Smell My Colours II, 2014

6 naked people, each wearing an animal mask, were sprayed with coloured scents. After the perfumance, they wandered among the public and invited them to smell them.

6 naakte personen met ieder een masker op in de vorm van een dier, werden geparfumeerd met gekleurde geuren. Na de perfumance wandelden ze door het publiek en lieten zich aan de aangebrachte geurkleuren op hun lichaam ruiken.

Etcetera, S.M.A.K., curator Godart Bakkers, Ghent, BE, 08.05.2014

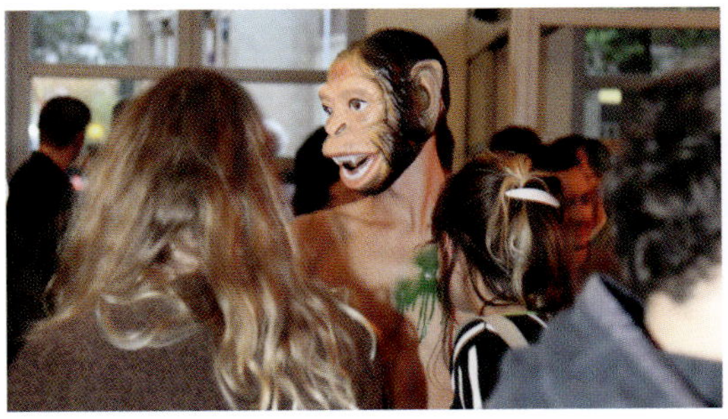

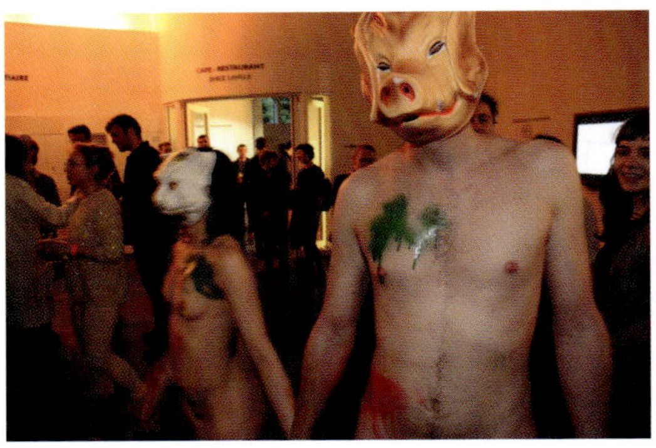

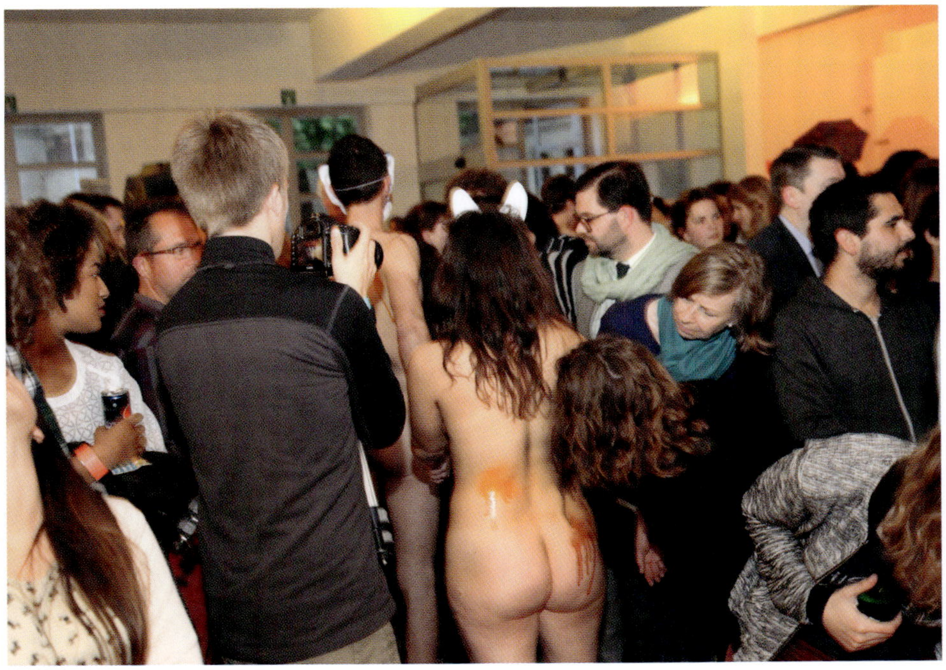

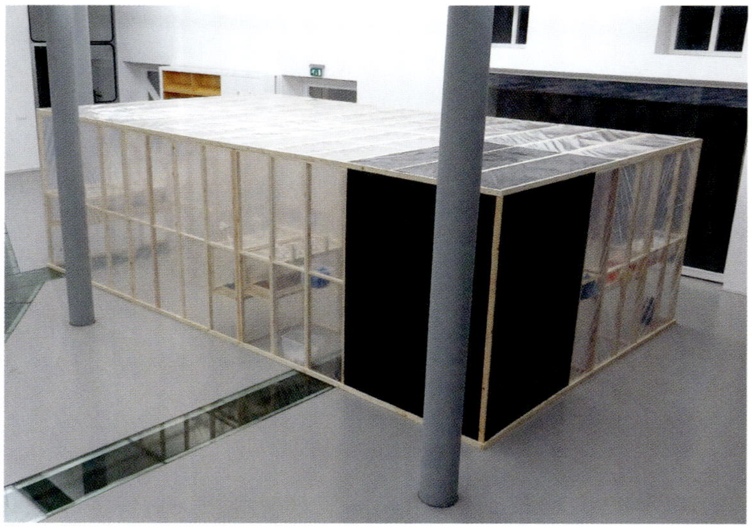

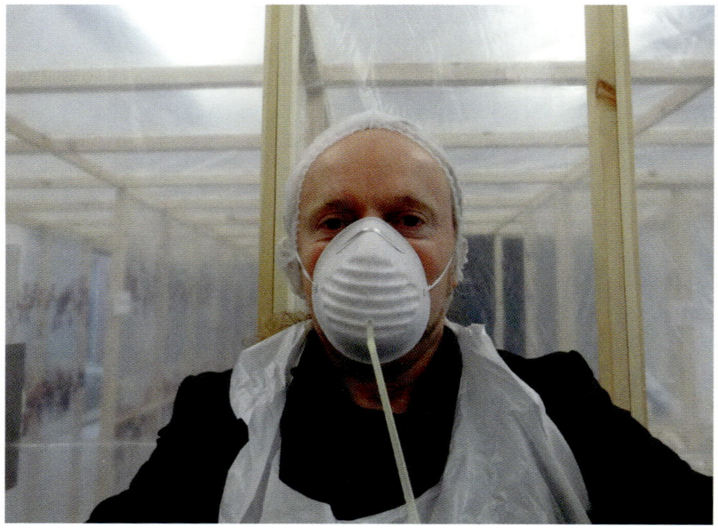

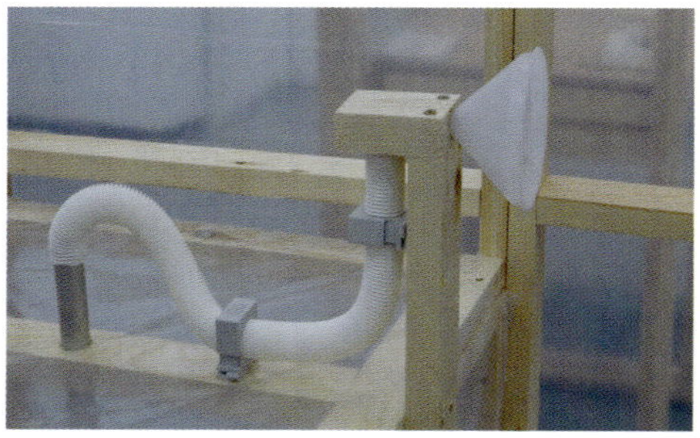

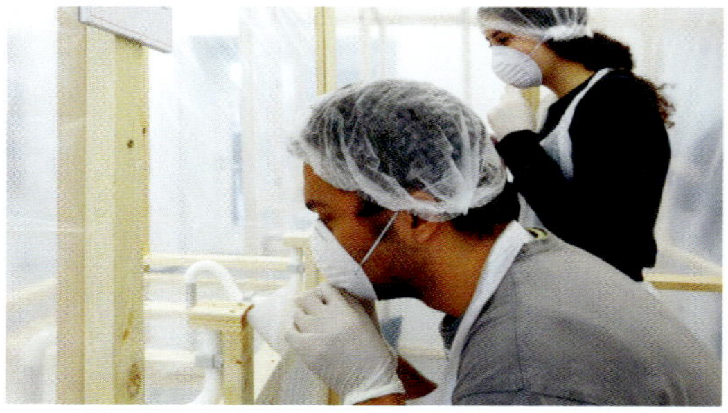

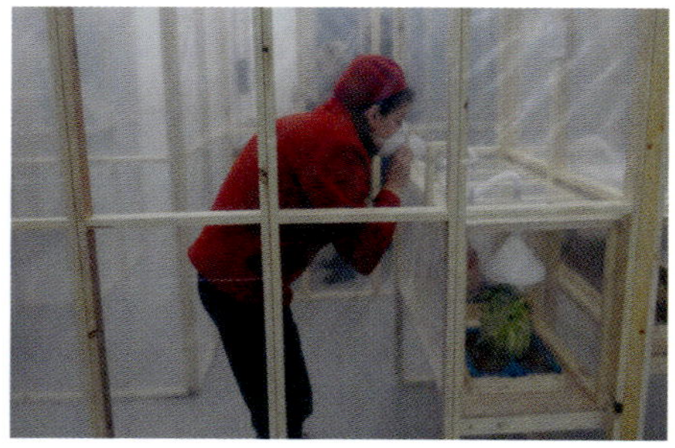

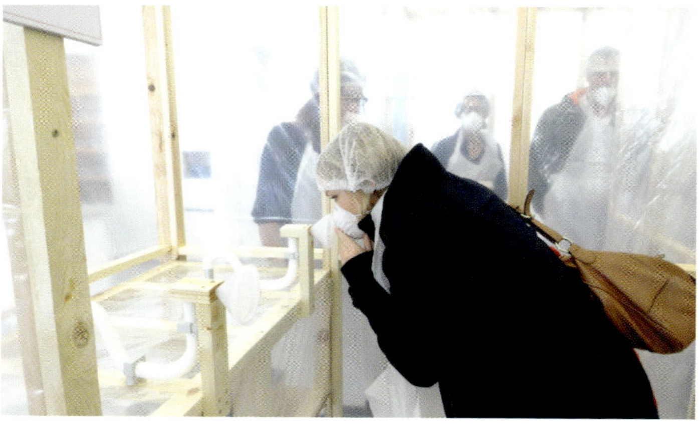

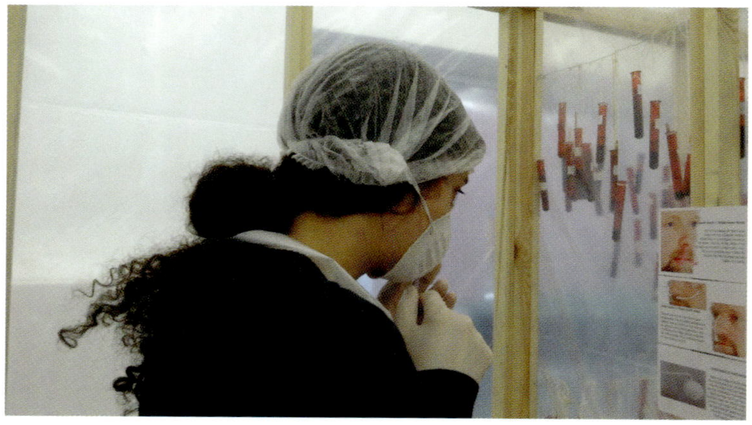

Smell Lab, 2013-2014

In the Smell Lab, visitors could enjoy 'scent engineered' plants and conduct experiments with smell.

In het Smell Lab kon men 'scent engineerde' planten ruiken en deden bezoekers experimenten met geur.

The Art of Smelling, Olfactory Art Research, Art Center Rozendaal 21, curator Yasmijn Jarram, Enschede, NL, 01.12.2013-02.03.2014

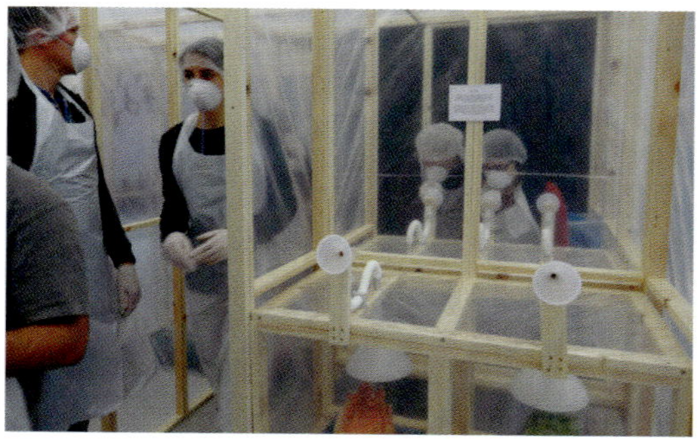

Pep & Straw, 2013

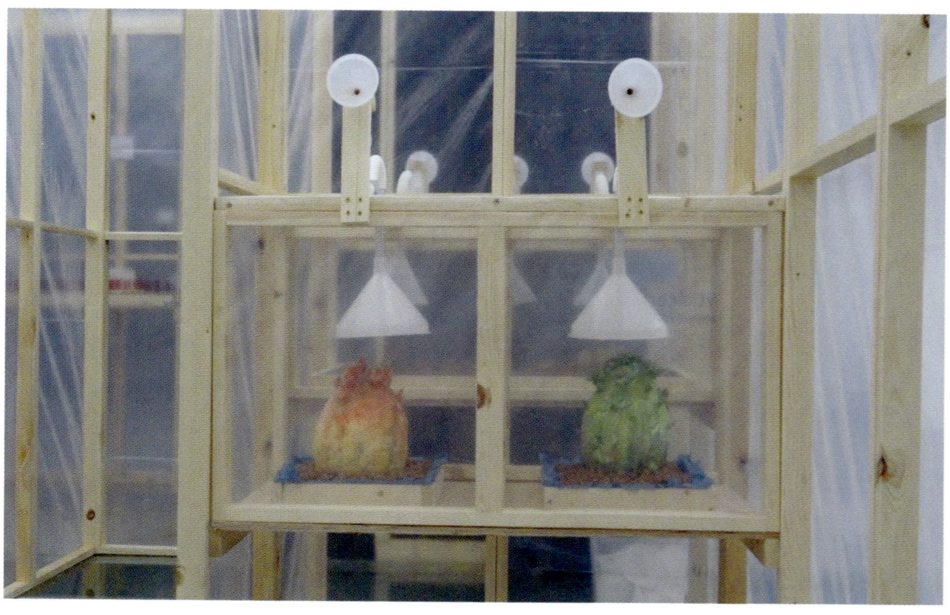

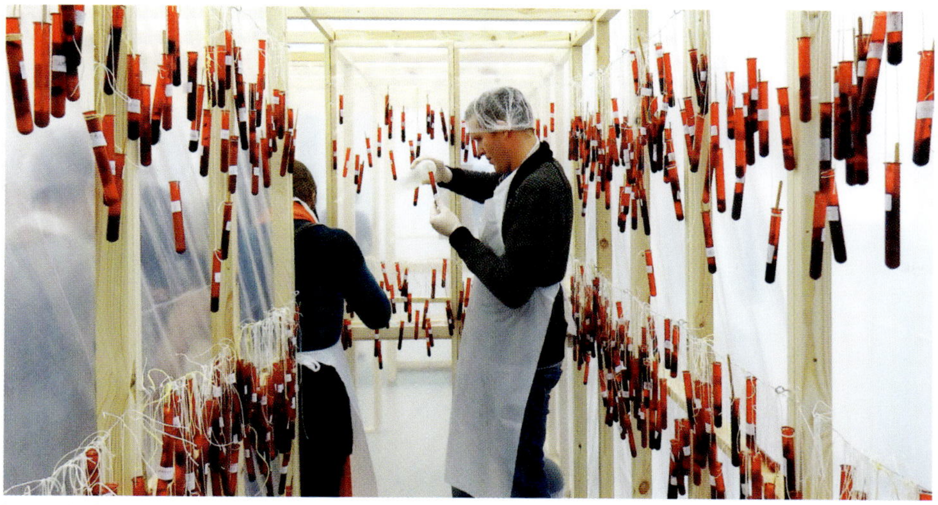

Interactive Smell Research

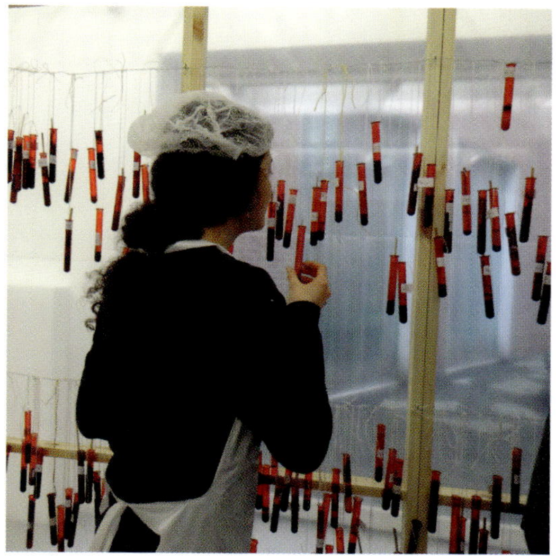

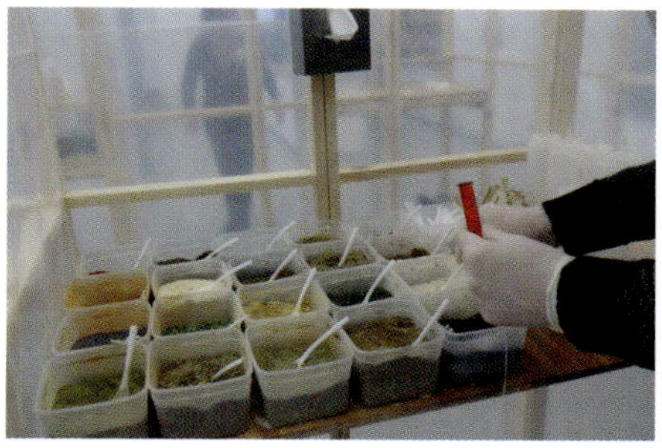

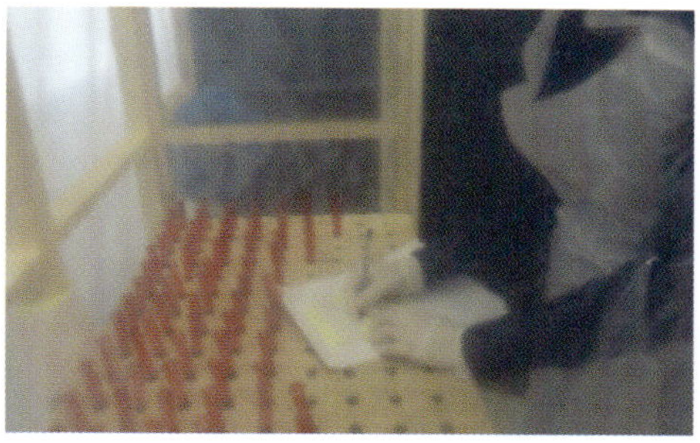

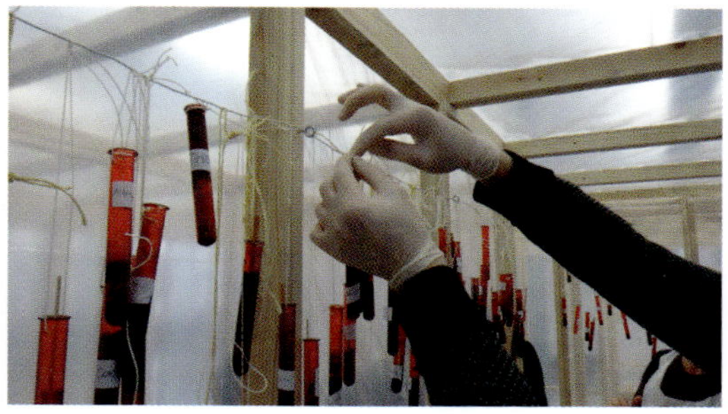

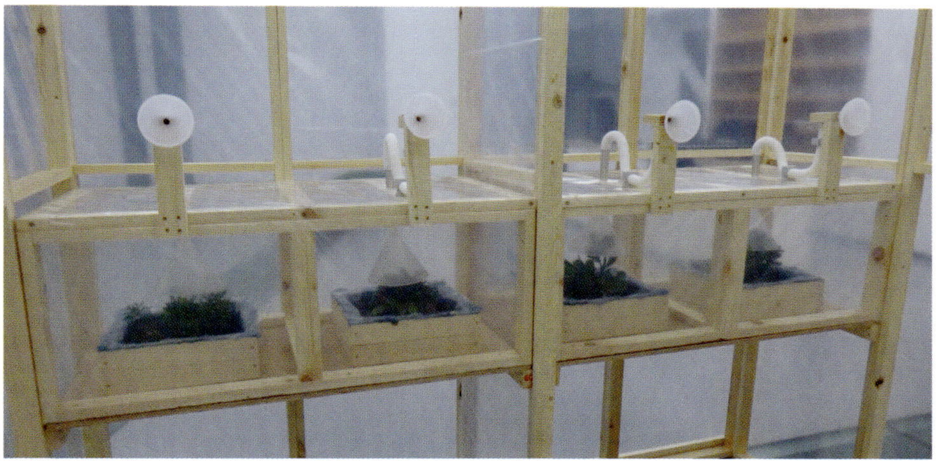

COG (Genetic Olfactory Manipulation)

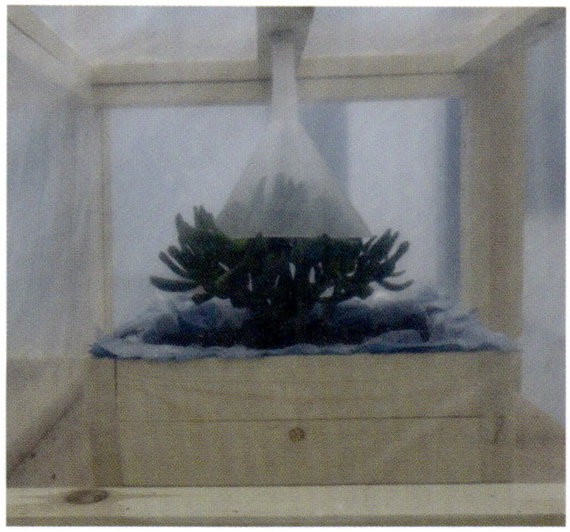

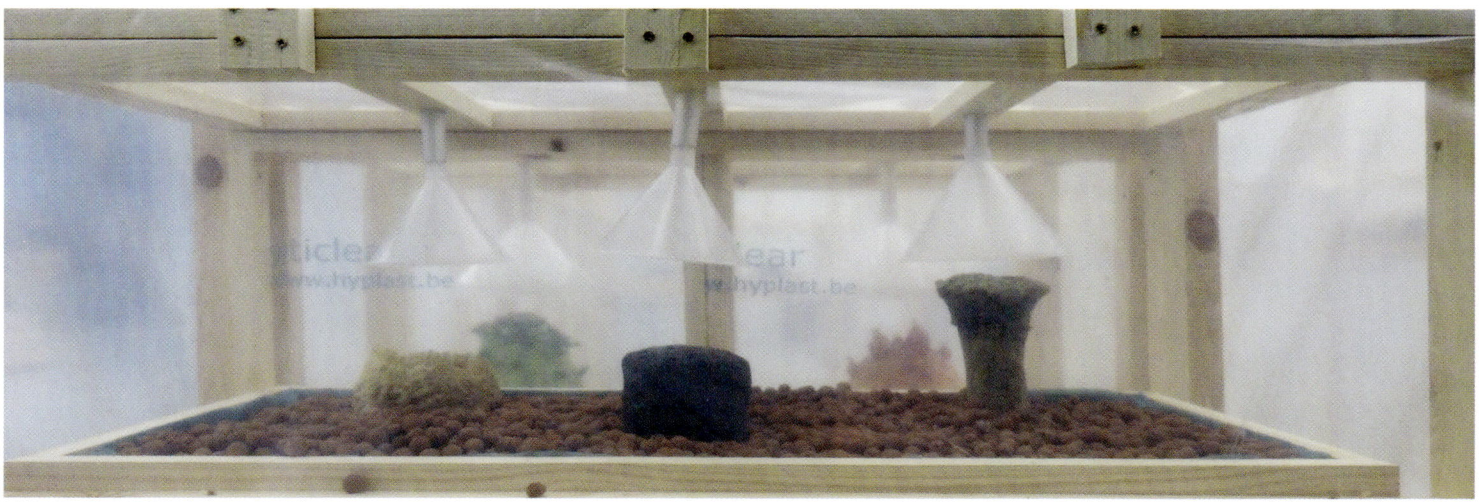

VBS (Visualisation By Smell)

PETER DE CUPERE

EXPERIMENTAL RESEARCH
Geur & Experiment

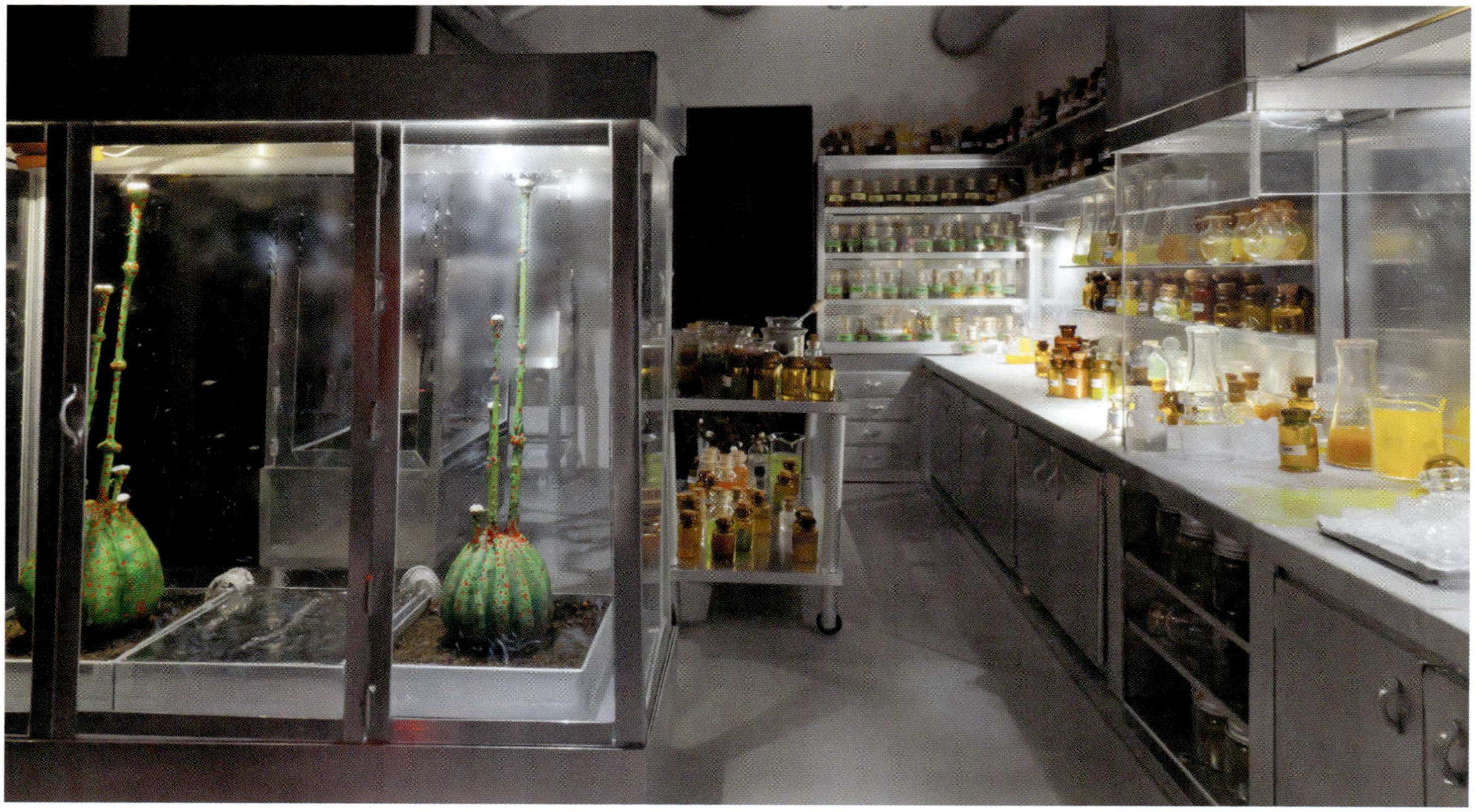

Foto © smart-pictures.be

Miniature Lab, 2012

Scale 1:7, 100 cm x 60 cm x 60 cm
Visitors can explore the different scents of the little scent sculptures and control the lights in the minilab. It was specially made for the project 'Museum to scale 1/7' by Ronny Van de Velde.

'Museum to scale' features more than one hundred exhibition rooms at a scale of 1/7. The exhibition gives an overview of Belgian art from the 20th and 21st centuries. 101 Belgian artists display their work in miniature rooms measuring 100 x 60 x 60 cm. Among the participating artists are Luc Tuymans, Jan Fabre, Jan De Cock, Koen Vanmechelen, Wim Delvoye and many more. 'Museum to scale' was on view in fall 2013 in the Royal Museum of Fine Arts Brussels, and later in the Baker Museum in Naples, Florida and Kunsthal Rotterdam.

Schaal 1:7, 100 cm x 60 cm x 60 cm
Bezoekers kunnen de verschillende geuren van de kleine geursculpturen ervaren en eveneeens het licht in het minilab bedienen. Deze installatie was speciaal gemaakt voor het project 'Museum to scale 1/7' van Ronny Van de Velde.

'Museum to scale' bestaat uit meer dan honderd artificiële kunstenaarsruimtes op een schaal van 1/7. De tentoonstelling geeft een beeld van de Belgische kunst van de 20ste en 21ste eeuw. 101 kunstenaars tonen hun werken in miniatuurruimtes op formaat 100 x 60 x 60 cm. Bij de deelnemende kunstenaars vinden we Luc Tuymans, Jan Fabre, Jan De Cock, Koen Vanmechelen en Wim Delvoye. 'Museum to scale' werd getoond in diverse internationale musea.

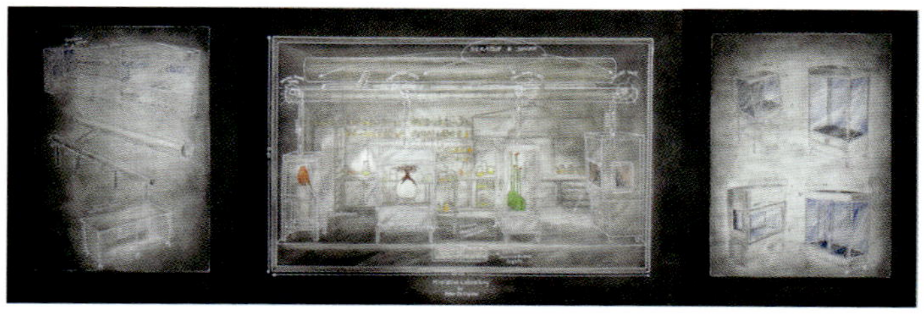

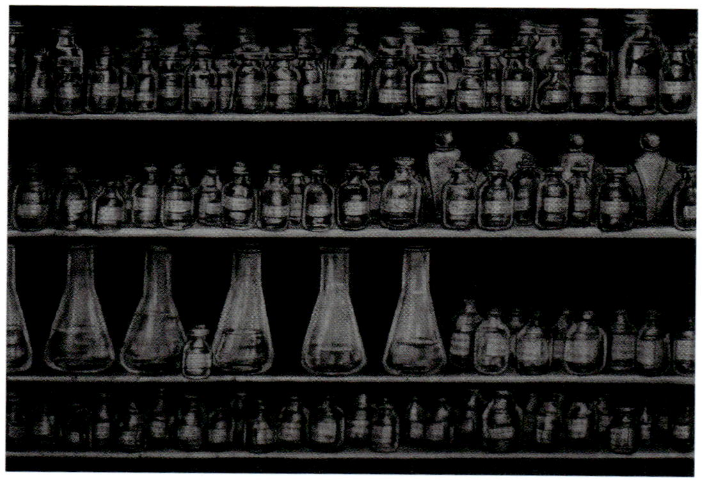

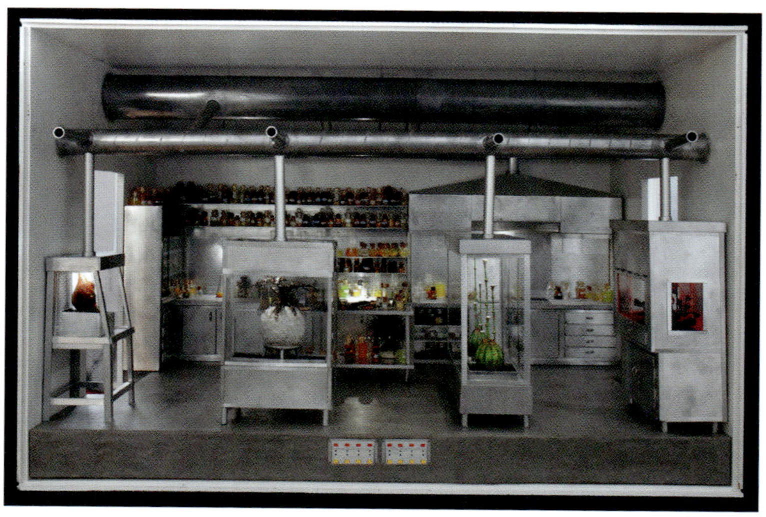

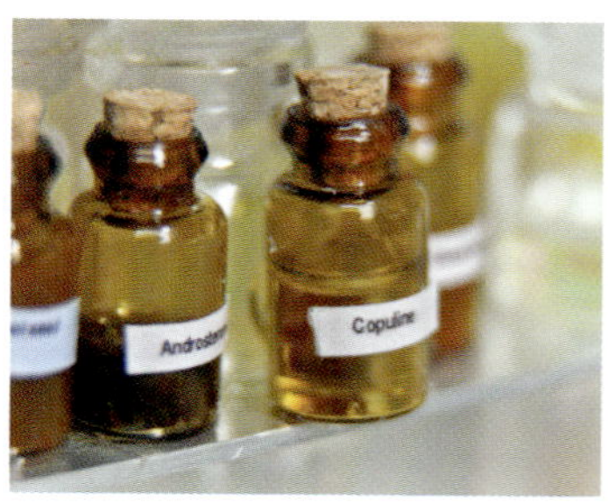

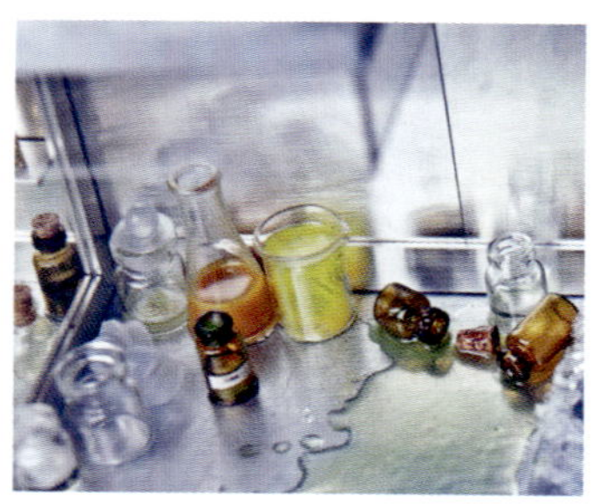

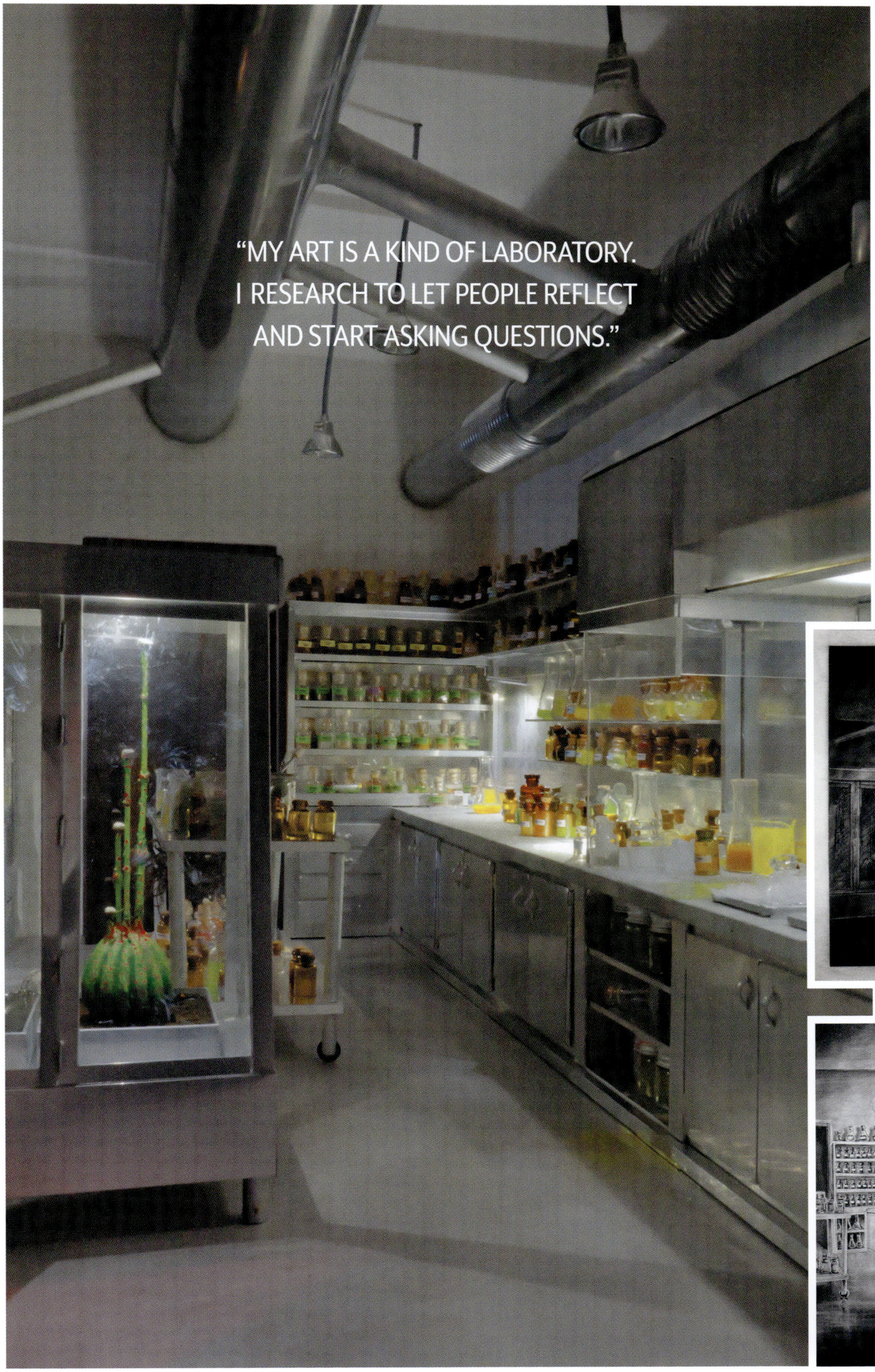

Museum to scale 1/7, Kunsthalle Rotterdam, curator Ronny Van de Velde, Rotterdam, NL 13.09.2014-14.12.2014

Museum to scale 1/7, The Baker Museum Naples, curator Ronny Van de Velde, Florida, USA 15.03.2014-31.07.2014

Museum to Scale 1/7, Royal Museums of Fine Arts of Belgium, curator Ronny Van de Velde, Brussels, BE 12.10.2013-02.02.2014

Brafa art fair, Tour & Taxis Brussels, Galerie Ronny Van de Velde, 21.01.2012-29.01.2012

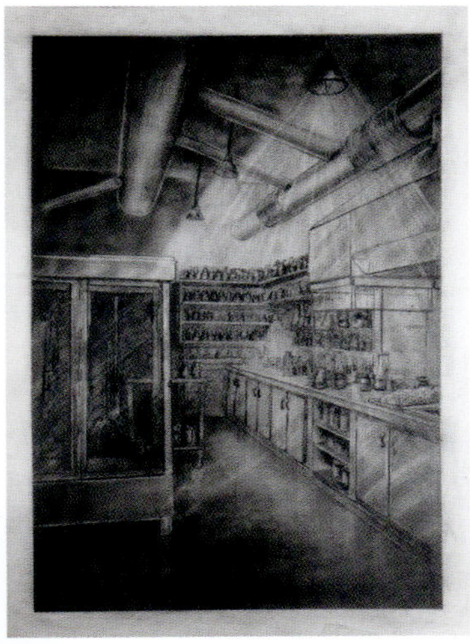

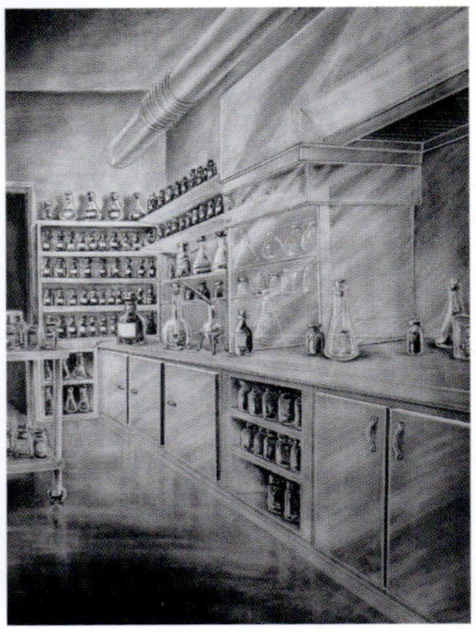

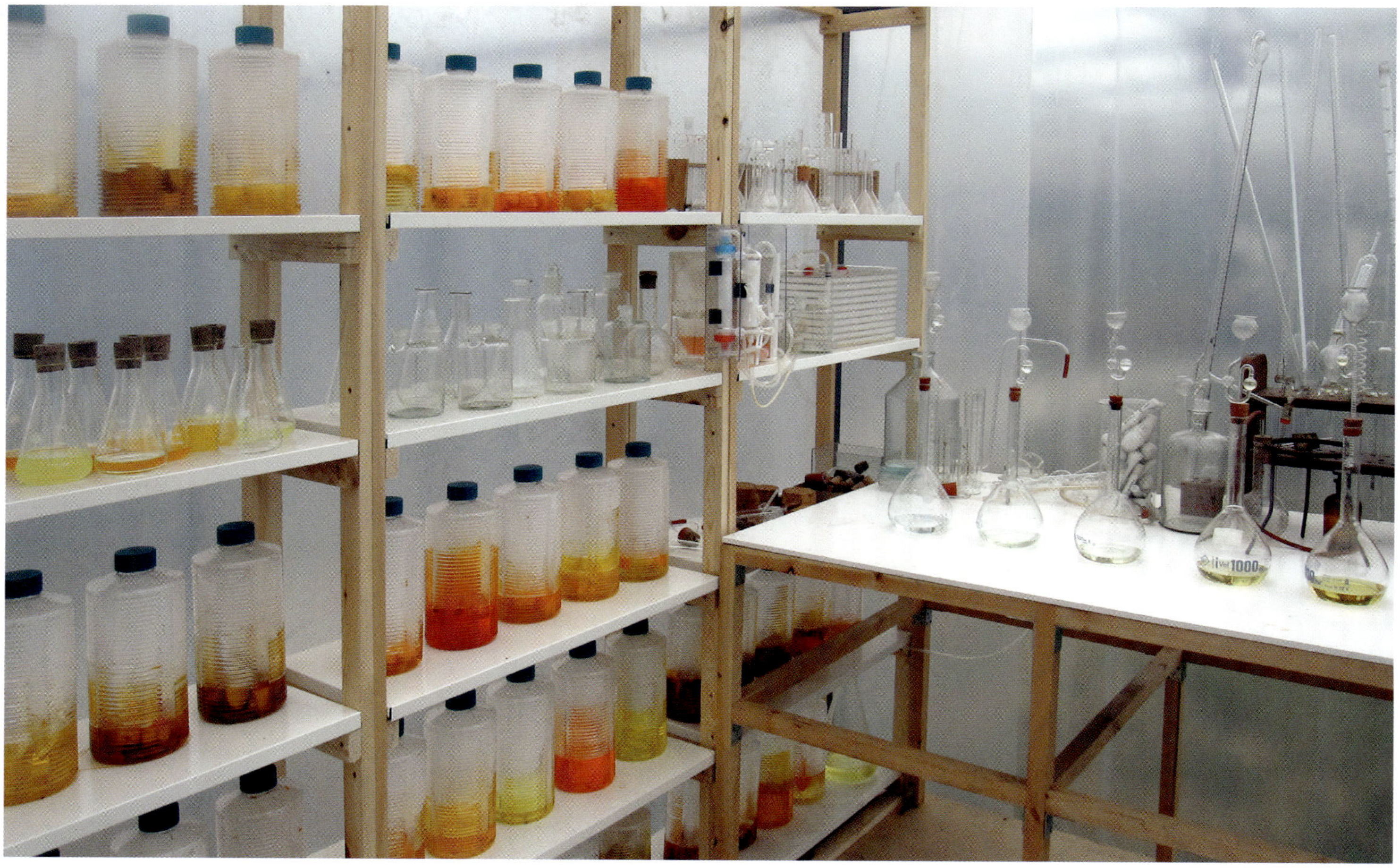

Experimental Lab, 2009

Smell experiments based on citrus fruit / Geurexperimenten op basis van citrusvruchten

Artificial Nature, Verbeke Foundation, Kemzeke, BE, 23.05.2009-15.11.2009

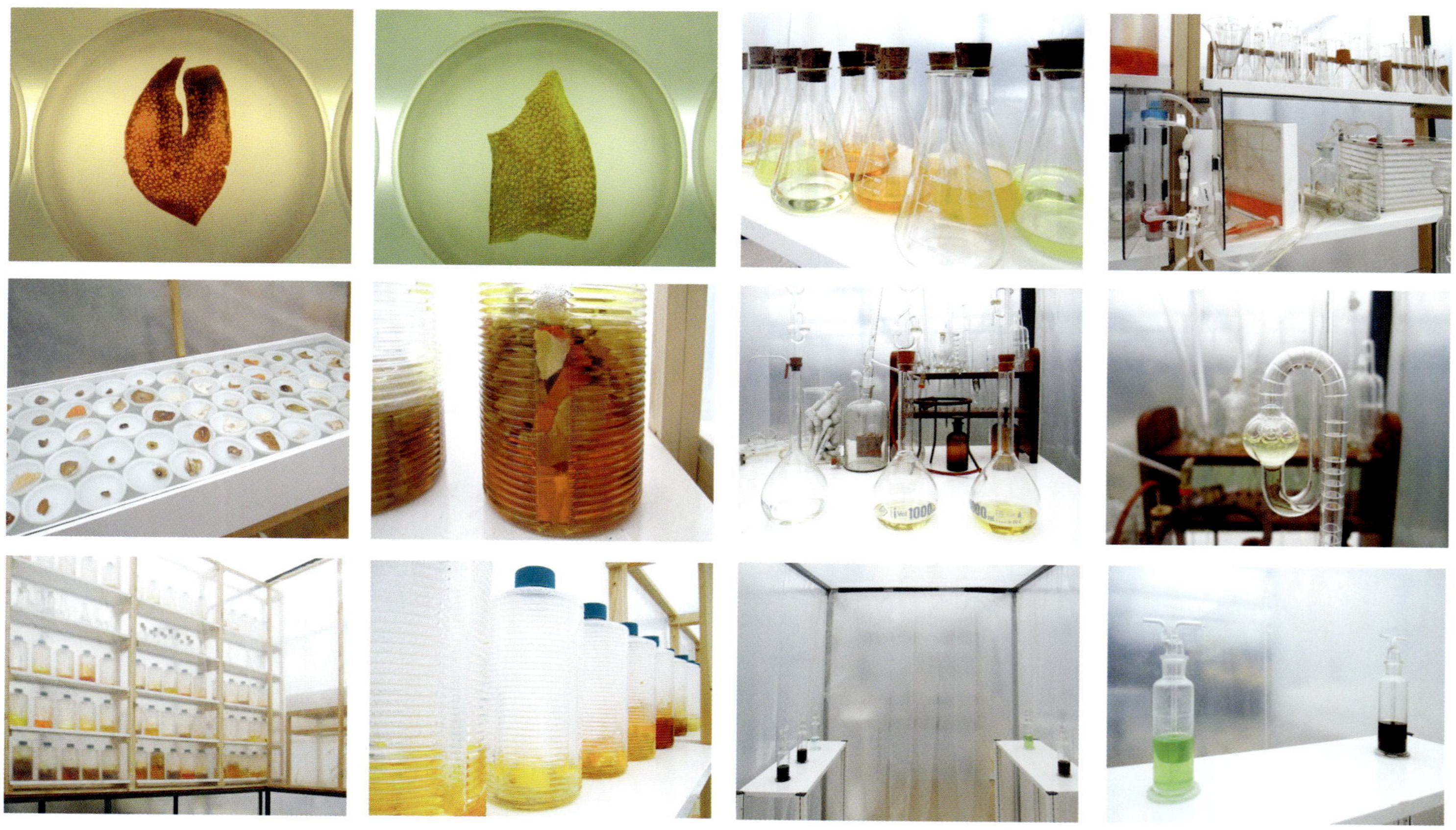

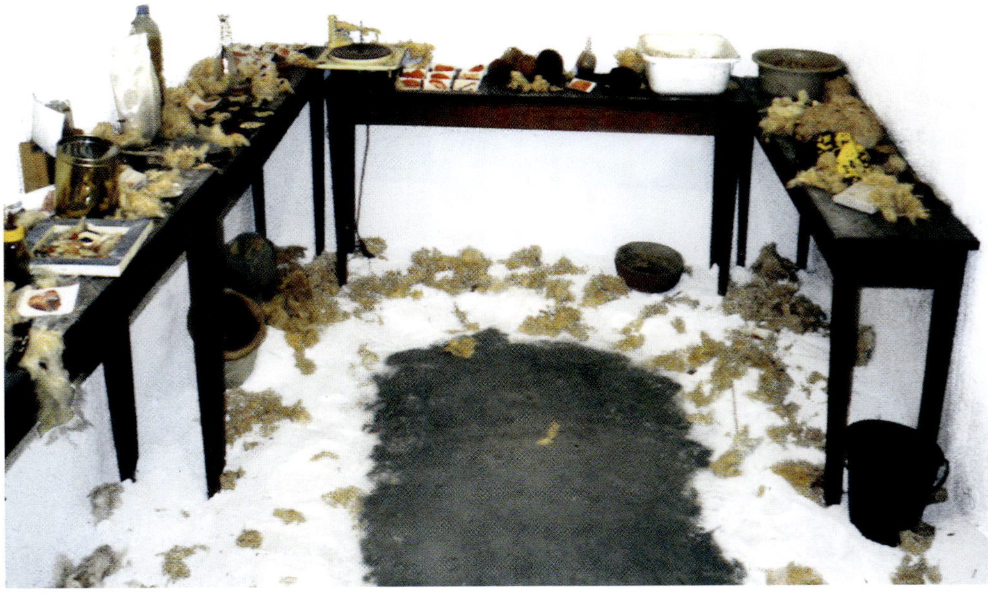

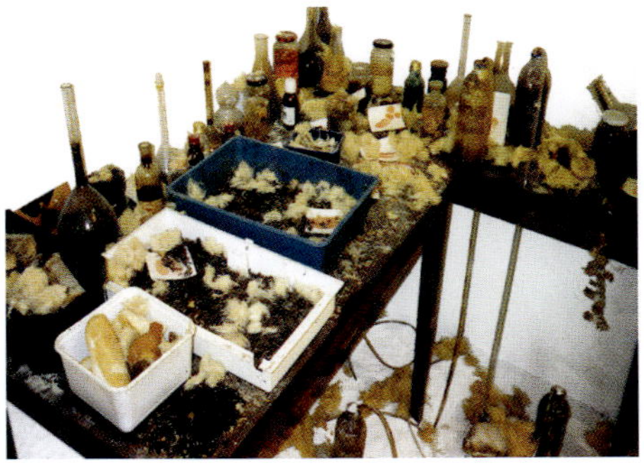

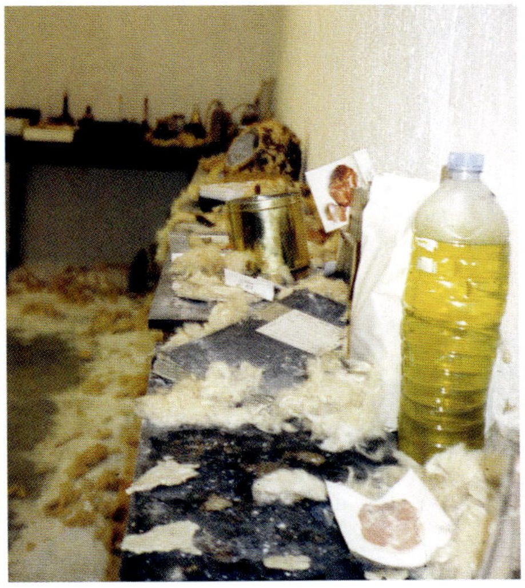

Aura Seminalis, 1997-1999

300 cm x 555 cm x 230 cm

Changing experiments in soap room (440 kg of soap on walls, ceiling and floor)

Levende experimenten in een zeepkamer (440 kg zeep uitgesmeerd op de muren, plafond en vloer)

Peter de Cupere, One-man exhibition in the association of the S.M.A.K., Ghent, BE, 07.05-06.06.1999
Collection: S.M.A.K., Ghent, BE

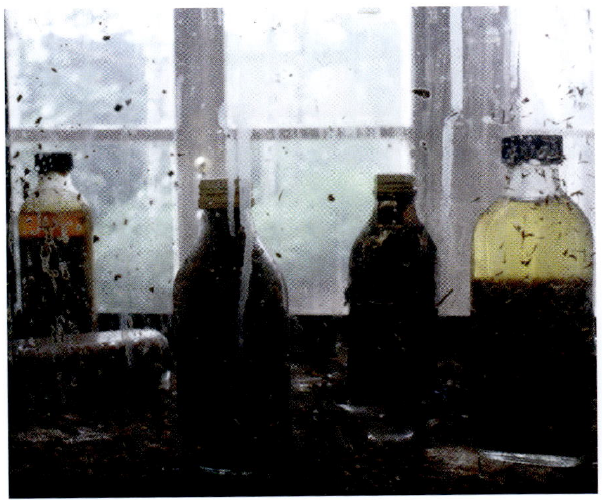

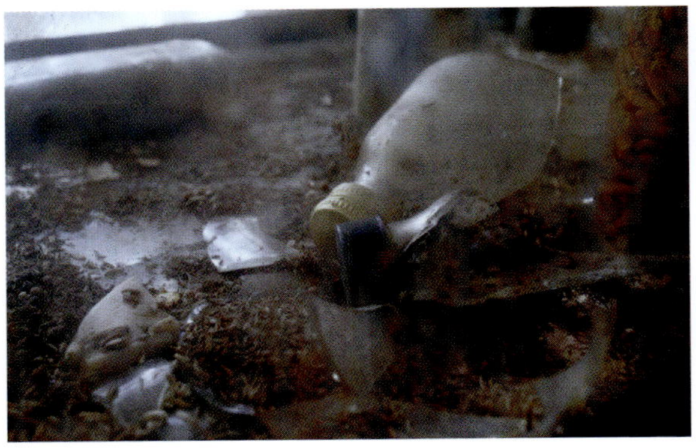

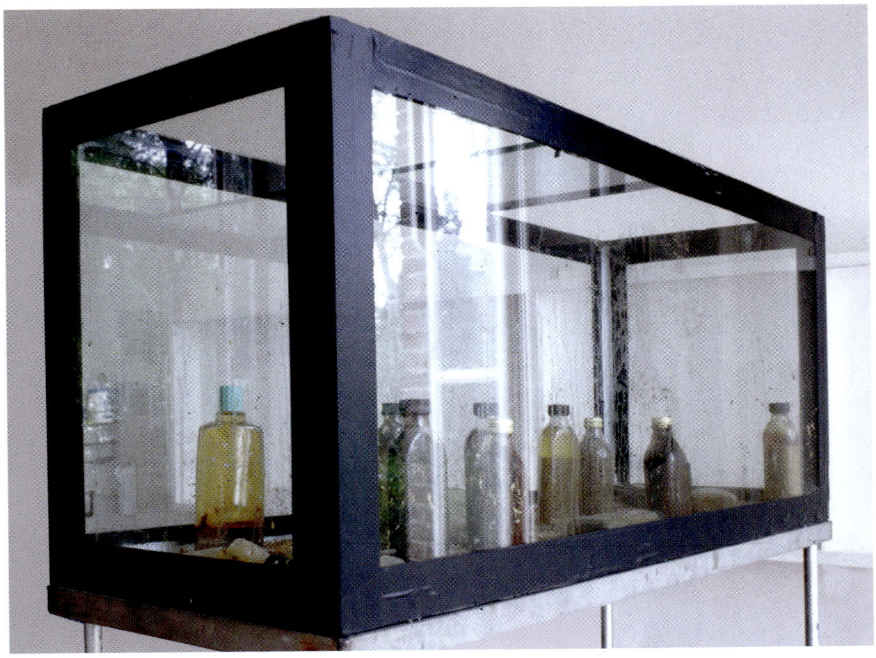

Exploding Bottles, 1996-1997

Bottles filled with spices and water, will explode by fermentation at different time.

Flessen gevuld met kruiden en water exploderen op verschillende tijdstippen door de fermentatie.

Collection: S.M.A.K. Ghent, Belgium (1999)
Peter de Cupere, One-man exhibition in the association of the S.M.A.K., Ghent, BE, 07.05-06.06.1999

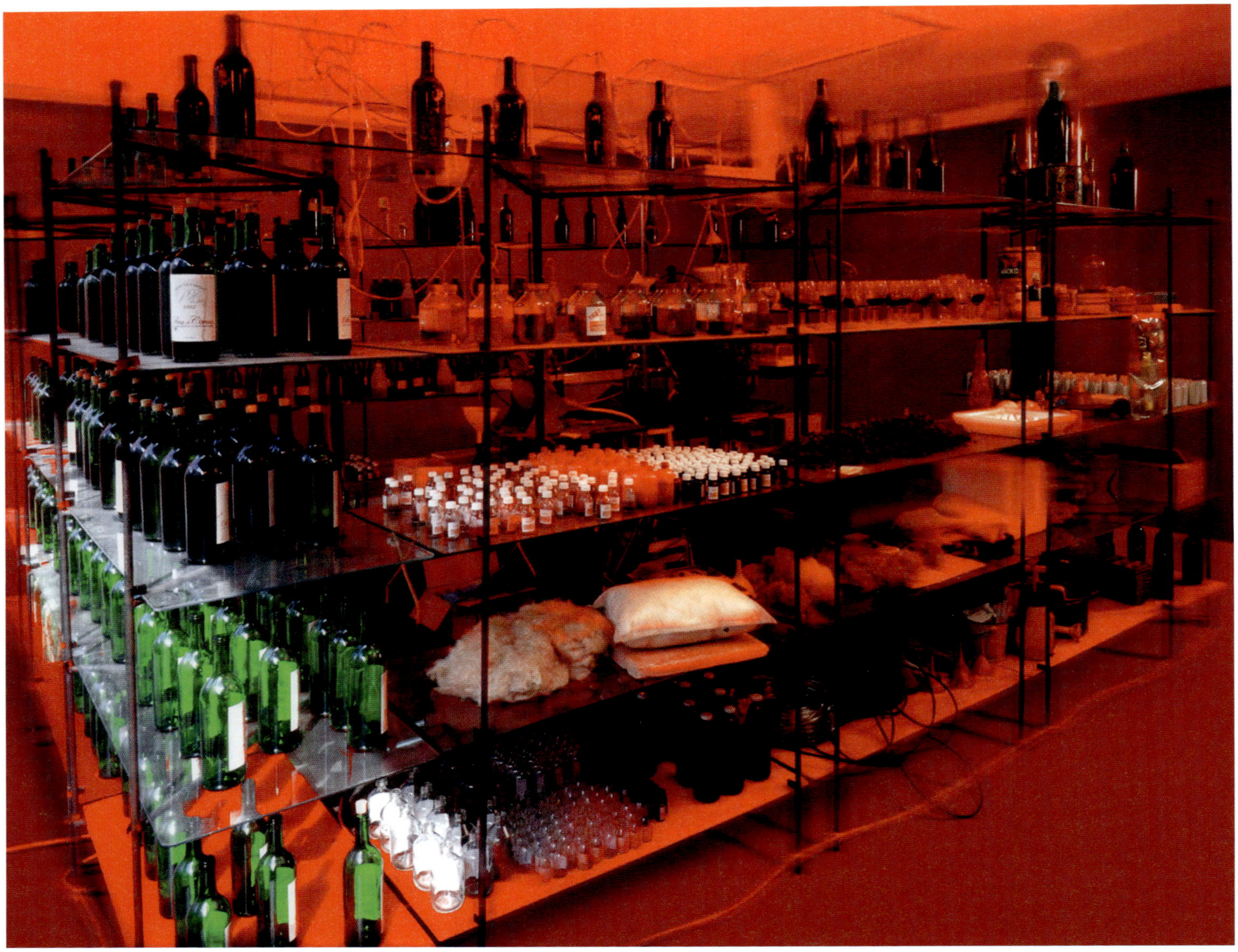

Grand Vin d'Anvers, 2002

±385 cm x 500 cm x 500 cm

Wine Smell Installation. Wine made of dried raisins, not drinkable, coloured, total installation, meekrap-red coloured room.

Wijn-geurinstallatie. Wijn gemaakt van gedroogde rozijnen, niet drinkbaar en gekleurd. De ruimte is geschilderd in rubine rood.

Van Laere Contemporary Art, Antwerp, BE, 07.03-13.04.2002

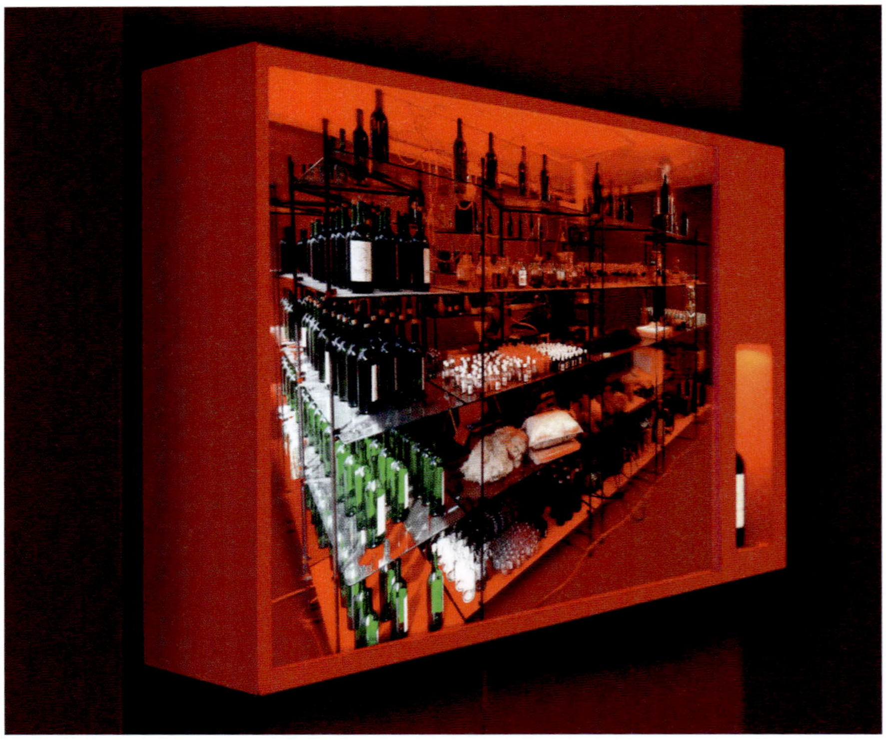

Light Box Grand Vin d'Anvers, 2002

95 cm x 150 cm x 30 cm

'The Collector's House', St.-Lucas Stichting, Brussels, BE
curator Filip Luyckx, 16.01-22.03.2003

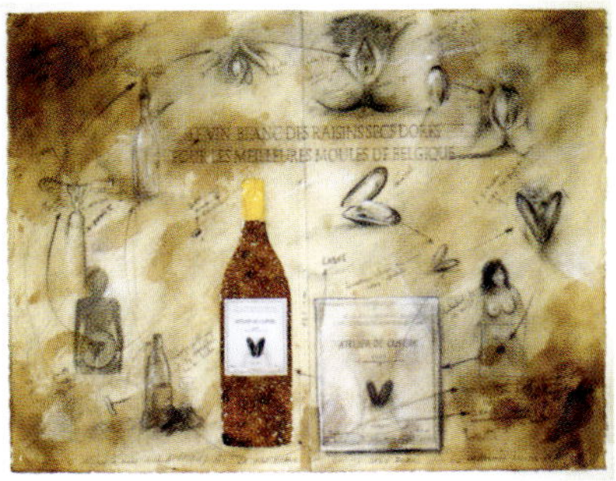

Drawing Le Vin Blanc Des Raisins Secs
Dores Pour Les Meilleures Moules De Belgique, 2000

55 cm x 68,5 cm

Drawing combined with dried raisins. Edition of 100 ex.

Tekening gecombineerd met gedroogde rozijnen. Editie op 100 ex.

Edition for 'Save the Mosselpot' of Marcel Broodthaers, 2001
S.M.A.K., 26 jan., Editions of Panamarenko, Luc Tuymans, Jan Fabre, Jacques Charlier, Jan Van Imschoot, Berlinde De Bruyckere, Peter de Cupere

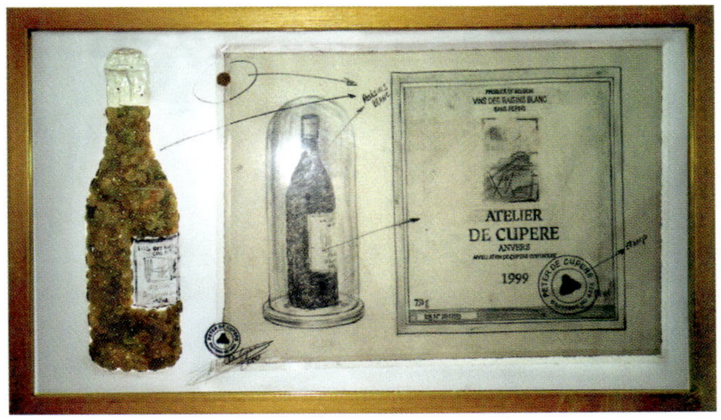

White Wine Bottle, Atelier de Cupere, 2000

Drawing with white wine bottle made of dried raisins

Tekening met een witte wijnfles gemaakt van gedroogde rozijnen

Van Laere Contemporary Art, Antwerp, BE, 2000

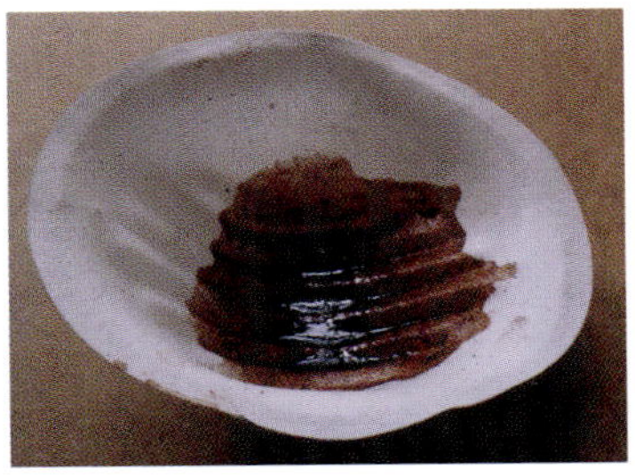

Mask, 1999

Mask with dried red wine

Masker met gedroogde rode wijn

Multiple, ed. 50 ex. 1 A.P.
presentation in S.M.A.K., Ghent, BE
1999

2 Raisins 1 Reason, 2014

Multiple 100 ex.
Variable measures / Variabele dimensies

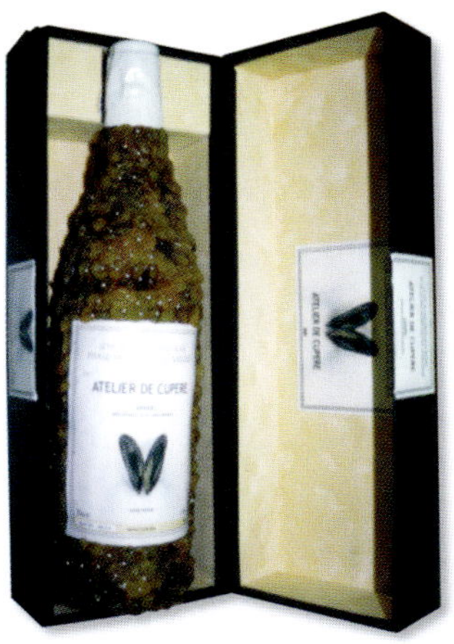

Wine Bottle, Atelier de Cupere, 1999-2000

Bottle wine made of dried raisins

Wijnfles gemaakt van gedroogde rozijnen

3 ex., 1 A.P.

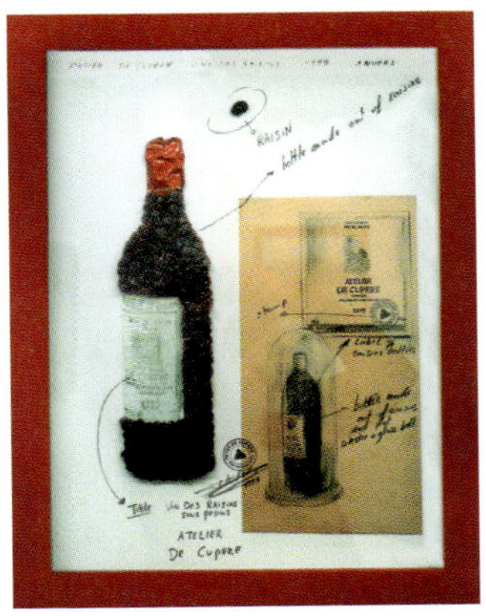

Red Wine Bottle, Atelier de Cupere, 2000

Drawing with red wine bottle made of dried raisins

Tekening met een rode wijnfles gemaakt van gedroogde rozijnen

Van Laere Contemporary Art, Antwerp, BE
2000

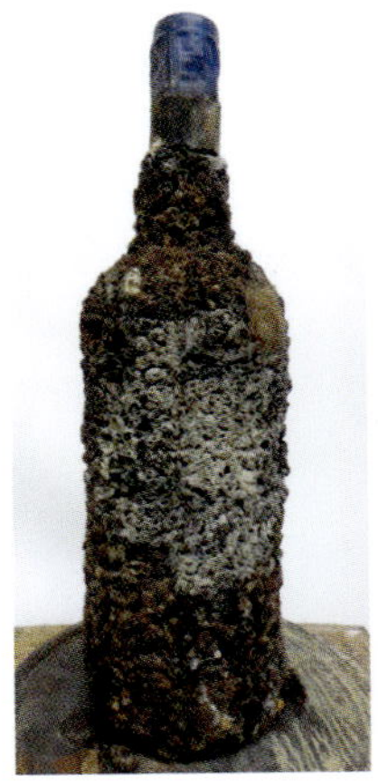

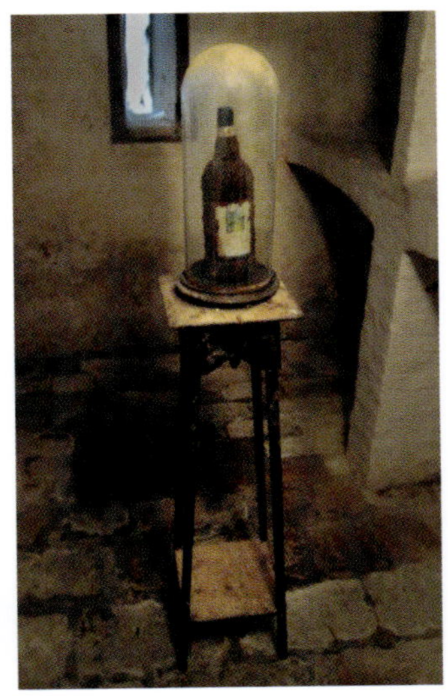

Wine Bottle, 1999-2001

Bottle wine made of dried raisins

Wijnfles gemaakt van gedroogde rozijnen

Smell the Castle, Castle Beauvoorde, curator Annemie Morisse, Beauvoorde, BE 15.07.2007-30.08.2007
C'est Beau, C'est Belge, Gallery Barbara Farber La Serre, Trest, FR 07.04-30.06.2001

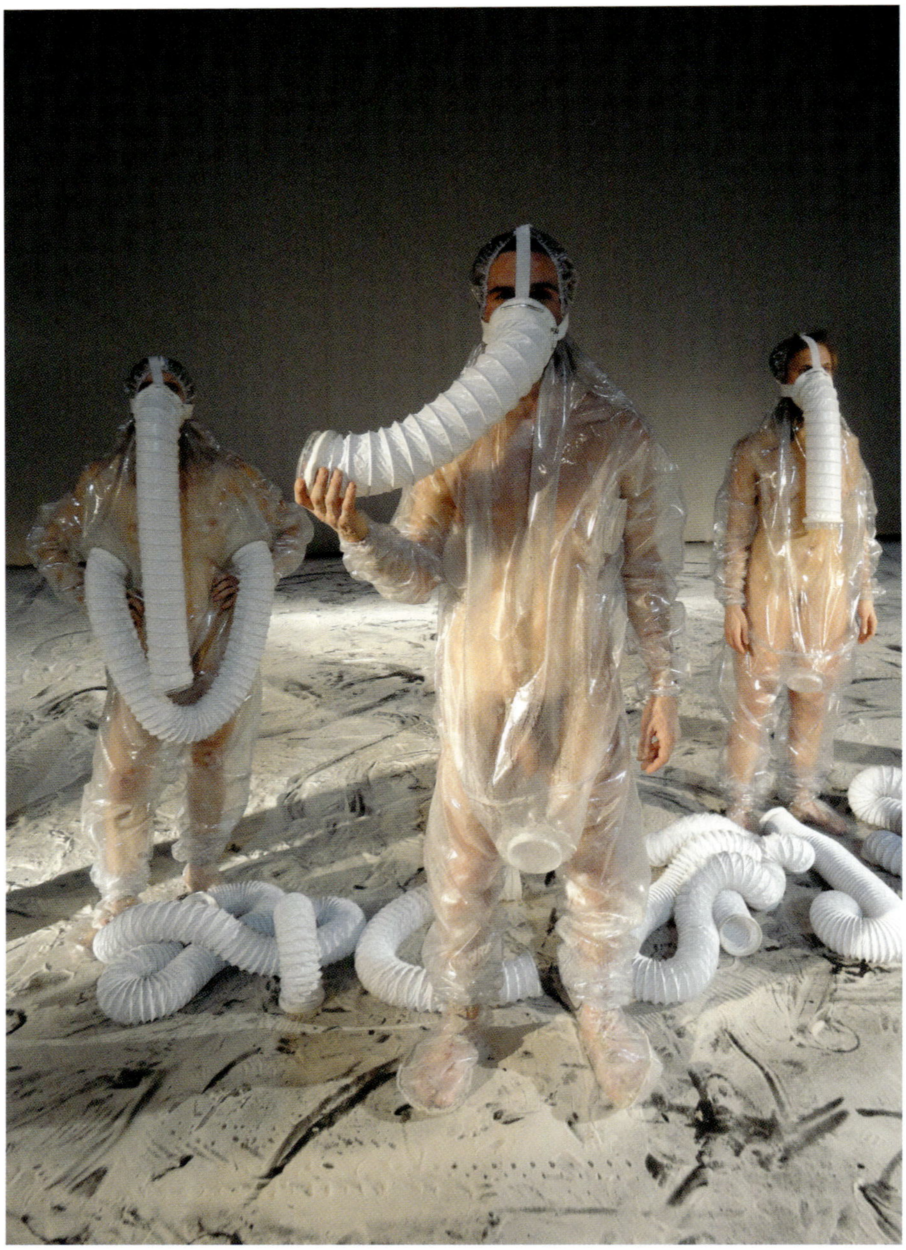

Sweat, 2010

Dance performance with five dancers. The sweat was collected in special costumes and distilled after the event. The scent of the sweat was later spread on the dance lab's walls. The sweat is protected by a glass box which the visitor can smell via a small opening. Prior to the performance, the artist prepared a different four course dinner for each dancer (examples of a few of the in total twenty different dishes prepared; pre-course, soup, main course, dessert).

This work was launched in Troubleyn, Smell Dance Performance: SWEAT, org. Troubleyn, curator Jan Fabre, 11.12.2010.

Dansperformance met 5 dansers; het zweet van de dansers wordt in de speciale kostuums opgevangen welke daarna gedistilleerd werden. De zweetgeur werd op de muur van het danslabo aangebracht. Beschermd door een glazen box kan de bezoeker via een kleine opening de zweetgeur waarnemen. Voor de performance werd door de kunstenaar voor iedere danser een verschillende 4-gangen maaltijd gemaakt (voorbeelden van een paar gerechten van in totaal 20 verschillende bereidingen, voorgerecht, soep, hoofdgerecht, nagerecht).

Inhuldiging van nieuwe werken in Troubleyn, Smell Dance Performance: SWEAT, org. Troubleyn, curator Jan Fabre, 11.12.2010

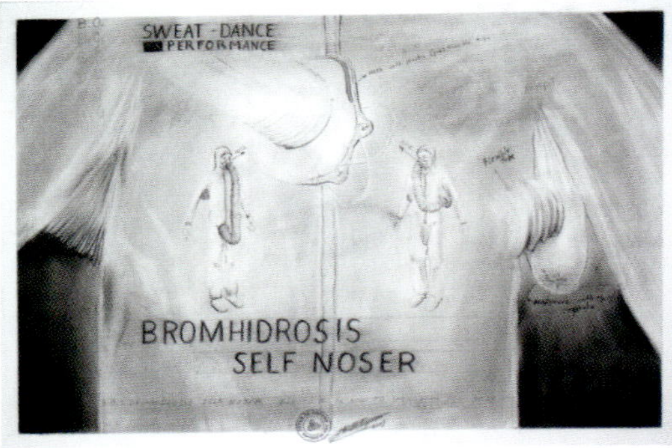

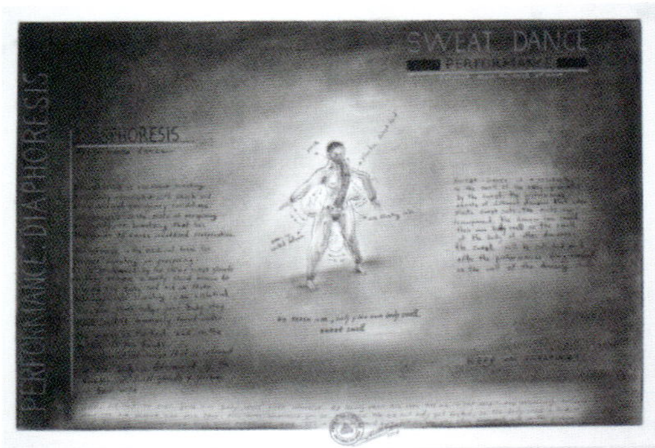

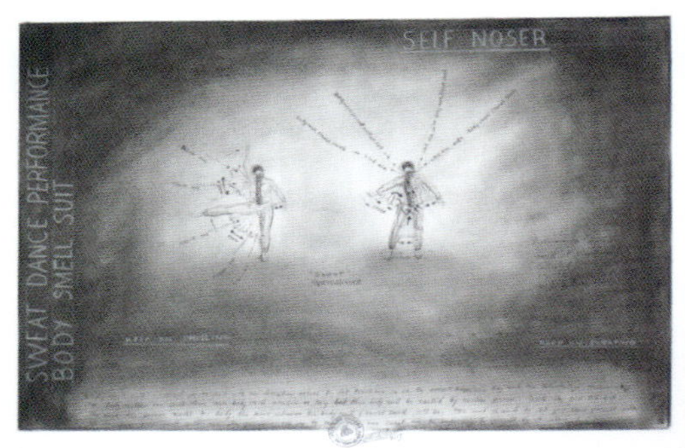

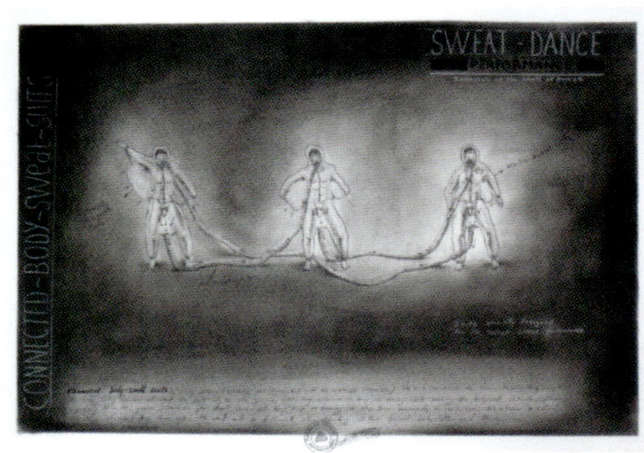

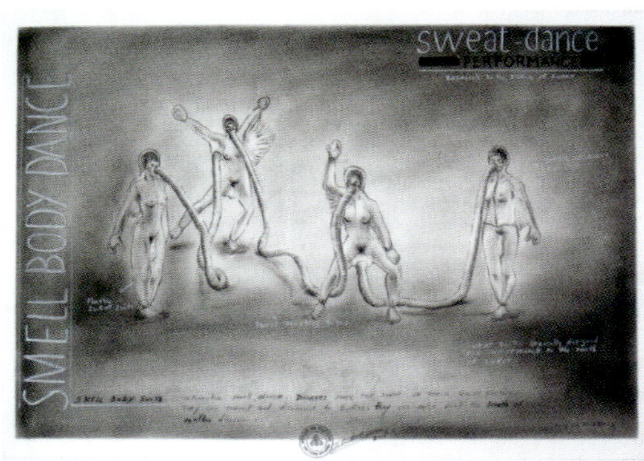

Drawings Sweat Dance, 2009

Framed / Ingekaderd 72,5 x 52 cm

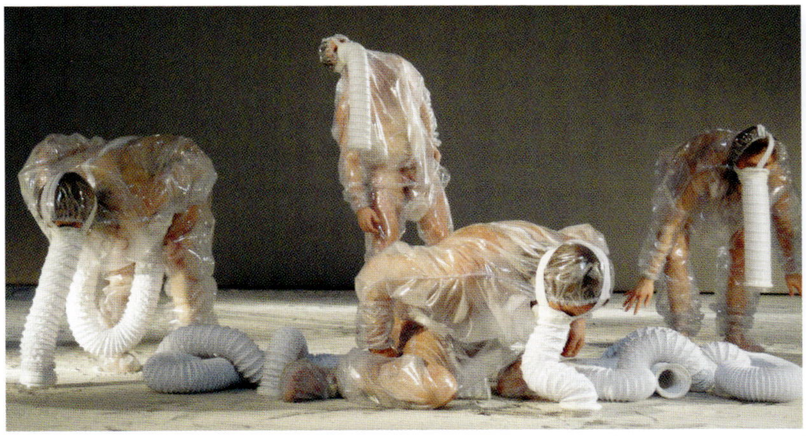

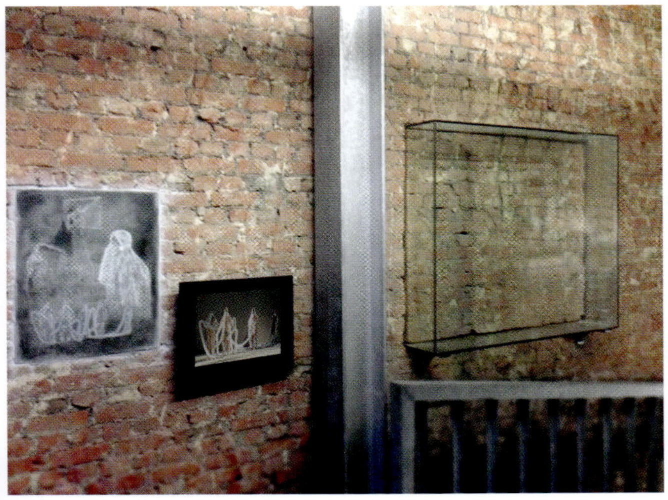

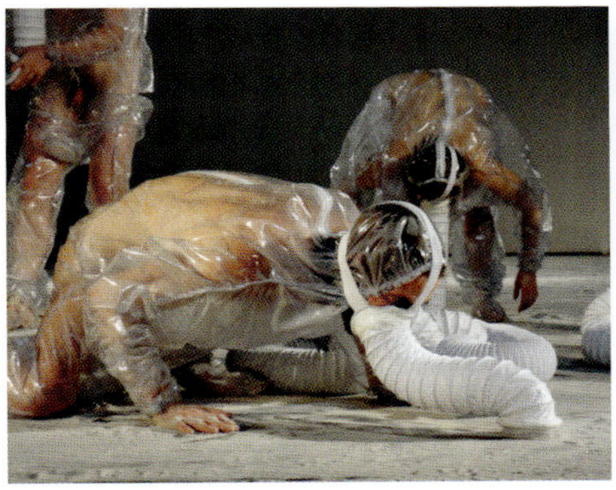

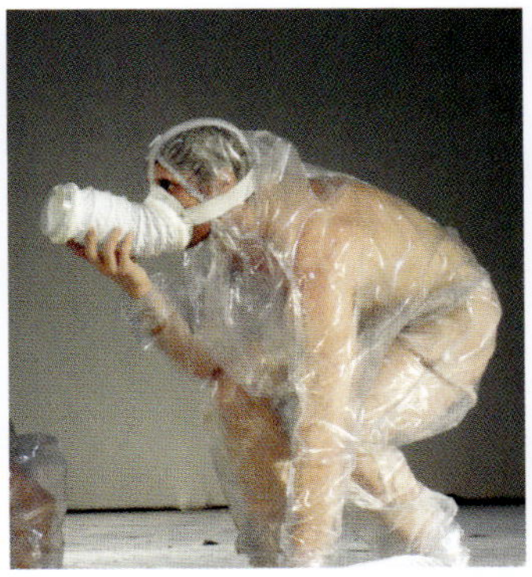

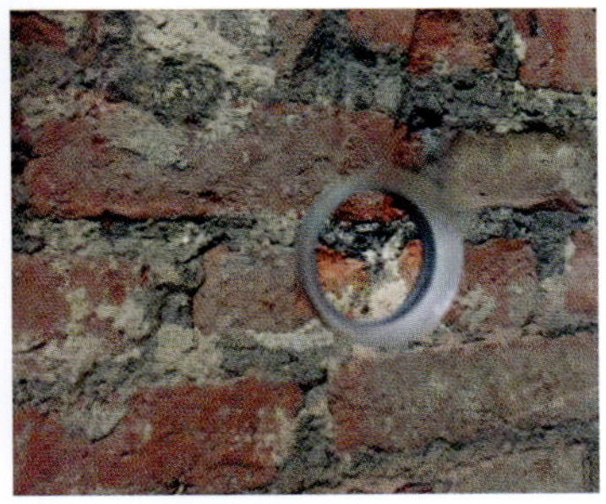

Sweat, 2010

In situ installation of Sweat Drawing on stone, monitor and glassbox with a hole in the glass to smell the sweat.

In situ installatie van Sweat Tekening op baksteen, met monitor en glazen box met een perforatie in het glas om het zweet te ervaren.

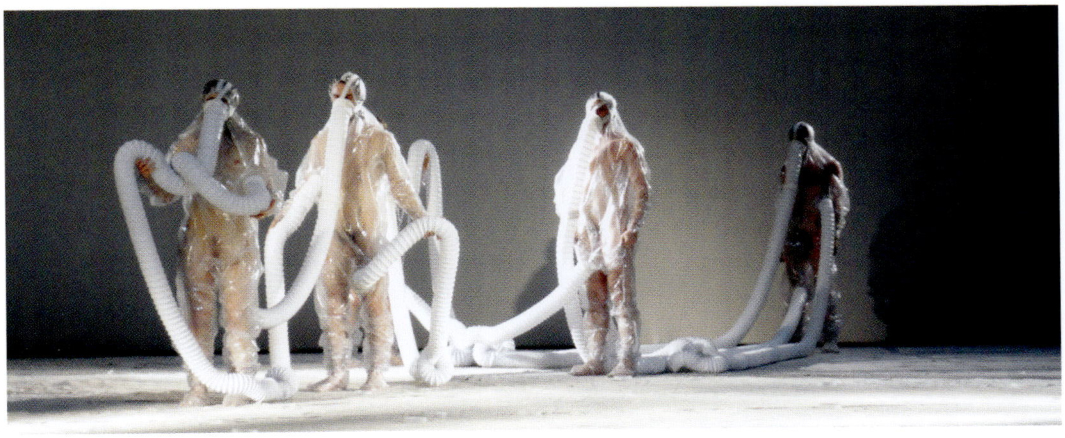

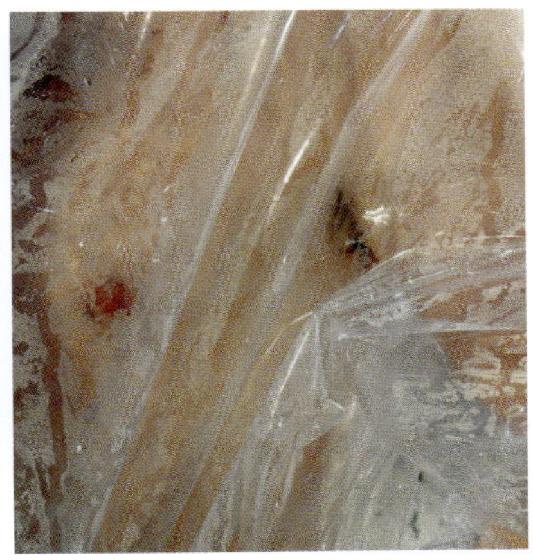

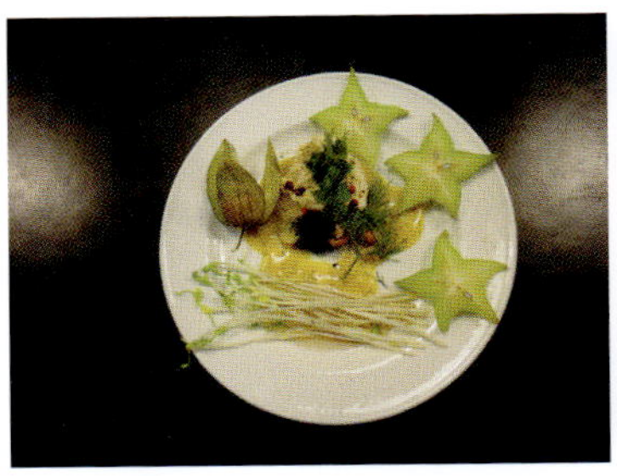

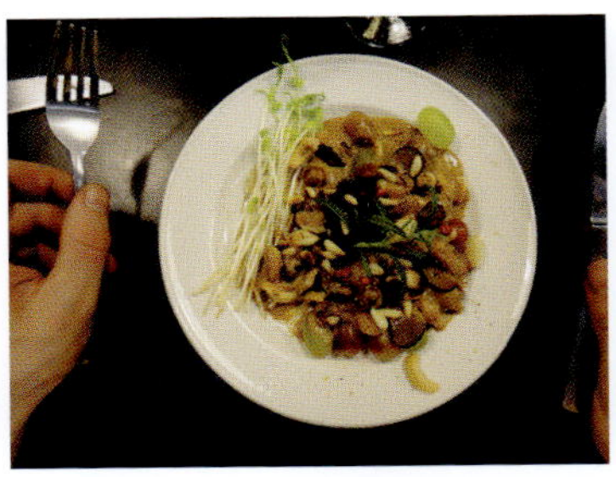

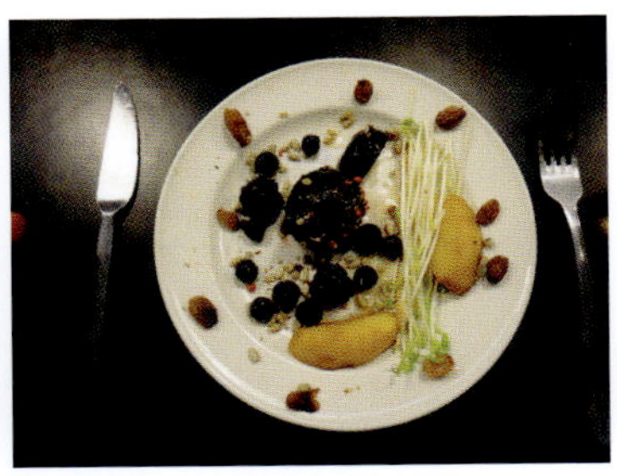

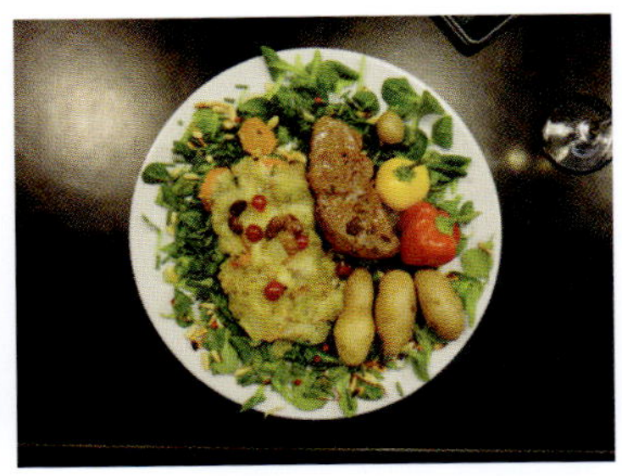

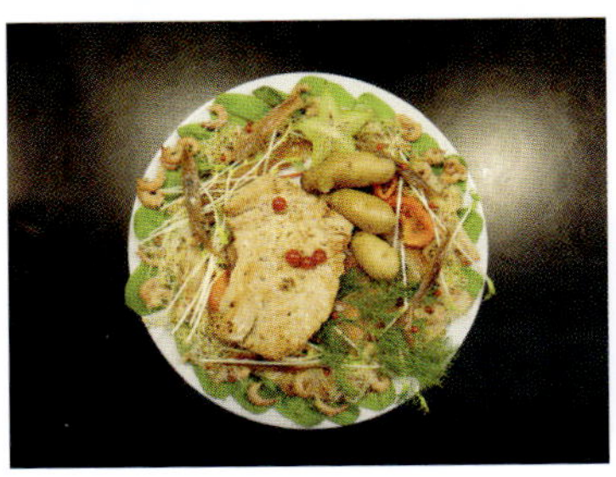

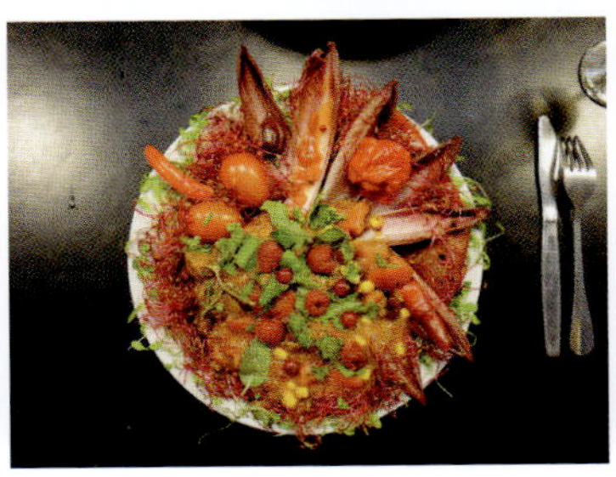

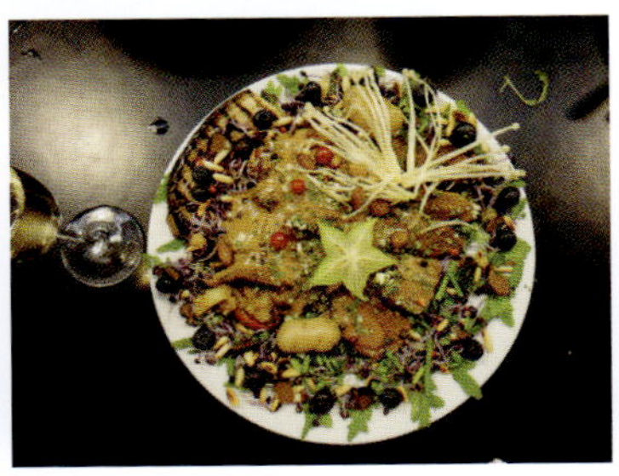

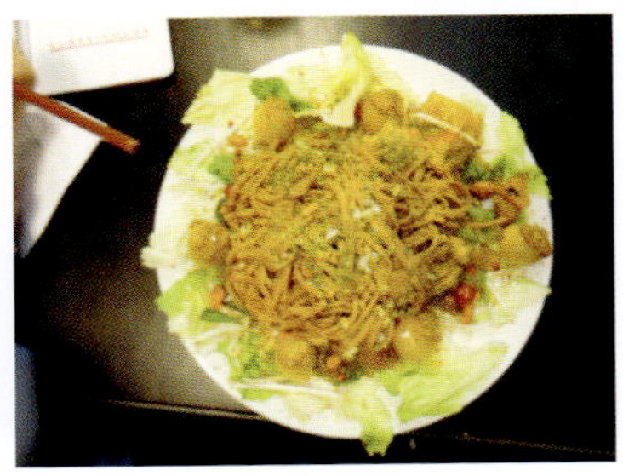

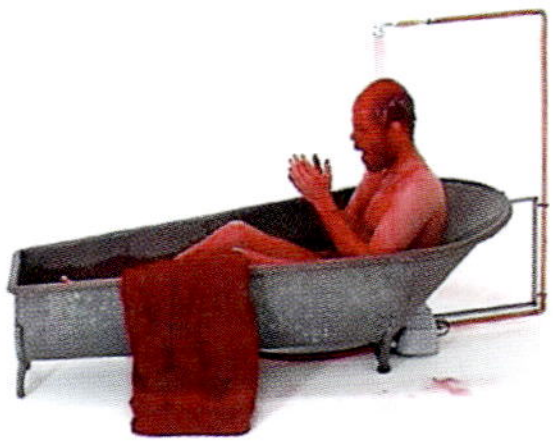

1

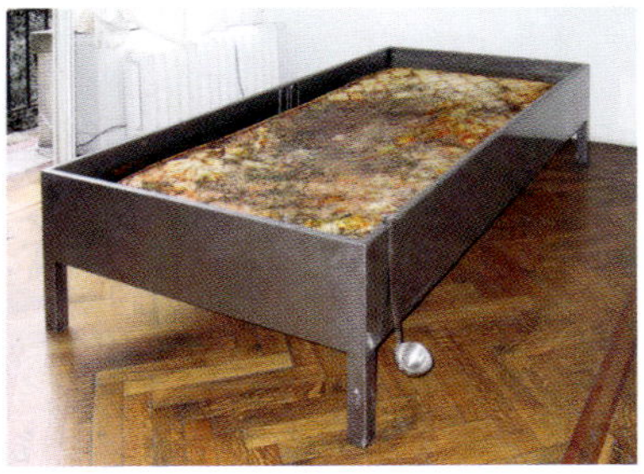

2

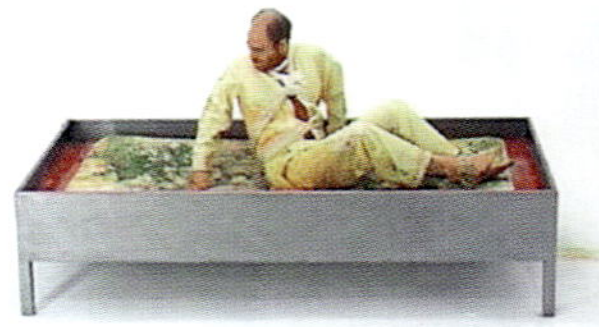

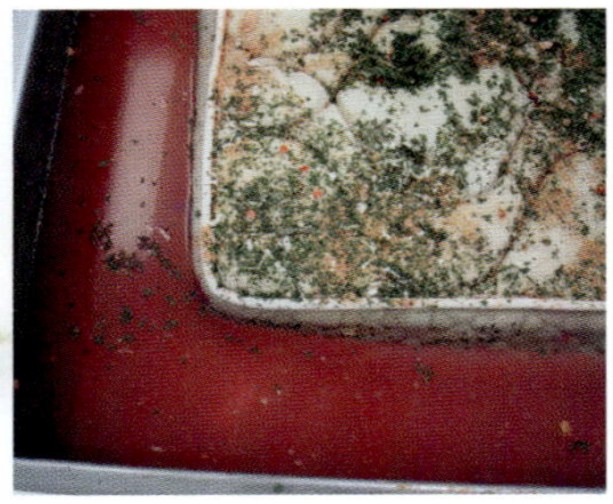

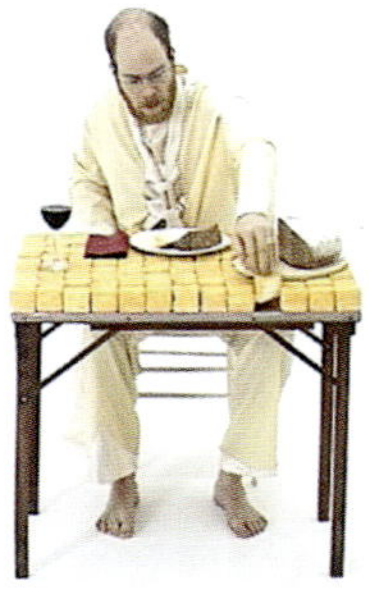

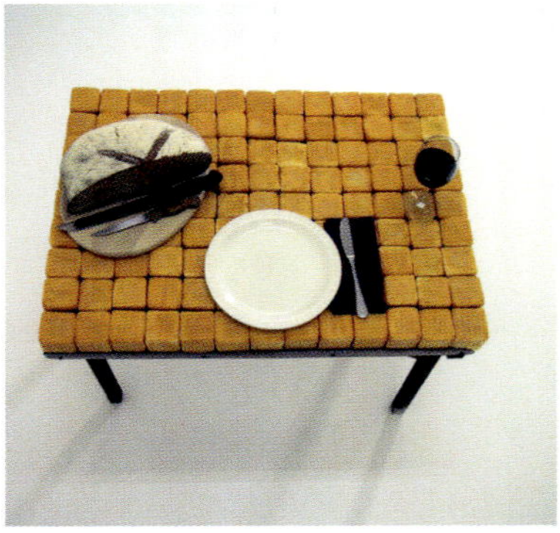

3

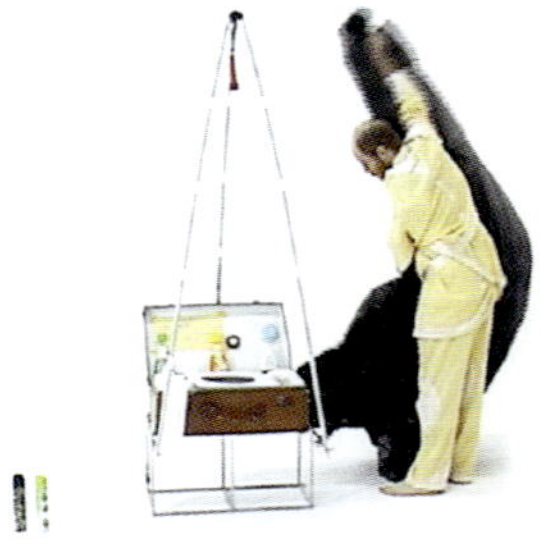

4

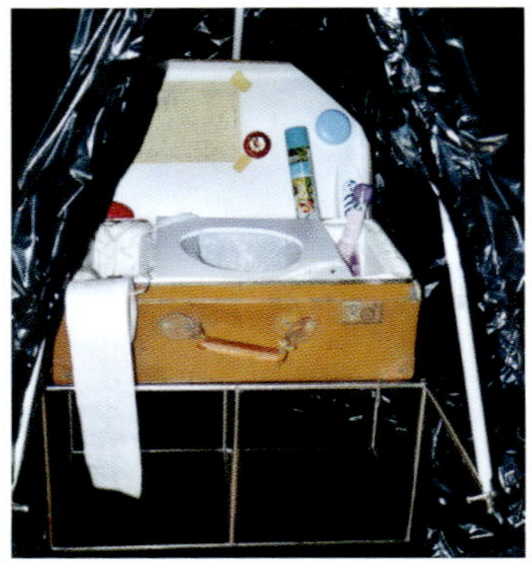

1. Wine Bath, 2002-2003

Old iron bath filled with wine / Oud ijzeren bad gevuld met wijn

2. Hot Mattress, 2002-2003

Bedframe made of steel, mattress, soup, spices, heater
Boiling of the mattress to make mattress soup of it.

Metalen bed, matras, soep, kruiden, verwarmingselement
Koken van de matras om er soep mee te maken.

3. Cheese Table, 2002-2003

Table covered with 130 Herve-cheeses

Tafel bedekt met 130 kazen van Herve

4. Toilet Suitcase, 2002-2003

The Collector's House, St.-Lucas Stichting,
curator Filip Luyckx, Brussels, 17.01.2003-22.03.2003

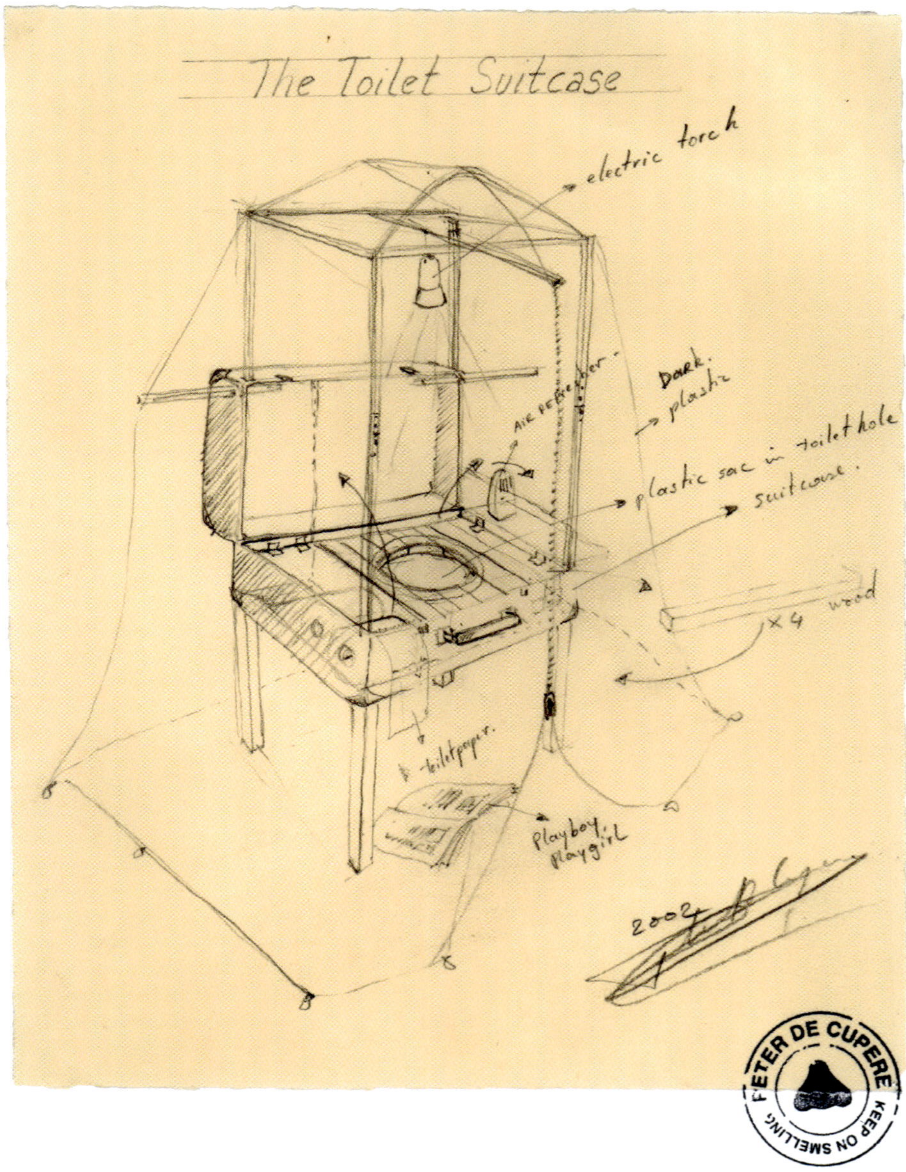

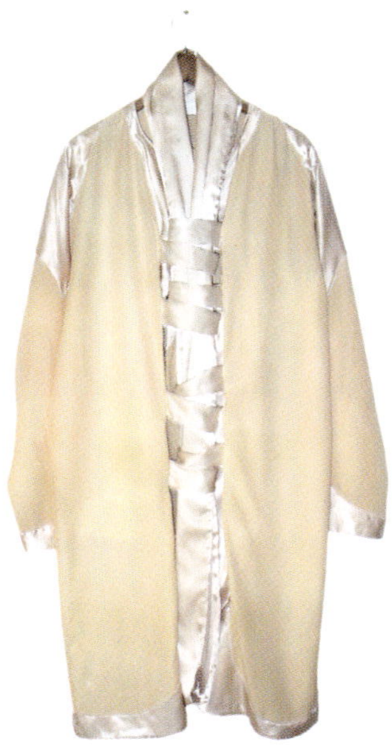

Pyjama designed by the artist and realized by his mother.
Pyjama ontworpen door de kunstenaar en afgewerkt door zijn moeder.
Video performance of The Collector's House, 2002

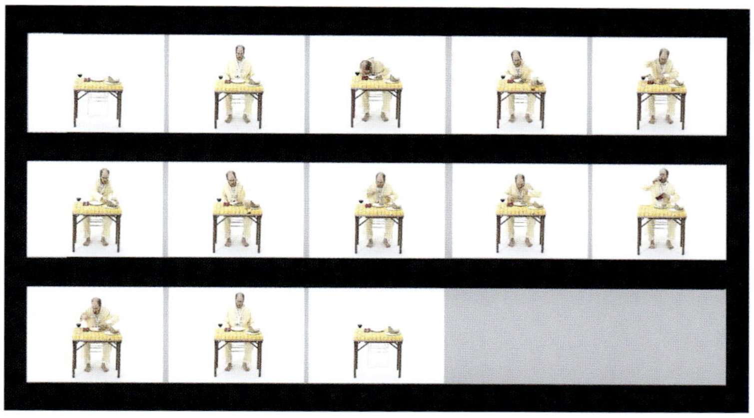

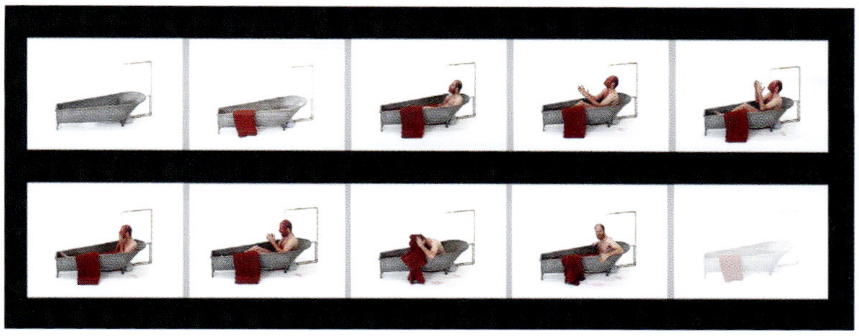

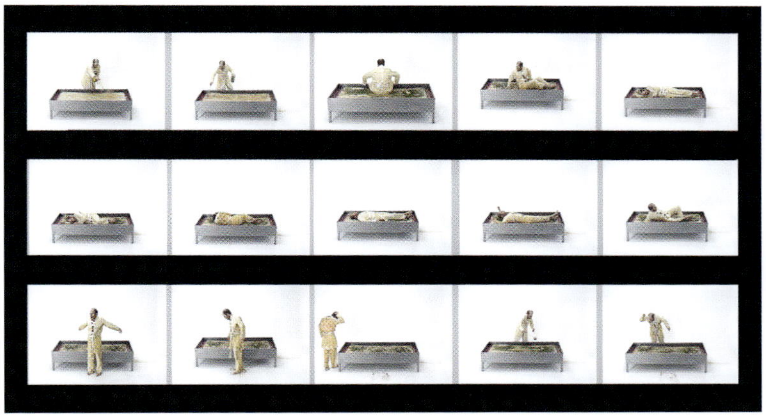

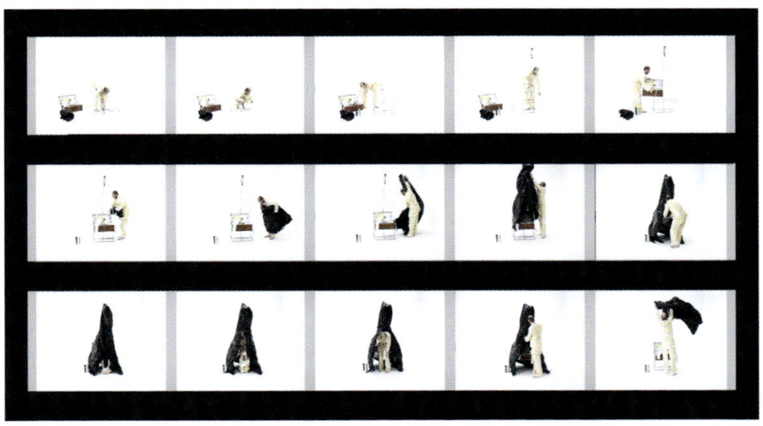

Video: The Collector's House

720 x 576, 12 min. 32 sec.

The Collector's House, St.-Lucas Stichting, curator Filip Luyckx, Brussels, BE
17.01.2003-22.03.2003

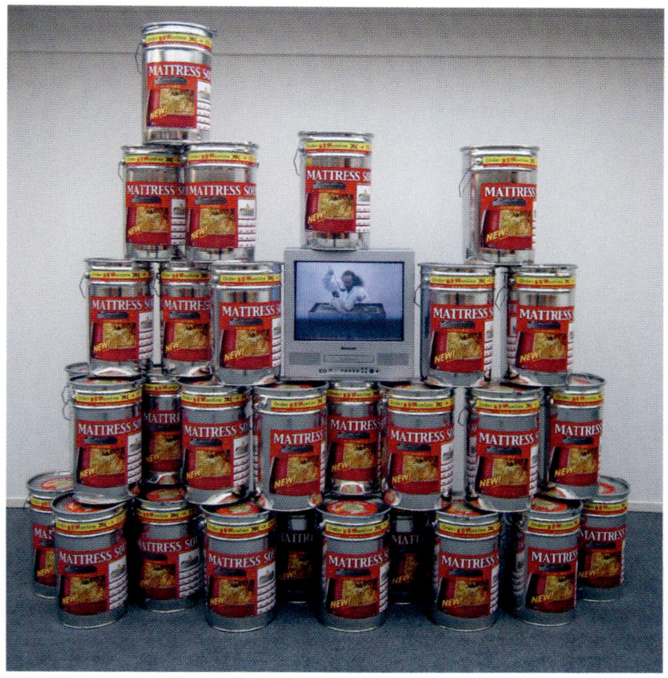

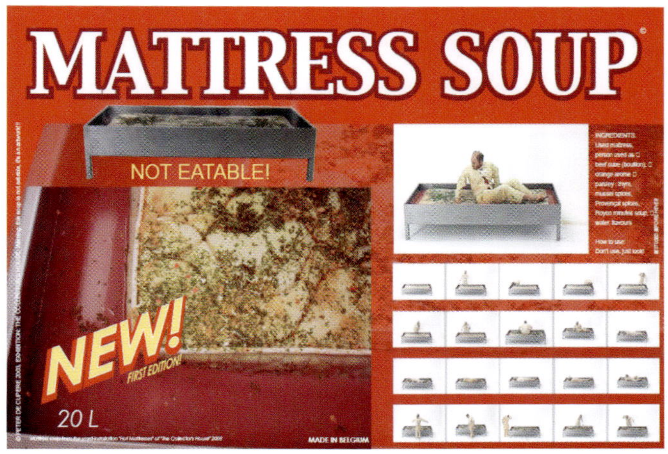

Video Mattress Soup, 2003

720 x 576, 3 min. 13 sec.

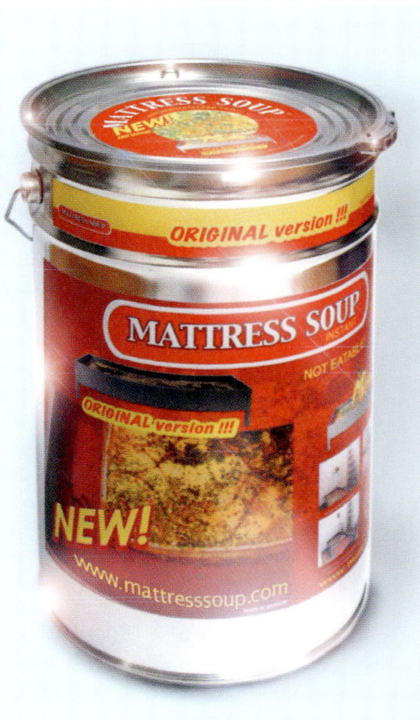

Mattress Soup, 2003

Edition of 25,
47 cm x 30,5 cm Ø

De Gustibus, Broel Museum, curators Lieven Van Den Abeele, Veerle Van Durme & Anne Petre, ING Kortrijk, BE
14.02.2007-29.04.2007

The Collector's House, St.-Lucas Stichting, curator Filip Luyckx, Brussels, BE
17.01.2003-22.03.2003

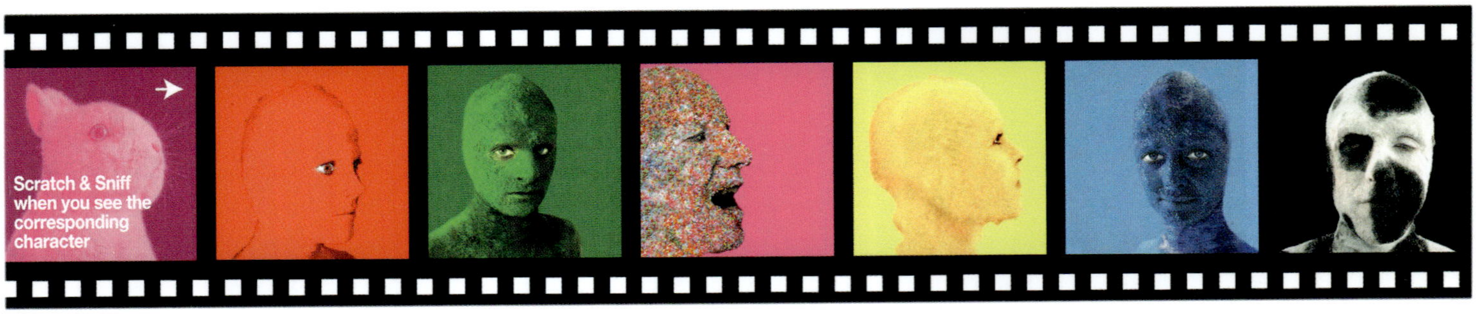

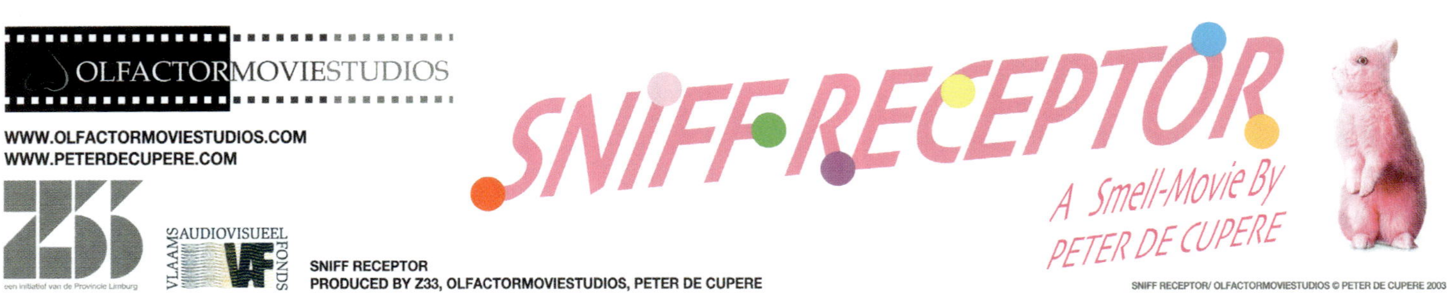

Scratch & Sniff kaart

Sniff Receptor, Smell-Movie, 2003

duration: 12 min.
5 actors, 4 professional contemporary
dansers. 150 figurants

The first Belgian olfactory movie. Using scratch and sniff cards, the viewer experienced the experimental, short, colourful film with an added olfactory dimension. The film sets were also presented during the exhibition to permit the visitors to smell the odours directly.

Eerste Belgische geurfilm. Via scratch & sniff kaarten kan de kijker de experimentele kleurrijke kortfilm olfactorisch waarnemen. Tijdens de tentoonstelling kon men de filmsets bezoeken waar men ook de geuren kon waarnemen.

Olfactormoviestudios.com, Smell-movie Sniff Receptor, Productie & tentoonstelling: Z33 Hasselt, curator Jan Boelen, productiemanager Danny Bierset, 08.11.2003-25.01.2004

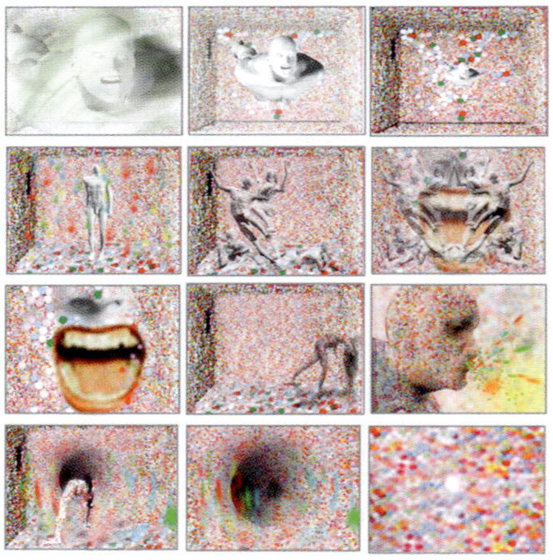

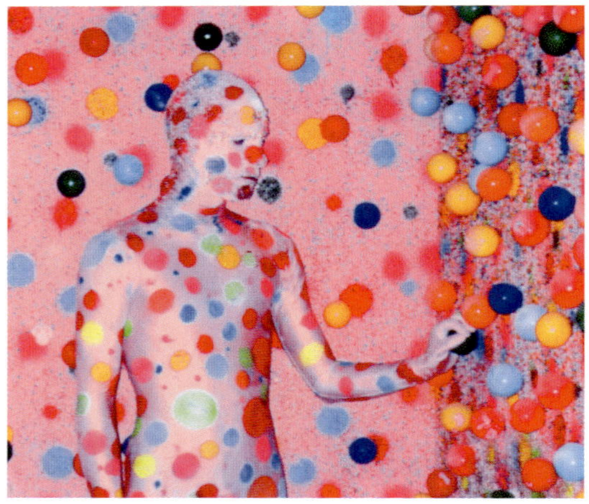

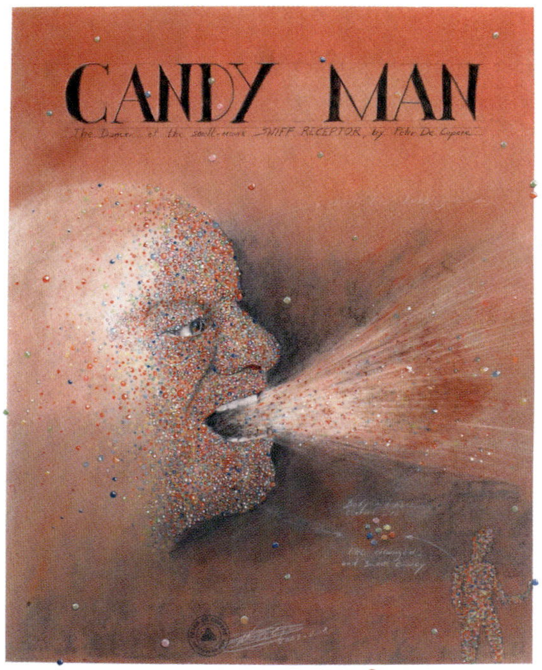

Drawing Candy Man, 2003

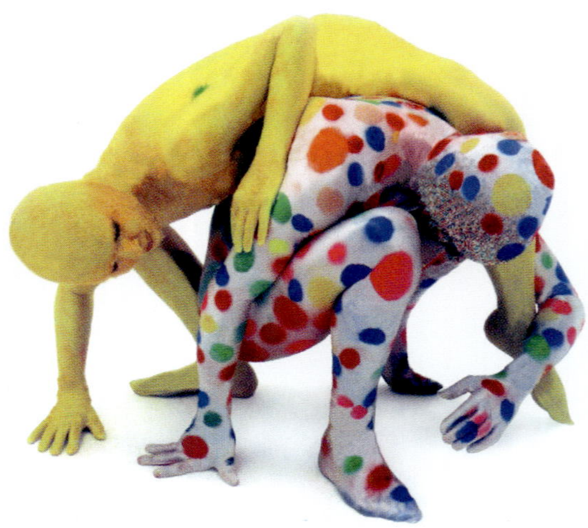

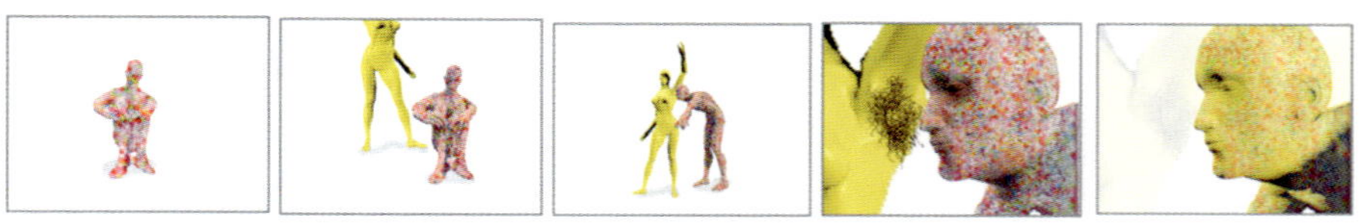

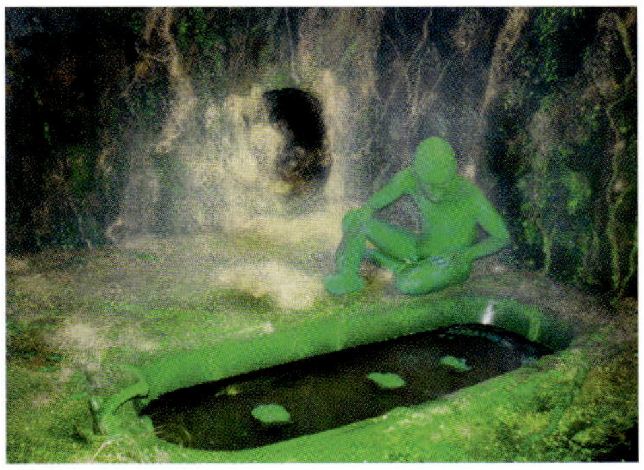
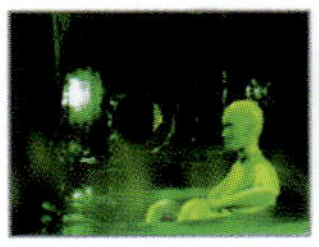
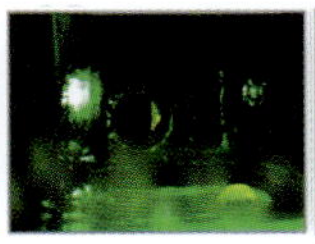
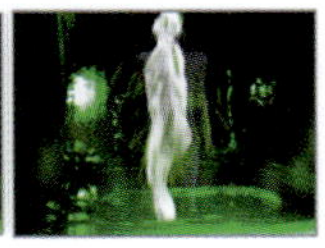
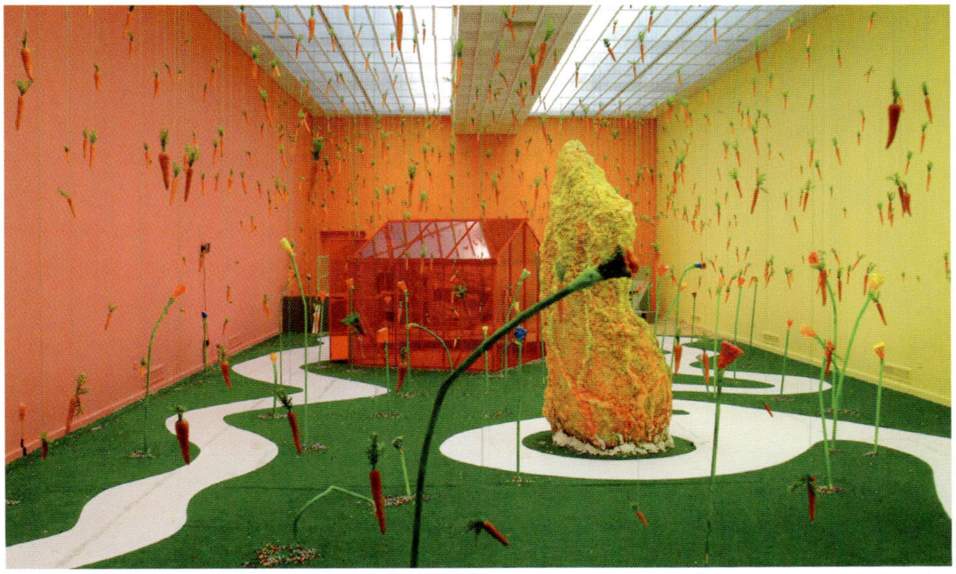

Exhibition view

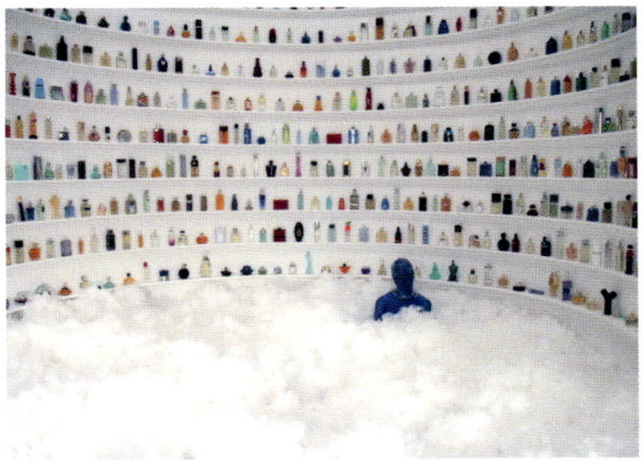
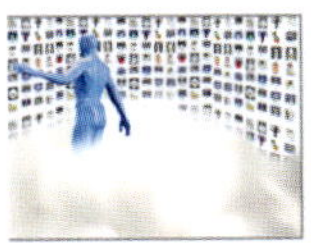
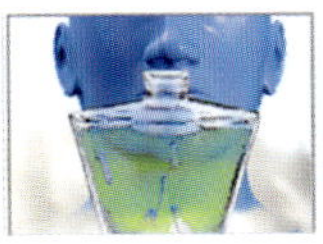
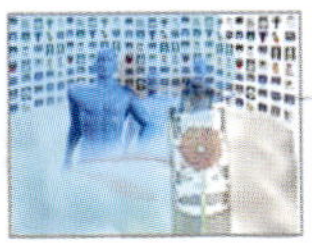
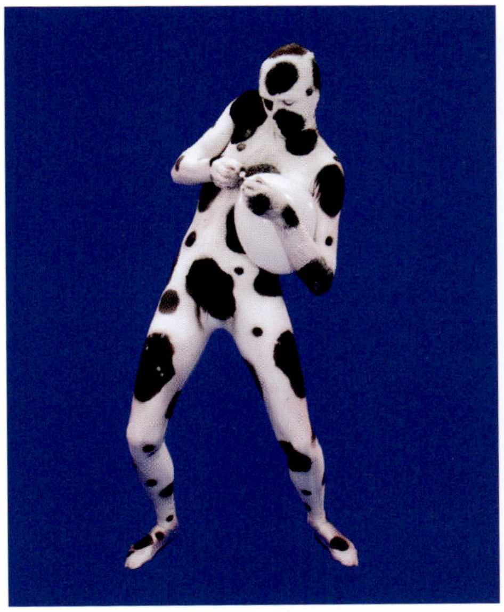
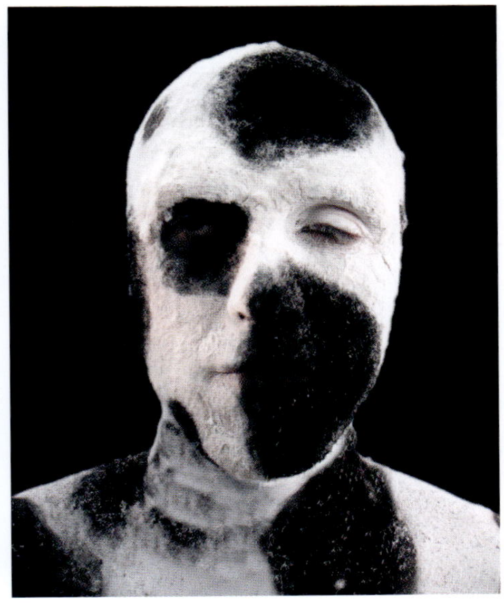
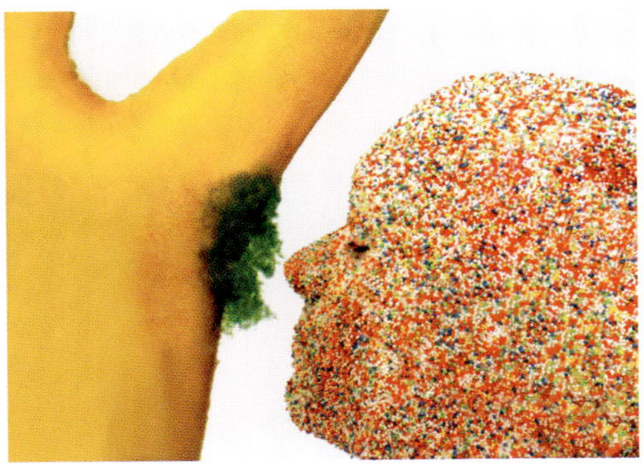
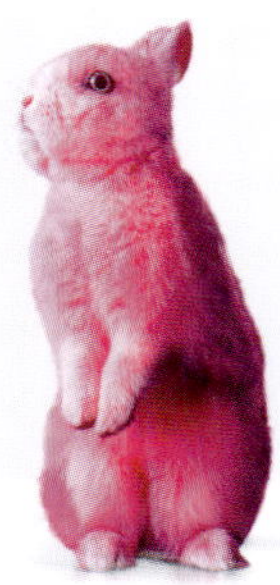
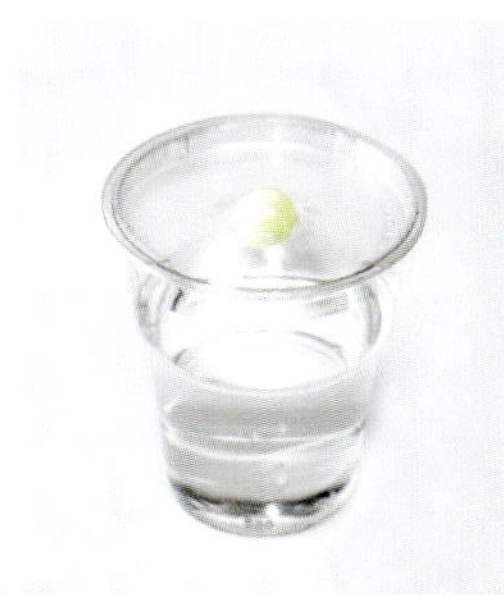

Smell Drink, 2003

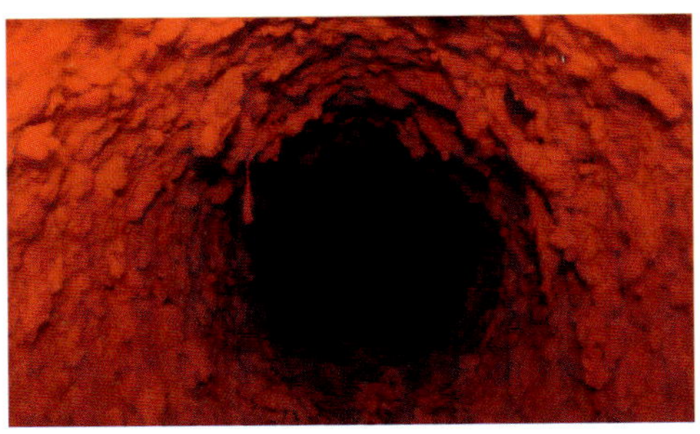
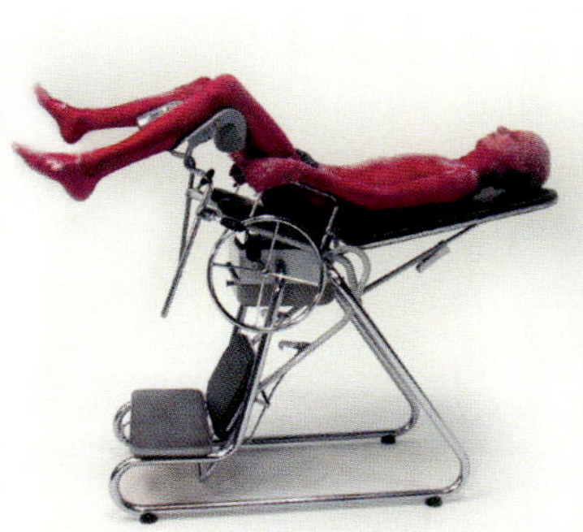
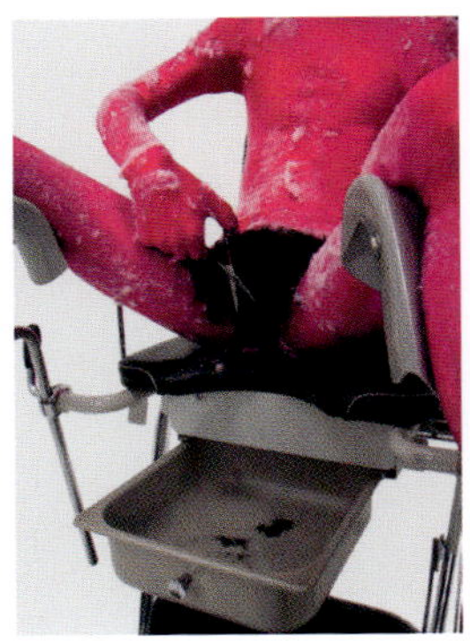
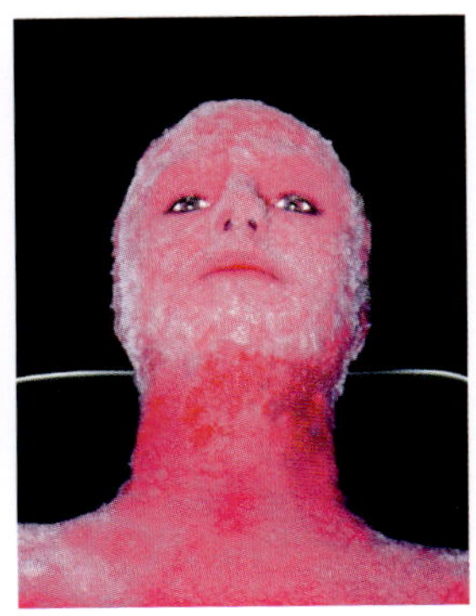

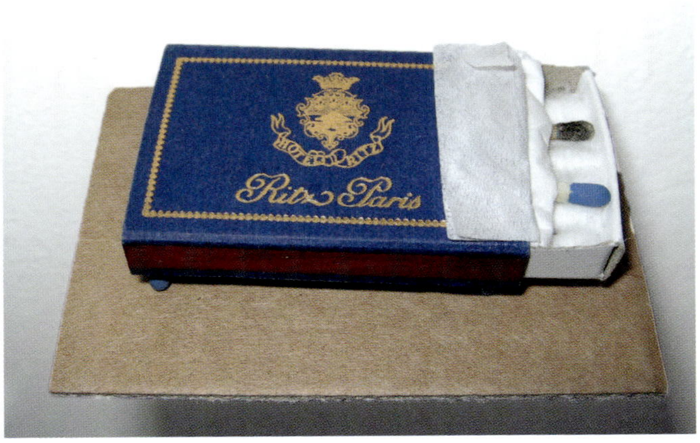

Ritz Paris, 2005

Tennis Nose

Clown nose made in the shape of a tennisball combined with the shape of the nose of the artist and the smell of grass.

Clownsneus gemaakt in de vorm van een tennisbal in combinatie met de vorm van de neus van de kunstenaar en een grasgeur.

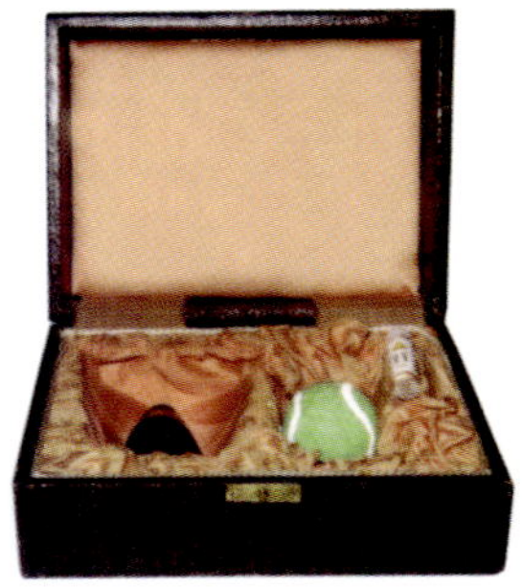

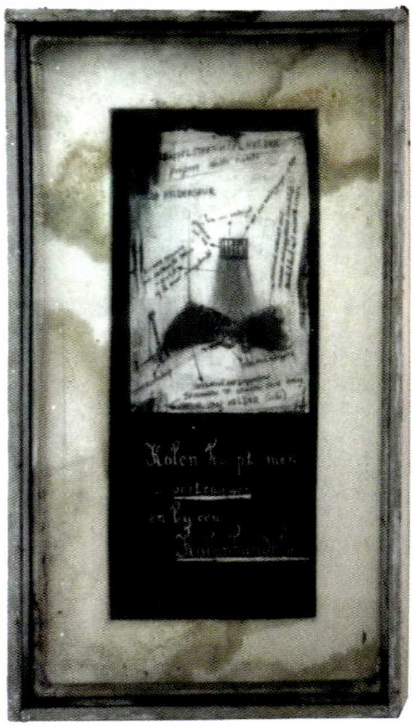

Drawing Cellar Odor

Concept to imitate the scent of an ancient cellar via potatoes painted with black latex paint, which are then constructed like a coal mountain. The latex prevents the potato to have direct aircontact so it starts rotting and the smell of an old coal cellar is popping up.

Concept om de geur van een oude kelder na te maken. Om de geur na te maken worden aardappelen met een latex verf zwart gemaakt en zoals steenkool op een hoop gelegd. De latex sluit deels de aardappel van de lucht af waardoor deze na een tijd begint te rotten en een muffe geur afgeeft welke lijkt op de geur van een oude kolenkelder.

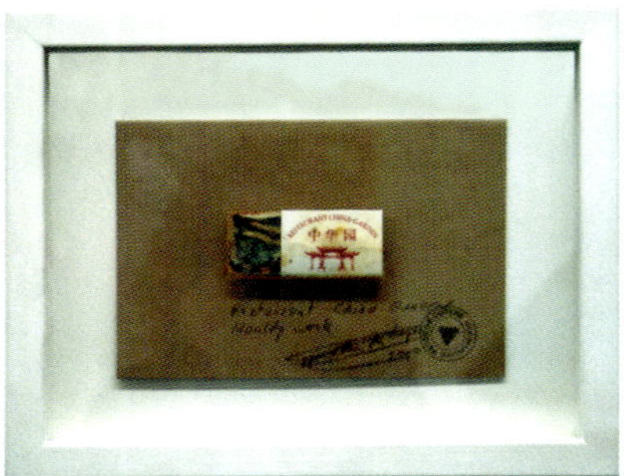

Restaurant China Garden, 2000

This artwork was made during a dinner in a Chinese restaurant in Hanne-Münden, Germany during the build up of the exhibition 3 Raümen, 3 Flüshen, curated by Jan Hoet. During the meal a box of matches was presented with the name of the restaurant 'Restaurant China Garden'. Peter de Cupere put part of his food in the small box together with two matches and framed the little piece when he was back in Belgium. Meanwhile the food started to mould and visually it looked like a small greyish kitchen garden. The two matches symbolise Chinese chopsticks.

Dit werk werd gemaakt tijdens een etentje in een Chinees restaurant in Hanne-Münden, tijdens de opbouw van de tentoonstelling *3 Raümen, 3 Flüshen* waar Jan Hoet curator was. Iemand vroeg aan de ober tijdens het eten naar lucifers. Op het luciferdoosje stond de naam van het restaurant 'Restaurant China Garden'. Peter de Cupere stak een overschot van het eten van op zijn bord in het luciferdoosje samen met twee lucifers en kaderde het bij zijn terugkomst in België in. Ondertussen was het voedsel in het luciferdoosje gaan beschimmelen. Visueel leek dit op een kleine groen grauwe moestuin. De twee lucifers staan symbool voor Chinese eetstokjes.

Peter de Cupere, Smellcom Happening, Smell Kiss Performance, rockconcert Admiral Freebee, Van Laere Contemporary Art, Antwerp, BE, 14.09-21.10.2000

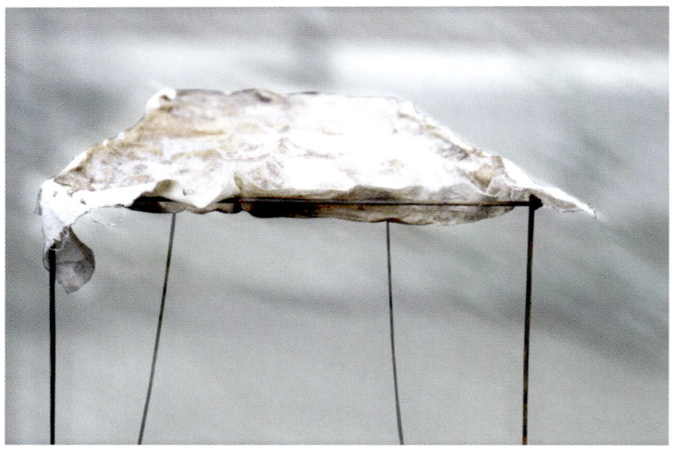

Small Small Garden, 1997-1999

±150 cm x 100 cm x 50 cm

Metal, canvas and mould

Metaal, canvas en schimmel

Collection: S.M.A.K., Ghent, BE

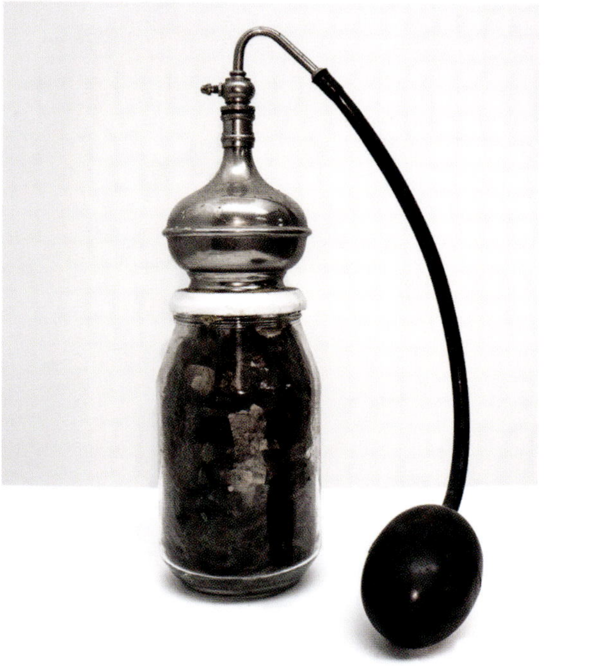

Dust Perfume, 1996-1999

Collected dust from the workshop of the artist at HISK.

Door de jaren heen selectief verzameld stof uit het kunstenaarsatelier in het HISK.

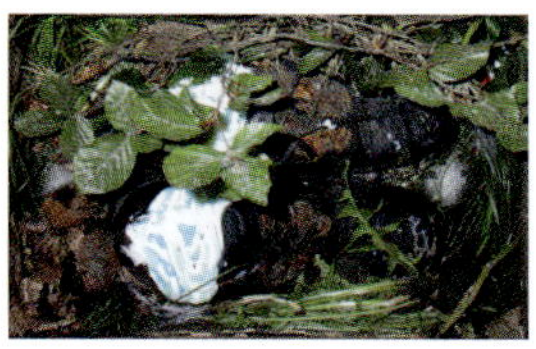

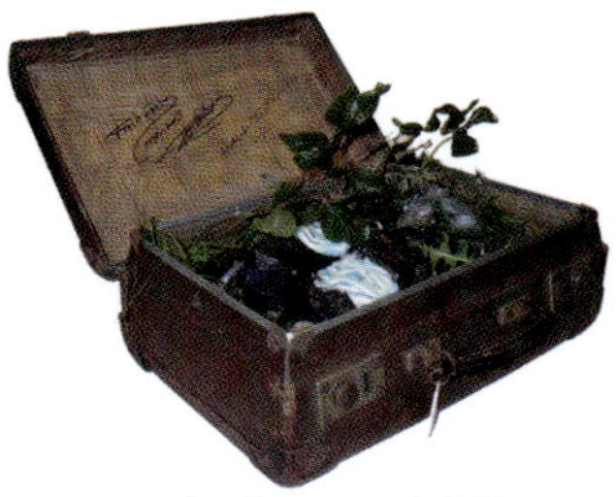

My Fresh Shoes, 1998-2003

Shoes filled with toothpaste are standing on a pile of grass and different plants and branches in a suitcase.

Schoenen met tandpasta gevuld staan in een koffer op aarde met gras en verschillende planten en takken.

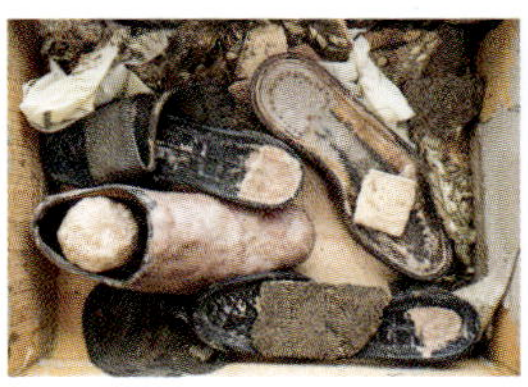

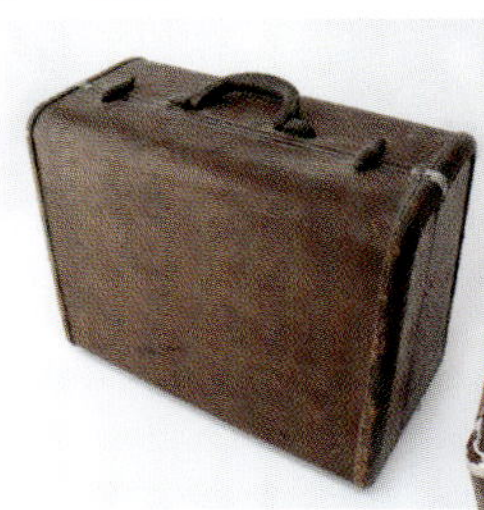

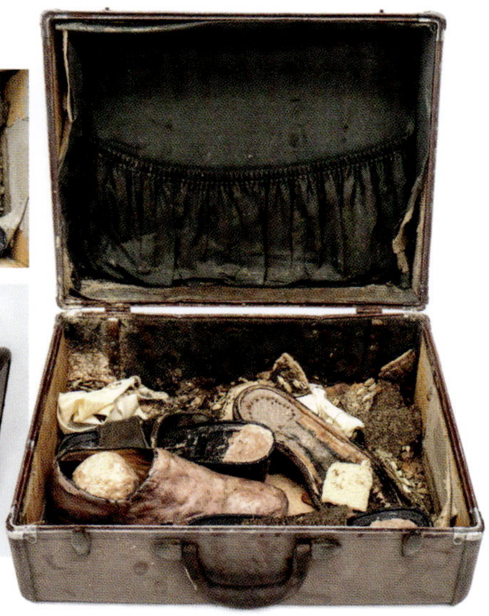

My Fresh Feet, 1996-1997

Perfumance by the artist, his feet put in shoes with soap and/or herbs.

Perfumance van eigen voeten met zeep en/of kruiden in schoenen.

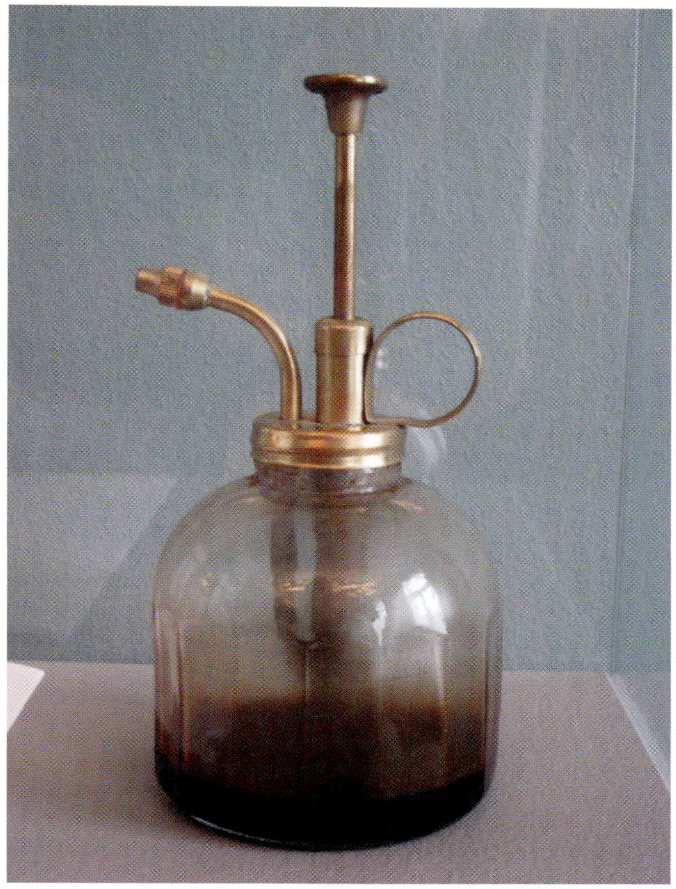

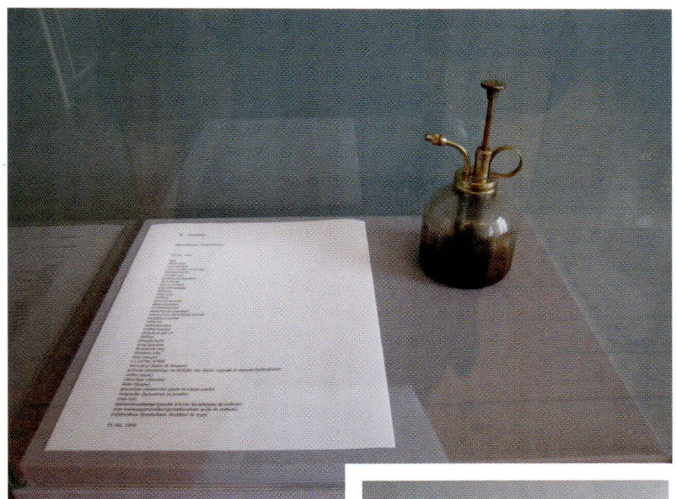

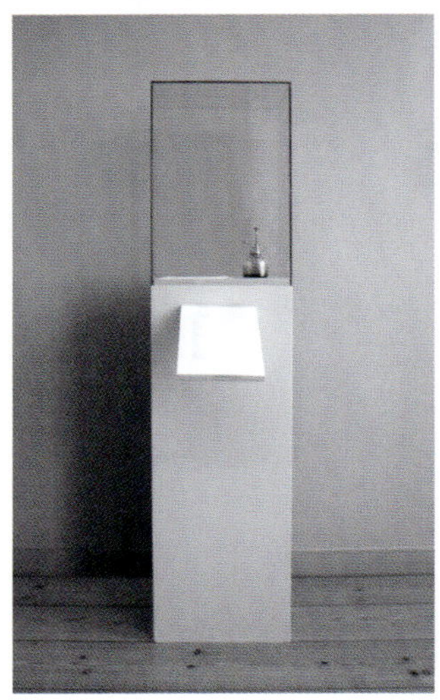

G-Perfume, 1996-1997

Perfume made of leftover food. A list of the ingredients of the food scraps illustrates the complexity of the perfume. The letter G stands for Garbage.

Parfum gemaakt van overgebleven voedselresten. Een lijst met de ingrediënten van overgebleven voedsel illustreert de complexiteit van het parfum. De letter G staat voor *Garbage*.

De Gustibus, Broel Museum, curators Lieven Van Den Abeele, Veerle Van Durme & Anne Petre, ING Kortrijk, BE 14.02.2007-29.04.2007

EE-Braille, 1992

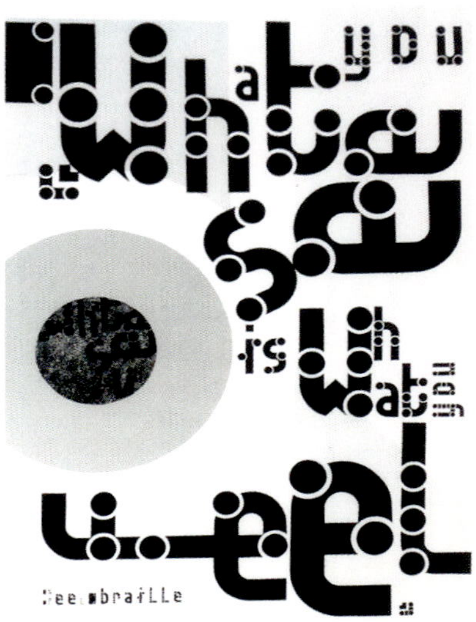

A font based on braille. The letters EE represent See and FeeL. Both sighted and blind people can read the letters. Braille script is used as the basis for this font, designed at the Kunsthogeschool PHIKO (art school in Hasselt). Today, PHIKO is known as the PXL-MAD School of Arts, where Peter de Cupere is also an instructor and conducts research into how smell gives context to a work of art.

Here you can see an example of a creative reworking of the font. This does mean that it loses its function of allowing blind people to read. To be able to use it as a braille script as well, the letters must be in a particular pattern.

Lettertype gebaseerd op het brailleschrift. De letters EE staan voor See en FeeL. Zowel zienden als blinden kunnen de letters lezen. Als basis werd het brailleschrift genomen. Het lettertype werd ontworpen in de Kunsthogeschool Phiko. Phiko is vandaag de PXL-MAD school of Arts waar Peter de Cupere ook docent is en onderzoek doet naar hoe geur context geeft aan het kunstwerk.

Hier zie je een voorbeeld van een creatieve verwerking van het lettertype. Hierdoor verliest het wel zijn functie van het blindelings te kunnen lezen. Om het ook als brailleschrift te kunnen lezen moeten de letters in een bepaald stramien staan.

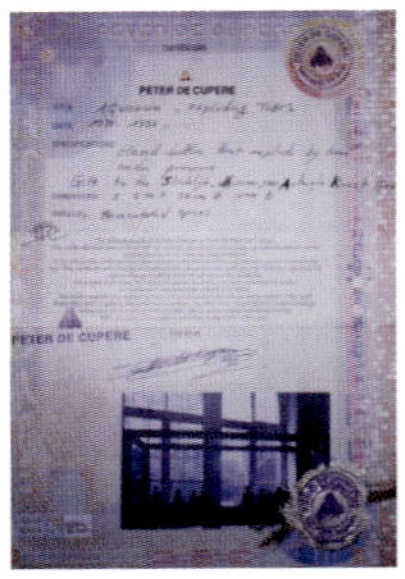

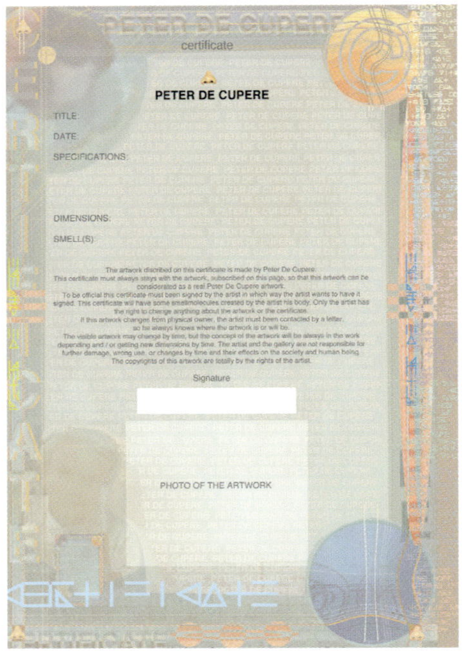

Certificate / Certificaat

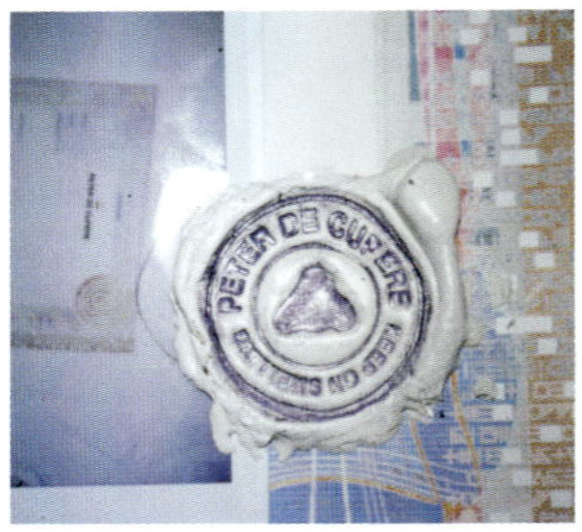

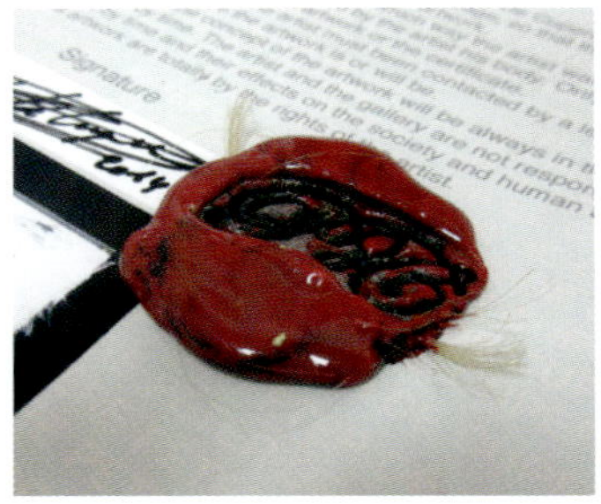

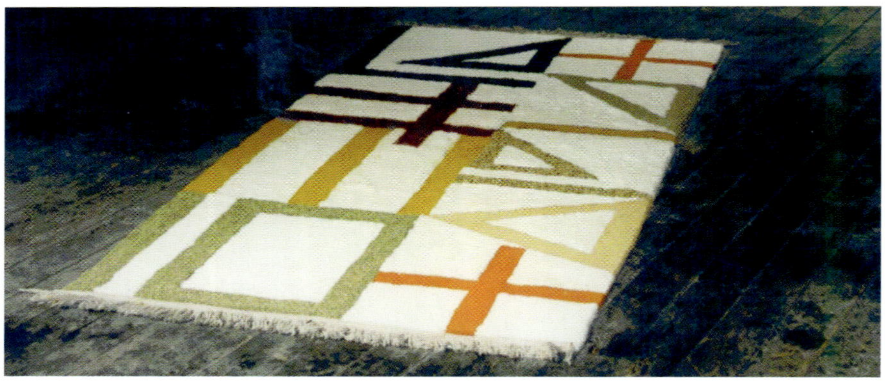

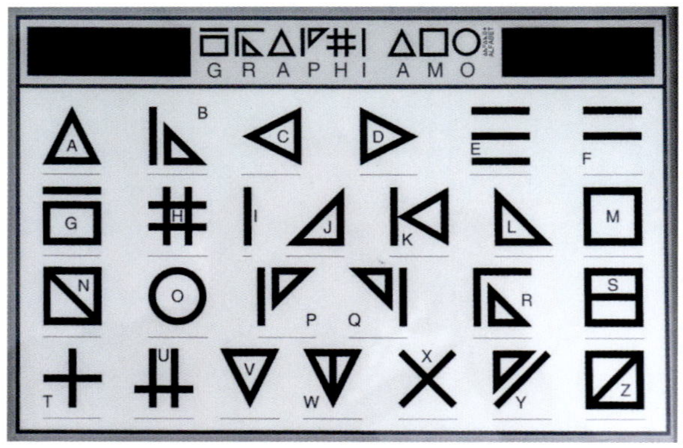

Het Graphi'AMO alfabet, 1994-1995

The Graphi'AMO alphabet, (grafein = Greek for writing, amo = Latin for I love) developed in December '94 – March '95 is not a functional but a pictorial (visual) alphabet based on three basic geometric shapes: triangle, square and circle, which may in some cases be combined with a line.
The alphabet consists of just 26 letters, no numbers and no punctuation marks. The latter two can be imagined to be unnecessary, since they can also be written out in letters. In words, the letters are written up against each other, and there is no line spacing. There is a space between the words. If the punctuation marks are typed out, a space is also added.
The letters were also used as smell letters. The font was used among other things as a basis for making scent carpets of herbs. The font is still used by the artist as a background for his certificates for works. The certificates are supplied only for artworks where the work cannot be signed by the artist. The certificate comprises a photo of the work along with a description. It is signed, stamped with lacquer into which the artist's DNA (hair, nails) was mixed. The certificate is also decorated with a thin golden or silver line, visible on both front and back.

Final Year Students Fine Arts, Sint-Lukas Brussel, Moving Art Studio, Brussels, BE, 14-28.06.1996

Het Graphi'AMO alfabet (grafein = grieks voor schrijven, amo = latijn voor houden van) ontwikkelt in dec. '94 - maart '95, is geen functioneel, maar een picturaal alfabet (visueel) gebaseerd op de drie geometrische basisfiguren, driehoek, vierkant, cirkel welke eventueel gecombineerd worden met een lijn.
Het alfabet bestaat alleen uit 26 letters, géén cijfers, géén leestekens. Deze laatste twee kan men fictief als overbodig beschouwen, vermits ze ook uitgeschreven kunnen worden in letters. In woorden worden de letters tegen elkaar aangeschreven, ook bestaat er geen interlinie tussen twee zinnen. Er is een spatie tussen woorden. Als er leestekens getypt worden ontstaat er ook een spatie.
De letters werden ook als geurletters gebruikt. Het lettertype diende o.a. als basis om geurtapijten van kruiden te maken. Het lettertype wordt door de kunstenaar nog steeds gebruikt als achtergrond op zijn certificaten van werken. Deze certificaten worden alleen bij kunstwerken meegeleverd waar geen *signature* van de kunstenaar kan opstaan. Het certificaat bevat dan een foto van het werk gecombineerd met een omschrijving van het werk. Het werd ondertekend, gestempeld met lak waarin DNA (haar, nagel) van de kunstenaar werd verwerkt. Het certificaat is ook voorzien van een dunne gouden of zilveren lijn welke zowel op de voorzijde als de achterzijde zichtbaar zijn.

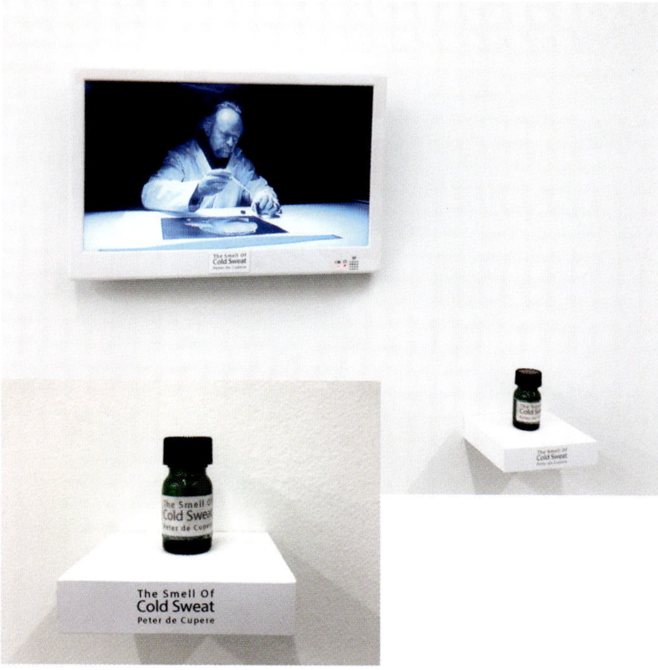

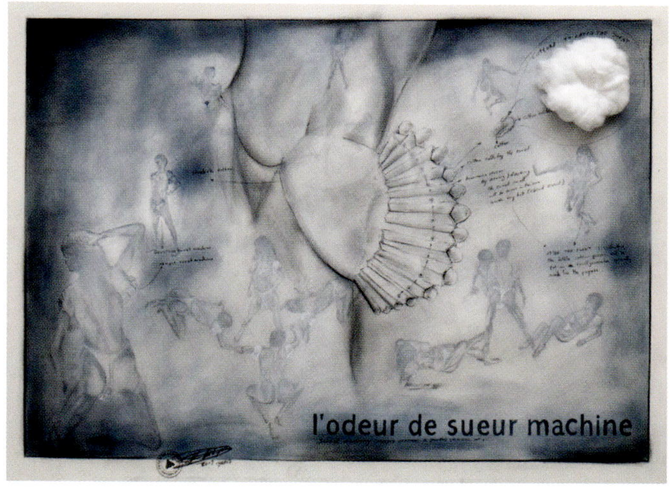

The Smell Of Cold Sweat, 2015

Black/White Video HD, 1 min. combined with the scent of cold sweat.

Zwart/Wit Video HD, 1 min. gecombineerd met de geur van koud zweet.

A Belgian Politician, Marion de Cannière Art Space, curators Lieven Segers, Tom Liekens, Antwerp, BE, 21.02.2015-21.03.2015

l'Odeur de Sueur Machine, 2009

Pastel, graphite, charcoal, pencil, natural cotton wool, dried smell of sweat activated while drawing the artwork. The cotton was put under the armpits of the artist while he was drawing.

Pastel, grafiet, houtskool, potlood, natuurlijke watten, opgedroogde zweetgeur van tijdens het tekenen van de tekening. De watten werden tijdens het tekenen onder de oksels gestoken.

Sweat Drawings

Drawings made with the artist's own sweat following the activity depicted. For example, after intense sex or sports, the artist made a drawing on paper using his own sweat. Since sweat is virtually colourless, the images are very vague. What remains once dry is what creates the partly visible drawing.

Variable dates and dimensions.

Tekeningen gemaakt met eigen zweet na de afgebeelde daad op de tekening. Zo werd er na intense sex met eigen zweet op een papier getekend of na het sporten werd dit eveneens met het zweet nagetekend.
De beelden zijn heel vaag daar zweet praktisch kleurloos is. Het is het restant dat achterblijft dat de tekening deels zichtbaar maakt.

Variable datums en afmetingen.

Sex Smells Geruch einer antitranspiranten Gesellschaft, Kunstverein Wolfsburg, curator Jennifer Bork, Wolfsburg, DE 02.09–06.11.2016

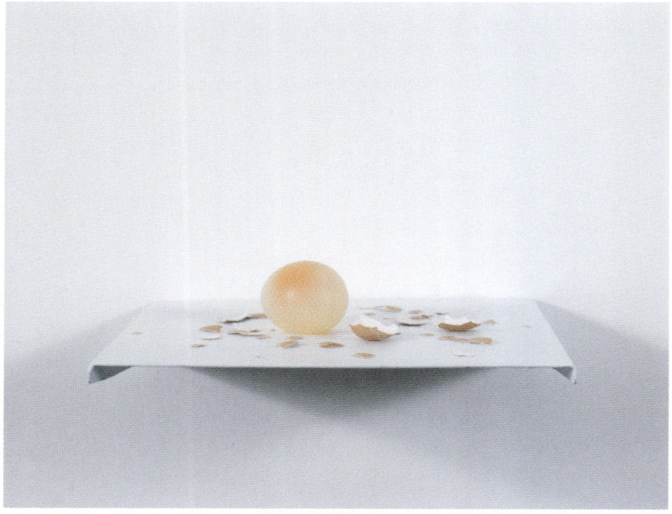

Soft Egg, 1997-2004

Edition of 5 + 1 A.P.

Egg with shell peeled off, The smell of a fresh egg.

Gepeld ei met de geur van een vers ei.

Garbage City, Van Laere Contemporary Art, Antwerp, BE, 20.05.2004-03.07.2004

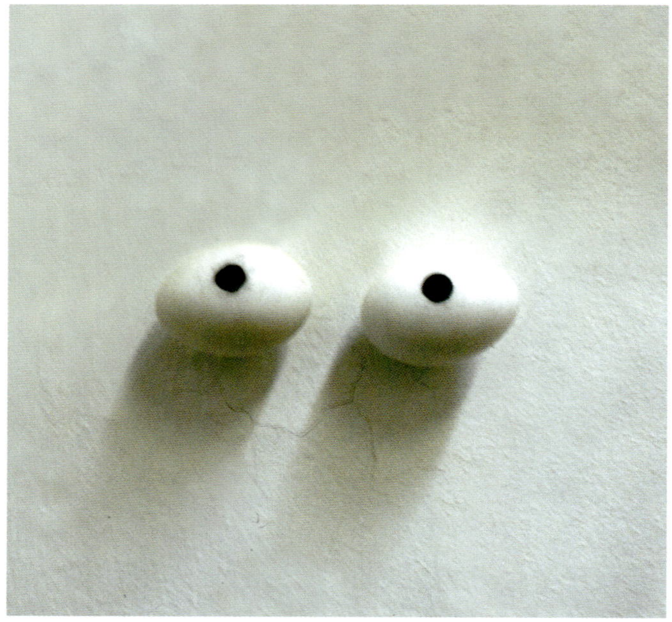

Look those smells, 1998

Two empty eggs with holes. The inside of the eggs are painted black, emanating an egg smell.

Twee lege eierschelpen waarvan de binnenzijde zwart geschilderd is en een eigeur verspreid wordt.

Black Beauty smell happening, Van Laere Contemporary Art, Openingsspeech Jan Hoet and rockconcert Admiral Freebee, Antwerp, 03.06-07.07.1999

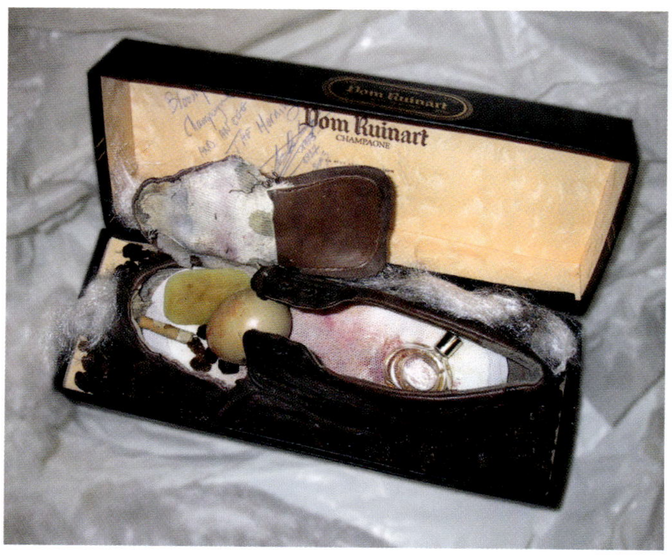

Bloody Champagne And An Egg In The Morning, 1993-1997-2003

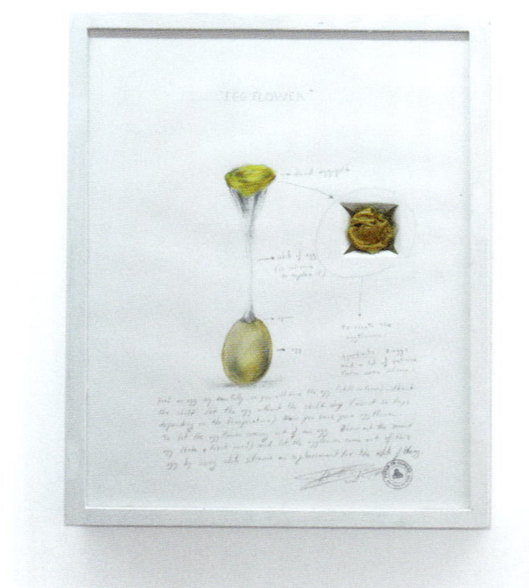

Egg Flower, 2005

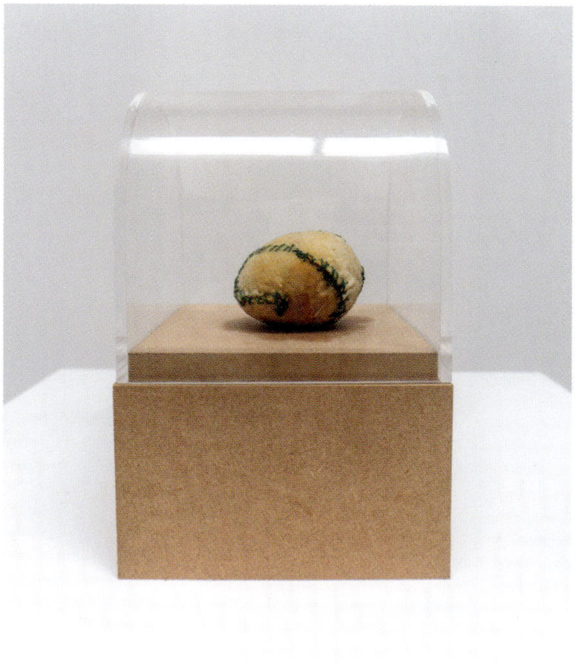

Egg, 1996

Out of the serie, Chicken egg with chicken skin wrapped around it, green thread
Variable dimensions & versions

Uit serie, kippenei met een wikkel van kippenhuid met groene draad
Variabele afmetingen & versies

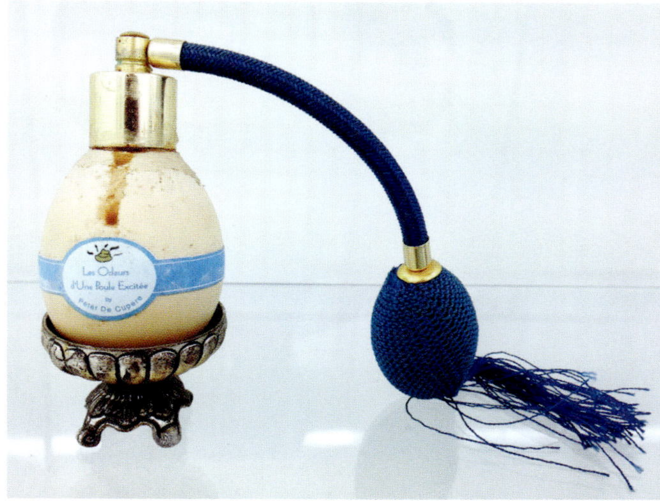

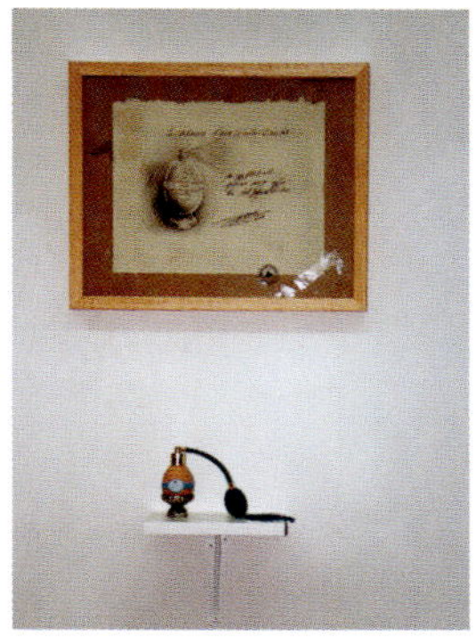

Les Odeurs d 'une Poule Excitée, 2000

Perfume made of chicken excrement
in an egg acting as a perfume bottle

Parfum gemaakt met ontlasting van kippen,
bewaard in een ei als parfumflesje

Perfume Bottles in Art History, The Olfactory,
Hasselt, BE, 19-20-22.09.2014
Peter de Cupere, Smellcom Happening, Smell
Kiss Performance, rockconcert Admiral Freebee,
Van Laere Contemporary Art, Antwerp, BE
14.09-21.10.2000

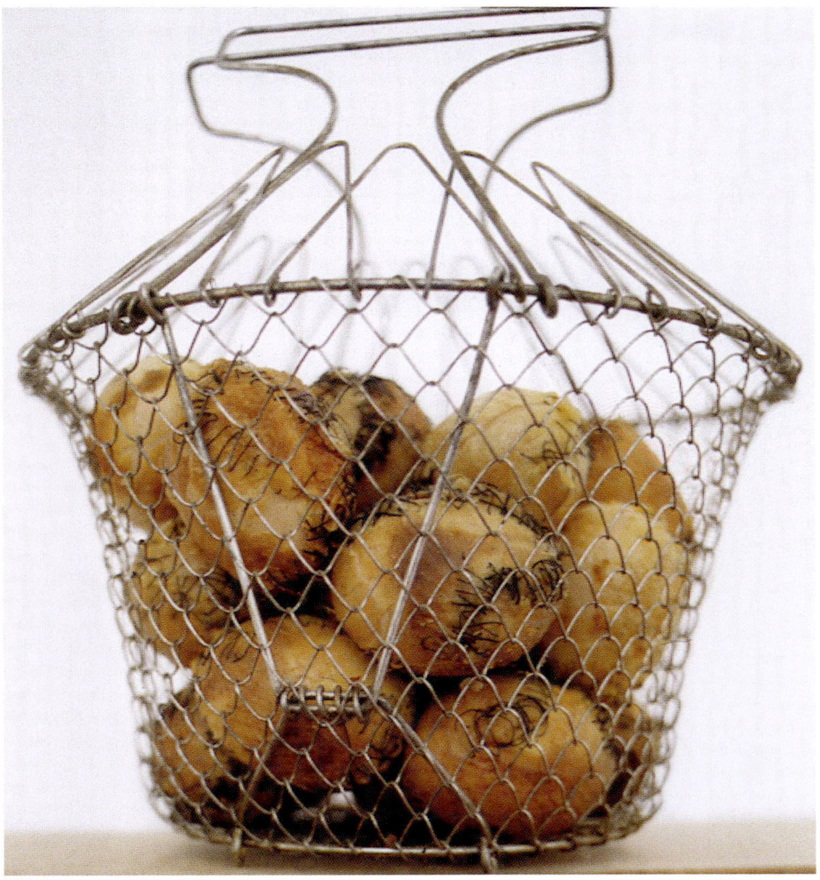

Eggs, 2000

23 eggs with chicken skin sewn around them.

23 eieren met kippenvel rond de eieren genaaid.

Collection: S.M.A.K., Ghent, BE
Black Beauty smell happening, Van Laere Contemporary Art, Openingsspeech Jan Hoet
and rockconcert Admiral Freebee, Antwerp, 03.06-07.07.1999

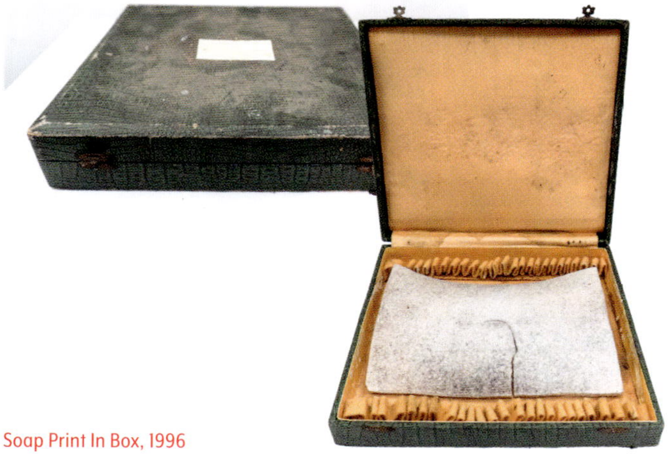

Soap Print In Box, 1996

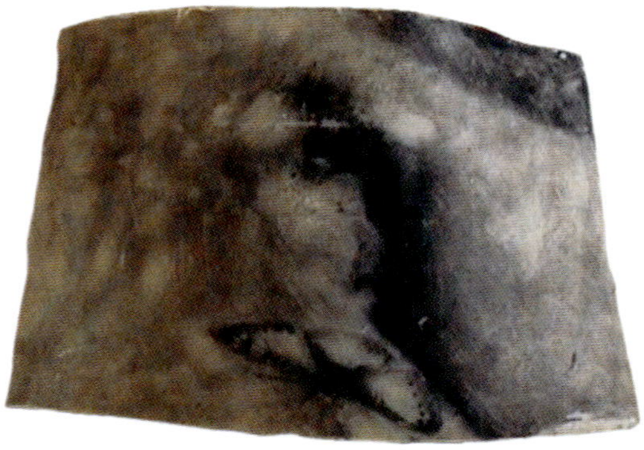

Soapprint, 1996

Computerprint on soap / Computerprint op zeep

Black Beauty smell happening, Van Laere Contemporary Art, Openingsspeech Jan Hoet and rockconcert Admiral Freebee, Antwerp, 03.06-07.07.1999

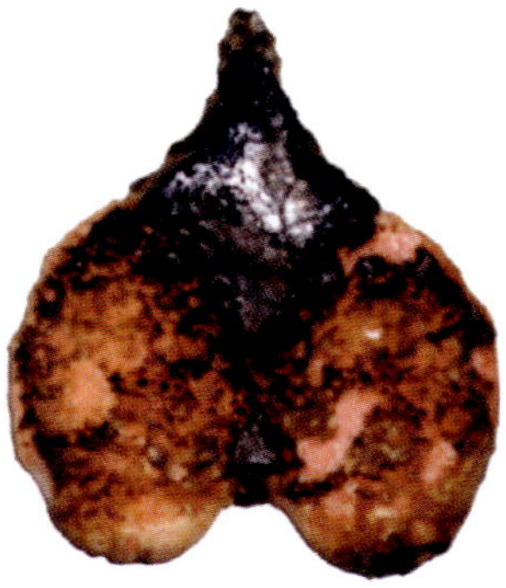

Cellulitis 2, 2000

2 burned soap pieces

2 verbrande stukken zeep

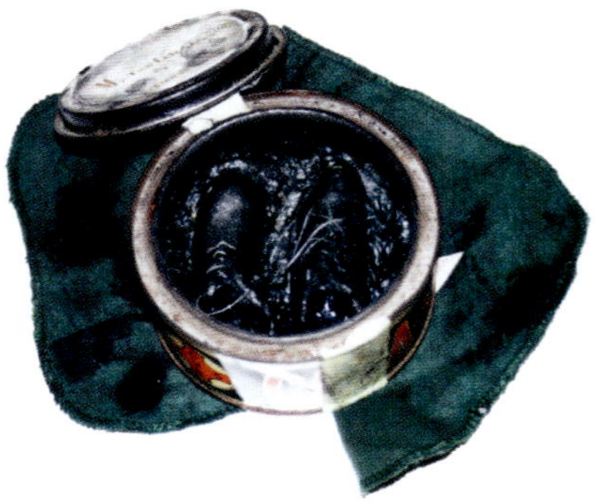

My Two Left Shoes, 2000

Two left shoes made of black shoe cream in a 'Ca va seul'- can

Twee linkse schoenen gemaakt van zwarte schoensmeer in een 'Ca va seul' blik

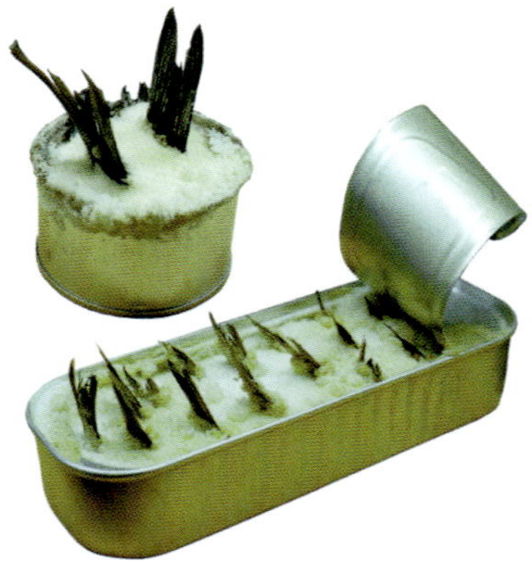

Fish in Salt, 1996-1997

Fish, salt, lemon fragrance, sardine cans

Vis, zout, citroengeur, sardienenblik

Black Beauty smell happening, Van Laere Contemporary Art, Openingsspeech Jan Hoet and rockconcert Admiral Freebee, Antwerp, 03.06-07.07.1999

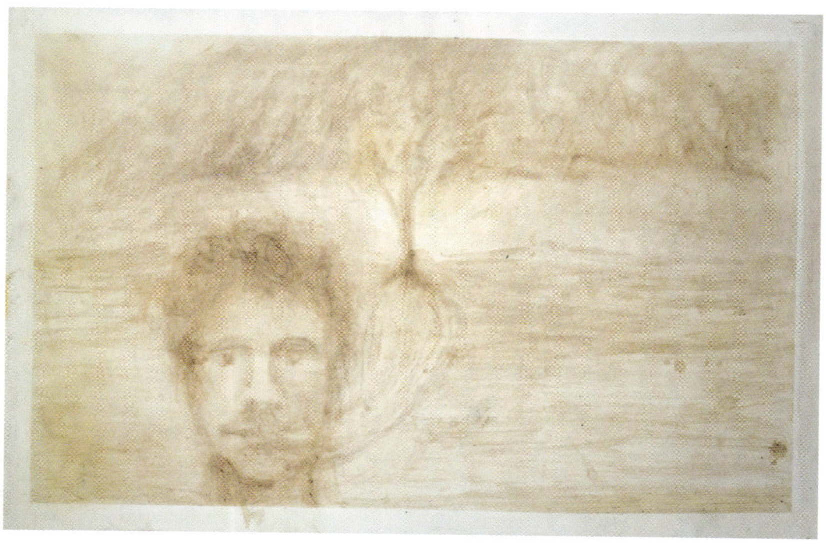

Olive Drawing, 2011

65 cm x 102 cm

Drawing made with olive oil, black & green olives

Tekening gemaakt met olijfolie van zwarte en groene olijven

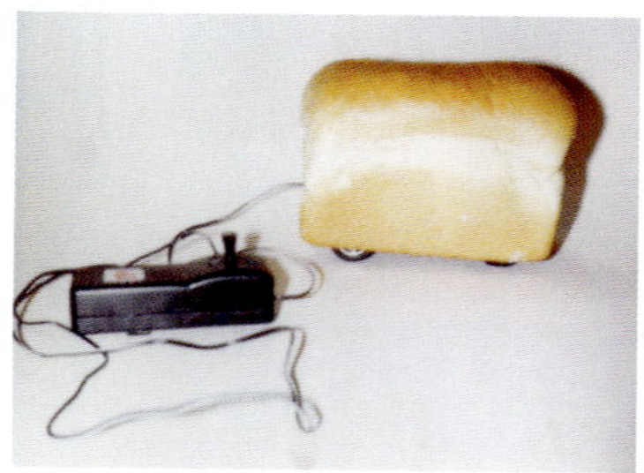

Running after daily bread, 1997

Old bread, car on remote control, bread fragrance

Oud brood, auto op afstandsbediening, broodgeur

Black Beauty smell happening, Van Laere Contemporary Art, Openingsspeech Jan Hoet and rockconcert Admiral Freebee, Antwerp, BE 03.06-07.07.1999

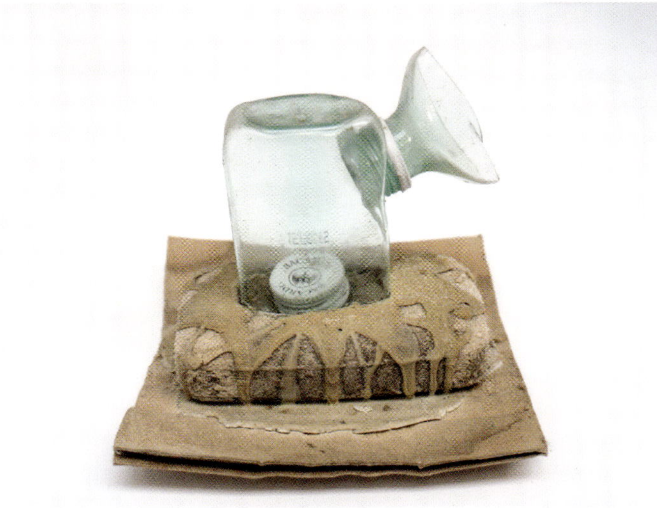

Flight To N .Y., 1998

Soap experiment with little plastic empty Bacardi bottle from a flight to N.Y.

Zeepexperiment met een klein leeg plastieken Bacardiflesje van de vlucht naar N.Y.

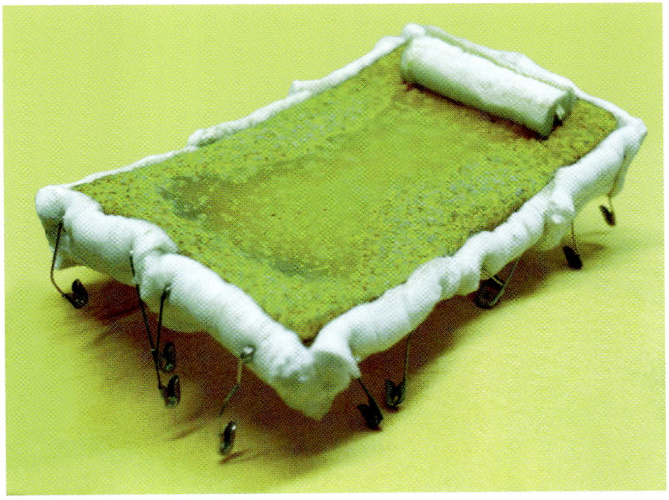

Nose Bed, 1996-1998

Computerprint of nose in soap, tampons, safety pins, pepper, lemon smell

Computerprint van een neus in zeep, tampons, veiligheidsspelden, peper en citroengeur

Peter de Cupere, Black Beauty smell happening, Van Laere Contemporary Art, Openingsspeech Jan Hoet and rockconcert Admiral Freebee, Antwerp, 03.06-07.07.1999

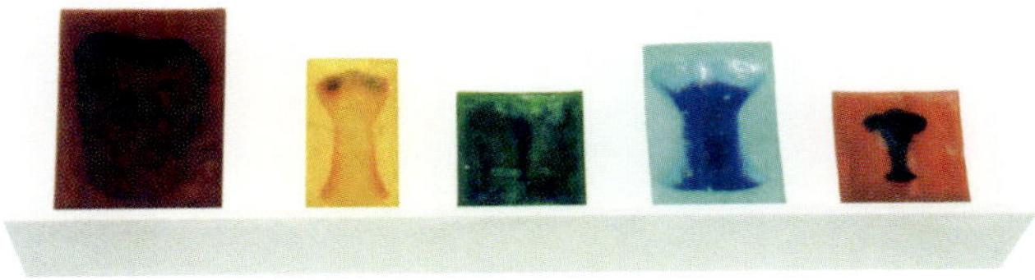

Soap Nose Vases, 1996

Prints of nose vases in a soap mold

Prints van neusvazen in zeep gegoten

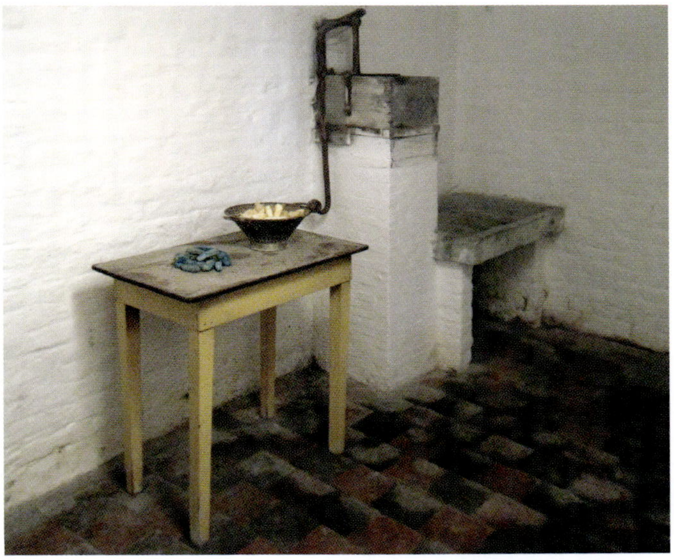

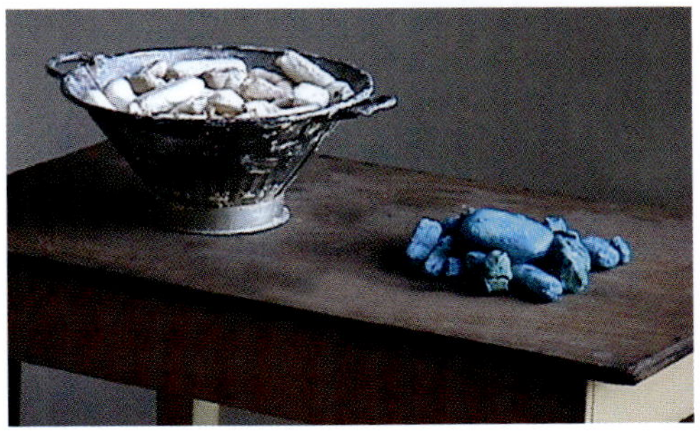

Cleaning, 1997

Smell the Castle, Castle Beauvoorde, curator Annemie Morisse, Beauvoorde, BE, 15.07.2007-30.08.2007

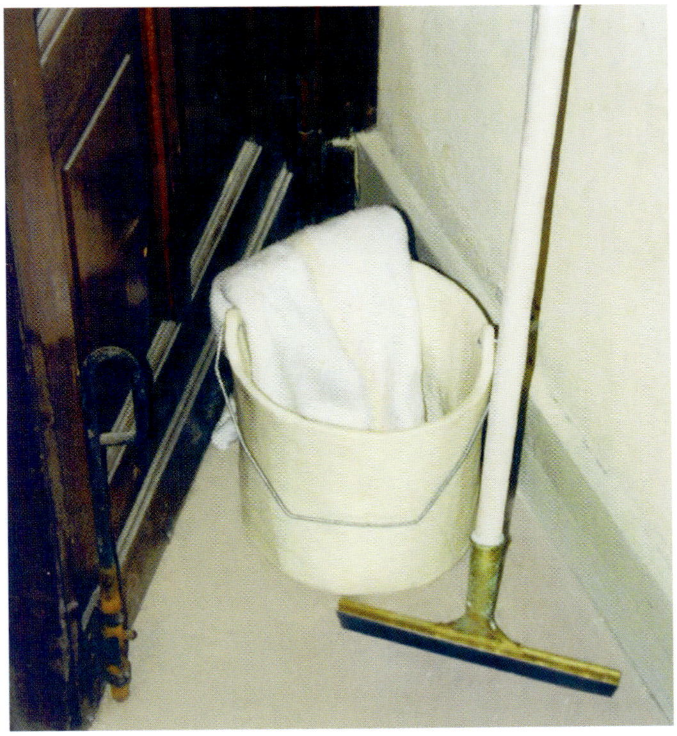

Clean House, 1995-1996

Bucket and cleaning brush made of soap

Emmer en aftrekker gemaakt van zeep

Final Year Students Fine Arts, Sint-Lukas Brussel, Moving Art Studio, Brussels, BE 14-28.06.1996

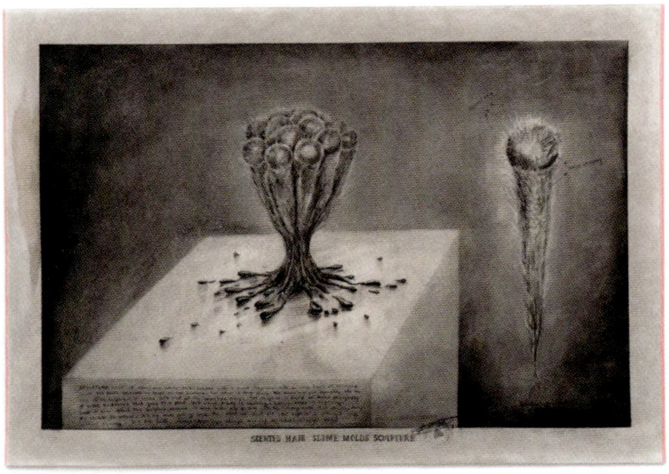

Scented Hair Slime Molds Sculpture, 2012

48 cm x 68 cm

Charcoal, graphite / Houtskool, grafiet

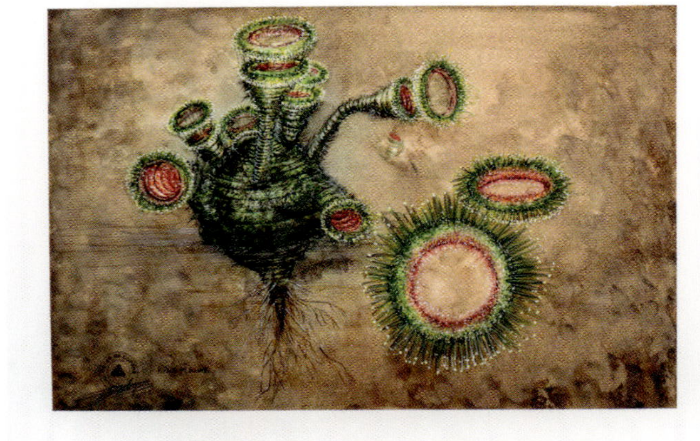

Ring Flower, 2012

39,5 cm x 57 cm

Watercolour / Aquarel

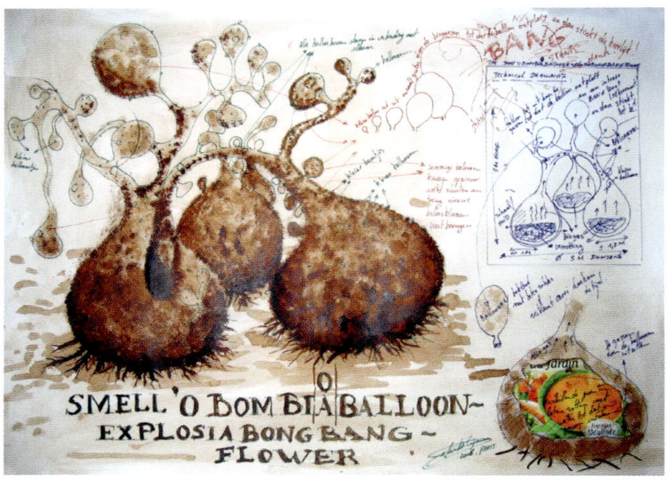

Smell'o Bom Biaballoon Explosia Bong Bang Flower, 2006

Watercolour, pencil / Aquarel, potlood

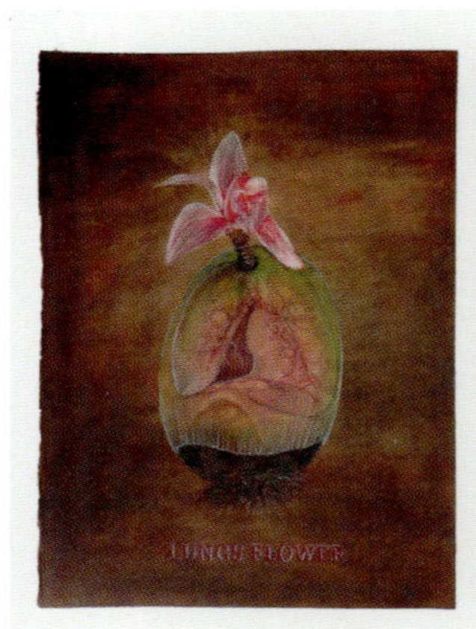

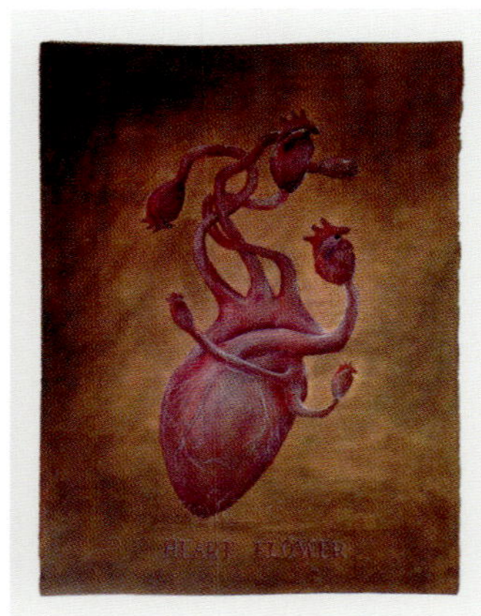

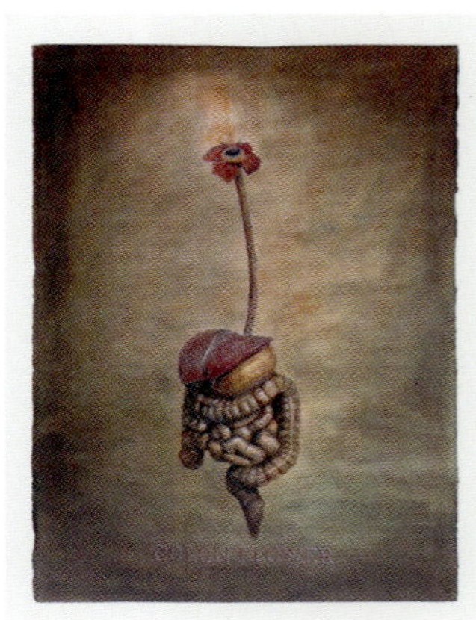

Organ Flowers, 2013

56 cm x 42 cm

Pastel, charcoal, colour pencils

Pastel, houtskool, kleurpotloden

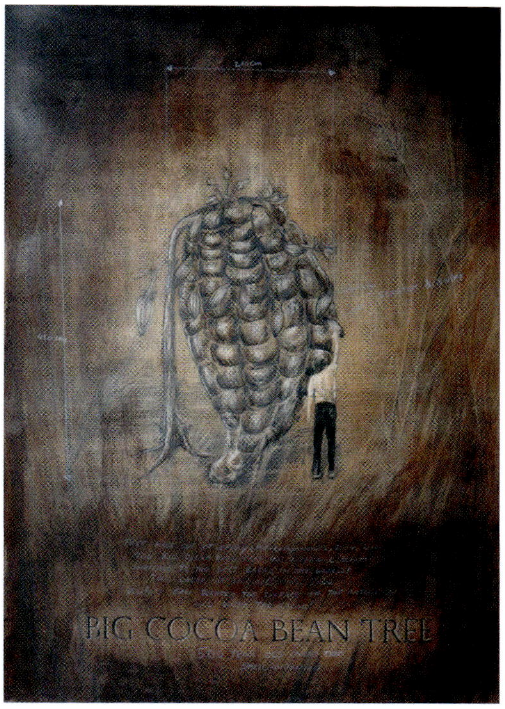

Big Cocoa Bean Tree, 2011

Framed / Ingekaderd 67,5 cm x 51 cm

Pastel, charcoal, graphite

Pastel, houtskool, grafiet

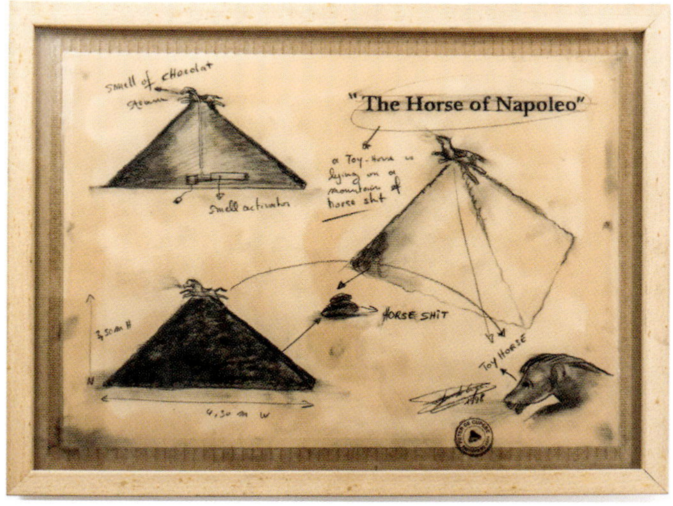

The Horse of Napoleo, 1998

39,5 cm x 53 cm

Concept drawing for an installation for a 350 cm high mountain, made of faeces and fertilizer from horses. A toy soldier is standing on the top of the mountain.

Concepttekening voor een installatie met een 350 cm hoge berg van gedroogde paardenuitwerpselen & paardenmest, waarop een speelgoedpaardje staat. Uit de mond van het speelgoedpaardje komt de geur van chocolade.

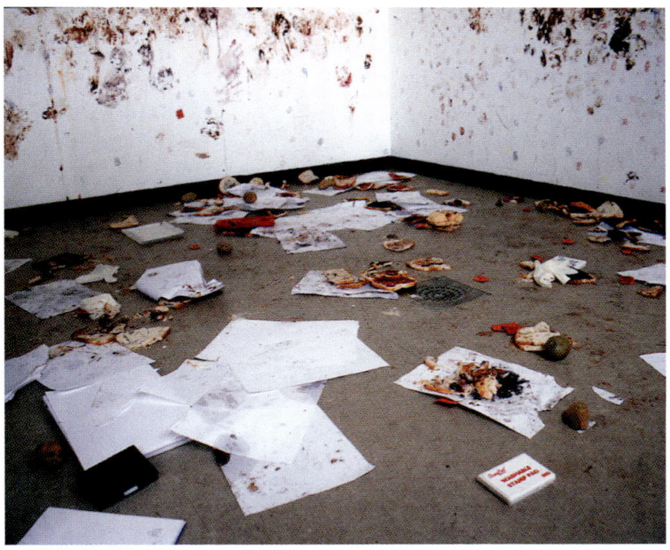

Chocojam, 1999

±320 cm x 450 cm x 350 cm

Installation of happening with six children (2,5 years young) who put stamps of choco, jam, bread, ink pads, etc., on the walls. In the room is a very intensif smell of cocoa.

Opbouw van een happening met zes kinderen van twee en een half jaar die stempels van choco, confituur, brood, inkt op de muur plaatsen. In de kamer is er een zeer sterke geur van cacao.

Kussen, Gallery, VUB, Free University Brussels, BE, 07-29.10.1999

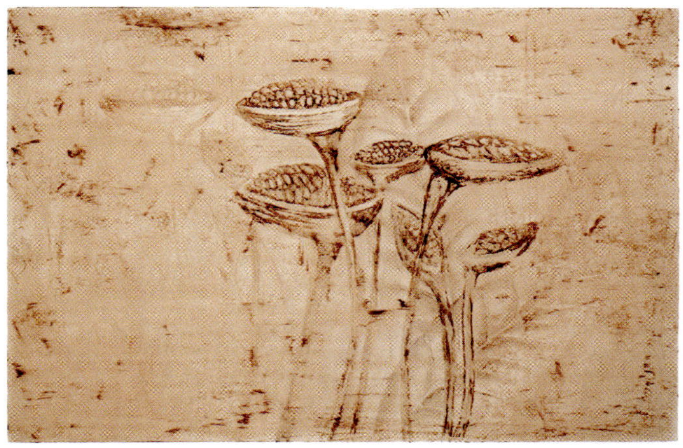

Cacao Drawing, 2015

65 cm x 95 cm

Drawing made with cacao on paper

Tekening gemaakt met cacao op papier

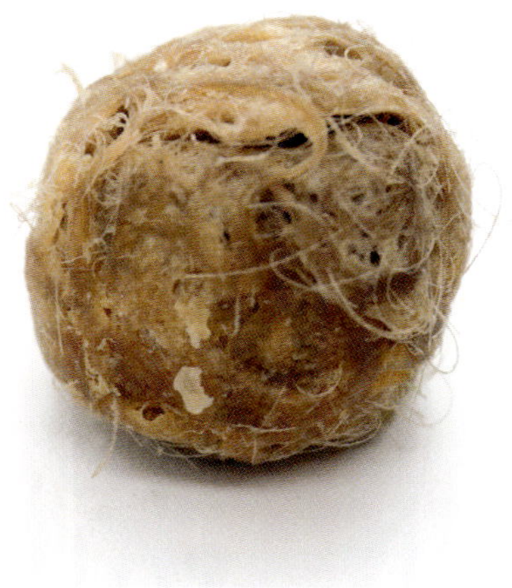

Soap Hair Ball, 1997
3,5 cm Ø
Soap & hair under a glass bell 17 cm x 10 cm
Zeep en haar onder glazen stolp 17 cm x 10 cm

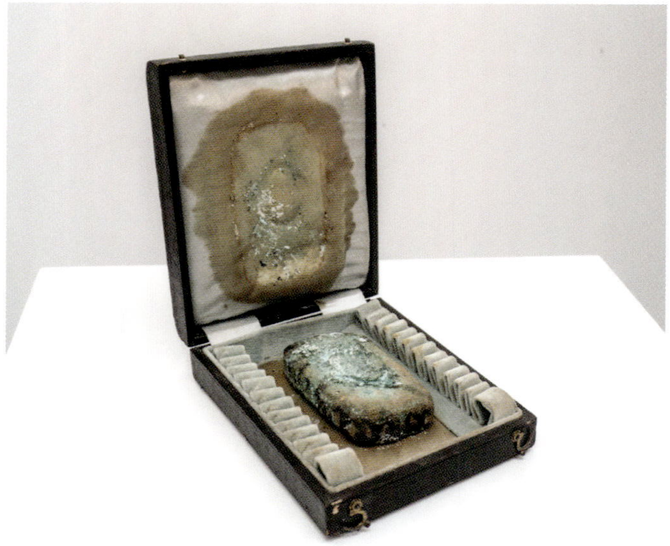

Soap Jewel, 1996-1997
Box open 18 cm x 18 cm x 14 cm
Soap experiment in oxidation process
Zeepexperiment met oxidatie

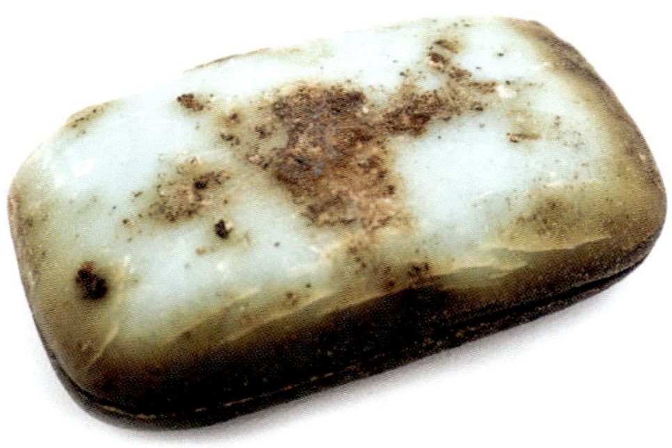

Rusted Soap, 1996-1997
2 cm x 8,5 cm x 5,5 cm
Soap experiment in oxidation process under a glass bell 18,5 cm x 12 cm
Geoxideerd zeep experiment onder glazen stolp 18,5 cm x 12 cm

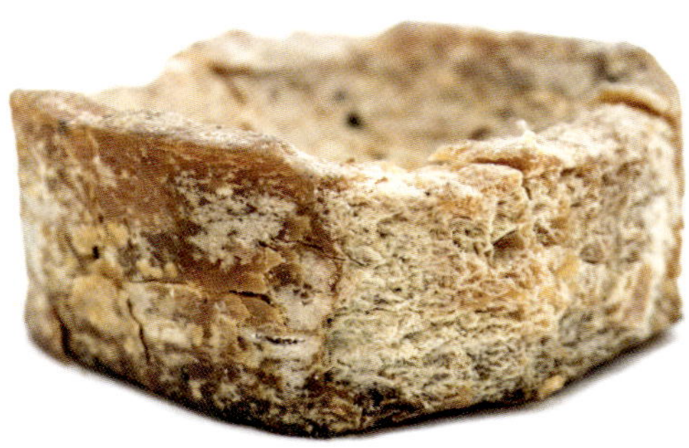

Soap Ashtray, 1997
3 cm x 7,5 cm x 7,5 cm
Ashtray made of soap
Assenbak gemaakt van zeep

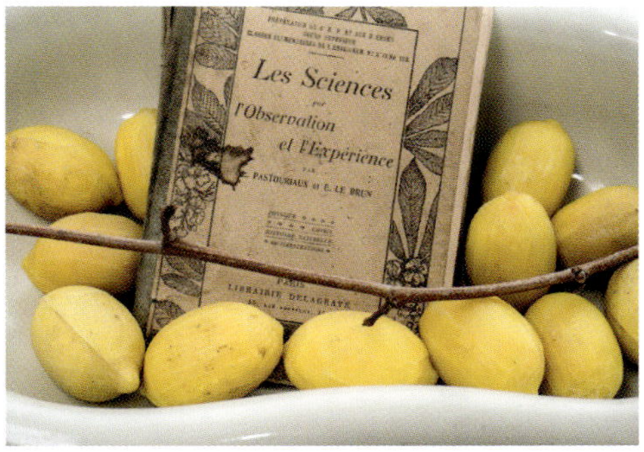

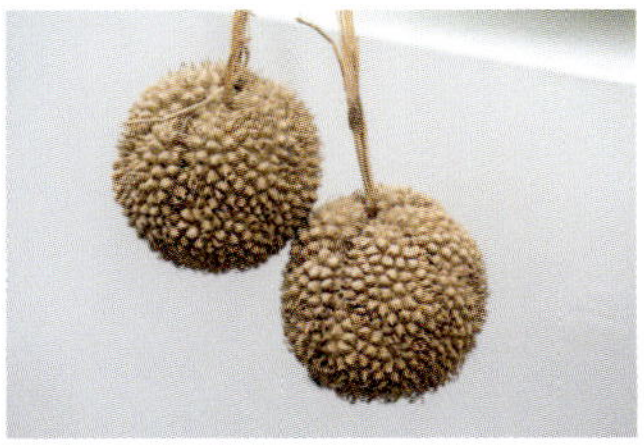

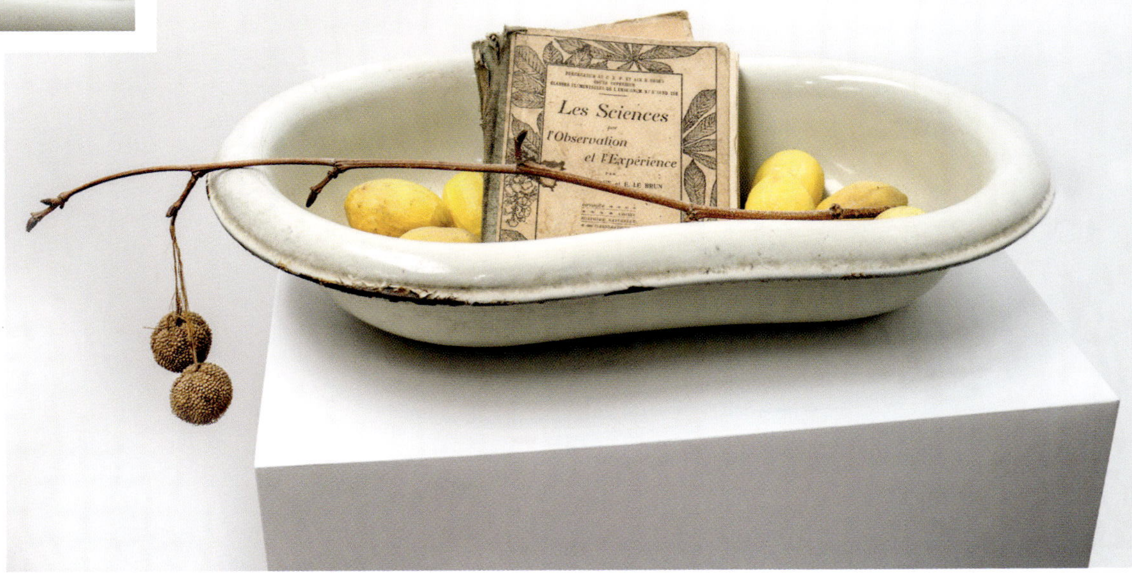

Les Sciences par l'Observation
et l'Experience, 1999-2000

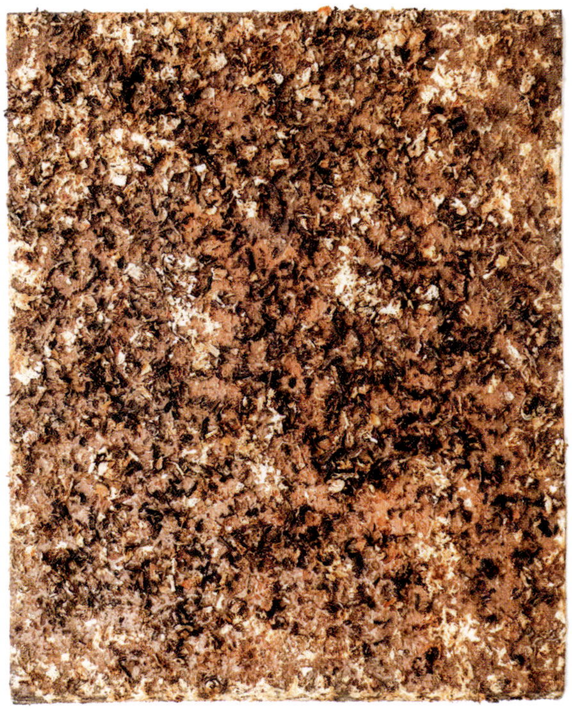

Hot Chili Painting, 1997

34,5 cm x 28 cm

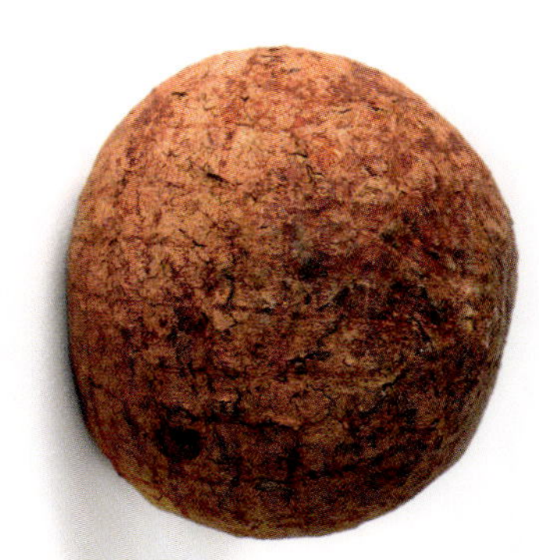

Piri Piri Nose, 1996

13 cm Ø x 10,5 cm

A large clown nose made out of 100 % piri piri. When you put the piri piri nose on your own nose, the intense sensory perception makes you cry.

Een grote clownwneus gemaakt uit 100% piri-piri. Wanneer je de *Piri Piri Nose* op je eigen neus steekt, prikkelt de piri-piri zo intens dat je tranen in je ogen krijgt.

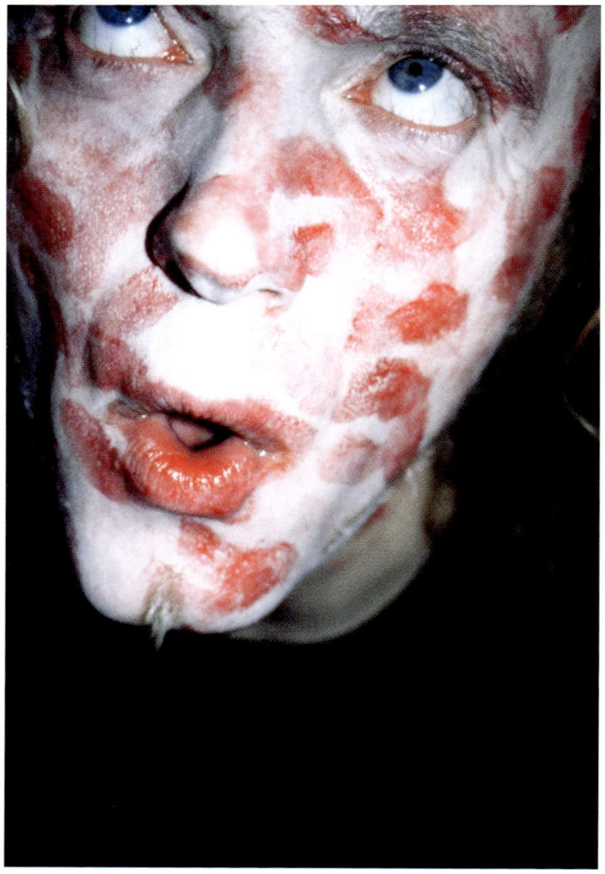

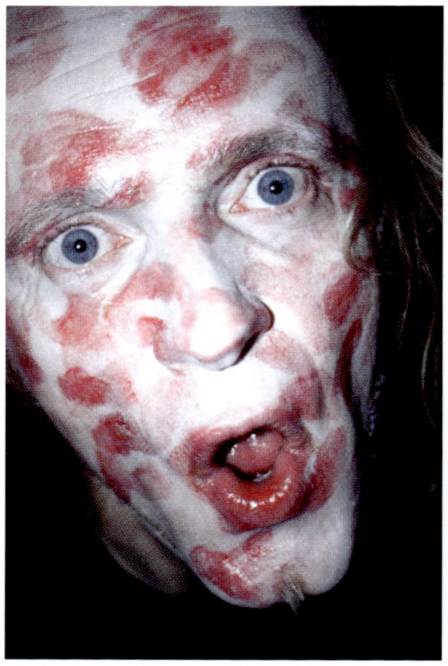

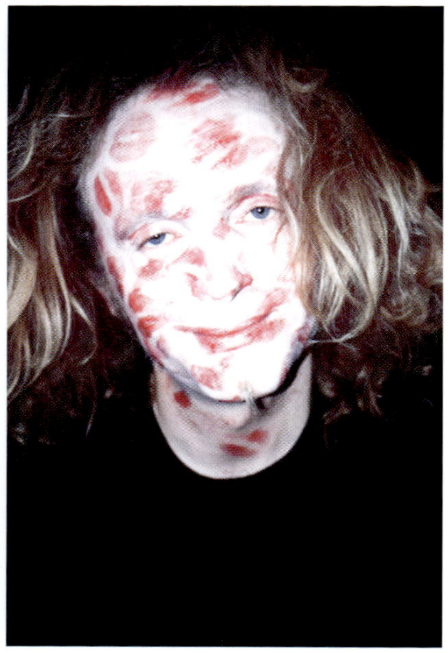

Kiss Perfumance, 2000

The face of the artist is painted white. Scented kisses with the smell of strawberry are given to him.

Het gezicht van de kunstenaar is wit geschilderd. Hij wordt overladen met kussen met aardbeigeur.

Cat Smells Cat

'Cat Smells Cat' are experiments with cats to see how they react on different smells in combination with Actinidine and/or 4aα, 7α, 7aα-Nepetalactone.

Actinidine and 4aα, 7α, 7aα-Nepetalactone are cat attractant and have a characteristic effect on cats. The chemical interacts as a vapour at the olfactory epithelium.

Nepetalactone is an organic compound first isolated from the plant catnip, (Nepeta cataria).

Actinidine is a pyridine derivative found in the essential oil of valerian (Valeriana officinalis) root and Actinidia polygama (silver vine).

Cat Smells Cat is a tribute to the beauty of cats in love or hate.

In honour of my cat.

Cat Smells Cat omvat een reeks experimenten om vast te stellen hoe katten reageren op verschillende geuren in combinatie met Actinidine en/of 4aα, 7α, 7aα-Nepetalactone.

Actinidine en/of 4aα, 7α, 7aα-Nepetalactone hebben een onweerstaanbare aantrekkingskracht met specifieke effecten op katten.

Het olfactorisch epiteel wordt gestimuleerd door de chemische samenstelling.

Nepetalactone is een organisch component dat geïsoleerd wordt uit kattenkruid (Nepeta cataria).

Actinidine is een pyridine derivaat dat men kan winnen uit de wortel van valeriaan en Actinidia polygama (kiwi-achtigen).

Cat Smells Cat is een eerbetoon aan de schoonheid van katten zowel in tijden van liefde als haat.

Uit liefde voor mijn kat.

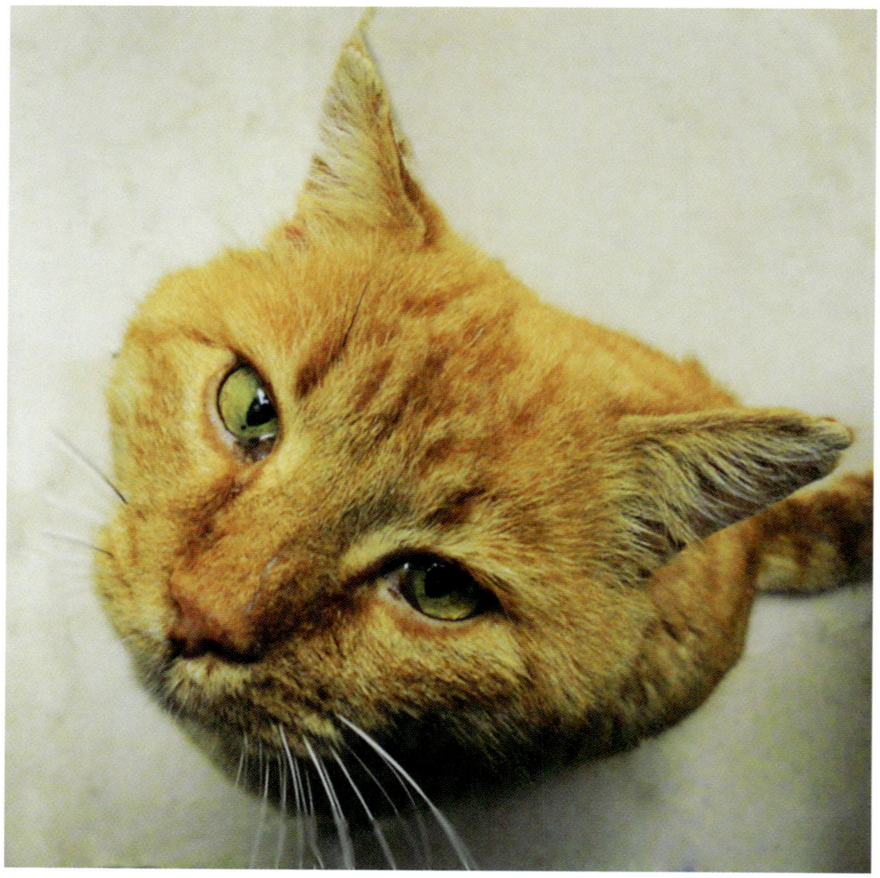

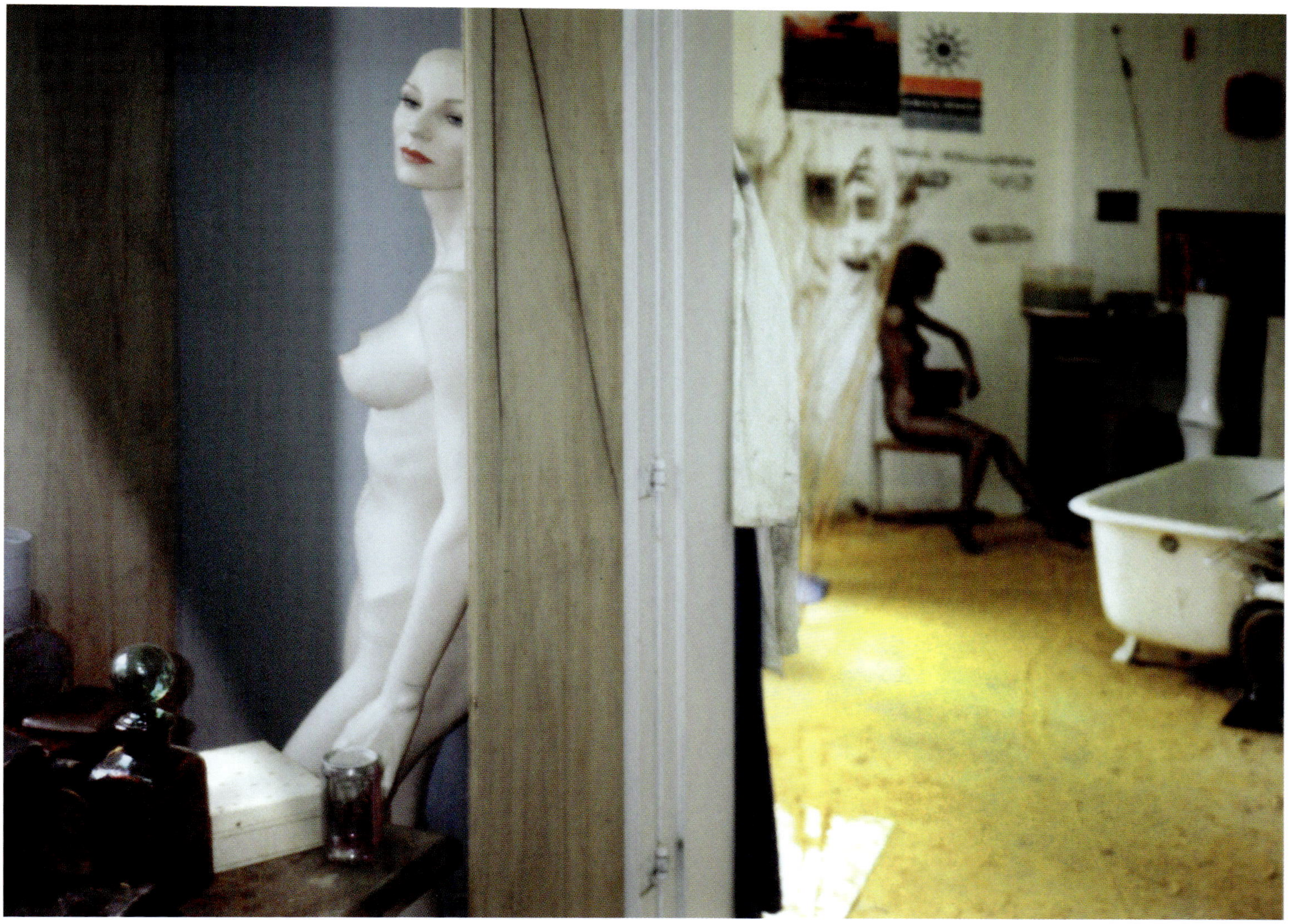

Studio experiments in HISK, 1996-1999

Spices on the ground and different works in progress

Kruiden op de grond en diverse kunstwerken in aanmaak

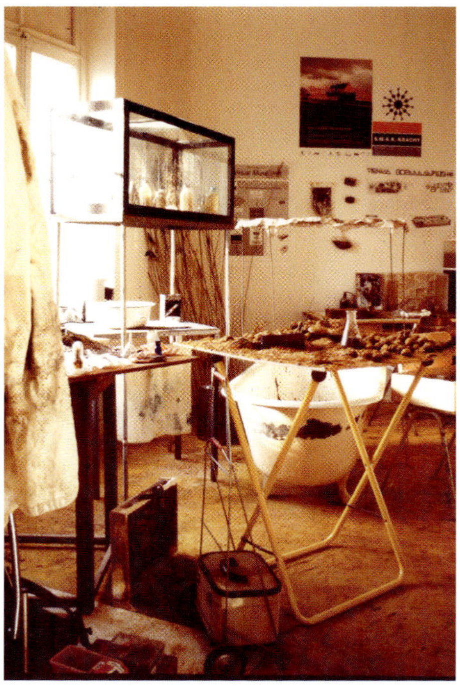

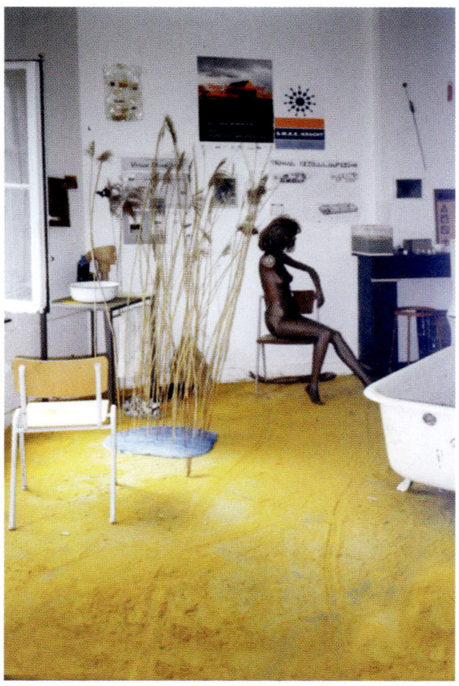

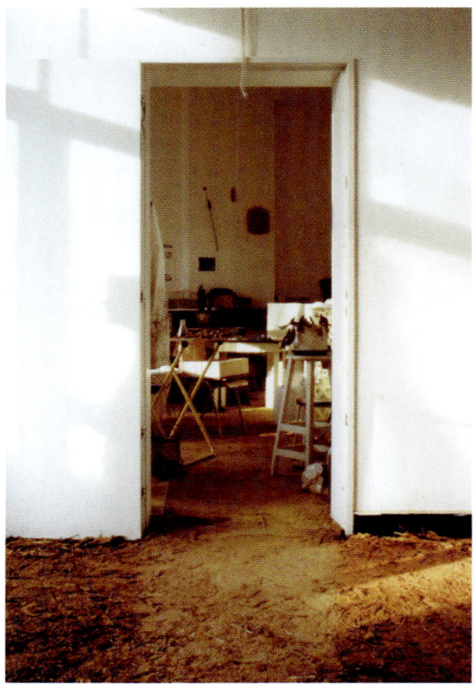

PETER DE CUPERE

LOOK, THOSE SMELLS
Geur in twee dimensies

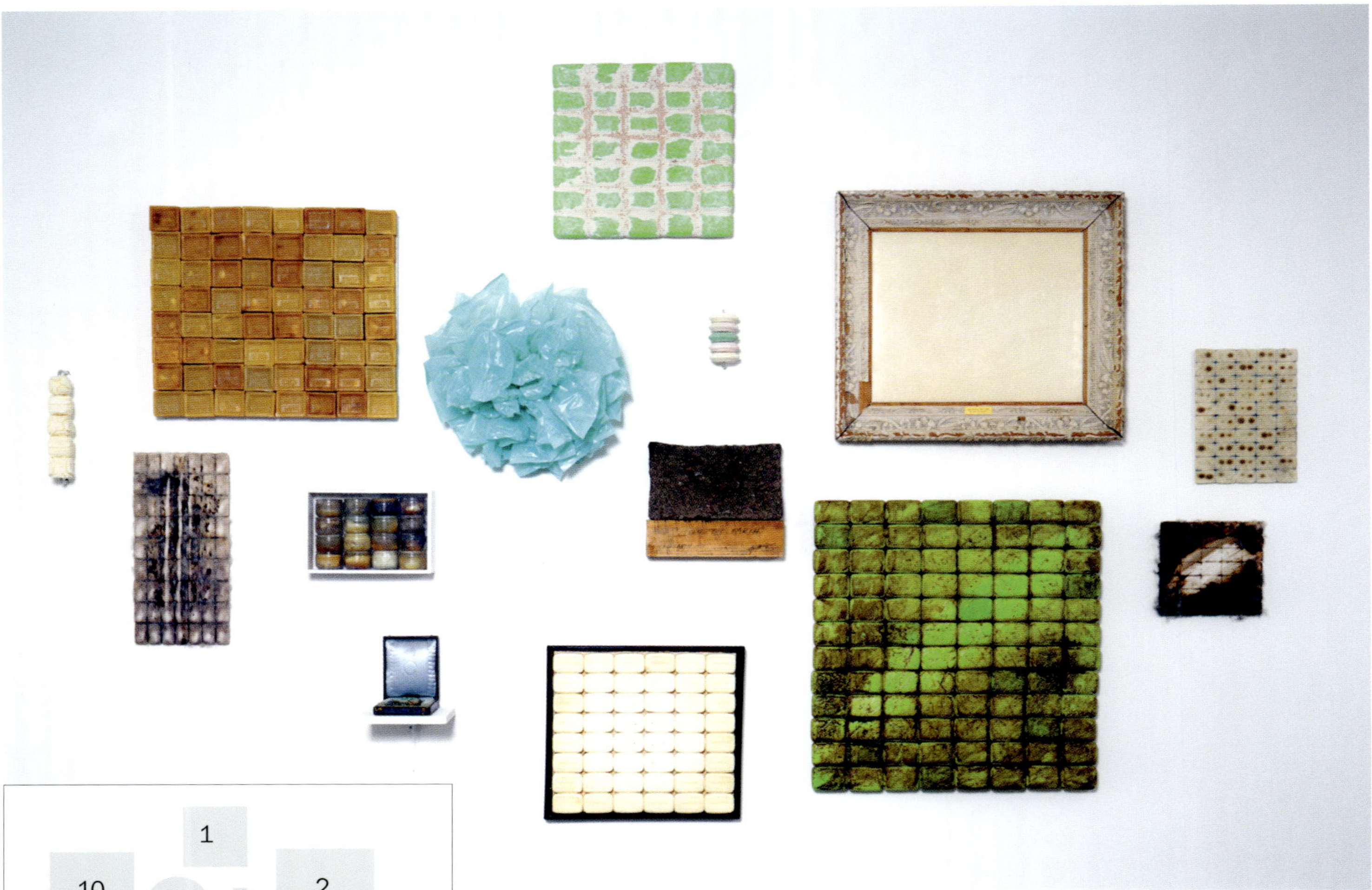

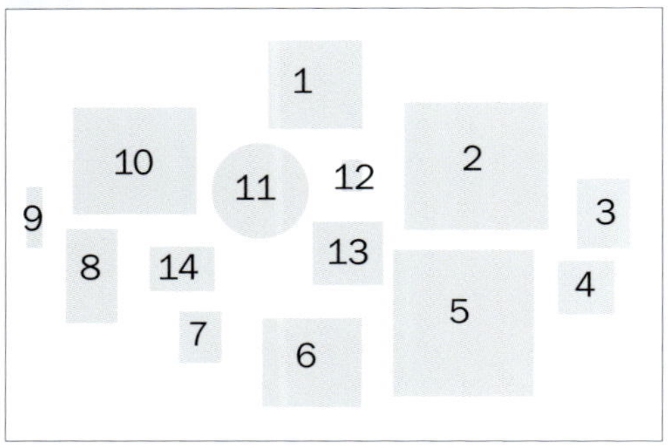

Different Soap Paintings from 1996-2002

Perfume happening, rockconcert Admiral Freebee,
Van Laere Contemporary Art, Antwerp, BE, 07.03 -13.04.2002

1. Broken Line, 2001
   35 pieces of soap, silicones and seed / 35 stukken zeep, siliconen en zaad
2. Soap Mirror, 2001
   Old cadre with surface of white soap / Oude kader met witte zeep
3. Spot Soap Painting 5 x 10, 1998
4. Washed Soap Painting 5 x 7, 2000-2002
5. Green Washed Soap Painting 8 x 12, 2001
   96 pieces of painted soap / 96 stukken beschilderde zeep
6. Toilet Soap Painting 6 x 8, 2000-2002
7. Soap Jewel, 1996-1997
8. Clean Nails 7 x 9, 2001
9. Soap Progress Painting 1 x 5, 2001
10. Sunlight 8 x 8, 2000
11. Pregnancy, 1999
    Plastic painting, smell of babypowder / Plastieken schilderij, geur van babypoeder
12. Soap Colour Composition 1 x 5, 1999
13. Clean The Earth, 2002
    Earth Soap Painting, 50 % earth, 50 % soap
    Aarden zeepschilderij met 50% aarde en 50% zeep
14. Untitled, 1998-1999
    15 pots with soap and fermentated food (eggs, etc.)
    15 potten met zeep en gefermenteerd voedsel (eieren, etc.)

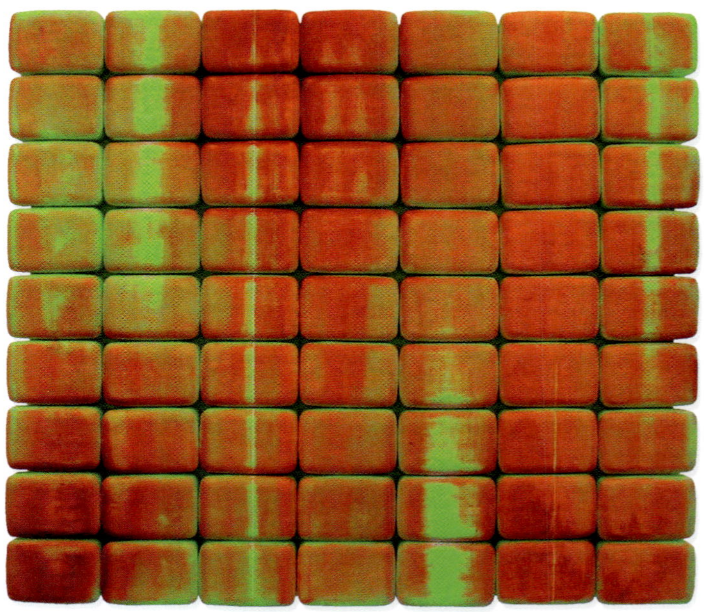

Soft Red-Green Soap Painting, 2001

63 pieces of painted soap / 63 stukken beschilderde zeep

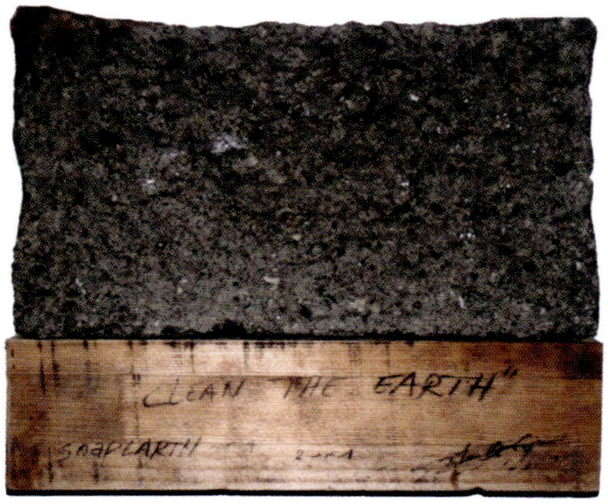

Clean the Earth, 2002

50 % soap & 50 % earth

50% zeep & 50% aarde

Earth Soap Painting

100 cm x 100 cm

Painting made from 50 % soap & 50 % earth

Schilderij gemaakt van 50% zeep & 50% aarde

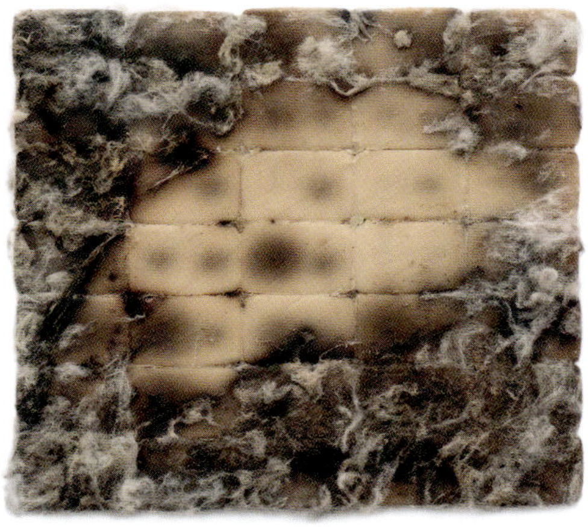

Washed Soap Painting 5 x 7, 2000-2002,

23,5 x 26,5 cm

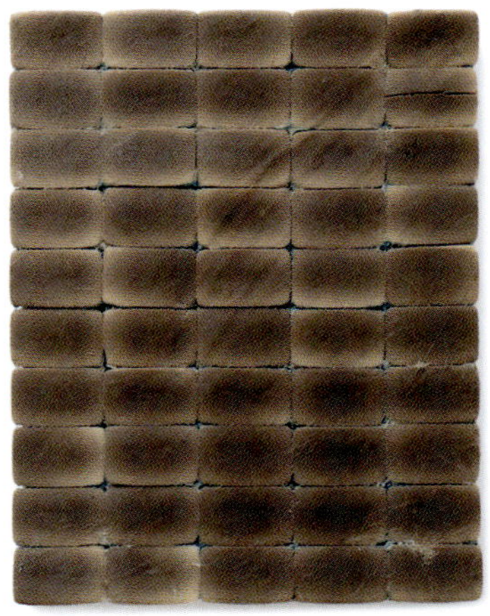

Changed Spot Soap Painting 5 x 10, 1998

33,5 cm x 26,5 cm

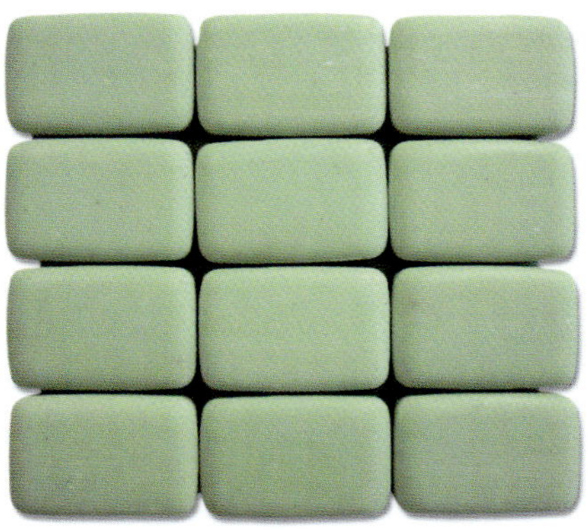

Green Soap Painting 3 x 4, 2002

12 pieces of soap / 12 stukken zeep

Perfume happening, rockconcert Admiral Freebee,
Van Laere Contemporary Art, Antwerp, BE, 07.03-13.04.2002

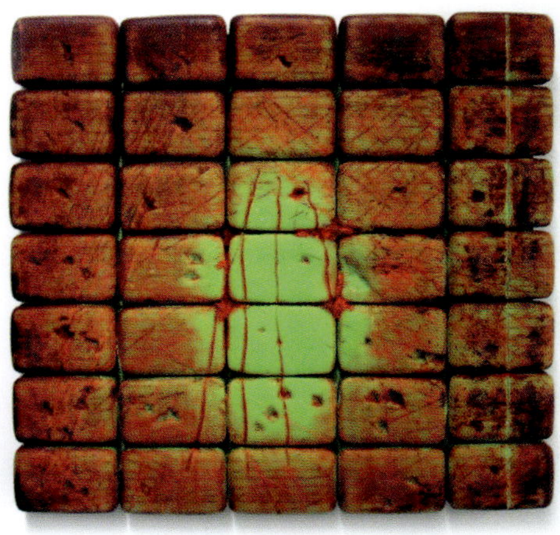

Red Scratch Wash Soap Painting 5 x 7, 2001

35 pieces of painted soap / 35 stukken geschilderde zeep

Soap TV, 1996-1997

An old TV set was covered with red, semi-transparent soap. Live soap opera series were shown with the sound distorted. The soap smelled of roses or strawberries.

Op een oude TV werd rode half doorzichtige zeep aangebracht. Er werden 'live soap series' getoond waarbij het geluid vervormd werd. De zeep rook naar rozen of aardbeien.

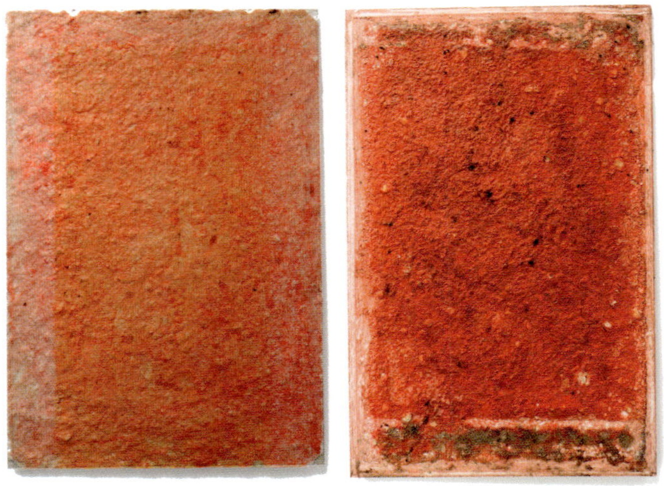

Experimental Soap Paintings, 2001

73 cm x 48 cm

Earth and Milk Soap Painting Objects, 2002

2 experimental soap paintings as objects

2 experimentele zeepschilderijen die ook objecten zijn.

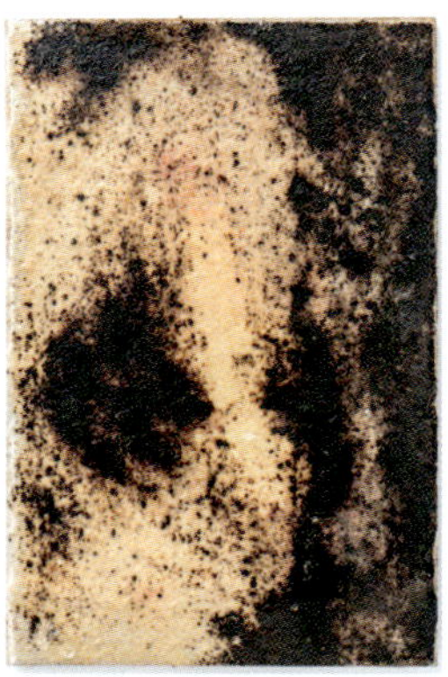

Experimental Soap Paintings, 2001

73 cm x 48 cm

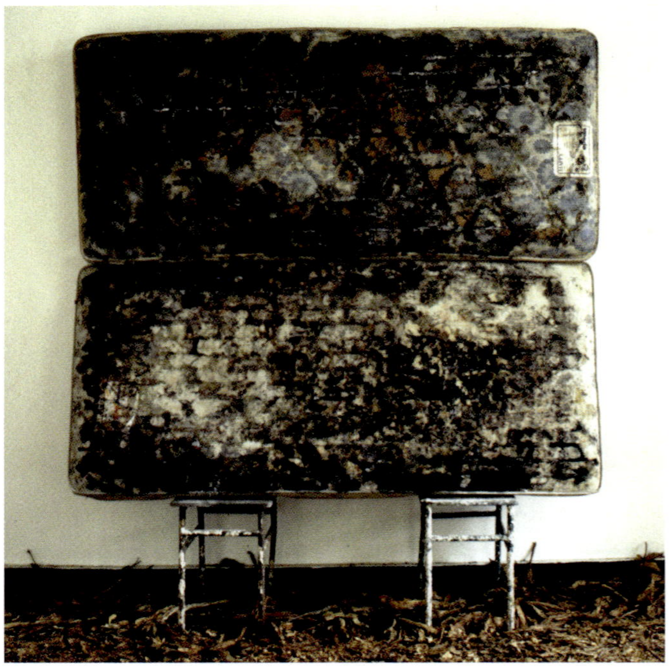

Mouldy Mattresses I, 1997-1999

2 mouldy mattresses on 2 chairs standing on dried Havana tobacco leaves

2 beschimmelde matrassen op twee stoelen op gedroogde Havana tabaksbladeren

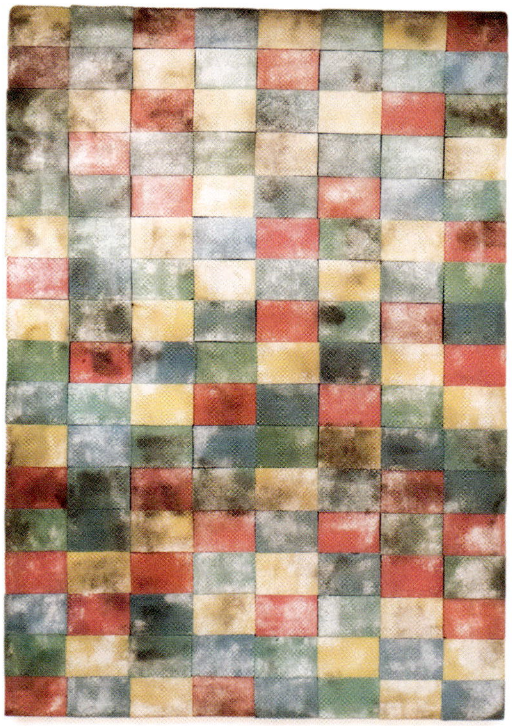

Wash Painting 17 x 8, 2001
117 cm x 80 cm
136 pieces of used sponges, 'Dash' soap
136 gebruikte sponsen met Dash zeep

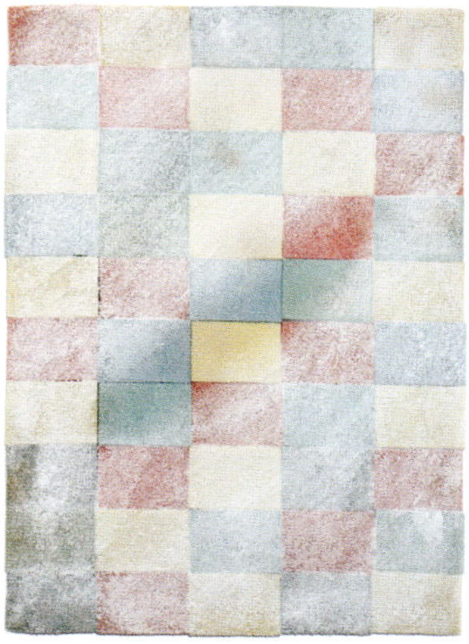

Wash Painting 10 x 5, 2001
69 cm x 50 cm
50 pieces of used sponges, 'Dash' soap
50 gebruikte sponsen met Dash zeep

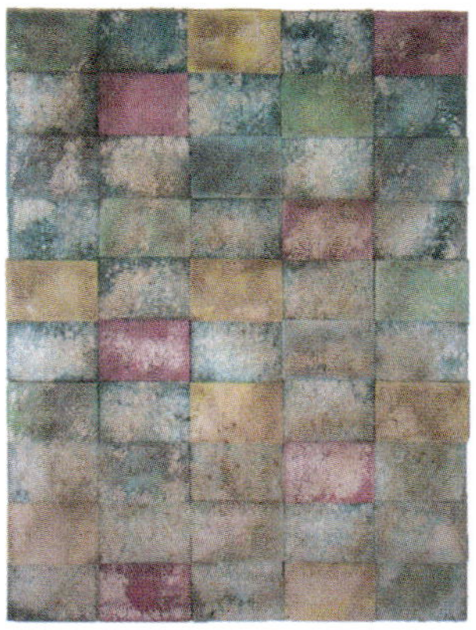

Wash Painting 10 x 5, 2001
69 cm x 50 cm
50 pieces of used sponges, 'Dash' soap
50 gebruikte sponsen met Dash zeep

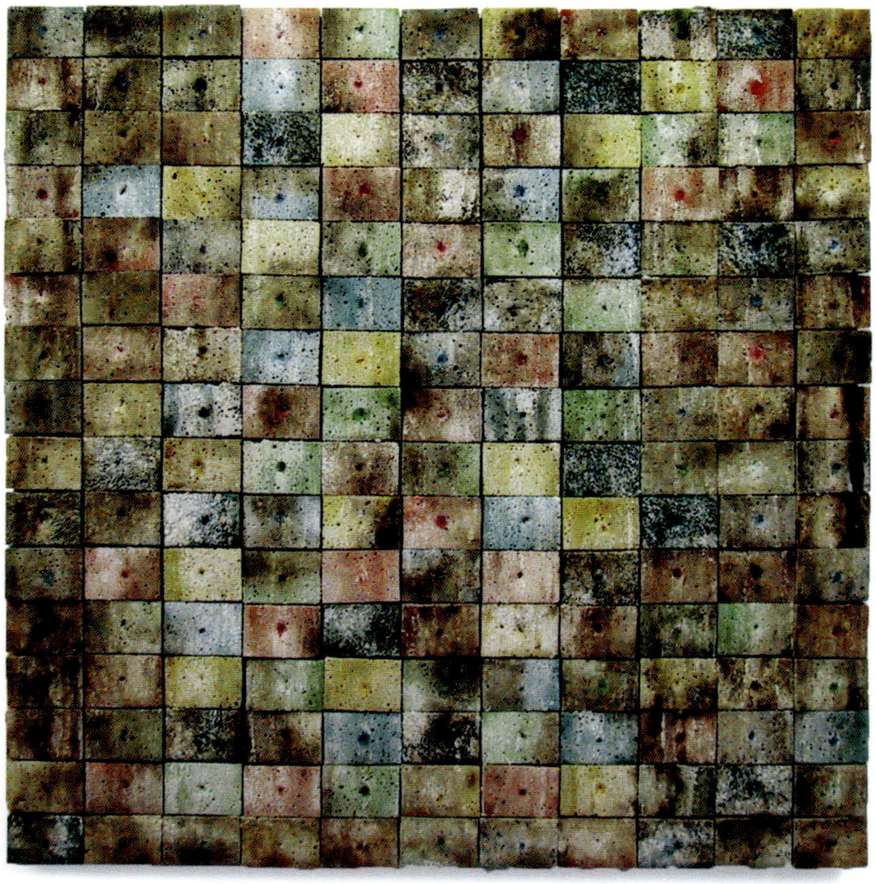

Wash Painting 11 x 16, 2001

In 2001, the artist-in-residence at the Academy of Arts in Berlin produced various Wash Paintings. The Wash Paintings were made by cleaning the studio with cheap sponges before using it for the first time. Instead of rinsing the sponges out each time, they were set aside to be used later for painting. The resulting works were sometimes given an extra layer of washing powder.

Als artist in residence in Akademie der Kunsten in Berlijn in 2001 werden verschillende *Wash Paintings* gerealiseerd. De Wash Paintings ontstonden door met goedkope sponsen het pas betreden atelier te kuisen. In plaats van de sponsen telkens uit te spoelen werden ze opzij gezet om achteraf een schilderij mee te maken. De gerealiseerde werken kregen dan soms een extra laag waspoederzeep.

Perfume happening, rockconcert Admiral Freebee,
Van Laere Contemporary Art, Antwerp, BE, 07.03-13.04.2002

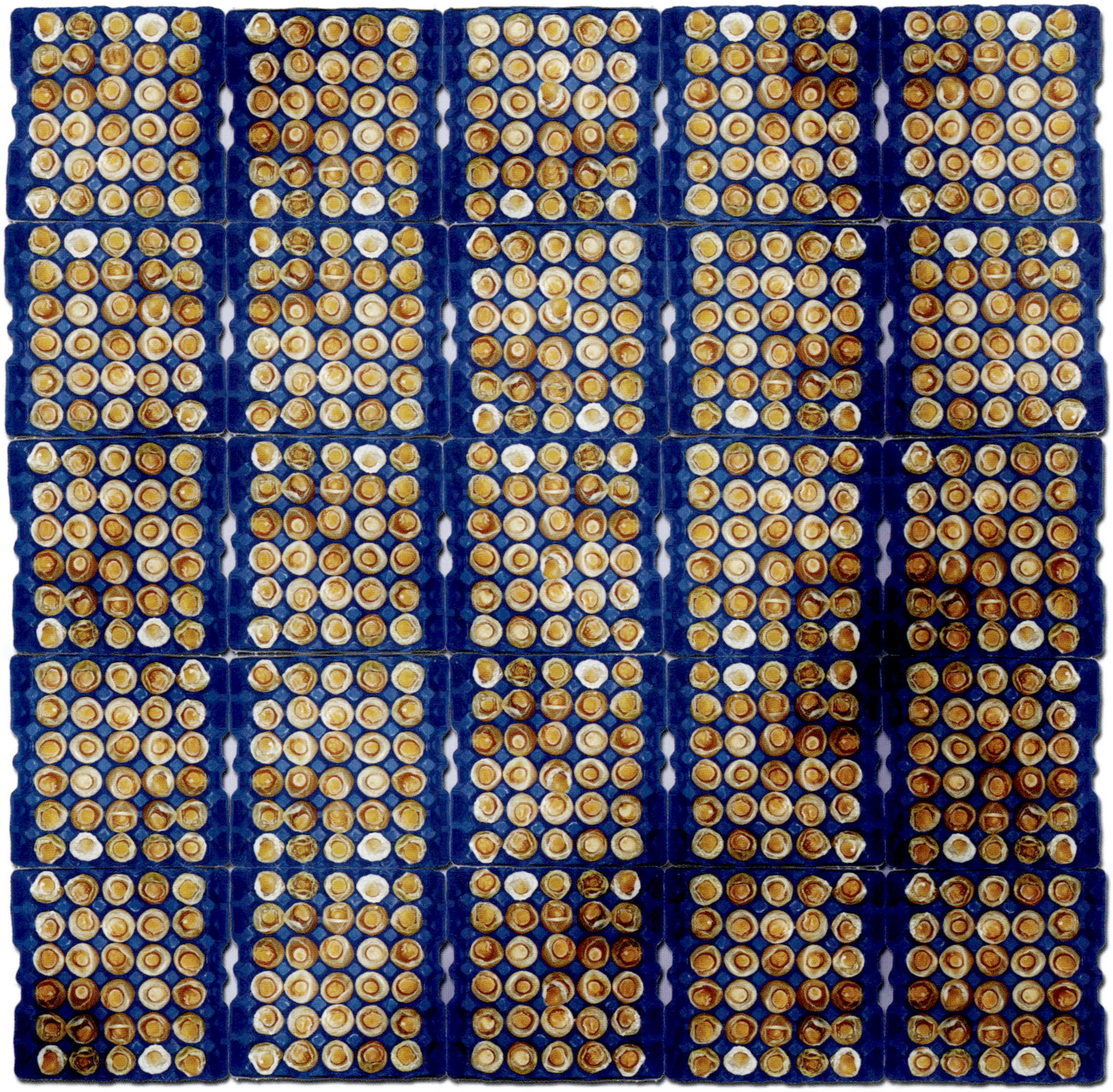

Blue Egg Painting (B750), 2000

750 dried eggs in blue egg holders

750 gedroogde eieren in blauwe eierkartons

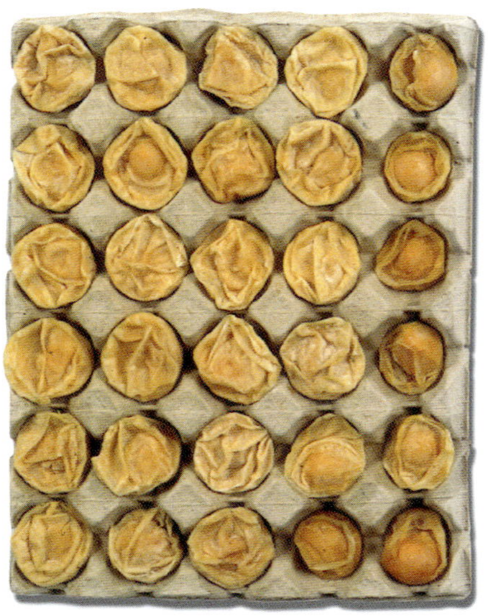

First Egg Painting, 1998

30 dried eggs in egg holder
30 gedroogde eieren in eierkarton

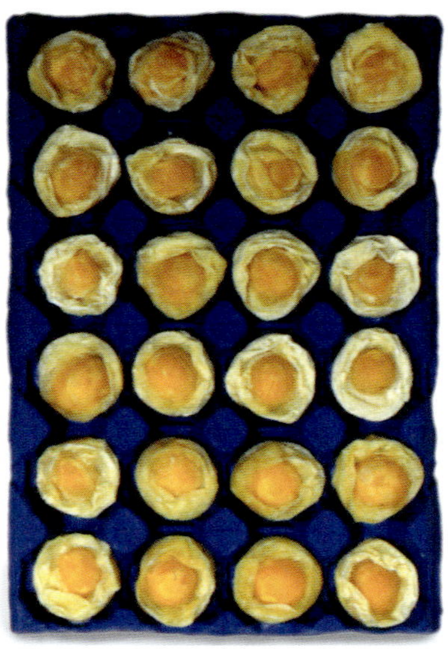

Blue Egg Painting (B24), 2000

24 dried eggs in blue egg holder

24 gedroogde eieren in blauw eierkarton

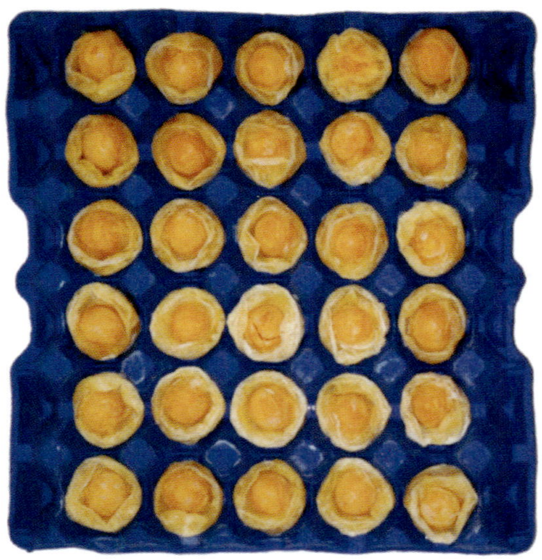

Blue Egg Painting (B30), 2000

30 dried eggs in blue egg holder

30 gedroogde eieren in blauw eierkarton

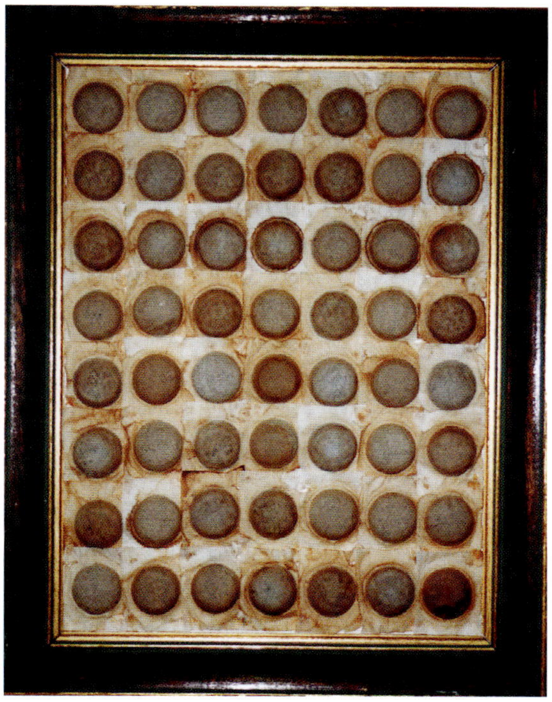

Good Morning Darling, a Cup of Coffee, 2000
61 cm x 47,5 cm
56 Illy coffee pads / koffiepads

Smell Seat, 1998
41,5 cm x 37,5 cm x 7,5 cm
Babypowder smell, old seat (±100 year), 2 versions
Geur van babypoeder, antiek zetelvlak (±100 jaar), 2 versies

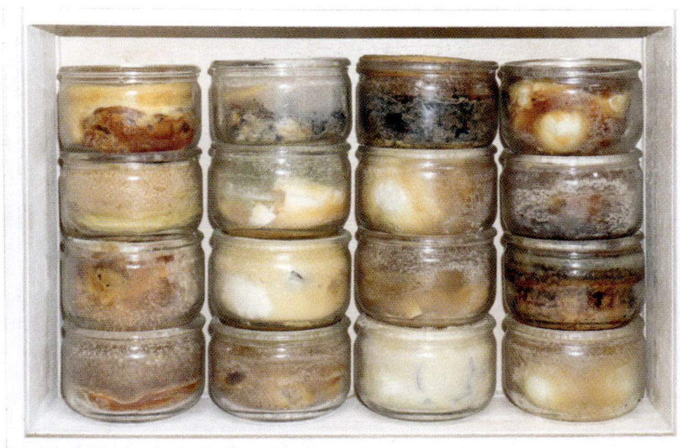

Status of artwork in 2016

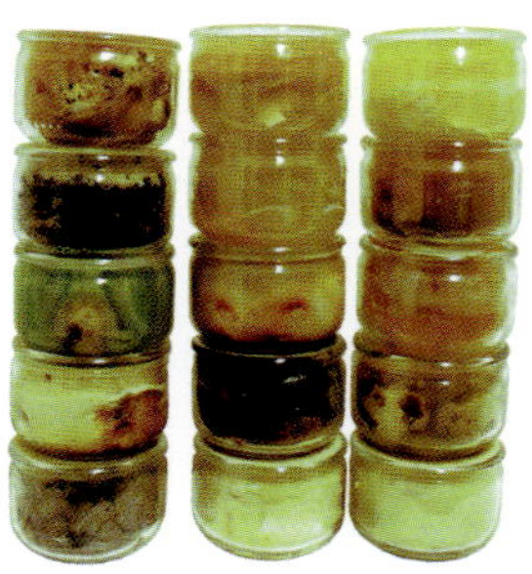

Status of artwork in 1998-1999

Untitled, 1998-1999
20.5 cm x 31 cm x 9 cm
15 pots with soap and fermentated food (eggs, etc.)
15 potten met zeep en gefermenteerd voedsel (eieren, etc.)

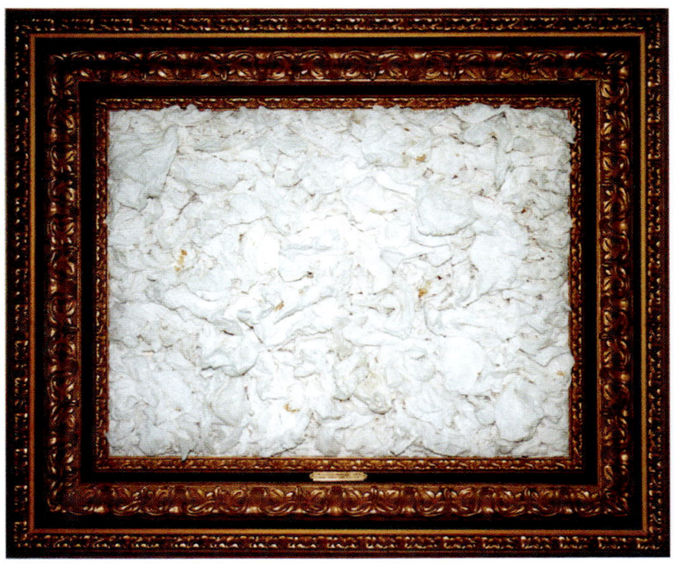

Winter Landscape, 1999-2000
207 used handkerchiefs of paper, eucalyptus smell
207 gebruikte papieren zakdoekjes, geur van eucalyptus

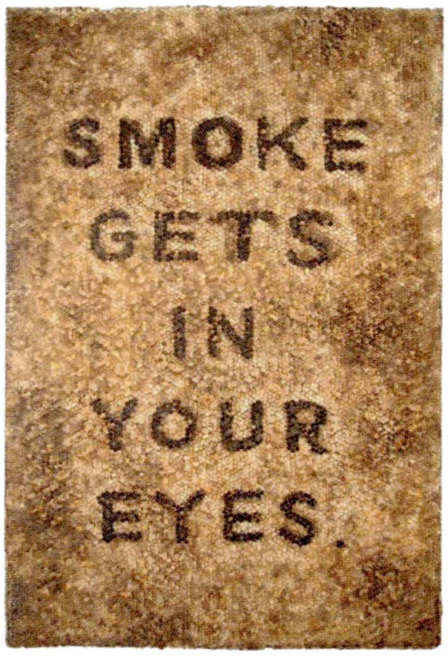

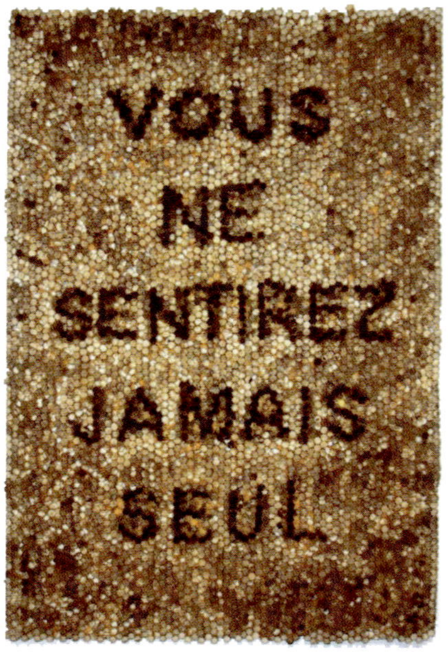

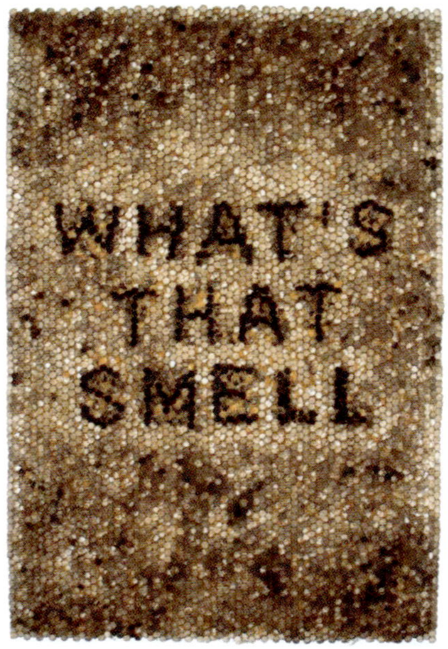

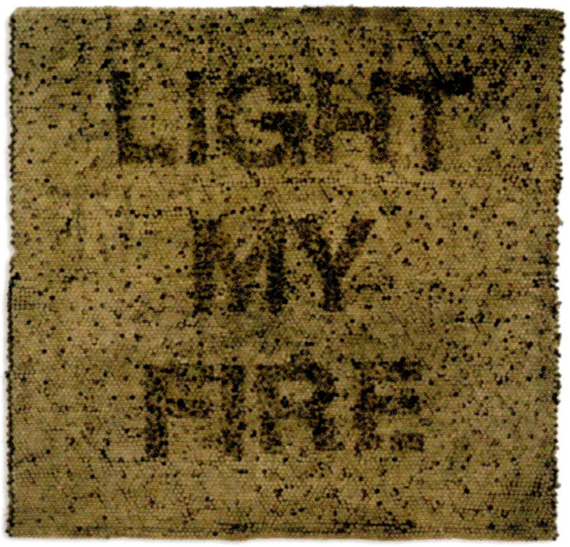

Cigarette Smoke Bacon Paintings, 1999-2010

Selection of cigarette paintings, different sizes

Selectie van schilderijen met sigarettenpeukjes, verschillende formaten

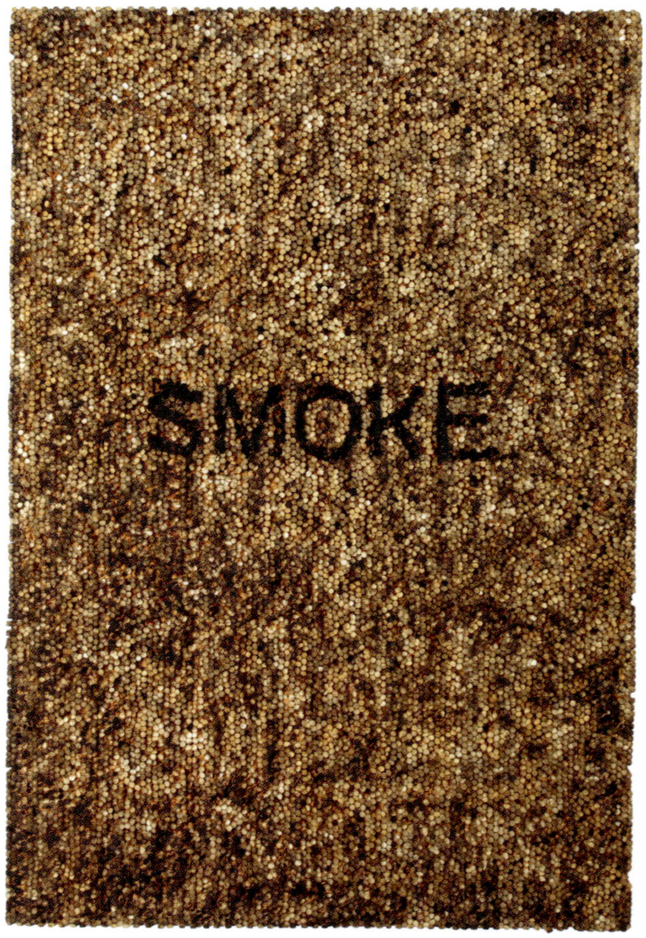

Smoke, 2000

124 cm x 84 cm

Cigarette butts
with bacon-smoke smell

Sigarettenpeukjes met een
geur van gerookt spek

Once Upon a Time, M HKA,
curators Bart De Baere,
Guillaume Bijl, Antwerp, BE
20.12.2003-29.02.2004

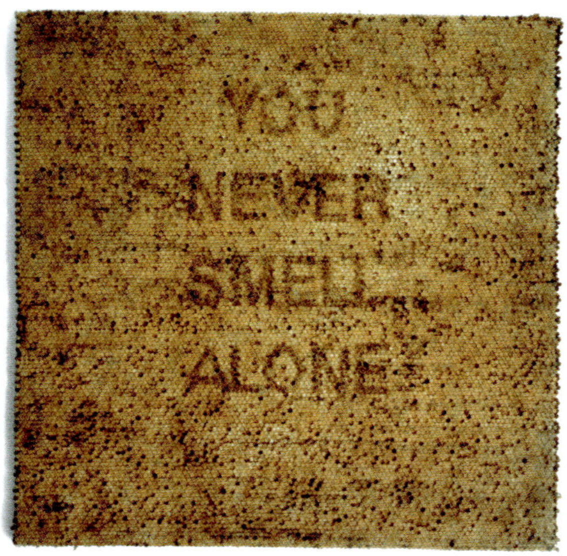

You Never Smell Alone, 1999

100 cm x 100 cm: 15.000

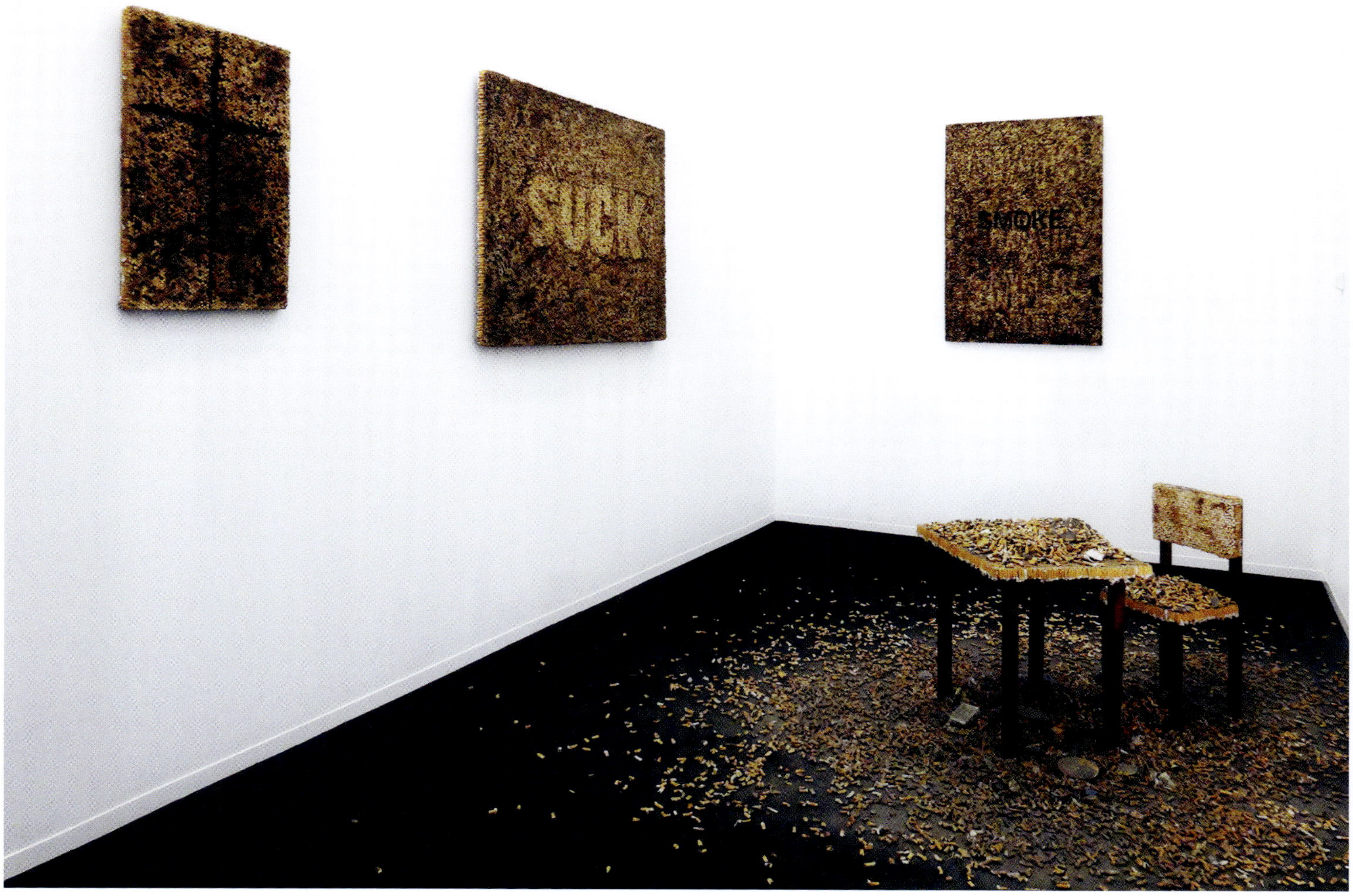

The Art of Smelling, Olfactory Art Research,
Art Center Rozendaal 21, Enschede, NL
01.12.2013-02.03.2014

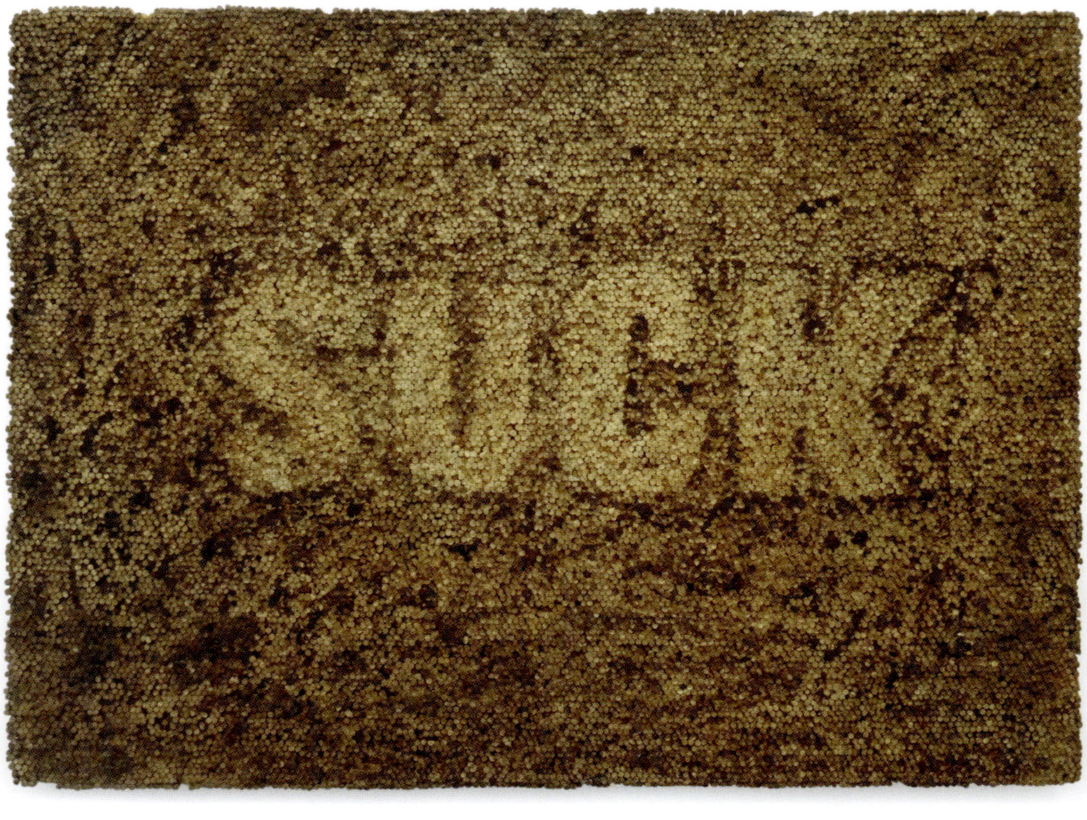

Suck, 2010

139 cm x 102 cm

Cigarette butts
with bacon-smoke smell

Sigarettenpeukjes met
een geur van gerookt spek

Artist Project, Art Brussels,
Artexis, curators Karen Renders
& Nele Verhaeren, Brussels, BE
22.04.2010-25.04.2010

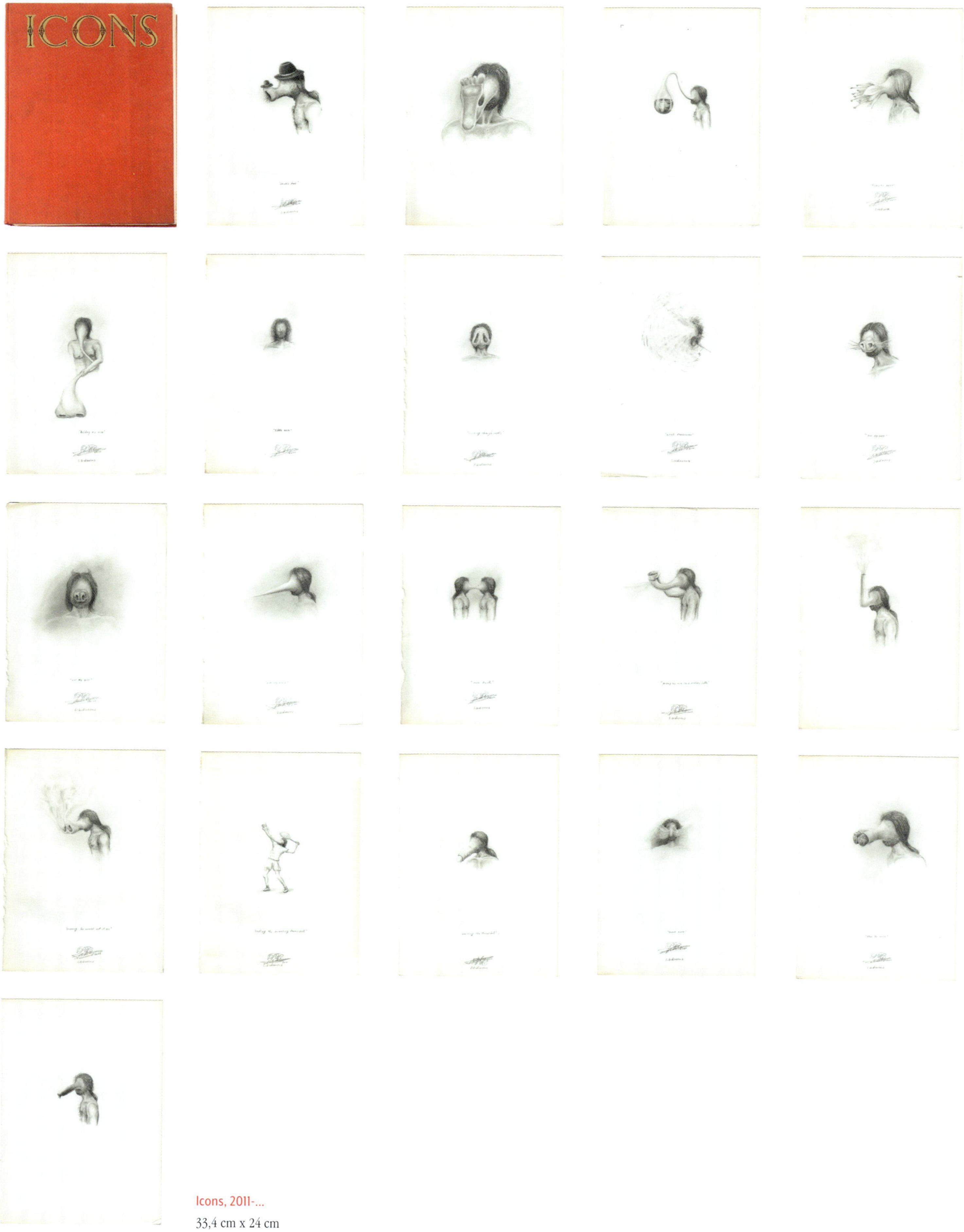

Icons, 2011-...

33,4 cm x 24 cm

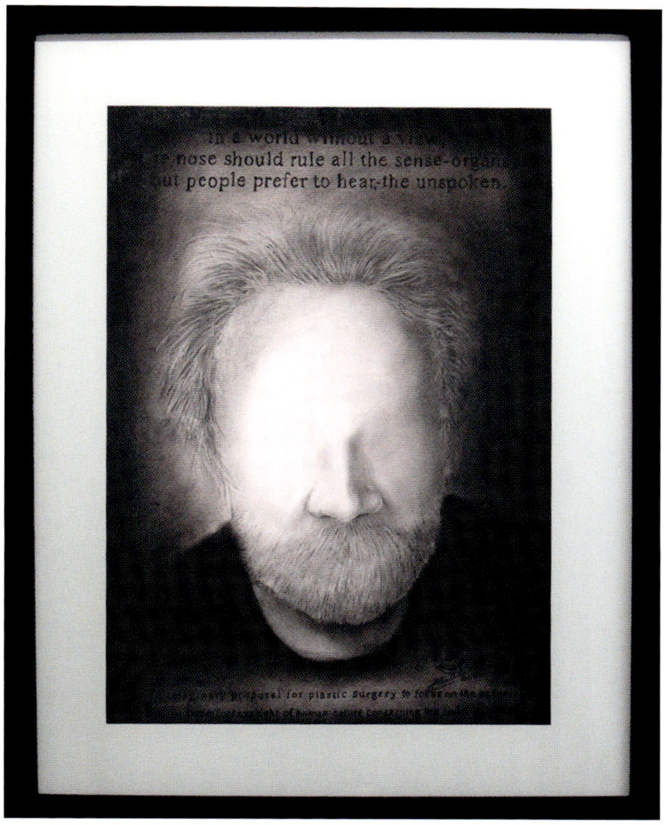

Nose Face ... The Unspoken, 2004

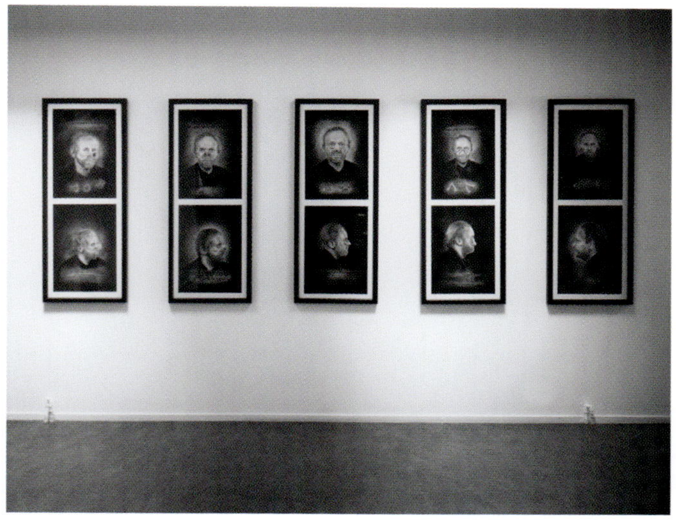

Nose-X's, 2004

Drawings / Tekeningen

Garbage City, Van Laere Contemporary Art, Antwerp, BE, 20.05.2004-03.07.2004

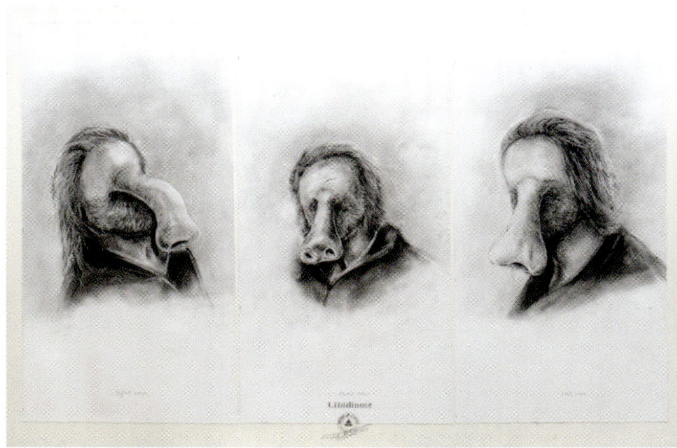

Libidinose, 2011

65 cm x 96 cm

Charcoal, graphite / Houtskool, grafiet

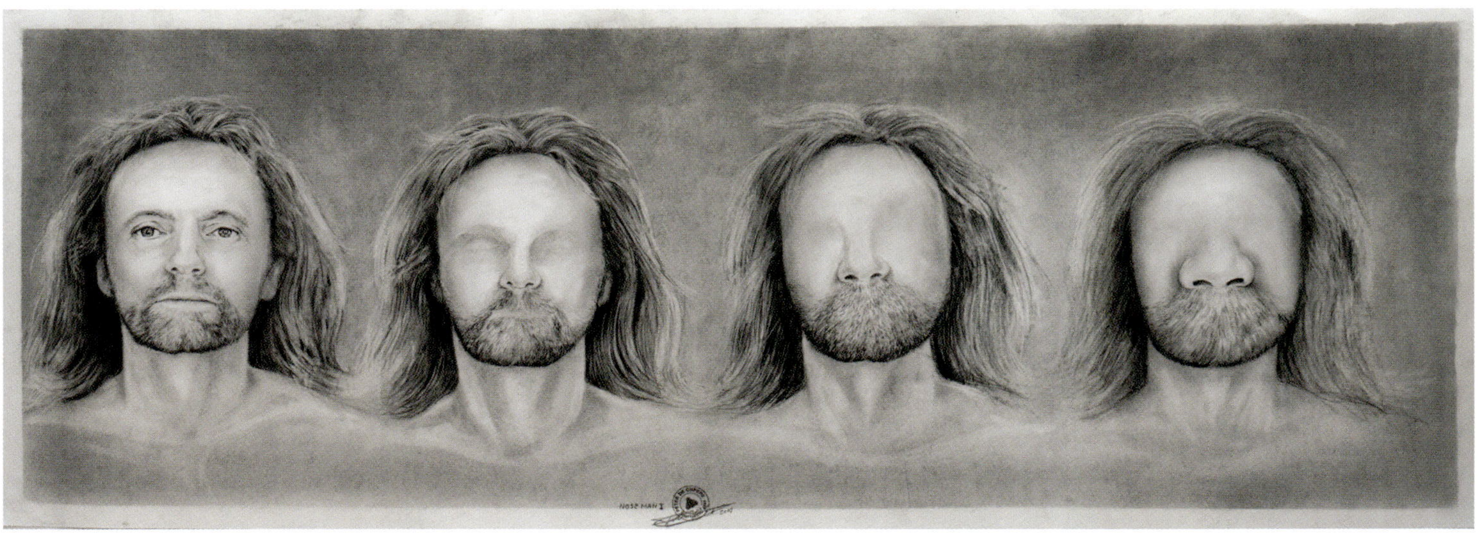

Nose Man 1, 2009

52,5 cm x 128 cm

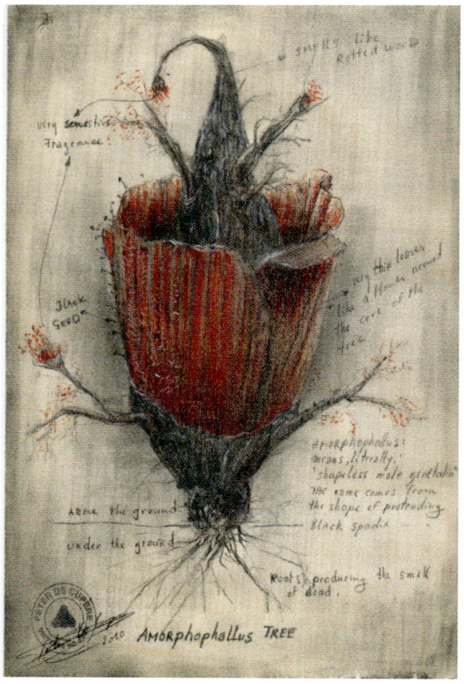

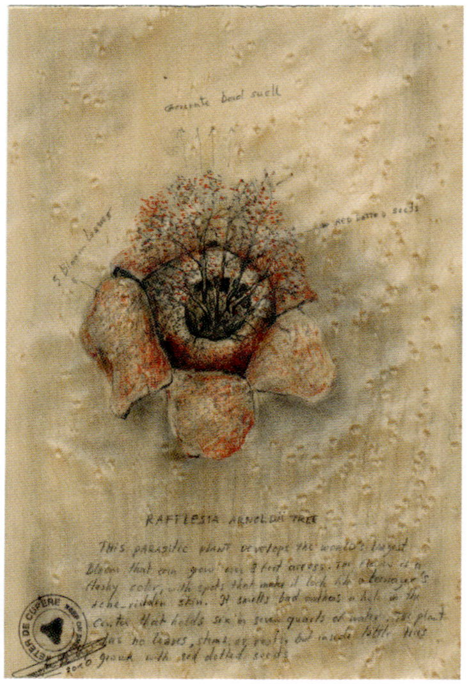

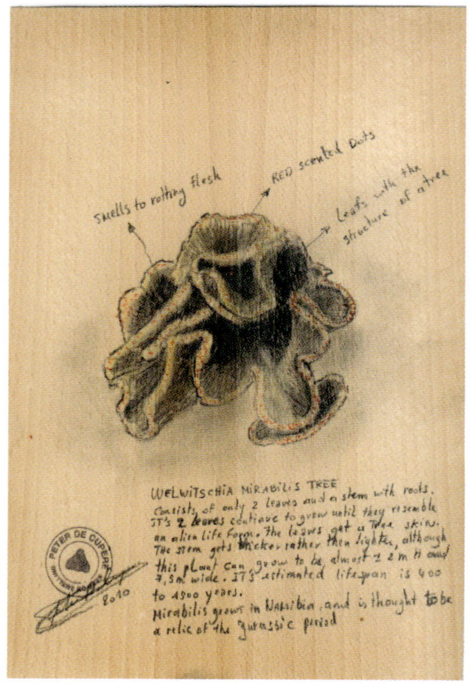

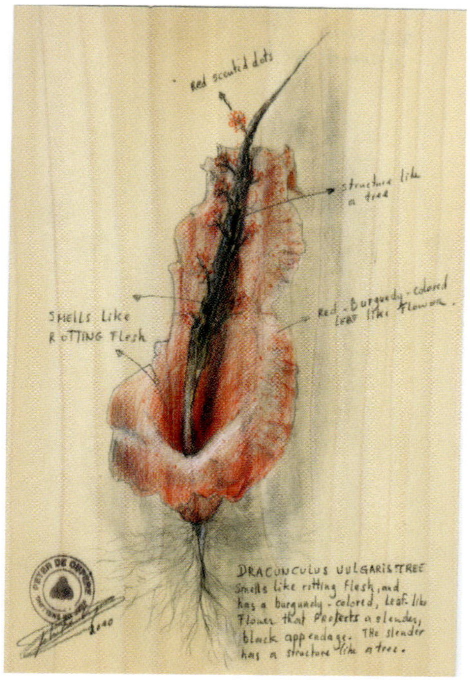

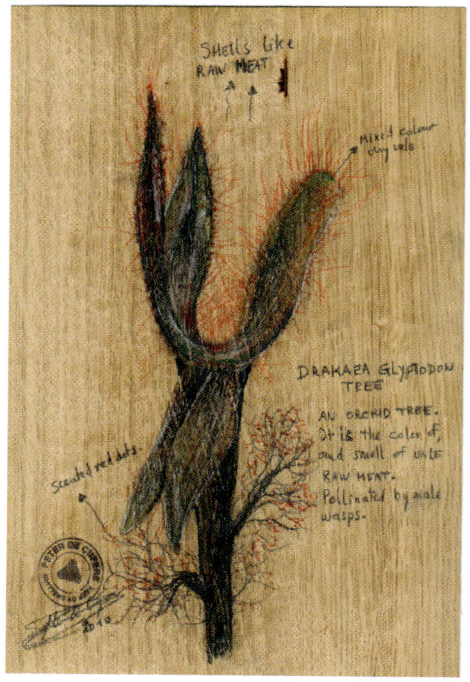

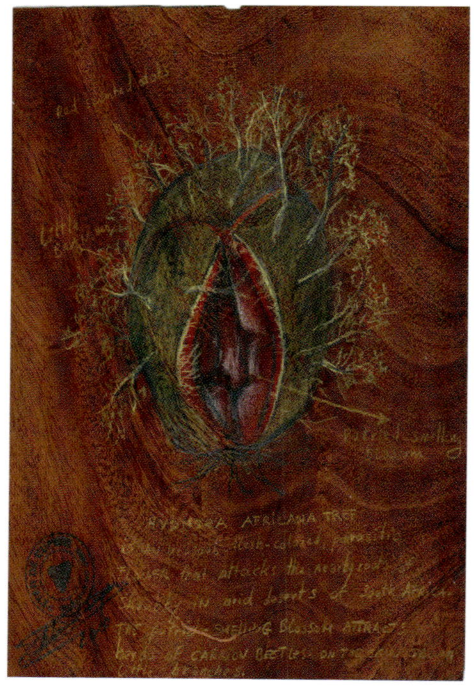

Drawings Flowers On Wood Veneer, 2010

±29 cm x 21 cm

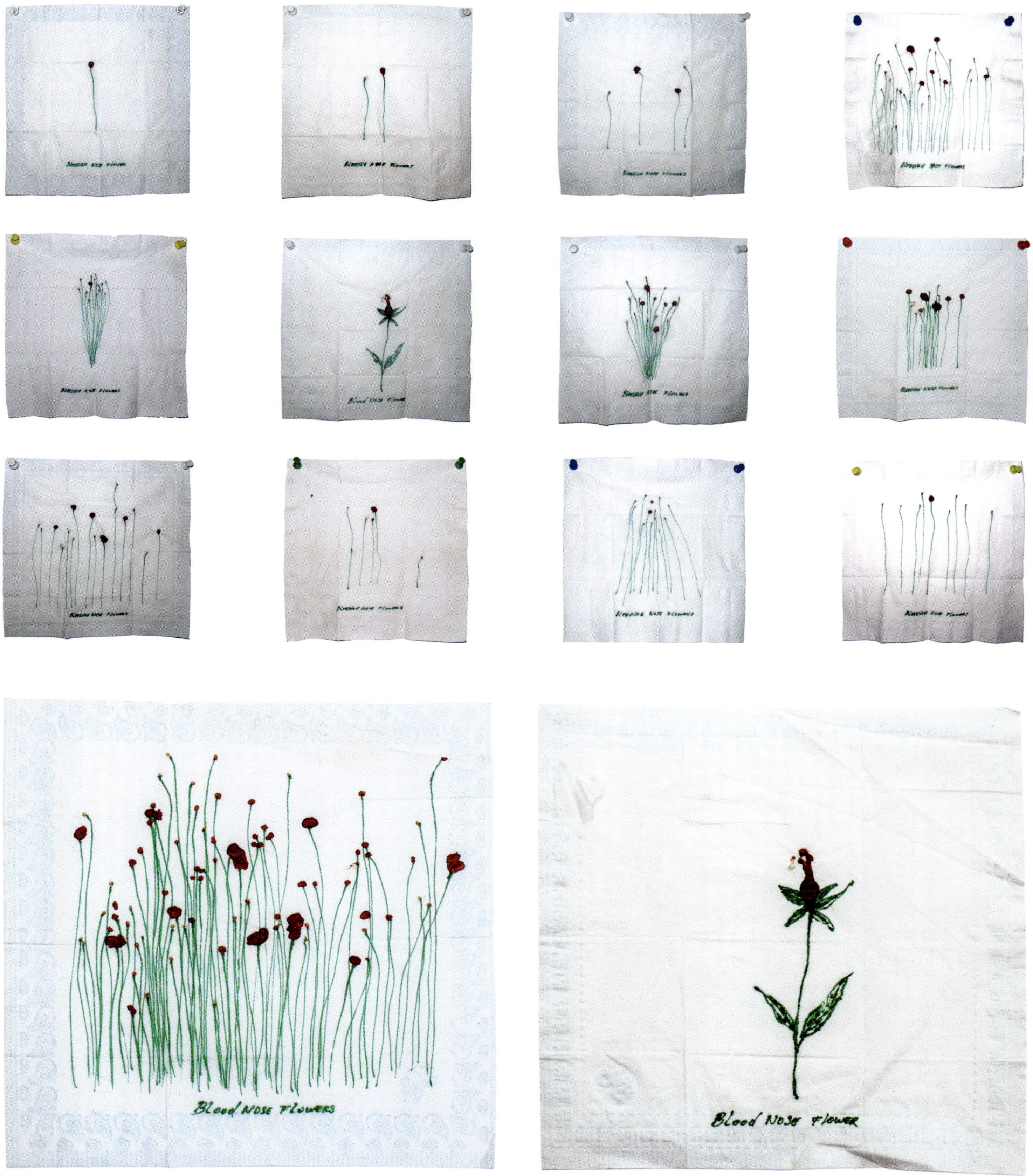

Bleeding Nose Flowers, 2005

A selection of drawings painted with the result of nosebleed combined with a green marker on paper tissues

Selectie van tekeningen met het bloed van een bloedneus op papieren zakdoekjes gecombineerd met groene viltstift

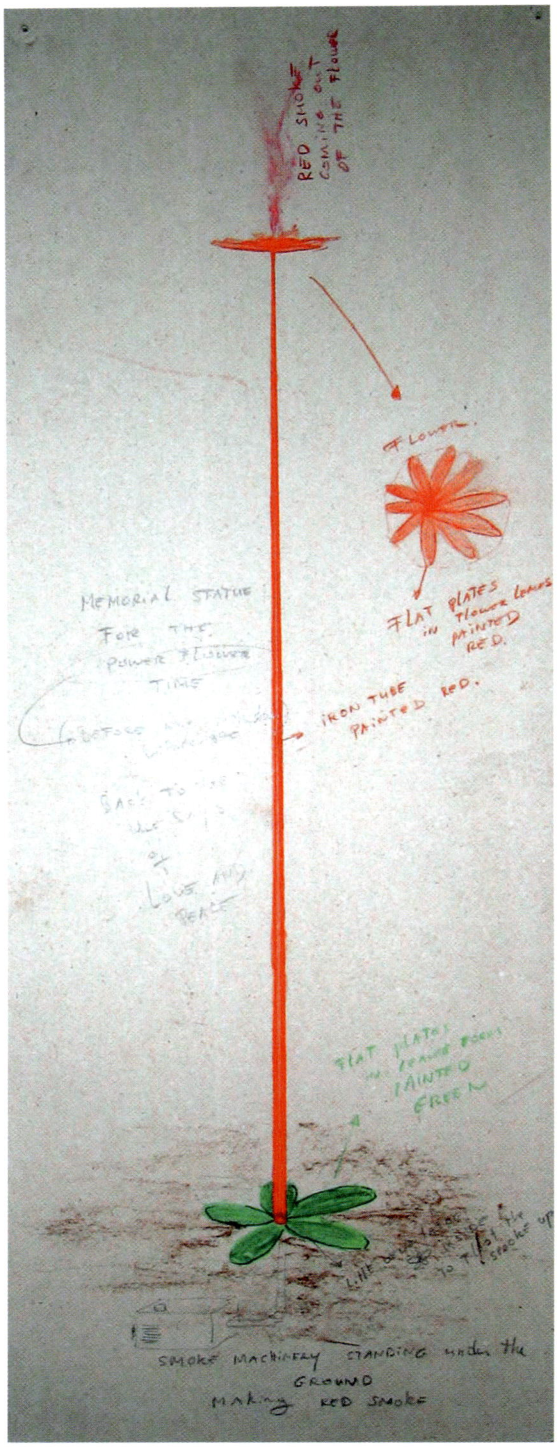

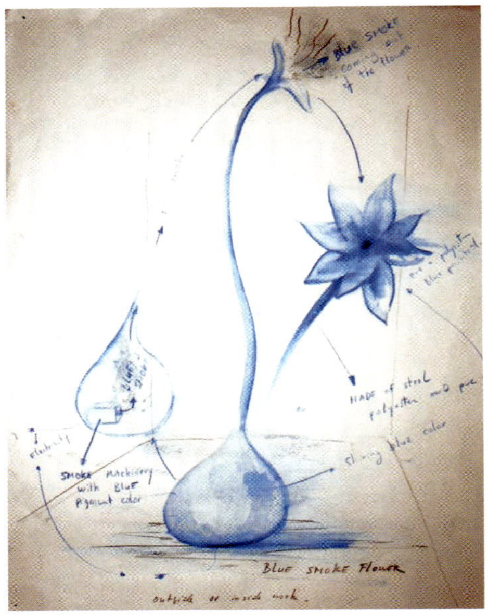

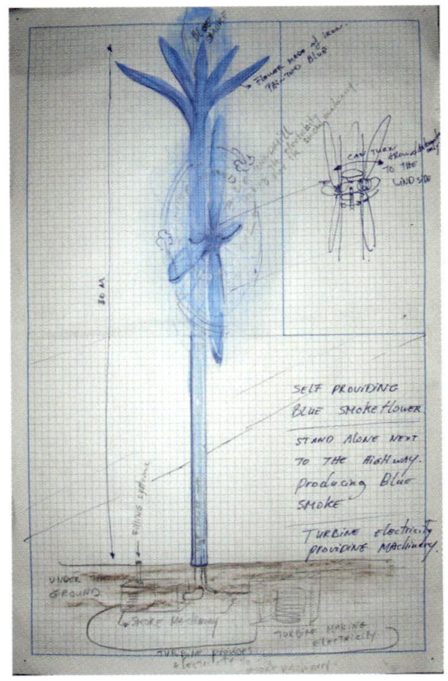

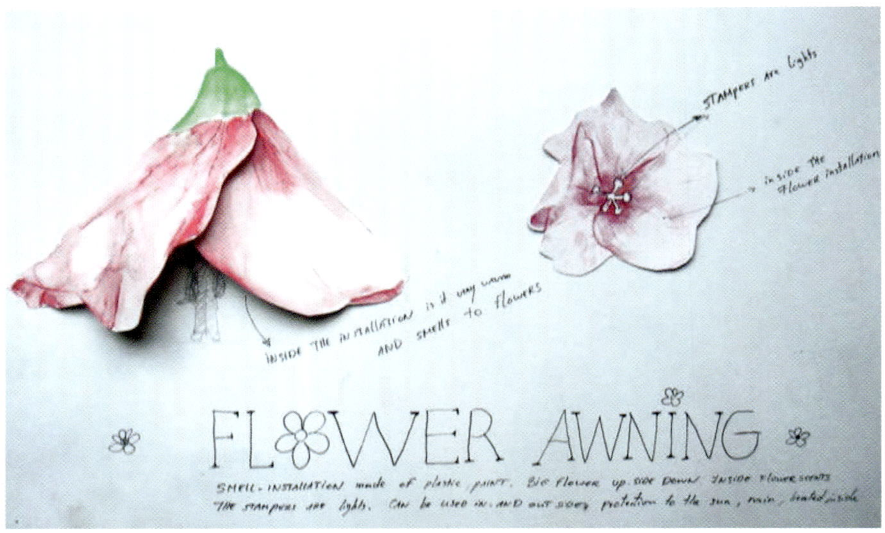

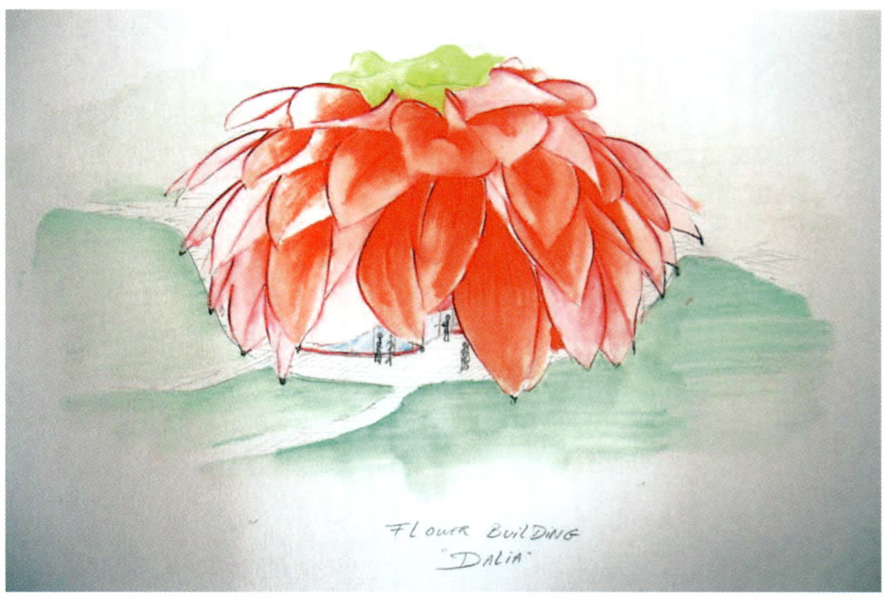

A Selection of Concept Flower Drawings

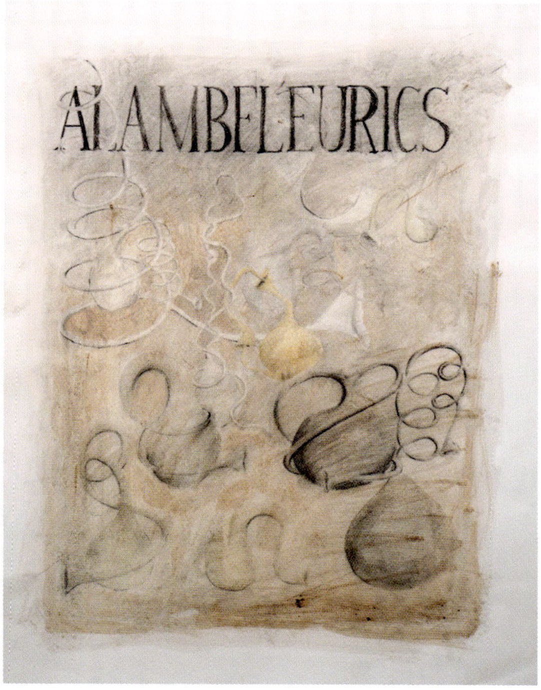

Alambfleurics Visual, 2005

50 cm x 40 cm

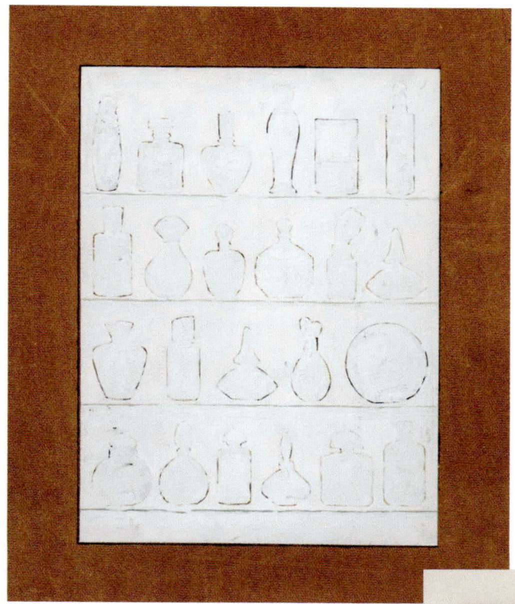

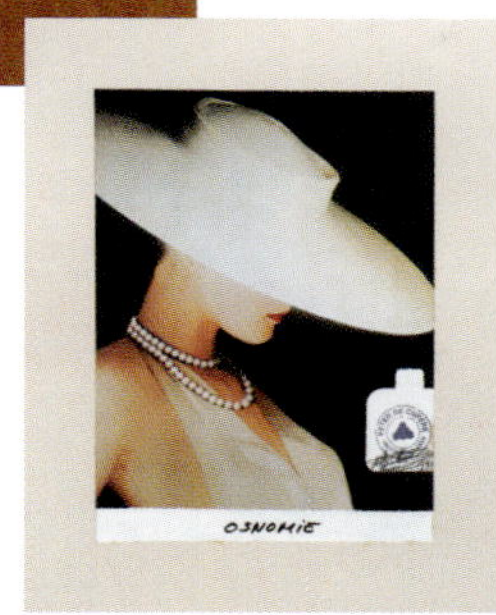

Osnomie, 1998

34 cm x 27 cm

Front & back / Voorkant & achterkant

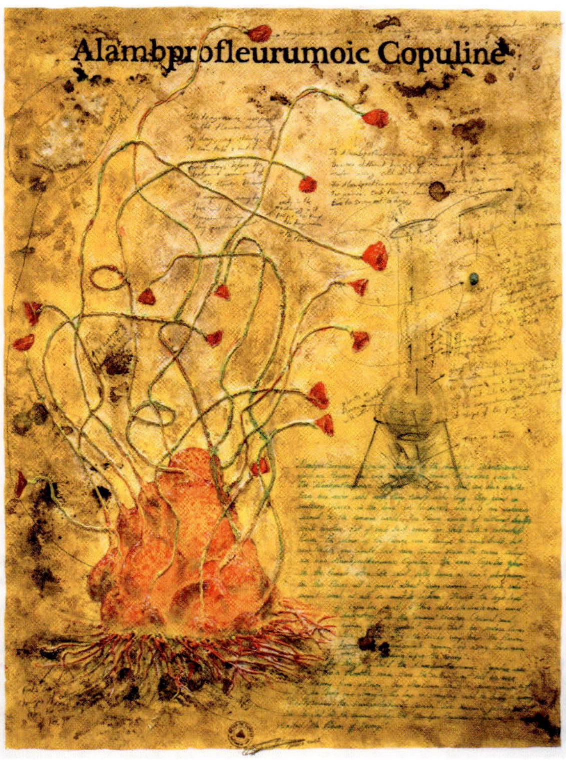

Drawing Alambprofleurumoic Copuline, 2005

91 cm x 70 cm

Splash Perfume Flower Field, 2011

76 cm x 56 cm

Drawing made with the smell of cassis & peach with cheap perfume as an additive.

Een tekening gemaakt met de geur van cassis & perzik aangelengd met een goedkope parfumgeur.

Perfume & Scent Drawings, 1984-...

Peter de Cupere began experimenting with smells as a child. As a 14-year-old boy, he was already making drawings with cheap perfume, drinks, tea, coffee and wine. Later on he also made drawings with sweat, among other things.
The drawings were made on light paper. Once they were dry, they left a slight trace. The smells disappeared, but the memory of the smell can be summoned up again via the image.

Al in zijn jeugdjaren experimenteerde Peter de Cupere met geuren. Zo maakte hij als jonge knaap op 14-jarige leeftijd reeds tekeningen met goedkoop parfum, drank, thee, koffie en wijn en op later leeftijd werden er ook tekeningen gemaakt met o.a. zweet.
De tekeningen werden op licht papier gemaakt. Eénmaal dat ze droog waren, lieten zij een licht spoor achter. De geuren verdwenen, maar de herinnering aan de geur kan hij blijvend via het beeld terug oproepen.

Perfume Drawing, Alchemie de Rochas, 2001

Drawings with perfume & green pencil

Tekeningen met parfum & groen potlood

77 cm x 56,5 cm (big perfume drawing / groot formaat)
56 cm x 34,5 cm (small perfume drawings / klein formaat)

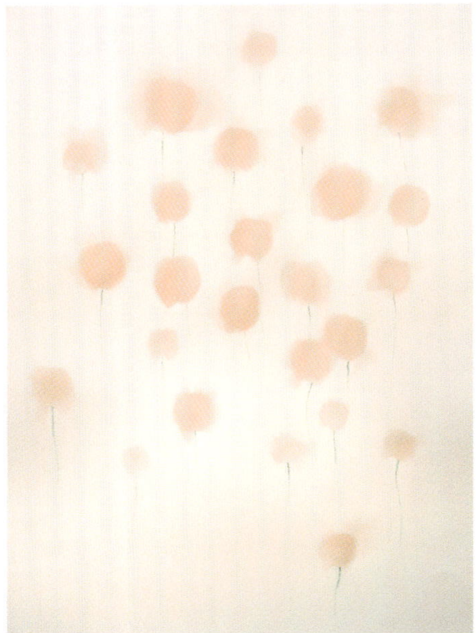

Perfume Drawing, Jardins de Bagatelle Guerlain, 2001

Drawings with perfume & green pencil

Tekeningen met parfum & groen potlood

77 cm x 56,5 cm (big perfume drawing / groot formaat)
56 cm x 34,5 cm (small perfume drawings / klein formaat)

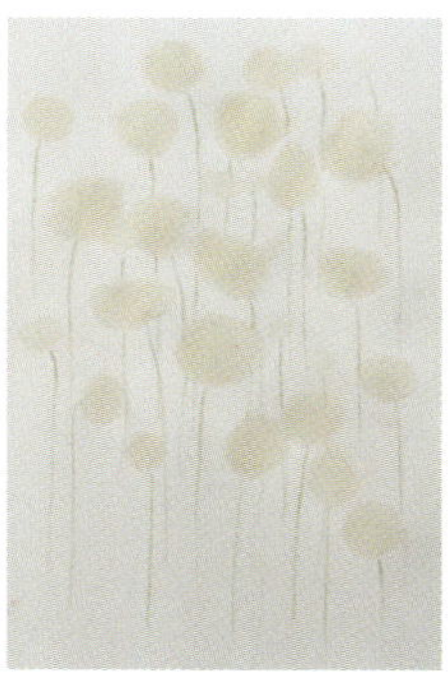

Perfume Drawing, Obsession Calvin Klein, 2001

Drawings with perfume & green pencil

Tekeningen met parfum & groen potlood

77 cm x 56,5 cm (big perfume drawing / groot formaat)
56 cm x 34,5 cm (small perfume drawings / klein formaat)

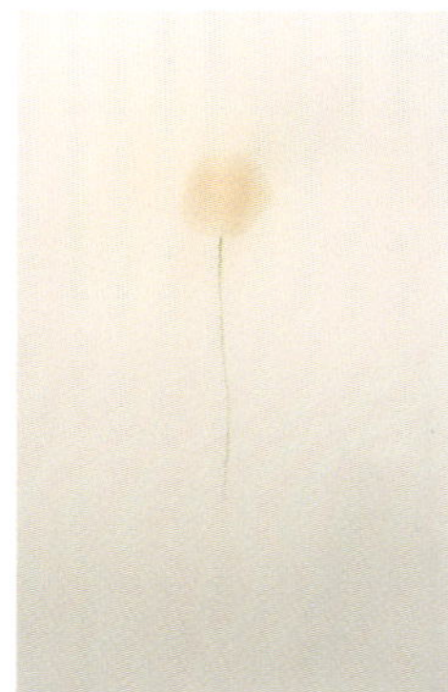

Perfume Drawing, Spellbound, 2001

Drawings with perfume & green pencil

Tekeningen met parfum & groen potlood

77 cm x 56,5 cm (big perfume drawing / groot formaat)
56 cm x 34,5 cm (small perfume drawings / klein formaat)

PETER DE CUPERE

SCENT & SEXUALITY
Geur & Sexualiteit

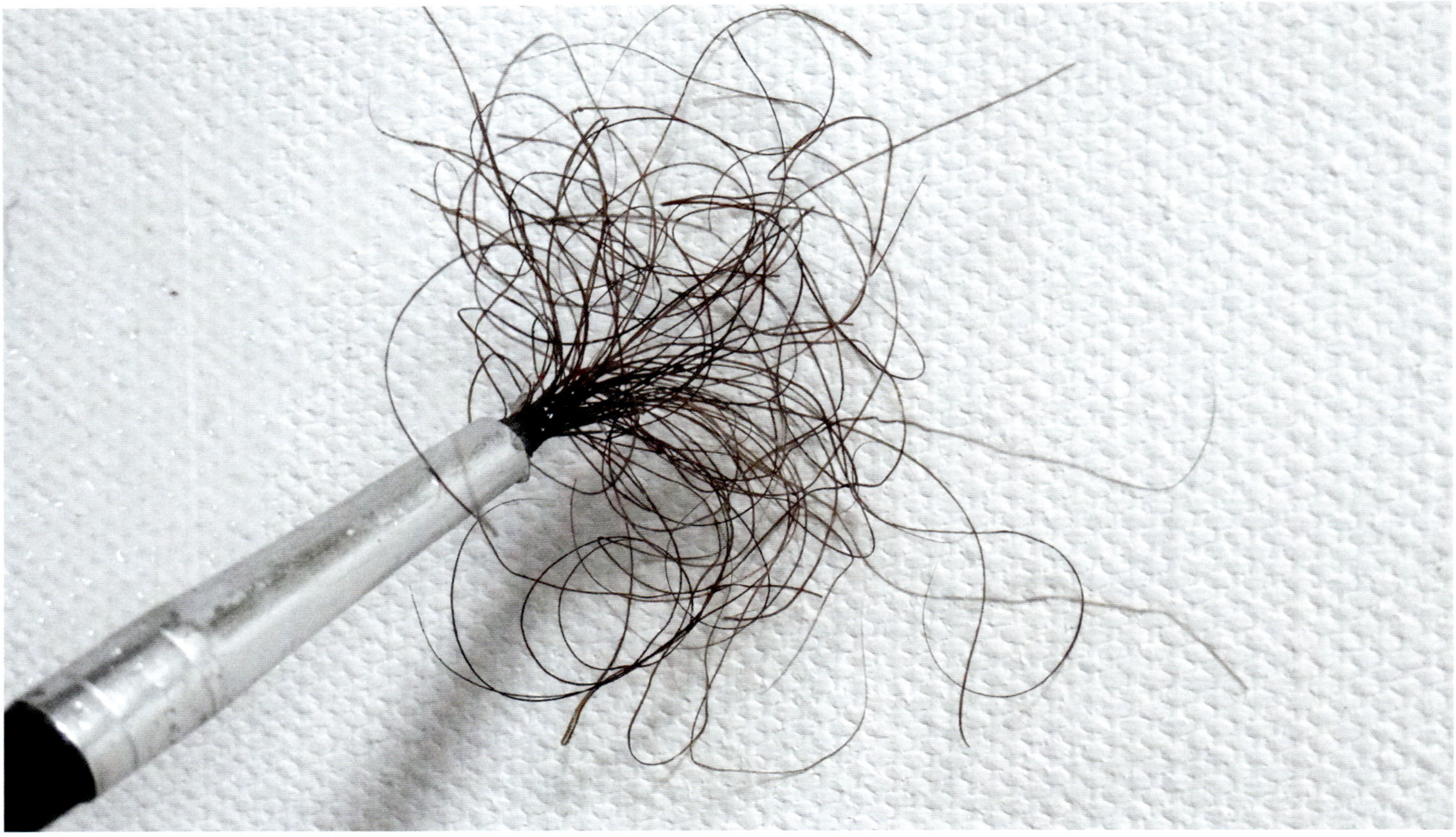

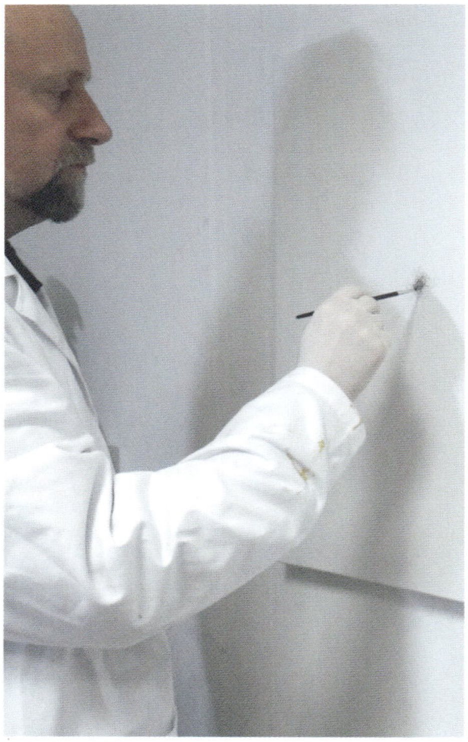

There's Something in the Air, Villa Rot, curator Caro Verbeek, Burgrieden-Rot, DE, 22.03.2015-28.07.2015
Sense of Smell, Symposium, Moti Museum, Breda, NL, 02.12.2014

The Paintbrush of Gustave Courbet, 2014

On October 23th 2014, Peter de Cupere showed the work 'Deflowering' for the first time (In The Olfactory at the M HKA, Antwerp). In this work a Madonna statue made out of frozen holy water melted and slowly released the scent of a vagina. 'Deflowering' received a lot of reaction all over the world.

After publication of an article in the Huffington Post entitled 'Olfactory Artist Has Crafted A 'Holy Water' Sculpture That Smells Like Vagina', it was shared worldwide over hundreds of news sites. The reactions were vividly enthusiastic. The artist received more than a thousand 'personal' e-mails from women who thanked him because he dared to express himself about the 'wonderfulness' of femininity as an artist and as a man. What one rarely dares to say, was said.

A lot of reactions also derived from the freedom as a woman to express herself and to be seen as an equal to man. The artist, through this work, questioned the low position of women in religion. He also mentioned that in some religions, women are still not equal to men, though he emphasized that this concerns a minority of religions. However, that this is still possible in 2014-2016 and that it is still a sensitive topic to talk about, also proved itself in the many reactions in which one blamed the artist to be seeking sensation.

Art in which religion is questioned, is still a sensitive item, especially when the position of the woman is questioned. There were not only positive reactions, but as it is with good art, there were also negative reactions. This shows that talking about female liberties is still a sensitive issue for many and remains a taboo. Or a previously created taboo. Because, be real and tell yourself; every woman has a vagina, just as every man has a penis. Why is this still so sensitive in the present time? Is it because religion stays conservative, while art thinks progressively and goes with the flow? Why does a small statue of about 20 cm of height creates so much response.

The printing of genitals in art was once also taboo. Gustave Courbet was the first artist who showed the female vagina in all its glory as a statement. For some, this work of art is the first work in which the painting does not require only to be looked at, but also makes a statement in combination with the title as a complete work. 'L'Origine du Monde' (1866) shows us as described by the title where the origin of our existence is derived from.

One can also see this work as an anti-religious work in which no god is seen as the origin of the world, but human kind. It speaks for itself that the work made quite an appearance and was provocative in its time. Now it belongs as one of the masterpieces to the collection of the 'Musée d'Orsay' in Paris!

De Cupere made a proper pencil in which he replaced the hairs of the pencil by pubic hairs and as paint, the smell of vagina. The work received the title 'The Paintbrush of Gustave Courbet'.

Of course 'The Paintbrush of Gustave Courbet' is a reference to the work 'L'Origine du Monde' and can thus be seen as a tribute. The work is also a tribute to the feminine and more specifically to the female fantasies and pleasure. Nothing as creative to start with an empty canvas and to brush down your desires with the smell of vagina! The paintbrush of Gustave Courbet is not only an object of sculpture, but also a painting in its utmost extreme meaning reduced to the basic instrument being a pencil and its paint.

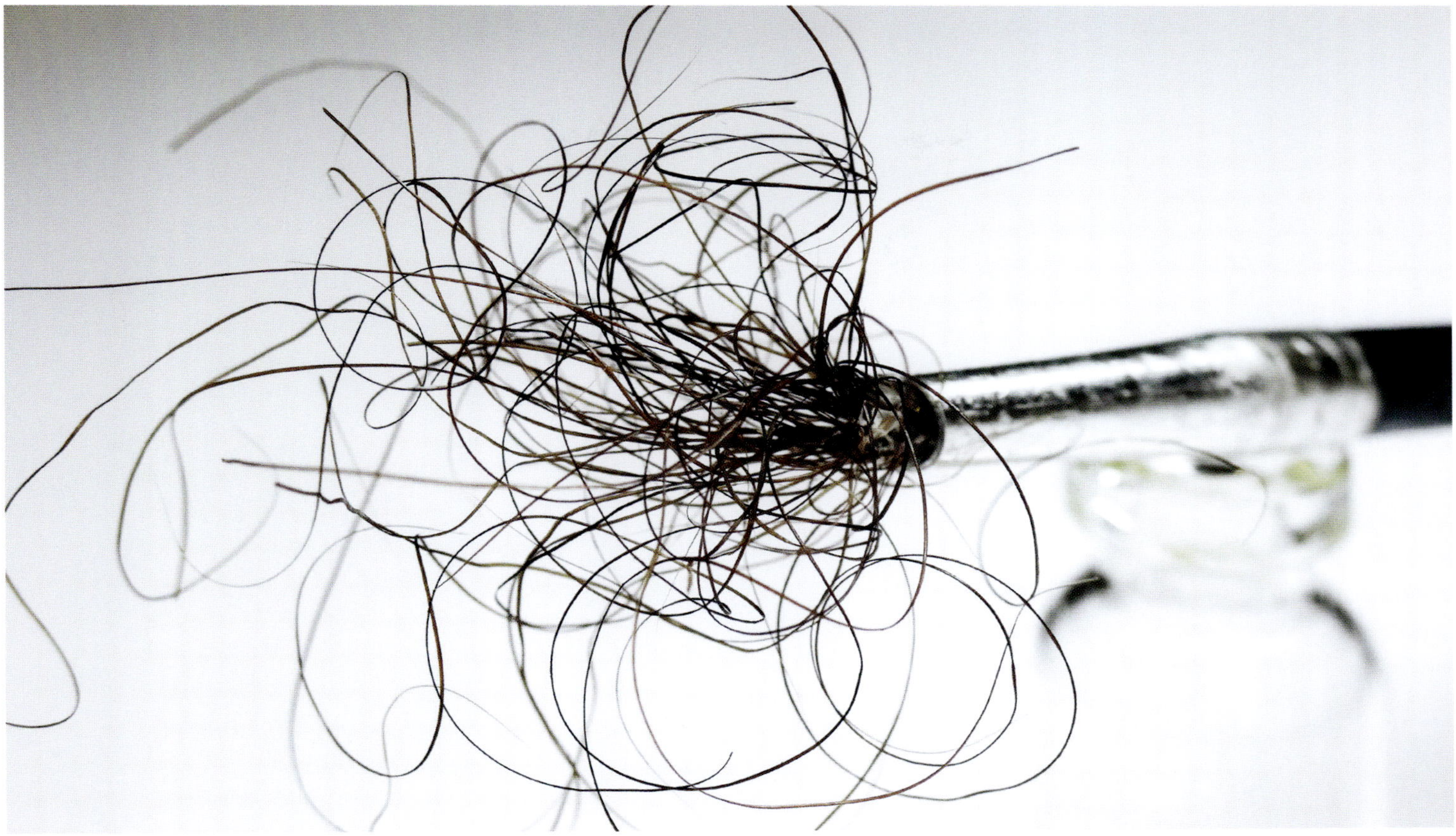

Op 23 oktober 2014 toonde Peter de Cupere voor de eerste keer het werk 'Deflowering' waarbij een madonnabeeldje gemaakt uit bevroren en gewijd water wegsmolt en langzaam de geur van vagina vrijgaf. 'Deflowering' kreeg reactie van over heel de wereld.

Na de publicatie van een artikel in de Huffington Post met als titel 'Olfactory Artist Has Crafted A 'Holy Water' Sculpture That Smells Like Vagina', werd dit wereldwijd gedeeld over honderden nieuwswebsites. De reacties waren laaiend enthousiast. De kunstenaar kreeg meer dan 1.000 'persoonlijke' emails van vrouwen die hem dankten omdat hij als kunstenaar en als man zich durfde te uiten over de 'heerlijkheid' van het vrouwelijke. Wat men zelden durfde uit te spreken, werd nu uitgesproken.

Vele andere commentaren reageerden in relatie tot de vrijheid om zich als vrouw te uiten en gelijkgesteld te worden aan de man. De kunstenaar stelde namelijk met dit werk de positie van de vrouw in verschillende religies in vraag. Hij haalde aan dat de vrouw in sommige religies nog steeds niet gelijkgesteld wordt aan de man. De vraag die zich stelt, is of het hier om een minderheid van religies gaat. Maar dat dit feit in 2014-2016 nog steeds een thema is en gevoelig ligt, bleek ook uit de vele reacties waarbij men de kunstenaar verweet sensatie te zoeken.

Kunst die zich kritisch uit over de positie van de vrouw in onze maatschappij en waarbij religie in vraag wordt gesteld, blijft soms weinig bespreekbaar.

Er waren dus niet alleen de positieve reacties, maar zoals het meestal bij sterke kunst hoort, ook sterke tegenreacties. In hoeverre is het praten over vrouwelijke vrijheden nog steeds een taboe? Of eerder een gecreëerd taboe. Iedere vrouw heeft een vagina, net zoals iedere man een penis heeft. Ligt de gevoeligheid in de conservatieve wereld van religies, terwijl kunst progressief denkt en actief meegaat met zijn tijd? Waarom roept een klein beeldje van 20 cm grootte zoveel respons op?

Ooit was het afbeelden van genitaliën in de kunstwereld een taboe. Gustave Courbet was de eerste kunstenaar die als statement de vrouwelijke vagina in volle glorie durfde af te beelden. Voor sommigen is dit werk zelfs het eerste werk waarbij een schilderij niet louter visueel bekeken diende te worden, maar waarbij de combinatie met de titel van heel het werk een statement maakte. 'L'Origine du Monde' (1866) toont zoals de titel het beschrijft, waar de oorsprong van ons bestaan ligt. Men kan dit werk als een anti-religieus werk zien waarbij niet een god als oorsprong van de wereld wordt gezien, maar wel de mens. Het spreekt voor zich dat het werk opgemerkt werd en in zijn tijd sterk provoceerde. Nu behoort het werk als één van de topstukken in de collectie van het Musée d'Orsay in Parijs!

Peter de Cupere heeft 'L'Origine du Monde' van Gustave Courbet als uitgangspunt genomen om te antwoorden op de reacties op 'Deflowering'. Veel mannelijke reacties reageerden met de melding dat vaginageur onmogelijk kunst kan zijn!

De Cupere maakte een zelfontworpen penseel waarbij hij de penseelharen construeerde met schaamharen en als verf een extract van de geur van vagina gebruikte. Het werk kreeg de titel 'The Paintbrush of Gustave Courbet'.

'The Paintbrush of Gustave Courbet' verwijst uiteraard naar 'L'Origine du Monde' en kan zo als een eerbetoon gezien worden aan de schilder. Verder schenkt het penseel ook eer aan het vrouwelijke en meer bepaald vrouwelijke fantasieën en vrouwelijk genot. Niets zo creatief om te starten met een leeg canvas en je verlangens neer te schilderen met vaginageur! 'The Paintbrush of Gustave Courbet' is niet alleen een object of een sculptuur, maar ook een schilderij dat in zijn meest extreme betekenis herleid is tot een basisinstrument voor de kunstenaar, zijnde een penseel en bijbehorende verf.

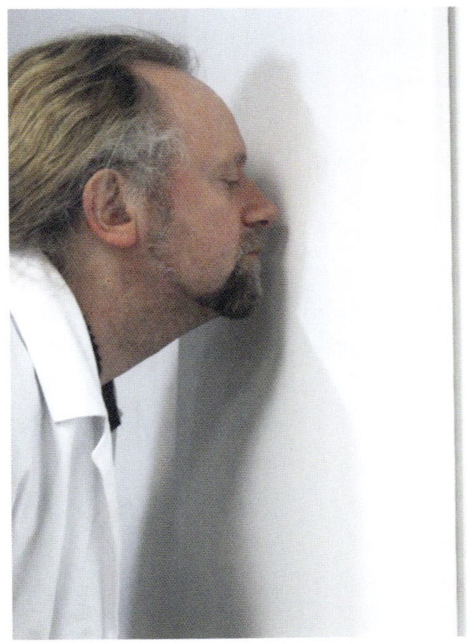

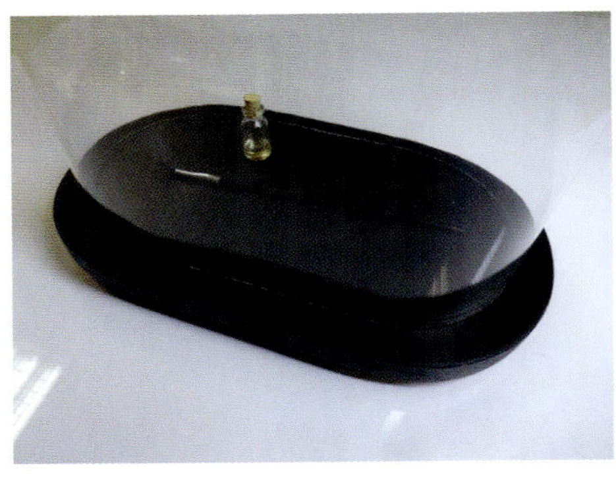

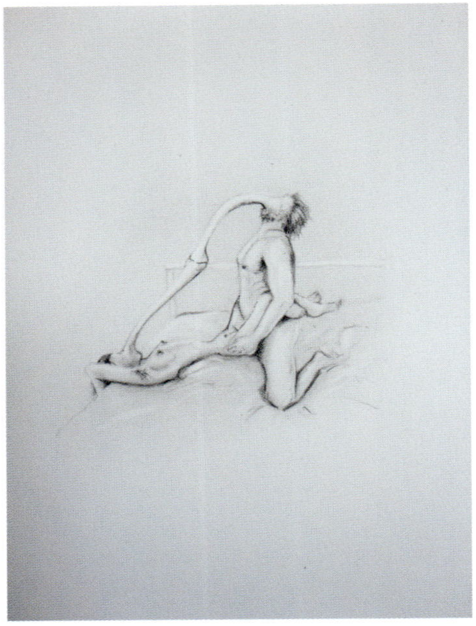

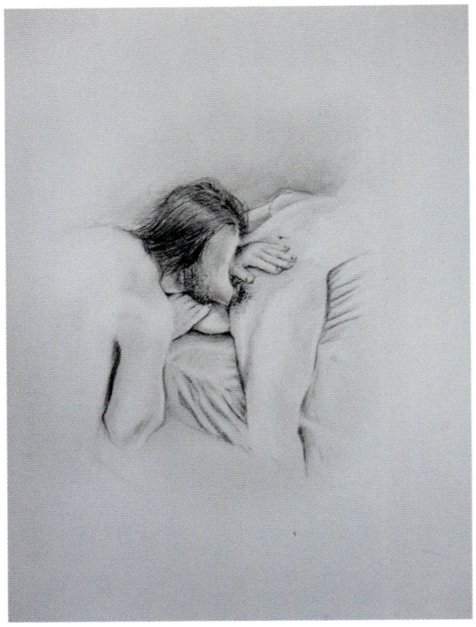

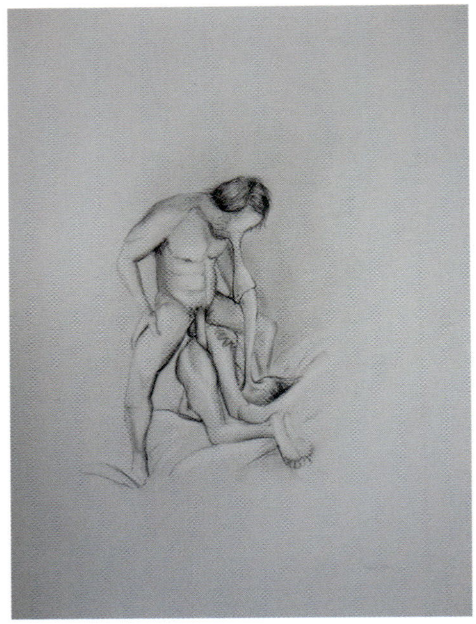

Drawing Libidonosus Stories, 2011

42 cm x 32 cm

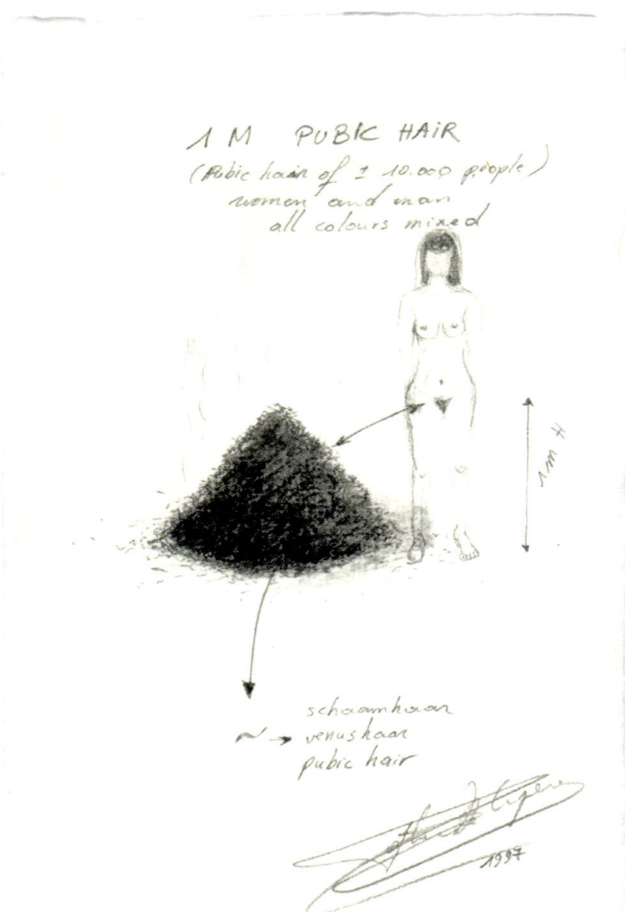

1 M Pubic Hair, 1997

Drawing

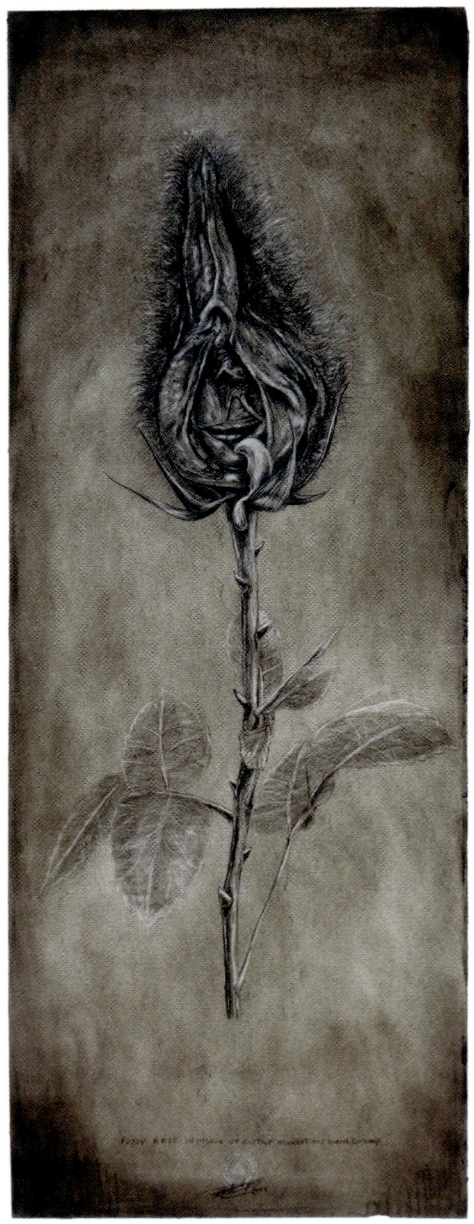

Drawing Pussy Rose In Honour of Gustave Courbet and Marcel Duchamp, 2014

100 cm x 40 cm

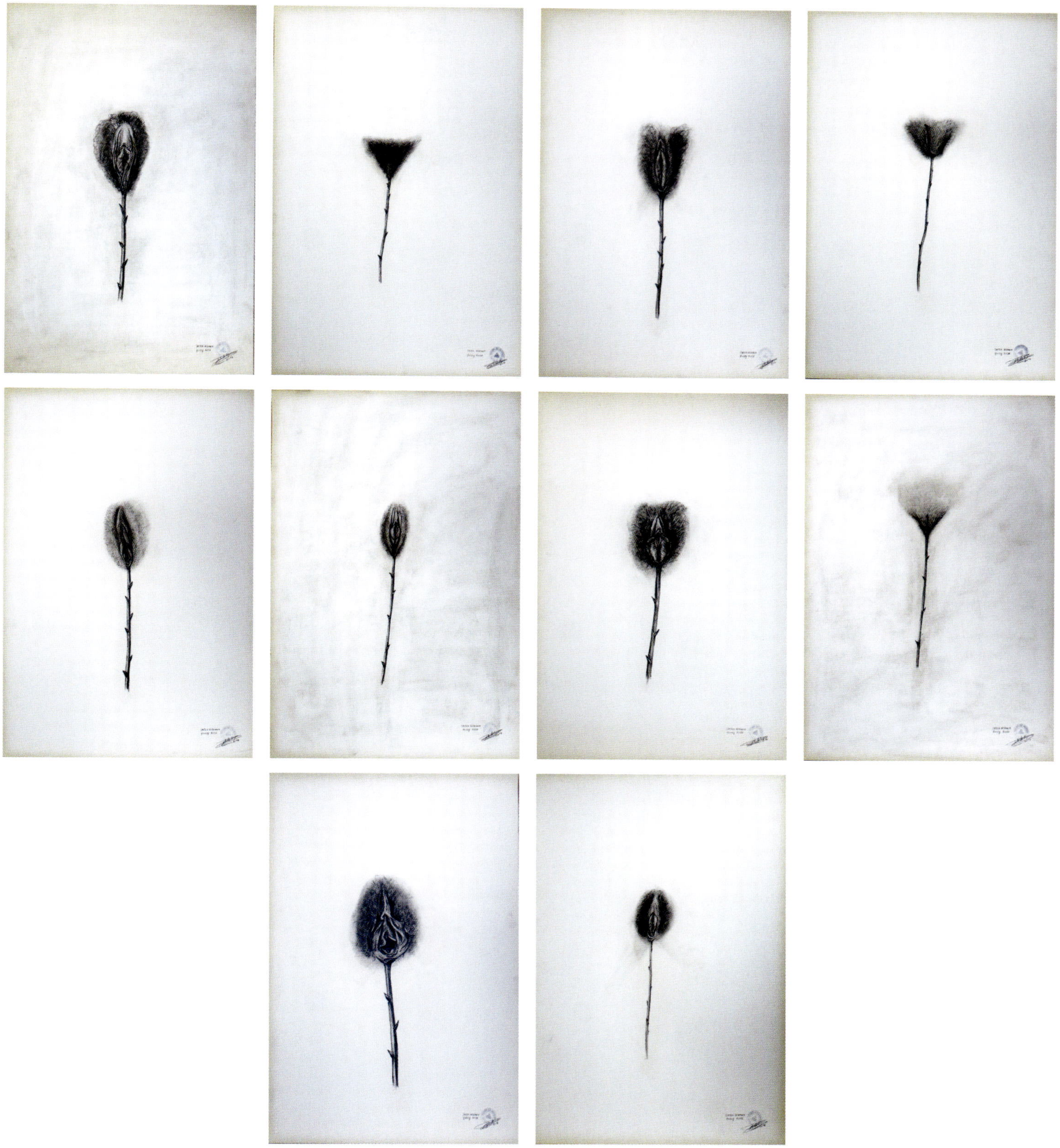

Drawings Pussy Rose Flowers, 2014
Framed / Ingekaderd 72,5 cm x 52,5 cm
Graphite, charcoal
Grafiet, houtskool

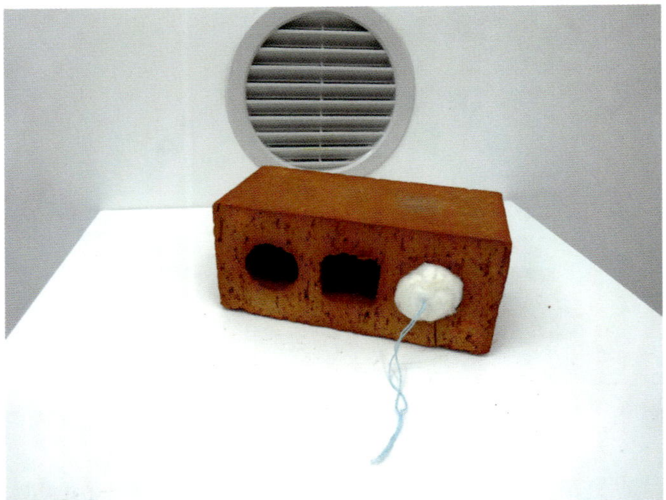

The Scented Brick, 2014

Brick with tampon. The tampon smells of an imitation vagina odour.
The work is about homeliness and the effect of cocooning.

Baksteen met tampon. De tampon ruikt naar een nagemaakte vaginageur.
Het werk gaat over huiselijkheid en het effect van cocoonen.

The Scented Brick, The Olfactory, Hasselt, BE, 13.10.2014

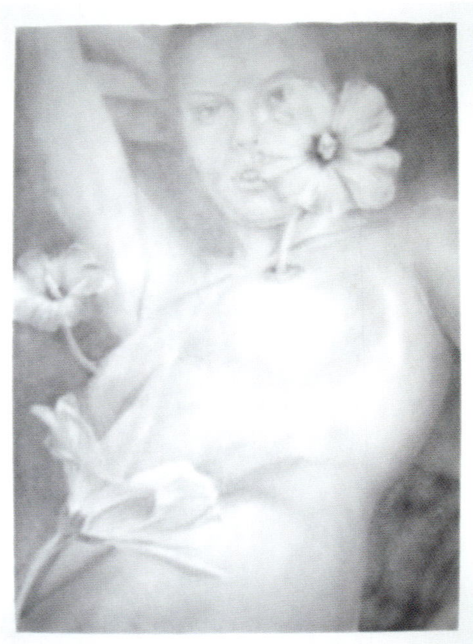

Flower Woman, 2005

Drawing with graphite & charcoal

Tekening met grafiet & houtskool

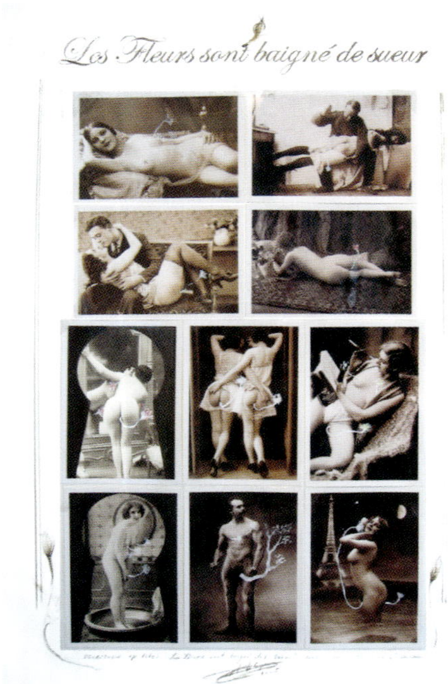

Les Fleurs Sont Baigné De Sueur, 2005

Framed / Ingekaderd 72,5 cm x 52 cm

Flowers and trees have been drawn on old Parisian postcards, growing from vaginas, breasts, bottoms and penises.

Op oude Parijse postkaarten werden bloemen en bomen getekend, ontluikend uit de vagina, borsten, kontje of penis.

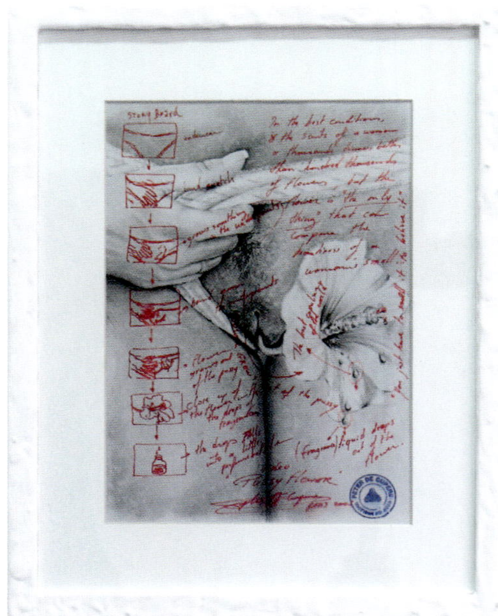

Pussy Flower, 2003

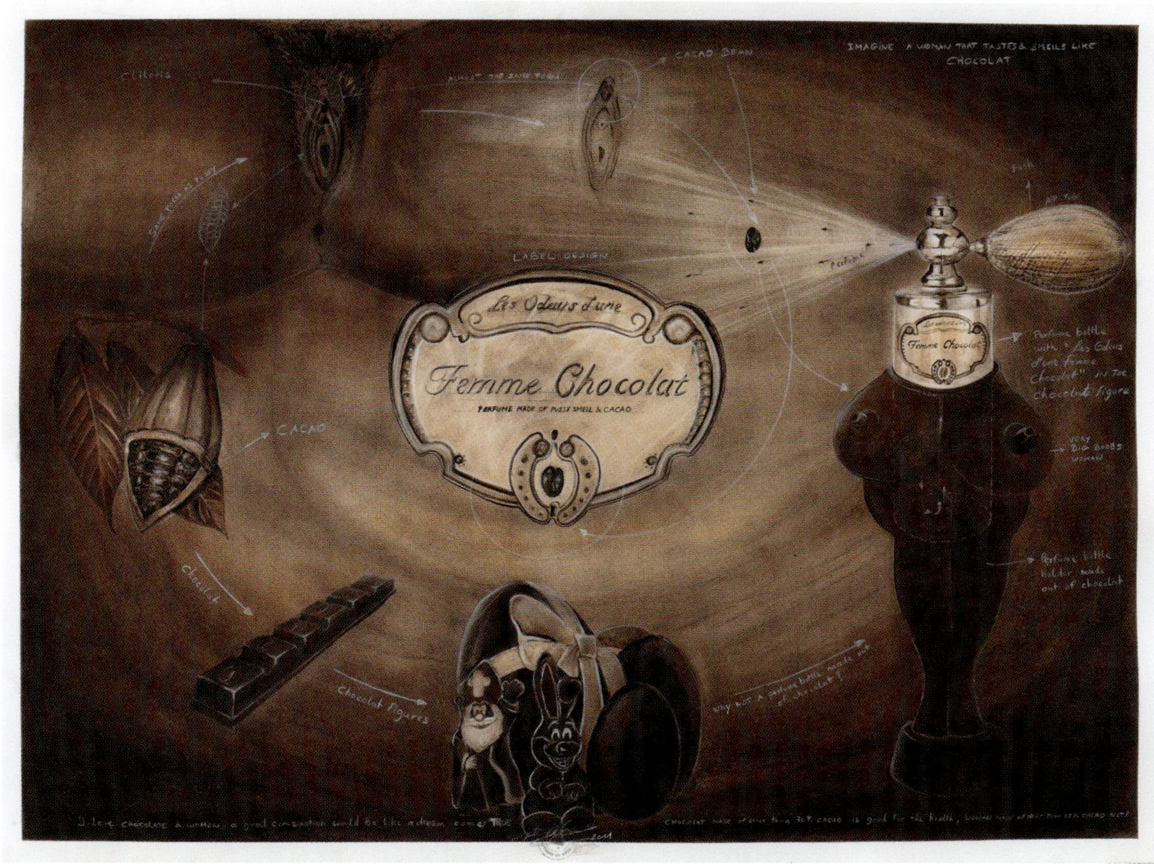

Drawing Femme Chocolat, 2011

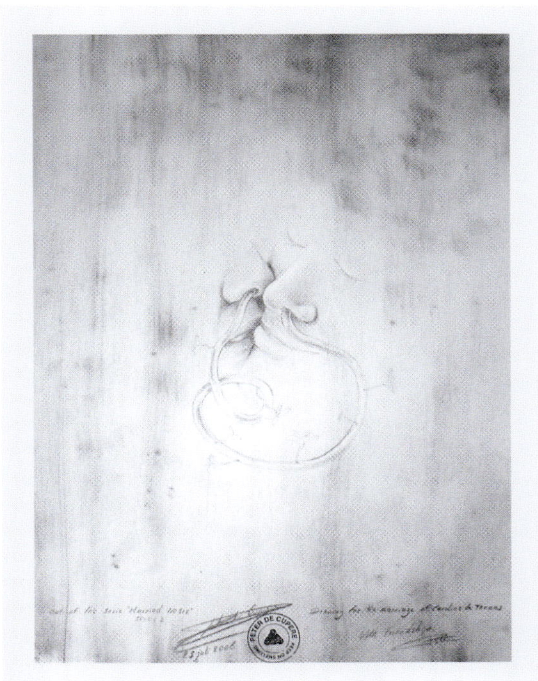

Married Noses, 2006

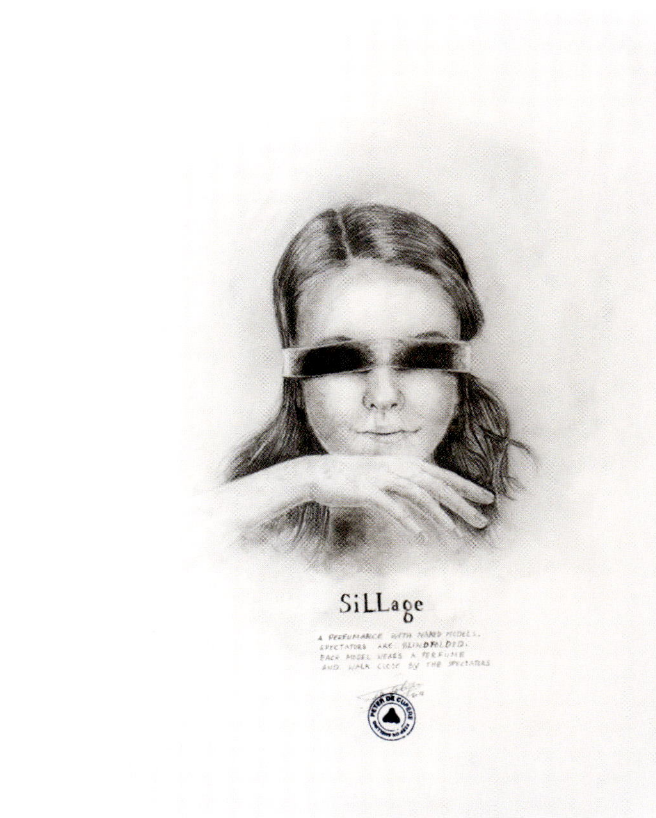

Drawing Sillage, 2016

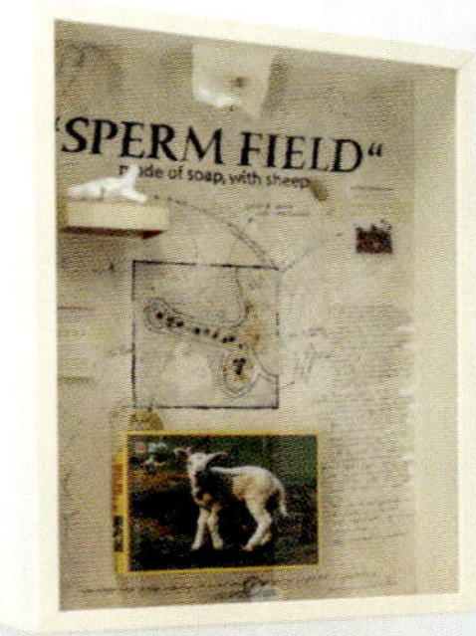

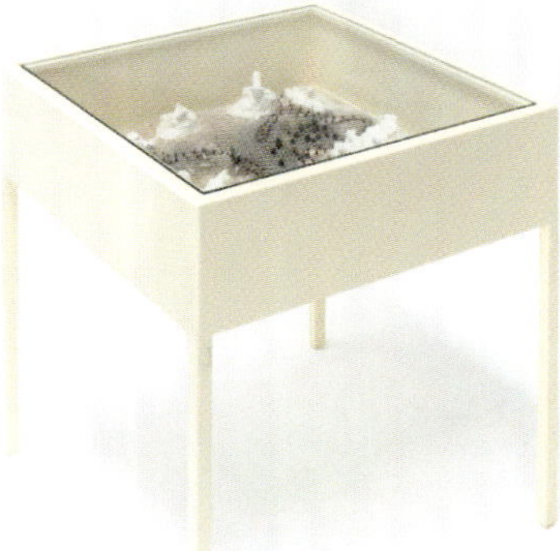

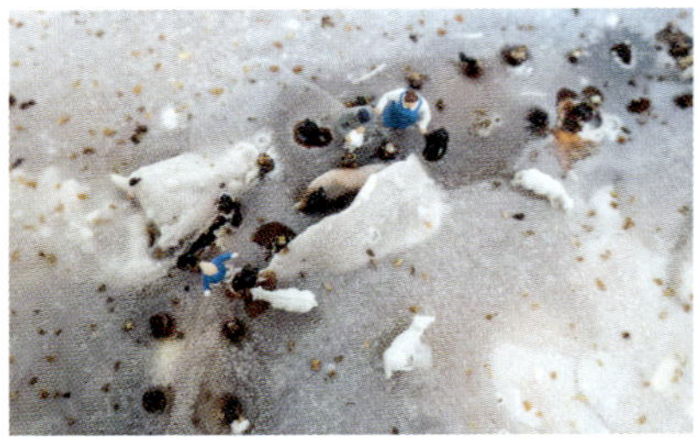

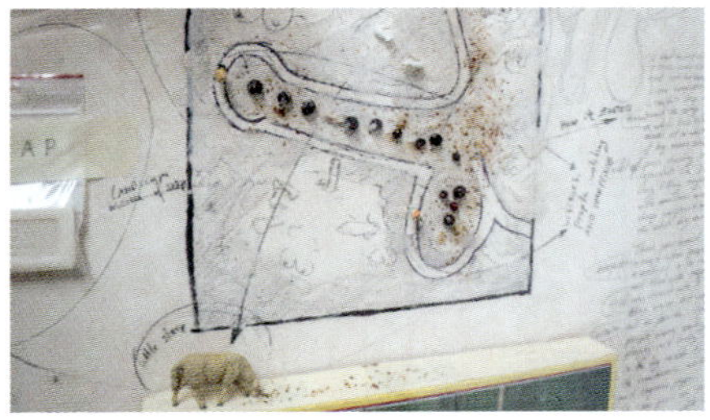

Sperm Field Made of Soap, 2005

Mixed smell media
Drawing, 80 cm x 60,5 cm x 15,5 cm
Model, 55 cm x 50 cm x 50 cm

Visualisation of an imaginary Sperm Field, through which man tries to find his way in a world dominated by the male sex. Exaggerated male power references the identity of our world in which the male of the species still occupies a position of power when compared to the female.
Sperm Field is made from soap, symbolising catharsis. However it is soiled with cranberries and red peppers. The sheep is a metaphor for the existing world's powerlessness. The path to be followed is the phallus, which in our society still determines the world view. This work was made as a reaction to the still revolving inequality between man and woman in our society, despite the progress of emancipation. Regardless of the explicit maleness of Sperm Field, the interpretation of the work can differ depending on how open the viewer approaches the work.

Visualisatie van een denkbeeldig spermaveld waar de mens zijn weg zoekt in een wereld beheerst door het mannelijk geslacht. Het overdreven mannelijk vermogen als verwijzing naar de identiteit van onze wereld waarin de man nog altijd een machtspositie inneemt ten opzichte van de vrouw.
Spermfield is gemaakt uit zeep als verwijzing naar een catharsis, maar wordt bevuild door veenbessen en rode pepertjes. Het schaap geeft de onmacht aan van de bestaande wereld. Het te volgen pad is de falus waarop onze maatschappij nog steeds het wereldbeeld bepaalt. Het werk is gemaakt als reactie op de nog steeds terugkerende ongelijkheid tussen man en vrouw in onze maatschappij, ondanks de vooruitgang in emancipatie. Ondanks het uitgesproken mannelijk karakter van Spermfield kan de interpretatie verschillen afhankelijk van de open ingesteldheid van de kijker.

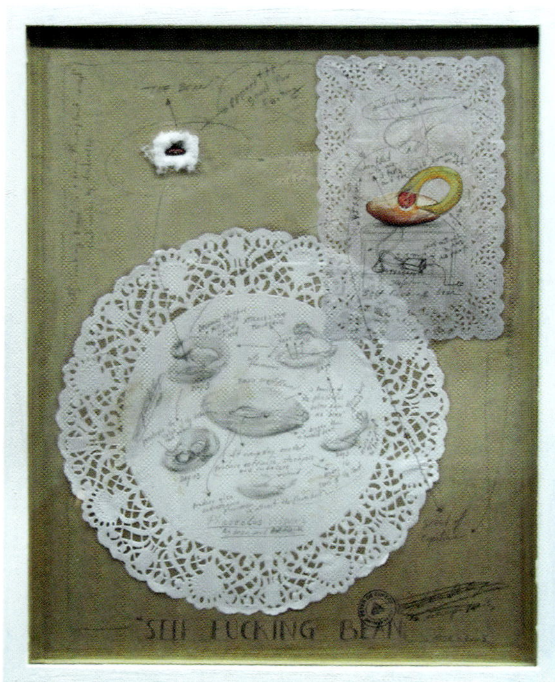

Self Fucking Bean, 1998-2005

Drawing

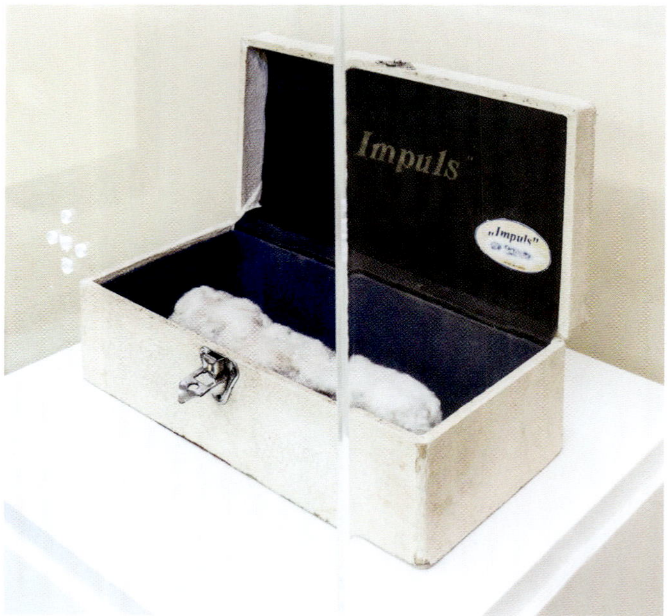

Soft Condom Impuls, 2000

Latex condom covered with cotton wool smelling to babypowder

Latex condoom bekleed met katoenen watten ruikend naar babypoeder

Van Laere Contemporary Art, perfume happening and rockconcert Admiral Freebee, Antwerp, BE, 07.03-13.04.2000
Sniff Your Jail, Justice Court Tongeren, curators, Paul Morrens, Johan Smets, Tongeren, BE, 14.05.2016-19.06.2016

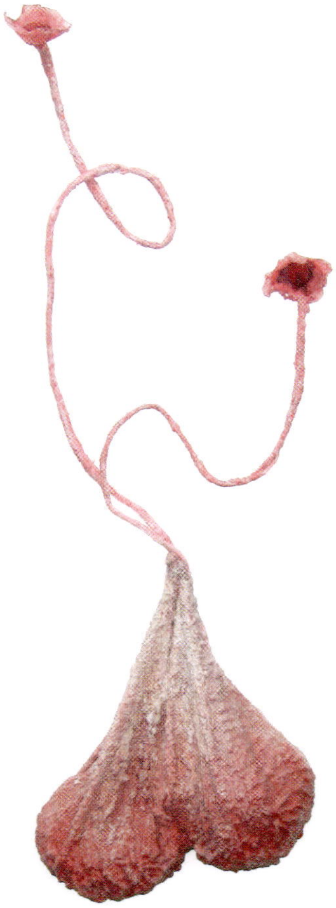

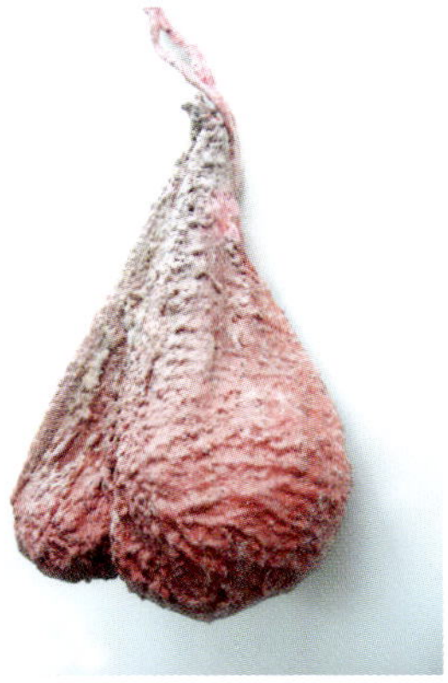

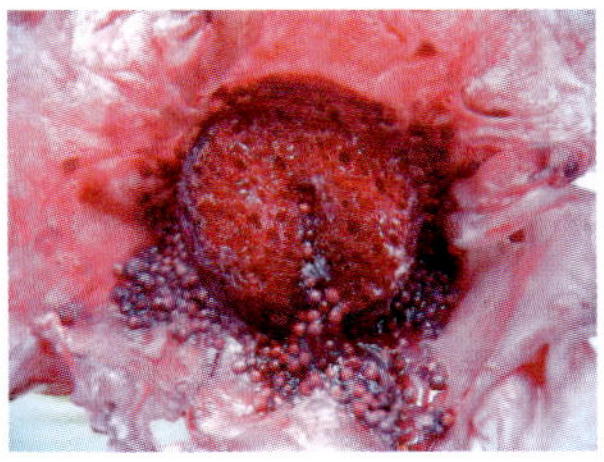

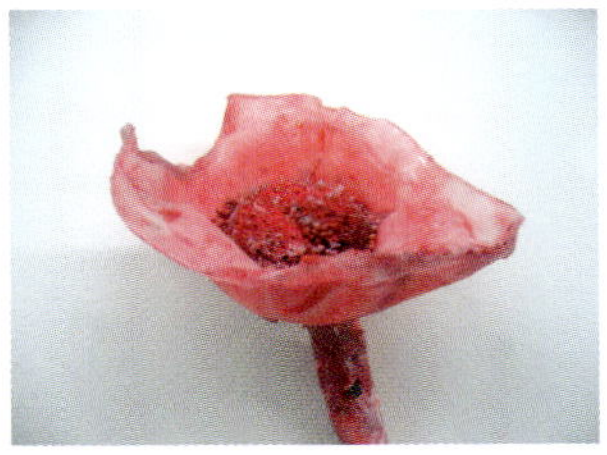

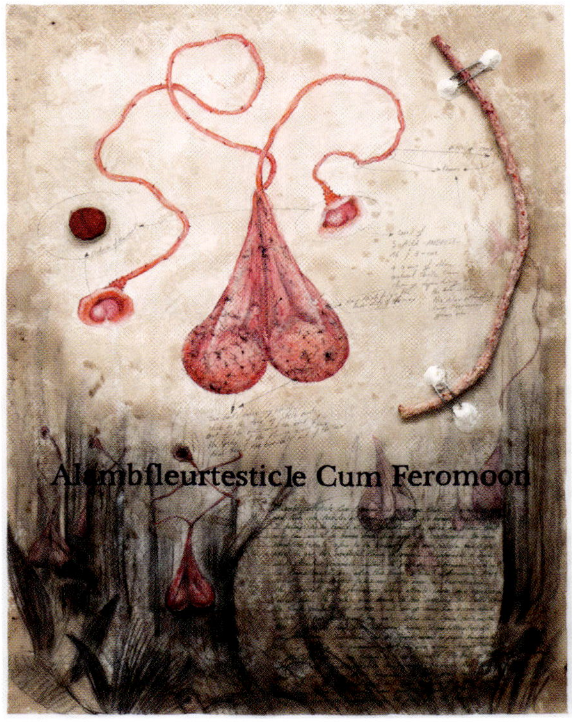

Alambfleurictesticle Cum Feromoon, 2005

Drawing 91 cm x 70 cm
Scent sculpture

Peter de Cupere, Sergio De Beukelaer & Maryam Najd, Van Laere Contemporary Art, Antwerp, BE, 26.01.2006-11.03.2006

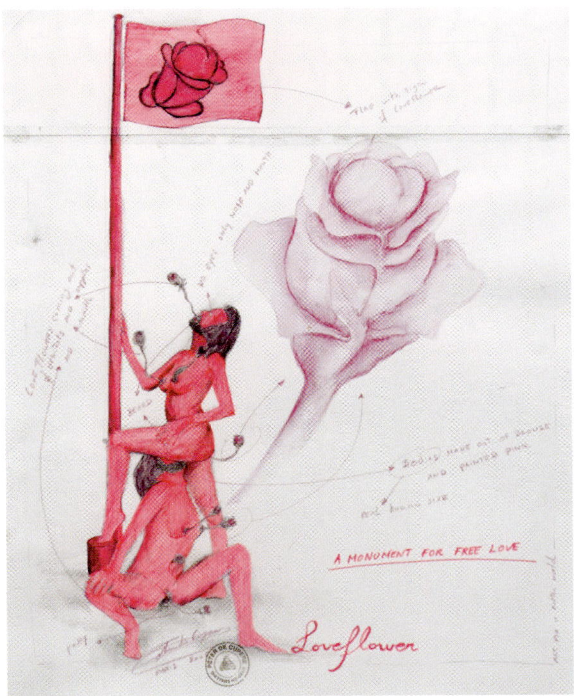

Love Flower, 2005

50 cm x 40 cm

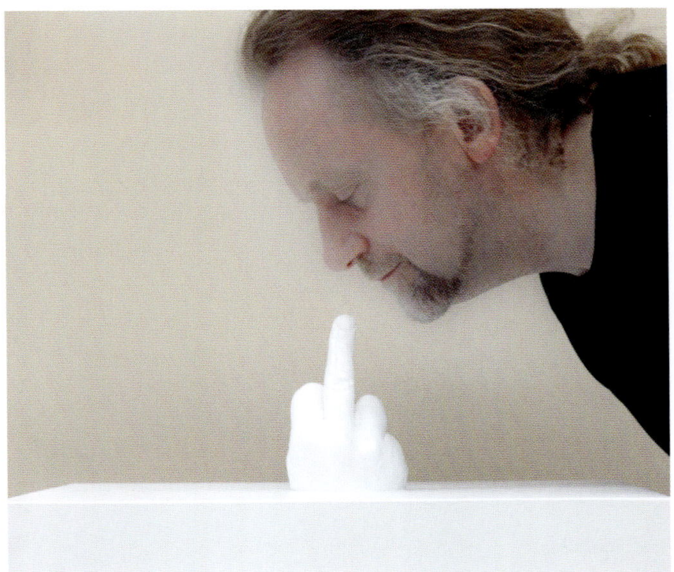

Sniff My Finger, 2016

Smelling middle finger. Smell the finger and discover the lovely scent.

Geurende middelvinger. Ruik aan de vinger en ontdek de heerlijke geur.

Sniff Your Jail, org. Balie Tongeren, curators Paul Morrens, Johan Smets, Justice Palace Tongeren, BE, 14.05.2016-19.06.2016

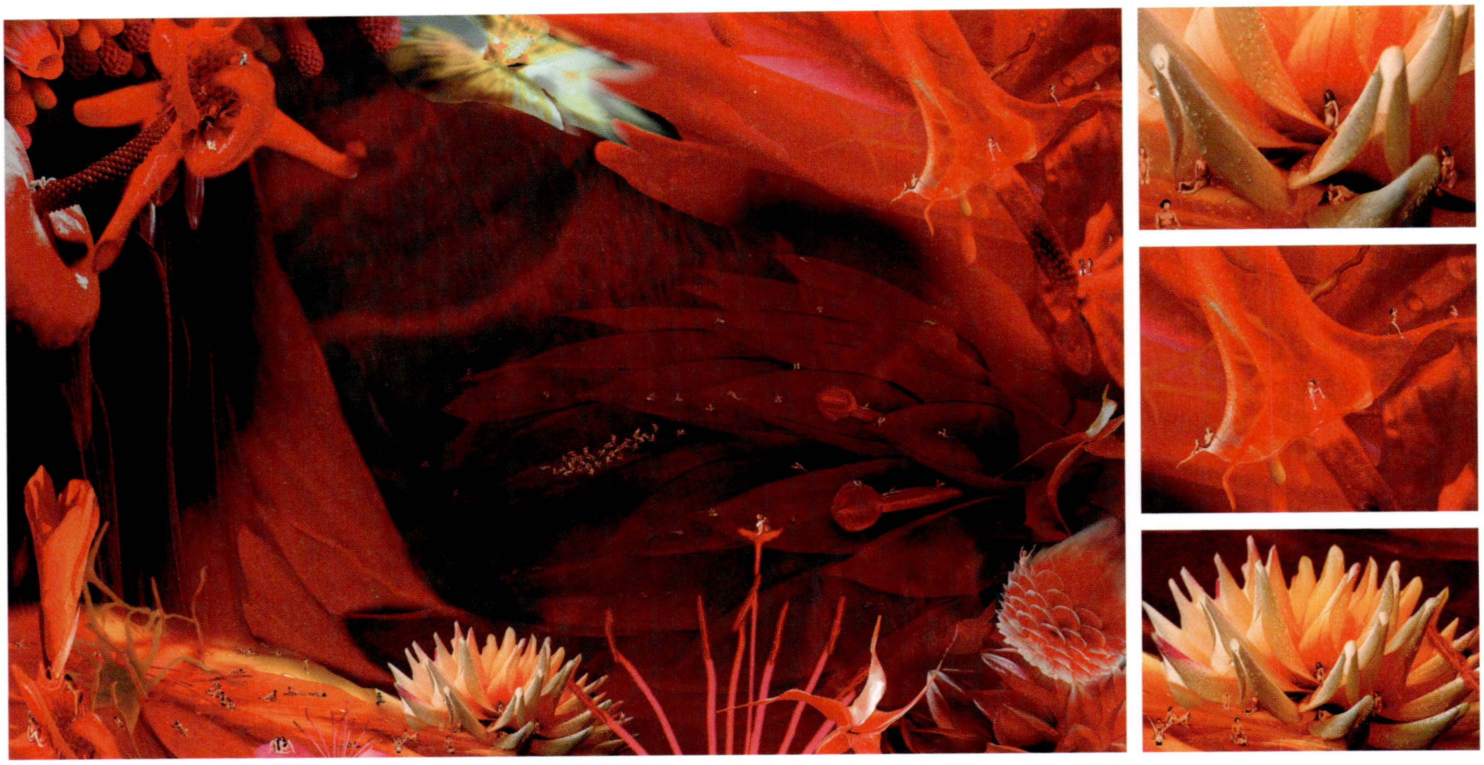

A Flower World of Sexual Fantasies 1, 2005
150 cm x 100 cm
Digital collage / Digitale collage

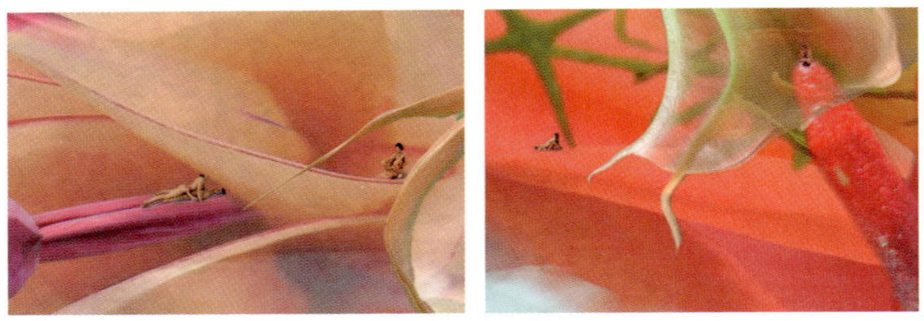

A Flower World of Sexual Fantasies 2, 2005
150 cm x 100 cm
Digital collage / Digitale collage

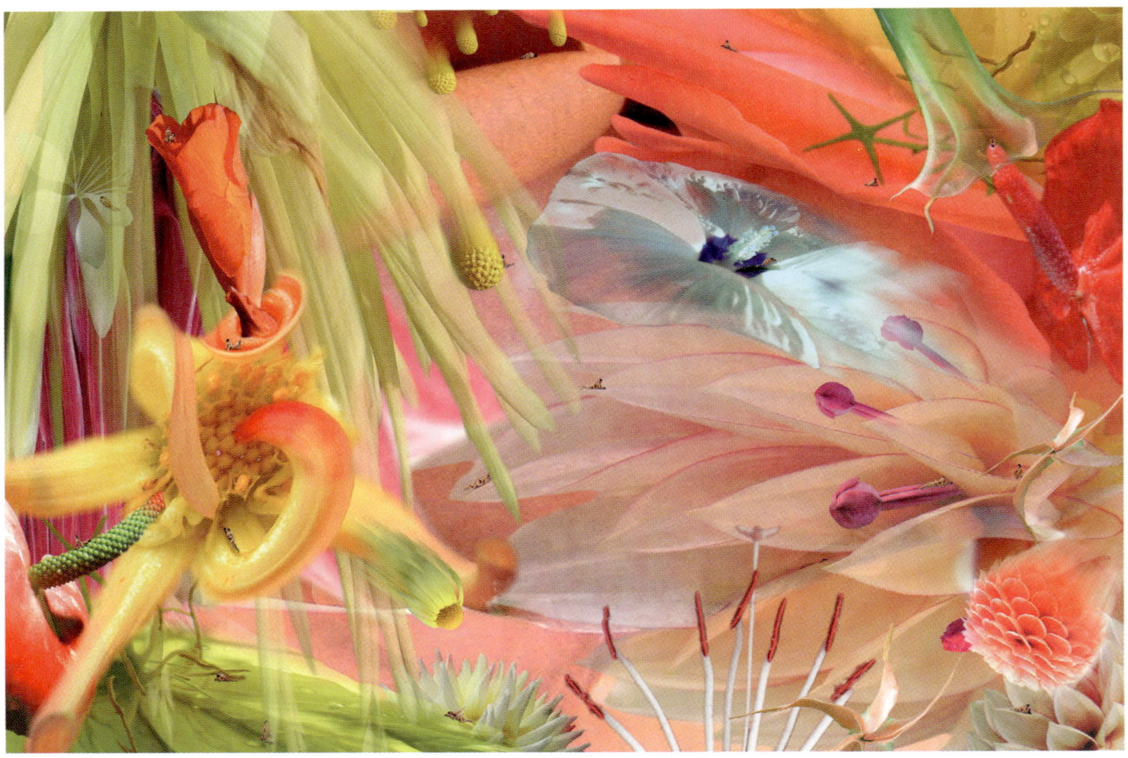

PETER DE CUPERE

COLLABORATIONS
Samenwerkingsverbanden

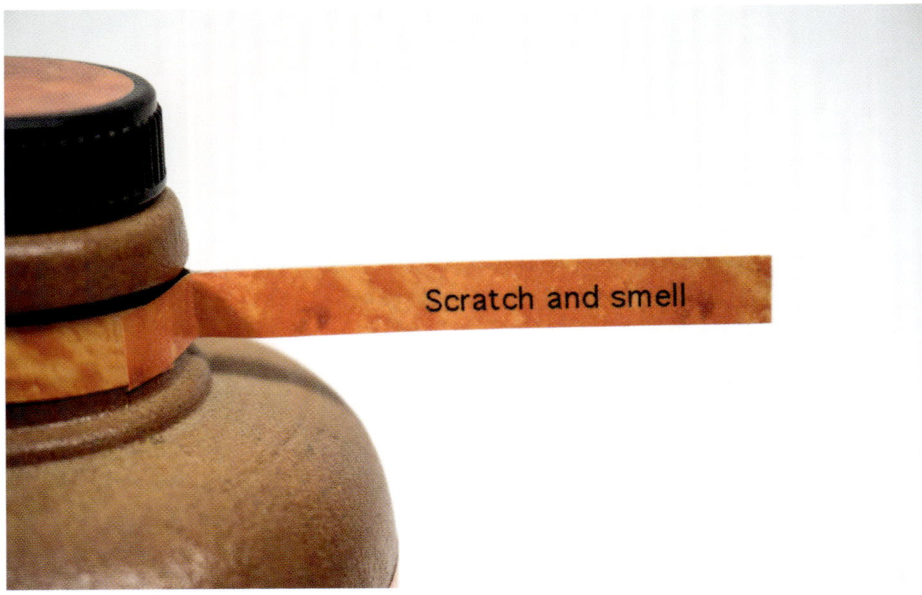

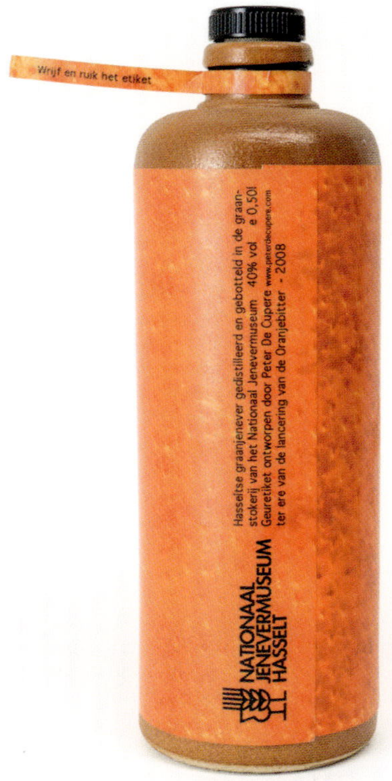

Scratch & Sniff Ticket Oranjebitter, 2008

Ticket design for the National Gin Museum in Hasselt, Belgium, for the launch of the Oranjebitter gin. The Oranjebitter is made by master distiller Jan Kempeneers. Peter de Cupere also designed the label to mark his solo exhibition Olfactology Lab, The Orange Bulb Alambfleurics in the National Gin Museum (curator Davy Jacobs, 26.04.2008-31.08.2008)

Labelontwerp voor de lancering van de jenever Oranjebitter voor het Nationaal Jenevermuseum te Hasselt. De Oranjebitter werd gemaakt door meester-stoker Jan Kempeneers. Peter de Cupere ontwierp ook het etiket naar aanleiding van zijn solotentoonstelling Olfactology Lab, The Orange Bulb Alambfleurics in het Nationaal Jenevermuseum, (curator Davy Jacobs, 26.04.2008-31.08.2008)

O'Hasselt
Eau d'Hasselt

O'Hasselt, 2014

Along with the master distiller Jan Kempeneers of the National Gin Museum in Hasselt, a smell has been developed for Hasselt. O'Hasselt, Eau d'Hasselt, is the first in a series of city smells that will in each case be named O' + the name of the city. The perfume is made and displayed in The Olfactory, which has been transformed into a smell laboratory for the occasion.

Samen met de meester-stoker Jan Kempeneers van het Nationaal Jenevermuseum te Hasselt werd een geur voor de stad Hasselt ontwikkeld. O'Hasselt, Eau d'Hasselt, is de eerste geur in een reeks stadsgeuren die telkens de naam O' + de stadsnaam zullen verkrijgen. Het parfum werd gemaakt en voorgesteld in The Olfactory, welke voor deze gelegenheid was omgebouwd tot een tijdelijk geurlabo.

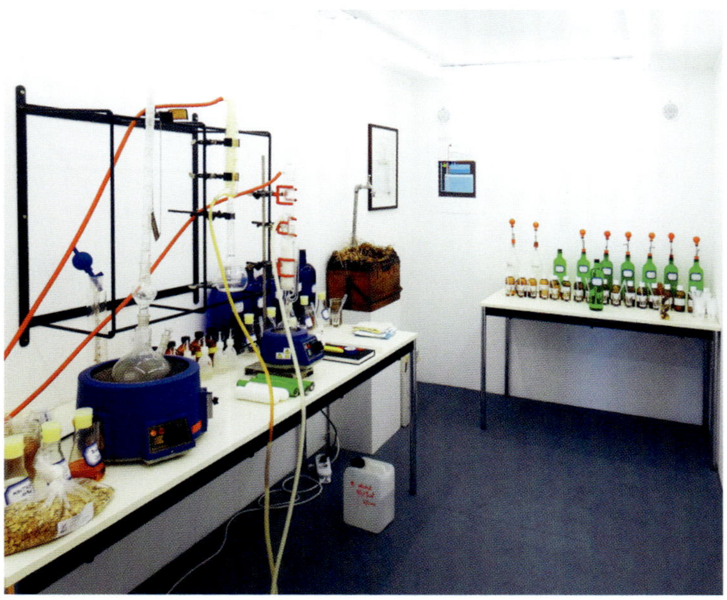

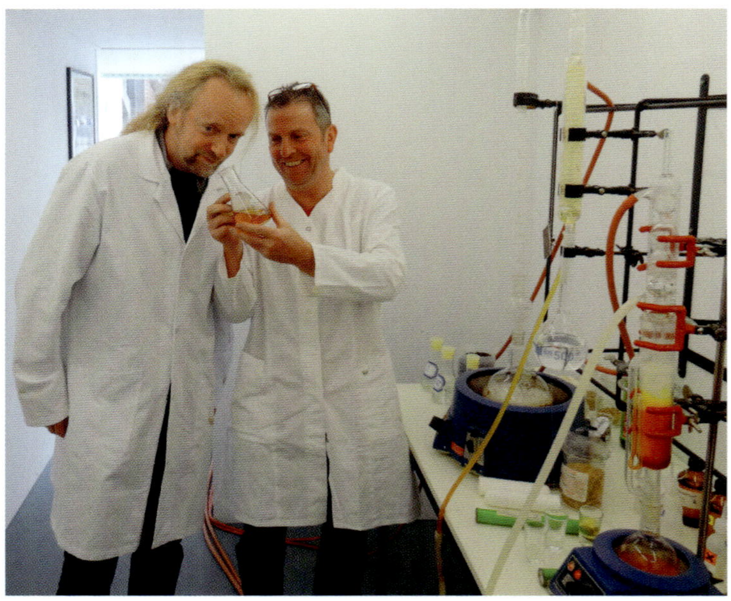

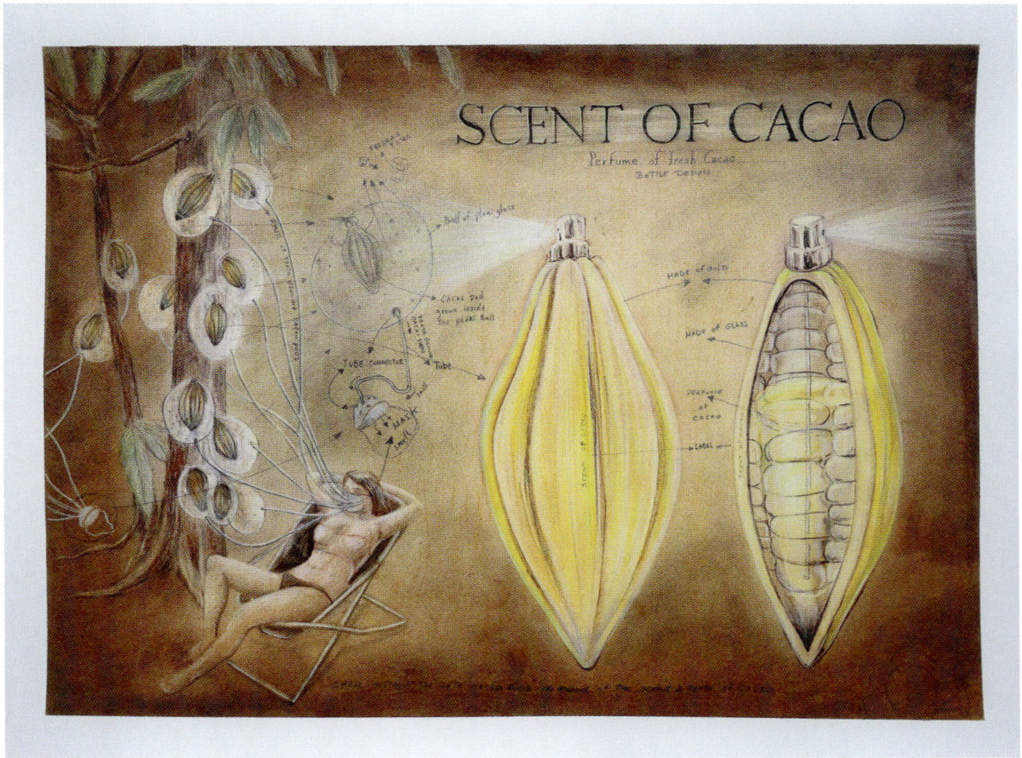

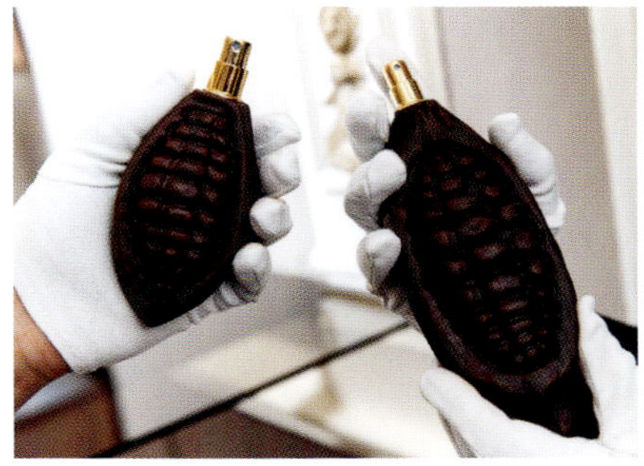

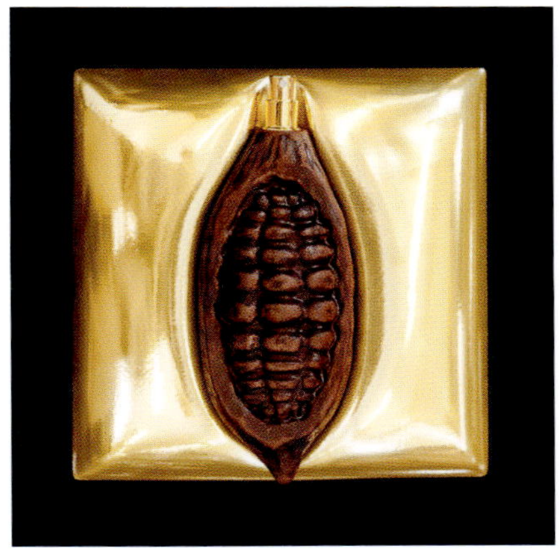

Drawing Scent of Cacao, 2011

51 cm x 67,5 cm

Cocoa 5 Senses, 2015

Peter de Cupere, in collaboration with Patrick Mertens and Inge Lijnen for 'The Chocolate Experience'. Boon developed a chocolate perfume bottle in the shape of a cocoa bean. The starting point of the design was taken from the drawing 'Scent of Cacao'.

'Cocoa 5 Senses' is an 'Eau de Cocoa' that can be sprayed onto the hand as an edible perfume. The underlying idea is the five senses. The shape and structure are perceived by the senses of sight and touch, the sense of taste by feasting on the delicious Belgian chocolate, and the sense of smell by the intense scent of the 'Eau de Cocoa' known as 'Cocoa 5 Senses'. The sound of cracking the bottle with your teeth, as well as the spontaneous expression of emotions, regale the fifth sense. The perfume also symbolizes the story of 'Bean to Chocolate'.
The perfume was presented, together with the *Cocoa Mask*, at the 2015 World Fair in Milan. Several Belgian collaborative ventures between artists and chocolatiers were on display. The event was sponsored by Callebaut and organized by the vzw Gluon, a non-profit organisation that brings artists together with scientists and the business world to produce new creations.

Peter de Cupere ontwikkelde samen met Patrick Mertens en Inge Lijnen van Boon *The Chocolate Experience*, een chocoladen parfumflesje in de vorm van een cacaovrucht. Als vertrekpunt voor het ontwerp werd de tekening *Scent of Cacao* uit 2011 genomen.
In de chocoladen parfumfles zit de geur 'Cocoa 5 Senses', een 'Eau de Cocoa' dat als een eetbaar parfum op de huid verstoven kan worden. Het uitgangspunt zijn de vijf zintuigen. De vorm en structuur worden waargenomen door het zien en het voelen, de smaak door het smullen van de heerlijke Belgische fijne chocolade en de geur is intens waarneembaar dankzij de 'Eau de Cocoa' met de naam 'Cocoa 5 Senses'.
Het geluid van het kraken van de fles tussen de tanden, maar ook het uiten van de emoties vervolledigen het vijfde zintuig. Daarnaast symboliseert het parfumflesje ook het verhaal van 'Bean to Chocolate'.
Het parfum werd samen met *Cocoa Air Mask* gepresenteerd op de wereldexpo in Milaan in 2015. Meerdere Belgische samenwerkingsverbanden tussen kunstenaars en chocolatiers werden er getoond. Het event was gesponsord door Callebaut en werd georganiseerd door vzw Gluon, een non-profit organisatie die kunstenaars samenbrengt met de wetenschaps- en bedrijfwereld om zo te komen tot nieuwe creaties.

Una Grande Abbuffata, World Expo Milan, Belgian Pavilion, org. Gluon, curator Christophe De Jaeger, Milan, IT, 19-20.09.2015

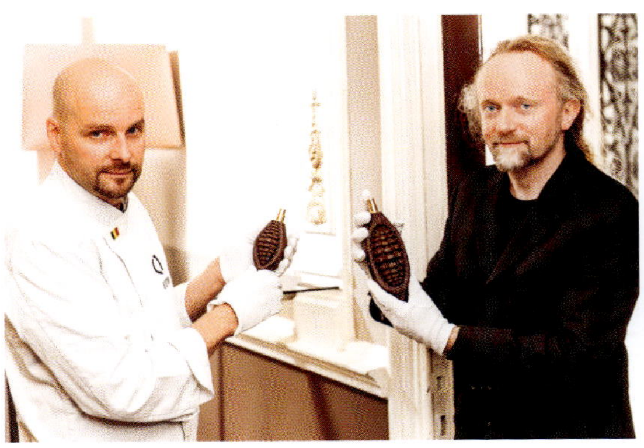

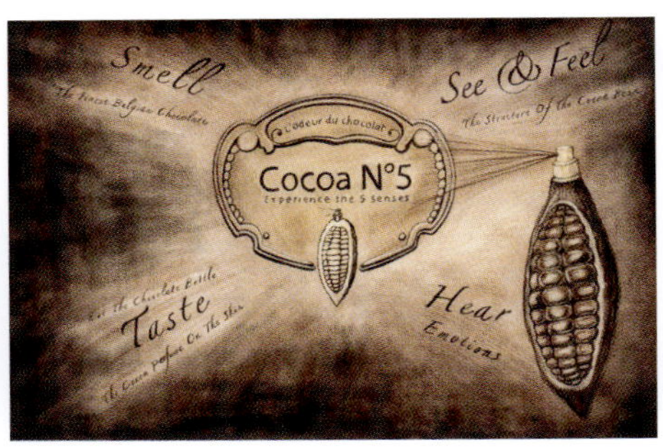

Drawing Cocoa N°5, 2011

Eerste ontwerptekening

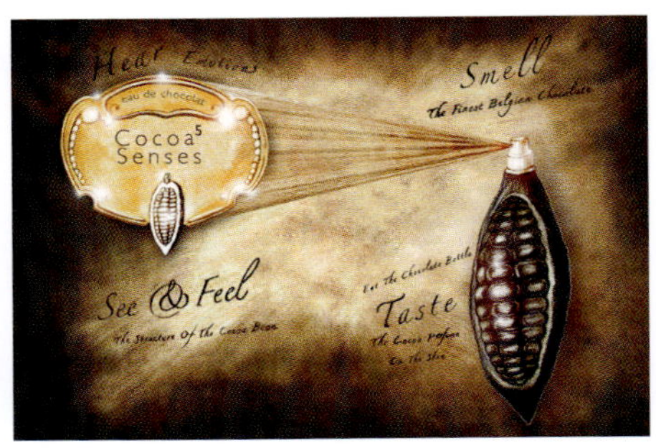

Drawing Cocoa 5 Senses, 2011

Definitief ontwerp

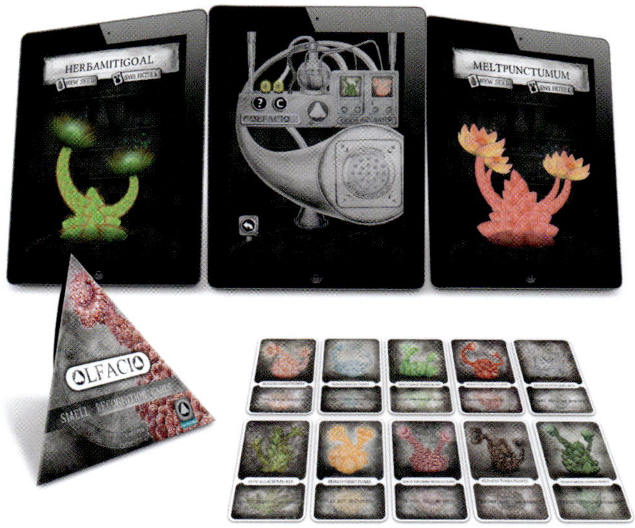

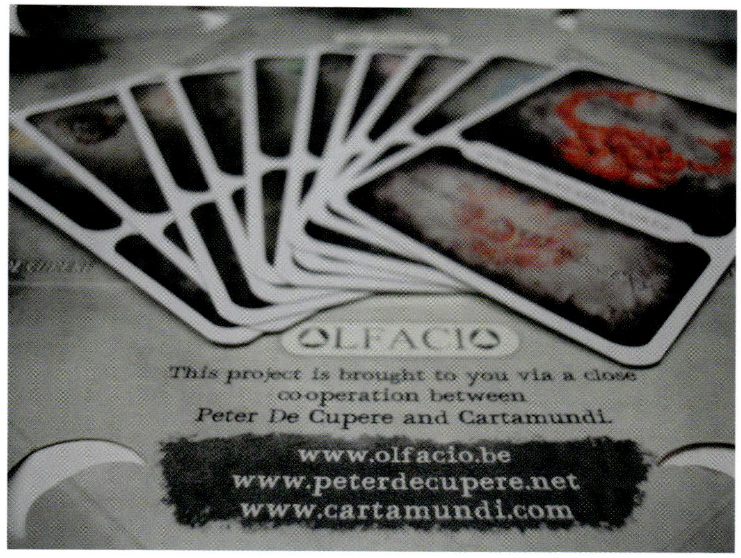

Olfacio, 2012

Olfacio is the first smell recognition app for the iPad.
In 2012, Peter de Cupere together with Cartamundi brought a special set of playing cards to market. Olfacio consists of ten cards with ten different imaginary flowers, each with its own seductive scratch & sniff scent. The accompanying Olfacio App for the iPad recognizes the scent of the cards. By combining cards, one can cross-fertilise plants and sow a seed that will grow into a new type of flower.
The collaboration between the artist Peter de Cupere and Cartamundi came about thanks to the non-profit association vzw Arteconomy.
Cartamundi is a world leader in making playing cards and board games.

Olfacio is de eerste geurherkennings app voor de iPad. In 2012 bracht Peter de Cupere samen met Cartamundi een speciale kaartenset op de markt. Olfacio bevat tien kaarten met tien verschillende denkbeeldige bloemen, elk met hun eigen verleidelijke scratch & sniff geur. De bijhorende Olfacio App voor de iPad herkent de geur van de kaarten. Door kaarten te combineren, kan men de planten kruisen en een eigen zaadje planten dat uitgroeit tot een nieuwe soort bloem. De samenwerking tussen kunstenaar Peter de Cupere en Cartamundi kwam er dankzij vzw Arteconomy.
Cartamundi is wereldleider op het gebied van spelkaarten en het produceren van gezelschapsspellen.

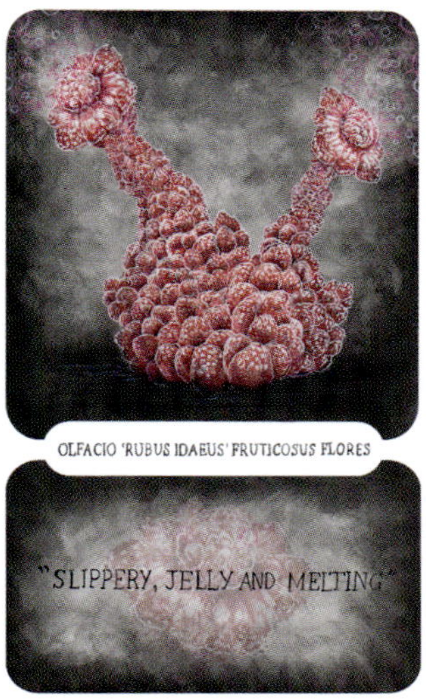

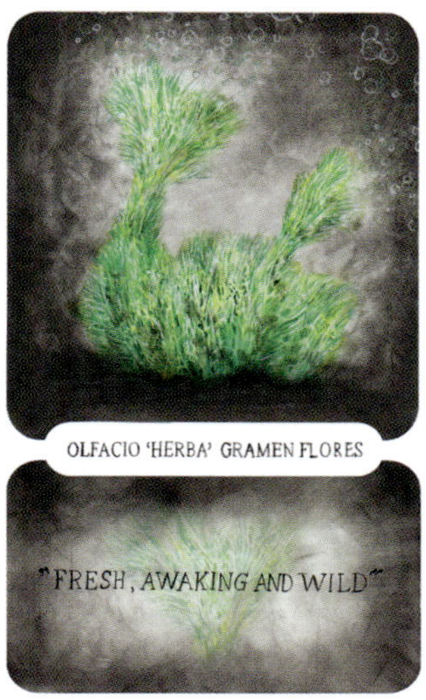

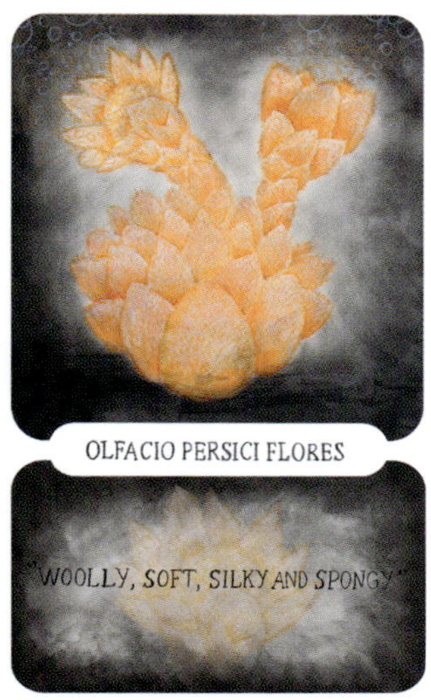

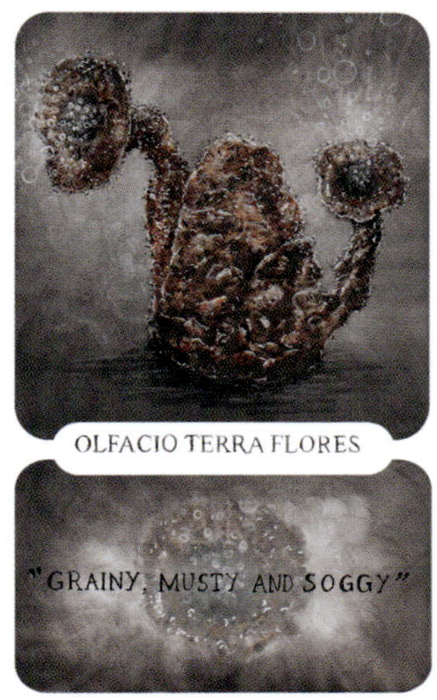

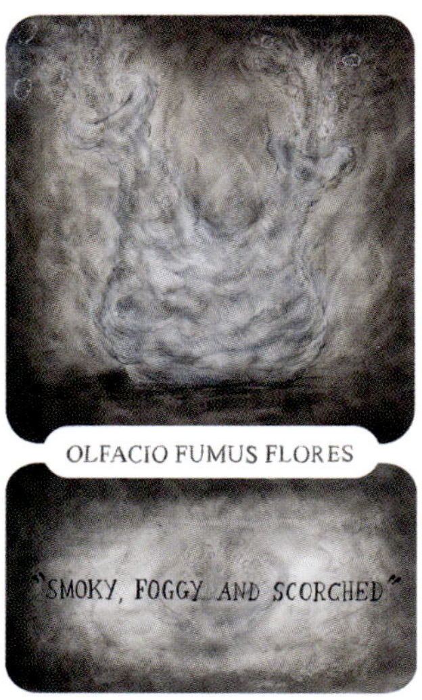

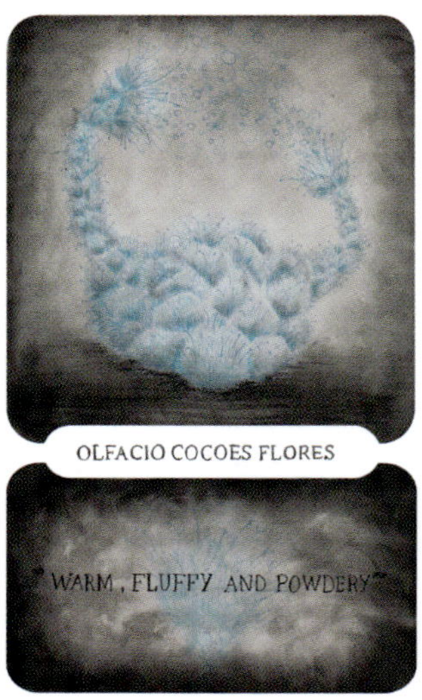

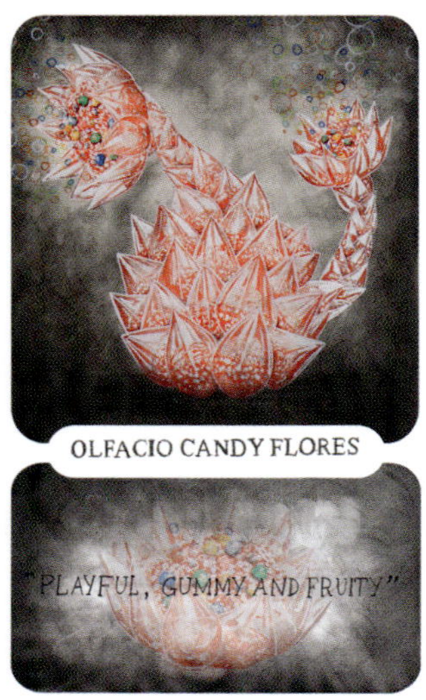

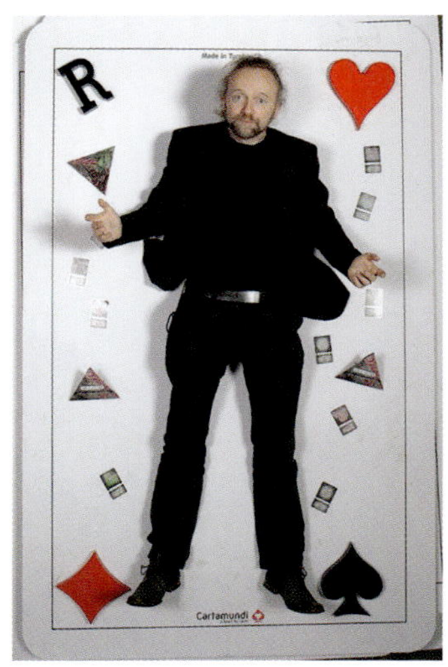

PETER DE CUPERE

BIOGRAPHIES & COLOPHON
Biografieën & Colofon

CURRICULUM VITAE / BIOGRAPHY

PETER DE CUPERE

Born, November 21, 1970, Leuven, Belgium
Lives and works in Antwerp & Hasselt, BE

Professional

- Olfactory Artist
- Founder of The Olfactory vzw, www.theolfactory.org
- Phd Researcher about the use of scents in art, PXL-MAD School Of Arts, UHasselt, Hasselt, BE and VUB, Brussels, BE
- Coordinator and tutor Masterstudio Art Sense(s) Lab, Open Lab at PXL-MAD School of Arts, Hasselt, BE

Studies

- 1996-1999: HISK, Higher Institute for Fine Arts, graduated June 21, 1999, Laureate in the Fine Arts
- 1994-1996: St.-Lukas Brussels, graduated June 30, 1996, Master in the Fine Arts, Studio Printmaking, thesis: Computer and Smell
- 1989-1993: Phiko, graduated June 30, 1993, Publicity Graphic Design (Phiko is now the PXL-MAD School of Arts)

SOLO EXHIBITIONS

2016–2017

- Eens was ik een mens (Is This Mankind), De Warande, curator Annelies Nagels, Turnhout, BE, 10.09.2016-22.01.2017
- Sillage, Fashion Museum, collaboration with Kóan Jeff Baysa, invited by Kenneth Ramaekers and Pieter Jan Valgaeren, TradeMarks, Stadstriënnale Hasselt-Genk, Hasselt, 01.10.16 - 08.01.17
- Touch Logos, PXL-MAD School of Arts, TM TradeMarks, curator Pieter Jan Valgaeren, Stadstriënnale Hasselt-Genk, Hasselt, 01.10.16 - 08.01.17

2016

- Sniff Your Jail, org. Balie Tongeren, Justice Palace Tongeren, BE, 14.05.2016-19.06.2016

2015

- 5 Piazze, 5 Sensi, Scent City Walk, org. Associazione Canecapovolto, curator Chiara Canali, Palermo, IT, 25.07.2015

2014

- The Olfactory, 33 olfactory art exhibitions in 7 weeks, Hasselt, Antwerp, Brussels, Ghent, BE, 15.09.-30.10.2014

2013–2014

- The Art of Smelling, Olfactory Art Research, Art Center Rozendaal 21, curator Yasmijn Jarram, Enschede, NL, 01.12.2013-02.03.2014

2012–2014

- Cultural Odor Generator, C-Mine, Genk, BE, April 2012-April 2014

2010

- Olfactory Tree, Pocketroom, curator Wim Waumans, Antwerpen, BE 12.09.2010-31.10.2010 / Special Nocturne Kiss Nature Smell Happening, 21.10.2010

2008

- Olfactology Lab, The Orange Bulb Alambfleurics, Nationaal Jenevermuseum, curator Davy Jacobs, Hasselt, BE, 26.04-31.08.2008.

2007

- Smell the Castle, Castle Beauvoorde, curator Annemie Morisse, Beauvoorde, BE 15.07-30.08.2007
- Air Polluter, De Brakke Grond, curator Fleurie Kloostra, Amsterdam, NL 09.06-15.07.2007

2005

- Open Studio, Cité International des Arts, Paris, FR, 21.12-22.12.2005
- The scent of information and paper, Culturama 2005, Stadsbibliotheek Henry Van de Velde, Leuven, BE, 17.02-19.02.2005

2004

- Garbage City, Van Laere Contemporary Art, Antwerp, BE, 20.05-03.07.2004
- Olfactiano VII, scent piano, Beursschouwburg, curator Guido Minne, Brussels, BE 10.11-21.11.2004

2003–2004

- Olfactormoviestudios.com, Smell-Movie Sniff Receptor, Z33, curator Jan Boelen, Hasselt, BE, 08.11.2003-25.01.2004

2003

- The Collector's House, St.-Lucas Stichting, curator Filip Luyckx, Brussels, 17.01.2003-22.03.2003

2002

- Smell Castle & Park, Castle of Poeke, curator Christa Vyvey, Helikon vzw, Poeke, BE 18.08-25.08.2002
- Peter de Cupere, perfume happening, rockconcert Admiral Freebee, Van Laere Contemporary Art, Antwerp, BE, 07.03 -13.04.2002

2000

- Peter de Cupere, Smellcom Happening, Smell Kiss Performance, rockconcert Admiral Freebee, Van Laere Contemporary Art, Antwerp, BE, 14.09-21.10.2000

1999

- Peter de Cupere, Black Beauty smell happening, Van Laere Contemporary Art, Openingsspeech Jan Hoet and rockconcert Admiral Freebee, Antwerp, BE 03.06-07.07.1999
- Peter de Cupere, Solo Exhibition, Vereniging, S.M.A.K., Ghent, 07.05-06.06.1999

1998–1999

- Mentha Piperita, Museum of Middle Africa Tervuren, BE, Oct. 1998 - Nov. 1999

GROUP EXHIBITIONS

2016

- Unidentical Twins, Rotary Izegem, curator Gery Van Tendeloo, Kortrijk, BE 08.09-06.10.2016
- Sex Smells Geruch einer antitranspiranten Gesellschaft, Kunstverein Wolfsburg, curator Jennifer Bork, Wolfsburg, DE, 02.09-06.11.2016

2015–2016

- The Importance of Being.., Museu de Arte Moderna, curator Sara Alonso Gómez, organized by Bruno Devos, Rio de Janeiro, BR, 17.12.2015-28.02.2016
- Jazz Age. The Roaring 20s, Fashion Museum Hasselt, curator Kenneth Ramaekers, Hasselt, BE, 12.09.2015-13.03.2016
- Schone Kunsten, Cacaofabriek, curator Ageeth Boermans, Helmond, NL 20.12.2015-24.01.2016
- Van Gogh & Malevich versus Next Door, Living Tomorrow, curator Barbara Dietrich, Vilvoorde, BE, 27.11.2015-30.06.2016

2015

- XII Bienal de La Habana, curator Jorge Fernández, co-curator, Sara Alonso Gómez, Havana, Cuba, 22.05-22.06.2015
- The Importance of Being..., Museo de Arte Contemporáneo, curator Sara Alonso Gómez, organized by Bruno Devos, Buenos Aires, AR, 17.07-04.10.2015
- Belle Haleine - The Scent of Art, Museum Tinguely, curator Mrs. Annja Müller-Alsbach, Basel, CH, 10.02-17.05.2015
- Vormidable, Vlaamse Hedendaagse Beeldhouwkunst, Museum Beelden aan Zee, Lange Voorhout, curator Stef van Bellingen, Den Haag, NL, 20.05-30.08.2015
- There's Something in the Air, Villa Rot, curator Caro Verbeek, Burgrieden-Rot, DE 22.03-28.07.2015
- Anders Abstract, Mondriaanhuis, Amersfoort, NL, 30.05-18.10.2015
- Aandacht, Aandacht (Attention, Attention), C-Mine, curator Annelies Nagels, Genk, BE, 15.09-15.11.2015
- Manufracture, Images and thoughts that matter, PXL-MAD, Hasselt, BE 24.09-27.10.2015

- Una Grande Abbuffata, World Expo Milan, Belgian Pavilion, org. Gluon, curator Christophe De Jaeger, Milan, IT, 19-20.09.2015
- De Negende Maand, Munthuis Tongeren, org. Stad Tongeren, BE 05.09-27.09.2015
- In the lee of the in-between, Kunstenfestival Watou, curator Jan Moeyaerts, Watou, BE, 04.07-30.08.2015
- The Smell of War, 100 years WWI, Castle De Lovie, curator Peter de Cupere, Poperinge, BE, 30.04-31.08.2015
- Aandacht, Aandacht (Attention, Attention), Warande, curator Annelies Nagels, Turnhout, BE, 25.03-24.05.2015
- A Belgian Politician, Marion de Cannière Art Space, curators Lieven Segers, Tom Liekens, Antwerp, BE, 21.02-21.03.2015
- The Importance of Being..., Museo Nacional de Bellas Artes de Cuba, curator Sara Alonso Gómez, organized by Bruno Devos, Havana, CU, 13.02-26.04.2015
- Panamarenko versus Next Door, Living Tomorrow, curator Barbara Dietrich, Vilvoorde, BE, 30.01-30.06.2015
- Art Eco, CC Strombeek, Strombeek-Grimbergen, curator Luk Lambrecht, BE 09.01-12.02.2015

2014–2015

- East Wing Biennial, Courtauld Institute of Art, London, UK, January 2014-July 2015
- Green Light District, Buda Fabriek, curator Christophe De Jaeger, Kortrijk, BE 08.11.2014-08.02.2015

2014

- Marta Museum in Motion, Marta Museum, curator Franziska Brückmann, Herford, DE, 08.06-15.06.2014
- Museum to scale 1/7, The Baker Museum Naples, curator Ronny Van de Velde, Florida, USA, 15.03-31.07.2014
- Bad Moon Festival, Kievitsnest, curator Jan Van Woensel, Antwerp, BE, 30.11.2014
- Van de sokkel, Hof De Bist, CC Ekeren, curators Johan Pas, Christine Clinckx, Kris Van Dessel, Ekeren, BE 25.10-26.10.2014
- Museum to scale 1/7, Kunsthal Rotterdam, curator Ronny Van de Velde, Rotterdam, NL, 13.09-14.12.2014
- Off Senses/Future Senses, Gemak, The Hague, NL, 01.08-27.09.2014
- Blood, Artisit, Alden-Biesen, curator Joannes Késenne, Lut Maris, BE 04.06-30.08.2014
- Next Door, Living Tomorrow, curator Barbara Dietrich, Vilvoorde, BE 12.05-31.12.2014
- Etcetera, S.M.A.K., curator Godart Bakkers, Ghent, BE, 08.05.2014
- Art(F)Air, MAS, curator Flor Beckx, Antwerpen, BE, 26.04.2014
- Lupercalia, Theatre Tinnenpot, Vermeylenfonds, curator Willem Elias, Gent, BE 15.02.2014

2013–2014

- Middle Gate, curator Jan Hoet, Geel, BE, 29.09.2013-19.01.2014
- Museum to Scale 1/7, Royal Museums of Fine Arts of Belgium, curator Ronny Van de Velde, Brussels, BE, 12.10.2013-02.02.2014

2013

- The Mind Of The Artist, Gallery Ronny Van de Velde, Knokke, BE, 02.08-06.10.2013
- Kortrijk Vlaandert, curator Hilde Van Canneyt, Kortrijk, BE, 04.07-18.08.2013
- Urban Explorers Festival, Scent City Trail, Dordrechts Museum, Dordrecht, NL 11.05-12.05.2013
- An Inside View, PXL-MAD School of Arts, Hasselt, BE, 30.04-30.05.2013

2012–2013

- Nature Now, CBK Drenthe, De Nieuwe Kolk, curator Toos Arends, Assen, NL 24.09.2012-08.01.2013

2012

- Creativity World Biennale, Rio de Janeiro, BR, 20.11-25.11.2012
- Brafa, Tour & Taxis, project Miniature Museum, Gallery Ronny Van de Velde, Brussels, BE, 21-29.01.2012
- Lupercalia, Theatre Tinnenpot, org. Vermeylenfonds, Ghent, BE, 15.02.2012
- Efemeer, Museum van Deinze & Leiestreek, curator William Ploegaert, Deinze, BE 01.07-07.10.2012
- Preview Futures, Het Gemak, Den Haag, NL, 01.06-16.06.2012
- Kanal, Ondernemen is een kunst, Prov. West-Vlaanderen, curators Christa Vyvey, Michel Dewilde, Ingelmunster- Roeselare, BE, 23.06-31.10.2012
- Art Economy, Turnhout Cultural City 2012, org. Arteconomy, Turnhout, BE 09.11-11.11.2012
- Festival of Creativity, Turnhout Cultural City 2012, org. Flanders DC, Turnhout, BE 09.11-11.11.2012
- 10 Years Z33, Z33 Art Center, curator Jan Boelen, Hasselt, BE, 10-11.11.2012

2011

- Creativity World Forum, Ethias Arena, curator Nora Weytens, Hasselt, BE 16.11-17.11.2011
- Goesting naar nog (appetite for more), Kasteel Le Paige, curator André van Hove, Herentals, BE, 26.11-18.12.2011
- The art of social network, Vrijzinnig Ontmoetingscentrum Hasselt, curators Fred Eerdekens, Herman Maes, Hasselt, BE, 01.10-16.10.2011
- Sound & Smell interventions, Artisti in Isola Comacina with Aurora Dal Mas, Italy, IT 26.06.2011
- Un Autre Monde, J.J. Grandville, Félicien Rops Museum, curator Ronny Van De Velde, Namur, BE, 25.06-11.09.2011
- Nietsvermoedend in het park, Pocketroom, curator Wim Waumans, Antwerp, BE 26.06.2011-01.09.2011
- Breathtaking, Exhibition for a good charity. On the last day, all artworks auctioned for the benefit of the mucosal association, an organization dedicated to patients with cystic fibrosis, Ghent, BE, 17.03-20.03.2011

2010–2011

- Crossover, The Royal Flemish Academy of Science and Arts, curator Sven Vanderstichelen, Brussels, BE, 11.12.2010 - 30.01.2011
- (when will they finally see) The power of drawing, Galerie Geukens & De Vil, Antwerpen, BE, 09.12.2010-22.01.2011

2010

- Festival De Wereld van Witte de With, Rotterdam, NL, 09.06-12.09.2010
- Artist Project, Art Brussels, Artexis, curators Karen Renders & Nele Verhaeren, Brussels, BE, 22.04-25.04.2010
- Inauguration new works of artists in Troubleyn, Smell Dance Performance SWEAT, Troubleyn, curator Jan Fabre, Antwerp, BE, 11.12.2010
- Sun-Light, org. Phidias & 5-Art, curator Christa Vyvey, Veurne, BE, 19.06-12.09.2010
- Green Summer, Verbeke Foundation, Kemzeke, BE, 29.05-31.10.2010

2009–2010

- From Memory, Museum Dr. Guislain, Ghent, BE, 10.10.2009 - 02.05.2010
- Everyone curator, art integration, org. Verbeke Foundation, Izegem, BE 20.12.2009 - 20.12.2010

2009

- Het Zelfde en het Andere, Zebrastraat, org. Unie Vrijzinnige Verenigingen, curator Willem Elias, Ghent, BE, 27.09-25.10.2009,
- IAMAI, org.Kunstenlab Deventer, Aktuele Kunst Hengelo (AkkuH) and Kunstvereniging Diepenheim, curator Koen Bril, Deventer, NL, 06.06-01.09.2009
- Artificial Nature, Verbeke Foundation, Kemzeke, BE, 23.05-15.11.2009

2008–2009

- Living landscape, Museum Groeneveld, NL, October 7, 2008-May 31, 2009

2008

- The Hands of Art, George Wittenborns Guestbook, S.M.A.K. Stedelijk Museum voor Actuele Kunst, with 21st Century additions initiated by Ronny Van de Velde, Ghent, BE 26.01-16.03.2008
- True Love, De Markten, org. Kunst in Huis, Brussels, 14.11-21.12.2008
- Exoten, Beelden op de Berg 2008, University Wageningen, org. Urban Aesthetics, curator Kim Knoppers, Wageningen, NL, 07.06-21.09.2008
- The Hands of Art, George Wittenborns Guestbook, Museum Marta Herford, with 21st Century additions initiated by Ronny Van de Velde, Herford, DE, 26.03-01.06.2008
- Trends, Sint-Barbaracollege, Ghent, BE, 01.03-15.03.2008

2007–2008

- So Close / So Far Away, Be-part, curator Hilde Teerlinck, Waregem, BE 11.11.2007 - 27.01.2008

2007

- NANO NU, Flemish Parliament, org. M HKA & Viwta, curator Edwin Carels, Brussels, BE 09.11-10.11.2007
- De Gustibus, Broel Museum, curators Lieven Van Den Abeele, Veerle Van Durme and Anne Petre, ING Kortrijk, BE, 14.02-29.04.2007
- Storm op komst, Warande, Turnhout, BE, 30.03-15.04.2007

2006

- Leere & Vision, Museum Marta Herford, curator Maïté Vissault, Herford, DE, 26.05-07.07.2006
- Déjeuner sur l'herbe, curator Stef Van Bellingen, Vlaamse Ardennen, BE 25.06-30.07.2006
- Dis-moi +, MAMAC, Musée d'Art Moderne et d'Art Contemporain, org. Les Brasseurs, Liège, BE, 21.04-04.06.2006
- 25 years Brakke Grond, curator Fleurie Kloostra, Amsterdam, NL, 07.06-10.06.2006
- ARCO, Art fair Madrid, Van Laere Contemporary Art, Madrid, ES, 08.02-13.02.2006
- Peter de Cupere, Sergio De Beukelaer & Maryam Najd, Van Laere Contemporary Art, Antwerp, BE, 26.01-11.03.2006

2005

- Play Ground, HISK Higher Institute for Fine Arts, Flanders, Art Fair Lineart Ghent, curators Willem Elias, Sven Vanderstichelen, Ghent, BE, 01-06.12.2005
- Grinding away at the Boundaries, festival Neusis, Urbino, IT, 09-11.06.2005
- Hit you with a flower, Atelier Van Lieshout, Jim Butler, Victoria Civera, Sergio De Beukelaer, Peter de Cupere, Bojan Fajfric, Nicolas Provost, Edward Lipski, Maryam Najd, Peter Rogiers, Thomas Schütte, Serse, Su-mei Tse, Juan Uslé, Franz West, Van Laere Contemporary Art, Antwerp, BE, 01.07-31.08.2005
- De Nachten, De Singel Antwerp, Villanella, Scent Concerts, Antwerp, BE, January

2004

- Mariages, MOMU, Museum for Fashion, curator Lieve Van Gorp, Antwerp, BE 17.09-12.12.2004
- Mo(NU)ment@Bornem, Monumental vzw, curator Ruth Renders, Bornem, BE 09.05-28.08.2004

2003-2004

- Once Upon a Time, Muhka, curators Bart De Baere, Guillaume Bijl, Antwerp, BE 20.12. 2003-29.02.2004

2003

- Tracer, Museum Pam Ename, curator Edith Doove, Ename, BE, 13.09-02.11.2003
- Don't think twice, it's all right, Van Laere Contemporary Art, Antwerp, BE 01.07-31.08.2003

2002

- Quattro Vendi, curator Letitzia Ragglia, Manciano, IT, 16.03-20.06.2002
- Akademie der Künsten, invited by Dieter Appelt, Berlin, DE, March-April 2002
- Flirt, Smart Project Spaces, Amsterdam, curators Thomas Peutz, Una Henry, NL 16.02-31.03.2002
- Metamorphosis, Peter de Cupere, Berlinde De Bruyckere, Peter Buggenhout, Johan Tahon, curator Christa Vyvey, vzw Phidias, Barcelona, ES, February-April
- Peter de Cupere, Hans Op de Beeck, Koen van den Broek, Sergio De Beuckelaer, curator Paul Morrens, Justice Court Antwerpen, Antwerp, BE, 21-28.11.2002
- Tussen kunst en kitsch, Culture Centre De Breughel, curator Martine Geerts Gerkenberg-Bree, BE, 19-21.09.2002
- Overbruggen, Brugge Culture City 2002, NICC Brugge, BE, 12.09-17.11.2002
- Summerdays, Van Laere Contemporary Art - Antwerp, BE, 10.07-10.09.2002
- Metamorphosis, Peter de Cupere, Berlinde De Bruyckere, Peter Buggenhout, Johan Tahon, Lieu d'Art Contemporain, curator Christa Vyvey, vzw Phidias, Sejean-Perpignan, FR, January-March

2001-2002

- Artist in Residence, Akademie der Künste, Berlin, DE, 06.10.2001-30.11.2002

2001

- Sonsbeek 9, curator Jan Hoet, Arnhem, NL, 03.06-23.09.2001
- Aller Retour, Le Lieu Unique, Nantes, FR, 11.10-21.11.2001
- Silhouettes 'n' Shadows, Fundament Foundation, Tilburg, NL, 01.09-28.10.2001
- C'est Beau, C'est Belge, Gallery Barbara Farber La Serre, Trest, FR, 07.04-30.06.2001
- Metamorphosis, Peter de Cupere, Berlinde De Bruyckere, Peter Buggenhout, Johan Tahon, vzw Phidias, curator Christa Vyvey, Rome, IT, 23.03 -17.04.2001
- Cutting Edge, confrontation Dieter Appelt - Peter de Cupere, curator Bart De Baere, Van Laere Contemporary Art, ARCO - Artfair Madrid, ES, 13-19.02.2001

2000-2001

- Metamorphosis, Peter de Cupere, Berlinde De Bruyckere, Peter Buggenhout, Johan Tahon, Galleria d'Arte Moderna, curator Christa Vyvey, San Gimignano, IT Dec. 2000 - Jan. 2001

2000

- 3 Raümen, 3 Flüshen, curator Jan Hoet, Hanne-Münden, DE, 10.06-30.09.2000
- Over The Edges, S.M.A.K., curator Jan Hoet, co-curator Giacinto Di Pietrantonio, Ghent, BE, 01.04-30.06.2000
- 3º Biennale d'Art Contemporain de Louvain-La-Neuve, curator Philippe Braem, Louvain-La-Neuve, BE 13.05-12.06.2000
- In honour of Fernand Khnopff, Museum of Fine Arts, Ghent, BE, 15.10-30.11.2000
- Kinderspel, Waarschoot, BE, 04-26.11.2000
- Diasporical Thoughts, Liebaert Projects vzw, Tacktoren, Kortrijk, BE, 10.10-21.11.2000
- Over The Edges, S.M.A.K., curator Jan Hoet, co-curator Giacinto Di Pietrantonio, Ghent, BE, 01.04-30.06.2000
- Dust & Dirt, Witte Zaal in cooperation with S.M.A.K., curator Jan Hoet, Ghent, BE 01.03-08.04.2000

1999

- S.M.A.K. KRACHT, Witte Zaal, org. S.M.A.K., curator Jan Hoet and students, Ghent, BE 21.01-21.02.1999
- Kussen, Gallery VUB, Free University Brussels, BE, 07-29.10.1999
- Bouillon, Higher Institute for Fine Arts Flanders, Antwerp, BE, 11-22.06.1999

1998

- Voor het verdwijnt, en daarna (Before it disappears, and after), SMAK, curator Jan Hoet, Watou, BE, 29.06-06.09.1998
- Spring 98, Jong Talent in Antwerpen, Koningin Fabiolazaal, Antwerpen, BE 10.04-03.05.1998

1997

- Peter de Cupere, Rik Van de Wouwer, Abel Joseph Gallery, curator Kevin Freitas, Brussels, BE, 13.03-26.04.1997

1996

- Final year students Fine Arts Sint-Lukas Brussel, Moving Art Studio, Brussels, BE 14-28.06.1996

LECTURES

2016
- 2nd World Congress on Olfaction & Issues, Politecnico di Milano, Digital Olfaction Society, Milano, IT, 23-24.05.2016
- Experts @ Your Service, PXL Hogeschool, Hasselt, BE, 29.04.2016
- Smell Your Earth! Smell as Stakeholder for Sustainability and Energy, Earth Day, Vlaamse Energiemaatschappij, Brussel, BE, 22.04.2016

2015
- Olfactory art and other smelly businesses, Mediamatic, Odorama, Lecture organized by Caro Verbeek, Amsterdam, NL, 08.10.2015

2014
- I am hurt, Art in the Waiting Room, Zebrastraat, org. David vzw, Gent, BE, 13.12.2014
- Artist talk, Museum to Scale 1/7, Kunsthal Rotterdam, NL, 07.12.2014
- Doctoral School Behavioral Science & Humanities, Campus UHasselt, Oude Gevangenis, Hasselt, BE, 03.04.2014
- Academy Guests, KASK, Antwerpen, BE, 14.03.2014
- Sense of Smell, Symposium, Moti Museum, Breda, NL, 02.12.2014
- Olfacio, lecture, Buda-Fabriek, Kortrijk, BE, 06.11.2014

2013
- Olfactology Lab, The Use of Smell in Art, lecture, 101th College Art Association, Session Olfactory Art, Hilton Hotel, New York, US, 16.02.2013
- The Use of Smell in Art, Design and Games, lecture, 1st World Conference Digital Olfaction, Ritz-Carlton Hotel, Berlin, DE, 11-12.04.2013
- Sense of Smell, 48 hours Sweatshop, Communication & Multimedia Design, £ Avans CMD, Breda, NL, 29.10.2013
- When Scent Makes Seeing, When Seeing Makes Scent, lecture, Symposium Beyond Art and Design, Mad-Faculty, Hasselt, BE, 07.03.2013

2011
- Olfactology Lab, lecture, Creativity World Forum Hasselt, BE, 16.11.2011
- Olfactology Lab, Lecture, Pecha Kucha Night in Ostend, BE, 10.09.2011

2010
- Do it, Smell it, lecture and debate with Peter de Cupere, Jim Drobnick (Ontario College of Art and Design, Toronto), Caro Verbeek (art historian and curator), Yolanda van Ede (University of Amsterdam), Adam Tasi (Smartnose, Amsterdam), Valentina Hulsman, Sue Corke, Circle of Senses (Aroma DJ/VJ), Stedelijk Museum - Amsterdam, NL, 23.09.2010
- Olfactory Art, debate, Festival De Wereld van Witte de With, with Peter de Cupere, Caro Verbeek (art historicus) and Garmt Dijksterhuis (professor Sensory Science, Unilever). Moderation: Hans Kennepohl., org. Arminius, Rotterdam, NL, 10.09.2010
- Olfactology Lab, lecture, The Royal Flemish Academy of Belgium for Sience and the Arts, Brussels, BE, 21.04.2010

PROJECTS, ART INTEGRATIONS, WORKSHOPS

2015
- Roten, Installation in Situ, Eau de Leie, Texture Museum, Sylvie De Coster, Kortrijk, BE June 2015
- Sweat, edition presentation, Free University Brussels VUB, Brussels, BE, 09.01.2015

2014
- Open Studios, Studio Peter de Cupere, org. NICC, Antwerp, BE, 07.09.2012
- Just another day, workshop, Artez Studium Generale, Arhnem, NL, 14.02.2014

2012
- Olfacio, the first smell recognition app for the iPad, collaboration with Cartamundi, project organised bij Arteconomy
- Open Studios, Studio Peter de Cupere, org. NICC, Antwerp, BE, 09.09.2012

2007
- NanoLove Perfumance, Nano Now, Flemish Parliament, Brussels, BE, 9-10.11.2007
- Smell Me Perfumance, Smell-happening at the opening of the exhibition Smell Castle, Beauvoorde, BE, 15.06.2007

2004–2005
- Smelloflowers, Art integration, Sensire Den Ooiman, Arhnem, NL
- Scent concerts with the Olfactiano through Belgium, different locations, BE

2004
- Olfactory concert 'Smellsonate for city of Brussels', Beursschouwburg, curator Guido Minne, Brussels, BE, 10.11-21.11.2004

2003
- Smellballoon-performance by Onashita, smell-me happening, opening exhibition Sniff Receptor, Z33 Hasselt, BE, 08.11.2003
- The Pink lady 974 A+, Pam Ename exhibition 'Tracer', Ename, BE, 13.09-02.11.2003

2002
- Flirt, Smart Project Spaces, Amsterdam, NL, 16.02.2002

2001
- Edition for the 'Mosselpot' of Marcel Broodthaers, S.M.A.K., Editions of Panamarenko, Luc Tuymans, Jan Fabre, Jacques Charlier, Jan Van Imschoot, Berlinde De Bruyckere, Peter de Cupere, Ghent, BE, 26.01.2001

2000
- Perfumance 'Dr. Smellart', 'Over The Edges', S.M.A.K., Ghent, BE, 24.06.2000

1999
- Smellcom Happening, Ericsson Nocturne in The Museum of Contemporary Art, BE S.M.A.K., Ghent, September, 1999
- Saltreedboat on lemon smell, Artintegration, Ministery of the Flemish Government, Copernicus Building Antwerp, BE, 1999
- Noses, Noses & Noses, Art integration, Children Clinic Free University Brussels, BE inauguration 07.05.1999

CURRICULUM VITAE AUTHORS

KÓAN JEFF BAYSA

Kóan Jeff Baysa is a physician, contemporary art collector, curator, designer, writer, critic, Whitney Museum Independent Study Program, Helena Rubinstein curatorial Fellow, and a member of AICA, the association of international art critics.
He is curator at the Art & Olfaction Institute in Los Angeles.
www.artandolfaction.com

He specialises in designing and producing projects and events that appose and contextualise seemingly disparate subjects.
A contributing writer for the online publication ArtSlant, and contributing writer and art editor for the now online contemporary culture periodical, aRUde. He has written for Art Asia Pacific, Flavorpill, Ctrl+P Journal of Contemporary Art, the Scent Marketing Institute Newsletter, and is the Pacific editor for d'Art International (Toronto). He was also invited as an international fashion journalist to Madrid Fashion Week 2012.

He has curated shows for the London Biennale, LA International Biennial, Chinese Biennial, Whitney Museum, Canon Corporation, The United Nations, and has organised and participated in art events throughout the US and in Paris, Cork, London, Abu Dhabi, Dubai, Tuzla, Sarajevo, Beirut, Beijing, Bandung, Hong Kong, Manila, Santiago, Singapore, Cologne, Seoul, St. Petersburg, Madras, Mexico City, and Yokohama. On the boards of The Vera List Center for Art and Politics at The New School University and the Art Omi International Artist Colony, he has presented lectures at the Whitney Museum of American Art and MoMA in New York, The Phillips Collection and The National Academy of Sciences in Washington DC, and is on the advisory panels for MuseCPMI, and Art and Med in Los Angeles, and the Streaming Museum, a cybersite with public exhibition spaces on all seven continents.

WILLEM ELIAS

Willem Elias is president of the HISK (Higher institute for Fine Arts, BE) and doctor in Philosophy (VUB, Free University of Brussels). Furthermore he studied pedagogy and museology at the University of Leiden.

As emeritus, from 1st October 2016, professor at the Free University Brussels in the faculty of cultural education, where he will be teaching the course 'culture philosophy'.
As an art critic (AICA), member of ICOM and president of the Higher Institute of Fine Arts (HISK) Flanders.

Member of the Royal Flemish Academy of Belgium for Arts and Sciences.
Author of: 'Aspects of Belgian Art after '45', Ghent, Snoeck, 2006, 2008, which can be consulted on: http://belgischekunst.be. Furthermore he is author of numerous catalogues and monographies about Belgian artists. Who wants to drown in the complexity of the modern art, can do this by reading his 'Signs at the wall', VUBPress, 2011.
Who wants to be introduced to it, simply explained, can better read his 'Modern Art', Luster, 2012.

HSUAN L. HSU

Hsuan L. Hsu is a Professor of English at the University of California, Davis. He is the author of Geography and the Production of Space in Nineteenth–Century American Literature (Cambridge), Sitting in Darkness: Mark Twain's Asia and Comparative Racialization (NYU), as well as several articles on film, environmental humanities and contemporary art.

ASHRAF OSMAN

Curator, architect and consultant on olfactory and socially engaged art. Founder–Director of ARTINECT; an agency that connects art and people both virtually and physically.
Co–founder of the SCENT CULTURE INSTITUTE; a think–tank focusing on the sense of smell in culture, business and society. Osman was born and raised in Lebanon, educated and experienced in the US and is now continuing his adventure in Switzerland. Always on the lookout for what's next.
www.scentculture.institute – www.artinect.com

RUTH RENDERS

Ruth Renders is specialised in Art and Film studies and worked as an exhibition maker and coordinator for several art institutes and projects. Her interest and expertise is focused on immaterial and audiovisual art and film. She is a board member of the scenarist guild and the digital Film and Image Bank Azura.
Ruth Renders wrote several articles about Peter de Cupere, amongst other 'Fasten your Nostrils', but also 'The Scent Borders of Paris' in which she discusses the photographic works made by Peter de Cupere in Paris (2005). The work 'Scent Borders of Paris' was not recorded in this book since it is a very expansive oeuvre in itself. Since 2005 Peter de Cupere is photographically registering the odor senses of society. You can find works and the text of Ruth Renders on his website.

CARO VERBEEK

Caro Verbeek is an olfactory art historian, curator and researcher. She is affiliated to the VU University, Mediamatic and the Rijksmuseum, Amsterdam.

Caro Verbeek (1980) is an art historian and a curator with a focus on the lower senses. Her aim is to (re)construct a more sensory history of art by collecting and (re)creating historical scents and tactile impressions. She is currently working on her PhD on art historical smells at VU University, with IFF (International Flavours & Fragrances) and the Rijksmuseum, Amsterdam. Furthermore she teaches the preliminary course 'The Other Senses' at the Royal Academy of Arts (The Hague) and creates olfactory tours and interventions for museums (for example: Biblical Museum, Amsterdam, Van Abbemuseum, Eindhoven). Verbeek curates the only scent platform in the Netherlands called 'Odorama' at Mediamatic, Amsterdam. Her books and articles include 'Scented Colours' (Routledge, 2016) 'Something in the Air – Scent in Art' (Villa Rot, 2015) and 'Inhaling Memories' (Senses & Society, 2013). Verbeek lectures regularly at venues worldwide such as TedX (Groningen, 2016), MSA Modernism Studies (Boston, 2015), Centre for Sensory Research, (Montreal, 2015), Goldsmiths' (London, 2014), CAA Conference (New York, 2013) and Erasmus University (2012).
www.caroverbeek.nl

PETER DE CUPERE

Peter de Cupere is a lecturer at the PXL–MAD School of Arts in Hasselt. He is the joint founder of the *Open Lab* where he teaches the use of the near senses, smell, taste and touch in the *Senses Lab*.
He also started up the English Master Fine Arts Programme *Art Sense(s) Lab* to promote the use of smell, taste and touch as a medium for the work of art. He is a PhD student at the PXL–MAD School of Arts, University of Hasselt, and VUB, and is researching into the use of smell as a context and/or concept for the work of art.

Peter de Cupere got all the rights to represent the works of Caflo Yrot. At the moment of writing he is working on an overview website (www.cafloyrot.com) where most of his works will be presented together with the audio files of the interviews with the son of Caflo Yrot.
www.peterdecupere.net

CURRICULUM VITAE AUTEURS

KÓAN JEFF BAYSA

Kóan Jeff Baysa is een arts, verzamelaar van hedendaagse kunst, curator, ontwerper, schrijver, criticus, Whitney Museum Independent Study Program, Helena Rubinstein Curatorial Fellow, en lid van AICA, de vereniging van internationale kunstcritici. Hij is een curator aan de Art & Olfaction Institute in Los Angeles. www.artandolfaction.com

Hij specialiseert in projecten rond ontwerpen en produceren, en evenementen die zich verzetten tegen en die schijnbaar afstandelijke onderwerpen contextualiseren. Een meewerkende schrijver voor de online publicatie ArtSlant, en een meewerkende schrijver en kunsteditor voor het nu online hedendaags culturele magazine, aRUde. Hij heeft geschreven voor Art Asia Pacific, Flavorpill, Ctrl+P Journal of Contemporary Art, de Scent Marketing Institute Newsletter, en hij is editor voor d'Art International (Toronto). Hij was uitgenodigd als een internationaal modejournalist bij de Madrid Fashion Week 2012.

Hij was curator voor shows voor de Londen Biennale, LA Internationaal Biennale, Chinese Biennale, Whitney Museum, Canon Corporation, De Verenigde Naties, en hij heeft deelgenomen aan kunstevenementen doorheen de VS en in Parijs, Cork, Londen, Abu Dhabi, Dubai, Tuzla, Sarajevo, Beiroet, Peking, Bandung, Hong Kong, Manilla, Santiago, Singapore, Keulen, Seoul, St. Petersburg, Madras, Mexico City en Yokohama. Hij zetelt in de raad van bestuur bij het Vera List Center for Art and Politics bij The New School University en de Art Omi International Artist Colony. Hij heeft toespraken gehouden bij het Whitney Museum of American Art en het MoMA in New York, The Phillips Collection en The National Academy of Sciences in Washington DC, en hij zetelt in de raadgevende panels voor MuseCPMI, en Art and Med in Los Angeles, en het Streaming Museum, een cybersite met publieke tentoonstellingsruimtes op alle 7 continenten.

WILLEM ELIAS

Willem Elias is voorzitter van het HISK (Hoger Instituut voor Schone Kunsten) en doctor in de Wijsbegeerte (VUB).
Verder studeerde hij aan de Rijksuniversiteit te Leiden pedagogie en museologie.

Is als emeritus vanaf 1 oktober 2016 gewoon hoogleraar aan de Vrije Universiteit Brussel in het vakgebied culturele educatie, waar hij de cursus cultuurfilosofie blijft doceren.
Is kunstcriticus (AICA), lid van ICOM en voorzitter van het Hoger Instituut voor Schone Kunsten (HISK) Vlaanderen.

Lid van de Koninklijke Vlaamse Academie van België voor Wetenschappen en Kunsten.
Auteur van: 'Aspecten van de Belgische Kunst na '45', Gent, Snoeck, 2006, 2008, raadpleegbaar op: http://belgischekunst.be.
Verder is hij auteur van talrijke catalogi en monografieën over Belgische kunstenaars. Wie wil verdiepen in de complexiteit van de moderne kunst kan dit door het lezen van zijn 'Tekens aan de wand', VUBPress, 2011.
Wie er simpel uitgelegd kennis wil mee maken, leest beter zijn 'Moderne kunst', Luster, 2012.

HSUAN L. HSU

Hsuan L. Hsu is een Professor Engels aan de Universiteit van Californië, Davis. Hij is de schrijver van 'Geography and the Production of Space in Nineteenth-Century American Literature' (Cambridge), Sitting in Darkness; Mark Twain's Asia and Comparative Racialization (NYU), zowel als verscheidene artikels over film, milieuwetenschappen en hedendaagse kunst.

ASHRAF OSMAN

Curator, architect en consultant rond olfactorische en sociaal geëngageerde kunst. Stichter-Directeur van ARTINECT; een agentschap dat kunst en mensen verbindt, zowel virtueel als fysiek. Medeoprichter van het Geur Cultuur Instituut; een denktank geconcentreerd op het zintuig van de geur in cultuur, zaken en de maatschappij. Osman is geboren en opgegroeid in Libanon, opgeleid en ervaring opgedaan in de VS en zet zijn avontuur nu verder in Zwitserland. Altijd uitkijkend naar wat het volgende is.
www.scentculture.institute – www.artinect.com

RUTH RENDERS

Ruth Renders is Kunst– en Filmwetenschapster en werkte als tentoonstellingsmaker en coördinator voor diverse kunstinstituten en –projecten. Haar interesse en expertise gaat uit naar immateriële en audiovisuele kunst en film. Ze is bestuurslid van de Scenaristengilde en de digitale Film– en Beeldbank Azura. Ruth Renders schreef eerder verschillende teksten over Peter de Cupere, waaronder 'Fasten your Nostrils', maar ook 'The Scent Borders of Paris' waarin ze het fotografisch werk van Peter de Cupere gemaakt in Parijs (2005) bespreekt. Het werk 'Scent Borders of Paris' werd niet opgenomen in dit boek daar het op zich al een heel uitgebreid oeuvre is. Sinds 2005 registreert Peter de Cupere de geurgrenzen van de maatschappij op fotografische wijze. Je vind hiervan werk en de tekst van Ruth Renders terug op zijn website.

CARO VERBEEK

Caro Verbeek is een olfactorisch kunsthistoricus, curator en onderzoeker. Ze is verbonden aan Vrije Universiteit, Mediamatic en het Rijksmuseum, Amsterdam.

Caro Verbeek (1980) is een kunsthistoricus en een curator met een focus op de lagere zintuigen. Haar doel is om te (re)construeren; een meer zintuiglijke kunstgeschiedenis door het verzamelen en re(creëren) van historische geuren en voelbare indrukken. Ze werkt momenteel aan haar doctoraat over kunsthistorische geuren aan de Vrije Universiteit, samen met IFF (International Flavours & Fragrances) en het Rijksmuseum, Amsterdam. Daarnaast doceert ze de voorlopige cursus 'De Andere Zintuigen' aan de Koninklijke Academie van Kunst (Den Haag) en maakt ze olfactorische rondreizen en tussenkomsten voor musea (bijvoorbeeld: Bijbels Museum, Amsterdam, Van Abbemuseum, Eindhoven). Verbeek is curator van het enige geurplatform in Nederland, genaamd 'Odorama' bij Mediamatic, Amsterdam. Haar boeken en artikels omvatten 'Geurende Kleuren' (Routledge, 2016), 'Iets in de lucht, Geur in Kunst' (Villa Rot, 2015) en 'Herinneringen inademen' (Senses & Society, 2013). Verbeek geeft regelmatig lezingen wereldwijd zoals bij TedX (Groningen, 2016), MSA Modernism Studies (Boston, 2015), Centrum voor Zintuiglijk Onderzoek (Montreal, 2015), Goldsmiths' (London, 2014), CAA Conference (New York, 2013) en Erasmus Universiteit (2012).
www.caroverbeek.nl

PETER DE CUPERE

Peter de Cupere is docent aan de PXL–MAD School of Arts in Hasselt. Hij is mede-oprichter van het *Open Lab* waar hij het gebruik van de nabije zintuigen, geur, smaak en tastzin in het *Senses Lab* doceert.
Daarnaast heeft hij de Engelstalige Master Fine Arts Programme *Art Sense(s) Lab* opgestart om het gebruik van geur, smaak en tastzin als medium van het kunstwerk te promoten. Hij is doctoraatsstudent aan de PXL–MAD School of Arts, UHASSELT (Universiteit Hasselt) en VUB (Vrije Universiteit Brussel) en doet een onderzoek naar het gebruik van geur als context en/of concept van het kunstwerk.

Peter de Cupere heeft al de rechten om de werken van Caflo Yrot voor te stellen. Op het moment van dit schrijven werkt hij aan een overzichtswebsite (www.cafloyrot.com) waar de meeste van zijn werken worden voorgesteld samen met de audiofragmenten van de interviews met de zoon van Caflo Yrot.
www.peterdecupere.net

The release of this publication coincides with the exhibition *Peter de Cupere: 'Eens was ik een mens' (Is This Mankind)*, curated by Annelies Nagels, co–curated by Tom Viaene at De Warande in Turnhout, Belgium, 10 September 2016-22 January 2017.

Deze uitgave is gepubliceerd naar aanleiding van de tentoonstelling *Peter de Cupere: 'Eens was ik een mens' (Is This Mankind)*, met curator Annelies Nagels en co–curator Tom Viaene in De Warande te Turnhout, van 10 september 2016 tot 22 januari 2017.

Peter de Cupere, Scent in Context, Olfactory Art
was made possible through the generous support of:
is mogelijk gemaakt met de genereuze steun van:
/ De Vlaamse Gemeenschap
/ De Warande, Turnhout
/ Bruno Devos, Stockmans Publishers
/ The Olfactory VZW.

Since 2008, until date of this publication, is artist Peter de Cupere not represented by any art gallery.

Sinds 2008, tot vandaag, wordt Peter de Cupere niet vertegenwoordigd door een galerie.

Peter de Cupere Official Website	www.peterdecupere.net
Project websites	www.olfactoryartmanifest.com www.theolfactory.org www.scentconcerts.com www.blindsmellstick.com
Exhibition websites	www.thesmellofwar.be
Community website	www.olfactoryart.net
Collaboration websites	www.olfacio.be www.cocoa5.com
Educational websites	www.artsenseslab.be www.sense-it-mad.be www.pxl-mad.be

About this book / Over dit boek

Not all his works are published in this book. Peter de Cupere has chosen to show a wide range of works to give an impression of his art and how it evolved through the years. Hereby he has chosen not to order his works chronological but by the content of the work. What he wants to express, is said or evoked by the work.

Niet alle werken van de kunstenaar zijn gereproduceerd in deze uitgave. Peter de Cupere heeft verkozen een ruime selectie van zijn werk te tonen om een overzicht te bieden van zijn kunst en zijn praktijk en hoe deze de laatste 20 jaar geëvolueerd zijn. De afgebeelde kunstwerken zijn niet in chronologische volgorde weergegeven maar wel op basis van hun context. Wat de kunstenaar wil weergeven, wordt uitgedrukt via het kunstwerk.

Peter de Cupere wishes to thank / Peter de Cupere dankt:

- Nancy Slangen, Dora Maes, Christiane De Meyer, Robert De Cupere, Annelies, Veerle, Erik, Jozef, Evelyn & Emily De Cupere, Ronny, Kerstin, Dario & Timo Beelen, Paul Morrens
- The authors: Willem Elias, Caro Verbeek, Ashraf Osman, Ruth Renders, Hsuan Hsu, Kóan Jeff Baysa
- De Warande, Annelies Nagels, Tom Viaene, and the whole exhibition team
- Bruno Devos, Stockmans Publishers, Wouter Van der Wangen
- The Flemish Government for their support
- IFF International, Bernardo Fleming, Meabh Mc Curtin, Gregoire Hausson, Christian Alori, for the support of the fragrances for the works Dead Body Bullets, Blood Helmet, Heroes Also Die, The Smell of a Stranger (Biennial of Havana)
- IFF, Christophe Laudamiel for the support of the perfume Evolution Man, 2004
- Scabal for the sponsorship of the custom-made suits for Evolution Man, 2004
- Paris XL for the sponsorship of the perfumes for the exhibition Olfactormoviestudios.com, 2003 (Sniff Receptor)
- Katoen Natie, Fernand & Karine Huts, Moortgat – Duvel – Vedett, Stad Hasselt, PXL Hogeschool, PXL–MAD School of Arts, UHasselt, VUB, M KHA, Zebrastraat, Alain Liedts & Françoise Meesen for the sponsorships and support of The Olfactory, 2014
- All his friends from his HISK period (1996-1999) and after.
- Every curator, art critic, art organizer, institute, museum, gallery mentioned in the book and CV and those I forgot to mention
- The Promoters of his Phd at the PXL-Mad School of Arts, UHasselt and VUB, Willem Elias, David Huycke and his doctoral committee Koen van den Broek, Koenraad Van Cleempoel, Sofie Gielis and the coordinator of PXL-MAD Research Bert Willems
- His research interns since 2014 at the PXL-MAD: Jorden Boulet, Sarah Reynders, Lien Hillen, Elissa De Groote, Brigitte Wendrickx, Emma Rankin, Jonas Nelissen, Yanna Gilles
- His art students and alumni of the PXL-MAD School of Arts in Hasselt, BE
- The Managing Director of the PXL University College Ben Lambrechts, the Directors Geert Masuy, Paul Martens, Astrid Hannes, Dave Hendriks, Heidi Croes
- The Department Head of PXL-MAD School of Arts Erwin Goegebeur. Erica Cselotei, Stijn Maes and all his other fantastic colleagues
- The Dean of Architecture and Art of UHasselt Rob Cuyvers
- The city of Hasselt and Genk, BE
- All art lovers and art collectors for their passion for Peter de Cupere's art
- Every buyer of the book for their interest in his work. Hope you enjoyed it in a lovely scented way
- Everyone he forgot to thank.

Colophon / Colofon

Text / Tekst	Willem Elias, Caro Verbeek, Ashraf Osman, Ruth Renders, Hsuan Hsu, Kóan Jeff Baysa
Concept	Bruno Devos, Peter de Cupere
Design / Vormgeving	Wouter Van der Wangen, Bruno Devos
Production / Productie	Stockmans
Printing / Druk	De Bie Printing, Stockmans (Duffel)
Binding / Boekbinder	Sepeli, Frank Vermeulen
Paper / Papier	Arctic Volume White 170 gsm
Font / Lettertype	ITC Garamond Light Narrow, Mr Eaves XL Mod Nar OT Regular
Scents / Geurinkt	Schubert International
Translations / Vertalingen	ElaN Languages, Akira Translations

ISBN 9789077207338
EAN 9789077207338

Printed in / Gedrukt in EC
Published by / Uitgegeven door Stockmans
In cooperation with / In samenwerking met Peter de Cupere

Smart Pictures: pag. 31, 38 (top), 67, 98, 161, 181, 182, 184, 196, 197, 263, 265, 270 (under), 271, 281 (middle & under), 283, 284, 285, 290, 291, 319, 331, 336 (top right), 361, 363, 393 (top right), 396, 397, 452 (under right), 453 (under right)
Steven De Vries: pag. 60 (top), 374 (top & right)
Frederik Buyckx: pag. 18, 58
Marco Mertens: 310 (top left), 457 (top right, under left)
Michiel Pauwels: pag. 28
Dirk Pauwels: pag. 342 (top)
Michaël Depestele: pag. 27 (under), 287 (top)
Ricardo Cruz: pag. 43 (middle), 382 (top & under), 383 (top right)
Liesbeth Driessen: pag. 393 (under)

Bruno Devos, voor Giulia en Ella

Note for the reader

The texts were written in either English or Dutch and translated in the other language. Some expressions can change by the translation. To safeguard the language and tone of all authors, the author's initial choice of spelling has been maintained as much as possible.

The editorial staff has done its utmost to identify and mention sources and beneficiaries of the text and images used.

Artist and publisher have made every effort to secure permission to reproduce the listed material, illustrations and photographs. We apologize for any inadvert errors or omissions. Parties who nevertheless believe they can claim specific legal rights are invited to contact the publisher and/or the artist.

Nota voor de lezer

Alle teksten werden origineel geschreven in Engels of Nederlands en vertaald naar de andere taal. Sommige uitdrukkingen of tekstgedeelten kunnen door de vertaling aangepast zijn. Om de taal en schrijfwijze van de auteurs te beschermen, werd de originele spellingswijze gehanteerd.

De redactie heeft zijn uiterste best gedaan om bronnen en rechthebbenden van tekst– en beeldmateriaal dat wordt gebruikt te achterhalen en te vermelden.

Kunstenaar en uitgever hebben alles in het werk gesteld om de rechten van de eigenaars van teksten, beelden, illustraties en foto's te vrijwaren. Wij verontschuldigen ons voor mogelijke vergissingen of weglatingen. Partijen die zich aangesproken voelen om een recht uit te oefenen, nodigen wij vriendelijk uit om ofwel uitgever of kunstenaar te contacteren.

This book has been enriched and scented with *scratch & sniff* layers. Images which have been varnished and ready for scratch & sniff, are indicated with a small icon, a copy of Peter de Cupere's nose. Depending on how this publication is conserved and how many times the reader scratches the images, the smell will disappear gradually and in time.

Dit boek is verrijkt met beelden die voorzien zijn van een geurlaag via *scratch & sniff* toepassing. De illustraties die met geurinkt bewerkt zijn, hebben een icoontje naast het beeld met een kopie van de neus van de kunstenaar. Afhankelijk van de wijze waarop deze uitgave bewaard wordt en het aantal keer dat de lezer op de illustraties wrijft, zal de geur geleidelijk en met de tijd verdwijnen.

KEEP ON SMELLING !